FOUNDATIONS OF TAXATION LAW

15TH EDITION

Foundations of Taxation Law provides a clear and comprehensive introduction to the policy, principles and practice that underpin the Australian taxation system.

Designed as a guide for law and business students as well as tax practitioners, the text blends policy issues, taxation theory, black letter law and commercial practice into a succinct general principles text.

Topics are presented in a logical and structured order and are cross-referenced to specific provisions in the legislation and relevant cases so that readers are able to easily find the source of the law. The text includes approximately 400 examples as well as dozens of diagrams and tables that condense the law and help clarify difficult concepts.

This edition contains expanded technical and policy discussion of several areas of law. It has been substantially revised and restructured to take account of the many important legislative reforms, case law developments and announcements that have occurred over the last 24 months. Some of the new topics covered include:

- the March and October 2022 and May 2023 Budget announcements
- the OECD's two-pillar solution on global tax reform
- the corporate collective investment vehicle regime
- the proposed tax on earnings on superannuation balances over $3m
- the skills and training and technology investment boosts
- the small business energy incentive
- the digital games tax offset
- the share buy-back reforms
- the ATO Charter
- the state and territory land tax, payroll tax and stamp duty changes
- the new ruling on residency tests for individuals
- the multinational tax transparency reporting rules
- the public beneficial ownership register requirements, and
- the denial of deductions for payments to associates for intangibles in low corporate tax jurisdictions.

Stephen Barkoczy is a Professor in the Faculty of Law at Monash University.

Cambridge University Press acknowledges the Australian Aboriginal and Torres Strait Islander peoples of this nation. We acknowledge the traditional custodians of the lands on which our company is located and where we conduct our business. We pay our respects to ancestors and Elders, past and present. Cambridge University Press is committed to honouring Australian Aboriginal and Torres Strait Islander peoples' unique cultural and spiritual relationships to the land, waters and seas and their rich contribution to society.

STEPHEN BARKOCZY

FOUNDATIONS OF TAXATION LAW

15TH EDITION

CAMBRIDGE
UNIVERSITY PRESS

CAMBRIDGE
UNIVERSITY PRESS

Shaftesbury Road, Cambridge CB2 8EA, United Kingdom

One Liberty Plaza, 20th Floor, New York, NY 10006, USA

477 Williamstown Road, Port Melbourne, VIC 3207, Australia

314–321, 3rd Floor, Plot 3, Splendor Forum, Jasola District Centre, New Delhi – 110025, India

103 Penang Road, #05–06/07, Visioncrest Commercial, Singapore 238467

Cambridge University Press is part of Cambridge University Press & Assessment, a department of the University of Cambridge.

We share the University's mission to contribute to society through the pursuit of education, learning and research at the highest international levels of excellence.

www.cambridge.org
Information on this title: www.cambridge.org/highereducation/isbn/9781009458832

First published by CCH Australia 2009
Eighth edition published by Oxford University Press 2016
Fourteenth edition published by Cambridge University Press & Assessment 2022
Fifteenth edition 2024

Cover and text designed by Sardine Design
Typeset by Integra Software Services Pvt. Ltd

A catalogue record for this publication is available from the British Library

A catalogue record for this book is available from the National Library of Australia

ISBN 978-1-009-45883-2 Paperback

Additional resources for this publication at www.cambridge.org/highereducation/isbn/9781009458832/resources

Please be aware that this publication may contain several variations of Aboriginal and Torres Strait Islander terms and spellings; no disrespect is intended. Please note that the terms 'Indigenous Australians', 'Aboriginal and Torres Strait Islander peoples' and 'First Nations peoples' may be used interchangeably in this publication.

FOREWORD TO THE FIRST EDITION

Foundations of Taxation Law is an impressively ambitious project impressively executed. The aim of the book is said in the preface to be to provide a 'concise' introduction to the policy, principles and practice of the Australian federal taxation system. Anyone acquainted with that system will appreciate how large and difficult a task that is. Stephen Barkoczy has brought to bear many years of teaching and practice in tax in the production of this substantial contribution to the literature on tax law, policy and practice in Australia. His teaching skills are evident in the exposition of complex and difficult issues in a systematic and clear language reflecting the kinds of questions which students might frequently have asked him. The text, however, is thoroughly informed by many years of practice and experience in tax law, policy and practice. The value of this book lies not only in its clarity and breadth of coverage. Readers will find throughout the book further references to pursue in more detail the many concepts and issues considered by the author. Teachers in taxation will undoubtedly find useful as a teaching tool both the text and the many detailed further references. They will also find particularly useful the study questions helpfully provided throughout the text at the end of various sections. They are designed to assist students in their understanding of the issues explained in the text and, as a teaching tool, will be very useful to the other teachers of taxation in Australia as a vehicle for discussion and application of principles.

It is particularly heartening to see a text of this kind directed to the student. There are many texts on tax law for practitioners designed, with varying degrees of success, to provide practical answers to difficult problems. Some publications for practitioners can do little more to assist the practitioner than gather together as much relevant information as possible and provide some statement of the law. *Foundations of Taxation Law* is directed to a different kind of enquiry, namely, that of the student wishing to understand what the rules are about. Tax law has developed over the years to become a complex system of many interacting rules. The complexity and size of the rules makes its teaching as a system a difficult task. The practitioner consulting a practice text or commentary may be presumed to have sufficient knowledge before looking up the text. For the student the task is different and more difficult. It is that enterprise that Stephen Barkoczy has undertaken with impressive results in this text.

On a personal note, it is particularly gratifying that this text should be written by one's own former student of many years ago. The text is a great credit to the author and I commend it to students of taxation in Australia.

The Hon. Tony Pagone AM KC

CONTENTS

PREFACE

AIMS AND OBJECTIVES

Taxation law is a vast and complex area of law that is continually evolving. As a consequence, it can be an overwhelming and challenging subject to study and research. The aim of this book is to provide a guide to the policy, principles and practice that underpin the Australian taxation system. The book focuses on the key components covered in many introductory and advanced taxation law courses studied at Australian universities. It is designed to be used by undergraduate and postgraduate students as well as students undertaking professional qualifications with accounting bodies, law societies and the Taxation Institute of Australia. The book is also intended to serve as a general reference guide for taxation academics and researchers, as well as practising lawyers and accountants who require a succinct and user-friendly explanation of fundamental taxation law concepts.

CONTENT AND STRUCTURE

The main emphasis of the book is on Commonwealth taxes, particularly income tax, goods and services tax, fringe benefits tax and superannuation taxes. It also examines various state and territory taxes, as well as a number of levies and charges. The book is divided into 13 parts containing 41 chapters. To make the book more accessible to readers, I have adopted the approach of focusing on general principles. My objective is to provide a broad overview of the foundations of the taxation system rather than an exhaustive explanation of all its intricate principles and exceptions. In this regard, I have been selective in the topics covered and have intentionally divided them into 'consumable chunks' that can be easily digested by a reader. At the same time, I have tried to ensure that the book addresses most areas of general importance and does not over-simplify the law or skirt around harder issues. The book is therefore more comprehensive than many other introductory guides and goes into deeper detail on several topics. I have purposely tackled difficult areas of law that I believe are of significant practical importance and are not always adequately covered in other general books. For instance, the book has detailed chapters dealing with topics such as superannuation, employee share schemes, consolidated groups, investment incentives, business restructures, international taxation, Double Taxation Agreements, base erosion and profit shifting, accruals taxation and the taxation of financial transactions. Although these areas are outside the scope of most basic tax courses, they are important for advanced courses and are critical for obtaining a broad understanding of the Australian taxation regime. They are also particularly important areas for academics and practitioners.

While the book does not purport to provide a complete picture of Australia's tax laws, it covers a lot of ground, including discussion of many hundreds of legislative provisions, cases and rulings. The discussion in the chapters should serve as a solid set of principles around which readers can progressively build their general understanding of the law. The discussion should also provide a useful road map for navigating the complex web of interconnected provisions in the tax legislation and for making sense of the extensive body of case law in the field. Hopefully, by using this book, readers will be able to tread more confidently through the tax law maze and be able to better 'see the wood for the trees'.

The book is the product of many years of researching, practising and lecturing in the field of taxation law, and it undoubtedly demonstrates my own biases about what I think is important for students, academics and practitioners to understand about the subject. I have tried to blend policy issues, taxation theory, technical 'black letter law' and commercial practice into a succinct, principled text. Although the book is primarily a legal text, it does not focus exclusively on legal issues. The discussion also touches on a wide range of social, economic, political and international comparative issues. Taxation law, perhaps more than any other area of law, is affected by these broader considerations, and I firmly believe that it needs to be approached with these perspectives in mind.

In writing the book, I have been conscious of the pressures placed on students and practitioners who have to grapple with large amounts of complex information located in different places in short time frames. For this reason, I have endeavoured to develop topics in a logical and structured order and clearly signpost and break up core concepts into their constituent elements. I have also extensively cross-referenced the discussion to specific legislative provisions and cases so that readers are able to easily find the source of the law. The book is peppered with examples, diagrams and tables that condense the law and help clarify difficult concepts.

QUESTIONS, ONLINE RESOURCES AND LECTURER SLIDES

To assist students with their exam preparation, the book contains a set of questions at the end of each chapter that are linked to the topics covered in that chapter. The questions test fundamental issues that students need to understand in order to properly grasp key concepts. They can also be used by lecturers as a basis for tutorial discussions. The questions have been designed in such a way that they examine core issues from both a practical (calculation and problem-based) perspective as well as a conceptual (theoretical and policy-based) perspective.

Online resources are available on the Cambridge University Press Higher Education website at www.cambridge.org/highereducation/isbn/9781009458832/resources. Student resources are freely available and include a list of references to selected government reports, taxation rulings, books and articles for those interested in conducting further research. The list of references should be particularly useful to students conducting research for their assignments. Lecturers can also gain access to a set of over 1,000 PowerPoint slides that are directly cross-referenced to topics covered in the chapters. The slides are designed as a handy teaching aid and can be obtained once your account is granted access.

CHANGES IN THE 15TH EDITION

This book has evolved considerably over the years. The 15th edition has undergone considerable restructuring and has been substantially revised to take account of many important legislative reforms, case law developments, administrative changes and policy announcements that have occurred over the last 24 months. It contains extensive analysis of the March and October 2022 and May 2023 Budget measures as well as discussion of many important new developments, such as the introduction of the new corporate collective investment vehicle regime, the skills and training and technology investment boosts and the digital games tax offset. There is also detailed discussion of the proposed new tax on earnings on superannuation balances over $3m and the proposed share buy-back reforms. The new ATO Charter, which replaces the Taxpayers' Charter, is examined as well as various land tax, payroll tax and stamp duty changes.

Special attention has been devoted to a number of significant international tax developments, including the ATO's new ruling on residency tests for individuals and the OECD's landmark two-pillar solution on global tax reform. There is also discussion of the proposed multinational tax transparency reporting and public beneficial ownership register requirements as well as the proposed anti-avoidance rule that denies significant global entities deductions for payments to associates for intangibles in low corporate tax jurisdictions.

The book contains discussion of dozens of additional cases, including recent decisions, such as *Adcon Resources Vic Pty Ltd v FC of T*; *Aurizon Holdings Ltd v FC of T; FC of T v Balasubramaniyan*; *B&F Investments Pty Ltd v FC of T*; *Bosanac v FC of T*; *FC of T v Carter & Ors; Cerrah v TPB Construction*; *Forestry, Maritime, Mining and Energy Union & Anor v Personnel Contracting Pty Ltd*; *Del Castillo v FC of T*; *Dua v FC of T*; *FFYS v FC of T*; *Hornsby Shire Council v Cth & Anor*; *Gough & Anor v TPB*; *FC of T v Guardian AIT Pty Ltd ATF Australian Investment Trust*; *Guttikonda & Anor v FC of T*; *H&B Auto Repair Centre Pty Ltd v FC of T*; *DFC of T v Huang*; *Hyder & Ors v FC of T*; *JHKW v FC of T*; *JMC Pty Ltd v FC of T*; *Kais Jewellery (Syd) Pty Ltd v FC of T*; *Khanna v FC of T*; *Lakes Oil NL v ISA*; *FC of T v Landcom*; *Logic Accountants & Tax Professionals Pty Ltd & Anor v TPB*; *Messenger Media and Information Technology Pty Ltd v FC of T*; *Plaskitt v TPB*; *FC of T v PricewaterhouseCoopers*; *Shaw v FC of T*; *Stark v FC of T*; *Thanabalasingam v TPB*; *Tomkinson v TPB*; *TPB v Ordiales*; *TPB v Williams*; *FC of T v Virgin Australia Airlines Pty Ltd*; *R v Willmott*; *Wood v FC of T*; *Worsley v TPB* and *YDXM v FC of T*.

There is also expanded policy and technical discussion of several areas of law as well as many new and updated examples, questions and diagrams. Certain topics have been consolidated and the chapter order has been reorganised and streamlined. Unless otherwise stated, the discussion in the book is generally based on the law in force as at July 2023.

ACKNOWLEDGEMENTS

I would like to thank my copyeditor, Ellie Gleeson, and the production, editorial and marketing staff at Cambridge University Press, especially Lucy Russell, Jodie Fitzsimmons and Alison Dean, for their valuable input into this new edition. I would also like to acknowledge the student research assistants who helped with previous editions of this book, especially from Sylvester Urban (third edition), Tamara Wilkinson (fifth edition), Jonathan Bisset and Antony Berger (ninth edition) and Radomir Jovanovic (11th edition). My special thanks are also extended to my former lecturer, the Hon Tony Pagone AM KC, for the lessons I learned from him and for taking the time to write the foreword to the first edition of this book. Most importantly, however, I would like to recognise the support of my family, for whom this book has been written.

Stephen Barkoczy
November 2023

ABOUT THE AUTHOR

Stephen Barkoczy, BA, LLB, M Tax Law, PhD

Stephen Barkoczy is a Professor in the Faculty of Law at Monash University and Chair of the Innovation Investment Committee of Industry Innovation and Science Australia. He is also a member of the International Faculty of the Institute for Austrian and International Tax Law at the Vienna University of Economics and Business. Stephen has published, practised and lectured widely in the areas of taxation, superannuation and venture capital investment law. He is the author/co-author of many books and the recipient of numerous teaching awards, including the 2008 Prime Minister's Award for Australian University Teacher of the Year.

KEY TO ABBREVIATIONS

A$	Australian dollars
AASB	Australian Accounting Standards Board
AAT	Administrative Appeals Tribunal
AATA	*Administrative Appeals Tribunal Act 1975*
ABA	Additional Benefits Agreement
ABN	Australian Business Number
ABS	Australian Bureau of Statistics
AC	Appeal Cases (House of Lords)
ACA	Allocable cost amount
ACC	Australian Crime Commission
ACCC	Australian Competition and Consumer Commission
ACCU	Australian carbon credit unit
ACNC	Australian Charities and Not-for-profits Commission
ACT	Australian Capital Territory
ADF	Approved deposit fund
ADI	Authorised deposit-taking institution
ADJRA	*Administrative Decisions (Judicial Review) Act 1977*
AFC	Applicable functional currency
AFCA	Australian Financial Complaints Authority
AFM	Available fraction method
AFOF	Australian fund of funds
AFP	Australian Federal Police
AFSL	Australian financial services licence
AFTS	Australia's Future Tax System
AGD	Attorney-General's Department
AGS	Australian Government Solicitor
All ER	All England Law Reports
AMIT	Attribution managed investment trusts
AMLCTFA	*Anti-Money Laundering and Counter-Terrorism Financing Act 2006*
AMLCTFR	*Anti-Money Laundering and Counter-Terrorism Financing Rules*
ANTS	A New Tax System
APA	Advance pricing arrangement
APRA	Australian Prudential Regulation Authority
ARFN	Australian registered fund number
ASIC	Australian Securities and Investments Commission
ASX	Australian Securities Exchange
AT	Australian Tax
ATC	Australian Tax Cases
ATD	Australian Tax Decisions
ATI	Adjusted tainted income

ATO	Australian Taxation Office
AUSTRAC	Australian Transaction Reports and Analysis Centre
BAS	Business Activity Statement
BCT	Business continuity test
BEPS	Base erosion and profit shifting
BTO	Beneficiary tax offset
BTWG	Business Tax Working Group
CA	*Customs Act 1901*
CCIV	Corporate collective investment vehicle
CFC	Controlled foreign corporation
CFE	Controlled foreign entity
CGC	Commonwealth Grants Commission
CGT	Capital gains tax
CLR	Commonwealth Law Reports
COAG	Council of Australian Governments
COT	Continuity of ownership test
CPB	Capital protected borrowing
CPI	Consumer Price Index
CR	Class Ruling
CRS	Common reporting standard
CSF	Crowd source funding
CTA	*Customs Tariff Act 1995*
DA	*Domicile Act 1982*
DASP	Departing Australia superannuation payment
DBTP	Death benefit termination payment
DGTO	Digital games tax offset
DICTO	Dependant invalid and carer tax offset
DIS	Decision Impact Statement
DPP	Director of Public Prosecutions
DPT	Diverted profits tax
DTA	Double Taxation Agreement
EA	*Excise Act 1901*
ECCT	Excess concessional contributions tax
EDCI	Eligible designated concession income
ENCCT	Excess non-concessional contributions tax
ERF	Emissions Reduction Fund
ESIC	Early stage innovation company
ESS	Employee share scheme
ESVCLP	Early stage venture capital limited partnership
ETA	*Excise Tariff Act 1921*
ETBT	Excess transfer balance tax
ETP	Employment termination payment
ETS	Emissions trading scheme
EU	European Union
EVCI	Eligible venture capital investment
FATCA	*Foreign Account Tax Compliance Act*
FBT	Fringe benefits tax
FBTA	*Fringe Benefits Tax Act 1986*

FBTAA	*Fringe Benefits Tax Assessment Act 1986*
FBTACA	*Fringe Benefits Tax (Application to the Commonwealth) Act 1986*
FC of T	Federal Commissioner of Taxation
FCR	Federal Court Reports
FDT	Franking deficit tax
FIF	Foreign investment fund
FITO	Foreign income tax offset
FLA	*Family Law Act 1975*
FLP	Foreign life assurance policy
FMD	Farm Management Deposit
FRE	Forex realisation event
FRG	Forex realisation gain
FRL	Forex realisation loss
FTC	Foreign tax credit
G20	Group of 20 Finance Ministers and Central Bank Governors
GDP	Gross domestic product
GFC	Global financial crisis
GIC	General interest charge
GloBE	Global anti-base erosion
GST	Goods and services tax
GST Regs	*A New Tax System (Goods and Services Tax) Regulations 2019*
GSTA	*A New Tax System (Goods and Services Tax) Act 1999*
GSTD	Goods and Services Tax Determination
GSTICA	*A New Tax System (Goods and Services Tax Imposition—Customs) Act* 1999
GSTIEA	*A New Tax System (Goods and Services Tax Imposition—Excise) Act 1999*
GSTIGA	*A New Tax System (Goods and Services Tax Imposition—General) Act 1999*
GSTR	Goods and Services Tax Ruling
GSTTA	*A New Tax System (Goods and Services Tax Transition) Act 1999*
HELP	Higher Education Loans Program
HESA	*Higher Education Support Act 2003*
HFE	Horizontal fiscal equalisation
IAS	Instalment Activity Statement
ICIJ	International Consortium of Investigative Journalists
ID	Interpretative Decision
IGT	Inspector-General of Taxation
IGTO	Inspector-General of Taxation and Taxation Ombudsman
IIR	Income inclusion rule
IISA	Industry Innovation and Science Australia
IMF	International Monetary Fund
IMR	Investment manager regime
IPO	Initial public offering
IRDA	*Industry Research and Development Act 1986*
IRS	Internal Revenue Service
ISA	Innovation and Science Australia
IT	Income Tax Ruling
ITA	*Income Tax Act 1986*
ITAA22	*Income Tax Assessment Act 1922*
ITAA36	*Income Tax Assessment Act 1936*

ITAA97	*Income Tax Assessment Act 1997*
ITAR15	*Income Tax Assessment (1936 Act) Regulation 2015*
ITAR21	*Income Tax Assessment (1997 Act) Regulations 2021*
ITC	Input tax credit
ITDIRWTA	*Income Tax (Dividends, Interest and Royalties Withholding Tax) Act 1974*
ITRA	*Income Tax Rates Act 1986*
ITTPA	*Income Tax (Transitional Provisions) Act 1997*
ITZ	Indirect tax zone
JITSIC	Joint International Tax Shelter Information Centre
LBTP	Life benefit termination payment
LCBTO	Loss carry back tax offset
LCR	Law Companion Ruling
LCT	Luxury car tax
LCTA	*New Tax System (Luxury Car Tax) Act 1999*
LCTICA	*A New Tax System (Luxury Car Tax Imposition—Customs) Act 1999*
LCTIEA	*A New Tax System (Luxury Car Tax Imposition—Excise) Act 1999*
LCTIGA	*A New Tax System (Luxury Car Tax Imposition—General) Act 1999*
LIC	Listed investment company
LITO	Low-income tax offset
LLC	Limited liability company
LTBR	Long-term bond rate
MAP	Mutual agreement procedure
MBLA	*Major Bank Levy Act 2017*
MEC	Multi-entry consolidated
MIS	Managed investment scheme
MIT	Managed investment trust
ML	Medicare levy
MLA	*Medicare Levy Act 1986*
MLI	*Multilateral Convention to Implement Tax Treaty Related Measures to Prevent Base Erosion and Profit Shifting*
MLS	Medicare levy surcharge
MLSFBA	*A New Tax System (Medicare Levy Surcharge—Fringe Benefits) Act 1999*
MNE	Multinational enterprise
MRRT	Minerals resource rent tax
MRRTA	*Minerals Resource Rent Tax Act 2012*
MT	Miscellaneous Taxation Ruling
NAI	Notional attributable income
NFRC	National Federation Reform Council
NRAS	National Rental Affordability Scheme
NSW	New South Wales
NT	Northern Territory
NZLR	New Zealand Law Reports
OBU	Offshore banking unit
OECD	Organisation for Economic Cooperation and Development
OECD MTC	OECD *Model Tax Convention on Income and on Capital*
PAYG	Pay As You Go
PDF	Pooled development fund
PDV	Post, digital and visual

PE	Permanent establishment
PR	Product Ruling
PRRT	Petroleum resource rent tax
PRRTAA	*Petroleum Resource Rent Tax Assessment Act 1987*
PRRTICA	*Petroleum Resource Rent Tax (Imposition—Customs) Act 2012*
PRRTIEA	*Petroleum Resource Rent Tax (Imposition—Excise) Act 2012*
PRRTIGA	*Petroleum Resource Rent Tax (Imposition—General) Act 2012*
PS LA	Practice Statement Law Administration
PSB	Personal services business
PSE	Personal services entity
PSI	Personal services income
PST	Pooled superannuation trust
PTG	Policy Transition Group
QAPE	Qualifying Australian production expenditure
QFA	Qualifying forex account
R&D	Research and development
RBA	Running balance account
RBL	Reasonable benefit limit
RBT	Review of Business Taxation
RPS	Redeemable preference shares
RSA	Retirement savings account
RSAA	*Retirement Savings Accounts Act 1997*
RSAR	*Retirement Savings Account Regulations 1997*
RSE	Registrable superannuation entity
RSPT	Resource super profits tax
SAM	Simplified accounting method
SAPTO	Seniors and pensioners tax offset
SBE	Small business entity
SBSCH	Small Business Superannuation Clearing House
SBT	Same business test
SCD	Superannuation Contributions Determination
SCR	Superannuation Contributions Ruling
SENCCTA	*Superannuation (Excess Non-Concessional Contributions Tax) Act 2007*
SETBTIA	*Superannuation (Excess Transfer Balance Tax) Imposition Act 2016*
SG	Superannuation guarantee
SGAA	*Superannuation Guarantee (Administration) Act 1992*
SGC	Superannuation guarantee charge
SGCA	*Superannuation Guarantee Charge Act 1992*
SGCLIEA	*Superannuation (Government Co-contribution for Low Income Earners) Act 2003*
SGD	Superannuation Guarantee Determination
SGR	Superannuation Guarantee Ruling
SHASA	Superannuation Holding Account Special Account
SISA	*Superannuation Industry (Supervision) Act 1993*
SISR	*Superannuation Industry (Supervision) Regulations*
SME	Small and medium sized enterprise
SMSF	Self managed superannuation fund
SMSFR	Self Managed Superannuation Funds Ruling
SR (NSW)	State Reports (New South Wales)

SSA	*Social Security Act 1991*
SSSCCIA	*Superannuation (Sustaining the Superannuation Contribution Concession) Imposition Act 2013*
STP	Single touch payroll
STTR	Subject to tax rule
TAA	*Taxation Administration Act 1953*
TAR17	*Taxation Administration Regulations 2017*
TASA	*Tax Agent Services Act 2009*
TBRL	Temporary budget repair levy
TCSA	Tax cost setting amount
TD	Taxation Determination
TFN	Tax file number
TIEA	Tax Information Exchange Agreement
TLIP	Tax Law Improvement Project
TOFA	Taxation of financial arrangements
TPB	Tax Practitioners Board
TPRS	Taxable Payments Reporting System
TR	Taxation Ruling
TSA	Tax sharing agreement
UN	United Nations
UN MTC	United Nations *Model Tax Convention Between Developed and Developing Countries*
UPE	Ultimate parent entity
US MTC	United States *Model Income Tax Convention*
UTPR	Undertaxed payment rule
VAT	Value added tax
VCA	*Venture Capital Act 2002*
VCLP	Venture capital limited partnership
VCMP	Venture capital management partnership
WET	Wine equalisation tax
WETA	*New Tax System (Wine Equalisation Tax) Act 1999*
WETICA	*A New Tax System (Wine Equalisation Tax Imposition—Customs) Act 1999*
WETIEA	*A New Tax System (Wine Equalisation Tax Imposition—Excise) Act 1999*
WETIGA	*A New Tax System (Wine Equalisation Tax Imposition—General) Act 1999*

ACKNOWLEDGEMENTS

The author and Cambridge University Press would like to thank the following for permission to reproduce material in this book.

Images on pages 831 and 832 © Board of Taxation and reproduced with permission. The Board of Taxation's report was published (and therefore these recommendations were developed) prior to the onset of the COVID-19 pandemic, and the Board notes that the extent to which these recommendations will be reflected in the proposed legislation is as yet undetermined.

Extracts from *Commonwealth Law Reports* (CLR): Reproduced with permission of Thomson Reuters (Professional) Australia Limited, legal.thomsonreuters.com.au.

Extracts from *Australian Tax Cases* (ATC), *Australian Tax Decisions* (ATD): Reproduced with permission of Wolters Kluwer.

Extracts from Australian Taxation Office: © Australian Taxation Office for the Commonwealth of Australia.

Extracts from The Board of Taxation, *Reforming Individual Tax Residency Rules—A Model for Modernisation* (2019), https://taxboard.gov.au/sites/taxboard.gov.au/files/migrated/2019/12/Tax-Residency-Report.pdf: © Commonwealth of Australian 2019, reproduced under Creative Commons Attribution 3.0 Australia (CC BY 3.0 AU), https://creativecommons.org/licenses/by/3.0/au/deed.en.

Extracts from the Australian Government (The Treasury), *Black Economy Taskforce: Interim Report—March 2017* (2017), https://treasury.gov.au/sites/default/files/2019-03/BE_IR.pdf: © Commonwealth of Australian 2017, reproduced under Creative Commons Attribution 3.0 Australia (CC BY 3.0 AU), https://creativecommons.org/licenses/by/3.0/au/deed.en.

Extracts from Australian Commonwealth legislation: Sourced from the Federal Register of Legislation. Reproduced under Creative Commons Attribution 4.0 International. For the latest information on Australian Government law please go to https://www.legislation.gov.au.

Every effort has been made to trace and acknowledge copyright. The publisher apologises for any accidental infringement and welcomes information that would redress this situation.

PART A

INTRODUCTION TO TAXATION AND AUSTRALIA'S TAX SYSTEM

1 TAXATION PRINCIPLES AND THEORY

[1.1] Introduction

Taxation is an ancient and ubiquitous concept that forms one of the central pillars around which civilisation has been built. In his 1925 treatise, *Taxation in Australia*, Stephen Mills noted that one of the certainties of history is that 'no structural society has ever arisen without taxation'. Taxation plays a critical role in society and has the capacity to affect the lives of everyone within it. As the United States Supreme Court observed in *Dobson v Commissioner* (1943) 320 US 489 (at 494–495): 'No other branch of law touches human activities at so many points'.

History vividly highlights that while taxation has brought great prosperity to nations, it has also fuelled bitter conflicts. Taxation can invoke passionate emotions in people about their rights and obligations and is a topic on which rational people often have diametrically opposed views. Ultimately, taxation is a powerful instrument that governments use to fund their activities and shape their economies. Without it, they would not be able to survive. While the features of taxation have evolved considerably over the years, taxation remains a fundamental characteristic of the modern nation state and an integral part of the overarching architecture that lies behind the economic systems of every developed country in the world. Its inescapable and pervasive nature was recognised long ago by Benjamin Franklin who famously wrote: 'In this world nothing can be said to be certain but death and taxes'.

What is taxation?

The *Oxford English Dictionary* defines a 'tax' as:

> A compulsory contribution to the support of government, levied on persons, property, income, commodities, transactions, etc.

One of the earliest Australian judicial pronouncements on the notion of taxation is found in *R v Barger* (1908) 6 CLR 41, where Griffith CJ, Barton and O'Connor JJ said (at 68):

> The primary meaning of 'taxation' is raising money for the purposes of government by means of contributions from individual persons.

Taxes come in a variety of forms and are also known by different names, such as duties, levies, tariffs and charges. The etymology of the word 'tax' can be traced to the Latin word *taxare*, meaning evaluate, estimate, or assess.

Taxation is the principal means by which governments raise revenue. Without taxation, governments would be unable to finance their operations or deliver the many public goods and services they provide to the community. Other ways that governments can raise revenue include:

- charging fees for rendering services or granting licences
- imposing fines for breaches of the law, and
- generating returns from their assets and investments.

Taxes are a special kind of impost that can be distinguished from fees and fines on the basis that they are imposed on the community at large and are not specifically connected with the receipt of any particular services, the granting of any special rights or privileges, or the breach of any law by the payer. Taxpayers are compelled by law to pay taxes and are obliged to do so even though they may not necessarily receive any direct benefits in return. In *Architecture of Australia's Tax and Transfer System*, the Australian Treasury recognised (at 11):

> A core characteristic of a tax is that there is no clear and direct link between the payment of the tax and the provision of goods and services to the taxpayer. The funds that the government raises from taxes may be used to provide goods or services to the community as a whole, and this may provide a benefit to the taxpayer, but the payment will still be considered a tax if there is no direct relationship between the amount of the payment and the benefit to the taxpayer.

Similar observations were made by the Australian Bureau of Statistics in *Australian System of Government Finance Statistics: Concepts, Sources and Methods*, where it is noted that although 'taxpayers expect provision of government services in return for the taxes they pay', there is 'usually no direct link between taxes paid by an individual taxpayer and the government services consumed by that taxpayer'.

What is taxation law?

Taxation law is the body of law that governs an entity's liability to pay tax to the government. It covers the rules that establish the incidence of tax and the tax base (ie who and what is subject to tax). It also extends to the rules relating to the administration and enforcement of the tax system, including the rules dealing with the collection and recovery of tax.

Australia, like other developed countries, has a vast body of taxation law. The primary source of this law is found in the many thousands of pages of tax legislation enacted by the Commonwealth, state and territory parliaments and the many hundreds of cases handed down by the courts and tribunals that have interpreted the statutory provisions over the years. Australia's extensive body of statute and common law is complemented by a broad array of administrative rulings, guidelines, and practice statements issued by the relevant revenue authorities.

Australia's taxation laws operate subject to the *Commonwealth Constitution* and the terms of its international treaties, including many Double Taxation Agreements ('DTAs') entered into with foreign countries.

Why study taxation law?

Taxation law is an extremely important and useful area of law to study, but is also incredibly challenging because of its voluminous nature, technical complexity and constant reform. Taxation law is particularly worth studying because of its wide social and economic impact and its practical relevance to all sorts of commercial transactions. It also raises interesting theoretical, ethical and philosophical issues, making it a discipline worth examining for purely academic purposes.

Taxation law does not operate in a vacuum. It intersects with many other areas of law, including aspects of commercial law, property law, corporate law and administrative law. Taxation is the major source of finance for most governments, and it affects all sorts of employment, business and investment dealings. In the commercial world, taxation is of great importance as it heavily influences the ways that entities are structured, investments are held and arrangements are financed. It is, frankly, impossible to properly appreciate how the government and the economy function without understanding basic notions of taxation. Each day, many millions of transactions are entered into that have taxation consequences.

Taxation is also a topical current affairs issue that features prominently in the media—stories relating to taxation appear frequently in daily newspapers and news broadcasts. The financial press, in particular, is peppered with articles on taxation. The pervasive nature of taxation means that it intrudes on many aspects of everyday life. It is therefore not surprising that people have strong and passionate views about taxation and that it is a perennial political issue that has the capacity to polarise public opinion. History vividly illustrates that taxation policies have the capacity to make or break governments and that good tax policies can lead to economic prosperity, while bad tax policies can result in social and political unrest.

On a personal level, having knowledge and skills in taxation law can be beneficial as it opens up many employment opportunities in the tax profession (in both the public and private sectors) as well as in related fields of law, accounting, business and finance. Understanding how the tax system works helps people run their businesses, plan their personal finances and comply with their reporting and other obligations under the law. Taxation awareness also provides people with a better appreciation of political and economic issues and enables them to engage more effectively in public debate in these areas.

What is the aim of this book?

This book introduces the policy, principles and practices that underpin the Australian tax system. It is designed to be used by students studying taxation law and as a general reference guide for taxation academics, researchers and practitioners. The aim of the book is to explain the foundations of Australian taxation law in a clear, concise, straightforward and structured manner without oversimplifying the law or avoiding discussion of complex concepts that have important practical ramifications.

More than 100 different taxes are levied in Australia. This book focuses on Commonwealth taxes, particularly income tax, goods and services tax ('GST'), fringe benefits tax ('FBT') and a range of superannuation taxes. It also touches on some of the main state, territory and local government taxes.

Although the book is designed as a legal text, it does not just present the reader with a bunch of technical rules. The objective is to place taxation law in its proper commercial context and to synthesise the legal analysis with discussion of related social, political, economic and policy issues. By weaving in these broader perspectives, taxation law can be better understood, and its practical relevance better appreciated.

How is this book structured?

This book is divided into 13 parts, consisting of 41 chapters. Each chapter commences with a broad introduction to the topics covered, followed by a detailed discussion of the core legal principles. Although the chapters deal with discrete topics, they are closely linked and comprehensively cross-referenced to show how the rules interrelate. The chapters are peppered with diagrams, tables and examples to synthesise the law, explain complex concepts and illustrate practical situations. There is also a set of questions at the end of each chapter that test many of the key issues covered.

The book is supported by online resources, available on the Cambridge University Press Higher Education website at www.cambridge.org/highereducation/isbn/9781009458832/resources. Student resources are freely available and include a list of references to selected government reports, taxation rulings, books and articles for those interested in conducting further research. In addition, a set of over 1,000 PowerPoint slides that are directly cross-referenced to topics covered in the chapters are available to lecturers who use the book, along with answers and worked examples to all end-of-chapter questions.

Conceptual framework for studying taxation law

Before launching into a detailed examination of how Australia's tax system works, it is useful to first establish a conceptual framework for studying taxation law. In particular, it is important to recognise the historical setting in which taxes have operated and the kinds of taxes that have been levied by governments over the years. It is also important to understand the basic structural features of taxes as well as the jurisdictional constraints and international settings in which they operate. As taxation has wide-ranging social, political, economic and policy dimensions, these aspects also need to be considered in parallel with any legal analysis. This chapter canvasses some of these broader issues and lays the theoretical foundations for the detailed technical discussion contained in the rest of the book.

[1.2] Historical background

Taxation is deeply rooted in history. Records of taxation date back in antiquity to the times of the earliest civilisations. Evidence of taxation can be found on an inscription on an ancient Sumerian tablet from the city of Lagash (located in what is now Iraq) which warns: 'You can have a Lord, you can have a King, but the man to fear is the tax collector'. The Bible also contains many notable references to taxation. The following passage from Paul's *Epistle to the Romans* (13:7–8) is a good example:

> Pay to all what is owed to them: taxes to whom taxes are owed, revenue to whom revenue is owed, respect to whom respect is owed, honour to whom honour is owed.

While it is impossible to precisely determine when the first taxes commenced to be levied, it is clear that by the times of the ancient Egyptians, taxation was already well established in society. During the reign of the Pharaohs, taxes were collected by public officials, called *scribes*, on behalf of the Pharaoh's chief minister, known as the *vizier*. Taxes were paid in kind and levied on items such as grains from harvests, livestock and cooking oil. The ancient Egyptians also paid taxes with their own labour by working on construction projects like the pyramids and serving in the army.

In ancient Greece, the concept of benefaction was deeply rooted in society and the wealthy proudly made voluntary payments, known as *liturgies*, to fund public projects. In times of crisis, such as war, an additional wealth tax, known as *eisphorá*, was levied. The ancient Greeks also collected customs duties at their harbours and levied excise duties on products such as olive oil. They also paid taxes on their slaves and levied a per capita 'poll tax', known as *metoikion*, on foreigners.

The ancient Chinese also had their own unique tax system. Various kinds of agriculture, land and poll taxes were imposed during the Shang, Zhou, Qin and Han dynasties. It was usually the role of local magistrates, who were appointed by the imperial court, to collect taxes in their regions. Like the ancient Egyptians, the ancient Chinese also paid taxes with their labour by working on projects like the Great Wall and providing military service to their emperors.

During the Roman Empire, customs duties (*portoria*), sales taxes (*centesima rerum venalium*), land taxes (*tributum soli*) and poll taxes (*tributum capitis*) all featured prominently. In addition, there were also inheritance taxes (*vicesima hereditatium*) and taxes on owners who freed their slaves (*vicesima libertatis*). Taxation was largely decentralized and many early taxes were collected by *publicani* who were professional 'tax farmers' that bid at auctions for the right to collect taxes in the provinces and had the right to retain any excess for themselves.

In medieval England, the main taxes were property taxes, such as the *geld* and *tallage*, and death and inheritance taxes, such as the *heriot* and *relief*. These taxes were imposed alongside other peculiar feudal taxes, such as the *scutage* (which was payable by knights to commute military service owed to their lords) and the *merchet* (which was payable by serfs for a woman's right to marry). The famous *Domesday Book*, commissioned by William the Conqueror in 1086, was the first recorded survey of property holdings in England and was expressly undertaken for the purpose of assessing taxes.

Although taxes are nowadays usually paid in money, this has not always been the case, especially before the wide use of currency as a medium of exchange. In the Middle Ages, for example, it was common for peasants to pay taxes by contributing a percentage of their crops and agricultural produce to their landlords. This often left the poor with little to live off and even led to uprisings like the English Peasants Revolt of 1381. It also contributed to the creation of legendary stories, such as that of Robin Hood who, with his Merry Men from Sherwood Forest, stole back taxes collected by the Sheriff of Nottingham so that they could be returned to the poor. Another well-known tale is that of Lady Godiva who rode naked on horseback through the centre of town to persuade her husband, Leofric, the Earl of Mercia, to lower taxes on the people of Coventry.

During the Middle Ages, taxes were also levied by religious orders. The ancient *tithe*, which can trace its origins back to biblical times, is an example of such a tax. This tax derives its name from the old English word for 'one-tenth', as it originally involved a contribution of one-tenth of a person's earnings (usually taken from the produce from their land). People who did not pay the *tithe* to the Catholic Church were at risk of excommunication. While nowadays it is usually only governments that raise taxes, it is interesting to note that religious taxes still exist in some places. An example is the *Kirchenbeitrag* levied by the Catholic Church on its members in Austria.

Over the years, almost every kind of product has been taxed in some form or another, including even the most basic commodities, such as sugar and salt. The fact that taxes can be imposed on virtually anything is vividly illustrated by bizarre taxes such as the urine tax (*vectigal urinae*), which was first imposed by the Roman emperor Nero, and later his successor Vespasian, in the first century AD. Urine was a valuable commodity as it contained ammonia and could be used in a number of chemical processes, including cleaning garments, tanning leather and fertilizing crops. The tax was payable on the purchase of urine collected from public sewers. Vespasian's son, Titus, allegedly criticised his father for imposing such a disgusting tax, to which his farther famously responded by holding up a gold coin and remarking '*pecunia non olet!*' (money does not stink!).

Another colourful illustration of an unusual tax is the beard tax levied in Russia during the time of Peter the Great. The tax required men to pay for the right to have a beard and was part of the Tsar's efforts in modernising Russian society to fit more into line with Western Europe. A token was issued to those who paid the tax (which could be as high as 100 rubles for wealthy merchants). Those who refused to pay the tax or produce a token could be forcibly shaved in public.

The English window tax levied between 1696 and 1851 is yet another peculiar tax. The tax was imposed on property owners and was payable at rates that varied according to the number of windows in a dwelling. The aim was to tax the wealthy, who were more likely to have larger houses with more windows. Critics, however, cynically viewed it as a tax on daylight, and some property owners simply bricked up their windows to avoid the tax. Earlier on, between 1662 and 1689, a hearth tax (also known as a 'chimney tax') was levied in England at the rate of two shillings for every hearth or stove in a dwelling. The origins of the hearth tax date back to the Byzantine Empire where a similar tax, known as *kapnikon*, was levied on households.

History contains many examples that demonstrate the effects taxation can have on behaviour. A good illustration is the Dutch property tax levied during the 16th and 17th centuries, which was calculated according to the width of buildings. Not surprisingly, this led to the construction of many narrow multi-storey houses that are characteristic of the ones still seen today alongside the canals in Amsterdam.

It is fascinating to note that there have even been great archaeological discoveries related to taxation. The most notable example is the famous Rosetta Stone discovered by a French soldier serving under Napoleon near the Nile. The Rosetta Stone, which has been prominently displayed at the British Museum since the early 1800s, contains inscriptions in Egyptian hieroglyphics, Demotic script and ancient Greek. The inscriptions were the key to deciphering hieroglyphics, which ultimately unveiled to the modern world many of the hidden mysteries of ancient Egypt. Less well known, however, is the fact that the Rosetta Stone contained a decree recording a tax immunity granted by King Ptolemy V to the priesthood. This led Alvin Rabushka from the Hoover Institute at Stanford University to quip: 'Which is why, of course, it was engraved in stone and not written on papyrus.'

[1.3] Kinds of taxes

Income tax

The most important and widely imposed modern tax is income tax. As its name suggests, income tax is a tax on income (ie earnings). Income tax was first introduced in Great Britain in 1799 by Prime Minister William Pitt to fund the war against Napoleon. The tax was repealed for a short time in the early 1800s following the signing of the *Treaty of Amiens*. However, renewed fighting resulted in Henry Addington, who had replaced William Pitt as Prime Minister, reintroducing income tax in 1803. Income tax continued to be levied until 1816 (one year after Napoleon's defeat by the Duke of Wellington at the Battle of Waterloo). It was subsequently reintroduced for budgetary reasons in 1842 by Robert Peel and it has continued to be levied in the United Kingdom ever since.

The introduction of income tax was radical and controversial at the time. Taxing income was regarded by many as an inappropriate intrusion by government into the personal affairs of its citizens, and was criticised as being a tax on the fruits of labour that discouraged work. Despite these objections, income tax was found to be an effective and practical way to raise revenue. Personal income tax is now levied by almost every country in the world (some notable exceptions include the Bahamas, the United Arab Emirates, the Cayman Islands, Oman, Qatar, Monaco, Brunei and Vanuatu).

One of the first countries to follow the United Kingdom in imposing income tax was the United States, which levied income tax from 1862 to 1872 to pay for the Civil War. Congress reintroduced income tax in 1894. However, the United States Supreme Court held in *Pollock v Farmers' Loan & Trust Co* (1895) 157 US 429 that the legislation imposed a 'direct tax' and therefore breached the provisions of the Constitution, which required direct taxes to be apportioned among the states. This eventually led to the *Sixteenth Amendment to the Constitution* in 1913, which allows Congress to levy income tax without apportionment among the states. Income tax is the bedrock of the United States tax system and has been the largest single source of federal revenue for many decades. Income tax is also levied by more than 40 states and is, subject to certain limitations, generally allowed as a deduction in calculating federal income tax.

In Australia, income tax was introduced by the Commonwealth in 1915 to support the country's World War I effort. Earlier on, the colonies (which subsequently became the states) had already introduced their own income taxes. The Commonwealth and the states levied income tax in parallel until the middle of World War II, when the Commonwealth took over the income tax field as a consequence of the introduction of its Uniform Tax Scheme [4.2]. Ever since, income tax has remained Australia's major source of federal tax revenue.

Although Australia was influenced by the United Kingdom's income tax laws, Australia did not adopt the United Kingdom's 'schedular' model for its legislation. Under the United Kingdom legislation amounts were only taxed if they fell within one of six schedules. The schedules covered items such as rents from land and buildings (sch A), farming profits (sch B), interest and annuities from public funds (sch C), trading and professional profits and income not covered by the other schedules (sch D), employment income, annuities and pensions (sch E) and dividend income (sch F). Each schedule had its own computation rules. As a result, different rates of tax could be charged on different categories of income, and deductions relating to one category of income could not be applied against income of another category.

By contrast, Australia's income tax legislation does not use schedules to assess taxpayers. Instead, income tax is simply levied on a taxpayer's 'taxable income', which is calculated as the taxpayer's 'assessable income' less 'deductions' [8.4]. Different rates of tax do not apply to different categories of income and there are no general quarantining rules which specify that deductions relating to particular categories of income can only be applied against income of the same category. Australia's income tax legislation is therefore based on a 'global' model, as it generally allows all kinds of income and deductions to be set off against each other. For historical and constitutional reasons, Australia's income tax laws are not all contained in one Act. Instead, there are several distinct pieces of income tax legislation, including the *Income Tax Assessment Act 1997* ('*ITAA97*') and the *Income Tax Assessment Act 1936* ('*ITAA36*'), which determine how a taxpayer's taxable income is calculated, and the *Income Tax Act 1986* ('ITA') and the *Income Tax Rates Act 1986* ('*ITRA*'), which impose income tax and set out the rates of tax payable [8.2].

Despite the underlying structural differences between the Australian and United Kingdom income tax legislation, Australia has nevertheless borrowed certain concepts from the United Kingdom. Most importantly, like the United Kingdom, Australia distinguishes between 'income' and 'capital' amounts, and the Australian courts have drawn considerably on the United Kingdom jurisprudence in this area to help characterise various receipts. Australia also followed the United Kingdom in introducing a statutory CGT regime, which forms an integral part of its overarching income tax system [17.1].

Consumption taxes

In addition to income tax, most countries also impose some form of consumption tax. A consumption tax is a tax whose economic incidence falls on the consumer (eg through the increased cost of goods or services). It is the antithesis of income tax, as it taxes consumption rather than earnings.

The most widely encountered consumption tax is value added tax ('VAT'). VAT was first imposed in France in 1954 and has been adopted throughout the European Union ('EU'). It is a requirement for EU membership that Member States impose VAT at a minimum rate of at least 15% (reduced rates are allowed for certain supplies).

Australia began to levy its own version of VAT, known as goods and services tax ('GST'), on 1 July 2000 [7.1]. Interestingly, it was the last of the Organisation for Economic Cooperation and Development ('OECD') countries to do so (apart from the United States, which still does not have a VAT/GST).

VAT/GST is directed at taxing the value that has been added to the supply of goods and services. Registered entities (which include most entities that carry on business) charge VAT/GST on supplies they make and are generally allowed credits for VAT/GST charged on their acquisitions. The cost of VAT/GST is ultimately borne by end consumers who are not registered and, therefore, not entitled to credits for the VAT/GST charged on their acquisitions.

VAT/GST may be contrasted with sales tax, which is a much older and more traditional form of consumption tax. Sales tax is imposed on the sale of goods and is payable by the seller, who adds the tax to the price charged for the goods so that the burden of the tax is ultimately passed on to the purchaser. In the United States, many states impose retail sales tax. To ensure that this tax is charged only on retail sales and not on wholesale sales, registered persons who acquire goods for resale (ie not for their own consumption) provide a resale certificate to the seller, which enables them to acquire the goods free of sales tax.

In 1930, Australia introduced a wholesale sales tax. The tax was levied at the last point of wholesale sale of goods (eg from wholesaler to retailer). From the point of view of end consumers, wholesale sales tax was a 'hidden tax', as it was charged by wholesalers rather than retailers. The cost of the tax was nevertheless embedded in the price of the goods charged by retailers. As a result of the introduction of GST, wholesale sales tax was repealed from 1 July 2000. One of the main reasons for replacing sales tax with GST was that GST is levied on a much broader base, as it applies to the supply of goods and services (not just to the sale of goods).

Other taxes

A wide range of other kinds of taxes are also levied around the world. For example, many countries impose customs duties (on the importation and exportation of goods) and excise duties (on the production and manufacture of goods).

It is also common for countries to levy land taxes (on the ownership of real estate) and estate duties (on the assets of deceased estates). These taxes are forms of wealth taxes as they are levied on the value of a person's property. There are also several kinds of employment taxes, including payroll taxes (on the payment of wages) and fringe benefits taxes (on the provision of non-salary remuneration). In addition, there are many varieties of transactional taxes, such as stamp duties (on the execution of certain documents), gambling taxes (on betting at casinos, races and lotteries), financial taxes (on bank deposits and withdrawals), bed taxes (on accommodation provided in hotels) and road taxes (on the use of highways).

Some countries also impose taxes on profits from the exploitation of their natural resources. In 1987, Australia introduced a petroleum resource rent tax ('PRRT') on profits from petroleum projects [4.3]. In 2012, the Gillard Labor Government introduced a minerals resource rent tax ('MRRT') on profits from iron ore and coal mining projects [5.6]. At the same time, it also introduced a carbon tax on large greenhouse gas emitters to combat climate change [5.6]. The Abbott Liberal–National Coalition Government, however, abolished both the MRRT and carbon tax in 2014.

Mix of taxes

As each nation has the sovereign right to determine its own tax system, virtually anything can be made the subject of taxation. In *R v Barger* (1908) 6 CLR 41, Griffith CJ, Barton and O'Connor JJ recognised (at 68):

> The power to tax necessarily involves the power to select the subjects of taxation. In the case of things the differentiation or selection is, in practice, usually made by reference to objective facts or attributes of the subject matter, so that all persons or things possessing those attributes are liable to the tax. The circumstance that goods come from abroad or from a particular foreign country, or that particular processes or persons have been employed in their production, or that they possess certain ingredients, are instances of attributes which have been chosen for the purpose of differentiation.

Ultimately, each country determines who and what it subjects to tax and the particular attributes of its tax system. Each country inevitably adopts its own mix of taxes designed to suit its particular needs and circumstances. While there are many similarities between tax systems around the world, there are also many differences in the ways that taxes can operate, making each country's tax system unique.

[1.4] Functions of taxation

Taxation's revenue-raising function

The most important and immediately recognisable role of taxation is its revenue-raising role. It is widely acknowledged that without taxation, a government would not be able to properly function. As the United States Supreme Court said in *Nicol v Ames* (1899) 173 US 509 (at 515):

> The power to tax is the one great power upon which the whole national fabric is based. It is as necessary to the existence and prosperity of a nation as is the air he breathes to a natural man. It is not only the power to destroy, but the power to keep alive.

At the most basic level, taxes redirect economic resources from citizens to governments for use in their spending programs. Taxation therefore involves diverting wealth from the private sector to the public sector. Governments use revenue raised from taxes to fund the public service and defence force, to provide a legal system and law enforcement, to construct roads and airports, to run hospitals and education institutions, and to pay social security benefits. Without taxation, governments could not provide their citizens with the many kinds of goods and services that they have come to expect. Government spending is often justified on the basis that in a capitalist society, certain 'merit' goods and services may not necessarily be adequately provided by the free-market, and it is therefore both necessary and appropriate for the government to intervene and provide these things to make society a better place.

Taxation's social and political functions

It is important to understand that taxation is a powerful political engineering device that governments can use as either a 'carrot' or a 'stick' to promote their objectives. For instance, in Australia, the Federal Government provides a range of tax concessions under various 'tax expenditure programs' [1.5] to encourage particular kinds of investment, such as private retirement savings under the superannuation regime [19.1]. On the other hand, it imposes excise duties on cigarettes, not only to raise revenue, but also to discourage smoking and thereby reduce the nation's health costs. Similarly, it imposes the MLS on high-income earners who do not have private health insurance to encourage them to take out appropriate cover in order to lessen the burden on the publicly funded health system [8.8]. The benefit of a concession or the burden of taxation can thus be a useful tool in sculpting social behaviour.

Taxation's economic functions

Taxation also has important microeconomic ramifications. For instance, taxing particular goods adds to their cost, making them more expensive than similar kinds of untaxed goods. Taxation can therefore be used to modify consumer behaviour by encouraging spending on one product rather than another. Governments around the world have frequently used taxation to protect their domestic industries by taxing imported goods more heavily than locally produced goods. This provides the local goods with a competitive advantage over the imported goods which, in turn, encourages spending on local products. A government's ability to tax goods will, of course, be subject to its obligations under any international agreements it has entered into (eg under the World Trade Organization's General Agreement on Tariffs and Trade).

Governments also often use taxation as a macroeconomic device to speed up or slow down their countries' economies. Higher taxation usually leads to less spending as taxpayers have less disposable income. This typically has a deflationary effect on the economy. Lower taxation, on the other hand, usually results in increased spending as taxpayers have more disposable income. This, in turn, can have an inflationary effect on the economy.

Taxation's redistribution function

Taxation can also operate as a mechanism for creating economic equality between citizens. It can be used by governments to make their citizens richer or poorer. A tax system that taxes the rich so that the government can give to the poor promotes a more egalitarian society, redistributing wealth among citizens, which can result in a more level 'playing field'.

A more cynical way of looking at taxation is that it is simply a form of state-based confiscation which interferes with individual freedoms and rights. Some people complain that they pay a lot of tax, but get little direct benefits in return from the government. However, this kind of argument fails to recognise the fact that taxation enables a government to provide a range of services that can benefit society as a whole, and therefore make the state a better place to live. For instance, although some taxpayers might not directly use the public health system, they indirectly benefit from it as other members of society are cared for and public health, in general, is protected. Likewise, people without children should not complain that their taxes are being used to fund schools and universities, as public education has broad-ranging spillover benefits for the community.

Without taxation, living conditions within a country would be quite different. It would be up to each person to provide for themselves, since no one could rely on state-funded goods and services. Society would be more polarised, and wealth more concentrated. Those less able to support themselves would suffer, and the community as a whole would arguably be worse off.

Perspectives on taxation

Ultimately, taxation is one of the greatest powers a government has over its citizens. From a government's perspective, taxation enables the state to benefit from the fortunes of its citizens and the enterprises that they carry on. From a citizen's perspective, taxation is a cost of undertaking transactions, owning property, carrying on business and earning income. While taxation is one of the major factors that can affect a citizen's wealth, it also pays for the privileges associated with the kind of society in which they live. Accordingly, although taxation has been cynically described by some as a form of 'legalised robbery', it is more appropriate to view taxation, as Sabine observed in *A Short History of Taxation*, as 'part of the price of civilisation'. In the words of Justice Oliver Wendell Holmes (Jr) in *Compania General de Tabacos De Filipinas v Collector of Internal Revenue* (1927) 275 US 87 (at 100): 'Taxes are what we pay for civilized society.'

[1.5] Tax expenditures

In addition to its obvious revenue-raising function, governments also use their tax systems to provide incentives and financial assistance. Professor Surrey, in his seminal work, *Pathways to Tax Reform: The Concept of Tax Expenditures*, identified this aspect of the tax system as the system of 'tax expenditures'. Surrey recognised that tax systems contain two conceptually and functionally distinct components. One of these comprises the provisions that make up the 'normative tax structure' (ie the 'benchmark tax system' for collecting revenue) and the other comprises the provisions designed to effect government spending (ie the system of 'tax expenditures').

Tax expenditures may in turn be divided into two broad categories:

- 'tax incentives' (designed to induce certain activities or behaviour), and
- 'tax concessions' (designed to provide welfare assistance to those in need).

Tax expenditures are deviations from the benchmark tax system that are designed to benefit targeted taxpayers. They can be delivered in a number of ways. For instance, under the income tax system, tax expenditures may be provided to taxpayers by granting them special tax exemptions, tax deductions, tax offsets or reduced tax rates [27.1]. In addition, taxpayers may be provided with timing benefits. For example, they may be allowed to defer bringing income to account until a future year or be allowed to bring forward deductions into the current year. They may also be granted additional time to pay tax, allowing them more time to use the money they have earned.

Tax expenditure reporting

The Commonwealth Government has traditionally published annual *Tax Benchmarks and Variations Statements* (formerly known as *Tax Expenditures Statements*). In 2023, it published its *Tax Expenditures and Insights Statement*. These publications provide detailed information on the Government's tax expenditures as required under s 16 of the *Charter of Budget Honesty Act 1998*. They are designed to increase transparency and allow greater scrutiny of the tax system. In particular, they provide data on tax benchmarks and variations to such benchmarks. Tax benchmarks represent the standard taxation treatments that apply to similar taxpayers or activities. Special tax treatments may give rise to a positive or negative variation from the benchmark. A positive variation reduces tax payable relative to the benchmark. A negative variation increases tax payable relative to the benchmark. Tax incentives and concessions are positive variations as they reduce the tax that would otherwise be payable by taxpayers under the benchmark tax system.

A 'revenue forgone' approach is generally used to measure the cost of positive variations. This approach essentially compares the difference in tax paid as a result of the provision of a particular tax concession relative to the tax that would have been paid under the benchmark tax system if the tax concession had not been available (assuming taxpayer behaviour remained unchanged). A 'revenue gain' approach is also sometimes used to measure the cost of certain tax concessions. This approach takes into account potential changes in taxpayer behaviour that would arise if a tax concession were abolished.

Tax expenditure programs

Over the years, tax expenditures have become more prevalent in Australia, and several intricate tax expenditure programs have been developed by the Federal Government. Some of the main tax expenditure programs examined in this book include:

- the superannuation program (which provides tax incentives to encourage retirement savings) [19.2]
- the early stage investors ('ESI'), pooled development fund ('PDF'), venture capital limited partnership ('VCLP') and early stage venture capital limited partnership ('ESVCLP') programs (which provide tax incentives to encourage venture capital investment) [27.2]–[27.4]
- the research and development ('R&D') program (which provides tax incentives to encourage research and development activities) [27.5], and
- the film production program (which provides tax incentives to encourage Australian film production) [27.6].

The rationale for introducing these programs is that they address market failures and promote private investment in areas considered to be publicly desirable.

Tax expenditures are also provided to support specific categories of taxpayers. For instance, to support farmers, the Government provides a range of tax incentives to people who carry on 'primary production businesses' [25.2]. Likewise, to support taxpayers who operate small businesses, a range of special tax concessions are provided to small business entities ('SBEs') [8.7].

Tax expenditures may also be used to achieve broader economic objectives. For example, to stimulate economic activity during the global financial crisis ('GFC') and the COVID-19 pandemic, the Government provided a range of temporary tax incentives [1.13].

Tax expenditures clearly come at a cost as governments collect less revenue from those taxpayers who benefit from the concessions. Australia's largest tax expenditures are the CGT main residence exemption [17.11] and the superannuation concessions [19.2]. Together, these concessions make up more than half the estimated cost of all Australia's tax expenditures.

Tax expenditures versus direct spending

It is important to realise that there is arguably no difference between providing tax concessions and providing subsidies or grants—both are forms of government spending. Collecting less tax because a concession is in place ultimately achieves the same result as collecting ordinary amounts of tax under the benchmark tax system and then redistributing the revenue as subsidies or grants. While the subsidy or grant is a 'direct' form of government spending, tax expenditures are an 'indirect' form of government spending.

Arguments for and against tax expenditure programs

Advocates of tax expenditure programs argue that they are efficient as they overcome 'double handling' issues (ie the government does not need to first collect tax and then distribute it as a subsidy or grant). Instead, the government simply collects less tax from those who enjoy the benefit of the relevant tax expenditure. However, others argue that such programs are often poorly targeted and can provide benefits to unintended recipients. In this regard, it is sometimes said that the tax law is a 'blunt' instrument for achieving a government's policy objectives.

Furthermore, where tax expenditures are provided in the form of income tax exemptions or deductions, the value of such concessions differs between taxpayers depending on their respective tax rates. Taxpayers subject to higher tax rates stand to benefit more than taxpayers on lower tax rates, and this produces what Surrey referred to as an undesirable 'upside-down effect'.

Another significant argument against tax expenditures is that they add considerably to the volume and complexity of the tax law. Tax expenditures create exceptions to general rules, and these exceptions inevitably increase the size of the tax legislation and reduce its simplicity. The fact that tax expenditures are 'hidden' in the tax legislation also means that they may be confused with the provisions that make up the benchmark tax system and may be overlooked when reforms are being considered. Many critics of tax expenditures argue that because they are embedded within the tax law, they are less visible and therefore often escape the same rigorous scrutiny that other government spending programs experience. As a consequence, their effectiveness in achieving policy objectives may not be as closely monitored and this can result in inefficient and costly programs remaining in existence.

[1.6] Structural features of taxes

Although taxes vary greatly in their design and coverage, most taxes share four basic structural features:

1. **Taxpayers**. Each tax regime subjects particular 'taxpayers' to tax. Taxpayers are the legal entities (eg individuals or companies) who are liable to pay the tax and who are penalised if it is not paid. In Australia, income tax is payable by 'income earners' [8.4], GST is payable by 'suppliers' and 'importers' [7.3] and FBT is payable by 'employers' [18.2].
2. **Tax base**. Each tax regime has its own 'tax base'. The tax base consists of some form of property, transaction, activity or concept upon which the tax is imposed. In Australia, income tax is

imposed on 'taxable income' [8.4], GST is imposed on 'taxable supplies' and 'taxable importations' [7.3] and FBT is imposed on 'fringe benefits taxable amounts' [18.2].

3. **Tax periods.** Each tax regime has its own 'tax periods'. Taxpayers are required to pay tax on amounts that fall within the tax base during the relevant period. The tax period can be of any length of time (eg a month, a quarter, or a year). In Australia, the income tax period is the 'income year' (ie the 'financial year'—1 July to 30 June) [8.3]. Monthly or quarterly tax periods apply in the case of GST [7.4]. An annual period that runs from 1 April to 31 March applies in respect of FBT [18.2].
4. **Tax rates.** Each tax regime has its own 'tax rates' which are applied to the relevant tax base. Depending on the nature of the tax and the kind of taxpayer involved, tax rates may be set at a single rate (ie flat rate) or at differing rates (eg rates that vary with the level of the tax base). In Australia, companies generally pay income tax at the flat rate of 30%, unless they are 'base rate entities', in which case they pay income tax at the flat rate of 25% [22.3]. Individuals, on the other hand, pay income tax at progressive 'marginal rates' of up to 45%, and they are also generally required to pay the Medicare levy at the rate of 2% ('ML') if they are residents [8.8]. GST is imposed at a flat rate of 10% [7.3]. FBT is imposed at a flat rate of 47% [18.2].

Proportional, progressive and regressive taxes

Taxes may be described as being either 'proportional', 'progressive' or 'regressive':

- **Proportional taxes.** These taxes (also known as 'flat' taxes) are imposed at the same rate on all taxpayers. In Australia, the GST is an example of a proportional tax—it is levied at a flat rate of 10%.
- **Progressive taxes.** These taxes are imposed at rates that increase with the amount of the tax base. In Australia, income tax is an example of a progressive tax—individuals pay income tax at rates that increase depending on the amount of their taxable income.
- **Regressive taxes.** These taxes are imposed at rates that decrease with the amount of the tax base and are quite rare.

Direct and indirect taxes

In describing taxes, economists often distinguish between 'direct' and 'indirect' taxes:

- **Direct tax.** A tax is a direct tax if the economic burden of the tax is borne by the person who pays the tax.
- **Indirect tax.** A tax is an indirect tax if the person who pays the tax is able to pass the economic burden of the tax on to third parties.

The cost of income tax is borne by the person who earns the income and is therefore a direct tax. In contrast, the cost of GST, although paid by the supplier of goods or services, is ultimately borne by the consumer through the increased price charged for those goods or services by the supplier and is therefore an indirect tax.

[1.7] Tax systems and national stability

The design of a country's tax system and the way taxation revenue is collected and redistributed reflect much about a country's values and the demands and expectations of its citizens. The amount of taxes collected from a citizen less the amount of benefits the citizen obtains from the redistribution of taxation revenue ultimately affects the citizen's wealth and prosperity. The 'tax-transfer' system therefore has a direct bearing on living standards.

In designing tax systems, governments obviously need to focus on ensuring that they collect the desired amount of revenue. However, they also need to consider a broad range of social, economic and political factors to ensure that this is done in the most effective way. As the Finance Minister of King Louis XIV, Jean Baptiste Colbert, cynically observed:

> The art of taxation consists in so plucking the goose as to obtain the largest amount of feathers with the least amount of hissing.

It is widely accepted that a country's tax system underpins its social, economic and political stability. Governments that impose taxes that are perceived to be 'unfair' are often faced with political strife. At the extreme, even wars have erupted over disputes about taxation. The famous phrase 'no taxation without representation' encapsulated the complaints of the American colonists in the mid-1700s. The colonists argued that taxes were imposed by Great Britain without their consent as they were not represented in the British Parliament. One of the events that sparked the American Revolution was the Boston Tea Party in 1773, which was a revolt against Great Britain over its import tariffs.

Taxation was also a contributing factor to the demise of the *Ancien Régime* in France, where the cost of wars and extravagant spending by the monarchy over the years had put pressure on the royal budget. During the *Ancien Régime*, society was divided into three classes: the 'first estate' (the clergy), the 'second estate' (the nobility) and the 'third estate' (the commoners). It was the third estate that bore the brunt of taxation, as the first and second estates were largely exempt from most taxes. One of the most unpopular taxes was the *taille*, which had been introduced by Charles VII in the fifteenth century to pay for the Hundred Years' War. The *taille* was a land tax payable by peasants and therefore fell disproportionately on the poorest members of society. French citizens were also subject to the *capitation*, which was a poll tax levied on all adults other than the clergy. Another unpopular tax was the *vingtième*, which was introduced by Louis XV in 1749 and levied at the rate one-twentieth of a person's income. The *taille*, *capitation* and *vingtième* were all abolished following the French Revolution in 1789.

The American and French Revolutions highlight how protests against taxation can spill over into civil unrest and result in great social change. Another famous example is the legendary Salt March led by Mahatma Gandhi in 1930. The march was an act of peaceful civil disobedience (*satyagraha*) against Britain's monopoly on the manufacture and sale of salt in India. Under the *Salt Act 1882*, Indians were forced to buy salt, which was subject to tax, from the colonial government even though salt was freely available from the sea. Gandhi and his followers marched over 200 miles from Sabarmati Ashram to Dandi on the Arabian Sea to protest against the tax. When he got to Dandi, Gandhi defiantly picked up some salty sand from the sea and proclaimed that with this act he was 'shaking the foundations of the British Empire'. The *satyagraha* encouraged others across India to defy the law and resulted in over 60,000 people, including Gandhi, being arrested. The Salt March was widely regarded as an important catalyst for uniting Indians and one of the first steps in paving the path to India's independence in 1947.

Events such as those described above demonstrate that governments need to take great care in who and what they decide to tax. History vividly highlights that it is in a government's interests to develop tax systems that are popular (or at least acceptable) in the eyes of the community that bears the burden of payment. There are many notable instances of unpopular taxes that have created problems for governments. A good illustration is the 'community charge' (better known as the 'poll tax') introduced by Britain's Conservative Government in the late 1980s. The poll tax was designed to fund local government and replaced a rates system imposed on the rental value of housing. It was imposed at a flat rate per person with some limited exemptions. The tax was viewed by a large portion of the British population as manifestly unfair, and it prompted mass protests and riots which ultimately contributed to Margaret Thatcher's resignation as Prime Minister in 1990.

Governments usually tread cautiously before introducing new taxes as politicians are acutely aware that taxation is unpopular. Ultimately, in democratic countries, it is the citizens who will have the last say about taxes as they have the power to vote governments out of office. As a general rule, the community will accept taxation more willingly if it sees the justification for a tax and considers that its level is appropriate and the burden is shared fairly among those who are liable to pay it. Although most citizens would naturally prefer to pay as little tax as possible, they have also come to expect a certain level of government services and generally accept that taxes play a critical role in funding such things.

[1.8] Australia's economy and the design of its tax system

Australia is a developed country that is known for its strong rule of law, stable political system and open economy. It is a member of the OECD and plays an active role in international forums, such as the G20, WTO and APEC. The country has enjoyed one of the highest living standards in the world and, until the outbreak of the COVID-19 pandemic, benefited from over 100 consecutive quarters of economic growth without a recession. Australia also traditionally performs well on many global indicators—it is ranked 5th in the United Nations' Human Development Index, 14th in the World Bank's Ease of Doing Business Rankings and 20th in the Central Intelligence Agency's GDP (Purchasing Power Parity) Rankings. It is also one of the few countries in the world that has a 'AAA' credit rating from all three major credit rating agencies (Standard & Poor's, Moody's and Fitch). The continuing challenge is to maintain these standards in the rapidly changing and competitive international economic environment.

Black swan events

Although Australia is widely regarded as a 'lucky country', it is a part of the global economy and can be exposed to 'black swan' events at any time. This has been vividly highlighted by the COVID-19 pandemic, which created a huge contraction in economic activity around the world and plunged many countries, including Australia, into recession in 2020. The pandemic created unprecedented global turmoil, resulted in national borders being closed and wiped off hundreds of billions of dollars from the value of international financial markets. International travel, trade and commerce came to a virtual halt, and many jobs were lost as businesses were shut down and supply and demand chains were disrupted. The unprecedented scale of the crisis forced many governments, including the Australian Government, to launch expensive stimulus packages to try to cushion the impact of the virus on their economies.

In its January 2021 *World Economic Outlook Update*, the International Monetary Fund ('IMF') described the COVID-19 pandemic as 'a crisis like no other' and estimated that global growth would contract by approximately 3.3% in 2020. Because of Australia's border closures, strict quarantining rules and geographic isolation, it was able to control exposure to the virus better than most countries. The disruption caused by the pandemic has, nevertheless, been profound.

In its April 2023 *World Economic Outlook Update*, the IMF projected that global growth would fall from 3.4% in 2022 to 2.8% in 2023 and then rise to 3.0% in 2024. Factors that have affected global growth include supply disruptions, lockdowns in China and significant inflation concerns. The IMF has nevertheless predicted that global inflation has peaked and it expects the rate to fall from 8.7% in 2022 to 7% in 2023 and then to 4.9% in 2024.

Even before the outbreak of the pandemic, the world economy was only just really recovering from the 2008 GFC. In Europe, countries such as Greece, Italy, Portugal and Spain have been struggling with high levels of debt. Banks have also generally been adopting tighter lending practices, making it harder for businesses to raise finance. Over the last couple of years, interest rates have been rising as central banks try to curb inflation brought about by a long period of low interest rates and quantitative easing policies. This has put added pressure on many borrowers and adds to the risk of a global recession. Despite the lessons learned from the GFC, recent events indicate that the world banking system is again showing signs of stress. In 2023, Silicon Valley Bank in the United States failed, and this sparked fears of further contagion which jittered financial markets.

International events, such as the United Kingdom's departure from the EU and the threat of trade wars, particularly between the United States and China, have also fuelled economic uncertainty. The war in Ukraine, which resulted in economic sanctions against Russia, spooked financial markets and added to recession fears. Not only has the war destabilised and fragmented the world economy, but it has also led to a humanitarian crisis. In addition, ongoing geopolitical tensions elsewhere in the world, such as in the Middle East, South China Sea, Korean Peninsula and Kashmir border continue to have the potential to result in flashpoints that can rapidly escalate and disrupt international markets and trade at any time.

Mining, tourism and education

Australia's economic future is inextricably entwined with international events and business and investment conditions. Its economic future will, no doubt, be heavily influenced by how its major trading partner, China, recovers from the COVID-19 pandemic and whether it can continue its trajectory of economic growth. Australia is rich in natural resources, such as iron ore, coal, natural gas, gold, silver, copper, nickel and zinc. Iron ore and coal, in particular, are Australia's leading exports, and the country therefore benefited greatly during the mining boom. Higher commodity prices leading up to 2008, fuelled particularly by demand from China, resulted in mining companies making increased profits, which translated into greater tax revenues from the mining industry. However, increased supply coupled with the economic slowdown caused by the GFC led to a subsequent weakening of commodity prices. Although the iron ore price regained some momentum during 2000 to 2022, it was showing signs of weakness again in mid-2023. It is therefore not clear whether a strong iron ore price is sustainable in the long term. A weakening economic growth outlook in China presents downside risk for commodity prices and this would have a negative effect on Australia's terms of trade. If commodity prices fall, Australia will not be able to continue to rely as heavily as it has in the past on revenue from mining companies to drive economic growth.

Australia's economic prosperity is also heavily dependent on tourism. Statistics from Tourism Australia indicate that in 2018/19, tourism directly employed 660,000 Australians (5% of the workforce) and was Australia's fourth-largest exporting industry. During this period, 9.3 million international visitors arrived in Australia and spent $44.6 billion. Australia's tourism industry was severely hit by the COVID-19 pandemic as international travel literally 'fell off a cliff'. In April 2019, there were 700,400 arrivals into Australia, whereas in April 2020 this figure dropped to 2,260, representing a staggering 99.7% fall. While Australia has reopend its borders, its tourism industry is still recovering from the effects of the pandemic.

Prior to the COVID-19 pandemic, Australia provided education to over 600,000 international students (Australian Government, *International Student Data*, April 2020). The pandemic affected international enrolments and placed pressures on education institutions that relied on overseas students for funding. The fall in international student numbers during the COVID-19 crisis resulted in job losses in the education sector and had damaging flow-on effects for the broader Australian economy. Fortunately, for the January–December 2022 period, Australia's international student numbers had risen to 619,371, which is 8% more than in the same period in the previous year (Australian Government, *International Student Data*, December 2022). As education is the country's fourth largest export, it is important to ensure that the country remains a key destination for international study in the wake of the crisis.

Science and technology

To succeed in the twenty-first century and stay ahead of many rapidly advancing developing countries, Australia needs to be a leading knowledge-based economy. Science and technology have become more important than ever and are key drivers of economic growth. As Innovation and Science

Australia noted in its 2018 report, *Australia 2030: Prosperity through Innovation—A Plan for Australia to Thrive in the Global Innovation Race*:

> Australia needs to find new sources of growth and improve productivity to maintain our standard of living. The biggest growth opportunities will come from knowledge intensive companies that innovate and export, as they are the most profitable, competitive and productive.

Although Australia has a reputation for being a 'clever country' with good universities and talented researchers that have developed many ground-breaking inventions and technologies, the reality is that it has often failed to capitalise on these opportunities. Many Australian discoveries end up being commercialised overseas with profits going offshore. Australia needs to ensure that its innovation ecosystem supports talented entrepreneurs to develop new businesses and commercialise their innovations. This requires investment in R&D and the development of a domestic venture capital market large enough to meet the financing needs of Australia's entrepreneurs. While Australia has attempted to address some of these challenges through various initiatives, such as the Turnbull Government's 2015 *National Innovation and Science Agenda* [5.7], it still has a long way to go to compete with thriving innovation hubs like Silicon Valley, New York, Shenzhen, Singapore and Tel Aviv.

Electronic economy

Australia, like many other countries, is also confronting the challenge of dealing with cross-border digital transactions. The electronic economy has become more important than ever and its growth comes with increasing challenges for digital security. Threats of cyberattacks and online scams are always lurking in the background. The electronic economy also places stresses on Australia's tax system and exposes it to the risk of revenue leakage. Technological developments contribute to the ease with which taxpayers can mobilise capital and transfer it offshore. Transactions involving cryptocurrencies, such as Bitcoin, cause particular concern because they are difficult to trace and can facilitate tax evasion and money laundering.

Ageing population

Like many other Western countries, Australia is also confronting the demographic challenges of an ageing population. An ageing population means a shrinking proportion of people in the workforce who are able to earn income and pay taxes and an increasing proportion of older people who are expected to live longer and require costly healthcare and welfare support. In its *2023 Intergenerational Report*, the Australian Government predicted that life expectancy at birth would increase from 81.3 years for men and 85.2 years for women in 2022/23 to 87.0 years for men and 89.5 years for women in 2062/63. The percentage of Australians aged 65 years and older is expected to rise from 17% in 2022/23 to 23% in 2062/63. At the same time, the proportion of the population participating in the workforce is projected to decline from 66.6% in 2022/23 to 63.8% in 2062/63.

Having an ageing population means that the Government needs to ensure that it has the right policies to encourage people to save for their retirement. If retirees do not have sufficient private savings, they will need to rely on public pensions for support. This can be extremely costly to provide and places additional pressure on the Government to raise taxes. Ensuring that Australia has an effective retirement income strategy is therefore critical. While Australia has a well-established and broad-based superannuation system, the reality is that many people approaching retirement do not have sufficient superannuation savings. Recent global shocks, such as the GFC and COVID-19 pandemic, have adversely affected superannuation savings making it harder for superannuation funds to generate returns, which jeopardises retirement lifestyles. At the same time, the cost of providing superannuation concessions to encourage retirement savings is expensive and the Government needs to ensure that the system remains fiscally sustainable.

Climate change

As Australia is the driest inhabited continent on the planet, it is also likely to incur significant costs in coping with climate change. Evidence of this is found in the 2019/20 'Black Summer' bushfire crisis (which burnt over 45 million acres of land and destroyed over 2,000 homes) and the 2022 NSW and Queensland floods (which resulted in over 25,000 homes and businesses being flooded). Adverse environmental and ecological issues can negatively impact many sectors, including agriculture, which supports a significant portion of the Australian workforce and is critical for the nation's food security and exports.

To combat climate change, the Labor Government is seeking to boost renewable energy so that Australia can transition from its dependence on fossil fuels. However, this transition will be challenging given that Australia has traditionally relied heavily on coal and gas for its energy needs. It is, nevertheless, critical in helping reduce Australia's greenhouse gas emissions and achieve its obligations under the Paris Agreement, which is a binding international treaty that came into force in 2016 and has been entered into by over 190 members of the United Nations Framework Convention on Climate Change. The goal of the Paris Agreement is to keep the rise in mean global temperature to well below 2°C above pre-industrial levels. The aim is to reach 'net-zero' emissions (ie a balance between greenhouse gas emissions produced and greenhouse gas emissions removed from the atmosphere) by 2050.

Infrastructure, housing, cost of living and employment

Being a large country with a population of only about 25 million people, Australia also faces unique challenges in maintaining and upgrading its vast national infrastructure. The cost of transporting goods as well as building roads, railways, ports, power grids, pipelines and communication systems is likely to be higher in Australia than in smaller, more densely populated countries. At the same time, housing affordability issues in the large capital cities where the population is concentrated place pressure on younger families who often struggle to acquire their first home.

Household debt in Australia has been increasing and rising interest rates during 2022 and 2023 have contributed to cost of living pressures, particularly for those people with large mortgages. Increased levels of unemployment during the peak of the COVID-19 crisis also placed great strains on the community and increased the risk of people defaulting on their loans. In its July 2020 *Economic and Fiscal Update*, the Government noted that 709,000 jobs were lost in the June 2020 quarter, and it forecast the unemployment rate to peak at around 9.25% in the December 2020 quarter. Fortunately, the 2021 Budget Papers revealed that thanks to the Government's $291 billion stimulus package, which included expensive subsidies like the fortnightly 'JobKeeper Payment' [6.3], Australia's employment levels were stronger than originally expected. This was subsequently confirmed in Australian Bureau of Statistics ('ABS') figures, which indicate that the unemployment rate for May 2023 was 3.5% (ABS, *Labour Force, Australia, May 2023*). This rate is even lower than the 5.1% rate in February 2020, immediately before the pandemic hit Australia. Unemployment reached its highest levels of 7.4% at the peak of the pandemic in mid-2020.

Government debt and fiscal sustainability

An important issue confronting Australia, like many other countries around the world, is that it has been facing rising levels of government debt. When the Rudd Labor Government was elected in 2007, it inherited a surplus of $39.958 billion from the Howard Coalition Government. However, over the Rudd and Gillard Labor Government periods, this surplus turned into a deficit. According to the 2023 Budget Papers, government net debt had reached $159.594 billion (10.4% of GDP) in 2012/13 and $209.559 billion (13.1% of GDP) in 2013/14. Net debt continued to grow during the Abbott, Turnbull and Morrison Coalition Government periods, with net debt rising from $245.817

billion (15.1% of GDP) in 2014/15 to $515.650 billion (22.3% of GDP) in 2021/22. Not surprisingly, the massive stimulus initiatives implemented by the Morrison Government to support the Australian economy during the COVID-19 crisis contributed significantly to this debt. The following table shows net debt levels and their percentage of Australia's GDP over recent years.

Financial Year	Net debt	Percentage of GDP
2012/13	$159.594 billion	10.4%
2013/14	$209.559 billion	13.1%
2014/15	$245.817 billion	15.1%
2015/16	$303.467 billion	18.3%
2016/17	$322.320 billion	18.3%
2017/18	$341.961 billion	18.6%
2018/19	$373.566 billion	19.2%
2019/20	$491.217 billion	24.8%
2020/21	$592.221 billion	28.5%
2021/22	$515.650 billion	22.3%
2022/23 (estimate)	$548.581 billion	21.6%

Bourgeoning net debt places Australia's 'fiscal sustainability' at risk. The *2023 Intergenerational Report* defines fiscal sustainability as 'the Government's ability to manage its finances so it can meet its spending commitments, now and in the future'. Fiscal sustainability is important for maintaining economic stability, improving economic performance and ensuring future generations do not inherit an unmanageable tax burden for government services provided to the current generation.

While Australia's net debt as a percentage of GDP is relatively moderate by international standards, it places pressure on future budgets. As Australia has a 'fiat currency' (ie a currency that is not backed by a commodity like gold), modern monetary theorists argue that it can simply repay its debt by 'printing money'. Mainstream macroeconomic theorists, however, criticise this approach saying that it devalues the currency and leads to inflation. They argue that the conventional and more prudent way for governments to address their debt issues is to either increase revenue through taxation or decrease spending.

Policy decisions affecting the design of Australia's tax system

The many issues and challenges outlined above need to be carefully considered in policy decisions affecting the design of the Australian tax system. In making these decisions, the threats of international tax competition also need to be taken into account. If Australia does not have an internationally competitive tax system, it will struggle to attract foreign investment, which is vital for providing capital to industry and generating employment. Many countries in the region have lower tax rates than Australia and offer generous investment incentives, which may encourage businesses to relocate overseas. At the same time, Australia needs to protect its tax base from international tax avoidance practices, especially those employed by large multinational enterprises that seek to divert their profits through tax havens. It therefore needs a robust tax system with rules that are difficult to circumvent coupled with effective enforcement measures to ensure that Australia collects its fair share of tax. Unless Australia has a 'good' tax system, living standards and the country's future economic prosperity are likely to suffer.

[1.9] Features of a good tax system

In his famous 1776 treatise *The Wealth of Nations*, Adam Smith, the renowned Scottish economic philosopher, expressed the following views about taxation:

- The subject of every state ought to contribute towards the support of the government, as nearly as possible, in proportion to their respective abilities; that is, in proportion to the revenue which they respectively enjoy under the protection of the state.
- The tax each individual is bound to pay ought to be certain, and not arbitrary. The time of payment, the manner of payment, and the quantity to be paid, ought all to be clear and plain to the contributor, and to every other person.
- Every tax ought to be levied at the time, or in the manner in which it is most likely to be convenient for the contributor to pay it.
- Every tax ought to be so contrived as both to take out and to keep out of the pockets of the people as little as possible, over and above what it brings into the public treasury of the state.

Smith's 'maxims' have become foundation stones for the design of a good tax system and are still often referred to today by policymakers. Whether or not a tax system is 'good' obviously involves a qualitative judgment. Although people naturally have different opinions about what constitutes a good tax system, there are some generally accepted criteria by which tax systems may be evaluated. These criteria, evolving out of Smith's work, have been extensively discussed in the academic literature and closely analysed in government papers and reports, such as the Asprey Committee's *Full Report* (1975), Treasury's *Reform of the Australian Tax System: Draft White Paper* (1985) and the Review of Business Taxation's *A Tax System Redesigned* (1999). The following discussion outlines some commonly articulated views regarding tax system design and focuses on what are, arguably, the key attributes of a good tax system.

Fiscal and policy objectives

Obviously, one of the key measures by which a tax system is judged is whether it meets the government's fiscal targets. A good tax system should collect the amount of revenue that the government has set out to collect; otherwise, it will fail in its primary objective. From a government's perspective, it is vital that the cost of its spending programs is balanced against the revenue it receives. In this regard, governments need to be able to forecast the amount of tax they will collect each year and predict how variables, such as economic factors, may impact on revenue collection. If their estimates are incorrect, they risk falling into funding deficits.

The difficulties that governments face in predicting tax revenue can be illustrated by a simple example. Suppose a government imposes a fuel excise at a flat rate on petroleum products. If oil prices rise during the year, revenue will increase (resulting in a windfall), but if oil prices drop during the year, revenue will be lower (resulting in a shortfall). As oil prices depend on extraneous economic factors, many of which are outside a government's control, it is impossible to know exactly how much tax will be collected. Governments therefore need to take account of a range of variables when undertaking their fiscal modelling.

The Commonwealth, state and territory governments publish annual Budget Statements that contain economic data, including details of their respective revenues and expenditures. These statements also contain their fiscal outlooks for coming years based on various assumptions. If the economic modelling in these statements is wrong, they may miss their forecasts. Governments that do not collect sufficient revenue from their taxes inevitably end up having to either borrow money to fund their spending programs or cut the services they provide their citizens.

A good tax system is, however, not just about collecting the right amount of revenue. It should also operate in harmony with the government's broader socio-economic policy agenda. Ideally, a country's tax system should support the government to achieve optimal outcomes, such as increased productivity, employment growth, improved welfare and higher living standards. A country's tax system should also not unduly interfere with the advancement of the country's broader economic imperatives, such as boosting national savings, encouraging investment and supporting business activity.

Simplicity, certainty and stability

Most people would agree that simplicity and certainty are desirable features of a good tax system. If these criteria are not met, taxpayers will find it difficult to comply with the tax laws and apply them to their specific circumstances. Likewise, revenue authorities will find it difficult to administer and enforce the tax laws. Ideally, tax laws should be clear, unambiguous and uncomplicated. They should therefore not be bogged down in complex and voluminous legislation that is difficult to comprehend or navigate. Ultimately, taxpayers and revenue authorities should be able to identify the incidence of tax and calculate tax liabilities with ease and certainty.

Unfortunately, the reality is that tax laws are often highly complex and they are frequently criticised for this reason. Australia's income tax legislation, in particular, is notorious for containing many long and cryptic technical provisions that are difficult to understand. Even senior judges have been open critics of the legislation. In an article appearing on the front page of the *Australian Financial Review* on 21 January 2011, Justice Keane (a former High Court Justice) was reported as saying: 'Opening the *Tax Act* is like entering the door of a parallel universe.'

The Federal Government has acknowledged that the Australian tax system is too complicated. In its 2015 *Re:think* discussion paper, it identified a number of reasons for this, stating (at 2):

> One reason is the prevalence of tax concessions aimed at assisting particular groups. Another reason is the regular 'patching' of the law to fix narrow problems or provide certainty for taxpayers and transactions without fully considering consequences for the system as a whole. Overly risk-averse attitudes from policy advisers and administrators, combined with complex legislative drafting styles, have also led to complexity.

Complexity in the tax system is problematic as it can divert time and resources away from productive activities. Governments should therefore strive to simplify their tax systems where possible. It is also prudent for them to periodically review their tax laws to ensure that they continue to meet their fiscal and policy objectives. Where a country's tax laws are failing to have their desired effect, they should be amended or repealed. It is, nevertheless, also important to recognise that continual reform of a country's tax system can contribute to uncertainty about its operation. It is therefore generally desirable for a country to maintain relatively stable tax laws, as this allows business and investment decisions to be made with confidence. Frequently changing tax laws can have a negative impact on the economy, as taxpayers will be reluctant to make commercial and financial decisions where their tax impact is not clear.

Transparency and integrity

It is widely accepted that a good tax system should be transparent. Revenue authorities have considerable statutory responsibilities and powers, and their actions should be closely monitored by government and be subject to parliamentary scrutiny. At the same time, tax laws should be administered free of political interference and in accordance with the rule of law. Revenue authorities should interpret and apply tax laws consistently, so that taxpayers in similar circumstances are treated equally. While it is important that revenue authorities can readily enforce tax laws if they are breached, the rights of taxpayers also need to be closely protected. As there is often a great imbalance between the resources of revenue authorities to prosecute tax disputes and the capabilities of taxpayers to defend themselves, it is imperative that taxpayers are treated fairly and not denied natural justice. In particular, taxpayers should be able to contest their tax assessments before the courts if they believe they have been incorrectly assessed.

It is also desirable for taxation statistical data to be readily accessible, as this helps promote transparency in the tax system and foster community engagement. The availability of up-to-date and accurate statistics enables a tax system to be analysed and evaluated by academics and other commentators, who may be able to identify issues that need to be addressed. This can contribute significantly to future tax reform.

A good tax system also needs to be robust and resilient to ensure that it is not open to abuse. A country's tax laws should therefore be designed in such a way that they are difficult to avoid or evade. A tax system with loopholes will not be respected by taxpayers and will result in revenue leakage, as some people will inevitably choose to exploit the weaknesses in the system. To protect the government's revenue base, tax laws need to be drafted tightly so they cannot be easily manipulated. Appropriate anti-avoidance rules in the legislation can provide added protection and serve as an integrity measure to prevent abuse of the general provisions. In addition, to ensure compliance, it is important for tax laws to be vigorously enforced. Tax administrators and law enforcement agencies need to have appropriate resources and powers to pursue and prosecute tax cheats.

Efficiency and flexibility

Another generally accepted feature of a good tax system is that it should be efficient, in the sense that it should have low collection and compliance costs. Taxes that are expensive for a government to collect, or cumbersome, time-consuming or costly for taxpayers to comply with, are inefficient, as they divert resources from productive activities. In designing an optimal tax system, government efficiency requirements should be carefully balanced against taxpayer compliance obligations to ensure that the tax laws operate both fairly and effectively. The Australian Government in its 2015 *Re:think* tax discussion paper noted that the annual cost of administering the Commonwealth tax system was around $3.6 billion and that taxpayer compliance costs were around $40 billion.

Linked to the concept of efficiency is the concept of flexibility. A good tax system should be able to cope with, and where necessary, respond to, changes in economic circumstances without requiring major overhauls. For example, if a tax system is not broad-based and is skewed towards taxing commodities, then a fall in commodity prices will have a major impact on revenue collection. For this reason, governments usually impose many different kinds of taxes with broad tax bases to spread risk. Having a broad tax mix also ensures the burden of taxation is spread more widely among the community and does not fall disproportionately on only certain persons. However, having many different kinds of taxes adds to the overall complexity of the tax system and increases compliance costs for taxpayers. Governments should bear this in mind in deciding on their overall tax mix.

Neutrality

It is often argued that a good tax system should be neutral, in the sense that it should not distort commercial decisions or skew the market mechanism. Taxes can interfere with the way markets operate, as they affect the cost of the activities or products upon which they are imposed. Tax laws that increase or decrease the attractiveness of one arrangement ahead of another can alter the way taxpayers choose to organise their affairs. A tax imposed on a particular product discourages spending on that product and makes similar products which are not taxed, or are taxed to a lesser extent, more attractive. For instance, if a tax is imposed on black shoes but not white shoes, consumers may buy more white shoes than black shoes, even if they actually prefer the latter. Likewise, taxing one kind of legal structure more concessionally than another is likely to lead to greater adoption of the preferentially taxed structure as a business or investment vehicle.

A tax system that contains inherent biases can affect market efficiency and result in tax considerations, rather than commercial considerations, driving economic activity and business decisions. This can have an adverse impact on a country's economic competitiveness and produce distorted commercial outcomes. To ensure that taxes do not drive a wedge between optimal business and investment decisions, they should generally have a neutral effect on similar kinds of underlying business and investment choices. However, the reality is that, in practice, many tax systems have built-in structural biases. For example, in Australia, resident individuals are generally fully assessed on interest earned from bank deposits, but are generally only assessed on half the capital gains made from investments that have been held for at least 12 months [17.8]. As a consequence, capital gains are treated more concessionally than income gains.

Governments nevertheless often intentionally design tax systems not to be neutral in order to achieve specific policy objectives. For instance, they may tax imported goods specifically to support locally produced products. Strictly, any tax will operate to discourage the activity upon which it is imposed, and any tax incentive will encourage the activity in relation to which it is provided. Tax expenditures, in particular, are often used to address market failures. For example, the Australian Government's ESVCLP program was introduced to address the failure of the market to provide venture capital to Australian early-stage businesses [27.4]. Investments made under this program benefit from tax exemptions and tax offsets that are not available for other kinds of investments.

While it is generally accepted that a tax system should not influence business decisions unnecessarily, fiscal neutrality is not something a government should pursue at all costs. In specific situations it may be appropriate to impose taxes or provide tax incentives for particular activities. A fiscal bias may be justified where a valid reason to change taxpayer behaviour exists. For instance, if the market is not operating at its optimal level, taxes or tax expenditures may be necessary to improve economic efficiency. A government may also have wider political or social goals that might best be achieved by creating distortions in the tax system. For example, it might consider that the best way of stopping its citizens from smoking—thereby reducing national health costs—is to tax cigarettes to make them less affordable.

Equity

Of the many hallmarks of a good tax system, the most important is generally considered to be equity. Equity is critical not only on moral grounds, but also because it is more likely that taxpayers will respect and support their tax system if it is perceived to be fair. It is widely accepted that taxpayers should bear responsibility for their appropriate share of the overall tax burden of the country in which they live, do business or make investments. This is often expressed as the simple principle that 'each taxpayer should pay their fair share of tax'. What is 'fair' between a wide range of taxpayers is, however, not necessarily straightforward. It ultimately depends on an equitable sharing of responsibilities between members of society, judged by reference to the general standards and norms of that society. Different interest groups and generations within society may have quite different perspectives on this subject, and their values may gradually shift over time. The reality is that fairness, like beauty, lies in the eye of the beholder.

It is generally acknowledged that the concept of equity has two important dimensions—horizontal equity and vertical equity. A tax is described as 'horizontally equitable' if people in similar economic circumstances are treated similarly. For instance, if A and B each derive $40,000 of income, they should each pay the same amount of tax. In contrast, a tax is described as 'vertically equitable' if people in different economic circumstances are treated differently, with those who are better off bearing a greater share of the burden. For instance, if A derives $100,000 of income and B derives $30,000 of income, A should pay more tax than B.

The notion of vertical equity is also sometimes referred to as the 'ability-to-pay' concept. According to this concept, the level of taxation should be linked to a person's wealth. Vertical equity is justified on the basis that those who have benefited the most from living in a particular country should contribute the most to their government. Some people, however, dispute this, arguing that to be fair, the level of taxation should be measured by reference to the degree of services and benefits a particular person receives from the government rather than their capacity to pay tax. But this argument ignores the fact that taxation is a social contribution imposed on the citizens of a state for the benefit of the state as a whole, rather than for the benefit of particular individuals.

Ultimately, the extent to which a tax is viewed as equitable depends on community perceptions. As a general rule, taxes are more readily accepted if the burden is spread widely among the community rather than directed at only specific groups. Taxes that adversely affect certain members of the community more than others are generally viewed unfavourably, particularly where the criterion of vertical equity is not satisfied (ie where the burden is placed on those less able to pay).

While flat taxes are administratively convenient, and may seem to be fair in that they are levied at the same rate on all taxpayers, they do not take a person's ability to pay into account. Flat taxes can operate regressively, as they impose a relatively greater burden on the income of poorer members of society than the wealthier ones. An example of a flat tax is the GST, which is presently imposed at a standard rate of 10% [7.1]. This tax is arguably more directly felt by poorer members of society. For instance, assume that because of the introduction of GST, the price of certain goods that previously cost $100 increases by 10%. The extra $10 payable represents a greater slice of a poor person's income than a rich person's income.

In contrast to the flat-rate GST, Australia has a progressive income tax system as the rates of tax increase with the level of a person's taxable income [8.8]. Income tax is therefore designed to fall more heavily on those with a greater ability to pay. However, in practice, it is not always easy to achieve fairness. For instance, while two people earning $100,000 may pay the same amount of income tax, one of those people might be single, while the other may have several children and a spouse to support. Accordingly, the burden of the tax is not felt uniformly by these two economic units.

[1.10] The tax unit

One of the basic issues to consider in the design of any tax system is who should be the subject of taxation. In other words, who is the appropriate 'tax unit' (ie taxpayer)?

Individuals and families

The Australian income tax system treats each individual as a separate tax unit. By taxing individuals rather than families, the income of spouses is not aggregated and taxed as if they were a single taxpayer, or split equally between them. Instead, each person pays tax as a separate unit on their own taxable income. This is the case, even though they may pool their resources.

In calculating a person's income tax liability, there is generally no account taken of any dependants whom they are required to support. A person with children does not pay income tax at lower rates than a person without children. Instead, support for families is available through the Department of Human Services, which provides means-tested social security payments such as the Family Tax Benefit and the Child Care Subsidy. The concept of a family is, however, not totally irrelevant for income tax purposes. A person may, for instance, be able to benefit from tax offsets for maintaining certain dependants [8.9]. Special thresholds and phase-in arrangements also exist for families in respect of the ML and MLS [8.8].

Legal entities and their members

As business and investment income is often earned through legal structures (eg partnerships, trusts and companies), governments need to consider how best to tax the income earned by these entities.

Should they be treated as separate taxpayers, or should their ultimate owners (the individuals who hold membership interests in the entities) be taxed instead?

Australia generally treats partnerships and trusts as 'flow-through entities', which means their income is not taxed at the entity level, but rather in the hands of their members. As a result, partnerships and trusts do not give rise to a separate taxing point. Instead, they simply operate as conduits. It is, therefore, usually the respective partners [23.3] or beneficiaries [24.5] who are taxed.

In contrast, Australia generally treats companies as 'opaque entities', which means that they are taxed as separate taxpayers from their members (eg shareholders). To prevent double taxation of corporate profits—once in the hands of the company and again when they are distributed to shareholders as dividends—Australia has adopted an 'imputation system' which provides resident shareholders with credits for Australian income tax paid by resident companies on their underlying profits [22.6].

[1.11] Sovereign right to tax

Each nation has the sovereign right to design its own tax system. Subject to any restrictions imposed under their respective constitutions, governments are generally free to determine the nature and scope of their country's tax laws and the persons whom they subject to tax.

Enactment, administration and adjudication of tax laws

A country's tax laws are made by its appropriate legislative body and its tax system is administered by its relevant revenue authority. In Australia, federal tax legislation is enacted by the Commonwealth Parliament under its powers in the *Constitution* [3.4] and the federal tax system is administered by the ATO, which is headed by the Commissioner of Taxation [6.3].

Disputes between taxpayers and revenue authorities concerning the application of a country's tax laws are litigated before the country's tribunals and courts. In Australia, Commonwealth tax disputes are heard, at first instance, by the Administrative Appeals Tribunal ('AAT') or the Federal Court. Appeals from these decisions may be available to the Full Federal Court and (with special leave) the High Court [38.5].

Some countries, such as the United States and Canada, have established specialist Tax Courts that deal exclusively with tax disputes. Specialist Tax Courts do not exist in Australia. The principal reason traditionally advanced for establishing such courts is that since tax legislation is so technical and complex, it is appropriate that tax cases should be heard by judges with special expertise in the field (see S Chapple, 'Income Tax Dispute Resolution: Can We Learn from Other Jurisdictions?' (1999) 2 *JAT* 312). Certain prominent Australian judges have, however, rejected the need for such courts on the basis that it is preferable for judges hearing tax disputes to have general law expertise to ensure that tax law is not divorced from the ordinary commercial and legal environment (see D Hill, 'Great Expectations: What Do We Expect from Judges in Tax Cases?' (1995) 69 *ALJ* 992). It has been pointed out that there is a risk that specialists may be too 'inward looking', and that knowledge of other areas of law can 'spark ideas' which someone with only limited or specialised expertise may not perceive (see M Kirby, 'Hubris Contained: Why a Separate Australian Tax Court should be Rejected' (2007) 42 *TIA* 161).

Fiscal convergence and divergence

While the tapestry of a country's tax system is a sovereign issue, countries are inevitably influenced by one another in designing their tax rules. Globalisation has contributed to increasing economic integration and fiscal convergence among nations. It is therefore not surprising to find many broad similarities between tax systems around the world. This is especially the case where countries have formal links (eg through membership of international organisations such as the OECD). Each country's tax system is, nevertheless, unique, and its architecture ultimately depends on the individual approach the country has adopted. While international influences often play an important part in the broad design of a country's tax rules, the tax policies it ultimately adopts will be most heavily influenced by its own particular social, political and economic factors.

Close economic and political relations between nations can help foster 'tax harmonisation' (ie the adoption of similar, although not necessarily identical, tax laws within different jurisdictions). Tax harmonisation can lead to economic and administrative efficiencies, but is usually difficult to achieve in practice, as it requires a coordinated approach to taxation policy between nations that often have competing interests.

Tax harmonisation is perhaps most evident in the EU, where it is a requirement of membership that each Member State impose VAT at the rate of at least 15% (reduced rates are allowed for certain supplies). In recent years, the EU has also had a limited degree of success in harmonising direct taxes (eg certain aspects of corporate and savings taxes). It is, however, extremely difficult to achieve broad-based tax harmonisation within the EU, as it does not have any general taxation powers of its own—these powers remain with the individual Member States. The introduction of 'directives' in the field of taxation requires unanimity of the EU Council of Ministers, composed of the 27 National Ministers of each of the Member States. Progress towards further integration of European taxes therefore remains a slow and drawn-out process.

One area where there has been significant cooperation between countries recently is in their approach to tackling the problem of international tax avoidance and tax evasion. This has been largely due to work undertaken by the OECD under its base erosion and profit shifting ('BEPS') project [33.3]. Many countries have adopted various actions recommended by the OECD to deal with the problem. For example, 100 jurisdictions have signed a new multilateral convention to upgrade their tax treaties to tackle BEPS [32.4]. In addition, over 130 jurisdictions have agreed to enter into a two-pillar agreement on international tax reform which will re-allocate the profits of the largest multinational enterprises to those countries where the profits are earned and ensure that they are subject to a minimum corporate tax rate of at least 15% [33.6].

[1.12] Jurisdiction to tax

General jurisdictional rules

Most countries' tax systems are based on a set of general rules that define the jurisdictional limits of their respective tax laws. A country's general jurisdictional rules may be cast narrowly or widely and often operate subject to numerous exceptions. The following discussion outlines the two main jurisdictional approaches used by countries around the world in relation to income tax. At the heart of these approaches is the requirement that there be some clear nexus between the taxing jurisdiction and either the taxpayer (the 'tax subject') or the income-generating transaction (the 'tax object').

- **Territorial (source-based) jurisdictional rules.** The narrow 'territorial' approach to income taxation focuses on the source of the income. Countries that adopt this approach only tax income sourced within their geographic borders, irrespective of where the taxpayer resides.
- **Worldwide (residence-based) jurisdictional rules.** The wider 'worldwide' approach to income taxation focuses on the taxpayer's country of residence. Countries that adopt this broader approach tax their residents on both their domestic and foreign source income, but only tax foreign residents on their locally sourced income.

Justifications for territorial and worldwide jurisdictional rules

The territorial and worldwide approaches to taxation produce different economic efficiencies. A territorial approach promotes 'capital import neutrality', as investments made in the source country are treated in the same manner regardless of where the investor resides. A worldwide approach promotes 'capital export neutrality', as it does not influence an investor's decision about where to make investments (ie at home or abroad).

The territorial approach to taxation can be justified on the basis that there is an economic connection between the taxpayer and the taxing jurisdiction. It is based on a link between the income earned and the source country. This link may exist for a variety of reasons, including the fact that the business or employment activities take place in the source country, or the property that generates the income is located there. A territorial approach is defensible on the grounds that it is fair that persons who benefit from earning income in a particular country should also contribute to the country's costs of providing the economic environment that enables their income-earning activities to take place.

The worldwide approach to taxation can be justified on the basis that there is a personal connection between the taxpayer and the taxing jurisdiction. It is founded on the rationale that, as residents of a particular country are usually based in the country and benefit from the broad range of public goods and services provided by their government, it is appropriate to tax them on their worldwide income, as these things support their way of life and overall economic activities, both locally and abroad. Moreover, as residents usually have a personal allegiance to the country in which they choose to reside, and are usually entitled to derive benefits from their government that are not necessarily also available to foreigners (eg various forms of social security), it is possible to justify applying wider jurisdictional rules to them.

Credits for foreign taxes to prevent double taxation

The practical problem with the worldwide approach is that it leads to double taxation, since a taxpayer's foreign income is taxed not only in their country of residence but also in the source country. To alleviate this problem, it is common for countries that adopt the worldwide approach to grant their residents credits for tax paid on foreign income in the source country. However, if credits for foreign taxes were granted in excess of the tax paid in the country of residence, the excess credits could be utilised to reduce the tax payable on the resident's domestic income. Accordingly, to counteract erosion of their domestic tax bases, countries generally cap credits for foreign taxes so that they cannot exceed the amount of tax that would otherwise be payable on the foreign income in the country of residence.

Australia's general jurisdictional rules and exceptions

Australia's general jurisdictional rules are based on the worldwide approach and are discussed in Chapter 30. Accordingly, Australian residents are generally taxed on their worldwide income, while foreign residents are generally taxed only on their Australian-sourced income [30.1]. At the same time, to prevent double taxation, Australia also provides a credit, known as the 'foreign income tax offset', for foreign taxes paid on income that is also assessed in Australia [31.3].

It is important to understand that while Australia's income tax laws are based on the worldwide approach, Australia does not have a 'pure' worldwide system of taxation, as its jurisdictional rules operate subject to numerous exceptions [31.4]–[31.10].

Like Australia, most developed countries tax their resident individuals on their worldwide income. The United States is a special case, as it not only taxes its residents on a worldwide basis but also taxes non-residents who are United States citizens on a worldwide basis. This results in the United States having one of the broadest jurisdictional rules of any developed country. To mitigate double taxation, United States citizens who reside outside the United States and are physically present in foreign countries for at least 330 days during any 12-month period may exclude a portion (up to US$120,000 for 2023) of their foreign income provided they lodge United States tax returns.

In contrast to Australia, jurisdictions that adopt the much narrower territorial approach to taxation, such as Singapore, Malaysia and the Special Administrative Regions of Hong Kong and Macau, generally only tax income that is sourced within the jurisdiction. Residents of these jurisdictions do not therefore generally pay tax on foreign income in their country of residence.

International taxation agreements

A country's general jurisdictional rules operate subject to the terms of any international tax agreements it has entered into with other countries. In practice, these agreements are made after lengthy negotiations between the respective governments. They are typically bilateral in nature, as it is much more difficult to achieve multilateral agreements. For this reason, these treaties are often referred to as 'Double Taxation Agreements' ('DTAs').

One of the main functions of DTAs is to address the problem of double taxation, which is widely recognised as a major impediment to cross-border trade and investment. In the field of income tax, double taxation arises where more than one country asserts taxing rights over the same income. For instance, this can easily occur in respect of business profits—both the country in which the taxpayer is a resident and the country in which the income is earned may seek to tax the profits. The country of residence may seek to tax the profits on the basis of a worldwide approach to taxation, while the country of source may seek to tax the profits on the basis of a territorial approach to taxation.

To prevent double taxation of income, one of the countries needs to surrender its taxing rights in favour of the other country. The problem is that countries naturally want to protect their revenue bases and are reluctant to unilaterally give up their taxing rights. Nevertheless, in order to promote international trade and investment, they may be prepared to surrender their taxing rights if appropriate reciprocal arrangements are in place. DTAs provide the framework for these arrangements. They also contain special tie-breaker rules that operate where a taxpayer would otherwise be a dual resident.

The main way that DTAs deal with the problem of double taxation is by allocating taxing rights between the respective countries (referred to as 'Contracting States') according to a set of agreed principles that are set out in the DTAs. Where both the country of residence and the country of source share taxing rights, the DTAs usually require the country of residence to provide relief in the form of a credit for the payment of foreign tax.

DTAs also contain exchange of information clauses designed to assist tax authorities in the relevant countries to administer their respective tax laws and prevent tax avoidance and tax evasion.

Australia has entered into DTAs with more than 40 countries. These DTAs are broadly based on the OECD *Model Tax Convention on Income and on Capital* and are examined in Chapter 32. Australia has also entered into Additional Benefits Agreements ('ABAs') and Tax Information Exchange Agreements ('TIEAs') with a number of jurisdictions with which it does not have DTAs. ABAs are essentially mini DTAs that only cover a limited number of topics [32.3]. TIEAs, on the other hand, are special bilateral agreements that contain rules for exchanging tax and financial information [33.2].

International tax enforcement

It is important to recognise that while countries have the sovereign right to determine the jurisdictional scope of their tax laws and can enact legislation that imposes liabilities on foreigners who earn income within their territories, it is quite another matter for governments to enforce their tax laws against such persons. As foreigners reside outside a country's borders and may have all their assets located abroad, it can be difficult to recover taxes from them. There is a general principle that countries do not enforce each other's tax laws (*Government of India, Ministry of Finance (Revenue Division) v Taylor* [1955] AC 491). This principle was recognised in *Rothwells Limited (In Liquidation) v Connell* 93 ATC 5106, where the Supreme Court of Queensland Court stated (at 5113) that it was 'a settled rule of private international law that the courts do not assist the enforcement of foreign revenue laws, or claims made under those laws'. To address this issue, many countries, including Australia, have entered into bilateral and multilateral international tax enforcement arrangements [33.10].

Withholding taxes

To avoid international tax enforcement issues from arising, many countries impose withholding taxes on certain payments made to foreigners. Entities that make such payments are generally required to withhold tax from the payments and remit the tax to their revenue authorities on behalf of the foreigners. Australia imposes withholding taxes on a range of payments made to foreigners (including, dividends, interest and royalties) [31.11].

[1.13] Level of taxation

It is difficult to compare the overall level of taxation in one country with that in another country as the mix of taxes in each country is often quite different. In order to determine how heavily a country's citizens are taxed, it is necessary to take account of all kinds of taxes imposed at every level of government—federal, state and local.

When comparing the level of taxation in Australia with that in other countries, it is simplistic merely to focus on the rates of tax imposed in each jurisdiction. Obviously, the amount of revenue collected by a government from a particular tax will also depend on a range of other factors, including whom it subjects to tax and how broadly its tax base is defined. For example, while CGT forms part of the Australian income tax base, not all countries around the world impose CGT. Countries that do not have a general CGT regime therefore have a much narrower tax base. It is worth noting that a number of countries located close to Australia in the Asia–Pacific region do not have a general CGT regime, including Singapore, Malaysia and New Zealand. By way of way contrast, capital gains are taxed in countries such as the United States and the United Kingdom. However, these countries' tax regimes differ from Australia's. For instance, in the United States, individuals pay different rates of tax on their short-term and long-term capital gains. Short-term capital gains arise on assets held for a year or less and are taxed at ordinary rates of up to 37%; while long-term capital gains arise on assets held for longer than a year and are taxed at concessional rates of up to 20%. Australia, on the other hand, imposes CGT at ordinary income tax rates, but generally provides individuals with a 50% discount on capital gains made on assets held for at least 12 months [17.8]. There are also many differences in CGT exemptions and reliefs. In the United Kingdom, for example, resident individuals generally only pay CGT on their overall capital gains above the 'annual exempt amount' (£6,000 for 2023/24). No corresponding allowance exists in Australia.

Australia's tax expenditure programs are also quite different from those in other countries. For instance, Australia provides tax concessions to encourage activities such as retirement savings, research and development, local film production and venture capital investment. Similar kinds of tax expenditure programs are not necessarily available in other jurisdictions. On the other hand, foreign countries may offer other forms of tax incentives that are not available in Australia. For instance, countries such as Singapore and Malaysia provide 'tax holidays' (ie exemptions from tax for specific periods) to encourage the establishment of pioneer enterprises and to promote the development of various industries. The vast differences that exist between tax systems make it very difficult to compare regimes.

Data on levels of taxation

Comparative data on levels of taxation be found in the OECD's *Revenue Statistics 1965–2021*, which measures tax revenue as a percentage of GDP for OECD countries. Measuring tax-to-GDP ratios is the traditional way of comparing the relative levels of taxes raised across different countries as it takes account of the size of their respective economies. It is interesting to note that Australia's tax-to-GDP ratio for 2020 was 28.5%, which was well below the OECD average of 33.6%. This suggests that Australia imposes a relatively lower tax burden than many other nations. In 2020, 7 OECD countries had tax-to-GDP ratios above 40%, namely Denmark (47.1%), France (45.3%), Italy (42.7%),

Belgium (42.5%), Sweden (42.3%), Austria (42.2%) and Finland (41.8%). The OECD countries that had tax-to-GDP ratios below Australia were South Korea (27.7%), Switzerland (27.5%), the United States (25.8%), Turkiye (23.9%), Costa Rica (22.7%), Ireland (19.9%), Chile (19.4%), Colombia (18.8%) and Mexico (17.8%).

Balancing level of taxation against provision of services

The level of taxation imposed by a government needs to be balanced against the level of services the government seeks to provide its citizens. Greater revenue raised from taxes allows a government to provide more public services. Taxpayers who complain about a lack of government services such as public hospital beds, childcare facilities, or funded university places need to recognise that these things come at a significant cost. If citizens want more government services, they need to be prepared to pay more taxes. As the OECD's *Revenue Statistics 1965–2021* indicate, Scandinavian countries are among the highest tax-to-GDP ratio countries. These countries, however, traditionally have a more socially orientated outlook than many other countries and are well known for their generous pension and welfare systems. A government's ability to provide social services comes at a cost, and it is not surprising that this is usually largely funded out of taxation revenue.

Increasing and decreasing levels of taxation

Governments may require different levels of taxation revenue at different times. For instance, in times of crisis, such as war or natural disaster, they may need to impose higher levels of taxation than they would impose at other times. Additional revenue may also be required to pay for major public infrastructure projects, such as the construction of freeways, telecommunication networks and hospitals. Governments may also be forced to increase taxes to repay their borrowings. This situation was recently faced by the Greek Government, which had to increase taxation as well as curb public spending (including controversially cutting government pensions) in order to address its sovereign debt crisis and comply with its Eurozone bailout conditions. These austerity measures placed considerable pressure on Greek citizens, who ultimately bore the cost of bailing out their government. Not surprisingly, this created much internal turmoil and resulted in protests and riots around the country. One of the most noticeable tax reforms was the increase of Greece's VAT rate from 21% to 24%. Greece was, however, not alone in increasing its VAT rate—several other countries adversely affected by the GFC also increased their VAT rates, including Hungary, Iceland, Ireland, Italy, Portugal, Spain and the United Kingdom. The cost of large stimulus packages, like those introduced by many countries around the world to counter the economic effects of the COVID-19 pandemic, is also likely to place pressure on governments to increase taxes in the future.

Governments can increase taxation by raising tax rates and widening their tax bases. They can also benefit from bringing forward the time at which tax is collected in order to gain early access to the revenue. Governments can also reduce tax spending by limiting the incentives and concessions provided under their tax expenditure programs. However, when governments increase taxation and cut back on tax expenditures it can have a negative effect on the country's economy, as it generally results in decreased private spending and investment. Paradoxically, this can dampen overall government revenues, as there may be fewer transactions to tax.

Reducing the level of taxation, on the other hand, encourages private spending and therefore stimulates the broader economy. During the GFC, several governments around the world introduced temporary tax incentives to encourage economic activity. One example was the introduction of the investment allowance in Australia, which provided a 'bonus deduction' at rates that ranged from 10% to 50% for entities that incurred eligible expenditure on tangible depreciating assets. To qualify for the bonus deduction, a taxpayer must have committed to investing in the asset during the period

13 December 2008 to 31 December 2009 (ie the height of the slowdown). The incentive, therefore, encouraged taxpayers to bring forward spending on income-producing assets that they may have otherwise deferred on account of the uncertainty caused by the crisis.

A broad range of temporary tax incentives were also recently introduced by many governments around the world to combat the economic effects of the COVID-19 pandemic (see OECD, *Tax Policy Reforms 2021: Special Edition on Tax Policy During the COVID-19 Pandemic*). Australia, for example, introduced various capital allowance incentives, including an incentive to allow businesses with annual turnover of less than $5 billion to fully expense the cost of their eligible depreciating assets [15.2].

By actively intervening in their economies during the GFC and COVID-19 crises, governments were simply applying the economic theories of John Maynard Keynes as set out in his seminal 1936 treatise, *The General Theory of Employment, Interest and Money*. Keynes advocated that increased government expenditures and lower taxes can stimulate demand and thwart a recession. In essence, governments were using fiscal stimulus measures to influence aggregate demand in order to prevent an economic slump.

Finally, it is also important to recognise that reducing the level of taxation makes a country more attractive to foreign investors. This, in turn, can provide a range of related economic benefits, such as enhanced business and employment opportunities. Through increased foreign investment, a country's pool of potential taxpayers is also broadened. Thus, when considering the level of taxation and the form it will take, governments need to carefully weigh up several factors, including the effect taxation has on a country's international competitiveness.

[1.14] QUESTIONS

1. What kinds of taxes were imposed in ancient times and what are the main kinds of taxes imposed today?
2. Is it correct to say that the only role of taxation is to raise government revenue? If taxation has other functions, what are they?
3. What is a 'tax expenditure program'? Provide some examples of such programs. What are some of the criticisms faced by such programs?
4. What structural features do tax systems have in common?
5. Provide some historical example of where taxation has led to national instability.
6. What are the characteristics of a 'good' tax system and what are some of the issues facing Australia that should be taken into account in designing its tax system?
7. Discuss the difference between a 'flow-through entity' and an 'opaque entity'.
8. Which bodies make, administer and adjudicate a country's tax laws?
9. How do Australia's general jurisdictional rules operate?
10. Why is it difficult to compare the levels of taxation in different countries? What benefits may flow from reducing the level of taxation?

TAX LAW RESEARCH AND INTERPRETATION 2

[2.1] Introduction

Taxation law is a vast and dynamic area of law that intersects with many other areas of law and is never static. Australia has dozens of tax statutes containing thousands of pages of complex and interconnected legislative provisions. In addition, the Australian courts and tribunals have handed down hundreds of significant tax decisions over the years. Many of these cases involve complex commercial factual situations that raise thorny legal issues.

Taxation law is also continually evolving and being reformed. Every year, several Bills are introduced into the Commonwealth, state and territory legislatures to address technical issues, fix loopholes, vary tax rates, alter incentives and adjust tax bases. It is therefore not surprising that one of the many challenges faced in studying and practising taxation law is keeping up with the constant barrage of changes and locating up-to-date legal resources.

This chapter introduces the primary sources of taxation law in Australia; namely, statute and common law [2.2]. It also outlines the main kinds of rulings and advice documents issued by the ATO [2.3]. These documents are important as they set out the Commissioner's views on the operation of the law and, in certain cases, can be binding. The chapter also discusses the vast range of secondary reference material that can be used to assist in researching and resolving tax problems [2.4]. It also identifies some of the key websites that are useful for conducting tax research [2.5]. The chapter concludes with a discussion of some basic rules of statutory interpretation, which are critical for understanding and applying tax legislation [2.6].

[2.2] Primary sources of tax law

Statute

Taxation is a creature of statute, rather than common law. Legislation is therefore the primary source of tax law. In Australia, tax legislation is enacted by the Commonwealth, state and territory legislatures. The Commonwealth Parliament's legislative powers are found in the *Commonwealth Constitution* and the process involved in enacting legislation is discussed at [3.3]. There are dozens of different tax and related statutes that make up the Commonwealth legislative scheme. These Acts span thousands of pages and contain many thousands of complex and technical interconnected provisions. The Office of Parliamentary Counsel, established under the *Parliamentary Counsel Act 1970* (Cth), has the role of drafting Commonwealth legislation and publishing such laws. Australia's tax laws are being continuously reformed with many Bills introduced into Parliament each year. Tax legislation is also complemented by a broad range of subordinate legislative instruments, including many different regulations and determinations [3.3]. There is, arguably, no other area of law that is as complex or as legislatively fertile as tax law.

Common law

Tax laws enacted by the Commonwealth, state and territory legislatures are interpreted by the courts in the many cases that come before them each year. Tax cases typically involve disputes between a particular taxpayer and either the Commissioner of Taxation (in matters involving Commonwealth taxes) or the relevant Commissioners of State or Territory Revenue (in matters involving state and territory taxes). These disputes usually concern the way in which specific provisions in the legislation apply to particular transactions, and arise because taxpayers and tax administrators have different interpretations of the law. Over time, a large body of case law concerning the interpretation of tax legislation has been developed by the courts. The amount of tax litigation is not surprising given that tax disputes often concern the operation of complex provisions and involve large sums of money. The common law is therefore, together with the tax legislation, an important source of law.

Doctrine of precedent

In reading any court decision, it is important to be aware of the doctrine of precedent (*stare decisis*). This doctrine requires courts to follow earlier decisions when making their rulings and was developed to promote consistency and certainty in the application of the law by the courts. According to the doctrine, the *ratio decidendi* of a higher court in a court hierarchy is 'binding' on a lower court in the same hierarchy. The *ratio decidendi* is the court's reasons for its decision in the particular case. It forms the legal principle derived from the judgment in the case which can then be applied to similar cases. While the *ratio decidendi* of a higher court must be followed by lower courts in the same court hierarchy, the *ratio decidendi* of a court in another court hierarchy (eg a foreign court) does not need to be followed, but may nevertheless have 'persuasive' authority. A court must make a ruling on a particular point of law for a *ratio decidendi* to arise and it is possible for one case to give rise to a number of separate *ratios*.

Ratio decidendi should be distinguished from *obiter dicta* which consist of comments made by judges in passing that are not essential or directly relevant to the decision in a case. *Obiter dicta* are not binding and only have persuasive authority. In practice, the weight that a court will give to *obiter dicta* will typically depend on the reputation of the judge who has made the comments and the jurisdiction and seniority of the court on which that judge sits. It is possible, and indeed common, for *obiter dicta* in one case to later form the basis of the *ratio decidendi* of another case (ie where it is applied by the court in arriving at its decision in the subsequent case).

It is important to understand, however, that the *ratio decidendi* of a case will not be binding on a lower court if the decision can be distinguished on some ground (eg due to material factual differences in the cases). Much time is therefore often spent in court arguing whether or not a particular decision is applicable. Even slight variations in factual situations may produce different legal outcomes. In some situations, there may be conflicting precedents that require a court to draw distinctions between cases to determine which decision is the most appropriate to follow.

Court hierarchy

In the Australian federal tax jurisdiction, the basic hierarchy of courts (from highest to lowest) is as follows:

- High Court (consisting of up to seven judges—the current members of the High Court are Gageler CJ, Beech-Jones, Gordon, Edelman, Steward, Gleeson and Jagot JJ)
- Full Court of the Federal Court (consisting of three judges), and
- Federal Court (consisting of one judge).

The Administrative Appeals Tribunal ('AAT'), which is strictly an administrative body as opposed to a judicial body, also hears tax cases. The *Taxation Administration Act 1953* (Cth) ('*TAA*') gives the AAT the power to review certain decisions (including reviewable objection decisions) made by the Commissioner of Taxation. Reviews are conducted in accordance with the rules set out in the *Administrative Appeals Tribunal Act 1975* (Cth) ('*AATA*') as modified by the *TAA*. Taxpayers may appeal tribunal decisions to the Federal Court on questions of law (s 44 *AATA*). The way in which the appeal process operates is examined at [38.5].

Reports

Decisions of the federal courts and tribunals can be accessed online [2.5] and are also reported in law reports, such as:

- *Australian Tax Cases* ('ATC'), which contain reports of AAT, Federal Court and High Court tax decisions handed down since 1969
- *Australian Tax Decisions* ('ATD'), which contain reports of tax decisions handed down between 1930 and 1969
- *Australian Tax Reports* ('ATR'), which contain reports of AAT, Federal Court and High Court tax decisions
- *Federal Court Reports* ('FCR'), which contain authorised reports of Federal Court decisions, and
- *Commonwealth Law Reports* ('CLR'), which contain authorised reports of High Court decisions.

[2.3] Taxation rulings and advice

The ATO publishes a broad range of advice and guidance documents outlining the Commissioner's views on the operation of the tax laws. The main form of formal advice comes in the form of 'rulings'. Since 1 July 1992, a 'binding ruling system' has operated in Australia [38.4]. Under this system, the Commissioner can issue 'public rulings' advising on the way a relevant provision in the tax law applies to entities generally or to a class of entities. The Commissioner can also issue 'private rulings' to taxpayers who request them about how the tax law applies to their existing or proposed schemes. Public and private rulings must be in writing and must state that they are public or private rulings.

The Commissioner is generally bound to apply the law as set out in a binding ruling unless he is satisfied that the ruling is incorrect and disadvantages the taxpayer, in which case he may apply the law in a way that is more favourable to the taxpayer (provided he is not prevented from doing so by any legal time limits). Taxpayers who rely on a binding ruling are protected from having to pay any tax shortfall (ie underpaid tax), penalties or interest in respect of the matters covered in the ruling if it turns out that the ruling is incorrect.

There are several different kinds of binding public rulings, which each have a distinct prefix, year and identification number. The rulings are sometimes updated by addenda, and may be withdrawn. The main kinds of binding public rulings are contained in the following series:

- **Taxation Rulings ('TRs').** These rulings are the principal series of binding public rulings. They cover many different topics, including income tax and FBT. An example of a taxation ruling is TR 2008/2, which provides guidance on income tax issues relating to activities in the horse industry.
- **GST Rulings ('GSTRs').** These rulings are used to provide guidance on GST. An example of a GST ruling is GSTR 2006/9, which deals with the meaning of the term 'supply' for GST purposes.
- **Product Rulings ('PRs').** These rulings are usually sought by promoters of investment products such as managed investment schemes ('MISs'). They are typically attached to the prospectus accompanying the schemes to provide certainty to potential investors about the ATO's views on the tax implications of the particular products being marketed. An example of a product ruling

is PR 2008/63, relating to the 2009 Timbercorp Forestry Project. Product rulings overcome the need for each investor in the scheme to individually apply for a private ruling. Provided the scheme is carried out as described in the product ruling, investors are able to rely on the ruling. The product rulings system is explained further in PR 2007/71.

- **Class Rulings ('CRs').** These rulings are sought by entities on the tax effect of particular arrangements on a class of taxpayers. Class rulings are often sought by companies to advise their shareholders of the ATO position on capital management and restructuring issues, such as share buy-backs, takeovers and demergers. An example of a class ruling is CR 2008/10, which deals with the tax consequences for Coca-Cola Amatil's shareholders of an off-market share buy-back undertaken by the company. As with product rulings, class rulings overcome the need for each shareholder to individually seek a private ruling about the arrangement. The class rulings system is explained further in CR 2001/1.
- **Law Companion Rulings ('LCRs').** These rulings set out the ATO's views on how recently enacted tax laws apply. They are usually developed at about the same time as a Bill is being drafted and are designed to provide certainty about the application of new laws. The law companion guidelines system is explained further in LCR 2015/1.

The ATO also issues determinations, which are typically shorter than most rulings and generally only address specific questions. The following determinations are binding on the Commissioner: Taxation Determinations ('TDs') and GST Determinations ('GSTDs').

Rulings and determinations issued before the binding ruling system was introduced (on 1 July 1992) are not binding on the Commissioner. This includes the old Income Tax Rulings ('ITs'). The ATO also publishes a range of non-binding superannuation rulings and determinations, such as Superannuation Guarantee Rulings ('SGRs'), Self-Managed Superannuation Fund Rulings ('SMSFRs'), Superannuation Guarantee Determinations ('SGDs'), Superannuation Contribution Determinations ('SCDs') and Self-Managed Superannuation Fund Determinations ('SMSFDs'). While taxpayers that rely on non-binding rulings are not protected from having to pay any tax shortfall, they are generally protected against having to pay certain penalties and, if they relied on the document reasonably and in good faith, they are also generally protected from having to pay interest.

The ATO also publishes Interpretative Decisions ('IDs'), which set out the way it has interpreted the law in particular instances, and Decision Impact Statements ('DISs'), which set out its views on the outcome of particular court and tribunal decisions. Furthermore, to provide guidance on ATO administrative practices and assist ATO staff in performing their duties, the ATO issues Practice Statements Law Administration ('PS LA'). More recently, the ATO has started to publish Practical Compliance Guidelines ('PCGs'), which provide broad guidance on significant administrative and compliance issues. IDs, DISs, PS LAs and PCGs are not binding on the Commissioner. They are, nevertheless, made publicly available for information and transparency purposes.

A large amount of general advice is also published on the ATO website. This includes bulletins, guidelines, taxpayer alerts, policy statements, media releases and consultative documents. Over the years, the ATO has also produced useful guidebooks and manuals detailing the practical operation of the tax laws (eg *Guide to the Debt and Equity Tests* and *Consolidation Reference Manual*). Practical information can also be obtained from ATO publications designed to assist taxpayers in compiling their tax returns (eg *Individual Tax Return Instructions*).

[2.4] Taxation reference material

In addition to legislation, cases and ATO rulings and advice, a vast array of secondary reference material can be used to research and resolve taxation issues. Some of the main kinds of publications that are frequently used by taxation practitioners, scholars and policymakers are discussed below.

Government publications

From time to time, the Government releases various papers, reports, research documents and exposure drafts in order to foster public awareness of an issue or as part of its consultative processes. For example, it is common for Treasury to issue an Exposure Draft Bill for public comment and submissions on important proposed alterations to the tax laws before a Bill is formally introduced into Parliament. The Exposure Draft Bill is usually accompanied by an Explanatory Memorandum. Likewise, the Bill that is eventually introduced into Parliament will also typically have its own Explanatory Memorandum. These documents are extremely useful as they explain how proposed laws are intended to operate and can assist with interpreting complex legislative provisions.

Many government publications also contain useful policy information and reform recommendations, which often form the basis of future tax laws. In the late 1990s, the Review of Business Taxation [5.4] published two important discussion papers (*A Strong Foundation* (1998) and *A Platform for Consultation* (1999)) as well as a major report recommending reforms to the Australian business tax system (*A Tax System Redesigned* (1999)). A number of significant papers and reports were also produced by the Henry Tax Review [5.5]. This included *Architecture of Australia's Tax and Transfer System* (2008) and *Australia's Future Tax System—Report to the Treasurer* (2009). More recently, the Abbott Government published its *Re:think* (2015) discussion paper [5.7].

Board of Taxation publications

The Board of Taxation, which is an advisory board that assists the Government in the development and implementation of the tax laws, has also published several interesting papers and reports over the years, including the following:

- *International Taxation—A Report to the Treasurer* (2003)
- *A Tax Transparency Code—A Report to the Treasurer* (2016)
- *Reforming Individual Tax Residency Rules—A Model for Modernisation* (2019), and
- *Review of GST on Low Value Imported Goods* (2021).

Professional publications

Professional bodies, such as those listed below, also produce a variety of tax publications:

- Taxation Institute of Australia
- Australian Tax Research Foundation
- Corporate Taxpayers' Association
- Chartered Accountants Australia and New Zealand
- Law societies in states and territories
- Law Council of Australia, and
- CPA Australia.

These bodies often make submissions or release consultative documents or research papers concerning various tax matters.

In addition, many law and accounting firms (particularly the larger firms) produce their own publications dealing with aspects of taxation law. These publications often have a useful practical focus.

Academic and professional journals and conference papers

Journal articles and conference papers are an excellent secondary research resource as they usually contain a focused and critical analysis of particular topics. The main specialist Australian tax journals are listed below.

Australian Tax Journals	
Australian Tax Forum	*Journal of the Australasian Tax Teachers Association*
Australian Tax Review	*Revenue Law Journal*
CCH Tax Week	*Taxation in Australia*
eJournal of Tax Research	*Tax Specialist*
Journal of Australian Taxation	*Weekly Tax Bulletin*

Tax articles can also be found in university law reviews (eg *Melbourne University Law Review*), law journals (eg *Australian Law Journal*) and accounting journals (eg *Charter*). Tax papers are also frequently presented at conferences conducted throughout the year by various professional bodies, including the Taxation Institute of Australia and CPA Australia. These papers often have a highly practical and current focus. Tax papers are also presented at academic conferences such as those conducted by the Australasian Tax Teachers Association and the Accounting Association of Australia and New Zealand. These papers are often more theoretical and policy-orientated in nature.

Journal and conference papers can be accessed via databases such as the Attorney-General's Information Service ('AGIS'), the Australian Public Affairs Information Service ('APAIS') and the Social Science Research Network ('SSRN').

Textbooks and casebooks

Textbooks are perhaps the most useful starting point in conducting tax research as they enable the reader to gain an overview and basic understanding of a particular issue. Textbooks usually provide a conceptual framework and introduction to the law and a structured discussion of the relevant legislation, cases and rulings in the area. There is also often a critical analysis and synthesis of the legal principles covered. The most widely used and comprehensive annually updated Australian taxation law textbooks designed for practitioners are Wolters Kluwer, *Australian Master Tax Guide*, and R Deutsch, M Friezer, I Fullerton, P Hanley and T Snape, *Australian Tax Handbook*. There are also several textbooks that focus on specialist areas, such as GST (eg P McCouat, *Australian Master GST Guide* and I Murray Jones, *Australian GST Handbook*) and superannuation (eg J Leow and S Murphy, *Australian Master Superannuation Guide* and S Jones, *Australian Superannuation Handbook*). The Australian Tax Research Foundation also publishes useful books containing in-depth research studies on particular taxation law topics.

Casebooks can also play a useful part in tax research. Casebooks generally provide the reader with the basic facts of a case as well as critical parts of the leading judgments (eg S Barkoczy, C Rider, J Baring and N Bellamy, *Australian Tax Casebook* (2021)). Some casebooks go beyond merely providing summaries and extracts of cases to also include commentary and questions (eg G Cooper, M Dirkis, M Stewart and R Vann, *Income Taxation Commentary and Materials* (2022)).

International resources

While the tax laws of each country vary dramatically, there are many common issues. For instance, many countries adopt similar concepts of income and deductions. They also usually base their jurisdictional rules on similar principles (eg residence and source) and have broadly similar kinds of international tax regimes (eg transfer pricing, accruals and withholding tax regimes). Likewise, many principles of tax theory are of universal concern—policy issues, such as what are the features of a good tax system and how should tax avoidance be tackled, are generally relevant to all jurisdictions. It is also interesting to look at alternative tax systems for comparative purposes. Foreign tax systems may provide useful benchmarking data and provide innovative ideas for tax reform. For these reasons, it is appropriate in many cases to extend one's research beyond Australia and investigate the international literature. This includes using books published by international publishers like Wolters Kluwer, LexisNexis and Thomson Reuters as well as those published by international organisations such as the OECD and the International Bureau of Fiscal Documentation. It also involves using specialist international tax journals such as the following:

International Tax Journals	
American Journal of Tax Policy	*Florida Tax Review*
Asia-Pacific Tax Bulletin	*Houston Business and Tax Law Journal*
ATA Journal of Legal Tax Research	*Intertax*
British Tax Review	*International Tax Journal*
Bulletin for International Taxation	*International Tax Review*
Canadian Current Tax	*New Zealand Journal of Taxation Law and Policy*
Canadian Tax Journal	*Pittsburgh Tax Review*
Columbia Journal of Tax Law	*Tax Law Review*
EC Tax Journal	*Tax Lawyer*
EC Tax Review	*Tax Notes International*
European Taxation	*VAT Monitor*
Fiscal Studies	*Virginia Tax Review*

[2.5] Online and electronic resources

Useful tax and related legal information from Australia and around the world can be obtained via the internet. For instance, many of the articles in the overseas journals mentioned at [2.4] can be conveniently accessed electronically using databases such as *LexisNexis*, *Westlaw*, *Kluwer Law Online* and the *IBFD Tax Research Platform*.

Without doubt, one of the most useful practical research tools is Wolters Kluwer's *CCH IntelliConnect*, which is an electronic database that provides access to a number of products, including the *Master Tax Guide* and a range of more detailed encyclopaedic services. These services contain key source material (eg legislation, cases and rulings) and extensive commentary regarding the law. *CCH IntelliConnect* allows rapid searches across numerous products and is particularly user-friendly as references are linked by hypertext. Another useful electronic library service is *Checkpoint*, which provides access to an array of tax and related publications published by Thomson Reuters.

The following table lists some useful websites for conducting tax research.

Australian Government	
Australian Border Force	www.abf.gov.au
Australian Business Register	www.abr.business.gov.au
Australian Charities and Not-for-profits Commission	www.acnc.gov.au
Australian Parliament	www.aph.gov.au
Australian Prudential Regulation Authority	www.apra.gov.au
Australian Securities and Investment Commission	www.asic.gov.au
Australian Taxation Office	www.ato.gov.au
Australian Transaction Reports and Analysis Centre	www.austrac.gov.au

Board of Taxation	www.taxboard.gov.au
Industry Innovation and Science Australia	www.industry.gov.au
Inspector-General of Taxation	www.igt.gov.au
myGov	www.my.gov.au
Tax Practitioners Board	www.tpb.gov.au
Treasury	www.treasury.gov.au/review
Australian Federal Courts and Tribunals	
High Court	www.hcourt.gov.au
Federal Court	www.fedcourt.gov.au
Administrative Appeals Tribunal	www.aat.gov.au
State and Territory Revenue Agencies	
ACT Revenue Office	www.revenue.act.gov.au
Queensland Office of State Revenue	www.treasury.qld.gov.au
Revenue NSW	www.revenue.nsw.gov.au
RevenueSA	www.revenuesa.sa.gov.au
RevenueWA	www.finance.wa.gov.au
State Revenue Office of Tasmania	www.sro.tas.gov.au
State Revenue Office Victoria	www.sro.vic.gov.au
Territory Revenue Office	www.treasury.nt.gov.au
Foreign Revenue Agencies	
Canada Revenue Agency	www.cra-arc.gc.ca
Hong Kong Inland Revenue Department	www.ird.gov.hk
Inland Revenue Authority of Singapore	www.iras.gov.sg
New Zealand Inland Revenue	www.ird.govt.nz
United Kingdom HM Revenue and Customs	www.hmrc.gov.uk
United States Internal Revenue Service	www.irs.gov
Legal Research Sites	
Australasian Legal Information Institute	www.austlii.edu.au
Federal Register of Legislation	www.legislation.gov.au
World Legal Information Institute	www.worldlii.org
Australian Tax Law Publishers	
Cambridge University Press	www.cambridge.org
Thomson Reuters	www.thomsonreuters.com.au
Wolters Kluwer	www.wolterskluwer.com/en_au
Australian Professional Bodies	
Association of Superannuation Funds of Australia Ltd	www.superannuation.asn.au
CPA Australia	www.cpaaustralia.com.au
Chartered Accountants Australia and New Zealand	www.charteredaccountantsanz.com

Law Council of Australia	www.lawcouncil.asn.au
National Tax and Accountants' Association	www.ntaa.com.au
Tax Institute	www.taxinstitute.com.au
Australian Law Firms	
Allens	www.allens.com.au
Ashurst	www.ashurst.com
Clayton Utz	www.claytonutz.com
Corrs Chambers Westgarth	www.corrs.com.au
Herbert Smith Freehills	www.herbertsmithfreehills.com
King & Wood Mallesons	www.kwm.com
MinterEllison	www.minterellison.com
Australian Accounting and Tax Advisory Firms	
BDO	www.bdo.com.au
Deloitte	www.deloitte.com.au
Ernst and Young	www.ey.com/en_au
KPMG	www.kpmg.com.au
Pitcher Partners	www.pitcher.com.au
PricewaterhouseCoopers	www.pwc.com.au
International Organisations	
International Bureau of Fiscal Documentation	www.ibfd.org
International Monetary Fund	www.imf.org
Organisation for Economic Co-operation and Development	www.oecd.org
Tax Justice Network	www.taxjustice.net

[2.6] Statutory interpretation

As taxation law is a creature of statute, statutory interpretation (ie the process of ascertaining the meaning of words and phrases used in legislation) is a critical aspect of everyday tax practice. Unfortunately, language is not always a precise tool for conveying ideas and there are often different views on the meaning of words in a statute. This is particularly the case where a statute deals with difficult technical concepts, such as those relating to taxation.

Legislative intention

It is for the courts to rule on the interpretation of tax legislation and, in doing so, they are required to give effect to the intention of Parliament as expressed by the terms of the statute. In *Cooper Brookes (Wollongong) Pty Ltd v FC of T* 81 ATC 4292, Mason and Wilson JJ recognised (at 4305) that the object 'is to ascertain the legislative intention by reference to the language of the instrument viewed as a whole'. Their Honours went on to explain that 'in performing that task, the courts look to the operation of the statute according to its terms and to legitimate aids to construction'.

In *Project Blue Sky v Australian Broadcasting Authority* (1998) 194 CLR 355, the High Court explained (at 381) that 'the process of construction must always begin by examining the context of the provision that is being construed'. The High Court noted that statutes consist of verbal formulas, where the literal meaning of words is not always the same as their legal meaning. In elaborating on this point, McHugh, Gummow, Kirby and Hayne JJ said (at 384):

> Thus, the duty of a court is to give the words of a statutory provision the meaning that the legislature is taken to have intended them to have. Ordinarily, that meaning (the legal meaning) will correspond with the grammatical meaning of the provision. But not always. The context of the words, the consequences of a literal or grammatical construction, the purpose of the statute or the canons of construction may require the words of a legislative provision to be read in a way that does not correspond with the literal or grammatical meaning.

The importance of reading words in their proper context, rather than in isolation, was recognised long ago in *Metropolitan Gas Co v Federated Gas Employees' Industrial Union* (1924) 35 CLR 449, where Isaacs and Rich JJ emphasised (at 455) that a 'canon of interpretation' was that 'every passage in a document must be read, not as if it were entirely divorced from its context, but as part of the whole instrument'.

More recently, in *Construction, Forestry, Maritime, Mining and Energy Union v Australian Building and Construction Commissioner* [2020] FCAFC 192, Allsop CJ explained (at [4]):

> Meaning is to be ascribed to the text of the statute, read in its context. The context, general purpose and policy of the provision and its consistency and fairness are surer guides to meaning than the logic of the construction of the provision.

In *Zheng v Cai* (2009) 239 CLR 446, the High Court stated (at 455) that attributing legislative intention is 'something of a fiction' that does not involve the attribution of a 'collective mental state to legislators' but rather 'the application of rules of interpretation accepted by all arms of government in the system of representative democracy'.

Ultimately, a statute has the meaning that Parliament intended it to have. The High Court in *Lacey v Attorney-General* (Qld) (2011) 242 CLR 573 explained (at 592) that this meaning is ascertained by reference to 'the rules of construction, common law and statutory, which have been applied to reach the preferred results and which are known to parliamentary drafters and the courts'. The High Court went on to state:

> The application of the rules will properly involve the identification of a statutory purpose, which may appear from an express statement in the relevant statute, by inference from its terms and by appropriate reference to extrinsic materials. The purpose of a statute is not something which exists outside the statute. It resides in its text and structure, albeit it may be identified by reference to common law and statutory rules of construction.

The following discussion introduces some of the basic statutory and common law rules that have been developed over the years to assist with the interpretation of legislation. However, before examining these rules, it is worth noting the words of Pearce in *Statutory Interpretation in Australia* (2019) who states (at 136):

> Legislation is, at its heart, an instrument of communication. For this reason, many of the so-called rules or principles of interpretation are no more than common-sense and grammatical aids that are applicable to any document by which one person endeavours to convey a message to another. Any inquiry into the meaning of an Act should therefore start with the question: 'What message is the legislature trying to convey in this communication?'

Legislative rules of statutory interpretation

The *Acts Interpretation Act 1901* contains a number of rules and presumptions for interpreting Commonwealth legislation. Some of the more important provisions in the Act are outlined below:

- **Acts read subject to the *Constitution*.** Section 15A states that every Act 'shall be read and construed subject to the *Constitution*, and so as not to exceed the legislative power of the Commonwealth'. Where any enactment would otherwise be in excess of that power 'it shall nevertheless be a valid enactment to the extent to which it is not in excess of that power'.
- **Construction that promotes the purpose or object of the Act.** Section 15AA states that in interpreting a provision of an Act, 'a construction that would promote the purpose or object underlying the Act (whether that purpose or object is expressly stated in the Act or not) shall be preferred to a construction that would not promote that purpose or object'.
- **Use of extrinsic material.** Section 15AB states that if any material not forming part of an Act is capable of assisting in ascertaining the meaning of a provision in the Act, consideration may be given to that material to:
  (a) confirm that the meaning of the provision is the ordinary meaning conveyed by the text taking into account its context and the purpose or object underlying the Act, or
  (b) determine the meaning of the provision when: (i) the provision is ambiguous or obscure; or (ii) the ordinary meaning conveyed by the text taking into account its context and the purpose or object underlying the Act leads to a result that is manifestly absurd or is unreasonable.

  Material that may be considered for the purposes of s 15AB includes:
  - documents attached to the Act
  - reports of a Royal Commission, Law Reform Commission or committee of inquiry or other similar body laid before Parliament before enactment
  - treaties or other international agreements referred to in the Act
  - explanatory memoranda relating to the Bill containing the provision, or any other relevant document, laid before Parliament by a Minister before enactment
  - Ministerial speeches made to Parliament moving the Bill, and
  - materials in the Journals of the Senate, Votes and Proceedings of the House of Representatives or in any official record of debates in Parliament.

  Only material existing at the time the relevant legislation was enacted should be considered under s 15AB. As Williams J of the Supreme Court of Queensland stated in *FC of T v Bill Wissler (Agencies) Pty Ltd* 85 ATC 4626 (at 4631):

  > I do not read s 15AB of the Acts Interpretation Act as permitting the Court to consider a statement made at a later point of time (say when the legislation was being amended) in order to discern the intention of the legislature when the original statute was passed. It is much easier to be wise after the legislation has been applied in practice and scrutinised by the courts. Such belated statements of legislative intent could hardly ever affect the proper construction of the language used in the statute.

- **Changes to style.** Section 15AC states that where an Act has expressed an idea in a particular form of words and a later Act appears to have expressed the same idea in a different form of words for the purpose of using a clearer style, the ideas shall not be taken to be different merely because different forms of words were used.
- **Relevance of examples.** Section 15AD states that where an Act includes an example of the operation of a provision, the example shall not be taken to be exhaustive and, if the example is inconsistent with the provision, the provision prevails.

2

Common law rules of statutory interpretation

Over the years, the courts have also devised a number of approaches to assist with the interpretation of legislation, including the following three basic rules:

1. **The literal rule.** The literal rule is the basic approach for interpreting legislation. According to this rule, the words of legislation are to be interpreted according to their natural and ordinary meaning. The essence of the literal rule was expressed by Higgins J in *Amalgamated Society of Engineers v Adelaide Steamship Co Ltd* (1920) 28 CLR 129 at (161) as follows:

   > The fundamental rule of interpretation, to which all others are subordinate, is that a statute is to be expounded according to the intent of the Parliament that made it; and that intention has to be found by an examination of the language used in the statute as a whole. The question is, what does the language mean; and when we find what the language means, in its ordinary and natural sense, it is our duty to obey that meaning, even if we think the result to be inconvenient or impolitic or improbable.

2. **The golden rule.** The golden rule is used where the literal rule produces an absurd, irrational, capricious or unjust outcome. It qualifies the literal rule and allows courts to interpret legislation in a common-sense way that avoids these results. The origins of the golden rule can be found in *Grey v Pearson* (1857) 10 ER 1216, where Lord Wensleydale stated (at 1234) that in construing statutes:

   > the grammatical and ordinary sense of the words is to be adhered to, unless that would lead to some absurdity, or some repugnance or inconsistency with the rest of the instrument, in which case the grammatical and ordinary sense of the words may be modified, so as to avoid that absurdity and inconsistency, but no farther.

3. **The mischief rule.** The mischief rule requires a court to interpret legislation in a way that addresses the mischief, harm or defect that the legislature intended to remedy. This rule is another qualification to the literal rule and can be traced back more than five centuries to the Court of Exchequer's decision in *Heydon* (1584) 76 ER 637. It is considered by many to be the origins of the modern 'purposive approach' discussed further below.

Traditional approach to interpreting tax legislation

The traditional approach adopted by the Australian courts to interpreting tax legislation, particularly around the time that Sir Garfield Barwick was Chief Justice of the High Court (1964–1981), was to use a strict literal approach. This approach is evident from his Honour's remarks in *FC of T v Westraders Pty Limited* 80 ATC 4357 (at 4358–4359):

> It is for the Parliament to specify, and to do so, in my opinion, as far as language will permit, with unambiguous clarity, the circumstances which will attract an obligation on the part of the citizen to pay tax. The function of the Court is to interpret and apply the language in which the Parliament has specified those circumstances. The Court is to do so by determining the meaning of the words employed by the Parliament according to the intention of the Parliament which is discoverable from the language used by the Parliament. It is not for the Court to mould or to attempt to mould the language of the statute so as to produce some result which it might be thought the Parliament may have intended to achieve, though not expressed in the actual language employed... Parliament having prescribed the circumstances which will attract tax, or provide occasion for its reduction or elimination, the citizen has every right to mould the transaction into which he is about to enter into a form which satisfies the requirements of the statute. It is nothing to the point that he might have attained the

> same or a similar result as that achieved by the transaction into which he in fact entered by some other transaction, which, if he had entered into it, would or might have involved him in a liability to tax, or to more tax than that attracted by the transaction into which he in fact entered. Nor can it matter that his choice of transaction was influenced wholly or in part by its effect upon his obligation to pay tax. Of course, the transaction must not be a pretence obscuring or attempting to supplant some other transaction into which in fact the taxpayer had earlier entered. Again, the freedom to choose the form of transaction into which he shall enter is basic to the maintenance of a free society.

Underpinning the strict literal approach is the basic principle that the intention to impose a tax must be shown by clear and unambiguous language and should not be inferred from ambiguous words. Gibbs CJ referred to this principle in *Western Australian Trustee Executor & Agency Co Ltd v C of ST (WA)* 80 ATC 4567 (at 4571):

> The established rule that no tax can be imposed on a subject by an Act of Parliament without words which clearly show an intention to lay the burden upon him does not mean that the court will strive to find loopholes where none are apparent; the words of the Act must be given a fair and reasonable construction, without leaning one way or the other. However, although, if the terms of the Act plainly impose the tax they should be given effect, equally if they do not reveal a clear intention to do so the liability should not be inferred from ambiguous words.

The courts have been prepared to depart from the literal meaning of a provision where doing so would give effect to the clear intention of Parliament. This occurred in *Cooper Brookes (Wollongong) Pty Ltd v FC of T* 81 ATC 4292, where a majority of the High Court construed a former poorly drafted anti-avoidance rule dealing with the carry forward of corporate losses according to its intent rather than its literal meaning so that its operation would not be 'capricious' or 'irrational'. Mason and Wilson JJ stated (at 4306):

> If the judge applies the literal rule it is because it gives emphasis to the factor which in the particular case he thinks is decisive . . . .
>
> On the other hand, when the judge labels the operation of the statute as 'absurd', 'extraordinary', 'capricious', 'irrational' or 'obscure' he assigns a ground for concluding that the Legislature could not have intended such an operation and that an alternative interpretation must be preferred. But the propriety of departing from the literal interpretation is not confined to situations described by these labels. It extends to any situation in which for good reason the operation of the statute on a literal reading does not conform to the legislative intent as ascertained from the provisions of the statute, including the policy which may be discerned from those provisions.

Modern approach to interpreting tax legislation

The modern approach to interpreting legislation is to adopt a construction that promotes the purpose or object of the statute. This 'purposive approach' is supported by s 15AA of the *Acts Interpretation Act* and requires the courts to have regard to the broader context of the legislation from the outset and not just when an ambiguity arises. In *CIC Insurance Ltd v Bankstown Football Club Ltd* (1997) 187 CLR 384, Brennan CJ, Dawson, Toohey and Gummow JJ stated (at 408):

> the modern approach to statutory interpretation (a) insists that the context be considered in the first instance, not merely at some later stage when ambiguity might be thought to arise, and (b) uses 'context' in its widest sense to include such things as the existing state of the law and the mischief which . . . one may discern the statute was intended to remedy.

In *Fox v Commissioner for Superannuation (No 2)* (1999) 88 FCR 416, Black CJ referred to this passage and explained (at 419–420):

> It was once thought that a statutory provision was to be interpreted literally unless its terms disclosed an ambiguity of meaning, in which case regard could be had to its context in order to discern the intention behind the provision's enactment and thereby resolve the ambiguity. This, however, is contrary to the modern approach to statutory interpretation...
>
> It follows that context must be considered at the beginning of any inquiry into the meaning of a statute, regardless of the apparent clarity of the literal terms of the relevant provision itself...
>
> Where a conflict exists between the constructions of a provision revealed by two principles of interpretation—here, by a literal reading and a purposive reading—a court 'must proceed with its primary task of extracting the intention of the legislature from the fair meaning of words by which it has expressed that intention', remembering always the mischief that the provision was enacted to address...

More recently, the modern approach was summarised by the High Court in *Sztal v Minister for Immigration and Border Protection* (2017) 262 CLR 362, where Keifel CJ, Nettle and Gordon JJ stated (at 368):

> The starting point for the ascertainment of the meaning of a statutory provision is the text of the statute whilst, at the same time, regard is had to its context and purpose... Context should be regarded at this first stage and not at some later stage and it should be regarded in its widest sense... This is not to deny the importance of the natural and ordinary meaning of a word, namely how it is ordinarily understood in discourse, to the process of construction. Considerations of context and purpose simply recognise that, understood in its statutory, historical or other context, some other meaning of a word may be suggested, and so too, if its ordinary meaning is not consistent with the statutory purpose, that meaning must be rejected.

Legal maxims

To assist in working out the meaning of particular words or phrases in a statute that may be ambiguous or unclear, the courts have often relied on various guiding principles that have been expressed in Latin maxims. The principles reflect a logical and common-sense approach to interpreting the language of a statute and are founded on basic grammatical and syntactic rules. Some commonly encountered maxims are outlined below:

- ***Noscitur a sociis***. This maxim supports a contextual approach to interpretation. It stands for the principle that a word or phrase should take its meaning from associated or accompanying words or phrases. In his 1937 book, *Law & Other Things*, Lord Macmillan vividly expressed the maxim as 'words of a feather flock together'. An illustration of where the maxim was applied is found in *Montgomerie v CIR (NZ)* (1965) 14 ATD 102, where the Supreme Court of New Zealand had to consider whether income of a trust had been 'applied' for the purposes of a provision in a New Zealand tax statute that contained the words 'pays or applies'. Barrowclough CJ said (at 107): 'The word "applied" is used in conjunction with "paid" and whilst of course it must have a somewhat different connotation, nevertheless, *noscitur a sociis*, and in my opinion the income cannot be said to be "applied" unless there is some dealing with it that is akin to payment—some parting with the possession and control of it.'
- ***Ejusdem generis***. This maxim means 'of the same kind'. It stands for the principle that where there is a list of specific things followed by a more general thing, the meaning given to the general thing should be restricted to cover the same class of things that are included in the specific

list. In *R v Regos* (1947) 74 CLR 613, Latham CJ explained that under this rule, 'general words may be restricted to the same genus as the specific words that precede them'. For example, in *Canwan Coals Pty Ltd v FC of T* 74 ATC 4231, the Supreme Court of NSW considered the phrase 'a railway, road, pipe-line or other facility' in a former *ITAA36* provision. It relied on the *ejusdem generis* rule to construe the words 'other facility' as referring only to those facilities upon which, or through which, relevant goods might be moved or conveyed. A reserve storage facility was therefore not such a facility, as it was not used for transport.

- ***Expressio unius est exclusio alterius***. This maxim can be translated as 'the expression of one is at the exclusion of others'. It suggests that where one class of thing is mentioned in a statute, then other classes of the same thing that are not mentioned should be excluded. Although this maxim can be useful in certain cases, the courts have warned that it should be applied with caution (see eg *FC of T v Barnes Development Pty Ltd* 2009 ATC ¶20-121; *State of Tasmania v Cth* (1901) 1 CLR 329; *Houssein v Under Secretary of Industrial Relations and Technology* (1982) 148 CLR 88).
- ***Generalia specialibus non derogant***. This maxim means 'the general does not detract from the specific'. Based on this maxim, a specific provision in a statute should override a general provision in the statute where those provisions are in conflict. The maxim has been considered in a number of tax cases, including the High Court decision in *FC of T v Gulland* 85 ATC 4765. In *Barker v Edger* [1898] AC 748, the Privy Council explained (at 754) that the maxim operates as follows: 'whenever there is a particular enactment and a general enactment in the same statute, and the latter, taken in its most comprehensive sense, would overrule the former, the particular enactment must be operative, and the general enactment must be taken to affect only the parts of the statute to which it may properly apply'.

It is important not to view the above maxims as rigid and inflexible rules, but rather as simply aids to construction. As Higgins J said in *Bank Officials' Association (South Australian Branch) v Savings Bank of South Australia* (1923) 32 CLR 276 (at 299), the maxims 'merely afford presumptions' and 'merely aid us in taking our bearings in the movement of our reason'.

The difficulty in relying on the maxims was noted in *Chief Executive Officer of Customs v Biocontrol Ltd* [2006] FCA 107, where the Federal Court warned that the *ejusdem generis* rule is 'no more than a guide to interpretation' that should be 'used cautiously'. Young J said (at [46]):

> There will be occasions when it is not appropriate to apply the rule having regard to the context and purpose of the particular statutory provision. There will also be occasions where the descriptive terms that precede the general words are so varied that it is futile to search for a single genus or class that can be of assistance in giving meaning to the general words. Conversely, there will be occasions where it is both sensible and appropriate to give meaning to the general words by identifying the class or genus that is indicated by the preceding particular words. All in all, the surest approach is to give meaning to general words which follow particular words in a statutory provision by determining the meaning of those words in their context and by reference to the purpose of the provision, in the same way as meaning is given to other words in a statute.

Defined terms and common expressions

Where legislation defines a particular term, the term must obviously be interpreted in accordance with its technical statutory definition. It is, therefore, important when interpreting legislation to check whether it contains any express definitions. Most tax statutes have lengthy definition sections. Examples of such provisions in Australia's tax statutes include: s 6 *ITAA36*, s 995-1 *ITAA97*, s 195-1 *GSTA* and s 136 *FBTAA*. Terms that are not specifically defined in the legislation should ordinarily be given their natural meanings.

When reading statutes, it is also important to note the distinctions that are generally drawn between commonly used expressions, such as the following:

- **'May' and 'shall'.** The word 'may' usually confers a discretionary power (ie it indicates that something is permissible or optional). The word 'shall', on the other hand, usually imposes an obligation or duty (ie it indicates that something is mandatory or compulsory).
- **'Means' and 'includes'.** The word 'means' indicates that a term has an exhaustive and restricted definition and that no other meaning can be attributed to it (ie it confines the scope of a definition). The word 'includes', on the other hand, indicates that a term has meanings outside those things specifically mentioned (ie it enlarges the scope of a definition).
- **'And' and 'or'.** The word 'and' when used in a list of words or phrases indicates that the words or phrases are to be read conjunctively (ie as cumulative requirements). The word 'or' when used in a list of words or phrases indicates that the words or phrases are to be read disjunctively (ie as alternatives).

[2.7] QUESTIONS

1. What are the primary sources of tax law?
2. What kinds of rulings does the ATO issue? What is the difference between a binding and a non-binding ruling?
3. Discuss the main kinds of secondary resource materials available for undertaking tax research. What are some of the main Australian tax journals?
4. Visit the ATO website—what kinds of information does it contain? Visit the parliamentary website—what tax Bills are currently before Parliament?
5. In what circumstances does s 15AB of the *Acts Interpretation Act 1901* (Cth) permit material that does not form part of an Act to be used to assist in ascertaining the meaning of a provision in the Act?
6. Explain the different connotations of the words 'means' and 'includes' when used in a definition provision. Provide some examples from the *ITAA97*.

CONSTITUTIONAL FRAMEWORK OF THE AUSTRALIAN TAX SYSTEM 3

[3.1] Introduction

In order to properly appreciate the framework in which Australia's tax laws operate, it is necessary to understand Australia's system of government and the constitutional setting within which the tax system functions. This chapter discusses how Australia's federal system of government evolved and how sovereign power is shared between the Commonwealth and states [3.2]. It also examines the *Commonwealth Constitution* [3.3] and focuses on the following provisions:

- s 51(ii) (which deals with the Commonwealth Parliament's taxation power) [3.4]
- s 53 (which deals with the Senate's powers in relation to taxation laws) [3.5]
- s 55 (which deals with the nature of laws imposing taxation) [3.6]
- s 81 and s 83 (which deal with the Consolidated Revenue Fund and appropriations of money from Treasury) [3.7]
- s 90 (which deals with the power to impose customs and excise duties) [3.8]
- s 96 (which deals with grants of financial assistance to the states) [3.9], and
- s 114 (which deals with the imposition of taxes on property belonging to the states) [3.10].

[3.2] Australian system of government

Australia has been inhabited by First Nations people for over 50,000 years. In 1788, Australia was colonised by Britain when Governor Phillip arrived with the First Fleet in Botany Bay to establish New South Wales ('NSW') as a penal colony. NSW was subsequently divided into a number of additional independent colonies: namely, Tasmania, originally called Van Diemen's Land (in 1825), South Australia (in 1836), Victoria (in 1851) and Queensland (in 1859). Western Australia originated as a separate free colony (in 1829). As the colonies were 'British settlements', the existing laws of Britain were transplanted, insofar as they were applicable, to the colonies under the 'doctrine of received law'. The British colonisers treated Australia as *terra nullius* (ie a land belonging to nobody) and did not recognise the existence of any customary laws of the First Nations people.

Over time, Britain eventually granted the colonies their own Constitutions with their respective Parliaments. This allowed the colonies to be self-governing, subject to oversight by the Westminster Parliament which retained the power to make laws for them. Although the colonies were independent, the colonists shared the same language and heritage. It was therefore not surprising that a bourgeoning movement to unite the colonies gradually evolved. This movement was motivated by a number of factors, including the desire to remove tariffs and promote free trade between the colonies. There was also a growing belief that the colonies would be stronger if they had a united defence force and immigration policy under a national government. A series of constitutional conventions involving representatives of the colonies were convened to consider federation in the 1890s. This eventually resulted in the production of a draft Bill containing the proposed *Commonwealth Constitution*. The colonies held referendums to vote on the draft Bill, and they voted in favour of its adoption. The draft Bill was then presented to the United Kingdom Parliament, which enacted it in the *Commonwealth of Australia Constitution Act 1900* (Imp). This legislation came into force on 1 January 1901 and established the Commonwealth of Australia as a self-governing dominion within the British Empire. The former colonies consequently became states within the federation and retained their own Constitutions, which also originated in United Kingdom legislation, but which now operated subject to the *Commonwealth Constitution*.

Legislative independence

Although federation created a unified nation, it was not an independence movement under which Australia sought to leave the British Empire and become a republic. Australia's historical ties with Britain remained firmly in place as the Commonwealth and states continued to be subject to the following common law doctrines:

- the 'doctrine of imperial supremacy', which gave the United Kingdom Parliament the power to legislate by paramount force for its dominions within the British Empire, and
- the 'doctrine of repugnancy', which was statutorily enshrined in s 2 of the *Colonial Laws Validity Act 1865* (Imp) and provided that colonial laws operated subject to United Kingdom laws and were void to the extent of any repugnancy (see *Union Steamship Co of New Zealand Ltd v Cth* (1925) 36 CLR 130).

The United Kingdom Parliament therefore retained the power to make laws for Australia and the states. It could therefore technically enact legislation expressed to apply to Australia and the states that would be effective notwithstanding anything expressed to the contrary in Commonwealth or state legislation.

The United Kingdom's power to legislate for the Commonwealth was subsequently restricted by the *Statute of Westminster 1931* (Imp), which was adopted in Australia by the *Statute of Westminster Adoption Act 1942* (Cth) and made retroactive to 3 September 1939 (the date the British Empire entered World War II). The *Statute of Westminster* had its genesis in the Balfour Declaration made at the 1926 Imperial Conference in London where it was declared that the Dominions would be autonomous communities within the British Empire. The *Statute of Westminster* provided that no Act of the United Kingdom Parliament passed after the commencement of the statute shall extend to a Dominion unless it expressly requested and consented to it (s 4). It also removed the doctrine of repugnancy and abolished the application of the *Colonial Laws Validity Act 1865* (Imp) to any Dominion law made after its commencement (s 2).

Under the *Statute of Westminster*, the definition of 'Dominion' included the Commonwealth, but made no reference to the states (s 1). The statute therefore did not apply to the states and it was only in 1986 that the states achieved full legislative independence when the United Kingdom and Commonwealth Parliaments (with the request of all state Parliaments) each passed their own versions of the *Australia Act 1986*. This legislation provided that no Act of the United Kingdom Parliament passed after its commencement shall extend to the Commonwealth, a state or a territory (s 1). It also abolished the doctrine of repugnancy and the application of the *Colonial Laws Validity Act 1865* (Imp) to any state law made after the commencement of the legislation and granted the state Parliaments the power to amend or repeal United Kingdom legislation in so far as it related to them (s 3).

Commonwealth and state sharing of power

As a consequence of federation, Australia has a system of government under which sovereign power is shared between a central Commonwealth Government and a number of state Governments. The Commonwealth of Australia consists of a union of six states (formerly the six colonies) and three internal and seven external territories. The internal territories include the Australian Capital Territory ('ACT') (which was ceded to the Commonwealth by NSW in 1911 for the purposes of forming the national capital) and the Northern Territory ('NT') (which was ceded to the Commonwealth by South Australia in 1911). The other internal territory is Jervis Bay (which was ceded by NSW in 1911 to serve as a seaport for the proposed national capital).

Each of the states, as well as the ACT and NT, has its own government. The Commonwealth Government is headed by the Prime Minister, state Governments are headed by their respective Premiers and the territory Governments are headed by their respective Chief Ministers. Each jurisdiction also has its own legislature. As is common in Westminster style democracies, the Commonwealth and all the states (other than Queensland) have bicameral parliaments (ie parliaments consisting of two chambers—a Lower House and an Upper House). Queensland abolished its Upper House (the Legislative Council) in 1922. The ACT and NT have unicameral legislatures (ie they only have Legislative Assemblies). The remaining territories are administered by the Commonwealth. The Commonwealth retains the power to legislate in the self-governing territories and can override their laws.

The terms under which sovereign power is shared between the Commonwealth and states is set out under the Commonwealth and state constitutions. While the *Commonwealth Constitution* provides that the Commonwealth Parliament can only enact laws that are within the specific heads of power set out in the *Constitution*, the state constitutions provide that the state parliaments have the power to make laws for their respective states subject to the provisions of the *Commonwealth Constitution*. The state parliaments therefore have plenary powers, which are only limited by the *Commonwealth Constitution* and the requirement of a requisite territorial nexus.

Coordination between Australian Governments

In 1992, the Council of Australian Governments ('COAG') was formed to manage matters of national significance that required coordinated action between the respective Australian governments. COAG usually met at least twice a year and its membership comprised the Prime Minister, state Premiers, territory Chief Ministers and the President of the Australian Local Government Association. In March 2020, a National Cabinet consisting of the Prime Minister, state Premiers and territory Chief Ministers was formed to deal with the COVID-19 pandemic. In May 2020, the National Cabinet agreed to establish the National Federation Reform Council ('NFRC') to replace COAG. The NFRC focuses on priority national reform issues and its members are the Prime Minister, state Premiers, territory Chief Ministers, Treasurers from all jurisdictions, and the President of the Australian Local Government Association.

[3.3] The *Commonwealth Constitution*

The *Commonwealth Constitution* is contained in the *Commonwealth of Australia Constitution Act 1900* (Imp), which came into force on 1 January 1901 when the former British colonies (now the six states) formed the Commonwealth of Australia [3.2]. The first eight sections of this legislation comprise 'covering clauses', while s 9 contains the actual provisions of the *Constitution*. The *Constitution* is divided into eight chapters comprising 128 sections that deal with the following matters:

- Chapter I deals with the Commonwealth Parliament
- Chapter II deals with the executive government
- Chapter III deals with the judicature
- Chapter IV deals with finance and trade
- Chapter V deals with the powers of the states
- Chapter VI deals with procedures for establishing new states
- Chapter VII deals with a range of miscellaneous matters, and
- Chapter VIII deals with procedures for the alteration of the *Constitution*.

Separation of powers

The *Commonwealth Constitution* is Australia's most important legal document as it sets out the legislative, executive and judicial powers of the Commonwealth. Legislative power involves making laws, executive power involves administering and enforcing laws, and judicial power involves interpreting and adjudicating laws. These three powers are dealt with under separate chapters in the *Constitution*, and are based on the 'separation of powers doctrine' advocated by Baron de Montesquieu in his 18th century political treatise, *De l'Esprit des Lois*.

The object of the separation of powers doctrine is to ensure that power is not vested in a single person or group of persons. The doctrine prevents the potential abuse of power by providing checks and balances on the various branches of government. While the doctrine underpins the *Constitution*, it is important to understand that Australia does not adopt a strict separation of powers doctrine like, for instance, the United States, but is instead modelled on the United Kingdom's 'Westminster system'. In Australia, the separation of powers is blurred because, like in the United Kingdom, there is an overlap between executive and legislative powers. As will be discussed further below, s 64 of the *Constitution* requires government ministers (who form part of the executive branch of government through their membership of the Federal Executive Council) to also be members of Parliament (which is the legislative branch of government). This overlap promotes the principle of 'responsible Government' by ensuring that the Executive is accountable to Parliament.

Legislative power

Section 1 of the *Constitution* vests Commonwealth legislative power (ie the power to make Commonwealth law) in the Commonwealth Parliament. The Commonwealth Parliament consists of three distinct bodies:

- **The House of Representatives** (also known as the 'Lower House'). The House of Representatives is composed of 151 Members elected by the people of the Commonwealth. Each Member represents their respective electorate. Electoral boundaries are adjusted from time to time to ensure they contain roughly similar numbers of voters (electorates therefore vary in size from a few square kilometres to over one million square kilometres). Members are elected under a preferential voting system for terms of three years (s 28). The political party (or coalition of parties) that has the most Members in the Lower House is the governing party and its leader is the Prime Minister.
- **The Senate** (also known as the 'Upper House'). The Senate is composed of 76 Senators (12 Senators for each of the six states, elected by the people of the respective states, and a further two Senators elected for each of the two territories, elected by the people of the respective territories). Although the Senate was originally a House that represented only the states, s 122 of the *Constitution* allows Parliament to legislate for Territory representation, and it did

so under the *Senate (Representation of Territories) Act 1973* (Cth). Senators are elected under a proportional representation system for terms of six years, with half-Senate elections occurring every three years.

- **The King** (represented by the Governor-General). As Australia is a 'constitutional monarchy', the British Monarch (King Charles III) is the Head of State. The Governor-General is appointed on the advice of the Australian Prime Minister. Australia's current Governor-General is His Excellency General the Honourable David Hurley AC DSC (Retd).

Enacting legislation

Members of Parliament initiate new laws by introducing Bills into Parliament. For a Commonwealth Bill to be enacted and become law, both Houses of Parliament must pass the Bill and it must also receive the assent of the Governor-General.

There are three readings of a Bill in each House of Parliament. At the first reading, the Bill is simply introduced and distributed among members for consideration. At the second reading, the member responsible for the Bill makes a speech explaining the reasons for its introduction. This is typically followed by debate. The Bill is then considered by the House in detail and may be referred to a select or standing committee, which may make recommendations to the House. Any proposed amendments to the Bill are then moved. At the third reading, the members vote on whether the Bill (with any proposed changes) should be passed. Once passed, the Bill proceeds to the other House for similar consideration.

The *Constitution* provides that each House determines whether a Bill should be passed by majority vote (ss 23, 40). In the House of Representatives, the member who is elected as Speaker does not vote unless the votes are equal, in which case he or she has the casting vote. In the Senate, the senator who is chosen as President is entitled to vote, and if the votes are equal, the Bill is not passed. Both Houses require a quorum of one-third of the members or senators to constitute a meeting and vote on a Bill (ss 22, 39).

After a Bill has been passed by both Houses, it is presented to the Governor-General for assent in the Monarch's name (s 58). Although the Governor-General can technically exercise his discretion to withhold assent or reserve the Bill for the Monarch's pleasure, in practice, the Governor-General generally always assents to a Bill. Once assent has been granted, the Bill becomes an Act and is given an Act number.

An Act operates from the date specified in the legislation. In practice, most Acts usually only operate prospectively. However, on certain occasions, Parliament has enacted retrospective legislation. For instance, it has does this in respect of anti-avoidance measures. A well-known example of retrospective tax legislation is the *Crimes (Taxation Offences) Act 1980* (Cth), which applies to 'bottom of the harbour' schemes [36.3]. The problem with retrospective legislation is that it can be unjust and contribute to uncertainty, as it can adversely impact on transactions that have already taken place and make people liable for offences and expose them to sanctions for non-compliance that they were unaware existed at the time of their actions. The Commonwealth Parliament's constitutional power to enact retrospective legislation was nevertheless confirmed long ago in *R v Kidman* (1915) 20 CLR 425, where the High Court stated (at 451):

> There are plenty of passages that can be cited showing the inexpediency, and the injustice, in most cases, of legislating for the past, of interfering with vested rights, and of making acts unlawful which were lawful when done; but these passages do not raise any doubt as to the power of the Legislature to pass retroactive legislation, if it sees fit.

Delegated legislation

It is common for Parliament to delegate legislative power to the Executive or some other body in order to reduce its busy workload. Delegated legislation, also known as 'subordinate legislation', must be made with Parliament's authority under a primary Act (often referred to as the 'enabling legislation'). For example, an Act may allow the Governor-General, a Minister, a government agency or public official (such as the Commissioner of Taxation) to prescribe certain regulations under the statute.

By delegating its legislative power, Parliament can focus on general principles and broader policy issues in a statute, while leaving detailed matters (eg those relating to administrative or technical issues) to other bodies. Delegated legislation allows laws to be made and amended more quickly than they would be if they had to be passed by Parliament and enables bodies that possess special knowledge or expertise in particular areas to make such laws.

There are many forms of delegated legislation, including regulations, proclamations, orders, notices, declarations and determinations. The *Legislation Act 2003* (Cth) requires these instruments to be registered in the Federal Register of Legislation managed by the Office of Parliamentary Counsel (s 15A). To ensure parliamentary oversight is maintained over subordinate legislation, such instruments must be laid before each House of Parliament within six sitting days of the House following registration (s 38). Each House has 15 sitting days after tabling to issue a notice of motion to disallow an instrument, and such a motion must be resolved or withdrawn within 15 sitting days after the notice is given (s 42). Legislative instruments that are not laid before each House within the prescribed time limit are automatically repealed.

Limitation on Commonwealth's legislative powers

Importantly, the Commonwealth Parliament can only enact laws that are within the specific heads of power listed in the *Constitution*. It cannot therefore legislate on every type of subject matter. In *R v Barger* (1908) 6 CLR 41, Griffith CJ, Barton and O'Connor JJ explained (at 67):

> The scheme of the Australian Constitution, like that of the United States of America, is to confer certain definite powers upon the Commonwealth, and to reserve to the States, whose powers before the establishment of the Commonwealth were plenary, all powers not expressly conferred upon the Commonwealth.

The Commonwealth Parliament's main powers are contained in s 51. This section sets out a list of areas in which the Commonwealth Parliament may, subject to the *Constitution*, 'make laws for the peace, order and good government of the Commonwealth'. The areas include trade and commerce (s 51(i)), taxation (s 51(ii)), postal services (s 51(v)), naval and military defence (s 51(vi)), currency (s 51(xii)), bankruptcy and insolvency (s 51(xvii)), and copyrights, patents and trademarks (s 51(xviii)). There is also an incidental power which covers matters incidental to the execution of any express power vested in the Parliament by the *Constitution* (s 51(xxxix)). In addition, the *Constitution* contains a reference power which authorises the Commonwealth Parliament to make laws with respect to matters referred to it by the states (s 51(xxxvii)). Laws enacted under this power 'extend only to those States by whose Parliaments the matter is referred, or which afterwards adopt the law'.

The powers in s 51 are concurrent powers, which means that both the Commonwealth and state parliaments can legislate on these subject matters. However, if an inconsistency exists between Commonwealth and state laws, the Commonwealth law prevails, and the state law is invalid to the extent of the inconsistency (s 109).

The Commonwealth Parliament also has a limited number of exclusive powers. This includes the powers mentioned in s 52 (eg the power to legislate in respect of Commonwealth places) and the power in s 90 (relating to customs and excise duties) [3.8]. The states cannot legislate on these matters.

Executive power

Section 61 of the *Constitution* vests Commonwealth executive power (ie the power to administer and enforce Commonwealth law) in the Governor-General, who exercises this power as the Monarch's representative. Section 64 gives the Governor-General the power to appoint Ministers who, as outlined above, are required to also be Members of Parliament. The Governor-General traditionally makes such appointments on the advice of the Prime Minister whom he or she also appoints. Although the office of the Prime Minister is not specifically mentioned in the *Constitution*, as indicated above, the Prime Minister is, by convention, always the leader of the political party (or coalition of parties) that controls the House of Representatives. The Prime Minister allocates portfolios (eg Treasury and Finance) to Ministers who are officially appointed by the Governor-General. Ministers are individually responsible for actions undertaken by their respective departments under the doctrine of 'Ministerial responsibility'.

When exercising executive power, the Governor-General usually does so on the advice and through the offices of his or her Ministers who are members of the Federal Executive Council (ss 62, 64). The Federal Executive Council is the body responsible for advising the Governor-General and has *de jure* executive power to implement the decisions made by the Government of the day. In practice, Government decisions are traditionally made by Cabinet. Although Cabinet is not mentioned in the *Constitution* and has no official legal status, it is a widely recognised institution in the Westminster system of government and is where policy decisions are made. Cabinet consists of the Prime Minister and his or her selected Ministers. Cabinet meetings are confidential and its records are kept secret for a specified period of time (generally between 20 and 30 years depending on the nature of the record and when it was made). Ministers are expected to support Cabinet decisions publicly to ensure Cabinet solidarity.

The Governor-General also has a limited number of 'reserve powers' which are not codified in the *Constitution*. When exercising these powers, the Governor-General does not need to act in accordance with Ministerial advice. As will be discussed further, one of these reserve powers is the power to dismiss a Prime Minister, which was exercised by the Governor-General in 1975 [3.7].

Judicial power

Section 71 of the *Constitution* vests Commonwealth judicial power (ie the power to adjudicate disputes about Commonwealth laws) in:

- the High Court of Australia
- such other federal courts that the Commonwealth Parliament creates (eg the Federal Court of Australia established under the *Federal Court of Australia Act 1976* (Cth)), and
- such other courts as the Commonwealth Parliament invests with federal jurisdiction (eg state courts invested with federal jurisdiction under the *Judiciary Act 1903* (Cth)).

High Court and Federal Court justices are appointed by the Governor-General in Council (ie by the Governor-General sitting with the advice of the Federal Executive Council) (s 63). They can only be removed from office by the Governor-General in Council on an address from both Houses of Parliament on the ground of proved misbehaviour or incapacity (s 72). Justices have tenure until the age of 70 but may resign beforehand by notifying the Governor-General in writing.

Changes to the *Constitution*

Although the *Commonwealth Constitution* is contained in a United Kingdom Act, Australia's constitutional links with the United Kingdom have been effectively cut following the enactment of the *Statute of Westminster Adoption Act 1942* and the *Australia Act 1986* [3.2]. Australia is therefore an independent nation that is free to amend its *Constitution*. Section 128, however, states that amendments to the *Constitution* must be approved by an absolute majority of both Houses of Parliament and must be approved in a referendum by a majority of voters, including a majority of voters in a majority of states. Of the 45 proposals for changes to the *Constitution* that have been put to the nation at referendums, only eight have been approved.

[3.4] Commonwealth taxation power

The Commonwealth Parliament has limited powers and can only enact laws that are within the specific heads of power listed in the *Constitution* [3.3]. The primary source of the Commonwealth Parliament's taxation power is found in s 51(ii), which must be read subject to the other provisions of the *Constitution*. Section 51(ii) provides that the Commonwealth Parliament has the power to make laws with respect to 'taxation; but so as not to discriminate between States or parts of States'.

Laws with respect to taxation

One of the earliest High Court cases to consider s 51(ii) was *R v Barger* (1908) 6 CLR 41. In this case, it was held that in determining whether an Act imposes a law with respect to taxation, a court must consider the substance of the Act, and should not be influenced by the name that Parliament gives it. As Higgins J observed (at 118):

> It is conceded on all sides that this Court is not to be bound by the name which Parliament has chosen to give to the Act, but is to consider what the Act is in substance—what it does, what it commands or prescribes.

Similar observations were made by Griffith CJ, Barton and O'Connor JJ, who said (at 75) that 'an inquiry into the purpose of an Act is not an inquiry into the motives of the legislature, but into the substance of the legislation'.

Thirty years later, in *Matthews v Chicory Marketing Board* (1938) 60 CLR 263, Latham CJ (at 276) described a levy imposed on a chicory grower under a Victorian Act as a tax because it was:

> a compulsory exaction of money by a public authority for public purposes, enforceable by law, and is not a payment for services rendered.

Although Latham CJ's statement has been frequently cited in subsequent cases, the High Court in *Luton v Lessels & Anor* 2002 ATC 4311 emphasised that the Chief Justice's words were not offered as a definition of a tax, but were simply the explanation of the features of the impost under consideration that justified the conclusion that it was a tax. As Gleeson CJ stated (at 4313), 'whether an exaction of money or the imposition of some other financial obligation is a tax involves an exercise in characterisation'.

On this basis, it has been recognised that while the characteristics mentioned by Latham CJ are important, they are not determinative of whether a law operates as a tax. For instance, it has been held that it is not essential that an exaction should be by a public authority for it to constitute a tax (*Australian Tape Manufacturers Association Ltd & Ors v Cth* (1993) 176 CLR 480; *Air Caledonie International & Ors v Cth* (1988) 165 CLR 462). Likewise, it has been held that the fact that money is not paid into the Consolidated Revenue Fund [3.7] does not prevent an exaction from being for public purposes (*Australian Tape Manufacturers Association Ltd & Ors v Cth* (1993) 176 CLR 480; *Northern Suburbs General Cemetery Reserve Trust v Cth* 93 ATC 4118). The corollary to this is that a payment is not necessarily a tax just because money is paid into the Consolidated Revenue Fund.

In *Australian Tape Manufacturers*, the High Court held that legislation requiring blank tape vendors to pay royalties to a collecting society, which were to be distributed among copyright owners who were members of the society in recompense for home copying of their sound recordings, was a law with respect to taxation. The fact that the royalty was not paid to a public authority, was not paid into the Consolidated Revenue Fund and recompensed one group of persons at the expense of another did not prevent the exaction from being characterised as a tax. In arriving at the conclusion that the royalty was a tax, the majority (Mason CJ, Brennan, Deane and Gaudron JJ) stated (at 507):

> It does not fall within any of the well-recognized descriptions of fees or charges which stand outside the concept of a tax. It is not a fee for a licence or privilege or for a service rendered; it

> is not a charge for the acquisition or use of property; and it is certainly not a fine or penalty. Moreover, it has the characteristics of an excise; it is imposed upon the vendors of blank tapes in respect of the sale of tapes and it is a charge which the vendor will, in the ordinary course of business, pass on to the purchaser . . .

Subsequently, in *Roy Morgan Research Pty Ltd v FC of T* 2011 ATC ¶20-282, an employer challenged the validity of the *Superannuation Guarantee (Administration Act) 1992* (Cth) ('*SGAA*') and the *Superannuation Guarantee Charge Act 1992* (Cth) ('*SGCA*'). The *SGAA* provided that where an employer failed to provide a prescribed minimum level of superannuation support for its employees, then any shortfall (together with an interest component and an administration component) became a charge levied on the employer by the *SGCA*. The charge was required to be paid into the Consolidated Revenue Fund and the amount of the charge (excluding the administration component) was then required to be paid out of the Consolidated Revenue Fund to a superannuation fund for the benefit of the relevant employee. The employer referred to Latham CJ's formulation in *Matthews v Chicory Marketing Board* and submitted that an essential element of a tax is that it be imposed for public purposes. The employer argued that the charge conferred a 'private and direct benefit' on employees and was therefore not for public purposes. The High Court, however, rejected this argument. The Court held that the charge was for public purposes because it was paid into the Consolidated Revenue Fund, wherein it loses its identity and becomes available to be appropriated by Parliament for any lawful purpose. French CJ, Gummow, Hayne, Crennan, Kiefel and Bell JJ explained (at [49]):

3

> It is settled that the imposition of a tax for the benefit of the Consolidated Revenue Fund is made for public purposes . . . That is not to say that the receipt of funds into the Consolidated Revenue Fund conclusively establishes their character as the proceeds of a tax. But it does establish in the present case that the Charge is imposed for 'public purposes' and thus, if other necessary criteria are met, as they are in this case, the Charge is a valid tax.

In *MacCormick v FC of T* 84 ATC 4230, the High Court indicated that to constitute a tax, an exaction must not be 'incontestable' or 'arbitrary'. Gibbs CJ, Wilson, Deane and Dawson JJ said (at 4237):

> For an impost to satisfy the description of a tax it must be possible to differentiate it from an arbitrary exaction and this can only be done by reference to the criteria by which liability to pay the tax is imposed. Not only must it be possible to point to the criteria themselves, but it must be possible to show that the way in which they are applied does not involve the imposition of liability in an arbitrary or capricious manner.

In *Giris Pty Ltd v FC of T* 69 ATC 4015, the High Court was called upon to rule on the validity of ss 99 and 99A *ITAA36* which dealt with the assessment of trustees [24.5]. Under s 99A(2), the Commissioner had a discretion not to assess a trustee under s 99A if he formed the opinion that it would be unreasonable to do so, in which case the trustee would be assessed at lower rates under s 99. In forming his opinion, the Commissioner was directed to have regard to certain circumstances, including 'such other matters, if any, as he thinks fit'. In the course of reaching its decision, the Court examined the notion of an 'incontestable tax'. Kitto J said (at 4021):

> The expression refers to a tax provided for by a law which, while making the taxpayer's liability depend upon specified criteria, purports to deny him all right to resist an assessment by providing in the courts that the criteria of liability were not satisfied in his case.

The High Court held that even though the trustee's liability depended on the exercise of an opinion of the Commissioner, this did not render the provisions invalid. As the Commissioner's opinion was open to judicial review (ie it was open to a court reviewing an assessment to determine whether the opinion was formed bona fide or arbitrarily), the tax was not incontestable and therefore fell within the scope of s 51(ii). The Court also concluded that the provisions did not constitute an inadmissible delegation of legislative power.

In *Luton v Lessels & Anor*, the High Court recognised that one of the key characteristics of a tax is that it has the purpose and effect of raising revenue for the government. A law can nevertheless still be characterised as a law with respect to taxation even if it operates to achieve another purpose. For instance, in *State Chamber of Commerce and Industry & Ors v Cth* 87 ATC 4745, the High Court held that the fringe benefits tax legislation was valid, even though it also operated to discourage the provision of fringe benefits.

Earlier on, in *Fairfax v FC of T* (1965) 14 ATD 135, the trustees of a superannuation fund challenged legislation which amended the *ITAA36* to make tax exemptions for superannuation funds conditional on the Commissioner being satisfied that trustees of the funds held a specified portion of their investments in public securities. The trustees contended that the amendment was beyond the Commonwealth's legislative powers as it was not a law with respect to taxation, but a law with respect to the investment of moneys of superannuation funds. The High Court, however, unanimously rejected this argument and held that the legislation was a valid exercise of the power under s 51(ii). Kitto J referred to *Barger's case* and held that even though the legislative purpose of the amendment was to induce superannuation funds to invest in public securities, and the raising of revenue was a 'secondary concern', the substance of the legislation must be determined by reference to the obligation it imposed, which was to pay tax. His Honour pointed out (at 137) that the question of constitutional validity under s 51 is always one of subject matter:

> Under that section the question is always one of subject matter, to be determined by reference solely to the operation which the enactment has if it be valid, that is to say by reference to the nature of the rights, duties, powers and privileges which it changes, regulates or abolishes; it is a question as to the true nature and character of the legislation: is it in its real substance a law upon, 'with respect to', one or more of the enumerated subjects, or is there no more in it in relation to any of those subjects than an interference so incidental as not in truth to affect its character?

Menzies J emphasised that constitutional validity of a law depends on its 'true nature and character' rather than its economic consequences or legislative motives. His Honour stated (at 143):

> Whether or not a law is one with respect to taxation cannot be determined by looking at its economic consequences, however apparent they must have been at the time of its enactment; nor is an enquiry into the motives of the legislature permissible.

Menzies J, nevertheless, went on to indicate that there may be laws that ostensibly impose tax which are not laws with respect to taxation and he provided the following example of such a law in his obiter dictum (at 143):

> a special prohibitive tax upon income derived from the sale of heroin or from the growing or treatment of poppies for the production of heroin may not be a law with respect to taxation but rather a law made for the suppression of the trade in that drug by imposing penalties described as taxes for participation in it. The reason for denying to such a law the character of a law with respect to taxation would not be either its economic consequences or the motive behind its enactment. It would simply be that its true character is not a law with respect to taxation.

Discrimination between states

Under s 51(ii), the Commonwealth does not have power to enact taxation laws that 'discriminate between States or parts of States'. A law discriminates between states where it treats a taxpayer in one state differently from a taxpayer in another state. For instance, in *Cameron v DFC of T* (1923) 32

CLR 68, the High Court held that regulations which placed different values on livestock according to the state in which the livestock was located discriminated between the states and therefore breached s 51(ii).

A law also discriminates between states where it places a particular disability or burden on the operations and activities of a state. In *Austin & Anor v Cth* 2003 ATC 4042, the High Court held that Commonwealth legislation which purported to make state judges personally liable for tax on notional state superannuation contributions placed a burden on the activities of the states, insofar as those activities included employing judges and retaining them in office. As a result, the legislation was found to be invalid as it exceeded the Commonwealth's legislative powers. McHugh J explained (at 4088):

> Here the federal law discriminates against State judicial officers in a way that interferes in a significant respect with the States' relationships with their judges. It interferes with the financial arrangements that govern the terms of their offices, not as an incidence of a general tax applicable to all but as a special measure designed to single them out and place a financial burden on them that no one else in the community incurs.

The operation of s 51(ii) was also considered by the High Court in *Fortescue Metals Group Ltd & Ors v Cth* 2013 ATC ¶20-405. This case concerned the constitutional validity of the mining tax ('MRRT') legislation [5.6]. The applicants argued that the legislation not only breached s 51(ii) of the *Constitution* as it discriminated between states, but also that it breached s 99 of the *Constitution*, which prohibits a 'law or regulation of trade, commerce or revenue' giving 'preference to one State . . . over another State'. The applicants submitted that as the legislation, in determining the tax liability of a miner, made allowances for mining royalties payable under state laws, MRRT liability could vary according to state royalty regimes. It was contended that this gave rise to a differential operation of the tax from state to state, which therefore discriminated between the states (contrary to s 51(ii)) and gave preferences to one state over another state (contrary to s 99).

The High Court unanimously rejected these arguments. French CJ indicated that the limitations imposed by ss 51(ii) and 99 did not prevent the enactment of uniform laws which had different effects in different states due to differences in the circumstances to which they applied, including different state legislative regimes. His Honour stated (at [34]):

> It is not controversial that a law which is uniform across the Commonwealth and does not in terms discriminate between States or parts of States can nevertheless have different effects between and within the States because the circumstances upon which it operates, including the different State legal regimes with which it interacts.

His Honour relied on *Cameron's case*, where Starke J said (at 79):

> A law with respect to taxation applicable to all States and parts of States alike does not infringe the Constitution merely because it operates unequally in the different States—not from anything done by the law making authority, but on account of the inequality of conditions obtaining in the respective States.

Similar views to those of French CJ were expressed by Hayne, Bell and Keane JJ, who held that the fact that a miner would pay a different amount of tax if that miner conducted identical operations in a different state does not demonstrate discrimination. In this regard, they stated (at [117]) that 'a law is not shown to discriminate between States by demonstrating only that it will have a different practical operation in different States because those States have created different circumstances to which the federal Act will apply by enacting different State legislation'. They went on to conclude that as the legislation did not discriminate between states, there was no preference of one state over another.

[3.5] Powers of the Houses of Parliament

The *Constitution* contains special rules relating to the way tax laws are required to be enacted. In particular, s 53 provides that 'proposed laws appropriating revenue or moneys, or imposing taxation shall not originate in the Senate'. It also provides that the Senate may not amend a proposed taxation law or appropriation law. As a result, all tax and appropriation Bills must originate in the House of Representatives. If the Senate is not satisfied with a tax Bill, it can either reject it outright or return it to the House of Representatives with a request that it be amended.

The historical origins behind s 53 can be traced to the famous slogan 'no taxation without representation' used by the colonists during the American War of Independence. A similar provision is contained in s 7 of Article 1 of the United States Constitution, which provides that: 'All Bills for raising revenue shall originate in the House of Representatives'.

Section 53 recognises the Lower House represents the people, whereas the Upper House represents the states. While s 53 ensures that the initiative to impose taxes lies with the House of Representatives, the reality is that a tax Bill will only become law if the political party that introduced the Bill has the votes to also get it passed by the Senate. There have been numerous occasions where the Senate has blocked the Government's tax Bills. There have also been many instances where significant amendments were required to be made to a Bill before it was passed by the Senate.

[3.6] Laws imposing taxation

Section 55 of the *Constitution* provides that laws imposing taxation shall deal only with the imposition of taxation, and any provision therein dealing with any other matter shall be of no effect. The section also provides that laws imposing taxation, except laws imposing duties of customs or of excise, shall deal with one subject of taxation only. Laws imposing duties of customs shall deal with duties of customs only, and laws imposing duties of excise shall deal with duties of excise only.

The purpose behind the enactment of s 55 is to prevent 'tacking'. In essence, it is designed to protect the Senate from any potential abuse arising from the operation of s 53, which prohibits the Senate from amending a proposed taxation law [3.5]. In *Harding v FC of T* (1917) 23 CLR 119, Issacs J explained this point (at 134):

> The prohibition mentioned was not inserted as a trap for the Commonwealth Legislature, and through them for the nation. It was intended as a genuine protection to the people of the Commonwealth, by guarding the Senate from compulsive acquiescence in one tax by the moral necessity of passing another distinct tax. To secure that end the test is unity of subject matter of taxation in each measure, so that each proposed tax may be fairly considered on its merits.

Section 55 is clearly breached where a law that imposes a tax is inserted in an Act dealing with other matters such as migration (*Air Caledonie International & Ors v Cth* (1988) 165 CLR 462) or copyright (*Australian Tape Manufacturers Association Ltd & Ors v Cth* (1993) 176 CLR 480).

The provision was not, however, violated in *Resch v FC of T* (1942) 66 CLR 198, where the High Court held that the *Income Tax Assessment Act 1922* (Cth) could deal with the taxation of both profits or gains of an income nature as well as profits or gains of a capital nature. Starke J said (at 213):

> the Parliament possesses power, without infringing the provisions of sec 55 of the Constitution, to bring to charge in an income-tax Act all profits and gains accruing to a taxpayer, without distinguishing whether the profit or gain should be regarded as a receipt on capital or on income or revenue account.

Because of s 55, Commonwealth tax laws are traditionally contained in several different Acts, rather than just a single statute. There are separate Acts dealing with income tax, GST and FBT, as well as a whole range of other taxes. In addition, the legislature typically enacts both Assessment Acts (which deal with the 'incidence of' or 'liability to' tax) and Taxing Acts (which 'impose' tax). Fullagar J explained this phenomenon in *Re Dymond* (1959) 101 CLR 11 (at 18) as follows:

> By reason of the provisions of sec 55 it has been the invariable practice since the establishment of the Commonwealth, when Parliament has proposed to levy a tax on any subject of taxation, to pursue that object by means of two separate Acts, the one of which actually imposes the tax and fixes the rate of tax, and the other of which provides for the incidence, assessment, and collection, of the tax . . . It is common to refer to the latter Act as the Assessment Act, and to the former as the Taxing Act.

As a consequence of s 55, the Commonwealth income tax, GST and FBT legislative schemes have been designed in a rather convoluted way as follows:

- **Income tax.** The *Income Tax Assessment Act 1936* (Cth) ('*ITAA36*') and *Income Tax Assessment Act 1997* (Cth) ('*ITAA97*') set out the liability to income tax, while the *Income Tax Act 1986* (Cth) ('*ITA*') imposes income tax at the rates prescribed under the *Income Tax Rates Act 1986* (Cth) ('*ITRA*').
- **GST.** The *A New Tax System (Goods and Services Tax) Act 1999* (Cth) ('*GSTA*') sets out the liability to GST, while the *A New Tax System (Goods and Services Tax Imposition—General) Act 1999* (Cth) ('*GSTIGA*'), the *A New Tax System (Goods and Services Tax Imposition—Excise) Act 1999* (Cth) ('*GSTIEA*') and the *A New Tax System (Goods and Services Tax Imposition—Customs) Act 1999* (Cth) ('*GSTICA*') impose GST at the prescribed rate.
- **FBT.** The *Fringe Benefits Tax Assessment Act 1986* (Cth) ('*FBTAA*') sets out the liability to FBT, while the *Fringe Benefits Tax Act 1986* (Cth) ('*FBTA*') imposes FBT at the prescribed rate.

The scope of s 55 was examined in *State Chamber of Commerce and Industry & Ors v Cth* 87 ATC 4745. In that case, certain entities unsuccessfully challenged the validity of the FBT legislation on the basis that it infringed s 55. The entities had argued that the *FBTA* dealt with more than one subject of taxation as it imposed tax on fringe benefits provided by employers as well as other persons (eg associates of employers) and because it dealt with separate categories of fringe benefits, applying different criteria to each benefit. The High Court, however, held that all fringe benefits constituted a 'unit of subject matter' and that s 55 had therefore not been breached.

Section 55 was also considered in *Luton v Lessels & Anor* 2002 ATC 4311. This case concerned the validity of the *Child Support (Assessment) Act 1989* (Cth) which imposed an obligation on certain persons to pay child support payments. The payments were required to be paid into the Consolidated Revenue Fund and were then transferred to a Child Support Reserve for use by the Registrar to make payments to registered payees. The High Court held that the legislation did not constitute a law imposing taxation as it did not have the purpose or effect of raising revenue for the Commonwealth. Rather, its purpose was to create private rights and liabilities, which took the exaction outside the description of a tax.

[3.7] Consolidated Revenue Fund and Appropriation Acts

Section 81 of the *Constitution* provides that revenue raised from Commonwealth taxes forms one Consolidated Revenue Fund to be appropriated for the purposes of the Commonwealth subject to the *Constitution*.

Under s 83, money may only be drawn from this fund under appropriation made by law. This is achieved by Parliament enacting Appropriation Acts that authorise the drawing of funds and that specify the amount of money that is to be used for a particular purpose. Thus, Appropriation Acts are vital in unlocking revenue raised from taxes so that this money can be dedicated to specific government purposes. It is standard practice for Appropriation Acts to be introduced into Parliament on an annual basis at the same time that the Treasurer delivers the Budget. This usually occurs in May each year. However, in 2019, it occurred in April due to the federal election and, in 2020, it was deferred to October due to the COVID-19 pandemic. In 2022, there were two Budgets: one delivered before the May federal election in March by the former Liberal-National Coalition Government, and the other delivered after the election in October by the new Labor Government [5.10].

The operation of ss 81 and 83 was considered in *Pape v FC of T & Ors* 2009 ATC ¶20-116. The plaintiff in this case sought a declaration that the *Tax Bonus for Working Australians Act (No 2) 2009* (Cth) was invalid. The Act provided that the Commissioner would make payments of between $250 and $900 to Australian residents whose 'adjusted tax liability' for 2007/08 was greater than nil and whose 'taxable income' for the year did not exceed $100,000. The purpose of the payments was to stimulate economic activity during the GFC. The plaintiff submitted that the legislation was not supported by any express or implied head of legislative power under the *Constitution* and that there had not been a valid appropriation under ss 81 and 83.

A majority of the High Court, however, rejected both these arguments. The majority held that the legislation was supported by s 51(xxxix) of the *Constitution*, as it was incidental to the exercise of the executive power in s 61. The majority also held that the payments were expenditure 'for the purposes of the Commonwealth' and therefore satisfied s 81. Furthermore, they held that the appropriation was valid as it was effected by s 16 of the *Taxation Administration Act 1953* (Cth) ('*TAA*'), which stated that where the Commissioner is required to pay an amount to a person under a provision of a taxation law of which he has the general administration, 'the amount is payable out of the Consolidated Revenue Fund, which is appropriated accordingly'.

The importance of the appropriation process and the way it could be put to political use was highlighted in the 'constitutional crisis' of 1975, which led to the sacking of the Whitlam Labor Government by Governor-General Sir John Kerr. The crisis was brought about by a deferral of action on Labor's Appropriation Bills in the Senate by the Liberal–Country Party Coalition, led by Malcolm Fraser. This effectively blocked supply of funds to the Government. The Coalition took this unprecedented step after various political scandals confronting Labor, including the 'Khemlani loans affair' in which the Government was accused of bypassing standard Treasury procedures in attempting to borrow money from the Middle East through a Pakistani broker. By deferring supply, the Coalition was trying to force Gough Whitlam to call an early election, which he refused to do. To resolve the deadlock before funding ran out, on 11 November 1975, the Governor-General exercised his rarely used 'reserve powers' to dismiss Gough Whitlam as Prime Minister and replace him with Malcolm Fraser as 'caretaker' Prime Minister. Shortly thereafter, the stalled Bills were passed by the Senate. Interestingly, despite the furore that had erupted in response to the sacking, the ensuing December 1975 election was resoundingly won by the Coalition.

[3.8] Exclusive power to impose customs and excise duties

Pursuant to s 107 of the *Constitution*, on the establishment of the Commonwealth of Australia in 1901, the state parliaments retained the powers of the former colonial parliaments, except to the extent that those powers were exclusively vested in the Commonwealth Parliament or withdrawn. Of particular importance to state parliaments is the constraint in s 90 of the *Constitution* which provides that the power to impose customs and excise duties is vested exclusively in the Commonwealth Parliament. A state Act that purports to impose a customs or excise duty is therefore invalid. As a result, although the state parliaments have the power to levy taxes under their respective constitutions, their powers are limited in that they are prohibited from imposing customs and excise duties.

Customs duty

A customs duty is a tax imposed on imports or exports of goods. As Starke J stated in *Commonwealth Oil Refineries Ltd v South Australia* (1926) 38 CLR 408 (at 438):

> Duties of customs under the Constitution are duties levied upon the importation or exportation of commodities into and out of the Commonwealth.

Excise duty

An excise duty is a tax imposed on a step in the production, manufacture or distribution of goods. A sales tax on goods is therefore a classic example of an excise duty.

One of the earliest pronouncements on the nature of an excise duty was made in *Peterswald v Bartley* (1904) 1 CLR 497, where Griffith CJ described such a duty (at 509) as 'a duty analogous to a customs duty upon goods either in relation to quantity or value when produced or manufactured'.

Subsequently, in *Parton v Milk Board (Vic)* (1949) 80 CLR 229, a majority of the High Court held that a Victorian milk levy charged on milk producers at one-tenth of a penny per gallon of milk sold or distributed was an excise. The majority held that a levy will be an excise if it taxes the production or manufacture of goods. Rich and Williams JJ took a broad view of this concept, stating (at 252):

> the production or manufacture of an article will be taxed whenever a tax is imposed in respect of some dealing with the article by way of sale or distribution at any stage of its existence, provided that it is expected and intended that the taxpayer will not bear the ultimate incidence of the tax himself but will indemnify himself by passing it on to the purchaser or consumer.

Likewise, Dixon J noted (at 260):

> A tax upon a commodity at any point in the course of distribution before it reaches the consumer produces the same effect as a tax upon its manufacture or production.

The High Court subsequently stated, in *Bolton v Madsen* (1963) 110 CLR 264 (at 271):

> It is now established for constitutional purposes duties of excise are taxes directly related to goods imposed at some step in their production or distribution before they reach the hands of consumers.

Over the years, a number of cases have come before the courts concerning whether licence fees imposed on persons seeking to carry on particular activities constitute excise duties. In *Capital Duplicators Pty Ltd v Australian Capital Territory (No 2)* 93 ATC 5053, ACT legislation required wholesalers and retailers of X-rated videos to hold licences for which they were required to pay monthly fees. The fees included an 'advance fee' (for initial licences) and a 'franchise fee' (for renewals). These fees were based on 40% of the wholesale values of videos sold during the month of the licence period (in the case of an advance fee) or during the month that occurred two months prior to the licence period (in the case of a franchise fee). A majority of the High Court characterised the licence fees as an excise. The majority found that the fees exceeded the cost of implementing the scheme and that the scheme was directed at raising revenue rather than creating a regulatory regime to protect the public. They also held that even though the franchise fee was based on sales made in a previous period, this did not prevent it from being an excise, as transactions in the past may well provide a reliable forecast of transactions that will occur during the currency of the licence.

A similar outcome was reached in *Ha & Anor v NSW & Ors* 97 ATC 4674, where a majority of the High Court held that a NSW Act, which imposed a licence fee on tobacco sellers based on the amount of tobacco sold, constituted an excise duty and was therefore invalid.

As an excise duty must relate to goods, as opposed to land, a tax on in-ground swimming pools which formed part of the land was found not to constitute an excise duty in *Mutual Pools and Staff Pty Ltd & Anor v FC of T* 92 ATC 4016.

[3.9] Financial assistance

Section 96 of the *Constitution* allows the Commonwealth Parliament to 'grant financial assistance to any State on such terms and conditions as the Parliament thinks fit'. The provision was inserted in the *Constitution* to protect the viability of the federation, particularly in the first few years of its existence, in case a state encountered financial distress.

General and special purpose grants

Section 96 allows the Commonwealth Parliament to make both 'general grants' (ie grants that are not tied to any conditions) and 'special purpose grants' (ie grants that are tied to specific conditions, such as the terms on which the states must use the funding). The provision has been used by the Commonwealth on many occasions. Its most important use in recent years has been to distribute GST revenue to the states under the revenue-sharing arrangements discussed at [4.4].

Wide scope of s 96

The courts have construed s 96 widely and have not restricted its operation to providing assistance in respect of only those areas that the Commonwealth can legislate on (eg the heads of power specified in s 51).

In *Victoria v Cth* (1926) 38 CLR 399, the High Court held that the Commonwealth could make grants to the states on the condition that they used the funds to construct certain kinds of roads approved by the Commonwealth. The grants were provided on the basis that the states were required to contribute towards the cost of the roads and would receive payments at such times, and on such conditions, as the Minister determined.

Subsequently, in *Victoria and NSW v Cth* (1957) 99 CLR 575, Dixon CJ (at 606) explained that *Victoria v Cth* was authority for the principle that s 96 can be used even though:

> (1) the State is bound to apply the money specifically to an object that has been defined, (2) the object is outside the powers of the Commonwealth, (3) the payments are left to the discretion of the Commonwealth Minister, (4) the money is provided as the Commonwealth's contribution to an object for which the State is also to contribute funds.

The broad interpretation given to s 96 means that it has the potential 'to wield enormous political power' in areas that would otherwise be beyond the Commonwealth Parliament's legislative authority (see S Joseph and M Castan, *Federal Constitutional Law: A Contemporary View* at 339). A classic illustration of where the provision was used to achieve a blatant political objective is found in *South Australia & Anor v Cth* (1942) 65 CLR 373. This case concerned the validity of the Uniform Tax Scheme, which was established by the Commonwealth to gain exclusive control of income tax during World War II. Under the scheme, grants would be provided to the states under the *State Grants (Income Tax Reimbursement) Act 1942* (Cth) provided they refrained from imposing income tax. In other words, to get the grants, the states had to effectively (although not legally) give up their income taxing rights, which they eventually ended up doing.

Limitations of s 96

In *WR Moran Pty Ltd v DFC of T* (1940) 63 CLR 338, the Privy Council held that the power to grant financial assistance under s 96 is not subordinate to the taxation power in s 51(ii), which contains a prohibition on taxation that discriminates between the states or parts of states [3.4]. Parliament may therefore make grants of financial assistance which benefit one state ahead of another. The Privy Council, nevertheless, warned that Parliament cannot exercise its powers in s 96 with complete disregard of the prohibition in s 51(ii). Their Lordships warned (at 350):

> Cases may be imagined in which a purported exercise of the power to grant financial assistance under s 96 would be merely colourable. Under the guise or pretence of assisting a State with money, the real substance and purpose of the Act might simply be to effect discrimination in regard to taxation. Such an Act might well be ultra vires the Commonwealth Parliament.

Although it is clear that s 96 allows the Commonwealth to provide financial assistance to the states in respect of areas that are outside its constitutional powers, it appears that the provision would not be able to be used by the Commonwealth to evade an express prohibition on its constitutional powers. In *A-G (Vic) (ex rel Black) v Cth* (1981) 146 CLR 559, Gibbs J said (at 593):

> It is one thing to say that the Parliament, by a condition imposed under s 96, could achieve a result which it lacks power to bring about by direct legislation, but quite another to say that the Parliament can frame a condition for the purpose of evading an express prohibition contained in the Constitution.

In addition, while *South Australia & Anor v Cth* shows that the Commonwealth is able to make grants conditional on the states refraining from exercising their constitutional powers, it is unlikely that the provision could be validly used to require a state to abdicate its constitutional powers (*Victoria and NSW v Cth* (1957) 99 CLR 575). A grant might, nevertheless, be made to a state on the basis that it refers certain of its legislative powers to the Commonwealth pursuant to the express referral power contained in s 51(xxxvii) of the *Constitution*.

It is important to note that while s 96 empowers the Commonwealth to grant financial assistance, it does not require a state to accept such assistance. If a grant is made on terms and conditions that a state is not prepared to accept, it can simply reject the grant.

[3.10] Prohibition on taxing property belonging to states

An important limitation on the Commonwealth Parliament's taxation power is contained in s 114 of the *Constitution* which provides that the Commonwealth cannot impose 'any tax on property of any kind belonging to a State'. Similarly, the states cannot, without the consent of the Commonwealth Parliament, impose any tax on property of any kind belonging to the Commonwealth.

The operation of s 114 was considered in *State of South Australia & Anor v Cth & Anor* 92 ATC 4066, where it was held that the Commonwealth could not subject a state superannuation fund to capital gains tax as such a tax was a tax on property belonging to the state. Mason CJ, Deane, Toohey and Gaudron JJ said (at 4070):

> a tax is properly characterised, for the purposes of s 114, as a 'tax on property' if, and only if, it is imposed upon a taxpayer by reference to a relationship between the taxpayer and the relevant property and the relationship is such that the tax represents a tax on the ownership or holding of the property in question.

Their Honours held that as capital gains tax was imposed on the disposal of assets, it had a sufficient nexus with property.

Five years earlier, in *State of Queensland v Cth* 87 ATC 4029, a majority of the High Court rejected the argument that the imposition of FBT in respect of car and housing fringe benefits provided by a state to its employees contravened s 114. Mason, Brennan and Deane JJ explained (at 4040) that 'the object of the section is to protect the financial integrity of the Commonwealth and the States by exempting each from taxation on its property by the other'. They held that the question of whether a tax is a 'tax on property' belonging to a state must be determined by 'matters of substance rather than mere form'. According to their Honours (at 4041):

> The section protects the property of a State from a tax on the ownership or holding of property but it does not protect the State from a tax on transactions which affect its property, unless the tax can be truly characterised as a tax on the ownership or holding of property.

Their Honours concluded that FBT on car and housing fringe benefits was imposed because the state, as employer, provided employees with a benefit 'in connection with' their employment, not because the state owned or disposed of any property. A similar conclusion was reached by Wilson J who characterised FBT as a transaction tax rather than a tax on property. His Honour held (at 4043) that 'making available to the employee a motor car for his use or a housing right does not shift the focus of the tax from the fringe benefit to the property in question'. According to his Honour, the involvement of the property of the state was merely 'fortuitous' and 'peripheral' to the operation of the legislation.

Section 114 was most recently considered in *Hornsby Shire Council v Cth & Anor* 2023 ATC ¶20-868. The case concerned the payment of 'notional GST' on the sale of a car by a Council. The notional GST had been paid pursuant to intergovernmental agreements made in 1999 and 2009, which provided that the Commonwealth would pay all GST revenue to the states and territories and that the Commonwealth, states and territories (and their authorities, which included the Council) would operate as if they were subject to the 'GST legislation' and would make 'voluntary or notional payments where necessary'. The Council sought restitution of the notional GST it had paid, arguing that it was a tax on property belonging to NSW. The High Court, however, rejected this and held that s 114 had not been breached as the inclusion of notional GST was a 'voluntary act' made in accordance with the intergovernmental agreements, and '[n]o federal law compelled or obliged the Council to include that notional GST'.

[3.11] QUESTIONS

1. How is sovereign power shared between the Commonwealth and states? In which bodies do the legislative, executive and judicial powers of the Commonwealth reside?
2. How does a Bill become law? Why does Parliament sometimes delegate its legislative power?
3. What is the primary source of the Commonwealth Parliament's taxation power? What are the characteristics of a law 'with respect to taxation'? Why did the High Court decide in *Fortescue Metals Group Ltd & Ors v Cth* 2013 ATC ¶20-405 that the mining tax legislation did not breach the *Constitution*?
4. What is the effect of s 53 of the *Constitution*?
5. What is the purpose behind s 55 of the *Constitution*? Provide examples of where the provision was breached. Why does the Commonwealth Parliament enact different kinds of Assessment Acts and Taxing Acts instead of just one General Taxation Act?
6. What is the 'Consolidated Revenue Fund' and what is the role of an Appropriation Act? On what basis did the High Court in *Pape v FC of T & Ors* 2009 ATC ¶20-116 conclude that the relevant legislation and appropriation was valid?
7. Discuss the difference between a customs duty and an excise duty. Can the states impose these duties?
8. What does s 96 of the *Constitution* allow the Commonwealth Parliament to do?
9. How does s 114 of the *Constitution* constrain the Commonwealth Parliament's taxation powers? Why was the section contravened in *State of South Australia & Anor v Cth & Anor* 92 ATC 4066 but not in *State of Queensland v Cth* 87 ATC 4029 or *Hornsby Shire Council v Cth & Anor* 2023 ATC ¶20-868?

AUSTRALIAN TAXES 4

[4.1] Introduction

Like other developed countries around the world, Australia imposes a broad mix of taxes on labour, capital and consumption. The Australian tax system is, however, complicated by the fact that Australia is a federation that includes six states and two mainland territories which all have their own legislatures that impose their own taxes. In addition, Australia also has more than 500 local government authorities which levy their own council rates.

In 2008, the Commonwealth Treasury's discussion paper, *Architecture of Australia's Tax and Transfer System*, identified at least 125 different taxes levied in Australia, with the 10 largest taxes accounting for more than 90% of all government revenue. Of the 125 taxes, 99 were levied by the Commonwealth Government, 25 by the state and territory governments, and 1 by local government. The Treasury's estimate of the number of taxes was based on equivalent state and territory taxes being counted as a single tax, even though they differed in terms of rates, thresholds and exemptions, and were paid to different authorities.

While taxes are levied at all levels of government in Australia, the following table shows that over 80% of all tax revenue in Australia is raised by the Commonwealth (ABS, *Taxation Revenue, Australia 2021–22*).

Total tax revenue by level of government for 2021/22	
Commonwealth	$550,609m
State and territory	$111,605m
Local Government	$20,811m
Total	$683,025m

In practice, the states and territories rely heavily on the Commonwealth for funding. All GST revenue collected by the Commonwealth is handed back to the states and territories under special revenue-sharing arrangements [4.4]. The states and territories also receive significant transfers from the Commonwealth. For example, the 2023 Budget Papers note that the states and territories are expected to receive around $179.9 billion in payments from the Commonwealth in 2023/24, which includes $87.4 billion for specific purposes (eg schools and hospitals) and $92.5 billion in general revenue assistance.

This chapter introduces Australia's complex and dynamic federal tax system. It commences with a brief history of taxation in Australia [4.2], followed by a short description of the main

Commonwealth [4.3], state and territory [4.4] and local government [4.5] taxes. The Commonwealth taxes will be examined in detail in subsequent chapters.

[4.2] Australia's tax history

Colonial taxes

The history of taxation in Australia can be traced back to colonial times. The first taxes imposed by the colonies were indirect taxes in the form of customs and excise duties. Taxes were levied on items such as beer, spirits, tobacco and certain luxury goods. Customs and excise duties were relatively easy to administer and were less controversial than many other forms of taxation. In addition, as they were imposed on items such as alcohol, they could be justified as 'sin' taxes that addressed the social evils facing the colonies. During the 1850s gold rush, a controversial licence fee was levied on gold miners. This licence fee played a significant role in sparking the revolt at the Eureka Stockade. Around the same time, estate duties also began to be levied by the colonies, commencing with the introduction of probate and administration fees in NSW in 1851. This was followed by the introduction of a succession tax in Tasmania in 1865 and death duties in Victoria in 1870. By the mid-1890s all colonies imposed some form of duty on deceased estates. Victoria was the first colony to impose land tax in 1877. The first colony to levy income tax was South Australia in 1884. Victoria and NSW introduced income tax in 1895. The other colonies only commenced levying income tax shortly after federation. Queensland and Tasmania introduced income tax in 1902, whereas Western Australia introduced income tax in 1907.

Early Commonwealth taxes

As a consequence of the formation of the Commonwealth of Australia in 1901, the colonies became states within the new federation [3.2]. Although the Commonwealth Parliament was granted the power to make laws with respect to taxation [3.4], the states retained the right to levy their own taxes (subject to the constraints of the *Commonwealth Constitution*), and they continued to independently do so.

The first taxes imposed by the Commonwealth were customs and excise duties in 1902. The states had given up their rights to levy such duties under s 90 of the *Commonwealth Constitution* [3.8]. The Commonwealth subsequently introduced other taxes, such as land tax in 1910 and death duty in 1914. It was, however, only in 1915 that the Commonwealth decided to impose income tax. This measure was prompted by pressures brought on by World War I and was regarded at the time as merely an interim measure. The *Income Tax Assessment Act 1915* (Cth) was the first Commonwealth Assessment Act. This Act was subsequently replaced by the *Income Tax Assessment Act 1922* (Cth) ('*ITAA22*'). Over these early years, the states continued to levy their own income taxes and there was little uniformity between the state and Commonwealth laws.

It was not until the 1930s depression era that hallmarks of a uniform income tax system began to emerge, with the replacement of the *ITAA22* by the *Income Tax Assessment Act 1936* (Cth) ('*ITAA36*'). This Act was adopted by the states as a model Assessment Act. However, as time progressed, amendments to the respective state Acts meant that differences inevitably developed between their legislation (including differences in the rates of tax charged). Eventually, the pressures of World War II prompted the Commonwealth to take over the income tax field exclusively and it did so through the introduction of a series of Acts which together became known as the 'Uniform Tax Scheme'. The constitutional validity of this scheme was upheld by the High Court in *South Australia & Anor v Cth* (1942) 65 CLR 373.

The most important components of the Uniform Tax Scheme were the *Income Tax Act 1942* (Cth) and the *States Grants (Income Tax Reimbursement) Act 1942* (Cth). The former Act imposed income tax at rates that were designed to raise revenue equal to the total revenue that had been raised in the preceding year through Commonwealth and state income taxes. The High Court held that this Act was authorised by the taxation power in s 51(ii) of the *Commonwealth Constitution* as 'it is not possible for this Court to impose limitations upon the Parliament as to the rate of tax which it proposes to impose upon the people' [3.4]. The latter Act authorised grants to the states that were approximately equal to the revenue they had received in previous years from the imposition of income tax. However, the states were entitled to this financial assistance only if the Commonwealth Treasurer was satisfied that they had not levied income tax. The Court held that s 96 of the *Constitution* allowed the Commonwealth to attach conditions on grants offered to the states [3.9]. The condition that states must not levy an income tax in order to obtain financial assistance was repealed in 1959. Nevertheless, in spite of this, no state has levied income tax since 1942. The position in Australia is therefore quite different from the position in countries such as the United States and Canada, where the state and provincial governments levy income tax in addition to federal income tax.

Modern Commonwealth taxes

The Commonwealth tax laws have evolved considerably since the middle of last century. Over this period, the income tax legislation has been amended on hundreds of occasions. In addition to the many detailed technical reforms that have been enacted over the years, there have also been many substantive changes to the law, particularly since the 1980s. Major reforms have included the introduction of new general anti-avoidance provisions in 1981 [37.1], the introduction of a CGT regime in 1985 [17.1], the introduction of an imputation system in 1987 [22.6] and the introduction of accruals measures for taxing the income of controlled foreign companies in 1990 [34.2].

In the mid-1990s, the Tax Law Improvement Project ('TLIP') resulted in a rewrite of a large portion of the provisions in the *ITAA36* and the introduction of the *ITAA97*, which now contains the bulk of Australia's income tax laws [8.2].

Significant business tax changes were introduced in the early 2000s under the A New Tax System ('ANTS') reforms [5.4]. These reforms substantially modernised the income tax laws and spawned a variety of new taxation regimes, such as the consolidation regime [26.1] and the debt and equity regime [29.9].

In addition to many changes in the field of income tax, there have also been many significant reforms in other areas of tax law over the years. Until the late 1970s, both the Commonwealth and the states imposed death duties. Queensland was the first state to abolish death duties in 1977. The Commonwealth and other states followed shortly thereafter.

In 1983, the Commonwealth introduced the Medicare levy ('ML') to fund the national health care system [8.8]. The ML has since been supplemented by the Medicare levy surcharge ('MLS'), which was introduced in 1997 [8.8].

The Commonwealth introduced FBT in 1986 [18.1]. It also introduced a number of different superannuation taxes over the years, commencing with the superannuation guarantee charge ('SGC') in 1992 [19.5].

A significant reform took place in 2000 when the antiquated sales tax regime, which had been introduced in 1930, was replaced with the much broader GST regime [7.1]. At the same time that GST was introduced, the Government also introduced two related indirect taxes, being the wine equalisation tax ('WET') and the luxury car tax ('LCT') [4.3].

In 2012, the Labor Government introduced the mining tax and the carbon tax [5.6]. Both these taxes were repealed by the Coalition Government in 2014. In the same year, the Coalition Government introduced a three-year temporary budget repair levy ('TBRL') on high-income earners as a means of tackling the budget deficit [5.7].

More recently, in 2017, the Coalition Government introduced the 'major bank levy', which is payable by Australia's largest banks [4.3]. In the same year, to increase the supply of housing, it introduced an annual 'vacancy fee' on foreigners who own unoccupied residential property that is not available for rent for at least 183 days in a year (pt 6A *Foreign Acquisitions and Takeovers Act 1975* (Cth)).

[4.3] Commonwealth taxes

It is useful to have a general understanding of the broad mix of taxes that currently exist in Australia before examining them in detail. The following discussion outlines the basic features of some of the main Commonwealth taxes and the legislation that governs their operation.

Income tax

Income tax (discussed in Chapter 8) is payable by a broad range of entities, including individuals, companies and trustees of superannuation funds. Taxpayers pay income tax on their 'taxable income' for an 'income year' (ie generally 1 July to 30 June). The rates of income tax depend on the nature of the taxpayer and are summarised below:

- **Individuals.** Resident individuals pay no income tax on the first $18,200 of their taxable income and then pay tax at progressive rates that range from 19% to 45% on the balance of their taxable income. Non-resident individuals pay income tax on their taxable income at progressive rates that range from 32.5% to 45% [8.8].
- **Companies.** Companies generally pay income tax on their taxable income at the rate of 30%. However, companies that are 'base rate entities' pay income tax on their taxable income at the rate of 25% [22.3].
- **Superannuation funds.** Trustees of superannuation funds generally pay income tax on the taxable income of a fund at the rate of 15% (if the fund is a 'complying superannuation fund') or 45% (if the fund is a 'non-complying superannuation fund') [19.14].

Income tax is levied under the *Income Tax Assessment Act 1936* (Cth) ('*ITAA36*'), the *Income Tax Assessment Act 1997* (Cth) ('*ITAA97*'), the *Income Tax (Transitional Provisions) Act 1997* (Cth) ('*ITTPA*'), the *Income Tax Rates Act 1986* (Cth) ('*ITRA*') and the *Income Tax Act 1986* (Cth) ('*ITA*').

Medicare levy and Medicare levy surcharge

The ML and MLS are payable by resident individuals [8.8]. These levies are collected together with income tax and are outlined below:

- **Medicare levy.** The ML was introduced to help fund Medicare, which is Australia's public health system. It is payable by resident individuals on their taxable income for an income year. The ML is generally payable at a flat rate of 2% but operates subject to phase-in rules for low-income earners. The ML is imposed under the *ITAA36* and the *Medicare Levy Act 1986* (Cth) ('*MLA*').
- **Medicare levy surcharge.** The MLS was introduced to encourage high-income earners to take out private health insurance in order to lessen the burden on Medicare. The MLS is payable by resident individuals who do not have private health insurance and have 'income for surcharge purposes' above specified amounts. The MLS is payable on the person's taxable income and reportable fringe benefits total for the income year. It is imposed at the rate of 1%, 1.25% or 1.5%, depending on the level of the person's income for surcharge purposes. The MLS is imposed under the *MLA* and the *A New Tax System (Medicare Levy Surcharge—Fringe Benefits) Act 1999* ('*MLSFBA*').

Fringe benefits tax

FBT (discussed in Chapter 18) is payable by employers on 'fringe benefits' provided to their employees. Most employment benefits, other than salary and superannuation, constitute fringe benefits.

Fringe benefits therefore arise where employers provide their employees with things such as cars, housing or overseas holidays as part of their remuneration packages. Employers are required to pay FBT on their 'fringe benefits taxable amount' for a 'year of tax' (ie 1 April to 31 March). FBT is imposed at the rate of 47% and is levied under the *Fringe Benefits Tax Assessment Act 1986* (Cth) ('*FBTAA*'), the *Fringe Benefits Tax Act 1986* (Cth) ('*FBTA*') and the *Fringe Benefits Tax (Application to the Commonwealth) Act 1986* (Cth) ('*FBTACA*').

Superannuation taxes

Australia imposes the following taxes under its superannuation regime (discussed in Chapter 19):

- **Superannuation guarantee charge ('SGC').** The SGC is imposed on employers that fail to provide minimum levels of superannuation support for their employees (generally 11% of their salary or wages for 2023/24) [19.5]. Superannuation support is measured on a quarterly basis and the SGC is based on the amount of any shortfall (plus interest and administrative components). The SGC is levied under the *Superannuation Guarantee (Administration) Act 1992* (Cth) ('*SGAA*') and the *Superannuation Guarantee Charge Act 1992* (Cth) ('*SGCA*').
- **Excess non-concessional contributions tax ('ENCCT').** ENCCT is imposed on members of superannuation funds that have 'excess non-concessional contributions' during a financial year and elect not to have appropriate amounts released from their superannuation funds [19.9]. It is imposed on their excess non-concessional contributions for the year at the rate of 47% and is levied under the *ITAA97* and the *Superannuation (Excess Non-Concessional Contributions Tax) Act 2007* (Cth) ('*SENCCTA*').
- **Division 293 tax.** Division 293 tax is imposed on members of superannuation funds with income above $250,000 during a financial year [19.10]. The tax is imposed at the rate of 15% on their 'taxable contributions' for the income year. It is levied under the *ITAA97* and the *Superannuation (Sustaining the Superannuation Contribution Concession) Imposition Act 2013* (Cth) ('*SSSCCIA*').
- **Excess transfer balance tax ('ETBT').** ETBT is imposed on individuals who are in the retirement phase of superannuation and have 'excess transfer balance earnings' [19.15]. Excess transfer balance earnings arise where the 'transfer balance' in an individual's 'transfer balance account' exceeds their 'transfer balance cap' for the financial year. The tax is imposed on the individual's 'notional earnings' at the rate of 15% (for the first breach) and 30% (for subsequent breaches). ETBT is levied under the *ITAA97* and the *Superannuation (Excess Transfer Balance Tax) Imposition Act 2016* (Cth) ('*SETBTIA*').

4

Goods and services tax

GST (discussed in Chapter 7) is a broad-based indirect tax that replaced the former sales tax regime on 1 July 2000. GST is charged at the rate of 10% on 'taxable supplies' and 'taxable importations' made by registered suppliers and importers. Registered entities are also generally entitled to 'input tax credits' ('ITCs') for the GST charged on their acquisitions and importations. The difference between an entity's GST liability and its ITC entitlements for a particular 'tax period' (typically a period of either one or three months) is used to determine its 'net amount', which is the amount of tax the entity must pay, or the amount of tax which is refunded to the entity, for the period.

GST is levied under the *A New Tax System (Goods and Services Tax) Act 1999* (Cth) ('*GSTA*'), the *A New Tax System (Goods and Services Tax Transition) Act 1999* (Cth) ('*GSTTA*'), the *A New Tax System (Goods and Services Tax Imposition—General) Act 1999* (Cth) ('*GSTIGA*'), the *A New Tax System (Goods and Services Tax Imposition—Customs) Act 1999* (Cth) ('*GSTICA*') and the *A New Tax System (Goods and Services Tax Imposition—Excise) Act 1999* (Cth) ('*GSTIEA*').

Wine equalisation tax and luxury car tax

WET and LCT were introduced at the same time as GST. This was because wine and luxury cars had been taxed at higher rates under the former sales tax regime and the Government wanted to continue to subject these products to higher taxation after it introduced GST. It did not, however, want to impose more than one GST rate and it therefore decided to levy separate taxes on wine and luxury cars. WET and LCT are, nevertheless, payable under the GST system as they are included in calculating the 'net amount' for GST purposes [7.4]. The way in which the taxes work is outlined below:

- **WET.** WET is levied on 'assessable dealings' in wine (eg wholesale sales and importations of wine). In general, WET is designed to apply at the last point of wholesale sale of wine (eg usually at the point a wholesaler makes a supply to a retailer). The tax is imposed at the rate of 29% of the 'taxable value' of the wine (ie usually the wholesale price or value of the wine excluding GST). Producers are allowed a rebate, in the form of a 'wine tax credit', for tax paid during a financial year of up to $350,000. WET is levied under the *A New Tax System (Wine Equalisation Tax) Act 1999* (Cth) ('*WETA*'), the *A New Tax System (Wine Equalisation Tax Imposition—General) Act 1999* (Cth) ('*WETIGA*'), the *A New Tax System (Wine Equalisation Tax Imposition—Customs) Act 1999* (Cth) ('*WETICA*') and the *A New Tax System (Wine Equalisation Tax Imposition—Excise) Act 1999* (Cth) ('*WETIEA*').
- **LCT.** LCT is levied on taxable supplies and taxable importations of luxury cars. Luxury cars are vehicles designed to carry loads of less than two tonnes and fewer than nine passengers and have a GST-inclusive value above the 'LCT threshold'. The LCT threshold for 2022/23 is $89,332 (for fuel-efficient cars) and $76,950 (for other cars). LCT is imposed at the rate of 33% on 10/11th of the amount by which the car's 'LCT value' exceeds the LCT threshold. The tax does not apply to certain cars (eg cars that are more than two years old, trucks, emergency vehicles and exports). LCT is levied under the *A New Tax System (Luxury Car Tax) Act 1999* (Cth) ('*LCTA*'), the *A New Tax System (Luxury Car Tax Imposition—General) Act 1999* (Cth) ('*LCTIGA*'), the *A New Tax System (Luxury Car Tax Imposition—Customs) Act 1999* (Cth) ('*LCTICA*') and the *A New Tax System (Luxury Car Tax Imposition—Excise) Act 1999* (Cth) ('*LCTIEA*').

Customs duty

Customs duty is payable by importers on the importation of goods into Australia. The rate of duty depends on the classification of the goods and is a percentage of their value. There are various methods for valuing goods. The most common method is the 'transaction value' method, which is simply based on the price paid for the goods converted into Australian dollars. Most goods are subject to the general tariff rate of 5%. Special exemptions and concessions apply to certain goods. For instance, travellers over 18 years of age can generally import up to $900 worth of goods and limited quantities of alcohol and tobacco under the duty-free concession. Customs duty is levied under the *Customs Act 1901* (Cth) ('*CA*') and the *Customs Tariff Act 1995* (Cth) ('*CTA*').

Excise duty

Excise duty is a tax on the production or manufacture of certain products in Australia, such as petroleum products, crude oil, tobacco, beer, spirits and other alcoholic beverages (other than wine, which is subject to WET). Producers and manufacturers must generally be licensed to deal in excisable goods. Excise duty is payable by the licensed producer or manufacturer at various rates depending on the nature of the product. For example, the excise rates for alcohol are based on alcoholic volume and are indexed twice a year. Excise duty is levied under the *Excise Act 1901* (Cth) ('*EA*') and the *Excise Tariff Act 1921* (Cth) ('*ETA*').

Petroleum resource rent tax

Petroleum resource rent tax ('PRRT') applies to profits from 'marketable petroleum commodities' (eg crude oil, natural gas, condensate, liquefied petroleum gas, ethane and shale oil) arising from off-shore petroleum projects as well as the North West Shelf and Bass Strait projects. PRRT is imposed at the rate of 40% on an entity's 'taxable profit' for a financial year in relation to a petroleum project. It is levied under the *Petroleum Resource Rent Tax Assessment Act 1987* (Cth) ('*PRRTAA*'), the *Petroleum Resource Rent Tax (Imposition—General) Act 2012* (Cth) ('*PRRTIGA*'), the *Petroleum Resource Rent Tax (Imposition—Customs) Act 2012* (Cth) ('*PRRTICA*') and the *Petroleum Resource Rent Tax (Imposition—Excise) Act 2012* (Cth) ('*PRRTIEA*').

Major bank levy

The major bank levy operates from 1 July 2017 and is payable on a quarterly basis by ADIs (ie 'authorised deposit-taking institutions' under the *Banking Act 1959* (Cth)). ADIs are financial institutions that are licensed by the Australian Prudential Regulation Authority ('APRA') to carry on banking activities. The major bank levy is payable by ADIs that have a 'total liabilities amount' that exceeds the levy threshold for the quarter. The levy threshold commenced at $100 billion for July-September 2017 and is subject to indexation. ADIs are required to pay a 0.015% levy on their 'applicable liabilities amount' for the quarter. An ADI's applicable liabilities amount for a quarter is basically its total liabilities for the quarter excluding Tier-1 capital, deposits protected under the ADI financial claims scheme and certain other amounts. Currently, Australia's five largest banks (Commonwealth Bank, Westpac, ANZ, National Australia Bank and Macquarie) pay the levy, which is imposed under the *Major Bank Levy Act 2017* (Cth) ('*MBLA*').

4

Summary of Commonwealth taxes

The following table summarises the basic features of the Commonwealth taxes discussed above.

Tax	Tax base	Tax period	Tax rates (2023/24)	Taxpayer	Legislation
Income tax	Taxable income	Financial year	Progressive rates from 0% to 45% (for resident individuals) and 32.5% to 45% for non-resident individuals) Flat rate of 25% (for companies that are base rate entities) and 30% (for other companies) Flat rate of 15% (for complying superannuation funds) and 45% (for non-complying superannuation funds)	Individuals, companies, superannuation fund trustees	*ITAA36* *ITAA97* *ITTPA* *ITA* *ITRA*
ML	Taxable income	Financial year	Flat rate of 2% (operates subject to thresholds and shading-in rules)	Resident individuals (and certain trustees)	*MLA* *ITAA36*

Tax	Tax base	Tax period	Tax rates (2023/24)	Taxpayer	Legislation
MLS	Taxable income and reportable fringe benefits total	Financial year	Flat rate of 1%, 1.25% or 1.5% (operates subject to thresholds and depends on level of income for surcharge purposes)	Resident individuals with high incomes for surcharge purposes	*MLA* *MLSFBA*
FBT	Fringe benefits taxable amount	FBT year (1 April to 31 March)	Flat rate of 47%	Employers	*FBTAA* *FBTA* *FBTACA*
SGC	Superannuation guarantee shortfall	Quarterly	Total individual superannuation guarantee shortfalls plus interest and administration components	Employers	*SGAA* *SGCA*
ENCCT	Excess non-concessional contributions	Financial year	Flat rate of 47%	Superannuation fund members	*ITAA97* *SENCCTA*
ETBT	Notional earnings	Excess transfer balance period	Flat rate of 15% or 30%	Superannuation fund members	*ITAA97* *SETBTIA*
Division 293 tax	Taxable contributions	Financial year	Flat rate of 15%	Superannuation fund members	*ITAA97* *SSSCCIA*
GST	Taxable supplies and taxable importations	Monthly or quarterly	Flat rate of 10%	Suppliers and importers	*GSTA* *GSTTA* *GSTIGA* *GSTICA* *GSTIEA*
WET	Assessable dealings in wine	Monthly or quarterly	Flat rate of 29% of taxable value	Dealers in wine (eg wholesalers)	*WETA* *WETIGA* *WETICA* *WETIEA*
LCT	Taxable supplies and taxable importations of luxury cars	Monthly or quarterly	Flat rate of 33% of 10/11th of the amount by which the car's LCT value exceeds the LCT threshold	Suppliers and importers of luxury cars	*LCTA* *LCTIGA* *LCTICA* *LCTIEA*
Customs duty	Importation of dutiable goods	Special rules	Different rates depending on nature of goods	Importers of dutiable goods	*CA* *CTA*
Excise duty	Production or manufacture of excisable goods	Special rules	Different rates depending on nature of goods	Producers and manufacturers of excisable goods	*EA* *ETA*

Tax	Tax base	Tax period	Tax rates (2023/24)	Taxpayer	Legislation
PRRT	Taxable profits	Financial year	Flat rate of 40%	Entities undertaking petroleum projects	*PRRTAA* *PRRTIGA* *PRRTICA* *PRRTIEA*
Major bank levy	Applicable liabilities amount	Quarterly	Flat rate of 0.015%	Large banks	*MBLA*

Commonwealth tax revenue

The 2023 Budget Papers indicate that Australia's total tax revenue was $550,412m in 2021/22 and is estimated to be $604,169m in 2022/23. In comparison, its total non-tax revenue (eg from interest, dividends, sales of goods and services and other sources) was $45,989m in 2021/22 and is estimated to be $49,598m in 2022/23. This shows that tax revenue constitutes more than 90% of the Australian Government's total revenue.

The following table lists the estimated revenue the Commonwealth expects to receive from its major taxes for 2022/23 and 2023/24. It shows that income tax from individuals and companies raises the most revenue, followed by GST.

Tax	2022/23 (estimated revenue)	2023/24 (estimated revenue)
Income tax (individuals)	$303,200m	$325,900m
Income tax (companies)	$140,800m	$131,100m
GST	$88,040m	$89,080m
Customs and excise duties	$43,330m	$47,360m
Superannuation fund taxes	$9,670m	$16,620m
FBT	$3,510m	$3,500m
PRRT	$2,230m	$2,770m
Major bank levy	$1,560m	$1,640m
WET	$1,170m	$1,160m
LCT	$1,150m	$860m

Commonwealth spending

The Commonwealth Government uses the revenue it raises from taxes and other sources to deliver a wide range of services. The following table sets out the Commonwealth Government's estimated expenses by function for 2022/23 and 2023/24. It indicates that over 50% of government spending each year is devoted to social security, welfare, health and education.

Expenses	2022/23 (estimated expenses)	2023/24 (estimated expenses)
General public services	$30,106m	$29,126m
Defence	$40,059m	$42,850m
Public order and safety	$7,384m	$7,434m

4

Expenses	2022/23 (estimated expenses)	2023/24 (estimated expenses)
Education	$45,876m	$48,258m
Health	$107,710m	$106,538m
Social security and welfare	$226,378m	$250,280m
Housing and community amenities	$7,135m	$7,940m
Recreation and culture	$4,840m	$4,776m
Fuel and energy	$8,953m	$13,008m
Agriculture, forestry and fishing	$3,185m	$5,034m
Mining manufacture and construction	$4,905m	$5,022m
Transport and communication	$13,461m	$17,508m
Other economic affairs	$14,935m	$12,447m
Other purposes	$128,309m	$133,743m
Total expenses	$644,788m	$684,085m

[4.4] State and territory taxes

The Australian states and territories levy their own taxes. These taxes are quite different from those imposed by the Commonwealth and are administered by their respective revenue agencies, namely:

- Revenue NSW
- State Revenue Office Victoria
- RevenueSA
- Queensland Office of State Revenue
- State Revenue Office of Tasmania
- RevenueWA
- ACT Revenue Office, and
- Territory Revenue Office.

While the states and territories generally impose similar kinds of taxes, the nature and scope of these taxes varies between jurisdictions (particularly with respect to rates, thresholds, concessions and exemptions). The three most important state and territory taxes are payroll tax, land tax and stamp duty. The broad features of these taxes are outlined below. The states and territories also impose other taxes (eg gambling taxes) and raise revenue by other means (eg by imposing royalties on mineral resources and issuing licences). In addition, to reduce congestion and encourage the use of public transport, some states (eg NSW and Victoria) impose parking space and congestion levies on off-street private and public parking spaces in specific parts of their capital cities.

Payroll tax

Payroll tax is imposed by all the states and territories under their respective payroll tax legislation. In 2007, the states and territories agreed to overhaul and modernise their legislation in order to achieve greater harmonisation. This resulted in the adoption of aligned provisions in key areas, with many common terms and concepts. While the jurisdictions now have largely identical legislation, each state and territory adopts different tax rates and thresholds.

Payroll tax is imposed on employers on the 'taxable wages' paid to their employees. Taxable wages are essentially those wages that are not specifically exempt. The term 'wages' is defined broadly in the legislation and generally includes salaries, bonuses, allowances, termination payments, superannuation contributions and fringe benefits. Wages paid by certain organisations, such as hospitals, religious institutions, charities, public benevolent institutions, municipal councils and schools are usually exempt.

In general, payroll tax is payable monthly and is levied only on those wages that relate to services rendered in the particular state or territory. Employers are required to register for payroll tax with their jurisdiction's revenue agency once their monthly payroll exceeds specified thresholds. If an employer pays wages in more than one state or territory, the thresholds are generally reduced in proportion to the ratio of the wages paid in each state or territory to the total Australian wages paid. For example, if 70% of an employer's total wages are paid in NSW, they are entitled to 70% of the threshold in NSW. Employers must generally lodge monthly returns as well as an annual return, which is usually due on 21 July (or 28 July in NSW). Ordinarily, payroll tax for each month is payable within seven days after the end of the month, although for the month of June, it is usually payable by 21 July (or 28 July in NSW).

Payroll tax is imposed at different rates in the respective states and territories. It is payable on wages that are taxable in the relevant jurisdiction (eg wages paid by an employer for services performed by an employee in the relevant state or territory). Only wages above the relevant state or territory annual wages thresholds are taxed. This means many small businesses do not pay payroll tax. In Queensland, WA and the NT, the thresholds are gradually tapered out once wages exceed the relevant thresholds. Some states grant rebates that reduce payroll tax in special cases (eg NSW, Queensland and Tasmania provide rebates for certain wages paid to apprentices and trainees). In addition, some states, such as Victoria and Queensland, have lower rates for regional employers.

To prevent companies splitting up their businesses so that they can benefit from separate thresholds, payroll tax legislation contains special 'grouping' rules that group 'related corporations' under the *Corporations Act 2001* (Cth) (ie companies that are in a holding/subsidiary relationship and companies that have a common holding company or common ultimate holding company). Grouping can also occur where one or more employees of a company perform duties under an agreement for another company, or where a person, or set of persons, commonly control multiple businesses. Under the grouping rules, only one member of the group may claim the threshold. This is typically the designated group employer or the member that lodges the group return.

The following table summarises the state and territory payroll tax legislation, rates and thresholds at 1 July 2023.

Jurisdiction	Legislation	Payroll tax rate	Monthly wages threshold	Annual wages threshold
New South Wales	*Payroll Tax Act 2007* (NSW)	5.45%	$95,082, $98,361, $101,639[1]	$1,200,000
Victoria	*Payroll Tax Act 2007* (Vic)	4.85%[2]	$58,333	$700,000[3]
Queensland	*Payroll Tax Act 1971* (Qld)	4.75% or 4.95%[4]	$108,333	$1,300,000[5]
Western Australia	*Payroll Tax Act 2002* (WA)	5.5%[6]	$83,333	$1,000,000
South Australia	*Payroll Tax Act 2009* (SA)	4.95%[7]	$125,000	$1,500,000
Tasmania	*Payroll Tax Act 2008* (Tas)	6.1%[8]	$95,890, $102,740, $106,164[1]	$1,250,000

Jurisdiction	Legislation	Payroll tax rate	Monthly wages threshold	Annual wages threshold
Australian Capital Territory	*Payroll Tax Act 2011* (ACT)	6.85%	$166,666	$2,000,000
Northern Territory	*Payroll Tax Act 2009* (NT)	5.50%	$125,000	$1,500,000[5]

[1] Monthly thresholds are based on the actual number of days in the month in NSW and Tasmania (ie 29, 30 or 31 days).

[2] A reduced rate of 1.2125% applies if at least 85% of the annual wages is associated with regional Victorian employees. Victoria is imposing (from 1 July 2023 to 30 June 2033) an additional 0.5% levy on businesses with annual payrolls above $10,000,000 and a further 0.5% levy on businesses with annual payrolls above $100,000,000.

[3] Victoria is increasing the annual wages threshold to $900,000 from 1 July 2024 and to $1,000,000 from 1 July 2025.

[4] The 4.75% rate applies to small employers with annual wages up to $6,500,000. The rate of 4.95% applies for large employers with annual wages over $6,500,000. Reduced rates apply to regional Queensland employers, namely 3.75% (for employers with annual wages up to $6,500,000) and 3.95% (for employers with annual wage over $6,500,000). To qualify, 85% of taxable wages must be paid to employees who reside in regional Queensland. From 1 January 2023, Queensland also imposes a mental health levy on employers with annual wages above $10,000,000.

[5] The thresholds in Queensland and the Northern Territory are tapered out and reduced by $1 for every $4 of wages over the relevant thresholds. For example, in Queensland the annual wages threshold of $1,300,000 is reduced to zero once the employer's annual taxable wages reach $6,500,000.

[6] Western Australian employers with annual wages between $1,000,000 and $7,500,000 reduce their taxable wages by a deductible amount calculated according to a tapering out formula.

[7] Variable rates (from 0% to 4.95%) apply to annual wages from $1,500,000 and below $1,700,000. The rate of 4.95% applies to annual wages of $1,700,000 or more.

[8] A reduced rate of 4.0% applies to annual wages from $1,250,001 to $2,000,000. The 6.1% rate applies to annual wages above $2,000,000.

During the COVID-19 crisis, the states and territories introduced a number of payroll tax reliefs, including special tax reductions, refunds, deferrals and waivers. Details of these concessions can be obtained from the relevant revenue agencies' websites [2.5].

Land tax

Land tax is levied by all the states and the ACT. The land tax legislation of each jurisdiction varies considerably. Generally, land tax is imposed on landowners annually, based on the 'taxable value' (usually the 'unimproved value') of land owned in the jurisdiction at midnight on a specific date in the preceding year (ie 30 June in Queensland, SA and WA; 1 July in Tasmania; and 31 December in Victoria and NSW). In the ACT, land tax is assessed quarterly and applies to leases of Crown land.

Land used as a person's principal place of residence or as primary production land is usually exempt from land tax provided certain conditions are met. Depending on the jurisdiction, exemptions may also apply to land used for certain other purposes (eg for charitable, religious or educational purposes, or as a hospital, aged care establishment or retirement village). To help with housing supply, some jurisdictions (eg Victoria and NSW) provide land tax relief for eligible 'build-to-rent' residential properties. Several jurisdictions granted land tax relief during the COVID-19 crisis. In addition, Victoria and NSW provided relief for those adversely affected by the 2019/20 bushfires.

Land tax is generally only imposed once the combined taxable value of land held by an entity in the jurisdiction exceeds a prescribed threshold amount. The thresholds and rates of tax differ greatly between jurisdictions and change from year to year. They also vary depending on the kind of entity owning the land (eg special rates may apply to certain trusts and companies). Grouping rules apply where land is held by related companies.

The following table sets out the legislation and the general rates of land tax at 1 July 2023.

Jurisdiction	Legislation	Taxable value of land	Land tax
New South Wales	*Land Tax Act 1956* (NSW) *Land Tax Management Act 1956* (NSW)	Nil to $969,000	Nil
		More than $969,001 to $5,925,000	$100 + 1.6% of the excess over $969,000
		More than $5,925,000	$79,396 + 2% of the excess over $5,925,000
Victoria[1]	*Land Tax Act 2005* (Vic)	Nil to $300,000	Nil
		$300,000 to $599,999	$375 + 0.2% of the excess over $250,000
		$600,000 to $999,999	$975 + 0.5% of the excess over $600,000
		$1,000,000 to $1,799,999	$2,975 + 0.8% of the excess over $1,000,000
		$1,800,000 to $2,999,999	$9,375 + 1.3% of the excess over $1,800,000
		$3,000,000 or more	$27,975 + 2.25% of the excess over $3,000,000
Queensland	*Land Tax Act 1915* (Qld)	Nil to $599,999	Nil
		$600,000 to $999,999	$500 + 1.0% of the excess over $600,000
		$1,000,000 to $2,999,999	$4,500 + 1.65% of the excess over $1,000,000
		$3,000,000 to $4,999,999	$37,500 + 1.25% of the excess over $3,000,000
		$5,000,000 to $9,999,999	$62,500 + 1.75% of the excess over $5,000,000
		$10,000,000 or more	$150,000 + 2.25% of the excess over $10,000,000
South Australia	*Land Tax Act 1936* (SA)	Nil to $668,000	Nil
		$668,001 to $1,073,000	$0.50 for every $100 or part of $100 above $668,000
		$1,073,001 to $1,561,000	$2,025 + $1.00 for every $100 or part of $100 above $1,073,000
		$1,561,001 to $2,500,000	$6,905 + $2.00 for every $100 or part of $100 above $1,561,000
		$2,500,001 or more	$25,685 + $2.40 for every $100 or part of $100 above $2,500,000
Western Australia[2]	*Land Tax Act 2002* (WA) *Land Tax Assessment Act 2002* (WA)	Nil to $300,000	Nil
		$300,001 to $420,000	$300
		$420,001 to $1,000,000	$300 + 0.25 cents for each $1 in excess of $420,000
		$1,000,001 to $1,800,000	$1,750 + 0.90 cents for each $1 in excess of $1,000,000

4

Jurisdiction	Legislation	Taxable value of land	Land tax
		$1,800,001 to $5,000,000	$8,950 + 1.80 cents for each $1 in excess of $1,800,000
		$5,000,001 to $11,000,000	$66,550 + 2.00 cents for each $1 in excess of $5,000,000
		$11,000,001 or more	$186,550 + 2.67 cents for each $1 in excess of $11,000,000
Tasmania	*Land Tax Act 2000* (Tas) *Land Tax Rating Act 2000* (Tas)	Nil to $99,999	Nil
		$100,000 to $499,999	$50 + 0.45% of the excess over $100,000
		$500,000 or more	$1,850 + 1.5% of the excess over $500,000

[1] From 1 January 2024, Victoria is decreasing the $300,000 threshold to $50,000 and introducing a fixed fee of $500 (for land with a taxable value between $50,000 and $100,000) and $975 (for land with a taxable value above $100,000). It is also increasing the rate by 0.1% (for land with a taxable value above $300,000).

[2] Western Australia also imposes a Metropolitan Region Improvement Tax on property subject to land tax in the Perth Metropolitan region at the rate of 0.14% of the excess taxable value over $300,000.

In NSW, Victoria, Queensland and the ACT, a surcharge applies to absentee and foreign owners. Broadly speaking, this generally covers individuals who are not Australian citizens and do not reside in Australia as well as foreign companies that are incorporated outside Australia or are foreign controlled. The surcharge for absentee owners is 4% in NSW, 2% in Victoria, Tasmania and Queensland, and 0.75% in the ACT. Victoria is proposing to increase its surcharge to 4% from 1 July 2024. In some jurisdictions, the surcharge does not apply to land with a taxable value below certain thresholds (eg $350,000 in Queensland).

Example Alex is an Australian resident who owns two residential investment properties (one in Queensland and the other in Tasmania) that each have a taxable value of $800,000.

His Queensland land tax is calculated as follows:

$2,500 = $500 (land tax on $600,000) + $2,000 (1% × $200,000)

His Tasmanian land tax is calculated as follows:

$6,350 = $1,850 (ie land tax on $500,000) + $4,500 (ie 1.5% × $300,000)

If Alex was a foreign citizen living overseas, he would also be liable for a surcharge in each state of $16,000 ($800,000 × 2%).

Stamp duty

Stamp duty is an antiquated impost that originated in England in 1694. Traditionally, stamp duty was a tax on 'instruments' (ie documents), such as conveyances and transfers of property. To prevent taxpayers avoiding stamp duty by not having transactions evidenced in writing, the stamp duty legislation requires certain transactions to give rise to the creation of documents, which can then be subject to the duty. Stamp duty takes its name from the fact that the duty was payable by purchasing actual stamps that had to be affixed to the relevant documents to show that duty had been paid. Stamp duty is now generally payable electronically through the relevant State Revenue Office's website.

In Australia, all of the states and territories have, for a long time, imposed stamp duty. However, over the years, their legislation had become quite parochial and diverse. To create some degree of harmony and to modernise their stamp duty systems, the ACT, NSW, Victoria, Queensland, Tasmania, and WA decided to adopt model Duties Acts. SA and the NT have retained their existing stamp duty legislation. While the Duties Acts are similar in nature, they contain characteristic differences, including differences in the rates of duty charged. Unlike traditional stamp duty legislation, which impose duty on documents, the Duties Acts charge duty on transfers of dutiable property and certain other specific transactions.

In the past, the states and territories levied stamp duty under many different heads of duty. As a consequence of the GST revenue-sharing arrangement entered into between the Commonwealth and states and territories (see below), several duties have been abolished (eg mortgage duty, lease duty, hire of goods duty and share transfer duty). The most important duty that continues to be collected by the states and territories relates to transfers and certain other transactions relating to land. The liability to pay duty is imposed on the transferee and arises at the time the transaction occurs. Duty is payable at progressive rates on what the Duties Acts refer to as the 'dutiable value' of the 'dutiable property'. The dutiable value is usually the greater of the GST-inclusive consideration for the transaction or the unencumbered value of the property. Stamp duty must be paid within prescribed time limits which, depending on the jurisdiction, is usually either 30, 60 or 90 days after the liability arises.

The table below sets out the legislation and general rates of duty at 1 July 2023 to transfers of dutiable property in the jurisdictions that have adopted Duties Acts and to conveyances of property in SA and the NT. The table operates subject to a number of qualifications and special rules. For example, several jurisdictions provide exemptions and reduced rates of stamp duty for eligible first home buyers and for principal places of residence. To qualify for these concessions, the value of the property must be below the prescribed threshold set by the jurisdiction and the buyer must generally live in the property for a specified time (usually 6 or 12 months).

Jurisdiction	Legislation	Dutiable value	Duty payable on dutiable value
New South Wales	*Duties Act 1997* (NSW)	Nil to $16,000	$1.25 for every $100
		$16,001 to $35,000	$200 + $1.50 for every $100 above $16,000
		$35,001 to $93,000	$485 + $1.75 for every $100 above $35,000
		$93,001 to $351,000	$1,500 + $3.50 for every $100 above $93,000
		$351,001 to $1,168,000	$10,530 + $4.50 for every $100 above $351,000
		$1,168,001 or more	$47,295 + $5.50 for every $100 above $1,168,000
		Residential property with a dutiable value over $3,305,000 is subject to 'premium duty' of $175,830 + 7% for every $100 (or part thereof) above $3,268,000	
Victoria	*Duties Act 2000* (Vic)	Nil to $25,000	1.4%
		$25,001 to $130,000	$350 + 2.4% on excess above $25,000
		$130,001 to $960,000	$2,870 + 6% on excess above $130,000

4

Jurisdiction	Legislation	Dutiable value	Duty payable on dutiable value
		$960,001 to $2,000,000	5.5%
		$2,000,000 or more	$110,000 + 6.5% on excess above $2,000,000
Queensland	*Duties Act 2001* (Qld)	Nil to $5,000	Nil
		$5,001 to $75,000	$1.50 for every $100 (or part thereof) above $5,000
		$75,001 to $540,000	$1,050 + $3.50 for every $100 (or part thereof) above $75,000
		$540,001 to $1,000,000	$17,325 + $4.50 for every $100 (or part thereof) above $540,000
		$1,000,001 or more	$38,025 + $5.75 for every $100 (or part thereof) above $1,000,000
Western Australia	*Duties Act 2008* (WA)	Nil to $120,000	$1.90 for every $100 (or part thereof)
		$120,001 to $150,000	$2,280 + $2.85 for every $100 (or part thereof) above $120,000
		$150,001 to $360,000	$3,135 + $3.80 for every $100 (or part thereof) above $150,000
		$360,001 to $725,000	$11,115 + $4.75 for every $100 (or part thereof) above $360,000
		$725,001 or more	$28,453 + $5.15 for every $100 (or part thereof) above $725,000
Tasmania	*Duties Act 2001* (Tas)	Nil to $3,000	$50
		$3,001 to $25,000	$50 + $1.75 for every $100 (or part thereof) above $3,000
		$25,001 to $75,000	$435 + $2.25 for every $100 (or part thereof) above $25,000
		$75,001 to $200,000	$1,560 + $3.50 for every $100 (or part thereof) above $75,000
		$200,001 to $375,000	$5,935 + $4.00 for every $100 (or part thereof) above $200,000
		$375,001 to $725,000	$12,935 + $4.25 for every $100 (or part thereof) above $375,000
		$725,001 or more	$27,810 + $4.50 for every $100 (or part thereof) above $725,000
South Australia	*Stamp Duties Act 1923* (SA)	Nil to $12,000	$1.00 for every $100 (or part thereof)
		$12,000 to $30,000	$120 + $2.00 for every $100 (or part thereof) above $12,000
		$30,001 to $50,000	$480 + $3.00 for every $100 (or part thereof) above $30,000
		$50,001 to $100,000	$1,080 + $3.50 for every $100 (or part thereof) above $50,000

Jurisdiction	Legislation	Dutiable value	Duty payable on dutiable value
		$100,001 to $200,000	$2,830 + $4.00 for every $100 or part of $100 above $100,000
		$200,001 to $250,000	$6,830 + $4.25 for every $100 (or part thereof) above $200,000
		$250,001 to $300,000	$8,955 + $4.75 for every $100 (or part thereof) above $250,000
		$300,001 to $500,000	$11,330 + $5.00 for every $100 (or part thereof) above $300,000
		$500,001 or more	$21,330 + $5.50 for every $100 (or part thereof) above $500,000
Australian Capital Territory	*Duties Act 1999* (ACT)	Nil to $200,000	$20 or $1.20 for every $100 (or part thereof), whichever is more
		$200,001 to $300,000	$2,400 + $2.20 for every $100 (or part thereof) above $200,000
		$300,001 to $500,000	$4,600 + $3.40 for every $100 (or part thereof) above $300,000
		$500,001 to $750,000	$11,400 + $4.32 for every $100 (or part thereof) above $500,000
		$750,001 to $1,000,000	$22,200 + $5.90 for every $100 (or part thereof) above $750,000
		$1,000,001 to $1,455,000	$36,950 + $6.40 for every $100 (or part thereof) above $1,000,000
		$1,455,001 or more	$4.54 for every $100 of the total transaction value
Northern Territory	*Stamp Duty Act 1978* (NT)	Nil to $525,000	Calculated according to the following formula: $0.06571441 \times V + 15\ V$ (where V is 0.1% of the property's value)
		$525,001 to $2,999,999	4.95%
		$3,000,000 to $4,999,999	5.75%
		$5,000,000 or more	5.95%

Example Jeff is an Australian resident who bought a residential investment property in Melbourne with a dutiable value of $500,000 on 1 July 2023. The stamp duty payable under the *Duties Act 2000* (Vic) is calculated as follows:

$25,070 = $2,870 (duty on $130,000) + $22,200 (6% × $370,000)

If Jeff also bought a residential investment property in Brisbane for the same amount on the same date, the stamp duty payable under the *Duties Act 2001* (Qld) is calculated as follows:

$15,925 = $1,050 (duty on $75,000) + $14,875 (duty of $3.50 for every $100 in $425,000)

4

Since both properties are investment properties, Jeff does not qualify for the first home buyer concession in relation to either property. If, on the other hand, the Melbourne property was Jeff's first home, he could claim the first home buyer exemption. This is because Victoria provides a full exemption from stamp duty to first home buyers who purchase a home for under $600,000, so long as they live in it for a continuous period of 12 months.

In addition to the standard rates of duty, all states levy additional duty on transfers of residential property to foreigners. The additional duty is imposed at the rate of 8% (in NSW, Victoria and Tasmania) and 7% (in Queensland, SA and WA).

In certain jurisdictions (eg NSW and Victoria), stamp duty relief is available on the purchase of replacement homes for people whose homes were destroyed in the 2019/20 bushfires. Exemptions from stamp duty also generally apply to transfers involving deceased estates and transfers on marriage breakdowns. Certain transfers of the family home between spouses and domestic partners are also exempt.

To lower the up-front cost of purchasing property, NSW introduced a new First Home Buyer Property Tax Option, which gives eligible first home buyers purchasing homes valued up to $1.5m or vacant land valued at up to $800,000 the choice to pay an annual property tax instead of stamp duty on the transfer. To qualify, a first home buyer must, within one year of the purchase of a new home, occupy a dwelling on the property and live in it for at least six months. Separate requirements apply to purchases of vacant land. The property tax rate is $400 plus 0.3% of the property's unimproved land value. If it is rented out, an investor rate of $1,500 plus 1.1% of the property's unimproved land value applies. The rates will be indexed annually from 2024/25.

Victoria is proposing to transition its stamp duty for transfers of commercial and industrial properties to an annual property tax from 1 July 2024.

Stamp duty is also payable on certain transfers of shares and units in companies and trusts that own interests in land. This type of duty is traditionally known as 'landholder duty' and is designed to prevent duty being avoided by transferring shares and units in an entity holding land rather than transferring the underlying land itself. Landholder duty is payable on acquisitions of significant interests in a 'landholder' (ie a company or unit trust). A person generally acquires a significant interest where they acquire 50% or more of the interests in a private company or trust, or 90% or more of the interests in a listed company or trust. In most jurisdictions, landholder duty only applies if the value of the land in the jurisdiction exceeds specified amounts. These amounts are $2m in NSW, Queensland and WA, $1m in Victoria, and $500,000 in Tasmania and the NT. No amounts are prescribed in SA or the ACT.

Other important stamp duties imposed by the states and territories include duty on insurance premiums and motor vehicle registrations and transfers.

GST revenue-sharing arrangements with the states and territories

Although GST is a federal tax, the Commonwealth agreed to redistribute all its GST revenue to the states and territories under the landmark *Intergovernmental Agreement on the Reform of Commonwealth–State Financial Relations* negotiated between the Prime Minister and the Premiers of the states and Chief Ministers of the territories in 1999. In exchange for receiving GST revenue, the states and territories agreed to abolish a number of their taxes, including bed taxes (from 1 July 2000), financial institutions duty (from 1 July 2001), debits tax (from 1 July 2005) and certain forms of stamp duty, such as duty on listed securities (from 1 July 2001).

Pursuant to the *Intergovernmental Agreement on Federal Financial Relations*, GST revenue is paid to the states and territories in accordance with the principle of 'horizontal fiscal equalisation' ('HFE'). According to this principle, the relevant state and territory governments 'should receive funding from the pool of GST revenue such that, after allowing for material factors affecting revenues and expenditures, each would have the fiscal capacity to provide services and the associated infrastructure at the same standard, if each made the same effort to raise revenue from its own sources and operated at the same level of efficiency'. The use of the HFE model means that GST revenue is not allocated to the states and territories on a per capita basis, but rather by reference to their relative fiscal capacities. The purpose of using the relative fiscal capacities of the states and territories to allocate GST revenue is to ensure that Australian citizens are able to enjoy a broadly similar standard of government services regardless of where they live. The Commonwealth Grants Commission ('CGC'), which was established during the Great Depression to assess special requests from the states for financial assistance, advises the Commonwealth on the relative fiscal capacities of the states and territories.

Originally, the HFE model was designed to bring the fiscal capacities of all the states and territories up to those of the strongest state or territory. In effect, this meant that the strongest states (traditionally Victoria and NSW) supported the weaker states and territories. Although this system initially worked in a relatively stable way, it did not function well in times of economic shock. In particular, the effects of the mining boom resulted in volatility in GST allocations, leading to complaints by certain states, such as Western Australia, about their allocation. As a consequence, the Turnbull Government instructed the Productivity Commission to undertake an inquiry into the HFE system. In May 2018, the Productivity Commission released its *Horizontal Fiscal Equalisation: Productivity Commission Inquiry Report*, which contained a number of recommendations that were largely accepted by the Government. The *Commonwealth Grants Commission Act 1973* (Cth) and the *Federal Financial Relations Act 2009* (Cth) were subsequently amended to create an updated HFE system for distributing GST revenue.

The new system aims to create a fairer and more sustainable way to distribute GST revenue that guards against economic shocks. Under the new arrangements, the HFE system will transition from full equalisation (equalised to the strongest state or territory) to reasonable equalisation (equalised to the stronger of NSW and Victoria) over a period of eight years commencing from 2019/20. A special feature of the new system is that it contains a 'GST relativity floor' to ensure that no state or territory will receive less than 70 cents per person per dollar of GST revenue for 2022/23 and 2023/24, and 75 cents per person per dollar of GST revenue for 2024/25 and later years.

[4.5] Local government taxes

There are more than 500 local governments (ie municipal councils) in Australia. These bodies are established under state and territory statutes. Local governments provide a broad range of community services, such as rubbish collection, health services, public libraries and sports and recreation facilities. Local governments receive Commonwealth and state funding to support their activities. They also impose their own taxes in the form of municipal rates. These rates are typically levied on the value of land in the relevant city or shire. Local governments use a range of different methods for valuing land (including unimproved and improved value methods). The rates of tax charged also vary considerably between the respective councils. Municipal rates usually operate subject to special exemptions (eg land owned by the state or Commonwealth governments) and special concessions (eg land owned by pensioners or used for farming purposes).

[4.6] QUESTIONS

1. What were some of earliest taxes levied in Australia?
2. Discuss the key features of the main Commonwealth taxes levied in Australia.
3. What is the tax base of each of the following taxes: income tax, GST and FBT?
4. How is GST revenue shared with the states and territories?
5. Discuss the key features of the main state, territory and local government taxes levied in Australia.

TAX POLICY, POLITICS AND REFORM

5

[5.1] Introduction

Tax laws are based on policies developed by governments, which take into account a broad range of social, economic and political considerations. It is impossible to properly understand how a country's tax system has evolved without taking these considerations into account. This chapter explores the political setting in Australia [5.2] and the process involved in formulating tax policies and implementing tax reform [5.3].

The chapter discusses various tax reviews that have shaped the Australian tax landscape and considers some of the more important tax reforms that have taken place over recent years. In particular, it discusses the Liberal–National Coalition Government's 'A New Tax System' ('ANTS') reforms, which resulted in a number of significant changes to the Commonwealth tax system in the early 2000s (including the introduction of GST from 1 July 2000) [5.4]. It also discusses the 'Henry Tax Review', which was commissioned by the Labor Government in 2008 to make recommendations for the design of 'Australia's Future Tax System' [5.5].

The chapter also examines some of the interesting events that have taken place in Australia's recent tax history and their impact on tax reform. In particular, it focuses on various measures that were introduced following the last five federal elections, being the 2010 election (which produced a minority Labor Government), the 2013, 2016 and 2019 elections (which produced Liberal–National Coalition Governments) and the 2022 election (which produced a Labor Government) [5.6]–[5.10].

[5.2] Political setting in Australia

Australia is a democratic country where tax policies are determined by the duly elected federal, state and territory governments. As discussed in Chapter 3, these governments make tax laws through legislation enacted by their respective parliaments. Over the last few decades, tax reform has become highly politicised, particularly at federal level, where election campaigns have been vigorously fought on ideological grounds. Understanding the political setting in which tax policies are framed is vital for appreciating how the Australian tax system has evolved into its current form.

Australian political parties

The two major political forces in Australia are the Australian Labor Party and the Liberal–National Coalition. Labor is a centre–left social democratic party with trade union affiliations. The Liberal–National Coalition is an alliance of centre–right conservative parties comprising the Liberal Party (the dominant party) and the National Party of Australia.

In addition to the major parties, a number of minor parties and independent candidates also contest elections. At federal level, it has been common for the minor parties and independents to hold the balance of power in the Senate. They have also become more successful in recent years at winning seats in the House of Representatives.

Australian governments

The political party that controls the Lower House of Parliament is the party that is able to form government. At federal level, the party that gains control of the House of Representatives rarely also has a majority in the Senate. As a result, the Government often has to rely on the cross-benchers in the Upper House to get controversial Bills through Parliament. This can lead to protracted negotiations and compromises to policies.

The table on the following pages shows the federal election results for the House of Representatives since 1983 and the respective governments and Prime Ministers that have held office since that time. The number of seats in the House of Representatives has changed over the years due to the redrawing of electoral boundaries. From 2019, there are 151 seats in the House of Representatives.

[5.3] Tax policy and reform

Stakeholders in the tax system

There are many different stakeholders in the Australian tax system, including:

- the Commonwealth, state and territory governments (who make tax laws, administer the tax system and collect tax revenue)
- taxpayers (who are required to comply with the tax laws and pay tax), and
- tax professionals (who provide advice on the tax laws and represent taxpayers in their dealings with government and before the tribunals and courts in tax disputes).

Each of these stakeholders has a vested interest in tax policy and ensuring that the tax system functions clearly, fairly and efficiently.

Lobby groups

In a democracy, like Australia, tax policy is not conceived in a vacuum. The development of tax policy involves both a political and a social process. Many lobby groups and industry associations have played important roles behind the scenes in shaping Australia's tax laws. These bodies are actively involved in vigorous debates about taxation and their views are often reflected in the Government's tax reforms. Some of the bodies that regularly make submissions to government on tax policy issues include the Australian Council of Social Service, the Australian Chamber of Commerce and Industry, the Business Council of Australia, the Corporate Taxpayers' Association, the Association of Superannuation Funds of Australia, the Taxation Institute of Australia, CPA Australia and Chartered Accountants Australia and New Zealand. Many individuals (including business people, academics and practitioners) also actively participate in the tax reform process. These people often make their own private submissions on tax reform and sit on advisory panels.

Parliament Number	Election Date	Labor Seats	Coalition Seats	Other Seats	Total Seats	Government	Prime Minister	Comments
33rd	5/3/1983	75	50	0	125	Labor	Bob Hawke (Labor)	23rd Prime Minister from 11/3/1983 to 20/12/1991
34rd	1/12/1984	82	66	0	148	Labor	Bob Hawke (Labor)	
35th	11/7/1987	86	62	0	148	Labor	Bob Hawke (Labor)	
36th	24/3/1990	78	69	1	148	Labor	Bob Hawke (Labor)	
							Paul Keating (Labor)	24th Prime Minister from 20/12/1991 to 11/3/1996 (took over in leadership spill)
37th	13/3/1993	80	65	2	147	Labor	Paul Keating (Labor)	
38th	2/3/1996	49	94	5	148	Coalition	John Howard (Liberal)	25th Prime Minister from 11/3/1996 to 3/12/2007
39th	3/10/1998	67	80	1	148	Coalition	John Howard (Liberal)	
40th	10/11/2001	65	82	3	150	Coalition	John Howard (Liberal)	
41st	9/10/2004	60	87	3	150	Coalition	John Howard (Liberal)	
42nd	24/11/2007	83	65	2	150	Labor	Kevin Rudd (Labor)	26th Prime Minister from 3/12/2007 to 24/6/2010
							Julia Gillard (Labor)	27th Prime Minister from 24/6/2010 to 27/6/2013 (took over in leadership spill)

Parliament Number	Election Date	Labor Seats	Coalition Seats	Other Seats	Total Seats	Government	Prime Minister	Comments
43rd	21/8/2010	72	72	6	150	Labor (minority in coalition with four cross-benchers)	Julia Gillard (Labor)	
							Kevin Rudd (Labor)	Returned as 26th Prime Minister from 27/6/2013 to 18/9/2013 (took over in leadership spill)
44th	7/9/2013	55	90	5	150	Coalition	Tony Abbott (Liberal)	28th Prime Minister from 18/9/2013 to 15/9/2015
							Malcolm Turnbull (Liberal)	29th Prime Minister from 15/9/2015 to 24/8/2018 (took over in leadership spill)
45th	2/7/2016	69	76	5	150	Coalition	Malcolm Turnbull (Liberal)	
							Scott Morrison (Liberal)	30th Prime Minister from 24/8/2018 (took over in leadership spill)
46th	18/5/2019	68	77	6	151	Coalition	Scott Morrison (Liberal)	
47th	21/5/2022	77	58	16	151	Labor	Anthony Albanese	31st Prime Minister from 23/5/2022

Shaping tax policy

Ultimately, tax policy is a matter for the Government to decide upon. In Australia, taxation has been a major political issue with many recent elections vigorously fought over tax policies. Political parties often promise tax reforms as important aspects of their election platforms. For this reason, the taxation landscape is never static.

Both the Treasury [6.2] and the ATO [6.3] play important roles in the development of federal tax policy. The Treasury is the central agency that analyses tax policy issues form a whole of economy perspective and is accountable for providing advice to the Government on tax law design. The ATO is the Government's principal revenue collection agency that administers the tax laws. The working arrangements between the Treasury and ATO are set out in *Treasury and the Australian Taxation Office—Tax and Superannuation Protocol.* While Treasury is accountable for tax costings and responsible for developing policy and drafting instructions for tax legislation to the Office of Parliamentary Counsel, it is required to work closely with the ATO, which collaborates in the costing process and is also involved in developing drafting instructions, reviewing draft legislation and advising on administrative and interpretive issues.

To help shape tax policy, the Government often relies on economic data obtained from agencies such as the Australian Bureau of Statistics ('ABS') and the Productivity Commission [6.2].

Designing and implementing tax laws

Since tax reform can be highly controversial, the process involved in implementing tax laws is an important and sensitive political issue that governments need to carefully consider. In Australia, there have been several occasions where the Government has been criticised for not consulting enough before introducing new tax measures. This has often resulted in the need for changes in policy and subsequent reforms. There has also been much criticism about the length of time it can sometimes take for legislation to be enacted following its announcement. Of particular concern is the practice known as 'legislating by press release', whereby new tax laws are given retrospective effect (usually backdated to the date of announcement). The problem with this practice is that announcements can sometimes be quite general and vague in nature. The precise effect of the tax laws cannot therefore be determined until the legislation has been passed by Parliament. In the meantime, taxpayers must enter transactions based on only their broad understanding of what the law may be like when eventually enacted.

In 2008, the Commonwealth established a Tax Design Review Panel to advise it on aspects of tax law design and implementation. The panel delivered a report, *Better Tax Design and Implementation*, in which it made a number of recommendations. A key recommendation was that the Government should consult with private sector experts on tax changes at the initial policy design stage, prior to any public announcement. In the case of substantive tax changes, it was recommended that a tri-partite team led by Treasury should be established. This team would have the carriage of the changes throughout the design phase and would include ATO officers and private sector experts. It was also proposed that the team should monitor the early implementation of the measures, identifying any legislative refinements required and ensuring that there are appropriate administrative products and guidance material available. The Government accepted the tri-partite recommendation. PS LA 2013/4 states that the tri-partite tax law design approach recognises 'that tax policy, law and administration are integrally related and interdependent' and 'that an optimal tax design process involves joint cooperation and collaboration between the Treasury, ATO and the private sector'. The tri-partite approach is depicted in the following diagram:

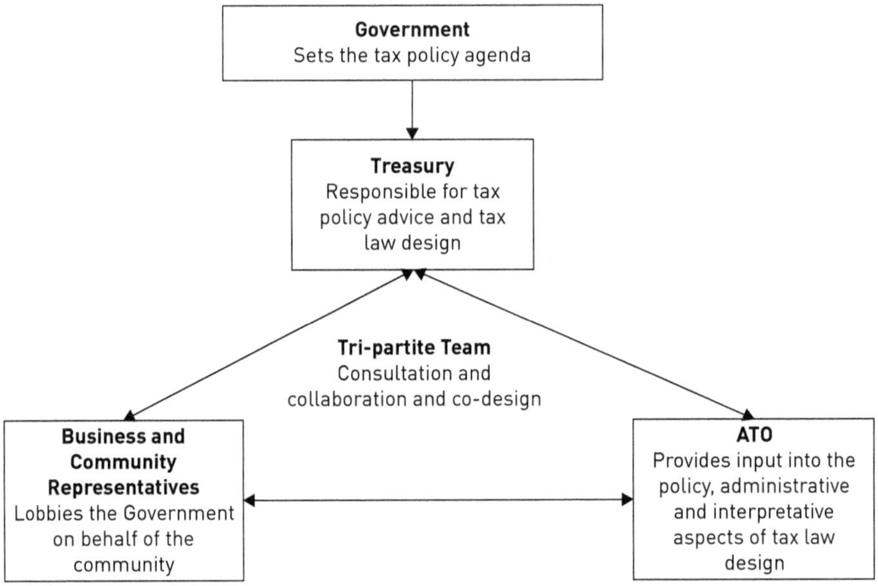

The Tax Design Review Panel also recommended that the Government should publish its plans for further consultation on announced tax measures and foreshadow Bills it plans to introduce into the next sittings of Parliament. It also recommended that tax changes be introduced within 12 months of announcement (six months for retrospective measures). In addition, it supported the establishment of the Tax Issues Entry System, under which the public could raise issues about the tax laws.

Tax reviews

The Australian tax system has been considerably shaped by the outcome of various tax reviews that have been commissioned by the Government over the years. The panels responsible for conducting the reviews consult extensively with stakeholders and receive numerous public submissions which they consider before reporting back to the Government with their recommendations.

The first formal review of the Australian tax system can be traced back to the 1920 Kerr Royal Commission, established by Prime Minister Hughes following World War I. The Royal Commission was charged with examining issues such as the equitable distribution of the tax burden, the harmonisation of state and Commonwealth taxation and the simplification of returns, objections and appeals. This Royal Commission was followed by the Ferguson Royal Commission, which was established in 1932 during the Great Depression to consider the simplification and standardisation of the country's tax laws.

Over the remainder of the 20th century, a number of committees were established to examine aspects of the tax system, including the Spooner Committee of 1950 (established to make recommendations on matters referred to the committee by the Treasurer) and the Ligertwood Committee of 1959 (established to deal with anomalies, inconsistencies, complexities and other defects in the income tax laws). Although the recommendations of these committees resulted in various changes to the tax system, they did not really produce any sweeping reforms. Significant reform proposals were, nevertheless, raised by the Asprey Committee, which had been established by the Liberal Government in 1972, but which ended up handing down its report under the Whitlam Labor Government in 1975. The Asprey Committee recommended a substantial widening of the income tax base through the introduction of a CGT regime and the introduction of a broad-based

GST regime to replace the wholesale sales tax regime. It took a further 10 years for CGT to eventually be introduced by the Hawke Labor Government in 1985. The Labor Government did not, however, have the political appetite at the time to also introduce a GST, which was only introduced some 15 years later by the Howard Liberal–National Coalition Government in 2000 as part of its ANTS reforms [5.4].

[5.4] A New Tax System reforms

Over the past few decades, there have been several tumultuous reforms to Australia's tax system, which have spawned hundreds of pages of new legislation and substantially changed the face of the tax landscape. A significant number of reforms were introduced by the Howard Liberal–National Coalition Government in the late 1990s and early 2000s. The most important changes were the ANTS reforms. These reforms had been foreshadowed by Treasurer Peter Costello in a paper entitled *Tax Reform—Not a New Tax—A New Tax System*, which was published shortly before the 1998 federal election.

GST, ABN and PAYG systems

The central pillar of the ANTS reforms was the introduction of the GST regime, which replaced the sales tax regime from 1 July 2000 [7.1]. The ANTS reforms also included the introduction of the ABN [39.3] and PAYG [39.4] systems.

Review of Business Taxation

Another important aspect of the ANTS reforms was the Review of Business Taxation ('RBT'). The RBT, chaired by John Ralph, was tasked with reviewing the business tax system. In 1999, the RBT delivered a major report, entitled *A Tax System Redesigned*, in which it made numerous reform recommendations. The Government implemented many of these recommendations, including the introduction of a number of new taxation regimes such as the uniform capital allowance [15.2], simplified imputation [22.6], consolidation [26.1] and debt and equity [29.9] regimes.

Interestingly, however, not all of the RBT's recommendations were accepted by the Government. For instance, it rejected the recommendation to abolish the FBT system and tax fringe benefits in the hands of employees rather than employers. The Government also decided not to proceed with an 'entity taxation regime' under which trusts would be taxed like companies. In addition, it did not proceed with a radical recommendation (known as 'Option 2') under which income tax liability would have been based on accounting concepts, such as cash flows and asset values, rather than traditional legal distinctions, such as income and capital.

Board of Taxation

The ANTS reforms also resulted in the establishment of the Board of Taxation. The Board has the role of advising the Government on tax reform. Its Charter states that its mission is 'to contribute a business and broader community perspective to improving the design of taxation laws and their operation'. The Board consists of up to 10 members and is currently chaired by Rosheen Garnon. Up to seven members are selected from business, the tax profession and the broader community. The Secretary to the Treasury, the Commissioner of Taxation and the First Parliamentary Counsel are also members of the Board. The Board undertakes community consultation and has been involved in many reviews and published numerous reports for the Government over the years [2.4]. It also maintains an online platform, known as 'Sounding Board +', which allows the community to contribute ideas on tax reform that might reduce red tape, result in compliance savings, and remove ambiguities in the laws.

[5.5] Australia's Future Tax System reforms

In 2007, a Labor Government, led by Kevin Rudd, replaced the former Liberal–National Coalition Government which had been in power for the preceding 11 years. The new Government was quick to ensure that tax reform remained squarely on the political agenda, and it decided to undertake a comprehensive 'root and branch' review of the tax system, which became known as the Australia's Future Tax System ('AFTS') review. The role of the review was to examine Australia's existing tax system and make recommendations 'to position Australia to deal with the demographic, social, economic and environmental challenges of the 21st century'. The idea for the review evolved out of the *2020 Summit* where it was suggested that the Government should examine measures to harmonise taxes, reduce inefficient taxes, ensure a progressive tax system and address negative interaction with the welfare system.

The Review Panel and AFTS Report

A Review Panel chaired by Dr Ken Henry, who was Secretary to the Treasury, was appointed to undertake the review. The panel was instructed to consider the competitiveness of Australia's tax system taking into account a range of challenges and opportunities, including the ageing population, the rise of emerging economies (such as China and India), and climate change. It was also instructed to look at simplifying the tax system and the interactions between federal, state and local government taxes. Importantly, any recommendations had to be made in the context of the Government's policy of not raising the GST rate or broadening the GST base, preserving the tax-free treatment of superannuation payments for those over 60, and its aspirational goals of reducing personal income tax rates.

The panel undertook extensive consultations and received many submissions. It released a number of papers before finally delivering its report to the Treasurer in December 2009. The report, *Australia's Future Tax System—Report to the Treasurer* ('AFTS Report'), was around 1,000 pages in length and contained 138 recommendations for reforming the Australian tax system. The recommendations covered a broad spectrum of issues relating to the following areas:

- personal taxation (including the tax treatment of income from savings, retirement incomes and wealth transfer taxes)
- investment and entity taxation (including the tax treatment of business entities and tax concessions for not-for-profit organisations)
- land and resource taxation (including stamp duty and charging for non-renewable resources)
- consumption taxation (including GST and payroll tax), and
- social and market outcome taxation (including environment, road transport, alcohol, tobacco and gambling taxes).

The AFTS Report also made numerous recommendations in relation to the transfer system. Some of the specific areas covered included income support payments, child care assistance, housing assistance and aged care funding. The report also contained recommendations relating to state tax reform and tax administration.

The Labor Government responded to the AFTS Report in May 2010. Surprisingly, however, it only accepted a small handful of the recommendations. The following discussion outlines the Government's response to the report and some of the interesting political events that followed.

New tax on Australian non-renewable resources

The most controversial and significant recommendation in the AFTS Report that was accepted by the Government was the proposal to introduce a new resource tax from 1 July 2012 (Recommendation 45). The AFTS Report noted (at 217–218) that 'Australia has the world's largest economically demonstrated reserves of brown coal, lead, mineral sands (rutile and zircon), nickel, silver, uranium and zinc and the second largest reserves of bauxite, copper, gold and iron ore'. The Government pointed out that Australia's minerals are non-renewable resources and argued that Australia had not adequately charged for these resources under the existing state and territory royalty arrangements. According to the Government, Australia's resources belong to all Australians, and the country should therefore share in the profits that mining companies make from extracting and selling them. On this basis, it decided that it would introduce a 'resource super profits tax' ('RSPT') on the exploitation of Australian non-renewable resources.

The RSPT was modelled on the PRRT and was proposed to apply to profits from all resource projects carried on in Australia at the rate of 40% (which was the same as the PRRT rate). Based on the strong demand for Australia's resources from countries such as China, the RSPT had the potential to raise significant revenue. However, it also had the potential to have a significant adverse impact on mining companies, and it was therefore not surprising that the mining industry strongly opposed the tax. Mining companies argued that, like other companies, they already paid income tax and it was unfair to increase their overall tax burden as this would significantly diminish the returns they could provide to their shareholders. The mining industry actively campaigned against the tax, and spent considerable effort advocating their views in the media. They warned that many mining projects would be shut down or suspended if the RSPT was introduced. They also argued that mining investment would go overseas where mining is taxed more concessionally, and this would result in jobs being lost in Australia. The heavy opposition to the RSPT was one of the catalysts that ultimately contributed to the Labor Government leadership spill which resulted in Kevin Rudd being replaced by Julia Gillard as Prime Minister in June 2010.

In light of the political backlash against the RSPT, the new Prime Minister immediately announced that she would consult with the mining industry on the details of the Government's resource tax arrangements. In July 2010, after only a couple of weeks of discussions with some of Australia's major mining companies (including BHP and Rio Tinto), the Government announced that it would replace the RSPT with a new 'minerals resource rent tax' ('MRRT') [5.6].

Significantly, the MRRT would only apply to iron ore and coal projects in Australia (not to all resource projects in Australia as was originally proposed under the RSPT). In addition, small miners with annual taxable profits below $50m (later increased to $75m) would not be subject to the tax. This meant that the number of companies affected by the tax would be reduced from 2,500 to around 320. The Government also promised to provide mining companies with a number of generous allowances that were not available under the RSPT. The Government set the 'headline' MRRT rate at 30%. It, however, also announced that this rate would operate subject to a 25% 'extraction factor' that would recognise the contribution of the miner's expertise to mining projects. This effectively meant that the 'actual' MRRT rate would be only 22.5% (ie 30% × 75%), which was a considerable back-down from the proposed 40% RSPT rate.

Reduction in the corporate tax rate

The AFTS Report also focused on the corporate income tax rate. The report noted that corporate tax rates had been falling across OECD countries over the last 30 years and that Australia's corporate tax rate of 30% was one of the highest rates among small to medium OECD countries (which had an average tax rate of around 25%). Australia's corporate tax rate was also significantly higher than the corporate tax rate in Singapore (17%) and Hong Kong (16.5%). It was also higher than the average corporate tax rate for the Asia–Pacific region (27.5%). On this basis, the Review recommended that Australia's corporate tax rate should be reduced from 30% to 25% in order to increase Australia's international competitiveness and stimulate economic growth by encouraging more investment and further employment (Recommendation 27).

However, the Government was not prepared to fund such a steep reduction of the corporate tax rate, particularly after it had spent considerable money to fund stimulus initiatives to combat the economic downturn caused by the GFC. Instead, in its response to the AFTS Report, the Government announced that it would reduce the corporate tax rate to 29% (from 2013/14) and then to 28% (from 2014/15). Special reductions were announced for SBEs [8.7], which would have their tax rate reduced to 28% (from 2012/13). The Government planned to fund its corporate tax rate reduction from the extra revenue it expected to raise from the RSPT. However, as it subsequently decided to replace the RSPT with the MRRT, it was evident that it would raise much less revenue than originally expected. As a consequence, in July 2010, the Government announced that it would only reduce the corporate tax rate to 29% and would not further reduce the rate to 28%. However, for the reasons outlined at [5.6], this reform did not eventuate.

Other recommendations

In its response to the AFTS Report, the Government also announced various changes to the capital write-off rules, including the introduction of an 'instant asset write-off' allowing SBEs an immediate deduction for the cost of depreciating assets valued under $5,000 (this figure was subsequently increased to $6,500) [15.2]. The report had actually recommended that the instant asset write-off should apply to depreciating assets valued under $10,000 (Recommendation 29).

Several superannuation reforms were also announced by the Government, including the progressive increase in the SGC rate from 9% to 12% [19.5] and the introduction of government co-contributions for concessional contributions relating to low-income earners [19.8]. Interestingly, these reforms were quite different to those recommended in the AFTS Report (Recommendations 18 to 24).

The Government also rejected a number of other recommendations in the report. For instance, it rejected recommendations to remove the ML (Recommendation 5), impose land tax on the family home (Recommendations 52 and 53), change the tax treatment of the not-for-profit sector (Recommendations 13, 41, 43 and 44) and abolish the LCT (Recommendation 80).

Surprisingly, the Government was conspicuously silent on the bulk of the remaining recommendations and was criticised in the media for this. In the 2010 Budget, which followed shortly after the release of the report, the Government announced additional reforms, some of which are discussed at [5.6]. However, before any of these reforms could be legislated, a federal election was set for August 2010.

[5.6] Tax reform following the 2010 election

The August 2010 federal election was one of the closest in history. The outcome was that neither of the major political parties obtained an outright majority of the 150 seats in the House of Representatives. As a consequence, neither party was able to form a government in its own right, producing the first 'hung Parliament' in 70 years. The Labor Party (led by Julia Gillard) and the Liberal–National Coalition (led by Tony Abbott) each ended up winning 72 seats. The remaining six seats were won by four independent candidates (Andrew Wilkie, Rob Oakeshott, Tony Windsor and Bob Katter), one National Party of Western Australia candidate (Tony Crook) and one Greens candidate (Adam Bandt). Immediately after the election results became known, both Labor and the Liberal–National Coalition sought to gain the support of these candidates to form a government. Eventually, after more than two weeks of protracted negotiations, Labor was successful in gaining the support of Andrew Wilkie, Rob Oakeshott, Tony Windsor and Adam Bandt to form a minority government with Julia Gillard as Prime Minister.

Tax Forum and the Business Tax Working Group

In garnishing support to form a minority government with the independents, Prime Minister Gillard promised to hold a National Tax Forum, which took place in October 2011. The forum was a televised discussion that involved around 180 representatives from community groups, businesses, governments, unions, academia and tax practice. It covered a broad range of topics and was designed to build on the AFTS review and prioritise the future tax reform agenda. One of the outcomes of the forum was that the Government established a Business Tax Working Group ('BTWG') to look at how Australia's tax system could be improved in order to make the most of the challenges and opportunities arising from the broader economic environment, including the 'patchwork economy' that had developed in the wake of the GFC.

The BTWG's first task was to consider the treatment of tax losses, which had been raised at the forum. In early 2012, it published its *Final Report on the Tax Treatment of Losses* which recommended that in addition to being able to carry forward tax losses, companies should be allowed to carry back tax losses within certain limits. The Government accepted this recommendation and enacted legislation that allowed companies to carry back up to $1m of tax losses each year.

The BTWG was also asked to consider ways of reducing the corporate tax rate. It released a discussion paper which recognised that a lower corporate tax rate would lead to greater investment in Australia and improve productivity. Various options for funding the reduction were canvassed, including changing the treatment of interest deductibility, capital allowances and R&D incentives. However, in its *Final Report* released in 2012, the BTWG was unable to recommend any revenue-neutral measures as it could not find general support from the business community for a further broadening of the tax base.

Labor Government reforms

The Gillard Government faced significant political challenges as, being a minority government, it had to rely on non-Labor members in the House of Representatives and Senate to get Bills enacted. It was nevertheless successful in introducing new marginal tax rates (which included a substantially increased tax-free threshold), increasing the ML rate from 1.5% to 2% to fund the National Disability Insurance Scheme and implementing a range of new superannuation measures. The Gillard Government was also successful in implementing its resource tax reforms (which resulted in the introduction of the MRRT from 1 July 2012) and its climate change reforms (which resulted in the introduction of a carbon tax on large greenhouse gas emitters from 1 July 2012). Both these reforms were extremely controversial and were vigorously opposed by the Liberal–National Coalition, which eventually repealed both taxes in 2014 after defeating Labor in the 2013 federal election [5.7]. Although neither the MRRT nor the carbon tax exist today, it is worthwhile examining how they operated given their unique and contentious nature.

Minerals resource rent tax

The MRRT was a significantly watered-down version of the Government's RSPT proposal [5.5]. It taxed profits from Australian iron ore and coal projects and was based on the PRRT, which taxed profits from petroleum projects [4.3]. Both the MRRT and the PRRT were designed to tax the 'economic rent' (ie positive cash flow) derived from resource projects. The taxes were based on a model developed by Ross Garnaut and Anthony Clunies Ross in the 1970s, which was, in turn, based on an earlier model developed by E Cary Brown in the United States in the 1940s. The difference between the two models was that, under the Brown model, where a project makes a loss (ie negative cash flow), the Government provides a refund for the loss. The Government therefore shares in losses and profits from projects at the same rate. Under the Garnaut–Clunies Ross model, on the other hand, there is no refund for a loss. Instead, negative cash flows are carried forward to be deducted against any positive cash flows in future years. To preserve the value of losses over time, they are uplifted by an interest rate. Unutilised losses from projects can also generally be transferred and offset against profits from other projects. The advantage of the Garnaut–Clunies Ross model over the Brown model was that it was a 'pure' profits tax as the Government did not have upfront costs for resource projects and did not share in the costs of projects that made losses.

Arguments for and against the MRRT

As the MRRT was levied on top of income tax, it naturally made iron ore and coal mining more expensive for companies operating in Australia and increased their compliance costs. Indeed, one of the principal arguments against the tax was that it resulted in miners operating in Australia being placed at a competitive disadvantage compared with miners operating overseas. Opponents to the tax argued that it would encourage miners to abandon, scale down or defer their Australian projects and instead undertake projects overseas. They contended that this would have a negative effect on the mining industry, which in turn would affect employment opportunities and overall mining revenues in Australia. They also maintained that it was unfair to single out miners and impose an additional tax on them when other industries, such as the banking and finance industry, did not have equivalent industry specific taxes.

From the Labor Government's perspective, however, the aim of the MRRT was to ensure that Australia received a greater share of the profits from projects involving the extraction of its non-renewable resources. By their very nature, these resources cannot be replaced and should be charged for appropriately. The MRRT was simply an additional cost imposed on mining companies for exploiting Australia's iron ore and coal deposits. The Government contended that these resources had been provided to mining companies too cheaply and belonged to all Australians who deserved to benefit more from them.

State taxation arrangements

At the time the MRRT was introduced, the states already had their own existing resource taxation arrangements. The Western Australian Government, for example, collected around $4 billion a year in mineral royalties under the *Mining Act 1978* (WA) and other legislation. The Commonwealth could not impose royalties on iron ore and coal as the resources technically belonged to the states, and s 114 of the *Constitution* prevented the Commonwealth from imposing taxes on property belonging to the states [3.10]. The MRRT was therefore designed to tax profits from projects *after* the resources had been extracted from the ground, so as not to breach s 114. The introduction of the MRRT did not prevent the states from continuing to charge mining royalties. However, to prevent double taxation, a royalty allowance (discussed below) reduced a miner's MRRT liability.

MRRT legislation

The MRRT was levied under the *Minerals Resource Rent Tax Act 2012* (Cth) ('*MRRTA*'). The *MRRTA* required a miner to pay MRRT equal to the sum of its MRRT liabilities for each of its mining project interests for an MRRT year (ie a financial year starting on or after 1 July 2012). A 'miner' was an entity that had a 'mining project interest' (ie a share of the output of an undertaking to extract 'taxable resources', which principally covered iron ore and coal). A miner's 'MRRT liability' for a mining project interest was calculated as follows:

$$\text{MRRT liability} = \text{MRRT rate} \times (\text{Mining profit} - \text{MRRT allowances})$$

As previously mentioned, the MRRT rate was 22.5%, which was a drastic reduction from the 40% rate initially proposed for the RSPT by the Labor Government.

A miner's 'mining profit' for a mining project interest was basically the excess of its mining revenue over its mining expenditure for the interest for the year. 'Mining revenue' was, broadly speaking, that part of the revenue the miner made from supplying, exporting or using extracted taxable resources (or things produced from them) that reasonably related to the form and place the resources were in at their 'valuation point'. 'Mining expenditure' essentially represented the costs of finding and extracting the taxable resources and getting them to their valuation point—it included expenses such as the capital cost of establishing mine shafts and drilling.

The *MRRTA* contained a number of allowances, including the following:

- **Mining loss allowance.** Miners were allowed to carry forward their unutilised losses and uplift those losses at the long-term bond rate ('LTBR') plus a further 7%. Miners could transfer their losses from particular projects to other projects.
- **Royalty allowance.** Miners that paid mining royalties to the Commonwealth, state and territory governments were provided with a credit for the royalties so that they were not effectively double taxed. Unused credits for royalties were carried forward and uplifted at the LTBR plus a further 7%. However, unlike losses, they were generally not transferable.
- **Starting base allowance.** Miners that had existing projects were provided with a starting base allowance for the value of their investments in those projects as at 1 May 2010. They could choose to use either a market value or a book value method for valuing such investments, with the book value starting base being uplifted at the LTBR plus 7%.

The allowances were more generous than those proposed under the RSPT. For example, under the RSPT losses and royalties could only be carried forward at the LTBR. The additional 7% loading under the MRRT created a higher hurdle before the tax applied. Further, whereas RSPT losses were not transferable between projects, MRRT losses could be transferred between projects. In addition, the *MRRTA* contained a special 'low profit offset', which ensured that miners with a group mining profit below $75m in an MRRT year were not required to pay any tax, and miners with group profits of between $75m and $125m in an MRRT year obtained a reduction in their tax liability.

5

Ultimately, due to the various allowances available to miners and the fact that the mining boom was coming to an end, the MRRT did not generate much revenue over its short period of existence. It therefore ended up being an ill-fated tax from both political and fiscal perspectives.

Carbon tax

The Gillard Government's climate change reforms were the product of a protracted political process. By way of background, the former Rudd Labor Government had originally proposed to introduce a 'carbon pollution reduction scheme' under which it would set a cap on carbon pollution and require large greenhouse gas emitters to acquire permits for their emissions. Under the scheme, the Government would issue a limited quantity of permits to emitters. Emitters that required additional permits would need to trade for such permits in the secondary market. In this way, the market would set the price for greenhouse gas emissions. Entities wishing to avoid having to pay for additional permits would, therefore, need to limit their emissions. The Rudd Government was, however, unable to enact legislation to implement the scheme before the 2010 election because the Liberal–National Coalition blocked its Bills in the Senate.

In 2011, the Gillard Government unveiled its *Clean Energy Future* reforms which included a two-stage plan:

- **Stage 1—fixed price period (carbon tax).** The first stage involved introducing a carbon tax (from 1 July 2012) which set a fixed price for carbon emissions.
- **Stage 2—flexible price period (ETS).** The second stage involved transitioning to an emissions trading scheme ('ETS') (from 1 July 2015) which used a flexible price for carbon emissions determined by the market.

The decision to introduce a carbon tax as the first stage of the plan was a significant change in policy as Prime Minister Gillard had previously stated that there would be no carbon tax. Ultimately, the decision was made because it was supported by the Greens whose votes were necessary to pass the legislation in the Senate.

Carbon pricing mechanism

Importantly, unlike most other taxes, the principal objective of the carbon tax and ETS was not to collect revenue, but to reduce greenhouse gas emissions. The carbon pricing mechanism required large-scale polluters to pay for every tonne of greenhouse gases they released into the atmosphere by surrendering 'eligible emissions units'. If an entity did not meet its obligation to surrender eligible emissions units by specified dates, it was subject to a non-deductible 'unit shortfall charge'.

The carbon pricing mechanism covered four of the six greenhouse gases counted under the Kyoto Protocol (ie carbon dioxide, methane, nitrous oxide and perfluorocarbon emissions from the aluminium sector). In general, it applied only to those entities that had facilities with direct greenhouse gas emissions of at least 25,000 tonnes of carbon dioxide emissions a year (excluding emissions from transport fuels and certain synthetic greenhouse gases). There were, however, different thresholds for certain facilities (eg special rules for natural gas retailers). There were also a number of exclusions from the regime (eg it did not apply to fuels used for household transport or light commercial vehicles).

Legislative framework, eligible emissions units and unit shortfall charge

The Government's climate change reforms were complex and contained in over a dozen pieces of legislation, including the following Acts:

- The *Clean Energy Act 2011* (Cth) established the carbon pricing mechanism and identified the greenhouse gas emissions to which it applied. It also set out the obligations of liable entities to surrender eligible emissions units.
- The *Clean Energy Regulator Act 2011* (Cth) established the Clean Energy Regulator, which was the statutory authority set up to administer the scheme and enforce the law.
- The *Carbon Credits (Carbon Farming Initiative) Act 2011* (Cth) established the 'carbon farming initiative' under which farmers and land managers who undertook eligible projects in Australia to increase carbon stored in soils or reduce greenhouse gas emissions from agriculture would be issued Australian carbon credit units ('ACCUs') that could be sold to businesses to offset their emissions.

Central to the carbon pricing mechanism was the concept of an 'eligible emissions unit'. The main kind of eligible emission unit was a 'carbon unit'. Carbon units were issued by the Clean Energy Regulator making electronic entries in the 'registry account' of the 'registered holder'. Each unit had a unique 'identification number' and 'vintage year'. For the ETS period, eligible emissions units would also include ACCUs (issued under the carbon farming initiative) and 'eligible international emissions units' (eg 'emission reduction units' from projects under the Kyoto Protocol).

During the carbon tax period, the cost of a carbon unit was set at a fixed price ($23.00 per tonne in 2012/13 and $24.15 per tonne in 2013/14). During the ETS period, an overall limit (ie cap) was to be placed on annual emissions. This was to be achieved by the Regulator issuing only a fixed number of carbon units each year. Some of the units would be sold at auction and a limited number would be allocated free of charge to help adversely affected industries make necessary transitions. Carbon units would then be able to be traded in the market, resulting in a flexible price (which would operate subject to a ceiling in the first three years of the ETS to reduce the risks for businesses). During the carbon tax period, the unit shortfall charge was 130% of the fixed price charged for units. During the ETS period, it was to be up to 200% of the benchmark average auction price for the relevant period. The object of the charge was to provide a clear financial incentive to acquire and surrender units.

Rationale for climate change policy

The Labor Government's policy for taking action on climate change and its mechanism for setting a carbon price was explained in *Securing a Clean Energy Future, The Australian Government's Climate*

Change Plan. This plan noted that there was unequivocal scientific evidence of global warming and that high levels of carbon pollution pose significant environmental and economic threats to Australia and the rest of the world. It also emphasised that Australia's carbon pollution levels were high and were rising. The Government's goal was to reduce carbon emissions from 2000 levels by 5% by 2020 and by 80% by 2050. The carbon pricing mechanism was aimed at supporting a global response to climate change and creating an economic incentive to reduce carbon emissions. It was also designed to make lower-polluting technologies more competitive and help transform the economy towards a 'clean energy future'. The Government accepted that the carbon pricing mechanism would modestly increase the cost of living (eg the cost of electricity and gas). To mitigate this, it introduced a household assistance package, which included income tax rate cuts.

Opponents of the carbon pricing mechanism argued that the carbon price was too high and would make Australian businesses less competitive when compared with businesses operating overseas in jurisdictions that do not have a similar impost. They pointed out that carbon pricing places an additional regulatory burden on Australian businesses and imposes additional costs that would inevitably be passed on to consumers who would experience an increase in their cost of living. They also contended that it would encourage polluters to go offshore where they could continue to emit greenhouse gases, resulting in the loss of Australian jobs and the problem simply being transposed overseas without achieving an overall reduction in global greenhouse gas emissions.

Replacement of carbon pricing mechanism

5

After defeating Labor in the 2013 federal election [5.7], the Liberal–National Coalition Government replaced Labor's climate change reforms with its *Direct Action Plan*, the centrepiece of which was the establishment of a $2.55 billion Emissions Reduction Fund ('ERF') designed to encourage greenhouse gas abatement activities through direct incentives rather than a tax or an ETS. The ERF is used to purchase ACCUs issued by the Clean Energy Regulator from bidders who propose to undertake approved greenhouse gas reduction projects. Each ACCU represents 1 tonne of greenhouse gas emissions savings. ACCUs are purchased using a competitive reverse auction process, which operates subject to a benchmark price above which ACCUs will not be purchased.

Labor Government's unlegislated tax reforms

While the Labor Government had been successful in introducing major tax reforms like the MRRT and carbon tax, not all the tax measures it had proposed ended up being legislated. In particular, in the 2012 Budget, the Government stated that it would not proceed with its proposal to reduce the corporate tax rate from 30% to 29% [5.5]. It also indicated that it would not proceed with its 2010 Budget commitments to introduce a 'standard deduction' (which would have provided individuals with an optional deduction of $1,000 as an alternative to claiming deductions for work-related and tax management expenses) and a 'savings incentive' (which would have provided individuals with a 50% discount on up to $1,000 of the interest earned from deposits with financial institutions). These reforms were abandoned to help the Government deliver a 2012/13 Budget surplus. However, for various reasons, including much less revenue collected from the MRRT than originally expected, the Government was unable to achieve a surplus and instead forecast a deficit of $19.4 billion for the fiscal year.

[5.7] Tax reform following the 2013 election

In early 2013, Prime Minister Gillard announced that a federal election would be held on 14 September 2013. In the meantime, the Government was struggling with various political issues and performing poorly in the opinion polls. It therefore seemed inevitable that Kevin Rudd, whom Julia Gillard had deposed as Prime Minister in 2010, would challenge her leadership. After much speculation, a leadership ballot was called in June 2013 and Kevin Rudd was once again elected Labor leader.

A few weeks after being sworn in as Prime Minister, Kevin Rudd announced a new federal election date, 7 September 2013. However, despite the change in Labor leadership, the 2013 election was convincingly won by the Liberal–National Coalition, led by Tony Abbott. The Coalition won 90 of the 150 seats in the House of Representatives. In the Senate, the Coalition held 33 seats, Labor held 25 seats, the Greens held 10 seats, and the minor parties and independents held the remaining 8 seats. As it did not control the Senate, the Coalition Government was required to rely on the support of the cross-benchers to pass its Bills. Nevertheless, in spite of some difficulties, it was successful in overturning many Labor reforms, including repealing the MRRT (from 1 October 2014) and the carbon tax (from 1 July 2014) [5.6]. The Coalition had vigorously opposed these taxes when it was in opposition and their scrapping was a central platform in its election campaign.

Abbott Government's 2014 and 2015 Budgets

The Abbott Government's first budget was delivered by Treasurer Joe Hockey in May 2014. The Treasurer foreshadowed a $29.8 billion deficit for 2014/15 and laid much of the blame for this on the policies of the former Labor Government. To address the budgetary position, the Treasurer introduced a three-year temporary budget repair levy ('TBRL') on high-income earners. The TBRL applied for the 2014/15 to 2016/17 income years and required resident and non-resident individuals to pay an additional 2% levy on so much of their taxable income as exceeded $180,000. As a consequence of the introduction of the TBRL, a number of other tax rates that were based on the top marginal rate were also increased by 2% for the 2014/15 to 2016/17 income years. This included various superannuation and withholding rates. The FBT rate was also increased by 2%, but only for the 2015/16 and 2016/17 FBT years.

Other changes made by the Abbott Government included the abolition of various tax offsets (such as the mature age worker tax offset) and the discontinuation of various tax incentive schemes (such as the National Rental Affordability scheme) [27.7]. The Government also proposed controversial changes to the Higher Education Loan Program [8.10] and delayed the timing of the progressive increases in the SGC rate introduced by the Labor Government [19.5]. The Budget also contained a number of cost-saving measures, including a contentious proposal for a $7 fee to be paid by patients who consulted a doctor. There was considerable opposition to a number of the reforms, and several measures were not legislated.

The Abbott Government's second budget was delivered in May 2015. This budget also contained a host of tax measures, but was considerably more benign than its first. A major highlight was that it included a number of significant tax concessions for taxpayers operating small businesses. One of these was a 1.5% reduction in the corporate tax rate (ie from 30% to 28.5%) for companies that were SBEs [22.3]. Another was an increase in the instant asset write-off threshold, allowing SBEs an immediate deduction for capital expenditure incurred on assets costing less than $20,000 that were acquired from 7.30pm 12 May 2015 to 30 June 2017 [15.2].

The Government also announced that it would amend the general anti-avoidance provisions in pt IVA *ITAA36* by introducing a targeted anti-avoidance rule aimed at large multinational companies that minimise tax by artificially avoiding having a taxable presence in Australia [37.8]. It also stated that it would extend the GST system to cover international supplies of digital products and services (such as movie and music downloads) imported by Australian consumers [7.18].

Change of Prime Minister

During the 2013 election campaign, Tony Abbott had campaigned strongly on Labor disunity resulting from the leadership feud between Kevin Rudd and Julia Gillard. Ironically, his term as Prime Minister only lasted two years due to a leadership spill in September 2015, which resulted in his rival, Malcolm Turnbull, successfully challenging him for leadership of the Liberal Party.

After Malcolm Turnbull was appointed Prime Minister, the direction of the Coalition Government's policies changed somewhat. In particular, the Turnbull Government decided not to proceed with a comprehensive White Paper on tax reform, which Tony Abbott had promised to take to the next federal election. As a precursor to the White Paper, the Abbott Government had released its *Re:think—Tax Discussion Paper* outlining various challenges facing Australia and opportunities to improve its tax system. The Abbott Government was also planning to issue a Green Paper with a set of reform options before releasing the White Paper with its final proposals. However, the Turnbull Government shelved this process and instead laid out the tax policies it would take to the 2016 election in the 2016 Budget.

In the meantime, the Turnbull Government launched its *National Innovation and Science Agenda*, which contained various initiatives aimed at boosting innovation and science to help Australia transition from the 'mining boom' to the 'ideas boom'. A number of new tax incentives to support entrepreneurs and their start-up companies were announced, including a 20% tax offset for investments made in early-stage innovation companies [27.2] and a 10% tax offset for capital contributed to ESVCLPs [27.4].

Turnbull Government's 2016 Budget

Given that the Turnbull Government had decided not to proceed with a White Paper, there was considerable interest in the direction it would take on tax reform in the 2016 Budget. In particular, there was much speculation that it might broaden the GST base and raise the GST rate. However, this was rejected shortly before the Budget.

In the 2016 Budget, Scott Morrison, who had replaced Joe Hockey as Treasurer after Malcolm Turnbull became Prime Minister, revealed that the deficit for 2015/16 was forecast to increase to $39.9 billion. This was more than double the deficit left by the preceding Labor Government and was attributed, in part, to the slowdown in the mining industry. To address the deficit, a number of significant tax savings measures were announced. They included major reforms to the superannuation regime to make it more sustainable [19.3] and the introduction of a diverted profits tax on multinationals [37.9]. At the same time, the Government also proposed to increase the SBE aggregated turnover threshold from $2m to $10m [8.7] and progressively reduce the corporate tax rate from 30% to 25% over 10 years [22.3].

However, before any reforms could be enacted, Parliament was prorogued due to the setting of an early election for 2 July 2016. The election was triggered on 9 May 2016 when the Prime Minister requested the Governor-General to dissolve both Houses of Parliament as a result of the Senate twice rejecting a Bill to restore the Australian Building and Construction Commission.

[5.8] Tax reform following the 2016 election

Not surprisingly, tax reform featured prominently as a major issue in the 2016 federal election campaign. The Coalition's tax policies were based on the measures that the Turnbull Government had announced in the 2016 Budget [5.7]. The Labor Party opposed a number of these policies—especially the cuts to the corporate tax rate for larger businesses, which it argued were unaffordable given the budgetary position. Labor said that if it was elected, it would address the budget deficit by retaining the TBRL [5.7], limiting negative gearing [12.3], reducing the CGT discount from 50% to 25% [17.8] and introducing its own superannuation reforms. Labor also campaigned heavily on Medicare and education issues.

As events turned out, the 2016 election was much closer than predicted. The Coalition, which had been tipped by most commentators to win the election, managed to just sneak over the line and win 76 of the 150 seats in the Lower House, allowing it to form government in its own right. Labor won 69 seats and the remaining five seats were won by the minor parties (the Greens, Katter's Australian Party and the Nick Xenaphon Team) and independents (Andrew Wilkie and Cathy McGowan).

In spite of the fact that the double dissolution of Parliament resulted in a full Senate election, neither of the major parties was able to gain a majority in the Upper House, where the balance of power was held by a number of cross-benchers. There were 30 Coalition senators, 26 Labor senators and 20 cross-bench senators (including nine from the Greens, four from One Nation and three from the Nick Xenophon Team).

The fact that the Coalition Government did not control the Senate meant that it faced challenges enacting legislation. The difficulties were illustrated in the implementation of some of its 2016 Budget reforms. For example, the Government was able to implement cuts to the company tax rate only after agreeing to a Senate request to make changes to its original proposal. The changes included removing tax cuts for companies with aggregated turnover above $50m [22.3].

The Government also had significant problems with its superannuation reforms, which included unpopular retrospective elements that were believed to have contributed to its reduced majority in Parliament. After the election, the Government consulted on these reforms and announced that it had decided to amend some key aspects of its 2016 Budget package. The amended package was eventually enacted, and the new superannuation reforms commenced operation from 1 July 2017 [19.3].

Turnbull Government's 2017 Budget

The 2017 Budget focused heavily on housing affordability, which had become a problem in Australia's major capital cities. To address this issue, a range of measures was announced. For example, in order to allow people to save for their first homes in a concessional tax environment, the Treasurer announced that individuals would be able to make contributions to their superannuation funds that they could subsequently withdraw (together with deemed earnings) to pay for a first home [19.12]. In addition, to make more housing stock available for growing families, the Treasurer announced that, from 1 July 2018, people aged 65 or over who want to 'downsize' would be allowed to contribute $300,000 from the proceeds of the sale of their homes to their superannuation funds without being subject to superannuation restrictions and caps [19.12].

The Treasurer also indicated that the CGT discount would be increased from 50% to 60% for resident individuals who invest in qualifying housing provided to lower-income tenants at below market rates [17.8]. He also announced that the Government would remove the main residence exemption for foreign and temporary residents from 9 May 2017 [17.11]. In addition, the immediate deduction available to SBEs for capital expenditure on assets costing less than $20,000 was extended to 30 June 2018 [15.2]. The main surprise in the 2017 Budget was the announcement of a major bank levy on Australia's largest banks [4.3].

Turnbull Government's 2018 Budget

The 2018 Budget forecast a deficit of $14.5 billion for 2018/19. However, it also indicated that the Australian economy was strengthening, and that the Government was on the verge of delivering its first surplus since 2007. Forward estimates forecast a surplus of $2.2 billion in 2019/20, $11 billion in 2020/21, and $16.6 billion in 2021/22. The forecast return to surplus over the coming years enabled the Government to promise some pre-election tax cuts for individuals under its Personal Income Tax Plan. This plan was the centrepiece of the budget and was to be introduced in three stages over seven years. The first stage applied from 1 July 2018 and consisted of a $3,000 increase in the top threshold of the 32.5% marginal tax rate [8.8] coupled with a new low and middle income tax offset ('LMITO') [8.9].

The Government also announced that it would extend (until 30 June 2019) the immediate deduction available to SBEs for capital expenditure on assets costing less than $20,000 [15.2] and that it would make changes (from 1 July 2018) to the R&D tax incentive [27.5]. It also announced additional measures to deal with the 'black economy', such as denying employers deductions (from 1 July 2019) for payments to employees where PAYG has not been withheld [14.7].

Change of Prime Minister

In August 2018, disunity within various ranks of the Coalition Government led to a leadership ballot, which resulted in Malcolm Turnbull being replaced by his former Treasurer, Scott Morrison, as Prime Minister. Following the leadership spill, Malcolm Turnbull resigned from Parliament, and a by-election was held for his seat of Wentworth in October 2018. Although Wentworth had always been a safe Liberal seat, it was won by independent candidate Dr Kerryn Phelps. As a consequence, the Coalition Government lost its one-seat majority in the House of Representatives and only retained 75 of the 150 seats.

Morrison Government's 2019 Budget

The 2019 Budget was delivered by the new Treasurer, Josh Frydenberg, on 2 April 2019 and laid out the Government's plans for the forthcoming election scheduled for 18 May 2019. The Treasurer forecast that the Government would deliver a surplus of $7.1 billion in 2019/20 (which, if achieved, would be the first surplus in over 10 years). He also announced changes to the Government's Personal Income Tax Plan previously announced in the 2018 Budget. The Treasurer stated that the Government would provide three additional rounds of tax cuts:

5

- The first round would operate from 1 July 2018 and involved increasing the maximum LMITO from $530 to $1,080 [8.9].
- The second round would operate from 1 July 2022 and involved increasing the top threshold of the 19% marginal tax rate from $41,000 to $45,000 and increasing the maximum low-income tax offset ('LITO') from $645 to $700 [8.9].
- The third round would operate from 1 July 2024 and involved lowering the 32.5% marginal tax rate to 30% [8.8].

The Treasurer also announced that the instant asset write-off would be extended to 30 June 2020 and the threshold would be increased to $30,000 for assets acquired after 7.30pm on 2 April 2019 to 30 June 2020. He also announced that businesses with aggregated turnover of between $10m and $50m would be entitled to the write-off [15.2].

Although the Government was able to enact its instant asset write-off reforms before the election, it did not have enough time to enact its tax cuts. In his budget reply speech, the opposition leader, Bill Shorten, indicated that if Labor won the election, it would honour the first round of the tax cuts, but would not proceed with the second or third rounds. He also confirmed that Labor planned to make a number of major changes to the tax system to make it 'fairer' and pay for its ambitious social policy initiatives, which included a Medicare Cancer Plan and Climate Change Action Plan [5.9].

[5.9] Tax reform following the 2019 election

The 2019 federal election was fought heavily on taxation issues, particularly Labor's ambitious tax reform agenda. Labor's tax changes were unquestionably the boldest tax reforms proposed by any opposition party in over 25 years and included the following proposals:

- **Denying franking credit refunds.** Labor proposed to deny refunds for excess franking credits [22.7]. This measure was directed at individuals and superannuation funds. It did not apply to tax-exempt charities, deductible gift recipients or entities covered by a 'Pensioner Guarantee'.

- **Limiting deductions for negative gearing.** Labor proposed to limit deductions for negatively geared investments [13.3]. This measure did not apply to investments acquired before the change or to future investments in new housing. Losses from negatively geared investments would be able to be carried forward and offset against any capital gains made on such investments.
- **Reducing the CGT discount for individuals.** Labor proposed to reduce the CGT discount on assets held by individuals for more than 12 months from 50% to 25% [17.8]. This measure did not apply to small business assets.
- **Reintroducing the TBRL.** Labor proposed to introduce an additional 2% levy on an individual's taxable income above $180,000. This measure was designed to effectively reintroduce the TBRL [5.7] and increase the top marginal tax rate from 45% to 47% (plus ML).
- **Introducing a minimum 30% tax rate on discretionary trust distributions.** Labor proposed to introduce a minimum 30% tax on discretionary trust distributions. This measure was designed to discourage families using discretionary trusts for tax minimisation purposes.
- **Introducing an investment guarantee.** Labor proposed to allow taxpayers operating businesses to deduct 20% of the value of eligible depreciable assets in the year of acquisition and then allow them to write off the balance under the ordinary capital allowance rules [15.2].
- **Making superannuation changes.** Labor proposed to make a number of superannuation changes, including lowering the non-concessional contributions cap from $100,000 to $75,000 [19.9], lowering the div 293 threshold from $250,000 to $200,000 [19.10], removing the five-year carry forward of the concessional contributions cap [19.9], removing the tax deductibility of personal contributions [19.9], and ending the freeze on the progressive increase in the SGC percentage [19.5].
- **Introducing a jobs deduction.** Labor proposed to provide companies with turnover of less than $10m that have been operating for more than two years an additional 30% deduction (capped at $50,000) for salaries paid to up to five new workers in the first year of their employment. The new employees needed to be unemployed for at least three months and be under 25 or over 55 years of age, or be parents or carers returning to work.
- **Limiting deductions for managing tax affairs.** Labor proposed to place a $3,000 cap on the amount individuals would be able to deduct each year for managing their tax affairs.
- **Implementing measures to tackle multinational tax avoidance.** Labor proposed to introduce a raft of measures to combat multinational tax avoidance. These measures included increasing penalties for promoting tax evasion and avoidance and allowing whistleblowers to share in the penalty tax (up to $250,000) payable by the entities they report.

In its election campaign, Labor focused on the need for change and attacked the leadership instability that had plagued the Coalition Government, which had been led by three different Prime Ministers (Tony Abbott, Malcolm Turnbull and Scott Morrison) over a period of less than six years. Although Labor had consistently led in the polls up to the date of the election, the Coalition surprisingly ended up winning the election, gaining a small majority in the new 151-seat House of Representatives. The Coalition won 77 seats, Labor won 68 seats, and the Greens and independents won the remaining 6 seats. The outcome meant that Labor's ambitious tax reform agenda would not proceed, and the Coalition Government was able to successfully enact its 2019 Budget tax cuts.

Morrison Government's 2020 Budget

Due to the COVID-19 pandemic, the Morrison Government deferred the 2020 Budget from May to October. In his grim Budget Speech, Treasurer Frydenberg emphasised the profound impact of the pandemic on the Australian economy. The Budget Overview described the pandemic as the 'worst global economic crisis since the Great Depression' and projected global growth to fall by 4.5% in 2020. It also noted that Australia was facing its first recession in almost 30 years. Not surprisingly, instead of delivering the surplus that the Treasurer had planned over a year ago, the Budget Papers forecast a deficit of $213.7 billion (11% of GDP) and net debt to reach $703.2 billion (36.1% of GDP) in 2020/21.

The 2020 Budget was a 'big spending budget' designed to support a private sector-led economic recovery. The measures announced were aimed at creating jobs and stimulating economic activity. They included:

- bringing forward tax cuts and the new low-income tax offset for individuals from 1 July 2022 to 1 July 2020 and retaining the LMITO for an extra year [8.9]
- introducing a temporary tax incentive to allow businesses with aggregated turnover of less than $5 billion to fully expense the cost of their eligible depreciating assets [15.2], and
- increasing the aggregated turnover threshold for certain small business concessions from $10m to $50m [8.7].

The Government also revised the R&D tax incentive to make it more attractive [27.5] and announced a temporary incentive allowing companies with aggregated turnover up to $5 billion to carry back their tax losses to previous income years [22.23]. It also announced various FBT and superannuation reforms.

Morrison Government's 2021 Budget

The Morrison Government's 2021 Budget was delivered in May 2021 and forecast an underlying deficit of $161 billion (7.8% of GDP) and net debt of $617.521 billion (30% of GDP) for 2020/21. The Government was, nevertheless, more upbeat about the economy than in the previous budget delivered just over six months earlier. Treasurer Frydenberg reported that the Australian economy had outperformed every major advanced economy in the world and had recovered quicker than anticipated with a lower unemployment rate than expected due to the $291 billion in economic support the Government had provided in response to the pandemic.

To stimulate the economy further, the Government announced a number of additional measures. This included an extension, for another year, of some temporary tax concessions announced in the 2020 Budget, such as the LMITO [8.9], the full expensing of eligible depreciating assets [15.2] and the carry back of corporate tax losses [22.23]. The Government also announced various superannuation reforms, such as removing the $450 salary and wages exemption from the superannuation guarantee scheme [19.5]. In addition, it proposed to introduce a 'patent box' regime that would tax companies at the concessional rate of 17% on their Australian owned and developed medical and biotechnology patent income. The aim was to encourage companies to base their medical and biotechnology R&D operations, and commercialise innovation, in Australia and retain their associated patent profits in Australia.

Morrison Government's 2022 Budget

The Morrison Government delivered its 2022 Budget in March 2022, only two months before the 2022 federal election. Treasurer Frydenberg emphasised that Australia had continued to outperform all major advanced economies and had a low unemployment rate of 4%. The considerable cost of the COVID-19 pandemic, nevertheless, continued to weigh heavily on its fiscal position. The Government estimated an underlying cash deficit of $78 billion (3.4% of GDP) in 2021/22. Net debt was estimated to rise to $631.477 billion (27.6% of GDP) in 2021/22 and $714.947 billion (31.1% of GDP) in 2022/23.

The Government warned that Australia was affected by global inflationary pressures resulting from elevated oil prices and supply chain disruptions. The Budget Papers forecast Australia's inflation to reach 4.25% for 2021/22. To ease the cost of living pressures, the Government reduced the fuel excise by 50% for six months, announced a one-off payment of $250 to individuals receiving social security payments, and increased the LMITO by $420 for 2021/22 [8.9]. It undertook to introduce a new 'technology investment boost' and a new 'skills and training boost' to support small businesses [27.8]. In addition, the Government said that it would extend its proposed patent box regime to also cover eligible patents linked to agricultural and veterinary chemical products as well as low-emissions technologies.

[5.10] Tax reform following the 2022 election

The 2022 federal election was held on 21 May 2022 and was won by the Labor Party led by Anthony Albanese. Of the 151 seats in the Lower House, Labor won 77 seats, the Liberal-National Coalition won 58 seats, the Greens won 4 seats, and independents and other parties won the remaining 12 seats. Although Labor holds a majority of seats in the House of Representatives, it does not have a majority in the Senate where it holds only 26 of the 76 seats. The remaining seats in the Senate are currently divided between the Coalition (31 seats), the Greens (11 seats), One Nation (2 seats), the Jackie Lambie Network (2 seats), United Australia Party (1 seat) and independents (3 seats). Labor therefore needs to rely on the cross-benchers in the Senate to get its Bills through Parliament.

The 2022 election was fought over a number of social and economic issues. Labor's campaign targeted Scott Morrison's increasing unpopularity with various sectors of the electorate, the bourgeoning debt that had grown under the Coalition Government and the increased cost of living and housing affordability facing Australians. Labor emphasised that even though the unemployment rate had dropped, Australia had emerged out of the pandemic facing rising inflation and falling real wages.

Labor's economic plan stated that it would drive productivity growth, expand capacity, grow wages and invest public money in a way that delivers economic value. Labor said that it would prioritise smart, responsible and targeted investments, trim wasteful spending in the public service and conduct a waste and rorts audit. Its aim was to reduce debt over time, while still delivering real outcomes for Australians in essential areas. Specifically, its policies focus on strengthening Medicare, improving aged care, making child care more affordable and addressing housing affordability. It plans to tackle climate change by reducing Australia's greenhouse gas emissions by 43% by 2030 to achieve 'net-zero' emissions by 2050 under the Paris Agreement [1.8]. As part of this goal, it intends to boost renewable energy under its Powering Australia plan.

Although Labor did not propose any large-scale tax changes, it flagged that it would close loopholes that allow multinationals to avoid tax.

Albanese Government's 2022 Budget

The Albanese Government's first budget was delivered in October 2022, only seven months after the Coalition Government's last budget. In his Budget Speech, the new Treasurer, Dr Jim Chalmers, warned that Australia was confronting the prospect of a third global downturn in a decade and a half—this time not as a result of a financial crisis or a pandemic, but a war driving inflation and higher interest rates around the world. Despite fears of a global recession, the Treasurer indicated that the Australian economy was expected to grow at a rate of 3.25% in 2022/23 before slowing to 1.5% in 2023/24. He also said that inflation was expected to peak at around 7.75%, while unemployment was expected to remain low at around 4.5% in 2023/24.

Given the economic conditions and global challenges, the Treasurer emphasised that the Budget would be responsible, affordable and targeted. The Budget contained various forms of cost-of-living relief as well as targeted investments in affordable housing and renewable energy. It also contained a number of technical tax reforms, including changes to the off-market share buy-back rules [22.10] and the introduction of new anti-avoidance rule to deny significant global entities tax deductions for payments to associates in relation to intangibles held in low-tax jurisdictions [33.7]. The Government also announced some small superannuation changes, including allowing people aged 55 or over to make downsizer contributions [19.12]. In addition, it announced an FBT exemption for electric vehicles [18.7].

Albanese Government's 2023 Budget

The Albanese Government's second budget was delivered by Dr Chalmers on 9 May 2023. Surprisingly, the Budget Papers forecast a surplus of $4.2 billion in 2022/23 (the first surplus since 2007/08). Factors that contributed to achieving this forecast included increased revenue from resource companies due to high commodity prices and increased taxes from individuals due to high employment and bracket creep. The Government, nevertheless, warned that Australia is facing a challenging economic environment in an uncertain world and it predicted that growth over the next two years will be the weakest in two decades (excluding the GFC and pandemic periods). It therefore forecast a return to a deficit of $13.9 billion in 2023/24. The Government noted that the global slowdown, persistent inflation, and higher interest rate environment were weighing heavily on the Australian economy.

To address these challenges, the Government announced a range of cost-of-living relief measures. In particular, it increased the base rate for JobSeeker payments and strengthened the Medicare system by increasing the incentive for doctors to bulk-bill patients. It is also partnering with the state and territory governments to provide energy bill relief to households. The Government also announced various measures to support affordable housing, including providing increased rental assistance and tax incentives to encourage 'build-to-rent' projects [15.7], [25.10].

The instant asset write-off threshold for SBEs, which was going to revert back to $1,000 following the end of temporary full expensing, was increased to $20,000 for 2023/24 [15.2]. To raise further revenue, the Government said it would limit deductible expenditure for PRRT projects. It also confirmed it will implement the BEPS two-pillar solution on global tax reform on or after 1 January 2024 [33.6]. The Government has, however, decided to abandon the Coalition's proposed patent box measures [5.9].

[5.11] QUESTIONS

1. How does the political setting in Australia affect the process of tax reform?
2. Identify some of the lobby groups that are frequently engaged in making submissions about the tax system.
3. Discuss some of the key changes that took place under the ANTS reforms.
4. What was the outcome of the Henry Tax Review?
5. Discuss the key differences between the RSPT and MRRT.
6. Explain the stages of the former Labor Government's carbon pricing mechanism.
7. Discuss some of the differences between the Labor and Coalition Governments' tax policies over recent years.

6 THE TREASURY, AUSTRALIAN TAXATION OFFICE AND TAX PROFESSION

[6.1] Introduction

Commonwealth Government revenue and expenditure generally falls within the Treasury portfolio. This chapter examines the portfolio and some of the key departments, agencies, authorities and boards that sit within it [6.2], including the ATO, which is Australia's principal tax collection agency [6.3]. The chapter also discusses the role of tax professionals in Australia and examines their duties and responsibilities and how they are regulated [6.4].

[6.2] The Treasury

Commonwealth executive power is vested in the Governor-General who appoints Members of Parliament as Ministers [3.3]. Each Minister has their own portfolio and is responsible to Parliament for actions undertaken under their authority, including any actions undertaken by their respective departments. The Treasurer is responsible for the Treasury portfolio. Australia has had over 40 Treasurer's since federation. Australia's first Treasurer was Sir George Turner from the Protectionist party. A list of Treasurers since the mid-1990s is set out below.

Treasurer	Party	Period of appointment
Dr Jim Chalmers	Labor	23/5/2022–
Josh Frydenberg	Liberal	24/8/2018–23/5/2022
Scott Morrison	Liberal	15/9/2015–23/8/2018
Joe Hockey	Liberal	18/9/2013–21/9/2015
Chris Bowen	Labor	27/6/2013–18/9/2013
Wayne Swan	Labor	3/12/2007–27/6/2013
Peter Costello	Liberal	11/3/1996–3/12/2007

As the Treasury portfolio is extremely large and complex, it is common for other Ministers to be appointed alongside the Treasurer to assist in the portfolio. These Ministers work closely with the Treasurer and share some of the workload. For example, under the Albanese Government, there is an Assistant Treasurer and Minister for Financial Services (Stephen Jones), an Assistant Minister for Competition, Charities and Treasury (Dr Andrew Leigh), and a Minister for Housing, Homelessness and Small Business (Julie Collins).

Given the size and scope of the Treasury portfolio, a number of important departments, agencies, authorities and boards fall within its ambit, including:

- **The Department of the Treasury.** This department develops, delivers and implements policy and advice for the Australian Government on issues such as the budget, financial sector, foreign investment, structural policy, superannuation, small business, housing affordability, the economy and taxation. The department also works with state and territory governments on key economic policy areas and manages federal financial relations. It is divided into five groups: Fiscal, Macroeconomic, Revenue, Markets and Corporate & Foreign Investment and is led by the Secretary to the Treasury (Steven Kennedy).
- **The Australian Taxation Office ('ATO').** The ATO is the agency that administers Australia's tax system as well as key aspects of its superannuation system. The ATO is headed by the Commissioner of Taxation (Chris Jordan).
- **The Australian Competition and Consumer Commission ('ACCC').** The ACCC is an independent statutory authority that administers the *Competition and Consumer Act 2010* (Cth). It covers issues such as competition, consumer protection and price monitoring. The chair of the commission is Gina Cass-Gottlieb.
- **The Australian Prudential Regulation Authority ('APRA').** APRA is the authority responsible for the supervision and prudential regulation of the banking, deposit taking, insurance and superannuation industries. The chair of APRA is John Lonsdale.
- **The Australian Securities and Investments Commission ('ASIC').** ASIC is Australia's corporate, markets, financial services and consumer credit regulator. It is an independent body established under the *Australian Securities and Investments Commission Act 2001* (Cth) that undertakes most of its work under the *Corporations Act 2001* (Cth). ASIC is responsible for licensing and monitoring financial services providers and regulating financial reporting, auditors and insolvency practitioners. The chair of ASIC is Joseph Longo.
- **The Australian Bureau of Statistics ('ABS').** The ABS is Australia's official statistical entity. It provides statistics on a wide range of economic, demographic, social and other matters. The bureau is led by the Australian Statistician, Dr David Gruen.
- **The Productivity Commission.** The Productivity Commission is Australia's independent research and advisory body on a range of economic, social and environmental issues. The chair of the commission is Michael Brennan.
- **The Commonwealth Grants Commission ('CGC').** The CGC advises the Australian Government on the equitable distribution of GST revenue to state and territory governments [4.4]. The chair of the commission is Michael Callaghan.
- **The Australian Accounting Standards Board ('AASB').** The AASB formulates and makes accounting standards that are used by Australian entities to prepare financial reports. The chair of the board is Dr Keith Kendall.
- **The Reserve Bank of Australia ('RBA').** The RBA is Australia's independent central bank and derives its powers under the *Reserve Bank Act 1959*. The RBA's role is to conduct Australia's monetary policy and issue its currency. The RBA sets the cash rate (ie the interest on overnight loans in the money market) to meet an agreed inflation target. It also works to maintain strong financial and efficient payments systems and seeks to promote employment and economic prosperity. The Governor of the RBA is Michelle Bullock.

[6.3] The Australian Taxation Office

Every tax system needs to be administered by an entity or organisation that has the power to ensure the tax laws are complied with and the correct amount of tax is collected. In Australia, the Commissioner of Taxation is responsible for administering the Commonwealth tax system and is the head of the ATO. The ATO can trace its origins back to 1910 and was formerly known as the Federal Taxation Office and Commonwealth Taxation Office.

Commissioner of Taxation

The Commissioner of Taxation is appointed by the Governor-General for a period of seven years (ss 4, 5 *TAA*). Over the years, there have been 12 Commissioners of Taxation as detailed below.

Commissioners of Taxation	
George McKay (1910–1916)	Edward Cain (1964–1976)
Robert Ewing (1917–1939)	William O'Reilly (1976–1984)
Lawrence Jackson (1939–1946)	Trevor Boucher (1984–1993)
Patrick McGovern (1946–1961)	Michael Carmody (1993–2005)
John O'Sullivan (1961–1963)	Michael D'Ascenzo (2005–12)
Daniel Canavan (1963–1964)	Chris Jordan (2013–present)

Sitting under the Commissioner are three Second Commissioners, who are also appointed by the Governor-General and have the same powers and functions as the Commissioner (except for his power or delegation and his responsibility to furnish an annual report to the Treasurer) (ss 4, 6D *TAA*). A number of Deputy Commissioners are also appointed under the legislation (s 7 *TAA*).

Duties and powers of the Commissioner of Taxation

The Commissioner has wide-ranging duties and powers in relation to a broad spectrum of Commonwealth taxes, including income tax, superannuation taxes, GST, FBT, WET, LCT, PRRT and excise duty. He is also the Registrar of the Australian Business Register [39.3]. The Commissioner is, however, not responsible for customs duty, which is the responsibility of the Australian Border Force Commissioner who is also the Comptroller-General of Customs.

The Commissioner may delegate his powers and functions under a Commonwealth law (other than his power of delegation) to a Deputy Commissioner or any other person (eg ATO officers) (s 8 *TAA*). The delegation must be in writing signed by the Commissioner. Delegated powers and functions exercised or performed by delegates are deemed to have been exercised or performed by the Commissioner.

As the Commissioner's powers are administrative in nature, he is bound to apply administrative law principles in discharging them. This means he must act lawfully and with procedural fairness. Procedural fairness is principally concerned with the fairness of the process by which a decision is made, rather than the fairness of the substantive decision actually made. Where the Commissioner has not acted with procedural fairness in making a decision, 'judicial review' may be available (unless that right is expressly removed by statute) [38.6].

ATO staff and offices

The ATO has an annual operating budget of $3.6 billion and is a vast organisation that employed 20,375 staff at 30 June 2022 (Commissioner of Taxation, *Annual Report 2021/22*). ATO staff undertake the practical day-to-day administration of the tax system and are engaged under the *Public*

Service Act 1999 (Cth) (s 4A *TAA*). The ATO's head office is located in Canberra, and it also has several branch and regional offices around Australia. The ATO is currently divided into the following groups: the Client Engagement Group, the Law Design and Practice Group, the Service Delivery Group, the Enterprise Solutions and Technology Group, and the Enterprise Strategy and Corporate Operations Group. Some of these groups are headed by Second Commissioners, while the respective divisions within the groups are usually headed by Deputy Commissioners.

Tax returns, assessments and collection

The ATO is involved in a broad range of activities, including processing tax returns, issuing assessments, collecting tax and ensuring that the taxation laws are complied with. In 2021/22, it collected \$516.690 billion in tax. The three largest components of this revenue, approximately 88% of net tax collections, consisted of income tax from individuals (\$259.052 billion), income tax from companies (\$124.358 billion) and GST (\$73.650 billion) (Commissioner of Taxation, *Annual Report 2021/22*).

Rulings

The ATO provides a broad range of rulings and guidance to taxpayers on the operation of the tax laws [2.3]. In particular, it can issue binding public and private rulings under divs 358 and 359 of sch 1 *TAA* [38.4]. Oral rulings are also permitted in limited cases under div 360 of sch 1 *TAA*. During 2021/22, the ATO issued 40 public rulings and 4,347 private rulings (Commissioner of Taxation, *Annual Report 2021/22*). In order to modernise its extensive suite of public rulings, the ATO implemented 'Project Refresh', which focused on reviewing its public rulings to ensure they were up to date. As a consequence of this project, a large number of rulings have been withdrawn, updated, rewritten or consolidated.

6

Audit powers

The onus is on taxpayers to disclose relevant information to the ATO when completing their income tax returns and other tax forms. In order to ensure that all required information has been provided accurately, the Commissioner has wide audit powers, including the power to gain access to places and documents and the power to require persons to provide evidence on oath [38.8]. Penalties usually apply where incorrect information has been provided in tax returns [41.2]. In addition, the general interest charge ('GIC') ordinarily applies where tax has been underpaid or not paid on time [40.8].

Recovery and remission powers

The Commissioner regularly institutes proceedings in the courts against taxpayers who have not paid their taxes and he has a broad range of enforcement powers at his disposal to recover tax debts [40.7]. He also has the power to release individuals from all or part of their tax liabilities in cases of serious hardship. In addition, he can remit penalties and interest, and allow taxpayers further time to pay their tax debts or to pay by instalments.

Remedial power

As the complexity of the tax laws can sometimes lead to anomalous outcomes, the Commissioner has been given a special remedial power that allows him to issue a legislative instrument to modify their operation. The power is contained in div 370 of sch 1 *TAA* and can only be used where:

- the modification is not inconsistent with the intended purpose or object of the provision
- the Commissioner considers the modification is reasonable, having regard to the intended purpose or object of the provision and whether the costs of complying with the provision are disproportionate to achieving the intended purpose or object, and

- the Department of the Treasury or the Department of Finance advises the Commissioner that any impact on the Commonwealth Budget would be negligible (s 370-5).

Confidentiality of taxpayer information

As the ATO gains access to sensitive information concerning taxpayers, strict secrecy obligations are imposed on ATO officers. It is only in very limited situations that they are permitted to divulge information that they have obtained in the course of their duties.

The rules relating to the confidentiality of taxpayer information are located in div 355 of sch 1 *TAA*. This division generally prohibits disclosure of information about an entity's tax affairs, except in specific circumstances. The broad policy behind div 355 is to only allow disclosure where the public benefit derived from the disclosure outweighs the entity's privacy.

It is an offence, punishable by imprisonment for up to two years, for a tax officer to make a record or disclose protected information acquired as a tax officer (ss 355-25, 355-30). There are, however, a number of important exceptions to this prohibition. For instance, the prohibition does not apply where the record or disclosure is made in the performance of the tax officer's duties (s 355-50), or where it is made to a Minister to enable him or her to exercise a power or perform a function under a taxation law (s 355-55). The making of records and disclosures are also permitted where they are made for specified government purposes (eg for the purposes of investigation or enforcement activities undertaken by ASIC) (s 355-65).

To improve transparency of the tax system, the Commissioner is required to make publicly available certain information obtained from the tax returns of specified corporate tax entities (s 3C *TAA*). In particular, he is required to report on entities that have total income equal to or exceeding $100m for the income year.

The information that must be disclosed includes details of the amount of their taxable income and income tax payable. The Commissioner publishes the information in annual reports available on the ATO's website. According to the *2020/21 Report of Entity Tax Information*, BHP Group Ltd had the greatest amount of taxable income ($30,322,876,470) and tax payable ($7,304,554,082) for the 2020/21 income year.

The Commissioner has also recently been granted the power to disclose tax debt information to registered credit reporting bureaus (ss 355-72, 355-215 *TAA*). This is designed to encourage entities to better manage their tax debts and, where they are unable to pay them on time, enter into appropriate arrangements with the ATO. The *Taxation Administration (Tax Debt Information Disclosure) Declaration 2019* sets out the criteria for disclosure. Broadly speaking, the measure applies to entities registered in the Australian Business Register [39.3] that have total tax debts of $100,000 or more for more than 90 days and fail to effectively engage with the Commissioner. The measure does not apply to deductible gift recipients, complying superannuation funds, registered charities or government entities. It also does not apply to entities that have already entered into arrangements to pay their tax debts by instalments and have been complying with such arrangements.

International cooperation

As the ATO deals with many international issues, it has developed close links with international organisations, such as the OECD and the Commonwealth Association of Tax Administrators. The ATO also shares certain information with other revenue authorities under its international exchange of information programs, which are underpinned by Australia's many Double Taxation Agreements ('DTAs') [32.1] and Tax Information Exchange Agreements ('TIEAs') [33.2].

Tax complaints and disputes

Taxpayers frequently complain about the tax system. In most cases, their complaints relate to the way in which they have been assessed or the way in which the Commissioner has exercised particular discretions under the legislation that may affect them. These kinds of disputes can be challenged under the legal system through the courts and tribunals in accordance with the appropriate appeal and review procedures [38.5]–[38.6].

Inspector-General of Taxation and Taxation Ombudsman

Complaints about general taxation administrative practices may be referred to the Inspector-General of Taxation and Taxation Ombudsman ('IGTO'), currently Karen Payne, who is an independent statutory officer appointed by the Governor-General.

The IGTO's functions and powers are conferred under the *Inspector-General of Taxation Act 2003* (Cth), which operates in conjunction with the *Ombudsman Act 1976* (Cth). The IGTO may investigate action taken by a tax official affecting an entity that relates to administrative matters under a taxation law at its own initiative or if the entity makes a complaint. In addition, the IGTO has the power to investigate systems to administer the taxation law established by the ATO or Tax Practitioners Board ('TPB') [6.4] and report to the Government on those investigations. The IGTO must undertake such investigations if directed by the Minister. The IGTO's functions do not, however, include the investigation of rules imposing or creating an obligation to pay tax. They also do not extend to advising on underlying tax policy, which is the role of the Board of Taxation [5.4].

The IGTO's strategic priorities are outlined in its *Corporate Plan 2023–26* and data on its investigations and complaints is published in its *Annual Reports* and *Quarterly Reporting Packs.* During the 2021/22 financial year, the IGTO received 1,314 complaints (*IGTO Annual Report FY22*). Over the years, the IGTO has undertaken a number of reviews relating to particular tax administration matters. Some of its recent publications include:

6

- *An Investigation into the Effectiveness of ATO Communication of Taxpayers' Rights to Complain, Review and Appeal* (2021)
- *The Future of the Tax Profession* (2019)
- *Review into Aspects of the Pay As You Go Instalments System* (2018), and
- *Review into the Taxpayers' Charter and Taxpayer Protection* (2016).

As the IGTO's role is essentially investigative in nature, it cannot compel the Commissioner of Taxation to take any particular course of action after an investigation or review. The Commissioner nevertheless tends to agree with the majority of the IGTO's recommendations and has generally sought to implement them.

Public accountability of the ATO

The activities of the ATO are subject to parliamentary scrutiny. As the ATO is an agency within the Treasury portfolio, the Treasurer, as the responsible Minister, is ultimately accountable to Parliament for the ATO's performance. The Commissioner reports directly to the Treasurer and is required to prepare an annual report on the ATO's operations (s 3B *TAA*). This report is tabled by the Treasurer in Parliament.

The Commissioner also regularly appears before parliamentary committees to answer questions about the administration of the tax system. The Joint Committee of Public Accounts and Audit is responsible for holding government agencies, such as the ATO, to account for the lawfulness and effectiveness of their operations. In addition, the Australian National Audit Office conducts financial and related audits of the ATO. The Commissioner is bound by the *Financial Management and Accountability Act 1997* (Cth) which contains the framework for dealing with and managing Commonwealth money and property.

Although the Commissioner reports to the Treasurer, he has statutory independence to administer the tax laws free from political interference. Government Ministers cannot therefore direct the Commissioner on the way that he must administer the tax laws.

ATO's role relating to foreign investment in residential real estate

The ATO has special functions in relation to regulating foreign investment in residential real estate. Foreign investors that seek to acquire interests in residential real estate in Australia are required to comply with the *Foreign Acquisition and Takeover Act 1975* (Cth). This legislation requires foreign investors to notify and seek approval from the Treasurer (through the Foreign Investment Review Board) before acquiring such an interest and to comply with any relevant conditions imposed on the acquisition. Applications are required to be submitted to the ATO via its website and are subject to fees. Foreign residents must register acquisitions and disposal of their interests on the Register of Foreign Ownership of Residential Real Estate maintained by the ATO. The Commissioner is responsible for monitoring compliance with the rules and can impose penalties for breaches. For example, in *FC of T v Balasubramaniyan* [2022] FCA 374, a $250,000 penalty was imposed on a foreign resident who had purchased multiple properties in Victoria in contravention of the rules.

ATO's role relating to the JobKeeper Payment scheme

In 2020, the ATO was given responsibility for administering the Commonwealth Government's JobKeeper Payment scheme. This scheme provided a temporary subsidy to businesses and not-for-profit entities adversely affected by the COVID-19 pandemic. The scheme was initially only available for six months (from 30 March 2020 to 27 September 2020). However, it was subsequently extended (with some variations) for another six months (from 28 September 2020 to 28 March 2021).

Under the scheme, eligible employers could apply to the ATO to receive fortnightly payments for each eligible employee that they employed. These payments were required to be paid to their employees and reported to the ATO via the single touch payroll ('STP') regime [40.4]. Employers were assessed on JobKepeer payments they received and could deduct payments made to their employees in the same way as they could deduct salary. Likewise, employees who received such payments were assessed on them in the same way as they were assessed on their salary [9.3].

An eligible employee was, basically, a resident who was an Australian citizen or permanent visa holder and who was a full-time or part-time employee or a long-term casual employee (ie someone who had been employed on a regular basis for longer than 12 months) of the employer as at 1 March 2020 or, from 3 August 2020, 1 July 2020.

To be eligible for payments from 30 March 2020 to 27 September 2020, employers had to have a prescribed fall in their projected GST turnover [7.3] for the quarter ending in June 2020 (or the quarter ending in September 2020 if they first sought payments in July 2020 or later). To be eligible for payments from 28 September 2020 to 3 January 2021, they must have had the prescribed fall in their actual GST turnover for the quarter ending in September 2020. To be eligible for payments from 4 January 2021 to 28 March 2021, they must have had the prescribed fall in their actual GST turnover for the quarter ending in December 2020. The prescribed fall was: 30% (for employers with aggregated turnover of up to $1 billion), 50% (for employers with aggregated turnover of more than $1 billion) and 15% (for not-for-profit entities).

The JobKeeper scheme also allowed eligible sole traders who had suffered the prescribed fall to apply for payments for themselves. Broadly speaking, sole traders who were actively engaged in their businesses were eligible for payments if they carried on business in Australia on 1 March 2020, had an ABN on 12 March 2020 and met certain tax return and/or GST return lodgment criteria.

From 30 March 2020 to 27 September 2020, the fortnightly JobKeeper payment was $1,500 per eligible employee or sole trader irrespective of the hours they worked. The fortnightly payments were reduced to:

- $1,200 (from 28 September 2020 to 3 January 2021) and $1,000 (from 4 January 2021 to 28 March 2021) for eligible employees who, in the four weeks of pay periods before 1 March 2020, were working in the business or not-for-profit for 20 hours or more a week on average, and for eligible sole traders who were actively engaged in the business for 20 hours or more per week on average in February 2020, and
- $750 (from 28 September 2020 to 3 January 2021) and $650 (from 4 January 2021 to 28 March 2021) for other eligible employees and eligible sole traders.

ATO Charter

The ATO makes decisions that affect millions of taxpayers. Given its significant powers and vast resources, there is usually a substantial imbalance of power between the ATO and taxpayers. It is critical that the ATO's processes are fair and that it is accountable for its actions. For many years, the ATO's policy on conducting its relationship with taxpayers was spelt out in the Taxpayers' Charter. The Taxpayers' Charter was recently reviewed in response to the IGTO's report, *An Investigation into the Effectiveness of ATO Communication of Taxpayers' Rights to Complain, Review and Appeal*. In June 2023, a new ATO Charter replaced the Taxpayers' Charter. The ATO Charter states the following:

- **Fair and reasonable treatment.** The ATO is committed to being fair, ethical and accountable. It undertakes to: treat taxpayers with courtesy, consideration and respect; act with honesty and integrity; be impartial and act in good faith; treat taxpayers as being honest unless it has reason to think otherwise, giving them an opportunity to explain; and work with their representatives (eg professional advisers).
- **Professional service.** The ATO recognises that a taxpayer's rights and obligations can be complex and it aims to provide reliable, accessible and useful information and services to help them understand their rights and obligations. It undertakes to: be responsive and provide timely, accurate and easy-to-understand information; work with the community to design products and services to be inclusive and easy-to-use; and provide services digitally except where an alternative approach is more appropriate.
- **Support and assistance.** The ATO recognises that it may be harder for taxpayers to meet their obligations if they are experiencing vulnerability, difficulties or a crisis. It undertakes to: listen to their circumstances and take them into account where possible; provide support during difficult times; and provide assistance if taxpayers need help understanding or accessing ATO services.
- **Security of data and privacy.** The ATO recognises the importance of privacy and security of personal information. It undertakes to: respect privacy and only disclose information where permitted by law; use multiple layers of cyber security and identity protection to keep data and online transactions safe; and use, acquire and share data ethically and lawfully.
- **Keeping taxpayers informed.** The ATO is committed to being transparent and accountable. It undertakes to: keep taxpayers informed; explain its decisions; communicate and explain their rights, obligations and review options; and give them access to their information, and information that helps the ATO make decisions, where appropriate.

The ATO Charter also sets out what the ATO expects of taxpayers. This includes: treating the ATO with courtesy, consideration and respect; being truthful and acting in accordance with the law;

meeting their obligations (including lodging and paying on time); keeping good records; and taking reasonable care in keeping their identity information safe. The ATO Charter also sets out steps taxpayers can take if they disagree with a decision or believe the ATO has not followed the Charter.

Like the Taxpayers' Charter, the ATO Charter is administrative in nature and is not designed to extend any rights or obligations under the law. Its role is principally to articulate expectations and values, improve professional service, and promote better engagement in the administration of the tax system.

ATO National Tax Clinics and Tax Help program

The Government recently established a National Tax Clinic program under which universities can apply to the ATO for grants to establish and operate independent *pro bono* clinics to assist people who cannot afford professional tax advice and representation. The clinics provide free tax advice to low-income individuals, small businesses, not-for-profit organisations, and charities. The services are provided by students studying tax-related courses under the supervision of qualified clinic managers.

Assistance is also provided to low-income earners through the ATO's Tax Help program. This program is available to individuals earning below $60,000 that have simple tax affairs. It consists of a network of ATO-trained community volunteers who help people with their tax returns and related matters. Tax Help can be accessed online, over the phone, or through centres across Australia.

[6.4] The tax profession

The tax profession plays an integral role in the tax system. The tax profession is made up largely of tax agents, many of whom are accountants, who advise taxpayers in relation to their tax affairs and assist with the preparation of their returns. Approximately 67.8% of taxpayers used tax agents for lodging their returns in 2021/22 (Commissioner of Taxation, *Annual Report 2021/22*). Lawyers are also heavily involved in advising taxpayers on the operation of the tax laws and representing them in tax disputes before the courts and tribunals. Over the years, as tax law has become more complex, tax advisers have become increasingly specialised in their areas of practice. For instance, it is not unusual in large accounting and law firms for practitioners to work exclusively in discrete areas, such as corporate tax, international tax, FBT or GST. The complexity of tax law has also led to the establishment of many specialist industry and university tax courses, including postgraduate tax qualifications such as Master of Taxation degrees.

Duties and responsibilities of tax professionals

Tax professionals have a duty to act in the best interests of their clients and ensure that their advice is accurate and up to date. Where they fail to properly discharge their duties, they may be exposed to liability for breach of contract and/or negligence (*Sacca v Adam & Anor* 83 ATC 4326; *Gadens Lawyers Sydney Pty Ltd v Symond* 2015 ATC ¶20-493).

Tax professionals also have an overriding obligation to act ethically and in accordance with the law. In particular, they need to ensure that their conduct does not breach any criminal laws. There have been several instances where tax professionals have been convicted of criminal offences. For example, in *R v Baldock* [2010] WASCA 170, the Court of Appeal of the Western Australia Supreme Court sentenced an accountant to three years jail for fraudulently under-remitting $6.9m in tax instalments withheld from employees of various entities. Likewise, in *Pearce & Ors v R* 2005 ATC 4319, the Court dismissed an appeal by accountants who had been convicted of conspiring to defraud the Commonwealth and sentenced to imprisonment for five years for their involvement in a mass-marketed tax evasion scheme.

Earlier on, in *R v Forsyth* (1990) 20 ATR 1818, a prominent barrister who had provided advice on the legality of a tax avoidance scheme was prosecuted for conspiracy to defraud the Commonwealth.

In this case, however, Hampel J directed the jury to acquit the barrister on the basis that there was insufficient evidence to convict him. His Honour held that knowledge by the accused of the alleged co-conspirators' unlawful purpose was an essential element of the charge of conspiracy against him. The written brief and instructions on which he advised and his written opinion were not capable of fixing him with knowledge of the scheme promoters' unlawful purpose. Hampel J stated that a barrister is 'bound to give advice in the field in which he or she practised, provided the advice is bona fide and not given dishonestly with the purpose of assisting a client's unlawful purpose'.

It is also important to be aware that where professional advisers have been involved in tax offences, this can lead to disciplinary actions being brought against them by their relevant professional bodies. For example, in *New South Wales Bar Association v Hamman* [1999] NSWCA 404 it was held that a barrister who had understated his income and defrauded the Commonwealth was unfit to practise and removed from the bar roll in order to protect the public. Likewise, a barrister who had been convicted for failing to lodge tax returns for 17 years was also found to be in a similar position in *New South Wales Bar Association v Somosi* (2001) 48 ATR 562.

Tax professionals should also be aware that special civil penalties apply to 'promoters' of 'tax exploitation schemes' under div 290 of sch 1 *TAA* [41.4].

Regulation of tax professionals

Given the important role that the tax profession plays in representing taxpayers, it is not surprising that there are special rules regulating the provision of tax advice. The conduct of lawyers is regulated under relevant state legislation, such as the *Legal Profession Uniform Law Application Act 2014* (Vic). Tax agents, on the other hand, were for many years regulated by state Tax Agents' Boards. The *Tax Agent Services Act 2009* (Cth) ('*TASA*') established a new national Tax Practitioners Board ('TPB'), which replaced the state boards. Since 1 March 2010, the TPB has been responsible for registering and regulating tax agents as well as 'BAS agents' (ie persons who provide Business Activity Statement services). There were 62,340 registered tax practitioners in Australia at 30 June 2022, comprising 45,333 tax agents and 17,007 BAS agents (TPB, *Annual Report 2021/22*).

Previously, the TPB was responsible for regulating 'tax (financial) advisers' (ie financial services licensees or their representatives who, in the course of giving advice, provided certain tax agent services for a fee). However, a new framework for regulating tax (financial) advice services was introduced from 1 July 2022. Under the new framework, providers of tax (financial) advice services are regulated by ASIC through its Financial Services and Credit Panel under the *Corporations Act 2001* (Cth).

Registration as a tax agent or BAS agent

Individuals, partnerships and companies can seek registration as tax agents or BAS agents under s 20-5 *TASA*. The TPB may impose conditions on a person's registration and may vary the conditions where appropriate (s 20-40). Fees are payable with registration applications. From 1 July 2023, these fees are $783 for tax agents and $156 for BAS agents (s 20-20, reg 22 *Tax Agent Services Regulations 2022*).

Section 20-5 provides that for an individual to be eligible for registration they must be over 18 years of age and satisfy the TPB that they are a 'fit and proper person'. They must also meet the prescribed qualification and relevant experience requirements contained in the *Tax Agent Services Regulations 2022* (Cth). In addition, they must maintain professional indemnity insurance and, in the case of renewal, have completed the TPB's continuing professional education requirements.

Fit and proper person requirement

In deciding whether an individual is a fit and proper person, the TPB must have regard to whether the individual is of good fame, integrity and character. It must also have regard to whether an event described in s 20-45 has occurred during the previous five years (eg the individual has been convicted of a serious tax offence or an offence involving fraud or dishonesty) and whether the individual has been an undischarged bankrupt or served a term of imprisonment during the previous five years (s 20-15).

In *Hourani v TPB* 2012 ATC ¶10-265, the AAT affirmed the TPB's decision to refuse to grant an applicant registration as a tax agent on the basis that he was not a fit and proper person because he was not of good fame, integrity and character. The applicant had, some years earlier, been involved in defrauding the ATO and clients of a former accounting firm. The AAT was not persuaded that he had rehabilitated himself and found that he failed to demonstrate any real insight into the seriousness of his earlier conduct.

Qualification and relevant experience requirements

The prescribed qualification and relevant experience requirements vary depending on whether the person is seeking registration as a BAS agent (regs 101 to 103) or a tax agent (regs 201 to 212). An individual is eligible for registration as a tax agent if they have been engaged in the equivalent of one year of full-time relevant experience in the last five years and satisfy one of the following:

- they hold a degree or postgraduate award from an Australian tertiary institution, or a degree or award that is approved by the TPB from an equivalent institution, in accountancy, and have successfully completed approved courses in Australian taxation law and commercial law
- they hold a degree or a postgraduate award from an Australian tertiary institution, or a degree or award that is approved by the TPB from an equivalent institution, in another discipline that is relevant to the tax agent services, and if the TPB considers it relevant to those services, have successfully completed approved courses in basic accountancy principles, Australian taxation law and commercial law, or
- they hold the academic qualifications required to be an Australian legal practitioner and have successfully completed approved courses in Australian taxation law and basic accountancy principles.

An individual is also eligible for registration as a tax agent if:

- they have been engaged in the equivalent of two years of full-time relevant experience in the last five years and hold a diploma or higher award from a registered training organisation, or equivalent institution, in accountancy and have successfully completed approved courses in Australian taxation law and commercial law
- they have been engaged in the equivalent of eight years of full-time relevant experience in the past 10 years and have successfully completed approved courses in basic accountancy principles, Australian taxation law and commercial law, or
- they have been engaged in the equivalent of eight years full-time relevant experience in the past 10 years and are a member of a recognised tax agent association.

Relevant experience includes work as, or under the supervision of, a registered tax agent and work as an Australian legal practitioner.

In *Thanabalasingam v TPB* [2021] AATA 5042, the AAT affirmed the TPB's decision to reject an application for registration as a tax agent on the basis that the applicant had not been engaged in the equivalent of one year of full-time relevant experience under the supervision of a registered tax agent in the preceding five years.

Continuing professional education requirement

The TPB's explanatory paper, TPB(EP) 07/2021, details the continuing professional education requirements that tax agents and BAS agents must satisfy. In general, tax agents are required to undertake at least 120 hours, and BAS agents are required to undertake at least 90 hours, of continuing professional education over a three-year period (with a minimum of 20 hours per year).

The continuing professional education should be relevant to the services the practitioner provides and should develop their relevant knowledge and skills. Any education should be provided by persons or organisations with suitable qualifications and/or practical experience.

Code of Professional Conduct for tax agents and BAS agents

The Code of Professional Conduct is contained in div 30 *TASA* and governs the ethical and professional standards and responsibilities of registered tax agents and BAS agents. Under the Code, a registered tax agent or BAS agent must:

- act honestly and with integrity (s 30-10(1))
- comply with the taxation laws in the conduct of their personal affairs (s 30-10(2))
- account to a client for money or other property received from or on behalf of a client that is held on trust (s 30-10(3))
- act lawfully in the best interests of a client (s 30-10(4))
- have in place adequate arrangements for the management of conflicts of interest that may arise in relation to the activities that are undertaken in the capacity of a registered tax agent or BAS agent (s 30-10(5))
- not disclose any information relating to a client's affairs to a third party without the client's permission (unless there is a legal duty to do so) (s 30-10(6))
- ensure that a tax agent service that they provide, or that is provided on their behalf, is provided competently (s 30-10(7))
- maintain knowledge and skills relevant to the tax agent services that the agent provides (s 30-10(8))
- take reasonable care in ascertaining a client's state of affairs, to the extent that ascertaining the state of those affairs is relevant to a statement the agent makes or a thing the agent does on behalf of the client (s 30-10(9))
- take reasonable care to ensure that taxation laws are applied correctly to the circumstances in relation to which advice is provided to a client (s 30-10(10))
- not knowingly obstruct the proper administration of the taxation laws (s 30-10(11))
- advise a client of the client's rights and obligations under the taxation laws that are materially related to the tax agent services provided (s 30-10(12))
- maintain the professional indemnity insurance that the TPB requires the agent to maintain (s 30-10(13)), and
- respond to requests and directions from the TPB in a timely, responsible and reasonable manner (s 30-10(14)).

The Treasury Laws Amendment (2023 Measures No 1) Bill 2023 proposes to extend the Code to state that a registered tax agent or BAS agent must:

- not employ, or use the services of, an entity to provide tax agent services on their behalf if they know, or ought reasonably to know, that the entity is a disqualified entity and the TPB has not given approval under s 45-5 to employ the entity (proposed s 30-10(15))
- not provide tax agent services in connection with an arrangement with an entity that they know, or ought reasonably to know, is a disqualified entity (proposed s 30-10(16)), and
- comply with any obligations determined by the Minister under s 30-12 (proposed s 30-10(17)).

The TPB has disciplinary powers to deal with breaches of the Code, including the power to terminate registration under div 40 of the Act. A widely-publicised illustration of where this power was recently used occurred in respect of a former PriceWaterhouseCoopers ('PWC') partner. The partner had been in confidential consultations with Treasury on improvement of the tax laws, including

6

discussions on new rules to stop multinationals avoiding tax by shifting profits from Australia to tax havens. An investigation by the TPB found that the partner made unauthorised disclosures of confidential law reform information to PWC partners and staff. The TPB found he failed to act with integrity, as required under his professional, ethical, and legal obligations, and terminated his registration for a period of two years. The TPB also found that PWC failed to properly manage conflicts of interest and ordered that the firm have processes and training to ensure such conflicts are adequately managed (TPB, *Media Release*, 23 January 2023). Treasury has subsequently referred this matter to the Australian Federal Police for investigation (Treasury, *Media Release*, 24 May 2023).

Under the Code, one of a tax agent's responsibilities is to comply with the taxation laws in the conduct of their personal affairs (s 30-10(2)). This is necessary to 'uphold the confidence and trust that the public are entitled to expect in the services offered by a registered tax agent': *Cleary v TPB* [2014] AATA 260. In *Shmuel v TPB* [2019] AATA 2168, the AAT noted that a tax agent's failure to comply with their personal tax obligations reflected adversely on their good fame and character and was sufficiently serious of itself to justify a finding that they failed to meet the fit and proper person requirement. As the AAT explained (at [23]):

> Complying with taxation obligations is a fundamental duty of a tax agent and goes to the heart of an agent's capacity and willingness to perform their function. A failure to comply with taxation obligations must raise serious doubt about the capacity and commitment of an agent to competently handle other people's taxation affairs.

In *Logic Accountants & Tax Professionals Pty Ltd & Anor v TPB* 2021 ATC ¶10-569, the AAT upheld the TPB's decision to terminate the registration of a company and its sole director for a period of two years on the basis they had breached the Code. The parties had failed to comply with their taxation obligations over several years by lodging 4 income tax and over 100 activity statements late and paying their tax late. They also failed to provide competent tax agent services and take reasonable care in ascertaining their clients' affairs and ensuring the taxation laws were complied with by lodging excessive and incorrect deduction claims on behalf of clients. The AAT found that the director had complete disregard for the taxation laws, did not demonstrate the level of knowledge and competence the public would expect of a registered tax agent, and was not a fit and proper person under s 20-5 of the Act. The decision was upheld by the Federal Court on appeal in *Logic Accountants & Tax Professionals Pty Ltd & Anor v TPB* 2022 ATC ¶20-838.

Another recent example regarding termination of registration due to poor compliance history is *Gough & Anor v TPB* 2022 ATC ¶10-640. In that case, the tax agent had for several years repeatedly failed to lodge income tax returns and activity statements on time. The AAT was satisfied that significant breaches of the Code had been committed and that the agent had demonstrated he was not of sufficient competence and integrity to hold the privilege of acting for clients and providing tax agent services.

There are countless other cases where tax agents have had their registration terminated on the basis that they breached the Code and were not fit and proper persons. Recent illustrations include:

- *Tomkinson v TPB* 2021 ATC ¶10-617, where the tax agent made a false declaration to the TPB relating to his outstanding tax obligations, failed to lodge over 20 activity statements for himself and a trust of which he was trustee, and failed to lodge income tax returns and meet his superannuation guarantee obligations
- *Norman v TPB* 2021 ATC ¶10-571, where the tax agent failed to act honestly as he did not declare to the TPB that he had an overdue tax debt, failed to provide tax agent services competently, and failed to take reasonable care that taxation laws were applied correctly in claiming deductions
- *Cerrah v TPB* 2022 ATC ¶10-613, where the tax agent made false declarations to the TPB, failed to lodge her tax returns on time and properly declare her income, and failed to comply with her continuing professional education requirements

- *Plaskitt v TPB* 2022 ATC ¶10-617, where the tax agent failed to manage conflicts of interests properly and allowed his partnership to engage in dishonest conduct and misappropriate a client's funds, and
- *Worsley v TBP* 2022 ATC ¶10-617, where the tax agent defaulted on taxation payment plans in breach of a stay order that he had been granted, failed to maintain the knowledge and skills relevant to the tax agent services he provided, and failed to respond to requests from the TPB in a timely, responsible and reasonable manner.

Civil penalties

The TPB has the power to apply to the Federal Court for civil penalties where a civil penalty provision has been breached. It can also seek an injunction from the Federal Court to restrain a contravention of a civil penalty provision.

The civil penalty provisions are contained in div 50 *TASA*. One of these provisions is s 50-5, which prohibits an entity from charging or receiving a fee or other reward for a tax agent service unless the entity is a registered tax agent (this rule does not apply to legal services provided by lawyers). A 'tax agent service' is defined as any service that relates to ascertaining or advising about the liabilities, obligations or entitlements of an entity under a taxation law, or that relates to representing an entity in its dealings with the Commissioner (s 90-5). The TPB's views on the meanings of the terms 'fee or other reward' and 'tax agent service' are set out in its information sheets (TPB(I) 40/2023 and TPB(I) 39/2023).

In *TPB v Ordiales* 2022 ATC ¶20-847, penalties were imposed on an individual who supplied tax agent services while unregistered. In 2010, the TPB warned the individual that such conduct was illegal and she gave assurances it would not happen again. However, between 2018 and 2021, she contravened s 50-5 another 636 times. She admitted preparing returns for family and friends, but said she did not request payment, rather they insisted on paying her. She received amounts ranging from $50 to $100 (totalling $48,865). The Federal Court imposed a penalty of $236 per contravention (totalling $150,096) and issued an injunction preventing her from engaging in such further conduct.

Similarly, in *TPB v Williams 2023* ATC ¶20-851, the Federal Court ordered that a former tax agent who continued to supply tax agent services for a fee after his registration lapsed and an interim injunction was issued ordering him not to do so should pay civil penalties of $80,000 and be sentenced to 10 days imprisonment for contempt of court. The Court also issued a final injunction (which he could only apply to vary or revoke after 10 years) prohibiting him from supplying tax agent services.

[6.5] QUESTIONS

1. Who is the current Treasurer and what areas does the Treasury portfolio cover?
2. Who administers the federal tax system? What are some of their duties and powers?
3. What rules exist to protect taxpayer confidentiality?
4. What agencies and bodies are involved in the tax process in Australia?
5. Discuss the independence and accountability of the Commissioner of Taxation.
6. What is the role of the TPB and what powers does it have?
7. What requirements must a person fulfil to become a registered tax agent?
8. Discuss the ethical and professional standards and responsibilities of registered tax agents under the Code of Conduct. Provide some examples of where it has been breached.

PART B

GOODS AND SERVICES TAX

7 GOODS AND SERVICES TAX

[7.1] Introduction

Goods and services tax ('GST') is one of Australia's most important and widely encountered taxes. According to the 2023 Budget Papers, GST is expected to raise approximately $88,042 billion in 2022/23, making it the second largest tax behind income tax. GST revenue is paid by the Commonwealth to the states and territories under special revenue-sharing arrangements [4.4].

GST is a broad-based transactions tax which, like the value added tax ('VAT') that operates in many jurisdictions overseas, generally applies at each stage of the supply chain. The way it basically works is that registered entities charge GST on their supplies (ie outputs) and are entitled to credits for GST charged on their acquisitions (ie inputs). The burden of GST is designed to ultimately fall on end consumers who are not registered and are therefore not entitled to any credits for GST charged on the things they acquire. These consumers therefore absorb the cost of GST in the price they pay for goods and services. For this reason, GST is often described as a consumption tax.

This chapter outlines the background to the introduction of GST [7.2] and explains the basic principles that underpin its operation [7.3]. The chapter focuses on the concepts of 'taxable supplies' [7.6] and 'creditable acquisitions' [7.8], which are the core building blocks of the GST system. It also discusses 'GST-free' and 'input taxed' supplies [7.7], as well as the accounting [7.9], adjustment [7.10] and record-keeping [7.11] rules. A number of special topics that are of practical importance are also examined, such as going concerns [7.12], financial supplies [7.13], leases and sales of residential land [7.14], the margin scheme [7.15] and importations [7.16].

[7.2] Background to the introduction of GST

The GST regime was introduced on 1 July 2000 to replace the former sales tax regime which had been in existence for the previous 70 years. Although GST and sales tax are both indirect taxes, they differ in many crucial respects. Sales tax was a narrow-based tax that was payable in respect of the sale and importation of certain goods. It was a single-level tax that was levied at the point of wholesale sale or importation. The rates of sales tax varied depending on the nature of the goods. Most goods were taxed at the general rate of 22%. Other goods were taxed at special rates (eg 12% or 32%). The sales tax regime also contained a large number of exemptions which resulted in some bizarre and arbitrary distinctions (eg toothpaste was subject to sales tax while toothbrushes were exempt).

GST was introduced in Australia to substantially broaden the indirect tax base so that not only goods, but also services, would be taxed. GST is payable at a flat rate of 10% on the supply of most goods and services made by registered entities. It is also imposed on most importations of goods. No GST is, however, payable on GST-free or input taxed supplies or on non-taxable importations.

Unlike sales tax, GST is a multi-level tax that is generally payable at each stage of the supply chain. To prevent GST having a cascading effect and to ensure that GST operates as a neutral tax in relation to dealings between registered entities (ie most business-to-business transactions), registered entities are generally entitled to recoup the cost of the GST that they have been charged. This recoupment is achieved by virtue of the 'input tax credit' ('ITC') mechanism which allows registered entities to claim ITCs for GST charged on things they acquire or import for the purposes of their 'enterprise' (eg their business). No ITCs are available to unregistered entities, such as final consumers, who therefore bear the ultimate economic cost of GST.

> ***Example*** A registered manufacturer supplies goods to a registered retailer for $110 (including $10 GST). The retailer then supplies the goods to an unregistered consumer for $220 (including $20 GST). The retailer is entitled to an ITC of $10 (ie the GST charged by the manufacturer is recouped by the retailer). The net cost of the goods to the retailer after the ITC is therefore $100. The consumer does not get any ITC. The net cost of the goods to the consumer is therefore $220 (ie the consumer bears the cost of the $20 GST).

Political background

The introduction of GST in Australia was an extremely controversial issue that involved many political twists and turns along the way. GST was first seriously proposed during the 1985 Tax Summit by Labor Treasurer Paul Keating. However, the idea was ultimately rejected by Prime Minister Bob Hawke who caved in to pressure from a number of lobby groups, including the trade union movement, that opposed GST.

In the 1993 federal election, John Hewson, who was the Liberal leader, resurrected the GST issue by making it the cornerstone of his highly publicised 'Fightback' election campaign. Paul Keating, who had succeeded Bob Hawke as Labor leader, however, ended up winning this election in what many considered to be a surprising outcome. Ironically, Keating's campaign victory was largely attributable to his vigorous opposition against the GST, which he had himself proposed in 1985.

The Coalition's 1993 election defeat led John Howard, who became Coalition leader in 1995, to vow that the Coalition would not introduce GST if it won the 1996 election. As it turned out, the Coalition ended up winning this election and kept its promise in relation to GST. However, by the time of the next election in 1998, the Coalition again proposed to introduce GST. Although the Coalition narrowly won this election, it did not have a majority in the Senate and it was therefore always going to be difficult for it to enact GST legislation. Nevertheless, after significant political manoeuvring, it eventually succeeded in passing its GST Bills through Parliament after gaining the support of the Democrats in the Upper House.

The Coalition had always intended to implement a broad-based GST with very few exceptions. However, to obtain the Democrats support, the Coalition was forced to make a number of political compromises, including making certain food GST-free. As a result of these compromises, Australia's GST system is not as broad-based as, for example, New Zealand's GST system.

International background

It is not surprising that Australia decided to replace its sales tax regime with a GST regime given that all OECD countries (other than the United States) already imposed GST or VAT. The following table sets out the years in which the respective OECD countries introduced their GST or VAT systems and the standard rates of tax presently charged in those countries. Some countries also impose reduced rates of GST or VAT on certain supplies (eg food and medical services). These countries have an asterisk (*) next to their standard rates.

Country (year introduced)	Standard GST/ VAT rates	Country (year introduced)	Standard GST/ VAT rates
Australia (2000)	10%	Japan (1989)	10%
Austria (1973)	20%*	Korea (1977)	10%
Belgium (1971)	21%*	Luxembourg (1970)	17%*
Canada (1991)	5%	Mexico (1980)	16%
Czech Republic (1993)	21%*	Netherlands (1969)	21%*
Denmark (1967)	25%	New Zealand (1986)	15%
Finland (1994)	24%*	Norway (1970)	25%*
France (1954)	20%*	Poland (1993)	23%*
Germany (1968)	19%*	Portugal (1986)	23%*
Greece (1987)	24%*	Slovakia (1993)	20%*
Hungary (1988)	27%*	Spain (1986)	21%*
Iceland (1989)	24%*	Sweden (1969)	25%*
Ireland (1972)	23%*	Switzerland (1995)	7.7%*
Israel (1976)	17%*	Turkiye (1985)	18%*
Italy (1973)	22%*	United Kingdom (1973)	20%*

In addition to the countries mentioned above, many non-OECD countries have also introduced GST/VAT regimes. This includes countries close to Australia, such as Singapore, which introduced GST in 1994 at the rate of 3% (the rate has progressively increased over the years and is 8% in 2023 and will be 9% in 2024). Interestingly, Malaysia introduced GST in 2015 at the rate of 6%. However, due to its unpopularity, the Malaysian Government reduced the GST rate to 0% and reintroduced a sales and services tax in 2018.

It is worth noting that Australia's GST rate is relatively modest when compared with the standard rates imposed in many other countries. Canada, Japan and Switzerland are the only OECD countries with lower rates (although note that in Canada, the provinces also levy GST). Australia has maintained its GST rate at 10% despite calls from some quarters that the rate should be increased. Raising the GST rate is a highly sensitive issue in Australia and none of the major political parties appears to have the political appetite to take this issue on.

[7.3] Basic principles of GST

Legislative scheme

A number of different Acts make up Australia's GST legislative scheme. The main statute is the *A New Tax System (Goods and Services Tax) Act 1999* (Cth) ('*GSTA*'). This Act determines an entity's liability to GST and its entitlement to ITCs. The *GSTA* operates in conjunction with the *A New Tax System (Goods and Services Tax) Regulations 2019* (Cth) ('*GST Regs*').

GST is imposed under the following Acts:

- the *A New Tax System (Goods and Services Tax Imposition—General) Act 1999* (Cth)—this Act is the main imposition Act and imposes GST in so far as it is neither a customs nor excise duty
- the *A New Tax System (Goods and Services Tax Imposition—Customs) Act 1999* (Cth)—this Act imposes GST in so far as it is a customs duty, and
- the *A New Tax System (Goods and Services Tax Imposition—Excise) Act 1999* (Cth)—this Act imposes GST in so far as it is an excise duty.

The reason for having three separate imposition Acts is to ensure that s 55 of the *Constitution* is not breached [3.6].

GST and ITCs

Australia's GST system is built around two key concepts: charging GST and claiming ITCs. The central provision is s 7-1 *GSTA* which provides:

- GST is payable on 'taxable supplies' [7.6] and 'taxable importations' [7.16], and
- ITCs arise on 'creditable acquisitions' [7.8] and 'creditable importations' [7.16].

At its most basic level, the GST system operates as follows:

- Registered entities (and entities that are required to be registered) that make taxable supplies must pay GST at the rate of 10% on the value of those taxable supplies. Entities (irrespective of whether or not they are registered or required to be registered) that make taxable importations must pay GST at the rate of 10% on the value of those taxable importations.
- Registered entities (and entities that are required to be registered) that make creditable acquisitions and creditable importations are entitled to ITCs for the GST charged on the things they acquire and import.

The GST and ITC rules tie in closely with the concept of registration [7.5], which is critical to the operation of the GST system. As a general rule, most entities that carry on business (unless they are very small) will be registered for GST, whereas end consumers will not be registered for GST.

GST is payable on the 'value' of a taxable supply at the rate of 10% [7.6]. The value of a taxable supply is basically its 'price' multiplied by 10/11. ACCC guidelines state that displayed prices for goods and services should generally be quoted on a GST-inclusive basis so that consumers know how much they need to pay prior to acquiring them. Where goods and services have been advertised for sale at a GST-exclusive price and no mention is made of extra GST being payable, this may breach the Australian Consumer Law (eg s 48 of sch 2 of the *Competition and Consumer Act 2010* (Cth)).

The following example illustrates how the basic GST and ITC rules work.

Example Raffer is registered for GST. He owns a sports shop selling tennis racquets. Raffer must charge GST on the tennis racquets he sells to his customers as the sales constitute taxable supplies. He is also entitled to ITCs for the GST charged on the tennis racquets he purchases from his suppliers as the purchases constitute creditable acquisitions.

If Raffer sells a tennis racquet for a price of $220, the value of the supply is $200 (ie $220 × 10/11) and he is required to charge $20 GST (ie $200 × 10%). This means that the net amount he would receive from the sale, after paying GST, is $200 (ie $220 – $20).

If Raffer purchased the tennis racquet from a GST registered wholesaler for a price of $110 (inclusive of $10 GST), he would be entitled to an ITC of $10. This means that his net cost for the acquisition, after taking into account the ITC, is $100 (ie $110 – $10).

Basic effect of GST

While GST is generally charged by registered entities on their supplies, such entities are also generally entitled to ITCs for GST charged on their acquisitions. The effect of this is that GST generally has a neutral effect on supplies between registered entities as the ITC entitlement of the acquirer wipes out the GST charged by the supplier.

Importantly, ITCs are not available for GST charged on things acquired or imported by entities that are not registered for GST. This means that end consumers are not able to claim ITCs. The effect of this is that GST operates as a de facto consumption tax as it is end consumers who ultimately bear the cost of the GST.

Example A timber supplier (T) supplies timber for $110 to a manufacturer (M) who uses the timber to build furniture. The manufacturer sells the furniture to a retailer (R) for $330. The retailer then sells the furniture to a consumer (C) for $770. T, M and R are registered for GST, but C is not. The consequences of the transactions for the parties are as follows:

Sale Proceeds		GST		ITC		Net Amount Payable to ATO
$110	T	$10	-	Nil	=	$10
$330	M	$30	-	$10	=	$20
$770	R	$70	-	$30	=	$40
	C	Nil	-	Nil	=	Nil

The total GST charged on the three supplies is $110 ($10 + $30 + $70) and the total ITC entitlements on the three acquisitions is $40 ($10 + $30). This means that the ATO has collected an overall net amount of $70 in tax. The burden of this tax is ultimately borne by C who, as the end consumer, is not entitled to an ITC for the GST charged by R.

GST is a transaction tax

Although GST is often described as a consumption tax, from a legal perspective, it is strictly speaking a transaction tax. This point was recognised by the Full Federal Court in *Sterling Guardian Pty Ltd v FC of T* 2006 ATC 4227 where Heerey, Dowsett and Conti JJ stated (at 4230):

> In economic terms it may be correct to call the GST a consumption tax, because the effective burden falls on the ultimate consumer. But as a matter of legal analysis what is taxed, that is to say what generates the tax liability (and the obligations of recording and reporting), is not consumption but a particular form of transaction, namely supply . . .

These comments were subsequently endorsed by the High Court in *FC of T v Reliance Carpet Co Pty Ltd* 2008 ATC ¶20-028.

Charging GST

The GST regime distinguishes between different kinds of supplies and importations. Registered entities (and entities required to be registered) only charge GST on their 'taxable supplies' [7.6]. They do not charge GST on their:

- 'GST-free supplies' (these supplies are commonly referred to in VAT jurisdictions as 'zero rated supplies'), or
- 'input taxed supplies' (these supplies are commonly referred to in VAT jurisdictions as 'exempt supplies').

A supply is 'GST-free' if it falls within div 38 *GSTA* (s 9-30(1)). A supply is 'input taxed' if it falls within div 40 *GSTA* (s 9-30(2)). The specific kinds of supplies that fall within div 38 and div 40 are outlined at [7.7]. Examples of GST-free supplies include supplies of medical services, supplies of certain food, and exports of goods. Examples of input taxed supplies include financial supplies and leases of residential premises.

Importers only charge GST on taxable importations. They do not charge GST on non-taxable importations [7.16].

The general rules relating to charging GST are summarised in the following table:

7

Supplies		Importations	
Kind of supply	**Is GST charged on the supply?**	**Kind of importation**	**Is GST charged on the importation?**
Taxable supply	Yes	Taxable importation	Yes
GST-free supply	No	Non-taxable importation	No
Input taxed supply	No		

Input tax credits

Registered entities (and entities required to be registered) are entitled to ITCs for GST charged on their creditable acquisitions [7.8] and creditable importations [7.16].

An entity makes a creditable acquisition where it acquires something for a 'creditable purpose', the supply of the thing to the entity was a taxable supply (ie GST was charged by the supplier), and the entity provided consideration for the supply. An item is acquired for a creditable purpose to the extent that it is acquired for the purpose of carrying on the entity's enterprise, but not to the extent that it is used to make input taxed supplies. This essentially means that ITCs are only available to the extent that an acquisition is for an entity's enterprise and is used by the entity to make taxable supplies or GST-free supplies.

The general rules relating to ITCs are summarised in the following table:

Acquisitions		Importations	
Kind of acquisition	**Is an ITC available for GST charged on a taxable supply?**	**Kind of importation**	**Is an ITC available for GST charged on a taxable importation?**
Acquisition used to make taxable supplies	Yes	Importation used to make taxable supplies	Yes
Acquisition used to make GST-free supplies	Yes	Importation used to make GST-free supplies	Yes
Acquisition used to make input taxed supplies	No	Importation used to make input taxed supplies	No

Different kinds of supplies and acquisitions

The following example illustrates the consequences that flow from making the different kinds of supplies and acquisitions mentioned above.

Example Doogie is a doctor who is registered for GST and operates a medical practice. He also owns a block of residential flats and a commercial office block that he leases to various tenants. Doogie therefore makes the following supplies:

1. **Taxable supplies.** Doogie's leases of the office premises constitute 'taxable supplies' under s 9-5 *GSTA* [7.6]. Doogie therefore has to charge GST on the rent. He is also entitled to ITCs for GST charged on acquisitions relating to his office block. For instance, if he pays a solicitor $2,200 (inclusive of GST) to prepare a lease, he would be entitled to an ITC of $200.
2. **GST-free supplies.** Doogie's supplies of medical services to his patients constitute 'GST-free supplies' under s 38-7 *GSTA* [7.7]. Doogie therefore does not have to charge GST on the provision of such services. He is, nevertheless, entitled to ITCs for GST charged on acquisitions relating to his medical practice. For instance, if he purchased a computer for $3,300 (inclusive of GST) from a department store for use in preparing his surgery's accounts, he would be entitled to an ITC of $300.
3. **Input taxed supplies.** Doogie's leases of the residential flats constitute 'input taxed supplies' under s 40-35 *GSTA* [7.7]. Doogie therefore does not have to charge GST on the rent. He does not, however, benefit from any ITCs for GST charged on supplies made to him relating to this enterprise. For instance, if he pays an electrician $1,100 (inclusive of GST) to repair the wiring in one of the flats, he would not be entitled to an ITC of $100.

GST turnover

An entity's 'GST turnover' is relevant for determining whether it meets certain thresholds that are important for determining its obligations and entitlements under the GST system. The key thresholds are:

- the tax period turnover threshold ($20m) [7.4]
- the electronic lodgment turnover threshold ($20m) [7.4]
- the instalment turnover threshold ($2m) [7.4]
- the registration turnover threshold ($75,000) [7.5]
- the cash accounting turnover threshold ($2m) [7.9], and
- the small enterprise entity turnover threshold ($2m) [7.17].

An entity's GST turnover meets a particular turnover threshold if:

- its current GST turnover (ie the value of supplies it has made, or is likely to make, during the 12 months ending at the end of the month), or
- its projected GST turnover (ie the value of supplies it has made, or is likely to make, during the month and the next 11 months),

is at or above the turnover threshold (ss 188-10, 188-15, 188-20 *GSTA*).

For the purposes of calculating an entity's current and projected GST turnover, the values of the following supplies are expressly ignored:

- input taxed supplies
- supplies that are not for consideration (other than certain supplies to associates), and
- supplies that are not made in connection with an enterprise carried on by the entity.

Since GST turnover is based on the 'value' (rather than the 'price') of supplies made or likely to be made, GST charged on these supplies is ignored.

Example On 1 January 2023, T Co wants to determine whether it meets the tax period turnover threshold of $20m. The value of the supplies T Co is likely to make for the 12 months ending on 31 January 2023 is $23m (which includes $4m of input taxed supplies) and the value of supplies it is likely to make up to 31 December 2023 is $24m (which includes $2m of input taxed supplies). T Co's current GST turnover is $19m and its projected GST turnover is $22m. As its projected GST turnover is over $20m, T Co meets the tax period turnover threshold.

[7.4] Net amount for a tax period and payment rules

Registered entities (and entities that are required to be registered) must subtract their ITCs from their GST and make certain adjustments to calculate their 'net amount' for a particular 'tax period' (ss 7-5, 7-15, 17-5, 17-10 *GSTA*). The net amount represents the amount of tax payable by the entity or the amount of refund the entity is entitled to receive in respect of the relevant tax period (s 7-15). 7

Tax periods

In general, an entity's 'tax period' is a period of three months (ending on 31 March, 30 June, 30 September and 31 December) (s 27-5 *GSTA*). However, entities with GST turnovers that meet the tax period turnover threshold of $20m [7.3] must use monthly tax periods (s 27-15). Entities with GST turnovers below $20m can elect to use monthly tax periods instead of quarterly tax periods (s 27-10).

Example A dentist who has GST turnover of $2m would ordinarily use tax periods of three months. The dentist could, however, elect to use monthly tax periods. In contrast, a company that has a GST turnover of $100m must use monthly tax periods.

Net amount

An entity is required to pay a positive net amount to the ATO and it is entitled to receive a refund for a negative net amount from the ATO (s 7-15(1)). Entities that are required to pay net amounts to the ATO must do so within a specified time after the end of the relevant tax period in accordance with rules contained in div 33 *GSTA*. Special arrangements apply to taxable importations [7.16].

In order to determine an entity's net amount for a tax period, it is necessary to set off its GST liabilities [7.6] against its ITC entitlements [7.8] for the tax period. In addition, it is necessary to take into account any 'increasing' and/or 'decreasing' adjustments that arise during the tax period (eg because an 'adjustment event' has occurred) [7.10].

The following formula identifies how an entity's net amount for a tax period is generally calculated.

Net Amount	=	GST [7.6]	−	Input Tax Credits [7.8]	+	Increasing Adjustments [7.10]	−	Decreasing Adjustments [7.10]

It is important to be aware that the LCT and WET systems are integrated with the GST payment and refund system [4.3]. As a result, any LCT and WET amounts that relate to a tax period are added or subtracted (as the case requires) from the net amount calculation set out above (s 17-5(2)).

Example Harry owns a hardware business and is registered for GST. He has tax periods of three months. In the 1 January to 31 March tax period, he charged GST on his taxable supplies of $100,000 and claimed ITCs of $40,000 for his creditable acquisitions. He also had an increasing adjustment for the tax period of $2,000 and a decreasing adjustment of $1,000. His net amount for the tax period is calculated as follows:

Net amount = $100,000 – $40,000 + $2,000 – $1,000
= $61,000

As the net amount is a positive amount, Harry must pay $61,000 to the ATO.

Assessment and payment rules

Entities are under an obligation to report their net amount for a tax period on their GST returns (s 31-5 *GSTA*). When an entity gives the Commissioner their return, the Commissioner is treated as having assessed the entity (s 155-15 *TAA*). He may also assess an entity at any time (s 155-5 *TAA*).

Entities may choose to lodge their GST returns and pay tax electronically (s 31-25). Entities with GST turnover that meets the electronic lodgment turnover threshold ($20m) [7.3] must lodge and pay tax electronically.

Entities with monthly tax periods must lodge their GST returns and pay any net amount owing within 21 days of the end of the relevant tax period (ss 31-10, 33-5).

Entities with quarterly tax periods must lodge their GST returns and pay any net amount owing for the relevant tax period as follows (ss 31-8, 33-3):

Quarter	Due date
1 July–30 September	28 October
1 October–31 December	28 February
1 January–31 March	28 April
1 April–30 June	28 July

Special rules for GST instalment payers

Certain entities may elect to pay GST by quarterly instalments under div 162 instead of under the ordinary quarterly arrangements described above (s 162-15). An entity is eligible to pay GST by instalments under div 162 if:

- it is an SBE [8.7], or it does not carry on business and has GST turnover that does not exceed the instalment turnover threshold ($2m) [7.3]
- it has not elected to use monthly tax periods under s 27-10 [7.4] and is not affected by a determination made by the Commissioner under ss 27-15 or 27-37 to use monthly or special tax periods, and
- it has been lodging returns over the previous four months, has complied with its GST return obligations, and is not in a net refund position (defined in s 162-5(3)) (s 162-5).

The effect of the election is that the entity is deemed to be a GST instalment payer and to have an instalment tax period that is the remainder of the financial year (ss 162-50, 162-55).

GST instalment payers are required to pay GST instalments equal to either their 'notified instalment amount' (calculated by the Commissioner: s 162-135) or their 'varied instalment amount' (calculated by the entity: s 162-140). These amounts represent estimates of the annual GST liability for the instalment tax period spread over the relevant payment periods (note that penalties may apply for underestimates of the varied instalment amount: s 162-175).

The instalments are generally required to be paid at the same time as ordinary quarterly instalments (s 162-70). However, unlike ordinary quarterly instalment payers, GST instalment payers must also complete an annual GST return that reconciles their annual GST liability with the instalments paid for the year (s 162-145). A GST instalment payer's 'net amount' for a GST instalment tax period is the amount that would otherwise be its net amount for the period less the sum of the instalments that have already been paid over the period (s 162-105). A positive net amount must be paid to the Commissioner by the time the return is required to be lodged (s 162-110). The Commissioner must refund a negative net amount (s 35-5).

Example Rex is a GST instalment payer. The Commissioner has calculated that he is required to pay quarterly instalments of $10,000 during the financial year. Rex pays each instalment on time. When he lodges his annual return, he calculates his GST liability for the year as $45,000. He must therefore pay an additional $5,000 on top of his four instalments of $10,000 for the year.

[7.5] Registration of entities

As a general rule, GST is only payable by, and ITCs are only available to, entities that are registered, or required to be registered, for GST [7.6]. The main exception to this general rule is that importers are required to pay GST regardless of whether they are registered, or required to be registered, for GST [7.16].

Definition of entity

An 'entity' is defined as an individual, a body corporate, a corporation sole, a body politic (eg a government), a partnership, an unincorporated association or body of persons (eg a club), a trust, or a superannuation fund (s 184-1(1) *GSTA*).

As a right or obligation cannot be conferred or imposed on an entity that is not a legal person, the trustee of a trust or superannuation fund is taken to be an entity consisting of the person who is, or the persons who are, the trustee or trustees at any given time (s 184-1(2)).

It should also be noted that a legal person can have a number of different capacities in which they do things. In each of those capacities, the person is taken to be a different entity for GST purposes (s 184-1(3)). For instance, a legal person may be trustee of a number of different trusts. The legal person would be treated as a separate entity in their own capacity and as a separate entity for each trust.

Supplies and acquisitions made by partners of a partnership in their capacity as partners, or by members of the management committee of an unincorporated association or body of persons in their capacity as members of that committee, are taken to be made by the relevant partnership, unincorporated association, or body, rather than the legal person who is the partner or member (s 184-5).

Registration requirements

An entity *may* be registered for GST if it is carrying on an enterprise (eg a business) [7.6] (s 23-10 *GSTA*). It *must* be registered for GST if it is carrying on an enterprise and its GST turnover meets the registration turnover threshold of $75,000 ($150,000 for a non-profit body) (ss 23-5, 23-15 *GSTA*; regs 23-15.01, 23-15.02 *GST Regs*).

The registration turnover threshold is designed to enable small entities to fall outside the GST system. This allows them to avoid compliance issues and having to charge GST on their supplies. However, it also means that they are not entitled to benefit from ITCs on their acquisitions.

Special registration rules require the following entities to register irrespective of their GST turnover:

- resident agents acting for non-residents that are registered or required to be registered (s 57-20 *GSTA*)
- representatives (eg liquidators) of incapacitated entities that are registered or required to be registered (s 58-20 *GSTA*), and
- suppliers of taxi travel (this includes Uber drivers: see *Uber BV v FC of T* 2017 ATC ¶20-608) (s 144-5 *GSTA*).

Example Arthur runs a flower stall at a weekend market. His GST turnover is $30,000. As he is carrying on an enterprise he may register for GST but does not need to do so as his GST turnover is below the $75,000 registration turnover threshold. However, if his GST turnover was $100,000, he would have to register for GST. If Arthur was a taxi driver, he would need to register for GST irrespective of his GST turnover.

Registration process

An entity that is required to be registered must apply in the approved form for registration within 21 days of being required to do so (s 25-1). An entity that is entitled to be registered, but not required to do so (eg an entity that is carrying on an enterprise but has turnover below $75,000), may apply for registration at any time. Applications can be made via the Australian Business Register website [2.5].

The Commissioner must register an entity if he is satisfied that it is carrying on an enterprise or intends to do so from a particular date (s 25-5(1)). He must also register an entity (even though it has not applied) if he is satisfied that the entity is required to be registered (s 25-5(2)). The Commissioner must notify the entity of the date of effect of its registration, its GST registration number, and the tax periods that apply to it (s 25-5(3)). Registration generally takes effect from the date specified in the application (which cannot be earlier than the date on which the entity commenced to carry on an enterprise) (s 25-10). The Commissioner can also backdate registration if he is satisfied that the entity was required to be registered earlier, in which case the GST rules apply from the earlier date (s 25-15).

Cancellation of registration

An entity that is registered and is not carrying on an enterprise must apply to the Commissioner in the approved form for cancellation of its registration within 21 days of it ceasing to carry on its enterprise (s 25-50). The Commissioner must cancel an entity's registration if it has applied for cancellation in the approved form, has been registered for at least 12 months, and he is satisfied that it is not required to be registered (s 25-55(1)). He must also cancel an entity's registration (even if it has not applied) if he is satisfied that the entity is not carrying on an enterprise and he believes on reasonable grounds that it is not likely to carry on an enterprise for at least 12 months (s 25-55(2)). The Commissioner may cancel an entity's registration if it has applied for cancellation in the approved form less than 12 months after being registered and he is satisfied that it is not required to be registered (s 25-57).

[7.6] Taxable supplies

Definition of taxable supply

Entities must pay GST on the taxable supplies they make (s 9-40 *GSTA*). A 'taxable supply' is defined in s 9–5 *GSTA* and contains both positive and negative elements. The positive elements provide that an entity makes a taxable supply if:

- the entity makes the supply for consideration
- the supply is made in the course or furtherance of an enterprise that the entity carries on
- the supply is connected with the indirect tax zone, and
- the entity is registered or required to be registered.

The negative elements provide that a supply is not a taxable supply to the extent that it is GST-free or input taxed.

The terms 'supply', 'consideration', 'enterprise' and 'connected with the indirect tax zone' as used in the positive elements of s 9-5 are discussed below. The concept of 'registration' has already been discussed at [7.5]. The terms 'GST-free' and 'input taxed' supplies are discussed separately at [7.7]. The diagram on the following page outlines the positive and negative elements of the taxable supply definition and sets out the key provisions which deal with these elements.

7

Supply

A 'supply' is defined as 'any form of supply whatsoever' (s 9-10(1) *GSTA*). A supply therefore takes on its ordinary dictionary meaning. The definition of a supply is also deemed to specifically include the following (s 9-10(2)):

- supplies of goods or services
- the provision of advice or information
- a grant, assignment or surrender of real property
- a creation, grant, transfer, assignment or surrender of any right
- a financial supply, and
- an entry into or release from an obligation to do anything, to refrain from an act, or to tolerate an act or situation.

In GSTR 2006/9, the ATO sets out a number of propositions concerning supplies. The ruling states that for every supply there must be a supplier and there must also generally be a recipient to whom the supply is made. These entities must be different entities because an entity cannot make a supply to itself. The ruling also notes that the supplier must actually do something to make a supply (ie there must be some positive act by the supplier). In *Westley Nominees Pty Ltd v Coles Supermarkets Australia Pty Ltd* 2006 ATC 4363, the Full Federal Court stated (at 4366) that:

> The concept of 'supply' in its ordinary meaning in s 9-10(1) . . . does seem to require some act of provision, furnishment, conferral or giving of some thing.

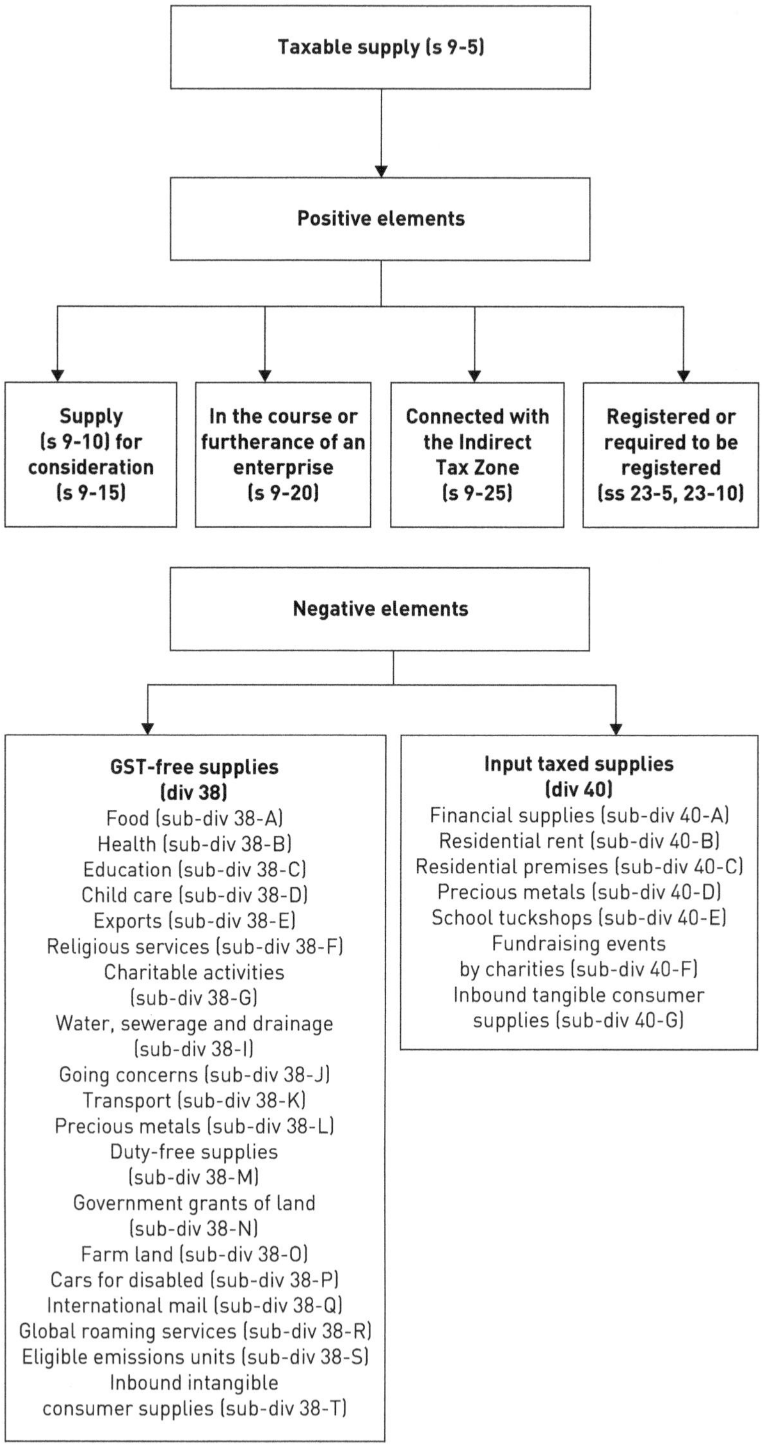

It is important to note that just because an entity receives money does not necessarily mean that it has made a supply. As the above passage indicates, an entity actually needs to provide something to make a supply.

Example Alf is registered for GST and owns a fitness centre that had to be closed for several weeks due to a COVID-19 lockdown. Alf received a state government support payment of $10,000 for being impacted by the lockdown. He completed an application confirming his eligibility to receive the payment, but did not enter into any binding obligation in return. Alf has not made any supply to the state government and is therefore not required to pay GST.

Promises as supplies

The concept of a supply was considered by the High Court in *FC of T v Qantas Airways Ltd* 2012 ATC ¶20-352. In this case, an airline had unsuccessfully argued that it was not liable to pay GST on forfeited pre-paid fares for domestic flights by passengers who failed to take their flights. The airline had argued that there was no taxable supply as the relevant 'supply' was the actual carriage of a passenger by air, which had not occurred. A majority of the High Court, however, rejected this argument and held that the relevant supply was the promise made by the airline to use its best endeavours to carry the passenger and their baggage.

The fact that a promise can be a supply is also illustrated in *ATS Pacific Pty Ltd & Anor v FC of T* 2014 ATC ¶20-449. This case concerned an Australian company that conducted an inbound tour operating business. It entered into contracts with non-resident travel agents relating to accommodation, car hire, transfers and other products which were provided by third party Australian providers to non-resident tourists. The non-resident travel agents selected the products from the taxpayer's website to form a package. The taxpayer then entered into contracts with the relevant Australian providers to provide the products to the non-resident tourists. The taxpayer charged a fee which included the cost of the products as well as a margin. The Full Federal Court held that the supplies made by the taxpayer were not the supplies of the products themselves, but rather the supplies of the promises that the Australian providers would provide the products to the non-resident tourists.

In *FC of T v MBI Properties Pty Ltd* 2014 ATC ¶20-474, the High Court concluded (at [33]) that 'it is wrong to consider that one transaction must always involve the making of just one supply'. The Court held that the concept of supply 'is of wide import' and stated (at [35]):

> A transaction which involves a supplier entering into and performing an executory contract will in general involve the supplier making at least two supplies: a supply which occurs at the time of entering into the contract, in the form of both the creation of a contractual right to performance and the corresponding entering into of a contractual obligation to perform; and a supply which occurs at the time of contractual performance, even if contractual performance involves nothing more than the supplier observing a contractual obligation to refrain from taking some action or to tolerate some situation during a contractually defined period.

7

On this basis, the Court found that in the case of a lease, there will generally be a supply which occurs at the time of entering the lease (being the grant and creation of contractual rights under the lease). There will also be at least one other supply which occurs progressively throughout the term of the lease (being the observation by the lessor of the express or implied covenant of quiet enjoyment under the lease).

Supply of money and digital currency

The concept of a 'supply' expressly excludes a 'supply of money or digital currency' unless the money or digital currency is provided as consideration for a supply that *is* a supply of money or digital currency (s 9-10(4)).

A supply of money or digital currency is not ordinarily treated as a supply because that would result in an unintended duplication of GST. Money and digital currency are generally only the consideration for a supply. They are not treated as separate supplies themselves (except where, for example, foreign exchange or digital currency exchange transactions are involved).

The term 'money' is defined widely to include things such as currency, promissory notes, bills of exchange, negotiable instruments, postal notes, money orders, payments by credit or debit card, credit or debit to an account or creation or transfer of a debt (s 195-1). It does not include a collector's piece, an investment article, an item of numismatic interest or currency with a market value above its stated value as legal tender. 'Digital currency' is also defined widely to cover fungible digital units of value provided as consideration for a supply that are either not denominated in any country's currency or not government-issued digital currency and that do not have a value based on the value of anything else (s 195-1). The definition is intended to capture cryptocurrencies such as Bitcoin.

Example Fred owns a bookshop and is registered for GST. He sells a book to John for $44. The sale of the book is a supply of goods by Fred and would therefore be subject to GST. The payment of money by John is not a separate supply.

Fred purchases a money order from a Post Office for $200. Fred makes a supply as he provides the $200 as consideration for a supply of money (ie the money order). The Post Office also makes a supply, as the money order is provided as consideration for a supply of money (ie the $200).

Court orders and out-of-court settlements

An important issue that arises is whether a supply can occur as a consequence of the making of a court order or an out-of-court settlement. This issue has been considered in a number of early GST cases.

In *Interchase Corporation Ltd v ACN 010 087 573 Pty Ltd & Ors* 2000 ATC 4552, the Supreme Court of Queensland held that a court order for the payment of damages in negligence would not involve the 'creation, grant, transfer, assignment or surrender of any right' or the 'entry into, or release from, an obligation' within the meaning in s 9-10(2). White J stated (at 4554) that: 'It is not easy to see how a court giving judgment or the payment of a judgment sum . . . could constitute a "supply"'. According to her Honour, when a judgment is satisfied, the debt created by the judgment is simply 'extinguished'.

A similar view was reached in *Shaw v Director of Housing & Anor (No 2)* 2001 ATC 4054 concerning a court order for damages for negligent misstatement. The Supreme Court of Tasmania held that to 'make' a taxable supply, there had to be some voluntary action. The release of the obligation to pay a judgment sum by the payment of that sum will occur regardless of whether the judgment creditor makes, or does, any act at all.

In GSTR 2001/4, the ATO accepts that a court in giving judgment does not make a supply and that the extinguishment of a judgment debt by its payment does not constitute a supply. The ATO, nevertheless, maintains that supplies can arise as a consequence of out-of-court settlements where there is:

- an earlier supply (eg where the subject of the dispute is an earlier transaction in which a supply was made by the parties), or
- a current supply (eg where a new supply is created requiring one party to provide the other party with something of substance).

Example In both of the following cases, X would be making a supply for consideration:

- **Earlier supply**. X supplies widgets to Y and a dispute arises about payment. The matter is settled on the basis that Y agrees to pay X $100 for the goods.
- **Current supply**. X sues Y for wrongful use of its trade name. The matter is settled on the basis that X grants Y a licence to use its trade name for three years in consideration of $100.

The ATO also indicates in GSTR 2001/4 that even where there is no earlier or current supply, the wide definition of supply usually results in out-of-court settlements crystallising one or more new supplies. As settlements typically ensure no further legal action is taken in relation to a dispute, the parties to such settlements are surrendering rights to pursue legal action and releasing each other from obligations in relation to the relevant disputes. They are therefore creating supplies under ss 9-10(2)(e) and (g). These kinds of supplies are referred to as 'discontinuance supplies'.

According to GSTR 2000/19, where a payment is received as consideration for the surrender of a right, it will be consideration for a separate supply (as opposed to an adjustment event [7.10]).

Example Payment by a manufacturer to a recipient to forego the right to have damaged goods supplied by the manufacturer repaired or replaced is consideration for a separate supply made by the recipient. It is not an adjustment event changing the consideration for the earlier supply [7.10].

In GSTR 2001/4, the ATO accepts (at [69]) that a discontinuance supply does *not* arise where a dispute is resolved by a court order, as in such case, 'it is the judgment of the court in the matter and its associated orders that "settles" the dispute'.

The ruling also notes that disputes often arise over incidents that do not relate to a supply (eg claims for damages arising out of property damage, negligence causing loss of profits, wrongful use of trade name, breach of copyright, termination or breach of contract or personal injury). According to the ruling (at [73]), the 'damage, loss or injury, being the substance of the dispute, cannot in itself be characterised as a supply made by the aggrieved party'. The reason for this is that 'the damage, loss, or injury, in itself does not constitute a supply under s 9-10'.

Consideration

'Consideration' is defined broadly. It includes any payment, or any act or forbearance, in connection with a supply of anything, or in response to or for the inducement of a supply of anything (s 9-15(1) *GSTA*). It does not matter whether the payment, act or forbearance was voluntary, or whether it was by the recipient of the supply (s 9-15(2)). Furthermore, it does not matter whether the payment, act or forbearance was in compliance with a court order or legal settlement (s 9-15(2A)).

Gifts, prizes, grants and subsidies

Mere gifts do not attract GST as they are not made for consideration. A gift arises where something is transferred voluntarily without any material benefit to the donor (*FC of T v McPhail* (1968) 117 CLR 111). A prize, on the other hand, may constitute consideration for a supply (GSTR 2002/3).

Example Bill owns a racehorse and enters it in a race. The horse wins the race and Bill receives a cash prize. The prize is consideration for a supply (ie entering the horse in the race).

Whether GST is payable in respect of a grant or subsidy depends on whether there is a sufficient nexus between the grant or subsidy and a supply made by the payee. A grant or subsidy will usually constitute consideration for a supply where it is made on the condition that the grantee does something specific in return for receiving the grant or subsidy. By way of contrast, a grant or subsidy made 'without any strings attached' would ordinarily be treated in the same way as a gift and would not be subject to GST. An undertaking to merely report on how a grant or subsidy is used does not normally attract GST (GSTR 2012/2).

Example Frank is a scientist who receives a research grant from the Government. If the terms of the grant provide that Frank must prepare a report of his research findings which the Government is allowed to commercially exploit, then the grant would constitute consideration for the supply of the research. In contrast, if a company receives a Government subsidy to improve its technological capabilities and is merely required to report on how it spends the funds, GST does not apply.

Dividends

Payment of a dividend by a company is not ordinarily regarded as consideration for a supply made by the company to its shareholders (GSTR 2002/2).

Deposits

Section 99-5 *GSTA* provides that a deposit held as security for the performance of an obligation is not treated as consideration for a supply unless it is forfeited or applied as consideration for a supply. The way in which a forfeited or applied deposit is treated is examined at [7.9].

Taxes, fees and charges

Division 81 *GSTA* provides that the payment of an Australian tax, fee or charge is deemed not to be the provision of consideration unless the tax, fee or charge is prescribed by regulations. Some of the fees and charges that have been prescribed by regulations include:

- a fee for parking a motor vehicle in a ticketed or metered parking space
- a toll for driving a motor vehicle on a road
- a fee for hire of, use of, or entry to a facility, except for an entry fee to a national park
- a fee for the use of a waste disposal facility, and
- a fee for the provision of information if the information is not required to be provided under an Australian law.

Example Bob owns an office building from which he operates his business. He pays local council rates of $2,000 in relation to the building. As the rates are an Australian tax and are not specifically prescribed by regulations, they do not constitute consideration and are therefore not subject to GST.

Bob also pays a daily toll of $2 for driving his car on a newly constructed highway. As the toll is prescribed by regulations, it is deemed to constitute consideration and is therefore subject to GST.

Enterprise

The concept of an 'enterprise' is central to the GST regime and is exhaustively defined in s 9-20.

Activities done in the form of a business

The definition of enterprise encompasses an activity or series of activities done in the form of a 'business' (s 9-20(1)(a)). The *GSTA* states that a business 'includes any profession, trade, employment, vocation or calling, but does not include occupation as an employee' (s 195-1). There have been many cases that have considered the meaning of a business for income tax purposes, and these cases are generally also relevant for GST purposes [9.4]. Broadly speaking, the cases indicate that a business will be carried on if the relevant activities are recurrent in nature and carried out in a systematic and organised manner for the purpose of profit.

Activities need not necessarily be undertaken on a large scale to constitute a business. This is illustrated in *Case 3/2013* 2013 ATC ¶1-052, where a person who tutored students between 10 and 25 hours per week was held to be carrying on activities in the form of a business. The case may, however, be contrasted with *D'Arcy v FC of T* 2008 ATC ¶10-041, where a full-time employee project manager who held interests of between 10% and 30% in eight mares and spent between 8 and 12 hours per week in horse breeding activities was found not to be carrying on an enterprise as his horse breeding activities had not been approached in a business-like way and were conducted for pleasure or recreation. What weighed heavily against the conclusion that the taxpayer was carrying on a business was the fact that his horse breeding activities were unlikely to return a profit within any reasonable timeframe.

In *Body Corporate, Villa Edgewater CTS 23092 v FC of T* 2004 ATC 2056, a body corporate that maintained the common property for the owners of apartments was found to be carrying on activities in the form of a business. The AAT consequently held that contributions made by its members to the fund it administered attracted GST, as the contributions were made in the course or furtherance of the enterprise that it carried on.

Activities done in the form of an adventure or concern in the nature of trade

An enterprise also includes activities done in the form of an 'adventure or concern in the nature of trade' (s 9-20(1)(b)). In *FC of T v Swansea Services Pty Ltd* 2008 ATC ¶1-003, the AAT relied on various income tax cases to hold (at [154]) that the 'acquisition of goods or property with the intention of a future sale, hopefully at a profit, will fall within the concept of an activity in the form of an adventure in the nature of trade'. The concept of a 'trading' activity is examined at [9.4].

Activities done on a regular or continuous basis, in the form of a lease, etc

An enterprise also extends to activities done 'on a regular or continuous basis, in the form of a lease, licence or other grant of an interest in property' (s 9-20(1)(c)). Lessors who regularly rent out their property will therefore be carrying on an enterprise even though they may not necessarily be carrying on a business.

> ***Example*** Frank owns a commercial building in a shopping centre that he leases to various retailers throughout the year. Frank's leasing activities constitute an enterprise.

7

Activities done by certain trustees, charities and the government

An enterprise also encompasses activities done by charities, trustees of complying superannuation funds and certain other funds, as well as activities done by the Commonwealth, states or territories (ss 9-20(1)(d) to (h)).

Exclusions—activities of employees and hobbies

The definition of enterprise specifically excludes the activities of an employee (s 9-20(2)). GST is therefore not charged by employees on the salary they receive for the services they provide their employers.

> ***Example*** Doug is employed by Francis as a cleaner. Doug's employment activities do not constitute an enterprise and he does not therefore charge GST for the services he provides Francis.

The pursuit of a hobby is also expressly deemed not to constitute an enterprise (s 9-20(2)). In *FC of T v Swansea Services Pty Ltd* 2009 ATC ¶20-100, the Commissioner unsuccessfully argued that a company that had invested over $4m on 225 antiques and 87 paintings over eight years, but had sold only three items during that period at a loss, was carrying on a hobby. The Federal Court held that it was open to the AAT to conclude that the company was carrying on an enterprise as there was evidence that its purpose was to acquire and hold antiques and artworks with a view to turning these to account when circumstances were right to derive a profit. The fact that the artworks were displayed or held at the premises of related entities did not convert the taxpayer's activities into a hobby.

Carrying on an enterprise

The 'carrying on' of an enterprise expressly includes activities done 'in the course of the commencement or termination of the enterprise' (s 195-1). This means that the acquisition or sale of an enterprise will be treated as acts done in the carrying on of the enterprise.

Example Bob is registered for GST and owns a milk bar. Bob sells the milk bar to Paul who is also registered for GST. The sale and purchase of the milk bar are acts done in the carrying on of both Bob and Paul's respective enterprises.

The carrying on of an enterprise does not, however, extend to mere preparatory or exploratory activities. This is illustrated in *Clayton & Anor v FC of T* 2013 ATC ¶10-321, which concerned a husband and wife who had purchased a property in 2003 on which they planned to start an ecotourism business. The taxpayers had undertaken market research, prepared a business plan and applied for permission to build cabins on the property. However, after encountering difficulties, they revised their business plan in 2008 to focus on organising wildlife tours and producing bush foods. No paying tourists visited the property until 2012. The issue before the AAT was whether the taxpayers could claim ITCs for acquisitions they made up to 2011. The AAT found that no business had come into existence by that time. As a result, the taxpayers were not carrying on an enterprise and were not entitled to any ITCs.

Connected with the indirect tax zone

A supply must be 'connected with the indirect tax zone' to be a taxable supply. This expression replaces the former expression 'connected with Australia', which applied until 1 July 2015. The change in terminology was made for technical reasons and was not intended to produce a significant alteration to meaning. Section 195-1 essentially defines indirect tax zone ('ITZ') to mean 'Australia' (within the meaning of the *ITAA97*), but not its external territories or certain specified offshore areas (such as the Joint Petroleum Development Area in the Timor Sea).

A supply of goods is 'connected with the ITZ' where:

- the goods are delivered, or made available, to the recipient in the ITZ
- the goods are removed from the ITZ, or
- the goods are imported into the ITZ (ss 9-25(1) to (3)).

In addition, from 1 July 2018, an 'offshore supply of low value goods' (ie goods valued up to $1,000) is connected with the ITZ if it is connected with the ITZ under sub-div 84-C [7.18] (s 9-25(3A)).

A supply of real property is connected with the ITZ if the property, or the land to which it relates, is in the ITZ (s 9-25(4)).

A supply of anything other than goods or real property (eg services and intangibles) is connected with the ITZ if the thing is done in the ITZ or the supplier makes the supply through an enterprise that the supplier 'carries on in the ITZ' (ss 9-25(5)(a) to (b)).

A supply of anything other than goods or real property that is not covered by ss 9-25(5)(a) or (b) is also connected with the ITZ if the thing is a right or option to acquire another thing, the supply of which would be connected with the ITZ (s 9-25(5)(c)).

In addition, a supply of anything other than goods or real property is connected with the ITZ if the recipient of the supply is an 'Australian consumer' (s 9-25(5)(d)). An Australian consumer is, basically, an Australian resident that is either: (a) not registered for GST; or (b) registered for GST and does not acquire the thing supplied solely or partly for the purpose of an enterprise it carries on (s 9-25(7)).

However, a supply is *not* connected with the ITZ if it falls within s 9-26 *GSTA*. This provision contains a special 'disconnection rule', which applies where the supplier is a non-resident, the supplier does not make the supply through an enterprise that it carries on in the ITZ, and the supply is covered by an item in the table in the provision (which relates to certain offshore intangible and other supplies). The disconnection rule, however, operates subject to s 57-7 *GSTA*, which 'switches off' s 9-26 in certain cases involving supplies made by non-residents through their resident agents. Basically, the aim of s 57-7 is to allow non-residents and their resident agents to agree in writing that supplies made through the resident agent will be connected with the ITZ, resulting in the agent being liable for GST under div 57 [7.18].

Amount of GST on taxable supplies

The amount of GST on a taxable supply is 10% of the value of the taxable supply (s 9-70 *GSTA*). The 'value' of the taxable supply is the price × 10/11 (s 9-75). 'Price' is the GST-inclusive monetary consideration for the supply, or, where consideration is not provided in money, the GST-inclusive market value of that consideration.

A short-hand way of calculating GST on a taxable supply is that it is simply 1/11th of the price.

Example A supplier sells goods to a customer for $110. The price of the goods is therefore $110. The value of the supply is $100 and the GST on the supply is $10. In other words, the GST is 1/11th of $110.

The supplier also sells goods to another customer in consideration of receiving a painting with a GST-inclusive market value of $3,300. The price of the goods is therefore $3,300. The value of the supply is $3,000 and the GST on the supply is $300. In other words, the GST is 1/11th of $3,300.

Where consideration for a supply is provided in foreign currency, the value of the supply is worked out by converting the foreign currency into Australian currency in accordance with rules contained in *Goods and Services Tax: Foreign Currency Conversion Determination 2018*. Where digital currency is involved, the digital currency must be converted into Australian currency in accordance with rules contained in *Goods and Services Tax: Digital Currency Determination 2019*.

Mixed supplies

Where a supply is partly a taxable supply and partly a GST-free or input taxed supply, the value of the part of the actual supply that is a taxable supply is the proportion of the value of the actual supply that the taxable supply represents (s 9-80).

Supplies that are fringe benefits

Employers that provide fringe benefits to their employees will often be making taxable supplies of the things they have provided [18.3]. Section 9-75(3) states that the price of a taxable supply that is a fringe benefit is limited to the recipient's payment or contribution towards the benefit. The aim of this rule is to ensure that GST is not payable by employers on taxable supplies of fringe benefits provided to employees except to the extent that the employee makes a specific payment or contribution towards receiving the benefit.

Example An employer provides an employee with a TV as a fringe benefit. The TV has a GST-inclusive market value of $5,500. The employee contributes $1,100 for the benefit. The price of the taxable supply is $1,100 (not $5,500) and the employer is therefore required to pay $100 GST.

[7.7] GST-free and input taxed supplies

GST is only payable on taxable supplies [7.6]. It is not payable on either GST-free supplies or input taxed supplies. It is therefore crucial to distinguish between these categories of supplies. The kinds of supplies that constitute GST-free and input taxed supplies are set out in ch 3 *GSTA*. According to ch 3:

- a supply is 'GST-free' if it falls within the categories of supplies listed in div 38 (or it is a right to receive such a supply) (s 9-30(1)), and
- a supply is 'input taxed' if it falls within the categories of supplies listed in div 40 (or it is a right to receive such a supply) (s 9-30(2)).

If a supply would otherwise fall within both the GST-free and input taxed categories, it is usually treated as a GST-free supply (s 9-30(3)).

Reasons for treating certain supplies as GST-free or input taxed

There are a number of different reasons why certain supplies have been classified as GST-free or input taxed. Some of these reasons are outlined below:

- **Consistency.** Some supplies have been treated as GST-free or input taxed to maintain consistency with approaches adopted overseas. For instance, Australia treats exports as GST-free as other countries also generally exempt their exports from GST/VAT. This ensures that Australian exporters are not disadvantaged when competing with foreign exporters in the international market.
- **Public policy.** Some supplies have been treated as GST-free or input taxed for public policy reasons. For instance, medical supplies, such as a consultation with a doctor, are treated as GST-free to ensure that health care costs are kept low.
- **Political compromise.** Some supplies have been treated as GST-free or input taxed because of political compromise. For instance, as mentioned at [7.2], in order to ensure the successful passage of the GST legislation through the Senate, the Government agreed to treat supplies of certain food as GST-free.

In addition, there are special reasons why financial supplies are input taxed [7.13].

GST-free supplies

Entities that are registered for GST (or required to be registered for GST) do not charge GST on their GST-free supplies but are nevertheless entitled to ITCs on their acquisitions that relate to making such supplies (see the diagram below). GST-free treatment therefore provides an entity with the most preferential tax treatment under the GST law.

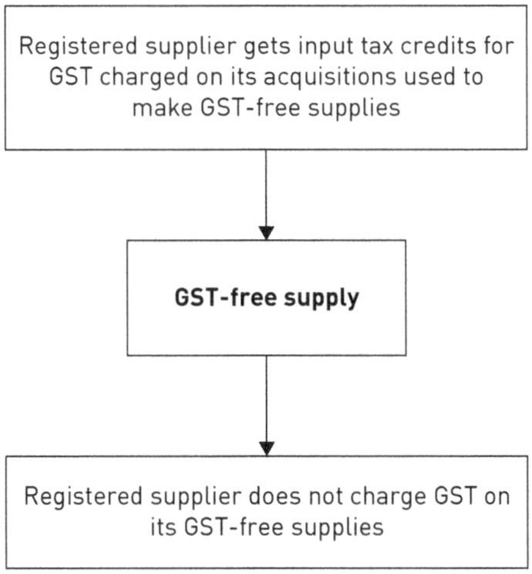

The following kinds of supplies are GST-free:

- **Food.** Supplies of food as defined in s 38-4 (s 38-2) and related packaging (s 38-6) are GST-free under sub-div 38-A. However, supplies of food are not GST-free if they are excluded by s 38-3. For example, the following supplies are excluded:
  - supplies of food for consumption on the premises from which it is supplied (eg restaurant food)
  - hot take-away food, and
  - food mentioned in sch 1 *GSTA* (eg specified prepared foods, confectionery, savoury snacks, ice creams, biscuits and certain bakery products).

  As a general rule, supplies of items such as fresh fruit, vegetables, eggs, meat and seafood are therefore GST-free. However, when these foods are sold as a prepared meal (eg as a packaged frozen dinner), they are usually taxable. Supplies of beverages are only GST-free if they fall within sch 2 *GSTA*. Some beverages that fall within sch 2 include milk products (but not flavoured milk), tea, coffee, certain fruit juices and non-carbonated water without additives.
- **Health.** Supplies of certain medical, health, hospital and residential and community care services, supplies of certain medical aids, appliances, drugs and medicinal products, and supplies of private health insurance are GST-free under sub-div 38-B. Examples of GST-free supplies therefore include medical treatment provided by a doctor, dental services provided by a dentist, the supply of prescription medicine by a pharmacist and the supply of a hearing-aid by a medical aids manufacturer.
- **Education.** Supplies of education courses, excursions, course materials and leases of curriculum related goods are GST-free under sub-div 38-C. An 'education course' is defined exhaustively in s 195-1 and covers a range of specifically defined courses, such as a 'pre-school course', a 'primary course', a 'secondary course', a 'tertiary course' and an 'English language course for overseas students'. It also covers a 'professional or trade course', which is a course that leads to a qualification that is an essential prerequisite for entry into, or commencement of practice of, a profession or trade in Australia. However, a professional conference or training seminar is not an education course.
- **Child care.** Supplies of child care by specified providers (eg registered carers) and certain related supplies are GST-free under sub-div 38-D.
- **Exports.** Supplies by way of export of goods, leases of goods for consumption outside the ITZ and supplies of things (other than goods or real property) for consumption outside the ITZ

are GST-free under sub-div 38-E. The GST-free treatment of exports ensures that Australian exports can remain competitive in international markets.

- **Religious services.** Supplies of services by religious institutions that are integral to the practice of that religion are GST-free under sub-div 38-F. This could cover, for example, bible study classes provided by a church.
- **Charities.** Certain supplies by charitable institutions, gift-deductible entities and government schools are GST-free under sub-div 38-G. Examples of some of these GST-free supplies include supplies for low-value consideration, supplies of second-hand goods and supplies relating to raffles, bingo and retirement village accommodation.
- **Water, sewerage and drainage.** Supplies of water, sewerage, drainage and septic tank services are GST-free under sub-div 38-I. However, a supply of water is not GST-free if it is supplied in a container or transferred into a container that has a capacity of less than 100 litres.
- **Going concerns.** Supplies of 'going concerns' (eg sales of businesses) are GST-free under sub-div 38-J provided the conditions discussed at [7.12] are satisfied.
- **Transport.** Supplies of passenger transport on international flights and sea voyages (as well as domestic legs of international flights and sea voyages) are GST-free under sub-div 38-K. GST-free treatment also extends to supplies involving the international transport of goods and supplies of insurance relating to such transport.
- **Precious metals.** Supplies of precious metals (eg gold, silver and platinum) by refiners of precious metals to dealers of precious metals are GST-free under sub-div 38-L (see further *ACN 154 520 199 (in liq) v FC of T* 2020 ATC ¶20-772).
- **Duty-free.** Supplies of airport shop goods through an inwards duty-free shop to a relevant traveller are GST-free under sub-div 38-M.
- **Government land grants.** Supplies by the Commonwealth, a state or a territory of freehold or long-term leasehold interests in unimproved land are GST-free under sub-div 38-N.
- **Farm land.** Supplies of potential residential land subdivided from land on which a farming business has been carried on for at least five years to an associate of the supplier for no consideration or below market value consideration are GST-free under sub-div 38-O. Supplies of land on which a farming business has been carried on for at least five years to a recipient that intends to carry on a farming business are also GST-Free.
- **Cars for the disabled.** Supplies of cars to certain disabled veterans and other persons are GST-free under sub-div 38-P.
- **International mail.** Supplies of services to foreign postal administrators for the delivery in, or transit through, the ITZ of international mail are GST-free under sub-div 38-Q.
- **Global roaming.** Certain telecommunication supplies relating to global roaming arrangements in the ITZ are GST-free under sub-div 38-R.
- **Eligible emissions units.** Supplies of eligible emissions units [5.6] are GST-free under sub-div 38-S.
- **Inbound intangible consumer supplies.** Inbound intangible consumer supplies [7.18] made by non-residents that are covered by a determination made by the Minister are GST-free under sub-div 38-T.

Input taxed supplies

Entities that are registered for GST (or required to be registered for GST) do not charge GST on their input taxed supplies and are generally not entitled to ITCs on their acquisitions that relate to making such supplies (see the diagram below). Entities that make input taxed supplies therefore enjoy the benefit of being able to sell goods and services without having to include GST in the price. However, as they do not get the benefit of ITCs, they are effectively in the same position as end consumers in respect of their acquisitions.

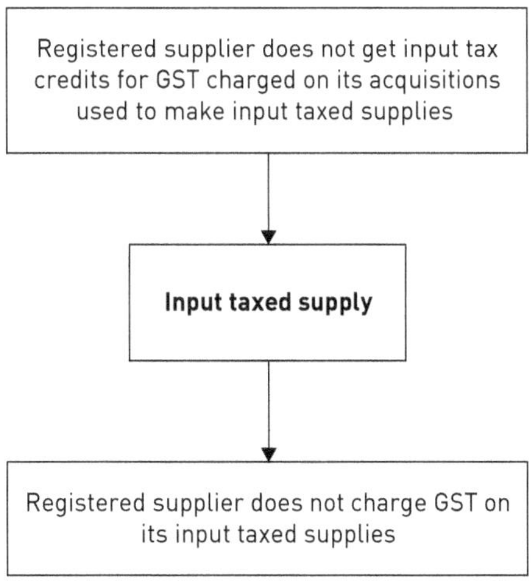

The following kinds of supplies are input taxed:

- **Financial supplies.** Financial supplies are input taxed under sub-div 40-A. A 'financial supply' is defined in div 40 *GST Regs* and includes things such as the making of loans and the issuing securities. The nature of a financial supply is examined at [7.13].
- **Leases of residential premises.** Supplies by way of lease, hire or licence of residential premises (other than commercial residential premises) are input taxed under sub-div 40-B. The term 'residential premises' is defined as land or a building that is occupied, or intended to be occupied, as a residence or for residential accommodation (s 195-1). 'Commercial residential premises' include a hotel, motel, inn, caravan park or a camping ground (s 195-1). Leases of residential premises are discussed further at [7.14].
- **Sales and long-term leases of residential premises.** Sales and long-term leases (ie leases for periods of at least 50 years) of real property are input taxed under sub-div 40-C, but only to the extent that the property is 'residential premises to be used predominantly for residential accommodation'. A sale or long-term lease is, however, not input taxed to the extent that the residential premises are commercial residential premises or new residential premises (other than those used for residential accommodation before 2 December 1998). Sales and long-term leases of residential premises are discussed further at [7.14].
- **Precious metals.** Supplies of precious metals (eg gold, silver or platinum) that do not fall within sub-div 38-L (see above) are input taxed under sub-div 40-D.
- **Tuckshops.** Supplies of food by a non-profit body through a tuckshop on school grounds are input taxed under sub-div 40-E provided the non-profit body chooses to have all its supplies of food through the shop treated as input taxed.
- **Fundraising.** Supplies in connection with certain fundraising events conducted by charities, gift-deductible entities and government schools are input taxed under sub-div 40-F.
- **Inbound intangible consumer supplies.** Inbound intangible consumer supplies [7.18] made by non-residents that are covered by a determination made by the Minister under s 40-180(2) are input taxed under sub-div 40-G.

[7.8] Creditable acquisitions

Entities are entitled to ITCs under s 11-20 *GSTA* for the creditable acquisitions that they make. The aim of providing an entity with an ITC for a creditable acquisition is to recoup the GST charged on the taxable supply made to the entity. The ITC is designed to neutralise the impact of GST on business-to-business transactions.

Creditable acquisition

According to s 11-5 *GSTA*, an entity makes a 'creditable acquisition' if:

- the entity acquires anything solely or partly for a creditable purpose
- the supply of the thing to the entity was a taxable supply
- the entity provides, or is liable to provide, consideration for the supply, and
- the entity is registered or required to be registered.

Acquisition

An 'acquisition' is defined as 'any form of acquisition whatsoever' (s 11-10(1)). An acquisition therefore takes on its ordinary dictionary meaning. The definition of an acquisition also expressly includes the following (s 11-10(2)):

- an acquisition of goods or services
- an acquisition of advice or information
- an acceptance of a grant, assignment or surrender of real property
- an acceptance of a grant, transfer, assignment or surrender of any right
- an acquisition of something the supply of which is a financial supply, and
- an acquisition of a right to require another person to do anything, or to refrain from an act, or to tolerate an act or situation.

An acquisition does not, however, include an acquisition of money (unless the money is provided as consideration for a supply that is a supply of money) (s 11-10(3)).

Creditable purpose

An entity acquires something for a 'creditable purpose' to the extent that the entity acquires it in carrying on its enterprise (s 11-15(1) *GSTA*).

However, a thing is not acquired for a creditable purpose to the extent that:

- the acquisition relates to making supplies that would be input taxed (s 11-15(2)(a)), or
- the acquisition is of a private or domestic nature (s 11-15(2)(b)).

Example Larry is the owner of a sports shop and is registered for GST. He purchased sports goods from a manufacturer for sale in his business for $1,100 (inclusive of GST). Larry acquired the sports goods for a creditable purpose as he acquired them in carrying on his enterprise. He is therefore entitled to an ITC for the GST charged by the manufacturer (ie $100).

Larry also owns a residential apartment and engages an estate agent to find a tenant for the apartment. The agent charges Larry a fee of $1,100 (inclusive of GST) for this service. Although the agent's services are acquired in carrying on an enterprise, the acquisition relates to a lease of residential premises, which is an input taxed supply. The agent's services have therefore not been acquired for a creditable purpose and Larry is therefore not entitled to any ITC for the GST charged by the agent.

In *Rio Tinto Services Ltd v FC of T* 2015 ATC ¶20-525, s 11-15(2)(a) operated to deny a mining company ITCs for acquisitions made by its GST group members in providing and maintaining residential accommodation in remote areas that were leased to its employees. The Full Federal Court found that the acquisitions were wholly related to the input taxed supplies of the premises even though the taxpayer's broader business was to profit from making taxable and GST-free supplies of iron ore.

Section 11-15(2)(a) operates subject to s 11-15(3) which provides that an acquisition is not treated, for the purposes of s 11-15(2)(a), as relating to making supplies that would be input taxed to the extent that the supply is made through an enterprise, or part of an enterprise, that the entity carries on outside the ITZ.

Section 11-15(2)(a) also operates subject to the exceptions in ss 11-15(4) and (5) which concern acquisitions that relate to making input taxed financial supplies [7.13].

Amount of input tax credit for a creditable acquisition

The ITC for a creditable acquisition is equal to the GST payable on the supply (s 11-25). However, where the acquisition is only partly creditable, the ITC is apportioned according to the following formula (s 11-30):

$$\text{Full input tax credit} \times \text{Extent of creditable purpose} \times \text{Extent of consideration}$$

Example Theo carries on business as a retailer. He is registered for GST and acquires a computer for $1,100 (inclusive of GST). If he uses the computer 100% for business purposes, the acquisition is fully creditable and he is entitled to an ITC of $100. If he uses the computer 80% for business purposes and 20% for private purposes, the acquisition is only partly creditable and he is entitled to an ITC of $80 = $100 × 80% × 100%.

Acquisitions that are not creditable acquisitions

7

An acquisition that is a 'non-deductible expense' is not a creditable acquisition (s 69-5(1) *GSTA*). A non-deductible expense is an expense that is not deductible for income tax purposes under any of the following provisions:

- s 26-5 *ITAA97* (penalties) [14.7]
- s 26-30 *ITAA97* (relative's travel expenses) [14.7]
- s 26-40 *ITAA97* (family maintenance expenses) [14.7]
- s 26-45 *ITAA97* (recreational club expenses) [14.7]
- s 26-50 *ITAA97* (leisure facility expenses) [14.7]
- div 32 *ITAA97* (entertainment expenses) [14.4]
- div 34 *ITAA97* (non-compulsory uniform expenses) [14.5], or
- s 51AK *ITAA36* (non-cash business benefits) [14.8].

[7.9] Accounting for GST and input tax credits

Cash or accruals

Entities must attribute GST and ITCs to tax periods under either a cash or accruals basis of accounting. The accruals basis applies unless an entity qualifies to use the cash basis. An entity can choose to use the cash basis if:

- it is an SBE [8.7]

- it does not carry on business and has GST turnover that does not exceed the cash accounting turnover threshold of $2m [7.3]
- it accounts for its income under the receipts method for income tax purposes [9.9], or
- each enterprise that it carries on is of a type that the Commissioner has determined in writing as being of a kind able to adopt a cash basis (s 29-40).

The Commissioner may also permit an entity to account on a cash basis if he is satisfied, having regard to the nature and size of the enterprise and the accounting system used, that it is appropriate to use the cash basis (s 29-45).

Cash basis entities attribute GST and ITCs to the extent that consideration is received or paid during a particular tax period (ss 29-5(2), 29-10(2)).

Accruals basis entities attribute GST and ITCs to the tax period in which any of the consideration for the supply is received, or an invoice is issued (if it is issued before any consideration is received) (ss 29-5(1), 29-10(1)).

Example A retailer with GST turnover of $1m would ordinarily use a cash basis of accounting. If in tax period 1, the retailer issued a tax invoice for $1,100 for goods supplied to a customer, the retailer would only need to remit GST in respect of the supply in tax period 1 if the customer actually paid for the goods in that period. If the customer only paid for the goods in tax period 3, the $100 of GST is payable in respect of tax period 3. If, however, the customer only paid one-half of the price in tax period 3, then only $50 of GST would be payable in respect of that period and the balance GST would be payable in respect of the period that the remaining consideration is received.

In contrast, a large retailer with GST turnover of $100m would use an accruals basis of accounting. If, in tax period 1, the retailer issued a tax invoice for $1,100 for goods supplied to a customer, the retailer would be required to pay GST of $100 in relation to that tax period. This is the case, even though the customer might only pay for the goods in tax period 3.

An entity is generally only entitled to claim an ITC for a creditable acquisition in relation to a tax period if it holds a tax invoice at the time of giving the Commissioner their GST return for the period (s 29-10(3)) [7.11]. The Commissioner can, however, waive this requirement. For example, he allows entities to claim ITCs based on corporate card statements in certain situations (*Goods and Services Tax: Waiver of Tax Invoice Requirement (Corporate Card Statements) No 2 Determination 2020*).

An entity generally ceases to be entitled to claim an ITC for a creditable acquisition if it has not claimed the ITC within four years after the day on which it was required to give the Commissioner a GST return for the tax period to which the ITC would be attributable under ss 29-10(1) or (2) (s 93-5). This rule operates subject to certain exceptions specified in s 93-10. Three recent examples of where s 93-5 applied are *JHKW v FC of T* 2022 ATC ¶10-643; *H&B Auto Repair Centre Pty Ltd v FC of T* 2022 ATC ¶10-651; and *Messenger Media and Information Technology Pty Ltd v FC of T* 2023 ATC ¶10-666. In all these cases, the AAT upheld the Commissioner's decisions to disallow ITCs claimed by taxpayers in BASs that had been lodged outside the four-year time limit.

Example A cash basis entity made a creditable acquisition in February 2023 but forgot to take this into account in its January–March 2023 quarterly return, which was required to be lodged by 28 April 2023. The taxpayer has until 28 April 2027 to claim the ITC.

Special rules for progressive and periodic supplies and acquisitions

Special attribution rules apply under div 156 *GSTA* to a supply or acquisition that is made for a period or on a progressive basis (eg a lease) if the consideration is also provided on such a basis. In such cases, each periodic or progressive component of the supply or acquisition is treated as a separate supply or acquisition (ss 156-5, 156-10).

> ***Example*** Larry owns a commercial property and entered into a 12-month lease of the property to Terry at a monthly rental of $11,000. Both Larry and Terry are registered for GST. Under ss 156-5 and 156-10, the GST charged by Larry and the ITC available to Terry in respect of each month's rental is attributed to the period in which the rent for the month is paid or an invoice is issued (if this occurs earlier). Without this special rule, assuming Larry and Terry are both accruals basis taxpayers, GST and ITCs for the whole 12-month rental period would be attributed to the tax period in which the first rental payment was made or invoice was issued (if this occurred earlier).

Special rules for deposits

The *GSTA* contains special rules relating to deposits. A deposit held as security for the performance of an obligation is not treated as consideration for a supply unless it is forfeited or applied as consideration for a supply (s 99-5). The GST relating to the payment of the deposit is attributable to the tax period in which the deposit was forfeited or applied as consideration for the supply (s 99-10). The application of this principle is illustrated in *FC of T v Reliance Carpet Co Pty Ltd* 2008 ¶ATC 20-028.

> ***Example*** Paula pays a $55 deposit to a computer retailer for the purchase of a new computer costing $2,200 (inclusive of GST) in tax period 1. Paula must pay the balance of the price owing under the contract in tax period 2. If Paula fails to complete the contract by the due date and the deposit is forfeited, the GST of $5 is attributable to tax period 2 (rather than tax period 1 as would ordinarily be the case under s 29-5).

7

[7.10] Increasing and decreasing adjustments

It is sometimes necessary to adjust the amount of GST that has been charged or the amount of ITC that has been claimed by an entity in relation to a particular transaction to ensure that the GST system operates appropriately. Adjustments are required where certain events occur after the transaction has been entered into that make the GST or ITC attributed in a previous tax period incorrect. These events can give rise to increasing and decreasing adjustments, which affect an entity's net amount for a tax period (s 17-5(2)) [7.4].

Increasing and decreasing adjustments arise in a number of situations, including where:

- an adjustment event occurs (div 19 *GSTA*)
- a bad debt is written off or is overdue for 12 months or more (div 21 *GSTA*), or
- the extent of creditable purpose in relation to an acquisition or importation has changed (div 129 *GSTA*).

Increasing and decreasing adjustments are generally attributable to the tax period in which the entity becomes aware of them (s 29-20(1)). However, if the entity accounts on a cash basis and is liable to provide consideration, the adjustment is attributable to the tax period in which the consideration is provided. If only part of the consideration is provided in a tax period, the adjustment is attributable to the extent that the consideration is provided in that tax period (s 29-20(2)).

Adjustment event (div 19 *GSTA*)

An adjustment event is any event that has the effect of:

- cancelling a supply or acquisition
- changing the consideration for a supply or acquisition, or
- causing a supply or acquisition to become or stop being taxable (s 19-10).

An adjustment event arises in respect of a supply where:

- one or more adjustment events in relation to the supply occur during a tax period
- GST on the supply was attributable to an earlier tax period (or, if the supply was not a taxable supply, would have been attributable to an earlier tax period had the supply been a taxable supply), and
- as a result of those events, the previously attributed GST amount for the supply no longer correctly reflects the amount of GST on the supply (s 19-40).

If the corrected GST amount is *greater* than the previously attributed GST amount, an increasing adjustment equal to the difference arises (s 19-50). If the corrected GST amount is *less* than the previously attributed GST amount, a decreasing adjustment equal to the difference arises (s 19-55).

An adjustment event arises in respect of an acquisition where:

- one or more adjustment events in relation to the acquisition occur during a tax period
- an ITC for the acquisition was attributable to an earlier tax period (or, if the acquisition was not a creditable acquisition, would have been attributable to an earlier tax period had the acquisition been a creditable acquisition), and
- as a result of those events, the previously attributed ITC amount for the acquisition no longer reflects the amount of the ITC on the acquisition (s 19-70).

If the previously attributed ITC amount is *greater* than the corrected ITC amount, an increasing adjustment equal to the difference arises (s 19-80). If the previously attributed ITC amount is *less* than the corrected ITC amount, a decreasing adjustment equal to the difference arises (s 19-85).

The following example illustrates how div 19 operates (further examples are found in GSTR 2000/19).

Example T Co is furniture manufacturer that supplies tables to furniture retailers. Both T Co and the retailers account for GST on an accruals basis. In tax period 1, T Co entered into a contract to sell five tables to one of its retailers for $2,200 each. T Co is therefore liable to pay GST of $1,000 (ie 5 × $200) in tax period 1 and the retailer is entitled to an input tax credit of $1,000 (ie 5 × $200) in tax period 1. In tax period 2, the retailer returned one of the tables and T Co provided the retailer a $2,200 refund. As a result, T Co has a decreasing adjustment of $200 in tax period 2 and the retailer has an increasing adjustment of $200 in tax period 2.

Bad debt is written off or overdue for 12 months or more (div 21 *GSTA*)

Section 21-5(1) provides that a decreasing adjustment arises where:

- an entity has made a taxable supply
- the whole or part of the consideration for the supply has not been received, and

- the entity writes off as bad the whole or a part of the debt, or the whole or a part of the debt has been overdue for 12 months or more.

The amount of the decreasing adjustment is 1/11th of the amount written off or 1/11th of the amount that has been overdue for 12 months or more.

Correspondingly, s 21-15(1) provides that an increasing adjustment arises where:

- an entity has made a creditable acquisition for consideration
- the whole or part of the consideration is overdue, and
- the supplier of the thing acquired by the entity writes off as bad the whole or a part of the debt, or the whole or a part of the debt has been overdue for 12 months or more.

The amount of the increasing adjustment is 1/11th of the amount written off or 1/11th of the amount that has been overdue for 12 months or more.

Adjustments do not arise under ss 21-5(1) and 21-15(1) if the relevant supplier or acquirer accounts on a cash basis (ss 21-5(2), 21-15(2)).

Where the whole or part of the amount written off, or the whole or a part of the debt has been overdue for 12 months or more, is recovered by the supplier, an increasing adjustment of 1/11th of the amount recovered arises for the supplier (s 21-10). Likewise, where the whole or part of the amount written off, or the whole or a part of the debt has been overdue for 12 months, is paid by the acquirer, a decreasing adjustment of 1/11th of the amount paid arises for the acquirer (s 21-15).

The following example illustrates how div 21 operates.

Example X Co is an electrical goods wholesaler that accounts for GST on an accruals basis. In tax period 1, it supplied electrical goods to an electrician and provided him with a tax invoice for $1,100. X Co is therefore liable for $100 of GST in tax period 1. The electrician did not pay for the goods and subsequently runs into financial difficulties. If, in tax period 4, X Co writes off the $1,100 as a bad debt, it has a decreasing adjustment of $100 (ie 1/11th of $1,100) for that tax period. If the electrician also accounts on an accruals basis, the electrician has a corresponding increasing adjustment of $100 (ie 1/11th of $1,100). If the electrician subsequently pays half the debt in tax period 7, the supplier will have an increasing adjustment of $50 (ie 1/11th of $550) and the electrician will have a corresponding decreasing adjustment of $50 (ie 1/11th of $550) in that tax period.

Changes in creditable purpose (div 129 *GSTA*)

The extent to which an acquisition or importation is for a creditable purpose affects the amount of ITC that the acquirer or importer is entitled to receive (ss 11-30, 15-25). Where the extent of creditable purpose changes due to subsequent events, adjustments may be required under div 129 (s 129-5).

Changes in creditable purpose must be measured over 'adjustment periods' (s 129-20). An adjustment period is a tax period that commences at least 12 months after the tax period to which the acquisition or importation is attributable and generally ends on the following 30 June. The number of adjustment periods varies depending on the GST-exclusive value of the acquisition or importation and whether or not it relates to business finance:

- For acquisitions and importations that relate to business finance, there are either one ($50,000 or less), five ($50,001–$499,999) or 10 ($500,000 or more) adjustment periods.
- For acquisitions and importations that do not relate to business finance, there are either two ($5,000 or less), five ($5,001–$499,999) or 10 ($500,000 or more) adjustment periods.

However, an adjustment cannot arise where the GST exclusive value of an acquisition or importation is $10,000 or less (for acquisitions or importations that relate to business finance) or $1,000 or less (for other acquisitions or importations) (s 129-10).

Entities are required to work out the extent to which they have applied the thing acquired or imported for a creditable purpose during the relevant adjustment periods (s 129-40). If the actual application of the thing is *less* than its intended or former application, an increasing adjustment arises for the adjustment period calculated under s 129-70 as follows:

$$\text{Increasing adjustment} = \text{Full input tax credit} \times \left[\begin{array}{c}\text{Intended or}\\ \text{former application}\end{array} - \begin{array}{c}\text{Actual}\\ \text{application}\end{array} \right]$$

If the actual application of the thing is *greater* than its intended or former application, a decreasing adjustment arises for the adjustment period calculated under s 129-75 as follows:

$$\text{Decreasing adjustment} = \text{Full input tax credit} \times \left[\begin{array}{c}\text{Actual}\\ \text{application}\end{array} - \begin{array}{c}\text{Intended or}\\ \text{former application}\end{array} \right]$$

The following example illustrates how div 129 operates (further examples are found in GSTR 2000/24).

Example Fred is a barrister and is registered for GST. On 5 December 2020, he purchased a computer for $4,400 (inclusive of GST). Fred intended to use the computer solely for business purposes and claimed an ITC of $400 in the tax period ending 30 December 2020. As the GST-inclusive value of the computer is under $5,000, there are two adjustment periods relating to the acquisition: adjustment period 1 (ending 30 June 2022) and adjustment period 2 (ending 30 June 2023). If, at the end of adjustment period 1, Fred determined that he actually used the computer only 60% of the time for business purposes and 40% for private purposes, he is liable for an increasing adjustment of $160 (ie $400 × (100% – 60%)) for the tax period ending 30 June 2022.

[7.11] Tax invoices and adjustment notes

Entities are required to hold tax invoices and adjustment notes at the time they lodge their GST returns for a relevant tax period in order to be able to claim ITCs and decreasing adjustments for the period (ss 29-10(3), 29-20(3) *GSTA*). These documents must be held for a period of five years after the completion of the relevant transaction (s 382-5 *TAA*) [40.2]. Tax invoices and adjustment notes are critical for the ATO's audit processes as they enable the ATO to match details of supplies and acquisitions made between relevant entities.

It is important to understand that tax invoices and adjustment notes simply record taxable supplies and adjustment events. The mere fact that an entity holds a tax invoice cannot be used to substantiate a creditable acquisition if no acquisition was actually made. In *Kais Jewellery (Syd) Pty Ltd v FC of T* [2022] AATA 425, the AAT noted it was inappropriate to use tax invoices as prima facie evidence that the transactions described in them occurred. The AAT pointed out that this was consistent with the view in *Bayconnection Property Developments Pty Ltd v FC of T*[2013] AATA 40 where the AAT stated (at 86):

> ... the reality is that a tax invoice does not *create* a taxable supply; it *records* one. If a taxable supply did not take place, then a 'tax invoice' is meaningless. In other words, documents that are so called 'tax invoices' cannot substantiate a creditable acquisition, *if in fact there was no supply or acquisition.*

Requirement to issue tax invoices and adjustment notes

Suppliers must generally issue tax invoices and adjustment notes in the approved form within 28 days of a request (ss 29-10(3), 29-20(3), 29-70(2), 29-75(2) *GSTA*). Suppliers are, however, not required to issue tax invoices where the value of the supply does not exceed $75 (s 29-80(1) *GSTA*; reg 29-80.01 *GST Regs*). There is no need to issue an adjustment note where the value of the adjustment is less than $75 (s 29-80(2) *GSTA*; reg 29-80.02 *GST Regs*).

Requirements of a tax invoice

Section 29-70(1) *GSTA* states that a 'tax invoice' is a document that complies with the following requirements:

- it is issued by the supplier of the supply or supplies, unless it is a recipient created tax invoice (issued by the recipient)
- it is in the approved form
- it contains enough information to enable the following to be clearly ascertained:
  - the supplier's identity and ABN
  - if the total price of the supply or supplies is at least $1,000 or if the document was issued by the recipient—the recipient's identity or ABN
  - what is supplied, including the quantity (if applicable) and the price of what is supplied
  - the extent to which each supply is a taxable supply
  - the date the document is issued
  - the amount of GST (if any) payable in relation to each supply
  - if the document was issued by the recipient and GST is payable in relation to any supply—that the GST is payable by the supplier
  - such other matters as the regulations specify, and
- it can be clearly ascertained from the document that the document was intended to be a tax invoice or, if it was issued by the recipient, a recipient created tax invoice.

The Commissioner's views on these requirements are contained in GSTR 2013/1.

7

Recipient created tax invoices

A 'recipient created tax invoice' is a tax invoice that the Commissioner has determined in writing may be issued by the recipient of a taxable supply rather than the supplier (s 29-70(3)). Recipient created tax invoices may be used in the industries identified by the Commissioner in *Recipient Created Tax Invoice Determination 2023* and GSTR 2000/10. They are typically used where it is more convenient for the recipient, rather than the supplier, to issue an invoice. Recipient created tax invoices can only be issued if both parties are registered for GST and they have entered into a written agreement that recipient created tax invoices will be issued in respect of particular supplies.

Example Leo authors fiction books and is registered for GST. He has an agreement with his publisher, who is also registered for GST, that in exchange for assigning copyright to the publisher, Leo will be paid a 10% royalty on the price of any books sold by the publisher. The Commissioner has determined that recipient created tax invoices can be issued in the publishing industry and Leo and his publisher have agreed in writing that the publisher will issue such invoices. During a particular tax period, the publisher sells $5,500 worth of books and pays Leo a royalty of $550. The publisher must issue a recipient created tax invoice for the supply made by Leo. Leo does not issue a tax invoice in respect of the supply to the publisher.

Document that may be treated as a tax invoice

A document issued by an entity to another entity may be treated by the other entity as a tax invoice if:

- it would comply with the requirements for a tax invoice but for the fact that it does not contain certain information, and
- all of that information can be clearly ascertained from other documents given by the entity to the other entity (s 29-70(1A)).

The Commissioner may also treat a particular document that is not a tax invoice as if it was a tax invoice (s 29-70(1B)). The circumstances in which the Commissioner will exercise the discretion to do this are set out in PS LA 2004/11 and GSTR 2013/1.

Adjustment notes

Section 29-75(1) *GSTA* states that an adjustment note:

- must be issued by the supplier
- must set out the ABN of the entity that issues it
- must contain such other information as the Commissioner determines in writing, and
- must be in the approved form.

As with tax invoices, the Commissioner may treat a particular document that is not an adjustment note as if it were an adjustment note.

[7.12] Going concerns

As mentioned at [7.6], the carrying on of an enterprise includes activities done 'in the course of the commencement or termination of the enterprise' (s 195-1). This means, for example, that the sale of a business would ordinarily give rise to a taxable supply by the vendor and a creditable acquisition by the purchaser. It may, nevertheless, be possible for the vendor and the purchaser to treat such a supply as a supply of a going concern, in which case the supply is GST-free under sub-div 38-J *GSTA*.

Supply of a going concern

A 'supply of a going concern' is GST-free provided:

- the supply is for consideration
- the recipient is registered or required to be registered, and
- the supplier and the recipient have agreed in writing that the supply is of a going concern (s 38-325).

For a supply to be a supply of a going concern, there must be an arrangement under which the supplier provides the recipient with all things necessary for the continued operation of an enterprise. The supplier must also carry on the enterprise until the day of the supply.

In *Aurora Developments Pty Ltd v FC of T* 2011 ATC ¶20-250, the Federal Court held that a supply of land by a property developer did not constitute a supply of a going concern as the property developer had abandoned its enterprise in relation to the property prior to settlement of the contract, which was the time of the supply. As a result, the supply of the land was not GST-free under s 38-325.

Consequences of treating a supply as a supply of a going concern

By electing to treat a supply as a supply of a going concern under s 38-325, the vendor does not charge GST on the supply. At the same time, the purchaser is not able to claim ITCs in relation to the acquisition (as no GST is charged on the supply since it is GST-free).

The benefit of electing to treat a supply as a supply of a going concern is that the purchaser's acquisition costs will be lower than would be the case if the supply was a taxable supply as the price will not include GST. The purchaser will therefore have lower financing costs than would otherwise be the case (assuming the purchaser borrows money to fund the acquisition). Furthermore, any stamp duty payable will also be lower as it will be based on GST-exclusive consideration.

Example Val owns a commercial property that is leased to a tenant. The leasing activity constitutes an enterprise (s 9-20(1)(c)). This means that Val could sell the property subject to the lease to a purchaser, Pam, as a supply of a going concern provided they agree in writing and are both registered for GST. In such a case, no GST would be charged by Val and no ITC would be available to Pam. Alternatively, Val could sell the property to Pam as a taxable supply. In such a case, GST would be charged by Val and an ITC would, ordinarily, be available to Pam.

If Val sells the property as a taxable supply and wants to receive net sale proceeds of $10m, Val would need to sell the property for $11m (inclusive of GST).

However, if the supply is a supply of a going concern under s 38-325, Val would only need to sell the property for $10m (as no GST is charged).

In both cases, Val would receive a net amount of $10m and Pam would pay a net amount of $10m. However, in the case of the taxable supply, Pam would need to temporarily finance the extra $1m of the purchase price (which she would be able to recoup as an ITC in the future). Pam would also have higher stamp duty costs on the transfer of the property as its value for stamp duty purposes would be $11m rather than $10m.

[7.13] Financial supplies

Financial supplies are input taxed (s 40-5 *GSTA*) [7.7]. As a result, entities that make financial supplies do not charge GST on such supplies.

Benedict has advanced two reasons why financial supplies are input taxed (see K Benedict, 'The Australian GST Regime and Financial Services: How Did We Get Here and Where Are We Going?' (2011) 9 *eJTR* 174):

- **Valuation reasons.** One reason for treating financial supplies as input taxed is that they are inherently difficult to value. The difficulties stem from the fact that entities that make financial supplies, such as banks, typically act as intermediaries between depositors and borrowers and charge fees based on margins spread over a vast number of transactions. It is difficult to apportion the margins between the individual supplies made by the bank and to determine the extent to which the charges represent fees for the bank's services as opposed to simply compensation for the use of money over time.
- **Theoretical reasons.** The other reason for treating financial supplies as input taxed is that financial supplies often relate to savings. From a theoretical perspective, savings should not be subject to GST as GST is intended to tax final consumption. Savings are only consumed when they are later applied for consumption. Taxing savings as well as consumption would therefore give rise to double taxation issues.

Meaning of financial supply

The definition of a financial supply is contained in div 40 *GST Regs*. Broadly, a financial supply is the provision, acquisition or disposal of an interest specified in the table in reg 40-5.09(3) (see below). To be a financial supply, the provision, acquisition or disposal of the interest must be for consideration, in the course of an enterprise, and connected with the ITZ. In addition, the supplier must be registered, or required to be registered, for GST and must be a 'financial supply provider' in relation to the supply. A financial supply provider is the entity that immediately before the supply owned or created the interest (reg 40-5.06).

The table in reg 40-5.09(3) refers to the following interests:

Item	An interest in or under . . .
1	An account made available by an Australian ADI in the course of: (a) its banking business within the meaning of the *Banking Act 1959*; or (b) its State banking business
2	A debt, credit arrangement or right to credit, including a letter of credit
3	A charge or mortgage over real or personal property
4	A regulated superannuation fund, an approved deposit fund, a pooled superannuation trust or a public sector superannuation scheme within the meaning of the *Superannuation Industry (Supervision) Act 1993*, or a retirement savings account within the meaning of the *Retirement Savings Accounts Act 1997*
5	An annuity or allocated pension
6	A life insurance business (within the meaning of the *Life Insurance Act 1995*): (a) which consists of the issuing of life policies (within the meaning of that Act); or (b) to which a declaration under subsection 12(2) or section 12A of that Act applies; or related reinsurance business
7	A guarantee
7A	An indemnity that holds a person harmless from any loss as a result of a transaction the person enters with a third party
8	Credit under a hire purchase agreement entered into before 1 July 2012 in relation to goods, if: (a) the credit for the goods is provided for a separate charge; and (b) the charge is disclosed to the recipient of the goods
9	Australian currency, the currency of a foreign country, digital currency or an agreement to buy or sell any of these 3 things
10	Securities, including: (a) a debenture described in paragraph (a), (b), (c), (e) or (f) of the definition of *debenture* in section 9 of the *Corporations Act 2001*; and (b) a document issued by an individual that would be a debenture if it were issued by a body corporate; and (c) a scheme described in paragraph (e), (i) or (m) of the definition of *managed investment scheme* in section 9 of the *Corporations Act 2001*; and (d) the capital of a partnership or trust
11	A derivative
12	An account made available by a non-resident in the course of carrying on banking business (within the meaning of the *Banking Act 1959*) in a foreign country in which the entity is authorised under the law of that country to carry on banking business
13	A foreign superannuation fund (within the meaning of the *Income Tax Assessment Act 1997*)

A financial supply does not, however, include a supply mentioned in the table in reg 40-5.12. The table covers a number of specific supplies, such as the supply of professional services (including advice relating to a financial supply), broking services, debt collection services, trustee services and custodian services.

Examples of what does and does not constitute a financial supply are provided in the tables in sch 2 of the *GST Regs*. Some common financial supplies include:

- opening and operating cheque, debit card, deposit and savings accounts
- borrowing and lending money
- granting mortgages over land or chattels
- providing guarantees and indemnities (but not a warranty for goods or a contract of insurance)
- transferring and issuing securities (eg shares, convertible notes, debentures, bonds, units in a unit trust), and
- entering into derivative arrangements (eg forward contracts and futures contracts).

Example Steve operates a cake shop and borrows $10,000 from a bank at an interest rate of 5% per annum to buy trading stock. The loan made by the bank constitutes the creation of a credit arrangement (GSTR 2002/2). It is therefore a financial supply, which is input taxed. As a consequence, the bank does not charge any GST on the loan. In addition, Steve is not entitled to any ITCs for his repayments as he has not made a creditable acquisition since the loan is not a taxable supply to him (s 11-5(2)(b)). If Steve defaults on the loan and the bank engages a law firm to recover the debt, the debt collection services provided by the law firm to the bank constitute a taxable supply, which is subject to GST.

A financial supply expressly includes an incidental financial supply (reg 40-5.08). An 'incidental financial supply' is defined in reg 40-5.10 and arises if something is supplied by an entity to a recipient directly in connection with a financial supply where:

- it is incidental to the financial supply
- it is provided around the same time as the financial supply, but not for separate consideration, and
- it is the usual practice of the entity to supply such things together with the financial supply in the ordinary course of its enterprise.

An incidental financial supply is treated as a financial supply even though it may also fall within the scope of reg 40-5.12.

Example A bank provides advice to a customer in respect of a housing loan made to the customer. So long as the advice is provided around the same time as the loan is made and a separate fee is not charged for the advice, the supply of the advice is an incidental financial supply and is therefore a financial supply.

Special input tax credits for acquisitions relating to financial supplies

Ordinarily, entities are not entitled to ITCs for acquisitions that relate to making financial supplies. This is because financial supplies are input taxed and acquisitions that relate to making such supplies are therefore not acquired for a 'creditable purpose' by virtue of s 11-15(2)(a) *GSTA* [7.8].

It is important to realise, however, that s 11-15(2)(a) operates subject to the exceptions in ss 11-15(4) and (5) which deal specifically with certain acquisitions that relate to making financial supplies. These exceptions are discussed below.

Section 11-15(4) exception—financial acquisitions threshold not exceeded

Section 11-15(4) contains the financial acquisitions threshold exception to s 11-15(2)(a). The purpose of this exception is to allow entities that make a relatively small amount of financial supplies (when compared with their taxable or GST-free supplies) to claim ITCs relating to those financial supplies.

Section 11-15(4) provides that an acquisition is *not* treated, for the purposes of s 11-15(2)(a) as relating to making financial supplies that would be input taxed if:

- the only reason it would be so treated is because it relates to making financial supplies, and
- the entity does not exceed the financial acquisitions threshold.

The 'financial acquisitions threshold' is calculated under div 189 and tested on a monthly basis. In essence, the financial acquisitions threshold is exceeded where, assuming that all 'financial acquisitions' made by an entity:

- during the 12 months ending at the end of the relevant month (ie current period), or
- during the relevant month and the next 11 months (ie future period),

were made solely for a creditable purpose, and either or both of the following apply in relation to either one of the above periods:

(a) the ITC entitlements relating to those financial acquisitions would exceed $150,000, or

(b) the ITC entitlements relating to those financial acquisitions would exceed 10% of the total ITCs to which the entity is entitled.

A 'financial acquisition' is defined in s 189-15 *GSTA* as an acquisition that relates to making financial supplies (other than a financial supply consisting of a borrowing).

The following diagram illustrates how the financial acquisitions threshold is tested:

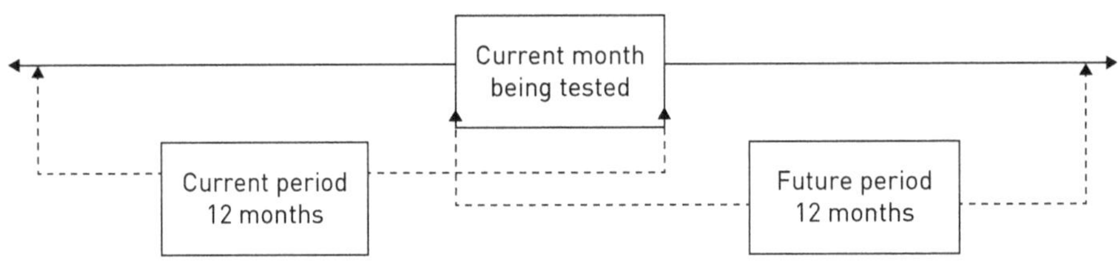

Example In March 2023, X Co calculates that its total acquisitions for the period 1 April 2022 to 30 March 2023 are $4,400,000, and that $330,000 of these acquisitions are financial acquisitions. For the purposes of div 189, X Co's ITCs for its total acquisitions for the current period amount to $400,000 and its ITCs for its financial acquisitions for the current period amount to $30,000.

X Co has not exceeded the financial acquisitions threshold for the current period because: (a) the $30,000 ITCs relating to financial acquisitions do not exceed $150,000; and (b) $30,000 is not greater than 10% of $400,000.

X Co also calculates that its total acquisitions for the period 1 March 2023 to 29 February 2024 are likely to be $7,700,000, and that $550,000 of these acquisitions are likely to be financial acquisitions. For the purposes of div 189, X Co's ITCs for its total acquisitions for the future period amount to $700,000 and its ITCs for its financial acquisitions for the future period amount to $50,000.

X Co has not exceeded the financial acquisitions threshold for the future period because: (a) the $50,000 ITCs relating to financial acquisitions do not exceed $150,000; and (b) $50,000 is not greater than 10% of $700,000.

As X Co has not exceeded the financial acquisitions threshold for either the current or future period, it is entitled to claim ITCs for the financial acquisitions it makes in March 2023.

Section 11-15(5) exception—borrowing expenses

Section 11-15(5) provides that an acquisition is *not* treated, for the purposes of s 11-15(2)(a) as relating to making financial supplies that would be input taxed to the extent that:

- the acquisition relates to a financial supply consisting of a borrowing, and
- the borrowing relates to the entity making supplies that are not input taxed.

The Explanatory Memorandum to the Bill that introduced this provision indicated that it was designed to ensure that where an entity borrows money and uses it to make taxable or GST-free supplies, it will be entitled to ITCs for its borrowing-related expenses. In other words, those expenses will not be treated as relating to making financial supplies that would be input taxed.

Example L Co carries on business leasing commercial buildings (ie making taxable supplies) and leasing residential buildings (ie making input taxed supplies). It borrows $1m to renovate some of its properties and pays $11,000 (inclusive of GST) to its lawyers for legal expenses relating to negotiating the loan. Of the $1m sum borrowed, $600,000 is used to renovate its commercial properties and $400,000 is used to renovate its residential properties. L Co is entitled to an ITC of $600 ($1,000 × 60%) in relation to the legal expenses.

Reduced credit acquisitions

Section 70-5 *GSTA* contains a special reduced credit acquisition rule. This rule allows reduced ITCs at the prescribed percentage (generally 75%) for reduced credit acquisitions that relate to making financial supplies (s 70-15 *GSTA*; reg 70-5.03 *GST Regs*).

'Reduced credit acquisitions' are acquisitions that fall within the tables in regs 70-5.02 and 70-5.02A. Some common examples of reduced credit acquisitions include:

- banking and cash management services (eg performing telephone and internet banking services)
- payment and fund transfer services (eg processing, settling and clearing transactions relating to cheques and credit and debit cards)
- debt collection services (eg providing debt recovery and litigation services), and
- securities transactions services (eg providing order placement and trade execution services).

An acquisition is not a reduced credit acquisition to the extent that an entity would otherwise be entitled to an ITC for the acquisition (s 70-5(1A)). Accordingly, no reduced ITC is available if the entity is already entitled to an ITC under ss 11-15(4) or (5) (discussed above).

The aim of the reduced credit acquisition rule is to provide some relief against the bias that exists in favour of in-sourcing (as opposed to out-sourcing) acquisitions by entities that make financial supplies. This bias arises because entities are not charged GST by their employees for their services but are generally charged GST by third parties for their services. Since entities that make financial supplies are not ordinarily entitled to ITCs for their acquisitions, it would be cheaper for them to have these things provided by their employees rather than third parties (as the GST charged by third parties cannot ordinarily be recouped). By granting entities that make financial supplies reduced ITCs, the incentive for them to in-source particular kinds of acquisitions is lessened.

Example Brett and Angie are registered for GST and carry on separate businesses as share traders. Each year they buy and sell many millions of dollars of shares. In the current tax period, Brett sold shares in X Co to Angie for $10m. No GST is payable by Brett in respect of the sale of the shares as it is a financial supply and is therefore input taxed. Angie is not entitled to an ITC in relation to the acquisition of the shares as no GST has been charged on the supply.

If Brett and Angie both used a broker to execute the sale and the broker charged each of them a commission of $11,000, the supply of the brokerage services would constitute a taxable supply and the broker would be liable for $1,000 GST on each of the supplies.

Assuming Brett and Angie do not qualify for ITCs under the *de minimis* exception to s 11-15(2)(a) in s 11-15(4), they would ordinarily not be entitled to ITCs for the brokerage services as those services are acquired for the purpose of their share-trading businesses which involve making input taxed financial supplies. However, under s 70-5, Brett and Angie are each entitled to a reduced ITC of $750 ($1,000 × 75%) in respect of the brokerage services as they are trade execution services which constitute reduced credit acquisitions under reg 70-5.02.

[7.14] Leases and sales of residential premises

Certain supplies of residential premises are input taxed under sub-divs 40-B and 40-C *GSTA* [7.7]. As a result, entities do not charge GST on these supplies and are not entitled to ITCs for GST charged on their acquisitions.

Leases of residential premises

Section 40-35 provides that supplies by way of lease, hire or licence of residential premises (other than a supply of commercial residential premises or a supply of accommodation in commercial residential premises provided to an individual by the entity that owns or controls the commercial residential premises) are input taxed. However, a supply is not input taxed under s 40-35 if it relates to a long-term lease (in such a case s 40-70 outlined below may apply).

Example Lisa owns a residential apartment in Melbourne which she leases to a tenant for one year. The lease of the apartment is an input taxed supply. Lisa does not therefore charge any GST on the lease. She is also not entitled to any ITCs. Accordingly, if an estate agent charged her $1,100 (inclusive of GST) for finding a tenant for the apartment, Lisa would not be entitled to any ITC in relation to the agent's fees.

Sales and long-term leases of residential premises

Sections 40-65 and 40-70 provide that sales and long-term leases of real property are also input taxed, but only to the extent that they are residential premises to be used predominantly for residential accommodation. However, a sale or long-term lease is not input taxed to the extent that the residential premises are:

- commercial residential premises, or
- new residential premises (other than those used for residential accommodation before 2 December 1998).

The sale or long-term lease of such premises will, therefore, ordinarily be a taxable supply provided the positive requirements of s 9-5 are met [7.6].

Example Dan is a property developer who sells a block of residential apartments that he has recently constructed to Pam. The sale is not input taxed under s 40-65, as it involves the sale of new residential premises. Assuming the positive requirements of s 9-5 are met, Dan is required to charge GST on the sale and is entitled to ITCs for the GST charged on its acquisitions relating to the building of the apartments. If Pam subsequently sells the apartment to a third party for use as residential accommodation, the sale will be input taxed as the property is no longer new residential premises. Pam will therefore not charge GST and will not be entitled to any ITCs for the GST charged by Dan.

Residential premises

'Residential premises' is defined as land or a building that:

- is occupied as a residence, or
- is intended to be occupied, and is capable of being occupied, as a residence (s 195-1).

The length of the term, or intended term, of occupation is irrelevant.

Whether premises are residential premises is determined by their physical characteristics (*Marana Holdings Pty Ltd & Anor v FC of T* 2004 ATC 5068). Whether premises are 'intended to be occupied' as a residence depends on the objective intention with which they are designed or built. This intention is reflected in their suitability for occupation as a residence (GSTR 2012/5).

In *Vidler v FC of T* 2010 ATC ¶20-186, the Full Federal Court held that vacant land containing no shelter or basic living facilities was not residential premises because it was not capable of being occupied as a residence or for residential accommodation.

Long-term lease

A 'long-term lease' is a supply by way of lease, hire or licence (including renewal or extension) for a period of at least 50 years if:

- at the time of the lease, etc, it was reasonable to expect that it would continue for at least 50 years, and
- unless the supplier is an 'Australian Government agency', the terms of the lease as they apply to the recipient are substantially the same as those under which the supplier held the premises (s 195-1).

7

Real property

Real property includes:

- any interest in or right over land (ie a legal or equitable interest or right, such as a fee simple interest: GSTR 2003/7)
- a personal right to call for or be granted any interest in or right over land (eg an option), or
- a licence to occupy land or any other contractual right exercisable over land (s 195-1).

Fixtures attached to land are part of the land. Chattels, on the other hand, are not part of the land. Where land is sold together with chattels, the consideration for the supply must be apportioned between these items.

To be used predominantly for residential accommodation

The words 'to be used predominantly for residential accommodation' were considered by the Supreme Court of NSW in *Toyama Pty Ltd v Landmark Building Developments Pty Ltd* 2006 ATC 4160.

The case concerned the sale of a disused house to a purchaser who intended to demolish the building and develop the land. The Court held that although the building was 'residential premises', the sale was not an input taxed supply as the purchaser did not intend to use it for residential accommodation. White J held that the words 'to be used predominantly for residential accommodation' require a prediction to be made about the future use of the premises and that the most important factor in making such a prediction is the intention of the purchaser.

A different approach was, however, adopted by the Full Federal Court in *Sunchen Pty Ltd v FC of T & Anor* 2010 ATC ¶20-229. In this case, a residential building was sold with approval for the construction of a block of flats to a property developer that ended up leasing the building instead of developing it. The Commissioner denied the taxpayer an ITC in respect of the purchase of the property on the basis that the supply to the taxpayer was an input taxed supply. The taxpayer argued that the supply should have been treated as a taxable supply as it had purchased the property with the intention of developing it in the future. The taxpayer submitted that *Toyama* was authority for the principle that a purchaser's subjective intention is the principal issue to consider in determining whether residential premises were 'to be used predominantly for residential accommodation'.

The Full Federal Court, however, declined to follow *Toyama* and instead accepted the Commissioner's argument that whether premises are 'to be used predominantly for residential accommodation' should be determined objectively by reference to the physical characteristics of the property as at the date of acquisition. Edmonds and Gilmour JJ held that the words 'to be used predominantly for residential accommodation' did not refer to use by any particular person, but described the attributes of the property (ie its characteristics in terms of its suitability). According to their Honours, the intention of the future owner, even if determined solely by reference to objective circumstances, was totally irrelevant.

The Commissioner's views on *Sunchen* are expressed in GSTR 2012/5, where it is stated (at [70]):

> The Commissioner considers that the observation made by Edmonds and Gilmour JJ in *Sunchen* . . . recognises that in the majority of instances, premises that possess characteristics suitable for residential accommodation will be used for that purpose. However, the actual use of such premises for a purpose other than residential accommodation does not prevent the premises from being residential premises to be used predominantly for residential accommodation.

Commercial residential premises exception

Neither leases nor sales of commercial residential premises are input taxed. The term 'commercial residential premises' is defined to mean:

- a hotel, motel, inn, hostel or boarding house
- premises used to provide accommodation in connection with a school
- ships mainly let out on hire or used for entertainment or transport in the ordinary course of a business
- a marina at which one or more of the berths are occupied, or to be occupied, by ships used as residences
- a caravan park or a camping ground, or
- anything similar to residential premises described above (s 195-1).

Example Tony is on holidays and spends $3,300 for accommodation at a large hotel on the Gold Coast. The hotel is commercial residential premises. The supply of the accommodation is therefore a taxable supply and the hotel operator is required to pay GST of $300.

In *ECC Southbank Pty Ltd (as Trustee for Nest Southbank Unit Trust) & Anor v FC of T* 2012 ATC ¶20-336, the Federal Court held that a sublease of student residential accommodation by an entity ('NSUT') that held a 99-year lease of the premises to another entity ('USLT') which leased the accommodation to tenants (principally students) was a supply of 'commercial residential premises' on the basis that the accommodation was similar to a hostel. The relevant accommodation consisted of more than 150 studio and shared apartments with common areas such as TV, games and group study rooms, a library and a 24-hour reception desk. The Court also held that USLT's supplies of the accommodation to the tenants constituted supplies of commercial residential premises provided to individuals by the entity that controlled the commercial residential premises. On this basis, the relevant supplies were treated as taxable supplies.

By way of contrast, in *FFYS v FC of T* 2021 ATC ¶10-608, an owner of a house on the Sunshine Coast that used the Airbnb online platform to source guests who paid to occupy a bedroom in the house was found not to be supplying commercial residential premises. The AAT held that while the bundle of services the owner was supplying was similar in some ways to the services and features of hotels, motels, inns, hostels and boarding houses, the physical configuration and layout and the absence of multiple occupancies was a key distinction that set aside the premises from being commercial residential premises.

New residential premises exception

A sale or long-term lease of new residential premises other than those used for residential accommodation before 2 December 1998 is also not input taxed. The term 'new residential premises' is defined as residential premises that:

- have not previously been sold as residential premises (other than commercial residential premises), and have not previously been the subject of a long-term lease
- have been created through substantial renovations of a building, or
- have been built to replace demolished premises on the same land (s 40-75(1)).

New residential premises do not, however, include premises that have been used only for input taxed residential rent purposes for at least five years since they were built, substantially renovated or replaced (s 40-75(2)).

In addition, residential premises are not new residential premises if they are created from residential premises that became the subject of a property subdivision plan and were not new residential premises immediately before the plan (s 40-75(2AA)).

7

GST withholding regime

A number of taxpayers in the property industry (particularly developers) have failed to remit GST on the sale of new residential premises or new subdivisions. This has sometimes been due to 'phoenixing' (ie where the companies that make the supplies are dissolved before they pay tax). To address this problem, sub-div 14-E of sch 1 *TAA* contains a GST withholding regime which operates from 1 July 2018.

The GST withholding regime applies to recipients of taxable supplies by way of sale or long-term lease of:

- new residential premises that have not been created through substantial renovations to a building and are not commercial residential premises, or
- potential residential land that is included in a property subdivision plan and does not contain any building that is in use for a commercial purpose (ss 14-250(1)(a), (2)).

Potential residential land is defined as land that it is permissible to use for residential purposes but does not contain any buildings that are residential premises (s 195-1 *GSTA*). The regime does not apply to taxable supplies of potential residential land if the recipient is registered for GST and acquires the land for a creditable purpose (ie it does not apply to business-to-business transactions) (s 14-250(1)(b)).

Under the GST withholding regime, the recipient of the taxable supply (ie the purchaser of the premises or land) is required to pay an amount to the Commissioner, representing the GST on the transaction. The amount is a proportion of either the 'contract price' (ie the price for the supply in the contract, not taking into account normal adjustments that may apply) or the 'price' of the supply (if there is no contract price) (s 14-250(7)).

If the 'margin scheme' [7.15] does not apply to the supply, the purchaser must pay 1/11th of the contract price or price (s 14-250(6)(b)). If the margin scheme applies to the supply, the purchaser must pay 7% of the contract price or price (or a greater amount determined by the Minister in a legislative instrument, being no more than 9% of the contract price or price) (ss 14-250(6)(a), (8)). Where supplies are made between associates for consideration that is less than the GST-inclusive market value of the supply, the purchaser must pay 10% of the GST-exclusive market value of the supply (s 14-250(9)).

If a supply is made to multiple recipients, each recipient is treated as receiving a separate supply in proportion to their interest in the property. The payment that each recipient is required to make is proportionate to their interest in the property (s 14-250(11)). However, if the recipients are joint tenants, they are treated as having received a single supply, and they each have an obligation to make the payment.

Amounts must generally be paid on the day on which any of the consideration for the supply (other than consideration provided as a deposit) is first provided (s 14-250(4)). This will generally be the date of settlement. However, if the supplier is an associate of the recipient and the supply is without consideration, it must be paid on the day on which the supply is made. The Commissioner may, by legislative instrument, vary the day by which a payment is to be made (s 14-250(5)). For example, where the consideration is provided in instalments, he could provide that payments be made by the end of the day on which each instalment is paid.

An entity that makes a taxable supply to which s 14-250 applies is entitled to a credit for the amount paid to the Commissioner by the recipient (ss 18-60(1), (2)). The credit arises when an assessment has been made of the supplier's net amount for the tax period in which the payment was made (s 18-60(3)). The credit only arises if the recipient has actually paid the amount to the Commissioner—it does not arise merely because an amount has been withheld from a payment to the supplier.

Example On 10 July 2023, Jill enters into a contract to acquire new residential premises for a contract price of $1.1m from Jack who is a developer registered for GST. Jill pays Jack a deposit of $220,000 on signing the contract and the balance $880,000 at settlement on 10 September 2023. Assuming the margin scheme is not used, and Jack and Jill are not associates, Jill must pay 1/11th of contract price to the Commissioner on 10 September 2023. She must therefore withhold $100,000 (ie 1/11th of $1.1m) from the balance owing to Jack. Jack is entitled to a credit of $100,000 against his net amount for the tax period in which the payment is made.

To help recipients comply with their GST withholding obligations, entities that make supplies of residential premises or potential residential land are required to provide a written notice to the recipient before making the supply stating whether the recipient will be required to make a payment under s 14-250 (s 14-255(1)). However, this rule does not apply to a supply of commercial residential premises or to a supply of potential residential land if the recipient is registered and acquires the land for a creditable purpose (s 14-255(2)). A penalty of 100 penalty units [41.1] applies if the notice is not provided (ss 14-255(4), (6)).

[7.15] Margin scheme

In certain cases, entities can use the concessional margin scheme in div 75 *GSTA* to calculate the GST payable on a taxable supply of real property instead of the general GST rules. The broad aim of the margin scheme is to ensure that GST only applies to the value added to real property after 1 July 2000 (rather than the total consideration for the supply).

Eligibility to use the margin scheme

The margin scheme can be used where an entity sells a freehold interest in land, sells a stratum unit, or grants or sells a long-term lease. In order to be able to use the margin scheme, the supplier and the recipient must agree in writing, on or before making the supply (or within such further period as the Commissioner allows), that the margin scheme is to apply (ss 75-5(1), (1A)). The margin scheme cannot be used where the supplier acquired the property through a supply that was ineligible for the margin scheme (s 75-5(2)). A supply is ineligible for the margin scheme if it falls within the categories of supplies mentioned in s 75-5(3). Supplies that fall within this provision include:

- supplies where the supplier acquired the property through a taxable supply on which GST was worked out without applying the margin scheme, and
- supplies where the supplier acquired the property as a GST-free supply of a going concern under sub-div 38-J from an entity that was registered or required to be registered and that acquired the property through a taxable supply on which the GST was worked out without applying the margin scheme.

> ***Example*** Alice and Bob are both registered for GST. Last year, Alice sold a commercial property to Bob as a taxable supply under the ordinary GST rules. If Bob subsequently sells the property to a third party, he cannot use the margin scheme as he acquired the property as a taxable supply on which the GST was worked out without using the margin scheme.

7

Calculating GST under the margin scheme

Under the margin scheme, the GST is 1/11th of the margin for the supply (s 75-10(1)). In general, the 'margin' for the supply is the amount by which the consideration for the supply exceeds the supplier's consideration for acquiring the property (s 75-10(2)). Importantly, in determining the supplier's consideration for acquiring the property, the value of other acquisitions relating to the property (eg capital improvements) is expressly disregarded (s 75-14). In *Sterling Guardian Pty Ltd v FC of T* 2006 ATC 4227, it was noted that a supplier would ordinarily be entitled to ITCs relating to capital improvements at the time those costs are borne.

There are special rules for calculating the margin where the property was acquired before 1 July 2000. In these circumstances, the margin is generally calculated as the amount by which the consideration for the supply exceeds an approved valuation of the property as at 1 July 2000, or an approved valuation of the property at the date the supplier became registered for GST where the supplier was not registered on 1 July 2000 (s 75-10(3)).

There are also separate integrity rules for calculating the margin in specific cases (such as where the property was acquired as a GST-free supply of a going concern under sub-div 38-J) (s 75-11).

No input tax credit for acquirer and no tax invoice

Where the margin scheme is used, the acquirer is deemed not to make a creditable acquisition and is therefore not entitled to any ITC in relation to the acquisition (s 75-20). In addition, the supplier is not required to issue a tax invoice (s 75-30).

Situations in which margin scheme is commonly used

The margin scheme is often used by developers when they sell residential land and buildings to unregistered purchasers. The advantage of using the margin scheme in this situation is that the GST charged by the developer is less than would otherwise be the case under the general GST rules. The fact that the purchaser is not entitled to an ITC under the margin scheme should be irrelevant as the purchaser would not be entitled to an ITC under the general GST rules. Using the margin scheme can therefore reduce the overall cost of residential land and buildings sold to unregistered purchasers.

Example David is a property developer and is registered for GST. In 2021, he acquired residential land for $1m from Vicky, who had lived on the property for the previous 20 years. No GST was charged on the supply of the land by Vicky and no ITC was therefore available to David.

David demolished the existing house on the land and built a new house on it at a cost of $660,000 (inclusive of GST). David claimed ITCs of $60,000 in relation to the demolition and construction works. In 2023, he sold the house for $3.3m to Penny for use as her home.

If David does not use the margin scheme, he would be required to pay GST of $300,000 ($3.3m × 1/11), as it is a supply of new residential premises. Penny would not be entitled to an ITC as she has not acquired the property for a creditable purpose.

If, however, David elects to use the margin scheme, he would only be required to pay GST of $209,091 (($3.3m – $1m) × 1/11). David would not be required to issue a tax invoice and Penny would not be entitled to an ITC.

Note that the GST withholding tax regime would also apply to the sale of the house [7.14]. Penny would therefore be required to withhold GST from the payment (s 14-250 *TAA*) and David would get a credit for the amount paid to the Commissioner by Penny (s 18-60 *TAA*).

The margin scheme was recently considered in *FC of T v Landcom* 2022 ATC ¶20-846, where the Full Federal Court held that the sale of four freehold interests in land under a single contract each constituted separate supplies (rather than a single supply). The Court pointed out that div 75 was concerned with the sale of a particular freehold interest in land. Where there was a supply of more than one interest, s 75-10 applied to each interest.

[7.16] Importations

Part 2-3 *GSTA* contains special rules relating to importations. These rules require entities to pay GST on their taxable importations (s 13-15) and allow them ITCs for their creditable importations (s 15-15).

Taxable importations

A taxable importation arises if goods are imported and 'entered for home consumption' within the meaning of the *Customs Act 1901* (Cth) (s 13-5). Importantly, for a taxable importation to arise, it is *not* necessary that the importer be registered for GST.

An importation is not a taxable importation to the extent that it is a 'non-taxable importation'. A non-taxable importation arises where, assuming the importation had been a 'supply', it would have been GST-free or input taxed [7.7].

Example Dora imports a motorised wheelchair. As supplies of wheelchairs are GST-free under sub-div 38-B, the importation is a non-taxable importation.

A non-taxable importation also arises where the importation falls within the provisions in pt 3-2 *GSTA* (s 13-10). For instance, provided certain conditions are satisfied, exported goods that are returned to the ITZ in an unaltered condition are treated as non-taxable importations under s 42-10. Likewise, goods that benefit from specified customs concessions under the *Customs Tariff Act 1995* (Cth) are treated as non-taxable importations under s 42-5.

Amount of GST on taxable importations

The amount of GST on a taxable importation is 10% of the 'value of the taxable importation' (s 13-20(1)). The value of the taxable importation is essentially the sum of the customs value of the imported goods, international transport and insurance costs, plus customs duty payable on the importation (s 13-20(2)).

> ***Example*** Glen imports a pair of skis for sale in his ski shop. The customs value of the skis together with insurance freight and customs duty amounts to \$2,000. Glen must pay GST of \$200 (\$2,000 × 10%) on the importation. Note that GST would be payable even if Glen was not registered for GST.

Creditable importations

An entity makes a 'creditable importation' if:

- the entity imports goods solely or partly for a creditable purpose
- the importation is a taxable importation, and
- the entity is registered or required to be registered (s 15-5).

Something is imported for a creditable purpose to the extent that it is imported in carrying on the entity's enterprise (s 15-10(1)). However, the thing is not imported for a creditable purpose to the extent that the importation relates to making supplies that would be input taxed (s 15-10(2)(a)) or is of a private or domestic nature (s 15-10(2)(b)).

7

Amount of input tax credit for a creditable importation

The ITC for a creditable importation is equal to the GST payable on the importation (s 15-20). However, where the importation is only partly creditable, the ITC is apportioned and calculated as follows (s 15-25):

$$\text{Full input tax credit} \times \text{Extent of creditable purpose}$$

> ***Example*** In the above example, Glen would be entitled to an ITC for the \$200 GST charged on the importation of the skis as he acquired the skis wholly for a creditable purpose (ie for sale in his ski shop).

Payment of GST on importations

The GST attribution and payment rules [7.4] are modified for importers under div 33 *GSTA*. GST is generally payable by an importer at the same time and in the same manner as customs duty (ie when the goods are entered for home consumption) (s 33-15(1)). However, div 33 of the *GST Regs* contains a special scheme which allows certain importers to defer their GST payments on taxable importations until they lodge their first GST return after the goods are entered for home consumption. An entity must apply to the Commissioner for approval to use the scheme. Approval is generally granted provided the entity is registered for GST, has an ABN, uses monthly tax periods, pays GST electronically and has a satisfactory compliance record.

[7.17] Special entities

The *GSTA* contains special rules that apply to particular kinds of entities. Some of these rules are outlined below.

GST groups (div 48 *GSTA*)

Two or more entities may become registered as a 'GST group' provided they satisfy specified membership requirements and agree in writing to form the GST group. One of the entities (which must be an Australian resident) must be nominated as the 'representative entity' and must notify the Commissioner in the approved form of the formation of the group (s 48-5).

The membership requirements for a GST group are contained in s 48-10. Essentially, companies may form a GST group only if they are members of the same 90% owned group (s 190-1). Other entities (eg individuals, trusts or partnerships) may generally only be included in a GST group if they have a 90% stake in a company that is a member of the GST group. For a recent illustration of where the 90% owned group requirements were not met, see *Adcon Resources Vic Pty Ltd v FC of T* 2022 ATC ¶10-639.

The consequence of becoming a GST group is that the group is treated as a single entity and intra-group transactions are generally ignored. In other words, no GST is charged, and no ITCs are available, in respect of supplies and acquisitions made between group members. It is only where supplies and acquisitions are made to and from third parties that GST and ITC issues arise for the group.

The GST obligations and entitlements for transactions involving supplies and acquisitions made by group members outside the group lie with the representative member of the GST group. The representative member must pay GST on any taxable supplies made by group members and is entitled to any ITCs for creditable acquisitions made by group members (ss 48-40, 48-45). It is also required to lodge the group's GST return (s 48-60).

> ***Example*** H Co owns 100% of the shares in S1 Co. S1 Co owns 100% of the shares in S2 Co. H Co, S1 Co and S2 Co form a GST group of which H Co is the representative member.
>
> If S2 Co supplies goods to S1 Co, the supply is not treated as a taxable supply and no GST is therefore charged by S2 Co and no ITC is available to S1 Co.
>
> If S1 Co makes a taxable supply to a third party, the GST is payable by H Co. Likewise, if S1 Co makes a creditable acquisition from a third party, H Co is entitled to the ITC.

Joint ventures (div 51 *GSTA*)

A GST joint venture may be formed by two or more entities involved in a joint venture for the exploration of mineral deposits or for a purpose specified in the *GST Regs* (s 51-5). The participants must satisfy certain participation requirements and agree in writing to the formation of the GST joint venture. They must also notify the Commissioner in the approved form of the formation of the GST joint venture.

The effect of becoming a GST joint venture is that the 'GST joint venture operator' nominated in the agreement is liable for GST on supplies and importations and entitled to ITCs on acquisitions and importations that it makes on behalf of participants in the joint venture in the course of activities for which the joint venture was entered into (ss 51-30, 51-35).

Branches (div 54 *GSTA*)

Ordinarily, a branch of an entity is not a separate entity. Nevertheless, a registered entity can apply to register a 'GST branch' provided the branch maintains an independent system of accounting and carries on an enterprise (s 54-5). The GST liabilities and ITC entitlements of a GST branch are calculated separately from those of the parent entity (ss 54-40, 54-45).

Dealers in second-hand goods (div 66 *GSTA*)

Ordinarily, ITCs are only available if GST has been charged on a supply, as this is a requirement for a creditable acquisition [7.8]. An entity that acquires second-hand goods for sale or exchange in the ordinary course of business is nevertheless generally entitled to claim ITCs even though the supply of the goods to the entity did not attract GST (s 66-5).

For example, this rule applies where a second-hand dealer acquires goods from an unregistered entity. The reason for allowing ITCs in these circumstances is that the unregistered entity would ordinarily have been charged GST when acquiring the goods but would not have been entitled to any ITCs as it is unregistered. The price the dealer in second-hand goods pays for the goods therefore includes the embedded GST. It is therefore reasonable to allow the second-hand dealer ITCs in relation to this underlying GST.

The amount of the ITC is 1/11th of the cost of the goods. However, where the cost of the goods is more than $300, the ITC cannot exceed the GST charged on any subsequent supply (s 66-10) and special attribution rules determine when the ITC can be claimed (s 66-15). In certain circumstances, a global accounting method may be used for calculating GST and ITCs in relation to second-hand goods (sub-div 66-B).

Associates (div 72 *GSTA*)

Ordinarily, a taxable supply only arises where something is supplied for consideration. Nevertheless, a supply made to an 'associate' (defined in s 195-1) for no consideration may still constitute a taxable supply if the associate is not registered or required to be registered and the associate acquires the thing supplied otherwise than solely for a creditable purpose (s 72-5). In this case, the value of the supply is the 'GST-exclusive market value' of the supply (s 72-10).

Further, a taxable supply to an associate for consideration that is less than GST-inclusive market value is deemed to be for its GST-exclusive market value unless the associate is registered or required to be registered and acquired the thing solely for a creditable purpose (s 72-70).

7

Simplified accounting methods for retailers (div 123 *GSTA*)

The Commissioner can create simplified accounting methods ('SAMs') for certain retailers and 'small enterprise entities', which they can use to calculate their net amounts (ss 123-5, 123-10, 123-15).

A small enterprise entity is basically:

- an entity that is an SBE or that would be an SBE if the aggregated turnover threshold for an SBE was $50m (instead of $10m) [8.7], or
- an entity that does not carry on a business but has GST turnover that does not exceed the small enterprise entity turnover threshold ($2m) [7.3] (s 123-7).

The Commissioner has created SAMs for food retailers who sell food that is both taxable and GST-free. In particular, under *Goods and Services Tax: Simplified Accounting Methods Determination 2017 for Retailers who sell Food—Business Norms, Stock Purchases and Snapshot Methods*, the Commissioner allows eligible food retailers to use one of three SAMs to calculate the taxable and GST-free supplies of their stock. Each method has its own special conditions which must be met before it can be used. Food retailers can only use the methods if they do not have adequate point-of-sale equipment (eg electronic scanners) to identify and record each separate supply as being taxable or GST-free. The three methods are outlined below:

- **Business norms method.** Under this method, an entity estimates its GST-free sales and GST-free purchases by applying standard percentages to their total sales and purchases of stock. The standard percentages are listed in the determination and differ depending on the type of business the entity conducts. For example, a cake shop that sells mainly cakes and pastries and does not operate as a café can use 2% for GST-free sales and 95% for GST-free purchases, while a hot bread shop can use 50% for GST-free sales and 75% for GST-free purchases.

> ***Example*** Carol owns a cake shop and chooses to use the business norms method. During the relevant tax period, she sold stock for $300,000 and purchased stock for $200,000. As the business norm for cake shop GST-free sales is 2% and for GST-free purchases is 95%, Carol can calculate her GST-free sales for the period as $6,000 (ie 2% of $300,000) and her GST-free purchases for the period as $190,000 (ie 95% of $200,000).

- **Stock purchases method.** Under this method, the percentage of an entity's GST-free sales is taken to be the same as the percentage of its GST-free purchases. The GST-free percentage must be calculated on an 'every tax period', 'two sample period', or '5% GST-free stock estimation' basis. The stock purchases method only applies to resellers and cannot be used by entities that convert GST-free items into taxable items. For example, it could be used by a grocer that sells the fruit and vegetables it purchased at the market, but not by a restaurant that converts GST-free food into taxable meals.

> ***Example*** Glen owns a grocery business and chooses to use the stock purchases method. He elects to work out the percentage of his GST-free purchases on an every-tax-period basis. During a relevant tax period, Glen sold $300,000 of stock and purchased $200,000 of stock which included $150,000 of GST-free stock. Glen's percentage of GST-free purchases is therefore 75% (ie $150,000/$200,000). Glen can use this percentage to calculate his GST-free supplies of stock for the period. As a consequence, his GST-free supplies for the period is $225,000 (ie $300,000 × 75%).

- **Snapshot method.** Under this method, the entity takes a snapshot of the percentages of its GST-free sales and GST-free purchases. The entity can then use the respective percentages to calculate its GST-free sales and GST-free purchases for every tax period. The snapshot percentages must be calculated on an 'every tax period', 'two sample period', or '5% GST-free stock estimation' basis. The snapshot method can be used by both resellers and converters.

> ***Example*** Max owns a milk bar and chooses to use the snapshot method. During the relevant snapshot period, Glen determined that he sold $400,000 of stock of which $100,000 was GST-free (ie 25% GST-free). He also determined that he purchased $500,000 of stock of which $250,000 was GST-free (ie 50% GST-free). For each tax period until another snapshot is taken, Max can treat 25% of his sales of stock as GST-free and 50% of his purchases or stock as GST-free.

In addition to the SAMs outlined above, eligible supermarkets and convenience stores can use the 'sales percentage method' set out in *A New Tax System (Goods and Services Tax) Act 1999 Simplified GST Accounting Methods Determination (No 29) 2015* and eligible restaurants, cafes and caterers can use the 'purchases snapshot method' set out in *A New Tax System (Goods and Services Tax) Act 1999 Simplified GST Accounting Methods Determinations SAM 2006/1*.

Gambling suppliers (div 126 *GSTA*)

To avoid GST being charged on every single gambling transaction, GST relating to gambling is accounted for under a global accounting system, which essentially taxes the 'gambling margin'.

Entities making gambling supplies (s 126-35) must calculate their 'global GST amount' (ie the total amount wagered less the total monetary prizes paid during a tax period multiplied by 1/11th) (s 126-10). Where the total monetary prizes paid exceeds the total amount wagered for the period, the excess is added to the total monetary prizes for the next period, ie any loss is carried forward (s 126-15). The global GST for a tax period is then added to the supplier's other GST liabilities less ITC entitlements to arrive at the net amount payable by the entity for the tax period (s 126-5).

Gambling supplies do not give rise to creditable acquisitions (s 126-30). This means that a professional punter does not get an ITC for 1/11th of the cost of a bet made at a casino.

Government departments (div 149 *GSTA*)

Although a government department is not an entity distinct from government, it can be separately registered (s 149-5), in which case it is treated as if it were a separate entity for GST purposes (s 149-15). A government department is, however, not required to be registered even if it carries on an enterprise and its turnover exceeds the registration turnover threshold (s 149-10).

[7.18] Reverse charge and other special rules

Ordinarily, it is the supplier that is required to charge GST on supplies. However, the *GSTA* contains a number of special rules that make someone other than the supplier liable for GST. The following discussion outlines some of these situations, together with a range of other special rules.

Supplies by agents (div 57 and sub-div 153-B *GSTA*) 7

Based on the general law of agency, where a principal makes supplies or acquisitions through an agent, it is the principal that is liable for GST or entitled to ITCs rather than the agent. This general rule is, however, subject to the following important qualifications:

- **Resident agent acts for non-resident principal.** Where a resident agent acts for a non-resident, it is the resident agent that is liable for any GST and entitled to any ITCs on supplies and acquisitions rather than the non-resident principal (div 57).
- **Principal and agent enter into agreement.** A registered principal and its registered agent may enter into a written agreement to treat specified supplies or acquisitions as if they were outside the agency arrangement. The effect of this is that the principal is treated as making supplies to, or acquisitions from, the agent and the agent is treated as making supplies to, or acquisitions from, third parties (sub-div 153-B).

Taxable supplies made by non-residents (div 83 *GSTA*)

Where a non-resident makes a taxable supply otherwise than through an enterprise that it carries on in the ITZ, it can enter into an agreement with the recipient of the supply (provided the recipient is registered or required to be registered) under which the recipient pays the GST on the supply rather than the supplier (s 83-5 *GSTA*). In such a case, the GST is 10% of the price of the supply (s 83-20).

Offshore intangible supplies by non-residents (sub-div 84-A *GSTA*)

To be a taxable supply, a supply must ordinarily be connected with the ITZ. However, a supply of something other than goods or real property (eg a supply of rights) that is not connected with ITZ is nevertheless treated as a taxable supply under s 84-5 if:

- the recipient of the supply acquires the thing supplied for the purpose of an enterprise that it carries on in ITZ (other than solely for a creditable purpose)
- the supply is for consideration, and
- the recipient is registered (or required to be registered). However, the supply is not a taxable supply to the extent that it is GST-free or input taxed.

Where a taxable supply arises under s 84-5, the recipient is liable to pay the GST in relation to the supply rather than the supplier (s 84-10). The GST payable is 10% of the price of the supply (s 84-12). The ITC to which the recipient may be entitled is calculated according to a special formula (s 84-13). Basically, this formula allows the recipient an ITC of 11/10th of the ITC it would have been entitled to, had the supply been a taxable supply under the normal rules.

Example A foreign computer company that does not carry on an enterprise in the ITZ grants a licence to use one of its programs for $1m to an Australian bank. The bank uses the program 80% for the purpose of making input taxed financial supplies and 20% for the purpose of making taxable supplies. The grant of the licence is not connected with the ITZ (s 9-25(5)) and would therefore ordinarily not be a taxable supply. However, as the bank acquires the licence for the purpose of an enterprise that it carries on in the ITZ and for a purpose that is not wholly creditable, the supply is treated as a taxable supply. Under the reverse charge rules in div 84, the bank must pay GST of $100,000 (ie $1m × 10%) (s 84-10). The bank is also entitled to an ITC of $22,000.

Inbound intangible consumer supplies (sub-div 84-B *GSTA*)

Subdivision 84-B operates from 1 July 2017 and deals with cross-border supplies of services and other intangibles made to Australian consumers. The subdivision is designed to ensure that GST is payable on things such as downloading of apps, games, movies and music from foreign websites in the same way that these things are subject to GST if they are downloaded from local websites. For this reason, it is sometimes referred to as the 'Netflix tax'.

Under sub-div 84-B, where an 'inbound intangible consumer supply' is made through an 'electronic distribution platform', the operator of the platform is treated as the supplier (s 84-55). It is therefore the operator of the platform (rather than the actual supplier) who will be liable for GST. Tax invoices and adjustment notes are not required to be issued for these supplies (s 84-50).

An 'inbound intangible consumer supply' is a supply of anything other than goods or real property where the recipient is an 'Australian consumer' and the thing is not done wholly in the ITZ or made wholly through an enterprise that the supplier carries on in the ITZ (s 84-65). An Australian consumer is, basically, an Australian resident that is either: (a) not registered for GST; or (b) registered for GST and does not acquire the thing supplied solely or partly for the purpose of an enterprise it carries on (s 9-25(7)) [7.6].

An 'electronic distribution platform' is a service (including a website or internet portal) that allows entities to make supplies available to end users and is delivered and made by means of electronic communication (s 84-70). However, a mere 'carriage service' or a service that simply provides access to a payment system is not an electronic distribution platform. This ensures that providers of ordinary telecommunications services or credit card services are not caught simply because a purchase occurs using their network.

Offshore supplies of low value goods (sub-div 84-C *GSTA*)

Subdivision 84-C operates from 1 July 2018 to ensure that offshore supplies of low value goods to consumers that are brought to the ITZ with the assistance of the supplier receive equivalent GST treatment to goods supplied within the ITZ.

An offshore supply of low value goods is connected with the ITZ if the recipient is a consumer of the supply (s 84-75(1)). An entity is a consumer if it: (a) is not registered for GST, or (b) is registered for GST and does not acquire the thing supplied solely or partly for the purpose of an enterprise it carries on in the ITZ (s 84-75(2)).

A supply of goods is a supply of low value goods if the customs value of the goods is $1,000 or less and the goods are not tobacco products or alcoholic beverages (s 84-79). The 'customs value' of goods is generally based on the value of the goods at the time of export under the *Customs Act 1901*. It excludes GST, transport and insurance costs.

A supply of low value goods is an offshore supply of low value goods if:

- the supply involves the goods being brought to the ITZ and the supplier delivers the goods into the ITZ, or procures, arranges or facilitates the delivery of the goods into the ITZ (s 84-77(1))
- the supply involves the goods being brought to the ITZ, is made through an electronic distribution platform and the operator of the platform delivers the goods into the ITZ, or procures, arranges or facilitates the delivery of the goods into the ITZ (s 84-77(2)), or
- the supply involves the goods being delivered to a place outside the ITZ and a 'redeliverer' (defined in s 84-77(4)) delivers the goods into the ITZ, or procures, arranges or facilitates the delivery of the goods into the ITZ (s 84-77(3)).

Generally speaking, if a supply of low value goods that is connected with the ITZ is made through an electronic distribution platform, the operator of the platform is treated as the supplier for GST purposes. Likewise, if a supply of low value goods is acquired by a consumer and brought to the ITZ with the assistance of a redeliverer, then the redeliverer is generally treated as the supplier for GST purposes.

Limited registration entities (div 146 *GSTA*)

Division 146 allows non-resident entities who make offshore supplies of low value goods that are connected with the ITZ because of sub-div 84-C to elect to be treated as 'limited registration entities'. Limited registration entities have simplified registration and reporting requirements. They cannot make creditable acquisitions or creditable importations and have quarterly tax periods regardless of their turnover.

[7.19] GST general anti-avoidance rules

Division 165 *GSTA* contains a set of general anti-avoidance rules designed to protect the integrity of the GST system. These rules have broad similarities with the general anti-avoidance rules in pt IVA *ITAA36* [37.3]. In essence, the object of div 165 is to deter entities from entering into 'schemes' (defined broadly in s 165-10) that reduce GST, increase refunds, or alter the time of payment of GST or refunds. An illustration of where div 165 applied is found in *FC of T v Unit Trend Services Pty Ltd* 2013 ATC ¶20-389.

Application

Basically, div 165 operates where:

- an entity (the 'avoider') gets a GST benefit from a scheme
- the GST benefit is not attributable to a choice expressly allowed by the legislation, and

- taking account the 12 matters set out in s 165-15, it is reasonable to conclude that either:
  - an entity that entered into or carried out the scheme, or part of the scheme, did so with the sole or dominant purpose of that entity or another entity getting a GST benefit from the scheme, or
  - the principal effect of the scheme, or part of the scheme, is that the avoider gets the GST benefit from the scheme directly or indirectly (s 165-5).

GST benefit

An entity gets a 'GST benefit' from a scheme if:

- the amount payable by the entity is less than (or payable later than), or
- the amount payable to the entity is more than (or payable earlier than),

it would be under the legislation if the scheme was not entered into (s 165-10).

Consequences

Where div 165 applies, the Commissioner can negate the GST benefit that the avoider gets from the scheme (s 165-40) and impose penalty tax on the avoider under sub-div 284-C of sch 1 *TAA* [41.2]. He also has the power to compensate another entity (the 'loser') that gets a 'GST disadvantage' from the scheme (s 165-45).

[7.20] Transitional arrangements

The *A New Tax System (Goods and Services Tax Transition) Act 1999* (Cth) contains special transitional rules relating to GST. Under these rules, GST is only charged to the extent that a supply or importation is made on or after 1 July 2000 and ITCs are only available to the extent that an acquisition or importation is made on or after 1 July 2000 (s 7).

Generally, the time at which something is supplied or acquired is when it is made available (in the case of goods or property) or performed (in the case of services and other things) (s 6). In *Central Equity Limited & Anor v FC of T* 2011 ATC ¶20-274, the Federal Court held that land sold under contracts entered into before 1 July 2000 was not 'made available' to the purchasers until settlement of the contracts. As settlement occurred after 1 July 2000, the sale of the land was subject to GST.

A special rule applies to rights granted on or after 2 December 1998 and before 1 July 2000. Such rights are deemed to be supplied on or after 1 July 2000 to the extent that they could reasonably be expected to be exercised after that date (s 11).

There is also a special rule for supplies made over periods that commence before 1 July 2000 but which terminate on or after that date. These 'progressive supplies' are deemed to be made continuously and uniformly over the relevant periods (s 12). Lease and hire arrangements that span 1 July 2000 can fall within this rule.

Supplies made after 1 July 2000 in respect of contracts that were made before 8 July 1999 (or before 2 December 1998 where the recipient was not entitled to a full ITC for the acquisition) were GST-free until the earlier of 1 July 2005 or a 'review opportunity' arose (ie an opportunity arose to change the consideration because of GST, or to conduct a general review, renegotiation or alteration of the consideration) (s 13). GST is payable on supplies made on or after 1 July 2005 under these contracts. However, special rules apply to supplies which would have been GST-free under s 13 if they were made immediately before 1 July 2005. Under these rules, GST liability is transferred from the supplier to the recipient if the recipient fails to accept an arbitrated offer to adjust the consideration to take account of GST (ss 15A to 15M).

Special transitional rules also apply to rights granted for life (s 14), funeral arrangements (s 15) and construction agreements (s 19).

[7.21] QUESTIONS

1. What are some of the differences between the GST and former sales tax regimes?
2. Explain the circumstances in which GST is charged and ITCs are available.
3. How is the 'net amount' for a tax period calculated? Why is this concept important?
4. Which entities use monthly tax periods and which entities use quarterly tax periods to account for GST? How do the GST payment rules operate?
5. In what circumstances must entities register for GST?
6. What is a 'taxable supply' and how is GST on a taxable supply calculated? Why is it important to distinguish between 'taxable supplies' and 'GST-free supplies' and 'input taxed supplies'? Provide some examples of these different kinds of supplies.
7. Discuss whether GST would apply to the following supplies:
   - the sale of fruit by a grocer
   - the sale of books by a newsagent
   - the sale of shares in a company
   - the supply of a meal at a restaurant
   - the provision of audit services by an accounting firm
   - the export of raw minerals by a mining company
   - the sale of a new residential home by a builder
   - the sale of a holiday home
   - the lease of a city office and a residential home
   - the provision of a medical consultation by a doctor
   - the sale of a business as a going concern
   - the supply of hospital care.
8. What is a 'creditable acquisition' and why is this concept important?
9. Discuss whether ITCs would be available for the following acquisitions:
   - the purchase of books by a bookshop from a publisher
   - the purchase of beef by a hamburger restaurant from a butcher
   - the purchase of a computer by a doctor for use in his surgery
   - the purchase of pipes by a plumber for use in repairing a sewer at a client's home
   - the purchase of a set of law reports by a solicitor
   - the purchase of shares and payment of brokerage fees by an investor
   - the purchase of a new home unit from a developer by a home-owner, and
   - the payment of fees to an electrician by a lessor of a residential property.
10. Mike owns a milk bar. The fridge he uses to store soft drinks broke down earlier this year. He contacted his friend Eric, who is an electrician, to repair the fridge. Eric spent two hours fixing the fridge. Eric's ordinary hourly rate is $110. However, instead of paying Eric $220 for his services, it was agreed that Mike would provide him with soft drinks worth $220. Assuming both parties are registered, discuss the GST implications of this arrangement. Would your answer differ if Eric repaired the fridge for free?

7

11. Betty is a baker who supplies cakes to restaurants. Andy is one of her customers who last year entered into a three-year contract with Betty for the supply of a certain number of fresh cakes each week for his restaurant. On 1 April this year, Andy decided to retire and he requested Betty to release him from his remaining obligations under the contract. Betty agreed to release Andy in consideration of him paying her $11,000. What are the GST implications of this transaction?
12. Explain the different ways entities attribute GST and ITCs under the cash and accruals basis of accounting. How does the GST law deal with deposits?
13. What are 'increasing adjustments' and 'decreasing adjustments' and why is it necessary to account for these under the GST system?
14. Fred purchased rocks from Barney for use in his gardening business for $11,000 (inclusive of GST). The rocks turned out to be of a poor quality and Fred sued Barney for damages. The matter was eventually settled by Barney paying Fred $4,400. How does GST apply to the settlement?
15. R Co is a large sports goods retailer. It purchases tennis racquets for $110 each from M Co, a large manufacturer of tennis products. R Co plans to sell the tennis racquets at a 200% mark-up to its customers. In January last year it purchased 100 racquets. However, in April, it discovered that 10 of these racquets had design faults and it returned them to the manufacturer and obtained a full refund. Discuss the GST consequences of this arrangement.
16. X Co is a resident company listed on the ASX. It has several shareholders. One of these shareholders is Trader Co (a large share-trading company that buys and sells many millions of dollars of shares each year). Another shareholder is Bill (an ordinary investor). Both of these shareholders use a broker, Busy Broker, to purchase and sell their shares in X Co. Busy Broker charges a 1% commission on any sale or purchase made. Last financial year, Trader Co and Bill each made one purchase and sale in X Co. Trader Co purchased 100,000 shares in X Co for $110,000 in January and sold the shares for $330,000 in February. Bill purchased 10,000 shares in X Co for $11,000 in January and sold the shares for $22,000 in April. Explain how the GST law applies to these transactions assuming only Trader Co and Busy Broker are registered for GST.
17. C Co is an Australian bank that brought an action against one of its customers for defaulting on a loan. The bank paid a law firm $88,000 to recover the debt from the customer. Discuss the GST implications of the transactions.
18. In what circumstances can the margin scheme be used? How is the GST calculated under the margin scheme? Is the acquirer entitled to any ITCs under the margin scheme?

PART C

INCOME TAX

8 INCOME TAX

[8.1] Introduction

Albert Einstein once stated that income tax is 'the hardest thing in the world to understand'. While this may be an overstatement, particularly to anyone who has tried to grapple with his theories of relativity, there is no denying that income tax is difficult and sometimes just as counterintuitive. The Australian income tax system, in particular, is considered to be among the most complex tax systems in the world. As Treasurer Peter Costello noted in the Howard Government's 1998 policy paper, *Tax Reform—Not a New Tax—A New Tax System* (at 6):

> The current tax system is unnecessarily complex. Income tax legislation has grown from about 120 pages to more than 7,000 as a result of 60 years of patching and filling. Over the past fifteen years there have been over 650 different tax policy changes announced.

Unfortunately, while consecutive governments have tried to simplify the tax laws, the income tax system continues to swell and 'grow new tentacles'. Although there have certainly been a number of positive efforts made at simplifying the tax laws over recent years, many reforms, while purporting to be simplification measures, have actually added a new level of complexity to the overall tax system. The introduction of the consolidation regime (discussed in Chapter 26) is a classic example of this phenomenon. Indeed, some cynics believe that the tax system displays a form of built-in entropy—the more the Government fiddles with it, the more complex it seems to become.

In order to properly understand how the income tax system works, it is necessary to adopt a structured approach that starts with the most basic elements of the regime. At the centre of every tax system are the statutes that govern their operation and contain the rules for calculating tax liability. This chapter introduces Australia's income tax legislation [8.2] and focuses on how a taxpayer's income tax liability is calculated [8.3]. It examines the concept of taxable income [8.4] and discusses how income tax interacts with GST and FBT [8.5]. The chapter outlines a number of special concepts relevant to calculating a taxpayer's tax liability [8.6] as well as the special rules that apply to SBEs [8.7].

It also examines the rates of income tax payable by different entities and focuses on the marginal tax rates and additional levies (eg Medicare levy ('ML') and Medicare levy surcharge ('MLS')) that apply to individuals [8.8]. Tax offsets [8.9], the Higher Education Loans Program ('HELP') [8.10] and the basic assessment, payment and collection rules [8.11] are also discussed. The chapter concludes with a detailed example showing the steps involved in calculating a taxpayer's income tax liability [8.12].

[8.2] Income tax legislation

Australia has a complex income tax legislative scheme. The most important income tax statutes are the *Income Tax Assessment Act 1936* (Cth) ('*ITAA36*') and the *Income Tax Assessment Act 1997* (Cth) ('*ITAA97*'). Together, these Acts determine the incidence of tax (ie who is taxed) and the tax base (ie what is taxed). The *ITAA36* and *ITAA97* are very long and complicated pieces of legislation that must be read in conjunction with other Acts, such as:

- the *Income Tax Act 1986* (Cth) ('*ITA*') (which imposes income tax)
- the *Income Tax Rates Act 1986* (Cth) ('*ITRA*') (which sets out the rates of income tax)
- the *Taxation Administration Act 1953* (Cth) ('*TAA*') (which contains provisions relating to the administration of income tax and other tax laws)
- the *Income Tax (Transitional Provisions) Act 1997* (Cth) ('*ITTPA*') (which deals with various transitional matters), and
- the *International Tax Agreements Act 1953* (Cth) (which incorporates Australia's international tax agreements with other countries).

The *ITAA36* and *ITAA97* also operate alongside the *Income Tax Assessment (1936 Act) Regulation 2015* (Cth) ('*ITAR15*') and the *Income Tax Assessment (1997 Act) Regulations 2021* (Cth) ('*ITAR21*'), while the *TAA* operates alongside the *Taxation Administration Regulations 2017* (Cth) ('*TAR17*').

Tax Law Improvement Project

For many years, the *ITAA36* was the only Assessment Act in existence. When originally introduced, this Act was just over 100 pages in length. However, over time, it had been amended on many occasions and had blown out in size. By the mid-1990s, the *ITAA36* had become 50 times longer, and was the largest single piece of Commonwealth legislation in existence. As a result of the constant barrage of amendments, what was once a relatively clear and logically structured piece of legislation had become cumbersome and difficult to navigate. The Act was frequently criticised for being framed in complex language and not being user-friendly. In *Case P132* 82 ATC 660, Dr Gerber colourfully remarked (at 662):

> I suspect that if a million monkeys were put in front of a million typewriters, by Wednesday one of them would come up with an improved version of the *Income Tax Assessment Act*.

To address the many problems with the *ITAA36*, the Labor Government established the Tax Law Improvement Project ('TLIP') in the mid-1990s. The aim of the TLIP was to redraft and simplify the *ITAA36*. Its underlying purpose was not to change the substance of the law, but rather to improve the way it was presented. Originally, it was intended that the TLIP team would rewrite the *ITAA36* by instalments over a period of about three years. However, this objective was not achieved. For reasons outlined below, only three instalments of the rewrite were enacted:

- the first instalment resulted in the enactment of the *ITAA97*, which commenced to operate from the 1997/98 income year
- the second instalment amended the *ITAA97* with general effect from the 1997/98 income year, and
- the third instalment amended the *ITAA97* with general effect from the 1998/99 income year.

The first instalment included a rewrite of the core provisions of the *ITAA36*, while the second and third instalments contained the rewrite of certain specific areas such as the trading stock provisions and the CGT provisions. Although many of the basic tax provisions and special rules are therefore now found in the *ITAA97*, whole portions of the tax law remain in the *ITAA36*. It is therefore necessary to work with two interrelating Acts that are written in completely different styles.

Style of the *ITAA97*

The fundamental objections to the *ITAA36* were that it was too long, complicated and difficult to navigate. To tackle these criticisms, the *ITAA97* adopts a new structure, plainer language, greater standardisation, a new numbering system and a revised layout:

- **Structure.** The *ITAA97* is arranged in a pyramid structure as illustrated by the diagram contained in s 2-5 which is set out below. As the diagram indicates, the general idea is that the Act starts with the central or core concepts at the top of the pyramid. Conceptually, the Act then progressively works its way through the general provisions to the more specialised topics further down the pyramid, with the base of the pyramid consisting of, among other things, the Dictionary definitions. The various layers of the pyramid correspond to specific chapters in the Act. Chapters of the Act are divided into Parts, which are broken down into Divisions and often Subdivisions, which are made up of the various sections.

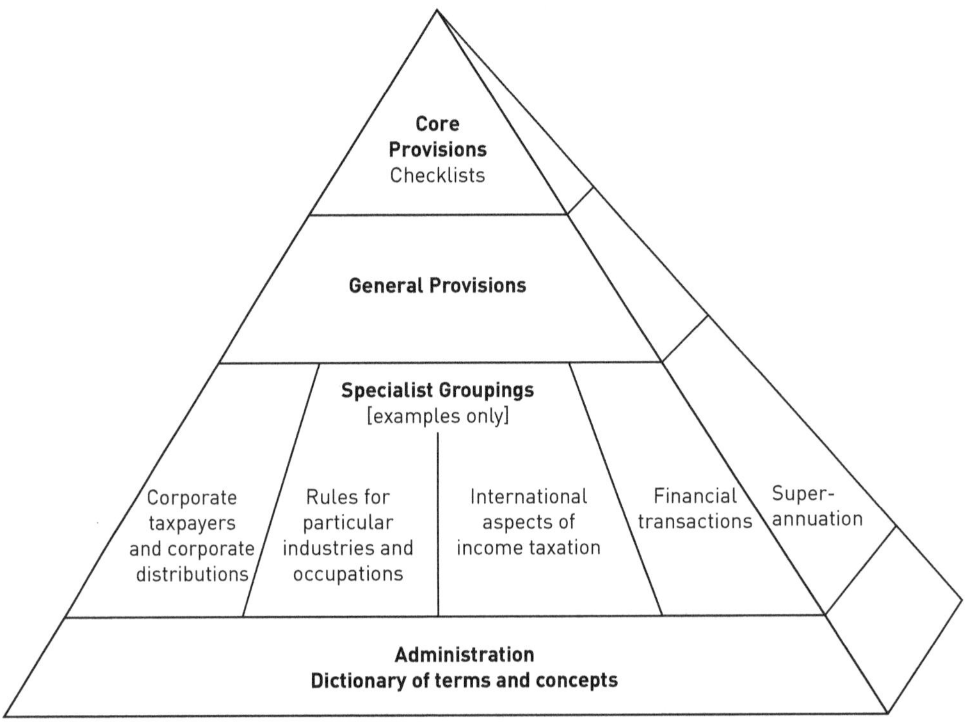

- **Language and standardisation.** In general, the *ITAA36* was drafted in a formal style whereas the *ITAA97* uses an informal style coupled with plainer and more direct language. For instance, throughout the Act the word 'you' is used instead of 'taxpayer'. The *ITAA97* also contains standardised common rules and definitions to avoid the duplication that often existed under the *ITAA36*.

- **Numbering.** The growth of the *ITAA36* completely overloaded its numbering system. For example, before the rewrite there were hundreds of sections between s 158 and s 161 resulting in cumbersome composite numbering (eg s 159GZZZZD). To provide space for future amendments, the *ITAA97* contains gaps in the sequence of numbering of Parts, Divisions, Subdivisions and sections. For example, s 15-15 is followed by s 15-20 (rather than s 15-16). The *ITAA97* also links the numbering of the various components of the Act. Thus, 'Part 3-5' refers to the fifth Part in Chapter 3.
- **Layout.** There are a number of unique layout features of the *ITAA97*. For instance, it includes Guides at the start of many divisions and subdivisions that provide an indication of the scope and nature of the operative provisions that follow. Guides often include a boxed theme statement (eg s 43-1) and sometimes include flowcharts, diagrams and other explanatory material (eg s 43-2). Although Guides actually form part of the Act, their effect is limited (s 950-150(2)). Further assistance is provided by cross-referencing notes and examples which accompany certain sections. Furthermore, to indicate that a term located in the body of the Act has been defined in the Dictionary in s 995-1, an asterisk (*) is placed in front of the term. The *ITAA97* also includes six alphabetical checklists covering taxable entities (div 9), assessable income (div 10), exempt income (sub-div 11-A), non-assessable non-exempt income (sub-div 11-B), deductions (div 12) and tax offsets (div 13). These checklists cross-refer to relevant provisions in the *ITAA36* and *ITAA97* and serve as useful indexes.

Continued operation of precedent and rulings

To reflect the fact that the *ITAA97* is essentially a rewrite of the *ITAA36*, a special provision has been inserted to ensure that mere differences in drafting style should not be taken to indicate differences in meaning. Section 1-3 *ITAA97* provides that if the *ITAA36* expressed 'an idea' in a particular form of words and the *ITAA97* 'appears to have expressed the same idea in a different form of words in order to use a clearer or simpler style', then 'the ideas are not to be taken to be different just because different forms of words are used'. This provision is designed to maintain, as far as appropriate, the wealth of judicial precedent that has developed over the years in interpreting the *ITAA36*. Furthermore, a note to s 1-3 indicates that special provision has also been made to ensure the continued operation of rulings issued by the Commissioner. Such rulings continue to have effect to the extent that the new law 'expresses the same ideas' as the old law (s 357-85 *TAA*).

TLIP superseded by ANTS reforms

The Labor Government was replaced with a Liberal–National Coalition Government in 1996. In its second term, the Coalition Government introduced its ANTS reforms [5.4]. These reforms resulted in significant policy changes being made to the income tax laws. As a consequence of these reforms, the TLIP rewrite (which was intended to be only cosmetic in nature) was derailed before it could be completed and absorbed into the greater tax reform agenda. Both the *ITAA36* and the *ITAA97* therefore remain in existence. Over the years, amendments have been made to both these Acts, with new regimes usually placed in the bourgeoning *ITAA97*. Although the *ITAA36* has been steadily shrinking, a substantial body of tax law remains in the *ITAA36* and the day that Australia will once again have a single Assessment Act is still some time away.

Coverage of the *ITAA36* and *ITAA97*

The *ITAA97* is the main Assessment Act. It is divided into chapters, which are broken down further into parts, divisions and subdivisions. The relevant chapters are as follows:

- **Chapter 1—Introduction and core provisions.** This Chapter contains a short preliminary part (pt 1-1) followed by a guide to the Act (pt 1-2) setting out how the legislation is arranged and structured. It contains the core provisions (pt 1-3) in the legislation, including the formula for working out how income tax is calculated. It deals with core concepts such as taxable income, assessable income and deductions. The Chapter concludes with a checklist (pt 1-4) that lists the provisions located elsewhere in the legislation relating to these Core concepts.

- **Chapter 2—Liability rules of general application.** This Chapter contains rules about assessable income (pt 2-1), deductibility (pt 2-5), capital allowances (pt 2-10), non-assessable income (pt 2-15), tax offsets (pt 2-20), trading stock (pt 2-25), employment-related payments (pt 2-40) and personal services income (pt 2-42).
- **Chapter 3—Specialist liability rules.** This Chapter contains rules about capital gains and losses (pt 3-1 and 3-3), corporate taxpayers and corporate distributions (pt 3-5), the imputation system (pt 3-6), financial transactions (pt 3-10), particular trusts (eg managed investment trusts) (pt 3-25), superannuation (pt 3-30), insurance business (pt 3-35), special taxpayers (eg small business entities and primary producers) (pt 3-45), roll-overs (pt 3-80), consolidated groups (pt 3-90) and value shifting (pt 3-95).
- **Chapter 4—International aspects of income tax.** This Chapter contains a range of international tax rules (pt 4-5), including: exemptions for foreign and Australian source income and gains (div 768 and 842), foreign income tax offset rules (div 770), foreign currency gains and losses rules (div 775) and thin capitalisation rules (div 820).
- **Chapter 5—Administration.** This Chapter contains record-keeping rules (pt 5-30) and various miscellaneous rules (pt 5-35).
- **Chapter 6—The Dictionary.** This Chapter contains interpretation rules and general rules relating to core concepts (such as foreign currency, entities, membership interests and debt and equity interests) (pt 6-1). It also contains a comprehensive dictionary with definitions of key terms (pt 6-5).

The *ITAA36* is much shorter than it used to be as many of its provisions have been rewritten and transferred into the *ITAA97*. The *ITAA36* is divided into Parts, which are broken down further into Divisions and Subdivisions. It also contains a number of schedules. The most important parts of the *ITAA36* are as follows:

- **Part I—Preliminary.** This Part deals with a range of preliminary matters and contains the general definition section.
- **Part II—Administration.** This Part gives the Commissioner of Taxation the role of administering the Act.
- **Part III—Liability to taxation.** This Part contains an eclectic mix of tax liability rules. For instance, it contains a number of miscellaneous assessment rules (eg relating to non-cash business benefits, annuities and dividends) and deduction rules (eg relating to pre-payments). It also contains the regimes for taxing certain entities, such as partnerships (div 5) and trusts (div 6), as well as the dividend, interest and royalty withholding tax rules (div 11A) and the share buy-back rules (div 16K).
- **Part IV—Returns and assessments.** This Part contains rules about tax returns and the making and amendment of assessments.
- **Part IVA—Schemes to reduce income tax.** This Part contains the important general anti-avoidance rule.
- **Part VA—Tax File Numbers.** This Part contains rules relating to TFNs.
- **Part VIIB—Medicare levy and surcharge.** This Part contains rules about the ML and MLS.
- **Part VIII—Miscellaneous.** This Part contains an array of miscellaneous rules relating to matters such as the appointment of public officers.

- **Part X—Controlled foreign companies.** This Part contains the controlled foreign companies ('CFC') attribution rules.
- **Schedules.** The end of the Act contains schedules dealing with special matters such as trust losses (sch 2F).

[8.3] Calculating income tax liability

Income tax is payable by a broad range of entities including individuals, companies and trustees of superannuation funds (ss 4-1, 9-1 *ITAA97*). Most entities are required to pay income tax on their 'taxable income' for the 'income year' (s 4-10).

Taxable income

An entity's taxable income for an income year is calculated under s 4-15 as follows:

$$\text{Taxable Income} = \text{Assessable Income} - \text{Deductions}$$

The respective elements that make up an entity's taxable income, namely assessable income and deductions, are themselves made up of further sub-elements, being 'ordinary income', 'statutory income', 'general deductions' and 'specific deductions'. These sub-elements are introduced at [8.4] and examined further in subsequent chapters.

Income year

For most entities, the income year is generally the same as the financial year (1 July to 30 June) (s 995-1 *ITAA97*). A company's income year is, however, the *previous* financial year (s 4-10(2) *ITAA97*).

The Commissioner may allow an entity to have an income year that does not end on 30 June (s 18 *ITAA36*). For instance, a company might seek a 'substituted accounting period' where balancing on 30 June is impractical because of its special business operations or because it is a subsidiary of a foreign company that might balance on a different date. The Commissioner's practice relating to substituted accounting periods is contained in PS LA 2007/21 which states (at [9]):

> The Commissioner considers that Parliament has required a taxpayer to obtain the Commissioner's leave to adopt a substituted accounting period because income tax, an annual tax, would be very difficult to administer if every taxpayer was able to nominate his or her own accounting period, with the result that no one period was normal or standard. Regard must be had to this legislative purpose. A decision to grant or withhold leave to adopt a substituted accounting period therefore involves a balancing of convenience to the taxpayer with the general public interest in efficient administration of the Act.

8

Income tax formula

Section 4-10(3) *ITAA97* contains the income tax formula. This formula lies at the heart of the income tax system and states that an entity's income tax liability for a financial year is calculated as follows:

$$\text{Income tax} = (\text{Taxable income} \times \text{Rate}) - \text{Tax offsets}$$

The elements and sub-elements of the income tax formula, and the places where they are discussed in this book, are set out in the following diagram:

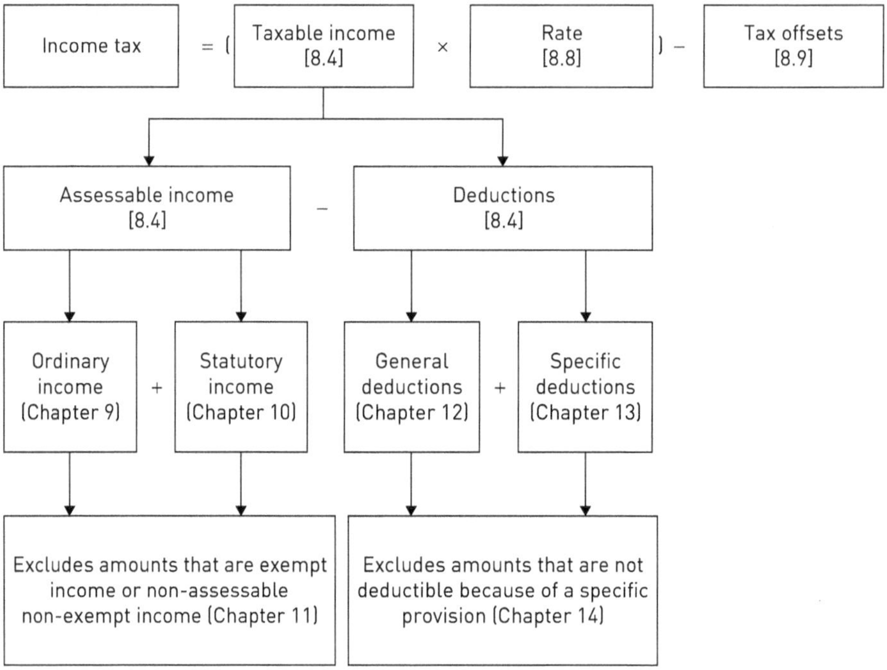

It is evident from the income tax formula that there are a number of steps involved in calculating an entity's income tax liability for an income year:

- The first step is to calculate the entity's taxable income for the year. As the diagram illustrates, an entity's taxable income for an income year is calculated by subtracting its deductions for the year from its assessable income for the year. These elements (and their respective sub-elements) are discussed at [8.4].
- The second step is to multiply the entity's taxable income for the year by the relevant tax rate to arrive at the entity's 'basic income tax liability'. The tax rates differ depending on the nature of the entity and are discussed at [8.8].
- The third step is to subtract the entity's tax offsets from its basic income tax liability. There are many different kinds of tax offsets which are provided for a range of policy reasons. Some of the main tax offsets are discussed at [8.9].

Additional levies payable by individuals

Certain entities must pay additional levies on top of their income tax (s 90-1 *TAA*). In particular, resident individuals are generally required to pay the ML and, if they are high-income earners and do not have private health insurance, they must also pay the MLS [8.8]. In addition, individuals who have outstanding HELP debts relating to their tertiary studies may be required to repay these debts under the income tax system [8.10]. An individual's overall tax liability is therefore calculated as follows:

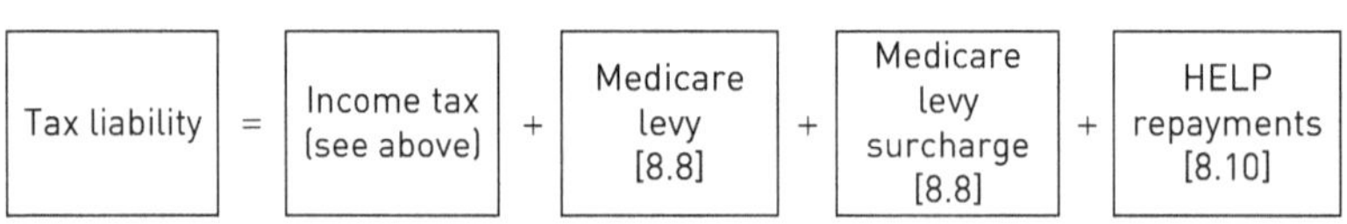

Tax losses

It is important to realise that entities do not always have taxable income for an income year. Some entities may instead have a 'tax loss' for the year. An entity has a tax loss for an income year where its deductions exceed its assessable income and net exempt income for the year (s 36-10 *ITAA97*) [13.15]. Income tax is not payable by an entity that has a tax loss. Instead, the tax loss can generally be carried forward and claimed as a deduction in calculating its taxable income in future income years (ss 36-15, 36-17 *ITAA97*). Special rules apply to companies [22.22] and trusts [24.9], which are generally required to satisfy certain tests to carry forward their tax losses.

[8.4] Taxable income

'Taxable income' is the central concept upon which income tax is levied. An entity's taxable income for an income year is calculated by subtracting its 'deductions' for the income year from its 'assessable income' for the income year (s 4-15 *ITAA97*).

> ***Example*** Mandy has $90,000 of assessable income and $20,000 of deductions during 2023/24. Her taxable income for the year is therefore $70,000.

The concepts of assessable income and deductions are fundamental to the operation of the income tax system and a large portion of the provisions in the *ITAA36* and *ITAA97* are concerned with these concepts. The following discussion introduces the concepts, which are then examined in detail throughout this book.

Assessable income

The concept of assessable income is dealt with in div 6 *ITAA97*. 'Assessable income' consists of 'ordinary income' and 'statutory income' but does not include ordinary income or statutory income that is 'exempt income' or 'non-assessable non-exempt income' (ss 6-1, 6-15 *ITAA97*).

> ***Example*** Claire has $50,000 of ordinary income, $40,000 of statutory income, $30,000 of exempt income and $20,000 of non-assessable non-exempt income during an income year. Her assessable income for the year is $90,000 (ie $50,000 + $40,000).

Ordinary income

Ordinary income is included in a taxpayer's assessable income under s 6-5 *ITAA97*. The term 'ordinary income' is not defined in the legislation and therefore takes on its common law meaning. There is an extensive body of case law dealing with the concept of ordinary income and the relevant cases are examined in detail in Chapter 9. Some common examples of ordinary income include:

- salary and wages
- ordinary business receipts (eg proceeds from the sale of trading stock)
- interest received on a bank deposit, and
- rent derived from an investment property.

Section 6-5 operates subject to jurisdictional rules that are based on the concepts of residence [30.2] and source [30.3]. According to these rules, Australian residents are required to include in assessable income ordinary income derived directly or indirectly from all sources (whether in or out of

Australia) (s 6-5(2)). Foreign residents, on the other hand, are only required to include in assessable income ordinary income derived directly or indirectly from Australian sources and other ordinary income that a provision includes in assessable income on some basis other than having an Australian source (s 6-5(3)).

Statutory income

Amounts that are not ordinary income but are, nevertheless, included in assessable income under specific provisions in the legislation are referred to as 'statutory income' (s 6-10(2) *ITAA97*). There are many statutory income provisions in the *ITAA36* and *ITAA97*. A full list of these provisions is located in div 10 *ITAA97*. Some of the statutory income provisions discussed in this book include:

- s 27H *ITAA36* (annuities) [10.2]
- s 15-2 *ITAA97* (allowances in relation to employment) [10.3]
- s 15-3 *ITAA97* (return to work payments) [10.3]
- s 15-5 *ITAA97* (accrued leave transfer payments) [10.3]
- s 15-10 *ITAA97* (bounties and subsidies) [10.3]
- s 15-15 *ITAA97* (profit-making undertakings) [10.3]
- s 15-20 *ITAA97* (royalties) [10.3]
- s 15-25 *ITAA97* (lease payments) [10.3]
- s 15-30 *ITAA97* (insurance or indemnity for loss of assessable income) [10.3]
- s 15-35 *ITAA97* (interest on early payments of tax) [10.3]
- s 15-40 *ITAA97* (mining, quarrying or prospecting information) [10.3]
- s 15-50 *ITAA97* (work in progress payments) [10.3]
- ss 20-35, 20-40 *ITAA97* (recoupments) [10.4]
- s 40-285 *ITAA97* (balancing adjustments) [15.3]
- s 70-35 *ITAA97* (trading stock) [16.2]
- ss 82-10, 82-65 *ITAA97* (employment termination payments) [20.2]
- ss 83-10, 83-80 *ITAA97* (unused annual and long service leave) [20.3]
- s 102-5 *ITAA97* (net capital gains) [17.2]
- s 207-20 *ITAA97* (franking credits) [22.8]
- ss 301-20, 301-25, 301-35, 301-40 *ITAA97* (superannuation benefits) [19.16]
- s 44 *ITAA36* (dividends) [22.5]
- s 92 *ITAA36* (partnership income) [23.3], and
- ss 97, 98, 99, 99A *ITAA36* (trust income) [24.5].

The statutory income rules also operate subject to jurisdictional rules. Australian residents are required to include in assessable income statutory income from all sources (whether in or out of Australia) (s 6-10(4) *ITAA97*). Foreign residents, on the other hand, are only required to include in assessable income statutory income from Australian sources and other statutory income that a provision includes in assessable income on some basis other than having an Australian source (s 6-10(5) *ITAA97*).

Exempt income and non-assessable non-exempt income

An amount of ordinary income or statutory income is 'exempt income' if it is made exempt by a provision in the *ITAA36*, *ITAA97* or another Commonwealth law (s 6-20(1) *ITAA97*). Likewise, an amount of ordinary income or statutory income is 'non-assessable non-exempt income' if it is stated to be not assessable income and not exempt income by a provision in the *ITAA36*, *ITAA97* or another Commonwealth law (s 6-23 *ITAA97*).

Subdivisions 11-A and 11-B *ITAA97* contain lists of the provisions in the *ITAA36* and *ITAA97* that treat amounts as exempt income and non-assessable non-exempt income. A number of these provisions are discussed in Chapter 11 and various other chapters. Examples of exempt income include the income of registered charities and public educational institutions (s 50-5 *ITAA97*) [11.4]. Examples of non-assessable non-exempt income include GST charged on a taxable supply (s 17-5 *ITAA97*) and income that constitutes a fringe benefit (s 23L *ITAA36*) [8.5].

Rule to prevent double assessment

In the absence of a special rule to the contrary, an amount might be included in a taxpayer's assessable income under more than one provision. For instance, an amount may be 'ordinary income' (assessable under s 6-5 *ITAA97* [9.1]), as well as statutory income such as an 'annuity' (assessable under s 27H *ITAA36* [10.2]). To prevent double taxation, s 6-25 *ITAA97* provides that an amount is included only once in a taxpayer's assessable income. Unless the contrary intention appears, a statutory income provision prevails over the ordinary income provision.

Deductions

The concept of 'deductions' is dealt with in div 8 *ITAA97*. Deductions fall into two categories: 'general deductions' and 'specific deductions'.

General deductions

The general deduction provision is contained in s 8-1 *ITAA97*. This provision allows taxpayers to deduct losses and outgoings to the extent that they are incurred in gaining or producing their assessable income or are necessarily incurred in carrying on a business for the purpose of gaining or producing their assessable income. Certain kinds of losses and outgoings (eg losses and outgoings of a capital or private nature) are not deductible under s 8-1. The general deduction provision is discussed in detail in Chapter 12.

Specific deductions

Specific deductions are available under a range of provisions (s 8-5 *ITAA97*). These provisions are listed in div 12 *ITAA97* and are discussed in Chapter 13 as well as certain other chapters. The specific deduction provisions are designed to cover particular kinds of expenditure and other amounts that might not otherwise be deductible under the general deduction provision (eg certain kinds of capital expenditure). Some of the specific deduction provisions discussed in this book include:

- s 25-5 *ITAA97* (tax-related expenses) [13.2]
- s 25-10 *ITAA97* (repairs) [13.3]
- ss 25-15, 25-20, 25-110 *ITAA97* (lease-related expenses) [13.4]
- s 25-25 *ITAA97* (borrowing expenses) [13.5]
- s 25-35 *ITAA97* (bad debts) [13.6]
- s 25-40 *ITAA97* (losses from profit-making undertakings or plans) [13.7]
- s 25-45 *ITAA97* (losses caused by theft) [13.8]
- s 25-50 *ITAA97* (pensions, gratuities and retiring allowances) [13.9]
- s 25-55 *ITAA97* (payments for membership of associations) [13.10]
- ss 25-60, 25-65 *ITAA97* (election expenses) [13.11]
- s 30-15 *ITAA97* (gifts) [13.13]
- ss 36-15, 36-17 *ITAA97* (tax losses) [13.15]
- s 40-25 *ITAA97* (capital allowances) [15.2]
- s 40-285 *ITAA97* (balancing adjustments) [15.3]

- s 40-880 *ITAA97* (blackhole expenditure) [15.6]
- s 43-10 *ITAA97* (capital works) [15.7], and
- s 70-35 *ITAA97* (trading stock) [16.4].

Limiting provisions

The general and specific deduction provisions operate subject to any provisions in the *ITAA36* and *ITAA97* that deny or limit deductions. These provisions are discussed in Chapter 14. For example, div 900 *ITAA97* denies deductions for certain expenditure that is not substantiated by written records [14.2] and div 32 *ITAA97* denies deductions for certain entertainment expenditure [14.4].

Rule to prevent double deductions

In the absence of a special rule to the contrary, it would technically be possible for an amount to be deductible under more than one provision. For instance, expenditure on repairs may satisfy the requirements of both the general deduction provision [12.1] and the specific deduction provision in s 25-10 *ITAA97* [13.3]. To prevent taxpayers obtaining the benefit of double deductions for the same loss or outgoing, s 8-10 *ITAA97* provides that if two or more provisions allow deductions in respect of the same amount (whether for the same income or different income years) the taxpayer can only obtain a deduction under the provision that is most appropriate.

Foreign currency translated into Australian currency

In calculating a taxpayer's taxable income, any amounts received or paid in foreign currency must be converted into Australian currency using the currency translation rules in div 960 *ITAA97* [35.2]. This ensures that a standard unit of account is used to calculate a taxpayer's assessable income and deductions.

[8.5] Reconciling income tax with GST and FBT

Before examining how the income tax system operates, it is appropriate to consider the relationship between income tax and other Commonwealth taxes examined in this book, especially GST (discussed in Chapter 7) and FBT (discussed in Chapter 18). In particular, it is important to be aware there are special reconciliation rules to ensure that income tax does not inappropriately overlap with these taxes. The reconciliation rules exclude certain amounts from a taxpayer's assessable income and deny deductions for certain kinds of expenditure. In essence, their aim is to prevent double taxation or double benefits from occurring.

GST reconciliation rules

The GST regime requires registered entities to charge GST on their taxable supplies [7.6] and allows them ITCs for their creditable acquisitions [7.8].

Under the general income tax rules, a taxpayer's assessable income would ordinarily include GST charged on taxable supplies and the taxpayer would ordinarily be entitled to deductions for ITCs on their creditable acquisitions. However, to ensure that the income tax and GST rules do not overlap, GST and ITCs are dealt with exclusively under the GST regime. This is achieved by removing GST and ITCs from the amounts that are included in a taxpayer's assessable income and deductions. The main provisions that do this are:

- s 17-5 *ITAA97*, which provides that an amount is non-assessable non-exempt income to the extent that it includes an amount relating to GST payable on a taxable supply [7.6], and
- s 27-5 *ITAA97*, which provides that a deduction is not allowable to the extent that a loss or outgoing includes an amount relating to an ITC [7.8].

Example C Co (a chocolate manufacturer) and S Co (a supermarket) are both registered for GST. C Co sells chocolates to S Co for $11,000 (inclusive of $1,000 GST). In calculating their assessable income and deductions from this transaction, C Co and S Co respectively ignore the GST charged on the supply and the ITC available on the acquisition. Accordingly, C Co is assessed on only $10,000 (rather than $11,000) and S Co is entitled to deduct only $10,000 (rather than $11,000).

It is also important to note that s 17-5 treats an increasing adjustment [7.10] that relates to a supply as non-assessable non-exempt income and s 27-5 denies a deduction for a loss or outgoing that relates to a decreasing adjustment [7.10].

Separate GST reconciliation rules apply under the capital allowance [15.2]–[15.3] and CGT [17.6]–[17.7] regimes.

FBT reconciliation rules

The FBT regime taxes employers on 'fringe benefits' provided to their employees [18.1]. Fringe benefits cover most forms of non-salary remuneration provided in respect of an employee's employment (eg the use of a car). Fringe benefits do not, however, include 'exempt benefits' (eg certain minor benefits) [18.3].

Under the general income tax rules, the receipt of a fringe benefit or an exempt benefit would ordinarily be assessable income in the hands of the employee under s 6-5 *ITAA97* as it would constitute ordinary income, being a reward for the employee's services [9.3]. To ensure that the income tax and FBT rules do not overlap and that employees are not also assessed on fringe benefits and exempt benefits, such benefits are dealt with exclusively under the FBT regime. This is achieved pursuant to:

- s 23L(1) *ITAA36*, which provides that income which is a fringe benefit is non-assessable non-exempt income, and
- s 23L(1A) *ITAA36*, which provides that income which is an exempt benefit (other than a benefit to which s 15-70 *ITAA97* applies [10.3]) is exempt income.

Example Bill employs Ben as a salesperson and provides him with a car fringe benefit. Bill is required to pay FBT in respect of the benefit. Ben does not, however, pay any income tax in respect of the benefit as it is non-assessable non-exempt income under s 23L(1).

[8.6] Special concepts and terms

Special concepts

Although taxable income [8.4] is the central concept on which income tax is levied, there are a number of other special concepts that are also relevant in calculating a taxpayer's tax liability. These concepts comprise various interconnected elements that often tie in with FBT and superannuation concepts discussed in Chapters 18 and 19. The key concepts and their relevance are outlined below:

- **Rebate income.** Rebate income is relevant for determining a taxpayer's entitlement to certain tax offsets [8.9]. A taxpayer's rebate income for an income year is the sum of their:
  - taxable income for the income year
  - reportable superannuation contributions for the income year
  - total net investment loss for the income year, and
  - adjusted fringe benefits total for the income year (s 6(1) *ITAA36*).

- **Adjusted taxable income.** Adjusted taxable income is relevant for determining a taxpayer's entitlement to certain tax offsets [8.9] as well as their entitlement to government superannuation co-contributions [19.8]. A taxpayer's adjusted taxable income for an income year is the sum of their:
  - taxable income for the income year
  - adjusted fringe benefits total for the income year
  - total net investment loss for the income year
  - reportable superannuation contributions for the income year
  - tax-free pension or benefit for the income year, and
  - exempt foreign income for the income year,

  less their deductible child maintenance expenditure for the income year (s 995-1 *ITAA97*; sch 3 *A New Tax System (Family Assistance) Act 1999* (Cth)).
- **Income for surcharge purposes.** Income for surcharge purposes is relevant for determining a taxpayer's entitlement to the private health insurance tax offset [8.9] and their liability to pay the MLS [8.8]. A taxpayer's income for surcharge purposes for an income year is the sum of their:
  - taxable income for the income year
  - reportable fringe benefits total for the income year
  - reportable superannuation contributions for the income year, and
  - total net investment loss for the income year,

  less the amount of any superannuation benefit for which they are eligible for a tax offset under s 301-20(2) *ITAA97* [19.16] (s 995-1 *ITAA97*).
- **Repayment income.** Repayment income is relevant for determining a taxpayer's liability to make HELP repayments [8.10]. A taxpayer's repayment income for an income year is the sum of their:
  - taxable income for the income year
  - total net investment loss for the income year
  - reportable fringe benefits total for the income year
  - exempt foreign income for the income year, and
  - reportable superannuation contributions for the income year (s 154-5 *Higher Education Support Act 2003* (Cth)).
- **Reportable employer superannuation contributions.** Reportable employer superannuation contributions are relevant for determining a taxpayer's reportable superannuation contributions and their entitlement to certain superannuation deductions and tax offsets [19.7]. A taxpayer's reportable employer superannuation contributions for an income year is basically their 'salary sacrifice' contributions for the year (ie the amount of employer superannuation contributions made for a taxpayer's benefit which the taxpayer had the capacity to influence). It does not include contributions required to be made by employers under the superannuation guarantee scheme [19.5] or contributions made pursuant to an 'industrial instrument' as defined in s 995-1 *ITAA97* (s 16-182 *TAA*).
- **Reportable superannuation contributions.** Reportable superannuation contributions are relevant for determining a taxpayer's rebate income, adjusted taxable income, income for surcharge purposes and repayment income. A person's reportable superannuation contributions for an income year is the sum of their reportable employer superannuation contributions for the year and their deductible personal superannuation contributions under sub-div 290-C *ITAA97* for the year [19.7] (s 995-1 *ITAA97*).

- **Reportable fringe benefits total.** Reportable fringe benefits total is relevant for determining an employee's income for surcharge purposes and repayment income. An employee's reportable fringe benefits total for an income year is the sum of their 'reportable fringe benefits amounts' for the income year. This amount must exceed $2,000 and is, basically, the taxable values of the fringe benefits (other than excluded benefits) provided to the employee for the FBT year ending on 31 March during the relevant income year multiplied by a gross-up factor of 1.8868 [18.4] (ss 5E, 5F, 135N, 135P *FBTAA*; s 995-1 *ITAA97*).
- **Adjusted fringe benefits total.** Adjusted fringe benefits total is relevant for determining an employee's rebate income and adjusted taxable income. An employee's adjusted fringe benefits total for an income year is basically the taxable values of the fringe benefits provided to the employee for the year. More specifically, it is the sum of their 's 57A employer fringe benefits total' and their 'other employer fringe benefits total' (s 6(1) *ITAA36*; sch 3 *A New Tax System (Family Assistance Act) 1999* (Cth); ss 57A, 135P, 135Q *FBTAA*).
- **Total net investment loss.** Total net investment loss is relevant for determining an individual's rebate income, adjusted taxable income, income for surcharge purposes and repayment income. An individual's net investment loss for an income year is the amount by which their deductions attributable to financial investments and rental property for the income year exceed their gross income from those activities for the year (s 995-1 *ITAA97*).

Special terms

In addition to the special concepts outlined above, the income tax legislation contains hundreds of special terms. The meanings of these are usually set out in the main definition sections in the legislation (eg s 6 *ITAA36*; s 995-1 *ITAA97*). These sections either define the terms outright or cross-refer to other provisions where they are defined. There are, however, some terms that do not have statutory definitions and therefore take their ordinary meanings. Three important terms that come up in many places in this book are 'associate', 'arm's length' and 'market value'.

Associate

The term 'associate' is defined widely in s 318 *ITAA36* (s 995-1 *ITAA97*). There are different definitions for associates of natural persons (s 318(1)), companies (s 318(2)), trustees (s 318(3)) and partnerships (s 318(4)). For example, an associate of a natural person includes the person's relative, the person's partner, a partnership in which the person is a partner, the trustee of a trust in which the person or their associates can benefit, and a company that is sufficiently influenced by, or in which a majority voting interest is held by, the person and/or their associates.

Arm's length

The legislation does not contain a general definition of the term 'arm's length'. Section 995-1 *ITAA97* nevertheless states that in determining whether parties deal at arm's length, any connection between them and any relevant circumstance should be considered. Broadly speaking, a transaction is considered to be at arm's length where its terms and conditions would have been agreed to by independent parties acting in their own commercial interests (TR 2002/2).

Market value

The legislation does not contain a general definition of the term 'market value', and this expression therefore usually takes its ordinary meaning. It is important to recognise that the concept of market value differs from other concepts such as 'price' or 'cost'. In *Spencer v Cth* (1907) 5 CLR 418, Issacs J said (at 441) that to arrive at the value of land:

> we have . . . to suppose it sold then, not by means of a forced sale, but by voluntary bargaining between the plaintiff and a purchaser, willing to trade, but neither of them so anxious to do so that he would overlook any ordinary business considerations.

A similar approach was adopted in relation to the value of shares in *Abrahams v FC of T* (1944) 70 CLR 23, where Williams J stated (at 29):

> the court should endeavour to ascertain . . . the price which a willing but not anxious vendor could reasonably expect to obtain and a hypothetical willing but not anxious purchaser could reasonably expect to have to pay for the shares if the vendor and purchaser had got together and agreed on a price in friendly negotiation.

According to the ATO website, market value is 'the estimated monetary worth of an asset on the open market at a particular time'. It is based on 'the most valuable use of the asset (which may be different to how it is currently used)' and 'the amount that a willing buyer and seller would agree to in an arm's length transaction'. The website refers to the ATO's *Market Valuation for Tax Purposes* guide, which adopts the International Valuation Standards Council's definition of market value, being the 'estimated amount for which an asset or liability should exchange on the valuation date between a willing buyer and a willing seller in an arm's length transaction, after proper marketing and where the parties had each acted knowledgeably, prudently and without compulsion'.

The guide outlines three internationally-defined approaches for valuing an asset:

- **The market approach.** This approach relies on comparing market prices in transactions involving comparable assets at the valuation date.
- **The income approach.** This approach estimates the risks and return of an asset based on the income or cashflows it can be expected to generate in the future.
- **The cost approach.** This approach involves estimating the market cost of replicating an asset in a similar condition as at the valuation date.

The guide states that the valuation approach must be reasonable, supported by evidence, suitable for tax purposes, replicable, well-documented and exclude buyer or seller transaction costs.

Importantly, an asset's market value is reduced by any ITCs to which the entity would be entitled assuming they had acquired the asset for a creditable purpose (s 960-405 *ITA97*). In addition, in working out the market value of a non-cash benefit, anything that would prevent or restrict its conversion to money is disregarded (s 960-410 *ITAA97*).

[8.7] Small business entities

The income tax laws contain a range of special rules that apply to certain entities. In particular, a number of special tax concessions apply to small business entities ('SBEs'). As a large portion of individuals, companies and trustees that operate businesses in Australia are SBEs, it is important to understand the nature of these entities and identify the tax concessions available to them.

Nature of an SBE

An entity is an SBE for an income year if it carries on business during the year and:

- its aggregated turnover for the previous year was less than $10m, and/or
- its aggregated turnover for the current year is likely to be less than $10m (s 328-110(1)).

However, an entity is not an SBE under the second requirement if it carried on a business in each of the two preceding years and its aggregated turnover for each of those years was $10m or more (s 328-110(3)).

An entity is also an SBE for an income year if it carries on business during the year and its aggregated turnover for the current year is actually less than $10m (s 328-110(4)).

Aggregated turnover

An entity's 'aggregated turnover' is generally based on the combined 'annual turnover' of the entity, its 'connected entities' and its 'affiliates' for the particular income year (ss 328-115(1), (2)). These terms have the following meanings:

- **Annual turnover.** An entity's 'annual turnover' is the total ordinary income (excluding GST) that it derives in the income year in the ordinary course of business (s 328-120).
- **Connected entity.** An entity is 'connected' with another entity if it controls the other entity or is controlled by the other entity, or they are under common control (s 328-125(1)). For this purpose:
  - An entity controls another entity that is not a discretionary trust if the entity and/or its affiliates own, or have the right to acquire the ownership of, interests in the other entity that carry between them the right to receive at least 40% of any distribution of the income or capital by the other entity. An entity also controls a company if the entity and/or its affiliates own, or have the right to acquire the ownership of, equity interests in the company that carry between them the right to exercise, or control the exercise of, at least 40% of the voting power in the company (s 328-125(2)).
  - An entity controls a discretionary trust if a trustee of the trust acts or could reasonably be expected to act in accordance with the directions of wishes of the entity, its affiliates, or the entity together with its affiliates (s 328-125(3)). For an example of where this applied, see *Gutteridge & Anor v FC of T* 2013 ATC ¶10-347. An entity (other than an exempt entity or deductible gift recipient) also controls a discretionary trust if, for any of the four previous income years, the trustee paid or applied for the benefit of the entity and/or its affiliates 40% of the income or capital paid or applied by the trustee for that year (ss 328-125(4), (5)).

  The Commissioner has a discretion to treat an entity as not controlling another entity in certain cases where the ownership interests are between 40% and 50% (s 328-125(6)).
- **Affiliate.** An 'affiliate' of an entity is an individual or company that acts, or could reasonably be expected to act, in accordance with the entity's directions, or in concert with the entity (s 328-130(1)). However, an individual or company is not an affiliate of an entity merely because of the nature of the business relationship the entity and the individual or company share (s 328-130(2)).

An entity's aggregated turnover excludes the amounts set out in s 328-115(3). For example, it excludes amounts derived by an entity from a connected entity or an affiliate. The reason for this is that aggregated turnover is calculated as if all the entities were a single entity, so transactions between them should be ignored.

Example Lucy runs a marketing business and earns income of $220,000 (including $20,000 GST) during the income year. She also earns $10,000 in wages working as a part-time employee tennis coach and $30,000 in rent from leasing a residential investment property. Lucy's annual turnover is $200,000 as only her business income (excluding GST) is taken into account. If Lucy also owns all the shares in X Co, she controls the company, which is a connected entity. If X Co derives income of $880,000 (including $80,000 GST) from a business that it carries on during the year, then its annual turnover is $800,000. Lucy's aggregated annual turnover will therefore be $1m ($200,000 + $800,000).

Tax concessions available to SBEs (and certain other businesses)

Prior to 1 July 2016, the aggregated turnover threshold for SBEs was $2m (instead of the current $10m). The $2m threshold has been retained for the small business CGT concessions [17.9]. There is also a special $5m threshold that applies to the small business income tax offset [8.9]. In addition, a variety of higher thresholds (eg $50m, $500m and $5 billion) have been introduced at various times to enable larger businesses to also benefit from certain concessions. The relevant concessions and thresholds are set out below.

Concession	Aggregated turnover threshold
Small business income tax offset (sub-div 328-F *ITAA97*) [8.9]	$5m
Instant asset write-off (sub-div 328-D *ITAA97*) [15.2]	$10m
Accelerated depreciation (sub-div 40-BA *ITTPA*) [15.2]	$500m
Temporary full expensing (sub-div 40-BB *ITTPA*) [15.2]	$5 billion
Small business pooling (sub-div 328-D *ITAA97*) [15.4]	$10m
Immediate deduction for start-up expenses (sub-div 40-I *ITAA97*) [15.6]	$50m
Simplified trading stock rules (sub-div 328-E *ITAA97*) [16.6]	$50m
Small business CGT concessions (div 152 *ITAA97*) [17.9]	$2m
Loss carry back tax offset (div 160 *ITAA97*) [22.23]	$5 billion
Skills and training boost (s 328-445 *ITTPA*) [27.8]	$50m
Technology investment boost (s 328-455 *ITTPA*) [27.8]	$50m
Small business restructure roll-over relief (div 152 *ITAA97*) [28.2]	$10m
Advance payment deduction concessions (s 82KZM *ITAA36*) [29.10]	$50m
Two-year amended assessment periods (s 170 *ITAA36*) [38.3]	$50m

[8.8] Income tax rates and levies payable by individuals

Section 5 of the *Income Tax Act 1986* (Cth) ('*ITA*') imposes income tax at the rates set out in the *Income Tax Rates Act 1986* (Cth) ('*ITRA*'). The *ITRA* prescribes different rates of tax for different entities. Some entities, like companies and trustees of superannuation funds, pay tax at flat rates. Companies generally pay tax at the rate of 30%, unless they are 'base rate entities', in which case they pay tax at the rate of 25% [22.3]. Trustees of complying superannuation funds generally pay tax at the rate of 15%, while trustees of non-complying superannuation funds generally pay tax at the rate of 45% [19.14].

Individuals, on the other hand, pay tax at rates that vary depending on the level of their taxable income and residency status. In addition, they may be required to pay certain levies. The following discussion focuses on the tax rates and levies payable by individuals.

Income tax rates payable by individuals

Individuals are required to pay income tax on their taxable income at 'marginal rates' that increase in steps (known as 'brackets') as their taxable income increases (s 12 and sch 7 *ITRA*). The progressive nature of the marginal rate structure reflects the principle of vertical equity (ie that persons who earn more income should pay more tax) [1.9].

Different marginal rates apply to 'residents' (pt I of sch 7 *ITRA*) and 'prescribed non-residents' (pt II of sch 7 *ITRA*). A resident is defined as a person who is not a prescribed non-resident (s 3(1) *ITRA*). A prescribed non-resident is a person who, at all times during the income year, was a non-resident (other than a person who, at any time during the year, was paid assessable pensions and benefits under the *Social Security Act 1991* (Cth) or the *Veterans' Entitlements Act 1986* (Cth)). The rules for determining whether an individual is a resident or non-resident are examined at [30.2].

Resident individuals benefit from a 'tax-free threshold' upon which they pay no tax. The tax-free threshold is $18,200 and is apportioned where an individual is a resident for only part of the income year (ss 16–20 *ITRA*). Resident individuals pay tax on so much of their taxable income that exceeds the tax-free threshold at marginal rates that range from 19% to 45%. Unlike residents, prescribed non-residents do not benefit from any tax-free threshold. Instead, they pay tax on their taxable income at marginal rates that range from 32.5% to 45%.

Since 1 July 2017, special marginal rates have applied to 'working holiday makers' (pt III of sch 7 *ITRA*). The special rates are colloquially referred to as the 'backpacker tax'. Working holiday makers do not benefit from a tax-free threshold and are subject to tax on their 'working holiday taxable income' at rates that range from 15% to 45%. A working holiday maker is a person who holds a subclass 417 (Working Holiday) or subclass 462 (Work and Holiday) visa or a special bridging visa allowing them to work in Australia (s 3A(1) *ITRA*). Their working holiday taxable income is, generally speaking, their assessable income derived from sources in Australia, less any deductions that relate to that income (s 3A(2) *ITRA*). The High Court recently held in *Addy v FC of T 2021* ATC ¶20-803 that the working holiday maker rates are not applicable where they contravene a 'non-discrimination article' contained in a DTA that Australia has entered into with another country [32.7].

Over the years, the marginal rates of tax payable by individuals have changed on many occasions. The following tables set out the marginal rates for the 2020/21 and subsequent income years. Note that while the tax rates for 2020/21 to 2023/24 have remained the same, new rates will apply for 2024/25 and subsequent income years.

2020/21 to 2023/24 individual tax rates					
Residents		**Non-residents**		**Working holiday makers**	
Taxable income	**Tax**	**Taxable income**	**Tax**	**Taxable income**	**Tax**
0 to $18,200	Nil	0 to $120,000	32.5% on excess over 0	0 to $45,000	15% on excess over 0
$18,201 to $45,000	19% on excess over $18,200	$120,001 to $180,000	$39,000 plus 37% on excess over $120,000	$45,000 to $120,000	$6,750 plus 32.5% on excess over $45,000
$45,001 to $120,000	$5,092 plus 32.5% on excess over $45,000	$180,001 and over	$61,200 plus 45% on excess over $180,000	$120,001 to $180,000	$31,125 plus 37% on excess over $120,000
$120,001 to $180,000	$29,467 plus 37% on excess over $120,000			$180,000 and over	$53,325 plus 45% on excess over $180,000
$180,001 and over	$51,667 plus 45% on excess over $180,000				

2024/25 and later income years individual tax rates					
Residents		**Non-residents**		**Working holiday makers**	
Taxable income	**Tax**	**Taxable income**	**Tax**	**Taxable income**	**Tax**
0 to $18,200	Nil	0 to $200,000	30% on excess over 0	0 to $45,000	15% on excess over 0
$18,201 to $45,000	19% on excess over $18,200	$200,001 and over	$60,000 plus 45% on excess over $200,000	$45,001 to $200,000	$6,750 plus 30% on excess over $45,000
$45,001 to $200,000	$5,092 plus 30% on excess over $45,000			$200,001 and over	$53,250 plus 45% on excess over $200,000
$200,001 and over	$51,592 plus 45% on excess over $200,000				

Example Betty (a resident) and Theo (a non-resident) each earn $200,000 of taxable income in 2023/24. Their income tax liabilities for 2023/24 are calculated as follows:

Resident individual (Betty)

Income tax at 0% on the first $18,200 of taxable income	Nil
Income tax at 19% on the next $26,800 (ie $45,000 – $18,200) of taxable income	$5,092
Income tax at 32.5% on the next $75,000 (ie $120,000 – $45,000) of taxable income	$24,375
Income tax at 37% on the next $60,000 (ie $180,000 – $120,000) of taxable income	$22,200
Income tax at 45% on the next $20,000 (ie $200,000 – $180,000) of taxable income	$9,000
Total income tax on taxable income of $200,000	$60,667

Prescribed non-resident individual (Theo)

Income tax at 32.5% on the first $120,000 of taxable income	$39,000
Income tax at 37% on the next $60,000 (ie $180,000 – $120,000) of taxable income	$22,200
Income tax at 45% on the next $20,000 (ie $200,000 – $180,000) of taxable income	$9,000
Total income tax on taxable income of $200,000	$70,200

Additional levies payable by individuals

In addition to paying income tax at the marginal rates set out above, resident individuals are also generally required to pay the ML. Resident individuals on high incomes who do not have private health insurance are also liable to pay the MLS.

Medicare levy

The ML was introduced in 1983 to help fund Medicare (Australia's public health care system). The ML is payable by resident individuals (s 251S *ITAA36*; s 5 *MLA*). It is not payable by prescribed persons as defined in s 251U *ITAA36* (eg defence force members). It is also not payable by non-resident individuals or other entities such as companies and trustees of superannuation funds.

Example In the previous example, as Betty is a resident, she would be required to pay the ML, but as Theo is a non-resident, he would not be required to pay the ML.

From the 2014/15 income year, the ML is imposed at the rate of 2% on a taxpayer's taxable income (s 6 *MLA*). It was previously imposed at the rate of 1.5% and was increased by 0.5% to fund the National Disability Insurance Scheme.

To assist lower income earners, the ML is not payable where a taxpayer's taxable income is below certain thresholds (ss 7 to 9 *MLA*). The thresholds for 2023/24 were not available at the time of writing this chapter. The thresholds for 2022/23 are set out in the table below and depend on whether the taxpayer is single or part of a family and whether they qualify for the seniors and pensioners tax offset ('SAPTO') [8.9]. The family income threshold is based on the combined income of the taxpayer and their spouse. It increases by $3,760 for each child or student dependant. The ML also operates subject to phase-in rules where a taxpayer's taxable income falls between certain amounts. Where these rules apply, the ML is 10% of the excess of the taxpayer's taxable income over the threshold amount.

Medicare levy thresholds and phase-in limits for 2022/23			
Taxpayer	**Threshold**	**Phase-in limits**	**Full levy of 2%**
Singles	$24,276	$24,277 to $30,345	$30,346
Families (no children)	$40,939	$40,940 to $51,173	$51,174
Families (1 child)	$44,699	$44,700 to $55,873	$55,874
Families (2 children)	$48,459	$48,460 to $60,573	$60,574
Families (3 children)	$52,219	$52,220 to $65,273	$65,274
Singles eligible for SAPTO	$38,365	$38,366 to $47,956	$47,957
Families eligible for the SAPTO	$53,406	$53,407 to $66,757	$66,758

Example Curly is a single resident with taxable income of $100,000 in 2022/23. As his taxable income is above the full levy figure of $30,346, his ML for the year is $2,000 (ie $100,000 × 2%).

Larry is a single resident with taxable income of $20,000 in 2022/23. As his taxable income is below the threshold amount of $24,276, his ML for the year is nil.

Moe is a single resident with taxable income of $25,276 in 2022/23. As his taxable income is above the threshold amount of $24,276, but below the phase-in limit of $30,346, his ML for the year is $100 (ie [$25,276 – $24,276] × 10%).

Medicare levy surcharge

The MLS is payable in addition to the ML and was introduced to encourage resident individuals to take out private health insurance to reduce the burden on the Medicare system. The MLS only applies if the individual's or family's income for surcharge purposes [8.6] exceed specified thresholds and they are not covered by private health insurance for any part of the year. Taxpayers who have appropriate levels of health insurance throughout the year are therefore not liable to pay the MLS.

The MLS is payable on a taxpayer's taxable income and reportable fringe benefits total for the income year [8.6]. It is pro-rated where the person is covered by private health insurance for part of the year. It is also adjusted in certain cases (eg where the person is a member of a couple for only part of the year) (ss 8B to 8D *MLA*; ss 10 to 16 *MLSFBA*).

The MLS is imposed at the rate of either 1%, 1.25% or 1.5%, depending on the individual's or family's income for surcharge purposes [8.6]. The MLS rates for 2023/24 are set out below.

Medicare levy surcharge rates for 2023/24					
Income for surcharge purposes	Singles	$0 to $93,000	$93,001 to $108,000	$108,001 to $144,000	More than $144,000
	Families*	$0 to $186,000	$186,001 to $216,000	$216,001 to $288,000	More than $288,000
Rate		0%	1%	1.25%	1.5%

* The income for surcharge thresholds for families are increased by $1,500 for each additional dependant child after the first child.

Example Greta is a single resident who does not have any private health insurance during 2023/24. She has taxable income of $200,000, a reportable fringe benefits total of $10,000 and reportable superannuation contributions of $20,000. Her income for surcharge purposes is therefore $230,000. She is liable to pay the MLS on her taxable income and reportable fringe benefits total, amounting to $210,000. Her MLS is therefore $3,150 (ie $210,000 × 1.5%).

Some points about income tax rates and levies

The preceding discussion showed that individuals pay income tax on their taxable income at marginal rates (plus the ML and MLS where applicable). Conceptually, a taxpayer's marginal tax rates should be distinguished from their:

- 'average tax rate' (which is calculated by dividing the taxpayer's total tax liability by their taxable income), and
- 'effective tax rate' (which is calculated by dividing the taxpayer's total tax liability by their 'economic income', which includes their exempt income).

Example Tom is an Australian resident who has private health insurance. During 2023/24, he has taxable income of $130,000 as well as exempt income of $20,000. Tom must pay income tax on his taxable income (which does not include his exempt income) at the following marginal rates:

- 0% on the first $18,200 of his taxable income
- 19% on his taxable income above $18,200 up to $45,000 (ie 26,800 × 19% = $5,092)
- 32.5% on his taxable income above $45,000 up to $120,000 (ie $75,000 × 32.5% = $24,375), and
- 37% on his taxable income above $120,000 up to $130,000 (ie $10,000 × 37% = $3,700).

Tom's income tax liability is therefore $33,167 (ie $5,092 + $24,375 + $3,700). In addition, he must also pay the ML at the flat rate of 2% on his taxable income (ie $130,000 × 2% = $2,600). Tom's total tax liability is therefore $35,767 (ie $33,167 + $2,600).

Tom's marginal tax rates should be contrasted with his:

- average tax rate of 27.513% (which is calculated by dividing his total tax liability by his taxable income (ie $35,767/$130,000)), and
- effective tax rate of 23.844% (which is calculated by dividing his total tax liability by his economic income, which includes both his taxable income and exempt income (ie $35,767/$150,000)).

The following additional points should also be noted:

- **Top tax rate.** The 'top tax rate' payable by resident individuals in Australia is effectively 47% (ie 45% plus 2% ML). This rate is even higher if an individual is also required to pay the MLS (ie it can be as high as 48.5%). As will be discussed in subsequent chapters, various other taxes, such as FBT [18.2], certain superannuation taxes [19.9] and certain withholding taxes [39.4] are also based on the 47% top tax rate. Interestingly, Australia's top tax rate is much higher than the top tax rates in several neighbouring countries, such as New Zealand (39%), Malaysia (30%) and Singapore (22%). It is also much higher than the top tax rate in the United States (37%).
- **Bracket creep.** Since the marginal tax rates payable by individuals are not automatically indexed for inflation, 'bracket creep' can easily occur. Bracket creep arises where, as a result of a person's income increasing from year to year due to inflation, they are pushed into higher marginal tax rate brackets. The result is that while the person's income may have kept pace with inflation, their overall spending power has actually decreased because they are required to pay more tax.
- **Fluctuating levels of taxable income.** As income tax is an annual tax, individuals with fluctuating levels of taxable income from year to year can be pushed into higher marginal tax rate brackets in 'good years' but do not get any adjustment for this in 'bad years'. This results in them paying greater overall tax than taxpayers who have steady levels of taxable income. For example, a taxpayer that has $250,000 of taxable income in Year 1 and Year 3 but only $50,000 of taxable income in Year 2 and 4, will pay more tax over the four years than a taxpayer that earns $150,000 over each of those years, even though their average annual taxable income over the period is the same. To address this issue, special averaging rules apply to certain taxpayers, namely primary producers (eg farmers) [25.2] and special professionals (eg authors, inventors, performing artists and sportspersons) [25.3].
- **Income splitting.** Individuals who are subject to high tax rates may seek to minimise their tax liabilities by splitting income with their associates (eg family members) or earning income through associated entities (eg companies) which pay tax at lower rates. Taxpayers should, however, be careful when considering these strategies as they may not always be tax-effective. Splitting income with minors (ie children under 18) can be particularly problematic as penalty rates of tax apply to their 'eligible taxable income' [25.4]. Income splitting arrangements may also be caught by a number of specific anti-avoidance provisions (discussed in Chapter 36) or fall within the operation of the general anti-avoidance rule in pt IVA *ITAA36* (discussed in Chapter 37).
- **Income tax liability reduced by LITO.** While individuals pay tax at the standard marginal rates outlined above, their tax liability is reduced by tax offsets [8.9]. In particular, it is important to be aware that resident individuals on low incomes can benefit from the low-income tax offset ('LITO'), which reduces their tax liability by up to $700.

[8.9] Tax offsets

Tax offsets (sometimes also referred to as 'rebates' or 'credits') are an import element of the tax formula [8.3]. Tax offsets are subtracted from the income tax payable on a taxpayer's taxable income (s 4-10(3) *ITAA97*). Tax offsets are therefore quite different from deductions, which are subtracted from a taxpayer's assessable income to calculate their taxable income. In other words, while a $1 tax offset reduces a taxpayer's tax payable by an amount of $1, a $1 deduction only reduces a taxpayer's tax payable by an amount of $1 multiplied by the taxpayer's tax rate.

Types of tax offsets

The *ITAA36* and *ITAA97* contain many different types of tax offsets. A list of these tax offsets is contained in s 13-1 *ITAA97*. Many tax offsets have complex eligibility criteria and operate subject to exclusions and phase-out rules. Great care must therefore be taken in working out whether a person qualifies for a tax offset and in calculating the amount of the tax offset.

In general, tax offsets can only reduce a taxpayer's basic income tax liability. This means that any excess tax offsets are usually not refundable and cannot be applied to reduce a taxpayer's other tax liabilities (eg GST, FBT, ML or MLS) (s 160AD *ITAA36*). Refunds may nevertheless be available for tax offsets that fall within the special 'refundable tax offset rules' in div 67 *ITAA97*. Some of the main refundable tax offsets are:

- the private health insurance tax offset (sub-div 61-G *ITAA97*) [8.9]
- the franking credit tax offset for individuals and complying superannuation entities (div 207 *ITAA97*) [22.8]
- the R&D tax offset for entities with aggregated turnover under $20m (div 355 *ITAA97*) [27.5], and
- the film production tax offset (div 376 *ITAA97*) [27.6].

The difference between refundable and non-refundable tax offsets is illustrated below.

Example Fred is a resident who has taxable income of $180,000 in 2022/23. His income tax liability is therefore $51,667 and his ML liability is $3,600 (ie $180,000 × 2%).

If Fred is entitled to a non-refundable tax offset of $60,000, he would pay no income tax, but would still be required to pay the ML of $3,600.

If, however, Fred was entitled to a refundable tax offset of $60,000, he would pay no income tax or ML and would be entitled to a tax refund calculated as follows:

$$\$4{,}733 = \$60{,}000 - (\$51{,}667 + \$3{,}600)$$

Although most tax offsets are non-refundable, the excess unused amount of certain non-refundable tax offsets may be carried forward into later income years under special rules in div 65 *ITAA97*. The kinds of tax offsets that can be carried forward are listed in div 63 *ITAA97* and include:

- the early-stage investor tax offset (sub-div 360-A *ITAA97*) [27.2]
- the ESVCLP tax offset (sub-div 61-P *ITAA97*) [27.4], and
- the R&D tax offset for entities with turnover of $20m or more (div 355 *ITAA97*) [27.5].

Where a taxpayer is entitled to more than one tax offset for an income year, the tax offsets are applied in the order set out in the table in s 63-10 *ITAA97*.

The following discussion outlines some common tax offsets and divides them into four groups.

1. Concessional tax offsets

A large number of tax offsets are concessional in nature. These tax offsets are usually linked to the taxpayer's personal and family circumstances and are often means-tested. Some of the main concessional tax offsets are outlined below.

Low-income tax offset

In order to provide targeted tax relief to low-income earners, a non-refundable low-income tax offset ('LITO') is provided to resident individuals with taxable income up to $66,667 (s 61-110 *ITAA97*). For the 2020/21 and subsequent income years, the LITO is up to $700, but is phased-out where the taxpayer's taxable income exceeds $37,500. The following table sets out how the LITO is calculated (s 61-115 *ITAA97*):

LITO for the 2020/21 and subsequent income years	
Taxable income	**LITO**
Not more than $37,500	$700
Exceeds $37,500 but does not exceed $45,000	$700 less 5% of the excess over $37,500
Exceeds $45,000 but does not exceed $66,667	$325 less 1.5% of the excess over $45,000

Example Bill is a resident who has $40,000 of taxable income in 2022/23. He is eligible for a LITO calculated as follows:

$$\$575 = \$700 - [(\$40,000 - \$37,500) \times 5\%]$$

Previously, in addition to being entitled to the LITO, resident individuals with taxable income of up to $126,000 were also entitled to a non-refundable low- and middle-income tax offset ('LMITO') (former s 61-105 *ITAA97*). The LMITO was available from 2018/19 to 2021/22 and was calculated as follows (former s 61-107 *ITAA97*):

Former LMITO for the 2018/19 to 2021/22 income years		
Taxable income	**LMITO for 2018/19 to 2020/21**	**LMITO for 2021/22**
Not more than $37,000	$255	$675
Exceeds $37,000 but does not exceed $48,000	$255 plus 7.5% of the excess over $37,000	$675 plus 7.5% of the excess over $37,000
Exceeds $48,000 but does not exceed $90,000	$1,080	$1,500
Exceeds $90,000 but does not exceed $126,000	$1,080 less 3% of the excess over $90,000	$1,500 less 3% of the excess over $90,000

Dependant invalid and carer tax offset

8

Subdivision 61-A *ITAA97* contains the non-refundable dependant invalid and carer tax offset ('DICTO'). This tax offset assists taxpayers maintain certain dependants who are genuinely unable to work because of invalidity, or because of their care obligations (s 61-5).

A taxpayer may be entitled to the DICTO for an income year if they contribute to the maintenance of another individual who is: their spouse; their parent or spouse's parent; or their child, brother or sister or spouse's brother or sister (who is at least 16 years of age) (s 61-10(1)). The other individual must be an Australian resident (unless they are the taxpayer's spouse or child, in which case they will qualify if the taxpayer has a domicile in Australia). They must also meet certain requirements to ensure the tax offset is only available where the other individual is genuinely unable to work due to invalidity or carer obligations. The requirements will be satisfied if the individual is paid a disability support pension or a special needs disability support pension or an invalidity service pension (s 61-10(2)). The requirements will also be satisfied if the individual is the taxpayer's parent, or the taxpayer's spouse's parent, and is being paid a carer allowance or carer payment in relation to provision of care to the taxpayer's child, brother or sister, or the brother or sister of their spouse, who is at least 16 years of age (s 61-10(3)).

Generally, a taxpayer can only claim the DICTO if the combined adjusted taxable income of the taxpayer and their spouse is below a prescribed limit ($104,432 for 2022/23) (s 61-20).

However, if the taxpayer claims the DICTO for a spouse, only the taxpayer's adjusted taxable income is taken into account.

The maximum tax offset to which a taxpayer is entitled in respect of another individual is $2,943 (for 2022/23) and $3,152 (for 2023/24) (s 61-30). This amount is reduced by $1 for every $4 by which the dependant's adjusted taxable income exceeds $282 (s 61-45). The tax offset therefore completely cuts out where the dependant's adjusted taxable income for the year reaches $12,054 (for 2022/23) and $12,890 (for 2023/24).

A taxpayer may receive more than one tax offset provided each amount relates to a different individual (s 61-10(5)). The tax offset is reduced in certain cases, such as where a taxpayer has shared care arrangements for a child (s 61-35), or where the taxpayer contributes to the maintenance of the other individual for only part of the year (s 61-40).

Example Fred and Ginger are married residents. Ginger does not work during 2023/24 as she cares for her invalid brother who receives a disability support pension. Fred's adjusted taxable income is $90,000 and Ginger's adjusted taxable income is $4,282. Fred can claim the DICTO in respect of Ginger. The maximum tax offset of $3,152 is reduced by $1 for every $4 by which Ginger's adjusted taxable income exceeds $282. This means it is reduced by $1,000 (ie ($4,282 – $282)/4). Fred's tax offset in respect of Ginger is therefore $2,152 (ie $3,152 – $1,000).

Private health insurance tax offset

Residents who take out a complying private health insurance policy with a registered health insurer may be entitled to a refundable private health insurance tax offset under sub-div 61-G *ITAA97*. The amount of the tax offset is a percentage of the premium paid for the policy. It can be claimed directly from the insurer by way of a reduction in the premium or from the ATO when lodging a tax return.

The rate of tax offset is based on an age-based tier structure designed to ensure that those with a greater capacity to pay for private health insurance receive less government support. The tier structure depends on the individual's or family's income for surcharge purposes [8.6] and ties in with the MLS thresholds [8.8]. The rates are normally adjusted in April each year. The current rates are set out below.

Private health insurance tax offset rates for 2023/24					
Income for surcharge purposes	Singles	Up to $93,000	$93,001 to $108,000	$108,001 to $144,000	More than $144,000
	Families*	Up to $186,000	$186,001 to $216,000	$216,001 to $288,000	More than $288,000
Age of single person or oldest person in a family	Less than 65	24.608%	16.405%	8.202%	0%
	65 to less than 70	28.710%	20.507%	12.303%	0%
	70 and above	32.812%	24.608%	16.405%	0%

* The income for surcharge purposes thresholds for families are increased by $1,500 for each additional child dependant after the first child.

Example Rebecca is a 40-year-old single resident who paid $2,000 for private health insurance in April 2023. If her income for surcharge purposes was $100,000, she would be entitled to a refundable tax offset of $328.10 (ie $2,000 ×16.405%). However, if her income for surcharge purposes was only $70,000, she would be entitled to a refundable tax offset of $492.16 (ie $2,000 × 24.608%).

Zone tax offset

Individuals who are residents of prescribed remote areas of Australia may be eligible for a non-refundable zone tax offset under s 79A *ITAA36*. The tax offset compensates taxpayers for the higher costs of living in isolated areas. There are two zones: Zone A (more harshly affected areas) and Zone B (less harshly affected areas). A higher tax offset is available for individuals who are residents of Zone A. Higher tax offsets apply for persons who are residents of 'special areas' within these zones. A person is taken to be a resident of a particular area if they have their 'usual place of residence' in the area for more than half of the income year. This means, for example, that fly-in fly-out workers whose usual place of residence is outside a zone cannot claim the tax offset even if they were in the zone for more than half of the year.

Defence force tax offset

Australian Defence Force personnel serving in specified overseas locations may be eligible for a non-refundable overseas defence force tax offset under s 79B *ITAA36*.

Seniors and pensioners tax offset

Individuals who receive certain social security pensions, such as the age pension and disability support pension may be entitled to the non-refundable seniors and pensioners tax offset ('SAPTO') under s 160AAAA *ITAA36*. The SAPTO is means-tested and operates subject to phase-out rules that are based on the level of the individual's rebate income [8.6]. Different figures apply to a single person, a partner of a couple, and a partner of a couple who have to live apart due to illness. The maximum tax offset for 2023/24 is set out in the table below. It is reduced by 12.5 cents for each dollar that the individual's rebate income exceeds the shading-out threshold and is completely phased out when their rebate income reaches the cut-out threshold. Although the SAPTO is non-refundable, individuals may, in certain cases, transfer excess tax offsets to their spouses (regs 9 to 12 *ITAR15*).

SAPTO for 2023/24 income year			
	Maximum tax offset	**Shading-out threshold**	**Cut-out threshold**
Single person	$2,230	$32,279	$50,119
Partner of a couple	$1,602	$28,974	$41,790
Partner of an illness separated couple	$2,040	$31,279	$47,599

Example Amy is a single, aged pensioner. In 2023/24, her rebate income is $30,000. As this is below the shading-out threshold of $32,279, she is entitled to the maximum SAPTO of $2,230 for the income year. However, if her rebate income was $42,297, her SAPTO would be calculated as follows:

$$\$980 = \$2,230 - [(\$42,279 - \$32,279) \times 0.125]$$

8

Beneficiary tax offset

Individuals who receive other kinds of social security payments, such as the JobSeeker payment or Youth Allowance, may be eligible for a non-refundable beneficiary tax offset ('BTO') under s 160AAA(3) *ITAA36*. Like the SAPTO, the BTO is means-tested and operates subject to phase-out rules which depend on the level of the individual's rebate income [8.6].

2. Averaging tax offsets

Some tax offsets reduce a taxpayer's tax liability by averaging down or limiting the rates of tax payable on special kinds of income. A number of these tax offsets are outlined below.

Superannuation tax offsets

Individuals who receive certain superannuation or death benefits may be entitled to various tax offsets under divs 301 and 302 *ITAA97*, which ensure that the tax payable on particular elements of their benefits do not exceed specified rates [19.16].

Primary production tax offset

Individuals who carry on primary production businesses may be entitled to a tax offset under div 392 *ITAA97* to ensure that their taxable income is averaged over periods of up to five years [25.2]. The tax offset is designed to smooth out their tax liabilities to take into account seasonal fluctuations.

Termination payment tax offsets

Individuals who receive certain employment termination, unused annual leave and unused long service leave payments may be entitled to tax offsets under div 82 [20.2] and div 83 [20.3] *ITAA97*. The tax offsets are designed to ensure that the tax payable on these payments does not exceed specified rates.

Income arrears tax offset

Individuals who have received eligible lump sums consisting of certain income that has accrued in earlier income years (eg salary that accrued more than 12 months before it is paid) may be eligible for a tax offset under s 159ZRA *ITAA36*. The tax offset is designed to alleviate the bunching effect that this has on their taxable income in the year the income is derived.

Medicare levy surcharge lump sum arrears tax offset

Individuals who have an increased MLS liability because they have received eligible lump sums that have accrued in earlier income years may be eligible for a tax offset under sub-div 61-L *ITAA97* to reduce their additional MLS liability.

3. Incentive-related tax offsets

Certain tax offsets are provided as incentives to encourage particular kinds of investment and business activities. The main incentive-related tax offsets are outlined below.

Superannuation spouse tax offset

To encourage superannuation investment, taxpayers may be entitled to non-refundable tax offsets of up to $540 for making contributions to their spouses' superannuation funds under s 290-230 *ITAA97* [19.7].

Research and development tax offset

To encourage investment in R&D, companies that qualify as 'R&D entities' are entitled to tax offsets under div 355 *ITAA97* for expenditure relating to their R&D activities [27.5]. The rate of the tax offset, and whether or not it is refundable, depends on the company's aggregated turnover [8.7].

Film production tax offsets

To encourage Australian film investment, companies are entitled to refundable tax offsets under div 376 *ITAA97* for their qualifying Australian production expenditure ('QAPE') [27.6]. There are three tax offsets: the producer offset' (which provides a 40% tax offset for QAPE on a feature film and a 30% tax offset for QAPE on other films); the location offset (which provides a 16.5% tax offset for QAPE on large-scale international films produced in Australia); and the post, digital and visual ('PDV') offset (which provides a 30% tax offset for QAPE on post, digital and visual effects production).

Angel and venture capital tax offsets

To encourage angel investment, sub-div 360-A *ITAA97* provides a 20% non-refundable tax offset to eligible investors who subscribe for shares in early stage innovative companies [27.2]. In addition, to encourage venture capital investment, sub-div 61-P *ITAA97* provides a 10% non-refundable tax offset to limited partners who contribute capital to ESVCLPs [27.4].

Digital games tax offset

To support the development of the digital games industry, div 378 *ITAA97* provides a refundable 30% tax offset (capped at $20m) to eligible companies that spend at least $500,000 on 'qualifying Australian development expenditure' [27.9].

Small business income tax offset

A non-refundable small business income tax offset is available under sub-div 328-F *ITAA97* to individuals who are SBEs or whose assessable income includes a share of the net income of an SBE that is *not* a corporate tax entity (eg a partnership or trust). For the purposes of sub-div 328-F, in working out whether an entity is an SBE, the individual's aggregated turnover must be less than $5m (rather than $10m) [8.7] (s 328-357).

Section 328-360(1) provides that the tax offset is 16% of the amount worked out under the following formula:

$$\frac{\text{Your total net small business income for the income year}}{\text{Your taxable income for the income year}} \times \text{Your basic income tax liability for the income year}$$

8

However, if the amount worked out under s 328-360(1) exceeds $1,000, the tax offset is limited to $1,000 (s 328-360(2)).

An individual's 'total net small business income' for the income year is so much of the sum of the following as does not exceed the individual's taxable income for the income year:

- the individual's net small business income for the income year, and
- the individual's share of an SBE's (other than a corporate tax entity's) net small business income for the income year that is included in the individual's assessable income reduced by any deductions attributable to that share.

An SBE's 'net small business income' is defined in s 328-365. It is basically the entity's assessable income for the income year that relates to carrying on a business (disregarding any net capital gain and any personal services income not produced from conducting a personal services business [36.5]) less deductions that are attributable to that assessable income. If the result is less than zero, its net small business income is nil.

Example Alice is an SBE who qualifies for the small business income tax offset. In 2023/24, her taxable income is $90,000, which means her basic income tax liability is $19,717. If her taxable income included total net small business income of $10,000, she would be entitled to a tax offset of $350.52, calculated as follows:

$$\$350.52 = 16\% \times \$10{,}000/\$90{,}000 \times \$19{,}717$$

However, if her total net small business income was $70,000, her tax offset would be limited to $1,000. This is because the amount calculated below exceeds the $1,000 limit:

$$\$2{,}453.67 = 16\% \times \$70{,}000/\$90{,}000 \times \$19{,}717$$

4. Credit-related tax offsets

To prevent double taxation, some tax offsets provide taxpayers with credits for taxes that have already been paid. There are two important credit-related tax offsets.

Franking credit tax offset

Resident entities that receive franked distributions from companies are generally eligible for a tax offset equal to the franking credit allocated to the distribution under s 207-20 [22.7]. The franking credit represents the tax paid by a company on its underlying profits used to fund the distribution. The aim of the tax offset is to ensure that a company's underlying profits are not taxed twice—once in the hands of the company and again in the hands of shareholders when they are distributed as dividends.

Foreign income tax offset

Taxpayers who receive foreign income that is assessable in Australia are entitled to a non-refundable tax offset under div 770 *ITAA97* for foreign tax they have paid on such income [31.3]. The tax offset cannot generally exceed the Australian tax paid on the foreign income. The aim of the tax offset is to prevent income being taxed twice—once overseas and again in Australia.

[8.10] Higher Education Loan Program

The HELP is the Commonwealth Government's student loan program established under the *Higher Education Support Act 2003* (Cth) ('*HESA*'). It replaced the former Higher Education Contribution Scheme ('HECS') established under the *Higher Education Funding Act 1988* (Cth). Under HELP, the Government provides loans to eligible students who are not able to pay their course fees when they enrol in tertiary courses. These loans are paid directly to the tertiary institution (rather than the student). There are a variety of different HELP loans, including:

- HECS-HELP (to help eligible Commonwealth supported tertiary students pay their student contribution amounts)
- FEE-HELP (to help eligible fee-paying tertiary students pay their tuition fees)
- OS-HELP (to help eligible Commonwealth supported tertiary students study overseas), and
- VET Student Loans (to help eligible students enrolled in certain higher-level vocational education and training courses pay their tuition fees).

The Government has introduced a cap on the total amount of HECS-HELP, FEE-HELP and VET Student Loans that students can access. The cap is known as the 'combined HELP loan limit' and is indexed annually. For 2023, the cap is $162,336 (for medicine, dentistry, veterinary science and aviation students) and $113,028 (for other students). The cap is renewable, which means that students are able to re-borrow once they have repaid their HELP loans. A separate cap applies to OS-HELP loans. For 2023, the maximum OS-HELP loan for a six-month study period is $7,348 (for study outside Asia) or $8,817 (for study in Asia, plus an extra $1,172 if study of an Asian language is undertaken in preparation for such study).

Repayment of HELP loans

HELP loans are indexed annually and can be repaid at any time. Where a person has a HELP loan and their repayment income [8.6] for the income year has reached a threshold amount ($48,361 for 2022/23 and $51,550 for 2023/24), they must repay their HELP loan by paying an additional charge levied on top of their income tax liability. The rate at which they must repay their HELP loan varies depending on their repayment income for the income year. The HELP repayment rates and repayment income levels for 2022/23 and 2023/24 are set out below:

HELP repayment rates		
Repayment income 2022/23	**Repayment income 2023/24**	**Repayment rate**
Below $48,361	Below $51,550	Nil
$48,361 to $55,836	$51,550 to $59,518	1.0%
$55,837 to $59,186	$59,519 to $63,089	2.0%
$59,187 to $62,738	$63,090 to $66,875	2.5%
$62,739 to $66,502	$66,876 to $70,888	3.0%
$66,503 to $70,492	$70,889 to $75,140	3.5%
$70,493 to $74,722	$75,141 to $79,649	4.0%
$74,723 to $79,206	$79,650 to $84,429	4.5%
$79,207 to $83,958	$84,430 to $89,494	5.0%
$83,959 to $88,996	$89,495 to $94,865	5.5%
$88,997 to $94,336	$94,866 to $100,557	6.0%
$94,337 to $99,996	$100,558 to $106,590	6.5%
$99,997 to $105,996	$106,591 to $112,985	7.0%
$105,997 to $112,355	$112,986 to $119,764	7.5%
$112,356 to $119,097	$119,765 to $126,950	8.0%
$119,098 to $126,243	$126,951 to $134,568	8.5%
$126,244 to $133,818	$134,569 to $142,642	9.0%
$133,819 to $141,847	$142,643 to $151,200	9.5%
$141,848 and above	$151,201 or more	10.0%

Example Bob has a HELP loan of $10,000. His repayment income for 2023/24 is $80,000. He must therefore repay $3,600 (ie $80,000 × 4.5%) of his HELP loan. This amount is added to his income tax and ML liability for the year. The repayment reduces his outstanding HELP loan to $6,400 (ie $10,000 – $3,600). Note that if Bob's HELP loan was $3,000, he would only be required to repay $3,000 (not $3,600).

Foreign residents

Foreign residents are required to repay their HELP loans at the same rates as Australian residents if their 'assessed worldwide income' (ie their repayment income and foreign sourced income converted into Australian currency) exceeds the minimum repayment threshold set out above (ss 154-16, 154-17 *HESA*; s 4 *Student Loans (Overseas Repayment Levy) Act 2015* (Cth)). This ensures that foreign residents who may be earning substantial amounts of income overseas but not much Australian income do not escape repaying their HELP loans. To assist with enforcement, HELP debtors who leave Australia for more than six months are required to register with the ATO. Failure to do so can result in penalties.

[8.11] Assessment, payment and collection of income tax

Tax returns and assessments

After the end of each income year, taxpayers are required to lodge income tax returns with the ATO containing information necessary to calculate their tax liabilities for the relevant year (ie details of their assessable income, deductions and tax offsets) [38.2]. Taxpayers are assessed on the basis of the information contained in their returns as well as any other information that is available to the Commissioner. The Commissioner issues formal notices of assessment to most taxpayers, including individuals, advising them of their tax liability. However, 'full self-assessment taxpayers' (see below) do not receive formal notices of assessment. Instead, the returns they lodge are deemed to be assessments made by the Commissioner (s 166A(3) *ITAA36*). These taxpayers therefore self-assess their income tax liability when lodging their returns [38.3].

The Commissioner also has the power to issue amended assessments to taxpayers. Amended assessments are typically issued after the ATO has conducted a tax audit and discovered that a taxpayer has understated their tax liability. Taxpayers can also request the Commissioner to amend their assessments (eg where they have discovered that they have made a mistake by omitting to disclose income or claim a deduction). The Commissioner's power to amend assessments operates subject to strict time limits (except where fraud or evasion is involved) [38.3].

Payment of income tax

The time income tax is due and payable differs depending on whether or not the taxpayer is a 'self-assessment entity'. A self-assessment entity is defined in s 995-1 *ITAA97* as a 'full self-assessment taxpayer' within the meaning of s 6(1) *ITAA36* (ie a company [22.2], or the trustee of a public trading trust [25.9], superannuation fund, approved deposit fund ('ADF') or pooled superannuation trust ('PST') [19.4]). The payment rules operate as follows:

- **Self-assessment entities (eg companies and trustees of superannuation entities).** Income tax is due and payable by self-assessment entities on the first day of the sixth month after the end of the income year (s 5-5(4) *ITAA97*).
- **Other entities (eg individuals).** Income tax is due and payable by other entities 21 days after the 'return day' (ie the day that the taxpayer is required to lodge his or her tax return for the income year) (s 5-5(5) *ITAA97*). However, if a taxpayer's return is lodged on or before the return day and the Commissioner gives the taxpayer a notice of assessment after the return day, income tax is due and payable 21 days after the giving of the notice (s 5-5(6) *ITAA97*).

Where the Commissioner amends an assessment, any extra income tax resulting from the amendment is due 21 days after the day on which the Commissioner gives the taxpayer the notice of amended assessment (s 5-5(7) *ITAA97*).

If an amount of income tax is unpaid after the time it is due, the taxpayer is also liable to pay the general interest charge ('GIC') on the unpaid amount (s 5-15 *ITAA97*). The GIC is calculated on a daily compounding basis and is designed to compensate the Commonwealth for the loss of the use of the tax during the period that it remains unpaid [40.8].

When income tax becomes due and payable, it becomes a debt owed to the Commonwealth payable to the Commissioner in the manner specified in the *TAR17*. Rules governing the collection and recovery of income tax are contained in pt 4-15 of sch 1 *TAA* [40.7].

PAYG tax collection system

A taxpayer's actual income tax liability for an income year can only be precisely determined once the income year has ended. The reason for this is that assessable income may be earned, or deductions may be incurred, right up until the end of the income year. It is therefore not possible to accurately calculate a taxpayer's taxable income for the year until all amounts have been properly accounted for. Until such time, a taxpayer cannot be assessed for income tax. In spite of this, income tax is nevertheless collected from, or on behalf of, taxpayers during the income year (ie before they are formally assessed) under the 'Pay As You Go' ('PAYG') system [39.4]. The PAYG system allows the ATO to collect tax progressively during the income year based on a taxpayer's expected or estimated tax liability for the year, rather than their actual tax liability for the year.

The PAYG system has both withholding and instalment collection rules. For example, employers are required to withhold tax at specified rates from salary paid to their employees and they are required to remit PAYG withholding amounts to the ATO. Self-employed people, on the other hand, are required to pay PAYG instalments to the ATO based on their instalment income, or their 'notional' or 'estimated' tax liabilities. The PAYG system also ties in with the TFN [39.2] and ABN [39.3] systems, which are used to identify taxpayers and their businesses.

Amounts withheld or paid under the PAYG system are generally credited against the taxpayer's actual tax liability for the year when the taxpayer is finally assessed (ss 18-15, 45-30 *TAA*). In the meantime, however, the taxpayer cannot utilise those funds as they have been paid to the ATO. As the amounts collected under the PAYG system usually differ from the taxpayer's actual assessed tax liability for the income year, the taxpayer may be required to pay a balancing amount (where insufficient PAYG has been collected for the year) or may be entitled to a refund (where too much PAYG has been collected for the year).

Example Don is an employee who, after filing his tax return for an income year, is assessed to pay income tax plus ML of $40,000. If his employer has already withheld $38,000 in PAYG from his salary, this amount is credited against Don's tax liability for the year and he will only be liable to pay the balance $2,000 to the Commissioner. If his employer had instead withheld $45,000 in PAYG, Don would be entitled to a refund of $5,000.

[8.12] Sample income tax calculation

Calculating a taxpayer's income tax liability is quite a straightforward mathematical task involving the application of the tax formula at [8.3]. In practice, the difficulty that arises is determining what amounts fall within the respective elements of the formula (ie determining what amounts constitute assessable income, deductions and tax offsets). These concepts are explored in detail in subsequent chapters. However, before proceeding any further, it is useful to provide an illustration of the way an individual's income tax and related tax liabilities are calculated.

Example Fred is a single 40-year-old resident who does not have private health insurance and has an outstanding HELP debt of $45,000. During 2022/23, he earned salary of $140,000 from which his employer withheld PAYG of $42,000. He also derived rent of $10,000 from his residential investment property and made a net capital gain during the year of $30,000. Fred is a shareholder in a company and received a $7,000 dividend from the company which had $1,000 of franking credits allocated to it. He is also a beneficiary of a family trust and was presently entitled to $10,000 of the income of the trust estate.

Fred is entitled to the following deductions: $800 (for the cost of a professional development seminar he attended), $700 (for the decline in value of the computer he uses in his study at home for work-related matters), $6,000 (for repairs to the fence of his investment property) and $500 (for fees charged by his accountant to prepare his previous year's tax return). He is also entitled to franking credit tax offset of $1,000 in relation to the partly franked dividend he received.

Fred's tax liability for the 2022/23 income year is calculated as follows:

Step 1	**Calculate assessable income**		
	Salary: s 6-5 *ITAA97* [9.1]	$140,000	
	Rent: s 6-5 *ITAA97* [9.1]	$10,000	
	Net capital gain: s 102-5 *ITAA97* [17.2]	$30,000	
	Dividend: s 44(1) *ITAA36* [22.4]	$7,000	
	Franking credit: s 207-20 *ITAA97* [22.8]	$1,000	
	Trust amount: s 97 *ITAA36* [24.5]	$10,000	
	Total assessable income		$198,000
Step 2	**Calculate deductions**		
	Self-education seminar: s 8-1 *ITAA97* [12.1]	$800	
	Computer depreciation: s 40-25 *ITAA97* [15.2]	$700	
	Repairs: s 25-10 *ITAA97* [13.3]	$6,000	
	Tax-related expenses: s 25-5 *ITAA97* [13.2]	$500	
	Total deductions		$8,000
Step 3	**Calculate taxable income (Step 1 – Step 2)**		$190,000
Step 4	**Calculate basic income tax liability on $190,000 of taxable income at the 2022/23 resident individual tax rates** $51,667 on the first $180,000 of taxable income plus $4,500 on the next $10,000 of taxable income [8.8]		$56,167
Step 5	**Calculate tax offsets**		
	Franking credit tax offset: s 207-20 *ITAA97* [22.8]	$1,000	
	Total tax offsets		$1,000
Step 6	**Calculate income tax liability after subtracting tax offsets (Step 4 – Step 5)**		$55,167
Step 7	**Add ML** Taxable income of $190,000 × 2%		$3,800

Step 8	**Add MLS** Income for surcharge purposes of $190,000 × 1.5%	$2,850
Step 9	**Add HELP repayment** Repayment income of $190,000 × 10%	$19,000
Step 10	**Subtract credit for PAYG withheld by employer**	$42,000
Step 11	**Calculate total outstanding tax liability (Step 6 + Step 7 + Step 8 + Step 9 – Step 10)**	$38,817

[8.13] QUESTIONS

1. What was the aim of the TLIP? Why are there two Income Tax Assessment Acts?
2. Why is an asterisk placed in front of certain terms used in the *ITAA97*? Where is the 'Dictionary' located? What is the role of s 1-3 *ITAA97*?
3. What is the formula for calculating a taxpayer's income tax liability? Where does this formula come from? What additional levies may be payable together with income tax?
4. What is the difference between taxable income, ordinary income and statutory income? What kinds of ordinary income and statutory income are not assessable income?
5. How does the income tax system interact with the GST and FBT regimes?
6. Discuss the meanings of the following concepts and explain why they are important: rebate income, adjusted taxable income, income for surcharge purposes and repayment income.
7. What requirements must an entity satisfy to be classified as an SBE?
8. What rates of tax do companies and complying superannuation funds generally pay? What are the differences between the tax rates for resident and non-resident individuals?
9. Tom is a single resident who does not have private health insurance. During the current income year, he earned assessable income of $240,000 and incurred deductions of $20,000. Calculate his tax liability.
10. What is the difference between a 'deduction' and a 'tax offset'? Which tax offsets are 'refundable'?
11. Max is a resident who has taxable income of $40,000 in the current income year. Calculate his LITO.
12. George is an SBE who has taxable income of $140,000 (including total net small business income of $20,000) in the current income year. Calculate his small business income tax offset.
13. Barry has a HELP loan of $20,000. His repayment income for 2022/23 is $80,000. Calculate his HELP repayment liability. How much would he have to pay if his HELP loan was only $1,000?

PART D

INCOME

9 ORDINARY INCOME

[9.1] Introduction

Section 6-5 *ITAA97* provides that a taxpayer's assessable income includes 'income according to ordinary concepts' (called 'ordinary income'). Section 6-5 is based on former s 25(1) *ITAA36*, which was rewritten as a consequence of the TLIP rewrite [8.2]. Like its predecessor, s 6-5 contains different assessment rules for 'residents' and 'foreign residents'. These rules provide that:

- a resident is required to include in assessable income ordinary income derived directly or indirectly from all sources, whether in or out of Australia, during the income year (s 6-5(2)), and
- a foreign resident is required to include in assessable income ordinary income derived directly or indirectly from all Australian sources during the income year, as well as other ordinary income that a provision includes in assessable income on some basis other than having an Australian source (s 6-5(3)).

The rules for determining whether a taxpayer is a resident or a foreign resident are discussed at [30.2]. The way in which the source of income is determined is examined at [30.3].

Ordinary income is not defined in the legislation and therefore takes on its common law meaning. Over the years, there have been many cases that have examined this concept. Although the majority of these cases concern former s 25(1), they are equally relevant for the purposes of s 6-5. This chapter discusses the leading Australian cases that have considered the meaning of ordinary income [9.2]–[9.6]. It also examines a number of foreign authorities that have been influential in the development of the Australian jurisprudence in this field. As ordinary income must be 'derived' by a taxpayer in order to be assessable, the chapter also examines what is meant by this term [9.7].

Section 6-5 operates subject to the other provisions in the legislation. As a result, ordinary income that is exempt income or non-assessable non-exempt income is not included in assessable income (ss 6-1, 6-15, 6-20, 6-23 *ITAA97*). This means, for example, that to the extent that a taxpayer's ordinary income includes GST on a taxable supply, the income is not assessable because it is non-assessable non-exempt income under s 17-5 *ITAA97* [8.5]. Likewise, ordinary income that is a fringe benefit under the *FBTAA* is not assessable because it is non-assessable non-exempt income under s 23L *ITAA36* [8.5]. The concepts of exempt income and non-assessable non-exempt income are examined separately in Chapter 11.

It is important to note that s 6-5 is not the only provision dealing with assessable income. An amount that is not ordinary income may still be assessable income if it is statutory income. Statutory income is discussed in Chapter 10.

[9.2] Characterising income

The concept of income has been examined by the courts on hundreds of occasions, particularly in cases dealing with former s 25(1) *ITAA36*. The courts have, nevertheless, been reluctant to provide a comprehensive definition of the term. Instead, judges have traditionally adopted a process of 'characterisation' in which they weigh up various factors to determine whether or not an amount constitutes income.

In *GP International Pipecoaters Pty Ltd v FC of T* 90 ATC 4413, the High Court stated (at 4420):

> To determine whether a receipt is of an income or of a capital nature, various factors may be relevant. Sometimes, the character of receipts will be revealed most clearly by their periodicity, regularity or recurrence; sometimes, by the character of a right or thing disposed of in exchange for the receipt; sometimes, by the scope of the transaction, venture or business in or by reason of which money is received and by the recipient's purpose in engaging in the transaction, venture or business.

While many factors may be relevant in determining whether or not an amount is income, it is important not to over-complicate matters by viewing income as a highly technical or artificial concept. As Jordan CJ stated in *Scott v Commissioner of Taxation* (1935) 35 SR (NSW) 215 (at 219):

> The word 'income' is not a term of art, and what principles are to be applied to ascertain how much of those receipts ought to be treated as income, must be determined in accordance with the ordinary concepts and usages of mankind . . .

Gain concept

At the most basic level, income is simply a form of financial gain. Economists usually define income by reference to the 'Schanz-Haig-Simons' formulation. According to this definition, a person's income for a period is determined by reference to the person's change in wealth over the period plus his or her consumption during the period. The economists' model of income treats all financial gains, whether realised or not, as income. The courts, on the other hand, generally only recognise realised financial gains as income. This means that until a gain is 'crystallised', there is nothing to tax even though a person's wealth may have actually increased in the meantime. For example, a person who trades in shares may have acquired shares in a company which have increased in value over the period of ownership. Even though the trader's wealth has grown over this period, it is only when the shares are eventually disposed of that the trader will derive any income for tax law purposes.

The tax law also draws important distinctions between different kinds of gains. Not all realised financial gains will necessarily be of an income nature. In characterising particular amounts, the Australian courts distinguish between 'income' and 'capital' gains. As the diagram below illustrates, only income gains are assessable under s 6-5 *ITAA97*. Capital gains are only assessable if they are caught by a statutory income provision [10.1]. In the majority of cases, capital gains will be assessed under the CGT regime discussed in Chapter 17.

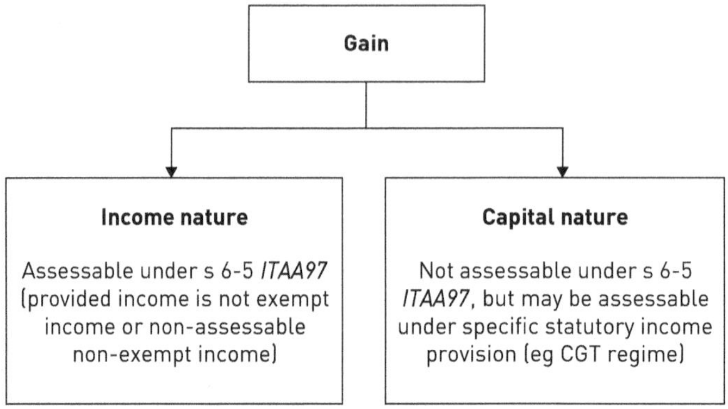

Accretion, flow and trust concepts of income

Although the term income is widely used in tax legislation around the world, its meaning is not uniformly understood. Different countries have adopted different notions of income. The United States courts, for example, have adopted a broad 'accretion' concept, which recognises any realised accretion to wealth as being of an income nature. Australia, on the other hand, like a number of other Commonwealth countries, has adopted a narrower approach. The Australian courts essentially combine a 'trust' concept of income with a 'flow' (sometimes also referred to as a 'source') concept of income.

The trust concept is derived from United Kingdom trust law principles. Under trust law, a person holding a life estate in certain property has the right to benefit from income derived from the property (eg rent) during their lifetime, but is not entitled to dispose of the property (eg the land), which is held for the benefit of the remainderman. Trust law therefore draws fundamental distinctions between the 'income' of an estate and the 'corpus' (or 'capital') of the estate.

The flow concept is closely related to the trust concept. The essence of the flow concept is depicted in the colourful 'fruit and tree' metaphor of the United States Supreme Court in *Eisner v Macomber* (1920) 252 US 189, where Pitney J stated (at 251):

> The fundamental relation of 'capital' to 'income' has been much discussed by economists, the former being likened to the tree or the land, the latter to the fruit or the crop; the former depicted as a reservoir supplied from springs, the latter as the outlet stream, to be measured by its flow during a period of time.

Under the flow concept, returns generated from the exploitation or use of capital assets are ordinarily of an income nature. Examples of income therefore include:

- rent arising from a lease of land
- interest received on a loan of money
- royalties derived from the grant of a licence to use copyright, and
- dividends received in respect of shares.

These items all represent the 'fruit' (ie income) from the exploitation of the 'tree' (ie the underlying capital asset). Equally, rewards received from the exploitation of human capital (ie the fruits of a person's labour, such as salary and wages) are also typically treated as income. For similar reasons, the ordinary proceeds of a business (eg receipts from the sale of trading stock) are also of an income nature.

By way of contrast, a gain made from the realisation (eg sale) of a capital asset is not usually of an income nature. This proposition finds support in a subsequent passage from *Eisner v Macomber*, where it was stated (at 207) that income is a gain 'severed from' capital as opposed to a gain 'accruing to' capital:

> [Income is] *not* a gain *accruing* to capital, not a *growth or increment* of value *in* the investment; but a gain, a profit, something of exchangeable value *proceeding from* the property, *severed from* the capital however invested or employed, and *coming in*, being '*derived*', that is, *received or drawn by* the recipient (the taxpayer) for his *separate* use, benefit and disposal . . .

As the United States legal scholar, Henry Campbell Black, stated in his 1913 work, *A Treatise on the Law of Income Taxation under Federal and State Laws*, income tax 'is not a tax upon accumulated wealth, but upon its periodic accretions'. It is, as Black went on to explain, 'a tax on earnings'.

Quality in the hands of the recipient, reliance and regularity

The High Court in *FC of T v McNeil* 2007 ATC 4223 emphasised (at 4227) that whether an amount is income 'depends upon its quality in the hands of the recipient, not the character of the expenditure by the other party'. The source of this principle can be found in earlier High Court pronouncements made in cases such as *Scott v FC of T* (1966) 117 CLR 514 (at 516) and *GP International Pipecoaters Pty Ltd v FC of T* 90 ATC 4413 (at 4419).

The courts have also frequently stated, in cases like *Hayes v FC of T* (1956) 96 CLR 47 (at 55) and *FC of T v Harris* 80 ATC 4238 (at 4240), that the motives of the payer may be relevant, but are seldom, if ever, decisive in characterising a receipt. The case law clearly establishes that it is the recipient's (rather than payer's) perspective which is critical in determining whether amounts received are of an income or capital nature. On this basis, it is not surprising that in characterising receipts, the courts have often focused on factors such as the regularity with which they occur to determine their nature. Payments that arise frequently, especially where taxpayers can reasonably rely on receiving them, are likely to be income in nature. This is the case even though they may not necessarily be connected directly with any specific services rendered by the taxpayer.

For instance, in *Keily v FC of T* 83 ATC 4248, the Supreme Court of South Australia held that an aged person's pension paid by the Government under the *Social Security Act 1947* (Cth) was of an income nature as the pension exhibited the features of 'recurrence, regularity and periodicity' and the pensioner had a continuing expectation of receiving the payments.

An identical outcome was reached in *FC of T v Inkster* 89 ATC 5142, where the Full Federal Court held that weekly workers compensation payments received by a former employee who had contracted asbestosis were income. The Court pointed out that although periodicity alone may not determine the character of the payments, it is an important factor. Furthermore, even though the payments were not in substitution of lost wages as the taxpayer had already retired, additional circumstances, such as the fact that the payments were intended to supplement whatever other income the taxpayer enjoyed, made it clear that they were of an income nature.

Similarly, in *FC of T v Blake* 84 ATC 4661, the Supreme Court of Queensland held that a regular subsidy paid by a bank to a former employee on top of his fortnightly pension was of an income nature. Carter J pointed out that the taxpayer had been in receipt of the payment for some years and had a reasonable expectation that he would receive the increments to his pension every fortnight. The fact that the payments were made at the discretion of the bank and were reviewed annually did not prevent the subsidies from being treated as income.

By way of contrast, amounts received infrequently and unexpectedly (eg windfalls) are often capital in nature, especially if they are not connected with any current income-earning activity undertaken by the taxpayer. This principle is illustrated in *FC of T v Harris* 80 ATC 4238, where a former bank employee was held not to be assessable on a lump sum payment of $450 received from his former employer as a goodwill gesture to offset the effects of inflation on his pension. The Full Federal Court noted that the payment was not a product of the taxpayer's past service and characterised it as a gift.

However, one must be careful not to jump to conclusions about the character of a gain simply based on whether or not the payments received are periodic. There have been instances where one-off lump sum payments have been found to be of an income nature, such as where they arise from isolated profit-making schemes (*FC of T v The Myer Emporium Ltd* 87 ATC 4363) [9.5]. Equally, there have also been instances where periodic payments have been treated as capital, such as where they represent instalments for the purchase price of a capital asset (*Foley v Fletcher* (1858) 157 ER 678) [9.6]. Periodicity is therefore just one of the many factors that should be taken into account in the characterisation process.

Income must 'come in' and be 'money' or 'convertible into money'

Ordinarily, for something to be income it must 'come in' to a taxpayer and be received as money or in a form that is convertible into money—otherwise there is no 'gain' that can be taxed. This principle can be traced back to the longstanding decision in *Tennant v Smith* [1892] AC 150, which concerned whether a bank's agent was required to pay income tax on the value of free accommodation that he had received. The bank had provided the agent with a house where he lived and where he was bound to transact after-hours banking business. The House of Lords held that the privilege of the free residence should not be taken into account in calculating his income, as it was not something the agent could convert into money, given that he was prohibited from sub-letting the premises. In a frequently cited passage, Lord Macnaghten stated (at 164):

> [Income tax] is a tax on what 'comes in'—on actual receipts . . . No doubt if [the taxpayer] had to find lodgings for himself he might have to pay for them. His income goes further because he is relieved from that expense. But a person is chargeable for income tax . . . not on what saves his pocket, but on what goes into his pocket.

Based on *Tennant v Smith*, benefits that merely save expenditure and cannot be converted into cash have generally been held not to constitute income. This is illustrated in *FC of T v Cooke & Sherden* 80 ATC 4140, where soft drink retailers that were provided with free overseas holidays by a soft drink manufacturer as part of a sales incentive scheme were not assessed on the value of the holidays, as the holidays were not transferable and could not be converted into money. Similarly, in *Payne v FC of T* 96 ATC 4407, an employee of a firm of accountants was not assessed on the value of airline tickets that she had redeemed under a Qantas frequent flyer program, as the tickets were not transferable and not convertible into money.

It is important to note that the taxpayers in *Cooke & Sherden* and *Payne* had not provided any services to the entities that provided them with the benefits. The benefits could not therefore be treated as income from personal exertion [9.3]. Similarly, the benefits were not received in the ordinary course of any business carried on by the taxpayers. These cases may be contrasted with *FC of T v Unilever Australia Securities Ltd* 95 ATC 4117, which is authority for the principle that where a saving of expenditure arises in the ordinary course of a taxpayer's business, it may give rise to an income amount [9.4].

Income must come from 'outside sources'—the 'mutuality' principle

In order for income to 'come in' to a taxpayer, it must obviously come from 'outside' sources—taxpayers cannot derive income from themselves. Accordingly, subscriptions to clubs or associations by their members do not ordinarily constitute income of the clubs or associations, even though they may be unexpended at the end of the income year. This principle is known as the 'mutuality principle' and is illustrated in *The Bohemians Club v FC of T* (1918) 24 CLR 334. In this case, the High Court held that an unincorporated association that operated as a social club was not assessable on subscriptions received from its members that were unexpended at the end of the year. Griffith CJ explained (at 337–338):

> A man is not the source of his own income . . . A man's income consists of moneys derived from sources outside of himself. Contributions made by a person for expenditure in his business or otherwise for his own benefit cannot be regarded as his income unless the legislature expressly so declares.

In *Municipal Mutual Insurance Ltd v Hills* (1932) 16 TC 430, it was held that the mutuality principle will only apply if there is 'complete identity' between the contributors and participants (ie all the contributors to the common fund must be entitled to participate in the surplus and all participators in the surplus must be contributors to the common fund).

The identity principle was explained by the Full Federal Court in *Coleambally Irrigation Mutual Co-operative Ltd v FC of T* 2004 ATC 4835 in the following terms:

> The identity required is not an identity between individuals, but an identity between classes, and all that is required is a reasonable relationship between what a member contributes, and the member's expected participation in the common fund.

Coleambally Irrigation illustrates that where members are prohibited from participating in the surplus, the mutuality principle cannot apply. The case concerned a non-trading co-operative that was established to provide irrigation infrastructure for its members. The taxpayer's activities were funded by 'sinking fund' contributions paid by its members. The *Co-operatives Act 1992* (NSW), however, prohibited the taxpayer from giving returns or distributing any surplus to members on winding up. The Full Federal Court held that the mutuality principle did not apply because the sinking fund contributions no longer belonged to the members who paid them, as it was clear that they could not get their payments back.

Following the *Coleambally Irrigation Case*, s 59-35 *ITAA97* was enacted to allow non-profit entities whose constituent documents prevent them from making distributions to their members to treat certain income from their members as non-assessable non-exempt income.

Importantly, not all receipts of an entity from its members will necessarily fall within the mutuality principle. In certain cases, a club may actually be trading with its members, in which case its ordinary trading receipts will be treated as income (*FC of T v Australian Music Traders Association* 90 ATC 4536; *Sydney Water Board Employees' Credit Union Ltd v FC of T* 73 ATC 4129; *Royal Automobile Club of Victoria v FC of T* 73 ATC 4153). The key issue is whether the transaction between the club and its members constitutes a trading transaction (in which case the receipts will be income) or simply a contribution to a common fund which may result in a surplus (in which case the receipts will not be income).

Statutory non-cash rules

The common law principle that income must be something that is received as money or that is convertible into money needs to be considered in the context of the express statutory rules contained in ss 21 and 21A *ITAA36*.

Section 21 provides that where, upon any transaction, any consideration is paid or given otherwise than in cash, the money value of that consideration shall be deemed to have been paid or given. It is important to realise, however, that while s 21 deems non-monetary consideration to be converted into its money value, it is not an assessment provision in its own right and does not make something income that is not income. The aim of s 21 is to ensure that the money value of 'in kind' payments is taken into account for tax purposes where the amount would otherwise be of an income nature. The provision is clearly directed at barter transactions and would apply, for example, where a lawyer provides legal services to a builder that 'pays' the lawyer by repairing his fence. The lawyer will be deemed to have been paid the money value of the repairs and would be assessed on this amount under s 6-5 *ITAA97* as the consideration would constitute income according to ordinary concepts.

Section 21A(1) provides that 'in determining the income derived by a taxpayer', a 'non-cash business benefit' that is not convertible into cash shall be treated as if it were convertible into cash.

A 'non-cash business benefit' is defined as property or services provided wholly or partly in respect of, or in relation directly or indirectly to, a business relationship (s 21A(5)). For this purpose, 'services' is defined widely and covers things such as arrangements relating to the performance of work and lending of money. Importantly, the definition of non-cash business benefits does not, however, cover property or services provided in respect of an employment relationship as such benefits are usually fringe benefits and are therefore taxed under the FBT regime discussed in Chapter 18 rather than the income tax regime.

It is the arm's length value of the benefit reduced by any contribution made by the recipient which must be brought to account. Any conditions that would restrict the conversion of the benefit into cash are disregarded (s 21A(2)).

Example As part of a business arrangement, a furniture manufacturer provides the managing director of an advertising company with a table that has an arm's length value of $10,000. Under the arrangement, the managing director is not permitted to sell or transfer the table. The provision of the table is a non-cash business benefit and the restriction on its conversion is disregarded. The managing director is therefore assessed on $10,000.

The value of the benefit is reduced to the extent that the recipient of the benefit would otherwise have been entitled to a deduction for its cost had the recipient paid for it (s 21A(3)).

Example Under a business arrangement, an insurance company provided a self-employed insurance agent with a 1 year interest free loan of $100,000 on 1 July 2023. The loan was applied as follows: $60,000 was used to purchase a home for the agent and $40,000 was used for developing his business. The agent has received a non-cash business benefit. Assuming interest would have normally been charged on the loan at 10% pa, the arm's length value of the benefit is $10,000 (ie $100,000 × 10%). However, as interest on the portion of the loan used to develop his agency business would be deductible under s 8-1 *ITAA97* [12.1]—the 'otherwise deductible rule' in s 21A(3) reduces the value of the benefit. The agent is therefore assessed on $6,000 (ie ($10,000 – $4,000) × 10%).

The value of the benefit is also reduced to the extent that it is non-deductible entertainment expenditure of the provider (s 21A(4)). 'Non-deductible entertainment expenditure' is entertainment expenditure that is not deductible under s 32-5 *ITAA97* [14.4] and that would otherwise be deductible under the general deduction provision in s 8-1 *ITAA97* [12.1] (s 21A(5)).

The broad aim of s 21A is to ensure that a benefit does not escape being treated as income merely because it is a non-cash business benefit that is not convertible into cash. The section was inserted to deal with practices that developed as a result of cases like *Cooke & Sherden*, where taxpayers were provided with business benefits that had restrictions placed on their convertibility into money.

Where the total non-cash business benefits derived by a taxpayer in a year of income do not exceed $300, the income is exempt (s 23L(2) *ITAA36*).

Categorising income

The line that separates income from capital can sometimes be quite fine. As Sir Wilfred Greene MR observed in *IRC v British Salmson Aero Engines Ltd* [1938] 2 KB 482 (at 498), 'in many cases it is almost true to say that the spin of a coin would decide the matter almost as satisfactorily as an attempt to find reasons'. Notwithstanding these remarks, the distinction between income and capital is not arbitrary. While the outcome of a case depends on its particular facts, the courts have developed a number of guiding principles for differentiating between these two forms of gains. These principles are typically weighed up against each other to characterise the nature of the particular gains.

For discussion purposes, it is convenient to divide the concept of income into four broad categories:

1. **Income from personal exertion.** This category covers remuneration from employment (*Dean & Anor v FC of T* 97 ATC 4762) and rewards from rendering personal services (*Brent v FC of T* 71 ATC 4195) [9.3].
2. **Income from business.** This category covers the ordinary proceeds of a business (*Blockey v FC of T* (1923) 31 CLR 503) and gains from trading activities (*Californian Copper Syndicate Ltd v Harris (Surveyor of Taxes)* (1904) 5 TC 159) [9.4].
3. **Income from profit-making schemes.** This category covers gains from isolated schemes that are entered into with the purpose of making a profit (*FC of T v The Myer Emporium Ltd* 87 ATC 4363) [9.5].
4. **Income from property.** This category covers amounts such as rent from a lease (*Adelaide Fruit and Produce Exchange Co Ltd v DFC of T* (1932) 2 ATD 1) and interest on a sum of money (*Riches v Westminster Bank Ltd* [1947] AC 390) [9.6].

The four categories of income outlined above are used purely for classification purposes and are not intended to be an exhaustive list. They are depicted in the following diagram and discussed in detail throughout this chapter.

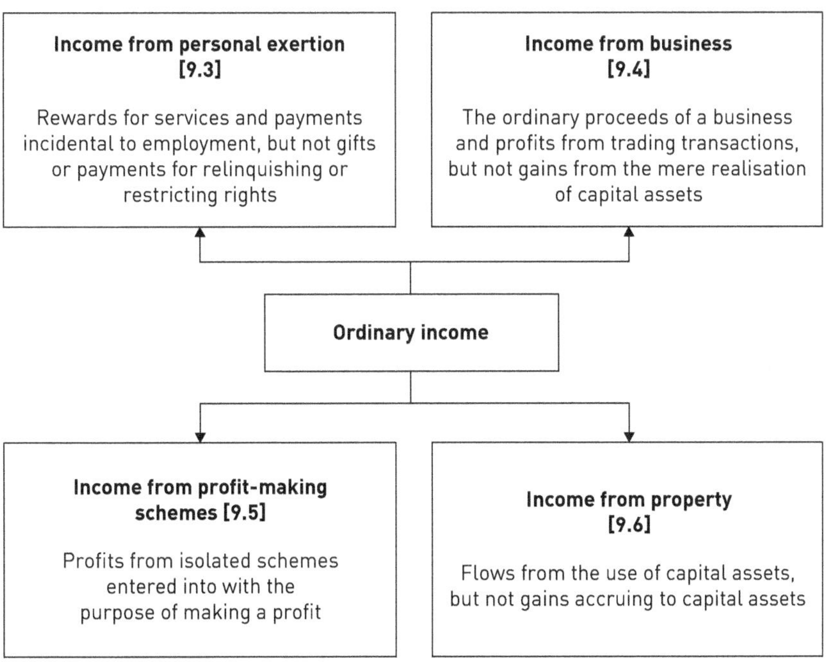

[9.3] Income from personal exertion

Reward for services

In *Eisner v Macomber* (1920) 252 US 189, the United States Supreme Court observed (at 207) that 'income may be defined as the gain derived from capital, from labor, or from both combined'. On this basis, just as income is often the flow from a capital asset, it can also be the product of a taxpayer's personal exertion and efforts.

Remuneration received by an employee is a classic example of an income receipt. This is illustrated in *Dean & Anor v FC of T* 97 ATC 4762, which concerned the character of one-off retention payments made to two key employees of a company. The payments were made in consideration of the employees agreeing to remain employed by the company for a period of 12 months following a takeover of the company, and they had to be refunded on a proportionate basis if the employees retired within the period. The Federal Court held that the payments were salary or wages, as they constituted remuneration for services rendered, and were therefore clearly of an income nature.

The fact that rewards received for services rendered are of an income nature is also illustrated in *Brent v FC of T* 71 ATC 4195. This case concerned payments received by the wife of the convicted 'Great Train Robber' for granting a media company the exclusive right to publish her life story. The taxpayer had entered into an agreement with the company pursuant to which she was paid money in consideration of making herself available for interviews with its journalists. The High Court found that the amounts she received for doing this were of an income nature. Gibbs J pointed out that the taxpayer had not disposed of a capital asset, nor did she assign any copyright in the manuscript which, in fact, had been produced by the journalist. The special information she possessed did not constitute a property right that gave rise to any copyright. On this basis, she had simply been rewarded for her services and should be assessed accordingly.

Voluntary payments that relate to professional activities

Importantly, the fact that payments may have been voluntarily made by the payer does not necessarily mean that they are not income in the hands of the recipient. So long as the payments have a sufficient connection with the recipient's income-earning activities, they are usually treated as income even though the payer may not have been under any legal requirement to make them.

In *Calvert v Wainwright* (1947) 27 TC 475, for example, tips received by a taxi driver were found to be of an income nature even though the passengers were under no obligation to pay them. The Court concluded that the tips were clearly remuneration for services rendered and should therefore be assessed. On a similar basis, tips received by a railway dining car waiter (*Penn v Spiers & Pond Ltd* [1908] 1 KB 766) and a railway porter (*Western Railway Co v Helps* [1918] AC 141) have also been treated as income receipts.

Likewise, in *Moorhouse (Inspector of Taxes) v Dooland* [1955] 1 All ER 93, collections received from the crowd by a professional cricketer for 'meritorious performances' were also held to be of an income nature. The United Kingdom Court of Appeal found that the collections were part of the cricketer's professional earnings and were expressly provided for under his contract. The Court distinguished the earlier case of *Seymour v Reed* [1927] AC 554, in which a professional cricketer had received gate money collected by his club from a benefit match that it had organised to mark his retirement. The House of Lords characterised the payment as a personal gift or testimonial rather than a product of his employment.

Payments that are incidental to employment

For a payment to be income of an employee, it is not essential that the payment be made by their employer. Payments made by third parties are usually of an income nature where they are sufficiently incidental to a taxpayer's employment.

In *Kelly v FC of T* 85 ATC 4283, a professional footballer received a $20,000 cash award from a television station ('Channel 7') for being awarded his League's 'best and fairest' player. The Supreme Court of Western Australia considered that there was a sufficient nexus between the receipt and the taxpayer's employment for it to constitute income. Franklyn J pointed out that the payment had been made to the taxpayer because of the pursuit of his career as a professional footballer and his playing of the game to the best of his ability. His employment with his club 'caused' the payment as it allowed him to play professional football which rendered him eligible to win the award.

The award in *Kelly's Case* was assessable because it was clearly linked to the taxpayer's employment. An award or prize received by a taxpayer that has no link to employment would not generally be of an income nature unless it arises in the course of carrying on a business, in which case it would constitute an ordinary business receipt. This was the case in *FC of T v Stone* 2005 ATC 4234, where a professional athlete was assessed on sponsorships and prize money that she received [9.4]. The ATO's views on the treatment of prizes are set out in IT 167, which states (at [3]–[5]):

> In the absence of any unusual features, it is considered that no liability to tax would ordinarily arise where a member of the general public participates casually in a competition and wins a prize. A windfall gain of this nature would not have the character of income.
>
> On the other hand, if a taxpayer makes regular appearances in radio or television programmes (whether as an artist or as a participant in some form of competition), the reward received for appearing on the programme would form part of his assessable income . . .
>
> A prize or an award won in circumstances where it is an incident of the taxpayer's income-producing activities (eg a 'best player' award won by a professional footballer in a newspaper competition) or where it is part of the proceeds of a business conducted by the taxpayer (eg a prize won by an author in a literary competition) would have the character of income.

Payments to induce employment

Payments made to induce an employee to work for an employer are generally of an income nature. In *Pickford v FC of T* 98 ATC 2268, the taxpayer was employed by E Ltd and held options to acquire shares in his employer's parent company under an employee share scheme. The options would lapse if the taxpayer ceased employment with E Ltd. The taxpayer was subsequently approached to take up employment with another company, W Ltd. The taxpayer resigned from his job with E Ltd and was paid a lump sum of $20,000 by W Ltd to compensate him for the loss of the 'potential capital gain' that may have been available to him in relation to the shares to which he would have been entitled under the employee share scheme. The AAT treated the payment as ordinary income on the basis that it was an inducement for the taxpayer to enter the employment of W Ltd and an incident of his income-earning activities as an employee. As the AAT pointed out, it was one of the main attractions of his overall salary package.

Payments that are a substitute for salary

Payments made to persons by their former employers have been held to be of an income nature where they can be relied upon as substituting or supplementing income that they might have otherwise received. For example, in *FC of T v Dixon* (1952) 86 CLR 540, the High Court held that a taxpayer who had enlisted in the army on the understanding that he would receive a supplement from his former civilian employer to make up the difference between his previous civilian wage and his military wage was assessable on the relevant payments. Fullagar J concluded that the payments were of an income nature as they were a 'substitute' for the wages that he would have otherwise received. Dixon CJ and Williams J reached a similar conclusion on the basis that the taxpayer was able to enlist with the 'expectation' that he could depend on receiving wages that were not less than the wages he would have otherwise received as a civilian. Their Honours emphasised (at 556) that 'if payments are really incidental to an employment, it is unimportant whether they come from the employer or somebody else'.

Deferred payments

A reward for services does not necessarily need to be paid when the services are performed to be treated as income. This is illustrated in *Blank v FC of T* 2016 ATC ¶20-587, which involved a taxpayer who was employed by a company ('GA') that was a wholly-owned subsidiary of another company ('GI'). The taxpayer participated in an 'employee profit participation scheme' under which GI's profits were distributed to employees. The scheme involved a number of complex agreements, including an Incentive Profit Participation Agreement which provided that, in addition to receiving any salary or bonuses, the taxpayer would, 'in consideration of the services to be rendered' by him to GA, receive 'deferred compensation'. The deferred compensation was payable after termination of his employment and was based on GI's profits and the number of Profit Participation Units ('PPUs') allocated to the taxpayer. The taxpayer ceased employment with GA in December 2006 and, on 15 March 2007, he executed a declaration relinquishing his claim to payments with respect to the PPUs in consideration of becoming entitled to receive US$160m payable in 20 quarterly instalments from GI.

The High Court held that the payments were of an income nature and assessable under s 6-5 when received by the taxpayer. The Court concluded that the payments were deferred compensation for services rendered and were a recognised incident of his employment. The fact that the payments were made after the termination of his contract of service, separately from his salary or bonuses and by an entity other than his employer, did not detract from this characterisation.

Payments for underpaid wages

In the same way that wages received by employees are ordinarily of an income nature, payments received by former employees for underpaid wages are also generally of an income nature. This is illustrated in *Guttikonda & Anor v FC of T* 2022 ATC ¶10-630, which concerned two taxpayers who had been employed by various 7-Eleven franchisees and had not been paid wages in accordance with the relevant awards. 7-Eleven established an independent panel to investigate the underpayments by its franchisees and created a program for lodging claims. The taxpayers made claims for underpaid wages and, upon signing various deeds relating to each 7-Eleven franchise they worked at, the taxpayers received lump sum payments from a company associated with 7-Eleven called Independent Claims ('IC'). The taxpayers argued that the payments were capital in nature as they were received as consideration for the surrender of valuable rights. They contended that, because the receipts comprised payments made by IC under the deeds, their character fell to be assessed having regard only to the terms of the deeds and the nature of the consideration given by them under the deeds. The AAT, however, concluded that the payments were of an income nature as there was an obvious nexus between the gross amounts agreed to be paid by IC to the taxpayers and the services they had provided to their former employers. The AAT pointed out that, however these payments were described, they were the product of the services provided by the taxpayers during their employment with the franchisees.

Payments that are personal gifts

By way of contrast, payments made to former employees or service providers are generally not of an income nature if they can be traced to some personal relationship that exists between the payer and the recipient rather than to the provision of any specific services rendered in the past. In such cases, the payments may be characterised as personal gifts, rather than as remuneration.

This principle is illustrated in *Hayes v FC of T* (1956) 96 CLR 47, which concerned an accountant who received shares in a company from the former owner of the business for whom he had previously worked and who had since become a close friend. The High Court found that the accountant had been remunerated for his services in the past and held that as it was impossible to relate the receipt of the shares to any specific income-producing activity on his part, the shares constituted a capital receipt.

A similar illustration is found in *Scott v FC of T* (1966) 117 CLR 514. The taxpayer in this case was a solicitor who had acted for Mr Freestone for many years. After Mr Freestone's death, the taxpayer acted for his wife. The taxpayer was paid £10,000 by Mrs Freestone out of her husband's estate. The evidence indicated that the payment was made to the taxpayer as a gift, as a result of personal friendship. The High Court held that any connection between the £10,000 and the taxpayer's provision of services was too indirect for the amount to be regarded as a product of his services. Windeyer J observed (at 526):

> An unsolicited gift does not . . . become part of the income of the recipient merely because generosity was inspired by goodwill and the goodwill can be traced to gratitude engendered by some service rendered.

Both *Hayes* and *Scott* were distinguished in *Brown v FC of T* 2002 ATC 4273. In that case, the taxpayer (a retired government Minister) had introduced Mr Ray, the principal of an Australian development company ('Monacorp'), to the principals of a Japanese development company, which ended up purchasing Monacorp's land for $21m. A company related to Monacorp subsequently transferred a townhouse it had developed on the Gold Coast to the taxpayer. The taxpayer contended that this was a mere gift and pointed to the fact that he had become friends with Mr Ray. The Full Federal Court, however, found that the benefit was assessable as it went beyond mere gratitude and had been received in lieu of a $1m commission payable to the taxpayer for the introduction services he had rendered to Monacorp.

Payments for relinquishing rights

Although amounts received for rendering services are of an income nature, amounts received for relinquishing rights are often of a capital nature. Authority for this proposition can be found in the United Kingdom case of *Jarrold v Boustead* (1964) 41 TC 701, where lump sum payments received by rugby players for giving up their amateur status were held to constitute capital receipts. Lord Denning MR distinguished payments received for playing in a match from 'signing-on' fees for giving up a 'permanent advantage'. While the former payments would constitute income, the latter payments would be capital sums.

The proposition also finds support in another United Kingdom decision, *Pritchard v Arundale* [1972] Ch 229. This case concerned the character of an inducement (in the form of shares) paid to an accountant to leave private practice and work for a company. In somewhat strained reasoning, the Court held that the consideration for the shares was not a reward for the rendering of future services by the taxpayer, but his undertaking to serve the company and thereby give up his secure livelihood. The Court pointed out that his employment was not to commence for six months and he might have died before any services were rendered. On this basis, the receipt was characterised as being of a capital nature.

Payments for entering into restrictive covenants

Payments received for entering into restrictive covenants are also generally of a capital nature as demonstrated by *Higgs (Inspector of Taxes) v Olivier* [1951] 1 Ch 899. This case concerned a famous actor who, under a contract made in 1943, had been engaged by a film company to produce, direct and act in the film *Henry V*. The film was not as popular as expected, and it was decided that the best way of promoting the film would be for the taxpayer to refrain from appearing in any other film for a period of time. Accordingly, in 1945, an agreement was entered into pursuant to which the taxpayer undertook not to produce, direct or act in another film for 18 months in consideration of being paid a lump sum amount of £15,000. The English High Court held that the 1943 and 1945 agreements could not be read together and the £15,000 could not therefore be treated as further remuneration for the actor's services under the earlier agreement. The payment was not an ordinary incident of the taxpayer's vocation and was, in fact, made so that he would forgo his rights to act and thereby make a profit. In other words, the payment was not made in consideration of the taxpayer agreeing to perform work, but in consideration of the taxpayer agreeing *not* to perform work. It was therefore capital in nature.

A related case is *FC of T v Woite* 82 ATC 4578, which concerned a South Australian professional footballer who, for $10,000, signed an agreement with the North Melbourne football club under which he undertook that if he ever decided to play football in Victoria he would not play for a club other than North Melbourne. The South Australian Supreme Court held that the $10,000 was a capital receipt paid to restrict the taxpayer from entering into a contract with another club. The restriction was not incidental to his playing football, as it did not affect his ability to play in South Australia. Importantly, Mitchell J noted that the agreement did not bind the taxpayer to play for North Melbourne. If it had bound him to play for North Melbourne, her Honour indicated that she would have found it difficult not to treat the amount as income.

It is important to recognise that in both of the preceding cases the taxpayers did not provide any services for entering into the restrictive covenants. Where, on the other hand, there is a relationship between a restrictive covenant and services provided by a taxpayer, it is likely that the receipt will be of an income nature. For example, in *Reuter v FC of T* 93 ATC 4037, an accountant had been engaged by a merchant bank ('Rothwells') to advise on the takeover of John Fairfax Ltd by one of its clients ('Tryart'). Rothwells had, in the meantime, encountered financial difficulties and was forced to obtain a credit facility from another company ('BML'). Rothwells gave a charge over its interests in the Tryart agreement (including the right to a 'success fee') as security for the facility. In addition, BML arranged for $8m of the funds to be paid to the accountant. In return, the accountant covenanted that he would not, without the prior approval of BML, make any claim against BML or any other party in relation to his interest in the Tryart agreement (which included an entitlement to share in the success fee). The accountant submitted that the $8m payment was of a capital nature as it was received for temporarily giving up his rights to sue under the Tryart agreement. The Federal Court, however, held that there was a sufficient relationship, not being a merely temporal relationship, between the payment and the taxpayer's services to give it the character of income. The payment was so closely associated with the services he performed that it could be concluded it was a product of his services.

[9.4] Income from business

One of the most deeply entrenched principles of tax law is that gains flowing from trading transactions, or that represent the 'ordinary proceeds' or 'ordinary incidents' of a business activity, are income in nature. The origins of this principle can be traced back to early United Kingdom cases, such as the landmark decision in *Californian Copper Syndicate Ltd v Harris (Surveyor of Taxes)* (1904) 5 TC 159.

The *Californian Copper* principle

Californian Copper concerned a company that sold its copper-bearing land to another company in consideration of being allotted shares in that company. The taxpayer was unsuccessful in arguing that it should not be assessed on the profit made from the transaction on the basis that it had merely substituted one capital asset (the land) for another capital asset (the shares). The Court of Exchequer found that, from its inception, the taxpayer was endeavouring to profit from the sale of its land and this was evidenced by the fact that it never had sufficient funds to mine the land. The profitable sale of the land was therefore not the mere substitution of one investment for another, but rather an assessable trading transaction. In arriving at this conclusion, the Court laid down the following important statement of principle (at 165–166):

> It is quite a well settled principle in dealing with questions of assessment of Income Tax, that where the owner of an ordinary investment chooses to realise it, and obtains a greater price for it than he originally acquired it at, the enhanced price is not profit . . . assessable to Income Tax. But it is equally well established that enhanced values obtained from realisation or conversion of securities may be so assessable, where what is done is not merely a realisation or change of investment, but an act done in what is truly the carrying on, or carrying out, of a business. The simplest case is that of a person or association of persons buying and selling lands or securities speculatively, in order to make gain, dealing in such investments as a business, and thereby seeking to make profits. There are many companies which in their very inception are formed for such a purpose, and in these cases it is not doubtful that, where they make a gain by a realisation, the gain they make is liable to be assessed for Income Tax . . .
>
> What is the line which separates the two classes of cases may be difficult to define, and each case must be considered according to its facts; the question to be determined being—Is the sum of gain that has been made a mere enhancement of value by realising a security, or is it a gain made in an operation of business in carrying out a scheme for profit-making?

The above passage, which has been widely cited in the income tax jurisprudence in both Australia and the United Kingdom, clearly recognises that the tax law draws an important distinction between:

- gains arising from the realisation of an 'ordinary investment' (which are capital in nature), and
- gains arising from 'trading transactions' and 'profit-making schemes' (which are income in nature).

Although the basic principle to be derived from *Californian Copper* is straightforward in theory, it can be difficult to apply in practice as it is often unclear whether an asset has been held as an 'ordinary investment' or for 'trading' or 'profit-making' purposes. The line that separates an 'ordinary investor' from a 'trader' or 'speculator' can be quite blurred in borderline cases. The outcome in each case will depend on the particular factual circumstances involved.

Trading transactions

An early Australian adaptation of the *Californian Copper* principle is found in *Blockey v FC of T* (1923) 31 CLR 503. This case concerned a taxpayer who had purchased wheat scrip with the intention of selling it at a profit when the opportunity arose. The High Court held that the taxpayer was assessable on the profit he made from the sale of the wheat scrip as it constituted the proceeds of a business. Issacs J said (at 508–509):

> A mere realization of property though producing profit does not, as I have said, produce income. It is a mere enlargement of capital. But if a man, even in a single instance, risks capital in a commercial venture—say, in the purchase of a cargo of sugar or a flock of sheep—for the purpose of profit making by resale and makes profit accordingly, I do not for a moment mean to say he has not received 'income' which is taxable.

There are many other illustrations of speculative transactions that have given rise to income receipts. A well-known United Kingdom example is *Edwards v Bairstow & Anor* [1955] 3 All ER 48, where the House of Lords held that taxpayers who had purchased a spinning plant with the sole intention of quickly reselling it at a profit should be assessed on the profit as the transaction was an 'adventure in the nature of trade'. Another example is *Rhodesia Metals Ltd (In Liq) v Taxes Commissioner* [1940] 3 All ER 422, where the Privy Council held that a company was assessable on the profit it made from the sale of mining claims because it had acquired the claims for 'resale at a profit'.

Without doubt, the most memorable case on point is *Rutledge v IRC* (1929) 14 TC 490. This case concerned a moneylender who opportunistically purchased one million rolls of toilet paper from a bankrupt German firm while on a business trip to Berlin. Shortly after returning to England, he sold the whole consignment to one person making a profit of over £10,000. In deciding that the profit should be taxed on the basis that it involved an adventure 'in the nature of trade', Lord Sands pointed out the obvious (at 497):

> The nature and quantity of the subject dealt with exclude the suggestion that it could have been disposed of otherwise than as a trade transaction. Neither the purchaser nor any purchaser from him was likely to require such a quantity for his private use.

Mere realisation of a capital asset

The decision in *Californian Copper* recognises that 'trading transactions', like those outlined above, must be distinguished from transactions involving the 'mere realisation of capital assets'. A long line of cases establish that gains made outside the ordinary course of business from the mere realisation of capital assets are of a capital nature.

One of the earliest Australian authorities on this point is *Ruhamah Property Co Ltd v FC of T* (1928) 41 CLR 148. This case concerned a family company that made a profit from the sale of certain properties. The properties had been gifted to the company by the head of the family. The company held the properties for some nine years, during which time it derived rental income from them. The High Court held that the profit from the sale of the properties was of a capital nature as it involved the 'mere realisation of a capital asset' as opposed to the 'carrying on or carrying out any scheme of profit-making'. Knox CJ, Gavan Duffy, Powers and Starke JJ stated (at 154):

> A man has capacity to sell his property, but he may be realising it and changing his form of investment and not engaging in a profit-making scheme. So it is with a company with power to sell: it may be realising its property and changing the form of investment. Much must depend on whether the company has taken the property into its trade and traded in it: whether it conducted a trading concern as opposed to a mere realisation . . . The nature of the company, the character of its assets, the nature of the business carried on by it and the particular sale or realisation are all relevant to the issue.

A similar conclusion to that reached in *Ruhamah Property* was arrived at some years later in the famous case of *Scottish Australian Mining Co Ltd v FC of T* (1950) 81 CLR 188. This case concerned a company that had carried on a coal-mining business from a large parcel of land that it had purchased in the late 1860s. Many decades later, after the main coal seam had been exhausted, the company decided to dispose of the land and, in order to achieve an attractive sale price, decided to develop it. The company subdivided the land, constructed roads on the land, built a railway station on the land, and granted some of the land to public institutions, schools and hospitals. It also set aside part of the land for use as a park. The High Court held that, despite the scale of the activities undertaken by the company, it had not engaged in the business of selling the land, but had merely taken 'the necessary steps to realise the land to its best advantage'. Williams J stated (at 195):

> The facts would, in my opinion, have to be very strong indeed before a court could be induced to hold that a company which had not purchased or otherwise acquired land for the purpose of profit-making by sale was engaged in the business of selling land and not merely realizing

> it when all that the company had done was to take the necessary steps to realize the land to the best advantage, especially land which had been acquired and used for a different purpose which it was no longer businesslike to carry out.

Many other cases involving disposals of land have produced identical outcomes to those mentioned above. One well-known illustration is *Statham & Anor v FC of T* 89 ATC 4070. In this case, a farm had been acquired by Mr Aderman in 1970 so that he could raise his family in a rural environment and engage in some farming. He subsequently sold a half share in part of the farm to a company owned by his sister and brother-in-law. The co-owners attempted to raise cattle on the property, but abandoned this objective for various reasons, including a deterioration of Mr Aderman's health and the depressed cattle market. In 1979, the property was subdivided, and the lots were sold by agents between 1980 and 1986. In the meantime, Mr Aderman had died and his estate was assessed on the profit from the sale of the lots. The Full Federal Court held that the profit was not assessable as no business or profit-making scheme had been carried on. The Court found that what had occurred was 'the mere realisation, by the most advantageous means, of the asset which the owners had on their hands when they abandoned the intention of farming the subject property'.

Another illustration is *Casimaty v FC of T* 97 ATC 5135, which concerned a taxpayer that had purchased a large property in 1955 upon which he conducted a farming business. As a consequence of growing debt and ill-health, the taxpayer undertook a series of eight subdivisions between 1975 and 1993 and sold a large portion of his property. The Federal Court found that the taxpayer was not carrying on a business of subdividing land or a profit-making undertaking or scheme, with the result that the profit made from the transactions was of a capital nature.

The above cases demonstrate that the courts are less likely to find that a taxpayer is carrying on a speculative trading activity in respect of an asset where the asset has been used for some other underlying purpose (eg for leasing, mining or farming purposes). In these circumstances, the profitable sale of the asset will usually (although not necessarily always) be treated as constituting the mere realisation of the asset rather than an essential part of some underlying business or profit-making scheme.

Venturing an asset into a trading activity

As mentioned above, the line that separates the mere realisation of an asset from a business or trading activity is not always clear. In many instances, there will be cases that lie close to the border. The most well-known example of this is found in *FC of T v Whitfords Beach Pty Ltd* 82 ATC 4031. The taxpayer was a company formed by three fishermen which had acquired land in 1954 to provide the fishermen with access to fishing shacks on the beach. Several years later, the fishermen sold their shares in the company to a group of companies that intended to develop and sell the land. The land was subsequently rezoned, subdivided and sold by the taxpayer at a profit. The High Court found that the taxpayer had gone beyond merely realising an asset and had ventured into a land development business. Gibbs CJ held (at 4039) that when the development companies purchased the fishermen's shares, the taxpayer was 'transformed from a company which held land for the domestic purposes of its shareholders to a company whose purpose was to engage in a commercial venture with a view to profit' and that after the change in control, the company existed solely for the purpose of carrying on the business. A similar conclusion was reached by Mason J, who said (at 4047):

> I do not agree with the proposition . . . that sale of land which has been subdivided is necessarily no more than the realization of an asset merely because it is an enterprising way of realizing the asset to the best advantage. That may be so in the case where an area of land is merely divided into several allotments. But it is not so in a case such as the present where the planned subdivision takes place on a massive scale, involving the laying-out and construction

> of roads, the provision of parklands, services and other improvements. All this amounts to development and improvement of the land to such a marked degree that it is impossible to say that it is mere realization of an asset.

Mason J went on to indicate that he had difficulty with Williams J's decision in *Scottish Australian Mining*, stating (at 4048):

> The taxpayer there, after giving up its mining business in 1924, devoted itself to the subdivision of its land. This entailed the construction of roads, the building of a railway station, the granting of land to public institutions such as schools and churches and the setting aside of land for parks. I should have been inclined to the view that the taxpayer had ceased to carry out its mining business and that it had commenced to carry on the business of land development.

It is important to be aware that Mason J's criticisms of Williams J's decision in *Scottish Australian Mining* concerned his Honour's factual findings. As the Full Federal Court pointed out in *Statham* (at 4075), Mason J 'questioned the conclusion reached by Williams J on the facts of the case, but did not cast doubt on his Honour's statement of principle'. As a matter of law, the two cases can therefore sit comfortably together even though they arrive at different outcomes.

The decision in *Whitfords Beach* was followed some years later in *Crow v FC of T* 88 ATC 4620. This case involved a farmer who had borrowed heavily to purchase five large blocks of land over the years 1965 to 1975. The taxpayer used much of the land for farming, grazing and growing crops, but ended up subdividing most of the land. Between 1 July 1967 and 30 June 1981, the taxpayer sold 51 allotments making a net profit of $388,288. The Federal Court held that the taxpayer was assessable on the profit as he was carrying on a business of land development. It was acknowledged that the taxpayer intended to use the land for at least some time as a farm. However, the Court also noted that when the taxpayer purchased the land, he knew that he was financially committed to his creditors and would have to sell some portion of the land to repay his debts. Lockhart J did not accept that when purchasing the land, the taxpayer did so without the thought of subdivision and sale. His Honour distinguished *Scottish Australian Mining* on its facts and stated (at 4626):

> In this case the purchase of the various properties and the subsequent subdivision and sale of parcels of land involved transactions which were repetitive and systematic and had the characteristics of a continuing business of land development. The decision in *Scottish Australian Mining Company Ltd v FC of T* . . . whatever its status following the observations of Gibbs CJ on the one hand and Mason and Wilson JJ on the other in the *Whitfords Beach case* . . . does not assist the taxpayer on the present facts, being distinguishable by the period in which the property in question in that case had been operated as a mine prior to its subsequent subdivision and sale over an extended period.

Carrying on a business

The cases establish the principle that where a taxpayer is carrying on a business, the 'ordinary proceeds' or 'ordinary incidents' of the business will be of an income nature. Determining whether or not a taxpayer is actually carrying on a business is, however, not always straightforward and can be quite difficult to ascertain in borderline cases.

The difficulties that exist in distinguishing between 'business transactions' and other transactions arise because there is no categorical rule as to what is precisely required for activities to constitute a 'business'. There is merely an inclusive definition of the term in s 995-1 *ITAA97*, which states that a business 'includes any profession, trade, employment, vocation or calling, but does not include occupation as an employee'. The resolution of what constitutes a business has therefore been left to the courts to determine on a case-by-case basis. As Hill J stated in *Evans v FC of T* 89 ATC 4540 (at

4554), whether a business is being carried on depends on 'questions of fact and degree'. His Honour later observed, in *FC of T v Radnor Pty Ltd* 91 ATC 4689 (at 4702), that it is 'a question of impression' and he pointed out (at 4700) that 'there is no single factor that can be isolated as determinative of the question whether a taxpayer is carrying on a business' since there are 'a multitude of things which together make up the carrying on of a trade'. Earlier on, in *Martin v FC of T* (1953) 90 CLR 470, Webb J noted (at 474):

> The test is both subjective and objective: it is made by regarding the nature and extent of the activities under review, as well as the purpose of the individual engaging in them . . . the determination is eventually based on the large or general impression gained.

In practice, the courts consider a broad range of factors to determine whether or not a taxpayer is carrying on a business, including the scale and magnitude of the activities undertaken and whether they are carried out in a systematic and commercial manner. The larger the size of the taxpayer's operations and the more organised and commercially orientated they are, the more likely the activities will constitute a business. Factors such as employment of staff and investment in office space, equipment and advertising will usually clearly support the conclusion that a business is being carried on. Likewise, the frequency of transactions will also be a relevant consideration. Transactions that occur regularly are more likely to be business transactions than isolated events. The courts also focus closely on the existence of any profit motive. Where activities are undertaken with the intention of making a profit, it is likely that a business exists. By way of contrast, activities undertaken for pleasure rather than financial reward (eg a hobby or pastime) are more likely not to constitute a business.

In *Spriggs v FC of T; Riddell v FC of T* 2009 ATC ¶20-109, the High Court summarised the position (at [59]) in the following terms:

> The existence of a business is a matter of fact and degree. It will depend on a number of indicia, which must be considered in combination and as a whole. No one factor is necessarily determinative. Relevant factors include, but are not limited to, the existence of a profit-making purpose, the scale of activities, the commercial character of the transactions, and whether the activities are systematic and organised, often described as whether the activities are carried out in a business-like manner.

Small scale activities can constitute a business

It is important to realise that activities do not necessarily need to be carried out on a large scale to constitute a business. Even activities carried out on a very small scale can constitute a business. This is vividly illustrated in *FC of T v Walker* 85 ATC 4179, where a real estate agent was found to be carrying on a goat breeding business even though he started with only one Angora goat, which was being artificially inseminated. Similarly, in *Thomas v FC of T* 72 ATC 4094, a barrister who had planted 30 avocado trees and 75 macadamia trees was found to be carrying on a business of primary production.

Short-term activities can constitute a business

Shields v FC of T 99 ATC 2037 shows that even activities undertaken for only a short period of time, while a taxpayer is otherwise gainfully employed, can constitute a business. The taxpayer in this case was a full-time employee of a finance company who, for a period of two months, bought shares in Australian banks that were about to pay franked dividends at 'cum dividend' prices. The taxpayer then sold the shares after the banks paid the dividends at 'ex-dividend' prices. The spread between the 'cum dividend' and 'ex-dividend' prices gave rise to arbitrage opportunities, which the taxpayer sought to exploit. The AAT concluded that the careful and systematic way in which the taxpayer bought and sold shares, and the degree of repetition and substantial turnover involved in the transactions, pointed to the fact that he was carrying on a business.

Athletic pursuits can constitute a business

Even athletic pursuits undertaken by a person who is otherwise gainfully employed may constitute a business. This is illustrated in *FC of T v Stone* 2005 ATC 4234, which concerned a police officer who competed as a javelin thrower at national and international sporting events and who, during 1998/99, received prize money ($93,429), appearance fees ($2,700), grants ($27,900) and payments from sponsors for promoting their products ($12,419). The High Court held that, taken as a whole, the athletic activities undertaken by the taxpayer constituted a business. As a result, the amounts she received during the year were of an income nature. This was the case even though the taxpayer had argued that her motivation was not to make money, but rather to excel at her sport, represent her country and win medals. Gleeson CJ, Gummow, Hayne and Heydon JJ explained their reasoning as follows (at 4242–4243):

> What the taxpayer received from her sponsors were fees for the services she provided. . . . But the sponsorship arrangements show not only that the taxpayer made those arrangements to assist her pursuit of athletic activities but also that she was able to make them because of her pursuit of those activities . . . Taken as a whole, the athletic activities of the taxpayer . . . constituted the conduct of a business. She wanted to compete at the highest level. To do that cost money—for equipment, training, travel, accommodation. She sought sponsorship to help defray those costs. She agreed to accept grants that were made to her and agreed to the commercial inhibitions that came with those grants so that she might meet the costs that she incurred in pursuing her goals. Although she did not seek to maximise her receipts from prize money, preferring to seek out the best rather than the most lucrative competitions, her pursuit of excellence, if successful, necessarily entailed the receipt of prizes, increased grants, and the opportunity to obtain more generous sponsorship arrangements.

Illegal activities can constitute a business

The fact that activities may be illegal does not prevent them from constituting a business. This principle was established long ago by the United Kingdom cases of *Partridge v Mallandaine* (1886) 2 TC 179 (which concerned a taxpayer involved in illegal gambling activities) and *Lindsay & Ors v IRC* (1933) 18 TC 43 (which concerned taxpayers involved in illegal sales of whisky). In *Lindsay*, Lord Morrison made the following point (at 58):

> It is, in my opinion, absurd to suppose that honest gains are charged to tax and dishonest gains escape . . . The burglar and the swindler, who carry on a trade or business for profit, are as liable to tax as an honest business man, and, in addition, they get their desserts elsewhere.

The principle that illegal activities can constitute a business in the same way as legal activities was accepted in Australia in *FC of T v La Rosa* 2003 ATC 4510. This case concerned a taxpayer involved in an illegal drug dealing business who was allowed deductions for money that had been robbed from him during an attempted drug deal. The Full Federal Court pointed out that the purpose of the tax laws was to tax taxable income, not punish wrongdoing. Although the reasoning applied in *La Rosa* was technically correct, the decision was, understandably, highly controversial. It is therefore not surprising that shortly after the case was decided, s 26-54 *ITAA97* was introduced to expressly deny deductions for losses and outgoings that relate to the commission of certain offences [14.7].

Gambling activities can constitute a business

In most cases, gambling activities are usually regarded as a mere 'hobby' or 'pastime' rather than a business. There have, nevertheless, been instances where the courts have treated taxpayers who were heavily involved in gambling to be carrying on businesses as professional gamblers. Where taxpayers are found to be carrying on gambling businesses, they will be assessable on their winnings under s 6-5 *ITAA97* and will correspondingly be allowed deductions for their losses under s 8-1 *ITAA97* [12.1]. Where, however, taxpayers are found to be merely engaged in a hobby or pastime, their winnings and losses will usually be ignored for tax purposes.

In *Trautwein v FC of T* (1936) 56 CLR 196, a taxpayer who was involved in the hotel industry and had a keen interest in horse racing devoted a substantial portion of time to betting. The taxpayer had established a horse breeding and stud farm and expended considerable money racing his own horses and leased horses. He frequently attended races and regularly and systematically placed large bets on carefully selected horses after making extensive enquiries from trainers and others in the industry. He also occasionally employed others to place and settle his bets. The High Court held that, having regard to the system, extent, frequency, continuity and volume of the betting transactions, the taxpayer's activities 'were part and parcel of the carrying on of a horse-racing business'. On this basis, the taxpayer, who had made losses from his betting activities, was entitled to deduct those losses.

A similar finding concerning the activities of a taxpayer was reached by the High Court in *Prince v FC of T* (1959) 12 ATD 45. This case concerned a retired bookmaker who maintained a horse training establishment and gambled heavily and systematically. Menzies J concluded that the taxpayer had applied his wide and extensive knowledge of the horse-racing industry, which had been derived from his previous vocation as a bookmaker, for the purpose of maximising his profits. The extent, system and organisation of the taxpayer's gambling activities went beyond the vigorous pursuit of a hobby or pastime. He carried on his gambling activities for the purpose of profit, rather than for pleasure or the satisfaction of addiction so often present in gambling. As a consequence, the taxpayer was assessable on his winnings under former s 25(1) *ITAA36*.

Trautwein and *Prince* should be contrasted with *Martin v FC of T* (1953) 90 CLR 470, *Babka v FC of T* 89 ATC 4963 and *Brajkovich v FC of T* 89 ATC 5227, in which the Courts reached opposite conclusions about the nature of the taxpayers' gambling activities.

The taxpayer in *Martin* ran hotel and farming businesses that occupied most of his time. He also placed a considerable number of bets on horse races, from which he derived substantial winnings. The taxpayer usually attended only one racecourse and usually placed no more than one bet on each race. He also raced and bred his own horses, employed trainers and kept records of his betting activities. The High Court held that, despite these factors, it could not be concluded that the taxpayer's betting activities constituted any more than the normal activities of a person who derived pleasure from the pursuit of horse racing. The Court indicated that, to constitute income from carrying on a business, it must be established that the taxpayer was more involved than a person merely vigorously pursuing a hobby or pastime. The evidence must establish a systematic and organised approach towards gambling with a clear profit-making purpose and a design to eliminate the element of chance.

In *Babka,* a retired public servant spent considerable time on betting activities (predominantly from horse racing, but also from gambling at casinos and on lotteries). He had no business premises, did not employ any assistants, had never owned a racehorse, did not subscribe to any betting information service, and did not maintain a line of credit with any bookmaker. He also did not maintain any accounting records (although he did have a racing notebook, which detailed bets that he had placed and the relevant odds). The Federal Court held that the taxpayer was not engaged in the business of gambling but was merely a 'keen follower of the turf'. Hill J was of the view that the fact that a retired person devotes a considerable amount of time to betting activities does not turn what is otherwise a pastime into a betting business. Furthermore, just because a taxpayer follows a betting system 'will not require the conclusion that his activity constitutes a business'.

Finally, *Brajkovich* concerned a taxpayer who had retired and gambled heavily on horse races, card games, two-up and football games. As in *Martin* and *Babka*, the Full Federal Court found that the taxpayer was not carrying on a gambling business. What is useful about *Brajkovich* is that the Full

Federal Court outlined six criteria against which gambling cases are generally examined to determine whether a taxpayer is carrying on a business. The factors are as follows:

- whether the betting is conducted in a systematic, organised and business-like way
- its scale, ie the size of the wins and losses
- whether the betting is related to, or part of, other activities of a business-like character (eg breeding horses)
- whether the bettor appears to engage in his activity principally for profit or principally for pleasure
- whether the form of betting chosen is likely to reward skill and judgment or depends purely on chance, and
- whether the gambling activity in question is of a kind which is ordinarily thought of as a hobby or pastime.

The Commissioner's views on whether gambling activities constitute a business are contained in IT 2655. The ruling states (at [6]):

> The Commissioner accepts that it is possible for a mere punter to be carrying on a business of betting or gambling but considers that it will be rare for a taxpayer with no connection with racing other than betting to be carrying on a business of betting or gambling.

Ordinary proceeds of a business

Once it has been established that a taxpayer is carrying on a business, the next step is to determine what amounts the taxpayer is assessed on. The case law establishes that a taxpayer who carries on a business is assessed on the 'ordinary proceeds of the business'. This is the case even though the taxpayer may use such proceeds for capital purposes. The point is vividly illustrated in *GP International Pipecoaters Pty Ltd v FC of T* 90 ATC 4413, which involved a company that had been established to perform a pipe coating contract. Under the contract, the company received payments to construct a plant, which it required to have in order to coat the pipes. It was held that the payments relating to the establishment of the plant were assessable, as they were received for the performance of the taxpayer's obligations under the contract. The fact that the payments received would be used to pay for the construction of a capital asset did not make them capital in nature.

Whether or not amounts are the 'ordinary proceeds' of a taxpayer's business is a factual question. In many cases, the answer will be obvious. For instance, amounts received from the sale of soft drinks by a milk bar owner are of an income nature as the soft drinks are clearly the owner's trading stock. On the other hand, the proceeds from the sale of the milk bar owner's other business assets, such as amounts received for the sale of the equipment, premises and goodwill when the owner exits the business, will ordinarily be of a capital nature.

Ultimately, what constitutes the ordinary proceeds of a business will depend on whether a court adopts a broad or a narrow approach to characterising the particular taxpayer's business operations. The following discussion outlines the approaches adopted by the courts in some of the leading cases.

Business restructuring and restraint cases

As a general rule, amounts arising from the restructure of a taxpayer's business are not regarded as ordinary proceeds of the business and are therefore usually treated as being of a capital nature. For instance, in *FC of T v Merv Brown Pty Ltd* 85 ATC 4080, a clothing wholesaler had sold import quotas, which enabled it to benefit from concessional customs duty rates on certain clothing that it imported. The quotas were sold because the taxpayer wanted to reorganise its business and exit certain unprofitable lines of clothing. The Full Federal Court held that the quotas were an essential part of the taxpayer's 'income-earning mechanism' and the proceeds from the sale of the quotas were therefore capital receipts. The sale of the quotas was markedly different from the ordinary sales of clothing to its customers, which clearly would have been a normal incident of the taxpayer's business.

Likewise, payments received under trade-tie arrangements that constrain the way that a taxpayer can conduct business are also usually treated as being of a capital nature. Authority for this principle can be found in *Dickenson v FC of T* (1958) 98 CLR 460. This case concerned the owner of a service station business who had previously sold many different brands of petrol. The taxpayer entered into an exclusive arrangement with Shell to only sell its brand of petrol for a period of 10 years. The taxpayer also undertook that he would not establish a new service station business within five miles of his existing business for a period of five years without also agreeing to sell Shell products. A majority of the High Court held that the two payments of £2,000 which the taxpayer received under the agreements made with Shell were capital receipts as they were inducements to enter into trade-tie arrangements that constituted a substantial change to the capital structure of the taxpayer's business. Dixon CJ pointed out that there was nothing recurrent about the payments and they were not natural or ordinary incidents of the taxpayer's garage and service station business.

Banking, insurance and investment cases

In most instances, profits made by taxpayers from the sale of their income-earning assets are not of an income nature as they are merely realising capital assets or changing their investments. An important exception to this general rule, however, can be found in a number of cases involving banking, insurance and investment companies. The courts have generally taken a broad view of the ordinary business activities of these kinds of entities, with the result that they are usually assessed on profits made from the realisation of their securities and other investments. These assets, although not technically 'trading stock', may nevertheless be regarded as 'revenue assets'.

In *Punjab Co-operative Bank Ltd, Amritsar v ITC Lahore* [1940] AC 1055, the Privy Council held that a bank was assessable on profits made from the sale of securities which it realised to pay withdrawals by its depositors. This decision was reached on the basis that the sales arose out of what was truly the carrying on of its ordinary banking activities. The Privy Council found that a bank must keep enough liquid assets, including securities, on hand to meet any demand by its depositors and that the realisation of such assets is a normal transaction carried out in a banking business.

The reasoning in *Punjab* was followed in *Colonial Mutual Life Assurance Society Ltd v FC of T* (1946) 73 CLR 604, which concerned a mutual life assurance society that invested its funds in various stocks and debentures. The taxpayer adopted the policy of investing in those securities that it believed would provide it with the most effective yield, and it sometimes substituted securities to achieve this goal. The High Court found that the taxpayer should be assessed on the profit arising from the realisation of its investments. Williams J stated (at 619):

> an insurance company . . . is undoubtedly carrying on an insurance business and the investment of its funds is as much a part of that business as the collection of the premiums. The purpose of investing the funds . . . is to obtain the most effective yield of income. The diminution or increase in the capital value of the investment between the date of purchase and that of maturity, and the apportionment and deduction or addition over the intervening period of that diminution from or increase to the interest actually payable on the investment is a material ingredient in the ascertainment of this yield.

The *Colonial Mutual* decision was applied in *London Australia Investment Co Ltd v FC of T* 77 ATC 4398 to an investment company that sold and purchased shares on a considerable scale. The taxpayer's decision to sell and purchase shares was made with the object of obtaining the best dividend returns. The High Court held that the gains made by the taxpayer from the sales of its shares should be included in its assessable income, even though it did not acquire the shares for the primary purpose of profiting from their sale. Gibbs J held (at 4404) that the sales of the shares were a 'normal operation in the course of carrying on the business of investing for profit'. Likewise, Jacobs J found that the taxpayer's investment policy envisaged regular and frequent sales of shares which, coupled with the very large scale of its activities, led to the conclusion that the sales of shares were part of its business operations. His Honour stated (at 4411):

> The evidence taken as a whole strongly supports a conclusion that a purpose or intention or expectation implicit in the carrying into effect of its investment policy was that shares acquired would be resold if and when an occasion arose which would make it desirable so to do . . . The fact that enlargement of dividend income was the dominant purpose does not gainsay the existence of a concurrent purpose of resale if and when that resale would throw up a profit which could be used to enlarge the dividend income. The massive scale of the activities in the years in question practically compels the inference that the investment policy was one which in its inception and throughout the course of carrying it into effect would in the expected state of the rising market require frequent and regular realisations of shares whenever they rose in market price before dividends from them were increased.

In *GRE Insurance Ltd v FC of T*; *Unitraders Investments v FC of T* 92 ATC 4089, the Full Federal Court held that an insurance company was assessable on profits made from the sale of shares to its subsidiary. Northrop, Davies and Jenkinson JJ explained (at 4091) that 'the profits of insurance companies, as with the profits of banks, are derived from the investment of their circulating capital'. Their Honours went on to state (at 4094) that because 'these profits arose from equities which had been held as part of the investment portfolio of the insurance business, the profits made were in that sense normal and ordinary profits of the insurance business'.

Similar outcomes have also arisen where:

- an insurance company made a profit from the sale of its investments which were available for realisation as and when required for its insurance business (*RAC Insurance Pty Ltd v FC of T* 90 ATC 4737)
- an insurance company made a profit from the sale of shares that it had held as part of an investment portfolio and which constituted the 'necessary reserve fund' out of which its insurance business expenses could be met (*The Chamber of Manufacturers Insurance Ltd v FC of T* 84 ATC 4315)
- a life insurance company made a profit from the sale of a number of flats that it originally intended to hold as long-term investments, but which provided an unsatisfactory return (*Australasian Catholic Assurance Co Ltd v FC of T* (1959) 100 CLR 502), and
- a subsidiary of an insurance company made a profit from the sale of investment properties that were to be held so long as they generated satisfactory rental returns (*CMI Services Pty Ltd v FC of T* 90 ATC 4428).

It is important to realise that each case needs to be determined according to its particular facts and not all profits made by banks, investment and insurance companies from the sale of their investments will therefore necessarily be of an income nature. This is demonstrated by *National Bank of Australasia Ltd v FC of T* 69 ATC 4042, which concerned a bank that had acquired shares in a pastoral company in the course of merging with another bank ('QNB'). Prior to the merger, QNB had a substantial banking business in Queensland and had developed substantial goodwill in the pastoral industry, with branches in pastoral towns and a lending policy designed to assist rural areas. The pastoral company had been formed to take over properties that secured loans which had gone bad. The taxpayer did not want to appear as if it had 'swallowed' QNB and wanted to retain its custom. It accordingly acquired the shares in the pastoral company to maintain its market image. Several years later, the shares were sold at a profit. The High Court held that the profit was not of an income nature, as it did not arise from the carrying on of the taxpayer's banking business. Kitto J found that the taxpayer had planned to hold the shares for an indefinite period and the purchase was neither dictated nor influenced by the hope of making a profit on sale. His Honour explained (at 538):

> The purchase of the shares bore no resemblance to an investment of banking funds, made to earn income pending a need for their deployment in the making of advances and the like; it bore no resemblance to an investment by way of erecting a second or third line of defence against a time of stringency or emergency. It was an acquisition, not of the kind that might be repeated in the course of the profit-earning process, but made once and for all for the sake of enhancing, even if only for the time being, the profit-earning potential of the enterprise as a whole.

The *National Bank Case* is easily distinguishable from *Punjab* on the basis that the pastoral shares were not acquired for the purpose of realisation in the ordinary course of the taxpayer's banking business and were therefore not 'revenue assets', but 'capital assets'.

The *Punjab*, *Colonial Mutual* and *London Australia cases* have also been distinguished in other cases, such as *Trent Investments Pty Ltd v FC of T* 76 ATC 4105. In this case, the NSW Supreme Court held that a company was not assessable on the profit made from realising its shares, as it was not conducting an investment business. This was found to be the case even though it adopted 'portfolio management principles', which necessarily required it to switch from poorly performing stock to growth stock. Mahoney J explained (at 4108) that the taxpayers in the earlier cases were assessed 'not because of the systematic and businesslike manner in which the investments [were] made and managed, but because of the relationship of the investment activities to the main business of the taxpayer'.

Trent was followed by the Full Federal Court in *FC of T v Radnor Pty Ltd* 91 ATC 4689, which involved a company that operated as the investment vehicle for a number of trusts that had been established for a disabled person. The company was held not to be conducting a business of dealing in shares, but rather of investing in shares for dividends. This was the case even though it employed a professional fund manager for making its investments.

Likewise, in both *FC of T v Equitable Life and General Insurance Co Ltd* 90 ATC 4438 and *AGC (Investments) Ltd v FC of T* 92 ATC 4239, the Courts held that subsidiaries of insurance companies were not carrying on insurance activities, with the result that the profits made on the sale of their investments were on capital account.

Share trading cases

A thorny issue that often arises is whether individuals who buy and sell shares are carrying on business as 'share traders', or whether they are simply 'investors' who are merely realising their assets (ie swapping one investment for another). Although each case needs to be determined on its facts, as a broad 'rule of thumb', taxpayers that hold shares for a medium to long time frame for their dividend yield are likely to be treated as investors, while taxpayers that regularly buy and sell shares in substantial volumes on a systematic basis for the purpose of making a profit are likely to be regarded as share traders. Ultimately, difficulties will arise in borderline cases where it will be a question of impression and degree that determines whether the taxpayer is trading in shares or merely investing in them. Many factors need to be balanced to determine whether share transactions are of an income or capital nature.

In *Shields v FC of T* 99 ATC 2037 (discussed above), the AAT found that a person who carefully and systematically bought and sold shares in circumstances where substantial repetition and turnover was involved was carrying on a share trading business. Interestingly, the Tribunal found that the person was a share trader even though he was otherwise gainfully employed and only carried on his trading activities for a relatively short time frame.

Similarly, in *Case* 10/2011 2011 ATC ¶1-037, a businessman who managed a large portfolio of shares using a margin loan facility provided through a broker was found to be trading in shares. The taxpayer's strategy was to make short-term profits from selling shares, and he relied on the broker's online research tools and other information to identify companies he thought were undervalued. During the 2007/08 income year, he only sold two tranches of shares (worth around $300,000) and acquired large parcels of shares (worth around $1.5m). The reason the taxpayer had not sold many shares during the year was due to the GFC. Instead of crystallising his losses, he had decided to wait for a rebound in share prices and continued buying shares whose prices were falling to 'average down' his costs. The AAT held that the taxpayer was carrying on a share trading business in the 2007/08 year even though he only made a few sales during the year. The AAT found that his activities were conducted on a relatively large scale (at least in value) and that he had a systematic strategy. According to Senior Member McCabe (at [27]):

> The fact he did not end up selling many of the shares during that period was an accident of history that can be explained in particular by the impact of the GFC. He was an opportunist who bought and sold when opportunities arose. As it happened, the unexpected events of 2007–2008 meant there were more opportunities to buy than there were to sell.

In contrast, in *Smith v FC of T* 2010 ATC ¶10-146, the AAT found that a person who was highly qualified in finance and who bought and sold a large number of shares over a period of a few years while employed in the finance industry was a mere investor. The Tribunal concluded that there was no plan, repetition or regularity in the taxpayer's buying and selling of the shares. He did not set budgets and targets or have a clear profit motive. He also held the shares for longer periods than would be expected of a trader and did not necessarily take profits as they arose.

In *Hartley v FC of T* 2013 ATC ¶10-333, a full-time council employee who spent some 15 hours per week in the share market argued that he was engaged in the business of share trading, and was therefore entitled to various deductions relating to that activity. The taxpayer had entered into 40 transactions with turnover of $934,575 in 2010/11 and 25 transactions with turnover of $385,938 in 2011/12. The AAT considered that in determining whether the taxpayer was carrying on a business, the following factors identified in *Case* X86 90 ATC 621 (at 629) were relevant:

> (a) the nature of the activities and whether they have the purpose of profit-making;
> (b) the complexity and magnitude of the undertaking;
> (c) an intention to engage in trade regularly, routinely or systematically;
> (d) operating in a business-like manner and the degree of sophistication involved;
> (e) whether any profit/loss is regarded as arising from a discernible pattern of trading;
> (f) the volume of the taxpayer's operations and the amount of capital employed by him;
>
> and more particularly in respect of share traders:
>
> (a) repetition and regularity in the buying and selling of shares;
> (b) turnover;
> (c) whether the taxpayer is operating to a plan, setting budgets and targets, keeping records;
> (d) maintenance of an office;
> (e) accounting for the share transactions on a gross receipts basis;
> (f) whether the taxpayer is engaged in another full-time profession.

The AAT found that while the matter was 'finely balanced', the factors weighing against the existence of a share trading business were more significant than those weighing in favour of such a business. In particular, although various factors supported the conduct of a business (eg the taxpayer's turnover in gross terms was quite large, particularly having regard to his salary; he maintained an office in his home specifically for the purpose of conducting his share activities; and he kept records of transactions for the purposes of doing accounting and tax calculations), these factors were outweighed by other factors which pointed against the conduct of a business (eg the taxpayer's purchases and sales of shares were not regular or routine; there appeared to have been little in the way of a plan or in terms of setting budgets and targets; his trading and background research was unsophisticated; and he was engaged in another full-time profession).

The factors in *Case X86* were once again considered by the AAT in *Devi v FC of T* 2016 ATC ¶10-419. This case concerned a taxpayer who worked approximately 25 to 30 hours per week as a casual child care employee earning some $40,000 a year. The taxpayer argued that she had commenced a share trading business in her spare time in July 2010. During 2010/11, she made 71 purchases (valued at approximately $380,000) and 37 sales (valued at approximately $215,000) in 20 companies. The AAT held that the Commissioner had correctly denied the taxpayer a deduction for a $20,000 loss she made on her share transactions in the income year, on the basis that she was not carrying on a share trading business. In arriving at this conclusion, the AAT applied the *Case X86* factors as follows:

(a) **Nature of the activities and profit-making purpose**. Although the sole purpose of the taxpayer's activities was to make a profit rather than carry on a hobby, this motivation was consistent with both a share trading business and share investment. This factor was therefore neutral.

(b) **Complexity and magnitude of undertaking**. While the magnitude of the transactions pointed in favour of the taxpayer carrying on a share trading business, particularly as the total sales and purchases was substantial compared to her wages, there was nothing complex about the transactions. The taxpayer did not have any risk-management strategy in place, lacked expertise or formal qualifications, undertook little research and relied upon her husband's advice. The factors were therefore finely balanced.

(c) **Intention to engage in trade regularly, routinely or systematically**. The taxpayer's transactions were regular only in the first six months of the income year. This gave the impression that she started by investing all the available funds and later slowed down and took a passive approach. This factor therefore pointed against a share trading business.

(d) **Operating in a business-like manner and the degree of sophistication involved**. While the taxpayer had a home office and the necessary electronic equipment to undertake the transactions, the same would have been required to make share investments. Similarly, the records she kept would have been required to track her transactions for tax purposes irrespective of whether she was conducting a share trading business or share investment activities. The taxpayer had a CommSec subscription and claimed to have read financial newspapers and watched business programs. However, these were unsophisticated business tools that could have also been used for share investing. This factor therefore pointed against a share trading business.

(e) **Profits/losses arising from a discernible pattern of trading**. Although the taxpayer claimed to follow a pattern of selling shares, she failed to produce evidence of this. In addition, her business plan was not detailed, and contained general statements such as 'buy a stock if analysts have strong recommendation and is moving up'. The taxpayer's transactions were more substantial in the first six months and infrequent in the remaining six months of the income year. A share trader is expected to turn over a larger volume of shares on a more regular and systematic basis. This factor therefore pointed against a share trading business.

(f) **The volume of the taxpayer's operations and the amount of capital employed**. Having regard to the taxpayer's financial position, the amount of capital involved in her share transactions was not insubstantial. Nevertheless, this factor was consistent with both carrying on a share trading business and share investment. The factor was therefore neutral.

(g) **Specific share trading factors.** The factors which favoured the taxpayer carrying on a share trading business were that the turnover was substantial, particularly having regard to her wages, and that she maintained a home office for undertaking the transactions. However, the factors which pointed against such a business were that the transactions were not regular and systematic, they were very basic and lacked sophistication, there was no demonstrated pattern of trading, and the taxpayer had no skills or experience in shares. Overall, the specific share trading factors weighed heavily against her carrying on a share trading business.

The ATO's website contains information about the factors it will consider in determining whether or not a taxpayer is carrying on a share trading business. The ATO states that '[t]he intention to make a profit is not, on its own, sufficient to establish that a business is being carried on' and that '[i]t would be reasonable to expect a share trading business to involve the study of daily and longer-term trends, analysis of a company's prospectus and annual reports, and the seeking of advice from experts'. While the ATO indicates that the higher the volume of purchases and sales, the more likely it will be that a taxpayer is carrying on a business, it does not consider the amount of capital invested by a taxpayer to be a crucial factor. The ATO therefore recognises that it is possible to carry on business with a relatively small amount of capital and, correspondingly, to invest a substantial amount of capital and not be a share trader.

Leasing cases

The courts have sometimes taken broad views of the business activities of taxpayers engaged in leasing activities to find that they are assessable on not only the rent received under their leases, but also on the profits derived from sales of their leased equipment. For instance, in *Memorex Pty Ltd v FC of T* 87 ATC 5034, the Full Federal Court held that the taxpayer was in the business of not only leasing computer equipment, but also selling the equipment, with the result that the profits it made from sales to customers of previously leased equipment were of an income nature.

Similarly, in *FC of T v GKN Kwikform Services Pty Ltd* 91 ATC 4336, a company that carried on the business of leasing scaffolding was found to be assessable on profits it made from 'compensation payments' received from its customers in relation to non-returned scaffolding. The Full Federal Court held that the profits were a regular, ordinary and expected incident of the taxpayer's business of hiring out scaffolding.

In contrast, the courts have held that where the evidence indicates that the leased equipment has not been acquired for the purpose of resale, any gains arising from the disposal of such equipment will usually be of a capital nature. This is what occurred in both *FC of T v Hyteco Hiring Pty Ltd* 92 ATC 4694 (where the taxpayer made a profit on the sale of previously leased forklift trucks) and *FC of T v Cyclone Scaffolding Pty Ltd* 87 ATC 5083 (where the taxpayer made a profit on the sale of previously leased scaffolding equipment).

Lease incentive cases

Striking illustrations of situations in which the courts have adopted broad views of the business activities of taxpayers are found in two well-known lease incentive cases, *FC of T v Cooling* 90 ATC 4472 and *FC of T v Montgomery* 99 ATC 4749. In both these cases, solicitors were held to be assessable on payments received from landlords as inducements to move their respective firm's business premises. Such payments, perhaps surprisingly, were found to be received in the ordinary course of the solicitors' business activities. In *Cooling*, Lockhart, Gummow and Hill JJ stated (at 4484):

> Where a taxpayer operates from leased premises, the move from one premises to another and the leasing of the premises occupied are acts of the taxpayer in the course of its business activity just as much as the trading activities that give rise more directly to the taxpayer's assessable income.

Interestingly, the opposite outcome was reached by the Privy Council in *CIR (NZ) v Wattie & Anor* (1999) 1 NZLR 529 in relation to similar kinds of lease incentive payments received by a firm of accountants in New Zealand.

Intellectual property and know-how cases

The courts have frequently had to grapple with cases involving gains made on the sale and licensing of intellectual property rights and 'know-how'. Like the other cases discussed above, whether such gains are of an income or capital nature depends on whether they arise in the ordinary course of the taxpayer's business or involve the mere realisation of capital assets.

In *Ducker (Inspector of Taxes) v Rees Roturbo Development Syndicate Ltd* [1928] AC 132, the taxpayer was formed to acquire, develop and exploit certain patents. Although the taxpayer's main business involved deriving royalties from licensing its patents, it also contemplated selling the patents (even though it actually preferred not to do so if this could be avoided). The taxpayer made a profit from selling its patents to a foreign company as a consequence of an option being exercised under its licensing agreements. The House of Lords held that the profit was assessable, as the sale of patents was a line of business that the taxpayer was prepared to undertake and not 'a mere accidental dealing'.

By way of contrast, in *Moriarty (Inspector of Taxes) v Evans Medical Supplies Ltd* [1957] 3 All ER 718, the taxpayer carried on a worldwide business as a drug manufacturer and had an agency in Burma. In 1953, the taxpayer entered into an agreement with the Burmese Government under which it was paid £100,000 to provide the Government with secret processes and ancillary know-how necessary to enable it to establish its own pharmaceutical factories and commence drug production. The House of Lords held that this payment was a capital receipt. According to Viscount Simonds, the £100,000 sum was received for parting with a capital item, namely its secret processes, which would effectively bring the taxpayer's Burmese agency to an end.

Evans Medical Supplies Ltd was distinguished on the basis of its facts five years later in *Rolls Royce Ltd v Jeffrey (Inspector of Taxes)* [1962] 1 All ER 801, where the House of Lords took a much broader view of the taxpayer's business operations. This case involved a taxpayer that designed and manufactured aircraft engines. Over a period of seven years, the taxpayer entered into a series of 'licence agreements' with various countries that were unwilling to purchase its engines because they wanted to manufacture their own engines. Under the agreements, the taxpayer supplied drawings and manufacturing data to the various countries, and agreed to teach their technicians. Payments under the licence agreements included lump sums given 'as consideration for the rights granted' in respect of the taxpayer's aero-engine know-how. The House of Lords held that these payments were of an income nature. It found that the taxpayer was not disposing of a capital asset under the licence agreements, but was exploiting its know-how in the best way possible in countries where it could not directly manufacture or sell engines. The supply of know-how was undertaken by the taxpayer on a regular and systematic basis over a period of years and was either a trading activity in itself or a mere extension of its principal business operations.

Rolls Royce Ltd may be contrasted with *Kwikspan Purlin System Pty Ltd v FC of T* 84 ATC 4282, which concerned a taxpayer that owned the patent for an invention used in the building industry. The taxpayer received four separate 'once and for all' lump sum payments totalling $535,000 in consideration of granting exclusive licences to various companies to use its invention in defined geographical areas around Australia and for giving assistance to enable the system to be sold and manufactured. The Supreme Court of Queensland held that the taxpayer was not in the business of dealing in patents but had merely realised a capital asset. Campbell J stated (at 4287):

> the fact that several licences were granted for different places in Australia is the same as if one licence had been granted for the whole of Australia. No element of repetitiveness was present in the real sense ...

Debt defeasance cases

The decision in *Tennant v Smith* [1892] AC 150 [9.2], is authority for the principle that a benefit that merely results in a saving of expenditure is not usually of an income nature. A saving of expenditure (eg the reduction of a liability) may, nevertheless, be treated as income if it arises in the ordinary course, or as an ordinary incident, of the taxpayer's business operations (*International Nickel Australia Ltd v FC of T* 77 ATC 4383 and *Warner Music (Australasia) Pty Ltd v FC of T* 96 ATC 5046).

The proposition that a saving of expenditure may constitute an ordinary business gain is illustrated in *FC of T v Unilever Australia Securities Ltd* 95 ATC 4117. In this case, a finance company had raised finance under debentures issued in 1967 and 1979. The taxpayer was obliged to repay the principal amounts owing under the debentures when they matured some 20 years later. In the meantime, interest was also payable. In 1987, the taxpayer entered into a 'debt defeasance arrangement' with LGFA pursuant to which LGFA agreed to repay the principal amounts owing under the debentures on maturity ($7.385m) in exchange for receiving a present payment ($6.031m). The Full Federal Court held that the difference between the payment which the taxpayer made to LGFA and the amount it would have otherwise had to pay under the debentures (ie the saving of approximately $1.354m) was a 'profit' that constituted income according to ordinary concepts, since it arose in the ordinary course of the taxpayer's business as a finance company.

The decision in *Unilever* may be contrasted with the High Court decision in *FC of T v Orica Ltd* 98 ATC 4494, which also involved a similar kind of debt defeasance arrangement. In *Orica*, however, the taxpayer was found not to be carrying on a business as a finance company. As a result, the difference between the amounts owing under its debentures ($98.662m) and the amount it paid to a third party to take on the liability to discharge the debentures at maturity ($62.309m) was held not to be of an income nature.

[9.5] Income from profit-making schemes

While it is clear that gains made in the ordinary course of carrying on a business are income in nature, it does not necessarily follow that gains made from transactions entered into *outside* the ordinary course of business are always capital in nature. The High Court in *FC of T v The Myer Emporium Ltd* 87 ATC 4363 established that gains made from isolated or extraordinary transactions may, nevertheless, be of an income nature where they arise from business operations or commercial transactions entered into by taxpayers with the intention or purpose of making a profit. As will be discussed, the corollary to this is that losses from such transactions will usually be deductible (*Greig v FC of T* 2020 ATC ¶20-733) [12.3].

The first strand of *Myer*

In *Myer*, the taxpayer carried on a retail trading and property development business and also acted as a finance company for other companies in its group. In order to obtain funding to diversify its operations, the taxpayer entered into the following transactions:

- On 6 March 1981, the taxpayer lent $80m to Myer Finance, a shelf company that it had acquired a few weeks earlier. The loan agreement provided that Myer Finance was required to repay the loan 'on but not prior to' 30 June 1988 and that interest at the commercial rate of 12.5% per annum was to be payable on the loaned funds on dates set out in the agreement. The total interest payable amounted to $72m.
- On 9 March 1981, the taxpayer assigned to Citicorp (a company with accumulated tax losses) 'the moneys due or to become due as the interest payments and interest thereon' in consideration of Citicorp paying the taxpayer a lump sum of $45.37m on that day.

The issue in *Myer* was whether or not the $45.37m received by the taxpayer constituted income. The taxpayer argued that the right to interest which it assigned to Citicorp was a 'chose in action'. According to the taxpayer, it had merely realised a capital asset in an isolated transaction outside the ordinary course of its business. The High Court, however, rejected this argument and held that the $45.37m was of an income nature. The Court was not prepared to view the loan and the assignment as separate transactions. Instead, it viewed the two transactions as interrelated, since it found that the taxpayer would not have made the loan to Myer Finance unless it knew in advance that Citicorp would pay for the assigned interest. Viewed from the taxpayer's perspective, the two transactions were integral elements of an overall profit-making scheme.

Mason ACJ, Wilson, Brennan, Deane and Dawson JJ indicated (at 4367) that the important proposition to be derived from *Californian Copper* [9.4] was that:

> a receipt may constitute income, if it arises from an isolated business operation or commercial transaction entered into otherwise than in the ordinary course of the carrying on of the taxpayer's business, so long as the taxpayer entered into the transaction with the intention or purpose of making a relevant profit or gain from the transaction.

Their Honours then went on to state (at 4366–4367):

> Although it is well settled that a profit or gain made in the ordinary course of carrying on a business constitutes income, it does not follow that a profit or gain made in a transaction entered into otherwise than in the ordinary course of carrying on the taxpayer's business is not income. Because a business is carried on with a view to profit, a gain made in the ordinary course of carrying on the business is invested with the profit-making purpose, thereby stamping the profit with the character of income. But a gain made otherwise than in the ordinary course of carrying on the business which nevertheless arises from a transaction entered into by the taxpayer with the intention or purpose of making a profit or gain may well constitute income. Whether it does depends very much on the circumstances of the case. Generally speaking, however, it may be said that if the circumstances are such as to give rise to the inference that the taxpayer's intention or purpose in entering into the transaction was to make a profit or gain, the profit or gain will be income, notwithstanding that the transaction was extraordinary judged by reference to the ordinary course of the taxpayer's business. Nor does the fact that a profit or gain is made as the result of an isolated venture or a 'one-off' transaction preclude it from being properly characterized as income . . . The authorities establish that a profit or gain so made will constitute income if the property generating the profit or gain was acquired in a business operation or commercial transaction for the purpose of profit-making by the means giving rise to the profit.

This passage has been coined the 'first strand of *Myer*' and has been widely cited in many subsequent decisions. For the first strand of *Myer* to apply, the taxpayer must have a 'not insignificant' purpose (although not necessarily the sole or dominant purpose) of making a profit from the transaction at the time of entering into it (*FC of T v Cooling* 90 ATC 4472). Where this requirement is absent, the first strand of *Myer* does not apply (*Henry Jones (IXL) Ltd v FC of T* 91 ATC 4663; *SP Investments Pty Ltd v FC of T* 93 ATC 4170).

Accordingly, the first strand of *Myer* did not apply in *Westfield Ltd v FC of T* 91 ATC 4234, where a company that was in the business of designing, constructing, leasing and managing shopping centres made a profit from selling certain land to AMP. The Full Federal Court reached this conclusion because it found that the taxpayer had acquired the land with the intention of developing it as a shopping centre, rather than for the purpose of selling it at a profit. According to the Court, where a transaction occurs outside the taxpayer's ordinary business activities, in order for the first strand of *Myer* to apply, the transaction that generates the profit must be a commercial transaction and at the time the transaction was entered into there must have been a purpose of profit-making by the very means which gave rise to the profit actually made. The crux of the Court's judgment is found in the following passage of Hill J (at 4243):

> While a profit-making scheme may lack specificity of detail, the mode of achieving that profit must be one contemplated by the taxpayer as at least one of the alternatives by which the profit could be realised. Such was the case in *Steinberg*. But, even if that goes too far, it is difficult to conceive of a case where a taxpayer would be said to have made a profit from the carrying on, or carrying out, of a profit-making scheme, where, in the case of a scheme involving the acquisition and resale of land, there was, at the time of acquisition, no purpose of resale of land, but only the possibility (present, one may observe, in the case of every acquisition of land) that the land may be resold. . . . As the court observed in *Myer*, in the passage already set out, the property, which generates the gain, must be acquired in an operation of business or commercial transaction:
>
> > '. . . *for the purpose of profit-making by the means giving rise to the profit*.' (emphasis added)

Westfield may be contrasted with *Moana Sand Pty Ltd v FC of T* 88 ATC 4897, which concerned a taxpayer that had acquired beachside land in 1958 for the purpose of carrying on the business of selling sand. The taxpayer also intended that, once the sand had been sold and the land became 'ripe for subdivision', it would sell the land to a related company which would subdivide the land or, if more advantageous, to a third party. Council approval to subdivide the land was never granted and the land was rezoned and eventually resumed by the Coast Protection Board in 1979. The taxpayer was paid $500,000 for the resumption of the land ($370,000 was received in 1979/80 and the balance was received in the following income year). The Commissioner assessed the taxpayer for the 1979/80 income year on $370,000 less the cost of the land and certain other expenses on the basis that it constituted a profit within the principle in *Myer*. The Full Federal Court held that, even though the profit arose out of an isolated transaction, it was of an income nature as the taxpayer had acquired the land not only to sell the sand, but also to subsequently sell the land at a profit. The Court was not concerned that the taxpayer had not intended to dispose of the land in the particular way that it did, since the resumption of the land fulfilled its ultimate purpose, which was to make a profit from its sale.

A profit-making purpose was also found to exist in *McCurry v FC of T* 98 ATC 4487. This case concerned two brothers who, in 1986, used their own money, together with a bank loan, to purchase land on which an old house stood. They removed the house and took out an additional loan to construct three townhouses on the land. Prior to completion in mid-1987, the townhouses were advertised for sale, but no sale eventuated. The taxpayers and other members of their family then moved into two of the townhouses. Although, when purchasing the property, the brothers had in mind the possibility that they would rent out the townhouses, at no time was any attempt made to do this. The townhouses were readvertised in mid-1988 and were eventually sold in December 1988, resulting in each taxpayer making a net profit of $75,811.

The Federal Court held that the profit made by the taxpayers fell within s 25(1) *ITAA36*, as it was derived from a profit-making undertaking or scheme. Davies J pointed out that it was the main or dominant purpose of the scheme which was important in determining whether a profit-making undertaking or scheme exists. His Honour stated (at 4491):

> It is not inconsistent with there being a profit-making undertaking or scheme that two possible ends were in mind, one, that of deriving a profit on resale and the other of deriving regular income. It does not matter that the taxpayers had in mind these two alternatives provided that the possibility of making a profit by the development of the land and its resale was the predominant factor which actuated the transaction.

His Honour concluded that of the two actuating factors the brothers had in mind, the possibility of reselling the developed property at a profit was the dominant one. Davies J also held (at 4493) that the profit-making scheme was not abandoned even though the townhouses had also been used for another purpose, as 'the sale of the units always remained an option for the brothers, notwithstanding that, for some period, when it was convenient to do so, the units were used for another purpose'.

A similar outcome recently arose in *McCarthy v FC of T* 2021 ATC ¶10-573, where the AAT held that a profit from the subdivision of a residential property in Perth was assessable under s 6-5 *ITAA97*. The property was purchased in August 2016 and an application to subdivide the property was made in November 2016. The taxpayer argued that, at the time she acquired the property with her husband, they planned to rent it out for the long term and only abandoned this plan after it proved to be financially unsustainable. She argued that the reason the application to subdivide the property occurred soon after purchase was due to uncertainty about future approvals. The AAT, however, agreed with the Commissioner's assessment that the acquisition of the property was a commercial transaction entered into with the intention or purpose of generating a profit or gain from its subdivision and sale. The AAT held that the claim that the couple intended to hold the property as a rental investment was not supported by the evidence. The taxpayer made no enquiries to ascertain the rental value of the property and made no calculation as to whether the rent could service the $750,000 loan use to purchase the property, which was in excess of the purchase price, giving rise to the inference that the additional funds were to be used for the subdivision. The AAT held that the actions taken by the couple were equally, if not more, consistent with an intention to subdivide and sell the property. It was clear that at the time of purchase it was firmly part of their considerations that an option was to subdivide the property.

The second strand of *Myer*

It is important to note that there was also another line of reasoning in *Myer*, which led the High Court to conclude that the taxpayer was assessable on the $45.37m. The High Court held that where a future right to interest is converted into a present lump sum amount, the present lump sum amount will be of an income nature since it replaces the future interest which, when derived, would have been treated as income. This principle, which has become known as 'the second strand of *Myer*', finds support in various cases involving compensation payments [9.7] and was expressed in the following terms by the High Court (at 4371–4372):

> If the lender sells his mere right to interest for a lump sum, the lump sum is received in exchange for, and ordinarily as the present value of, the future interest which he would have received. This is a revenue not a capital item—the taxpayer simply converts future income into present income . . .
>
> By a transaction consisting in the making of a loan and a sale of the right to interest on the money lent, the lender acquires at once a debt and the price which the sale of the right has fetched. The price of the right is the lender's compensation for being kept out of the use and enjoyment of the principal sum during the period of the loan and, like the interest for which it is exchanged, it is a profit. It is immaterial that the lender receives the profit not from the borrower but from the other party to the transaction, and it is immaterial that the profit is received immediately and not over the period of the loan.

The second strand of *Myer* was applied in *Henry Jones (IXL) Ltd v FC of T* 91 ATC 4663, which concerned a taxpayer that owned trademarks relating to a canned fruits business run by its subsidiary. As the business was not sufficiently profitable, it was decided that the business would be disposed of. Negotiations were entered into with two companies ('SPC' and 'Ardmona'). However, these companies were not prepared to pay a lump sum for the business. Instead, a licence agreement was entered into in December 1981, which gave SPC and Ardmona the right to use the taxpayer's trademarks for 10 years in consideration of payment of an annual royalty. As the taxpayer still wanted to realise a lump sum, in May 1982, it sold its rights under the licence agreement (including the right to receive royalties) to Citicorp for $7.5m. The Commissioner assessed this amount under both the first and second strands of *Myer*. The Full Federal Court, however, held that the first strand of *Myer* did not apply, as the taxpayer had not entered into the licence agreement with the purpose of making a profit from its sale. Rather, it entered into the agreement because this was the only arrangement acceptable to SPC and Ardmona. The Court, nevertheless, found that the $7.5m was of an income nature based on the second strand of *Myer* as this sum was received in substitution of the future royalties payable under the agreement.

A similar outcome was reached in *SP Investments Pty Ltd v FC of T* 93 ATC 4170. This case concerned the trustee of a trust estate that, in 1964, had acquired a 15% interest in royalties from an iron ore venture. Many years later, the taxpayer assigned its interest in the royalties, for a period of just over seven years, to a finance company for almost $4m. The Full Federal Court again found that the first strand of *Myer* could not apply to the arrangement, as the taxpayer had not acquired the interest in the royalties for the purpose of making a profit from the assignment. It, nevertheless, concluded that the second strand of *Myer* applied to the arrangement. In doing so, the Court noted that while *Myer* and *Henry Jones* both involved assignors who had been carrying on businesses, the fact that the trustee was not carrying on a business, did not prevent the second strand from applying.

Historical cost concept of profit

In *Myer*, one of the reasons put forward by the taxpayer as to why it should not be assessed on the $45.37m was that it had not made any 'profit'. The taxpayer submitted that the $45.37m it received under the transaction was merely an amount equal to the value of the chose in action that it assigned. The High Court, however, rejected this 'economic equivalence' argument and held that the accounting basis to be used for calculating profits and losses under the tax legislation was 'historical cost'. On this basis, the Court found that the taxpayer had, indeed, made a $45.37m profit on the $80m loan. The High Court explained this as follows (at 4370):

> once the two transactions are seen as integral elements in one profit-making scheme, it is apparent that Myer made a relevant profit, that profit being the amount payable on the assignment. As a result of the two transactions Myer, having lent $80,000,000 on 6 March 1981 repayable in accordance with the terms of the loan agreement, had profited by 9 March 1981 to the extent of the first interest payment received on 6 March 1981 and the sum of $45,370,000 paid for the assignment, the principal on the loan being intact.

[9.6] Income from property

Amounts received from the exploitation or use of capital assets

The 'flow concept' [9.2] supports the principle that amounts received from the exploitation or use of a capital asset are ordinarily of an income nature. On this basis, rent received by a lessor from the lease of property is income as it represents the 'fruit' from the exploitation of the 'tree' (ie the leased asset). This principle is illustrated in *Adelaide Fruit and Produce Exchange Co Ltd v DFC of T* (1932) 2 ATD 1, where the Supreme Court of South Australia held that a company that owned a market with enclosed shops and surrounding covered space for stalls was assessable on the rent it received as it constituted income from property.

For similar reasons, interest received on a loan will also generally be treated as being of an income nature as it represents the lender's return from allowing a borrower to use their money over a period of time. Support for this principle is found in *Federal Wharf Co Ltd v DFC of T* (1930) 44 CLR 24, where the High Court held that interest is of an income nature as it compensates lenders for being deprived of the use of funds which could otherwise be invested to earn income.

TD 2017/11 states that where interest is earned on bank accounts, the person who beneficially owns the money is assessable on the interest. In the case of joint bank accounts, the account holders are assessable in proportion to their beneficial interests. There is a presumption that joint account holders beneficially own the money in equal shares, unless evidence exists to the contrary.

Amounts received from the sale or realisation of capital assets

By way of contrast, gains made on the sale or realisation of capital assets are not ordinarily of an income nature. This principle is illustrated in a number of the cases discussed at [9.4], such as *Ruhamah Property Co Ltd v FC of T* (1928) 41 CLR 148 and *Scottish Australian Mining Co Ltd v FC of T* (1950) 81 CLR 188. It is also exemplified by the early English case of *Foley v Fletcher* (1858) 157 ER 678, where the Court of Exchequer held that vendors who had sold their land for instalments of £768 payable every six months over a period of 30 years were not assessable on the amounts received, as they had merely parted with a capital asset for consideration that was payable over a fixed period of time.

Distinguishing between gains severed from capital and accruing to capital

The decision in *Foley v Fletcher* sits comfortably alongside the passage cited at [9.2] from *Eisner v Macomber* (1920) 252 US 189, where the United States Supreme Court stated that income is a gain 'severed from' capital as opposed to a gain 'accruing to' capital. The High Court referred to this passage in *FC of T v McNeil* 2007 ATC 4223 to conclude that the proceeds from the disposal of 'sell-back rights' received by a shareholder in a company constituted income of the shareholder. The sell-back rights had been issued as part of a share buy-back undertaken by the company. The company issued one sell-back right for every 20 shares held by a shareholder. The sell-back rights operated as a 'put option' requiring the company to buy back its shares for $16.50 per share. They were issued to a custodian who held the rights for the benefit of the shareholders. Shareholders could direct the custodian to realise their sell-back rights by a specified date, otherwise the custodian was required to transfer them to a merchant bank that was required to exercise the rights and account for the proceeds to the custodian as trustee for the shareholders. The taxpayer, who had not provided any direction to the trustee, received a sum of money for the realisation of her sell-back rights. The High Court concluded that the proceeds were of an income nature as the shareholder's shares in the company remained 'untouched' by the issue of the rights. In other words, the shareholder had not given up any profit-yielding asset to receive the rights.

Income streams

Although the proceeds from the sale of a capital asset are not ordinarily of an income nature, it is important to realise that it is possible for a taxpayer to convert what would otherwise be capital consideration into an income stream. This is vividly illustrated in *Egerton-Warburton & Ors v DFC of T* (1934) 51 CLR 568, which concerned a taxpayer that owned land upon which a farming business was carried on. The taxpayer entered into an agreement to sell the land to his two sons (subject to reserving the right to live in the dwelling situated on the land). Under the agreement, the sons agreed to pay the taxpayer an annuity of £1,200 for the rest of his life. After the taxpayer's death, an annuity of £1,000 would be payable to his widow for the rest of her life together with a £10,000 payment, which would be divided among his three daughters and the children of a deceased daughter. The taxpayer was unsuccessful in arguing that, like in *Foley v Fletcher*, the relevant payments he received were capital instalments for the sale of his land. The High Court held that the annuity paid to the taxpayer could not be characterised as 'mere instalments of purchase money' paid for the sale of the land. The payment in this case was characterised as being of an income nature since, unlike in *Foley v Fletcher*, it could not be determined what 'fixed gross amount' would be payable to the taxpayer, as it depended upon how long he would live. Rich, Dixon and McTiernan JJ outlined (at 573) the legal principles in the following passage:

> A transaction by which an owner of capital assets disposes of them for a consideration which includes annual payments may serve the double purpose of converting a capital asset into money and of converting the money, which otherwise would be capital, into income. In other words, the annual payments are not necessarily deferred payments of principal, they may be income the right to which has been purchased by an outlay of capital. In the ordinary case of the purchase of a life annuity for cash, the annuity is income into which the capital laid out has been transformed . . .
>
> On the other hand, where the purchase price of property sold is payable by instalments spread over a long period of time, the instalments, but not the interest on the unpaid balance, are capital. 'In the one case there is an agreement for good consideration to pay a fixed gross amount and to pay it by instalments; in the other there is an agreement for good consideration not to pay any fixed gross amount, but to make a certain, or it may be an uncertain, number of annual payments. The distinction is a fine one, and seems to depend on whether the agreement between the parties involves an obligation to pay a fixed gross sum' (per Walton J, *Chadwick v Pearl Life Insurance Co* [1905] 2 KB 507 at 514).

The decision in *Egerton-Warburton & Ors* was followed half a century later in *Moneymen Pty Ltd v FC of T* 91 ATC 4019. *Moneymen* concerned a taxpayer that had sold its milk processing and pasteurising business. As part of the arrangement, the taxpayer entered into a 20-year milk supply contract with one of the purchasers under which it was entitled to be paid, for a specified number of gallons of milk supplied each day, at the purchaser's highest relevant milk price. In 1974, the taxpayer transferred its milk supply contract to another company. The consideration for the transfer was an amount payable to the taxpayer over the remaining term of the contract based on a proportion of the net price payable for a specified quantity of milk supplied each month. The Full Federal Court held that, even though the contractual rights under the milk supply contract were a structural asset, the payments received by the taxpayer were of an income nature. Relying on *Egerton-Warburton & Ors*, the Court concluded that a taxpayer may sell a capital asset for a stream of income, in which case the consideration received will be of an income nature. According to the Court, the issue in the case was not whether the payments were an 'annuity', but whether there had been an agreement to pay a 'fixed gross amount' by instalments or merely an agreement to make a number of annual payments. The Court found that at no time was there ever any ascertained purchase price payable for the rights sold by the taxpayer and, on this basis, the case was indistinguishable from *Egerton-Warburton*.

Interestingly, another reason why the monthly payments in *Moneymen* were treated as income was because, viewed objectively, they were a substitute for the income which the taxpayer could have derived had it continued to produce milk and not assigned its rights under the milk supply contract. According to the Full Federal Court, the formula for calculating the monthly payments suggested that they were intended to compensate the taxpayer for at least some of the profits that it would have otherwise derived. This reasoning sits comfortably alongside the second strand reasoning of the High Court in *Myer* [9.5]. It also ties in with the discussion regarding the character of compensation receipts [9.7].

Premiums

While it is clear that rent is of an income nature, 'premiums' can be more difficult to characterise. In *Australian Mercantile Land and Finance Co Ltd v FC of T* (1929) 42 CLR 145, Rich J described a premium as 'a reward to the lessor for the grant of the particular interest or benefit obtained by the lessee'. Premiums are ordinarily regarded as capital receipts as they are usually received as lump sum payments for the grant of a lease, rather than as periodic payments for the use of the premises over the term of the lease.

Premiums may, nevertheless, be of an income nature where they constitute the ordinary proceeds of a business. For example, in *Kosciusko Thredbo Pty Ltd v FC of T* 84 ATC 4043, a taxpayer entered into a 45-year lease of part of the Kosciusko State Park, which it set about developing as a skiing and tourist resort. As part of the development, the taxpayer constructed apartments which it sub-let at substantial premiums for long periods of time lasting almost the entirety of the unexpired period of the head lease. The Supreme Court of NSW held that the taxpayer was assessable on the premiums it received for the subleases as they constituted ordinary income. The Court found that the transactions were 'repetitive and recurrent' and constituted an 'essential ingredient' of its business, which involved selling subleases.

[9.7] Compensation amounts and reimbursements

Taxpayers often receive compensation payments where they suffer commercial and other kinds of losses. The character of a compensation receipt will usually depend on what the amount is received for. Payments that replace, substitute or compensate a taxpayer for the loss of revenue items, or amounts that would have been received on income account, are generally of an income nature. In contrast, payments that replace, substitute or compensate a taxpayer for the loss, destruction or sterilisation of capital assets are generally of a capital nature. These broad principles are illustrated in the following diagram and discussed further below.

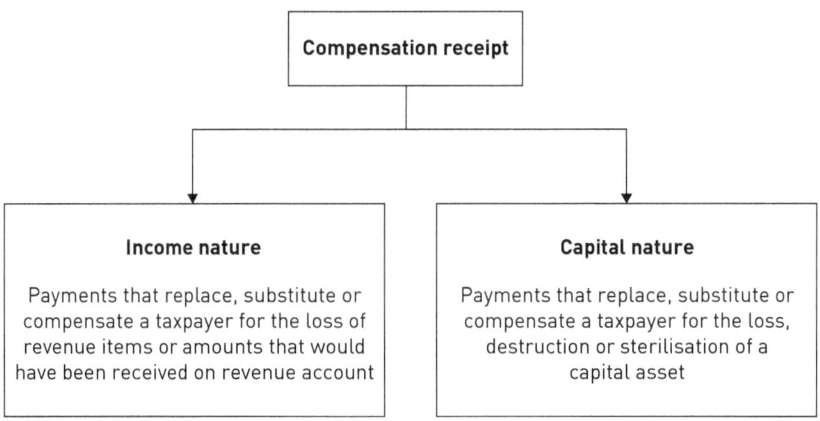

Compensation for loss of the use of money

Compensation received in the form of 'interest' for the temporary loss of the use of money will generally be of an income nature [9.6]. In *Federal Wharf Co Ltd v DFC of T* (1930) 44 CLR 24, the High Court held that interest paid under the *Harbors Act 1913* (SA) on a sum of money owed to a company as compensation for the compulsory acquisition of its land was income. The Act computed interest 'from the time when the Minister entered into occupation . . . to the time when compensation is paid'. Rich J characterised the interest (at 28) as an income receipt on the basis that it was 'recompense for loss of the use of capital during a period of time in which it would earn income'.

A similar conclusion was reached in *Riches v Westminster Bank Ltd* [1947] AC 390, where a court awarded a taxpayer damages in relation to a dispute over a sum of money. The damages included interest on the money from the date the cause of action arose to the date of judgment. The House of Lords held that the interest was of an income nature.

The above cases should, however, be distinguished from *Whitaker v FC of T* 98 ATC 4285, where the Full Federal Court held that 'pre-judgment interest' received in a personal injury claim made against a doctor by a patient who had been left blind after an operation was capital in nature. The Court distinguished *Federal Wharf* on the following basis (at 4295):

> Receiving compensation for the compulsory acquisition of a capital asset which would have been put to a revenue use is quite different from compensation for damages for personal injury. The latter is compensation for not having received damages when they should have been paid, where the plaintiff should not be treated as having invested the judgment moneys in such a way as to earn taxable income. Interest is awarded in cases of this kind because the plaintiff has been deprived of the use of his money, not because he has forgone investment opportunity.

The Court, nevertheless, held that 'post-judgment interest' payable on the outstanding judgment amount was properly characterised as being of an income nature as it was disconnected with the underlying action for personal injury.

Like interest, the courts have also treated gains arising from the maturity of discounted bills of exchange as being of an income nature. In *FC of T v Hurley Holdings (NSW) Pty Ltd* 89 ATC 5033, a company involved in the hotel industry used funds that it had available from the sale of assets to purchase a discounted bill of exchange for $442,199 in January 1983. The bill had a face value of $500,000 and matured in January 1984. The Federal Court held that the $57,801 discount on the bill was assessable income of the taxpayer. Gummow J followed *Myer* and held that the fact that the purchase of the bill was an isolated transaction did not deprive the $57,801 from being of an income nature. His Honour held that the taxpayer sought to invest its funds and the discount compensated the taxpayer for the loss of the use of the money during the term of the bill.

Although in the majority of cases the amount a lender receives over and above the amount lent will usually be regarded as interest and therefore treated as being of an income nature, there is no general rule that this will always be the case. In special circumstances, the excess may be a premium, which is capital in nature. Authority for this proposition comes from the United Kingdom case of *Lomax v Peter Dixon & Son Ltd* [1943] 1 KB 671. The taxpayer in this case had lent funds to a Finnish company just before World War II, when it was risky to make such loans. The Finnish company issued notes to the taxpayer at a discount of 6% and was also required to pay a premium in addition to interest on the notes. The House of Lords accepted that the notes were issued at a reasonable rate of interest and held that the discount and premium were capital in nature as they compensated for the risk of non-payment of the principal. Lord Greene MR summed up his conclusion in three propositions (at 683):

> (1) Where a loan is made at or above such a reasonable commercial rate of interest as is applicable to a reasonably sound security there is no presumption that a 'discount' at which the loan is made or a premium at which it is payable is in the nature of interest. (2) The true nature of the 'discount' or the premium (as the case may be) is to be ascertained from all the circumstances of the case, and, apart from any matter of law which may bear on the question (such as the interpretation of the contract), will fall to be determined as a matter of fact by commissioners. (3) In deciding the true nature of the 'discount' or premium in so far as it is not conclusively determined by the contract, the following matters together with any other relevant circumstances are important to be considered, namely, the term of the loan, the rate of interest expressly stipulated for, the nature of the capital risk and the extent to which, if at all, the parties expressly took or may reasonably be supposed to have taken the capital risk into account in fixing the terms of the contract.

Compensation for loss of trading stock

Compensation payments have been treated as income where they are received for the loss of trading stock. A good illustration of this principle is found in *FC of T v Wade* (1951) 84 CLR 105, where a farmer was assessed on compensation he received for the loss of his cows that had been destroyed by a public authority. As Dixon and Fullagar JJ stated (at 112) 'moneys recovered from any source representing items of a revenue account must be regarded as received by way of revenue'.

Compensation for loss of income under insurance policies

In *FC of T v Smith* 81 ATC 4114, a medical practitioner employed by a hospital was injured in an accident and received amounts under a personal disability insurance policy. The High Court held that these payments were of an income nature. Gibbs, Stephen, Mason, Murphy and Wilson JJ conceded that while the policy insured the taxpayer against loss of the ability to earn income, which was a capital asset, the payments were paid in 'substitution for income' and therefore took the place of a revenue receipt. Relying on a similar metaphor to that used by the United States Supreme Court in *Eisner v Macomber* (1920) 252 US 189, their Honours stated (at 4116):

> If the ability to earn is the tree, and income the fruit thereof, a policy of insurance against impairment of the fruit-bearing capacity of the tree may well take the form of providing the fruit until such time as the tree recovers its proper role. The degree of correspondence, if any, between the moneys payable under the policy and the actual pecuniary loss of revenue suffered by the insured is a relevant factor, but it is not necessary to look for an indemnity measured with any precision against the loss. Any fruit is better than none, whether or not it represents adequate compensation for the loss.

Compensation for losses under statutory schemes

It is common under statutory compensation schemes for taxpayers to receive amounts for 'loss of income' or 'earning capacity'. The treatment of such payments is illustrated in two contrasting cases: *Tinkler v FC of T* 79 ATC 4641 and *FC of T v Slaven* 84 ATC 4077. Both cases involved taxpayers injured in car accidents who received a series of payments under s 25 of the *Motor Accidents Act 1973* (Vic). *Tinkler* involved the original version of s 25, which provided compensation for 'loss of income' and required the Board to make payments calculated according to a statutory formula that took into account four-fifths of the taxpayer's average weekly earnings. *Slaven* involved an amended version of s 25, which provided compensation for 'deprivation or impairment of earning capacity' and required the Board to take into account not only a taxpayer's loss of earnings, but also other factors such as their vocation, the nature of their injury, and medical evidence relating to the injury. In *Tinkler*, the Federal Court held that the payments were of an income nature as they were a substitute for the wages the taxpayer would have earned if the accident had not taken place. In *Slaven*, the Federal Court held that the payments were of a capital nature as their essential character was compensation for the loss of the taxpayer's earning capacity.

Compensation for cancellation of employment contracts

Amounts received as compensation for the loss of salary due to the cancellation of employment contracts have usually been treated as income. This principle is illustrated in *C of T (Vic) v Phillips* (1936) 55 CLR 144, where a managing director of a theatre company who retired before the end of his contract was paid 'by way of compensation' the same amounts at the same times that he would have otherwise been entitled to receive as salary if he had not retired. The High Court held that the payments he received 'must be regarded as of the same nature as the payments which they replace'. As the payments replaced 'salary', they were of an income nature.

Phillips was followed in *Allman v FC of T* 98 ATC 2142, where the AAT held that an airline pilot whose employment had been wrongly terminated because he turned 60 should be assessed on the damages received to compensate him for the loss of his wages.

A different outcome was, however, reached in the early NSW Supreme Court case of *Scott v C of T (NSW)* (1935) 35 SR (NSW) 215. In this case, the chair of a statutory board that had been dissolved was not assessed on compensation that he received under the relevant statute on the basis that the amount was paid because his office had been 'abolished'. Jordan CJ explained (at 219):

> a price received as a consideration for going out of business . . . or compensation received for being prevented from carrying on business any further, or for being prevented from continuing employment, are not income, according to the natural meaning of the word. The sum in question in the present case was compensation made payable because the appellant's office had been abolished before the period for which he had been appointed to hold it had expired, and was measured by the amount of damages which he would have been entitled to recover if he had been wrongfully dismissed.

In *Bennett v FC of T* (1947) 75 CLR 480, the managing director of a radio company was paid a sum of £12,255 in three instalments over three years to change the terms of his appointment. The taxpayer had initially been appointed for seven years under an indenture made in 1935, which gave him sweeping powers that allowed him to effectively control the company's business. Following a change in the shareholding of the company, he was reappointed under new indentures made in 1936, which provided him with the same annual remuneration but removed his effective control of the company and required him to comply with directions given to him by the other directors. Williams J concluded that the payments were of a capital nature on the following basis (at 485):

> the substance of the matter is that the sum of £12,255 was a lump sum payable by instalments as compensation for the cancellation of the indenture of 24 August 1935, and such payments are of a capital nature unless the compensation is some form of equivalent for the loss of the income which the taxpayer would have earned under the agreement but for its cancellation, as in the case of the payments in *Commissioner of Taxes (Vict.) v Phillips* . . . The payments in the present case are simply payments made as part of the consideration for the [taxpayer] agreeing to cancel one agreement under which he had certain rights and entering into a fresh agreement under which he had different rights. Adapting the words of Lord MacMillan in *Van Den Berghs Ltd v Clark* . . . the congeries of the rights which the [taxpayer] enjoyed under the agreement and which for a price he surrendered was a capital asset.

Compensation for closing down or sterilisation of a capital asset

The courts have treated compensation amounts received for the closing down or the 'sterilisation' of profit-yielding assets as capital. The classic case on this point is *Glenboig Union Fireclay Co Ltd v IRC* (1922) 12 TC 427. This case concerned a taxpayer that was in the business of manufacturing and selling fireclay. The taxpayer had mining rights over fields adjacent to a railway line. The railway company that owned the line sought to prevent the taxpayer from mining the land in order to protect its line from being undermined. The railway company eventually paid the taxpayer £15,316 as compensation for the taxpayer ceasing to further work its fields. This amount was calculated by reference to the future profits which it was considered that the taxpayer could have derived from the fields over the next two and a half years before the fireclay would have been exhausted. The House of Lords characterised the compensation payment as a capital receipt on the basis that it was received for the 'sterilisation' of a capital asset. Lord Buckmaster explained the Court's conclusion in the following terms (at 463):

> In truth the sum of money is the sum paid to prevent the [taxpayer] obtaining the full benefit of the capital value of that part of the mines which they are prevented from working . . . It appears to me to make no difference whether it be regarded as a sale of the asset out and out, or whether it be treated merely as a means of preventing the acquisition of profit that would otherwise be gained. In either case the capital asset of the Company to that extent has been sterilised and destroyed, and it is in respect of that action that the sum of £15,316 was paid.

A similar outcome was reached in Australia in *Federal Coke Co Pty Ltd v FC of T* 77 ATC 4255, but for different reasons. This case concerned a company that produced coke, which it supplied to its parent, Bellambi. Bellambi then sold the coke to its customers. One of its customers, Le Nickel, was unable to accept the full amount of coke it had ordered. A settlement was reached between Bellambi and Le Nickel under which it was decided that Le Nickel's purchasing obligations would be reduced in consideration of it agreeing to pay $1m compensation. As a result, the taxpayer's market for coke was reduced. For this reason, and also because the taxpayer was under pressure from the Department of Health to mitigate pollution at its plant, the taxpayer's coke business was closed down. In the meantime, Bellambi had received advice that if it received the payment for varying the contract, the payment would be of an income nature. It was consequently agreed that, instead of Bellambi receiving the payment, Le Nickel would pay the amount to the taxpayer for having to close down its business. The taxpayer, however, was not a party to this agreement. The Full Federal Court held that, in the hands of the taxpayer, the payment was a 'windfall gain' in the nature of a gift. Bowen CJ pointed out that the taxpayer had not given any consideration for the payment and it was not the product of any business or income-producing activities which it had carried on.

Federal Coke should be viewed as a special case that turned on its particular facts. While the decision is considered to be a correct application of the law in the circumstances, it is arguable that the Commissioner may have been able to obtain a different outcome if he had, instead, assessed Bellambi on the basis that it had actually derived the compensation payment under the 'constructive receipt rule' formerly contained in s 19 *ITAA36* and now contained in s 6-5(4) *ITAA97* [9.9].

Compensation for cancellation of trading contracts

Amounts received for the loss of business profits due to the cancellation of trading contracts are usually treated as income. This principle is illustrated in *Heavy Minerals Pty Ltd v FC of T* (1966) 115 CLR 512, which concerned a taxpayer that was engaged in the business of mining and selling rutile. The taxpayer had entered into forward contracts for the sale of its product with its customers. However, in 1958, the world rutile market collapsed, and the taxpayer's customers sought to be released from their contracts. The High Court held that the amounts received by the taxpayer for agreeing to cancel the contracts were of an income nature. In reaching this conclusion, Windeyer J found that, unlike its mining tenements and plant, the cancelled contracts were not capital assets of the taxpayer.

Likewise, provided a taxpayer's capital assets have not been permanently impaired, a compensation payment that fills a 'hole in profits' will usually be of an income nature. This is demonstrated by *Liftronic Pty Ltd v FC of T* 96 ATC 4425, which concerned a taxpayer that sold, installed and maintained lift systems. The taxpayer had purchased defective equipment from Hyundai and successfully brought an action for breach of contract in the Supreme Court of NSW as a result of which it was awarded a sum of money for loss of profits. The Federal Court characterised this amount as income. In arriving at this conclusion, Foster J noted (at 4442):

> the breaches of Hyundai did not destroy the goodwill or earning capacity of Liftronic. They did not take away 'the whole structure, [its] profit making apparatus' . . . Those income earning assets of Liftronic were not 'sterilised and destroyed' . . . They were temporarily impaired . . . There was no destruction of these assets but 'a mere restriction of . . . trading opportunities'. This restriction created a 'hole in profits' which the award of damages was intended to fill.

Compensation for cancellation of structural contracts

Compensation amounts received in respect of the cancellation of 'structural' contracts that are integral to the way that a taxpayer conducts its business operations are usually of a capital nature. For instance, in *Van den Berghs Ltd v Clark (Inspector of Taxes)* [1935] AC 431, the House of Lords held that payments received by a manufacturer of margarine products, in relation to the cancellation of agreements that regulated the way in which it shared profits with a rival and the way in which it conducted its business both in the United Kingdom and abroad, were capital in nature. In the course of delivering the Court's judgment, Lord Macmillan stated (at 442):

> The three agreements which the [taxpayer] consented to cancel were not ordinary commercial contracts made in the course of carrying on their trade; they were not contracts for the disposal of their products, or for the engagement of agents or other employees necessary for the conduct of their business; nor were they merely agreements as to how their trading profits when earned should be distributed as between the contracting parties. On the contrary the cancelled agreements related to the whole structure of the [taxpayer's] profit-making apparatus. They regulated the [taxpayer's] activities, defined what they might and what they might not do, and affected the whole conduct of their business. I have difficulty in seeing how money laid out to secure, or money received for the cancellation of, so fundamental an organisation of a trader's activities can be regarded as an income disbursement or an income receipt.

Compensation for cancellation of agency agreements

Consistent with the principle outlined in *Van den Berghs*, amounts received for the cancellation of agency agreements have been treated as capital receipts where the agency agreements are fundamental and necessary to the continued operation of the taxpayer's business. This proposition is illustrated in *Californian Oil Products Ltd (in liq) v FC of T* (1934) 52 CLR 28, which concerned an oil products distributor that received 10 half-yearly payments of £7,000 each for the cancellation of its exclusive agency arrangement with its supplier. The High Court found that the amounts were received for the abandonment of the only business that the taxpayer conducted and were therefore of a capital nature.

In contrast, amounts relating to the cancellation of agency agreements have been treated as income receipts where the agreements are not integral to the continued operation of the taxpayer's business as a whole. This proposition is illustrated in *Allied Mills Industries Pty Ltd v FC of T* 89 ATC 4365, which concerned a taxpayer that conducted a large food manufacturing and distribution business. The taxpayer had been appointed by Arnotts as the sole distributor of its Peek Frean's biscuits. Arnotts subsequently wanted to take over the distribution of the biscuits and paid the taxpayer a lump sum amount of $372,700 to cancel the distribution agreement. The Full Federal Court held that this payment was of an income nature as, taking into consideration the size, structure and activities of the taxpayer as a whole, the taxpayer had not parted with or received payment for a structural asset, nor had it ceased to carry on business. The Court found that the distribution agreement was entered into in the ordinary course of the taxpayer's overall business and the amount paid to terminate it was for loss of anticipated profits.

Compensation for personal injury

Compensation payments received for personal injury, such as the loss of one's sight from an operation, are usually treated as being capital in nature (*Whitaker v FC of T* 98 ATC 4285). A similar principle extends to payments received for the loss of reputation. In *FC of T v Sydney Refractive Surgery Centre Pty Ltd* 2008 ATC ¶20-081, a corporation that carried on a laser eye surgery business was awarded damages for defamation. The Full Federal Court held that the damages were of a capital nature, even though the amount was calculated by reference to lost profits, as the damages were received for impairment of the taxpayer's earning capacity. According to the Court, an injury to a corporation's reputation diminishes its capacity to earn because it reduces its ability to induce others to do business with it and therefore affects its capital asset.

Compensation payments that are undissected lump sums

The courts are generally prepared to apportion compensation receipts where it is possible to dissect them into distinct income and capital components (*Federal Wharf Co Ltd v DFC of T* (1930) 44 CLR 24). However, where this is not possible (eg in cases relating to unliquidated claims that have mixed elements which are not readily identifiable), the entire amount received is usually treated as a capital receipt.

In *McLaurin v FC of T* (1961) 104 CLR 381, the taxpayer, a grazier, received a lump sum payment of £12,350 to settle a damages claim relating to a fire that damaged his land, fences and livestock. The Commissioner was unsuccessful in treating a portion of the settlement amount (which the payer had allocated to income items) as being of an income nature in the hands of the taxpayer. Dixon CJ, Fullagar and Kitto JJ held (at 391) that while it is appropriate to apportion a single payment or receipt of a mixed nature into income or non-income components where the receipt 'is in settlement of distinct claims of which some at least are liquidated' or 'are otherwise ascertainable by calculation', it is not appropriate 'where the payment or receipt is in respect of a claim or claims for unliquidated damages only and is made or accepted under a compromise which treats it as a single, undissected amount of damages'. Their Honours held that, in such a case, the amount must be 'considered as a whole' and, on this basis, they treated the entire amount as being of a capital nature.

A similar result arose in *Allsop v FC of T* (1965) 113 CLR 341, which concerned a lump sum settlement amount received by an interstate road carrier in respect of licence fees he had paid to the State of NSW under an Act which had subsequently been proved to be invalid. The settlement sum was paid by the Motor Transport Commissioner and released the Commissioner from any liability in respect of the licence fees and any other claims under the invalid legislation. It was accepted that the taxpayer may also have had claims for unlawful interference to his vehicles and business. The High Court held that the entire amount received was of a capital nature as no part of it could be attributed solely to the refund of fees.

In *FC of T v Spedley Securities Ltd* 88 ATC 4126, the taxpayer, a merchant bank, had been engaged by Santos to secure a $65m loan in consideration for being paid a commission, being a percentage of the loan amount. Santos terminated its agreement after the taxpayer had completed most of the work required to arrange the loan. The evidence indicated that the cancellation of the agreement might have caused damage to the taxpayer's reputation, as it might have indicated that Santos had lost confidence in the taxpayer. Under a deed of discharge, Santos paid the taxpayer a lump sum amount of $200,000 in full satisfaction of all rights the taxpayer had against Santos in relation to the termination of the agreement. The deed of discharge did not separately identify how this amount was allocated between the taxpayer's loss of reputation and its loss of commission. The Full Federal Court relied on *McLaurin* and *Allsop* to conclude that no basis of apportionment is available to dissect a lump sum where the component representing the compensation for the damage to the taxpayer's goodwill and the component representing the loss of commission cannot be separately identified. On this basis, the Court treated the entire lump sum as capital.

Another case dealing with the same point is *FC of T v CSR Ltd* 2000 ATC 4710. This case concerned a public company that had become subject to numerous asbestos related injury claims arising out of its business activities. The taxpayer had taken out insurance policies, the obligations under which had been assumed by the New Zealand Insurance Group ('NZI'). The taxpayer sought to be indemnified under the policies, but NZI disputed the claim. The matter was eventually settled by NZI paying $100m to the taxpayer in return for the taxpayer granting it various releases. The taxpayer argued that the $100m was received as consideration for the release of a number of rights, including rights to damages on capital account. The taxpayer submitted that when it became known that NZI declined to indemnify the taxpayer, the taxpayer suffered damage to its reputation (including its credit rating) and goodwill and there was also a significant fall in its market capitalisation. The High Court accepted the taxpayer's submission and followed *Allsop* and *McLaurin* to hold that the $100m was entirely of a capital nature.

Reimbursements and refunds

An issue that is loosely related to the characterisation of compensation payments is the treatment of reimbursements and refunds. A well-known United Kingdom case that considered the treatment of reimbursements is *Hochstrasser (Inspector of Taxes) v Mayes* [1960] AC 376. In this case, an employer had established a housing scheme to assist married male employees who were required to transfer to new work locations. Under the scheme, employees that had entered into 'housing agreements' were reimbursed for losses arising on the sale of their homes. The House of Lords held that a £350 payment received by an employee under the scheme was not taxable under sch E of the *Income Tax Act 1952* (UK), which levied income tax on profits from employment. The Court held that the payment did not fall within sch E as it was not in the nature of a reward for services rendered by the employee. Lord Denning characterised the reimbursement as compensation received for a loss that the taxpayer incurred as a consequence of his employment and as being analogous to indemnification received for workplace injuries. Lord Cohen pointed out that although employment was the *causa sine qua non* (necessary precondition) for the benefit, it was not the *causa causans* (the actual cause).

The leading Australian case dealing with reimbursements is *FC of T v Rowe* 97 ATC 4317. This case concerned a taxpayer who had received an ex gratia payment from the Queensland Government to reimburse him for legal costs that he had incurred in relation to a successful action he had brought against the local council for wrongful dismissal. The taxpayer had been allowed a deduction for his legal costs. The issue before the High Court was whether the reimbursement of these costs should be included in his assessable income. The Court held that the reimbursement was not of an income nature as it was in no sense a reward for his services. The Court also made it clear that there is no common law rule in Australia that reimbursements of deductible expenses are necessarily of an income nature.

Refunds of previously deductible amounts have, nevertheless, been treated as income where they are the ordinary proceeds of the taxpayer's business. This is illustrated in *HR Sinclair & Son Pty Ltd v FC of T* (1966) 114 CLR 537, which involved a timber merchant that obtained timber from state forest reserves under licences granted by the Forests Commission. The taxpayer was required to pay timber royalties to the Forests Commission in respect of timber removed at rates determined in accordance with a formula specified in the licences. For the 1957 to 1960 income years, the taxpayer had paid royalties at a rate specified by the Forests Commission. However, throughout this period it claimed that the Forests Commission had miscalculated the formula and set the royalties at an excessive rate. The Forests Commission ultimately accepted the taxpayer's objections and paid the taxpayer a refund in November 1960. The High Court held that the refund was an ordinary business receipt of the taxpayer and was therefore of an income nature.

Division 20 *ITAA97* contains special statutory income rules that deem certain kinds of recouped expenditure to constitute assessable income [10.4].

[9.8] Calculating income

For an amount to constitute income a taxpayer must realise a gain [9.2]. This raises the important question of how the gain should be calculated—should it be calculated before, or after, taking into account expenses? In other words, is the taxpayer's income simply the gross amount that comes in to the taxpayer ignoring any expenses incurred by the taxpayer to derive that amount, or is it the net profit that has arisen after taking into account expenses incurred by the taxpayer to derive that profit?

Gross basis for calculating income

In most cases, a taxpayer's income is calculated on a gross basis. This approach is consistent with the flow concept [9.2]. The gross basis typically applies to income derived from personal exertion, business and property. A taxpayer's income therefore includes amounts such as the gross salary received from employment, the ordinary proceeds from carrying on a business (*GP International Pipecoaters Pty Ltd v FC of T* 90 ATC 4413) and the gross rental received under a lease (*FC of T v Citibank Ltd & Ors* 93 ATC 4691). Expenses incurred in deriving such amounts are not relevant in calculating the taxpayer's income, but may be separately deductible under either the general or specific deduction provisions in the legislation provided the requirements of those provisions are fulfilled.

Example Sam operates a retail business selling furniture purchased from manufacturers. Sam's income includes the gross amount that he receives from selling his trading stock (eg the tables and chairs). He is therefore assessed on this amount under s 6-5 (less any GST: s 17-5 *ITAA97* [8.5]). The amount Sam pays to purchase his trading stock is not taken into account in calculating his income. Instead, this amount is separately deductible under the general deduction provision in s 8-1 (less any ITCs: s 27-5 *ITAA97* [8.5]).

Net basis for calculating income

In special cases, a taxpayer's income is calculated on a net basis. This approach is consistent with the economic notion of income and focuses on the profit derived from a transaction. The net basis has been applied by the courts in calculating gains made by banks, insurance and investment companies from the realisation of their investments which, although not considered to be trading stock, were nevertheless treated as being held on revenue account (*Punjab Co-operative Bank Ltd, Amritsar v ITC Lahore* [1940] 4 All ER 87; *Colonial Mutual Life Assurance Society Ltd v FC of T* (1946) 73 CLR 604; *London Australia Investment Co Ltd v FC of T* 77 ATC 4398) [9.4]. Likewise, the net basis also applied to taxpayers who made profits from carrying out isolated schemes (*FC of T v The Myer Emporium Ltd* 87 ATC 4363; *Moana Sand Pty Ltd v FC of T* 88 ATC 4897; *McCurry v FC of T* 98 ATC 4487; *McCarthy v FC of T* 2021 ATC ¶10-573) [9.5]. Where the net basis applies, taxpayers do not get separate deductions for their expenses, since these amounts would generally be taken into account in determining their profit from the relevant transaction.

Example An insurance company invests a large portion of the premiums it receives in the share market. It sells some of its shares in order to pay amounts owing under insurance claims. Assuming the shares are treated as revenue assets (but not as trading stock), the net profit on the sale of the shares will form the insurance company's income. In calculating the net profit, the cost of purchasing the shares is subtracted from the amount received for selling the shares. The amount incurred to acquire the shares is not a separate deduction as it has already been taken into account in calculating the profit.

[9.9] Derivation of income

Section 6-5 *ITAA97* requires taxpayers to include in their assessable income for an income year the ordinary income 'derived' during the income year. It is therefore necessary to determine when a taxpayer derives income so that it can be allocated to the appropriate income year for accounting purposes. In *Brent v FC of T* 71 ATC 4195, Gibbs J observed (at 4200) that the tax legislation 'does not define the word "derived" and does not establish a method to be adopted as a general rule to determine the amount of income derived by a taxpayer'. His Honour then went on to state that, in the absence of any specific statutory provision, the derivation of income is determined 'by the application of ordinary business and commercial principles'. Factors such as accounting evidence and practice will therefore be relevant.

Methods of accounting for income

There are two commercially accepted methods for determining when income is derived. These methods operate subject to any specific statutory timing rules (such as those discussed in Chapter 29 relating to various financial transactions).

- **The cash basis.** Under the cash basis (also known as the 'receipts basis'), income is derived when cash or its equivalent (eg a cheque or something that is convertible into cash) is received. Section 6-5(4) provides that in working out whether a taxpayer has derived an amount of ordinary income, the taxpayer is taken to have received the amount as soon as it is applied or dealt with on the taxpayer's behalf. This 'constructive receipts' rule operates, for example, where an amount owing to a taxpayer by a debtor is paid directly to the taxpayer's creditor instead of the taxpayer. In such a case, the taxpayer is taken to have 'received' the amount under s 6-5(4) and is therefore treated as having derived the income under the cash basis of accounting.
- **The accruals basis.** Under the accruals basis (also known as the 'earnings basis'), income is derived when it has been earned. Income is taken to have been 'earned' when a debt comes into existence. Typically, this will arise once the relevant services have been performed, or the relevant goods have been delivered, and a bill has been rendered by the taxpayer to the customer. The fact that the customer may not yet have paid for the services or goods is generally irrelevant.

Example

- **Cash basis.** Tom is an employee who, in Year 2, received salary for work that he performed for his employer in Year 1. Assuming the cash basis applies, Tom derives the salary in Year 2 (even though it relates to work he performed in Year 1).
- **Accruals basis.** Jerry carries on a business selling phones. In Year 1, he sold a phone to a customer under an 'easy pay plan', which allowed the customer to pay for the phone in Year 2. Assuming the accruals basis applies, Jerry derives the income from the sale of the phone in Year 1 (even though the customer only pays for it in Year 2).

In practice, the difficulty that arises is determining which method of accounting applies. In *C of T (SA) v The Executor Trustee and Agency Co of South Australia Ltd* (1938) 63 CLR 108 (*Carden's Case*), Dixon J stated (at 154) that the method of accounting to be adopted by a taxpayer is that which 'is calculated to give a substantially correct reflex of the taxpayer's true income'. Similarly, in *Ballarat Brewing Co Ltd v FC of T* (1951) 82 CLR 364, Fullagar J noted (at 369) that the method to be used is the one that most accurately represents the 'truth and reality of the situation'.

These nebulous, yet frequently cited, statements are not very helpful, and merely indicate that each case needs to be determined on its particular facts. Although each case is unique, it is nevertheless possible to identify some broad principles that have emerged from the case law about which method of accounting is usually most appropriate to apply in particular circumstances. The following discussion examines the approach taken by the courts in specific cases.

Employees and sole traders

It is generally accepted that employment income (eg salary and wages) is derived on a cash basis. Authority for this principle is found in *Roszkiewicz v FC of T* [2019] AATA 931, which concerned an employee who had been paid salary and wages in July 2016 relating to employment she conducted in June 2016. The AAT held that the salary and wages was derived in the 2016/17 income year, rather than the 2015/16 income year, as it was 'common practice' for an employee's income to be assessed on a receipts basis. According to the AAT, the income only 'came home' to the taxpayer when she received it in the 2016/17 income year, and there were no relevant circumstances that would justify it to be treated differently.

A similar outcome was reached in *Blank v FC of T 2016* ATC ¶20-587, where the taxpayer was assessed on deferred compensation amounts payable in 20 quarterly instalments following his retirement on the basis that the amounts were a recognised incident of his employment. The High Court held that the taxpayer was a receipts-based taxpayer and was therefore assessable on the instalments in the income years in which they were received by him.

The cash basis is also usually the appropriate method to be used for determining when income is derived by individuals who conduct business as sole practitioners. This is illustrated in *Carden's case*, which concerned the estate of a deceased doctor who had been engaged in sole practice until his death. The High Court accepted that, up to the time of his death, the income of the doctor had been properly accounted for on a cash basis.

Carden's Case was followed by the Supreme Court of Victoria in *FC of T v Firstenberg* 76 ATC 4141. This case concerned the income of a sole practising solicitor who employed a secretary. McInerney J held (at 4152) that 'in the case of a one-man professional practitioner the essential feature of income 'derived' is receipt'. According to his Honour (at 4155), the accruals basis of accounting would represent 'an artificial, unreal, an unreasonably burdensome method' of calculating the taxpayer's income.

The cash basis of accounting was also found to apply to a chartered accountant engaged in sole practice in *FC of T v Dunn* 89 ATC 4141. Davies J contrasted *Carden's Case* with *Henderson's Case* (discussed below) and stated (at 4147):

> In order to determine the actual appropriateness of an accounting method, regard must be had to the nature and particular circumstances of the taxpayer's income and enterprise. A cash receipts basis may be the correct method of determining the income come home to a taxpayer such as a medical practitioner who is unwilling to pursue vigorously the recovery of fees from patients or clients who have difficulty in meeting the charges rendered. See *Carden's case*. On the other hand, if income is derived from an enterprise having substantial fixed and circulating capital, trading stock, employees and the like, then an accruals basis of accounting may be appropriate to reflect the ongoing derivation of income by the complex organisation. See *Henderson's case*.

Davies J also referred to *Firstenberg* but cautioned that it was an overstatement to conclude that the case was authority for the principle that all sole practitioners are assessed on a cash basis. His Honour expressed the following view on this matter (at 4151):

> There is no principle of law or binding authority to the effect that a sole practitioner is to be assessed on a cash receipts basis. The matter depends upon the nature and incidents of the

> income earning enterprise, upon current accounting principles and practice and upon current perceptions in the field in which the taxpayer gains his income. These matters may differ from time to time. There may be relevant differences between different occupations, between different periods and between different taxpayers in the same field of occupation.

Professional partnerships

In contrast to the position relating to sole practitioners, the accruals basis is usually the appropriate method of accounting for the income of professional partnerships. The leading case on this point is *Henderson v FC of T* 70 ATC 4016. The case concerned an accountancy partnership that had 19 partners and employed 295 staff (including 150 accountants). Until 30 June 1964, the firm lodged its accounts on a cash basis. In 1964 it swapped to an accruals basis, and continued to use that method in subsequent years. The Commissioner, however, refused to accept the change of accounting method. The High Court nevertheless held that the accruals basis was the appropriate method of accounting for the firm's income for the income years ending 30 June 1965 and 30 June 1966. In arriving at this conclusion, the High Court considered that the size, structure and method of operation of the firm were all relevant factors it could take into account.

Importantly, the High Court also concluded that once it was established that the firm's income should be accounted for on an accruals basis, it was not appropriate to include in the firm's assessable income for the income years ending 30 June 1965 and 30 June 1966 any receipts which related to earnings in respect of services provided and completed by the firm in previous years. The practical effect of this was that the taxpayer was not assessed on fees outstanding but uncollected as at 30 June 1964. In other words, as a consequence of the change in its basis of accounting, these fees (which, if the firm had continued to account for its income on a cash basis, would have been assessed in the year that they were received) completely escaped being taxed.

The High Court was not prepared to accept the argument that some kind of adjustment should be made to the taxpayer's income to account for the fact that certain fees were not taxed because of the change in accounting basis. Barwick CJ explained (at 4019) that 'there cannot be any warrant in a scheme of annual taxation upon the income derived in each year of taxation for combining the results of more than one year in order to obtain the assessable income for a particular year of tax'. Accordingly, once the Court had decided that the accruals basis of accounting applied in respect of the particular years of income in question, only earnings relating to those years could be included in the relevant tax computations.

Sole trader forms a partnership (change in accountancy basis)

The outcome in *Henderson's Case* relating to the change in accounting basis should be confined to the special circumstances of that case and should not be applied more generally to situations where a sole practitioner subsequently forms a partnership.

In *Dormer v FC of T* 2002 ATC 5078, the taxpayer had, until 30 June 1997, conducted an accountancy practice as a sole practitioner and accounted for his income on a cash basis. He subsequently formed a partnership with two of his former employees, and the practice thereafter returned its income on an accruals basis. The Commissioner assessed the taxpayer on amounts that he received in the 1997/98 and 1998/99 income years in respect of debts relating to his sole practice (these debts had not been transferred to the partnership). The taxpayer argued that he should not be assessed on these amounts, based on *Henderson's Case*. The Full Federal Court, however, concluded that *Henderson's Case* did not apply, as it involved income of the *same* business. In contrast, the business carried on by the taxpayer as a sole practitioner was different from the business he carried on in partnership. As a result, the taxpayer continued to be assessable on the receipts arising from his former practice.

The fact that the receipts of the taxpayer's business as a sole practitioner continued to be assessable after the change in practice structure is a sensible outcome. If this were not the case, cash-basis taxpayers could simply avoid paying tax by ceasing to carry on their businesses and collecting their debts immediately afterwards. It was clear that the debtors of the taxpayer's former practice remained liable for their debts to the taxpayer and the taxpayer could have presumably sued to recover those debts even though he had commenced a new partnership business. It was therefore appropriate for the taxpayer to be liable to pay tax on those debts when they were received, even though his other income was brought to account on an accruals basis.

Dormer's Case demonstrates that there are situations in which a taxpayer may derive some income on a cash basis and other income on an accruals basis in the same income year. For instance, this could occur where a partner (eg in a legal or accounting firm) also earns salary income (eg from employment as a lecturer at a university). While their partnership income would be accounted for on an accruals basis, their salary income would be accounted for on a cash basis.

Impediments to enforcement

Another illustration of where the accruals basis of accounting applied to a professional partnership is found in *Barratt & Ors v FC of T* 92 ATC 4275. This case concerned a pathology partnership consisting of five partners. The practice employed many staff and also operated through associated service companies that owned diagnostic equipment and employed technicians. What is interesting about this case is that the Full Federal Court held that the accruals basis applied to the pathology practice even though it was prevented, under the *Medical Practitioners Act 1938* (NSW), from instituting recovery proceedings for its fees until six months had expired from the time the patients had been sent their bills. The Court held that *Henderson* should not be interpreted as deciding that an amount cannot be derived unless it is presently recoverable. The Court found that the pathology practice's debts had come into existence when the bills were rendered to the patients. The fact that recovery action could only be commenced in respect of the bills six months after service was merely an 'impediment to enforcement'.

Barratt's case is authority for the principle that just because legislation may prevent recovery action from being instituted until a certain period of time has elapsed, this does not necessarily mean that income has not been 'earned' until the end of that period.

Trading businesses

As a general rule, the accruals basis of accounting applies to taxpayers that carry on trading businesses in much the same way as it applies to taxpayers that carry on professional partnerships.

In *J Rowe & Son Pty Ltd v FC of T* 71 ATC 4157, the taxpayer operated a retail store and sold household goods on credit terms for periods of up to five years. The High Court held that the taxpayer had derived the full price of the goods sold on credit terms in the year of sale. In arriving at this conclusion, the High Court rejected the taxpayer's submission that the income from the credit sales was derived over the period for which the credit was allowed. Menzies J stated (at 4160):

> I consider income from the sale of stock is derived when the stock is sold and a debt is created. It need not be payable in the income year.

Conditional contracts

The importance of determining the time at which a debt is created for the purpose of ascertaining when income is derived under the accruals basis of taxation is illustrated in *Gasparin v FC of T* 94 ATC 4280. This case concerned the sale, under conditional contracts, of subdivided land held by a land developer as trading stock. The Full Federal Court was of the view that the income from the sale of the allotments was derived not when the contracts became unconditional, but at settlement when a debt accrued to the vendor. The Court held that, as a general rule, under an executory contract for the sale of land, unpaid purchase money does not become a debt until the contract has been completed by the execution and acceptance of a conveyance. Prior to settlement, the vendor is not entitled to sue for the purchase money as a debt, but is merely entitled to sue for damages or specific performance.

Unbilled services

Another important case that deals with the issue of when a debt has been created is *FC of T v Australian Gas Light Co & Anor* 83 ATC 4800. This case concerned the activities of two gas companies which were governed by legislation and regulations that controlled the price at which they could sell gas. The companies could only demand payment from their customers where they had rendered accounts, which were based on quarterly meter readings. However, due to the large number of customers involved, these readings and the invoicing of accounts based on the readings were spread over the year. As a result, as at 30 June of any year, a substantial number of customers' quarterly periods had not expired, and their meters had not been read. These customers did not therefore receive their accounts until the following financial year.

The Commissioner assessed the taxpayers on the estimated value of the unbilled gas that had been supplied up to 30 June. The Full Federal Court, however, held that the assessments were incorrect. According to the Court, the reading of the meters and the invoicing of customers were 'conditions precedent' to demanding payment and 'their claims against customers for current liabilities for gas had not matured into recoverable debts'. The value of the unbilled gas did not therefore represent income derived by the taxpayers.

In IT 2095, the ATO seeks to confine the scope of the *Australian Gas Light* decision to its facts. The ruling states the decision 'will only have application to utility companies . . . whose operations are controlled by legislation which prohibits recovery of debts until an account for the gas supplied has been rendered.' Whether the decision will be so narrowly interpreted by the courts is questionable. It is arguable that it may in fact have a broader scope and apply more generally to situations where taxpayers are required to undertake some further steps before becoming entitled to payment for goods and services that they have supplied.

Advance payments

It is quite common for taxpayers to receive payments in advance for services that they have not yet provided. This raises the question whether the income from such services is derived at the time payment is received or only once the services have been performed. The issue was considered in the landmark case of *Arthur Murray (NSW) Pty Ltd v FC of T* (1965) 114 CLR 314, which involved a taxpayer that received advance payments for the provision of a course of dance lessons. The High Court held that the pre-paid tuition fees were derived in the year that the lessons were provided, rather than the year the fees were received. In other words, the Court found that the income was earned on an accruals, rather than cash, basis. An important feature of this case was that, for its own accounting purposes, the taxpayer placed the unapplied balance of the fees in a 'suspense account' and only drew on this account as it provided the relevant lessons. Furthermore, although the taxpayer's agreements with its students provided that no refunds were available, it adopted the practice of providing refunds where not all lessons were taken. On this basis, the High Court concluded that it could not be said that the taxpayer treated the pre-paid receipts as income. Barwick CJ, Kitto and Taylor JJ explained the position as follows (at 319):

> The possibility of having to make such a payment back . . . is an inherent characteristic of the receipt itself. In our opinion it would be out of accord with the realities of the situation to hold, while the possibility remains, that the amount received has the quality of income derived by the company.

In *Country Magazine Pty Ltd v FC of T* (1968) 15 ATD 86, a magazine publisher had accounted for its income from magazine subscriptions on a cash basis and therefore brought to account the full amounts that it had received each year for its subscriptions. However, following the *Arthur Murray Case*, it realised that it should have accounted for its income on an accruals basis. Accordingly, in its tax return for the 1966 income year, it deducted from the amount it received for subscriptions during that year an amount for 'subscriptions in advance' (which related to magazine issues that would not be published until the subsequent year). It also sought to exclude from its assessable income for the year an amount relating to subscriptions that became due during the year, but which it had already brought to account in the 1965 year under its previous cash basis of accounting.

The High Court held that the taxpayer could not exclude this amount from its assessable income in the 1966 income year since, under the accruals basis of accounting, it constituted income of that year. Kitto J indicated that the taxpayer could not turn what was assessable income of one year into assessable income of another year. His Honour pointed out that the Commissioner was obliged to assess taxpayers on all the income they derived during an income year and had no discretion to exclude any portion of such income on the basis that it had been mistakenly included in a previous year's return. Accordingly, the correct course of action for the taxpayer to adopt in these circumstances in order to avoid double taxation should have been to instead seek an amended assessment for the prior year.

Refunds provided after the end of the year

In appropriate circumstances, the amount of income derived by a taxpayer from its trading activities in a particular year should take account of refunds that the taxpayer is likely to provide in a subsequent year. This principle is illustrated in *Ballarat Brewing Co Ltd v FC of T* (1951) 82 CLR 364, which concerned a brewing company that sold products on terms that allowed its customers a 'discount' and a 'rebate' on the agreed gross purchase price if they fulfilled certain conditions. These conditions included prompt payment for the liquor supplied (due on the 28th day of the month following the month of delivery) and compliance with certain business practices. The evidence indicated that it was very rare that discounts or rebates were not in fact given to customers. On this basis, the High Court held that the taxpayer, in calculating its income, had properly taken the discounts and rebates into account in relation to the year in which the products were sold rather than, as the Commissioner had submitted, in the year in which they were actually allowed. Fullagar J explained that the taxpayer's approach was correct as it brought to account amounts which the taxpayer, in the light of past experience, would almost certainly receive; whereas the Commissioner's approach brought to account amounts which the taxpayer would almost certainly not receive. In other words, the taxpayer's method of accounting was closer to the 'truth and reality' of the situation.

Income which is subject to a dispute

The issue of when amounts that are the subject of a dispute are derived was considered in *BHP Billiton Petroleum (Bass Strait) Pty Ltd & Anor v FC of T* 2002 ATC 5169. The taxpayers in this case were joint venturers who supplied natural gas to buyers through a pipeline. Under the contracts, the gas became the property of the buyers on delivery. The buyers were invoiced monthly and were obliged to pay for the gas according to an agreed formula, which could be adjusted for any increase or decrease in taxes attributable to the production or supply of gas. In 1991, the PRRT was extended to cover the taxpayers' operations, and the taxpayers sought to pass on the tax to the buyers in their monthly invoices. The buyers, however, disputed the taxpayers' rights to pass on the tax. The dispute was eventually settled, following arbitration and the institution of court proceedings, by the buyers paying the taxpayers two lump sums: one for past claims and the other for future claims relating to the pass-on amounts. The Commissioner contended that the income relating to the pass-on amounts was derived either when the gas was delivered or when the buyers were invoiced.

The Full Federal Court, however, held that the income relating to the pass-on amounts was only derived when the dispute was settled as the amounts were not capable of being measured with sufficient reliability until such time. The Court found no Australian authority requiring a taxpayer who is assessed on an accruals basis to account for trading income that is the subject of a dispute in the year that the goods are sold. The Court stated (at 5187):

> As should by now be clear a principle which requires the taxpayer to account for disputed income in the year goods are sold conflicts with accounting practice. That practice regards income to be derived when the dispute is concluded, whether through arbitration, litigation or settlement. The only justification for the principle for which the Commissioner here contends is one that proceeds on the fiction that a successful litigant was always going to be successful and was always going to receive the amount which the arbitral or litigation result achieves. The Court should be slow to adopt a fiction in preference for reality in a case such as the present. The deferral of derivation until the conclusion of the dispute (or perhaps receipt if that occurs earlier) avoids the difficulties which arise where the accounts of the year in which the trader sells goods cannot be reopened and where the availability of a deduction for a bad debt may be the subject of doubt. It avoids too the unfairness to a taxpayer in being required to pay tax immediately where recoverability of what is owed to the taxpayer and which is the fund out of which the tax might be expected to be paid, is, as a result of a bona fide dispute, outside the control of the taxpayer.

[9.10] QUESTIONS

1. Discuss whether any of the following items constitute income:
   - salary and a performance bonus received by an employee
   - a tip received by a waiter
   - interest derived from a bank deposit
   - rent received from an investment property
   - a gift received under a will of a deceased relative
   - frequent flyer points received by an employee relating to work-related travel
   - a birthday gift received from a close friend who is also a former employer
   - proceeds received from the sale of the goodwill of a restaurant business
   - proceeds from the sale of food by a supermarket
   - a prize received by a competitor on a quiz show
   - gambling winnings of a regular punter
   - proceeds from the sale of used furniture at a garage sale
   - a free overseas holiday received by a retailer from a manufacturer
   - returns to members of excess funds raised by a tennis club for a club house renovation
   - a prize from a radio station to a professional footballer for being named best player.
2. Why were the taxpayers in *FC of T v Cooke and Sherden* 80 ATC 4140 not assessed in relation to the overseas holidays? Does s 21A *ITAA36* overcome the decision?
3. It has been said that 'a mere saving of expenditure does not constitute income'. Discuss whether you agree or disagree with this statement and provide cases to support your arguments.

4. Why were the payments in *Calvert v Wainwright* (1947) 27 TC 475; *Moorhouse (Inspector of Taxes) v Dooland* [1955] 1 All ER 93; and *FC of T v Dixon* (1952) 86 CLR 540 of an income nature, but the payments in *Hayes v FC of T* (1956) 96 CLR 47 and *Scott v FC of T* (1966) 117 CLR 514 not of an income nature?
5. Are all receipts of a taxpayer that carries on a business income in nature?
6. Explain the respective outcomes reached by the courts in the following sale of land cases: *Californian Copper Syndicate Ltd v Harris (Surveyor of Taxes)* (1904) 5 TC 159; *Scottish Australian Mining Co Ltd v FC of T* (1950) 81 CLR 188; *FC of T v Whitfords Beach Pty Ltd* 82 ATC 4031; *Statham & Anor v FC of T* 89 ATC 4070; *Casimaty v FC of T* 97 ATC 5135; *Moana Sand Pty Ltd v FC of T* 88 ATC 4897; *Crow v FC of T* 88 ATC 4620; *McCurry & Anor v FC of T* 98 ATC 4487; and *McCarthy v FC of T* 2021 ATC ¶10-573.
7. What factors do courts take into account in determining whether a person is a share trader?
8. What is the 'first strand' of the decision in *FC of T v The Myer Emporium Ltd* 87 ATC 4363? Did the courts apply the first strand in any of the following cases: *FC of T v Cooling* 90 ATC 4472; *Westfield Ltd v FC of T* 91 ATC 4234; *Henry Jones (IXL) Ltd v FC of T* 91 ATC 4663 and *SP Investments Pty Ltd v FC of T* 93 ATC 4170? If the first strand did not apply in some of these cases but amounts were nevertheless assessable, on what basis was this so?
9. In 1979, a doctor who lived and worked in Sydney purchased a 20-acre parcel of rural land on the outskirts of the city for $100,000. Over the years, he used the property as a 'hobby farm' for growing fruit trees and as a 'weekend retreat' for relaxation. Recently, the surrounding area has become more developed and the property has increased in value. The doctor has also recently run into financial difficulties as a result of a malpractice suit and he is considering selling the property. Would he be required to include any amount in his assessable income as a result of the sale? Would your answer be different if he had originally purchased the property with the intention of selling it at a profit when land prices had risen sufficiently? Also, would your answer be different if he had decided to develop the property three years ago and subdivided it into 20 one-acre allotments and constructed roads and buildings on it and sold off the allotments separately over a period of one year?
10. On 1 July 2022, Ross purchased land with an old factory on it for $2.2m from a manufacturing company that was selling its assets because of financial difficulties. Ross bought the land because his friend had told him a technology company was planning to build a research centre on the adjoining site. Ross was confident the land would rise in value after this was made public, and he wanted to make a quick profit from selling the land. To maximise his profit, he paid $220,000 to a demolition company to remove the old factory, as the land was more valuable as a vacant site. Ross also planned to make money out of selling the bricks from the demolished factory. He sold these for $110,000 in January 2023. A few months later, after the technology company announced its intention to build the centre, Ross sold the property for $4.4m. Discuss whether any amounts are assessable under s 6-5 *ITAA97*.
11. Is it possible to reconcile the different outcomes reached by the courts in *FC of T v Unilever Australia Securities Ltd* 95 ATC 4117 and *FC of T v Orica Ltd* 98 ATC 4494?
12. Contrast the decisions in *Egerton-Warburton & Ors v DFC of T* (1934) 51 CLR 568 and *Foley v Fletcher* (1858) 157 ER 678.
13. Explain why the payments received in *Heavy Minerals Pty Ltd v FC of T* (1966) 115 CLR 512 and *Allied Mills Industries Pty Ltd v FC of T* 89 ATC 4365 were regarded as income while the payments in *Glenboig Union Fireclay Co Ltd v IRC* (1922) 12 TC 427; *Van den Berghs Ltd v Clark (Inspector of Taxes)* [1935] AC 431 and *Californian Oil Products Ltd (in liq) v FC of T* (1934) 52 CLR 28 were treated as capital.

14. Why did the courts not apportion the receipts in *Allsop v FC of T* (1965) 113 CLR 341, *McLaurin v FC of T* (1961) 104 CLR 381 and *FC of T v Spedley Securities Ltd* 88 ATC 4126?
15. Why is it important to determine when income is derived? Explain the difference between the 'cash' and 'accruals' basis of accounting.
16. John is a self-employed accountant. He owes his plumber $5,000 for repairs to his bathroom. John requests one of his clients, who owes him $5,000 for accounting services, to pay this amount directly to his plumber. Has John derived any income?
17. Betty is a barrister who received $110,000 in fees during the current income year (80% related to services provided during the current year and 20% related to services provided in the previous year). Betty is also owed $33,000 by solicitors who have not paid her outstanding fees for court appearances this year. How much income has Betty derived this year?
18. Freddie is an experienced stockbroker who provides courses teaching other stockbrokers how to improve their trading skills. In January 2023, Fannie paid $1,320 for a 12-month course of lessons. There are 12 lessons in the course (each offered on the first day of each month over the duration of the course). Although the terms of the contract between Freddie and Fannie states that no refunds are available, Freddie typically provides refunds for the unexpired portions of a course if a student decides to quit part-way through. How should Freddie account for the course fees?

STATUTORY INCOME 10

[10.1] Introduction

A taxpayer's assessable income includes not only amounts that are ordinary income [9.1], but also amounts that are 'statutory income' (s 6-10(1) *ITAA97*). Statutory income comprises those amounts that are deemed by the legislation to be assessable income, but are not necessarily income according to ordinary concepts.

There are more than 100 statutory income provisions in the *ITAA36* and *ITAA97*. A useful list of these provisions is contained in div 10 *ITAA97*. This chapter focuses on:

- s 27H *ITAA36* (which relates to annuities) [10.2]
- div 15 *ITAA97* (which contains a variety of miscellaneous provisions) [10.3], and
- sub-div 20-A *ITAA97* (which deals with the recoupment of deductible expenditure) [10.4].

A number of other statutory income provisions are discussed in subsequent chapters.

Like the ordinary income rules, the statutory income provisions operate subject to jurisdictional rules. These rules provide that:

- a resident's assessable income includes statutory income from all sources, whether in or out of Australia (s 6-10(4) *ITAA97*), and
- a foreign resident's assessable income includes statutory income from all Australian sources, as well as other statutory income that a provision includes in assessable income on some basis other than having an Australian source (s 6-10(5) *ITAA97*).

The rules for determining whether a taxpayer is a resident or a foreign resident are discussed at [30.2]. The way in which the source of income is ascertained is discussed at [30.3].

As with ordinary income, to the extent that statutory income is exempt income [11.2] or non-assessable non-exempt income [11.3], it is excluded from assessable income (ss 6-1, 6-15, 6-20, 6-23 *ITAA97*). This means, for example, that to the extent that a taxpayer's statutory income includes GST on a taxable supply, it is not assessable as it constitutes non-assessable non-exempt income by virtue of s 17-5 *ITAA97* [8.5].

[10.2] Annuities

Section 27H(1) *ITAA36* includes in a taxpayer's assessable income, the amount of an annuity derived during the year of income less, where the annuity has been purchased, the deductible amount.

Definition of annuity

An 'annuity' is exhaustively defined in s 27H(4) *ITAA36*. The definition covers an annuity within the common law meaning of the term as well as certain other payments. The definition of annuity, however, expressly excludes 'an annuity that is a qualifying security for the purposes of div 16E' [29.12] and a 'superannuation income stream' [19.4].

Under the common law, an annuity is a form of periodic payment that is usually purchased (eg from an insurance company) and paid in regular intervals over a period of years or over a person's lifetime.

However, not all periodic payments are necessarily annuities. In many cases, periodic payments are simply repayments of capital with interest (eg repayments under a loan). In *Australia and New Zealand Savings Bank Ltd v FC of T* 93 ATC 4370, Hill J indicated that, in determining whether a payment is an instalment of an annuity or part repayment of capital with interest, the court must have regard to form rather than substance. His Honour explained (at 4389):

> There is good reason why the question whether a particular payment is an instalment of an annuity or part repayment of capital with interest must be determined as a matter of form, rather than substance. In every case where a term annuity is involved, the substance of the transaction will involve an investment of a capital sum by an investor to produce a return to the annuitant, calculated by reference to that capital sum to which is applied an agreed or defined percentage interest rate. So, too, some endowment life policies . . . may fairly be said to involve in substance the investment of a capital sum to be returned at a later date with interest. But neither all term annuities, nor all endowment insurance policies will be loans.

Where a person receives periodic payments under an agreement and it is not possible to identify any fixed gross sum payable under the agreement, this will often point to the conclusion that the payments are an annuity. A good illustration of this is the periodic payments that were made to the taxpayer in *Egerton-Warburton & Ors v DFC of T* (1934) 51 CLR 568 [9.6].

In *Chadwick v Pearl Life Insurance Co* [1905] 2 KB 507, Walton J said (at 514):

> It is obvious that there will be cases in which it will be very difficult to distinguish between an agreement to pay a debt by instalments and an agreement for good consideration to make certain annual payments for a fixed number of years. In the one case there is an agreement for good consideration to pay a fixed gross amount and to pay it by instalments. In the other there is an agreement for good consideration not to pay any fixed gross amount, but to make a certain, or it may be uncertain, number of annual payments. The distinction is a fine one and seems to depend on whether the agreement between the parties involves an obligation to pay a fixed gross sum.

The difficulty in distinguishing between annuities and instalment payments for the fixed price of a capital asset is illustrated in *IRC v Ramsay* [1935] 1 All ER 847. This case concerned a taxpayer who purchased a dental practice in London. The 'primary price' payable under the agreement was £15,000. The taxpayer was required to pay a deposit of £5,000 and, over each of the next 10 years, the taxpayer was required to pay the vendor, as 'capital sums', 25% of the net profits of the practice to make up the balance of the primary price. The agreement provided that the vendor was entitled to the full amount of the annual payments, even though the aggregate amounts payable might exceed the primary price. Conversely, if the aggregate amounts payable were less than the primary price, the vendor was required to accept the amounts payable in full satisfaction of the amount owing to him.

The House of Lords held that the annual payments were capital instalments of the fixed purchase price payable under the agreement and were therefore not deductible to the taxpayer. Lord Wright MR stated (at 853):

> this is not the case of an annuity or a series of annual payments. It is a case in which a capital lump sum has been stipulated as the price of a piece of property, and it is none the less so because the payment of that sum is to be made by instalments, instalments at certain specific periods, no doubt, but not instalments of a fixed price.

Deductible amount

Where an annuity has been purchased, it will comprise both an underlying interest component and an underlying capital component, even though, for legal purposes, such components are blended together into a single fused payment. To prevent taxpayers being assessed on the capital component of such payments, the amount of an annuity that is assessable is reduced by the portion of the annuity that consists of the 'deductible amount'. This amount is calculated according to the formula in s 27H(2) *ITAA36*. The formula is designed to ensure that taxpayers are not taxed on that portion of an annuity which represents the annualised return of their capital purchase price. The deductible amount formula is:

$$\frac{A(B-C)}{D}$$

For the purposes of the formula:

- 'A' is the taxpayer's share of the annuity in relation to the year of income
- 'B' is the amount of the 'undeducted purchase price' of the annuity
- 'C' is the 'residual capital value' in relation to the annuity or nil (where no such amount exists), and
- 'D' is the 'relevant number' in relation to the annuity (ie where the annuity is payable for a fixed term, it is the term of the annuity; where the annuity is payable for the lifetime of a person, it is the person's 'life expectation factor' according to the applicable Australian Life Tables set out in reg 7 *ITAR15*; or, otherwise, it is a number determined by the Commissioner taking into account specified factors).

Example On 3 May 2021, when Pam was 61 years old, she paid $300,000 to purchase an annuity of $18,000. The annuity is payable annually for the rest of her life and, on her death, a lump sum of $80,000 is payable to her husband. The applicable *Australian Life Tables* indicate that Pam has a life expectation factor of 26.03 years. The deductible amount is calculated under s 27H(2) as follows:

$$\begin{aligned}\text{Deductible amount} &= \frac{A(B-C)}{D}\\ &= \frac{1(\$300{,}000-\$80{,}000)}{26.03}\\ &= \$8{,}451\end{aligned}$$

Pam is required to include $9,549 (ie $18,000 – $8,451) in her assessable income each year under s 27H(1).

10

[10.3] Miscellaneous provisions in div 15 *ITAA97*

Division 15 *ITAA97* contains a diverse range of statutory income provisions. Some of these provisions are discussed below.

Allowances

Section 15-2 *ITAA97* includes in a taxpayer's assessable income the value to the taxpayer of all allowances, gratuities, compensations, benefits, bonuses and premiums provided to the taxpayer in respect of, or for or in relation directly or indirectly to, any employment of or services rendered by the taxpayer.

Section 15-2 is based on former s 26(e) *ITAA36*, which was drafted in similar terms. For the provision to apply, there must be a sufficient nexus between a benefit and the taxpayer's employment or services rendered. This will arise where the benefit is a 'product', 'incident' or 'consequence' of the taxpayer's employment or services, but not where it is extraneous to such activities (eg where it is in the nature of a gift).

In *Smith v FC of T* 87 ATC 4883, the taxpayer was employed by a bank. The bank had an 'encouragement to study' policy, under which it made payments to staff who completed various subjects and courses. The evidence indicated that the benefit of this policy for the bank was to provide it with better-qualified staff. The taxpayer was assessed under former s 26(e) in respect of payments he received from the bank in relation to a four-year management certificate course he had completed. A majority of the High Court held that these payments fell within former s 26(e), as they were sufficiently connected with the taxpayer's employment to be a product, incident or consequence of employment. Brennan J stated (at 4890):

> I am quite unable to say that the allowance was paid for considerations extraneous to the employment. On the contrary, the allowance was paid because it was an incentive to an employee to improve his skills to his own advantage and to the anticipated advantage of the bank. The relationship between the employment of the appellant and the payment of the allowance was substantial. In my opinion, the employment was a direct cause of the payment. It follows that the allowance was paid 'in consequence of' the employment, and thus was paid 'in respect of . . . or in relation . . . to' the employment.

Employment is not, however, a mandatory requirement for s 15-2 to apply. A benefit that is not related to employment, but which nevertheless arises from services performed by a taxpayer, can satisfy the provision's nexus requirement. This is illustrated in *FC of T v Holmes* 95 ATC 4476, where a taxpayer was assessed on a reward received for salvaging a distressed ship. The Full Federal Court referred to *Smith* and held that the payment fell squarely within former s 26(e), as it was clearly received in recognition of the services performed by the taxpayer.

The nexus requirement is not satisfied where the benefit is provided by a third party who is not the taxpayer's employer under a separate contractual arrangement in circumstances where the taxpayer has provided no services for the benefit. This is illustrated in *Payne v FC of T* 96 ATC 4407 [9.2], which concerned an employee of a firm of accountants who redeemed airline tickets under Qantas' frequent flyer program. The tickets were found not to be income according to ordinary concepts on the basis that they were not transferable and not convertible into money. In addition, former s 26(e) did not apply to include the value of the benefit in the taxpayer's assessable income. The Federal Court held that although the taxpayer earned frequent flyer points by taking flights in the course of her employment, which were paid for by her employer, this was insufficient to treat the tickets as being provided 'in respect of', or 'for or in relation directly or indirectly to', her employment. The Court also found that the taxpayer did not provide any services to the airline, which instituted the scheme for its own benefit. It noted that the employer played no part in the scheme, as it did not pay for, or encourage, its employee's participation in it.

In practice, the scope of s 15-2 is very limited as it does not apply to amounts assessable as ordinary income under s 6-5 *ITAA97* [9.1], superannuation lump sums [19.16], employment termination payments [20.2], unused annual leave and long service leave payments [20.3], dividends [22.5], non-share dividends [29.9] and employee share scheme interests [21.2] (s 15-2(3)).

It also operates subject to s 23L *ITAA36*, which treats 'fringe benefits' as non-assessable non-exempt income and 'exempt benefits' under the *FBTAA* as exempt income [8.5]. As a result, most benefits provided in respect of employment will fall outside the operation of s 15-2 as they will usually be either fringe benefits or exempt benefits [18.3].

Return to work payments

Section 15-3 *ITAA97* includes in a taxpayer's assessable income amounts received under an arrangement for the purpose of inducing the taxpayer to resume work or provide services to any entity. These amounts are assessable irrespective of how they are described and regardless of who pays them.

> ***Example*** Bert recently resigned from employment with P Ltd because he did not like his working hours. Ernie is P Ltd's major shareholder and paid Bert $50,000 to recommence work with the company. Bert is required to include the $50,000 in his assessable income under s 15-3.

Accrued leave transfer payments

Section 15-5 *ITAA97* includes in a taxpayer's assessable income accrued leave transfer payments received by the taxpayer. An 'accrued leave transfer payment' is defined in s 26-10(2) *ITAA97* and covers payments made in respect of an individual's leave made by the individual's former employer to his or her current employer under an Australian law, or under an award, order, determination or industrial agreement under such a law.

> ***Example*** Issac's employee, Albert, is transferred to a new employer, Max. Isaac pays Max $1,000 for Albert's unused long service leave under the terms of an industrial agreement. Max is required to include the $1,000 in his assessable income.

Bounties and subsidies

Section 15-10 *ITAA97* includes in a taxpayer's assessable income a bounty or subsidy received in carrying on a business which is not ordinary income under s 6-5 *ITAA97*. Although the terms 'bounty' and 'subsidy' are not defined in the legislation, dictionary definitions indicate that a bounty is something that is 'generously bestowed' (eg a gratuity), while a subsidy is a payment, often made by a government, to provide assistance.

The predecessor of s 15-10 (former s 26(g) *ITAA36*) was considered in *First Provincial Building Society Limited v FC of T* 95 ATC 4145. This case concerned a payment made by the Queensland Government to a building society following the winding up of a statutory contingency fund to which the taxpayer and other building societies had made contributions. The Full Federal Court held that the payment was a subsidy and, as it lacked the necessary connection with the taxpayer's business activities to constitute ordinary income, was assessable under former s 26(g).

Former s 26(g) also applied in *Reckitt & Colman Pty Ltd v FC of T* 74 ATC 4185, where a manufacturer of household, pharmaceutical and other products was assessable on a Commonwealth R&D grant that it had received.

Profit-making undertakings or plans

Section 15-15 *ITAA97* includes in a taxpayer's assessable income profit arising from the carrying on or carrying out of a profit-making undertaking or plan. The provision does not apply to a profit that is ordinary income under s 6-5 *ITAA97* or that arises from the sale of property acquired on or after 20 September 1985 (which is the date that CGT was introduced [17.1]).

In *XCO Pty Ltd v FC of T* 71 ATC 4152, the High Court considered the predecessor of s 15-15 (former s 26(a) *ITAA36*), which applied to 'profit-making schemes'. Gibbs J indicated that a scheme is not a 'profit-making scheme' simply because it yields a profit when none was intended. A profit-making scheme is a 'plan devised in order to obtain a profit', and a scheme only answers that description if the taxpayer carries it out with the purpose of making a profit.

Earlier on, in *FC of T v Williams* 72 ATC 4188, a taxpayer who subdivided and sold land was found by the High Court not to be assessable on any profit from the sale under former s 26(a). This was because she had acquired the land as a gift from her husband rather than for the purpose of profit making by sale or as part of a profit-making scheme.

The practical need for s 15-15 is questionable as a profit arising from the carrying out of a profit-making scheme or plan would usually constitute ordinary income in accordance with the decision in *FC of T v The Myer Emporium Ltd* 87 ATC 4363 and would therefore be assessable under s 6-5 [9.5].

Royalties

Section 15-20 *ITAA97* states that a taxpayer's assessable income includes an amount that is received 'as or by way of royalty within the ordinary meaning of "royalty" (disregarding the definition of royalty in s 995-1) if the amount is not assessable as ordinary income under s 6-5'. In other words, s 15-20 is directed at assessing amounts that are 'royalties' within the common law (but not statutory) definition of the term and that are of a capital (rather than income) nature.

At common law, a 'royalty' is a payment for the use of an asset that is calculated by reference to the amount that the asset is used or exploited. An example of a royalty is found in *McCauley v FC of T* (1944) 69 CLR 235. This case concerned a dairy farmer who entered into an agreement with a purchaser to sell the right to cut and remove the standing milling timber then growing on his land 'at or for a price of royalty of three shillings for each and every 100 superficial feet of such milling timber so cut'. The High Court held that the amounts received by the taxpayer were royalties as they were payable by reference to the quantity of timber cut or removed from the land.

McCauley may be contrasted with *Stanton v FC of T* (1955) 92 CLR 630, where co-owners of land entered into an agreement with a sawmiller, under which they agreed to sell to the sawmiller for £17,500 (payable by instalments) 'five hundred thousand super feet of millable pine timber' and 'two million five hundred thousand super feet of millable hardwood timber' with the right to cut and remove the timber from the land. The agreement provided that, should there be insufficient timber on the land, a proportionate rebate would be available to the sawmiller. The High Court held that the payments were not royalties. Under the agreement, the full price was payable whether or not the timber had in fact been removed from the land. In contrast to *McCauley*, the payments in this case did not depend upon the quantity of the timber cut or removed from the land.

The concept of a royalty is extended by the statutory definition in s 995-1 *ITAA97*, which defines a royalty by reference to the definition in s 6(1) *ITAA36*. This provision deems that a royalty expressly includes a broad range of payments, however described or computed, that are received as consideration for things such as:

- the right to use any copyright, patent, design or model, plan, secret formula or process, trademark or other like property or right
- the use of, or the right to use, any industrial, commercial or scientific equipment, or
- the supply of scientific, technical industrial or commercial knowledge or information.

The extended definition would now also cover the circumstances in *FC of T v Sherritt Gordon Mines Limited* 77 ATC 4365. In that case, a Canadian company entered into an agreement to provide an Australian company with technical information and assistance to practise its 'Sherritt system' for mining nickel. The agreement provided that the taxpayer would be paid 'a percentage of the aggregate sales value of the nickel and by-products produced . . . by the practice of the Sherritt system' spread over 15 years. A majority of the High Court concluded that the payments were not royalties under the ordinary meaning of that term as they were consideration for the provision of technical assistance and information. The majority pointed out that the fact that the taxpayer had the right to use and sell products produced as a result of using the system was no more that recognition of the consequence which automatically flowed from the provision of the technical assistance and information. The payments were also outside the scope of the former extended definition of royalties, which was based on the definition in art 10(5) of the United Kingdom DTA and was therefore restricted to payments between Australian and United Kingdom residents.

It is clear that payments that are not calculated by reference to the use or exploitation of an asset can constitute royalties under the current extended definition in s 995-1. This means that amounts that are of a capital nature may be royalties under s 995-1. It is important to realise, however, that s 995-1 is only a definition provision and not an assessment provision. Consequently, given the fact that s 15-20 expressly disregards the s 995-1 definition of royalty, it is difficult to envisage specific situations where s 15-20 applies, as most common law royalty amounts would ordinarily be caught by s 6-5, since they represent the flow from some capital asset and would therefore usually constitute income according to ordinary concepts [9.2].

Payments made to members of a copyright collecting society

Section 15-22 *ITAA97* includes in a member of a copyright collecting society's assessable income payments made to the member by the society. This provision does not, however, assess any part of the payment that represents an amount on which the directors of the society (as trustees) are assessed under ss 98, 99 or 99A *ITAA36* [24.5]. Where s 15-22 applies, the payment is not also assessable as a royalty under s 15-20 (s 15-20(2)).

Payments of resale royalties by the resale royalty collecting society

Section 15-23 *ITAA97* includes in a taxpayer's assessable income payments made by the resale royalty collecting society under s 26 of the *Resale Royalty Right for Visual Artists Act 2009* (Cth). This Act entitles visual artists to a royalty payment on the sale price of any commercial resale of their original works of art over $1,000.

Amounts received for lease obligation to repair

Section 15-25 *ITAA97* includes in a lessor's (or former lessor's) assessable income amounts that are received from an entity (eg a lessee) for failing to comply with a lease obligation to repair premises that have been used by the entity for income-producing purposes and that are not assessable as ordinary income under s 6-5.

Insurance or indemnity for loss of assessable income

Section 15-30 *ITAA97* includes in a taxpayer's assessable income amounts received by way of insurance or indemnity for the loss of amounts that would have been included in assessable income and that are not ordinary income under s 6-5.

Interest on overpayments and early payments of tax

Section 15-35 *ITAA97* includes in a taxpayer's assessable income interest payable under the *Taxation (Interest on Overpayments and Early Payments) Act 1983* (Cth) on overpayments and early payments of tax [40.8].

Mining, quarrying or prospecting information

Section 15-40 *ITAA97* includes in a taxpayer's assessable income amounts received for providing mining, quarrying or prospecting information to another entity if the taxpayer continues to hold the information and the amount received is not ordinary income under s 6-5.

Work in progress amounts

Section 15-50 *ITAA97* includes in a taxpayer's assessable income 'work in progress amounts' received by the taxpayer. This provision is discussed in detail at [23.4].

Funeral policy payments

Section 15-55 *ITAA97* includes in a taxpayer's assessable income the amount of a benefit provided to the taxpayer by a life insurance company under a funeral policy issued after 31 December 2002 to pay for the funeral of an insured person. The assessable amount is reduced by premiums that are reasonably related to the benefit and fees included in the insurance company's assessable income under s 320-15(1)(k) *ITAA97*. This is designed to ensure that the assessable amount represents the investment return on the policy. Section 15-55 does not apply to benefits that are assessable as ordinary income under s 6-5 or as statutory income under another section.

Reimbursed car expenses

Section 15-70 *ITAA97* includes in a taxpayer's assessable income a reimbursement of 'exempt car expense payment benefits' under s 22 *FBTAA* [18.10]. Section 15-70 is aimed at taxing the reimbursement (on a cents per kilometre basis) of an employee's fuel costs paid by his or her employer. This kind of reimbursement is not subject to FBT in the hands of the employer as it is an 'exempt benefit' [18.3].

Bonuses on life insurance policies

Section 15-75 *ITAA97* includes in a taxpayer's assessable income any amount received as or by way of bonus on a life insurance policy, other than a reversionary bonus. A reversionary bonus is a bonus that is paid on maturity or surrender of a life insurance policy. A reversionary bonus may, nevertheless, be assessable under s 26AH *ITAA36*. Section 26AH treats a reversionary bonus on a life insurance policy as: fully assessable (if it is received within eight years); two-thirds assessable (if it is received in the ninth year); one-third assessable (if it is received in the tenth year); and non-assessable (if it received after the tenth year). Bonuses that are assessable under s 26AH are subject to a special tax offset under s 160AAB *ITAA36*.

[10.4] Recoupments of deductible amounts

Subdivision 20-A *ITAA97* contains a special regime designed to reverse the benefit of deductions allowed for certain losses and outgoings that have subsequently been recouped. The regime applies to 'assessable recoupments' as defined in s 20-20 *ITAA97*. An amount is not an assessable recoupment to the extent that it is ordinary or statutory income because of a provision outside sub-div 20-A.

Basically, assessable recoupments are amounts received by way of 'insurance' or 'indemnity' for any deductible loss or outgoing. They also include recoupments received for losses or outgoings that fall within the list of specific deduction provisions contained in s 20-30 *ITAA97*. This list includes provisions such as s 25-5 (tax-related expenses) [13.2], s 25-35 (bad debts) [13.6], s 25-60 (election expenses) [13.11] and div 40 (capital allowances) [15.2].

Subdivision 20-A includes an assessable recoupment (up to the amount of the relevant loss or outgoing in respect of which it is received) in a taxpayer's assessable income as follows:

- Where the whole of the loss or outgoing is deductible in a single income year, the assessable recoupment is assessed in the year it is received (unless it is received before the deduction year, in which case it is assessed in the deduction year) (s 20-35).
- Where the loss or outgoing is deductible over two or more years, the assessable recoupment is assessed in the year it is received, but only to the extent that it does not exceed the amounts that have been deducted up to that year. Any excess is then assessed in future years on the same basis (s 20-40).

Special rules apply where a loss or outgoing is only partially deductible (s 20-50).

Example

Loss or outgoing deductible in single income year
In Year 1, X Co writes off a bad debt owed to it by one of its customers of $10,000 and claims a deduction for this amount under s 25-35 [13.6]. In Year 2, X Co recovers $4,000 of the debt from the customer. The $4,000 is an assessable recoupment which is included in X Co's assessable income in Year 2 under s 20-35.

Loss or outgoing deductible over two or more years
At the beginning of Year 1, Y Co acquires machinery for use in its factory for $5m. Y Co depreciates the machinery on a prime cost basis over five years ($1m each year) under the capital allowance rules in div 40 [15.2]. If in Year 2, Y Co recoups $4m of its expenditure, it must include the following amounts in its assessable income over the relevant years under s 20-40.

Income year	Capital allowance deduction under div 40	Assessable recoupment	Assessable income under s 20-40
Year 1	$1m	Nil	Nil
Year 2	$1m	$4m	$2m
Year 3	$1m	Nil	$1m
Year 4	$1m	Nil	$1m
Year 5	$1m	Nil	Nil

The operation of sub-div 20-A was considered in *Denmark Community Windfarm v FC of T* 2018 ATC ¶20-646, where the Full Federal Court held that a grant received under the Commonwealth's Renewable Remote Power Generation Program was an assessable recoupment under s 20-20. The grant was paid in instalments and provided in respect of 50% of the eligible costs incurred by the taxpayer for construction of two wind turbines in Denmark. The taxpayer claimed deductions for the decline in value of the turbines under div 40 [15.2]. The Court found that the grant was an 'indemnity' as it had 'the character of compensation for a liability loss or expense incurred'. The Court rejected the taxpayer's argument that it was not able to deduct an amount for the loss or outgoing as the deductions it claimed under div 40 were for the decline in value of the relevant assets rather than for the expenditure incurred in constructing them. According to the Court, this was too narrow a reading of the words in sub-div 20-A, which were 'sufficiently broad to pick up a depreciation deduction under div 40'.

Subdivision 20-A was also considered in *Dessent v FC of T* 2021 ATC ¶10-572. In this case, the taxpayer's rental property, which was being used as a café, suffered storm damage. The taxpayer's insurer paid him $250,000 as settlement for loss of rent and other benefits under his insurance policy. The AAT held that the payment was an assessable recoupment under s 20-20.

[10.5] QUESTIONS

1. Why were the receipts in *Egerton-Warburton & Ors v DFC of T* (1934) 51 CLR 568 assessable but the receipts in *IRC v Ramsay* [1935] 1 All ER 847 capital?
2. Bill owns a large parcel of land on which there are many tall pine trees. Bill intends to use the land for grazing sheep and therefore wants to have it cleared. He discovers that a logging company is prepared to pay him $1,000 for every 100 metres of timber they can take from his land. Discuss the tax consequences of this arrangement. Would your answer differ if he was simply paid a lump sum of $50,000 for granting the logging company a right to remove as much timber as required from his land?
3. Larry leased his building to Terry to conduct a hotel business. The lease requires Terry to repair any damage to the building at the end of the lease. Terry fails to repair damage to the walls of the premises and instead pays Larry $2,000 for the damage. Discuss the tax treatment of this payment.
4. J Co owns a retail business and has claimed a deduction for a $20,000 bad debt that it has written off in the current income year. What happens if some of this debt is recouped in a subsequent income year?

EXEMPT INCOME AND NON-ASSESSABLE NON-EXEMPT INCOME 11

[11.1] Introduction

It is common for income tax systems around the world to contain a broad range of exemptions. From a policy perspective, there are many reasons why governments provide exemptions. The most obvious is to grant concessional treatment to certain 'deserving' entities. Tax exemptions may be total or partial and are usually provided because the relevant entities serve some social, community or philanthropic purpose that the government wishes to support. By providing particular entities with tax exemptions, the government delivers support to them indirectly (ie via tax expenditures) rather than directly (ie via grants or subsidies).

Clearly, providing tax exemptions comes at a cost, since governments do not collect revenue from the benefiting entities. However, this needs to be balanced against the fact that many of these entities provide important services to the community, which governments might otherwise feel they would have to provide themselves. By supporting such entities under their tax systems, governments can relieve themselves (either wholly or partly) from having to directly provide certain services that may, in any case, be best delivered through the private sector.

As tax exemptions can be costly, governments need to carefully budget for them, and ensure they are directed at only those entities that they are seeking to benefit. If an exemption is cast too widely, there is a risk that unintended bodies will fall within its parameters. Tax exemption provisions therefore often contain a number of qualifying conditions, and sometimes specify additional criteria (eg registration requirements) that must be satisfied before an entity can benefit from the exemption.

Australia's income tax legislation contains two kinds of exemptions: one relates to 'exempt income' and the other relates to 'non-assessable non-exempt income'. It is important to determine whether amounts are exempt income or non-assessable non-exempt income for the following reasons:

- exempt income and non-assessable non-exempt income are not included in a taxpayer's assessable income (s 6-15 *ITAA97*) [8.4], and
- losses or outgoings incurred in gaining or producing exempt income or non-assessable non-exempt income are not deductible (s 8-1(2) *ITAA97*) [12.4].

It is also necessary to distinguish between exempt income and non-assessable non-exempt income because exempt income (but not non-assessable non-exempt income) is taken into account in working out the amount of a tax loss under s 36-10 *ITAA97* [13.15].

In addition, a capital gain or capital loss made by a taxpayer from a CGT asset used solely to produce exempt income and certain forms of non-assessable non-exempt income is disregarded for CGT purposes (s 118-12 *ITAA97*) [17.4].

It should also be noted that certain entities that are exempt from tax may also be eligible for other concessions, such as deductible gift recipient status [13.13] and refundable franking credits [22.8]. They may also benefit from special concessions under the GST and FBT regimes.

This chapter outlines some of the main provisions in the *ITAA36* and *ITAA97* that render amounts exempt income [11.2] and non-assessable non-exempt income [11.3]. It also focuses on some of the most important and commonly encountered exemptions contained in div 50 *ITAA97* [11.4]–[11.10].

[11.2] Exempt income

An amount of ordinary income or statutory income is 'exempt income' if it is made exempt by a provision in the *ITAA36* or *ITAA97* or another Commonwealth law (s 6-20 *ITAA97*). Ordinary income is also exempt income to the extent that it is expressly or by implication excluded from being assessable income.

Classes of exempt income

The *ITAA36* and *ITAA97* are peppered with provisions that exempt particular kinds of ordinary and statutory income. Subdivision 11-A *ITAA97* contains a list of these provisions. The list divides exempt income into two classes:

- **First class.** The 'first class' (s 11-5) exempts the income of certain entities, irrespective of the nature of their income. Examples of this kind of exempt income include the income of:
  - registered charities (eg the Salvation Army) (s 50-5 *ITAA97*) [11.4]
  - religious institutions (eg the Catholic Church) (s 50-5 *ITAA97*) [11.4]
  - scientific institutions (eg the College of Surgeons) (s 50-5 *ITAA97*) [11.4]
  - public educational institutions (eg Monash University) (s 50-5 *ITAA97*) [11.4]
  - community service associations (eg senior citizens associations) (s 50-10 *ITAA97*) [11.5]
  - employee and employer associations and trade unions (eg the Australian Council of Trade Unions) (s 50-15 *ITAA97*) [11.6]
  - municipal corporations and local governing bodies (eg local councils) (s 50-25 *ITAA97*) [11.7]
  - public hospitals (eg the Royal Melbourne Hospital) (s 50-30 *ITAA97*) [11.8], and
  - animal racing, sports, musical and art societies and clubs (eg local tennis clubs) (s 50-45 *ITAA97*) [11.9].
- **Second class.** The 'second class' (s 11-15) exempts specific kinds of income. Examples of this kind of exempt income include:

- exempt benefits under the *FBTAA* (s 23L(1A) *ITAA36*) [8.5]
- non-cash business benefits that do not exceed $300 (s 23L(2) *ITAA36*) [9.2]
- PDF dividends (s 124ZM *ITAA36*) [27.3]
- interest on a judgment debt for personal injuries (s 51-57 *ITAA97*)
- foreign earnings derived by residents from eligible foreign service for a continuous period of not less than 91 days (s 23AG *ITAA36*) [31.4]
- allowances received by members of the defence force (s 51-5 *ITAA97*)
- scholarships and educational allowances paid to full-time students (s 51-10 *ITAA97*)
- income and gains from eligible venture capital investments (ss 51-52, 51-54 *ITAA97*) [27.4]
- certain social security and veterans payments (div 52 *ITAA97*), and
- payments under the Territories Stolen Generations Redress Scheme (s 53-30 *ITAA97*).

Example A registered charity earns $1,000 of interest from a bank deposit. Although the interest is ordinary income, it is not assessable income as it constitutes exempt income under s 50-5 *ITAA97*.

Special conditions and exceptions

Many of the exemptions outlined above operate subject to special conditions. In particular, in order to be able to treat their ordinary or statutory income as exempt, many of the entities mentioned in the first class of exemption are required to satisfy special conditions set out in div 50 *ITAA97* [11.10]. In addition, certain forms of income mentioned in the second class of exemption are only exempt if they meet the special requirements contained in divs 51 and 52 *ITAA97*.

[11.3] Non-assessable non-exempt income

An amount of ordinary income or statutory income is 'non-assessable non-exempt income' if it is stated to be non-assessable non-exempt by a provision in the *ITAA36* or *ITAA97* or another Commonwealth law (s 6-23 *ITAA97*).

Subdivision 11-B *ITAA97* contains a list of provisions that treat amounts as non-assessable non-exempt income. Two important provisions that have already been discussed are s 17-5 *ITAA97* (which treats GST payable on a taxable supply as non-assessable non-exempt income) and s 23L(1) *ITAA36* (which treats income that is a fringe benefit as non-assessable non-exempt income) [8.5]. The object of these provisions is to ensure that GST and FBT do not inappropriately overlap with income tax.

Example S Co owns a sports shop and is registered for GST. It sold golf clubs to a customer for $330 (including $30 GST). Although the company's ordinary income is $330, its assessable income is only $300 as the GST on the taxable supply is non-assessable non-exempt income under s 17-5 *ITAA97*.

Some other provisions that deem amounts to be non-assessable non-exempt income include:

- ss 82-10 and 82-65 *ITAA97* (tax-free component of employment termination payments [20.2])
- s 83-170 *ITAA97* (genuine redundancy payments) [20.4]
- ss 83-235 and 83-240 *ITAA97* (foreign termination payments) [20.5]
- ss 301-10, 301-15, 301-30 and 301-90 *ITAA97* (superannuation benefits) [19.16]
- ss 302-60 and 302-65 *ITAA97* (superannuation death benefits) [19.16]
- s 380-35 (National Rental Affordability Scheme payments) [27.7]

- s 768-5 *ITAA97* (foreign equity distributions of resident companies) [31.6]
- s 768-910 *ITAA97* (foreign source income of a temporary resident) [30.4]
- s 23AH *ITAA36* (foreign branch income of resident companies) [31.5]
- s 23AI *ITAA36* (attributed CFC income) [34.5]
- s 23AK *ITAA36* (attributed FIF income) [34.5]
- s 44(4) *ITAA36* (demerger dividends) [28.4], and
- s 128D *ITAA36* (amounts subject to withholding tax) [31.11].

There are also a number of miscellaneous provisions in div 59 *ITAA97* that deem particular amounts to be non-assessable non-exempt income. For example, s 59-30(1) provides that an amount received by a taxpayer is non-assessable non-exempt income if they must repay it in a later income year and they cannot deduct the repayment for any income year.

The Government has also recently enacted the following provisions that make certain COVID-19 related payments non-assessable non-exempt income:

- s 59-96 *ITAA97* (payments received by individuals that are 'COVID-19 disaster payments' within the meaning of the *COVID-19 Disaster Payment (Funding Arrangements) Act 2021* (Cth))
- s 59-97 *ITAA97* (payments received by SBEs under eligible state and territory grant programs), and
- s 59-98 *ITAA97* (payments received by SBEs under eligible Commonwealth grant programs).

In addition, s 59-99 *ITAA97* deems certain government disaster recovery grants made to small businesses and primary producers in relation to various floods and storms to be non-assessable non-exempt income.

[11.4] Registered charities and religious, scientific and public educational institutions

Section 50-5 *ITAA97* exempts the ordinary and statutory income of registered charities. It also exempts the ordinary and statutory income of religious, scientific and public educational institutions. The term 'institution' has its ordinary meaning and covers 'an establishment, organisation, or association, instituted for the promotion of some object' (*Young Men's Christian Association of Melbourne v FC of T* (1926) 37 CLR 351). To qualify for the exemptions, the relevant entities must satisfy special conditions discussed at [11.10].

Registered charities

For many years, the ATO was responsible for determining whether an entity was a charity. The *Australian Charities and Not-for-profits Commission Act 2012* (Cth) established the Australian Charities and Not-for-profits Commission ('ACNC'), which now has the role of regulating and registering charities. To be registered with the ACNC, entities need to satisfy certain conditions, including satisfying the definition of charity, complying with various standards and having an ABN. The *Australian Charities and Not-for-profits Commission (Consequential and Transitional) Act 2012* (Cth) ensures that entities that were previously endorsed as charities by the ATO are automatically registered with the ACNC. There are around 60,000 registered charities in Australia according to the ACNC website [2.5].

In determining whether an institution is a 'charity', it has been necessary to rely on the common law meanings of 'charitable' and 'charitable purpose' which have evolved over hundreds of years. To modernise the law and provide greater certainty for both institutions and regulators, the *Charities Act 2013* (Cth) introduced statutory definitions of these terms. The definitions are largely based on existing common law concepts with certain modifications. They apply for the purposes of all Commonwealth legislation from 1 January 2014.

Common law definition of charity

Under the common law, an institution is 'charitable' if it is maintained for 'charitable purposes'. The notion of a charitable purpose has its origins in English law and can be traced back to the categories of charitable purpose set out in the preamble to the *Statute of Charitable Uses 1601* (UK) (also known as the *Statute of Elizabeth*). In *The Commissioners for Special Purposes of the Income Tax v Pemsel* [1891] AC 531, Lord Macnaghten classified these categories into 'four heads':

- the relief of poverty
- the advancement of education
- the advancement of religion, and
- other purposes beneficial to the community.

The cases establish that for a purpose to be charitable it must come 'within the spirit and intendment' of the *Statute of Elizabeth* and it must be for the 'public benefit'. The common law concept of charitable purpose has also been extended by the *Extension of Charitable Purpose Act 2004* (Cth) which includes, for example, the provision of child care services on a non-profit basis.

In *FC of T v Word Investments Limited* 2008 ATC ¶20-072, the High Court indicated that in determining whether an institution is charitable, a court must focus on its 'main or predominant or dominant objects, as distinct from its concomitant or incidental or ancillary objects'. Accordingly, so long as an institution's main objects fall within one of the above four heads, the fact that it also has incidental or ancillary objects should not prevent it from being classified as a charitable institution.

TR 2011/4 states that the objects of an institution should be determined by objectively weighing up all of its features. These features can be ascertained from things such as its history, its governing documents, its activities, its policies and any legislation governing its operation. The ruling goes on to provide that an institution that carries out its activities for the private profit of its members is not charitable, because it does not satisfy the public benefit requirement. Likewise, an institution that has the purpose of carrying on a business or commercial enterprise, where that purpose is an end in itself, is not charitable.

Over the years, many court decisions have considered whether particular institutions are established or maintained for charitable purposes. Some noteworthy cases are outlined below:

- In *Property Services Industry Training Advisory Board Ltd v FC of T* 99 ATC 2076, an industry training advisory board that provided vocational training in the property security industry was found to be charitable as it satisfied the advancement of education criteria.
- In *Tasmanian Electronic Commerce Centre Pty Ltd v FC of T* 2005 ATC 4219, a company that was owned by the State of Tasmania and the University of Tasmania and was established to assist Tasmanian businesses adopt electronic commerce and compete in the electronic marketplace was found to be charitable as its objects were beneficial to the community.
- In *Victorian Women Lawyers' Association Inc v FC of T* 2008 ATC ¶20-035, an incorporated association whose principal objective was to remove barriers and increase opportunities for participation by, and advancement of, women in the Victorian legal profession was found to be a charitable institution as its objects were beneficial to the community. The Federal Court held that the association was charitable even though its activities included social events and networking functions that could benefit its members, as those activities were plainly directed towards its principal objective.
- In *FC of T v Word Investments Limited* 2008 ATC ¶20-072, a company incorporated for the purpose of raising funds for a charity involved in translating the Bible into indigenous languages was held to be a charitable institution even though it did not carry on religious work itself, and raised funds by undertaking commercial activities. The High Court held that the purpose for which the funds were raised was the salient point, not the way in which they were raised.

The company was simply using commercial methods to raise money for its charitable objects, which was to support an organisation that had charitable purposes.

- In *Aid/Watch Incorporated v FC of T* 2010 ATC ¶20-227, an organisation that was involved in promoting the effectiveness of Australian and multinational aid in foreign countries was held to be charitable as its activities were beneficial to the community. The High Court held that the organisation was charitable even though it had political objects (ie influencing the way agencies administered aid programs). The Court held (at [48]) that 'in Australia there is no general doctrine which excludes from charitable purposes "political objects"'.

Statutory definition of charity

Under the *Charities Act 2013* (Cth), an entity is a 'charity' if:

- it is a 'not-for-profit entity'
- all of its purposes are 'charitable purposes' that are for the 'public benefit' (or are ancillary or incidental purposes that further or aid those purposes)
- it does not have any 'disqualifying purposes', and
- it is not an individual, a political party or a government entity (s 5).

It is clear from the definition that to be a charity an entity cannot have an independent non-charitable purpose. An entity which has a purpose of carrying on a commercial enterprise as an end in itself cannot therefore be charitable. However, an entity may be charitable if its purposes are all charitable and it merely carries on an ancillary or incidental commercial enterprise to further its charitable purposes rather than as an end in itself.

A 'charitable purpose' is defined as any of the following purposes:

- advancing health
- advancing education
- advancing social or public welfare
- advancing religion
- advancing culture
- promoting reconciliation, mutual respect and tolerance between groups of individuals that are in Australia
- promoting or protecting human rights
- advancing the security or safety of Australia or the Australian public
- preventing or relieving the suffering of animals
- advancing the natural environment
- any other purpose beneficial to the general public that may reasonably be regarded as analogous to, or within the spirit of, any of the purposes mentioned above
- promoting or opposing a change to any matter established by law, policy or practice in relation to one or more of the purposes mentioned above (s 12).

A 'disqualifying purpose' is defined as the purpose of engaging in activities that are unlawful or contrary to public policy, or the purpose of promoting or opposing a political party, candidate or office (s 11).

A purpose an entity has is for the 'public benefit' if the achievement of the purpose would be of public benefit and the purpose is directed to a benefit that is available to members of the general public or a sufficient section of the general public (s 6).

In determining the purposes of an entity, regard must be had to its governing rules, activities and other matters. Benefits are not restricted to material benefits—they may be tangible (eg accommodation for the homeless) or intangible (eg spiritual benefits from religious services).

Certain purposes are deemed, in the absence of evidence to the contrary, to be for the public benefit, namely: preventing and relieving sickness, disease or human suffering; advancing education; relieving the poverty, distress or disadvantage of individuals or families; caring for and supporting the aged or individuals with disabilities; and advancing religion (s 7).

The requirement that a purpose be directed to a benefit that is available to members of the general public may be disregarded if the purpose is relieving the 'necessitous circumstances' of one or more individuals who are in Australia (s 8). The public benefit is also deemed to be satisfied where an entity's purpose relates to native title or traditional land rights that benefit only indigenous persons and that purpose would otherwise not be for the public benefit only because such persons are related (s 9).

Religious institution

The meaning of a religious institution was considered in *The Church of the New Faith v Commissioner of Pay-roll Tax (Vic)* 83 ATC 4652, which concerned an exemption from payroll tax for religious institutions. The High Court held that Scientology was a religion and that the Church of the New Faith was a religious institution. The judges identified various indicia of a religion. Mason ACJ and Brennan J said that there were two main criteria:

- belief in a supernatural Being, Thing or Principle, and
- the acceptance of canons of conduct in order to give effect to that belief (which do not offend against ordinary laws).

In the course of their judgment, Mason ACJ and Brennan J also made the following comments (at 4666) about the legal nature of a religion:

> The truth or falsity of religions is not the business of officials or the Courts. If each purported religion had to show that its doctrines were true, then all might fail. Administrators and Judges must resist the temptation to hold that groups or institutions are not religious because claimed religious beliefs or practices seem absurd, fraudulent, evil or novel; or because the group or institution is new, the number of adherents small, the leaders hypocrites, or because they seek to obtain the financial and other privileges which come with religious status. In the eyes of the law, religions are equal. There is no religious club with a monopoly of State privileges for its members. The policy of the law is 'one in, all in'.

Scientific institution

To be a scientific institution, an institution's main objects must be 'scientific' (ie they must relate to the advancement of science). A scientific institution can include an organisation established for professionals engaged in a particular field of science. For instance, it has been held that a College of Surgeons whose members were surgeons and which held scientific meetings and maintained a surgical library and published a surgical journal was a scientific institution (*Royal Australasian College of Surgeons v FC of T* (1943) 68 CLR 436). On the other hand, where the main purpose of an institution is 'professional', rather than 'scientific', it will not qualify (*Australian Dental Association (NSW Branch) v FC of T* (1934) 3 ATD 114).

In *Australian Tea Tree Oil Research Institute Ltd (in Liq) & Anor v FC of T* 2008 ATC ¶20-066, the Federal Court held that research companies established to investigate the benefits of tea tree oil did not qualify as scientific institutions. Edmonds J found that the taxpayers had been brought into existence to undertake research for reward under contracts which provided the research results to the participants in the scheme for commercial exploitation. According to his Honour, the taxpayers' activities were directed at a commercial endeavour rather than for any public benefit. His Honour indicated (at [225]) that for an entity to be a scientific institution, the results of its activities 'should be freely available to the community at large'.

Public educational institution

An institution is an educational institution if its main objects involve imparting knowledge, skills or instruction through training or teaching. In *Chesterman v FC of T* (1923) 32 CLR 362, Isaacs J indicated (at 386) that the term 'education' should be interpreted widely and connotes 'imparting knowledge or assisting and guiding the development of body or mind'.

To be 'public', an institution must be open to the community or, at least, a particular section of the community. In *Taxpayers' Association of NSW v FC of T* 2001 ATC 2096, an association whose fee-paying members were principally accountants and small business owners and which provided its members with taxation information in the form of a fortnightly journal, an annual summary, seminars and telephone advice was found not to be a public educational institution. The AAT held that the association's members could not be described as a section of the community.

[11.5] Community service associations and clubs

Section 50-10 *ITAA97* exempts the ordinary and statutory income of a society, association or club established for community service purposes (except political or lobbying purposes). To qualify for the exemption, the entity must satisfy certain special conditions discussed at [11.10].

TD 93/190 states that the term 'community service purposes' has a broader meaning than 'other purposes beneficial to the community' (which relates to 'charitable purposes' [11.4]) and that altruistic purposes are an essential element of the concept. According to the ruling, an association that carries out activities for the welfare of the community or any members of the community by reason of, for example, age (eg a senior citizens association) would qualify.

In *FC of T v Wentworth District Capital Ltd* 2011 ATC ¶20-253, members of a small country town had established a company that provided banking services to the community (under arrangements entered into with Bendigo Bank) following the closure of Westpac Bank's branch in the town two years earlier. The company was established to facilitate face-to-face banking in circumstances where the next closest bank was some 30 kilometres away. The Full Federal Court held that the main or dominant purpose for which the company was established was a community service, being the delivery of face-to-face banking, and that its income was therefore exempt under s 50-10.

[11.6] Employer and employee associations and trade unions

Section 50-15 *ITAA97* exempts the ordinary and statutory income of employee or employer associations and trade unions. An entity is only exempt from tax under s 50-15 if it satisfies the relevant special conditions discussed at [11.10].

In *Associated Newsagents Co-operative Ltd v FC of T* 70 ATC 4030, the High Court held that a co-operative society that sold goods (eg stationery) to its members, which were newsagents, was not an employer association under former s 23(f) *ITAA36* (the predecessor of s 50-15). This conclusion was reached on the basis that the members were not required to be employers and were not associated in such capacity. Their association arose from them being newsagents rather than employers. The Court also concluded that the taxpayer was not a trade union even though it was registered as an industrial union under the Industrial Arbitration Acts (NSW).

In *Norsemen Amalgamated Distress and Injustices Fund v FC of T* 95 ATC 4227, the Federal Court considered whether an unincorporated association in which all males employed by Central Norseman Gold Corporation were required to be members was a trade union. The association's objects were to raise money by compulsory levy and other means to provide financial assistance to sick or injured members or to fight injustice to members. The Federal Court described a trade union (at 4230) as an organisation 'formed by workers to further the interests of the workers in their employment and although part of the meaning of the term may include an organisation formed to provide financial aid to union members suffering adversity, the latter meaning is ancillary to, and dependent upon, the principal meaning described'. The Court held that although the taxpayer's constitution made oblique reference to the employer/employee relationship, it was not a trade union as it was not directed to the protection of employees in their employment or in furtherance of their interests in employment.

[11.7] Municipal corporations, local governing bodies, public authorities and constitutionally protected funds

Section 50-25 *ITAA97* exempts the ordinary and statutory income of a 'municipal corporation', a 'local governing body', a 'public authority' constituted under an Australian law and a 'constitutionally protected fund'. Unlike the other exemptions considered in this chapter, there are no special conditions that must be met for this exemption to apply.

The terms 'municipal corporation' and 'local governing body' cover a body such as a local council.

A public authority is, essentially, a body that performs some function of government—it is a government agency or instrument set up to exercise control or power for the public advantage or to execute a function in the public interest (*FC of T v Bank of Western Australia & Ors* 96 ATC 4009; *Coal Mining Industry Long Service Leave (Funding) Corp v FC of T* 99 ATC 4326).

A 'constitutionally protected fund' is basically a fund established under a state Act and is listed in the table in reg 995-1.03 *ITAR21* (s 995-1 *ITAA97*). For example, the definition covers state superannuation funds such as those established for judges under the *Judges' Pensions Act 1953* (NSW) and the *Supreme Court Act 1986* (Vic) [19.4]. The reason for exempting such funds is to ensure that s 114 of the *Constitution*, which prohibits the Commonwealth from taxing property belonging to a state, is not breached [3.10].

[11.8] Public hospitals, hospitals carried on by societies or associations and private health insurers

Section 50-30 *ITAA97* exempts the ordinary and statutory income of public hospitals, hospitals carried on by societies or associations, and private health insurers within the meaning of the *Private Health Insurance Act 2007* (Cth). These entities are only exempt from tax under s 50-30 if they satisfy the relevant special conditions discussed at [11.10].

In *O'Connell v Council of the City of Greater Newcastle* (1941) 41 SR (NSW) 190, the Court indicated that a public hospital was a hospital that was conducted primarily for the benefit of ordinary members of the public, or an appreciably important class of such members, rather than for private profit. A hospital does not necessarily need to be under public control to be a public hospital. It is the purposes to which the hospital is directed, not the manner in which it is controlled, that determines whether it is a public hospital.

[11.9] Animal racing, art, sport, literature and music societies, associations and clubs

Section 50-45 *ITAA97* exempts the ordinary and statutory income of a society, association or club established for the encouragement of animal racing, art, a game of sport, literature or music. To qualify for the exemption, the entity must satisfy the relevant special conditions discussed at [11.10].

The terms 'animal racing', 'art', 'game of sport', 'literature' and 'music' are not defined in the legislation and therefore take on their ordinary meanings.

The issue of whether a club qualified for exemption as a sports club under the predecessor of s 50-45 (ie s 23(g)(iii) *ITAA36*) was considered by the Full Federal Court in *Cronulla-Sutherland Leagues Club Ltd v FC of T* 90 ATC 4215. This case concerned a club whose objects included the promotion and development of rugby league football. The taxpayer was connected with a related rugby club, which it assisted with funding and facilities. The taxpayer owned a large clubhouse that included a gymnasium, squash courts, poker machines, bars, restaurants and an auditorium. The Federal Court held that the taxpayer did not qualify for the exemption as its main object was to operate as a social club rather than a sports club. Beaumont J explained (at 4244) 'although it is not necessary that the promotion or encouragement of the sport or game be the only, or exclusive, object, in order to qualify for the exemption . . . the institution must have, as its predominant purpose, the promotion or encouragement of the sport or game'.

The Court also pointed out that the question of whether a club was established for the encouragement or promotion of a sport should be examined on an 'annual basis'. Beaumont J said (at 4243) 'it is necessary to look at the taxpayer, and its activities, year by year, and not merely at the time of its incorporation . . . although the intentions of the promoters of the taxpayer may be relevant in determining the purpose for which the taxpayer was incorporated, it is necessary to look at the taxpayer's actual activities, since the purpose of its incorporation can be ascertained from what it did'. This passage indicates that, depending on the way a club conducts its activities from time to time, it might qualify for the exemption in one year but not in another year.

Cronulla-Sutherland Leagues Club was distinguished a few years later by the Federal Court in *Terranora Lakes Country Club Ltd v FC of T* 93 ATC 4078. This case concerned a large club that had approximately 4000 members. The club owned a clubhouse, sports ground and sporting complex. It also held an interest in a time-share resort. The club promoted various sports and pastimes (eg cricket, tennis, softball, touch football, golf, clay-pigeon shooting and horse riding). The club also provided a range of social activities (eg dining facilities, bars and poker machines available at the clubhouse). Hill J concluded that the club was eligible for the exemption under former s 23(g)(iii) *ITAA36* as it was established for the purpose of the promotion of sport. His Honour found that, in the relevant year of income, although the social activities of the club were extensive and provided it with substantial revenue, they were pursued as a means of financing the broad range of sporting activities offered by the club. According to his Honour, the social activities were neither predominant nor equal in importance to the sporting activities, even though they were vital to the survival of the club.

Cronulla-Sutherland Leagues Club was again distinguished by Hill J in *St Marys Rugby League Club Ltd* 97 ATC 4528. The objects of the club in that case included promoting rugby league in the St Marys district, providing financial support to rugby league clubs and providing sporting, social and recreational facilities to its members. The club fielded more than 30 teams in competitions in the district and operated a clubhouse that included a restaurant, a bar, a hairdressing salon, auditoriums and poker machines, which produced the majority of its profits. The club's constitution ensured that it was largely controlled by current or former footballers, and it spent approximately one-fifth of its annual net income on football-related grants. Hill J held that the exemption under former s 23(g)(iii) *ITAA36* was available to the club as its main object or purpose was the encouragement or promotion of a sport. His Honour found that although the club's social and gambling activities were significant in their own right, they were subordinate to its encouragement and promotion of rugby league football in the St Marys district. While Hill J recognised that the club's gambling activities generated the majority of its profits, his Honour pointed out (at 4533) that 'statistics do not necessarily tell the whole story'. He went on to explain:

> It requires little space and even less effort on the part of the Club to derive this profit. It takes a great deal more time and effort to put on the field week after week some 32 rugby league teams involving some 450 players, not to mention fielding a first grade team and a reserve grade team in the Metropolitan Cup competition.

According to Hill J, the constitution, activities, history and control of the club characterised it as one that had as its main object or purpose the encouragement or promotion of rugby league football. There was 'an intensity of activity directed towards football' which tipped the balance in favour of the club.

[11.10] Special conditions for exemptions

Most of the entities examined at [11.4]–[11.9] will be exempt from tax on their ordinary or statutory income only if they satisfy certain special conditions. These conditions are contained in div 50 *ITAA97* and differ depending on the nature of the entity.

To qualify for exemptions under s 50-5 [11.4], s 50-50 requires a charitable or religious institution to satisfy one of the following four requirements and s 50-55 requires a scientific or education institution to satisfy one of the first three of the following four requirements:

- it has a physical presence in Australia and, to that extent, incurs its expenditure and pursues its objectives principally in Australia
- it meets the description and requirements in item 1 of the table in s 30-15 *ITAA97* [13.13]
- it is a prescribed institution which is located outside Australia and is exempt from income tax in the country in which it is resident
- it is a prescribed institution that has a physical presence in Australia but which incurs its expenditure and pursues its objectives principally outside Australia.

An additional special condition applies to charitable institutions under s 50-52. This section requires a charitable institution to be 'endorsed' by the Commissioner as an entity that is exempt from income tax under sub-div 50-B *ITAA97*. The Commissioner must endorse an entity as exempt from income tax if it is entitled to be endorsed and has applied for endorsement under div 426 of sch 1 *TAA* (s 50-100). An entity is entitled to be endorsed as exempt from income tax if it meets the requirements in s 50-110 (which includes a requirement that it has an ABN).

To qualify for exemption under s 50-10 [11.5] or s 50-45 [11.9], s 50-70 requires that the relevant society, association or club not be carried on for the purpose of profit or gain of its individual members. In addition, one of the following requirements must also be satisfied:

- it has a physical presence in Australia and, to that extent, incurs its expenditure and pursues its objectives principally in Australia
- it meets the description and requirements in item 1 of the table in s 30-15 *ITAA97* [13.13]
- it is a prescribed institution which is located outside Australia and is exempt from income tax in the country in which it is resident.

To qualify for exemption under s 50-15 [11.6] an employee or employer association or trade union must be located in Australia and incur its expenditure and pursue its objectives in Australia. It must also comply with all the substantive requirements in its governing rules and apply its income and assets solely for the purposes for which it is established. An employee or employer organisation must also be registered or recognised under the *Fair Work (Registered Organisation) Act 2009* (Cth) or an Australian law relating to the settlement of industrial disputes.

To qualify for exemption under s 50-30 [11.8], private health insurers and hospitals carried on by societies or associations must not be carried on for the profit or gain of their individual members. In addition, a public hospital and a hospital carried on by a society or association must satisfy one of the following requirements in s 50-55:

- it has a physical presence in Australia and, to that extent, incurs its expenditure and pursues its objectives principally in Australia
- it meets the description and requirements in item 1 of the table in s 30-15 *ITAA97* [13.13]

- it is a prescribed institution which is located outside Australia and is exempt from income tax in the country in which it is resident.

[11.11] QUESTIONS

1. Why is it important to identify whether ordinary income or statutory income is exempt income or non-assessable non-exempt income? Where is the list of exempt income and non-assessable non-exempt income provisions located in the *ITAA97*?
2. What do ss 50-5 and 50-30 *ITAA97* and ss 23L and 128D *ITAA36* treat as non-assessable non-exempt income?
3. Discuss the meaning of 'charity' and provide some examples of charities.
4. What are the key attributes of a religious institution?
5. What sections exempt trade unions and municipal corporations from income tax?
6. What kinds of hospitals are exempt from income tax?
7. Why did the taxpayer in *Cronulla-Sutherland Leagues Club Ltd v FC of T* 90 ATC 4215 not qualify for a tax exemption? On what basis have subsequent cases distinguished this case?

PART E

DEDUCTIONS

12 GENERAL DEDUCTIONS

[12.1] Introduction

To arrive at their taxable income for an income year, taxpayers subtract their deductions from their assessable income [8.4]. Most deductions fall within the general deduction provision in s 8-1 *ITAA97*. Section 8-1 replaces former s 51(1) *ITAA36*, which was drafted in similar terms, but was rewritten in 1997 as a consequence of the TLIP rewrite [8.2]. This chapter examines the general deduction provision and the extensive body of case law that has considered it.

Section 8-1 has two positive limbs and four negative limbs. The positive limbs are contained in s 8-1(1), which states:

> You can deduct from your assessable income any loss or outgoing to the extent that:
> (a) it is incurred in gaining or producing your assessable income; or
> (b) it is necessarily incurred in carrying on a business for the purpose of gaining or producing your assessable income.

The negative limbs are contained in s 8-1(2), which states:

> However, you cannot deduct a loss or outgoing under this section to the extent that:
> (a) it is a loss or outgoing of capital, or of a capital nature; or
> (b) it is a loss or outgoing of a private or domestic nature; or
> (c) it is incurred in relation to gaining or producing your exempt income or non-assessable non-exempt income; or
> (d) a provision of this Act prevents you from deducting it.

As there are two distinct limbs of s 8-1, there is a two-step process involved in dealing with the provision. The first step is to determine the extent that a loss or outgoing falls within either of the two positive limbs. The second step is to determine the extent that the loss or outgoing is excluded under any of the four negative limbs. Obviously, it is only necessary to proceed to the second step if the first step has been satisfied. As Gleeson CJ, Gaudron and Gummow JJ observed in *Steele v DFC of T* 99 ATC 4242 (at 4247), 'it only becomes necessary to consider the exceptions to s 51(1) if it has already been concluded, or accepted by hypothesis, that one or more of the positive limbs applies'.

Although each of the two positive limbs and each of the four negative limbs of s 8-1 are alternatives, the potential exists for overlap. For instance, a loss or outgoing may fall within both the first and second positive limbs. Similarly, a loss or outgoing may be both capital and private in nature and therefore fall within the first two of the negative limbs.

This chapter commences with a discussion of the nature of a loss or outgoing [12.2] followed by a detailed discussion of the positive [12.3] and negative [12.4] limbs of s 8-1. The meaning of the term 'incurred' and issues relating to the timing of deductions are examined at [12.5]. The chapter then builds on this framework to explore how the general deduction provision has been applied to some common kinds of losses and outgoings. In particular, it focuses on clothing [12.6], travel [12.7], management [12.8], self-education [12.9], home office [12.10], rent and licence fees [12.11], interest [12.12], legal [12.13], and trade-tie [12.14] expenses.

It is important to be aware that a loss or outgoing that fails to satisfy the requirements of the general deduction provision may, nevertheless, still be deductible if it satisfies the requirements of a specific deduction provision. The specific deduction provisions are discussed in Chapter 13 and various other chapters.

[12.2] Loss or outgoing and apportionment

Loss or outgoing

Both the positive and negative limbs of s 8-1 *ITAA97* deal with a 'loss' or 'outgoing'. These terms are not defined in the legislation and therefore have their ordinary meanings.

A 'loss' arises where a taxpayer's financial resources have been diminished. For instance, a loss can occur where a taxpayer's money has been stolen (*Charles Moore & Co (WA) Pty Ltd v FC of T* (1956) 95 CLR 344, *FC of T v La Rosa* 2003 ATC 4510). Losses can also arise where bills and notes are issued at a discount to the face value for which they are redeemed (*Coles Myer Finance Ltd v FC of T* 93 ATC 4214, *FC of T v Energy Resources of Australia Ltd* 96 ATC 4536).

An 'outgoing', on the other hand, involves some form of payment, outlay or expenditure. Examples of outgoings include the payment of interest under a loan (*Fletcher & Ors v FC of T* 91 ATC 4950) and the payment of a premium under an insurance policy (*FC of T v Smith* 81 ATC 4114).

To the extent that

The words 'to the extent that' as used in relation to both the positive and negative limbs of s 8-1 *ITAA97* ('to the extent to which' as used in former s 51(1) *ITAA36*) indicate that in certain circumstances a loss or outgoing may need to be apportioned, in which case the loss or outgoing will only be partly deductible.

This is illustrated in *Ure v FC of T* 81 ATC 4100, where the Full Federal Court held that interest expenditure incurred by a taxpayer on a loan used for both income-producing and private purposes should be apportioned between those objects. Deane and Sheppard JJ stated (at 4108):

> In considering the deductibility, pursuant to s 51(1), of the interest paid by the taxpayer, it is important to be mindful of the fact that an outgoing which is claimed to have been incurred in earning assessable income is only deductible, pursuant to the subsection, 'to the extent to which' it was so incurred and 'to the extent to which' it cannot properly be characterized as being of a private or domestic nature. Where an outgoing was partially so incurred or

> should be partially so characterized, the subsection requires apportionment between what, not being of a private or domestic nature, should properly be regarded as incurred in earning the assessable income and what should not.

The issue of apportionment also arose in *Ronpibon Tin NL & Tongkah Compound NL v FC of T* (1949) 78 CLR 47 in relation to two Australian companies that had operated tin mines in Siam and Malaya and also derived investment income from Treasury bonds and fixed deposits. The income from their mining operations was exempt from Australian tax under former s 23(q) *ITAA36* [31.3], but their investment income was subject to Australian tax. During World War II, Siam and Malaya were overrun by the Japanese and the taxpayers had to close their mines. Although the taxpayers ceased to derive mining income, they continued to derive investment income. They also continued to incur directors' fees and administrative expenses in relation to their Melbourne offices. The Commissioner allowed the companies a deduction under s 51(1) *ITAA36* for a portion of their expenses. For example, the Commissioner allowed Ronpibon Tin to deduct an amount equal to 2.5% of its investment income on the basis that he had previously used this figure as a convenient means of apportioning the company's expenses between the exempt and assessable components of its income. The company, however, challenged the continued use of this method, arguing that it was no longer appropriate following the cessation of its mining operations.

The High Court held that it was inappropriate for the Commissioner to 'arbitrarily' choose an apportionment figure. Latham CJ, Rich, Dixon, McTiernan and Webb JJ explained (at 59):

> The reason why the Commissioner has adopted the practice of allowing two and one-half per cent on income from investments as a deduction is no doubt because generally speaking it has been found to produce an adequate allowance and because he is forced by the exigencies of administration to provide his assessors with some fixed rule.
>
> But it is a more or less arbitrary expedient to which it is scarcely possible to resort judicially when the Court is called upon to decide an appeal from an assessment. The Court must make an apportionment which the facts of the particular case may seem to make just . . .

According to the High Court, it was necessary to determine as a matter of fact what proportion of the relevant companies' expenses were actually incurred in gaining their assessable income, and it remitted the case back to the trial judge to rule on this issue. In the course of delivering their judgment, Latham CJ, Rich, Dixon, McTiernan and Webb JJ noted (at 59) that there are at least two kinds of items of expenditure that require apportionment:

> One kind consists in undivided items of expenditure in respect of things or services of which distinct and severable parts are devoted to gaining or producing assessable income and distinct and severable parts to some other cause. In such cases it may be possible to divide the expenditure in accordance with the applications which have been made of the things or services. The other kind of apportionable items consists in those involving a single outlay or charge which serves both objects indifferently. . . . With the latter kind there must be some fair and reasonable assessment of the extent of the relation of the outlay to assessable income. It is an indiscriminate sum apportionable, but hardly capable of arithmetical or rateable division because it is common to both objects.

Interestingly, although both s 8-1 *ITAA97* and former s 51(1) *ITAA36* clearly contemplate apportionment, the concept of apportionment has not always been a feature of Australia's general deduction provision. The former general deduction provision in s 23(1)(a) *Income Tax Assessment Act 1922* (Cth) ('*ITAA22*'), which operated subject to s 25(e) of that Act, only allowed deductions for losses or outgoings that were 'wholly and exclusively' incurred in gaining or producing assessable income.

The way in which the courts have apportioned outgoings under s 8-1 and former s 51(1) is considered further in a number of the cases discussed at [12.3].

[12.3] Positive limbs

Establishing a nexus between a loss or outgoing and the positive limbs

In order to come within the positive limbs of s 8-1 *ITAA97*, there must be a sufficient connection or link between a loss or outgoing and the gaining or production of the taxpayer's assessable income, or the carrying on of the taxpayer's business. In other words, there must be a sufficient 'nexus' between the loss or outgoing and either one of the positive limbs.

The courts have traditionally adopted a broad view of the 'nexus' requirement and, in so doing, have not required a particular loss or outgoing to be matched with the production of a specific amount of assessable income. Authority for this principle can be found in comments made in the High Court decision in *C of T (NSW) v Ash* (1938) 61 CLR 263, which concerned former s 23(1)(a) *ITAA22*. Latham CJ indicated that to justify a deduction, it is not necessary to show a connection between an outgoing and any particular item of income. It is sufficient if the outgoing is a 'step towards the production of income'. His Honour illustrated this point with the following example (at 272):

> Payment of weekly wages to a salesman cannot be allocated to particular items of goods sold by him, but moneys paid for wages are clearly a proper deduction of a shopkeeper.

The courts have also held that, for an expense to be deductible in a particular year, it does not necessarily have to actually produce income in that year. Expenditure designed to earn income in future years is, therefore, prima facie deductible. This point was recognised by the High Court in *FC of T v Smith* 81 ATC 4114, where a doctor was allowed deductions under s 51(1) *ITAA36* for premiums paid under a personal disability insurance policy that provided him with a monthly indemnity of $600 for any period that he sustained a total disability. Gibbs, Stephen, Mason and Wilson JJ stated (at 4117):

> The section does not require that the purpose of the expenditure shall be the gaining of the income of that year, so long as it was made in the given year and is incidental and relevant to the operations or activities regularly carried on for the production of income.

A similar observation was made by the High Court in *Fletcher & Ors v FC of T* 91 ATC 4950, where Mason CJ, Brennan, Deane, Dawson, Toohey, Gaudron and McHugh JJ indicated (at 4957):

> the reference in [s 51(1)] to '*the* assessable income' is not to be read as confined to assessable income actually derived in the particular tax year. It is to be construed as an abstract phrase which refers not only to assessable income derived in that or in some other tax year but also to assessable income which the relevant outgoing 'would be expected to produce'.

Accordingly, provided a loss or outgoing is, in the general sense, directed at gaining or producing the taxpayer's assessable income or carrying on the taxpayer's business for the purpose of gaining or producing assessable income, it will satisfy the requirements of the positive limbs.

Pragmatic and commercial approach to determining nexus

In practice, the courts have adopted a pragmatic and commercial approach to the nexus issue. An early illustration of this is found in *W Nevill & Co Ltd v FC of T* (1937) 56 CLR 290, where the High Court allowed a company a deduction, under former s 23(1)(a) *ITAA22*, for a resignation payment made to one of its joint managing directors. Prior to July 1930, the company only had a single managing director. In July 1930, it appointed an additional managing director for five years at an annual salary of £1,500. However, joint management did not work, and the company's business decreased. As a consequence, in March 1931, the company entered into an agreement to pay the additional director £2,500, by a series of promissory notes, as consideration for him agreeing to resign.

The Court held that although the payments did not produce assessable income when viewed in isolation, they were made 'for the purpose of increasing the efficiency of the company and therefore increasing its income-producing capacity'. In this regard, Latham CJ stated (at 301):

> No expenditure, strictly and narrowly considered, in itself actually gains or produces income. It is an outgoing, not an incoming. Its character can be determined only in relation to the object which the person making the expenditure has in view. If the actual object is the conduct of the business on a profitable basis with that due regard to economy which is essential in any well-conducted business, then the expenditure . . . is an expenditure incurred in gaining or producing the assessable income.

Another early example of the practical approach of the courts is found in *Herald and Weekly Times Ltd v FC of T* (1932) 48 CLR 113. In this case, a majority of the High Court allowed a newspaper publisher deductions under former s 23(1)(a) *ITAA22* for costs it incurred in defending and settling an action brought against it for alleged defamatory articles that had been published in its newspaper. Gavan Duffy CJ and Dixon J held that the requisite link between the costs and the taxpayer's income-producing activities existed for the following reasons (at 118):

> None of the libels or supposed libels was published with any other object in view than the sale of the newspaper. The liability to damages was incurred, or the claim was encountered, because of the very act of publishing the newspaper. The thing which produced the assessable income was the thing which exposed the taxpayer to the liability or claim discharged by the expenditure. It is true that when the sums were paid the taxpayer was actuated in paying them, not by any desire to produce income, but, in the case of damages or compensation, by the necessity of satisfying a claim or liability to which it had become subject, and, in the case of law costs, by the desirability or urgency of defeating or diminishing such a claim. But this expenditure flows as a necessary or a natural consequence from the inclusion of the alleged defamatory matter in the newspaper and its publication.

The outcome in *Herald and Weekly Times* may be contrasted with the outcome in *C of T (NSW) v Ash* (1938) 61 CLR 263, which concerned a lawyer who had incurred expenditure to settle an action brought against him by his clients. The clients were seeking to recover money that had been fraudulently misappropriated by the taxpayer's former partner who had, in the meantime, become bankrupt. The High Court held that the taxpayer was not entitled to a deduction for the payment under former s 23(1)(a) *ITAA22* as it was made to discharge a personal liability. Dixon J explained (at 283):

> In my opinion the loss inflicted upon the taxpayer by his fraudulent partner takes no place in the subsequent carrying on of his practice. It was simply a loss or depletion of his general resources as a result of his undertaking the risk of such a liability when by entering into partnership each partner armed the other with an authority which he might impose liabilities upon him.

The 'in the course of' and 'incidental and relevant' tests

The courts have indicated that the 'nexus' requirement is satisfied where a loss or outgoing is incurred 'in the course of' gaining or producing assessable income. In *Amalgamated Zinc (De Bavay's) Ltd v FC of T* (1935) 54 CLR 295, Dixon J stated (at 309):

> The expression 'in gaining or producing' has the force of 'in the course of gaining or producing' and looks rather to the scope of the operations or activities and the relevance thereto of the expenditure than to purpose in itself.

Similar comments were made by Latham CJ, who stated (at 303):

> The phrase 'losses and outgoings actually incurred in gaining or producing the assessable income' may, in relation to outgoings, be read as meaning that the outgoings must be an expenditure which has an effect in gaining or producing income . . . in order to make the section intelligible it must, in my opinion, be read as meaning 'losses and outgoings actually incurred in the course of gaining or producing the assessable income'.

In *W Nevill & Co Ltd v FC of T* (1937) 56 CLR 290, Dixon J indicated (at 305) that an outgoing is incurred in the course of gaining or producing assessable income where it 'is incidental and relevant to the operations or activities regularly carried on for the production of income'. These comments were subsequently expanded on, in *Ronpibon Tin NL v FC of T* (1949) 78 CLR 47 by Latham CJ, Rich, Dixon, McTiernan and Webb JJ, who stated (at 56–57):

> For expenditure to form an allowable deduction as an outgoing incurred in gaining or producing the assessable income it must be incidental and relevant to that end. The words 'incurred in gaining or producing the assessable income' mean in the course of gaining or producing such income . . . In brief substance, to come within the initial part of the sub-section it is both sufficient and necessary that the occasion of the loss or outgoing should be found in whatever is productive of the assessable income or, if none be produced, would be expected to produce assessable income.

In *Charles Moore & Co (WA) Pty Ltd v FC of T* (1956) 95 CLR 344, the High Court allowed the proprietor of a department store a deduction for a loss of money arising from a robbery that had occurred while its employees were taking the previous day's takings to the bank. The Court held that the loss had a sufficient connection with the taxpayer's income-producing activities. Dixon CJ, Williams, Webb, Fullagar and Kitto JJ reiterated that the words 'incurred in gaining or producing the assessable income' mean 'in the course of gaining or producing assessable income' and went on to state (at 349):

> In the case of a large department store such as the taxpayer carries on, the ordinary course of business requires that, day by day and as soon as may be, the takings shall be deposited in the bank. It is as necessary to the conduct of the business as it is to place goods on the shelves or to deliver them to customers. They are all operations in the course of gaining or producing the assessable income by means of carrying on the business . . .

Their Honours then explained (at 351):

> The phrase 'incidental and relevant' when used in relation to the allowability of losses as deductions do not refer to the frequency, expectedness or likelihood of their occurrence or the antecedent risk of their being incurred, but to their nature or character. What matters is their connection with the operations which more directly gain or produce the assessable income.

The 'character' test

It is clear from *Charles Moore & Co* that in determining whether an outgoing is incurred 'in the course of' gaining or producing assessable income, in the sense that it is 'incidental and relevant' to that end, it is necessary to focus on the 'nature' or 'character' of the loss or outgoing.

The importance of this principle is vividly illustrated in the seminal case of *Lunney & Hayley v FC of T* (1958) 100 CLR 478, where the High Court denied deductions under s 51(1) *ITAA36* for the cost of fares incurred by two taxpayers on travel between their homes and workplaces. Lunney was an employee ship joiner who worked 14 miles away from his home and travelled to work by bus, whereas Hayley was a dentist who resided eight miles from his surgery and travelled there by train.

The majority of the Court found that the expenditure was not incurred in gaining or producing assessable income or in carrying on a business, but merely arose as a necessary consequence of the taxpayers 'living in one place and working in another'. Williams, Kitto and Taylor JJ explained (at 498–499):

> The question whether the fares . . . are deductible under s 51 should not and, indeed, cannot be solved simply by a process of reasoning which asserts that because expenditure on fares from a taxpayer's residence to his place of employment or place of business is necessary if assessable income is to be derived, such expenditure must be regarded as 'incidental and relevant' to the derivation of such income . . . It is, of course, beyond question that unless an employee attends at his place of employment he will not derive assessable income and, in one sense, he makes the journey to his place of employment in order that he may earn his income. But to say that expenditure on fares is a prerequisite to the earning of a taxpayer's income is not to say that such expenditure is incurred in or in the course of gaining or producing his income. Whether or not it should be so characterised depends upon considerations which are concerned more with the essential character of the expenditure itself than with the fact that unless it is incurred an employee or a person pursuing a professional practice will not even begin to engage in those activities from which their respective incomes are derived.

Lunney & Hayley demonstrates that the mere fact that an outgoing is a prerequisite to the earning of assessable income is not sufficient, by itself, to render the outgoing deductible—whether an outgoing is deductible depends instead on its 'essential character'.

Accordingly, just because an employer requires an employee to incur an expense, this does not necessarily mean that the expense is deductible to the employee. This principle is illustrated in *FC of T v Cooper* 91 ATC 4396, where a professional rugby player who was instructed by his coach to increase his normal food and drink intake by consuming additional quantities of steak, potatoes, bread and beer was denied a deduction for his additional food and drink costs by a majority of the Full Federal Court. Lockhart J explained (at 4403) that the expenditure was not deductible because of its character:

> The taxpayer incurred the expenditure on additional food and drink for the purpose of increasing his weight and thus to play professional football and earn assessable income. But its character as the cost of additional food and drink is neither relevant nor incidental to the training for and playing of football matches, which is the activity by which he gained assessable income. The expenditure was not incurred in or in the course of that activity. The taxpayer was paid money to train for and play football, not to consume food and drink. His income-producing activities did not include the consumption of food and drink.

A similar view was adopted by Hill J who stated (at 4414):

> The income-producing activities to be considered in the present case are training for and playing football. It is for these activities that a professional footballer is paid. The income-producing activities do not include the taking of food, albeit that unless food is eaten, the player would be unable to play. Expenditure on food, even as here 'additional food' does not form part of expenditure related to the income producing activities of playing football or training.

Hill J then went on to conclude that, even if the direction to consume more food and drink was a direction lawfully given to the taxpayer under his contract, it does not follow that the expenditure must be deductible. His Honour said (at 4414):

> An employer may require an employee to travel to and from work by a particular mode of transport, but the fact that the employee is required, as a term of his employment, to incur a

> particular expenditure does not convert expenditure that is not incurred in the course of the income-producing operations into a deductible outgoing. If it did, then, no doubt, employers would be besieged by employees with requests that the employer should require the particular expenditure to be incurred.

Characterising outgoings by reference to objective advantages obtained

The courts traditionally characterise outgoings by reference to the legal rights or advantages that a taxpayer obtains from incurring the expenditure. In this regard, the courts usually focus on the objective circumstances surrounding the outgoings. For example, where a taxpayer has incurred expenditure to acquire goods or services under a contract, the character of the outgoing will ordinarily be determined simply by reference to the contractual benefits obtained by the taxpayer and the objective relationship those benefits have to the taxpayer's income-producing or business activities.

This concept is illustrated in *Cecil Bros Pty Ltd v FC of T* (1964) 111 CLR 430. In this case, the High Court allowed deductions to a shoe retailer for the amounts it paid to acquire its trading stock from a company (Breckler) that had been interposed between the taxpayer and its usual suppliers. The shareholders in Breckler were relatives of the taxpayer's shareholders. Breckler had sold the goods to the taxpayer at a mark-up of approximately 10%. The Commissioner had denied the taxpayer deductions for so much of the amounts paid to Breckler as exceeded the amounts that it would have paid its usual suppliers for the goods. Owen J, however, held that as soon as it was established that the expenditure was incurred to purchase trading stock, it was not appropriate to apportion the outgoings. His Honour explained (at 434) that 'it is not for the court or the Commissioner to say how much a taxpayer ought to spend in obtaining his income'.

A similar conclusion was reached by the Full Federal Court in *FC of T v Phillips* 78 ATC 4361, which concerned a firm of accountants that had established a 'service trust' arrangement. Under the arrangement, a unit trust was established with a corporate trustee. Each of the partners (or their nominees) could subscribe for units in the trust proportionate to the partner's interest in the partnership. The non-professional activities of the partnership (eg secretarial and clerical services) were taken over by the trustee of the trust, which then provided these services back to the partnership at commercial rates. The partnership's equipment was also purchased by the trustee and leased back to the partnership at commercial rates. The Full Federal Court allowed the partnership deductions for the entire amounts paid to the trustee and did not require any apportionment to take account of the mark-ups charged by the trustee on the basis that the amounts paid were commercially realistic. In this regard, Fisher J stated (at 4368):

> The deductibility or otherwise . . . of expenditure can generally be determined by answering the question whether 'the circumstances of its expenditure give it the complexion of money laid out in furtherance of a purpose of gaining income' . . . The question is ultimately one of fact . . .
>
> A crucially important circumstance in the present matter is the unchallenged finding of the trial judge that the charges paid by the firm were realistic and not in excess of commercial rates. The services were essential to the conduct of the firm's business and the fact that the charges paid were commercially realistic raises at least the presumption that they were a real and genuine cost of earning the firm's income and the cost of that alone. It strongly supports the view that the expenditure was exclusively for business purposes. Without doubt the cost of acquisition of the services was 'necessarily incurred' in the sense that it was 'clearly appropriate or adapted for' the production of the assessable income . . .
>
> Doubtless the converse would apply, namely, if the expenditure was grossly excessive, it would raise the presumption that it was not wholly payable for the services and equipment provided, but was for some other purpose. Such is not the case here.

Although the arrangements in both *Cecil Bros* and *Phillips* had the effect of allowing the taxpayers to divert income to related parties through the relevant interposed entities, the courts did not focus on this aspect of the arrangements to characterise the outgoings. Instead, they simply focused on what the outgoings had objectively obtained—namely trading stock, secretarial and clerical services and the use of equipment. As all these things, viewed objectively, were ordinary business expenses of the taxpayers, the courts had no trouble in allowing them to deduct the full amount of their expenditure on these items, without looking any further into the transactions.

The final paragraph in the above passage from *Phillips*, however, indicates that, if the expenditure had been grossly excessive, a different conclusion would have been reached, since this would suggest that the outgoings might not be wholly incurred for deductible purposes.

The Commissioner's views on *Phillips*-style service trust arrangements are outlined in TR 2006/2 and in a guide entitled *Your Service Entity Arrangements*. These arrangements are discussed further at [36.6].

Characterising outgoings by reference to a taxpayer's subjective purpose

Although the cases discussed above indicate that the courts generally focus on objective criteria to characterise outgoings, there have also been certain cases where the courts have been prepared to take a taxpayer's subjective purpose into account.

In *Magna Alloys & Research Pty Ltd v FC of T* 80 ATC 4542 (discussed below), Brennan J stated (at 4547):

> Though purpose is not the test of deductibility nor even a conception relevant to a loss involuntarily incurred, in cases where a connection between an outgoing and the taxpayer's undertaking or business is affected by the voluntary act of the taxpayer, the purpose of incurring that expenditure may constitute an element of its essential character, stamping it as expenditure of a business or income-earning kind.

Subsequently, his Honour remarked (at 4548):

> But purpose is relevant to describe an element of connection between expenditure and a taxpayer's undertaking or business in cases where a taxpayer incurs expenditure or agrees to incur expenditure without any antecedent obligation to do so or where the occasion of the expenditure (unlike the purchase of trading stock) is not manifestly to be found in whatever is productive of assessable income or in whatever would be expected to produce assessable income, or in the carrying on of a business.

The importance that a taxpayer's subjective purpose can have in characterising an outgoing was revealed in *Ure v FC of T* 81 ATC 4100. The taxpayer in this case had borrowed money at commercial interest rates (of up to 12.5% pa) and on-lent the funds to his associates (his wife and a family company) at a much lower interest rate (of 1% pa). The funds were used to discharge mortgages on residential property beneficially owned by the taxpayer's company and to purchase a new family home. The taxpayer claimed a deduction for the entire interest expenditure he incurred on the borrowings. He contended that the interest had been incurred to gain assessable income in the form of the interest income that he received from the loans made to his associates. The Full Federal Court, however, concluded that the taxpayer's interest expenditure was only partly deductible. Essentially, the court only allowed the taxpayer a deduction for so much of the interest expenditure he incurred that did not exceed the interest income he received. In arriving at this conclusion, the court indicated that a taxpayer's motives (ie subjective purpose) for incurring an outgoing may, in certain circumstances, be decisive in characterising the outgoing. In this regard, Deane and Sheppard JJ stated (at 4110):

> One of the most difficult aspects of the problem of characterizing an outgoing is the assessment of what, if any, weight is to be given to indirect objects which a taxpayer had in mind

> in incurring the outgoing. Such objects form part of the relevant circumstances by reference to which the problem of characterization must be resolved. There is however no rigid principle which can be applied in determining what, if any, weight should be given to them. In the ordinary case, such as, for example, where the immediate object achieved by the outgoing is the production of assessable income which is commensurate with the amount of the outgoing or where it is clear that the outgoing was for the purchase of stock-in-trade or the acquisition of services or hire of equipment used in earning assessable income, indirect objects or motives of a personal or domestic character will plainly not prevent the characterization of the outgoing as having been incurred in earning assessable income . . . In other cases, the immediate object or effect of an outgoing will not suffice either to explain or to characterize it. In such cases, indirect objects or motives can assume a sometimes decisive importance.

Their Honours went on to conclude (at 4110):

> In the present case, it would be a misleading half-truth to say that the object which the taxpayer had in mind or the advantage which he sought in incurring the liability to pay interest at rates of 7.5% or more was the derivation by him of interest at the rate of 1% per annum by re-lending the money which he borrowed. That was, no doubt, an object which the taxpayer had in mind: it was an advantage which he sought. In the circumstances however, characterization of the outgoing cannot properly be effected by reference to that object or advantage alone. The incurring of the outgoing can only be explained by reference also to less direct objects and advantages which the taxpayer sought to achieve and which plainly were of paramount importance. These indirect objects or advantages were, in so far as the taxpayer was concerned, not of an income-earning character . . .

Brennan J reached a similar conclusion to Deane and Sheppard JJ regarding the interest expenditure and noted (at 4104) that there was 'an air of unreality about the proposition that the borrowed moneys were laid out wholly for the purpose of earning a return of 1% per annum'.

Ure was considered by the High Court a decade later in *Fletcher & Ors v FC of T* 91 ATC 4950. The taxpayers in *Fletcher* had entered into an arrangement under which they had borrowed a large sum of money for a period of up to 15 years to purchase an annuity. The arrangement was structured so that during the first five years of the scheme the interest outgoings would exceed the annuity income (resulting in substantial losses over this period), whereas during the last five years the annuity income would exceed the interest outgoings (resulting in substantial net income). The arrangement also allowed the taxpayers to terminate the scheme early, thereby allowing them to avoid the adverse tax consequences that would otherwise arise in its later years. The Commissioner disallowed deductions for so much of the interest payments incurred in the early years of the arrangement that exceeded the annuity income derived in those years.

The High Court held that the deductibility of the interest payments depended on whether or not the overall arrangement was expected to be terminated before substantial amounts of assessable income began to be derived in the final years of the arrangement. As this was a factual issue, the Court referred the case back to the AAT to resolve this issue. Before doing so, however, Mason CJ, Brennan, Deane, Dawson, Toohey, Gaudron and McHugh JJ made the following important observations (at 4957–4958) on the role that a taxpayer's subjective purpose may have in characterising an outgoing:

> it is commonly possible to characterise an outgoing as being wholly of the kind referred to in the first limb of s 51(1) without any need to refer to the taxpayer's subjective thought processes. That is ordinarily so in a case where the outgoing gives rise to the receipt of a larger amount of assessable income. In such a case, the characterisation of the particular outgoing as wholly of a kind referred to in s 51(1) will ordinarily not be affected by considerations of

> the taxpayer's subjective motivation. If, for example, a particular item of assessable income can be earned by making a lesser outgoing in one of two possible ways, one of which is a loss or outgoing of the kind described in s 51(1) and the other of which is not, it will ordinarily be irrelevant that the taxpayer's choice of the method which was tax deductible was motivated by taxation considerations or that the non-deductible outgoing would have been less than the deductible one. In such a case, the objective relationship between the outgoing actually made and the greater amount of assessable income actually earned suffices, without more, to characterise the whole outgoing as one which was incurred in gaining or producing assessable income. If the outgoing can properly be wholly so characterised, it 'is not for the Court or the commissioner to say how much a taxpayer ought to spend in obtaining his income, but only how much he has spent'. . . .
>
> The position may, however, well be different in a case where no relevant assessable income can be identified or where the relevant assessable income is less than the amount of the outgoing. Even in a case where some assessable income is derived as a result of the outgoing, the disproportion between the detriment of the outgoing and the benefit of the income may give rise to a need to resolve the problem of characterisation of the outgoing for the purposes of the sub-section by a weighing of the various aspects of the whole set of circumstances, including direct and indirect objects and advantages which the taxpayer sought in making the outgoing . . . Where that is so, it is a 'commonsense' or 'practical' weighing of all the factors which must provide the ultimate answer . . . If, upon consideration of all those factors, it appears that, notwithstanding the disproportion between outgoing and income, the whole outgoing is properly to be characterised as genuinely and not colourably incurred in gaining or producing assessable income, the entire outgoing will fall within the first limb of s 51(1) . . . If, however, that consideration reveals that the disproportion between outgoing and relevant assessable income is essentially to be explained by reference to the independent pursuit of some other objective and that part only of the outgoing can be characterised by reference to the actual or expected production of assessable income, apportionment of the outgoing between the pursuit of assessable income and the pursuit of that other objective will be necessary.

Ure and *Fletcher* demonstrate that the courts will have no hesitation in taking a taxpayer's subjective purpose into account to characterise 'colourable' and 'voluntary' outgoings where the amount of income produced is less than the amount of the outgoings incurred. Where the disproportion between these amounts can only be explained by reference to some non-income-producing purpose, the courts will apportion, or even disallow, the deductions.

For example, the courts have disallowed deductions where outgoings were found to be incurred for the purpose of securing 'tax advantages' rather than gaining assessable income. This occurred in *FC of T v Ilbery* 81 ATC 4661, where the Full Federal Court denied deductions for interest incurred by a taxpayer in relation to a pre-paid interest scheme. It also occurred in *Deane v FC of T & Croker v FC of T* 82 ATC 4112, where the Supreme Court of NSW denied deductions for losses incurred by taxpayers involved in a 'Curran' share trading scheme.

More recently, in *Spassked Pty Ltd v FC of T* 2003 ATC 5099, a holding company involved in a complex restructure was denied deductions for interest incurred on loans used to acquire shares in a subsidiary company. The Full Federal Court applied *Fletcher* and found that the evidence in the case indicated that no dividend was intended to be paid on the shares for an indefinite period of time. The Court stated (at 5121):

> Ordinarily, where a taxpayer borrows money for the purpose of acquiring shares carrying rights to a dividend the interest on the funds borrowed will be deductible without reference to subjective matters. But, equally, where no dividends are derived by the taxpayer from the investment and especially where, as here, it appears that no dividend was intended to be paid

> on those shares for an indefinite time, the result would be very different, for in such a case the occasion of incurring the interest in the year of income would not be found in gaining or producing assessable income at all.

Characterising outgoings where related party transactions are involved

The underlying reason why the interest expenditure in *Ure* was not fully deductible was that the taxpayer had on-lent the money he borrowed on a non-arm's length basis (ie to related parties at a non-commercial interest rate). As Brennan J aptly noted, the arrangement had an 'air of unreality' about it. This special feature certainly helps make the decision reached by the Full Federal Court appear intuitively correct. In other words, the blatant non-commercial nature of the arrangement and the fact that it involved transactions between related parties provided the perfect opportunity for the court to focus on the taxpayer's subjective purpose to characterise the interest outgoings.

It is important to realise, however, that just because a transaction involves related parties does not mean the outgoing should always be apportioned. In this regard, *Ure* may be contrasted with *FC of T v Janmor Nominees Pty Ltd* 87 ATC 4813, which also involved a related-party transaction, but which generated commercial returns. *Janmor Nominees* concerned a company that acted as the trustee of a doctor's family trust. The company purchased a property with borrowed money and leased it to the doctor (who was a director of the company) at a commercial rent. The property was used as the doctor's residence. It was purchased via the trust as the doctor believed that this would minimise death duties and provide him with asset protection and 'negative gearing benefits'.

The company included the rent received from the doctor in the assessable income of the trust estate and it claimed deductions for the interest incurred in respect of the loan (as well as certain other outgoings relating to the property such as borrowing expenses, insurance, rates and repairs). The Commissioner disallowed deductions for so much of the interest payments as exceeded the rent. The Full Federal Court, however, held that the interest payments were fully deductible. The Court found that, although the transactions were motivated by familial considerations, this was not conclusive of the character of the interest payments. According to the Court, the interest was incurred in the course of producing assessable income and the mere fact that the payments exceeded the rent was no reason for severing the outgoings into a portion that was incurred in gaining or producing assessable income and a portion that was not.

It was critical to the outcome in *Janmor Nominees* that rent was charged at commercial rates. Where non-commercial rent is charged to related parties, a different outcome is likely to arise. This is vividly demonstrated by the Federal Court decision in *Madigan v FC of T* 96 ATC 4640. The taxpayer in this case was a beneficiary of a family trust who was assessed on a share of the net income of the trust estate. The Commissioner had calculated the net income on the basis that the trustee was only allowed to deduct one-quarter of the outgoings relating to a property that had been leased to the taxpayer's father at approximately one-quarter of its market rental. The outgoings included interest payable on the loan used to purchase the property as well as expenses such as land tax, rates, insurance, repairs and maintenance costs. The taxpayer argued that the full amount of these outgoings should have been deductible in calculating the net income of the trust estate.

Hill J, however, held that it was appropriate to apportion the outgoings. According to his Honour, the explanation for the low rent lay in the 'private relationship' the persons occupying the premises had with the trustee. On this basis, it was not possible to say that the whole of the outgoings had the character of outgoings incurred in gaining or producing assessable income. Hill J was at pains to distinguish *Janmor Nominees* on the basis of its facts. His Honour noted (at 4643):

> The present case is not one where the only relevant fact is the excess of the outgoings over the assessable income derived in the year of income. Had that been the only matter, the

> outgoings may well have been deductible in full. There is more to the facts of the present case. Here there is a rental struck at only twenty-five percent of market rental in circumstances where the only explanation for such a transaction is to be found in the relationship between those occupying the premises on the one hand and the trustee on the other, as reflected in the trust deed.

According to Hill J, *Ure* supported the conclusion that the outgoings should be only partially deductible. Interestingly, his Honour acknowledged that the mere fact that the rent was below market value did not, by itself, prevent the outgoings from being fully deductible. Rather, it was the fact that the explanation for the low rent was found in the private relationship that existed between the trustee and the father, which indicated that the outgoings were not fully incurred in gaining assessable income. In this regard, his Honour stated (at 4643–4645):

> The fact that the outgoings exceeded the rent is of itself, as *Janmor* makes clear, not of great significance. The fact that the rental received was not identical with market value might also not preclude the deduction of the outgoings. For example, a property may be let to a good tenant at a lower than market rent on the basis that the tenant will look after the property. The mere fact that the rental is thus below market rental will not preclude deductibility of the whole of the outgoings. But where the circumstances are such that the explanation for the low rent lies in the private relationship which the persons occupying the premises have to the trustee, it is not possible to say that the whole of the outgoings have the character of outgoings incurred in gaining or producing assessable income. The explanation is to be found rather in private or non–income-earning considerations.

Nexus between loss or outgoing and the taxpayer's assessable income

It is clear from the use of the word 'your' in s 8-1 *ITAA97*, that a loss or outgoing incurred by a taxpayer is only deductible to the extent that the loss or outgoing relates to gaining or producing *the taxpayer's* assessable income. An outgoing incurred by one taxpayer to make income for another taxpayer is therefore not deductible as the nexus requirement is not satisfied.

It is important to recognise, however, that the courts have taken a broad view of the nexus requirement in cases involving arrangements between parent companies and their wholly owned subsidiaries. For instance, in *FC of T v Total Holdings (Australia) Pty Ltd* 79 ATC 4279, a parent company was allowed deductions for interest incurred on money that it borrowed and on-lent interest-free to its wholly owned subsidiary for use in the subsidiary's business. The Full Federal Court held that the loan was made to render the subsidiary profitable as soon as commercially feasible so that it could pay dividends to the parent. As a result, there was a sufficient nexus between the parent's interest expenditure and the gaining or producing of its assessable income. The fact that the parent received no interest income from the loan it made to the subsidiary did not prevent the parent from being able to claim deductions for its interest expenses.

Nexus with carrying on a business

For a loss or outgoing to be deductible under the second positive limb of s 8-1 *ITAA97*, it must be 'necessarily' incurred in carrying on the taxpayer's business. As a general rule, the courts have interpreted the word 'necessarily', as used in this context, quite liberally.

For instance, in *FC of T v Snowden & Willson Pty Ltd* (1958) 99 CLR 431, the High Court allowed a company deductions for costs incurred in defending itself before a Royal Commission that was investigating its business practices and in placing newspaper advertisements expressing 'its side of the story' to the public. Dixon CJ held (at 436) that expenditure is necessarily incurred in carrying on a business if it is 'dictated by the business ends to which it is directed, those ends forming part of or being truly incidental to the business'. According to his Honour 'logical necessity is not a thing to be predicated of business expenditure'. Similar observations were made by Fullagar J, who stated (at 444) that 'the man who is carrying on the business must be the judge of what is "necessary"'.

Snowden & Willson was followed in *Magna Alloys & Research Pty Ltd v FC of T* 80 ATC 4542. In this case, the Full Federal Court allowed a company deductions for legal expenses incurred in defending its directors and agents against charges that they had received secret commissions. Deane and Fisher JJ stated (at 4557):

> The requirement that the claimed outgoing be 'necessarily' incurred in carrying on the relevant business does not, in the context, mean that the outgoing must be either 'unavoidable' or 'essentially necessary'. Nor does the word 'necessarily' import a requisite of logical necessity. What is required is that the relevant expenditure be appropriate and adapted for the ends of the business carried on for the purpose of earning assessable income.

Their Honours then went on to conclude (at 4561):

> The interests of the taxpayer were inextricably involved with those of its directors and agents and it was plainly in the taxpayer's own interests that the directors and agents be properly represented. In these circumstances, the incurring of expenditure in providing adequate representation for the directors and agents was reasonably capable of being regarded as desirable and appropriate from the point of view of the pursuit of the business ends of the taxpayer's business.

In *FC of T v Visy Industries USA Pty Ltd* 2012 ATC ¶20-340, the Australian holding company of a group of manufacturing companies that operated in the United States was allowed a deduction for an indemnity fee incurred in relation to a currency hedging arrangement which it had entered into for a 'not insignificant' purpose of profit-making. The Full Federal Court found that the fee was of a revenue nature and had been necessarily incurred in carrying on its business even though it had not been incurred in the 'ordinary course' of that business. The Court stressed (at [60]) that s 8-1 'does not distinguish between outgoings incurred in carrying on a business and outgoings incurred in the ordinary course of carrying on a business'. Both kinds of outgoings fall within the second positive limb.

Losses arising under the first strand of *Myer*

The relationship between s 8-1 *ITAA97* and the first strand of *FC of T v Myer Emporium Ltd* 87 ATC 4363 [9.5] was recently considered in *Greig v FC of T* 2020 ATC ¶20-733. The case concerned a wealthy corporate executive who purchased over $30m of shares between 2008 and 2014. This included shares in a company called Nexus that ultimately failed and was placed into administration. The Nexus shares had been purchased in two phases. The first phase was purchased in February 2011 and sold at a loss in May 2011. The second phase was purchased between March 2012 and May 2014 and involved 64 separate acquisitions costing $11,851,762. These shares were compulsorily transferred to a third party for nil consideration after a litigation action brought against the administrators to prevent the transfer failed. The taxpayer initially treated all his share transactions as being on capital account. However, after obtaining financial advice, he adopted the position that the second phase of Nexus shares was on revenue account, and he claimed deductions for the losses arising on their transfer. The taxpayer argued that, unlike his other share transactions, these shares were purchased pursuant to a 'Profit Target Strategy', which involved acquiring undervalued shares that were likely to increase in value in a short space of time, and then quickly selling them at a profit.

A majority of the Full Federal Court (Steward and Kenny JJ; Derrington J dissenting) found that the losses on the Nexus shares were deductible under the first positive limb of s 8-1 as the taxpayer had acquired the shares in a business operation or commercial transaction with a view that they be sold at a profit in the short term. The majority stated (at [8]):

> It was common ground that, under *Myer Emporium*, a loss or outgoing incurred in gaining or producing assessable income is deductible under s 8-1(1)(a) of the ITAA 1997 if that loss or outgoing is incurred in a 'business operation or commercial transaction' entered into with the purpose of deriving profit or gain, even though the loss or outgoing was not incurred in the ordinary course of carrying on the taxpayer's business.

In arriving at the conclusion that the acquisition of the Nexus shares had the character of a business operation or commercial transaction, the majority took into account the fact that the taxpayer had a sophisticated plan to generate profits, acquired the shares in a systematic fashion on 64 occasions and had relied on advice from an advisory firm. The majority also held that there appeared to be no material difference between the taxpayer's object in relation to the second phase of Nexus shares and his object in relation to the other shares. Steward J stated (at [252]) that 'the inference should be drawn that all the shares were acquired for the purpose of profit-making and all bore the character of a business deal'. Kenny J concurred with this view and added (at [28]) that the taxpayer's attempt to isolate his acquisition of the Nexus shares from the rest of his share trading activities had 'a distinct air of unreality'.

Temporal connection

In determining whether there is a sufficient nexus for the purposes of s 8-1 *ITAA97*, the existence of a temporal connection between a loss or outgoing and the gaining of assessable income may be relevant. This does not, however, mean that contemporaneity between a loss or outgoing and the production of assessable income is an essential requirement of the general deduction provision. This point was recognised in *Steele v DFC of T* 99 ATC 4242 [12.12], where Gleeson CJ, Gaudron and Gummow JJ stated (at 4251):

> The temporal relationship between the incurring of an outgoing and the actual or projected receipt of income may be one of a number of facts relevant to a judgment as to whether the necessary connection might, in a given case, exist, but contemporaneity is not legally essential, and whether it is factually important may depend upon the circumstances of the particular case.

Temporal issues have arisen before the courts in two kinds of situations. The first situation concerns losses or outgoings that are incurred prior to the commencement of a business. The second situation concerns losses or outgoings that are incurred after the cessation of a business. These two situations are explored below.

Losses or outgoings incurred before the commencement of a business

It is well established that losses and outgoings which are 'preliminary' to the commencement of an income-producing or business activity are not incurred 'in the course of' such activity and are therefore not deductible under the general deduction provision.

This principle is illustrated in *Softwood Pulp and Paper Ltd v FC of T* 76 ATC 4439, which concerned a company that had incurred feasibility study and other costs to determine whether or not to establish a new paper production mill in South Australia. The Supreme Court of Victoria held that the costs were not deductible as 'the company had not reached a stage remotely near the carrying on of a business'. Menhennitt J stated (at 4450):

> Everything that was done in this case, up till the time when the project ceased, was . . . entirely preliminary and directed to deciding whether or not an undertaking would be established to produce assessable income.

> The project had not reached anything like the stage of doing anything in the course of gaining or producing assessable income. All that had happened was that certain tests had been made to ascertain whether or not the project would be feasible.

A similar outcome was reached in *Griffin Coal Mining Company Ltd v FC of T* 90 ATC 4870, where the Full Federal Court disallowed a coal mining company deductions for expenditure incurred in undertaking a feasibility study relating to the construction of a proposed aluminium smelter. The Court held that the expenditure did not relate to the taxpayer's existing business, but to the formation of a potential new source of income.

Likewise, in *Goodman Fielder Wattie Ltd v FC of T* 91 ATC 4438, a company that was collaborating in a research project relating to the development of monoclonal antibodies was denied deductions for its initial R&D expenditure on the project on the basis that its activities were of a 'provisional kind only'. Hill J referred to *Softwood Pulp and Paper Ltd* and explained that it was critical to the decision in that case that the taxpayer had not yet committed itself to the project nor made a final definitive decision to do so. For similar reasons, his Honour held that the taxpayer's initial R&D expenditure should not be deductible.

The facts of the preceding cases may be contrasted with those in *FC of T v Osborne* 90 ATC 4889, which involved a taxpayer that had leased land to grow chestnuts. The taxpayer purchased chestnut plants and seedlings and had ploughed and fertilised the soil in preparation for planting, but abandoned the project because it was uneconomical. The Full Federal Court held that the taxpayer had commenced carrying on a primary production business. His activities were more than preliminary endeavours and were conducted on a sufficient scale to be more than a hobby. The Court, nevertheless, denied deductions under s 51(1) for the costs incurred in preparing the soil for planting on the basis that they were of a capital nature.

Losses or outgoings incurred after the cessation of a business

It was originally considered that losses or outgoings that are incurred after the cessation of a business are not deductible as they are not sufficiently connected with the taxpayer's income-producing activities. Authority for this view can be traced back to the early High Court decision in *Amalgamated Zinc (De Bavay's) Ltd v FC of T* (1935) 54 CLR 295, which concerned former s 23(1)(a) *ITAA22*. The taxpayer in this case had carried on business mining and producing zinc, but had closed down its mine in 1924. Despite the closure, the taxpayer remained liable under legislation to make annual workers compensation contributions to a fund for the benefit of its former employees and their dependants. The taxpayer sought deductions for payments it made in the 1932 and 1933 income years. The High Court, however, denied the deductions on the basis that the payments were 'completely dissociated from' the gaining or producing of the taxpayer's assessable income in the relevant years. Latham CJ made the following remarks (at 303–304):

> It is true that, in cases of continuing businesses, it has been conceded . . . that expenditure may be allowed as a deduction though it produces and is possibly designed to produce results in the way of income in a future year and not in the year in relation to which income is being assessed [*Ward & Co v Commissioner of Taxes* (1923) AC 145]. So it has also been held that expenditure which has a direct relation to income of a past year can be deducted in a later assessment year where it is of such a character that, in a continuing business, it must be met from time to time as a part of the process of gaining assessable income [*Herald and Weekly Times Ltd v FC of T* (1932) 48 CLR 113]. But even this benevolent interpretation cannot assist the taxpayer in a case like this, where there has been a complete cessation of the income-producing operations out of which the necessity to make the outgoing arose.

The *Amalgamated Zinc* decision drew a clear distinction between a continuing business and a ceased business. The decision has, however, been distinguished in a number of subsequent cases and it is now no longer considered to reflect the current view of the courts on this issue.

An early case that distinguished *Amalgamated Zinc* was *Queensland Meat Export Co Ltd v FC of T* (1939) 5 ATD 176. In this case, a company that had closed down its meatworks in Brisbane for a number of years, because of competition from another abattoir, sought deductions for maintaining its Brisbane premises and plant in good working order. The Supreme Court of Queensland held that, unlike in *Amalgamated Zinc*, the taxpayer had not irrevocably terminated its business and intended to recommence operations when conditions improved. In the meantime, the company continued to operate from elsewhere. As the 'closure' of its meatworks was 'temporary' and as the premises were maintained in the hope that when conditions improved they would again be used for income-producing purposes, the expenditure was deductible under former s 23(1)(a) *ITAA22*. Douglas J explained (at 180):

> If money is so laid out in the hope that income may accrue from this works or plant in the future, or to maintain it in proper order for a reasonable time awaiting sale, it is a proper deduction against profits, even though the profits come from another plant.

Likewise, in *AGC (Advances) Ltd v FC of T* 75 ATC 4057, the High Court declined to follow *Amalgamated Zinc* to conclude that a company that had restructured its business as a consequence of a scheme of arrangement, and that had subsequently been taken over by another company, was allowed to claim deductions for losses incurred in relation to bad debts arising from its previous business activities. Mason J stated (at 4071–4072):

> It may be argued that if the taxpayer has ceased to carry on particular business, a loss subsequently sustained in relation to that business cannot be described accurately as a loss incurred in carrying on that business, or at any rate one incurred in carrying it on for the purpose of gaining or producing assessable income. But the soundness of the argument depends on what is meant by 'incurred'. A loss constituted by the writing off of a bad debt is no doubt incurred, in the sense that it is sustained, at the time when the debt is written off, and that may occur in a given case after the taxpayer has ceased to carry on as a going concern the business in which the debt was created. Yet even in such a case it may be correct to speak of the loss as having been incurred in the carrying on of the business. This is because the occasion for the loss is to be found in a transaction entered into in the carrying on of the business for the purpose of producing assessable income, that is, in the agreement by which the debt was created. Because the loss had its origin in such a transaction the loss may be said to be one which was incurred in the carrying on of the business for the purpose of producing assessable income, notwithstanding that its true character as a loss is not finally ascertained until the debt is written off.

Thus, according to Mason J, the critical issue to determine under the general deduction provision was not whether the taxpayer's business had ceased, but whether the 'occasion' of the loss or outgoing could be found in the carrying on of the taxpayer's business.

AGC was followed in *Placer Pacific Management Pty Ltd v FC of T* 95 ATC 4459, where a company was allowed deductions for expenditure incurred in settling a dispute with one of its customers concerning a faulty conveyor belt that it had supplied. The settlement occurred several years after the taxpayer had sold its conveyor belt business. The Full Federal Court held (at 4464):

> In our view *AGC* should be taken as establishing the proposition that provided the occasion of a business outgoing is to be found in the business operations directed towards the gaining or production of assessable income generally, the fact that that outgoing was incurred in a year later than the year in which the income was incurred and the fact that in the meantime

> business in the ordinary sense may have ceased will not determine the issue of deductibility. There is no relevant distinction to be drawn between losses and outgoings. Provided the occasion for the loss or outgoing is to be found in the business operations directed to gaining or producing assessable income, that loss or outgoing will be deductible unless it is capital or of a capital nature.
>
> On the facts of the present case the occasion of the loss or outgoing ultimately incurred in the year of income was the business arrangement entered into between [the taxpayer] and [the customer] for the supply of the conveyor belt which was alleged to be defective. The fact that the division had subsequently been sold and its active manufacturing business terminated does not deny deductibility to the outgoing. A finding to the contrary would lead to great inequity. Many businesses generate liabilities which may arise in the considerable future. Such liabilities are sometimes referred to as 'long tail liabilities'. To preclude deductibility when those liabilities come to fruition on the basis that the active trading business which gave rise to them had ceased would be unjust.

Placer Pacific is authority for the principle that provided the occasion of a loss or outgoing can be traced to business operations that were formerly carried on by the taxpayer for the purpose of gaining assessable income, the loss or outgoing is *prima facie* deductible. Expressed in another way, provided a taxpayer's business operations are the 'cause' of a loss or outgoing, the fact that these operations may have ceased in the meantime does not, by itself, preclude the taxpayer from claiming a deduction.

Placer Pacific was applied in *FC of T v Brown* 99 ATC 4600, which concerned a taxpayer who, together with his wife, had borrowed money from a bank to fund the purchase of a delicatessen business that they operated in partnership. They subsequently sold the business, but continued to pay interest on the loan as the sale proceeds were insufficient to discharge their outstanding debt. The Commissioner denied deductions for the interest payments made after the sale of the business on the basis that the sale severed the nexus between the carrying on of the business and those payments. The Full Federal Court, nevertheless, concluded that the occasion for the interest payments was to be found in the loan entered into by the partnership in carrying on its business for the purpose of producing assessable income. It held that the cessation of business did not operate to break the nexus between the carrying on of the business and the incurring of the interest liability.

Lee, Nicholson and Merkel JJ noted that there may come a time, between the cessation of a business and the payment of interest, such that in the circumstances, the payment is no longer sufficiently proximate to the activities of the business to be deductible, with the consequence that those activities no longer provide the occasion for the outgoing. Their Honours did not, however, elaborate further on precisely when such a time would arise. Instead, they indicated that a 'commonsense' or 'practical' weighing of all the factors was required to resolve this issue. Their Honours' *obiter dicta*, nevertheless, contained the following caution (at 4608):

> Had the loan agreement in question been a 'roll over' business loan facility which entitled the taxpayer conducting the business, on the date of each monthly payment, to elect to repay the principal and thereby avoid incurring liability for interest or to 'roll over' the loan and continue to be liable for interest, that may have been a different situation. In that circumstance there may be considerable force in a contention that the occasion of the liability was the election to 'roll over' the loan on each monthly payment date, rather than any liability arising under the terms of the original loan agreement establishing the terms of the 'roll over' facility. In such a case the cessation of the business or sale of the income-producing asset acquired with the borrowed funds might properly be regarded as breaking the nexus . . .

A case that has similarities with *Brown*, but which also involved the refinancing of a loan, is *FC of T v Jones* 2002 ATC 4135. In this case, the taxpayer and her husband had taken out loans to acquire equipment used in a trucking business that they had carried on in partnership since 1967. The husband died in 1992, after which time the taxpayer returned to her former employment as a nurse. In the meantime, she continued to be liable to pay interest on an outstanding loan from the ANZ bank. In 1996, she refinanced the loan with another institution at a lower interest rate. The Full Federal Court followed *Brown* to conclude that the taxpayer was entitled to a deduction for the interest payments she incurred after the cessation of the partnership business in 1992. Importantly, the Court also held that the refinancing of the loan in 1996 did not break the nexus between the interest outgoings and the business. Indeed, the Court expressly stated that 'when an original borrowing is refinanced, the new financing takes on the same character as the original borrowing'. This principle was based on the 'refinancing principle' established in *FC of T v Roberts & Smith* 92 ATC 4380 [12.12].

The case law therefore demonstrates that the mere fact that outgoings are incurred after the cessation of a business does not necessarily preclude them from being deductible. Where, however, outgoings relate to the 'disposal' of a business (as opposed to the 'carrying on' of a business), it seems that they will not satisfy the requirements of the general deduction provision.

This principle is illustrated in *Peyton v FC of T* (1963) 109 CLR 315, which concerned a taxpayer who had sold his hotel business. Under the terms of his lease, the taxpayer was required to obtain the lessor's consent to transfer the lease to the purchaser. The lease also provided that such consent would be given only if the taxpayer carried out any repairs or renovations required by the lessor's architect, and that if this work had not been completed prior to the transfer, the lessor was entitled to be paid an amount for the estimated cost of such work. The issue before the High Court was whether the taxpayer could deduct an amount paid to the lessor for the estimated cost of the work. The Court held that the outgoing was not incurred in gaining or producing the taxpayer's assessable income, but in parting with his business and, on this basis, the outgoing should not be deductible.

Negative gearing

It is important to understand that there is no requirement in the tax legislation to quarantine deductions available under s 8-1 *ITAA97* against particular categories of assessable income. This is important for taxpayers who have 'negatively geared' investments (ie where the expenses relating to their investments exceed the income generated from them). A taxpayer who owns an income-producing investment property can therefore generally deduct their revenue losses and outgoings relating to the property (eg interest on borrowings to acquire the property) against not just the rent received from leasing the property, but also against any other forms of assessable income they might earn. This means that if their interest expenses on their investment property mortgage exceed their rental income, they will generally be able to apply the excess against, for instance, their salary or business income.

Negative gearing was a key issue in the 2016 and 2019 federal election campaigns [5.9]. In both these elections, Labor had campaigned heavily on introducing quarantining rules to limit tax deductions for negative gearing. Under Labor's proposal, taxpayers would be able to offset losses from new investments (eg in shares and properties) against income from those investments, but any excess losses would need to be carried forward and offset against the capital gains made from such investments in future years. However, the Coalition Government, which won the 2019 election, made it clear it would not change the law on negative gearing. The Albanese Labor Government has not deviated from this position. As a result, taxpayers with investment losses that are deductible under s 8-1 can continue to apply those losses against their non-investment income.

[12.4] Negative limbs

Even though a loss or outgoing may satisfy the nexus requirements of the positive limbs of s 8-1 *ITAA97*, it will not be deductible under s 8-1 if it falls within one of the four negative limbs of the provision.

First negative limb: Capital losses and outgoings

The first negative limb of s 8-1 denies a deduction for a loss or outgoing to the extent that 'it is a loss or outgoing of capital or of a capital nature'. 'Capital' losses or outgoings need to be distinguished from 'revenue' losses or outgoings. Only revenue losses or outgoings may be deducted under s 8-1. Over the years, the courts have spent considerable time and effort in distinguishing between 'revenue' and 'capital' losses or outgoings and they have developed various judicial tests to assist them in this process. The three leading tests (discussed below) are:

1. the 'once and for all' test
2. the 'enduring benefit' test, and
3. the 'business entity' test.

Although these tests can be quite helpful in distinguishing between revenue and capital amounts, they are only broad rules of thumb. As Lord Pearce said in *BP Australia Ltd v FC of T* (1965) 112 CLR 386 (at 397):

> The solution to the problem is not to be found by any rigid test or description. It has to be derived from many aspects of the whole set of circumstances some of which may point in one direction, some in the other. One consideration may point so clearly that it dominates other and vaguer indications in the contrary direction. It is a commonsense appreciation of all the guiding features which must provide the ultimate answer. Although the categories of capital and income expenditure are distinct and easily ascertainable in obvious cases that lie far from the boundary, the line of distinction is often hard to draw in border line cases; and conflicting considerations may produce a situation where the answer turns on questions of emphasis and degree. That answer 'depends on what the expenditure is calculated to effect from a practical and business point of view, rather than upon the juristic classification of the legal rights, if any, secured, employed or exhausted in the process' . . .

1. Once and for all test

The 'once and for all' test stands for the principle that expenditure that is incurred 'once and for all' will usually be capital in nature, whereas expenditure that is incurred 'regularly' will usually be revenue in nature.

The once and for all test can be traced to the United Kingdom decision in *Vallambrosa Rubber Co Ltd v Farmer* (1910) 5 TC 529, which concerned a taxpayer that owned and operated a rubber estate in Malaya. The taxpayer had claimed deductions for its 'general expenditure' relating to the estate. Such expenditure included expenditure on weeding, pest control and superintendence of the estate. However, as only one-seventh of the trees on the estate were producing rubber at the time, the Inland Revenue Commissioners only allowed the taxpayer deductions for one-seventh of its general expenditure. According to the Commissioners, the remaining six-sevenths of the expenditure was capital in nature. The Court of Session, however, rejected this argument and allowed the taxpayer to deduct the entire amount of its general expenditure. The Court held that, since the general expenditure was incurred on items that the taxpayer would have to meet every year, the expenditure was of a revenue nature. Lord Cullen stated (at 536):

> Now, I don't say that this consideration is absolutely final or determinative, but in a rough way I think it is not a bad criterion of what is capital expenditure as against what is income expenditure to say that capital expenditure is a thing that is going to be spent once and for all, and income expenditure is a thing that is going to recur every year.

2. Enduring benefit test

The 'enduring benefit' test is authority for the proposition that where expenditure is incurred to bring into existence an asset of a lasting nature, it will usually be capital in nature.

The enduring benefit test finds its roots in the United Kingdom decision in *British Insulated & Helsby Cables Ltd v Atherton* [1926] AC 205, which concerned a taxpayer that established a pension fund for the benefit of its employees. The House of Lords held that the sum of £31,784, which the taxpayer had spent to set up the fund, was of a capital nature as it brought into existence an asset of 'enduring benefit'. In this regard, Viscount Cave stated (at 213):

> When an expenditure is made, not only once and for all, but with a view to bringing into existence an asset or an advantage for the enduring benefit of a trade, I think that there is very good reason (in the absence of special circumstances leading to the opposite conclusion) for treating such an expenditure as properly attributable not to revenue but to capital.

Based on the enduring benefit test, United Kingdom courts have generally tended to treat expenditure that does not give rise to a new asset or alter an existing asset as being of a revenue nature (*Southern v Borax Consolidated Ltd* [1940] 4 All ER 412; *C of T v Nchanga Consolidated Copper Mines Ltd* [1964] 1 All ER 208). The Australian courts, on the other hand, have not strictly adhered to this approach and have been prepared, in certain cases, to treat expenditure that does not give rise to a new asset or alter an existing asset as being of a capital nature. This outcome is due largely to the operation of the 'business entity' test.

3. Business entity test

The 'business entity' test distinguishes between losses and outgoings that relate to the taxpayer's 'profit-yielding structure' and losses or outgoings that relate to 'the process of operating it'. Expenditure relating to the establishment, organisation, enlargement, extension or protection of a business entity is usually treated as capital in nature, whereas expenditure incurred in operating the business is usually treated as revenue in nature.

The business entity test was developed by Dixon J in *Sun Newspapers Ltd v FC of T* (1938) 61 CLR 337. This case concerned the deductibility of certain payments made by a taxpayer that published newspapers in Sydney. The taxpayer had paid £86,500 by instalments to a rival publisher in consideration of the rival selling its interest in a newspaper that it published to the taxpayer and agreeing not to produce a rival newspaper for a period of three years within a 300-mile radius of Sydney. The High Court held that the payments were of a capital nature as they strengthened and preserved the taxpayer's business organisation, which the taxpayer feared would be impaired due to the competition it faced from its rival.

In characterising the payments, Dixon J distinguished between expenditure that relates to the business entity (which he considered to be of a capital nature) and expenditure that relates to the process by which a taxpayer earns their income (which he considered to be of a revenue nature). In a famous passage, his Honour stated (at 359–360):

> The distinction between expenditure and outgoings on revenue account and on capital account corresponds with the distinction between the business entity, structure, or organization set up or established for the earning of profit and the process by which such an organization operates to obtain regular returns by means of regular outlay, the difference between the outlay and returns representing profit or loss. . . . As general conceptions it may not be difficult to distinguish between the profit-yielding subject and the process of operating it. In the same way expenditure and outlay upon establishing, replacing and enlarging the profit-yielding subject may in a general way appear to be of a nature entirely different from the continual flow of working expenses which are or ought to be supplied continually out of the returns or revenue.

Dixon J then went on to provide guidelines to help in distinguishing between the two kinds of expenditure. His Honour indicated (at 363) that there were 'three matters' to be considered:

> (a) the character of the advantage sought, and in this its lasting qualities may play a part, (b) the manner in which it is to be used, relied upon or enjoyed, and in this and under the former head recurrence may play its part, and (c) the means adopted to obtain it, that is, by providing a periodical reward or outlay to cover its use or enjoyment for periods commensurate with the payment or by making a final provision or payment so as to secure future use or enjoyment.

In his dissenting judgment in *Hallstroms Pty Ltd v FC of T* (1946) 72 CLR 634, Dixon J elaborated further on the capital/revenue distinction (at 647):

> the contrast between the two forms of expenditure corresponds to the distinction between the acquisition of the means of production and the use of them; between establishing or extending a business organization and carrying on the business; between the implements employed in work and the regular performance of the work in which they are employed; between an enterprise itself and the sustained effort of those engaged in it.

Dixon J's comments in both *Sun Newspapers* and *Hallstroms* have since been widely accepted and endorsed by the Australian courts. The business entity test is now the leading Australian pronouncement on the distinction between capital and revenue expenditure and it has been relied on in many subsequent cases discussed further on in this chapter.

In applying the business entity test, the Australian courts have taken a broad view of capital expenditure and have been prepared to treat as capital in nature expenditure that protects the taxpayer's business entity even though it may not result in the taxpayer acquiring a new asset or altering an existing asset. This principle is illustrated in cases such as *Broken Hill Theatres Pty Ltd v FC of T* (1952) 85 CLR 423 and *PBL Marketing Pty Ltd v FC of T* 85 ATC 4416 [12.13].

Second negative limb: Private or domestic losses or outgoings

The second negative limb of s 8-1 denies a deduction for a loss or outgoing to the extent that it is a loss or outgoing of a 'private or domestic nature'. The terms 'private' or 'domestic' are not defined in the legislation and therefore have their ordinary meaning. A loss or outgoing will be of a 'private' nature where it is of a 'personal' nature. A loss or outgoing will be of a 'domestic' nature where it concerns household affairs.

In the Supreme Court decision in *FC of T v Janmor Nominees Pty Ltd* 86 ATC 4681, Murphy J indicated (at 4687) that the second negative limb appears to have been inserted as a 'matter of caution'. Earlier, in *FC of T v Hatchett* 71 ATC 4184 [12.9], Menzies J stated (at 4186):

> It must be a rare case where an outgoing incurred in gaining assessable income is also an outgoing of a private nature. In most cases the categories would seem to be exclusive.

Ultimately, as cases such as *Lunney & Hayley v FC of T* (1958) 100 CLR 478 and *FC of T v Cooper* 91 ATC 4396 illustrate, whether a loss or outgoing is of a private or domestic nature or whether it is an income-producing or business expense will ultimately depend on the essential character of the loss or outgoing [12.3].

A classic example of a private or domestic outgoing is found in *Lodge v FC of T* 72 ATC 4174. In this case, the High Court denied deductions to a law clerk for nursery fees paid to have her child minded so that she could undertake work. Relying on *Lunney & Hayley*, Mason J pointed out (at 4175–4176) that for expenditure to be deductible 'it is not enough to show that the expenditure was an essential prerequisite to the derivation of assessable income'. According to his Honour, the nursery fees were 'neither relevant nor incidental' to the activities by which the taxpayer gained her income.

The decision in *Lodge* has been followed in several subsequent cases, including *Martin v FC of T* 84 ATC 4513, *Hyde v FC of T* 88 ATC 4748 and *Jayatilake v FC of T* 91 ATC 4516. These cases establish the principle that child care costs are not ordinarily characterised as income-producing expenses even though they may be necessary to enable a taxpayer to maintain a job. Rather, such costs are inherently of a private or domestic nature.

Another useful illustration of a private or domestic outgoing is found in *Fullerton v FC of T* 91 ATC 983. This case concerned expenses incurred by a taxpayer in moving with his family to a new home in another city because his job was relocated. The Federal Court held that even though, as a practical matter, it was necessary for the taxpayer to live near where he worked, the expenditure was not deductible as it related to a domestic or family arrangement.

There have also been a number of cases where taxpayers have tried to claim deductions for expenditure relating to a second property that they own or lease and use when working far away from their home. However, the expenditure in these cases has generally been characterised as being of a private or domestic nature.

For example, in *Case* X4 90 ATC 116, a radiologist who had a practice in a town located over 100 km from a capital city, but also worked in the city and travelled there on a regular basis, had purchased a house in the inner suburbs which he used for work as well as for occasional family purposes at weekends. The AAT held that the taxpayer was not entitled to deductions for outgoings relating to the property (such as interest, rates and insurance) as the essential character of the expenditure was of a private or domestic nature. According to the AAT, the outgoings were incurred because the taxpayer had decided to establish a 'second home' or 'home away from home'. Importantly, the AAT considered that the outgoings were not deductible even though it acknowledged (at 121):

> It is undoubtedly the case that if the applicant had adopted a different course and merely put up at a convenient hotel when in the city on business, the hotel account would fall within the positive limbs of s 51(1) and be allowable as a deduction, not being outgoings of a private or domestic nature.

In the course of delivering its decision, the AAT referred to *FC of T v Charlton* 84 ATC 4415, which concerned a pathologist who lived in Melbourne and was posted by the Health Department to work in Bendigo. To avoid excessive travel and fatigue, the taxpayer leased a flat in Bendigo for five months. For one month during this period he was also required to work in Wangaratta. The taxpayer used the flat during weekdays and returned to be with his family in Melbourne on weekends. The taxpayer claimed a deduction for the rent payable on the flat on the basis that it was maintained purely for work. The Supreme Court of Victoria, however, relied on *Lunney & Hayley* for the principle that, as the taxpayer had chosen to live in Melbourne, the rent was dictated not by his work but by private considerations. Interestingly, although the court denied deductions for the bulk of the rent, it allowed a deduction for the rent relating to the one-month period that the taxpayer worked in Wangaratta on the grounds that the circumstances of that work made the taking of rest at Bendigo necessary. The Court concluded that the keeping of a flat during that month was therefore incidental to his work and dictated by his income-producing activity.

In another related case, *FC of T v Toms* 89 ATC 4373, a logging contractor worked in forests which were more than 100 km away from his home in Grafton. The taxpayer claimed that it was too far to travel to work each day and he therefore lived in a caravan in a camp near the forests during the weekdays and travelled home on weekends. The caravan was also used for storing equipment and as a temporary shelter when the weather was bad. The taxpayer claimed deductions for various living expenses (eg heating, lighting and additional food costs associated with living in the camp) as well as deductions for depreciation relating to the caravan. The AAT allowed the taxpayer deductions for certain weekly amounts. However, on appeal, the Federal Court relied on *Charlton* to conclude that the taxpayer's living expenses were not deductible as they were not dictated by his work, but by private considerations. The Federal Court nevertheless also acknowledged that the use of the caravan for storing equipment and as a shelter was not so slight that it should be disregarded. It therefore decided that the taxpayer should be entitled to some allowance for depreciation of the caravan, even though its predominant use was not for the purpose of gaining assessable income. The case was referred back to the AAT to determine the appropriate apportionment.

TR 1999/10 states (at [328D]) that the 'prevailing principle' derived from cases like *Charlton* and *Toms* is that 'where a taxpayer's expenses are incurred because of a choice they made about where to live, the expenses are of a private or domestic nature and are, therefore, not deductible'. There are, nevertheless, certain situations in which the Commissioner will allow taxpayers deductions for expenses relating to an additional property. For example, TR 1999/10 states (at [328I]) that Members of Parliament can claim deductions for 'financing, holding and maintaining an additional property which they purchase or rent if it is occupied by them as accommodation in the course of travelling for work, except to the extent the expenses are of a capital, private or domestic nature'. The ruling, however, goes on to point out (at [328J]) that Members 'may claim such expenses only if the travel is required in undertaking their duties, rather than because of a choice the Member has made as to where to live, and they are working away from home for relatively short periods and have a permanent home elsewhere'.

Third negative limb: Losses or outgoings incurred in gaining exempt income or non-assessable non-exempt income

The third negative limb of s 8-1 denies a deduction for a loss or outgoing to the extent that the loss or outgoing is incurred in relation to gaining or producing a taxpayer's exempt income [11.2] or non-assessable non-exempt income [11.3].

The third negative limb is a curious exclusion, as a loss or outgoing that is incurred in gaining or producing exempt income or non-assessable non-exempt income would not seem to be able to satisfy the positive limbs of s 8-1 in any case as such income is not assessable income under ss 6-1(3) and (4) *ITAA97*. The exclusion therefore appears to be superfluous. This observation is supported by the High Court's comments on s 51(1) *ITAA36* in *Ronpibon Tin NL v FC of T* (1949) 78 CLR 47, where Latham CJ, Rich, Dixon, McTiernan and Webb JJ stated (at 55–56):

> to except losses and outgoings to the extent to which they are incurred in relation to the gaining or production of exempt income seems to except something from the primary description which could not fall within it. For exempt income can never be assessable income. They are mutually exclusive categories.

Fourth negative limb: Losses or outgoings that are not deductible

The fourth negative limb of s 8-1 denies a deduction for a loss or outgoing to the extent that the loss or outgoing is not deductible under a provision of the *ITAA36* or *ITAA97*. This means that s 8-1 operates subject to the other provisions in the legislation. For instance, a deduction would be denied for a loss or outgoing to the extent that it relates to an ITC as s 27-5 *ITAA97* expressly makes such a loss or outgoing not deductible [8.5]. A range of other provisions that deny or limit deductions are discussed in Chapter 14.

[12.5] Meaning of 'incurred' and timing of deductions

It is clear from the words of s 8-1 *ITAA97* that a loss or outgoing must be 'incurred' in order to be deductible. Unless special statutory rules (such as those discussed in Chapter 29) determine otherwise, a loss or outgoing will usually be deductible in the year it is incurred.

Importance of the existence of a liability

In determining whether a loss or outgoing has been incurred, the courts focus on whether or not a liability exists, rather than whether or not it has been discharged. Payment is therefore not a prerequisite for an amount to have been incurred. This is clear from Latham CJ's comments in *W Nevill & Co Ltd v FC of T* (1937) 56 CLR 290, where his Honour pointed out (at 302):

> the word used is 'incurred' and not 'made' or 'paid'. The language lends colour to the suggestion that, if a liability to pay money as an outgoing comes into existence, the quoted words of the section are satisfied even though the liability has not been actually discharged at the relevant time.

Completely subjected to the loss or outgoing

One of the leading decisions on the meaning of incurred is *FC of T v James Flood Pty Ltd* (1953) 88 CLR 492. This case concerned the deductibility of an amount that an employer had set aside to meet its anticipated future holiday pay obligations. The award provided that the taxpayer's employees were only entitled to receive holiday pay after 12 months of continuous service. An employee's entitlement could be lost in certain circumstances (eg where the employee died or was involved in an unauthorised strike or absenteeism). The High Court denied the taxpayer deductions for the amount it had set aside to meet the holiday pay of employees who had not yet completed the requisite period of service. The Court found that no liability to make holiday payments had been 'incurred' at such time—the taxpayer simply faced the possibility that it might have to incur a loss or outgoing in the future. Dixon CJ, Webb, Fullagar, Kitto and Taylor JJ held that, under former s 51(1) *ITAA36*, no deduction is available for a loss or outgoing unless the taxpayer 'has completely subjected himself' to the loss or outgoing. Their Honours stated (at 506):

> It may be going too far to say that he must have come under an immediate obligation enforceable at law whether payable presently or at a future time. It is probably going too far to say that the obligation must be indefeasible. But it is certainly true that it is not a matter depending upon 'proper commercial and accountancy practice rather than jurisprudence.'

Presently existing liability and definitive commitment

Nilsen Development Laboratories Pty Ltd v FC of T 81 ATC 4031 also related to provisions made by a taxpayer for its employees' leave entitlements. In this case, the taxpayer's employees were entitled to periods of leave proportionate to their period of service and were not subject to any qualifying period. On the basis of these facts, the taxpayer sought to distinguish *James Flood*. The High Court held, however, that it was only when an employee took leave that an accrued liability to pay arose and an outgoing was incurred. The Court found that even though the leave entitlements were indefeasible and would inevitably need to be met by the taxpayer at some stage, the taxpayer was not under any obligation to make the payments until its employees actually took leave. In other words, although it was certain that a liability would arise in the future, such a liability had not crystallised at the relevant time. Barwick CJ indicated that a loss or outgoing must 'come home' to the taxpayer for it to be incurred. The Chief Justice went on to state (at 4037) that 'what is clearly necessary is that there be a presently existing liability'.

Nilsen demonstrates that, no matter how certain it is that a loss or outgoing will arise in the future, in order for the loss or outgoing to have been incurred, it must have crystallised in the sense that it must have 'accrued' or 'come home' to the taxpayer so as to create a 'presently existing liability'. This point is also illustrated in *Ogilvy & Mather Pty Ltd v FC of T* 90 ATC 4836, where an advertising agency was denied deductions for advertisements placed with media outlets which had not been paid for, but which had, nevertheless, passed various 'non-cancellation periods'. Sweeney and Ryan JJ explained their reasoning (at 4844–5) as follows:

> The effect of the commencement of a 'non-cancellation period' was to preclude Ogilvy & Mather from unilaterally avoiding the obligation to pay for the advertisement. However, that is not to say that the liability was incurred, in the sense that Ogilvy & Mather was 'definitively committed' to discharge it, from the moment when the non-cancellation period commenced . . . it was publication of the advertisement which definitively committed the agency to the liability, even though payment was not due . . . until the thirtieth day of the month following that in which the advertising was published, broadcast or telecast.

The issue of whether an outgoing was incurred was also considered in *Merrill Lynch International (Australia) Ltd & Ors v FC of T* 2001 ATC 4541. This case concerned a group of companies involved in the banking and securities industry that adopted the calendar year as their income year. The taxpayers paid discretionary bonuses to their staff under various remuneration schemes. In exercising the discretion to pay bonuses, several factors were considered, including the employee's performance. Bonus payments were widely paid in the industry, and the taxpayers' senior management regarded the payments as a 'certainty', while the remaining professional staff held an expectation that they would be paid. Every year, the taxpayers' New York head office determined the amount of the bonus pool, which was communicated to the taxpayers, who then assessed the likely bonuses to be paid and recorded the aggregated amounts in their accounting records. The taxpayers unsuccessfully sought deductions in relation to the 1994 income year for bonuses that had been paid in 1995. The first time employees were informed about the bonuses to be paid for the 1994 year was around 24 January 1995, and the head office had not communicated the amounts available for the 1994 year until mid-January 1995.

The Federal Court held that in order for the bonuses to be incurred in the 1994 income year, the taxpayers must have completely subjected themselves, or definitively committed themselves, to make the payments to their employees by the end of the year. Lindgren J held that a legal approach should be adopted to determine this issue. His Honour indicated that a contractual promise to pay bonuses must be distinguished from a contractual promise to exercise the discretion to pay bonuses reasonably, fairly and in good faith. According to his Honour, the taxpayers would have been completely subjected to or definitively committed to pay the bonuses if there was at least a contractual promise to pay them. However, being bound by contractual terms to exercise a discretion in good faith, reasonably and fairly did not give rise to a legal liability to make a payment for which deductions could be claimed.

Mere impending, threatened or expected liabilities are not incurred

A liability is not incurred where it is merely a 'possibility'. This is illustrated in *Emu Bay Railway Co Ltd v FC of T* (1944) 71 CLR 596, which concerned a company that had issued debenture stock. Under the relevant deed, interest at 5% per annum was payable on the stock and 'was a charge upon and payable only out of' the taxpayer's annual net income. The deed also provided that the interest was to be payable half-yearly and constituted a cumulative liability from year to year. Although the taxpayer made a loss in the 1939 year, it nevertheless sought a deduction for an amount equal to 5% of its issued debenture stock for that year. A majority of the High Court held that no liability had come into existence during the relevant year, since the company did not have any net income during the year. Latham CJ explained this (at 606) in the following terms:

> As there has never been any such net income, the interest which the company claims is allowable as a deduction did not become payable, has not become a debt, and may never become a debt . . . As things stand at present, the interest has not become payable, and all that can be said is that there exists at the present time the possibility of a liability accruing

> in the future, such possibility depending, not only upon the derivation of net income, but also on the amount of such income derived.

The outcome in *Emu Bay* may be contrasted with the earlier decision in *New Zealand Flax Investments Ltd v FC of T* (1938) 61 CLR 179 where the High Court allowed a taxpayer deductions for so much of the interest relating to bonds it had issued that was 'referable' to the year in question. The different outcomes in the cases can be explained on the basis that in *Emu Bay*, the liability was contingent on there being 'annual net income' available, whereas in *New Zealand Flax*, the taxpayer owed 'a definite liability' to its bondholders. In the course of delivering his judgment in *New Zealand Flax*, Dixon J made the following statement (at 207) which has been quoted in many subsequent cases:

> 'Incurred' does not mean only defrayed, discharged, or borne, but rather it includes encountered, run into, or fallen upon. It is unsafe to attempt exhaustive definitions of a conception intended to have such a various or multifarious application. But it does not include a loss or expenditure which is no more than impending, threatened, or expected.

Use of referability principle to determine when an outgoing is deductible

The 'referability principle' in *New Zealand Flax* was applied in *FC of T v Australian Guarantee Corporation Ltd* 84 ATC 4642 to a finance company that was allowed deductions for accrued interest on debentures which it had issued notwithstanding that no interest was payable until redemption (20 years from the issue date). The Full Federal Court referred (at 4660) to an 'ordinary rule that interest accrues due on a daily basis, even if payment is deferred to a future date'. In arriving at this conclusion, the Court followed *Alliance Holdings Ltd v FC of T* 81 ATC 4637, which concerned a finance company that had borrowed money from the public secured by deferred interest debenture stock. Under the arrangement, no interest was payable until the debenture stock matured. The NSW Supreme Court nevertheless considered that a present obligation to repay the interest to the stockholder came into existence at the time the contract was made, even though the interest was payable in the future. Woodward J held (at 4643) that 'the contract was one to pay interest which accrued from day to day' and that the liability should be deductible accordingly.

The leading illustration of the referability principle is found in *Coles Myer Finance Ltd v FC of T* 93 ATC 4214. This case concerned a corporate group's finance company, which had drawn and sold bills of exchange and promissory notes. Some of the bills and notes drawn in the income year ending 30 June 1984 matured in the following income year. The High Court was required to determine whether the taxpayer was allowed deductions for the discounts in respect of the bills and notes in the income year ending 30 June 1984, in the year of income ending 30 June 1985, or over both years.

A majority of the Court concluded that the discounts were deductible over both years. Mason CJ, Brennan, Dawson, Toohey and Gaudron JJ found that a presently existing liability to pay the face value of the bills and notes on maturity had been incurred at the time the bills and notes were drawn. Their Honours then went on to conclude, however, that this liability was 'properly referable' to both the income years ending 30 June 1984 and 30 June 1985. On this basis, they held that the discounts should be deductible on a 'straight line basis' over both years. In other words, just because the liability had been incurred in one year, did not necessarily mean that the outgoing was fully deductible in that year. Their Honours explained (at 4222):

> The acceptance by this court of the jurisprudential analysis of s 51 does not compel the conclusion that, once a taxpayer subjects itself in the year of income on revenue account to a present legal liability to pay in a future year of income an amount which generates, or gives rise to, a net loss or outgoing, the net loss or outgoing is deductible in full in the year of income. The relevance of the present existence of a legal liability on the part of the taxpayer to meet the bills and notes at a future date is that it establishes that the taxpayer has 'incurred',

> in the year of income an obligation to pay an amount which gives rise to a net loss or outgoing, being the recurrent cost of acquiring working or circulating capital. But there remains the question: 'how much of that net loss or outgoing is referable to the year of income?'

This passage indicates that there is a 'two-step approach' in determining when an outgoing is deductible. The first step involves an application of jurisprudential principles (ie determining whether a loss or outgoing has been 'incurred'). The second step is concerned with 'referability' (ie a 'matching principle' based on accounting concepts). Their Honours continued (at 4222):

> In ascertaining what is the taxpayer's net income or profit for a particular year of income, it is proper to set against the taxpayer's gross income or profit for that period the net losses or outgoings referable to that period. Under s 51(1), a loss or outgoing is a deduction only to the extent to which it is incurred in gaining or producing the assessable income. That provision has been described as: 'a statutory recognition and application of the accountancy principle which all the accountants who gave evidence referred to as the matching principle' to use the words of Menhenitt J in *RACV Insurance Pty Ltd v FC of T* . . . Apportionment of the cost over two years of income therefore accords with both accounting principle and practice and the statutory prescription.

New Zealand Flax, *Australian Guarantee*, *Alliance Holdings* and *Coles Myer* share a common feature in that they all concerned financing costs. This raises the issue of whether 'matching' is confined to this kind of case alone, or whether it has broader application. The issue was examined in *FC of T v Woolcombers (WA) Pty Ltd* 93 ATC 5170, which concerned a wool trader that had entered into forward contracts for the purchase of its trading stock from woolgrowers. Contracts were entered into up to nine months before shearing and provided that property in the wool passed to the taxpayer upon payment for the wool, which was to occur 14 days after delivery. The taxpayer claimed a deduction in the 1987/88 income year for its estimated liability under the forward contracts it made during that year. None of the wool purchased by the taxpayer under these contracts was sold in that year. The Commissioner denied the deduction on the basis that no outgoing had 'come home' to the taxpayer in the relevant year. In the alternative, he argued that if an outgoing had been incurred, based on *Coles Myer*, the outgoing was properly referable to the following year when the benefit of the liability in respect of the wool was put to profitable advantage.

The Full Federal Court held that the taxpayer had, in fact, incurred an outgoing and that the estimate of its liability under the forward contracts was fully deductible in the 1987/88 year. Beaumont, French and Foster JJ distinguished the finance cases on the following basis (at 5181):

> In *Coles Myer*, because of the special nature of the financing transaction, it was held . . . that apportionment was appropriate. Likewise, in the financial arrangements considered in *Australian Guarantee*, apportionment of the total sum of the interest was proper. But there are no similar features in the present matter, which concerns a relatively simple forward contract for sale without any financing aspect; no question arises here of a liability accruing daily, as interest does, or otherwise accruing periodically.

The Full Federal Court upheld the earlier decision of Lee J at first instance (93 ATC 4342), where his Honour had concluded that an outgoing incurred in acquiring trading stock could not be equated with a loss incurred by a financier involved in a moneylending business. According to Lee J, accounting concepts may assist, but are not determinative of when a loss or outgoing is deductible. In this respect, his Honour stated (at 4349):

> the need for the loss or outgoing to be 'properly referable' . . . to the income year in which it is sought to be deducted requires the loss or outgoing not to be so anomalous to the revenue operations of the taxpayer as to affect a distortion in the result of those operations in the relevant income year.

Although *Woolcombers* limits the practical scope of the matching principle, it is clear from *Merchant v FC of T* 99 ATC 4221 that the matching principle is not just confined to financing costs. In *Merchant*, the Federal Court applied the matching principle to rent and management fees relating to a pine tree plantation arrangement, with the result that the taxpayer was only entitled to deduct a percentage of the rent and management fees in the year that they were incurred.

It is considered that there are good reasons for treating rent and management fees on a similar footing to financing costs, as they are all 'periodic expenditures'. Financing costs relate to the use of money over a period, rent relates to the use of property over a period and management fees relate to the obtaining of services over a period. These kinds of expenditures are distinguishable from expenditure incurred in purchasing assets such as trading stock. On this basis, it is submitted that the decisions in *Merchant* and *Woolcombers* can sit comfortably alongside each other.

A liability is not incurred if it is subject to further performance

Woolcombers was distinguished in *FC of T v Malouf* 2009 ATC ¶20-099. This case concerned a taxpayer that had entered into a contract on 25 June 1999 for the purchase of land and the development of a retirement village. The taxpayer paid a deposit of \$6.5m on entering the contract and was required to pay the residue of \$33.25m on settlement when Stage 1 of the development had been completed. The Full Federal Court held that the taxpayer was only entitled to deduct the deposit in the 1999 income year. This was because a pecuniary liability to pay the residue had not been incurred at the time of entering into the contract—it would only arise upon settlement. The Court pointed out that *Woolcombers* involved an 'unconditional agreement', whereas the present case depended on 'further performance by the vendor'. As Sundberg, Jessup and Middleton JJ explained (at 9566):

> The major portion of the value which the taxpayer obtained under the contract related to a development which did not exist at the time the contract was entered into by the parties . . . The contract was not an unconditional agreement subject to defeasance by unforeseen events. The taxpayer's obligation to pay under the contract was dependent upon further performance by the vendor, and upon the happening of events which were anticipated but were under the control of neither party.

A liability can be incurred even if it is not known when it will be discharged

Coles Myer was distinguished in *FC of T v Citylink Melbourne Ltd* 2006 ATC 4404. *Citylink* involved a taxpayer that had entered into contracts with the State of Victoria to construct and maintain 'the Link' roads system. During the 'concession period', which ran for more than 30 years, the taxpayer was entitled to charge tolls for the use of the roads. The taxpayer was also required to pay concession fees to the state in accordance with terms set out in a Concession Deed. At the end of the concession period, the infrastructure and all other rights relating to the project would revert to the state. The Concession Deed required the taxpayer to pay concession fees for approximately 25 years. The base concession fee of \$95.6m was payable semi-annually. A separate Master Security Deed provided that the concession fees could be satisfied by the taxpayer issuing Concession Notes, which were not payable until a specified date several years in the future. Clause 1.9 of the Master Security Deed also provided that the state could not present the Concession Notes for payment while there was an outstanding Project Debt or insufficient money in a Distributions Account to make payments. The effect of this was that the payment date for the Concession Notes depended on the project's financial returns.

In the income years ending 30 June 1996, 1997 and 1998, the taxpayer issued Concession Notes to the state and claimed deductions for the concession fees under s 51(1) *ITAA36* and s 8-1 *ITAA97*. The Commissioner contended that the concession fees were not incurred in gaining or producing the taxpayer's assessable income in the relevant income years. The Commissioner submitted that no outgoings had been incurred, as payment was not possible until clause 1.9 of the Master Security Deed had been satisfied. This had not occurred in the relevant income years, which meant that the taxpayer's liability to pay the fees was 'contingent'. In the alternative, he contended that the nominal amount of each concession fee should be apportioned over the income years from the date when such fee was incurred until the date upon which it would fall due for payment.

A majority of the High Court held that the fees were incurred in the income years in which they were claimed, as the taxpayer was definitively committed and had completely subjected itself to the liability in respect of those fees. Crennan J, who delivered the majority judgment, emphasised that a liability can be incurred in a particular year, even though it is not discharged in that year and even though the taxpayer does not know the precise date the liability will be satisfied. She indicated that 'a condition affecting the timing of the discharge of a liability (but not the creation of the liability) does not render the liability contingent in any business or commercial sense'. The crux of her Honour's reasoning on this point is found in the following passage (at 4425–6):

> The conclusion will be reached here that the concession fees were incurred in the years of income. On a semi-annual basis, the [taxpayer] was subjected to a contractual liability to pay the concession fees. The liability arose as and when each concession fee became due. That is when the outgoing was encountered or run into . . . These facts exemplify a situation where a liability is 'incurred' in the year of income but not 'discharged' in that same year . . . Clause 1.9 of the Master Security Deed is directed at conditions precedent to the timing of the discharge of the liability, not to the coming into existence of the liability. Here the liability comes into existence in the year of income. The deferral of the time for its discharge cannot alter this conclusion, nor can the length of time of the deferral . . .

Crennan J also found that the concession fees were referable to the relevant income years in question and should not be apportioned over a number of years. Her Honour distinguished *Coles Myer* on the following basis (at 4427):

> The facts here are distinguishable from *Coles Myer*, which concerned outgoings referable to an advantage spread over two years. The semi-annual liability for concession fees here does not secure the [taxpayer's] rights under the Concession Deed for future years. Each concession fee, like any periodic licence fee, is payable for its period. Other concession fees become due in each successive year. Accordingly, straight line apportionment is not an appropriate accounting basis for calculating the deductibility of the concession fees.

A liability can be incurred even if it cannot be precisely ascertained

The fact that the amount of a liability cannot be precisely ascertained does not necessarily mean that the liability is 'contingent' and therefore not deductible. In certain cases, taxpayers may be able to claim deductions for estimated liabilities.

The leading case on this point is *RACV Insurance Pty Ltd v FC of T* 74 ATC 4169. The issue in this case was whether a third-party personal insurer could claim deductions for amounts it had set aside to cover claims it anticipated would arise out of car accidents that arose during the income year but were unreported at the end of the income year. Menhennitt J allowed the taxpayer deductions for its reasonable estimate of such claims. His Honour held that a loss or outgoing is incurred once the events giving rise to a liability occur. He found (at 4183) that, under the policies, there was an 'unanswerable liability to indemnify the driver of the vehicle once the personal injury occurs' and that the liability was not dependent on notice of the injury or of the accident or upon a claim being made by the driver for indemnity. Menhennitt J distinguished *James Flood* pointing out (at 4182) that the circumstances of that case were 'in marked contrast with the position where an absolute liability to indemnify arises under an insurance policy upon the happening of events which result in the death of or bodily injury to a third person'. According to his Honour, the fact that the quantum of the loss or outgoing is a matter of estimate and that the amount may have to be adjusted in the light of later events did not preclude the loss or outgoing from being incurred.

The *RACV* decision was applied three years later in *Commercial Union Assurance Co of Australia Ltd v FC of T* 77 ATC 4186. As in *RACV*, the taxpayer was an insurance company that claimed deductions for estimates of unreported insurance claims at the end of the relevant year. However, unlike *RACV*, the relevant policies often contained a clause stating that, unless the insured provided the insurer notice of the relevant event giving rise to a claim within a specified time, the insured would be in breach of the policy, with the result that the insurer could technically avoid liability. Newton J found that, given that the taxpayer's general practice was never to rely on such a clause, as a matter of 'commercial reality', it had completely subjected itself to liability under the policies and had therefore incurred the relevant amounts claimed.

The principles developed in the preceding cases were found to be equally applicable to a self-insurer in *Australia & New Zealand Banking Group Ltd v FC of T* 94 ATC 4026, where the Full Federal Court allowed a bank deductions for its estimate of its workers' compensation liabilities in relation to both reported but 'unpaid claims' as well as 'unreported claims'. The Court found that, under the relevant statutory scheme, from the moment that an employee suffered an injury in the course of his or her employment, a presently existing liability to make payments in the future arose. This meant that liabilities relating to injuries sustained during a particular year would be incurred in that year, even though no claim may have been made until a subsequent year and the amount of such a claim may only be precisely quantifiable at some future time.

The principles discussed above were also applied by the Privy Council, in *C of IR (NZ) v Mitsubishi Motors New Zealand Ltd* 95 ATC 4711, to a manufacturer in relation to its expected liabilities under warranty claims. The taxpayer sold new cars through franchised dealers and agreed to indemnify the dealers against the cost of warranty claims made against them by their customers. The warranties covered a period of 12 months or 20,000 km (whichever occurred first) and required the purchaser to notify the dealer of a defect 'as soon as reasonably possible within 21 days of becoming aware of the defect'. The Privy Council held that the taxpayer was entitled to a deduction for its reasonable estimate of its costs under expected warranty claims in the year that the cars were sold. According to the Privy Council, in the light of all the surrounding circumstances, a legal obligation to make payments in the future had accrued to the taxpayer at the time the cars were sold. In delivering the judgment of the Court, Lord Hoffman reviewed the leading Australian cases and drew a distinction between expenditure which was 'definitely committed' even though it was only capable of estimation at the relevant time and mere 'contingent liabilities'. His Lordship stated (at 4715):

> although the jurisprudential approach prevents one from treating an aggregate of contingent liabilities as a statistical certainty, it does not rule out statistical estimation of facts which have happened but are unknown. Thus in *RACV Insurance Pty Ltd v Commissioner of Taxation* . . . an insurance company carrying on accident business was allowed to make a deduction from its premium income of an estimated sum to represent its liabilities 'incurred but not reported'. These liabilities were not in law contingent. The accidents which gave rise to the company's liability had happened but the company did not know about them. A similar decision was reached in *Commercial Union Assurance Co of Australia*

> *Ltd v FC of T*. . . . Both cases were cited with approval in the High Court of Australia by Mason J (with whom Aickin J and Wilson J agreed) in *Nilsen Development Laboratories Pty Ltd v FC of T*. . . . The learned judge distinguished them from the cases on contingent liabilities because the accidents which gave rise to the liabilities under the policies had occurred during the relevant year of account.

[12.6] Clothing expenses

On many occasions, taxpayers have sought deductions for the cost of purchasing clothing. The main issue that arises in these cases is whether such expenditure is of an income-producing or private nature.

As a general rule, the cases indicate that the cost of acquiring 'conventional' items of clothing, such as a suit, is not deductible under s 8-1 *ITAA97* as such expenditure is inherently private in nature. Hill J stated in *Mansfield v FC of T* 96 ATC 4001 (at 4008):

> It can be said that generally expenditure on ordinary articles of apparel will not be deductible, notwithstanding that such expenditure is necessary to ensure a suitable appearance in a particular job or profession. An employed solicitor may be required to dress in an appropriate way by his or her employer, but that fact alone would not bring about the result that the expenditure was deductible.

The courts have, nevertheless, allowed deductions for the cost of clothing in special circumstances. For instance, in *FC of T v Edwards* 94 ATC 4255, a taxpayer was allowed deductions for the cost of additional clothing (including hats, gloves and formal evening wear) required for her job. The taxpayer was employed as personal secretary to the Governor of Queensland's wife, and was required to accompany the Governor's wife on official occasions. The taxpayer attended more than 150 public engagements throughout the year and was required to dress appropriately at each of these events. On many occasions she had to change her attire several times a day. The Full Federal Court upheld the finding of the AAT (*Case 31/93* 93 ATC 359) that the taxpayer's expenditure on additional clothing was not of a private nature. In this regard, the Tribunal had stated (at 362):

> There is nothing about the additional changes of clothes in a work day for this taxpayer which serve a private purpose. Her personal requirements of modesty, decency and warmth are met by her first set of clothes for the day. Her additional changes of clothing throughout the day solely serve work-related purposes which enable the taxpayer to attend the wife of her employer in the performance of her duties at many different types of functions as Personal Secretary. The expenditure on the additional clothing is incurred in the course of gaining the income. Although not determinative of the issue, it is a relevant consideration that she makes the additional changes of clothes because the employer requires her to wear them.

The courts have also allowed deductions for the cost of clothing where the clothing is required to have special features or where harsh working conditions result in frequent damage to the clothing. For instance, in *Mansfield v FC of T*, the Federal Court allowed a flight attendant to deduct the cost of her shoes (which were required to be a half-size larger than her normal shoes because of cabin pressure) and the cost of her pantyhose (which frequently laddered owing to the confined spaces in which she worked).

Likewise, in *Morris v FC of T* 2002 ATC 4004, the Federal Court allowed a number of taxpayers who were engaged in various outdoor occupations (including a surveyor, a builder, a physical education teacher and a professional tennis umpire) deductions for the cost of sun protection items such as sunhats, sunglasses and sunscreens. Goldberg J held that there was a substantial and close nexus, a 'real connection', between the taxpayers' outgoings on sun protection items and their income-producing activities. His Honour explained this in the following terms (at 4423–4424):

> The applicants' evidence was that the sun protection items were necessary to enable them to perform their employment duties, that these items increased productivity and provided protection from exposure to the sun and ultraviolet radiation which can cause sunburn and skin cancer. . . . These factors, therefore, provide a substantial and close nexus between an applicant's expenditure on sun protection items and his or her income producing activities. Working outside in conditions of exposure to the sun and ultraviolet radiation forms part of the activities undertaken by each of the applicants for the production of their assessable income. Accordingly, there is a real connection between an applicant's production of assessable income and his or her expenditure on items such as sun protection items which increase productivity and provide protection while carrying out work activities. That is to say, an applicant's income-producing activities include the use of the sun protection items.

For similar reasons, the cost of work-related protective clothing (eg helmets worn by construction workers) is ordinarily deductible. Likewise, the cost of 'compulsory' uniforms is also generally deductible as there is a clear nexus with the taxpayer's income-producing activities. Division 34 *ITAA97*, however, contains special statutory restrictions relating to the deductibility of costs incurred on 'non-compulsory' uniforms [14.5].

[12.7] Travel expenses

It is common for taxpayers to seek deductions for their travel expenses. In order for these expenses to be deductible, they must be able to be characterised as working or business expenses. Private travel expenditure is not deductible.

Distinction between travel 'on work' and travel 'to work'

The cost of travelling 'in the course of' work is usually deductible as such outgoings have the necessary connection with a taxpayer's income-producing or business activities. For instance, a salesman who travels from one customer to another to sell products would be entitled to deductions for his travelling costs. Travelling is part of the salesman's job and the expenses are therefore incurred in the course of performing his work. As Lord Wilberforce recognised in the House of Lords decision in *Taylor v Provan* [1975] AC 194 (at 215) 'if a man has to travel from one place of work to another place of work, he may deduct the travelling expenses of this travel, because he is travelling on his work'.

There is, however, an important distinction between travelling 'on work' and travelling 'to work'. This point is illustrated in *Lunney & Hayley v FC of T* (1958) 100 CLR 478, where the High Court held that the cost of travelling between home and a person's usual place of work is generally not deductible [12.3]. Ordinarily, such expenditure is not incurred 'in the course of' any income-earning or business activities, but rather in simply getting to the place where such activities are performed. It is merely a 'prerequisite' to earning assessable income and a consequence of 'living in one place and working in another'.

The ATO relied on *Lunney & Hayley* in TR 2021/1 to state that, subject to limited exceptions, employees are not entitled to deductions for expenditure incurred in travelling between their home and regular place of work. The ATO states the reason for this is that the expenditure is explicable by reference to where the employee lives in relation to where they report for work. The expenditure is not incurred in the course of gaining or producing their assessable income but is of a private nature.

The fact that the employee may choose to perform some work tasks at home or conduct some work activities while travelling (eg responding to emails) does not convert the travel into part of their employment. Likewise, travel costs are not deductible where an employee travels to their regular place of work from another location in which they undertake private activities (eg a café or holiday location). Moreover, the fact that an employee's home may be some distance from their work (eg where they live in Melbourne and work in Sydney) does not change the position that travel between home and work is generally not deductible (see further *FC of T v Charlton* 84 ATC 4415; *FC of T v Toms* 89 ATC 4373 [12.4]).

It is important to note, however, that *Lunney & Hayley* only dealt with travel between a person's home and their usual place of work. It did not consider the situation where an employee's duties of employment require them to travel from their home to some other work location (eg to attend a client's premises or another office of their employer). In such cases, TR 2021/1 indicates that the costs of such travel may be deductible provided the occasion for the expenses is the taxpayer's employment.

The facts in *Lunney & Hayley* were distinguished in *John Holland Group Pty Ltd v FC of T* 2015 ATC ¶20-510. This case concerned taxpayers in the construction industry who paid for their employees to fly between Perth and Geraldton on a rostered basis to work on rail projects. The employees travelled between their homes and Perth airport at their own expense, but all other expenses were paid by their employers. The Commissioner assessed the employers to FBT on the basis that the flights constituted 'residual fringe benefits' [18.18]. The employers, however, argued that the taxable value of the fringe benefits should be reduced to nil under the 'otherwise deductible rule' in s 52 *FBTAA* [18.4] on the basis that the cost of the flights, if incurred by the employees, would have been deductible to them under s 8-1 *ITAA97*.

At first instance, the Federal Court, held that the employees would not have been entitled to deductions for the cost of the flights under s 8-1 on the basis that the object of the travel was to enable them to live where they chose (ie away from their place of work) and was therefore of a similar character to the outgoings incurred in *Lunney & Hayley*. On appeal, however, the Full Federal Court (Edmonds, Logan and Pagone JJ) reversed this decision and held that the expenditure would have been deductible to the employees under s 8-1. Edmonds J explained that the reason for this was because from the time that they checked in at Perth airport, they were travelling 'in the course of their employment', subject to the directions of their employers, and were being paid for this. The situation subsisted until they disembarked at Perth airport at the end of their rostered work. Accordingly, at no time during the relevant period were they travelling 'to work'—instead, they were travelling 'on work'. Pagone J pointed out (at [64]) that *Lunney & Hayley* concerned '"ordinary people" paying fares "to enable them to go day by day to their regular place of employment or business and back to their homes"; it was not about the specific demands occasioned by employment that required, as part of the employment, travel to a remote place'.

Earlier on, *Lunney & Hayley* was also distinguished in *FC of T v Wiener* 78 ATC 4006. In this case, a teacher employed by the Education Department was required to teach between five different schools during the week. The Commissioner allowed the teacher deductions for car expenses incurred in travelling between the schools, but not for car expenses incurred in travelling between home and the first and last school she attended each day. The Supreme Court of Western Australia, however, held that the Commissioner had wrongly denied the taxpayer deductions for this expenditure. Smith J found that the taxpayer's employment was inherently itinerant and that she was travelling in the performance of her duties from the moment she left home to the moment she returned. His Honour stated (at 4010):

> Viewed objectively, it does not seem to me to be open to question that the taxpayer would not have been able to perform her duties without the use of her motor vehicle. On four of the five

> working days the taxpayer's contract of employment required her to teach at not less than four different schools and to comply with an exacting timetable which kept her on the move throughout each of those days. The nature of the job itself made travel in the performance of its duties essential, and it was a necessary element of the employment that on those working days transport be available at whichever school the taxpayer commenced her teaching duties and that transport remained at her disposal throughout each of those days.

Similarly, in *FC of T v Ballesty* 77 ATC 4181, the Supreme Court of NSW allowed deductions to a part-time professional rugby league player for the cost of travelling between his home and various grounds where he had training sessions and matches. Waddell J explained his reasons for reaching this conclusion as follows (at 4184):

> I accept the taxpayer's evidence that it was necessary for him to travel in his own vehicle to matches and to training sessions in order to produce his best form. I would expect that the considerations upon which he relies to justify the use of his motor vehicle would be present in some form or other in most cases where a person earns income by engaging in high-level sporting activity. The occasion of the expenditure was, therefore, the necessity to comply with the terms of his contract and to fit himself to make the best contribution he could to the winning of the match or to the success of the training sessions to or from which he was travelling.

Taxpayers have also been allowed deductions for the cost of travelling between home and work where they are involved in 'stand-by' or 'on-call' duties (*FC of T v Collings* 76 ATC 4254; *Owen v Pook* [1970] AC 244). They have also been granted deductions for the cost of travelling between home and work where it is necessary for them to transport bulky goods between these places. For instance, in *FC of T v Vogt* 75 ATC 4073, a musician who transported instruments (trumpet, horn, acoustic bass, electric bass and amplifiers), upon which he practised at home, to the places where he performed was allowed deductions for the cost of travelling between home and work. Waddell J held that the expenditure had the essential character of an income-producing outgoing for the following reasons (at 4078):

> Firstly, the expenditure was incurred as part of the operations by which the taxpayer earnt his income. Secondly, it was essential to the carrying on of those operations: there was no other practicable way of getting his instruments to the places where he was to perform. Thirdly, in a practical sense, the expenditure should be attributed to the carriage of the taxpayer's instruments rather than to his travel to the places of performance. The mode of his travel was simply a consequence of the means which he employed to get his instruments to the place of performance, that is by carrying them in the motor vehicle which he drove.

Travel between two unrelated places of work

The cost of travelling between two unrelated places of work is generally not deductible under s 8-1 *ITAA97* in the same way that the cost of travelling between home and work is also generally not deductible. The reason why travel between two unrelated places of work is ordinarily not deductible under s 8-1 is that such an outgoing is not incurred 'in the course of' deriving income from either activity. Authority for this principle comes from *FC of T v Payne* 2001 ATC 4027, where the High Court denied a taxpayer deductions for the cost of travelling between his home (where he operated a deer farm business) and the airport (where he worked as a pilot). Gleeson CJ, Kirby and Hayne JJ explained (at 4030):

> The taxpayer's travel occurred in the intervals between the two income-producing activities. The travel did not occur while the taxpayer was engaged in either activity. To adopt and adapt

the language used in *Ronpibon*, neither the taxpayer's employment as a pilot nor the conduct of his business farming deer occasioned the outgoings for travel expenses.

The principle that travel between two unrelated places of work is generally not deductible must, however, now be read subject to s 25-100 *ITAA97* (which was introduced after the decision in *Payne* was handed down). This section allows deductions for the cost of 'travel between workplaces'. However, deductions are only available if the travel is directly between two places where income-producing activities are carried on and neither place is the taxpayer's home. The provision would, therefore, not have allowed Payne a deduction for his travel costs, as he was travelling to and from his home.

Travel to find new work

Whether or not the cost of travelling to find new work is deductible depends on the circumstances of each case. A distinction is usually drawn between expenditure incurred in travelling to get new business clients and expenditure incurred in travelling to get new employment. A self-employed builder who regularly goes from place to place to provide quotes to potential clients who wish to renovate their homes would usually be entitled to a deduction for his or her travelling costs as this expense would be incurred in the ordinary course of business. In contrast, an employee who incurs expenditure on travelling to a job interview for potential future employment would ordinarily not be entitled to a deduction for his or her travel costs as the expenditure is incurred in the course of 'getting', rather than 'doing', work.

On this basis, the High Court in *FC of T v Maddalena* 71 ATC 4161 held that a taxpayer who earned his living as an electrician and professional rugby player was not entitled to deduct costs associated with travelling to a new football club for interviews to obtain a playing contract as such expenditure came at a point 'too soon' to any income-earning activities. In delivering his judgment, Menzies J drew an important distinction between expenses incurred by an employee in travelling to find new employment and expenses incurred by a principal in travelling to find new contracts. His Honour stated (at 4163):

> Had the taxpayer claimed as a deduction the expenses of changing from one job to another as an employee electrician his outlay would not have been an allowable deduction. The expenditure would have been incurred in getting, not in doing, work as an employee. It would come at a point too soon to be properly regarded as incurred in gaining assessable income. Nor would the expenditure have been an outgoing in carrying on a business. There is a difference of first importance for present purposes between an electrician who seeks work as an employee and an electrician who seeks contracts to do work as a principal. In the former case the electrician would not have a business; in the latter he would. In the latter, therefore, what he spent to obtain contracts to do electrical work would be properly regarded as an outgoing of his business. There is, however, a clear distinction between the two cases.

Car expenses

Although the circumstances in which taxpayers qualify for deductions for travel expenses is generally determined under s 8-1, there are special rules in div 28 *ITAA97* for calculating the deductions that can be claimed where travel involves the use of a car. These rules apply to individuals as well as partnerships that include at least one individual. They prescribe two methods for claiming car expenses: the 'cents per kilometre method' and the 'logbook method'. Taxpayers can use whichever method provides them with the best result and are permitted to change methods from year to year and use different methods for different cars (s 28-20). The two methods are depicted in the following diagram and explained further below.

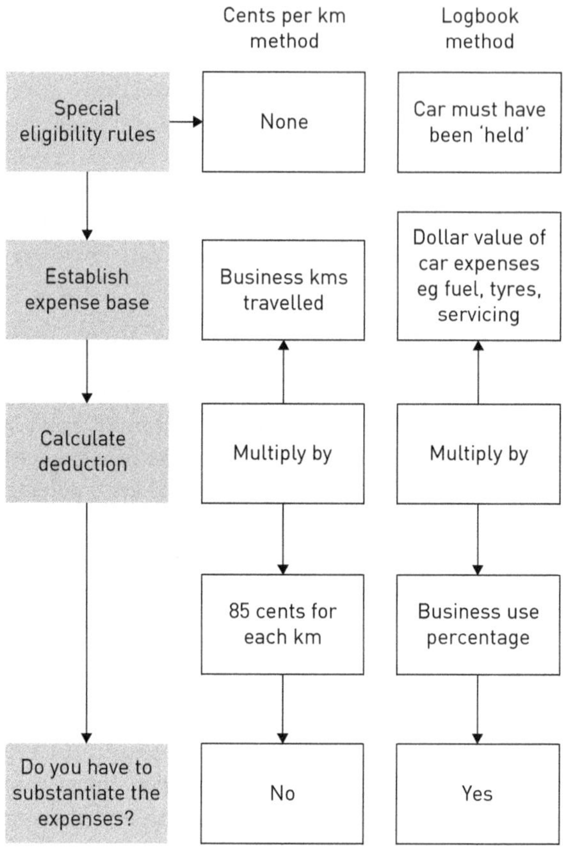

Cents per kilometre method

The cents per kilometre method is contained in sub-div 28-C and allows a taxpayer to determine the deduction for car expenses by multiplying the business kilometres the car travelled during the income year (up to a maximum of 5,000 kilometres) by a specified rate (85 cents per kilometre for 2023/24). Taxpayers using this method are able to estimate the number of business kilometres travelled during a year and do not need to comply with any substantiation rules.

Example Penny is a salesperson who travels 4,000 business kilometres in her car in 2023/24. She can claim a deduction for her car expenses of \$3,400 (ie 4,000 × 85 cents).

Logbook method

The logbook method is contained in sub-div 28-F and allows a taxpayer to deduct each car expense they incur during the income year by multiplying the expense by the 'business use percentage'. The business use percentage is designed to estimate the income-producing use of the car for the year. It is determined using logbook records kept by the taxpayer for a continuous period of 12 weeks under sub-div 28-G.

A logbook must contain details of each journey made during the logbook period. The entry must specify the day the journey began and ended, the car's odometer readings at the start and end of the journey, the number of kilometres travelled on the journey, and why the journey was made (eg for income-producing or for private purposes).

The following details must also be entered in the logbook:

(a) when the logbook period begins and ends
(b) the car's odometer readings at the start and the end of the period
(c) the total number of kilometres that the car travelled during the period
(d) the number of kilometres that the car travelled, in the course of producing the taxpayer's assessable income on journeys recorded in the logbook, and
(e) the number of kilometres referred to in para (d), expressed as a percentage of the total number referred to in para (c) (ie the 'business use percentage').

Each entry must be made at, or as soon as possible after, the start or end of the journey or relevant period.

> ***Example*** Jack is a courier and has kept a logbook to determine the business use percentage of his car for the last income year. His logbook showed that he travelled a total of 15,000 kms during the year, which included 12,000 kms were for business-related purposes. His business use percentage is therefore 80% (ie 12,000/15,000 × 100). Jack's total car expenses for the year (comprising registration, insurance premiums, repairs, servicing, depreciation, fuel and oil costs) amounted to $10,000. He is therefore entitled to a deduction of $8,000 (ie $10,000 × 80%).

[12.8] Management expenses

The deductibility of management fees was considered by the High Court in *Spriggs v FC of T*; *Riddell v FC of T* 2009 ATC ¶20-109. This case concerned two professional footballers, Spriggs (an AFL player) and Riddell (a Rugby League player), who had paid their agents management fees to represent them in negotiating their respective playing contracts, as a consequence of which they also obtained promotional work in the form of sponsorships, endorsements and media appearances. The Commissioner argued that it was necessary to separate the taxpayers' playing activities from their non-playing activities. According to the Commissioner, the management fees were incurred in obtaining 'new employment' and the fees should, therefore, not be deductible based on *FC of T v Maddalena* 71 ATC 4161 [12.7]. The High Court, however, rejected this argument and allowed deductions for the management fees under both of the positive limbs of s 8-1 *ITAA97*. It held that neither Spriggs nor Riddell were exclusively employees of their clubs and were 'engaged in the business of commercially exploiting their sporting prowess and associated celebrity'. The Court noted that there was a 'synergy' between their playing and non-playing activities and it would be artificial to separate the income from those activities. On this basis, the Court distinguished *Maddalena* on the grounds that it concerned a contract of employment involving a taxpayer that was not carrying on a business.

The High Court also rejected the Commissioner's submission that the management fees were of a capital nature as they were incurred to procure the taxpayers' playing contracts which were 'structural assets'. The Court held that even if the management fees were paid solely for negotiating the playing contracts, those contracts were 'revenue assets' as they were not 'lasting assets' but were of a 'relatively short-term nature and subject to renewal'. It was noted that each of the taxpayers entered into a number of contracts with different clubs in the course of their businesses and the management fees were a recurrent expenditure in respect of those revenue assets.

[12.9] Self-education expenses

Self-education expenses can include a range of different kinds of outgoings, such as:

- the cost of registration, travel to and accommodation at professional conferences

- the cost of course fees for undertaking a tertiary course, and
- the cost of study-related materials (eg calculators, textbooks and stationery).

The main issue that arises under s 8-1 *ITAA97* in respect of self-education expenses is whether the expenses have a sufficient link to the taxpayer's income-producing activities. To be deductible under s 8-1, the self-education expenses must also be of a revenue nature. Self-education expenses that are of a capital nature (eg the cost of purchasing a computer for study purposes) are not deductible under s 8-1, but may be deductible under the capital allowance regime in div 40 *ITAA97* [15.2].

Self-education expenses linked to current occupation

Self-education expenses usually satisfy the nexus requirement in the positive limbs of s 8-1 where they are incurred to maintain or increase a taxpayer's skills in an occupation in which the taxpayer is currently engaged. This is especially the case where the expenditure enhances the taxpayer's chances of promotion or prospects for earning greater income.

In *FC of T v Finn* (1961) 106 CLR 60, an architect employed by the Western Australian Government was allowed deductions for expenses he incurred in travelling overseas for almost one year to study architecture. During his trip, he made voluminous notes and photographs, made many sketches and wrote up reports. A portion of his expenditure was also met by his employer. The High Court found that the tour was incidental and relevant to his employment. Dixon CJ pointed to the fact that the knowledge sought and obtained by the taxpayer improved his chances of advancement in his job. His Honour also noted that his employer viewed the tour as a distinct advantage to his work. In the course of his judgment, Windeyer J expressed the following general rule about self-education expenses (at 70):

> Generally speaking . . . a taxpayer who gains income by the exercise of his skill in some profession or calling and who incurs expenses in maintaining or increasing his learning, knowledge, experience and ability in that profession or calling necessarily incurs those expenses in carrying on his profession or calling.

Similarly, in *FC of T v Hatchett* 71 ATC 4184, a primary school teacher was allowed deductions for costs incurred in having his thesis typed for his Teacher's Higher Certificate. Completion of the Teacher's Higher Certificate enabled the taxpayer to transfer to a higher salary scale and was needed for senior teaching appointments. The High Court held that, although the thesis typing expenditure had no effect on the taxpayer's assessable income in the year it was incurred, there was a plain connection between the obtaining of the certificate and his assessable income in future years. Moreover, the expenditure was not of a capital nature. As Menzies J stated (at 4186):

> There has been some suggestion that to equip the taxpayer's mind in order that he may have higher earning capacity is an affair of capital . . . This is, I think, a misunderstanding. It seems to me that it would be wrong to consider any of the expenditure here under consideration as an outgoing of capital or of a capital nature. An outlay is of that character when it is expended to obtain what can properly be described as capital in the economic sense . . . However, since human capacity is entirely different from 'capital', it is not necessary . . . to consider more closely the references to capital in s 51.

In *FC of T v Highfield* 82 ATC 4463, a dentist who carried on general practice was successful in claiming deductions for certain costs (including course fees, travel and accommodation expenses) relating to undertaking a Master of Science in Periodontics degree in London. The taxpayer had undertaken the degree to enable him to perform more periodontic work in his general practice and potentially specialise in the field. The NSW Supreme Court held that the expenses were necessarily incurred in carrying on his business as the purpose in going to London was to use the knowledge he obtained in the advancement of his practice as a general practitioner. In this regard, Lee J held (at 4471–4472):

> The additional knowledge and skills acquired in obtaining the degree would give to the respondent additional ability as a general practitioner which would justify him, in a commercial sense, in charging higher fees for the periodontic work and at the same time he would reasonably be entitled to expect that those charges would be acceptable to his patients because of his additional skill. Once it is accepted that the respondent at all relevant times intended to continue his general practice, the objective factors earlier referred to in regard to his practice and the periodontic component of it and the higher fees chargeable because of the respondent's skill in periodontics, in my view, established of themselves the necessary connection between the whole of the expenditure and the gaining of assessable income. It is not for the Court to decide what is and what is not appropriate for the respondent to do by way of carrying on his practice.

The fact that undertaking the course would allow the taxpayer to charge higher fees for his services was clearly a factor that the Court in *Highfield* took into account in reaching the conclusion that the self-education expenses were deductible. It is important to realise, however, that it is not a prerequisite for the deductibility of self-education expenses to show that the expenditure will necessarily result in extra income being earned by the taxpayer. It is sufficient if the expenditure has been incurred with the object of improving the taxpayer's 'proficiency' in his or her current occupation. This principle is illustrated in *FC of T v Studdert* 91 ATC 5006, where the Federal Court allowed deductions to a flight engineer for the cost of undertaking flying lessons as the lessons would improve his performance in his current job and increased his prospects for promotion. Hill J stated (at 5014):

> Where an outgoing is shown to contribute or to be likely to contribute to increased income, it will normally be the case that the necessary connection will exist between the outgoing and the activities of the taxpayer which more directly contribute to the gaining or production of assessable income. . . . However, it is not necessary for an outgoing to be deductible that a taxpayer be able to show a likelihood of increased income. In the present context, were this to be so, it would mean that a person who had reached the peak of his income-producing position, would never be entitled to a deduction for self-education expenses. Thus, the Commissioner of Taxation, having no public service office to which he could ordinarily expect to be promoted, could never obtain a deduction for a course of instruction that could be shown to better equip him in the performance of his duties as Commissioner. So to state the problem is to expose the fallacy in the argument. If the Commissioner were to undertake a course which would be objectively seen as improving or tending to improve his proficiency in his office, that would better equip him so to do, there is no reason to suppose that a deduction would not be allowable for expenditure which he incurred on such a course. There would be a relevant (or to use the words of Menzies J in *Hatchett* a perceived) connection between the outgoing and the activities of his office which more directly produce his assessable income . . .

Self-education expenses that enable a taxpayer to work more efficiently and better fulfil their job responsibilities are therefore usually deductible. This is the case even though the expenditure may relate to undertaking a course that is not a specific requirement of the taxpayer's job and is not a term of his or her employment. For instance, in *FC of T v Wilkinson* 83 ATC 4295, an air traffic controller was allowed deductions for the cost of undertaking flying lessons even though the lessons were not an essential requirement of his employment. As flying training made air traffic controllers more efficient and assisted with their prospects of promotion, the Supreme Court of Queensland held that a perceived connection existed between the expenditure and the taxpayer's assessable income. Williams J stated (at 4303):

> [The taxpayer] incurred the expenditure in question in order to better equip himself to fulfil his responsibilities as an air traffic controller. One of his main motives (if not the sole motive) was to improve his prospects of promotion and advancement in grade and salary. He became better equipped to carry out the duties of his employment. It is indisputable on the evidence that the obtaining of flying qualifications and experience, the consequential greater appreciation of the responsibility of an air traffic controller, and the consequential increase in efficiency, made advancement in the service more certain . . . The obtaining of a pilot's licence went beyond 'improving mind and body'; there was a 'perceived connection' between the outgoing and obtaining assessable income, in that the obtaining of the licence made it 'inherently likely' that the respondent would be promoted and receive a higher salary.

Self-education expenses not linked to current occupation

By way of contrast to the cases outlined above, self-education expenses relating to an occupation that a taxpayer is not presently engaged in are ordinarily not deductible. The reason for this is that the expenditure does not have a sufficient nexus with the taxpayer's income-earning activities. Thus, a medical student who is not yet practising as a doctor would usually be denied a deduction for the cost of his or her textbooks. This principle is confirmed in TR 98/9, which states that deductions are not available for self-education expenses if the study is to enable a taxpayer to get employment, to obtain new employment or to open up a new income-earning activity. The ruling relies on the High Court decision in *FC of T v Maddalena* 71 ATC 4161 [12.7] for the conclusion that such expenses are incurred at a point too soon to be regarded as incurred in gaining or producing assessable income.

In *FC of T v Roberts* 92 ATC 4787, the Federal Court relied on *Maddalena* to conclude that a mining engineer should be denied deductions for costs incurred in pursuing an overseas Master of Business Administration qualification. The taxpayer had been retrenched as a mine manager by his Australian employer and undertook studies in the United States for two years. On his return to Australia, he was employed by another company as a mine manager at an increased salary. Cooper J held that the self-education expenditure had been incurred to obtain 'new' employment rather than 'in the course of' employment. His Honour stated (at 4798):

> In my view, the expenditure in the present case falls squarely within the statements of Barwick CJ and of Menzies J in *Maddalena* . . . : they are moneys which were spent to obtain a new employment, albeit one in a better position and on higher wages. Being the cost to an employee of obtaining his employment, they do not form an outgoing incurred in the course of earning the wages payable in the employment. To use the phrase employed by Hill J in *Cooper*, those expenses cannot be described as 'working expenses'. It cannot be said that the taxpayer in the present case, in reliance upon the conditions of his employment, spent money to earn more: cf *Hatchett*. Nor can it be said that, at the time the expenses were incurred, the taxpayer was acting within the scope of his office, and therefore in the gaining of his salary: cf *Finn*.

A similar outcome was reached in *Elder v FC of T* 2007 ATC 2370, where a taxpayer who had previously worked in the oil and gas industry, but who described himself as a professional investor, was denied deductions for undertaking Masters degrees in finance, business and accounting at various universities. The AAT found that the taxpayer was not seeking to maintain or increase existing professional skills but to attain those skills. The expenses were incurred too soon and were of a capital nature. The AAT explained (at 2375):

> In this case, expenditure incurred by Mr Elder . . . related to the attaining of Masters degrees in subjects in which he did not appear to have had any prior qualifications. It would appear that it was not a matter of Mr Elder seeking to maintain or increase existing professional skills but to attain those skills. It is difficult to see how the obtaining of these degrees and attaining the knowledge within them so as to provide Mr Elder with skills to become a successful investor can be said to have been incurred in gaining or producing his assessable income. At best, they are a prelude to investment and incurred at a point too soon.

In *Ting v FC of T* 2015 ATC ¶10-386, a full-time maths and science teacher sought deductions under s 8-1 for expenses relating to undertaking a part-time Diploma in Management. The taxpayer's primary motivation for undertaking the course was to obtain a future position as a leading teacher or school principal. The Commissioner originally denied deductions for all six subjects in the course, but after proceedings commenced, allowed deductions for four of the subjects. He nevertheless maintained that expenses relating to two subjects (Financial Accounting and Marketing) were not deductible. The AAT confirmed that the expenses were not deductible as they did not have the necessary connection with the production of the taxpayer's assessable income. The AAT found that taxpayer's role was essentially pedagogical in nature and that the course did not improve or maintain his teaching skills nor was it a condition of his employment. The course was too tenuously connected to his income-producing activities for the expenses to be deductible. The AAT pointed out that leading teachers had a management role, which was materially different from a classroom teacher, and that promotion to such a position would result in an entirely different job. The expenses were 'incurred in getting, not doing' work and came at a point too soon to be regarded as incurred in gaining assessable income.

More recently, in *YDXM v FC of T* 2022 ATC ¶10-636, an officer in the army was denied deductions for self-education expenses relating to units undertaken in a post-graduate law degree. The taxpayer submitted that his studies improved his skills as an officer and also led to his promotion from Captain to Major. The AAT, however, held that the units did not have the 'necessary relevant and incidental connection' to the gaining or producing of his income and found that there was no 'real connection' between the units and his increased income. While his studies were viewed favourably, they were not required for promotion.

Self-education expenses linked to government allowances

Notwithstanding the decisions in the previous cases, there has been a notable case where self-education expenses were deductible to a taxpayer even though the taxpayer did not have any current employment or business. In *FC of T v Anstis* 2010 ATC ¶20-221, a full-time student who was undertaking a teaching degree was allowed deductions for the cost of textbooks, student administration fees, travel expenses in visiting schools and supplies for children during her teaching rounds. The taxpayer received a 'Youth Allowance', which was payable if a person satisfied the Secretary of the relevant Commonwealth Department that they were enrolled in a course at an educational institution, undertaking at least three-quarters of normal full-time study, and making satisfactory progress towards completing the course.

Both the Federal Court (*Anstis v FC of T* 2009 ATC ¶20-098) and the Full Federal Court (*FC of T v Anstis* 2009 ATC ¶20-142) held that the taxpayer's expenses were a necessary incident of deriving her assessable income from the Youth Allowance. The Full Federal Court rejected the Commissioner's arguments that the taxpayer's activities as a student were 'qualifying activities' akin to the activity of travelling from home to work to put oneself in a position to earn assessable income (as in *Lunney*) and were incurred at 'a point too soon' to be deductible (as in *Maddalena*). The Court also did not accept the Commissioner's contention that, as the taxpayer would have undertaken her course in any event, the essential character of the expenditure was 'linked to study' rather than to the Youth Allowance.

On appeal, the High Court held that the concept of 'gaining or producing' income is wider than merely 'earning' income. The Court said the term 'gain' means not only to 'earn or obtain (a living)' but also to 'obtain, secure or acquire' or to 'receive'. Similarly, the term 'produce' means to 'bring (a thing) into existence' and is not limited to bringing something into existence by mental or physical labour. According to the Court, the taxpayer gained or produced her Youth Allowance income by virtue of her statutory entitlement to payment. This right would be retained so long as she maintained her qualification for the payment. The Court pointed out that the taxpayer's reason or motive for incurring the outgoings (eg to obtain a qualification to undertake future employment as a teacher) was not determinative of whether those outgoings were incurred in gaining or producing income. Rather, the 'occasion of the outgoings' was to be found in what the taxpayer did to gain or produce the Youth Allowance payment (ie in what was 'productive' of her assessable income). The outgoings were deductible because they were incurred in the course of establishing or retaining her statutory right to payment.

The High Court also confirmed that the expenditure was not of a private nature. In reaching this conclusion, the Court referred to *Finn*, where Windeyer J observed (at 70):

> Outgoings incurred for the genuine purpose of acquiring or maintaining knowledge and skill in a vocation do not become an outgoing 'of a private nature' simply because the taxpayer got pleasure and satisfaction in increasing his knowledge and attainments.

On this basis, it followed that the outgoings did not lose their connection with the Youth Allowance simply because the taxpayer might have been studying for other reasons.

Statutory restrictions on deductibility of self-education expenses

In response to the decision in *Anstis*, the Government enacted s 26-19 *ITAA97*, which denies deductions for self-education expenses that relate to gaining 'rebatable benefits' (ie certain government assistance payments like Youth Allowance) [14.7].

Another statutory restriction on the deductibility of self-education expenses is found in s 26-20 *ITAA97*, which denies deductions for certain study-related payments (eg student contribution amounts and HECS-HELP repayments) [14.7].

In addition, former s 82A *ITAA36* previously denied deductions for the first $250 of 'expenses of self-education'. However, this provision was repealed from the 2022/23 income year.

[12.10] Home office expenses

As a general rule, a home does not constitute business premises and taxpayers are, therefore, not ordinarily entitled to deductions under s 8-1 *ITAA97* for expenses such as rent paid to lease their homes or interest paid on their home loans. This is the case even though they might maintain a study in their homes in which they work.

In *Handley v FC of T* 81 ATC 4165, a barrister who had a home study in which he worked for approximately 20 hours per week was denied deductions for interest paid on his home loan as well as rates and insurance premiums relating to the premises. Mason J characterised the expenditure as private or domestic in nature, stating (at 4173):

> Here the study is a room in the taxpayer's home, not separate from it in any way, having no distinctive physical characteristics, readily capable of other use for family purposes, and in fact used for non-professional purposes from time to time. Moreover when used for professional work it is ordinarily used only for professional work that can be done at home, in the evenings and at weekends, eg working on briefs and preparing opinions. Expenditure related to the study is therefore referable to the home. The 'essential character of the expenditure', to take up the expression used in *Lunney v FC of T* (1958) 100 CLR 478 at p 497 is therefore that of a 'capital, private or domestic nature'.

Likewise, in *FC of T v Forsyth* 81 ATC 4157, a barrister who paid rent to the trustee of his family trust (which owned the family home) was disallowed deductions for the rent that related to his home study. The High Court found that the barrister only used the study for 'convenience', not through 'compulsion', and, on this basis, considered that the rent was not incidental or relevant to the gaining or production of his assessable income.

Importantly, in both *Handley* and *Forsyth* the taxpayers also maintained their own chambers in town and therefore had places of work away from their homes. The position is not as straightforward where a taxpayer does not have separate business premises. Expenses relating to the maintenance of a home study may be deductible where the taxpayer's home is also their place of business.

For instance, in *Swinford v FC of T* 84 ATC 4803, the Supreme Court of NSW held that a self-employed scriptwriter was entitled to deductions for a portion of the rent paid in relation to her flat, on the basis that she dedicated a separate room in the flat for use as her study. The taxpayer wrote her scripts in this room and did not have separate business premises like the barristers. David Hunt J distinguished *Handley* and *Forsyth* on the following basis (at 4806):

> There can be no doubt that, as a result of those two cases, it will be difficult (perhaps impossible) for any taxpayer to obtain a deduction where his home office is a study used in those circumstances. It is, however, to take a very large step further to say that, as a result of those decisions, no deduction will be available in relation to a home office as a matter of law . . . In my view, the accuracy of the Commissioner's submission depends upon what is meant by a 'home office'. The area designated as such . . . may either constitute business premises notwithstanding the physical association of that area with the taxpayer's home, or it may be only part of the taxpayer's home (such as a study) used for business purposes as a matter of convenience. Whilst in most cases a home office will not constitute business premises unless, like the doctor's surgery, it is physically distinct from the area used as a home, I would not be prepared to say that a home office cannot, as a matter of law, amount to business premises.
>
> The present case, in my opinion, is clearly distinguishable from what was being considered in *Handley* and in *Forsyth*. The work done by the taxpayer in the present case was not done at her home rather than elsewhere as a matter of convenience. This was the only place where she did carry out her writing activities. This was the base, and the only base, of the taxpayer's operations . . .

Irrespective of whether the home is a place of business, taxpayers are generally able to depreciate the cost of items such as desks and bookshelves used at home for work purposes and they are generally entitled to deductions for the work-related proportion of their heating and electricity costs (*FC of T v Faichney* 72 ATC 4245).

ATO's views on home office expenses

In TR 93/30, the ATO distinguishes between:

- 'occupancy expenses' (eg rent, interest, rates and insurance premiums), and
- 'running expenses' (eg heating, cooling, lighting and depreciation).

The ruling states that where the home office is a 'place of business', a relevant proportion of both kinds of expenses may be deducted. Where, however, the home office is simply used 'in connection with the taxpayer's income-earning activities, but does not have the character of a place of business', only a relevant proportion of the running expenses may be deducted.

PCG 2023/1 recognises that while expenses associated with a taxpayer's home are inherently private in nature and generally not deductible, an exception arises where they incur additional running expenses as a result of working from home. The guideline indicates that deductions for additional running expenses can be claimed in respect of energy expenses (eg for heating, cooling and lighting);

home and mobile phone, internet and data expenses; stationery and office supply expenses; and the decline in value of depreciating assets used for work (eg office furniture and equipment) as well as repairs and maintenance of those assets.

PCG 2023/1 states that from 1 July 2022 taxpayers may use one of two methods to claim their additional running expenses:

- **Actual cost method.** This method allows employees to claim the actual work-related portion of all their additional running expenses.
- **Revised fixed rate method.** This method allows employees to claim 67 cents for each hour worked at home during the relevant income year for all their additional running expenses.

In order to use the actual cost or revised fixed rate methods, taxpayers must be working from home to fulfil their employment duties (not just carrying out minimal tasks, such as occasionally checking emails or taking phone calls), incur additional running expenses as a result of working from home, and have records that show they have incurred those expenses. To use the revised fixed rate method, taxpayers must also have kept records of the number of hours worked from home (eg diary notes).

Example Alan works from his home study several days per week. He has kept a diary that shows he worked a total of 500 hours from home during 2022/23. When working from home, Alan uses the heater in the study, which uses 1 kilowatt per hour of energy. Allan's electricity bills indicate he pays 30 cents per kilowatt for electricity. Under the actual cost method, Alan can claim a deduction of $150 for his heating costs (ie 500 hours × 30 cents per kilowatt hour).

While working in his study, Alan also uses a chair and desk that he purchased as well as a laptop computer provided by his employer. He also uses his own home internet connection. Under the actual cost method, Alan can claim a deduction of a portion of his home internet costs as well as a portion of the depreciation of his chair and desk under div 40 *ITAA97* [15.2]. He cannot, however, claim a deduction for the depreciation of the laptop as he does not own it.

Alternatively, if Alan chooses to use the revised fixed rate method, he can claim a deduction of $335 (ie 500 × 0.67 cents for hour) for all his additional running expenses.

It is important to note that the ATO states that a taxpayer does not incur additional running expenses if other members of their household (who are not working from home) are in the same room as the taxpayer while the taxpayer is working from home.

Example If, in the previous example, Alan worked from his lounge room where his wife and children also watch TV, he could not claim a deduction for any additional heating costs as a result of working in that room.

[12.11] Rent, royalty and licence fee expenses

Rent

Rent is a payment made for the use of an asset (eg land or a chattel) for a particular period of time. It must be distinguished from a payment made to acquire the asset outright. While rent paid for the use of an asset is ordinarily a revenue expense, the cost of acquiring the asset is generally capital in nature as it provides an enduring benefit. Accordingly, under s 8-1 *ITAA97*, taxpayers are generally entitled to deduct rent paid to lease their office premises but are not entitled to deduct the cost of purchasing those premises.

As a general rule, deductions are allowed for the payment of rent provided the only immediate advantage secured by the taxpayer from making the payment is the use of an income-producing asset over the term of the lease.

The leading case dealing with the deductibility of rent is *FC of T v South Australian Battery Makers Pty Ltd* 78 ATC 4412. In this case, the taxpayer's parent company ('ABM') wanted to establish a factory in South Australia. It entered into an agreement with the South Australian Housing Trust ('SAHT'), which owned land in South Australia. Under the agreement, SAHT agreed to build a factory on its land and lease it to ABM for 16 years at an annual rent of 10% of the capital cost of the project. SAHT also granted ABM an option to purchase the development for a price that was calculated in accordance with an 'amortisation factor', which effectively applied a portion of the rent against the cost of the project. ABM assigned its interest in the lease to the taxpayer (which used the development for its manufacturing business) and it assigned its interest in the option to PO (which was a company associated with ABM's overseas parent company).

The Commissioner was of the view that, as the rent paid by the taxpayer reduced the exercise price of the option, a deduction for a portion of the rent should be denied on the grounds that it was of a capital nature, being part of the purchase price for the development. A majority of the High Court, however, allowed the taxpayer to deduct the entire rent paid on the basis that the only interests the taxpayer had acquired by making the payments were those of a lessee. There was nothing to indicate that any advantage that PO might obtain by exercising the option was an advantage that the taxpayer would also obtain from paying the rent.

Similar outcomes were reached by the Full Federal Court in *FC of T v Metal Manufactures Ltd* 2001 ATC 4152 and *Eastern Nitrogen Ltd v FC of T* 2001 ATC 4164. These cases both concerned financing arrangements involving the sale and leaseback of manufacturing plants that were situated on land owned by the relevant taxpayers. In both cases, the taxpayers had sold their respective plant to third parties and leased the plant back from them. Although the lease agreements did not give them any express right to repurchase the plant, the taxpayers expected that they would be able to buy the plant back from the lessors for their respective residual values at the end of the lease periods. In both cases, the courts found that, since the only advantages obtained by the taxpayers from the payments of rent were the benefits they enjoyed as lessees of the plant, the payments were of a revenue nature and fully deductible.

Royalties and licence fees

Royalties and licence fees are other kinds of periodic payments that, like rent, are usually treated as being of a revenue nature. For example, in *Cliffs International Inc v FC of T* 79 ATC 4059, the High Court held that a mining company that paid royalties to mine iron at the rate of 15 cents per ton could deduct those payments as they were revenue outgoings. Likewise, in *FC of T v Citylink Melbourne Ltd* 2006 ATC 4404, the High Court held that licence fees paid for the right to exploit income-producing assets (ie the use of roads) over a period of time were deductible revenue outgoings as the taxpayer did not obtain any permanent ownership rights in relation to those assets [12.5].

Payments to secure a licence or lease

Although payments of rent and licence fees are usually of a revenue nature, payments that are made for the purposes of securing a lease or licence (eg premiums) are likely to be capital in nature. In *Star City Pty Ltd v FC of T* 2009 ATC ¶20-093, the Full Federal Court held that a large pre-payment of 'rent' totalling $120m made by a taxpayer under a 99-year lease of a casino was not deductible under s 8-1 *ITAA97* on the basis that it was of a capital nature since it was directed at securing the casino licence and the exclusive right to operate the casino in NSW for a period of 12 years. Goldberg J (with whom Dowsett and Jessup JJ concurred) referred to *Hallstroms Pty Ltd v FC of T* (1946) 72 CLR 634 and found (at [71]) that the payment related to 'the character and organisation of the profit-earning business' and was not 'an incident in the operation by which it is carried on'. Some of the factors that led his Honour to conclude that the payment was of a capital nature included the following:

- the payment was a lump sum made in advance
- the payment was not refundable if the lease was terminated
- there was disparity between the rent payable in each of the first 12 years of the lease ($15m) and the rent payable in each of the remaining 87 years of the lease ($250,000), and
- various documents drafted by the taxpayer's solicitors referred to the payment as reflecting part of the 'premium' paid by the taxpayer to obtain the licence.

Payments to secure lower rent under a lease

Payments made for the purposes of securing lower rent under a lease can also be capital in nature. In *Mussalli & Ors v FC of T* 2021 ATC ¶20-792, the taxpayers had entered into various agreements relating to the lease and operation of McDonald's restaurant franchises for periods of between 7 and 20 years. The taxpayers exercised options under the agreements to make upfront lump sum payments that reduced the rent payable from a 'higher percentage rate' to a 'lower percentage rate'. They claimed that these were for 'pre-paid rent' and should be deductible under s 8-1 *ITAA97* spread over a number of years in accordance with the special timing rules in s 82KZMD *ITAA36* [29.10].

The Full Federal Court denied the deductions on the basis that the payments were capital in nature. In doing so, it upheld the Federal Court's decision at first instance (2020 ATC ¶20-743), where Jagot J had found that the payments were one-off, non-refundable payments made in respect of each restaurant to secure an enduring advantage. According to Jagot J, the payments negated or extinguished any obligation to pay the higher percentage rent and did not, in fact, involve the payment of rent at all. Her Honour held (at [117]) that the payments secured 'the enduring advantage of acquiring a preferable business structure, being one which involved the payment of a lower percentage rent over the term'. According to her Honour, the payments were 'calculated to effect the acquisition of a right to operate the franchises on better terms as to rent than otherwise would have been the case' and 'were not concerned with the regular performance of the work', but 'with the profit-making structure of the business'.

The taxpayers had argued before the Full Court that a payment made to secure a reduction in a revenue outgoing should be treated as being on revenue account. McKerracher and Stewart JJ, however, rejected this and stated (at [93]) that there was 'no principle of general application that a lump sum paid to reduce or eliminate future revenue expenses is always to be characterised in the same way as the expenses for which it is substituted'.

Payments to secure ownership of assets

It is important to distinguish rent and licence fees from payments that result in the ownership of assets. For example, in *Ausnet Transmission Group Pty Ltd v FC of T* 2015 ATC ¶20-521, a taxpayer had paid statutory charges, amounting to over $177m, under the *Electricity Industry Act 1993* (Vic) in connection with a multi-billion dollar acquisition of the power assets of PNV (a State of Victoria-owned transmission company). The assets included a transmission licence, which was essential for conducting the taxpayer's transmission business. A majority of the High Court held that the statutory charges were capital in nature and therefore not deductible under s 8-1 *ITAA97*. The majority found that the statutory charges were a significant part of the consideration paid to acquire PNV's assets. The payments were significant liabilities that were not inherently recurrent and could not therefore be described as 'periodic licence fees'. The taxpayer assumed the liability to pay the charges in order to acquire the transmission licence, which was 'part of the structure of the business'. As French CJ, Kiefel and Bell JJ observed (at 66), without such a licence 'acquisition of the rest of the assets was pointless' and if it was revoked 'the whole business structure would collapse'.

The High Court reached a similar conclusion in *FC of T v Sharpcan Pty Ltd* 2019 ATC ¶20-715, where it held that $600,300 paid to the State of Victoria by a hotel operator for 18 gaming machine entitlements ('GMEs') was capital in nature and therefore not deductible under s 8-1. The GMEs were acquired at a government auction and gave the taxpayer the right to conduct gaming on machines at its premises for a period of 10 years (subject to forfeiture if the operating conditions were breached). The High Court found that as gaming at a venue was only lawful if the operator held GMEs, the GMEs were assets of an enduring advantage that were necessary for the structure of the taxpayer's business. Although the purchase price was paid in several instalments under a deferred payment agreement, the Court concluded that it was in the nature of a once and for all outgoing for the acquisition of an enduring asset. The Court distinguished *Citylink*, on the basis that the concession fees payable in that case were essentially periodic licence fees paid for the use of assets that were calculated, in part, according to the revenue generated from those assets. They did not give rise to any enduring advantage because they did not confer any 'permanent ownership rights' over the assets. The Court elaborated on the distinction as follows (at [22]):

> By contrast . . . the payments in respect of the GMEs were not in any sense in the nature of periodic licence fees. They were merely instalments of the purchase price 'for' the GMEs, which was payable once and for all upon the acquisition of the GMEs regardless of the amount of revenue which the GMEs might or might not generate.

The Court went on to conclude (at [33]):

> If a once-and-for-all payment is made for the acquisition of an asset of enduring advantage which, once acquired, forms part of the profit-earning structure of the business, the payment is incurred on capital account.

[12.12] Interest expenses

Interest expenditure is one of the most common forms of outgoing for which deductions are regularly sought under the general deduction provision. Interest is part of the cost of borrowing money, and it includes 'compound interest' (ie interest charged on 'ordinary interest') (*Hart & Anor v FC of T* 2002 ATC 4608). The nature of interest was described by Lee J in the Supreme Court decision in *Ure v FC of T* 80 ATC 4264 in the following terms (at 4273):

> As I have stated earlier interest is payment for the use of money. 'Interest is compensation for delay in payment . . . ' (per Farwell J in *Bond v Barrow Haematite Steel Co* (1902) 1 Ch. 353 at p 363). 'Interest, is in general terms, the return or compensation for the use or retention by one person of a sum of money, belonging to in a colloquial sense, or owed to another' (per Rand J in *Re Farm Security Act 1944* (1947) SCR (Canada) 394). 'Interest has been defined as compensation paid by the borrower to the lender for deprivation of use of his money' (see per Lord Wright in *Riches v Westminster Bank Ltd* (1947) 1 All E.R. 469 at p 472). '. . . The essence of interest is that it is a payment which becomes due because the creditor has not had his money at the due date. It may be regarded either as representing the profit he might have made if he had had the use of the money, or, conversely the loss he has suffered because he had not that use. The general idea is that he is entitled to compensation for the deprivation.' *Ridge Securities Ltd v IR Commrs* (1964) 1 All E.R. 275 per Pennycuick J at p 286.

Character of interest ordinarily depends on the use of the borrowed funds

One of the earliest High Court pronouncements regarding the deductibility of interest is found in *FC of T v Munro* (1926) 38 CLR 153. This case is famous for establishing what has become known as the 'use test'. It concerned a taxpayer who had borrowed money from a bank to make an interest-free loan to a company that he had established, and to acquire shares in the company for himself and his sons. The loan was secured by a mortgage over the taxpayer's rent-producing property. The taxpayer argued that the interest he incurred on the loan should be deductible under former s 23(1)(a) *ITAA22* since, if it was not paid, the lender would foreclose on his property, and he would not be able to derive any rental from it. The High Court, however, rejected this argument and held that the interest had not been 'wholly and exclusively' incurred in gaining the taxpayer's assessable income as required under s 25(e) *ITAA22*. Knox CJ stated (at 171):

> In this case the assessable income of the taxpayer was in no way referable to the transaction with the bank out of which the liability to pay interest arose, and the loan by the bank was in no way instrumental in or conducive to the production of the assessable income or that part of which consisted of the rents of the freehold property. The respondent was, before the mortgage was given, entitled to the whole of these rents, and he did not gain them nor were they produced in consequence of the payment of interest.

A similar conclusion was reached by Issacs J, who stated (at 197–198):

> Had the money borrowed been expended on the property so as to increase the rentals or so as to prevent depreciation which would have reduced the rentals, then it could have been properly said that the interest had been a means of gaining or producing the assessable income. But in employing the borrowed money for purposes independent of the property, leaving its condition entirely unaffected, that result cannot be postulated.

Subsequent cases have interpreted *Munro* as standing for the principle that the deductibility of interest payable on a loan will usually depend upon the objective use to which the borrowed funds are applied. As Deane and Sheppard JJ stated in *Ure v FC of T* 81 ATC 4100 (at 4109–4110):

> where the outgoing claimed as a deduction is interest paid on borrowed money, one cannot ordinarily look to the direct object or advantage which the outgoing was intended to achieve for the reason that that will ordinarily be the receipt of the borrowed money which is likely to be neutral in character. One must, of necessity, look more to the objects or advantages which the application and use of the borrowed money were intended to gain (*FC of T v Munro* (1926) 38 CLR 153 at 197).

Based on this principle, a taxpayer that borrows money for the purpose of using it to acquire an income-producing asset would ordinarily be entitled to claim a deduction for the interest payable on the loan. If, however, the taxpayer uses the borrowed funds for non-income-producing purposes, the interest payable on the loan would not be deductible. This is the case, even though the borrowings enable the taxpayer to retain income-producing assets which they might otherwise have had to sell.

In other words, it is clear from *Munro* that in characterising interest payments, the courts focus on the use to which the borrowed funds are applied rather than the nature of any security provided for the loan. On this basis, a taxpayer would be allowed deductions for interest incurred on borrowings used to purchase an income-producing property (even though the loan is secured by a mortgage over the taxpayer's private residence). The corollary to this is that interest incurred on borrowings used to purchase a non-income-producing property would not be deductible (even though the loan is secured by a mortgage over the taxpayer's income-producing property).

The principle established in *Munro* is illustrated in *Case* B11 70 ATC 46. The taxpayer in this case owned and lived in 'house A' and subsequently purchased 'house B' with the aim of making it his new family home. He borrowed money to buy house B and to discharge the existing loan relating to house A, which he retained and subsequently leased to tenants. The Commissioner allowed the taxpayer a deduction for the interest referable to that part of the borrowed funds used to discharge the existing loan in respect of house A but denied him a deduction for the balance of the interest. The taxpayer submitted that the balance should be deductible because the borrowed funds allowed him to retain ownership of house A, which produced rental income. However, relying on *Munro*, the Taxation Board of Review held that interest on a loan relates directly, and only, to the purpose for which the principal is put. The Board found that, in this case, the balance of the principal was applied towards purchasing the new family residence and the interest payable on this part of the funds should therefore not be deductible. The crux of the Board's reasoning is explained in the following passage (at 49):

> But it is only part of the truth to say that the purpose of the borrowing was to enable the taxpayer to retain ownership of A with a view to leasing it. The rest of the truth is that the borrowing also enabled him to acquire ownership of B with a view to occupying it as a family residence. He might have achieved one or other of those purposes without borrowing. For instance, he could, without borrowing, have vacated A and leased it and himself have become a tenant of another dwelling in which event the rent he paid would surely not be deductible from rent received; or he could have sold A and used the proceeds to buy B for his own occupation, in which event he would not be liable for any interest. But without borrowing he could not both retain ownership of A for letting and acquire B for his residence. Then is the taxpayer on the facts as they actually are entitled to a deduction of a further part of the interest ascertained on some basis of apportionment as being 'the extent to which' interest was 'incurred in gaining or producing' rents from A? We think the answer must be No. Suppose he had decided that he would continue to live in A but would buy B for letting to tenants, and to finance the purchase of B he had to mortgage either or both A and B. In that situation, the converse of what in fact happened, we think that interest paid on the borrowed money could not be apportioned so as to disallow any part of it—the whole of the interest would qualify for deduction. So here, where money borrowed was applied in paying for B used as his private home, no part of the interest paid thereon is deductible.

Munro's Case is often contrasted with *Begg v FC of T* (1937) 4 ATD 257, which concerned the deductibility of interest payments made by the executor of a large deceased estate that was being administered during the Great Depression. The executor was unable to sell the assets of the estate at reasonable prices in order to discharge the estate duties and other debts of the estate and he, therefore, decided to borrow money, secured over the income-producing assets of the estate, for this purpose. The South Australian Supreme Court found that the interest payments on the borrowings enabled the estate to retain income-producing assets that would otherwise have been sold at depression prices and, on this basis, it allowed deductions for the interest expenditure. Read ACJ distinguished *Munro* and held that it 'does not establish that interest which is paid on a loan raised on property which is already rent producing is not, under any circumstances, properly the subject of a deduction'.

According to his Honour, *Munro* turned on the basis that the moneys which the taxpayer had borrowed on the security of the property had nothing to do with the production of the assessable income. In contrast, in *Begg*, his Honour found that there was a 'real and substantial relation' between the interest paid on the borrowings and the production of the income of the estate, as it allowed the estate to be kept 'intact' and enabled the estate to continue to produce income.

With respect to his Honour, the reasoning in *Begg* is strained and the connection between the borrowings and income production is quite tenuous. The decision in *Begg* is certainly difficult to reconcile with *Munro* and the many cases that have subsequently followed *Munro*. In any event, the decision in *Begg* must now be considered to be highly questionable in the light of the Federal Court decision in *Hayden v FC of T* 96 ATC 4797.

Hayden concerned the deductibility of interest paid by the trustee of a deceased estate on borrowings used to fund a testator's family maintenance payment. As in *Begg*, the borrowings enabled the estate to retain income-producing assets. Spender J, however, declined to follow *Begg* and instead, relying on *Munro*, focused on the use of the borrowed funds to characterise the outgoing. Spender J found that the funds were used to discharge an obligation of the estate and he, therefore, held that no deduction should be allowed for the interest expenditure. According to his Honour, the case was no different from a case where an individual, in order to discharge an obligation such as school fees, borrows money on which interest is paid rather than sell income-producing assets and, from the proceeds, discharge the obligation. The payment of the school fees requires funds that might otherwise produce income. However, this does not make the interest incurred on the funds used to pay the school fees deductible.

Spender J's analogy represents a pragmatic and commonsense approach to dealing with the deductibility of interest. In essence, what his Honour was saying was that, for interest incurred on borrowings to be deductible, there must be a direct nexus between the use of the borrowings and the income-producing activities (rather than some tenuous link such as that which existed in *Begg*).

Refinancing principle

The 'use test' established in *Munro* was applied in *FC of T v Roberts & Smith* 92 ATC 4380. This case involved a law firm that had decided to reduce its partnership's capital account by an amount of $125,000. As the partnership did not have sufficient cash in the bank to pay this amount to the partners, it borrowed the amount from the bank. One of the partners in the firm, Mr Smith, received $25,000 as a result of the transaction and he applied this amount for his own private purposes. The issue before the Court was whether the interest payable to the bank on the loan was deductible. The Full Federal Court followed *Munro* and held that the character of interest is generally ascertained by reference to the objective use to which the borrowed funds are applied. Hill J, however, expressly indicated that a rigid tracing of funds is not always necessary to characterise interest. His Honour stated (at 4388–4389):

> let it be assumed that there are undrawn partnership distributions available at any time to be called upon by the partners. The partnership borrows from a bank at interest to fund the repayment to one of the partners who has called up the amount owing to him. That partner uses the moneys so received to purchase a house. A tracing approach, if carried beyond the payment of the partner, encourages the argument raised by the Commissioner in the present case that the funds were used for the private purpose of the partner who received them. But that fact will not preclude the deductibility of the outgoing. The funds to be withdrawn in such a case were employed in the partnership business; the borrowing replaces those funds and the interest incurred on the borrowing will meet the statutory description of interest incurred in the gaining or production by the partnership of assessable income.

His Honour then continued by drawing an analogy with the refinancing of a bank loan, stating (at 4389):

> In principle, such a case is no different from the borrowing from one bank to repay working capital originally borrowed from another; the character of the refinancing takes on the same character as the original borrowing and gives to the interest incurred the character of a working expense. Both these cases would equally satisfy the second limb of s 51(1). In no sense could the interest outgoing in either case be characterised as private or domestic. Similarly, where moneys are originally advanced by a partner to provide working capital for the partnership, interest on a borrowing made to repay these advances will be deductible, irrespective of the use which the partner repaid makes of the funds.

In the course of his judgment, Hill J noted that the Tribunal that had heard the case at first instance did not make any findings as to the composition of the 'capital account' (eg the extent to which the account represented capital invested by the partners). According to his Honour, the character of the interest payments could not be determined without such findings, and the case was therefore referred back to the Tribunal to determine the issue concerning the composition of the account. However, before making this order, Hill J noted (at 4390):

> If at least $125,000 of the amount in that account represents partnership capital . . ., undrawn profit distributions, advances by the partners or other funds which have actually been invested in the partnership and which the partners were entitled to withdraw . . ., then in my view the taxpayer is entitled to succeed. If, on the other hand, only a nominal amount in the capital account is so made up, then Mr Smith at least must fail. In between, a question may arise as to apportionment.

The decision in *Roberts & Smith* is supported by the earlier decision of *Yeung & Anor v FC of T* 88 ATC 4193. In *Yeung*, the Federal Court was concerned with the question as to whether interest on borrowings used to allow a family partnership to repay money previously advanced to the partnership on capital account by the head of the family should be deductible under s 51(1) *ITAA36*. In the course of concluding that the deductions should be allowed, Davies J made the following observations (at 4204):

> In an income-earning enterprise, both income and equity capital may be invested in assets directed to the earning of income. In such an event, if equity capital is repaid and loan capital replaces it, interest payable on the loan capital will ordinarily be an allowable deduction from the income derived from the assets. This is because the assets held represent the equity and the loan capital and, if the assets are directed to the earning of income, then both the loan capital and the equity capital which they represent are devoted to the earning of assessable income.

A few years after the *Roberts & Smith* decision was handed down, the ATO issued TR 95/25. The ruling states that interest on borrowings incurred by a partnership to fund the repayment of money originally advanced by a partner and used as partnership capital may be deductible to the extent that the partnership capital was employed in a business of the partnership carried on for the purpose of gaining assessable income. The ruling also indicates that the refinancing principle applies to companies in a similar way that it does to partnerships. In other words, interest may be deductible to a company on borrowings used to fund a repayment of share capital to shareholders where the capital was employed by the company for the purpose of deriving assessable income. The ruling, however, expressly states that the refinancing principle would not apply to joint owners of an investment property as they cannot withdraw capital and have no right to repayment of capital invested.

Interest is ordinarily a revenue outgoing

A number of cases have come before the courts concerning the issue as to whether interest expenditure is of a revenue or capital nature. A good starting point for discussing this issue is *Travelodge Papua New Guinea Ltd v Chief Collector of Taxes* 85 ATC 4432. *Travelodge* concerned interest payments made on loans used by a taxpayer to finance the construction of a hotel in Papua New Guinea. The interest was incurred over the four-year period that the hotel was being constructed. During this time, the taxpayer had not yet begun to produce any income from the hotel. The Collector of Taxes denied the taxpayer deductions for the interest on the basis that it was of a capital nature since it was incurred for the purpose of establishing a business structure. The Collector argued that this conclusion was supported by the fact that the taxpayer had capitalised the interest payments in its accounts. The National Court of Papua New Guinea, however, held that the interest payments were of a revenue nature and were therefore deductible. Bredmeyer J found that the interest was paid for the use of the money to build the hotel which, when completed, would generate assessable income. His Honour also concluded that the way in which outgoings are treated in the taxpayer's accounts is not necessarily determinative of their character.

Travelodge may be contrasted with *Wharf Properties Ltd v CIR (Hong Kong)* 97 ATC 4225, which concerned a property development company that had bought a tramway depot in Hong Kong as a development site in 1987. The site was only vacated by the tramway company in 1989. The Privy Council found that the interest payments made by the taxpayer over this two-year period on the moneys borrowed to purchase the property were of a capital nature. Their Lordships expressly rejected the contention that interest is always a revenue outgoing and held that 'the purpose of the loan during the period for which the interest payment was made is critical to whether it counts as a capital or revenue expense'. In this regard, their Lordships concluded (at 4228):

> In the present case, during the whole of the two years in question, the loan was clearly being applied for the purpose of acquiring and creating a capital asset rather than holding it as an income-producing investment. It follows that the interest was being expended for a capital purpose.

The reasoning in *Wharf Properties* has been soundly rejected in Australia in the landmark High Court decision in *Steele v DFC of T* 99 ATC 4242. The taxpayer in this case had acquired land in 1980 with the intention of building a motel on it. Although the taxpayer had plans drawn up and made council applications to construct the motel, the development never proceeded and the property was eventually sold in 1987. Over the period that she owned the land, the taxpayer incurred various holding costs including interest on the loan used to finance the purchase of the land. She also derived a small amount of income from the agistment of horses on the land. The issue before the Court was whether the taxpayer should be allowed a deduction for so much of her holding costs as exceeded her agistment income. This depended on a number of factors including whether the interest was of a revenue or capital nature.

A majority of the Court expressed the view that interest is ordinarily a revenue expense. Gleeson CJ, Gaudron and Gummow JJ stated (at 4248):

> As was explained in *Australian National Hotels Ltd v FC of T* ((1988) 19 FCR 234 at 239–241; 88 ATC 4627 at 4632–4633 per Bowen CJ and Burchett J), interest is ordinarily a recurrent or periodic payment which secures, not an enduring advantage, but, rather, the use of borrowed money during the term of the loan. According to the criteria noted by Dixon J in *Sun Newspapers Ltd and Associated Newspapers Ltd v FC of T* (1938) 61 CLR 337 at 359–363; 5 ATD 87 at 93–96 it is therefore ordinarily a revenue item. This is not to deny the possibility that there may be particular circumstances where it is proper to regard the purpose of interest payments as something other than the raising or maintenance of the borrowing and thus, potentially, of a capital nature.

Importantly, their Honours indicated (at 4248–4249) that the fact that a loan has been used to acquire a capital asset that has not yet begun to produce income does not mean that the interest payable on the borrowings should necessarily be treated as being of a capital nature:

> where interest is a recurrent payment to secure the use for a limited term of loan funds, then it is proper to regard the interest as a revenue item, and its character is not altered by reason of the fact that the borrowed funds are used to purchase a capital asset. The fact that the asset has not yet become, and may never become, income-producing may be relevant to a decision as to whether the case falls within the first limb of s 51(1). However, once it is determined, or accepted by hypothesis, that the interest is, during the relevant year, an outgoing incurred in gaining or producing the taxpayer's assessable income, (even though no assessable income

> is derived during that year, and no such income may ever be derived), the circumstance that the capital asset has produced no income is not a reason to conclude that the interest is an outgoing of a capital nature.

Their Honours went on to conclude (at 4249) that the decision in *Travelodge* was in accordance with Australian law, but the decision in *Wharf Properties* was not, as it 'turned upon legislation which may well have been regarded as materially different from the Australian legislation'. On this basis, the High Court reversed the earlier decision of the Full Federal Court (97 ATC 4239) in which a majority of judges had held that the interest payable by the taxpayer was capital in nature based on *Wharf Properties*. According to Gleeson CJ, Gaudron and Gummow JJ, the fact that the capital asset had not become, and may never become, income producing may be relevant, for the purposes of the positive limbs of s 51(1) *ITAA36*, in determining whether the expense was incurred in the course of gaining or producing assessable income. However, the fact that it produced no assessable income was not a reason to conclude that it was capital in nature.

Steele demonstrates that interest outgoings are not precluded from being deductible merely because they do not generate income in the year in which those outgoings are incurred. To be deductible, however, there must still be a sufficient connection between the incurring of the outgoings and the expectation that income will be produced at some time in the future (even though such income may never actually arise). This is a factual nexus requirement and is something that the High Court majority decided had to be remitted to the Tribunal to determine. According to Gleeson CJ, Gaudron and Gummow JJ (at 4251):

> The temporal relationship between the incurring of an outgoing and the actual or projected receipt of income may be one of a number of facts relevant to a judgment as to whether the necessary connection might, in a given case, exist, but contemporaneity is not legally essential, and whether it is factually important may depend upon the circumstances of the particular case.

Shortly after *Steele*, the Full Federal Court delivered its judgment in *FC of T v Firth* 2002 ATC 4346. This case concerned a taxpayer that had taken out 'protected equity investment loans' to purchase shares. The loans specified that, in the event of default, the lender's recovery rights were limited to enforcement against the shares purchased with the borrowed funds. The Commissioner denied the taxpayer deductions for a portion of the interest paid on the loans, being the difference between the interest paid by the taxpayer and the higher amount of interest that he would have paid had he been subject to interest at a specified rate published by the Commissioner. According to the Commissioner, the excess interest was a 'capital protection fee' as it was referable to the 'limited recourse' terms of the loans.

The Full Federal Court, however, held that it was not appropriate to apportion the interest because there was nothing to suggest that any part of it was attributable to any particular terms within the agreements. The limited recourse terms of the loans were integral parts of the loans and not severable from the other terms. On this basis, the entire interest was treated as being revenue in nature and therefore deductible under s 8-1 *ITAA97*. The case demonstrates that just because a loan may contain terms that limit a lender's right of recovery against the assets acquired with the borrowed funds, this does not necessarily make part of the interest capital in nature. To address the outcome in this case, the Government introduced div 247 *ITAA97* which deals with capital protected borrowing arrangements [29.7].

Special circumstances in which interest may be a capital outgoing

Although *Steele* indicates that the Australian courts generally treat interest as a revenue outgoing, the case does not rule out the possibility of interest being capital in nature in special circumstances.

For instance, in *Macquarie Finance Ltd v FC of T* 2005 ATC 4829 and *St George Bank Ltd v FC of T* 2009 ATC ¶20-103, the courts treated certain interest payments as capital outgoings. Both these cases concerned complicated financing arrangements involving banks that sought to satisfy the Reserve Bank of Australia's 'capital adequacy' regulatory requirements. These requirements had to be met in order for banks to maintain their banking licences. In essence, they required the banks to maintain a minimum ratio of capital to risk-weighted assets.

The *St George Case* concerned a bank that had acquired all the ordinary issued shares in another bank as part of a merger. Due to the outflow of cash required to pay for the shares, it was necessary for the taxpayer to raise further capital in order to satisfy the Reserve Bank's capital adequacy requirements. For this purpose, a Delaware limited liability company (LLC) was established. The taxpayer's two wholly owned Australian subsidiaries subscribed US$107m for the stock in LLC. LLC also issued US$250m preference stock in the United States upon which it was required to pay preferential dividends. LLC then loaned US$350m to the taxpayer in return for a debenture which required the taxpayer to pay interest to LLC. LLC applied the interest it received from the taxpayer to pay dividends to its security holders.

The issue in the case was whether the interest paid by the taxpayer was deductible under s 8-1 *ITAA97*. Both the Federal Court (at first instance) and the Full Federal Court (on appeal) applied the business entity test in *Sun Newspapers Ltd v FC of T* (1938) 61 CLR 337 to conclude that the interest payments were of a capital nature and were, therefore, not deductible.

The Full Federal Court held that 'the predominant purpose' underpinning the interest payments was the securing of a 'structural advantage' flowing to the taxpayer. Perram J, who delivered the leading judgment in the case, found that the interest was an essential element in an overall transaction that had the purpose of achieving the structural advantage of raising capital for the taxpayer to comply with the Reserve Bank's capital adequacy requirements. Compliance with these requirements was necessary to maintain the taxpayer's banking licence and had the immediate effect of improving the taxpayer's ability to withstand losses. It went to the 'heart' of the taxpayer's business as a bank, namely its continued ability to maintain the confidence of its depositors. It also had the effect of allowing the taxpayer to expand its operations where it would otherwise be prohibited from incurring further debts to make loans. These benefits were 'of a lasting character' for the taxpayer.

[12.13] Legal expenses

The principal issue that arises under the general deduction provision in relation to legal expenses is whether such expenses are revenue or capital in nature. For instance, this issue arose in *Hallstroms Pty Ltd v FC of T* (1946) 72 CLR 634, where the taxpayer, a refrigerator manufacturer, incurred legal expenses in opposing a rival manufacturer's application to extend its patent of a refrigerator. The taxpayer was planning to produce refrigerators based on this patent when it expired. A majority of the High Court (Latham CJ, Starke and Williams JJ) held that the legal expenses were of a revenue nature. The majority reached this conclusion on the basis that the legal expenses had not been incurred to acquire any asset since the taxpayer had the same rights as everyone else to manufacture refrigerators based on its rival's patent once it expired. Latham CJ stated (at 641–642):

> A right enjoyed in common with all persons is not a capital asset of any single person . . . [The taxpayer] did not acquire any asset or any right of any character when the petition of [its rival] was dismissed. It simply maintained its position as it already existed.
>
> Nor can it be said that the company, by making the expenditure, gained 'an enduring advantage'. It gained nothing—it merely succeeded in maintaining an existing position . . . In the present case the expenditure . . . was not incurred in relation to anything which can be called a capital asset—either to acquire it or even to protect it—but in order to maintain a common right.

It is clear from the above passage that the majority relied on the enduring benefit test for concluding that the expenditure was of a revenue nature. The minority (Dixon and McTiernan JJ), on the other hand, focused on the business entity test for concluding that the expenditure was of a capital nature. The minority found that the purpose of the legal expenses was to enable the taxpayer to carry into effect its plans for reorganising its business and producing a new refrigerator. As Dixon J stated (at 648):

> This appears to me to go to the character and organization of the profit-earning business and not to be an incident in the operations by which it is carried on.

Importantly, the fact that the expenditure did not result in any new asset being acquired by the taxpayer did not prevent the minority from holding that the expenditure was of a capital nature.

The business entity test, which was relied on by the minority in *Hallstroms*, has been applied in a number of subsequent cases dealing with the deductibility of legal expenses. For instance, in *Broken Hill Theatres Pty Ltd v FC of T* (1952) 85 CLR 423, a taxpayer that operated a theatre in Broken Hill was denied deductions for legal expenses it incurred in successfully opposing a rival's application for a theatre licence. The High Court relied on the business entity test to conclude that the advantage of being free from competition was capital in nature. According to the Court, the expenditure in this case was incurred 'for the purpose of preserving and protecting the company's business'. The fact that the legal expenses did not bring into existence any new asset for the taxpayer did not prevent the expenditure from being treated as capital.

Broken Hill Theatres was followed in *Sunraysia Broadcasters Pty Ltd v FC of T* 91 ATC 4530, where the Federal Court denied a taxpayer that operated an AM radio station in Mildura deductions for expenses incurred in applying for a supplementary FM radio licence. The taxpayer had enjoyed an effective monopoly in Mildura and applied for the FM licence because it feared that if a rival acquired such a licence, its form of horizontal programming involving local content would be under threat. Davies J concluded that the expenditure was capital in nature as it was designed to protect the taxpayer's business enterprise which was at risk.

A similar outcome was reached in *John Fairfax & Sons Ltd v FC of T* (1959) 101 CLR 30. This case involved a taxpayer that was attempting to take over a target company. An agreement had been reached under which a large number of shares in the target company were allotted to the taxpayer. In the meantime, a shareholder in the target company instituted court proceedings to declare the allotment void. The High Court relied on the business entity test to conclude that the legal expenses incurred by the taxpayer in opposing the proceedings were of a capital nature. According to Dixon CJ (at 36), the litigation was 'exclusively concerned with the organization and structure of the profit-earning enterprise'. A similar view was reached by Fullagar J, who held (at 41) that the legal expenses were incurred 'in the establishment, enlargement or alteration of the profit-making machine'.

Legal expenses were also held to be capital in nature in *PBL Marketing Pty Ltd v FC of T* 85 ATC 4416. The taxpayer in this case had an agreement with the Australian Cricket Board that gave it the exclusive right to organise the televising, merchandising and sponsorship of 'World Series Cricket' matches. A rival broadcaster had challenged the taxpayer's rights under the agreement in court proceedings. The NSW Supreme Court denied the taxpayer deductions for the legal expenses it incurred in opposing the proceedings. Yeldham J referred to the business entity test and stated (at 4422–4423):

> the character of the advantage sought from the expenditure of the legal costs in question, and the manner in which that advantage was to be used, demonstrate that the expenditure for which deduction is sought was an outgoing of a capital nature. The whole business

> of the [taxpayer] . . . depended entirely upon the existence of the agreement . . . and the exclusive rights which it gave to the [taxpayer] . . . That agreement is one without which . . . the [taxpayer] would not have any business. Thus the expenditure incurred in seeking to maintain or defend it is, in my view, an expenditure of a capital nature.

The *PBL Marketing Case* may be contrasted with *FC of T v Consolidated Fertilizers Ltd* 91 ATC 4677. In this latter case, the taxpayer, a fertiliser and pesticide manufacturer, had entered into an agreement with a United States company to acquire a licence to use certain technology. The taxpayer subsequently discovered that a scientist had commenced legal action against the United States company in relation to various patents that were relevant to this technology. The taxpayer incurred legal expenses to support the United States company in these proceedings and to seek an injunction to prevent the scientist from revealing information relating to the technology that had been licensed to the taxpayer. A majority of the Full Federal Court held that the taxpayer's legal expenses were of a revenue nature. The majority found that the expenditure had not been incurred to acquire an asset or enlarge its business as the taxpayer already possessed the 'profit-yielding subject' (ie the right to use the technology). Spender and Lee J stated (at 4688):

> a distinction must be made between expenditure incurred for the purpose of preserving and protecting a business as such, being expenditure for a particular purpose on an isolated occasion, and expenditure which the nature of business may require as part of the prudent management thereof.

In *FC of T v Chapman* 89 ATC 4246, the Federal Court allowed a trustee deductions for legal expenses and other costs incurred in opposing objections to the renewal of a planning consent to operate a quarry (the permit was renewable every five years). Pincus J held (at 4249) that the expenses were deductible on the following basis:

> the expenses are fairly comparable with those incurred by a business or professional man who has to pay a fee each year (or, for that matter, each five years) to renew a licence or certificate entitling him to carry on his business or practice. It could hardly be disputed that such a fee would be on revenue account. If, in a particular year, the applicant for renewal met opposition and found it necessary to engage lawyers to overcome it, in my view the same result would follow.

The deductibility of legal expenses was also considered by the High Court in *FC of T v Day* 2008 ATC ¶20-064. The focus of this case was not on the revenue/capital distinction, but on the nexus requirement under the positive limbs [12.3]. The issue was whether a customs officer was entitled to deductions for legal expenses incurred in defending himself against certain charges brought against him under the *Public Service Act 1922* (Cth). The Commissioner had denied the taxpayer deductions for these costs on the basis that the expenditure was incurred in defending conduct outside the performance of his duties and could not therefore be said to have been incurred 'in the course of' gaining or producing assessable income.

The Court referred to *Ronpibon Tin NL v FC of T* (1949) 78 CLR 47 [12.2] and held that in deciding whether the taxpayer should be allowed deductions, it was necessary to determine: 'is the occasion of the outgoing found in whatever is productive of actual or expected income?' A majority of the Court (Gummow, Hayne, Heydon and Kiefel JJ) held that a narrow approach should not be taken to answering this question. The majority held that the incurring of legal expenses with respect to charges against an officer for failure of duty 'must be considered in the context of the special position which such an officer holds, the extent of the duty owed by the officer and the legislative provision for the enforcement and regulation of such duty'. Their Honours concluded that the taxpayer's duties as an officer of the public service, and the possible consequences to him of internal disciplinary proceedings and action with respect to the continuation or termination of his service, formed part of what was 'productive of his assessable income'. The occasion of the legal expenses was found in his position as an officer and it followed that the expenditure was therefore deductible.

[12.14] Trade-tie expenses

The distinction between revenue and capital outgoings has been closely examined in certain cases dealing with trade-tie arrangements. The leading case is *BP Australia Ltd v FC of T* (1965) 112 CLR 386, which concerned a company that supplied petrol to service stations. The owners of the service stations had been selling competing brands of petrol from different pumps located on their sites. The pumps were owned by the respective suppliers and leased to the retailers at a nominal fee. In 1951, a rival supplier (Shell) introduced a 'solo site' plan under which it supplied petrol to service stations that dealt exclusively with it. Before the introduction of this plan, the taxpayer had pumps at around 4,000 sites. However, by the end of 1951, over 1,000 retailers had requested the taxpayer to remove its pumps from their sites. To stem further losses, the taxpayer, in cooperation with three other companies, entered into exclusive trade-tie arrangements with various retailers to sell their products for fixed periods that ranged from 3 to 15 years. The retailers were paid lump sum amounts to induce them to enter into the arrangements based on the estimated number of gallons of petrol they were expected to purchase. By 30 June 1952, the taxpayer had trade ties at 791 sites. The taxpayer claimed deductions under s 51(1) *ITAA36* for the amounts paid to the retailers. However, the Commissioner denied the deductions on the basis that they were capital in nature, arguing that they were made once and for all and produced an enduring benefit for the taxpayer's profit-making structure.

The Privy Council held that the payments were of a revenue nature. In arriving at this conclusion, the Privy Council analysed the three matters listed by Dixon J in *Sun Newspapers Ltd v FC of T* (1938) 61 CLR 337 (at 363) [12.4].

The Privy Council considered that the first matter, 'the character of the advantage sought', pointed to the payments being of a revenue nature. This was because the need or occasion for the payments was the sudden change in marketing in the petrol trade; the payments came out of the taxpayer's circulating capital and had to 'come back penny by penny with every order during the period' in order to reimburse the outlay; and the payments were of a recurrent nature made to meet a continuous demand in the trade.

The Privy Council also considered that the second matter, 'the manner in which the advantage is to be used, relied upon or enjoyed', pointed to the payments being of a revenue nature as the benefit was to be used in 'the continuous and recurrent struggle to get orders and sell petrol'. The agreements therefore became part of the ordinary process of selling.

While the Privy Council concluded that the third matter, 'the means adopted to obtain the advantage', did not clearly point to the payments being either revenue or capital, it is worth noting what their Lordships said about the length of the arrangements (at 399–400):

> Length of time, though theoretically not a deciding factor, does in practice shed a light on the nature of the advantage sought. The longer the duration of the agreements, the greater the indication that a structural solution was being sought. In this case the periods varied between three and fifteen years, but the average appears to be something just under five years and the predominant number of agreements was for a five-year period . . . That length of time appears to be neutral, and in itself indicates neither capital expenditure nor revenue by its mere length.

BP Australia was followed by the Full Federal Court in *National Australia Bank Ltd v FC of T* 97 ATC 5153. In this case, a bank entered into an agreement to secure the exclusive right to act as the lender under a Commonwealth defence force housing loan assistance scheme for a period of 15 years. Under the scheme, defence force members were entitled to receive a Commonwealth subsidy on interest paid on their home loans. The agreement required the taxpayer to pay the Commonwealth an upfront lump sum amount or $42m plus an annual formula-based amount for each year that a prescribed number of loans had been exceeded. The taxpayer claimed a deduction under s 51(1) *ITAA36* for the lump sum payment. However, the Commissioner denied the deduction on the ground that it was capital in nature based on *Sun Newspapers* and *Broken Hill Theatres Pty Ltd v FC of T* (1952) 85 CLR 423 [12.13]. According to the Commissioner, the payment excluded or limited competition and secured a monopoly over a specific class of business, thereby creating an enduring advantage for the taxpayer.

The Full Federal Court rejected the Commissioner's argument and held that the lump sum payment was of a revenue nature. The Court characterised the expenditure as a marketing expense which was not unlike a loan referral commission. It found that the payment did not confer on the taxpayer a monopoly over loans to defence force personnel or the acquisition of goodwill or anything of that nature. The payment did not enlarge the framework within which the taxpayer carried on its ordinary activities of borrowing and lending money. Rather, it was incurred as part of the process by which the bank operated 'to obtain regular returns by means of regular outlay' and was made in the expectation that it would be recouped out of profits made from loans and other products sold to defence force personnel. It was therefore not unlike the payments made in *BP Australia*, which were also on revenue account.

The above cases may be contrasted with the recent case of *FC of T v Healius Ltd 2020* ATC ¶20-766. The taxpayer was the head company of a corporate group. A subsidiary member of the group, Idameneo, owned and operated a chain of medical centres and provided premises, equipment and administrative services to doctors who, in turn, provided health care services to the public through the centres. Over a five-year period, Idameneo opened 18 new medical centres and entered into agreements with 505 doctors to join its centres. Idameneo paid the doctors lump sums in return for them agreeing to render their services exclusively from the centres for specified periods (usually five years) and entering into restrictive covenants preventing them from providing medical services from other locations (usually eight years). Under the agreements, Idameneo earned a percentage (usually 50%) of the fees rendered by the doctors and was responsible for collecting and banking fees and promoting the centres.

The Full Federal Court held that the lump sum payments made to the doctors were not deductible under s 8-1 *ITAA97* as they were of a capital nature. The Court rejected the taxpayer's argument that the payments were made to simply secure the doctors as Idameneo's customers. Rather, it held that the payments were made for the doctors to cease operating their existing practices, commence trading as part of the centres adopting Idameneo's mode of practice, and accept a restraint on establishing medical practices that would compete with the centres. The Court held that while the lump sums were not paid to acquire the goodwill of the existing practices, they secured arrangements that formed part of the profit-making structure of Idameneo's business. The arrangements enabled Idameneo to earn ongoing revenues and were the means by which it profited from the adoption of a mode of practice adopted by the doctors at its centres that formed an essential part of its business structure. The lump sums were paid to put in place that structure and they thereby created and protected the goodwill in the centres.

Jagot, Moshinsky and Colvin JJ distinguished *BP Australia*. They pointed out that whereas the service station owners could determine how they sold petrol, the doctors had detailed commitments regarding how they would conduct their practices. Furthermore, the prices charged by the service station owners for petrol was up to them—they did not need to adopt a particular method of charging or pay over a percentage of their revenues. Finally, unlike in *BP Australia*, Idameneo took on the responsibility for marketing the centres and attracting patients.

Their Honours also distinguished *National Australia Bank*. They pointed out that the lump sum payment in that case did not secure anything that might be added to the framework of the bank's business necessary to lend money to customers and was part of its trading activities. By contrast, it was not enough for Idameneo to build the centres and offer services, it also needed to secure arrangements with the doctors under which they would commit to its model. Without these commitments, it had no business.

[12.15] QUESTIONS

1. What are the 'positive' and 'negative' limbs of s 8-1 *ITAA97*? What is the difference between a 'loss' and an 'outgoing'? What is the effect of the words 'to the extent that' in s 8-1? What tests have the courts used to ascertain whether or not there is a sufficient nexus between a loss or outgoing and the positive limbs of s 8-1?
2. '*Amalgamated Zinc (De Bavay's) Ltd v FC of T* (1935) 54 CLR 29 is authority for the proposition that an outgoing incurred after the cessation of a business is not deductible.' Is this statement correct in light of: *AGC (Advances) Ltd v FC of T* 75 ATC 4057; *Placer Pacific Management Pty Ltd v FC of T* 95 ATC 4459; *FC of T v Brown* 99 ATC 4600; and *FC of T v Jones* 2002 ATC 4135?
3. Discuss the various tests developed by the courts for distinguishing between revenue and capital losses and outgoings.
4. In *Sun Newspapers Ltd v FC of T* (1938) 61 CLR 337, Dixon J indicated that there were three matters to take into account in distinguishing between revenue and capital expenditure. What are these matters and how have subsequent courts dealt with them?
5. What does the decision in *Coles Myer Finance Ltd v FC of T* 93 ATC 4214 establish about determining when a taxpayer is entitled to a deduction for a loss or outgoing? In that case, were the discounts on the bank bills and promissory notes deductible entirely in the income year in which they were issued? On what basis was *Coles Myer Finance Ltd* distinguished in *FC of T v Woolcombers (WA) Pty Ltd* 93 ATC 5170?
6. Is it possible to reconcile the decisions in *FC of T v Edwards* 94 ATC 4255 and *FC of T v Cooper* 91 ATC 4396?
7. Discuss the principle derived in *FC of T v Maddalena* 71 ATC 4161 and how it has been applied in subsequent cases.
8. Steve is a professional water polo player. He engages Jamie, who is a sports agent, to negotiate a three-year playing contract with a water polo club. In return, Jamie is entitled to a commission of 1% of all salary, sponsorships and endorsements that Steve receives. Can Steve deduct the commission paid to Jamie? Would your answer differ if Steve simply paid a lump sum of $10,000 for Jamie's services?
9. Yuri borrowed $100,000 from a bank at a commercial interest rate of 10% pa. He immediately lent the borrowed funds to the trustee of his family trust at an interest rate of 1% pa. The trustee used the funds to renovate a holiday home owned by the trust and used by Yuri's family. Is Yuri entitled to any deductions for his interest expenditure?
10. Fletch borrowed $500,000 from a bank at a commercial interest rate of 10% per annum to purchase a 'negatively geared' residential investment property. Immediately after acquiring the property, he engaged a real estate agent to advertise the property but was unable to secure a tenant for several months. Fletch's interest expenditure for the current year is expected to be three times the amount of the rent he will receive from the tenant. Is Fletch entitled to any deductions for his interest expenditure?

11. Brian is a self-employed builder who specialises in renovating residential properties. During the week, he travels from home to various building sites where he works. Sometimes he works at more than one site during a particular day. He usually carries his tools and some building products in the back of his truck. On weekends, he often goes to the homes of potential clients to quote for jobs. Only a small percentage of his quotes are accepted by clients as he charges quite a high fee for his services. Brian also wants to become an architect in the future and is enrolled in a part-time architecture course at university. He is required to pay fees for his course and he also purchases various textbooks and drawing materials for the course. What deductions can Brian claim?
12. Tony borrowed $1m from a bank at an interest rate of 10% per annum to purchase a large parcel of vacant land near a proposed airport site. He planned to operate a motel business on the site. Shortly after purchasing the land he engaged an architect to draw up plans for the construction of a motel. He approached his bank to raise additional finance of $10m to build the motel. However, given the size of the loan requested and his other financial obligations, the bank rejected his application. Tony then approached other banks but was unsuccessful in raising the funds required. Eventually, after five years, Tony decided to abandon his plans and he sold the land. Discuss whether any expenditure is deductible.
13. Tom is a bank clerk married to Betty, a history lecturer at an Australian university who specialises in ancient Egyptian history. In July 2018, Tom resigned from his job and started a new delicatessen business. He borrowed $700,000 from a bank at an interest rate of 10% pa. The loan was repayable over 10 years. He used $600,000 of the borrowings to purchase the goodwill and equipment of his new business. Tom lent the remaining $100,000 to his wife at an interest rate of 2% pa. Betty used $70,000 to renovate her holiday home and the balance $30,000 to undertake a comprehensive field study of the pyramids at Giza and a two-week intensive refresher course on Egyptian Pharaohs at the Cairo Museum. She plans to use the information gained from her overseas trip to write a textbook on the pyramids, which she hopes will be published commercially and prescribed as a textbook at various universities. If this is the case, it is very likely she will be promoted. Betty has kept a travel diary and all receipts relating to her expenditure. In the meantime, Tom's delicatessen business was unsuccessful, and after much deliberation, he sold it in January 2023 at a substantial loss. As the sale proceeds were insufficient to discharge his loan, he continued to pay interest on the borrowings. What deductions can Tom and Betty claim?
14. J Co is the trustee of Mr and Mrs Moore's family trust. J Co borrowed $1m at an interest rate of 10% per annum from a bank to purchase a residential property. J Co leased the property to Mr and Mrs Moore, who pay rent at commercial rates and use the property as their home. Last year, the interest payable by J Co was double the rent received from Mr and Mrs Moore. Is J Co entitled to any deductions? Would your answer differ if, instead of leasing the property to Mr and Mrs Moore, J Co leased the property to their daughter, Madge, at 50% of the commercial rent?
15. Sandra is an accountant employed by a chartered accounting firm in the city. She is undertaking a postgraduate degree in media studies for which she pays course fees of $2,000. She is undertaking this course as she hopes to eventually become a financial journalist once she has gained enough practical experience at her accounting firm. Sandra's employer requires her to dress appropriately at work and she spent $2,200 on purchasing a designer work suit. Sandra also has a part-time job at a night club which starts soon after her accounting job finishes on Friday nights. The night club is far away from the city and she drives her car to work on Fridays so that she can get to her part-time job in time. On all other days of the week, Sandra takes

a train between home and work and spends $44 per week on tickets. What deductions can Sandra claim?

16. B Co owns and operates a group of 30 dental centres across Australia with over 100 dentists working in them running their own private practices. B Co provides dentists with the use of surgeries at its centres, dental equipment, secretarial and administrative services, and billing and debt collection services. In exchange, dentists who join the centres must pay 40% of their fees to B Co. Dentists who work at the centres are required to enter into agreements whereby they agree to work at the centres for a fixed period of 4 years and agree not to perform dental work anywhere else for that period as well as an additional 2 years after leaving the centres. In exchange they are paid an up-front lump sum joining payment of $250,000. Pam operated her own dental practice for many years and decided to join the centres on 1 July 2023. B Co paid Pam $250,000 and billed $880,000 to patients for her dental work during 2023/24. B Co retained 40% of the fees and remitted the remaining 60% to Pam. Are B Co and Pam entitled to any deductions?

13 SPECIFIC DEDUCTIONS

[13.1] Introduction

Tax law contains a myriad of specific deduction provisions for particular kinds of expenditure that might not otherwise be deductible under the general deduction provision in s 8-1 *ITAA97* discussed in Chapter 12. This chapter focuses on some common specific deduction provisions. A range of other specific deduction provisions are examined elsewhere in this book (eg Chapter 15 deals with specific deductions under the capital allowance regime and Chapter 19 deals with specific deductions for superannuation contributions). Like the general deduction provision, the specific deduction provisions operate subject to any provisions that deny or limit deductions. These provisions are discussed in Chapter 14.

[13.2] Tax-related expenses

Section 25-5(1) *ITAA97* allows taxpayers deductions for expenditure to the extent that it is incurred in managing their 'tax affairs'. As a result, taxpayers are generally entitled to deductions for the cost of having tax agents complete their returns, objecting to assessments, requesting rulings and complying with tax audits.

Section 25-5(1) also allows deductions for certain other tax-related expenditure, such as expenditure in complying with an obligation imposed by a Commonwealth law relating to the tax affairs of an entity (eg complying with a notice under s 353-10 *TAA* to furnish information [38.8]). Payment of the GIC is also specifically deductible [40.8].

Deductions are, however, expressly denied for payments of income tax and PAYG amounts. Fees for tax advice paid to persons who are not 'recognised tax advisers' are also not deductible (s 25-5(2)). A 'recognised tax adviser' is defined as a registered tax agent or BAS agent or a legal practitioner (s 995-1).

Deductions are also denied to the extent that a provision in the *ITAA36* or *ITAA97* (except s 8-1) expressly prevents or limits a deduction under s 8-1 (s 25-5(3)). For example, if a taxpayer incurs expenditure on lunch with a tax agent to discuss their tax affairs, such expenditure would not be deductible as it constitutes 'entertainment expenditure' which is not deductible under s 32-5 *ITAA97* [14.4].

In addition, deductions are not available for capital expenditure. However, for this purpose, an amount is not capital expenditure merely because the tax affairs concerned relate to matters of a capital nature (s 25-5(4)). This means, for example, that a taxpayer could claim a deduction for expenditure incurred in applying for a private ruling on whether the cost of a capital asset may be depreciated under div 40 *ITAA97* [15.2].

The issue of what constitutes capital expenditure arose in *Drummond v FC of T* 2005 ATC 4783. The taxpayer in this case had engaged a solicitor to set up a superannuation fund and provide advice on the tax consequences of making a $500,000 contribution to the fund. The solicitor charged the taxpayer $450 to set up the fund and $49,550 for purported advice which the taxpayer sought to deduct. The AAT found that the letter of advice provided by the solicitor to the taxpayer did not actually contain any tax advice and even if some of the consideration had been paid for tax advice, the taxpayer had not discharged the onus of establishing the proportion that was deductible under s 25-5. On appeal, the Federal Court refused to remit the matter to the AAT to undertake an apportionment because the AAT proceedings had been conducted by the taxpayer on the basis that no apportionment was necessary. The Court, nevertheless, indicated that insofar as a fee is charged for advice from a recognised tax adviser as to the operation of the Commonwealth tax laws in relation to such a structure, it would be deductible under s 25-5. However, insofar as any amount is paid to establish and implement the structure, it would not be deductible as it does not relate to managing the taxpayer's tax affairs and is capital in nature as an enduring advantage is secured by a once and for all payment.

Property used by taxpayers in managing their tax affairs is deemed to be used for income-producing purposes (s 25-5(5)). On this basis, taxpayers are able to claim deductions under div 40 *ITAA97* for the decline in value of equipment, such as a computer, to the extent that it is used for storing tax information [15.2].

> ***Example*** Trevor paid his tax agent $1,000 to complete his previous year's income tax return. He also paid his solicitor $2,000 to draft an objection to an assessment. Both these costs are deductible under s 25-5(1). Trevor also paid $50,000 in income tax. This amount is not deductible under s 25-5(2).

[13.3] Repairs

Section 25-10 *ITAA97* provides deductions for expenditure (other than capital expenditure) on 'repairs' to premises and depreciating assets held or used for the purpose of producing assessable income. Where the relevant property is held or used only partly for such purpose, a 'reasonable' deduction is allowed.

Nature of a repair

The nature of a 'repair' has been discussed extensively in several court cases. In essence, a 'repair' involves restoring an asset to its previous condition. The object of a repair is to make good the deterioration in an asset through 'wear and tear' without changing its essential character. This can involve 'renewal or replacement of subsidiary parts of a whole' but not 'reconstruction of the entirety' (*Lurcott v Wakely and Wheeler* [1911] 1 KB 905, 923 (Buckley LJ)). In restoring an asset, it is not necessarily essential that identical materials be used. It is, however, essential that the function of the asset does not change.

A repair should be distinguished from an 'improvement', which involves making an item functionally better than it originally was. Likewise, a repair should be distinguished from a 'replacement', which involves substituting an original item with a new item. Although these distinctions may seem obvious, it is not necessarily always clear whether an item is being repaired, improved or replaced. In *W Thomas & Co Pty Ltd v FC of T* (1965) 115 CLR 58, Kitto J stated (at 72):

> The words 'repair' and 'improvement' may for some purposes connote contrasting concepts; but obviously repairing a thing improves the condition it was in immediately before repair. It may sometimes be convenient for some purposes to contrast a 'repair' with a 'replacement' or a 'renewal'. But repairs to a whole are often made by the replacement of worn-out parts by new parts. Repair involves a restoration of a thing to a condition it formerly had without changing its character. But in the case of a thing considered from the point of view of its use as distinct from its appearance, it is restoration of efficiency in function rather than exact repetition of form or material that is significant. Whether or not work done upon a thing is aptly described as a repair of that thing is thus a question of fact and degree.

Maintenance costs as opposed to acquisition costs

In *W Thomas & Co*, the taxpayer was denied deductions for the cost of extensive renovations undertaken on a dilapidated building which it had recently acquired. The renovations were necessary to make the building suitable for the taxpayer's business as a flour miller and grain merchant. The High Court held that where expenditure is incurred on an asset which, because of its state of disrepair, is not immediately capable of being put to use for its intended income-producing purpose, then the expenditure incurred in rendering the asset suitable for such purpose is capital in nature. Kitto J explained (at 72):

> Expenditure upon repairs is properly attributed to revenue account when the repairs are for the maintenance of an income-producing capital asset. Maintenance involves the periodic repair of defects that are the result of normal wear and tear in operation. It is an expense of a revenue nature when it is to repair defects arising from the operations of the person who incurs it. But if when a thing is bought for use as a capital asset in the buyer's business it is not in good order and suitable for use in the way intended, the cost of putting it in order suitable for use is part of the cost of its acquisition, not a cost of its maintenance.

W Thomas & Co has parallels with the earlier Scottish case of *Law Shipping Co Ltd v IRC* (1924) 12 TC 621, which concerned a taxpayer that had purchased a ship for £97,000 and spent £51,558 on repairs to make it seaworthy. The Court of Session treated the bulk of the repair costs as being of a capital nature. Lord Cullen (at 628) referred to the expenditure as being, in substance, 'an addition to the price'.

Both *W Thomas & Co* and *Law Shipping Co* illustrate that as a general rule costs incurred in fixing defects in an item which existed at the time of acquisition are usually of a capital nature in much the same way as the costs of acquiring the asset are of a capital nature. The rationale for this is that the defects are not attributable to wear and tear arising from the taxpayer's use of the asset and are, therefore, really costs incurred in improving the asset beyond the condition in which the taxpayer originally acquired it.

A different outcome was, however, reached in *Odeon Theatres Ltd v Jones* [1972] 1 All ER 681. This case concerned a company that had purchased a cinema in England in 1945. Due to wartime restrictions, cinema owners were only able to spend small amounts on repairs. As a result, even though the cinema was functioning when acquired by the taxpayer, it was in a state of disrepair. Between 1945 and 1954 the taxpayer incurred expenditure on 'deferred repairs and renewals' to the cinema. The issue in the case was whether the taxpayer could claim deductions for expenditure that was referable to work restoring dilapidations that had occurred prior to the time it acquired the cinema. The United Kingdom Court of Appeal held that the expenditure was deductible. The Court found that the expenditure would have been revenue in nature had it been incurred by the previous owners if not for wartime restrictions, and it pointed out that, unlike in *Law Shipping Co*, the taxpayer was able to put the asset to immediate use and its purchase price was not affected by the fact that it was in a state of disrepair. With respect, it is difficult to reconcile this case with the earlier cases discussed above, and the ATO has indicated in TR 97/23 that it considers the decision not to be authority in Australia as it is inconsistent with the High Court decision in *W Thomas & Co*.

Replacement of part of an asset as opposed to the entire asset

A repair often involves the replacement of parts of an asset with new parts. Even the replacement of large portions of an asset can constitute a repair, as long as the original asset remains in existence and is not effectively replaced with a new asset. This is illustrated in *Rhodesia Railways Ltd v CIT Bechuanaland* [1933] AC 368, where the owner of a 588 mile-long railway line was allowed deductions for expenditure incurred in renewing some 74 miles of track with new sleepers, rails and fastenings. The Privy Council held that the expenditure was a non-capital repair, as the renewals merely restored the line to its original condition. Lord Macmillan stated (at 374):

> The periodical renewal by section of the rails and sleepers of a railway line as they wore out by use is in no sense a reconstruction of the whole railway and is an ordinary incident of railway administration . . . The expenditure here in question was incurred in consequence of the rails having been worn out in earning the income of previous years on which tax had been paid without deduction in respect of such wear, and represented the cost of restoring them to a state in which they could continue to earn income. It did not result in the creation of any new asset; it was incurred to maintain the [taxpayer's] existing line in a state to earn revenue.

Rhodesia Railways may be contrasted with *Lindsay v FC of T* (1961) 106 CLR 377, in which deductions were denied for costs incurred for repairs made to a slipway owned by a partnership of ship repairers. Due to the unavailability of certain materials, a substantial proportion of the original slipway was demolished and replaced with a slightly longer slipway constructed out of concrete instead of timber. The High Court held that the extensive works went beyond a repair and constituted the acquisition of a new capital asset.

Restoration of an item as opposed to making it functionally better

Where expenditure incurred in relation to an asset leads to functional improvements in its quality, the outgoing will usually be regarded as an improvement rather than a repair and will therefore typically be of a capital nature. This is demonstrated in *FC of T v Western Suburbs Cinemas Ltd* (1952) 86 CLR 102, where a cinema operator was denied deductions for the cost of replacing the existing dilapidated celotex ceiling in one of its theatres with a new improved fibro ceiling. The High Court held that the expenditure was capital in nature, as the new ceiling provided a number of advantages over the old ceiling, including the likelihood of reduced repair bills. The Court also rejected the taxpayer's argument that it should be allowed a deduction for the 'notional cost' that it would have incurred if it had made repairs to the celotex ceiling, instead of replacing it with the fibro ceiling. Kitto J explained (at 107):

> when a taxpayer has two courses open to him, one involving an expenditure which will be an allowable deduction for income tax and the other involving an expenditure which will not be an allowable deduction, and for his own reasons he chooses the second course, he cannot have his income tax assessed as if he had exercised his choice the opposite way.

Example Bev owns a block of flats that she leases to tenants. One of the tenants accidentally damaged part of the picket fence at the front of the property while reversing his car out of the driveway. If Bev incurred expenditure to fix a couple of the broken pickets, she would be entitled to deduct the cost of the repairs under s 25-10. However, if Bev had instead completely rebuilt the picket fence or replaced it with a stronger brick fence, she would not be entitled to a deduction under s 25-10, as she would be replacing or improving the fence rather than repairing it.

[13.4] Lease-related expenses

Specific deductions are available for the following expenses relating to leases:

- **Expenses to repair leased premises.** Section 25-15 *ITAA97* allows a tenant to deduct an amount paid for failing to comply with a lease obligation to make repairs to premises that have been used for the purpose of producing assessable income.
- **Lease document expenses.** Section 25-20 *ITAA97* allows a tenant to deduct expenditure incurred for preparing, registering, or stamping a lease (or assignment or surrender of a lease) of property used for the purpose of producing assessable income. If the property is only used partly for such purpose, the deduction is apportioned.
- **Capital expenditure to terminate lease.** Section 25-110 *ITAA97* allows deductions for capital expenditure incurred to terminate a lease or licence if the expenditure is incurred in the course of carrying on a business or in connection with ceasing to carry on a business. A deduction of 20% of the expenditure incurred is available in the year the lease is terminated. Further deductions of 20% of the expenditure incurred are available in each of the next four income years.

[13.5] Borrowing expenses

Section 25-25 *ITAA97* provides deductions for expenditure incurred in borrowing money to the extent that the money is used for the purpose of producing assessable income. The aim of s 25-25 is to cover expenditure such as an 'establishment fee' paid to a bank for setting up an income-producing loan. This kind of expenditure is likely to be capital in nature and would therefore not be deductible under s 8-1 *ITAA97*.

Where the taxpayer uses the borrowed money solely for the purpose of producing assessable income, the taxpayer is entitled to deduct the 'maximum amount' worked out under the method statement in s 25-25(4) (s 25-25(2)). Where the taxpayer uses the borrowed money only partly for the purpose of producing assessable income, an appropriate portion of the 'maximum amount' is deductible (s 25-25(3)).

The method statement in s 25-25(4) is designed to ensure that borrowing expenses are deductible over the period of the loan (or the period of five years if this is shorter). A special rule ensures that borrowing expenses totalling $100 or less are deductible entirely in the relevant income year (s 25-25(6)).

Example Bill borrows $500,000 to purchase an investment property that he leases to tenants. The loan is for four years and commences on 1 September 2022. His bank charges him a $2,000 fee to establish the loan.

Bill's maximum amount for 2022/23 is calculated under s 25-25(4) as follows:

- **Step 1.** Work out the 'remaining expenditure'. For 2022/23, the remaining expenditure is the borrowing expenditure of $2,000. For future years, this amount is reduced by the maximum amount Bill could deduct for each earlier income year.
- **Step 2.** Work out the 'remaining loan period'. For 2022/23, the remaining loan period is the 'period of the loan', which is defined as the shortest of the following periods: the period of the loan as specified in the loan contract; the period starting on the day the money was borrowed and ending on the day it is repaid; and the period of five years starting on the day on which the money was borrowed. The remaining loan period is therefore four years (1,461 days). For future years, the remaining loan period is the period from the start of the relevant income year until the end of the period of the loan.
- **Step 3.** Divide Bill's remaining expenditure by his remaining loan period: $2,000/1,461 = $1.37.
- **Step 4.** Multiply the result from Step 3 by the number of days in the remaining loan period that are in the income year: $1.37 × 302 days = $413.74.

Bill is therefore entitled to a deduction for his borrowing expenses of $413.74 in 2022/23. If he only used 60% of the borrowed funds for the purpose of producing assessable income, his deduction would be $248.24 (ie $413.74 × 60%).

[13.6] Bad debts

Taxpayers that account for income on an 'accruals basis' derive income in the year that it is 'earned' (ie when a debt becomes due rather than when payment is received) [9.9]. It is therefore necessary to have some provision to deal with situations where debts go 'bad', otherwise taxpayers who are assessed on an accruals basis will have paid tax on amounts that they may never actually receive.

Section 25-35 *ITAA97* allows taxpayers to deduct a debt (or part of a debt) written off as bad in an income year if:

(a) it was included in the taxpayer's assessable income for the income year or an earlier income year, or

(b) it is in respect of money lent by the taxpayer in the ordinary course of the taxpayer's business of moneylending.

For examples of situations where a taxpayer has been found to be carrying on a business of moneylending, see *Fairway Estates Pty Ltd v FC of T* 70 ATC 4061; *FC of T v Bivona Pty Ltd* 90 ATC 4168; *FC of T v BHP Billiton Finance Ltd* 2010 ATC ¶20-169; and *FC of T v Ashwick (Qld) No 127 Pty Ltd & Ors* 2011 ATC ¶20-255.

Debt must exist

Deductions are only available under s 25-35 for debts that are in existence and not for debts that have been released, extinguished or compromised. For a debt to be in existence, a taxpayer must have some legal or equitable right to payment. In *GE Crane Sales Pty Ltd v FC of T* 71 ATC 4268, a company that had carried on a debt factoring business and encountered financial difficulties entered into a scheme of arrangement under which debts that were owed to it under factoring arrangements with its clients vested in the scheme manager. The High Court held that the taxpayer was not entitled to deductions under s 63 *ITAA36* (the predecessor of s 25-35) for amounts it claimed as bad debts because, at the time of writing off, no debts owing to the taxpayer existed in law or equity.

Debt must be bad

A debt has gone bad when it is reasonably regarded as irrecoverable. TR 92/18 states that whether a debt is bad 'is a matter of judgment having regard to all the relevant facts'. The Commissioner accepts that 'provided a bona fide commercial decision is taken by a taxpayer as to the likelihood of non-recovery of a debt, it will be accepted that the debt is bad'. A mere 'doubtful debt', however, is not a bad debt.

Debt must be written off

A bad debt is deductible in the year that it is physically written off in the taxpayer's books of account. The importance of writing off a debt in the year that it has gone bad is illustrated in *Point v FC of T* 71 ATC 4014. In this case, the taxpayer had, pursuant to a scheme of arrangement, released a debtor from repaying a debt in the income year ending 30 June 1964, but only wrote the debt off as bad in the following year. The High Court held that the taxpayer was not entitled to a deduction for the debt in either the income year ending 30 June 1964 (as the debt had not been written off in that year) or in the income year ending 30 June 1965 (as the debt was no longer in existence in that year).

Debt must be included in assessable income

Section 25-35 only applies to a taxpayer who is not a moneylender if an amount has been included in their assessable income. If an employer purports to pay an employee's salary with a dishonoured cheque, the employee would not be required to include any amount in their assessable income. This is because employees derive their income on a 'cash basis' when they are paid [9.9], and a dishonoured cheque is not considered to constitute payment (*Tilley v Official Received in Bankruptcy* (1960) 103 CLR 529). An employee in these circumstances would therefore not be able to claim any deduction under s 25-35 for a bad debt (TD 92/201).

Special rules for corporate and trust bad debts

Special anti-avoidance rules in sub-div 165-C *ITAA97* apply to bad debts of companies. These rules are designed to discourage trafficking in companies with bad debts, and broadly mirror the 'continuity of ownership test' ('COT') and 'business continuity test' ('BCT') rules that apply to companies in respect of their tax losses [22.22]. There is also a set of corresponding restrictions in sch 2 F *ITAA36* relating to bad debts of trusts which tie in with the carry forward trust loss provisions [24.9].

[13.7] Loss from profit-making undertaking or plan

Section 25-40 *ITAA97* allows a taxpayer to claim a deduction for a loss arising from the carrying on or carrying out of a profit-making undertaking or plan if any profit from that plan would have been assessable under s 15-15 *ITAA97* [10.3].

However, a loss is not deductible under s 25-40 if it arises in respect of the sale of property acquired on or after 20 September 1985 (ie the date CGT was introduced [17.1]).

Furthermore, a loss that arises in respect of property is only deductible if:

- the taxpayer has notified the Commissioner that the property was acquired for the purpose of profit-making by sale or for the carrying on or carrying out of a profit-making plan (the notice must generally be provided at or before the time the taxpayer lodged his or her income tax return for the year in which the property was acquired), or
- the Commissioner is satisfied that the taxpayer acquired the property for either of those purposes.

[13.8] Losses caused by theft

Section 25-45 *ITAA97* allows taxpayers to deduct a loss of money caused through theft, stealing, embezzlement, larceny, defalcation or misappropriation by their employee or agent. The loss must be discovered in the income year in which the deduction is claimed and the money must have been included in the taxpayer's assessable income for that income year or an earlier income year.

In *Lean v FC of T* 2010 ATC ¶20-159, the Full Federal Court held that s 25-45 can only apply where the money that is misappropriated is the same as the money that was included in the taxpayer's assessable income. If money that has been included in a taxpayer's assessable income is applied towards another investment which is subsequently misappropriated, the connection with the original money is broken.

Section 25-47(1) *ITAA97* allows a deduction for an amount (calculated under s 25-47(2)) where a depreciating asset held by a taxpayer has been disposed of and the proceeds are misappropriated by their agent or employee. This provision has been introduced for technical reasons because such an amount cannot be deducted under s 25-45 as the misappropriated proceeds are not included in the taxpayer's assessable income, but are instead taken into account in calculating the balancing adjustment under s 40-285 *ITAA97* [15.3].

[13.9] Pensions, gratuities and retiring allowances

Section 25-50 *ITAA97* allows taxpayers deductions for pensions, gratuities or retiring allowances that are paid during the income year to an employee, a former employee or a dependant of an employee or former employee. These payments are only deductible to the extent that they are paid in good faith in consideration of the employee's or former employee's past services in a business carried on by the taxpayer for the purposes of producing assessable income. A deduction is not available under s 25-50 if the payment is deductible under another provision in the legislation.

[13.10] Payments to associations

Section 25-55 *ITAA97* provides deductions for payments made for membership of a trade, business or professional association. The maximum amount deductible under s 25-55 for payments made in an income year to any one association is limited to $42. There is no requirement under s 25-55 that the membership of the association have a link with any income-producing or business activities carried on by the taxpayer.

Payments made for membership of a trade, business or professional association may also be deductible under s 8-1 *ITAA97* where the requisite nexus between the payments and the taxpayer's income-producing or business activities exists. Payments that are deductible under s 8-1 do not count towards the $42 limit under s 25-55 and there is no limit on the amount that can be deducted under s 8-1.

> ***Example*** Efraim is a retired accountant. He pays $500 as a yearly membership fee to an accountancy association. As Efraim is no longer earning income as an accountant, he is not entitled to deduct the membership fee under s 8-1. He is, nevertheless, entitled to deduct $42 under s 25-55. If Efraim had not retired and was still earning income as an accountant, he could deduct the full membership fee under s 8-1.

[13.11] Election expenses

Expenditure incurred in contesting an election for membership of the Commonwealth or state parliaments or the ACT or NT Legislative Assemblies is deductible under s 25-60 *ITAA97*.

Expenditure incurred in contesting a local government election is also deductible under s 25-65 *ITAA97*, subject to a limit of $1,000 per election. This limit may be exceeded in certain cases, such as where the expenditure has been recouped (in which case, the recoupment is disregarded in applying the $1,000 limit and is assessable under s 20-35 [10.4]).

Both s 25-60 and s 25-65 operate subject to s 25-70, which provides that no deduction is available under those provisions to the extent that the expenditure is incurred in respect of providing entertainment. This exclusion does not, however, apply where the entertainment is available to the public generally or where it is incurred in providing food or drink for the taxpayer (unless it would be concluded that the taxpayer has the purpose of enabling or facilitating entertainment to be provided to someone else).

[13.12] Work-related COVID-19 tests

Individuals may claim deductions under s 25-125 *ITAA97* for losses or outgoings to the extent that they are incurred in gaining or producing their assessable income and are incurred in testing for COVID-19 to determine whether they can attend or remain at their place of work. The test must be either a polymerase chain reaction test or a test included in the Australian Register of Therapeutic Goods (eg a rapid antigen test). Deductions are not available for capital losses or outgoings. However, given the consumable nature and repeated use of such tests, it is unlikely that they would be regarded as being of a capital nature.

[13.13] Gifts

Division 30 *ITAA97* provides deductions for certain 'gifts'. The deductions are concessional in nature as there is no requirement that the gifts have any relationship with the taxpayer's income-earning activities. There are two kinds of deductions available:

- sub-div 30-A provides deductions for gifts made during a taxpayer's lifetime to specified funds, authorities and institutions, and
- sub-div 30-DA provides deductions for gifts made to registered political parties, electoral candidates and members of legislative bodies.

Nature of a gift

A gift involves the voluntary transfer of property without any material benefit to the donor (*Cyprus Mines Corporation v FC of T* 78 ATC 4468). High Court authority for this principle can be found in *FC of T v McPhail* (1968) 117 CLR 111, where it was held that a parent who had contributed £15 to a school building fund in return for being charged reduced school fees had not made a gift of the £15 sum. Owen J stated (at 116) that to constitute gift, 'it must appear that the property transferred was transferred voluntarily and not as the result of a contractual obligation to transfer it and that no advantage of a material character was received by the transferor by way of return'.

A similar outcome was reached in *Leary v FC of T* 80 ATC 4438, which involved a taxpayer who had participated in a scheme under which he paid $10,000 to a public benevolent institution. Under the scheme, the taxpayer was provided with a 40-year loan of $8,500 through a company associated with the promoter of the scheme and the institution was required to pay 98.8% of the funds it received to the promoter. In disallowing the taxpayer a deduction for the $10,000 amount, Bowen CJ stated (at 4441) that 'the essential idea of a gift is the transfer of property by way of benefaction'.

In this case, the institution only retained $120 of the sum it received and the real motivation of the taxpayer was to obtain material benefits for himself rather than to benefit the institution.

Philanthropic gifts

Subdivision 30-A *ITAA97* is designed to encourage philanthropy and provides deductions for the kinds of 'gifts' specified in the table in s 30-15. The table identifies various categories of gift recipient, the type of gifts that can be made, the amount of deductions available, and any special conditions that must be fulfilled in order to qualify for deductions.

The following categories of gift recipient are mentioned in the table:

- funds, authorities or institutions covered in any of the tables in sub-div 30-B
- certain 'ancillary funds'
- the Australiana Fund, public libraries, museums and art galleries in Australia
- the Commonwealth (for the purposes of Artbank)
- the state and territory National Trusts and the Australian Council of National Trusts, and
- certain deductible gift recipients.

Different rules apply to each category of gift recipient. The following discussion focuses on the first category. To fall within this category, a fund, authority or institution must be covered by an item in the tables in sub-div 30-B *ITAA97*. These tables list a number of different kinds of funds, authorities and institutions and divide them into the following classes: health (s 30-20), education (ss 30-25 to 30-35), research (s 30-40), welfare and rights (ss 30-45 to 30-46), defence (s 30-50), environment (ss 30-55 to 30-60), industry, trade and design (s 30-65), the family (ss 30-70 to 30-75), international affairs (ss 30-80 to 30-86), sports and recreation (s 30-90), philanthropic trusts (s 30-95), cultural organisations (s 30-100), fire and emergency services (s 30-102) and other recipients (s 30-105). In some cases, the fund, authority or institution is described in general terms (eg a public or non-profit hospital, a public university, a public benevolent institution or a public fund established for charitable purposes). In other cases, a specific organisation is mentioned by name (eg Cancer Australia, Landcare Australia Ltd, the Australian Academy of Science, Amnesty International and the Scout Association of Australia).

The fund, authority or institution must be 'in Australia', and, if it is not specifically mentioned by name in sub-div 30-B, it must be endorsed under sub-div 30-BA as a 'deductible gift recipient' (s 30-17). To be endorsed as a deductible gift recipient, the entity is required to have an ABN [39.3] and satisfy certain conditions relating to the use of its funds. Charities are required to be registered with the ACNC [11.4].

Deductions are available under s 30-15 for gifts of money or property as long as the value of the gift is at least $2. Where the gift is money, the deduction is equal to the amount of money. Where the gift is property, the deduction is generally the lesser of the market value of the property on the day of the gift and the amount paid for the property. In the case of gifts of trading stock and shares in listed companies, the deduction is usually the market value of the item on the day of the gift. Special rules apply where the property was not purchased within the previous 12 months and is valued at more than $5,000. In this circumstance, the gift is based on the Commissioner's valuation of the property.

Political gifts

Subdivision 30-DA *ITAA97* allows deductions for certain contributions and gifts made to registered political parties, independent electoral candidates and independent members of Australian legislative bodies.

To be deductible the contribution or gift must be money or property purchased within the last 12 months, must be valued at $2 or more, must be made by an individual not in the course of carrying on a business, and must not be a testamentary contribution or gift (s 30-242). If the contribution or gift is money, the deduction equals the amount of money. If it is property, the deduction is the lesser of the market value of the property on the day of the gift and the amount paid for the property.

Taxpayers are not allowed to deduct more than $1,500 in an income year for their contributions and gifts to political parties. They are also not allowed to deduct more than $1,500 in an income year for their contributions and gifts to independent candidates or independent members (s 30-243).

[13.14] Conservation covenants

Division 31 *ITAA97* allows taxpayers deductions for entering into conservation covenants over land they own (s 31-5(1)). A conservation covenant is a covenant that restricts or prohibits activities on the land that could degrade its environmental value, is permanent and registered on the title to the land (if registration is possible), and is approved in writing by, or entered into under a program approved in writing by, the Environment Minister (s 31-5(5)).

The following conditions must be satisfied to claim the deduction:

- the covenant must be perpetual and the taxpayer must not receive any money, property or other material benefit for entering into the covenant
- the market value of the land must decrease as a result of entering into the covenant and the change in the market value of the land as a result of entering into the covenant must be more than $5,000 or the taxpayer must have entered into a contract to acquire the land not more than 12 months before entering into the covenant, and
- the covenant must have been entered into with either: a fund, authority or institution that meets the requirements of s 31-10; the Commonwealth, a state, a territory or a local governing body; or an authority of the Commonwealth, a state or a territory.

The taxpayer must also seek a valuation of the change in market value from the Commissioner (s 31-15).

The amount that is deductible is the difference between the market value of the land just before the taxpayer entered the covenant and its decreased market value just after that time, but only to the extent that the decrease is attributable to entering into the covenant (s 31-5(3)).

[13.15] Tax losses

Taxpayers sometimes make tax losses instead of taxable income during an income year [8.3]. Division 36 *ITAA97* generally allows taxpayers to carry forward their tax losses and claim deductions for them in subsequent income years. This means that a tax loss made in one year can reduce taxable income in future years. In the past, tax losses that had not been utilised within seven years automatically expired. This time limit has, however, been removed, with the result that tax losses can now be carried forward indefinitely. Nevertheless, from an economic perspective, as the benefit of a tax loss does not arise until such time as there is sufficient assessable income against which the loss can be applied, the value of a tax loss effectively erodes over time due to inflation.

Division 36 operates subject to special restrictions contained in div 165 *ITAA97* (relating to companies) [22.22] and sch 2 F *ITAA36* (relating to trusts) [24.9], which generally require companies and trusts to pass certain tests before they can carry forward their tax losses.

As a general rule, tax losses cannot be carried back into previous years. There is, however, one temporary exception to this rule contained in div 160 *ITAA97*, which allows eligible companies that have incurred tax losses in certain years to carry back their losses and set them off against their taxed profits in earlier income years. The loss carry back is delivered via a special refundable 'loss carry back tax offset' [22.23].

Calculating the amount of a tax loss

A taxpayer's tax loss for a particular income year is worked out under s 36-10 by adding up the taxpayer's deductions for the income year (excluding tax losses of earlier income years) and then subtracting from this amount the taxpayer's assessable income and net exempt income (as defined in s 36-20) for the year. Any amount remaining is the taxpayer's tax loss for the income year, which is called a 'loss year'. This can be expressed as follows:

Tax loss for an income year	=	Deductions for the income year (except tax losses for earlier income years)	–	Assessable income and net exempt income for the income year

Example In 2022/23, Kim had deductions of $60,000, assessable income of $30,000, and net exempt income of $20,000. Her tax loss for the year is therefore $10,000 (ie $60,000 – ($30,000 + $20,000)).

A taxpayer's tax loss for an income year is limited by s 26-55 *ITAA97* [14.7]. This provision prevents deductions under s 25-50 (pensions, etc) [13.9], div 30 (gifts) [13.13], div 31 (conservation covenants) [13.14] and s 290-150 (personal superannuation contributions) [19.7] from contributing to a tax loss.

Deduction of tax loss

The way in which a tax loss for a loss year may be deducted in a subsequent income year differs depending on whether or not the entity claiming the loss is a corporate tax entity.

Non-corporate tax entities

Taxpayers that are not corporate tax entities (eg individuals) are generally required to deduct a tax loss for a loss year first against their net exempt income for the income year, then against their assessable income for the income year. Any remaining tax loss is carried forward into the following income year (s 36-15).

Example In 2022/23, Sam had assessable income of $50,000, net exempt income of $10,000, and deductions of $80,000. He therefore made a tax loss of $20,000 (ie $80,000 – $50,000 – $10,000), which he can carry forward and claim as a deduction in the following year.

If, in 2023/24, Sam has assessable income of $60,000 and net exempt income of $15,000, his taxable income for the year, after taking into account the tax loss of $20,000, is $55,000 (ie $60,000 + $15,000 – $20,000).

Corporate tax entities

Taxpayers that are corporate tax entities may, subject to certain limitations, choose the amount of a tax loss to deduct in an income year provided they first apply the loss against their net exempt income for the year (s 36-17). The purpose of the choice is to ensure that a corporate tax entity's 'excess franking credits' (which are not refundable tax offsets [22.8]) are not wasted by its tax losses. In broad terms, a corporate tax entity has 'excess franking offsets' for a year if its franking tax offsets [22.8] for the year exceed the amount of income tax it would pay on its taxable income for the year if such tax offsets were disregarded (s 36-55).

The choice operates subject to the following limitations:

- if, disregarding its tax loss, the entity would have 'excess franking offsets' for the year, it must choose to deduct a nil amount (s 36-17(5)(a)), and
- if, disregarding its tax loss, the entity would not have 'excess franking offsets' for the year, it must not choose an amount that would result in it having excess franking offsets for that year (s 36-17(5)(b)).

Example X Ltd pays tax at the rate of 30%. During the income year, it has assessable income of $200m (consisting of a franked distribution of $70m, franking credits of $30m, and interest income of $100m). It has a tax loss of $150m from the previous year.

Section 36-17(5)(a) does not apply because, if X Ltd's $150m tax loss was disregarded, it would not have any excess franking offsets for the year since its franking offset ($30m) is less than the tax on its taxable income disregarding the offset ($60m = $200m × 30%).

Section 36-17(5)(b) applies and X Ltd would not be able to deduct the whole tax loss as this would result in it having excess franking offsets calculated as follows:

$$\text{Excess franking offsets} = \$30\text{m} - [(\$200\text{m} - \$150\text{m}) \times 30\%]$$
$$= \$15\text{m}$$

Therefore, the maximum tax loss that X Co could deduct is $100m, as this would result in it having no excess franking offsets:

$$\text{Excess franking offsets} = \$30\text{m} - [(\$200\text{m} - \$100\text{m}) \times 30\%]$$
$$= \text{Nil}$$

[13.16] QUESTIONS

1. Sandra paid $440 in fees to an accounting firm to prepare her previous year's tax return. She also paid the firm $1,100 to seek a private ruling about whether shares that she recently sold were subject to CGT. Is Sandra entitled to deductions for her expenditure?
2. Trevor recently purchased an investment property that was in poor condition. Before leasing it to tenants, he renovated the kitchen and replaced the front wood fence with a new brick fence. Can Trevor deduct these expenses?
3. John borrowed $500,000 from a bank to purchase shares in BHP. The loan is for a period of 20 years. To establish the loan, John was required to pay a $2,000 fee. Can John deduct the fee?
4. S Co is a large freight company. In the previous financial year, it billed one of its customers $1,100 for services that it had provided. S Co has recently discovered that the client is experiencing financial distress and will not be able to pay its bill. What action can S Co take from a tax perspective?
5. Gerry is a retired engineer whose only income is his superannuation pension. For many years, he has been a member of the Australian Engineer's Association. Can he deduct his $350 annual membership fee?
6. Julia spent $2,500 on her election campaign for a local council election. Can she deduct this expense?
7. In Year 1, Martha had assessable income of $60,000, net exempt income of $30,000, and deductions of $100,000. In Year 2, she has assessable income of $50,000 and net exempt income of $5,000. Calculate her tax loss and taxable income for the relevant years.

PROVISIONS THAT DENY OR LIMIT DEDUCTIONS 14

[14.1] Introduction

Even if a loss or outgoing fulfils the requirements of the general or a specific deduction provision, another provision may expressly deny or limit the deduction available to the taxpayer. For instance, an important provision that limits deductions is s 27-5 *ITAA97* [8.5]. As discussed, this section denies a deduction to the extent that a loss or outgoing includes an amount relating to an ITC [7.8] or a decreasing adjustment [7.10] under the GST law. This chapter examines a number of other common provisions that deny or limit deductions. These provisions have been enacted for a broad range of policy reasons and are scattered throughout the *ITAA36* and *ITAA97*.

[14.2] Substantiation

Division 900 *ITAA97* contains important 'substantiation rules' to assist the ATO with their tax audits and prevent fraudulent deduction claims. The substantiation rules require individuals to have written evidence of the following kinds of expenses in order to be able to claim deductions for them:

- 'work expenses' (ie expenses incurred in producing salary or wage income, certain PAYG withholding payments as well as travel and meal allowance expenses) (sub-div 900-B)
- 'car expenses' (ie expenses relating to a car such as fuel, maintenance and registration costs, etc) (sub-div 900-C), and
- 'business travel expenses' (ie expenses incurred in travelling away from home for at least one night to produce non-salary or wage income) (sub-div 900-D).

A person is not entitled to a deduction under either the general deduction provision or a specific deduction provision for any of the above expenses if he or she has not maintained appropriate written records to evidence the claim.

Written evidence

The evidence required under the substantiation rules is usually a 'receipt' or 'invoice' that contains prescribed information setting out:

- the name (or business name) of the supplier

- the amount of the expense
- the nature of the goods or services
- the date the expense was incurred, and
- the date of the document (ss 900-115, 900-120).

The strictness of these requirements is reduced in certain circumstances. For example, if the document does not show the date the expense was incurred, a bank statement or other reasonable independent evidence that shows when it was paid may be used. In addition, a taxpayer can self-record certain expenses under $10 where the total amount of these expenses is below $200 for the year (s 900-125). The self-recording of an expense is also permitted where the Commissioner considers it unreasonable for the taxpayer to obtain written evidence (s 900-130).

A taxpayer does not generally need to substantiate work expenses below $300 in total for the year (s 900-35).

Car expenses

Taxpayers that claim car expenses using the 'logbook method' [12.7] are required to maintain written evidence of those expenses (s 900-70). Fuel and oil expenses do not need to be substantiated by written evidence provided the taxpayer has maintained odometer records. In these circumstances, the Commissioner accepts a reasonable estimate of average fuel and oil costs based on business kilometres travelled (TD 97/19).

Travel records

Taxpayers that are away from their normal place of residence for six or more nights in a row must keep 'travel records' in accordance with sub-div 900-F to claim deductions for their travel expenses (s 900-85). Travel records must detail in English:

- the nature of the activity undertaken
- the day and approximate time when it began
- how long it lasted, and
- where the taxpayer engaged in the activity.

An activity must be recorded before it ends, or as soon as possible afterwards (s 900-150).

Travel allowance expenses

Special rules apply to 'travel allowance expenses' (ie losses or outgoings for accommodation, food, drink or incidentals incurred for travel that are covered by a travel allowance: s 900-30(2)). Taxpayers can deduct travel allowance expenses for travel within Australia without written evidence or travel records where the Commissioner considers that the total of the losses or outgoings claimed for travel covered by the allowance are reasonable (s 900-50(1)). They can also deduct travel allowance expenses for travel outside Australia without written evidence on the same basis as domestic travel with the exception that they are required to provide written evidence of losses or outgoings for accommodation (s 900-55). The Commissioner publishes annual rulings on what he considers to be reasonable amounts for travel allowance expenses. Travel records must be kept for overseas travel if the taxpayer is away from their normal place of residence for six or more nights in a row.

Maintaining records

Records of expenses under the substantiation rules must be kept for five years (s 900-165). Where records have been lost or destroyed, a complete copy of the document is treated as the original. If a taxpayer does not have such a copy, but the Commissioner is satisfied that the taxpayer took reasonable precautions to prevent the loss or destruction of the document, the deduction is not affected, provided the document was not written evidence (eg it was a logbook or travel record). If the document was written evidence (eg an invoice), the taxpayer must obtain substitute written evidence. However, if it is not reasonably possible to obtain substitute written evidence, the deduction is not affected (s 900-205).

Commissioner's discretion

The Commissioner has the discretion to allow deductions to a taxpayer who has not strictly complied with the substantiation rules if the nature and quality of the taxpayer's evidence to substantiate the claim satisfy the Commissioner that the taxpayer incurred the expense and is entitled to the deduction (s 900-195).

[14.3] Taxes

Deductions are expressly denied for the payment of certain taxes, including income tax (s 25-5 *ITAA97*) and GST (s 27-15 *ITAA97*). In addition, the following superannuation taxes are not deductible:

- superannuation supervisory levy (s 26-90 *ITAA97*) [19.4]
- SGC (s 26-95 *ITAA97*) [19.5]
- ENCCT (s 26-75 *ITAA97*) [19.9]
- div 293 tax (s 26-98 *ITAA97*) [19.10], and
- ETBT (s 26-99 *ITAA97*) [19.15].

Deductions are available for the payment of FBT [18.3] and payroll tax [4.4] provided the requirements of s 8-1 *ITAA97* are met.

> ***Example*** Harry owns a hardware business. He cannot deduct his annual income tax liability, nor the GST he charges on the supplies of his products. He can, nevertheless, deduct the FBT he pays on the fringe benefits provided to his employees, along with any payroll tax that he is liable to pay.

[14.4] Entertainment expenses

Section 32-5 *ITAA97* provides that deductions under s 8-1 *ITAA97* are denied to the extent that a loss or outgoing is incurred in providing entertainment. 'Entertainment' is defined as 'entertainment by way of food, drink or recreation' as well as 'accommodation or travel to do with providing entertainment by way of food, drink or recreation' (s 32-10). 'Recreation' includes 'amusement, sport or similar leisure-time pursuits' (s 995-1).

In *FC of T v Amway of Australia Ltd* 2004 ATC 4893, the Full Federal Court considered the predecessor of s 32-5 (s 51AE *ITAA36*) and held that whether food or drink constitutes entertainment is a matter of characterisation. All relevant circumstances must be considered, such as 'the locale where the food or drink is provided, the quality of the food or drink, the occasion for its provision, its cost and its nature'. According to the Court, expenditure on a gala dinner at a national seminar held at a luxurious holiday destination would be entertainment, but the provision during a working session by an employer of sandwiches or coffee and tea to an employee would not be entertainment. This approach is consistent with the approach outlined in IT 2675, where the Commissioner states that providing morning or afternoon tea (which can include light refreshments but not alcohol) to employees and their associates does not constitute the provision of entertainment.

Section 32-5 operates subject to a number of specific exceptions. The main exception is contained in s 32-20, which provides that entertainment expenditure incurred in providing a fringe benefit is generally deductible. FBT will, however, usually apply to such expenditure [18.1]. Other exceptions are contained in tables in s 32-30 to s 32-50, which are reproduced below.

Employer expenses (s 32-30)	
Section 32-5 does not stop a taxpayer from deducting a loss or outgoing for . . .	**But the exception does not apply if . . .**
providing food or drink to the taxpayer's employees in an 'in-house dining facility' (defined in s 32-55)	the food or drink is provided at a party, reception or other social function
providing food or drink to individuals (other than the taxpayer's employees) in an in-house dining facility	(a) the taxpayer chooses (under s 32-70) *not* to include in assessable income $30 for each meal provided in the in-house dining facility in the income year to an individual (other than the taxpayer's employee), or (b) the food or drink is provided at a party, reception or other social function
providing food or drink in a 'dining facility' (defined in s 32-60) to the taxpayer's employees who perform most of their duties in connection with: (a) the dining facility, or (b) a facility (of which the dining facility forms a part) for providing accommodation, recreation or travel	the food or drink is provided at a party, reception or other social function
providing food or drink to the taxpayer's employees under an 'industrial instrument' relating to overtime	
providing a facility for recreation on property the taxpayer occupies, if the facility is mainly operated for the taxpayer's employees to use	the facility is for: (a) accommodation, or (b) dining or drinking (unless it is a food or drink vending machine)
providing food or drink which would be a fringe benefit apart from ss 54, 58, 58N, 58S and 58T of the *FBTAA* (disregarding s 58P)	
providing a meal which would be a fringe benefit apart from ss 58A, 58F, 58L, 58LA and 58M of the *FBTAA* (disregarding s 58P)	
giving the taxpayer's employee an allowance that is included in his or her assessable income	(a) the employee is a relative of another of the taxpayer's employees, and (b) the taxpayer gives the allowance to the relative as the taxpayer's employee because: (i) he or she provides, or facilitates providing, entertainment to do with the other employee's employment, and (ii) the taxpayer expects the relative to do so

<table>
<tr><th colspan="2">Seminar expenses (s 32-35)</th></tr>
<tr><th>Section 32-5 does not stop a taxpayer from deducting a loss or outgoing for . . .</th><th>But the exception does not apply if . . .</th></tr>
<tr><td>providing food, drink, accommodation or travel to an individual (including the taxpayer) that is reasonably incidental to the individual attending a ‘seminar’ that goes for at least four hours</td><td>(a) the seminar is a business meeting, or
(b) the seminar’s main purpose is to promote or advertise a business (or prospective business) or its goods or services, or
(c) the seminar’s main purpose is to provide entertainment at, or in connection with, the seminar</td></tr>
<tr><th colspan="2">Entertainment industry expenses (s 32-40)</th></tr>
<tr><th>Section 32-5 does not stop a taxpayer from deducting a loss or outgoing for . . .</th><th>But the exception does not apply if . . .</th></tr>
<tr><td>providing entertainment for payment in the ordinary course of a business carried on by the taxpayer</td><td></td></tr>
<tr><td>providing entertainment in performing the taxpayer’s duties to his or her employer who carries on a business that includes providing that entertainment for payment</td><td></td></tr>
<tr><th colspan="2">Promotion and advertising expenses (s 32-45)</th></tr>
<tr><th>Section 32-5 does not stop a taxpayer from deducting a loss or outgoing for . . .</th><th>But the exception does not apply if . . .</th></tr>
<tr><td>providing entertainment if:
(a) the taxpayer provides it to an individual under a contract to supply him or her with goods or services in the ordinary course of the taxpayer’s business, and
(b) the taxpayer incurs the loss or outgoing to promote or advertise to the public his or her business or its goods or services</td><td></td></tr>
<tr><td>providing or exhibiting the taxpayer’s business’s goods or services if the loss or outgoing is incurred to promote or advertise those goods or services to the public</td><td></td></tr>
<tr><td>providing entertainment to promote or advertise to the public a business or its goods or services</td><td>some people have a greater opportunity to get the benefits of the entertainment than ordinary members of the public have</td></tr>
<tr><th colspan="2">Other expenses (s 32-50)</th></tr>
<tr><th>Section 32-5 does not stop a taxpayer from deducting a loss or outgoing for . . .</th><th>But the exception does not apply if . . .</th></tr>
<tr><td>buying food or drink to do with overtime work, if the taxpayer receives an allowance under an industrial instrument to buy the food or drink</td><td></td></tr>
<tr><td>providing entertainment free to members of the public who are sick, disabled, poor or otherwise disadvantaged</td><td></td></tr>
</table>

14

Example Tom is a self-employed accountant. He pays for a business lunch with his client at a restaurant owned by Jerry. Even though Tom and his client discuss business matters at the restaurant, the cost of the meal is not deductible to Tom because of s 32-5. Jerry is, however, entitled to a deduction for the cost of the food used in preparing the meal, as he is engaged in the business of providing entertainment and therefore falls within the exception in s 32-40.

A special anti-avoidance measure in s 32-75 *ITAA97* provides that if:

- a taxpayer incurs a loss or outgoing under an arrangement
- someone provides entertainment under the arrangement to the taxpayer or someone else, and
- s 32-5 would have prevented the taxpayer from deducting the loss or outgoing under s 8-1 if the taxpayer had incurred it in respect of providing that entertainment,

div 32 applies to the taxpayer as if they had incurred the loss or outgoing in providing that entertainment, to the extent the Commissioner thinks reasonable.

Example Ash owns a tennis shop business and pays $50,000 to sponsor a major tennis event. Under the same arrangement, she is provided with seats for herself and a guest at the women's final. Section 32-75 allows the Commissioner to treat Ash as having incurred so much of the $50,000 as he thinks reasonable in providing the entertainment.

[14.5] Non-compulsory uniform expenses

Division 34 *ITAA97* limits deductions relating to 'non-compulsory uniforms' for employees and individuals who receive certain 'withholding payments' (s 34-5). Such persons cannot deduct expenditure incurred in respect of non-compulsory uniforms unless:

- the expenditure is deductible under another provision in the legislation (eg s 8-1 *ITAA97*), and
- the design of the uniform is registered under div 34 *ITAA97* on the Register of Approved Occupational Clothing at the time the expenditure is incurred (s 34-10).

Division 34 does not prevent deductions for expenditure incurred in relation to 'occupation specific clothing' (eg a nurse's uniform) or 'protective clothing' (eg a construction worker's hard hat) (s 34-20).

A 'uniform' is defined as one or more items of clothing (including accessories) which, when considered as a set, distinctively identify the employee as a person associated (directly or indirectly) with the employer, or a group consisting of the employer and one or more 'associates' of the employer (s 34-15(1)).

A uniform is 'non-compulsory' unless the employer consistently enforces a policy requiring the taxpayer and other employees (except temporary and relief employees) who do the same type of work as the taxpayer to wear the uniform when working and not to substitute the uniform with any other clothing (s 34-15(2)).

Example Ted is employed by a bank. The bank encourages (but does not require) its employees to wear a bright pink open-neck shirt with the bank's name displayed on it. If the design of the shirt is not registered under div 34, Ted cannot deduct the cost of purchasing the shirt as it relates to a non-compulsory uniform.

[14.6] Non-commercial business losses of individuals

Division 35 *ITAA97* contains special rules directed at individuals that make losses from carrying on (either alone or in partnership) 'non-commercial businesses'. The rules prevent individuals from offsetting the excess deductions from their non-commercial business activities against their other assessable income for the year. Such 'losses' are 'deferred' and taken to be incurred in future years when they can be applied against assessable income from the same business activity (s 35-10(2)). Division 35 also applies to losses from 'pre-business' and 'post-business' activities that would otherwise be deductible under s 40-880 [15.6] (ss 35-10(2A), (2B)).

Deferral rule

Division 35 effectively quarantines an individual's deductions relating to a non-commercial business activity. This is a deviation from the general taxation rules, which ordinarily allow taxpayers to offset their deductions (no matter what kind) against all sorts of income.

The key provision is s 35-10(2), which states that if the amounts attributable to a business activity for an income year, which could otherwise be deducted in that year, exceed the assessable income from the business activity for the year, the excess is taken not to have been incurred in the year and is treated as if it was attributable to the activity for the next income year in which it is carried on.

Exceptions

The Commissioner has the discretion not to apply the deferral rule in s 35-10(2) if he is satisfied that it would be unreasonable to apply it (s 35-55). In *Bentivoglio v FC of T* 2014 ATC ¶10-374, the AAT held that it was unreasonable for the Commissioner to apply the rule in s 35-10(2) for the 2010 to 2013 income years in relation to medical practitioner who had been carrying on an olive growing and production business for 15 years because of a range of special circumstances, which included: a prolonged drought, infestations of olive trees by bugs, extraordinary challenges facing the olive oil industry and the illness of his wife.

The deferral rule also does not apply to a 'primary production business' or a 'professional arts business' where the taxpayer's assessable income (excluding capital gains) from other sources is less than $40,000 (s 35-10(4)).

Most importantly, the deferral rule is also not applicable where the sum of the taxpayer's taxable income (calculated ignoring deductions for excess non-commercial business losses), reportable fringe benefits total, reportable superannuation contributions, and total net investment loss [8.6] for the year is less than $250,000 *and* the taxpayer passes one of the following tests:

- **Assessable income test.** This test is passed if the taxpayer's assessable income from the business activity exceeds $20,000 for the year (s 35-30).
- **Profits test.** This test is passed if the business activity produced less deductions than assessable income in at least three of the last five years (ie it was profitable in at least three of the five years) (s 35-35).
- **Real property test.** This test is passed if the real property (excluding any dwelling used mainly for private purposes and tenant's fixtures) used on a continuing basis in carrying on the business in the income year has a total value of at least $500,000 (s 35-40).
- **Other assets test.** This test is passed if specified assets (ie depreciating assets, trading stock, leased assets and trademarks, patents, copyrights and similar rights) used on a continuing basis in carrying on the business in the income year have a total value of at least $100,000 (s 35-45).

Example

Adjusted income is less than $250,000 but none of the tests are passed
Sally is employed as an accountant. During 2022/23, she earned salary of $70,000. She also ran a small business selling flowers at a weekend market. In 2022/23 her business income was $10,000 and her business deductions were $15,000. Assuming the exceptions in div 35 do not apply, Sally is deemed to have incurred a $5,000 business loss in 2022/23. The deferral rule prevents her deducting this amount from her salary income. Her taxable income for the year is therefore $70,000 (rather than $65,000). She can, however, deduct the $5,000 loss against income earned from her business in future years.

Adjusted income is not less than $250,000 and one of the tests is passed
Keith is a self-employed doctor who earned $300,000 of income from his medical practice in 2022/23. He also owns a farm valued at $1m from which he conducts a farming business. In 2022/23, he made $10,000 of income from his farming activities and incurred $40,000 of deductible expenses in relation to those activities. Although Keith passes the 'real property test', he cannot apply the $30,000 loss from his farming activities against the income from his medical practice as his adjusted income is not less than $250,000. He therefore has taxable income of $300,000 for 2022/23 (rather than $270,000). Keith can, however, deduct the $30,000 loss against his future farming business income.

It is important to realise that div 35 is targeted at deferring an individual's excess deductions relating to 'business', 'pre-business' and 'post-business' activities. It is not directed at excess deductions relating to an individual's 'passive' investment activities. This means that div 35 does not apply to ordinary 'negative gearing' arrangements. It would therefore not defer deductions for the amount by which a taxpayer's interest expenditure on borrowings used to purchase an investment property exceed the rental from such property in a particular income year.

[14.7] Miscellaneous *ITAA97* provisions that deny deductions

Division 26 *ITAA97* contains a number of miscellaneous provisions that deny or limit deductions. Some of these provisions are outlined below, while others are examined in subsequent chapters:

- **Penalties.** Section 26-5 *ITAA97* denies deductions for the payment of penalties under Australian and foreign laws. The object of this provision is to prevent taxpayers benefiting under the income tax law for breaches of the general law. In any event, even if s 26-5 did not exist, penalties would ordinarily not be deductible. Support for this proposition is found in *Madad Pty Ltd v FC of T* 84 ATC 4739, where the Full Federal Court denied a company a deduction under s 51(1) *ITAA36* for a penalty incurred under the Trade Practices Act for engaging in resale price maintenance. It is also illustrated in *Mayne Nickless Ltd v FC of T* 84 ATC 4458, where the Supreme Court of Victoria denied a company that operated an armoured car business deductions under s 51(1) for parking and traffic fines. In both cases, the courts referred to *Herald and Weekly Times Ltd v FC of T* (1932) 48 CLR 113, where Gavan Duffy CJ and Dixon J stated (at 120):

  > The penalty is imposed as a punishment of the offender . . . Its nature severs it from the expenses of trading. It is inflicted on the offender as a personal deterrent, and it is not incurred by him in his character of trader.

Example A company that has been fined under Commonwealth legislation for engaging in misleading and deceptive conduct is not entitled to deduct the cost of the fine.

- **Leave payments.** Section 26-10 *ITAA97* provides that leave payments (eg long service leave, sick leave or annual leave) are only deductible in the income year that the payments are made. Employers are not entitled to deductions for mere 'provisions' relating to their employees' accrued leave entitlements. Leave payments are generally only deductible if they are paid to the individual to whom the leave relates (ie the employee) or to the individual's dependants or legal personal representative (in the case of death). In addition, 'accrued leave transfer payments' (ie payments made in respect of an individual's leave to another entity under an Australian, law, award, determination or industrial agreement) are also generally deductible.

Example Punch employs Judy in his puppet factory. He sets aside money as a provision for Judy's leave which she has not yet taken. Punch can only claim a deduction when he actually pays Judy.

- **Rebatable benefits.** Section 26-19 *ITAA97* denies deductions for a loss or outgoing to the extent that it is incurred in gaining or producing a 'rebatable benefit'. A rebatable benefit covers an assessable government assistance payment such as Youth Allowance and JobSeeker (s 160AAA *ITAA36*). Section 26-19 operates from 1 July 2011 and is designed to reverse the outcome in *FC of T v Anstis* 2010 ATC ¶20-221, where the High Court held that a student who incurred study expenses in gaining her assessable Youth Allowance was able to deduct those expenses under the general deduction provision [12.9].

Example Mavis is a full-time student who receives Youth Allowance while undertaking a teaching diploma. She cannot deduct expenses relating to undertaking teaching rounds for her course even though she needs to satisfactorily progress with her course in order to continue receiving Youth Allowance.

- **Assistance to students.** Section 26-20(1) *ITAA97* denies deductions for the payment of student contribution amounts under the *Higher Education Support Act 2003* (Cth) as well as repayments of HECS-HELP, FEE-HELP, OS-HELP and VET student loans [8.10]. The provision does not apply to expenditure incurred in providing a fringe benefit (s 26-20(2)). An employer who pays an employee's student contribution amount would therefore not be prevented from deducting the payment. The employer would, however, be liable to pay FBT on the provision of the benefit [18.3]. It is also worth noting that the ATO has ruled that s 26-20(1) does not deny a deduction for course fees paid by a student who has obtained a loan for those fees under FEE-HELP if the course is directly related to their current income-earning activities (ID 2005/26).

Example Dan works in an accounting firm as a trainee accountant and is also undertaking a part-time undergraduate accounting degree at university. He is not able to claim a deduction for payment of his student contribution amount relating to his course or any HECS-HELP repayments he makes. However, if his employer had paid his student contribution amount or HECS-HELP repayments, the employer could claim a deduction for the expenditure, but it would also constitute a fringe benefit upon which the employer would have to pay FBT.

- **Political contributions and gifts.** Section 26-22 *ITAA97* denies deductions for contributions and gifts made to political parties and individuals who are candidates for, or members of, Parliament and local government bodies. This prohibition does not apply to contributions and gifts that fall within sub-div 30-DA *ITAA97*, which allows deductions of up to $1,500 per year for certain political contributions and gifts made by individuals not in the course of carrying on a business [13.13].

Example P Co undertakes market research for political parties. To keep up its profile with the two main political parties, P Co contributes $10,000 to each of them. The gifts are not deductible.

- **Interest and royalties.** Section 26-25 *ITAA97* denies deductions for interest and royalty payments that are subject to 'withholding tax' under sub-div 12-F of sch 1 *TAA* where the payer has failed to withhold the relevant amounts from such payments [31.11].

Example An Australian publisher pays a royalty to a non-resident author but forgets to withhold tax from the payment. The royalty is not deductible to the publisher.

- **Relatives' travel expenses.** Section 26-30 *ITAA97* denies deductions to taxpayers involved in work-related travel for losses or outgoings relating to an accompanying relative's travel. This rule does not apply where the relative performs substantial work duties and it is reasonable to conclude that the relative would have accompanied the taxpayer even if he or she did not have a personal relationship. It also does not apply where the expenditure is incurred in providing a fringe benefit (in which case FBT will apply [18.1]).

Example Jeremy undertakes work-related travel and incurs expenditure on hotel accommodation which he shares with his wife who does not perform any work-related duties. He must apportion the cost of the hotel accommodation when claiming a deduction.

- **Travel related to use of residential premises as residential accommodation.** Section 26-31 *ITAA97* provides that a loss or outgoing is not deductible, insofar as it is attributable to travel, if it is incurred in gaining or producing assessable income from the use of residential premises as residential accommodation, and it is not necessarily incurred in carrying on a business. This provision was introduced to address concerns that many landlords had been claiming travel expenses that were of a private nature. The section is directed primarily at individuals and does not apply to specified entities, such as companies and non-self managed superannuation funds.

Example Louise is a lawyer who lives in Melbourne and owns a residential investment property on the Gold Coast. The property is leased to tenants through a local estate agent. Louise cannot deduct the cost of flights from Melbourne to the Gold Coast to inspect her property and meet with her agent.

- **Payments to related entities.** Section 26-35 *ITAA97* provides that deductions are only available for payments made to a 'related entity' (eg a relative) to the extent that the Commissioner considers the payments are reasonable.

Example Sally employs her son to work in her milk bar business. Sally can only deduct as much of the salary paid to her son as the Commissioner considers reasonable.

- **Family maintenance.** Section 26-40 *ITAA97* denies deductions for expenditure incurred in maintaining a spouse or child under 16 years of age.

Example Peter is a farmer. He cannot deduct the expenditure he incurs on food and lodgings provided to his 15-year-old son who works on the farm.

- **Recreational club expenses.** Section 26-45 *ITAA97* denies deductions for losses and outgoings relating to memberships of recreational clubs or rights to use recreational club facilities unless the expenditure is incurred in providing a fringe benefit (in which case FBT will apply [18.1]).

Example Bert is employed as a lawyer by a firm in Perth. To relieve himself from stress, he joins a gym and works out at lunchtime. The cost of Bert's monthly gym membership is not deductible. However, if his employer had paid for his gym membership, the payment would be deductible to his employer, but would also constitute a fringe benefit and be subject to FBT.

- **Leisure facilities and boats.** Section 26-50 *ITAA97* denies deductions for losses and outgoings relating to the acquisition or retention of rights to use leisure facilities and boats. This rule does not apply where the leisure facility or boat is held for use in the ordinary course of the taxpayer's business involving the provision of leisure facilities or the hiring of boats, or where the expenditure is incurred in providing a fringe benefit (in which case FBT will apply [18.1]).

Example Errol is the principal of an accounting firm and purchases a boat which he uses for entertaining clients on weekends. He cannot claim any deductions (eg depreciation) in respect of the boat. However, if he operated a business selling boats and purchased the boat for sale in his business, he would be entitled to deduct the cost of buying the boat as it would be his trading stock.

- **Bribes.** Sections 26-52 and 26-53 *ITAA97* deny deductions for 'bribes' made to foreign and Australian public officials. Broadly speaking, an amount is a bribe to a foreign or Australian public official to the extent that:
  (a) the taxpayer incurs the amount in, or in connection with: (i) providing a benefit to another person; (ii) causing a benefit to be provided to another person; (iii) offering to provide, or promising to provide, a benefit to another person; or (iv) causing an offer of the provision of a benefit, or a promise of the provision of a benefit, to be made to another person
  (b) the benefit is not legitimately due to the other person, and
  (c) the taxpayer incurs the amount with the intention of influencing a public official (who may or may not be the other person) in the exercise of the official's duties in order to: (i) obtain or retain business; or (ii) obtain or retain an advantage in the conduct of business that is not legitimately due to the taxpayer, or another person, as the recipient, or intended recipient, of the advantage in the conduct of business.

In the case of foreign public officials, certain benefits are expressly deemed not to constitute bribes (eg benefits of a minor nature incurred for the sole or dominant purpose of expediting or securing the performance of a routine government action of a minor nature). There is no equivalent exception for Australian public officials.

> ***Example*** M Ltd has tendered for a permit to operate a mine in a foreign country. Its managing director provides expensive gifts and a holiday to the close family members of the foreign official who is deciding the application. The cost of these gifts would not be deductible.

- **Expenses relating to illegal activities.** Section 26-54 *ITAA97* denies deductions for losses and outgoings to the extent that they relate to a physical element of an offence against an Australian law of which the taxpayer has been convicted of an indictable offence. This provision was enacted in 2005 in response to the decision in *FC of T v La Rosa* 2003 ATC 4510, where it was held that the fact a taxpayer carries on unlawful business activities does not prevent losses and outgoings arising in the course of such activities from being deductible [9.4].

> ***Example*** Bruce is a drug dealer and has been convicted of indictable drug trafficking offences. He cannot claim deductions for purchasing drugs from his suppliers.

- **Limit on deductions that contribute to a tax loss.** Section 26-55 *ITAA97* places a limit on the total amounts a taxpayer can deduct under s 25-50 (pensions, etc) [13.9], div 30 (gifts) [13.13], div 31 (conservation covenants) [13.14] and s 290-150 (personal superannuation contributions) [19.7]. The limit is designed to ensure that deductions under these provisions cannot contribute to the amount of a tax loss [13.15]. To avoid deductions under div 30 and div 31 being wasted due to the operation of s 26-55, sub-div 30DB *ITAA97* allows taxpayers to elect to spread their deductions for certain gifts and conservation covenants over 5 years.

> ***Example*** In 2022/23, Sally earned $70,000 of assessable income and incurred business deductions of $50,000. She also made a $25,000 personal superannuation contribution which she would ordinarily be able to deduct under s 290-150. However, Sally is only entitled to deduct $20,000 of the contribution, as it would otherwise produce a tax loss of $5,000. Sally's taxable income for the year is therefore nil, and she is not entitled to carry forward any loss into the subsequent year. If, on the other hand, the $25,000 deduction related to a conservation covenant instead of superannuation contributions, Sally could elect to claim a deduction of $20,000 in 2022/23 and the balance $5,000 in any of the next four income years.

- **Expenses associated with holding vacant land.** Section 26-102 *ITAA97* limits deductions relating to land where there is no substantial and permanent building or other structure that is in use or available for use on the land having a purpose that is independent of, and not incidental to, the purpose of any other structure or proposed structure. Basically, a loss or outgoing relating to holding such land (including interest on borrowings to acquire the land) is generally only deductible to the extent that the land is used to carry on a business. The provision is primarily targeted at individuals and does not apply to corporate tax entities, trustees of non-self managed superannuation funds, managed investment trusts and certain other entities.

It operates from 1 July 2019 and was introduced to address concerns that individuals were improperly claiming deductions for expenses, such as interest, relating to vacant land that they did not genuinely hold for income-producing purposes.

Example Sandy owns a block of land upon which she intends to eventually build a motel. The land is fenced but does not contain any building or other structure on it. Sandy incurs $20,000 in interest on borrowings used to purchase the land. These costs are not deductible under s 26-102. If, however, Sandy was operating a farming business on the land, she would be able to deduct these expenses.

- **Payments that do not comply with withholding obligations.** Section 26-105 *ITAA97* denies deductions where a taxpayer has failed to withhold PAYG from certain payments. The section applies to payments falling within the following provisions in sch 1 *TAA*: s 12-35 (payments to employees), s 12-40 (payments to directors), s 12-47 (payments to religious practitioners) and s 12-60 (payments under labour hire arrangements) [39.4]. It also applies to payments falling within s 12-190 (ie payments for supplies where the recipient has not quoted their ABN) [39.3].

Example Gretel employed Hans in her coffee shop. She paid him salary but failed to withhold PAYG as required under the *TAA*. Gretel cannot deduct the salary paid to Hans.

Deductions are also denied or limited under certain anti-avoidance regimes in the *ITAA97*, such as the 'forgiveness of commercial debts' [29.6], 'transfer pricing' [33.4], 'thin capitalisation' [33.5] and 'personal services income' [36.5] regimes.

[14.8] Miscellaneous *ITAA36* provisions that deny deductions

The *ITAA36* is peppered with a range of miscellaneous provisions that deny or limit deductions. Some of these provisions are outlined below:

- **Net capital gain expenses.** Section 51AAA(1) *ITAA36* denies a deduction where:
  (a) an amount is included in a taxpayer's assessable income under s 102-5 [17.2]
  (b) the taxpayer would otherwise be allowed a deduction under a provision listed in the table in s 51AAA(2) (eg s 8-1 *ITAA97*), and
  (c) if the amount had not been included in the taxpayer's assessable income, the deduction would not be allowable.

  The broad aim of s 51AAA is to deny deductions for expenditure incurred to generate assessable income by way of a net capital gain under the CGT regime discussed in Chapter 17.

Example Bill borrows money from a bank to purchase a holiday home which gives rise to a capital gain when it is subsequently sold. Bill cannot claim a deduction for the interest payable on the loan. He may, nevertheless, be able to include the interest in the cost base of his holiday home for the purposes of calculating his capital gain [17.6].

- **Reimbursements.** Section 51AH *ITAA36* denies deductions for expenses incurred by employees that have been reimbursed in circumstances where the reimbursement constitutes a fringe benefit or would constitute a fringe benefit if it was not an 'exempt benefit' under s 136(1)(g)

FBTAA [18.3]. Section 51AH does not apply to a 'cents per kilometre' reimbursement of car expenses (which is assessable under s 15-70 *ITAA97*) [10.3]. It also does not apply to deductions under the capital allowance rules in div 40 *ITAA97* [15.2].

Example George is an accountant employed by Tom. Tom asks George to visit a client's office in the suburbs for a meeting. George drives from work to the client's office. On the way, he purchases some stationery that he needs for taking notes. Tom reimburses George for his stationery and fuel costs (based on cents per kilometre rate). George is not entitled to a deduction for the cost of the stationery. He is, however, entitled to deduct his travel costs, but he will be assessed on the amount received for the reimbursement of his fuel costs under s 15-70.

- **Car expenses incurred by employees.** Section 51AF *ITAA36* provides that where an employer provides a car for the exclusive use of an employee or the employee's relative and that person is at any time during the relevant period entitled to use the car for private purposes, the employee is not entitled to a deduction for any car expense that relates to the car for the period. In these circumstances, the provision of the car would usually constitute a car fringe benefit [18.7].

Example Tom employs Jerry and provides him with a car for six months which can be used for private purposes. Jerry cannot claim any deductions for his petrol costs in respect of the car.

- **Private component of contributions for fringe benefits.** Section 51AJ *ITAA36* provides that employees who are provided with 'airline transport', 'board', 'loan', 'property', or 'residual' fringe benefits [18.3] may be denied deductions for amounts they contribute towards the cost of such benefits. The section applies where:
  - the employer or provider made an allowance for the employee's level of income-producing use of the benefit in calculating the amount of the contribution, and
  - the amount of the contribution would have been greater if it had been calculated without making such an allowance.

  In these circumstances, the employee is denied deductions to the extent that the contribution relates to, what is in effect, the private component of the benefit.

Example Laurel employs Hardy and provides him with a $100,000 loan, which constitutes a loan fringe benefit [18.9]. Assume the statutory interest rate for determining the taxable value of the loan fringe benefit is 10% and Laurel knows that Hardy will use 80% of the borrowings for income-producing purposes and 20% for private purposes. As FBT is effectively only payable on the private portion of a fringe benefit, and as Laurel does not want to pay any FBT, he charges interest at the rate of 2% per annum. In effect, the loan has been structured so that Hardy effectively pays interest at 0% per annum in respect of the $80,000 portion of the loan used for income-producing purposes and interest at 10% per annum in respect of the $20,000 portion of the loan used for private purposes. As Laurel has made an allowance for the income-producing use of the loan, s 51AJ applies, and Hardy is not entitled to any deduction in respect of the interest he pays on the loan, as it relates wholly to the private portion.

- **Non-cash business benefits.** Section 51AK *ITAA36* denies deductions to the extent that expenditure incurred under an agreement relates to a 'non-cash business benefit' that is not exclusively for use for the purpose of producing the taxpayer's assessable income.

> ***Example*** Max is a self-employed accountant. He purchases stationery costing $500 (exclusive of GST) for use in his practice. As part of the arrangement with the supplier, he is also provided with free fashion magazines worth $50 (exclusive of GST). Max will only be able to deduct $450.

- **Car parking expenses.** Section 51AGA *ITAA36* states that deductions are denied for expenses incurred by an employee in parking a car at parking facilities at, or in the vicinity of, his or her primary place of employment for more than four hours in total per day between the hours of 7am and 7pm if the car was used in connection with travel by the employee between his or her place of residence and primary place of employment. However, s 51AGA does not deny deductions for expenses that are excluded under regulations (eg certain disabled car parking facilities: reg 8 *ITAR15*).

> ***Example*** Carol travels from home to her primary place of work every Monday to Friday and parks her car at a parking station near work from 8am to 5pm each day. She is not entitled to deduct her car parking expenses unless they are excluded under regulations.

- **Tax avoidance schemes.** The *ITAA36* contains a variety of anti-avoidance provisions that deny or limit deductions. For example, s 177F allows the Commissioner to cancel deductions arising under schemes that fall within the general anti-avoidance provisions in pt IVA *ITAA36* [37.7]. There are also specific anti-avoidance provisions that deny or reduce deductions relating to certain 'pre-payment' (s 82KJ), 'tax deferral' (s 82KK) and 'recoupment' (s 82KL) schemes [29.11].

[14.9] QUESTIONS

1. What types of expenses do the substantiation rules in div 900 *ITAA97* apply to? What kinds of records satisfy these rules?
2. B Co owns a construction business. Can it deduct its income tax, FBT and payroll tax?
3. Barry is a barrister. On the days he is in court, he usually invites his instructing solicitors to lunch to discuss the cases he is working on. Over the last few months, Barry incurred $3,300 in restaurant bills. Can he deduct these expenses?
4. Wally works at a hamburger restaurant. His employer encourages, but does not require, him to wear a special pink shirt with a picture of a hamburger on the back. The design of the shirt is registered under div 34 *ITAA97*. Wally spent $88 to purchase the shirt. Can he deduct this expense?
5. Ted is employed by an accounting firm. To earn extra money, he established a small business selling handicrafts at the local market on weekends. In the first year of operating, he made a loss of $10,000. Can he offset this loss against his salary income of $80,000?
6. Bully Co breached the *Competition and Consumer Act 2011* (Cth) for misusing its market power in its business dealings and it incurred a large fine. Can it deduct the fine?
7. Kim works as a trainee accountant in a freight business while undertaking a part-time accounting degree. Can she deduct her HECS-HELP repayments relating to the degree?
8. Wally's employer reimburses him for the cost of stationery that he purchased for use at work. Can Wally deduct the cost of the stationery?

PART F

ASSET TAXATION RULES

15 CAPITAL ALLOWANCES

[15.1] Introduction

Capital expenditure is not deductible under the general deduction provision in s 8-1 *ITAA97* as it falls within the first negative limb of the section [12.4]. This means that capital expenditure can only be deductible if it satisfies the requirements of a specific deduction provision. The tax legislation contains a number of provisions that provide deductions for particular kinds of capital expenditure. Some of these provisions allow immediate deductions for capital expenditure, while others require capital expenditure to be written off over a number of years. Writing capital expenditure off over a number of years is justified on the basis that the expenditure usually provides taxpayers with benefits that extend beyond a single year. It is therefore appropriate to spread their deductions over more than one year to align the expenditure with the benefits received.

This chapter focuses on the 'capital allowance regime' in div 40 *ITAA97*, which allows taxpayers to deduct the cost of 'depreciating assets' that are used for a 'taxable purpose' over their 'effective lives'. The regime operates subject to special rules that allow SBEs and certain other entities to claim immediate deductions in particular cases [15.2]. It also contains 'balancing adjustment' rules that apply where taxpayers stop holding depreciating assets [15.3] and 'pooling' rules that allow groups of assets to be written off together as if they were a single asset [15.4]. There are also special rules that apply to primary producers and miners [15.5] as well as business-related 'blackhole' capital expenditure [15.6].

The chapter also examines the 'capital works regime' in div 43 *ITAA97*, which provides deductions for construction expenditure on 'capital works' (eg buildings and structural improvements) used for income-producing and other eligible purposes [15.7].

[15.2] Capital allowance regime

The central provision in div 40 is s 40-25(1), which provides that an entity can deduct an amount equal to the 'decline in value' for an income year of a 'depreciating asset' that it 'held' during the year.

The deduction available under s 40-25(1) is reduced in the following circumstances:

- **Reduction for assets not used wholly for a taxable purpose.** The deduction is reduced under s 40-25(2) by that part of a depreciating asset's decline in value attributable to the entity's use of the asset, or installation ready for use, for a purpose other than a 'taxable purpose'. An asset is applied for a 'taxable purpose' if it is applied for the purpose of producing assessable income, exploration or prospecting, mining site rehabilitation or environmental protection activities (s 40-25(7)).

Example Emily is an employee who held a depreciating asset used for work that had a decline in value for the income year of $1,000. If Emily used the asset 40% for a taxable purpose and 60% for a non-taxable purpose, she can deduct $400 (ie $1,000 – $600) for the income year.

- **Reduction for second-hand assets used in residential premises.** The deduction is reduced under s 40-27 by that part of the asset's decline in value that is attributable to producing assessable income from the use of residential premises to provide residential accommodation not in the course of carrying on a business, if:
  - the taxpayer did not hold the asset when it was first used, or first installed ready for use (other than as trading stock) by any entity, or
  - the asset was previously used, or installed ready for use, in the taxpayer's residence or for a non-taxable purpose.

  This reduction targets assets held by individuals and does not apply to assets held by companies, non-self managed superannuation funds and certain trusts.

15

Example Liz owns a residential apartment and furniture that she leases to tenants. She acquired the apartment and furniture on 1 July 2023 from the previous owner who had also leased the apartment and furniture to tenants. As the furniture is second-hand, s 40-27 prevents Liz from claiming deductions for its decline in value under s 40-25. If Liz had acquired new furniture from a retailer, s 40-27 would not apply and she would be able to claim deductions for its decline in value.

Depreciating asset

A 'depreciating asset' is defined in s 40-30(1) as an asset that has a limited 'effective life' and can reasonably be expected to decline in value over the time it is used. It, however, expressly excludes:

- land
- trading stock, or
- intangible assets (other than those intangible assets mentioned in s 40-30(2); namely: mining, quarrying or prospecting rights or information, intellectual property, in-house software, indefeasible rights to use international telecommunications submarine cable systems, spectrum licences and datacasting transmitter licences).

Some common examples of depreciating assets include:

- fridges used in a supermarket to store frozen food
- display cabinets used in a cake shop
- computers and furniture used in an office
- tools and trucks used by construction workers
- machinery and equipment used in a factory, and
- aircraft and ships used by airline and shipping companies.

Goodwill is not a depreciating asset as it is an intangible asset that is not mentioned in s 40-30(2). Goodwill is essentially the value of a business over the value of all its other assets, less liabilities. In *IRC v Muller & Co's Margarine Limited* [1901] AC 217, Lord Lindley described goodwill (at 235) as including 'whatever adds value to a business by reason of situation, name and reputation, connection, introduction to old customers, and agreed absence from competition'. In the same case, Lord Macnaghten said (at 223-4) that goodwill 'is the benefit and advantage of the good name, reputation, and connection of a business' and 'is the attractive force which brings in custom'. These observations were relied on by the High Court in *FC of T v Murry* 98 ATC 4585, where Gaudron, McHugh, Gummow and Hayne JJ explained (at 4) that goodwill 'is inseparable from the conduct of a business' and has three different aspects (property, source and value). According to their Honours, goodwill 'may derive from identifiable assets of a business, but it is an indivisible item of property, and it is an asset that is legally distinct from the sources—including other assets of the business—that have created the goodwill'.

Improvements or fixtures on land, whether removable or not, are treated as separate assets from the land for the purposes of div 40 (s 40-30(3)). Nevertheless, it is generally not possible to deduct amounts under div 40 in relation to expenditure on items such as buildings because div 40 does not apply to 'capital works' that are deductible under div 43 (or that would be deductible under div 43 but for certain reasons) (s 40-45(2)) [15.7].

Example Dorio operates a pizza restaurant and owns the following assets:

- ingredients for making pizzas
- the land, restaurant premises and goodwill of the business, and
- the tables, chairs, ovens and fridges used in the business.

Only the tables, chairs, ovens and fridges are depreciating assets.

Holder

The 'holder' of a depreciating asset is determined by reference to the table in s 40-40. The table identifies 10 different kinds of depreciating assets and the particular entities that are deemed to hold those assets. In the general case, the holder of a depreciating asset is its legal owner. In most cases, the legal owner of an asset is also its 'economic owner' (ie the entity able to access the asset's economic benefits while stopping others from doing the same). However, in some cases the legal owner of an asset will not be its economic owner. In these instances, it is the economic owner who is usually treated as the holder of the asset. For instance, under a 'hire purchase arrangement' the holder of the asset is the economic owner of the asset (the lessee) rather than the legal owner of the asset (the lessor).

Decline in value

The decline in value of a depreciating asset commences from the 'start time', which is usually the time when the entity first uses the asset, or has it installed ready for use, for *any* purpose (s 40-60).

An entity can choose to calculate the 'decline in value' of a depreciating asset using:

- a 'diminishing value method', or
- a 'prime cost method' (s 40-65).

Once a taxpayer has chosen to use a particular method to calculate the decline in value of a depreciating asset, the method cannot be changed (s 40-130). A taxpayer cannot therefore swap from one method to another in respect of the same depreciating asset. A taxpayer can, however, use different methods for different depreciating assets.

There is one prime cost method formula (s 40-75) and two diminishing value method formulas—one of these applies to assets acquired before 10 May 2006 (s 40-70) and the other applies to assets acquired after 9 May 2006 (s 40-72):

Diminishing value method (pre-10 May 2006 assets) : $\text{Base value} \times \frac{\text{Days held}}{365} \times \frac{150\%}{\text{Asset's effective life}}$

Diminishing value method (post-9 May 2006 assets) : $\text{Base value} \times \frac{\text{Days held}}{365} \times \frac{200\%}{\text{Asset's effective life}}$

Prime cost method : $\text{Asset's cost} \times \frac{\text{Days held}}{365} \times \frac{100\%}{\text{Asset's effective life}}$

The meanings of the terms used in the above formulas are outlined below.

Asset's effective life

Entities can choose to use the Commissioner's determination of an asset's effective life under s 40-100 or self-assess the asset's effective life under s 40-105 (s 40-95). The Commissioner's determination of the effective lives of a variety of different kinds of assets is set out in tables contained in *Income Tax (Effective Life of Depreciating Assets) Determination 2015* and TR 2022/1.

Where an entity self-assesses the effective life of an asset, it must estimate the period that the asset can be used for a taxable purpose (or for producing exempt income) having regard to reasonable wear and tear and assuming that the asset will be maintained in reasonably good order. If the entity concludes that it would be likely to scrap or abandon the asset before the end of this period, the effective life of the asset is deemed to end at such earlier time (s 40-105(2)). An entity may recalculate the effective life of an asset where its original estimate is no longer accurate (s 40-110).

Special rules exist to calculate the effective lives of certain assets. In particular, the following table specifies the deemed effective lives of certain intangible depreciating assets (s 40-95(7)).

Intangible depreciating asset	Effective life
Standard patent	20 years
Innovation patent	8 years
Petty patent	6 years
Registered design	15 years
Copyright (except copyright in a film)	The shorter of: (a) 25 years from when the taxpayer acquires copyright; or (b) the period until the copyright ends
A licence (except one relating to copyright or in-house software)	The term of the licence
A licence relating to a copyright (except copyright in a film)	The shorter of: (a) 25 years from when the taxpayer becomes licensee; or (b) the period until the licence ends
In-house software	5 years
Datacasting transmitter licence	15 years
Telecommunications site access right	The term of the right

Asset's cost

The cost of a depreciating asset is determined in accordance with sub-div 40-C *ITAA97*. There are two elements that make up the cost of an asset (s 40-175):

- **First element.** This element (usually calculated at the time an entity begins to hold the asset) is the amount that the entity is taken to have paid under s 40-185 to hold the asset (eg cash paid to acquire the asset).
- **Second element.** This element (calculated after the entity begins to hold the asset) is the amount the entity is taken to have paid under s 40-185 for each economic benefit that has contributed to bringing the asset to its present condition and location from time to time since it commenced to hold the asset (eg cash paid to transport or modify an asset).

In certain cases, the first and second elements of the cost of a depreciating asset are determined in accordance with market value and other special rules (ss 40-180, 40-190).

Importantly, the cost of a depreciating asset is reduced to the extent of any ITCs available to the entity in respect of its acquisition or importation (s 27-80). It is also generally reduced by decreasing adjustments (s 27-85) and increased by increasing adjustments (s 27-90) that relate to the asset. The cost of a depreciating asset is also generally reduced by any portion of its elements that are deductible under a provision outside div 40 (s 40-215).

Example Alice carries on a printing business and is registered for GST. On 1 July 2023, she acquired a photocopier for use in her business for $55,000 (including GST). On the same day, she also paid a courier company $1,100 (inclusive of GST) to have the photocopier delivered to her office. Alice is entitled to an ITC of $5,000 for the acquisition of the photocopier and an ITC of $100 for the delivery costs. These amounts are not included in the asset's cost. Therefore, the first element of the photocopier's cost is $50,000 and its second element is $1,000. The asset's cost is therefore $51,000.

To limit deductions relating to luxury cars, the first element of the cost of a car designed mainly for carrying passengers is reduced to the 'car limit' for the financial year in which it is first held if its cost exceeds that limit (s 40-230(1)). The car limit does not apply to cars used for transporting disabled people in wheelchairs for profit (eg modified taxis) or cars whose cost exceeds the car limit only because of modifications made to enable a disabled person to use it for a taxable purpose (eg for carrying on a business). The following table sets out the car limits over recent financial years.

Car limit				
2019/20	2020/21	2021/22	2022/23	2023/24
$57,581	$59,136	$60,733	$64,741	$68,108

Base value

The base value is the asset's cost (for the start year) or its opening adjustable value for the year and any element included in the second element of its cost for the year (for any later income year) (s 40-70). The 'opening adjustable value' of an asset for an income year is its adjustable value at the end of the previous year (s 40-85). The 'adjustable value' of a depreciating asset at a particular point of time is essentially the cost of the asset less any decline in value of the asset up until that time (s 40-85). The opening adjustable value of an asset is reduced by any ITCs available to the entity in respect of the acquisition or importation of the asset (s 27-80). It is also generally reduced by decreasing adjustments (s 27-85) and increased by increasing adjustments (s 27-90) that relate to the asset.

Example Following on from the previous example, the base value of Alice's photocopier on 1 July 2023 is $51,000. If the decline in value of the photocopier for 2023/24 is $10,200, the base value of the photocopier on 1 July 2024 is $40,800 (ie $51,000 – $10,200).

Days held

Days held means the number of days in the income year that the entity held the asset (ignoring any days that it did not use it or have it installed ready for use).

Example In the previous example, Alice acquired the photocopier on 1 July 2023. If she held the photocopier for the whole year, the days held would be 365. However, if she acquired the photocopier on 1 June 2024, the days held would be 30 days.

Comparing the diminishing value and prime cost methods

The following example compares the ways in which deductions for the decline in value of an asset are calculated under the diminishing value and prime cost methods.

Example C Co is a chocolate manufacturer and is registered for GST. On 1 October 2023, C Co installed a new machine in its factory. It purchased the machine for $110,000 (inclusive of GST) and uses it exclusively to manufacture a new variety of chocolate. When it acquired the machine, C Co estimated that it would have an effective life of 10 years. For depreciation purposes, the cost of the machine is deemed to be $100,000 (as C Co is entitled to an ITC of $10,000 in relation to the acquisition). Depending on which method of depreciation is chosen, the deduction for the decline in value of the machine over the next few years is calculated as follows:

Year	Diminishing value method	Prime cost method
2023/24	$\$100{,}000 \times \frac{365-92}{365} \times \frac{200\%}{10} = \$14{,}959$	$\$100{,}000 \times \frac{365-92}{365} \times \frac{100\%}{10} = \$7{,}479$
2024/25	$(\$100{,}000 - \$14{,}959) \times \frac{365}{365} \times \frac{200\%}{10}$ $= \$17{,}008$	$(\$100{,}000 - \$14{,}959) \times \frac{365}{365} \times \frac{100\%}{10}$ $= \$10{,}000$
2025/26	$(\$100{,}000 - \$14{,}959 - \$17{,}008) \times \frac{365}{365} \times \frac{200\%}{10}$ $= \$13{,}607$	$\$100{,}000 \times \frac{365}{365} \times \frac{100\%}{10} = \$10{,}000$
2026/27	$(\$100{,}000 - \$14{,}959 - \$17{,}008 - \$13{,}607)$ $\times \frac{365}{365} \times \frac{200\%}{10} = \$10{,}885$	$\$100{,}000 \times \frac{365}{365} \times \frac{100\%}{10} = \$10{,}000$

Assuming the machine continues to be used exclusively for income-producing purposes, C Co can continue to deduct the decline in value of the machine over the subsequent years until its cost is totally written off.

As mentioned above, the decline in value of a depreciating asset commences from the ‘start time’, which is usually the time the entity first uses the asset, or has it installed ready for use, for any purpose (s 40-60). This means that if a depreciating asset is used (or installed ready for use) for a non-taxable purpose, it will still decline in value, but no deductions will be available under s 40-25 until such time as it commences to be used (or installed ready for use) for a taxable purpose.

Example Max is an employee architect who acquired a printer on 1 July 2023 for $5,000 (disregarding GST). He uses the printer from 1 July 2023 to 30 June 2025 for private purposes. On 1 July 2025, he starts to use the printer exclusively for income-producing purposes and continues to use it for such purposes over the next few years. Max estimated that the printer has an effective life of five years and he has elected to use the prime cost method to determine its decline in value. Each year, the decline in value of the printer is therefore $1,000 (ie $5,000 × 365/365 × 20%). He cannot claim any deductions for the decline in value of the printer in the 2023/24 or 2024/25 income years as it is not used for a taxable purpose in those years. However, he can claim deductions of $1,000 in each of the 2025/26, 2026/27 and 2027/28 income years as the printer is being used for a taxable purpose in those years. No deductions are permitted beyond the 2027/28 income year as the cost of the printer is fully written off over five years.

It is also important to note that even though s 40-25(2) requires the deduction for the decline in value of a depreciating asset to be reduced to the extent that the asset is not used for a taxable purpose, this does not affect the calculation of the adjustable value of the asset.

Example Ted is an employee accountant. On 1 July 2023, he purchased a computer for $8,000 (disregarding GST). Throughout 2023/24, he used the computer 50% for a taxable purpose. If the computer's decline in value for the year is $2,000, Ted can only claim a deduction of $1,000 (ie 50% × $2,000). The adjustable value of the computer on 30 June 2024 is nevertheless $6,000 (ie $8,000 – $2,000).

Immediate deduction for non-business assets costing up to $300

Where the cost of an asset does not exceed $300 and the asset is used predominantly for the purpose of producing assessable income that is not income from carrying on a business, the decline in value of the asset is deemed to be the asset's cost (s 40-80(2)). This rule is designed to simplify the capital allowance regime by allowing assets costing up to $300 to be completely written off in the income year in which they start to be held. The rule does not apply to an asset that is part of a set of assets that the taxpayer starts to hold in the income year where the total cost of the set of assets exceeds $300. Furthermore, it does not apply where the total cost of the asset and any other identical asset that the taxpayer starts to hold in the income year exceeds $300.

Example Jerry is an employee photographer who purchased portable lights for work-related purposes for $290 (disregarding GST). Even though the lights may have an effective life of 10 years, Jerry can write off their total cost in the income year in which he commenced to hold them.

Immediate and accelerated deductions for business assets

Instant asset write-off for SBEs

Subdivision 328-D *ITAA97* contains an 'instant asset write-off' that allows SBEs [8.7] immediate deductions for the taxable purpose proportion of the adjustable value of depreciating assets costing less than a prescribed threshold (s 328-180). The threshold was originally set at $1,000 but has been increased on several occasions over the years to encourage spending on new assets (s 328-180 *ITTPA*). In particular, during the COVID-19 crisis, a special 'temporary full expensing' measure applied to assets first used or installed ready for use during the period 7.30pm on 6 October 2020 to 30 June 2023. This effectively meant that the threshold was unlimited during that period. In the 2023 Budget, the Government announced that the threshold will revert to $20,000 for assets first used or installed ready for use during the period 1 July 2023 to 30 June 2024. The following table summarises the relevant thresholds over recent years.

Period when asset first used or installed ready for use for a taxable purpose	Threshold
1 July 2023 to 30 June 2024	$20,000
7.30pm on 6 October 2020 to 30 June 2023	Unlimited
12 March 2020 to 7.30pm on 6 October 2020	$150,000
7.30pm on 2 April 2019 to 11 March 2020	$30,000
29 January 2019 to 7.30pm on 2 April 2019	$25,000
7.30pm on 12 May 2015 to 28 January 2019	$20,000
1 January 2014 to 7.30pm on 12 May 2015	$1,000
1 July 2012 to 31 December 2013	$6,500
1 July 2011 to 30 June 2012	$1,000

Example S Co is an SBE that operates a pizza restaurant. On 3 May 2020, it spent $100,000 (disregarding GST) on a new oven that it immediately commenced to use for baking pizzas. S Co could claim an immediate deduction for the cost of the oven as its cost was below the $150,000 threshold.

If S Co had, instead, purchased the oven on 1 January 2024 for $100,000 (disregarding GST), it would not be able to claim an immediate deduction for the cost of the oven as its cost is above the $20,000 threshold.

Temporary instant asset write-off for medium-sized businesses

On 2 April 2019, s 40-82 *ITAA97* was introduced to extend the instant asset write-off to medium-sized businesses. When s 40-82 was first introduced, it only applied to entities with an aggregated turnover of between $10m and $50m. However, due to the COVID-19 pandemic, it was extended from 12 March 2020 to entities with an aggregated turnover of between $10m and $500m. Basically, eligible entities were allowed immediate deductions for the taxable purpose proportion of depreciating assets costing less than:

- $30,000 for assets acquired from 7.30pm on 2 April 2019 to 11 March 2020 and first used or installed ready for use before 12 March 2020, and
- $150,000 for assets acquired from 7.30pm on 12 March 2019 to 31 December 2020 and first used or installed ready for use from 12 March 2020 to 30 June 2021.

> ***Example*** M Co is a computer parts manufacturer that had an aggregated turnover of $200m in 2020/21. On 5 August 2020, it spent $100,000 (disregarding GST) on a new machine that it immediately commenced to use for manufacturing computer parts. M Co could claim an immediate deduction for the cost of the machinery as it was below the $150,000 threshold.

Temporary full expensing for businesses with turnover up to $5 billion

To encourage additional investment during the COVID-19 pandemic, sub-div 40-BB *ITTPA* was enacted to temporarily allow most businesses to fully write off the cost of their eligible depreciating assets. The incentive applied to entities that were SBEs, or would be SBEs if the aggregated turnover threshold was $5 billion (instead of $10m), for the income year [8.7] (s 40-155 *ITTPA*). To be eligible, an entity had to start to hold the depreciating asset and start to use it, or have it installed ready for use, for a taxable purpose between 7:30pm on 6 October 2020 and 30 June 2023 (s 40-150 *ITTPA*).

Certain depreciating assets were excluded, such as those located outside Australia, those allocated to low-value or software development pools under sub-div 40-E *ITAA97* [15.4], and those deductible to primary producers under sub-div 40-F *ITAA97* [15.5] (ss 40-150(2) to (4) *ITTPA*). In addition, for entities that had an aggregated turnover of $50m or more, a depreciating asset was excluded if it was a second-hand asset or if the entity entered into a commitment to hold, construct or use the asset before Budget time (s 40-165 *ITTPA*).

> ***Example*** L Co is a mining company that had an aggregated turnover of $3 billion in 2022/23. On 9 August 2022, it purchased a new machine for $2m (disregarding GST) which it commenced to immediately use in its business. L Co could deduct $2m in 2022/23.

Temporary accelerated deductions for businesses with turnover under $500m

Prior to the introduction of full expensing, another measure used to stimulate business investment during the COIVD-19 pandemic was s 40-120 *ITTPA*. This provision allowed entities to calculate the decline in value of depreciating assets at accelerated rates where the following conditions were met:

- the income year was the year in which the entity started to use the asset, or had it installed ready for use, for a taxable purpose
- the entity had an aggregated turnover of less than $500m for the income year and would otherwise be an SBE [8.7], and
- the asset was covered by s 40-125 *ITTPA*.

An asset was generally covered by s 40-125 *ITTPA* if, in the period from 12 March 2020 to 30 June 2021, the entity started to hold the asset and started to use it, or have it installed ready for use, for a taxable purpose (s 40-125(1)). However, an asset was not covered by s 40-125 if it related to a contract entered into before 12 March 2020 (ss 40-125(2) to (6)), it was a second-hand asset (ie an asset previously held by another entity, other than as trading stock or for testing or trialling purposes) (s 40-125(7)), or it was used and located outside Australia (s 40-125(10)).

The accelerated rates were calculated under s 40-130 *ITTPA*, which worked out the decline in value of a depreciating asset as follows:

- **Start time occurred in the income year the entity started to use the asset.** If the asset's start time occurred in the income year in which the entity started to use the asset, or had it installed ready for use, for a taxable purpose (the 'current year'), the decline in value of the asset for the current year was the sum of the following amounts:

(a) 50% of the asset's cost at the end of the current year (disregarding any amount included in the second element of the asset's cost after 30 June 2021), and

(b) the amount that would be the asset's decline in value for the current year under div 40 *ITAA97* (assuming its cost was reduced by the amount worked out under paragraph (a) above) (s 40-130(2)).

- **Start time occurred in an earlier income year.** If the asset's start time occurred in an earlier income year, the decline in value of the asset for the current year was the sum of the following amounts:

(a) 50% of the asset's opening adjustable value for the current year and any amount included in the second element of its cost for that year (disregarding any amount included in the second element after 30 June 2021), and

(b) the amount that would be the asset's decline in value for the current year under div 40 *ITAA97* assuming: (i) for the diminishing value method—the asset's base value was reduced by the amount worked out under paragraph (a) above; or (ii) for the prime cost method—the asset's cost was reduced by the amount worked out under paragraph (a) above (s 40-130(4)).

15

Example Crafty Co had aggregated turnover of $300m in 2020/21. On 1 July 2020, it acquired machinery for $1m which it immediately commenced to use in its business. Ordinarily, the machinery could be written off at a diminishing value rate of 30%, which would result in a deduction of $300,000 in 2020/21. However, under the accelerated depreciation rates in s 40-130 *ITTPA*, it could claim a deduction of $650,000 in 2020/21. This amount is the sum of 50% of the machinery's cost (ie $500,000) and 30% of the remaining $500,000 (ie $150,000).

The accelerated rates could only be used once—in subsequent years, the decline in value of the asset falls under the general rules in div 40 *ITAA97* (s 40-135 *ITTPA*). The accelerated rates do not apply where the decline in value of the asset was worked out under s 40-82 *ITAA97* (see above) or sub-divs 40-E or 40-F *ITAA97* [15.5] (s 40-120(3) *ITTPA*).

[15.3] Balancing adjustments

Subdivision 40-D *ITAA97* contains 'balancing adjustment' rules that apply where a taxpayer disposes of a depreciating asset. The aim of these rules is to reconcile (ie 'balance') the deductions that have been claimed for the decline in value of an asset with any consideration received on the disposal of the asset. The rules may result in the taxpayer being required to include an amount in assessable income (where the taxpayer has 'over-depreciated' the asset) or being entitled to a deduction (where the taxpayer has 'under-depreciated' the asset).

Balancing adjustment event

Subdivision 40-D operates where a 'balancing adjustment event' arises in relation to a depreciating asset. Such an event occurs where an entity:

- stops holding a depreciating asset (eg sells it or loses it)
- stops using a depreciating asset for any purpose and expects never to use it again
- has not used a depreciating asset and decides never to use it, or
- changes its interests or holding in a depreciating asset (s 40-295).

Balancing adjustment

The balancing adjustment is basically calculated as follows:

- where the 'termination value' of the depreciating asset is more than its 'adjustable value' just before the balancing adjustment event—the difference is included in the entity's assessable income, and
- where the 'termination value' of the depreciating asset is less than its 'adjustable value' just before the balancing adjustment event—the difference is deductible to the entity (s 40-285).

The balancing adjustment is reduced to take account of any non-taxable use of the asset (s 40-290) and any reduction under s 40-27 (ie for second-hand assets used in residential premises) (s 40-291).

Adjustable value and termination value

As indicated earlier in the chapter, the 'adjustable value' of a depreciating asset is basically the cost of the asset less any decline in value of the asset up until the time of the balancing adjustment event (s 40-85). The cost of a depreciating asset is reduced by any ITCs available to the entity for its acquisition (s 27-80).

The 'termination value' of an asset depends on the nature of the balancing adjustment event (ss 40-300, 40-305). Generally, the termination value is based on the amount that an entity is taken to have received in respect of the balancing adjustment event (eg cash for the sale of the asset). However, in certain circumstances, market value or other special rules apply. The termination value must be reduced by any GST payable by the entity in relation to the balancing adjustment event (s 27-95(1)).

Example Johnny owns a tennis shop and purchased a stringing machine for $50,000 (exclusive of GST) on 1 July 2023. Johnny used the machine to string his customers' tennis racquets. Johnny estimated that the effective life of the machine is five years, and he claimed deductions for its decline in value at the prime cost rate of 20% (ie $10,000 per income year).

On 30 June 2025, Johnny sold the stringing machine. This constitutes a balancing adjustment event. At the time of sale, the 'adjustable value' of the stringing machine was $30,000 (ie $50,000 – $10,000 – $10,000).

If Johnny received $40,000 (exclusive of GST) for the sale of the stringing machine, he would be required to include $10,000 in his assessable income in 2024/25 as the termination value of the machine ($40,000) exceeds its adjustable value ($30,000) by $10,000.

If, however, Johnny received only $25,000 (exclusive of GST) for the sale of the stringing machine, he would be entitled to a deduction of $5,000 in 2024/25 as the termination value of the machine ($25,000) is less than its adjustable value ($30,000) by $5,000.

Balancing adjustment where car limit applies

Where a balancing adjustment happens in relation to a car that is subject to the car limit [15.2], the balancing adjustment is multiplied by a formula to reflect the fact that the full cost of the car has not been subject to the write-off (s 40-325).

Relief from the balancing adjustment rules

Relief from the operation of the balancing adjustment rules may be available in the following circumstances:

- **CGT roll-over relief (s 40-340).** Roll-over relief is available if a balancing adjustment event arises because a taxpayer disposes of an asset to another taxpayer, the disposal involves a 'CGT event' [17.3], and the conditions for specified kinds of CGT roll-over relief are satisfied [17.16]. The effect of the roll-over is that s 40-285 does not apply to the balancing adjustment event and the transferee can deduct the decline in value of the depreciating asset using the same method and effective life that the transferor was using (s 40-345).
- **Involuntary disposals (s 40-365).** A taxpayer can exclude an amount that is included in their assessable income as a result of a balancing adjustment event to the extent that they choose to apply the amount to reduce the cost of a replacement asset. A taxpayer can only make the choice if they stopped holding the asset because of certain circumstances (eg because the asset was lost or destroyed, or was compulsorily acquired by an Australian Government agency). The replacement asset must be used, or installed ready for use, for a taxable purpose and the taxpayer must be entitled to deduct an amount for it. Furthermore, unless the Commissioner otherwise allows, the replacement asset must start to be held by the taxpayer no earlier than one year before the balancing adjustment event occurred and no later than one year after the end of the income year in which the balancing adjustment event occurred.

[15.4] Pooling

Taxpayers may be eligible to use special 'pooling' rules to calculate the decline in value of certain depreciating assets instead of having to use the ordinary rules outlined at [15.2]. The benefit of pooling is that the decline in value of each asset does not need to be calculated separately. Instead, the pooled assets are written off together as if they were a single asset. There are three kinds of pools that can be established: 'low-value pools', 'software development pools' and 'general small business pools'.

Low-value pools

Subdivision 40-E *ITAA97* allows taxpayers to allocate 'low-cost assets' (ie assets costing less than $1,000) and 'low-value assets' (ie assets that have an opening adjustable value of less than $1,000) to a 'low-value pool' (s 40-425).

Assets that have been allocated to a low-value pool are written off at special diminishing value rates under s 40-440. The diminishing value rate of 18.75% applies to assets in the first year they are allocated to the pool. In subsequent years, the assets are written off at a diminishing value rate of 37.5%. The 37.5% rate assumes that the assets in the pool have an effective life of four years, while the 18.75% rate recognises that assets that have been allocated to the pool during the income year are only held for part of the year.

When allocating an asset to a low-value pool, a taxpayer must make a reasonable estimate of its taxable use percentage and calculate the decline in value based on this percentage (ss 40-435, 40-440). If a balancing adjustment event happens to a pooled asset, the closing balance of the pool for the year is reduced (but not below zero) by the taxable use percentage of the asset's termination value (any excess is included in the taxpayer's assessable income) (s 40-445).

Certain assets cannot be allocated to a pool. For instance, assets costing less than $300 that are used predominantly for the purpose of producing assessable income that is not income from carrying on a business cannot be allocated to a pool (s 40-425(4)). This is because these assets are deemed to have a decline in value equal to their cost and as a result they can be written off fully in the year that the expenditure is incurred [15.2]. In addition, to prevent duplication of the pooling rules, assets owned by SBEs and that are pooled under sub-div 328-D *ITAA97* (see below) cannot be pooled under sub-div 40-E (s 40-425(7)).

Example P Co is a large company that uses a pool to calculate the decline in value of its low-cost and low-value assets. On 30 June 2023, the closing balance of the pool was $10,000. During 2023/24, P Co acquired a low-cost asset for $500 (exclusive of GST), which it allocated to the pool. It estimated that this asset would be used 70% for a taxable purpose.

During 2023/24, it also allocated a low-value asset to the pool that it was previously writing off under the ordinary capital allowance rules. This asset was being used 80% for a taxable purpose and had an 'opening adjusted value' of $950 for the year.

The way that P Co calculates its deduction for 2023/24 in relation to the pool is set out below.

Asset	Amount included in pool	Decline in value for 2019/20	Deduction for 2019/20
Pool (closing balance on 30 June 2023)	$10,000	$10,000 × 37.5%	$3,750.00
Low-cost asset allocated to the pool	$350 (ie $500 × 70%)	$350 × 18.75%	$65.63
Low-value asset allocated to the pool	$760 (ie $950 × 80%)	$760 × 37.5%	$285.00
Totals	$11,110		$4,100.63
Pool (closing balance on 30 June 2024)	$7,009.37 (ie $11,110 – $4,100.63)		

Software development pools

Taxpayers can choose to allocate expenditure incurred on 'in-house software' for an income year to a 'software development pool' provided the in-house software is used solely for a taxable purpose (s 40-450).

'In-house software' is computer software or a right to use computer software that an entity acquires, develops, or has another entity develop and that is mainly for use in performing the functions for which the software was developed and is not deductible under a provision outside div 40 or div 328 (s 995-1).

Once a taxpayer chooses to create a software development pool, all expenditure incurred on in-house software for the income year must be allocated to the pool. Taxpayers are required to create a separate software development pool for each income year for which they incur expenditure on in-house software. Expenditure on in-house software in a software development pool that is incurred in a particular year is written off at the rates set out in the following table (s 40-455):

Income year	Expenditure that is deductible for the year
Year 1	Nil
Year 2	30%
Year 3	30%
Year 4	30%
Year 5	10%

General small business pools

SBEs are permitted to maintain 'general small business pools' under sub-div 328-D *ITAA97* and allocate depreciating assets costing more than the instant asset write-off threshold [15.2] to such a pool (s 328-185).

SBEs calculate deductions for their general small business pool by multiplying the 'opening pool balance' (worked out under s 328-195) by a diminishing value rate of 30% (s 328-190). A rate of 15% generally applies to depreciating assets in the first year they are allocated to the pool. However, this rate was increased to 57.5% for depreciating assets covered by s 40-125 *ITTPA* (s 328-182 *ITTPA*) [15.2].

When allocating an asset to a small business pool, the SBE must estimate its proportion of taxable purpose use and calculate the decline in value based on this proportion (s 328-205). If the balance in a small business pool at the end of an income year is less than the threshold amount, the SBE can deduct the entire balance of the pool (s 328-210).

[15.5] Primary producers and miners

The capital allowance regime contains special rules for primary producers and miners.

Under sub-divs 40-F and 40-G *ITAA97*, primary producers are entitled to immediate deductions for capital expenditure on 'fencing assets', 'water facilities', 'landcare operations' and 'fodder storage assets' (eg silos and tanks used to store grain and animal feed). They can also deduct the cost of 'horticultural plants' (eg live plants cultivated for their parts) at special rates that vary depending on their effective lives.

Under sub-div 40-H *ITAA97*, miners are entitled to immediate deductions for certain capital expenditure relating to exploration or prospecting, rehabilitation of mining or quarrying sites, and environmental protection activities. They are also allowed to deduct 'project amounts' (ie amounts relating to specified mining and transport capital expenditure) that have been allocated to a 'project pool' over the estimated life of the project under sub-div 40-I *ITAA97*.

[15.6] Business-related 'blackhole' capital expenditure

Section 40-880 *ITAA97* is a special provision within the capital allowance regime that deals with business-related 'blackhole' capital expenditure. The section is designed to operate as a 'provision of last resort' for granting deductions for business-related expenses that are not otherwise taken into account under the general provisions in the tax law.

Deduction over five years

Section 40-880 allows capital expenditure to be deductible in equal proportions over a period of five years starting with the year in which the expenditure is incurred. The deduction is available for capital expenditure incurred from 1 July 2005 that relates to a business that a taxpayer carries on, used to carry on, or proposes to carry on, for a 'taxable purpose' as defined in s 40-25(7) (eg for producing assessable income) [15.2].

A deduction is not available to the extent that the expenditure falls within any of the specific exclusions mentioned in the section. The most important exclusions are contained in s 40-880(5), which excludes expenditure to the extent that:

- it forms part of the cost of a depreciating asset held by the taxpayer
- it is deductible under another provision of the Act
- it forms part of the cost of land

- it is in relation to a lease or other legal or equitable right
- it would be taken into account in working out an assessable profit (eg under s 6-5) or a deductible loss (eg under s 8-1) of the taxpayer
- it could otherwise be taken into account in working out the amount of a capital gain or capital loss from a CGT event (eg it forms part of the cost base of a CGT asset)
- it would be non-deductible under another provision in the legislation if it were not of a capital nature
- it is not deductible under a provision in the legislation for a reason other than it being of a capital nature
- it is of a private or domestic nature, or
- it is incurred in gaining or producing exempt income or non-assessable non-exempt income.

> ***Example*** In the current income year, Raider Co incurred $500,000 of legal expenses in making an unsuccessful takeover bid for another company. The legal expenses are of a capital nature and are therefore not deductible under s 8-1. The legal expenses also do not result in Raider Co acquiring a depreciating asset and are not taken into account for CGT purposes. Raider Co is entitled to deduct the legal expenses under s 40-880. Raider Co can deduct $100,000 in the current income year and $100,000 in each of the next four income years.

Immediate deduction for start-up expenses

From 1 July 2015, taxpayers have been able to claim immediate deductions (rather than deductions over five years) for certain expenses associated with starting a new business. Section 40-880(2A) provides that capital expenditure is fully deductible in the income year in which it is incurred if it relates to a business that is proposed to be carried on and the expenditure is incurred:

- in obtaining advice or services relating to the proposed structure or the proposed operation of the business, or
- in payment to an Australian Government agency of fees, taxes or charges relating to establishing the business or its operating structure.

Immediate deductions are available to entities that are SBEs in the income year [8.7]. They are also available, for expenditure incurred on or after 1 July 2020, to entities that would be SBEs in the income year if the SBE aggregated turnover threshold was $50m (instead of $10m) (s 40-880(2B)).

> ***Example*** X Co is an SBE that is starting a new business. It paid a fee to ASIC for registering its business name as well a fee to a property consultant for advice on where to locate its new business premises. Both these expenses fall within s 40-880(2A).

[15.7] Capital works regime

Division 43 *ITAA97* allows taxpayers to deduct amounts for construction expenditure on capital works (being buildings, extensions, alterations and improvements to buildings) at the rate of either 2.5% over 40 years or 4% over 25 years (ss 43-10, 43-25).

Deductions are only available if the capital works are used for income-producing or other eligible purposes (eg R&D) during the income year. In addition, the construction must have commenced after specified dates, which differ depending on the nature of the capital works (s 43-20). Where construction commenced before 1 July 1997, there is an added requirement that, at the time of completion, the capital works must also have been intended to be used for the purposes specified in s 43-90.

Deductions are calculated separately for each individual capital works project. This means that if a building that has been constructed is later extended, the construction of the building is treated as a separate project from the construction of the extension. Construction expenditure does not include the cost of acquiring land or expenditure incurred in demolishing existing structures, levelling a site or landscaping (s 43-70).

Rate of write-off

Determining the rate of write off (ie 2.5% or 4%) is complex and depends on a range of factors, such as:

- the type of capital works
- the use of the relevant 'construction expenditure area' as defined in s 43-75, and
- the date when the capital works began as determined under s 43-80 (ie the date when construction commences, such as the pouring of foundations for a building).

The basic rules under s 43-25 are as follows:

- For capital works that began after 26 February 1992, the write-off rate is 2.5% (for parts used as described in the table in s 43-140) or 4% (for parts used as described in the table in s 43-145).
- For capital works that began before 27 February 1992, the write-off rate is 4% (if the capital works began after 21 August 1984 and before 16 September 1987) or 2.5% (in any other case).

The following table provides a rough guide of the general write-off rates that apply to certain kinds of capital works. The table operates subject to a number of exceptions and qualifications.

Type of capital works	Use/Activities	Date construction commenced	Rate
Non-residential buildings	Industrial	27 Feb 1992 onwards	4%
	Other	16 Sept 1987 onwards	2.5%
		22 Aug 1984 to 15 Sept 1987	4%
		20 July 1982 to 21 Aug 1984	2.5%
Residential buildings	Hotels, motels and guest houses used for short-term accommodation	27 Feb 1992 onwards	4%
		16 Sept 1987 to 26 Feb 1992	2.5%
		22 Aug 1984 to 15 Sept 1987	4%
		20 Aug 1979 to 21 Aug 1984	2.5%
	Other	16 Sept 1987 onwards	2.5%
		18 July 1985 to 15 Sept 1987	4%
Structural improvements		27 Feb 1992 onwards	2.5%

To support the supply of rental housing, the Government announced in the 2023 Budget that that it will increase the deduction rate from 2.5% to 4% for construction expenditure on eligible new 'build-to-rent' projects. The higher rate will apply where construction commences after 7:30pm on 9 May 2023 and the project consists of 50 or more apartments or dwellings available for rent to the general public. The dwellings must be retained under single ownership for at least 10 years before they can be sold and each lease must be of at least 3 years duration.

Commencement and ending of deduction

Deductions begin from the day capital works are first used for a relevant purpose and are pro-rated to the extent that any part of the capital works are not used for the requisite purpose during the year. Deductions are not allowed outside the period of 40 years (where the 2.5% rate is used) or 25 years (where the 4% rate is used). As a result, deductions are lost in relation to any construction expenditure not written off over this period.

Who can claim the deduction?

Generally, it is the owner of the building that is entitled to deductions (s 43-115). Subsequent owners claim deductions based on the construction expenditure of the original owner (the price paid by the subsequent owner for the building is irrelevant in calculating the deduction).

In practice it is not always possible for a new owner of a building to establish the original owner's construction expenditure, particularly where there have been several other owners in the meantime. In these circumstances, the ATO accepts an estimate of the construction expenditure by an appropriately qualified person (eg a quantity surveyor) (TR 97/25).

Example B Co is a manufacturing company that purchased land for \$2m on 1 January 2020. It commenced to build a factory on the land on 1 September 2020. Construction of the factory was completed on 12 July 2021 for a cost of \$10m (exclusive of GST). B Co commenced to use the factory for income-producing purposes from 1 August 2021.

As the factory is used for 'industrial activities', B Co can write off the \$10m construction costs at the rate of 4% from 1 August 2021. B Co is therefore entitled to a deduction in 2021/22 of \$366,027 (\$10m × 334/365 × 4%) and a deduction in 2022/23 of \$400,000 (\$10m × 365/365 × 4%).

If B Co sold the land to C Co on 1 July 2024 for \$20m (exclusive of GST), B Co cannot continue to claim any further deductions for the factory's construction costs. However, if C Co also uses the factory for income-producing purposes, C Co can write off the balance construction costs over the unexpired portion of the 25-year deduction period. On this basis, C Co is entitled to a \$400,000 deduction in 2024/25.

[15.8] QUESTIONS

1. What is a depreciating asset? Provide some examples of such assets. Explain the different ways that the decline in value of a depreciating asset may be calculated.
2. Barry is a barrister who purchased a desk for \$1,000, which he uses in his chambers. A computer terminal, which he acquired for \$4,400, is situated on the desk. There are also several bookshelves in his chambers which cost Barry \$3,300. On the bookshelves are law reports which he bought from another barrister for \$22,000. What deductions can he claim?
3. B Co is a large biscuit manufacturer. On 2 December 2023, it purchased a new machine for \$4.4m which it commenced to immediately use for producing biscuits. What deductions can it claim?
4. What is the role of a balancing adjustment? Provide some examples of balancing adjustment events.
5. R Co manufactures tennis balls. On 1 January 2024, R Co purchased a new machine for \$1.1m which it used to produce the tin cans in which it packages the tennis balls. At the time of acquiring the machine, R Co estimated that the machine would have an effective life of 10 years

before requiring replacement. Subsequently, on 1 January 2027, as a result of new technology, a better machine became available and R Co decided to sell the original machine for $330,000 and purchase a new machine for $2.2m. What are the tax consequences of these arrangements under div 40 *ITAA97*?

6. Explain how the pooling rules for low-value assets in sub-div 40-E *ITAA97* operate. What assets cannot be allocated to a pool under sub-div 40-E?
7. What is the purpose of s 40-880 *ITAA97*? Provide some examples of expenditure that falls within the provision and expenditure that is excluded from the provision.
8. Brett recently purchased a milk bar business. Can he claim a deduction under s 40-880 *ITAA97* for the amount paid to acquire the goodwill of the business?
9. Phil is a solicitor who owns his own legal practice. Three years ago, he purchased land for $2.2m near a new shopping centre. He spent $5.5m constructing an office building on the land and recently moved his practice into the building. Phil also spent $88,000 to purchase new furniture, computers and printers for his office. What deductions can Phil claim?

TRADING STOCK 16

[16.1] Introduction

Taxpayers that carry on trading businesses (eg manufacturers, wholesalers and retailers) buy and sell 'trading stock'. As trading stock is a 'revenue asset', buying and selling trading stock is dealt with under the ordinary income (s 6-5 *ITAA97*) [9.1] and general deduction (s 8-1 *ITAA97*) [12.1] provisions. In other words, subject to the GST reconciliation rules [8.5], the proceeds from selling trading stock is assessable under s 6-5 and the cost of purchasing trading stock is deductible under s 8-1.

This chapter examines the meaning of 'trading stock' [16.2] and the general treatment of trading stock under ss 6-5 and 8-1 [16.3]. It also discusses the operation of the special provisions in div 70 *ITAA97* that deal with accounting and valuing trading stock [16.4]–[16.6].

[16.2] Meaning of trading stock

Trading stock is defined in s 70-10 *ITAA97* to include anything produced, manufactured or acquired that is held for purposes of manufacture, sale or exchange in the ordinary course of business. It also expressly includes 'live stock' as defined in s 995-1(1) *ITAA97*. As the definition of trading stock in s 70-10 is merely inclusive, items that are trading stock within the ordinary meaning of that term will also constitute trading stock for the purposes of the tax law.

Virtually any tangible item can constitute trading stock so long as it is held by a taxpayer for the purpose of manufacture, sale or exchange in the ordinary course of business. Trading stock can, therefore, include land held by a land developer (*FC of T v St Hubert's Island Pty Ltd* 78 ATC 4104; *R&D Holdings Pty Ltd v DFC of T* 2006 ATC 4472) and shares held by a share trader (*Investment and Merchant Finance Corp Limited v FC of T* 71 ATC 4140; *Patcorp Investments Ltd & Ors v FC of T* 76 ATC 4225; *Wong v FC of T* 2012 ATC ¶10-247).

Other examples of trading stock include washing machines held by a whitegoods retailer, food held by a supermarket, and sports goods held by the owner of a sports shop. The raw ingredients used to manufacture products for sale also constitute trading stock, such as flour acquired by a bakery to make cakes and wood acquired by a cabinet maker to build cupboards. The ATO also treats packaging held for the purposes of sale of 'core' goods (eg boxes in which shirts are sold) as trading stock (TR 98/7).

It is important to realise, however, that not all goods held by the owner of a business will necessarily be trading stock—some goods will be capital assets. For instance, the fridge owned by a milk bar proprietor for storing milk is not held for the purposes of manufacture, sale or exchange in the ordinary course of business and is therefore not trading stock, but rather a depreciating asset. Consequently, the tax consequences arising from the purchase and sale of the fridge will be dealt with under the capital allowance rules [15.2]. By way of contrast, the milk stored in the fridge will be trading stock that will be dealt with under the general taxation rules.

Similarly, the land on which the milk bar premises is situated will be a CGT asset of the milk bar proprietor and will therefore be subject to the CGT rules [17.4]. A property developer, on the other hand, will treat its land as trading stock since the land is held for the purpose of sale. This demonstrates the critical point that whether or not an item is trading stock depends on the purpose for which it is held rather than its underlying nature. The same kind of item may therefore be trading stock of one taxpayer and a capital asset of another.

Example Jack regularly and systematically buys and sells large parcels of shares for the purpose of making a quick profit. Jack is likely to be carrying on business as a share trader, in which case the shares are his trading stock.

Jill acquires shares and holds them for a substantial period of time as an investment that yields dividends. Jill is unlikely to be a share trader and her shares are therefore capital in nature.

As trading stock must be held for the purposes of manufacture, sale or exchange, an item that is held for leasing purposes is not trading stock (*FC of T v Cyclone Scaffolding Pty Ltd* 87 ATC 5083). For example, the videos leased by the owner of a video library to its customers are not trading stock. It is also important to note that an item that was acquired for the purposes of manufacture, sale or exchange, but which is subsequently held for another purpose, will no longer constitute trading stock.

Trading stock does not include certain assets of complying superannuation entities [19.14], a div 230 financial arrangement [29.2], or a registered emissions unit (ss 70-10(2), 70-12).

[16.3] General treatment of trading stock

General principles

Amounts received from the sale of trading stock represent the ordinary proceeds of a business and therefore constitute ordinary income, which is assessable under s 6-5 *ITAA97* [9.1].

Expenditure incurred in purchasing trading stock is an outgoing necessarily incurred in carrying on a business and is expressly deemed not to be of a capital nature (s 70-25 *ITAA97*). As a result, such expenditure is usually deductible under the general deduction provision in s 8-1 *ITAA97* [12.1].

Expenditure incurred in purchasing trading stock is, however, only deductible in the year that it becomes 'trading stock on hand' (s 70-15 *ITAA97*). This reverses the common law position under which such expenditure would ordinarily be deductible in the year that it is incurred (*FC of T v Woolcombers (WA) Pty Ltd* 93 ATC 4342; *FC of T v Raymor (NSW) Pty Ltd* 90 ATC 4461).

Trading stock 'on hand'

For trading stock to be 'on hand', the taxpayer must have the power to dispose of it. This principle is derived from *Farnsworth v FC of T* (1949) 78 CLR 504, which concerned a fruit grower that was a member of the Australian Dried Fruits Association. The taxpayer delivered fruit to a packing house where it was mixed and packed with the fruit of other growers who were also members of the association. The High Court held that once the fruit was delivered to the packing house it ceased to be 'on hand' as the taxpayer had no power to dispose of the fruit and no power to direct or control the disposal of it by the packing house.

It is not technically necessary for a taxpayer to have legal ownership of trading stock for it to be on hand. This is illustrated in *FC of T v Suttons Motors (Chullora) Wholesale Pty Ltd* 85 ATC 4398. The taxpayer in this case was a car wholesaler and subsidiary company of 'SM' (a car retailer). Under a 'floor plan' arrangement designed to defer sales tax, the taxpayer obtained delivery of cars through 'GMAC' (a finance company related to the manufacturer). The cars were stored until sale at SM's showrooms. The taxpayer only purchased a particular car from GMAC when SM had entered into a contract to sell the car to a customer. Until such time, the car remained the property of GMAC. A majority of the High Court held that the cars were the taxpayer's trading stock on hand even though the taxpayer did not own the cars. The Court found that the cars were plainly in the possession and risk of the taxpayer's group and were held by the group for the purpose of being offered for sale in the ordinary course of the group's business.

Physical possession of trading stock is also not a prerequisite for trading stock to be on hand. This is demonstrated in *All States Frozen Foods Pty Ltd v FC of T* 90 ATC 4175, which concerned a taxpayer that was a wholesaler of frozen goods. At the end of the income year, goods that the taxpayer had purchased were en route to Australia in containers transported by ships. The Full Federal Court examined the contracts for the acquisition of the goods and concluded that the power to dispose of the goods passed to the taxpayer on receipt of a bill of lading. As the taxpayer had obtained a bill of lading in relation to the relevant goods that were in transit to Australia, those goods constituted its trading stock on hand.

Interaction with CGT and capital allowance rules

Capital gains and losses made in relation to trading stock are disregarded for CGT purposes (s 118-25 *ITAA97*) [17.4]. Similarly, deductions cannot be claimed under the capital allowance rules in respect of trading stock, as trading stock is not a depreciating asset (s 40-30(1)(b) *ITAA97*) [15.2]. These exclusions ensure that trading stock is taxed exclusively under the general tax rules in ss 6-5 and 8-1.

Interaction with GST rules

As taxpayers that sell trading stock are involved in carrying on a business, they will usually be registered for GST. The GST reconciliation rules will therefore apply to them [8.5]. Accordingly, to the extent that an amount received by a taxpayer in respect of the sale of trading stock represents GST charged on a taxable supply, it is non-assessable non-exempt income (s 17-5 *ITAA97*). Likewise, to the extent that an amount paid to acquire trading stock relates to an ITC, it is not deductible (s 27-5 *ITAA97*).

Example Raphael owns a music shop and is registered for GST. He purchases clarinets from a manufacturer for $110 each (inclusive of GST) and sells the clarinets for $440 each (inclusive of GST). Raphael can deduct $100 for the purchase of each clarinet (s 8-1) and is assessed on $400 from the sale of each clarinet (s 6-5). Raphael is not entitled to deduct the $10 ITC available in relation to the acquisition of each clarinet (s 27-5) and is not assessed on the $40 GST charged on the sale of each clarinet (s 17-5).

[16.4] Accounting and valuing trading stock

Division 70 *ITAA97* contains special rules for accounting and valuing trading stock on hand at the end of an income year. These rules can result in an additional amount being included in assessable income or being allowed as a deduction.

The rationale for the rules is that taxpayers may have acquired trading stock during the year (which means that they would have claimed deductions for the stock under s 8-1 *ITAA97*) but may not have sold all the trading stock by the end of the year (which means that they would not include amounts in assessable income for the stock under s 6-5 *ITAA97*). If special adjustments are not made, the calculation of a taxpayer's taxable income would be 'skewed', as it would not take into account the fact that the taxpayer retains some trading stock at the end of the year. In an economic sense, holding trading stock on hand at the end of the income year is similar to holding cash at the end of the income year—in both cases the taxpayer has an asset: in one case it is goods, in the other case it is money. Since no deduction would be available to a taxpayer for the cash held at the end of the year, some adjustment needs to be made for the fact that deductions have been available for acquiring trading stock that is still held at the end of the year. Without the adjustment, a taxpayer's taxable income would not reflect the taxpayer's true economic profit for the year.

Accounting for trading stock

Taxpayers must compare the value of their trading stock on hand at the start of the income year with their trading stock on hand at the end of the income year (s 70-35(1) *ITAA97*). Where there is a difference between these values, the following consequences arise:

- **Closing stock exceeds opening stock.** A taxpayer must include in assessable income the excess of the value of its trading stock on hand at the end of the year over the value of its trading stock on hand at the start of the year (s 70-35(2) *ITAA97*).
- **Opening stock exceeds closing stock.** A taxpayer is entitled to deduct the excess of the value of its trading stock on hand at the start of the year over the value of its trading stock on hand at the end of the year (s 70-35(3) *ITAA97*).

These rules are outlined in the following diagram:

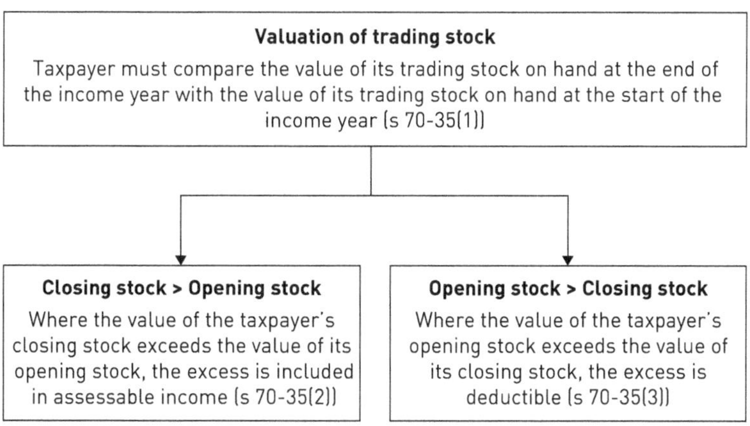

Valuing trading stock

A taxpayer can choose to value each item of stock on hand at the end of the income year based on its:

- 'cost' (ie the amount incurred in acquiring the item or bringing it into existence: *Philip Morris Ltd v FC of T* 79 ATC 4352)
- 'market selling value' (ie the amount for which the stock could be sold in the ordinary course of the taxpayer's business: *Australasian Jam Co Pty Ltd v FC of T* (1953) 88 CLR 23), or
- 'replacement value' (ie the amount the taxpayer would have to pay to replace the stock) (s 70-45(1)).

For the purposes of valuing trading stock at the end of the year, any ITCs that the taxpayer would have been entitled to claim (assuming the taxpayer had acquired the item solely for a creditable purpose) are disregarded (s 70-45(1A)).

A taxpayer may also elect to use a reasonable lower value for trading stock than the above values where the trading stock is 'obsolete' or there are 'other special circumstances' (s 70-50). According to TR 93/23, trading stock is obsolete where it is 'out of use, out of date, unfashionable or outmoded'.

Taxpayers can use different valuation methods for different items of stock and can switch between the different methods from year to year. However, the value of a particular item of trading stock at the start of the year must be the same as the value of that item in the immediately preceding year (s 70-40(1)). Where the item was not taken into account in a previous year (eg new stock), its opening year value is nil (s 70-40(2)).

Example Roger owns a tennis shop and is registered for GST. He purchased several tennis racquets for $70 each (disregarding ITCs) from a large wholesaler during 2022/23 for sale in his business. On 30 June 2023, each racquet had a replacement value of $80 and a market value of $90 (disregarding ITCs).

Roger can choose to value each tennis racquet on 30 June 2023 based on either its cost, replacement or market valuations (disregarding ITCs). In other words, each racquet may be valued at either: $70, $80 or $90.

The opening value of each racquet at the beginning of the 2023/24 income year is the same as its closing value in the 2022/23 income year. If a racquet's closing value in 2022/23 was $90 (ie market valuation was used), its opening value in 2023/24 must therefore also be $90.

Roger must revalue each racquet at the end of the 2023/24 income year. He can continue to use the same method of valuing the racquet as he used in the 2022/23 income year or change to another method. The closing value of the tennis racquet in the 2023/24 income year will automatically be its opening value in the 2024/25 income year.

[16.5] Interaction of div 70 with the general tax rules

The following example illustrates how the trading stock provisions in div 70 *ITAA97* tie in with the general income tax provisions in ss 6-5 and 8-1 *ITAA97*.

Example In Year 1, Klaus opened a new ski shop. He purchased 1,000 pairs of skis during the year for $330 each (inclusive of GST). The total cost for the skis was $330,000. He sold skis during the year at a 100% mark-up (ie for $660 each (inclusive of GST)). In Year 1, he sold 800 pairs of skis, leaving him with 200 pairs of skis at the end of the year. His total GST-inclusive revenue from the sale of the skis was $528,000 ($660 × 800). At the end of Year 1, he decided to value his trading stock at cost. The value of his trading stock at the end of Year 1 was $60,000 ($300 × 200). As he had no trading stock at the beginning of the year, the opening value of his trading stock was nil. Assuming there are no other relevant details, Klaus' taxable income for Year 1 is calculated as follows:

Assessable income	
Proceeds from sale of trading stock (ignoring GST: s 17-5): s 6-5 ($600 × 800)	$480,000
Value of closing stock less value of opening stock: s 70-35(2) ($60,000 – nil)	$60,000

Deductions	
Cost of purchasing trading stock (ignoring ITCs: s 27-5): s 8-1 ($300 × 1,000)	$300,000
Taxable income	$240,000

Note that the $240,000 taxable income represents the GST-exclusive profit of $300 on each of the 800 pairs of skis.

In Year 2, Klaus purchased another 500 pairs of skis for $330 each (inclusive of GST). The total cost for the skis purchased during the year was $165,000. He again sold skis at a 100% mark-up for $660 each (inclusive of GST). In Year 2, he sold 600 pairs of skis, leaving him with 100 pairs of skis at the end of the year. His total GST-inclusive revenue from the sale of the skis was $396,000 ($660 × 600). At the end of Year 2, he decided to again value his trading stock at cost. The value of his trading stock at the end of Year 2 was $30,000 ($300 × 100). The opening value of his trading stock in Year 2 was $60,000. Assuming there are no other relevant details, Klaus' taxable income for Year 2 is calculated as follows:

Assessable income	
Proceeds from sale of trading stock (ignoring GST: s 17-5): s 6-5 ($600 × 600)	$360,000
Deductions	
Cost of purchasing trading stock (ignoring ITCs: s 27-5): s 8-1 ($300 × 500)	$150,000
Value of opening stock less value of closing stock: s 70-35(3) ($60,000 – $30,000)	$30,000
Taxable income	$180,000

Note that the $180,000 taxable income represents the GST-exclusive profit of $300 on each of the 600 pairs of skis.

16

[16.6] Special trading stock rules

A number of special trading stock rules operate in addition to the basic rules discussed earlier in this chapter. Some of these rules are outlined below.

Trading stock not acquired at 'arm's length' for more than market value

Section 70-20 *ITAA97* provides that where trading stock is not acquired at 'arm's length' and for more than its market value, the trading stock is deemed to have been acquired for its market value. In determining whether parties are dealing with each other at arm's length, s 995-1 *ITAA97* directs that any 'connection between them' and any 'other relevant circumstance' are to be considered. Section 70-20 is relevant for both the acquirer and the seller, and is designed to deal with 'mark-up schemes' similar to the scheme entered into in *Cecil Bros Pty Ltd v FC of T* (1964) 111 CLR 430 [12.3].

Example Jack and Bob are brothers who carry on separate businesses selling used cars. In a non-arm's length transaction, Jack sells a car that has a market value of $50,000 (disregarding GST) to Bob for $90,000 (disregarding GST). By virtue of s 70-20, Jack is taken to have sold the car for $50,000 and is assessed on this amount under s 6-5 and Bob is taken to have acquired the car for $50,000 and is entitled to a deduction for this amount under s 8-1.

Item not originally held as trading stock becomes trading stock

Section 70-30(1) *ITAA97* provides that where a taxpayer owns an item but does not hold it as trading stock, and then starts to hold it as trading stock, the taxpayer is treated as if just before it became trading stock, they had sold the item to someone else for either its cost (worked out under ss 70(3) or (4)) or its market value, whichever the taxpayer elects, and immediately bought it back for the same amount.

> ***Example*** Alex owns a retail furniture business. He also has a desk in his home office which is a depreciating asset. On 8 December 2023, Alex decided to sell his home desk in his furniture retail business. The desk therefore ceases to be a depreciating asset and becomes trading stock. Depending on the election he makes, Alex is deemed to have sold the desk just before it became his trading stock for either its cost or market value and he is deemed to have bought it back for the same amount. He will therefore be able to claim a deduction under s 8-1 for this amount as the cost of his trading stock. The deemed sale will, however, also give rise to a balancing adjustment event under the capital write-off rules, which may result in a balancing adjustment arising under s 40-285 [15.3].

Trading stock disposed of outside the ordinary course of business

Section 70-90(1) *ITAA97* provides that where a taxpayer disposes of trading stock outside the ordinary course of business, their assessable income includes the market value of the item on the day of disposal. Correspondingly, s 70-95 *ITAA97* provides that the entity acquiring the item from the taxpayer is treated as having bought it for the same amount.

> ***Example*** John operated a music shop business, which he sold together with all his trading stock to Paul. John is required to include in his assessable income the market value of the trading stock on the date of sale. Paul is deemed to have bought the trading stock for the same amount and he can deduct this amount under s 8-1. If Paul subsequently gifts an instrument he held as trading stock to his sister, he would be assessed on the market value of the instrument on the day of the gift.

Fractional disposals of trading stock

Section 70-100 *ITAA97* provides that an item of trading stock is treated as having been disposed of outside the ordinary course of business if it stops being 'trading stock on hand' of an entity (the transferor) and immediately afterwards the transferor is not sole owner of the item but still has an interest in it. In such case, the transferor's assessable income includes the market value of the item on the day it stops being trading stock on hand of the transferor, and the entity or entities (the transferee) that own the item immediately afterwards are treated as having bought it for the same value on that day.

However, a special rule applies if, immediately after the item stops being trading stock on hand of the transferor, it becomes an asset of a business carried on by the transferee, *and* the entities that owned the item immediately beforehand have (between them) at least 25% of the interests in the item. In such case, the transferor and transferee can elect to treat the item as having been disposed of by the transferor, and bought back by the transferee, for what would have been its value as trading stock of the transferor at the end of an income year ending on the day of the disposal.

Example Steve owns a tennis shop business. He admits Rad as an equal partner on 5 May 2023, when the trading stock of the business has a market value of $70,000. The trading stock cost Steve $40,000 (disregarding GST), which he can claim as a deduction under s 8-1. No election is made under s 70-100, so Steve would be assessed on $70,000 (resulting in a net taxable amount of $30,000). The partnership would also be deemed to have bought the trading stock for $70,000.

However, as Steve and Rad continue to carry on the business, and as Steve continues to have a 50% interest in the trading stock, they can elect to treat Steve as having disposed of the trading stock for $40,000 (resulting in no net taxable amount). The partnership would also be deemed to have bought the trading stock for $40,000.

Owner of trading stock dies

Section 70-105 *ITAA97* provides that if the owner of trading stock dies, the market value of the stock at the date of death is included in the deceased's assessable income. In addition, the entity on which the trading stock devolves is treated as having bought the trading stock for its market value at that time.

However, if the business is carried on after the deceased's death and the trading stock continues to be held as trading stock of that business, the deceased's legal personal representative may elect instead to include in the deceased's assessable income the amount that would have been the value of the trading stock at the end of an income year ending on the deceased's death. In such a case, the entity on which the trading stock devolves is also treated as having bought it for the same amount.

Example Dave owned a hardware business and died on 8 June 2023. The market value of Dave's trading stock at the date of his death would ordinarily be included in his assessable income. If Dave's trading stock passes to his wife as the sole beneficiary under his will, she would be deemed to have bought the trading stock for its market value.

However, if Dave's wife takes over the business and holds the trading stock as trading stock of that business, Dave's legal personal representative could elect to instead include in Dave's assessable income the amount that would have been the value of the trading stock at the end of an income year ending on his death. In such case, his wife would also be treated as having bought the trading stock for the same amount and would be able to claim a deduction for this amount under s 8-1.

Item no longer held as trading stock

Section 70-110 *ITAA97* provides that where a taxpayer stops holding an item as trading stock, but still owns it, the taxpayer is treated as if just before the stock stopped being trading stock, they had sold it to someone else for its cost and immediately bought it back for the same amount.

Example Erin owns a computer sales store. On 5 May 2023, she took one of the computers home and began using it to maintain her business accounts. The computer therefore ceases to be trading stock and becomes a depreciating asset. Erin is treated as having sold the computer for its cost just before it stopped being her trading stock. This amount is required to be included in her assessable income under s 6-5. She is also deemed to have purchased the computer for the same amount and can start to claim deductions for its decline in value under s 40-25 [15.2].

Special rules for SBEs

To ease compliance burdens, s 328-285 *ITAA97* provides that entities that are SBEs [8.7], or that would be SBEs if the aggregated turnover threshold was $50m (instead of $10m), for an income year can choose not to account for changes in the value of their trading stock where the difference between the value of their trading stock on hand at the start of the income year and their reasonable estimate of the value of their trading stock on hand at the end of the income year is not more than $5,000.

Where an SBE has made a choice under s 328-285 for an income year, the value of their trading stock on hand at the end of the year is deemed to be the same as the value of their trading stock at the start of the year (s 328-295). The opening value of the SBE's trading stock for the subsequent year will therefore be based on this value.

> ***Example*** Nick is an SBE who operates a tennis stringing business from home. His trading stock comprises the strings that he uses for stringing racquets. The value of his trading stock on hand at the start of 2022/23 was $3,000, and he reasonably estimated that the value of his trading stock on hand at the end of the income year was $7,000. As the difference between these amounts does not exceed $5,000, Nick can choose not to account for the change in the value of his trading stock under s 70-35. If he does this, the opening value of his trading stock in 2023/24 will be $3,000 (not $7,000).

[16.7] QUESTIONS

1. What is 'trading stock' and why is it important to determine whether something is trading stock? Discuss what items owned by a milk bar proprietor would be trading stock and what items would not be trading stock. When is trading stock 'on hand' and why is this concept important?
2. Discuss the role of s 70-35 *ITAA97* and its relationship with ss 6-5 and 8-1 *ITAA97*.
3. S Co is a furniture retailer specialising in selling chairs. Its stock at the beginning of 2023/24 was valued at $2m. It purchased chairs from a manufacturer for $11m during the year. Its stock at the end of 2023/24 was valued at $5m. Its sales revenue for 2023/24 was $22m. Calculate S Co's taxable income for 2023/24.
4. In 2023/24, Wally opened a book shop. During the year, he purchased 10,000 books from various publishers for $110,000 and sold 4,000 books for $200,000. Calculate his taxable income for 2023/24.
5. Rick sells computers from his shop in Melbourne. He also has a personal computer which he uses at home for work and private purposes. On 4 January 2023, Rick took his personal computer to his shop and sold it to a customer. Subsequently, on 9 May 2023, he sold his business to Wayne (including all trading stock on hand at the date of sale). Wayne carried on the business until 5 October 2023, when he died. Under Wayne's will, all his assets passed to his wife, Wendy, who took over the business after his death. How do the trading stock rules apply to these transactions?
6. Mei-Ling and Pei-Ling are equal partners in a make-up manufacturing business. On 30 June 2023, they admit Xiao-Ling as an equal partner in the business, selling one-third of their interest in the partnership assets (including trading stock) to her. On 30 June 2023, the closing value at cost of the partnership's stock on hand was $30,000 and its market value was $50,000. Discuss the tax treatment of the trading stock.
7. Bob owns a grocery business and is an SBE. At the beginning of 2023/24, his opening stock was valued at $34,000. At the end of 2023/24 he estimated that his closing stock was valued at $30,000. What is the effect of Bob making a choice under s 328-285 *ITAA97*?

CAPITAL GAINS TAX 17

[17.1] Introduction

CGT was introduced by the Hawke Labor Government on 20 September 1985. Before this time, gains that were not of an income nature generally escaped tax unless they fell within a limited number of special statutory income provisions. One of these provisions was former s 26AAA *ITAA36*, which taxed profits made from selling property within 12 months of its purchase. However, taxpayers could easily avoid this provision by simply selling their property outside that period.

Many considered it unfair that income gains were taxed whereas capital gains generally escaped tax. For example, it was viewed as inequitable that taxpayers who earned salary and wages were taxed, but taxpayers who made capital gains from the realisation of their investments (eg shares and property) were not taxed. The CGT regime was designed to address this bias by bringing capital gains to account under a set of special statutory rules. These rules were originally contained in pt IIIA *ITAA36* and were loosely modelled on the United Kingdom's CGT legislation. In 1998, as part of the TLIP rewrite, pt IIIA was replaced with new provisions contained in pt 3-1 (ss 100-1 to 121-35) and pt 3-3 (ss 122-1 to 152-425) *ITAA97* [8.2].

The CGT regime is complex and spans hundreds of pages of legislation. A useful overview of the way CGT operates is outlined in div 100 *ITAA97*. This chapter examines the basic features of the CGT regime and focuses on its core elements. Interestingly, despite its name, the CGT regime does not technically assess amounts that are 'capital' at common law. Rather, it is a distinct statutory regime that includes a 'net capital gain' in a taxpayer's assessable income. A net capital gain is calculated under the steps contained in s 102-5 *ITAA97* [17.2]. These steps require a taxpayer's 'capital gains' for an income year to be set off first against their 'capital losses' for the year and then against any unapplied 'net capital losses' from earlier years. Any remaining capital gains that are 'discount capital gains' are then reduced by the appropriate 'discount percentage' [17.8]. Finally, any remaining capital gains that qualify for 'small business concessions' are then reduced under those concessions [17.9].

Taxpayers make capital gains and capital losses as a consequence of 'CGT events' [17.3]. There are more than 50 different kinds of CGT events, which each have their own rules for calculating capital gains and capital losses. The most common CGT event is 'CGT event A1' [17.10], which arises where a taxpayer disposes of a 'CGT asset' [17.4].

The CGT regime operates subject to numerous exemptions [17.5]. For example, capital gains and losses relating to assets acquired before the introduction of CGT (ie 20 September 1985) are generally disregarded. Likewise, capital gains and losses made in respect of a taxpayer's car or main residence are also usually disregarded. In addition, to prevent overlap with the general taxation rules, capital gains and losses relating to trading stock and depreciating assets are also generally disregarded.

The CGT regime has special rules that apply to foreign residents [17.12], deceased estates [17.13], investments [17.14] and options [17.15]. It also contains a number of roll-over provisions that allow taxpayers to defer CGT liability in certain circumstances [17.16].

[17.2] Net capital gains and net capital losses

Division 102 *ITAA97* contains the rules for working out whether a taxpayer has made a 'net capital gain' or a 'net capital loss' for an income year. These concepts are important because a net capital gain is assessable income, whereas a net capital loss is not deductible but may be carried forward to reduce a net capital gain in a future income year.

Net capital gain

Section 102-5 provides that a taxpayer's assessable income includes their 'net capital gain' for an income year. A taxpayer's net capital gain for an income year is worked out according to five steps:

- **Step 1:** Any 'capital gains' made during the income year are reduced by 'capital losses' made during the year [17.3].
- **Step 2:** Any remaining capital gains are then reduced by any 'net capital losses' from earlier years (see below).
- **Step 3:** Any remaining capital gains that are 'discount capital gains' are then reduced by the 'discount percentage' [17.8].
- **Step 4:** Any remaining capital gains that qualify for any of the 'small business concessions' are then reduced under those concessions [17.9].
- **Step 5:** The amount of any remaining capital gains is the taxpayer's net capital gain for the year.

Example During the income year, Betty made a capital gain of $20,000 on the sale of her shares in a company and a $4,000 capital gain on the sale of her units in a trust. Neither of these gains is a discount capital gain or eligible for the small business concessions. She also made a 'capital loss' of $5,000 on the sale of her land, and she has a 'net capital loss' carried forward from the previous year of $3,000.

Betty's net capital gain for the year, which must be included in her assessable income under s 102-5, is $16,000 calculated as follows:

Step 1: ($20,000 + $4,000) – $5,000 = $19,000
Step 2: $19,000 – $3,000 = $16,000
Step 3: Not applicable
Step 4: Not applicable
Step 5: $16,000

Net capital loss

A taxpayer makes a 'net capital loss' for an income year where the taxpayer's capital losses for the year exceed the taxpayer's capital gains for the year (s 102-10(1)). Taxpayers are not entitled to deductions for 'net capital losses' (s 102-10(2)). Net capital losses can, nevertheless, be carried forward to reduce net capital gains in future years (s 102-15). This reduction occurs under Step 2 of the s 102-5 formula outlined above.

Example Jenny makes capital gains of $100,000 and capital losses of $120,000 during an income year. As Jenny's capital losses exceed her capital gains, she has made a 'net capital loss' for the year of $20,000. This capital loss is not deductible but can be carried forward to reduce the amount of her net capital gains in future years.

Matters arising under div 102 *ITAA97*

The rules in div 102 raise three basic matters:

- First, as the net capital gain and net capital loss calculations in ss 102-5 and 102-10 require capital gains and capital losses to be set off against each other, it is necessary to understand how individual capital gains and capital losses are calculated. Capital gains and capital losses only arise if a 'CGT event' happens [17.3]. There are more than 50 different CGT events, which each have their own rules for calculating the respective capital gains and capital losses [17.10].
- Second, as Step 3 in s 102-5 requires 'discount capital gains' to be reduced by the 'discount percentage', it is necessary to understand which capital gains are discount capital gains and the amount of the discount percentage that applies to such gains. Basically, a discount capital gain is a capital gain made on a CGT asset that has been held for at least 12 months. The discount percentage is 50% for individuals and trusts and 33⅓% for complying superannuation entities [17.8].
- Third, as Step 4 in s 102-5 requires capital gains that qualify for the 'small business concessions' to be reduced under those concessions, it is necessary to identify the concessions and how they operate. There are four concessions: the 15-year exemption, the 50% reduction concession, the retirement concession and the small business roll-over concession. To qualify for these concessions, certain conditions must be satisfied [17.9].

It is important to note that since capital gains may be eligible for discounts and small business concessions under Steps 3 and 4, they are taxed preferentially to income gains which do not benefit from similar concessions.

The rules in div 102 also give rise to the following offsetting, quarantining and timing issues.

Offsetting issues

Under Step 1 and Step 2 in the formula in s 102-5, taxpayers can choose the order in which they reduce their capital gains by capital losses and net capital losses. Accordingly, in order to minimise the amount included in their assessable income, taxpayers should, so far as possible, choose to apply their capital losses and net capital losses against those capital gains that are not discount capital gains [17.8] and that do not qualify for any of the small business concessions [17.9]. The object of this strategy is to maximise the amount of capital gains that are eligible for concessional treatment under Step 3 and Step 4.

Example During the income year, Bill made the following 'capital gains':

- Capital gain of \$10,000 on the sale of his shares in X Co (this is *not* a 'discount capital gain').
- Capital gain of \$10,000 on the sale of his shares in Y Co (this is a 'discount capital gain' that is eligible for a 50% discount).

He also made a 'capital loss' of \$5,000 on the sale of his land and he has a 'net capital loss' from last year of \$3,000.

Bill's net capital gain under s 102-5 may be calculated as follows:

Step 1: (\$10,000 + \$10,000) – \$5,000 = \$15,000
Step 2: \$15,000 – \$3,000 = \$12,000
Step 3: \$12,000 – (\$10,000 × 50%) = \$7,000
Step 4: Not applicable
Step 5: \$7,000

The above calculations assume that the following has occurred:

1. Under Step 1, Bill has chosen to apply the \$5,000 capital loss against the \$10,000 capital gain on the X Co shares (rather than the \$10,000 capital gain on the Y Co shares). This leaves Bill with \$15,000 of capital gains consisting of a remaining \$5,000 capital gain on the X Co shares and a \$10,000 capital gain on the Y Co shares.
2. Under Step 2, Bill has chosen to apply the \$3,000 net capital loss against the remaining \$5,000 capital gain on the X Co shares (rather than the \$10,000 capital gain on the Y Co shares). This leaves Bill with \$12,000 of capital gains consisting of a remaining \$2,000 capital gain on the X Co shares and a \$10,000 capital gain on the Y Co shares.
3. Under Step 3, the \$10,000 capital gain on the Y Co shares is reduced by the discount percentage of 50%. This leaves Bill with a net capital gain of \$7,000 consisting of a remaining \$2,000 capital gain on the X Co shares and a discounted \$5,000 capital gain on the Y Co shares.

If Bill had, instead, chosen to apply the capital loss and the net capital loss against the \$10,000 capital gain on the Y Co shares (rather than the \$10,000 capital gain on the X Co shares), his net capital gain under s 102-5 would be calculated as follows:

Step 1: (\$10,000 + \$10,000) – \$5,000 = \$15,000
Step 2: \$15,000 – \$3,000 = \$12,000
Step 3: \$12,000 – (\$2,000 × 50%) = \$11,000
Step 4: Not applicable
Step 5: \$11,000

This example illustrates that in order to maximise the benefit of the CGT discount under Step 3, Bill is clearly better off applying the capital loss and net capital loss against the capital gain on the X Co shares, since that capital gain is not eligible for the CGT discount.

Quarantining issues

It is important to recognise that by requiring capital losses to be offset only against capital gains, capital losses are effectively 'quarantined' within the CGT regime. This means that a net capital loss cannot be applied against a taxpayer's other assessable income to reduce their taxable income. By way of contrast, there is no quarantining for net capital gains, as they are simply included in assessable income. Deductions can therefore be applied against a net capital gain to reduce the taxpayer's taxable income.

Example Pat earned salary of $70,000 and made a net capital loss of $20,000 during the income year. She cannot set her net capital loss off against her salary income since a net capital loss is not deductible. Her taxable income for the year is therefore $70,000 (not $50,000).

Rob made a net capital gain of $70,000 and incurred deductions under s 8-1 of $20,000 during the income year. He can apply the deductions against his net capital gain. His taxable income for the year is therefore $50,000.

Timing issues

As the CGT discount rules only apply to capital gains made on CGT assets that have been held for at least 12 months, taxpayers should consider deferring the disposal of assets that are liable to generate gains until they have held them for this period. Furthermore, as capital losses must be applied against capital gains, the time at which capital gains and capital losses arise is critical. Capital losses must be incurred in the year in which capital gains are made or in earlier income years to be applied against those capital gains. Where there are no capital gains in an income year against which capital losses can be offset, the capital losses must be carried forward into future years as a net capital loss. The net capital loss can only be utilised when capital gains are eventually made. The relative value of a net capital loss therefore erodes over time due to inflation. If no capital gains are made in the future, the net capital loss is wasted. Capital losses cannot be carried back into previous income years.

Example X Co makes a capital gain of $1m in Year 1 and a capital loss of $1m in Year 2. The capital loss in Year 2 cannot be carried back to reduce the capital gain in Year 1. X Co will therefore have to pay tax on its capital gain in Year 1. The capital loss in Year 2 forms a net capital loss to be carried forward into future years. However, if X Co never makes another capital gain, the net capital loss is wasted as it cannot be utilised.

Exceptions and modifications

The net capital gain and net capital loss rules outlined above operate subject to a number of exceptions and modifications listed in the table in s 102-30.

[17.3] Capital gains and capital losses

The first step in calculating a taxpayer's net capital gain or net capital loss for an income year is to work out the individual 'capital gains' and 'capital losses' that the taxpayer has made during the year and set these amounts off against each other (ss 102-5, 102-10 *ITAA97*) [17.2].

As previously discussed, capital gains and capital losses arise as a consequence of 'CGT events' happening (s 102-20). There are over 50 CGT events, ranging from 'CGT event A1' to 'CGT event L8'. Each of these CGT events has its own rules for calculating a capital gain or capital loss and for determining the time of the event.

The most common CGT event is 'CGT event A1', which arises where a taxpayer disposes of a 'CGT asset' [17.4]. The time of the event is when the taxpayer enters into the contract for the disposal, or, if there is no contract, when the change in ownership occurs. Under CGT event A1, the taxpayer's capital gain or capital loss is calculated by comparing the 'cost base' or 'reduced cost base' of the CGT asset [17.6] with the 'capital proceeds' from the disposal [17.7]. A taxpayer makes a capital gain where the capital proceeds from the disposal exceed the asset's cost base. A taxpayer makes a capital loss where the capital proceeds from the disposal are less than the asset's reduced cost base.

It is important to be aware that not all capital gains and capital losses that arise from CGT events are necessarily taken into account for CGT purposes. There are a number of circumstances where taxpayers are directed to disregard their capital gains and capital losses. The main situations where this occurs are outlined at [17.5]. For instance, capital gains and capital losses are generally disregarded if they are made in relation to assets acquired before 20 September 1985 (ie before the introduction of CGT). Capital gains and capital losses made in relation to cars, trading stock, depreciating assets and a taxpayer's main residence are also generally disregarded. In addition, in certain circumstances taxpayers may be able to 'defer' capital gains under various roll-over provisions [17.16].

CGT events

The following table is derived from s 104-5 *ITAA97* and summarises the CGT events. It describes each event, the time of the event, and the way in which a capital gain or capital loss from the event is calculated. Many of the CGT events outlined in the table are examined further at [17.10].

Event number and description	Time of event is:	Capital gain is:	Capital loss is:
A1 Disposal of a CGT asset (s 104-10)	when disposal contract is entered into or, if none, when entity stops being asset's owner	capital proceeds from disposal less asset's cost base	asset's reduced cost base less capital proceeds
B1 Use and enjoyment before title passes (s 104-15)	when use of CGT asset passes	capital proceeds less asset's cost base	asset's reduced cost base less capital proceeds
C1 Loss or destruction of a CGT asset (s 104-20)	when compensation is first received or, if none, when loss discovered or destruction occurred	capital proceeds less asset's cost base	asset's reduced cost base less capital proceeds
C2 Cancellation, surrender and similar endings (s 104-25)	when contract ending asset is entered into or, if none, when asset ends	capital proceeds from ending less asset's cost base	asset's reduced cost base less capital proceeds
C3 End of option to acquire shares, etc (s 104-30)	when option ends	capital proceeds from granting option less expenditure in granting it	expenditure in granting option less capital proceeds
D1 Creating contractual or other rights (s 104-35)	when contract is entered into or right is created	capital proceeds from creating right less incidental costs of creating it	incidental costs of creating right less capital proceeds

Event number and description	Time of event is:	Capital gain is:	Capital loss is:
D2 Granting an option (s 104-40)	when option is granted	capital proceeds from grant less expenditure to grant it	expenditure to grant option less capital proceeds
D3 Granting a right to income from mining (s 104-45)	when contract is entered into or, if none, when right is granted	capital proceeds from grant of right less expenditure to grant it	expenditure to grant right less capital proceeds
D4 Entering into a conservation covenant (s 104-47)	when covenant is entered into	capital proceeds from covenant less cost base apportioned to the covenant	reduced cost base apportioned to the covenant less capital proceeds from covenant
E1 Creating a trust over a CGT asset (s 104-55)	when trust is created	capital proceeds from creating trust less asset's cost base	asset's reduced cost base less capital proceeds
E2 Transferring a CGT asset to a trust (s 104-60)	when asset transferred	capital proceeds from transfer less asset's cost base	asset's reduced cost base less capital proceeds
E3 Converting a trust to a unit trust (s 104-65)	when trust is converted	market value of asset at that time less its cost base	asset's reduced cost base less that market value
E4 Capital payment for trust interest (s 104-70)	when trustee makes payment	non-assessable part of the payment less cost base of the trust interest	no capital loss
E5 Beneficiary becoming entitled to a trust asset (s 104-75)	when beneficiary becomes absolutely entitled	for trustee—market value of CGT asset at that time less its cost base; for beneficiary—that market value less cost base of beneficiary's capital interest	for trustee—reduced cost base of CGT asset at that time less that market value; for beneficiary—reduced cost base of beneficiary's capital interest less that market value
E6 Disposal to beneficiary to end income right (s 104-80)	the time of the disposal	for trustee—market value of CGT asset at that time less its cost base; for beneficiary—that market value less cost base of beneficiary's right to income	for trustee—reduced cost base of CGT asset at that time less that market value; for beneficiary—reduced cost base of beneficiary's right to income less that market value
E7 Disposal to beneficiary to end capital interest (s 104-85)	the time of the disposal	for trustee—market value of CGT asset at that time less its cost base; for beneficiary—that market value less cost base of beneficiary's capital interest	for trustee—reduced cost base of CGT asset at that time less that market value; for beneficiary—reduced cost base of beneficiary's capital interest less that market value

17

Event number and description	Time of event is:	Capital gain is:	Capital loss is:
E8 Disposal by beneficiary of capital interest (s 104-90)	when disposal contract entered into or, if none, when beneficiary ceases to own CGT asset	capital proceeds less appropriate proportion of the trust's net assets	appropriate proportion of the trust's net assets less capital proceeds
E9 Creating a trust over future property (s 104-105)	when entity makes agreement	market value of the property (as if it existed when agreement made) less incidental costs in making agreement	incidental costs in making agreement less market value of the property (as if it existed when agreement made)
E10 Annual cost base reduction exceeds cost base of interest in AMIT (s 104-107A)	when reduction happens	excess of cost base reduction over cost base	no capital loss
F1 Granting a lease (s 104-110)	for grant of lease—when entity enters into lease contract or, if none, at start of lease; for lease renewal or extension—at start of renewal or extension	capital proceeds less expenditure on grant, renewal or extension	expenditure on grant, renewal or extension less capital proceeds
F2 Granting a long-term lease (s 104-115)	for grant of lease—when lessor grants lease; for lease renewal or extension—at start of renewal or extension	capital proceeds from grant, renewal or extension less cost base of leased property	reduced cost base of leased property less capital proceeds from grant, renewal or extension
F3 Lessor pays lessee to get lease changed (s 104-120)	when lease term is varied or waived	no capital gain	amount of expenditure to get lessee's agreement
F4 Lessee receives payment for changing lease (s 104-125)	when lease term is varied or waived	capital proceeds less cost base of lease	no capital loss
F5 Lessor receives payment for changing lease (s 104-130)	when lease term is varied or waived	capital proceeds less expenditure in relation to variation or waiver	expenditure in relation to variation or waiver less capital proceeds
G1 Capital payment for shares (s 104-135)	when company pays non-assessable amount	payment less cost base of shares	no capital loss
G3 Liquidator or administrator declares shares or financial instruments worthless (s 104-145)	when declaration was made	no capital gain	shares' or financial instruments' reduced cost base
H1 Forfeiture of a deposit (s 104-150)	when deposit is forfeited	deposit less expenditure in connection with prospective sale	expenditure in connection with prospective sale less deposit
H2 Receipt for event relating to a CGT asset (s 104-155)	when act, transaction or event occurred	capital proceeds less incidental costs	incidental costs less capital proceeds

Event number and description	Time of event is:	Capital gain is:	Capital loss is:
I1 Individual or company stops being an Australian resident (s 104-160)	when individual or company stops being Australian resident	for each CGT asset the person owns, its market value less its cost base	for each CGT asset the person owns, its reduced cost base less its market value
I2 Trust stops being a resident trust (s 104-170)	when trust ceases to be resident trust for CGT purposes	for each CGT asset the trustee owns, its market value of asset less its cost base	for each CGT asset the trustee owns, its reduced cost base less its market value
J1 Company stops being member of wholly owned group after roll-over (s 104-175)	when the company stops	market value of asset at time of event less its cost base	reduced cost base of asset less that market value
J2 Change in relation to replacement asset or improved asset after a roll-over under sub-div 152-E (s 104-185)	when the change happens	the amount mentioned in s 104-185(5)	no capital loss
J4 Trust fails to cease to exist after a roll-over under sub-div 124-N (s 104-195)	when the failure happens	market value of asset less asset's cost base	reduced cost base of asset less asset's market value
J5 Failure to acquire replacement asset and to incur fourth element expenditure after a roll-over under sub-div 152-E (s 104-197)	at the end of the replacement asset period	the amount of the capital gain that you disregarded under sub-div 152-E	no capital loss
J6 Cost of acquisition of replacement asset or amount of fourth element expenditure, or both, not sufficient to cover disregarded capital gain (s 104-198)	at the end of the replacement asset period	the amount mentioned in s 104-198(3)	no capital loss
K1 As the result of an incoming international transfer of a Kyoto unit or an Australian carbon credit unit from your foreign account or your nominee's foreign account, you start to hold the unit as a registered emissions unit (s 104-205)	when you start to hold the unit as a registered emissions unit	market value of unit less its cost base	reduced cost base of unit less its market value
K2 Bankrupt pays amount in relation to debt (s 104-210)	when payment is made	no capital gain	so much of payment as relates to denied part of a net capital loss

17

Event number and description	Time of event is:	Capital gain is:	Capital loss is:
K3 Asset passing to tax-advantaged entity (s 104-215)	when individual dies	market value of asset at death less its cost base	reduced cost base of asset less that market value
K4 CGT asset starts being trading stock (s 104-220)	when asset starts being trading stock	market value of asset less its cost base	reduced cost base of asset less its market value
K5 Special capital loss from collectable that has fallen in market value (s 104-225)	when CGT event A1, C2 or E8 happens to shares in the company, or an interest in the trust, that owns the collectable	no capital gain	market value of the shares or interest (as if the collectable had not fallen in market value) less the capital proceeds from CGT event A1, C2 or E8
K6 Pre-CGT shares or trust interest (s 104-230)	when another CGT event involving the shares or interest happens	capital proceeds from the shares or trust interest (so far as attributable to post-CGT assets owned by the company or trust) less the assets' cost bases	no capital loss
K7 Balancing adjustment occurs for a depreciating asset that you used for purposes other than taxable purposes (s 104-235)	when balancing adjustment event occurs	termination value less cost times fraction	cost less termination value times fraction
K8 Direct value shifts affecting your equity or loan interests in a company or trust (s 104-250 and div 725)	the decrease time for the interests	the gain worked out under s 725-365	no capital loss
K9 Entitlement to receive payment of a carried interest (s 104-255)	when you become entitled to receive payment	capital proceeds from entitlement	no capital loss
K10 You make a forex realisation gain covered by item 1 of the table in s 775-70(1) (s 104-260)	when the forex realisation event happens	the forex realisation gain	no capital loss
K11 You make a forex realisation loss covered by item 1 of the table in s 775-75(1) (s 104-265)	when the forex realisation event happens	no capital gain	the forex realisation loss

Event number and description	Time of event is:	Capital gain is:	Capital loss is:
K12 Foreign hybrid loss exposure adjustment (s 104-270)	just before the end of the income year	no capital gain	the amount stated in s 104-270(3)
L1 Reduction under s 705-57 in tax cost setting amount of assets of entity becoming subsidiary member of consolidated group or MEC group (s 104-500)	just after entity becomes subsidiary member	no capital gain	amount of reduction
L2 Amount remaining after step 3A, etc of joining allocable cost amount is negative (s 104-505)	just after entity becomes subsidiary member	amount remaining	no capital loss
L3 Tax cost setting amounts for retained cost base assets exceed joining allocable cost amount (s 104-510)	just after entity becomes subsidiary member	amount of excess	no capital loss
L4 No reset cost base assets against which to apply excess of net allocable cost amount on joining (s 104-515)	just after entity becomes subsidiary member	no capital gain	amount of excess
L5 Amount remaining after step 4 of leaving allocable cost amount is negative (s 104-520)	when entity ceases to be subsidiary member	amount remaining	no capital loss
L6 Error in calculation of tax cost setting amount for joining entity's assets (s 104-525)	start of the income year when the Commissioner becomes aware of the errors	the net overstated amount resulting from the errors, or a portion of that amount	the net understated amount resulting from the errors, or a portion of that amount
L8 Reduction in tax cost setting amount for reset cost base assets on joining cannot be allocated (s 104-535)	just after entity becomes subsidiary member	no capital gain	amount of reduction that cannot be allocated

17

Order of application of CGT events

Given the broad variety of CGT events, the potential exists for more than one CGT event to apply in a particular situation. To address this problem, taxpayers are required to determine if a CGT event (other than CGT event D1 and H1) applies to their situation (s 102-25). If more than one CGT event applies, they are to use the CGT event that is most specific to their situation (see eg *Kafataris & Anor v DFC of T* 2015 ATC ¶20-523, where CGT event E1 applied ahead of CGT event A1 in a case involving a declaration of trust). If none of these CGT events apply, they are required to consider whether CGT event D1 applies or, if it does not, whether CGT event H1 applies. Special rules apply in relation to CGT events J2, K5 and K12, which may operate in addition to other CGT events.

Steps involved in dealing with capital gains and losses

The following diagram outlines the basic steps involved in dealing with capital gains and capital losses:

Determine whether there is a CGT event

There are over 50 CGT events that fall within the following 12 groups [17.3]:

- Disposals (sub-div 104-A)
- Use and enjoyment before title passes (sub-div 104-B)
- End of a CGT asset (sub-div 104-C)
- Bringing into existence a CGT asset (sub-div 104-D)
- Trusts (sub-div 104-E)
- Leases (sub-div 104-F)
- Shares (sub-div 104-G)
- Special capital receipts (sub-div 104-H)
- Australian residency rules (sub-div 104-I)
- CGT events relating to roll-overs (sub-div 104-J)
- Other CGT events (sub-div 104-K)
- Consolidated groups and MEC groups (sub-div 104-L)

↓

Determine the time of the CGT event

Each CGT event specifies the time of the CGT event [17.3]

↓

Determine whether a capital gain or capital loss arises under the CGT event

Each CGT event specifies how the capital gain or capital loss is calculated [17.3]

↓

Determine whether the capital gain or capital loss is disregarded

Capital gains and capital losses from CGT events relating to certain CGT assets are disregarded [17.5], eg:

- CGT assets acquired before 20 September 1985
- CGT assets that are collectables and acquired for $500 or less
- CGT assets that are personal use assets
- CGT assets that are depreciating assets
- CGT assets that are trading stock
- CGT assets that are not taxable Australian property of foreign and temporary residents
- CGT assets that are the taxpayer's main residence

↓

Determine whether roll-over relief applies

CGT relief may be available under various roll-over provisions [17.16]

[17.4] CGT assets

A number of key CGT events, including CGT event A1, happen in respect of 'CGT assets'. The concept of a CGT asset is dealt with in div 108 *ITAA97*, which contains a set of general rules (sub-div 108-A) as well as special rules relating to 'collectables' (sub-div 108-B) and 'personal use assets' (sub-div 108-C). There are also special rules that deem certain CGT assets that would otherwise be treated as single assets to be treated as 'separate assets' (sub-div 108-D).

Definition of CGT asset

A 'CGT asset' is defined broadly in s 108-5(1) as 'any kind of property' or 'a legal or equitable right that is not property'. Some common examples of CGT assets include: land, shares, options, debts and the goodwill of a business. Foreign currency and digital currency (eg Bitcoin) are also considered to be CGT assets (TD 2014/26). However, Australian currency, when used as legal tender, is not treated as a CGT asset as it merely serves as a medium of exchange to facilitate a transaction (TD 2002/25).

The issue of what constitutes 'property' was considered by the High Court in *Hepples v FC of T* 90 ATC 4497 in the context of the former CGT provisions in pt IIIA *ITAA36*. Gummow J referred (at 4516) to *The Queen v Toohey; Ex parte Meneling Station Pty Ltd* (1982) 158 CLR 327, in which Mason J had noted that while a statute may render some forms of property inalienable, it was nevertheless 'generally correct to say that a proprietary right must be capable in its nature of assumption by third parties'. Property is therefore ordinarily something that can be transferred to others and includes both 'tangible' items (such as land and equipment) and 'intangible' items (such as a copyright or a patent).

A right that is not property is a CGT asset if the right is legal or equitable in nature (ie it is recognised by a court exercising its legal or equitable jurisdiction). Examples of such rights would include the right of a patient to sue a doctor for negligence and the right of a beneficiary to sue a trustee for breach of trust. While such rights would not be proprietary in nature (as they would not be transferable), they would be enforceable in a court.

In *Excellar Pty Ltd v FC of T* 2015 ATC ¶10-391, the AAT held that an amount in a bank account was a CGT asset as it was a form of property, being a 'chose in action' of the depositor constituted by a debt owed to the depositor by the bank. Likewise, in *Coshott v FC of T* 2014 ATC ¶10-375, the AAT held that causes of action for negligence and breach of contract brought against a solicitor were also CGT assets.

The ATO considers that mere 'know-how' (ie knowledge or information) is not a CGT asset as it is neither a form of property nor a legal or equitable right (TD 2000/33). A licence or contractual right to use know-how would, however, be a CGT asset.

Collectables

A special quarantining rule applies to CGT assets that are 'collectables'. According to this rule, capital losses from collectables can only be applied against capital gains from collectables (s 108-10(1)).

There is also a low-value exemption for collectables, which provides that capital gains and capital losses made from collectables acquired for $500 or less are disregarded (s 118-10(1)).

The following CGT assets (provided they are kept mainly for the taxpayer's or their associates' personal use or enjoyment) are collectables:

- artwork, jewellery, antiques, coins or medallions
- rare folios, manuscripts or books, and
- postage stamps or first day covers (s 108-10(2)).

An interest in, debt arising from, or option or right to acquire, any of these assets is also a collectable (s 108-10(3)).

Example Bert recently acquired a gold ring for $400 and an antique chair for $2,000. These assets are both collectables. If he sold the gold ring for $800, he would disregard the capital gain as he acquired the ring for under $500. If he sold the antique chair for $1,500, he would make a loss of $500, but would only be able to apply this loss against a gain made on another collectable. He could not use the $500 loss to reduce a capital gain made on, for example, his shares as they are not collectables.

Where a taxpayer owns a 'set' of collectables that would ordinarily be disposed of together, then, if the taxpayer disposes of those items individually for the purposes of trying to obtain the s 118-10 exemption, the set of collectables is taken to be a single collectable and each of the disposals is treated as a disposal of part of that collectable (s 108-15).

Example Ernie recently acquired a rare encyclopaedia, consisting of three volumes, for $900. Under the apportionment rule in s 112-30, the cost base of each volume would be $300 [17.6]. Ordinarily, if Ernie sold each volume individually for $1,000, he would be able to disregard the capital gain under s 108-10, as each volume would be deemed to have been acquired for less than $500. However, assuming s 108-15 applies to treat the three volumes as a single collectable, the exemption in s 108-10 would not apply and he would therefore make a capital gain of $700 ($1,000 – $300) on the sale of each volume.

Personal use assets

To reduce compliance costs, special rules apply to CGT assets that are 'personal use assets'. Capital losses from 'personal use assets' are disregarded and therefore cannot be applied against capital gains (s 108-20(1)). Furthermore, a capital gain from a personal use asset is disregarded if the CGT asset was acquired for $10,000 or less (s 118-10(3)).

A personal use asset is essentially a CGT asset (other than a collectable) that is used or kept mainly for the taxpayer's or their associate's personal use or enjoyment (eg a home gym, TV or sofa). It also includes options or rights to acquire such assets, certain debts in respect of such assets, and non-income-producing/non-business debts (s 108-20(2)). Land, stratum units and buildings that are separate CGT assets under sub-div 108-D (see below) are excluded from the definition of personal use asset (s 108-20(3)).

Example Sara recently acquired a plasma TV for $8,000 and a new lounge suite for $9,000 for home use. If she sold the TV for $6,000, she would disregard the loss of $2,000 as it is made in respect of a personal use asset. If she sold the lounge suite for $13,000, she would disregard the gain of $4,000 as the lounge suite was acquired for under $10,000. If, however, Sara had acquired the lounge suite for $12,000, she would have to recognise the $1,000 gain.

Where a taxpayer owns a 'set' of personal use assets that would ordinarily be disposed of together, then, if the taxpayer disposes of those items individually for the purposes of trying to obtain the s 118-10 exemption, the set of personal use assets is taken to be a single personal use asset and each of the disposals is treated as a disposal of part of that asset (ss 108-25, 108-30).

Diagram of different kinds of CGT assets

The following diagram outlines the different kinds of CGT assets and the special rules that apply to them:

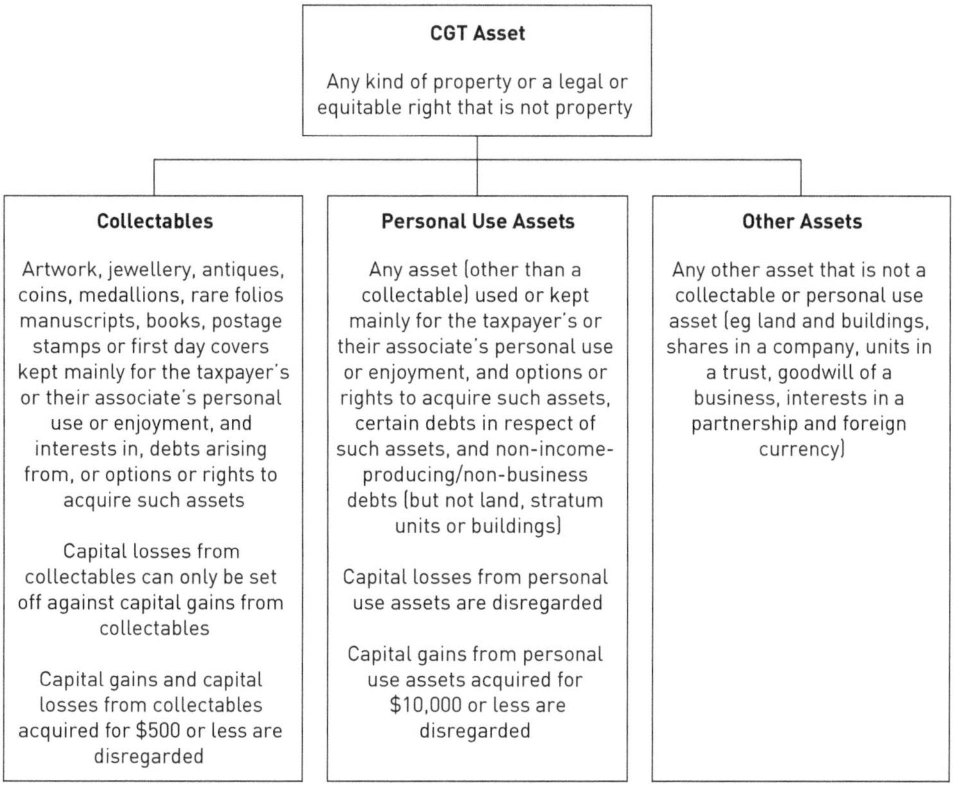

Separate CGT assets

Certain assets that would otherwise be treated as single assets are deemed to be separate assets under sub-div 108-D. These separate assets are examined below.

Buildings and structures

Under the general law, anything fixed to land becomes part of the land. Buildings and structures constructed on land are therefore generally treated as part of the land. However, for CGT purposes, s 108-55 treats certain buildings and structures as separate assets from the land. The rules differ depending on when the land was acquired:

- **Post-CGT land.** A building or structure on land acquired on or after 20 September 1985 is treated as a separate CGT asset from the land if one of the balancing adjustment provisions in sub-div 40-D *ITAA97* [15.3] or s 355-315 or s 355-525 *ITAA97* [27.5] apply to the building or structure (whether or not there is a balancing adjustment) (s 108-55(1)).
- **Pre-CGT land.** A building or structure that is constructed on land acquired before 20 September 1985 is also treated as a separate CGT asset if the construction contract was entered into on or after that day or, in the absence of a contract, construction commenced on or after that day (s 108-55(2)).

Example Bob owns two blocks of land: Block A (acquired on 5 May 2012) and Block B (acquired on 6 March 1982). In 2015, Bob builds a mill, which is subject to a balancing adjustment on its disposal, loss or destruction on Block A and a house on Block B. Both the timber mill and house are separate CGT assets from the land.

Adjacent land

Land acquired on or after 20 September 1985 that is adjacent to land acquired before 20 September 1985 is treated as a separate CGT asset if the post-CGT land and the pre-CGT land are amalgamated into one title (s 108-65).

Example Diana bought a block of land in May 1984 (ie before the introduction of CGT on 20 September 1985) and another block of land adjacent to the first block in June 1999. She amalgamated the titles to the two blocks into one title. The second block is treated as a separate CGT asset. Diana can make a capital gain or capital loss from that block if she sells the whole area of land.

Capital improvements

Capital improvements may be treated as separate CGT assets if they are either improvements to land (whether pre-CGT or post-CGT) or improvements to pre-CGT assets (not necessarily land).

A capital improvement to land is treated as a separate CGT asset from the land if one of the balancing adjustment provisions set out in s 108-55 apply to the improvement (s 108-70(1)).

A capital improvement made to a pre-CGT asset is treated as a separate CGT asset if, when a CGT event happens in relation to the pre-CGT asset, its cost base exceeds both:

- 5% of the capital proceeds from the event, and
- the 'improvement threshold' for the income year in which the CGT event happened as set out in the following table (ss 108-70(2), (3)).

Improvement threshold				
Income year	2020/21	2021/22	2022/23	2023/24
Threshold	$155,849	$156,784	$162,899	$174,465

If the improvement is a separate asset, the capital proceeds from the CGT event must be apportioned between the original pre-CGT asset and the improvement (s 116-40).

Capital improvements are not treated as separate CGT assets where they arose from a pre-CGT contract or, if there was no contract, they had a pre-CGT start date (s 108-70(4)).

Example Nick bought a sailing boat in June 1984 for $290,000 and installed a new mast (a capital improvement) in June 2010 for $45,000. He sold the boat in August 2023 for $580,000. The mast is not a separate CGT asset as its cost base ($45,000) is less than the 2022/23 improvement threshold ($174,465). The capital gain made on the sale of the boat is therefore disregarded as it was acquired before 20 September 1985.

However, if the mast had cost $180,000, it would be a separate CGT asset as its cost base exceeds $174,465 and is more than 5% of the capital proceeds from the CGT event ($580,000). Nick would be deemed to have acquired the mast in June 2010 for $180,000. To calculate his CGT liability in relation to the mast, he must apportion the capital proceeds from the CGT event under s 116-40 [17.7].

[17.5] Exemptions and special rules

Not all capital gains and capital losses made from CGT events fall within the CGT regime. Taxpayers are required to disregard capital gains and capital losses made in relation to particular kinds of CGT assets. These 'exemptions' have been granted for a broad range of policy reasons. The following discussion outlines some of the main exemptions in the *ITAA97*. It also examines a number of special CGT rules that apply to certain entities.

Pre-CGT asset exemption

To ensure that CGT does not have retrospective effect, capital gains and capital losses relating to CGT assets acquired before the introduction of CGT on 20 September 1985 are generally disregarded. The relevant pre-CGT asset exemptions are contained within the respective CGT events. For instance, for the purposes of CGT event A1, s 104-10(5) states that a capital gain or capital loss made on the disposal of a CGT asset acquired before 20 September 1985 is disregarded [17.10].

Example Ernie acquired land in 1983 for $100,000 and recently sold the land for $900,000. Ernie can disregard the $800,000 capital gain made on the disposal of the land as it was acquired before 20 September 1985.

Motor vehicle exemption

17

Capital gains and capital losses made in respect of cars, motorcycles and similar vehicles are disregarded under s 118-5.

A 'car' is defined as a motor vehicle that carries a load of less than one tonne and fewer than nine passengers (s 995-1). A large truck would therefore not fall within this exemption.

In practice, the exemption for cars, motorcycles and similar vehicles actually operates against taxpayers, as it is more likely that they would make losses rather than gains when they dispose of such assets.

Main residence exemption

Section 118-110 provides that a capital gain or capital loss made in relation to a dwelling that is a taxpayer's 'main residence' is disregarded. This provision operates subject to a number of qualifications and special rules [17.11].

As a taxpayer's home will often be their major asset, the main residence exemption is an important concession that comes at a significant cost to the Government. The exemption is often justified on the basis that it promotes home ownership, which is generally considered to be a good thing. It is also administratively efficient, as it reduces the need for taxpayers to comply with onerous record-keeping obligations in relation to costs incurred in maintaining and improving their homes, which are often held for many years. The main residence exemption nevertheless creates distortions as it encourages investment in private homes ahead of other assets, thereby increasing the cost of housing.

Personal use asset and collectables exemptions

The following exemptions apply to collectables and personal use assets:

- **Collectables.** Capital gains and capital losses made from 'collectables' acquired for $500 or less are disregarded (s 118-10(1)).

- **Personal use assets.** Capital losses from 'personal use assets' are disregarded (s 108-20(1)) and capital gains from personal use assets are disregarded if the asset was acquired for $10,000 or less (s 118-10(3)).

The exemptions are designed to minimise compliance costs by excluding certain assets acquired for low value from the general CGT rules. In addition, by disregarding capital losses from personal use assets, the revenue is protected as it is likely that taxpayers would generally make capital losses when they dispose of such assets.

Depreciating asset exemption

To ensure that gains and losses made in respect of depreciating assets are ordinarily dealt with under the capital allowance regime rather than the CGT regime, s 118-24 provides that capital gains and capital losses made from CGT events (that are also 'balancing adjustment events' [15.3]) that happen to 'depreciating assets' are generally disregarded. The exemption applies where the decline in value of the asset has been calculated under div 40 *ITAA97* or the deduction for the asset is calculated under div 328 *ITAA97* [15.2]. If the depreciating asset was not used wholly for a 'taxable purpose', a capital gain or capital loss may arise under CGT event K7 [17.3].

Example Fred owns a law firm and purchased a photocopier for use in his practice for $60,000. The photocopier is a depreciating asset and Fred claims deductions for its decline in value under div 40. If he sold the machine for $65,000, this would constitute a balancing adjustment event. The capital gain on the disposal of the photocopier is therefore disregarded under s 118-24. Any gain on the photocopier would need to be worked out under the balancing adjustment rules in s 40-285 [15.3].

Trading stock exemption

Capital gains and capital losses made in respect of CGT assets that are 'trading stock' at the time of the CGT event are disregarded under s 118-25. The reason for this exemption is that trading stock is a 'revenue asset' and it is therefore taxed under the general tax rules [16.2].

Example Bill operates a business selling boats. In the course of conducting his business, he makes a gain from selling a boat. The gain is disregarded for CGT purposes as the boat is Bill's trading stock. Bill is assessed on the proceeds from the sale of the boat under s 6-5 *ITAA97* and is entitled to a deduction for the cost of acquiring the boat under s 8-1 *ITAA97*.

Miscellaneous exemptions

The CGT regime also contains a number of miscellaneous exemptions. For instance, capital gains and capital losses made in relation to the following items are disregarded:

- decorations awarded for valour or brave conduct (provided the taxpayer has not paid money or given property to acquire it) (s 118-5)
- assets used solely to produce exempt income or certain forms of non-assessable non-exempt income (s 118-12)
- shares in PDFs [27.3] (s 118-13)
- carried interest payments [27.4] (s 118-21)

- div 230 financial arrangements [29.2] (s 118-27)
- gambling prizes and compensation or damages for personal and occupational injuries (s 118-37)
- foreign currency hedging contracts (s 118-55)
- rights under certain insurance policies (s 118-300)
- rights to benefits from superannuation funds, ADFs and RSAs [19.16] (ss 118-305, 118-310)
- segregated current pension assets of complying superannuation entities [19.14] (s 118-320), and
- eligible venture capital investments [27.4] (ss 118-405, 118-407, 118-410).

> ***Example*** Rob was injured at work and lost his vision. He received a compensation payment of $1m for his injuries from his employer. He also placed a $10 bet at the races and won $1,000. Both gains are disregarded under s 118-37.

Foreign and temporary residents exemptions

Foreign residents disregard capital gains and capital losses made from CGT events in relation to CGT assets that are *not* 'taxable Australian property' (s 855-10 *ITAA97*) [17.12]. A similar rule applies to temporary residents (s 768-915 *ITAA97*).

Deceased estates exemptions

Special rules in div 128 *ITAA97* disregard certain capital gains and capital losses made in respect of CGT assets relating to deceased estates (ss 128-10, 128-15) [17.13].

Granny flat exemption

Division 137 *ITAA97* provides that a CGT event does not happen on entering into, varying or terminating a 'granny flat interest' (ss 137-15, 137-20, 137-25). An individual has such an interest where they have a right to occupy a dwelling for life under an arrangement (s 137-10). To qualify for the exemption the individual must have reached pension age or have a disability. The arrangement must also be in writing indicating the parties intend to be legally bound and must not be of a commercial nature.

Roll-overs

Capital gains may also be disregarded where a 'roll-over' applies. There are a wide range of CGT roll-overs in divs 122 and 124 *ITAA97*, which are discussed in general terms at [17.16]. A number of specific roll-overs dealing with business, corporate and trust restructures are examined in Chapter 28.

Rule to prevent double taxation

To prevent duplication, a capital gain from a CGT event is generally reduced if, because of the CGT event, an amount (for any income year) is also included in the taxpayer's assessable income, exempt income, or non-assessable non-exempt income under a non-CGT provision (s 118-20 *ITAA97*). The capital gain is reduced to zero if it does not exceed the amount included. If the capital gain exceeds the amount included, it is reduced by the amount included. The rules operate subject to certain exceptions (eg a capital gain is not reduced by the amount of franking credits assessable under s 207-20 *ITAA97* [22.8], nor the amount that is a dividend under s 159GZZZP *ITAA36* [22.10]).

Example Barry acquired a CGT asset as part of a profit-making scheme. As a result of carrying out the scheme, Barry is required to include a profit of $30,000 in his assessable income under s 6-5. If he also made a capital gain of $30,000 from carrying out the scheme, the capital gain would be reduced to zero as it does not exceed the amount assessable under s 6-5.

Special entity rules

Division 106 *ITAA97* sets out special cases where a capital gain or capital loss is deemed to be made by someone other than the entity to which the CGT event happens. The special cases are outlined below.

- **Partnerships.** A capital gain or capital loss from a CGT event happening in relation to a partnership or one of its CGT assets is made by the partners individually, rather than the partnership (s 106-5). The treatment of such gains and losses is discussed further at [23.5].

Example Jerry and Dean are partners in a partnership that owns a parcel of land. If the land is sold, Jerry and Dean must each account separately for any gain or loss made in relation to their respective fractional interests in the partnership asset.

- **Bankrupts and liquidators.** The vesting of an individual's CGT assets in a trustee under the *Bankruptcy Act 1966* (Cth) (or similar foreign law) is ignored for CGT purposes. The CGT provisions apply to an act done by the trustee in relation to the individual's CGT assets as if the act had been done by the individual (s 106-30). Likewise, an act done by a liquidator of a company is deemed to have been done by the company (s 106-35).

Example Alpha Co has gone into liquidation and one of its assets is sold by its liquidator. Any capital gain or capital loss made on the disposal of the asset is made by Alpha Co, not the liquidator.

- **Absolutely entitled beneficiaries.** Where an entity is absolutely entitled to a CGT asset as against the trustee of a trust (disregarding any legal disability), the asset is treated as being the entity's asset (instead of an asset of the trust) and the CGT provisions apply to an act done by the trustee in relation to the asset as if the act had been done by the entity (instead of the trustee) (s 106-50).

Example Bert holds a block of land under a 'bare trust' for Ernie. Ernie is therefore absolutely entitled to the asset as against Bert. The land is treated as Ernie's land for CGT purposes and any capital gain or capital loss made on its disposal is deemed to be made by Ernie, not Bert.

- **Security holders.** An act done by an entity in relation to a CGT asset for the purpose of enforcing or giving effect to a security, charge or encumbrance the entity holds over the asset is deemed, for the purposes of the CGT provisions, as if the act had been done by the person who provided the security (s 106-60).

Example A bank holds a security over a borrower's property in relation to a loan that it has made. It exercises its rights to sell the property under its power of sale after the borrower defaults in repaying the loan. Any capital gain or capital loss made on the disposal of the property is deemed to be made by the borrower, not the bank.

Look-through earnout rights

Special rules in sub-div 118-I apply to 'look-through earnout rights'. Broadly speaking, look-through earnout rights are rights to future financial benefits created under arrangements involving the disposal of 'active assets' [17.9] that are provided within 5 years of such disposal, are not reasonably ascertainable at the time of their creation, and are contingent on the economic performance of the underlying asset (s 118-565). For example, these rights may arise where the purchaser of the goodwill of a business agrees to pay the vendor an upfront amount together with an additional amount 12 months later provided the business achieves specified sales targets. Alternatively, the vendor may agree to repay a certain amount 12 months later to the purchaser if the business does not reach such targets.

Any capital gain or capital loss arising under CGT event C2 (the cancellation or surrender of a CGT asset) or D1 (the creation of a CGT asset) occurring in relation to a look-through earnout right is disregarded (s 118-575). Instead, special rules require taxpayers to include the value of the financial benefits received or paid under look-through earnout rights in the cost base, reduced cost base, or capital proceeds of the underlying asset being disposed of [17.6]–[17.7].

[17.6] Cost base and reduced cost base

The 'cost base' of a CGT asset is used to calculate a capital gain from certain CGT events, while the 'reduced cost base' of a CGT asset is used to calculate a capital loss from certain CGT events. The general cost base and reduced cost base rules are contained in div 110 *ITAA97*. These rules are modified under special rules in div 112 *ITAA97*.

Cost base

The cost base of a CGT asset has five elements (s 110-25(1)):

- **First element.** The first element is the total of the money the taxpayer pays, or is required to pay, and the market value of any property the taxpayer gives, or is required to give, in respect of acquiring the asset (s 110-25(2)).
- **Second element.** The second element is the 'incidental costs' incurred by the taxpayer (s 110-25(3)). Incidental costs are costs incurred to acquire the asset or that relate to the CGT event. They include brokerage and agency fees, legal costs, transfer costs, stamp duty, advertising costs, valuation costs, search fees and borrowing expenses (s 110-35).
- **Third element.** The third element, which is applicable only to assets acquired after 20 August 1991 (but not to personal use assets or collectables: ss 108-17, 108-30), is the costs of owning the asset. These costs include: interest on money borrowed to acquire or refinance the asset; costs of maintaining, repairing or insuring the asset; and rates or land tax if the asset is land (s 110-25(4)).
- **Fourth element.** The fourth element is capital expenditure incurred to increase or preserve the asset's value or that relates to installing or moving the asset (s 110-25(5)). It does not include capital expenditure relating to goodwill (s 110-25(5A)).
- **Fifth element.** The fifth element is capital expenditure incurred to establish, preserve or defend the taxpayer's title to the asset or a right over the asset (s 110-25(6)).

Example In 2021, Barney purchased a holiday home near the beach for use by his family on weekends. The purchase price was $700,000 and Barney was required to pay $40,000 stamp duty on the transfer. He borrowed money from a bank to fund some of the purchase price and paid $20,000 in interest on the loan. Last year, he also paid $33,000 to a builder to renovate the kitchen. In addition, he paid $11,000 in legal costs to defend his title to the property against an adverse possession claim brought by his neighbour, who claimed that she owned part of his land.

The cost base of Barney's holiday home is $804,000, being the sum of:

- $700,000 (the first element of the cost base)
- $40,000 (the second element of the cost base)
- $20,000 (the third element of the cost base)
- $33,000 (the fourth element of the cost base), and
- $11,000 (the fifth element of the cost base).

Reduced cost base

The 'reduced cost base' of a CGT asset also has five elements (s 110-55(1)). The first, second, fourth and fifth elements of the reduced cost base mirror the respective elements of the cost base (s 110-55(2)). The third element is the amount that is assessable as a result of a 'balancing adjustment' taking place in relation to the asset or the amount that would be assessable if balancing adjustment relief under certain provisions (eg s 40-365 [15.3]) was not available (s 110-55(3)).

Amounts excluded from the cost base and reduced cost base

Certain kinds of expenditure are expressly excluded from being taken into account in determining the cost base and reduced cost base of a CGT asset. The main exclusions are outlined below:

- **Deductible or recouped expenditure.** The second and third elements of the cost base and reduced cost base do not include deductible or recouped expenditure (ss 110-40, 110-45, 110-55). Deductible expenditure is excluded because it is already taken into account under the general tax rules. Recouped expenditure is excluded because it has been recovered by the taxpayer so there is no need to include it in the respective elements.
- **Specific expenditure.** For a range of policy reasons, the cost base and reduced cost base elements do not include specific kinds of expenditure (eg expenditure relating to entertainment, bribes, penalties and illegal activities) (ss 110-38, 110-55).
- **Net input tax credits.** To prevent overlap with the GST rules, the cost base and reduced cost base of an asset, and any other amount that could be involved in the calculation of an entity's capital gain or capital loss must be reduced by any 'net input tax credit' available to the entity in relation to the amount (s 103-30). The 'net input tax credit' is the amount of any ITCs minus increasing adjustments plus decreasing adjustments that relate to the relevant acquisition or importation (s 995-1).

Example In October 2020, Betty (who is registered for GST) purchased a commercial office building for $990,000 (inclusive of GST), which she leases to a law firm. Betty was required to pay $40,000 stamp duty in respect of the transfer. She borrowed money from a bank to fund some of the purchase price and paid $20,000 in interest on the loan. Last year, she also paid $33,000 (inclusive of GST) to a builder to renovate the building.

The cost base of Betty's building is $970,000, being the sum of:

- $900,000 (the first element of the cost base)
- $40,000 (the second element of the cost base), and
- $30,000 (the fourth element of the cost base).

Note the following points:

- As Betty is registered for GST, she is entitled to an ITC of $90,000 in relation to the purchase of the office building (the first element of her cost base is therefore $900,000).
- As Betty is using the property for income-producing purposes, she is entitled to deduct the $20,000 interest paid to the bank (the third element of her cost base is therefore nil).
- As Betty is registered for GST, she is entitled to an ITC of $3,000 in relation to the amount paid to the builder for the renovation (the fourth element of her cost base is therefore $30,000).

Market value substitution rule

The cost base and reduced cost base rules operate subject to a 'market value substitution rule'. This rule provides that the first element of the cost base and reduced cost base of a CGT asset acquired from another entity is its 'market value' [8.6] at the time of acquisition if:

- the taxpayer did not incur expenditure to acquire it (eg the asset was received as a gift)
- some or all of the expenditure incurred to acquire it cannot be valued, or
- the taxpayer did not deal at arm's length with the other entity in connection with the acquisition (s 112-20).

Example Barney gifts land with a market value of $300,000 to Betty. The first element of the cost base or reduced cost base of the asset to Betty is $300,000.

Other modifications

There are a number of special modifications to the general cost base and reduced cost base rules. Some of the more important modifications are outlined below:

- **Split or changed asset rule.** Section 112-25 provides that where a CGT asset has been split or changed and the taxpayer remains the beneficial owner of the new asset, the split or change is not a CGT event and the cost base and reduced cost base of the new CGT asset is simply calculated by way of reasonable apportionment.

Example Rupert acquired 100 shares in X Co for $10 each. X Co undertook a share split under which it issued its shareholders two shares in exchange for each share they owned. Consequently, Rupert now owns 200 shares in X Co. The share split is not treated as a CGT event and the new shares have a cost base of $5 each.

- **Apportionment rule (only part of the expenditure relates to CGT asset).** Section 112-30(1) provides that where only part of the expenditure incurred in a transaction relates to the acquisition of a CGT asset, the first element of the cost base and reduced cost base of the asset is that part of the expenditure that is reasonably attributable to the acquisition of the asset.

> ***Example*** Hillary purchased 100 shares in X Co and 100 shares in Y Co from Bill for $3,000. At the time of acquisition, the X Co shares were worth twice as much as the Y Co shares. The cost base of the X Co shares is $2,000 and the cost base of the Y Co shares is $1,000.

- **Apportionment rule (CGT asset part of another asset).** Section 112-30(2) provides that if a CGT event happens to only part of a CGT asset, the cost base and reduced cost base of the asset must be apportioned. The cost base and reduced cost base of the CGT asset representing the part to which the CGT event happened is worked out as follows:

$$\text{Cost base or reduced cost base of asset} = \frac{\text{Capital proceeds for the CGT event happening to the part}}{\text{Those capital proceeds plus the market value of the remainder of the asset}}$$

> ***Example*** Popeye acquired a boat for $60,000 and sold the boat's motor to Olive for $20,000. If the market value of the remainder of the boat is $50,000, the cost of the motor would be calculated as follows:
>
> $$\$17{,}143 = \$60{,}000 \times \frac{\$20{,}000}{\$20{,}000 + \$50{,}000}$$
>
> The cost base of the remainder of the boat would be:
>
> $$\$42{,}857 = \$60{,}000 - \$17{,}143$$

- **Assumption of liability rule.** Section 112-35 provides that where a liability has been assumed in connection with the acquisition of a CGT asset, the cost base and reduced cost base of the asset includes the amount of that liability.

> ***Example*** Fannie sells land to Freddie for $100,000 subject to Freddie taking over a mortgage on the land with an outstanding liability of $99,000. The cost base of Freddie's land is $199,000.

- **Look-through earnout right rule.** Section 112-36 provides that the value of a look-through earnout right [17.5] is not included in the cost base or reduced cost base of a CGT asset. Instead, the first element of the asset's cost base and reduced cost base includes any financial benefit provided under such a right and is reduced by any financial benefit received under such a right.

> ***Example*** Jonathan purchases the goodwill of a business from Leo for $100,000 and is required to pay an additional $10,000 in 12 months if sales have reached a specified target within this period. Assuming the sales have reached this target and Jonathan pays Leo the additional $10,000, the cost base of the goodwill to Jonathan is $110,000.

Indexation of the cost base

At the time the CGT regime was introduced it was recognised that as capital gains accrue over a period of time it was appropriate to make an allowance for inflation when calculating such gains. As a consequence, special cost base indexation rules were inserted in the legislation that apply to assets held for more than 12 months. These rules were 'frozen' when the 'discount capital gains' rules were introduced on 21 September 1999 [17.8]. The indexation rules can, nevertheless, still be used to calculate capital gains on CGT assets acquired on or before 11.45am on 21 September 1999 (although the benefit of indexation does not extend beyond September 1999). The way indexation works is outlined below.

In what circumstances can indexation be used?

Indexation applies to the individual elements of the cost base of a CGT asset. The elements (other than the third element) of the cost base of a CGT asset acquired on or before 11.45am on 21 September 1999 may be indexed, provided the asset has been held for more than 12 months and a choice to index has been made (ss 110-36, 960-275(4), div 114 *ITAA97*).

The elements of the reduced cost base of a CGT asset *cannot* be indexed. This means that while indexation can reduce the amount of a capital gain that might otherwise arise, it can never operate to increase the amount of a capital loss.

Importantly, indexation cannot be used where a taxpayer chooses to use the discount capital gains treatment under div 115 *ITAA97* [17.8]. This prevents taxpayers from obtaining a double benefit. In practice, taxpayers choose to use the method which produces the lower net capital gain.

How is indexation calculated?

Indexation is calculated by multiplying the relevant element of the cost base by an 'indexation factor' (s 960-270). The indexation factor is generally calculated according to the following formula (s 960-275(2)):

$$\text{Indexation factor} = \frac{\text{Index number for quarter ending 30 September 1999}}{\text{Index number for quarter in which the expenditure was incurred}}$$

A special rule applies to calculate the indexation factor of the first element of the cost base of shares in companies or units in trusts that were acquired on or after 16 August 1989. The first element of the cost base of these assets is only indexed from the time that the relevant expenditure is paid (rather than when it is incurred). The indexation factor is therefore calculated as follows (s 960-275(3)):

$$\text{Indexation factor} = \frac{\text{Index number for quarter ending 30 September 1999}}{\text{Index number for quarter in which the expenditure was paid}}$$

The index numbers to be used in the above formulas are the quarterly All Groups Consumer Price Index ('CPI') numbers published by the Australian Statistician (s 960-280). These index numbers are set out in the following table:

Index numbers for quarters ending September 1985 to September 1999				
Year	**31 March**	**30 June**	**30 September**	**31 December**
1999	67.8	68.1	68.7	
1998	67.0	67.4	67.5	67.8
1997	67.1	66.9	66.6	66.8
1996	66.2	66.7	66.9	67.0
1995	63.8	64.7	65.5	66.0

17

Index numbers for quarters ending September 1985 to September 1999				
Year	31 March	30 June	30 September	31 December
1994	61.5	61.9	62.3	62.8
1993	60.6	60.8	61.1	61.2
1992	59.9	59.7	59.8	60.1
1991	58.9	59.0	59.3	59.9
1990	56.2	57.1	57.5	59.0
1989	51.7	53.0	54.2	55.2
1988	48.4	49.3	50.2	51.2
1987	45.3	46.0	46.8	47.6
1986	41.4	42.1	43.2	44.4
1985	37.9	38.8	39.7	40.5

The indexation factor must be worked out to three decimal places (rounded up if the fourth decimal place is five or more) (s 960-275(5)). An element of the cost base is not indexed if the indexation factor is one or less (s 960-270(2)). This is designed to prevent indexation reducing the element.

Example Company X acquired a CGT asset in March 1987 for $100,000. This is therefore the first element of Company X's cost base for the asset. If Company X sold the asset in January 2024 for $200,000, it would be able to index the first element of the cost base of the asset by an indexation factor of 1.517 (ie 68.7/45.3). The indexed cost base of the asset is therefore $151,700 ($100,000 × 1.517). Company X would, therefore, derive a capital gain of $48,300 ($200,000 – $151,700) in January 2024.

If Company X had instead sold the asset for $80,000, it would make a capital loss of $20,000 ($100,000 – $80,000). The reduced cost base of the asset is not indexed.

[17.7] Capital proceeds

The 'capital proceeds' from a CGT event is determined under div 116 *ITAA97*. In general, the capital proceeds from a CGT event is the sum of the money and/or the market value of the property that the taxpayer has received, or is entitled to receive, in respect of the CGT event happening (s 116-20(1)). Where the CGT event is also a 'supply' for GST purposes, the capital proceeds do not include any GST charged on the supply (s 116-20(5)).

Example Fred sold his shares in A Co to Wilma in consideration of being paid $200,000 in cash plus Wilma's shares in B Co worth $40,000. The capital proceeds from the disposal of the shares in A Co is $240,000.

Market value substitution rule

The general rule for calculating capital proceeds is modified by the 'market value substitution rule' (s 116-30). This rule provides that, subject to certain exceptions, the capital proceeds from a CGT event are replaced with the 'market value' [8.6] of the CGT asset that is the subject of the event where:

- no capital proceeds are otherwise received from the CGT event (eg the asset is disposed of by way of a gift)

- some or all of the capital proceeds cannot be valued, or
- the capital proceeds are more or less than the market value of the asset and either the parties did not deal with each other at arm's length or CGT event C2 is involved.

Example Barney gifts land with a market value of $300,000 to Betty. The capital proceeds from the disposal of the land is $300,000.

Other modifications

A number of other special modifications apply to the general capital proceeds rules. Some of the more important ones are outlined below:

- **Apportionment rule.** Section 116-40 provides that where a payment is received in connection with a transaction that relates to more than one CGT event, it is necessary to apportion the capital proceeds between the events so that the capital proceeds from each event is so much of the payment as is reasonably attributable to the event.

Example Jim sells his land and shares to Jenny for $200,000. As this involves two CGT events, the capital proceeds must be apportioned. The capital proceeds from the sale of the land is so much of the $200,000 as is reasonably attributable to the CGT event relating to the land. The capital proceeds from the sale of the shares is the balance of the capital proceeds.

- **Non-receipt rule.** Section 116-45 provides that where it is not likely that a taxpayer will receive some or all of the capital proceeds from a CGT event and this is not attributable to anything the taxpayer has done or omitted to do, then, provided reasonable steps have been taken to recover the unpaid amount, the capital proceeds are reduced by the unpaid amount.

Example Popeye sells a boat to Olive for $100,000, payable over a number of instalments. Olive pays the first two instalments of $10,000 each, but does not pay any of the balance instalments. After using his best efforts to try to find Olive, Popeye discovers that she has sailed overseas and cannot be located. The capital proceeds are reduced from $100,000 to $20,000.

- **Repayment rule.** Section 116-50 provides that the capital proceeds are reduced to the extent that the taxpayer repays any part of the capital proceeds or pays compensation that can reasonably be regarded as a repayment of part of the capital proceeds.

Example Andy sells a painting for $200,000 to Sam. Sam later sues Andy for misrepresenting the identity of the painter. As a result, Andy pays Sam $50,000 compensation. The capital proceeds are reduced from $200,000 to $150,000.

- **Assumption of liability rule.** Section 116-55 provides that the capital proceeds are increased if another entity acquires the CGT asset subject to a liability by way of security over the asset. The capital proceeds are increased by the amount of the liability that the other entity assumes.

Example Fannie sells land to Freddie for $100,000 subject to Freddie taking over a mortgage of the land with an outstanding liability of $99,000. The capital proceeds are increased to $199,000.

- **Look-through earnout right rule.** Section 116-120 provides that the capital proceeds from the disposal of a CGT asset does not include the value of a look-through earnout right [17.5]. Instead, the capital proceeds include any financial benefit received under such a right and are reduced by any financial benefit provided under such a right.

Example Leo sold the goodwill of his business to Jonathan for $100,000 and is required to repay $10,000 in 12 months if sales have not reached a specified target by then. Assuming the sales have not reached this target and Leo has repaid the $10,000, the capital proceeds from the sale of the goodwill is $90,000.

[17.8] Discount capital gains

Discount capital gains rules were introduced on 21 September 1999, when the cost base indexation rules were frozen [17.6]. Basically, the object of the discount capital gains rules is to provide a simpler method for taking inflation into account in respect of capital gains made on CGT assets held for at least 12 months. Importantly, the discount capital gains rules do *not* apply if a taxpayer has chosen to index the cost base of an asset.

The discount capital gains rules are contained in div 115 *ITAA97* and are taken into account under Step 3 of the method statement for working out a 'net capital gain' in s 102-5 *ITAA97* [17.2]. Step 3 requires a taxpayer's net capital gain to be reduced by the 'discount percentage' of any 'discount capital gains' remaining after Step 2 (ie after capital losses made during the income year and unapplied capital losses of previous years have been set off against capital gains made during the income year).

Discount capital gain

A 'discount capital gain' is a capital gain that satisfies the following requirements (s 115-5):

- the capital gain must be made by an individual, complying superannuation entity or trust (s 115-10)
- the capital gain must result from a CGT event happening after 21 September 1999 (s 115-15)
- the capital gain must have been calculated without taking indexation into account [17.6] (s 115-20), and
- the capital gain must result from a CGT event happening to a CGT asset acquired at least 12 months before the CGT event (the CGT event must not be a CGT event listed in s 115-25(3); namely, CGT event D1, D2, D3, E9, F1, F2, F5, H2, J2, J5, J6 or K10) (s 115-25).

In calculating the relevant 12-month period, the Commissioner excludes both the day of acquisition and the day on which the CGT event happens (TD 2002/10). This means that 'a period of 365 whole days (or in a leap year 366 whole days) must elapse between the day on which the CGT asset was acquired and the day on which the CGT event happens'. On this basis, if a taxpayer acquired an asset on 1 January 2022 and sold it on 1 January 2023, the 12-month requirement would *not* be satisfied.

Special rules determine the time at which CGT assets acquired under deceased estates [17.13] and certain roll-overs [17.16] are acquired (s 115-30).

It is important to note that the CGT discount only applies to capital gains. There is no CGT discount for capital losses. In addition, companies cannot benefit from the CGT discount as it is only available to individuals, complying superannuation entities and trusts.

Discount percentage

The 'discount percentage' for individuals and trusts is 50% (s 115-100(1)(a)). The discount percentage for complying superannuation entities is 33⅓% (s 115-100(1)(b)).

Example In January 2023, Ted sold a CGT asset he acquired in March 2020. The capital proceeds from the CGT event was $300,000 and the cost base of the asset was $200,000. He therefore made a capital gain of $100,000. Since Ted held the asset for more than 12 months, he can discount the capital gain by 50%. This means that his capital gain is reduced to only $50,000. Note that if Ted had held the asset for less than 12 months, he would not be able to discount the capital gain. Likewise, if the gain had been made by a company instead of an individual, no discount would be available.

Special rules for discount capital gains made by trusts

Sub-division 115-C *ITAA97* contains special rules that operate where trusts make capital gains that are eligible for the 50% CGT discount or the 50% reduction concession in sub-div 152-C *ITAA97* [17.9]. Under these rules:

- where a trust has a capital gain that has been reduced by *either* the 50% discount or the 50% reduction concession, the beneficiary is required to double their share of the gain
- where a trust has a capital gain that has been reduced by *both* the 50% discount and the 50% reduction concession, the beneficiary is required to quadruple their share of the gain.

17

The 'gross-up' effectively cancels the 50% CGT discount and/or 50% reduction concession that the trustee obtained at the trust level. The beneficiary is then able to offset their individual capital losses and unapplied net capital losses against the grossed-up capital gain. If the beneficiary is eligible to benefit from the CGT discount and/or the reduction concession, they can apply those concessions to the remaining capital gain.

The mechanics of sub-div 115-C are explained in more detail at [24.8].

Reduction of discount for foreign and temporary residents

The 50% discount available to individuals is reduced for any periods that they have been foreign or temporary residents after 8 May 2012 (s 115-105). The reduced discount percentage is calculated under s 115-115. In effect, the 50% discount is removed for capital gains that accrued to foreign and temporary residents after 8 May 2012. The 50% discount nevertheless remains for capital gains that accrued prior to 8 May 2012 provided the foreign or temporary resident obtains a market valuation of the asset as at 8 May 2012. Where an individual has been both an Australian resident and a foreign or temporary resident after 8 May 2012, the 50% discount is apportioned to ensure that it only applies to periods where they are an Australian resident.

Additional discount for affordable housing

The Government has introduced an additional CGT discount of up to 10% for resident individuals who invest in dwellings used to provide 'affordable housing' (s 115-125). The additional CGT discount applies from 1 July 2018 and is designed to encourage investment in residential dwellings that are provided to low-to-moderate income tenants at below the private market rental rate for at least three years.

A dwelling is used to provide affordable housing if the following conditions in s 980-5 *ITAA97* are met:

- the dwelling is 'taxable Australian real property' [17.13] and is residential premises that is tenanted or available to be tenanted and is not commercial residential premises
- the tenancy of the dwelling is exclusively managed by an 'eligible community housing provider' as defined in s 980-10 *ITAA97*
- the eligible community housing provider has given each entity that holds an ownership interest in the dwelling a certificate under s 980-15 *ITAA97*
- no entity is entitled to receive an NRAS incentive for the dwelling [27.7], and
- if an MIT [25.10] holds an ownership interest in the dwelling, none of the tenants have an interest in the MIT that passes the 'non-portfolio interest test' [31.10].

The additional discount is calculated under the following formula:

$$\frac{\text{Discount percentage that would apply to the discount capital gain apart from this section}}{5} \times \frac{\text{Affordable housing days}}{\text{Total ownership days}}$$

[17.9] Small business concessions

Division 152 *ITAA97* contains the small business concessions. These concessions are taken into account under Step 4 in s 102-5 to reduce the amount of a taxpayer's net capital gain [17.2].

Basic conditions

To qualify for the small business concessions, the basic conditions in s 152-10(1) must be satisfied. These conditions are summarised below:

- **CGT event and capital gain condition.** A CGT event must have occurred in relation to a CGT asset that would, if not for the concessions in div 152, result In the taxpayer making a capital gain (ss 152-10(1)(a), (b)).
- **Taxpayer condition.** At least *one* of the following must apply (s 152-10(1)(c)):
  - The taxpayer is a CGT small business entity ('CGT SBE') for the income year. A CGT SBE is an entity that would be an SBE for an income year if references in s 328-110 to $10m were references to $2m (s 152-10(1AA)). A CGT SBE is therefore essentially an SBE that has aggregated turnover under $2m [8.7].
  - The taxpayer satisfies the 'maximum net asset value' test in s 152-15. Broadly, this test is satisfied if the 'net value of the CGT assets' of the taxpayer, its 'connected entities' (defined in s 328-125 [8.7]) and its 'affiliates' (defined in s 328-130 [8.7]) does not exceed $6m. The 'net value of the CGT assets' of an entity is the amount by which the sum of the market values of those assets exceeds the sum of the liabilities related to those assets (s 152-20(1)). Certain assets are excluded, such as assets used by individuals solely for their personal use and enjoyment (eg their home), and rights to amounts payable out of a superannuation fund (s 152-20(2)).
  - The taxpayer is a partner in a partnership that is a CGT SBE for the income year.
  - The conditions in ss 152-10(1A) or (1B) are satisfied in relation to the CGT asset in the income year. Broadly, these conditions are satisfied if the taxpayer does not carry on a business but owns CGT assets that are used in businesses carried on by its affiliates or connected entities which are CGT SBEs.

- **Active asset test condition.** The CGT asset must satisfy the active asset test in s 152-35 (s 152-10(1)(d)). A CGT asset satisfies this test if it was an 'active asset' just before the CGT event (or if it relates to a business that ceased within the last 12 months before the time of that event or such longer period as the Commissioner allows, it is an active asset just before the business ceased). The CGT asset must have also been an active asset for at least half of the period it was owned (or for at least 7.5 years, if the asset was owned for more than 15 years). Broadly, an asset is an 'active asset' if the taxpayer owns it and:
  - it is used, or held ready for use, by the taxpayer, its affiliates or connected entities in the course of carrying on a business (if the asset is an intangible asset, such as goodwill, it must be inherently connected with a business that the entity, its affiliates or connected entities carry on) (s 152-40(1)), or
  - it is a share in a resident company or an interest in a resident trust, where the total market values of the active assets of the company or trust is 80% or more of the market values of all the assets of the company or trust (s 152-40(3)).

  However, an asset is not an active asset if it falls within s 152-40(4). This provision excludes certain assets such as financial instruments as well as assets mainly used to derive interest, annuities, rent, royalties or foreign exchange gains unless: (a) the asset is an intangible asset and has been substantially developed, altered or improved by the taxpayer so that its market value has been substantially enhanced; or (b) its main use for deriving rent was only temporary.

Example Zena owns a residential investment property that she leases to tenants. The property is not an active asset because she is not using it in carrying on a business. If, however, she owned a shop in a mall which she uses to sell handbags, it would be an active asset because she would be using it in carrying on a retail business.

17

The active asset condition was considered in *Eichmann v FC of T* 2020 ATC 20-762. The case concerned a taxpayer and his wife who operated a building, bricklaying and paving business through a family trust. They purchased land next to their family home and used it to store work tools, equipment and materials. The land had two sheds, high walls and a gate to secure the property. Although there was no business signage on the property, items were collected from the site on a daily basis and work vehicles and trailers were parked on it. In a private ruling, the Commissioner ruled that the land was not an active asset as there was no direct and immediate functional connection between the use of the asset and the carrying on of a business. On appeal, the Full Federal Court held that div 152 should be construed beneficially rather than restrictively to promote the purpose of the concessions. It held that the land was used in the course of carrying on the relevant business and was therefore an active asset. The Court explained (at 46):

> s 152-40(1)(a) does not require the use of the relevant asset to take place within the day to day or normal course of the carrying on of a business. Nor does the provision require a relationship of direct functional relevance between the use of an asset and the carrying on of a business. Such narrowing qualifications to the statutory test are not supported by the language of the provision, and are inconsistent with the need to construe that language beneficially.

More recently, in *Del Castillo v FC of T* 2022 ATC ¶10-660, the AAT held that a taxpayer who built multiple dwellings on a block of land for the purpose of deriving rental income was not entitled to the small business concessions as she was unable to satisfy the requirement that the property was an active asset. The AAT held that the exception in s 152-40(4) applied as the property was mainly used to derive rent. Given this finding, the AAT found it unnecessary to consider the additional question of whether she was carrying on a business.

Additional conditions if the CGT asset is a share in a company or an interest in a trust

If the CGT asset is a share in a company or an interest in a trust (the 'object entity'), the following additional conditions in s 152-10(2) must also be satisfied in order for a taxpayer to be able to qualify for the small business concessions:

- The shares or interests in the object entity must satisfy the active asset test in s 152-35 (see above) if the assumptions in s 152-10(2A) were made (s 152-10(2)(a)).
- Unless the taxpayer satisfies the maximum net asset value test in s 152-15 (see above), the taxpayer must have carried on a business just before the CGT event (s 152-10(2)(b)).
- The object entity must be a CGT SBE for the income year or satisfy the maximum net asset value test in s 152-15 (see above) (s 152-10(2)(c)).
- Just before the CGT event, either:
  - the taxpayer must be a 'CGT concession stakeholder' in the object entity, or
  - CGT concession stakeholders in the object entity must have a 'small business participation percentage' in the taxpayer of at least 90% (s 152-10(2)(d)).

A 'CGT concession stakeholder' is a 'significant individual' or the spouse of such a person (s 152-60). A 'significant individual' is an individual who has a 'small business participation percentage' of at least 20% in the object entity (s 152-55). An entity's 'small business participation percentage' is the sum of the entity's direct and indirect small business participation interests (defined in ss 152-70 and 152-75) in another entity (s 152-65).

Example Object Co carries on a small pizza restaurant business and all its assets are active assets. Camille owns 80% of the shares in Object Co and her husband, Humphrey, owns 5% of the shares in Object Co. The remaining 15% of the shares in Object Co are owned by third parties. If the shares in Object Co are sold and both Camille and Humphrey satisfy the 'maximum net asset value' test, they will qualify for the CGT concessions as they are both CGT concession stakeholders in Object Co. Camille is a CGT concession shareholder because she is a 'significant individual' in relation to Object Co, as she has a small business participation percentage of at least 20% in the company. Humphrey is a CGT concession shareholder because he is Camille's spouse. However, the third parties are not CGT concession stakeholders in Object Co as they do not have a small business participation percentage of at least 20% in the company. Consequently, they do not qualify for the concessions when they sell their shares.

Additional condition if the CGT event involves interests in partnerships

If the CGT event involves the creation, transfer, variation or cessation of a right or interest that would entitle an entity to:

- an amount of the income or capital of a partnership, or
- an amount calculated by reference to a partner's entitlement to an amount of income or capital of a partnership,

there is an additional condition in s 152-10(2C) that the right or interest must be a membership interest of the entity in the partnership immediately after the CGT event happens, or, if the CGT event involved the cessation of the right or interest, immediately before the CGT event happens.

The additional condition applies to CGT events happening after 7.30pm on 8 May 2018 and is targeted at '*Everett*-style' assignments [23.6]. It is designed to ensure that capital gains arising from CGT events involving the creation, transfer, etc of rights or interests in the income or capital of a partnership, without the underlying membership interest in the partnership, do not qualify for the concessions in div 152.

Concessions

Where the qualifying conditions outlined above are satisfied, taxpayers can choose to use the following concessions to disregard or reduce capital gains on their eligible CGT assets.

- **The 15-year exemption (sub-div 152-B *ITAA97*).** This concession allows individuals to disregard capital gains in respect of eligible active assets that they have owned for a continuous period of at least 15 years, provided they are over 55 years of age and are retiring or permanently incapacitated (s 152-105). Companies and trusts can also disregard capital gains in respect of eligible CGT assets that they have owned for a continuous period of at least 15 years, provided they had a 'significant individual' for at least 15 years and provided an individual who was a significant individual of the company or trust just before the CGT event was over 55 years of age and retiring or permanently incapacitated (s 152-110).
- **The 50% reduction concession (sub-div 152-C *ITAA97*).** This concession allows taxpayers to reduce their capital gains on eligible active assets by 50% (s 152-205).
- **The retirement concession (sub-div 152-D *ITAA97*).** This concession allows taxpayers to disregard their capital gains on eligible active assets (s 152-305). The concession operates subject to a lifetime 'CGT retirement exemption limit' of $500,000 (s 152-320). Taxpayers under 55 years of age must roll over the 'CGT exempt amount' into a complying superannuation fund or RSA.
- **The small business roll-over concession (sub-div 152-E *ITAA97*).** This concession allows taxpayers to roll over (ie defer) all or part of their capital gains on eligible active assets (s 152-410). However, if within the 'replacement asset period' (ie a period of generally up to one year before and two years after the CGT event: s 104-90), taxpayers do not acquire 'replacement assets' or do not incur expenditure on such assets that is at least equal to the capital gains that are deferred, CGT event J5 or J6 will occur and result in capital gains arising at the end of the replacement asset period (ss 104-197, 104-198) [17.3]. The practical effect of this is that taxpayers who do not acquire replacement assets can defer the taxation of their capital gains for two years. Where taxpayers acquire replacement assets, the capital gains on their original active assets are deferred until a change happens in relation to their replacement assets (eg the replacement assets are disposed of or stop being active assets) (s 104-185). When this occurs, CGT event J2 happens and the deferred capital gains on their original assets are effectively crystallised (s 104-185).

The concessions in sub-divs 152-C, 152-D and 152-E generally operate alongside each other (ie a taxpayer can elect to use more than one of the concessions to reduce their capital gains). They do not, however, apply where a taxpayer has claimed the 15-year exemption in sub-div 152-B as the capital gain is already completely disregarded (ss 152-215, 152-430).

The following example illustrates how the small business concessions can be used to reduce a taxpayer's net capital gain. It is important to note that as the concessions are applied under Step 4 in s 102-5, they arise *after* any CGT discount has first been applied under Step 3 in s 102-5 [17.8].

Example Tony is 49 years old. He established a business four years ago and sold it earlier this year. He made a capital gain of $2m (before the calculation of any CGT discount or small business concessions) on the disposal of the goodwill of the business. As Tony owned the goodwill for more than 12 months, he can claim the 50% CGT discount, which reduces the capital gain to $1m. Assuming he also qualifies for the small business concessions, he can use the 50% reduction concession to reduce the remaining $1m capital gain to $500,000. He can also avoid paying tax on the remaining $500,000 capital gain if he elects to use the retirement concession and roll over this amount into his superannuation fund.

If Tony chose not to apply the retirement concession and did not acquire any replacement asset within two years, he could defer the tax payable on the remaining $500,000 capital gain for two years. However, if Tony acquired a replacement asset (eg the goodwill of a new business) within this period, he would be able to defer the $500,000 capital gain on the goodwill of his old business until he disposes of the goodwill of his new business.

[17.10] CGT events

The CGT events mentioned in the table in s 104-5 [17.3] are divided into 12 groups:

- disposals (sub-div 104-A)
- use and enjoyment before title passes (sub-div 104-B)
- end of a CGT asset (sub-div 104-C)
- bringing into existence a CGT asset (sub-div 104-D)
- trusts (sub-div 104-E)
- leases (sub-div 104-F)
- shares (sub-div 104-G)
- special capital receipts (sub-div 104-H)
- Australian residency ends (sub-div 104-I)
- CGT events relating to roll-overs (sub-div 104-J)
- other CGT events (sub-div 104-K), and
- consolidated groups and MEC groups (sub-div 104-L).

The following discussion examines some of the most common CGT events; namely, A1, B1, C1, C2, C3, D1, D2, E1, E2, E4, E5, F1, F2, F3, F4, F5, G1, G3, H1, H2, K4 and K6. A number of other CGT events are discussed elsewhere (eg CGT event J2, J5 and J6 [17.9]; CGT event K3 [17.13]; CGT event E10 [25.10]; CGT event I1 [17.12]; CGT event K9 [27.4]; and CGT events L3, L4 and L6 [26.5]).

CGT event A1 (disposal)

CGT event A1 arises where a taxpayer 'disposes' of a 'CGT asset' (s 104-10(1)). A disposal occurs where there has been a 'change of ownership' of a CGT asset from one entity to another entity (s 104-10(2)). The sale or gift of a CGT asset is an obvious example of CGT event A1. The change of ownership required under CGT event A1 is a change in 'beneficial ownership'. A change of ownership for the purposes of CGT event A1 does not arise where there is merely a change of trustee as this, by itself, does not result in a change of beneficial ownership (only legal ownership). TD 2000/10 states that the splitting or merger of an asset (eg as a result of a share split or consolidation) does not result in a change in beneficial ownership, only a change in the 'form' of the original asset.

CGT event A1 occurs when the taxpayer entered into the contract for the disposal, or, if there is no contract, when the change of ownership occurs (s 104-10(3)). Determining the time at which a contract for the disposal of an asset is entered into was considered in *FC of T v Sara Lee Household*

& Body Care (Australia) Pty Ltd 2000 ATC 4378. This case involved an American company that had entered into a 'purchase and sale agreement' in May 1991 to dispose of pharmaceutical businesses operated by its subsidiaries in various countries. The terms of the agreement were amended by an 'amendment agreement' entered into in August 1991, which increased the sale price of the assets owned by its Australian subsidiary. The High Court held that the time of disposal of the Australian subsidiary's assets was in May 1991 (rather than August 1991) as the purchase and sale agreement was the source of the obligation to effect the disposal, and it was clear from the terms of the amendment agreement that the parties did not intend to rescind the earlier contract.

Under CGT event A1, a taxpayer makes a capital gain where the 'capital proceeds' from the disposal exceed the asset's 'cost base'. A taxpayer makes a capital loss where the 'capital proceeds' from the disposal are less than the asset's 'reduced cost base' (s 104-10(4)).

A capital gain or capital loss is disregarded if it relates to a CGT asset acquired by the taxpayer before 20 September 1985 (s 104-10(5)).

Example Mark purchased vacant land on 1 January 2023 for $1m. On 1 June 2023, he entered into a contract to sell the land to Cleo for $3m. The contract provided that settlement occurs on 1 August 2023, when Cleo is required to pay for the land and Mark is required to hand over the title deeds. The contract results in a change in ownership of the land. This constitutes a disposal under CGT event A1. The time of the CGT event is 1 June 2023, when the contract is entered into. Mark's capital gain is $2m, being the excess of the capital proceeds from the disposal ($3m) over the land's cost base ($1m).

CGT event B1 (use and enjoyment before title passes)

CGT event B1 occurs if a taxpayer enters into an agreement with another entity under which:

- the right to the use and enjoyment of an asset owned by the taxpayer passes to the other entity, and
- title in the asset will or may pass to the other entity at or before the end of the agreement (s 104-15(1)).

A hire purchase agreement and a terms contract for the sale of land are examples of where CGT event B1 may apply.

The time of this event is when the other entity first obtains the use and enjoyment of the asset (s 104-15(2)), rather than when there is an actual disposal at a later time.

The taxpayer makes a capital gain if the capital proceeds from the agreement are more than the asset's cost base. The taxpayer makes a capital loss if the capital proceeds are less than the asset's 'reduced cost base' (s 104-15(3)).

A capital gain or capital loss is disregarded if the asset was acquired before 20 September 1985 or if title in the asset does not pass at or before the end of the agreement (s 104-15(4)).

Example Anne acquired a holiday home on 1 January 2003 for $100,000. On 1 June 2023, she allowed Tony to live in the property for up to a year to see if he would be interested in purchasing it for $500,000. After living in the property for two months, Tony decided to purchase the property, and he entered into a contract with Anne on 5 August 2023. Anne makes a capital gain under CGT event B1 (rather than CGT event A1). The time of the CGT event is 1 June 2023 (rather than 5 August 2023).

CGT event C1 (loss or destruction of a CGT asset)

CGT event C1 occurs if an asset (or part of an asset) owned by a taxpayer is lost or destroyed (s 104-20(1)). Destruction of an asset includes involuntary actions and voluntary destruction by the owner (eg demolition), while loss of an asset includes an involuntary event which deprives the owner of the asset (eg theft). Roll-over relief may be available to defer the gain arising when an asset is involuntarily lost or destroyed [17.16].

The time of CGT event C1 is when compensation is first received for the loss or destruction, or, if no compensation is received, when the loss is discovered or the destruction occurred (s 104-20(2)).

A capital gain is made if the capital proceeds from the loss or destruction are more than the asset's cost base. A capital loss is made if the capital proceeds are less than the asset's reduced cost base (s 104-20(3)).

A capital gain or capital loss is disregarded if the asset was acquired before 20 September 1985 (s 104-20(4)).

> ***Example*** Graham acquired a factory on 1 December 2005. The factory was destroyed by fire on 1 January 2023 and he received compensation from his insurer on 8 July 2023. CGT event C1 occurred on 8 July 2023, when the payment was received.

CGT event C2 (cancellation or surrender of CGT asset)

CGT event C2 happens if a taxpayer's ownership of an intangible CGT asset ends by the asset:

- being redeemed or cancelled
- being released, discharged or satisfied
- expiring
- being abandoned, surrendered or forfeited
- in the case of an option—being exercised, or
- in the case of a convertible note—being converted (s 104-25(1)).

Examples of CGT event C2 include a share being redeemed, a debt being discharged or a contract expiring.

The time of CGT event C2 is when the taxpayer enters into the contract that results in the asset ending or, if there is no contract, when the asset ends (s 104-25(2)). A lease is taken to have expired even if it is extended or renewed (s 104-25(4)). As an asset ends when CGT event C2 happens, there is no acquisition of the asset by another person at that time.

The taxpayer makes a capital gain if the capital proceeds from the ending of the asset are more than the asset's cost base. The taxpayer makes a capital loss if capital proceeds are less than the asset's reduced cost base (s 104-25(3)).

A capital gain or capital loss is disregarded if the asset was acquired before 20 September 1985 (s 104-25(5)).

A capital loss flowing from the expiry, surrender, forfeiture or assignment of a lease (other than a lease granted for 99 years or more) is disregarded if the lease was not used solely or mainly to produce assessable income (s 118-40).

Capital gains and capital losses are also generally disregarded where rights to acquire shares or units are exercised (s 130-40) [17.14], where shares or units are acquired by converting a convertible interest (s 130-60) [17.14] and where an option is exercised (s 134-1) [17.15].

Example Julia purchased units in a trust on 1 December 2022 for $4,000. On 8 August 2023, her units were redeemed by the trustee for $5,000. As the capital proceeds exceed the cost base of the units, Julia makes a capital gain of $1,000 under CGT event C2 on 8 August 2023.

CGT event C3 (end of option to acquire shares or units)

CGT event C3 deals with the end of an option to acquire shares, units or debentures. This event occurs if an entity is granted an option by a company or the trustee of a unit trust to acquire shares or debentures of the company or units or debentures of the unit trust and the option ends in one of the following ways:

- it is not exercised by the latest time for its exercise
- it is cancelled, or
- it is released or abandoned (s 104-30(1)).

The time of this CGT event is when the option ends (s 104-30(2)).

The company or trustee makes a capital gain if the capital proceeds from the grant of the option are more than the expenditure incurred in granting it. The company or trustee makes a capital loss if the capital proceeds are less than the expenditure incurred (s 104-30(3)).

A capital gain or capital loss the company or trustee makes is disregarded if it granted the option before 20 September 1985 (s 104-30(5)).

Example On 1 September 2020, a company issued an option for $1,000 to a director to buy 5,000 shares in the company for $10 per share. The company incurred expenditure of $200 in granting the option. The option lapsed on 1 September 2023. The capital proceeds of $1,000 exceed the expenditure of $200, so the company makes a capital gain of $800 under CGT event C3 on 1 September 2023.

CGT event D1 (creating contractual or other rights)

CGT event D1 occurs if a taxpayer creates a contractual right or some other legal or equitable right in another entity (s 104-35(1)). Entering into restrictive covenants, exclusive trade ties and endorsement arrangements are examples of situations where CGT event D1 can occur.

CGT event D1 does not occur if:

- the taxpayer created the right by borrowing money or obtaining credit from another entity
- the right requires the taxpayer to do something that is another CGT event for the taxpayer
- a company issues or allots interests or shares, or grants an option to acquire equity interests or debentures in the company, or
- the trustee of a unit trust issues units in the trust, or grants an option to acquire units or debentures in the trust (s 104-35(5)).

The time of CGT event D1 is when the taxpayer enters into the contract or creates the other right (s 104-35(2)).

A capital gain arises if the capital proceeds from creating the right exceed the incidental costs incurred that relate to the CGT event. A capital loss arises if the capital proceeds are less than these incidental costs (s 104-35(3)).

The market value substitution rule [17.7] does not apply to capital proceeds received from CGT event D1.

> ***Example*** Jill sold her business to Jack. They entered into a contract on 5 May 2023 which provided that Jill would not operate a similar business in the same town for five years in consideration of Jack paying her $20,000. A contractual right was created in favour of Jack as he has an enforceable right against Jill. If Jill incurred legal costs of $1,500 in relation to drafting the agreement, she has made a capital gain on 5 May 2023 under CGT event D1 of $18,500 (ie $20,000 – $1,500).

CGT event D2 (granting an option)

CGT event D2 happens if a taxpayer grants an option or renews or extends an option the taxpayer had granted (s 104-40(1)). However, CGT event D2 does not apply to options granted, renewed or extended by a company or the trustee of a unit trust to acquire shares in the company or units in the unit trust or debentures of the company or unit trust (as CGT event C3 applies in this situation) (s 104-40(6)). CGT event D2 also does not apply to options relating to personal use assets or collectables [17.4] (s 104-40(7)).

The time of the CGT event is when the option is granted, renewed or extended (s 104-40(2)).

The taxpayer makes a capital gain if the capital proceeds from the grant, renewal or extension of the option are more than the expenditure incurred in the grant, renewal or extension. The taxpayer makes a capital loss if the capital proceeds are less than the expenditure incurred (s 104-40(3)). Any capital gain or capital loss will be disregarded if the option is exercised (s 104-40(5)).

> ***Example*** On 10 April 2023, Bob paid Sara $5,000 for a one-month option to buy Sara's property for $100,000. CGT event D2 occurs on 10 April 2023 and, assuming Sara incurred no expenses in granting the option, she has made a capital gain of $5,000. If Bob exercised the option on 1 May 2023, CGT event D2 is disregarded.

CGT event E1 (creating a trust over a CGT asset)

CGT event E1 occurs if a trust is created over a CGT asset by declaration or settlement (s 104-55(1)). However, this event does not happen if there is no real change in the underlying beneficial ownership of the asset, namely where:

- there is a sole beneficiary of the trust who is absolutely entitled to the asset as against the trustee and the trust is not a unit trust (eg a bare trust is created), or
- the trust is created by transferring the asset from another trust and the beneficiaries and the terms of both trusts are the same (s 104-55(5)).

In *Taras Nominees Pty Ltd as Trustee for the Burnley Street Trust v FC of T* 2015 ATC ¶20-483, a taxpayer that owned land in Richmond entered into a joint venture agreement with the owners of adjoining land to rezone and develop their properties. The taxpayer transferred legal title to its land to a trustee company to hold on trust for the benefit of the members of the joint venture. The Full Federal Court held that a settlement for the purposes of CGT event E1 had arisen as a result of the taxpayer transferring its legal title to the land to the trustee.

The time of CGT event E1 is when the trust over the asset is created (s 104-55(2)). The effect of this event is that the trustee is taken to have acquired the asset at the time when the trust is created (s 109-5(2)).

A taxpayer makes a capital gain if the capital proceeds from creating the trust are more than the asset's cost base. The taxpayer makes a capital loss if the capital proceeds are less than the asset's reduced cost base (s 104-55(3)).

If the taxpayer is the trustee and no beneficiary is absolutely entitled to the asset (disregarding any legal disability), the first element of the asset's cost base and reduced cost base is its market value when the trust is created (s 104-55(4)).

A capital gain or capital loss is disregarded if the asset was acquired before 20 September 1985 (s 104-55(6)).

Example Terry acquired land on 3 January 2023 for $1m. On 7 August 2023, he executed a deed declaring that he holds the land on trust for the benefit of his wife. CGT event E1 occurs when the trust is declared. If the market value of the land on 7 August 2023 was $1.2m, Terry makes a capital gain of $200,000.

CGT event E2 (transferring a CGT asset to a trust)

CGT event E2 happens if a taxpayer transfers a CGT asset to an existing trust (s 104-60(1)). However, this event does not happen if there is no real change in the underlying beneficial ownership of the asset (ie in similar circumstances to CGT event E1: see above).

The time of this event is when the asset is transferred (s 104-60(2)).

The taxpayer makes a capital gain if the capital proceeds from the transfer are more than the asset's cost base. The taxpayer makes a capital loss if the capital proceeds are less than the asset's reduced cost base (s 104-60(3)).

If the taxpayer is the trustee and no beneficiary is absolutely entitled to the asset, the first element of the asset's cost base and reduced cost base is its market value when the asset is transferred (s 104-60(4)).

A capital gain or capital loss is disregarded if the asset was acquired before 20 September 1985 (s 104-60(6)). 17

Example In consideration of being paid $2,500, Jed transferred an asset that he acquired last year for $2,000 to a trust. He makes a capital gain of $500 under CGT event E2.

CGT event E4 (capital payments for trust interest)

CGT event E4 happens where the trustee of a trust makes a payment to a taxpayer in respect of the taxpayer's unit or interest in the trust, and some or all of the payment (the 'non-assessable part') is not included in the taxpayer's assessable income (s 104-70(1)). The CGT event does not apply to a unit or interest in an AMIT [25.10] (s 104-70(1A)).

The non-assessable part typically consists of amounts that are associated with certain tax concessions that are not recognised for accounting purposes (eg the small business 50% reduction concession [17.9] and indexation [17.6]). However, certain tax-exempt amounts, tax-free amounts and CGT concession amounts are expressly excluded from the calculation of the non-assessable part (s 104-71).

The time of CGT event E4 is just before the end of the income year in which the trustee makes the payment. However, if another CGT event happens in relation to the unit or interest after the trustee makes the payment but before the end of the income year, the time of CGT event E4 is just before the time of that other CGT event (s 104-70(3)).

The taxpayer makes a capital gain if the total of the non-assessable parts of the payments made by the trustee during the income year is more than the cost base of the taxpayer's unit or interest (s 104-70(4)). If a taxpayer makes a capital gain, the cost base and reduced cost base of the taxpayer's unit or interest are reduced to nil (s 104-70(5)).

However, if the total of the non-assessable parts of the payments made by the trustee during the income year is not more than the cost base of the taxpayer's unit or interest, the cost base and reduced cost base are simply reduced by the amount of the non-assessable parts of the payments (s 104-70(6)).

A capital gain is disregarded if the unit or interest was acquired before 20 September 1985 (s 104-70(7)).

Example Heidi acquired a unit in a trust on 3 June 2020 for $20. She received a payment from the trustee of the unit trust of $100 on 5 May 2022, which included a non-assessable part of $30. As a result, Heidi made a capital gain of $10 (ie $30 – $20) under CGT event E4 on 30 June 2022 (ie just before the end of the 2022/23 income year). The cost base and reduced cost base of her unit is reduced to nil.

Peter acquired a unit in a trust on 8 October 2020 for $20. He received a payment from the trustee of the unit trust of $100 on 7 July 2023, which included a non-assessable part of $15. Peter does not make a capital gain. The cost base and reduced cost base of his unit is reduced to $5 (ie $20 – $15) on 30 June 2023.

CGT event E5 (beneficiary becoming entitled to a trust asset)

CGT event E5 happens if a beneficiary becomes absolutely entitled to a CGT asset of a trust as against the trustee. However, this event does not apply to a unit trust or a deceased estate (s 104-75(1)).

The time of CGT event E5 is when the beneficiary becomes absolutely entitled to the CGT asset (s 104-75(2)). The beneficiary is taken to have received the market value of the asset in exchange for the beneficiary's interest in the trust. Therefore, the event can apply to both the trustee and the beneficiary.

The trustee makes a capital gain if the market value of the asset at the time of this CGT event is more than the asset's cost base and a capital loss if the market value is less than the asset's reduced cost base (s 104-75(3)).

The beneficiary makes a capital gain if the market value of the asset at the time of the event is more than the cost base of the beneficiary's interest in the trust capital to the extent that it relates to the asset. If the market value is less than the reduced cost base of that interest, the beneficiary makes a capital loss (s 104-75(5)).

Any capital gain or capital loss made by the beneficiary from this CGT event is disregarded if the beneficiary's interest in the CGT asset was acquired for no expenditure (eg an interest in an asset bequeathed under a will). This exemption does not apply where the beneficiary's interest was acquired by way of an assignment from another entity (s 104-75(6)(a)).

A capital gain or capital loss is also disregarded if the beneficiary's interest in the asset was acquired before 20 September 1985 (s 104-75(6)(b)).

Example Betty is the trustee of a family discretionary trust. On 9 April 2023, she resolved that certain shares held by the trust were to be held absolutely for one of the beneficiaries. The shares had a market value of $5,000 and a cost base of $4,000. CGT event E5 occurs on 9 April 2023 and Betty makes a capital gain of $1,000 (ie $5,000 – $4,000).

CGT event F1 (grant of lease)

CGT event F1 occurs if a lessor grants, renews or extends a lease (s 104-110(1)). This event may apply to a lease granted, renewed or extended on or after 20 September 1985 even though the property subject to the lease is a pre-CGT asset.

Where a lease is granted, the time of CGT event F1 is when the contract for the lease is entered into or, if there is no contract, at the start of the lease. Where a lease is renewed or extended, the time of this CGT event is the start of the renewal or extension (s 104-110(2)).

The lessor makes a capital gain if the capital proceeds from the grant, renewal or extension are more than the expenditure incurred by the lessor on the grant, renewal or extension. If the capital proceeds are less than this expenditure, the taxpayer makes a capital loss (s 104-110(3)).

If the term of a lease is 50 years or more and the lessor instead chooses to apply the rules for CGT event F2 (see below), CGT event F1 will not apply (s 104-110(5)).

> ***Example*** On 7 In May 2023, Frank entered into a lease of his land to Elanor in consideration of receiving a premium of $50,000. He incurred $5,000 in legal costs for drafting the lease. Frank made a capital gain of $45,000 (ie $50,000 – $5,000) under CGT event F1 on 7 May 2023.

CGT event F2 (grant of long-term lease)

CGT event F2 deals with long-term leases. It occurs if a lessor grants, renews or extends a lease over land for a period of at least 50 years and the lessor chooses CGT event F2 to apply, rather than CGT event F1.

The time of this CGT event is when the lessor grants, renews or extends the lease (s 104-115(2)).

The lessor makes a capital gain if the capital proceeds from this CGT event are more than the cost base of the lessor's interest in the land. If the capital proceeds are less than the reduced cost base of that interest, the lessor makes a capital loss (s 104-115(3)). 17

A capital gain or capital loss is disregarded if the land was acquired by the lessor before 20 September 1985 (s 104-115(4)).

> ***Example*** Scarlett acquired a property on 5 June 2010 for $80,000. On 9 January 2023, she granted a 99-year lease of the property to Rhett for $100,000. Scarlett made a capital gain of $20,000 (ie $100,000 – $80,000) under CGT event F2 on 9 January 2023.

CGT event F3 (lessor incurs expenditure to vary lease)

CGT event F3 happens if a lessor incurs expenditure in obtaining a lessee's agreement to vary or waive a term of the lease. The lessor makes a capital loss equal to the amount of the expenditure it incurred (s 104-120(1)).

The lessor cannot make a capital gain from this event—it can only result in a capital loss. However, the amount received by the lessee will give rise to a capital gain under CGT event F4 (see below).

The time of CGT event F3 is when the term is varied or waived (s 104-120(2)).

This CGT event does not apply where the taxpayer has chosen to apply CGT event F2 (s 104-120(3)).

> ***Example*** On 1 July 2018, Les granted a 10-year lease of his property to Edna. On 4 May 2023, Les paid Edna $13,000 to have the term of the lease reduced to 4 years. Les made a capital loss of $13,000 under CGT event F3 on 4 May 2023.

CGT event F4 (lessee receives payment for varying lease)

CGT event F4 is the counterpart to CGT event F3. It occurs if a lessee receives a payment from a lessor for agreeing to vary or waive a term of the lease (s 104-125(1)). The lessee cannot make a capital loss from this event—it only gives rise to a capital gain.

The time of this CGT event is when the term is varied or waived (s 104-125(2)).

The lessee makes a capital gain if the capital proceeds from the event are more than the cost base of the lease at the time of the event. If the lessee makes a capital gain, the cost base of the lease is reduced to nil (s 104-125(3)). However, if the capital proceeds are less than the cost base of the lease, the cost base is reduced by the amount of the proceeds at the time of the event (s 104-125(4)).

A capital gain or capital loss is disregarded if the lease was granted before 20 September 1985, or, for a lease that has been renewed or extended, the last renewal or extension occurred before that day (s 104-125(5)).

Example Continuing the example under CGT event F3, assuming the cost base of Edna's lease was nil, she makes a capital gain of $13,000 when the term of the lease is reduced to four years on 4 May 2023.

CGT event F5 (lessor receives payment for varying lease)

CGT event F5 happens if a lessor receives a payment from the lessee for agreeing to vary or waive a term of the lease (s 104-130(1)).

The time of this CGT event is when the term is varied or waived (s 104-130(2)).

The lessor makes a capital gain if the capital proceeds from the event are more than the expenditure the taxpayer incurs in relation to the variation or waiver. The lessor makes a capital loss if the capital proceeds are less than this expenditure (s 104-130(3)).

A capital gain or capital loss is disregarded if the lease was granted before 20 September 1985. If the lease has been renewed or extended, the last renewal or extension must have occurred before that day (s 104-130(5)).

Example Donald owns a shopping centre and was paid $10,000 by the lessee of a shop for agreeing to change the terms of its lease. Donald incurred expenses of $1,000 for legal fees and $500 for a valuation in relation to the variation. Donald makes a capital gain of $8,500 under CGT event F5 when the terms of the lease are varied.

CGT event G1 (capital payment for shares)

CGT event G1 happens if:

- a company makes a payment to a shareholder in respect of a share that the taxpayer owns in the company (except where CGT event A1 or C2 happens in relation to the share)
- some or all of the payment is not a dividend [22.4], or taken to be a dividend under s 47 *ITAA36* [22.11], and
- the payment is not included in the shareholder's assessable income (s 104-135(1)).

The time of the CGT event is when the company makes the payment (s 104-135(2)).

CGT event G1 typically arises whenever a company returns non-assessable capital amounts to a shareholder without cancelling their shares [22.9]. Where the non-assessable amount is more than the share's cost base, the excess is a capital gain and the share's cost base/reduced cost base is reduced to nil (s 104-135(3)). Where the non-assessable amount is not more than the share's cost base, the share's cost base/reduced cost base is reduced by such amount (s 104-135(4)).

A capital gain is disregarded if the share was acquired prior to 20 September 1985 (s 104-135(5)). A payment made by a liquidator is also disregarded under this provision if the company ceases to exist within 18 months (s 104-135(6)). The payment will, instead, be part of the capital proceeds for CGT event C2 happening when the share ends.

Example Harry acquired a share for $1,000 in Y Co in January 2005. Y Co made a payment of $800 to Harry (this amount is not a dividend or otherwise assessable) in May 2023. The cost base of Harry's share is reduced from $1,000 to $200.

CGT event G3 (liquidator and administrator declarations)

CGT event G3 happens if a taxpayer owns shares in a company, or financial instruments issued or created by a company, and the company's liquidator or administrator declares in writing that they have reasonable grounds to believe that:

- for shares—there is no likelihood of shareholders receiving further distributions for their shares
- for financial instruments—the instruments have no value or only negligible value (s 104-145(1)).

The time of the CGT event is when the declaration is made (s 104-145(2)).

Where CGT event G3 applies, the taxpayer can choose to make a capital loss equal to the reduced cost base of their shares or financial instruments at the time of the declaration (s 104-145(4)). If the taxpayer makes the choice, the cost base and reduced cost base of their relevant shares or financial instruments are reduced to nil just after the declaration.

17

The object of CGT event G3 is to allow taxpayers to accelerate the crystallisation of their capital losses in respect of worthless shares or financial instruments in a company without having to wait until the winding up of the company is completed.

A taxpayer cannot choose to make a capital loss if the relevant shares or financial instruments were acquired before 20 September 1985 or were revenue assets at the time of the declaration.

Example Penny acquired a share in Y Co for $100 on 5 January 2010. Y Co encountered financial difficulties and was placed in liquidation. On 7 August 2023, the liquidator of the company made a written declaration that there is no likelihood that shareholders will receive any distributions in respect of their shares. Penny can claim a capital loss of $100 under CGT event G3 for the 2023/24 income year.

CGT event H1 (forfeiture of deposit)

CGT event H1 happens if a deposit is forfeited because a prospective sale or other transaction does not proceed (s 104-150(1)). The amount of the deposit is reduced by any part of the deposit that is repaid or any compensation that can reasonably be regarded as a repayment, provided the taxpayer cannot deduct such a payment.

The time of this CGT event is when the deposit is forfeited (s 104-150(2)).

The taxpayer makes a capital gain if the deposit is more than the expenditure incurred by the taxpayer in connection with the prospective sale or other transaction. The taxpayer makes a capital loss if the deposit is less than the expenditure incurred (s 104-150(3)). The expenditure incurred can include giving property but does not include any non-assessable recoupment of that expenditure (s 104-150(4)).

The Commissioner's position, following the decision in *Brooks v FC of T* 2000 ATC 4362, is that a deposit forfeited under a contract for the sale of land is assessable under CGT event H1 if it does not form part of a 'continuum of events' leading to a later disposal of the land. However, if there is a continuum of events, the forfeited deposit will be treated as part of the capital proceeds from the disposal (TR 1999/19).

Example Rita put her property on the market and a purchaser paid her a deposit of $25,000 under the contract of sale. The purchaser defaulted, and the deposit was forfeited. Rita then withdrew the property from sale. Rita makes a capital gain of $25,000 as a result of CGT event H1.

CGT event H2 (receipt for event relating to CGT asset)

CGT event H2 only applies if no other CGT event applies. This event happens if an act, transaction or event occurs in relation to a CGT asset owned by the taxpayer and it does not result in an adjustment being made to the asset's cost base or reduced cost base (s 104-155(1)).

The time of CGT event H2 is when the act, transaction or event takes place (s 104-155(2)).

A taxpayer makes a capital gain if the capital proceeds because of this CGT event are more than the incidental costs incurred by the taxpayer that relate to the event. The taxpayer makes a capital loss if the capital proceeds are less than those incidental costs (s 104-155(3)). The incidental costs can include the market value of any property given, but do not include any non-assessable recoupment of that expenditure (s 104-155(4)).

CGT event H2 does not apply in certain situations (eg where the act, transaction or event consists of the borrowing of money or the obtaining of credit from another entity, or it requires the taxpayer to do something that is another CGT event for the taxpayer). Other specific exceptions include where a company issues or allots shares, where the trustee of a unit trust issues units in the trust or where an option is granted (s 104-155(5)).

Example Toby owned land on which he intended to construct a manufacturing facility. A community organisation paid Toby $50,000 as an inducement to start construction early. No contractual rights or obligations were created by the arrangement. The payment was made because of an event (the inducement to start construction early) in relation to the land. Toby made a capital gain of $50,000 under CGT event H2 when the event took place.

CGT event K4 (CGT asset starts being trading stock)

CGT event K4 happens if:

- a taxpayer starts holding as trading stock a CGT asset that they already own but do not hold as trading stock, and
- the taxpayer elects under s 70-30(1)(a) to be treated as having sold the asset for its market value [16.6] (s 104-220(1)).

The time of the CGT event is when the taxpayer starts to hold the asset as trading stock (s 104-220(2)).

The taxpayer makes a capital gain from CGT event K4 if the asset's market value (just before it became trading stock) is more than its cost base. The taxpayer makes a capital loss if the asset's market value is less than its reduced cost base (s 104-220(3)).

A capital gain or capital loss is disregarded if the taxpayer acquired the asset before 20 September 1985 (s 104-220(4)).

> ***Example*** Rob acquired a CGT asset (which was not trading stock) on 5 May 2020 for $7,000. On 7 January 2024, he began to hold the asset as trading stock of his business and elected under s 70-30(1)(a) to be treated as having sold it for its market value. If the market value of the asset at that time was $10,000, Rob makes a capital gain of $3,000 under CGT event K4 on 7 January 2024.

CGT event K6 (pre-CGT share or unit interests)

CGT event K6 happens if:

- a taxpayer owns shares in a company or an interest in a trust acquired before 20 September 1985
- another CGT event (either A1, C2, E1, E2, E3, E5, E6, E7, E8, J1 or K3) happens in relation to the shares or trust interest
- there is no roll-over for the other CGT event, and
- just before the other CGT event happened:
  - the market value of the property of the company (other than trading stock) that was acquired on or after 20 September 1985, or
  - the market value of interests the company or trust owned through interposed companies or trusts in property (other than trading stock) that was acquired on or after 20 September 1985, is at least 75% of the net value of the company or trust (ss 104-230(1), (2)).

The time of CGT event K6 is when the other event occurs (s 104-230(5)). If a share or a trust interest is acquired by a taxpayer as a result of CGT event K6, it is acquired at the time of that CGT event (s 109-5).

A taxpayer makes a capital gain from CGT event K6 equal to that part of the capital proceeds from the disposal of the shares or units that is reasonably attributable to the amount by which the market value of post-CGT property exceeds the cost base of that property. This event cannot result in a capital loss (s 104-230(6)).

This CGT event does not apply to certain entities that have been continuously listed on an Australian or foreign stock exchange for at least five years before the other CGT event (s 104-230(9)). The CGT event also does not apply to 'demerged entities' [28.4] or where 'scrip for scrip' roll-over relief is available under sub-div 124-M *ITAA97* [28.3] (ss 104-230(9A) to (10)).

> ***Example*** In 1980, Bob acquired all of the shares in B Co for $100,000. He sold the shares for $1m earlier this year. This resulted in CGT event A1 happening in relation to the shares. However, as the shares were acquired before 20 September 1985, the capital gain is disregarded.
>
> Just before Bob sold the shares, B Co owned a block of land that it had acquired in 2020 for $600,000. The block of land is B Co's only asset and therefore represents 100% of the net value of the company.
>
> In these circumstances, CGT event K6 is triggered. Bob will make a capital gain equal to that part of the capital proceeds from the disposal of the shares that is reasonably attributable to the amount by which the market value of post-CGT property exceeds the cost base of that property (ie $400,000 = $1m – $600,000).

[17.11] Main residence exemption

Subdivision 118-B allows taxpayers to disregard capital gains and capital losses made from CGT events that happen to a 'dwelling' that is their 'main residence'. A partial exemption may be available if the dwelling was the taxpayer's main residence for only part of their 'ownership period'. Special rules apply where the taxpayer is an individual who acquired the interest in the dwelling as a beneficiary of a deceased estate or owned it as trustee of a deceased estate. Special rules also apply in other cases, such as where the dwelling is also used to produce assessable income. The following diagram is derived from s 118-105 and contains a useful map of the key provisions in sub-div 118-B which are discussed in detail below.

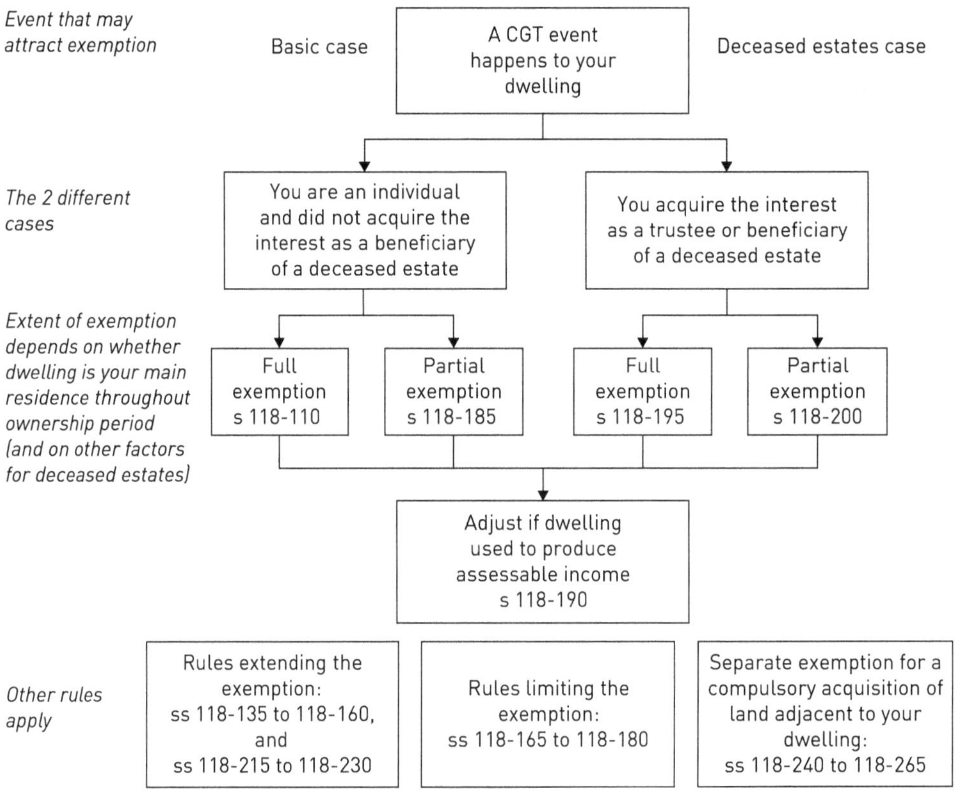

Basic case—full and partial exemptions for an individual's main residence

Section 118-110(1) provides that a capital gain or capital loss that an individual makes from a CGT event that happens in relation to a 'dwelling', or their 'ownership interest' in it, is disregarded if the dwelling was their 'main residence' *throughout* their 'ownership period' and they did not acquire their interest as a beneficiary in, or trustee of, a deceased estate.

Where the dwelling is the taxpayer's main residence for only *part* of their ownership period and they did not acquire their interest as a beneficiary in, or trustee of, a deceased estate, a partial exemption is available under s 118-185(1). In such case, the taxpayer's capital gain or capital loss is pro-rated and calculated under s 118-185(2) as follows:

$$\text{Capital gain or capital loss amount} \times \frac{\text{Non-main residence days}}{\text{Days in ownership period}}$$

Exemption no longer applies to certain foreign residents

New rules have been introduced to remove the main residence exemption for foreign residents. The new rules are contained in ss 118-110(3) and 118-185(3) and remove the full and partial exemptions if, at the time the CGT event happens, the taxpayer was an 'excluded foreign resident' or a foreign resident who does *not* satisfy the 'life events test'.

- **Excluded foreign resident.** An 'excluded foreign resident' is a foreign resident who, at the time of the CGT event, has been a foreign resident for a continuous period of more than six years (s 118-110(4)).
- **Life events test.** The 'life events test' is satisfied if, at the time of a CGT event, a foreign resident has been a foreign resident for a continuous period of six years or less and one of the following applies:
  - the foreign resident or their spouse has had a terminal medical condition that existed at any time during the period of foreign residency
  - the foreign resident's child has had a terminal medical condition that existed at any time during the period of foreign residency, and the child was under 18 years of age at such time
  - the foreign resident's spouse or child under 18 years of age has died during the period of foreign residency, or
  - the CGT event happens because of a matter referred to in s 126-5(1) involving the foreign resident and their spouse or former spouse (eg the CGT event happens as a result of a Family Court order relating to a relationship breakdown) (s 118-110(5)).

The new rules generally apply to CGT events occurring on or after 7.30pm on 9 May 2017. However, special transitional rules ensure that they do not apply to CGT events happening on or before 30 June 2020 where the foreign resident held an ownership interest in the dwelling throughout the period starting before 7.30pm on 9 May 2017 and ending just before the CGT event happens (s 118-110 *ITTPA*).

Dwelling, ownership period and ownership interest

A 'dwelling' includes a unit of accommodation that is a building, or is contained in a building, and consists wholly or mainly of residential accommodation. It also includes a unit of accommodation that is a caravan, houseboat or other mobile home, and any land immediately under the unit of accommodation (s 118-115). The ATO accepts that a dwelling can include more than one unit of accommodation, provided those units are used together as one residence (TD 1999/69). A dwelling also encompasses up to two hectares of 'adjacent land' (s 118-120). The ATO indicates that land does not have to be contiguous to the land on which a dwelling is situated to be adjacent land—it is sufficient if it is 'close to' or 'near' the dwelling (TD 1999/68).

A taxpayer's 'ownership period' is the period on or after 20 September 1985 when the taxpayer had an ownership interest in the dwelling or the land on which the dwelling is later built (s 118-125).

An 'ownership interest' includes a legal or equitable interest in, or right to occupy, land, as well as other specific interests, such as a licence or right to occupy a flat or home unit (s 118-130(1)).

A taxpayer has an ownership interest in land or a dwelling that they acquire under a contract from the time when they obtain legal ownership of it, or if the contract or a related contract gives them the right to occupy it at an earlier time, the earlier time (s 118-130(2)).

Generally speaking, a taxpayer obtains legal ownership of land or a dwelling at the time of settlement (rather than when they enter into the contract, as at such time they generally only obtain an equitable interest: *Lysaght v Edwards* (1876) 2 Ch D 499). A taxpayer will therefore have legal ownership of land or a dwelling from the date of settlement of the contract of purchase (or if they have a right to occupy it at an earlier time, that time) until the date of settlement of the contract of sale. This period is their ownership period (s 118-125).

> ***Example*** Betty is an Australian resident. She entered into a contract to purchase her home on 1 May 2020 and settlement occurred on 1 June 2020. She subsequently entered into a contract to sell her home on 2 July 2023 and settlement occurred on 2 August 2023.
>
> Betty is deemed to have acquired the home on 1 May 2020 and disposed of the home on 2 July 2023 as these were the dates she entered into the respective contracts (s 104-10). For the purposes of the main residence exemption, her 'ownership period' runs from 1 June 2020 to 2 August 2023 as this was the period she had an ownership interest in the dwelling (ss 118-125, 118-130).
>
> Assuming the dwelling was Betty's main residence throughout the ownership period, any capital gain or loss she makes from the sale would be disregarded under s 118-110.

Main residence

The term 'main residence' is not defined in the legislation. Whether or not a dwelling is a taxpayer's main residence is therefore a question of fact (see *Case 26/93* 93 ATC 320 and *Erdelyi & Anor v FC of T* 2007 ATC 2214). The ATO's *Guide to Capital Gains Tax* suggests a range of factors that may be relevant in resolving the issue, including the length of time the taxpayer lives in the dwelling (although the ATO notes there is no minimum period a person must live in a dwelling before it is considered to be their main residence). Other factors the ATO suggests may be relevant include the place where the taxpayer's belongings are kept and their family resides, and the place where their mail is delivered and they have their electoral roll address.

Ultimately, the answer will depend on the actual use of the dwelling. The mere intention of occupying a dwelling without actually doing so does not result in it becoming the main residence. This is illustrated in *Couch & Anor v FC of T* 2009 ATC ¶10-072, where a married couple acquired a property with the intention of living in it, but due to employment circumstances, ended up living elsewhere and renting it out instead. The AAT held that the gain made on the sale of the property was subject to CGT as an intention to occupy a property as a main residence was insufficient to give rise to the exemption.

Special rules

The basic rules outlined above operate subject to the following special rules:

- **Moving into a dwelling.** If a dwelling becomes a taxpayer's main residence by the time it was first practicable for the taxpayer to move into the dwelling after the taxpayer acquired it, the dwelling is treated as the taxpayer's main residence from when the taxpayer acquired the interest until it actually became the taxpayer's main residence (s 118-135). In *Chapman v FC of T* 2008 ATC ¶10-029 and *Caller & Anor v FC of T* 2009 ATC ¶10-116, it was held that s 118-135 did not apply to taxpayers who chose to rent out their dwellings prior to moving in to them, as they did not move in as soon as practicable. In *Caller*, the AAT stated (at [29]) that the expression 'by the time it was first practicable' should not be read down to mean 'by the time it was first convenient'.

> ***Example*** Alice is an Australian resident who entered into a contract to purchase her first home on 1 April 2023. Settlement occurred on 5 June 2023. In the meantime, Alice was involved in a car accident and only moved into the property after she was discharged from hospital on 7 July 2023. It is likely that Alice would be able to treat the dwelling as her main residence from 5 June 2023.

- **Separate CGT event for land.** The main residence exemption does not apply to a CGT event that happens in relation to land, or a garage, storeroom or other structure, if that CGT event does not also happen in relation to the dwelling that is the taxpayer's main residence (s 118-165).

Example Geoff is an Australian resident who owns land totalling less than two hectares on two titles ('title A' and 'title B'). If the dwelling that is the main residence is situated on title A, and Geoff sells title B separately, the main residence exemption does not extend to the disposal of title B.

- **Spouses with separate main residences.** If, during a period, a dwelling is the taxpayer's main residence and another dwelling is the main residence of the taxpayer's spouse (except a spouse living permanently separately and apart from the taxpayer), the taxpayer and the spouse can:
  - choose to treat one dwelling as their main residence for the period, or
  - nominate different dwellings as their main residences for the period.

  If they nominate different dwellings, the exemption operates as follows. If the taxpayer's interest in his or her nominated dwelling is not more than half of the total interests in the dwelling, it is taken to be the taxpayer's main residence during the whole of the period. If the taxpayer's interest in his or her nominated dwelling is more than half of the total interests in the dwelling, it is taken to be the taxpayer's main residence during only half of the period (s 118-170).

Example Greg and Lisa are married to each other and are Australian residents. Greg resides mainly in House A, while Lisa resides mainly in House B. Greg has an 80% interest in House A and Lisa has a 20% interest in House A. They each have a 50% interest in House B. Greg nominates House A as his main residence and Lisa nominates House B as her main residence. House A is taken to be Greg's main residence for half of the ownership period, while House B is taken to be Lisa's main residence for the entire ownership period.

If a capital gain of $100,000 is made on the disposal of House A, Greg can disregard $40,000 of the $80,000 capital gain he makes in relation to his 80% interest in House A (ie $100,000 × 80% × 50%). Lisa is assessed on the $20,000 capital gain relating to her 20% interest in House A (as it is not her nominated main residence).

If a capital gain of $100,000 is also made on the disposal of House B, Greg is assessed on the $50,000 capital gain relating to his 50% interest in House B (as it is not his nominated main residence). Lisa can disregard the $50,000 capital gain she makes relating to her 50% interest in House B.

- **Overlap when changing main residences.** If a taxpayer acquires a dwelling that is to become their main residence and the taxpayer still owns an existing main residence, both dwellings may be treated as the main residence for an overlapping period of up to six months. The overlapping period is the *shorter* of:
  - six months ending when the ownership interest in the existing main residence ends, or
  - the period between the acquisition of the new dwelling and the disposal of the old dwelling.

  This rule only applies if the taxpayer's existing main residence was the taxpayer's main residence for a continuous period of at least three months in the 12 months before it was disposed of. It must also not be used for income-producing purposes in any part of the 12-month period when it was not the taxpayer's main residence (s 118-140).

> ***Example*** Betty bought a new home under a contract that settled on 5 January 2023 and she immediately moved into it. She sold the old home in which she had been living for the previous five years under a contract that settled on 17 April 2023. Betty can treat both homes as her main residence for the period 5 January to 17 April 2023, even though she did not live in the old home during that period.

- **Absences.** If a dwelling that was a taxpayer's main residence ceases to be the taxpayer's main residence, the taxpayer may choose to continue to treat it as his or her main residence, provided the taxpayer does not treat any other dwelling as his or her main residence during this period. This rule operates subject to s 118-140 (see above). If the dwelling is not used for income-producing purposes, it can be treated as the taxpayer's main residence indefinitely. However, if the dwelling is used for income-producing purposes, the maximum period that the dwelling can be treated as the taxpayer's main residence is six years. If the dwelling once again becomes the taxpayer's main residence, the taxpayer is entitled to another maximum six-year period if the dwelling subsequently stops being the taxpayer's main residence (s 118-145).

> ***Example*** Terry is an Australian resident who bought a house in Melbourne under a contract that settled on 1 June 2013. He moved in immediately and used it as his main residence for three years. He was then posted to Sydney and lived with his brother in his brother's house in Sydney. He leased his Melbourne house to tenants for the next seven years until it was sold under a contract that settled on 1 June 2023. Ignoring any main residence exemption, Terry would have made a \$100,000 capital gain on the sale of the Melbourne house. If Terry chooses to use the exemption under s 118-145 and continues to treat the house as his main residence for six of the seven years while it was being leased, he would be able to treat the house as his main residence for a total of nine years (ie three years + six years). This means that his capital gain is calculated under the partial exemption in s 118-185 as follows:
>
> $$\$10,000 = \$100,000 \times \frac{365}{3,650}$$

- **Building or renovating a dwelling.** A taxpayer that has an ownership interest in land and builds, repairs or renovates a dwelling on the land can choose to treat the dwelling as if it was their main residence from the time they acquired their ownership interest in the land (s 118-150). The choice can only be made if the dwelling becomes their main residence as soon as practicable after the work is finished and continues to be their main residence for a period of at least three months. In addition, the choice only operates for the shorter of:
  - four years (or a longer time allowed by the Commissioner) before the dwelling becomes the taxpayer's main residence, or
  - the period starting when the taxpayer acquired their ownership interest in the land and ending when the dwelling becomes their main residence.

  Special rules apply where the taxpayer dies before the work is completed, before it is practicable to move into the dwelling, or before the three-month period ends (s 118-155).

Example Laszlo is an Australian resident who engages a builder on 1 September 2022 to build a house for him on vacant land that he has owned since 5 January 2013. The work was finished on 1 August 2024 and Laszlo moved into the house on 8 August 2024 (which was as soon as practicable after the work was finished). If he lived in the house for at least the next three months, he can treat it as his main residence from 8 August 2020 (ie four years immediately before the dwelling actually became his main residence).

- **Use of dwelling to produce assessable income.** Only a partial exemption is available where there is a CGT event in relation to a dwelling, or the taxpayer's ownership interest in it, if:
  - apart from s 118-190, because the dwelling was the taxpayer's main residence or someone else's during a period, the taxpayer would not make a capital gain or loss from the event, or would make a lesser capital gain or loss than if sub-div 118-B had not applied
  - the dwelling was used to produce assessable income, and
  - if the taxpayer had incurred interest on money borrowed to acquire the dwelling, the taxpayer could have deducted some or all of the interest (s 118-190).

  In such case, any capital gain or capital loss the taxpayer would have otherwise made from the CGT event is increased by an amount that is reasonable having regard to the extent to which they would have been able to deduct the interest.

Example Gemma is an Australian resident who works as a dentist. She acquired her main residence on 1 August 1990 for $2m and sold it 30 years later for $3m. Over her ownership period, she used the front three rooms in her home as a surgery. These rooms constituted 25% of the dwelling's floor area. Leaving aside s 118-190, Gemma would be able to disregard the $1m capital gain on the sale of her home under s 118-110. However, under s 118-190, it would be reasonable to increase the nil gain to $250,000 (ie 25% × $1m).

17

- **Special rule for first use to produce assessable income.** A special rule applies if a taxpayer would only get a partial exemption because the dwelling was used for the purpose of producing assessable income, that use occurred for the first time after 7.30pm on 20 August 1996, and a full exemption would have been available if a CGT event happened just before the first time (ie the 'income time') (s 118-192). In such a case, the dwelling is taken to have been acquired at the income time for its market value at that time.

Example Oscar is an Australian resident who acquired his main residence on 1 May 2000 for $500,000. On 1 May 2010, when his main residence had a market value of $800,000, he commenced conducting a full-time legal practice from home and used one of his rooms as an office to see clients. This room constituted 20% of the floor space of his home. He sold his home on 1 May 2023 for $1,800,000. Oscar's capital gain is calculated as follows:

$$\$200{,}000 = (\$1{,}800{,}000 - \$800{,}000) \times 20\%$$

Dwellings acquired from deceased estates

Subdivision 118-B *ITAA97* contains special rules relating to dwellings acquired under deceased estates. Most importantly, s 118-195 provides that a capital gain or capital loss from a CGT event that happens in relation to a dwelling may be ignored if the taxpayer is an individual who acquired their ownership interest in the dwelling as a beneficiary of a deceased estate or owned it as trustee of a deceased estate. The exemption only applies if the deceased was not an excluded foreign resident just before they died. In addition, the following two requirements must also be fulfilled.

The first requirement is that:

- the deceased must have acquired his or her ownership interest in the dwelling before 20 September 1985, or
- the deceased must have acquired his or her ownership interest in the dwelling after 20 September 1985, and the dwelling must have been the deceased's main residence just before death and must not then have been used for the purpose of producing assessable income.

The second requirement is that:

- the taxpayer's ownership interest must end within two years of the deceased's death (or such longer period as the Commissioner allows), or
- the dwelling must have been, from the deceased's death until the taxpayer's ownership interest ends, the main residence of one or more of:
  (a) the deceased's spouse other than a spouse who was living permanently separately and apart from the deceased (however, this paragraph is disregarded if the deceased was an excluded foreign resident just before their death)
  (b) an individual who had a right to occupy the dwelling under the deceased's will (however, this paragraph is disregarded if the deceased was an excluded foreign resident just before their death), or
  (c) the individual to whom the ownership interest passed as a beneficiary (however, this paragraph is disregarded if the individual was an excluded foreign resident at the time of the CGT event).

If an individual acquired their ownership interest in a dwelling as a beneficiary or trustee of a deceased estate and s 118-195 does not apply, they may nevertheless be entitled to a partial exemption under s 118-200. In such case, their capital gain or capital loss is calculated according to the following formula:

$$\text{Capital gain or capital loss amount} \times \frac{\text{Non-main residence days}}{\text{Total days}}$$

Example Ken is an Australian resident who acquired an ownership interest in a dwelling on 15 March 2002 which he used as his main residence until he died on 1 November 2003. After his death, his daughter, Barbara, who is also an Australian resident, acquired the dwelling as a beneficiary under his will and lived in it until it was sold on 1 November 2023. As the requirements of s 118-195 are satisfied, any capital gain or capital loss Barbara makes from the sale of the dwelling is disregarded.

[17.12] Australian and foreign residents

The CGT regime contains its own jurisdictional rules. Generally speaking, these rules ensure that the CGT regime applies more broadly to Australian residents than to foreign residents.

Australian residents

Subject to the operation of any specific exemptions, such as the main residence exemption [17.11], Australian residents are generally subject to CGT in respect of capital gains and capital losses from CGT events that happen to *any* CGT asset. There are, however, some important qualifications to this general rule. For example, resident companies generally disregard capital gains and capital losses that arise in respect of CGT assets that are not 'taxable Australian property' and are used wholly or mainly for the purpose of producing foreign income in carrying on a business through a permanent establishment [30.5] in a foreign country (s 23AH *ITAA36*) [31.5]. In addition, resident companies may, in certain cases, be able to reduce capital gains and capital losses made in relation to shares in foreign companies in which they hold a direct voting percentage of at least 10% (s 768-505 *ITAA97*) [31.7].

Example Lisa is an Australian resident. In May 2020, she acquired an investment property in Queensland and an investment property in Budapest as well as shares in an Australian company listed on the ASX and shares in a United States company listed on the NYSE. If Lisa sells her properties and shares, any gains or losses she makes from them will be subject to the CGT regime.

Foreign residents

Division 855 *ITAA97* contains special rules that apply to foreign residents. Foreign residents disregard capital gains and capital losses made from CGT events that happen in relation to CGT assets that are *not* 'taxable Australian property' (s 855-10). In other words, foreign residents are only subject to CGT in relation to CGT assets that *are* taxable Australian property and are not otherwise subject to a specific exemption. Similar rules apply to temporary residents [30.4] who, by virtue of s 768-915 *ITAA97*, are required to disregard capital gains and capital losses made from CGT events on the same basis as if they were foreign residents.

Taxable Australian property

There are three main forms of CGT assets that constitute taxable Australian property (s 855-15):

- **CGT assets that are taxable Australian real property.** This covers Australian land and rights to mine minerals in Australia (s 855-20).
- **CGT assets that are indirect Australian real property interests.** This covers membership interests held by an entity (the 'holding entity') in another entity (the 'test entity') that pass the 'non-portfolio interest test' and the 'principal assets test' (s 855-25). The 'non-portfolio interest test' is contained in s 960-195 and is passed if the holding entity and its associates (defined in s 318 *ITAA36* [8.6]) have direct participation interests (defined in s 960-190 *ITAA97* [31.6]) in the test entity of 10% or more. The principal assets test is contained in s 855-30 and is passed if the market value of the test entity's assets that are taxable Australian real property exceed the market value of the test entity's assets that are not taxable Australian real property.
- **CGT assets that are used in carrying on a business through a permanent establishment in Australia.** This covers, for instance, goodwill of a business carried on by a company through a branch in Australia.

A right or option to acquire any of the above CGT assets is also taxable Australian property.

Example Julio, a foreign resident who lives in Spain, recently sold his investment property in Sydney and his shares in Oz Co (which is an Australian resident company whose assets do not include any taxable Australian real property). The CGT regime applies to any capital gain or capital loss Julio makes in respect of his investment property as it is taxable Australian property. However, it does not apply to any capital gain or capital loss he makes in respect of his shares as the shares are not taxable Australian property.

If, however, Oz Co owned land in Australia (which had a market value of $2m) as well as other assets that are not taxable Australian real property (which had a market value of $1m), then if Julio owned at least 10% of the shares in Oz Co, he would be required to account for any capital gain or capital loss arising from the sale of the shares as they are indirect Australian real property interests.

17

Foreign residents capital gains withholding tax

Subdivision 14D of sch 1 *TAA* contains the foreign residents capital gains withholding tax regime. This regime applies where a foreign resident disposes of taxable Australian real property, an indirect Australian real property interest, or an option or right to acquire such property or interest (s 14-200(1)). It generally requires the purchaser to remit withholding tax equal to 12.5% of the first element of the CGT asset's cost base just after the acquisition (s 14-200(3)). The amount can be withheld from the payment made to the vendor and must be paid to the Commissioner on or before the purchaser becomes the CGT asset's owner (s 14-200(2)).

Withholding tax applies if:

- the purchaser knows or reasonably believes that the vendor is a foreign resident
- the vendor has an address outside Australia, or
- the purchaser is authorised to provide a related financial benefit to a place outside Australia (s 14-210).

Certain transactions are excluded (eg transactions involving taxable Australian real property or an indirect Australian real property interest where the market value of the asset is less than $750,000 (s 14-215(1)(a))).

In addition, a purchaser is not required to withhold tax in respect of a transaction if the vendor provides a 'clearance certificate' issued under s 14-220 that covers the time that the transaction was entered into (s 14-210(2)). Section 14-220 allows an entity to apply to the Commissioner to certify in writing that, based on the information before him, there is nothing to suggest that the entity is, or will be, a foreign resident during a specified period.

Likewise, a purchaser is not required to withhold tax in respect of a transaction if, before the purchaser pays the Commissioner, the vendor provides a declaration under s 14-225 that covers the time that the transaction was entered into (s 14-210(3)). Section 14-225 allows the vendor to declare, for a specified period, that it is, and will be, an Australian resident, or that specified CGT assets are membership interests but not indirect Australian real property interests. Penalties apply for knowingly or recklessly making declarations that are false or misleading in a material particular (s 14-230).

Withholding tax imposed under sub-div 14D is not a final tax. The vendor is required to lodge an income tax return and pay any outstanding tax. The vendor, however, receives a credit for the amount of withholding tax paid by the purchaser to the Commissioner (s 18-15).

Example Mei sells her penthouse apartment in Perth to Ethel for $4m on 7 July 2023. Ethel reasonably believes that Mei is a foreign resident living in Singapore. If Mei does not provide a clearance certificate or a residency declaration, Ethel must withhold $500,000 (ie $4m × 12.5%) from the amount paid to Mei and remit this to the Commissioner. Mei will receive a credit for the amount withheld. Accordingly, if she made a capital gain on the disposal of the apartment and would otherwise be required to pay tax of $700,000 on the capital gain, she will only have to pay the balance of $200,000.

Changing residency status

Special CGT rules apply where taxpayers change their residency status. These rules are outlined below.

Foreign residents becoming Australian residents

Where foreign residents become Australian residents, special rules apply to each CGT asset (other than pre-CGT assets or taxable Australian property) which they owned just before becoming residents (s 855-45). The relevant assets are deemed to be acquired at the time they became residents, and the first element of the cost base and reduced cost base of such assets is deemed to be their market value at that time. This means the entitlement to any discount will only arise if they held the assets for at least 12 months from becoming residents [17.8].

Example Ivana was a foreign resident who became an Australian resident on 1 May 2022. She acquired a hotel in Russia on 5 January 2005. As the hotel is not in Australia, it is not taxable Australian property. However, as Ivana is now a resident, she will be required to account for any gain or loss on the sale of the hotel. Ivana is deemed to have acquired the hotel on 1 May 2022 for its market value. If the market value of the hotel was $10m on 1 May 2022 and it was sold for $13m on 3 January 2023, Ivana would make a capital gain of $3m. She would not be entitled to any CGT discount even though she actually owned the hotel for more than 12 months as it has been less than 12 months since she became a resident.

Australian residents ceasing to be Australian residents

Where a taxpayer ceases to be an Australian resident, CGT event I1 [17.3] is triggered (s 104-160). In such a case, the taxpayer is effectively deemed to have disposed of their CGT assets that are not taxable Australian property for their market value at the time they ceased being a resident. The taxpayer makes a capital gain if the market value of the asset (at the time of the event) is more than its cost base, and they make a capital loss if that market value is less than the asset's reduced cost base (s 104-160(4)). The capital gain or capital loss is disregarded if the asset was acquired before 20 September 1985 (s 104-160(5)).

Individual taxpayers can choose under s 104-165 to disregard a capital gain or capital loss arising from all CGT assets covered by CGT event I1. If they make this choice, each of those assets is taken to be taxable Australian property until the earlier of the time that a CGT event happens in relation to the asset (if the CGT event involves the taxpayer ceasing to own the asset) or the time the taxpayer again becomes an Australian resident.

Example Luc has been an Australian resident all his life. On 1 July 2017, he left Australia to live permanently in Vietnam and therefore ceased to be an Australian resident. At the time of ceasing residency, he owned an investment property in Vietnam. The property was acquired on 5 February 2010 for $1m and had a market value of $1.5m on 1 July 2017. If Luc does not make a choice under s 104-165, he is deemed to have made a capital gain of $500,000 under CGT event I1 in respect of the Vietnam property on 1 July 2017. If, on the other hand, Luc made a choice under s 104-165, the capital gain is disregarded and the Vietnam property is taken to be taxable Australian property. If he subsequently sold the property for $3m on 7 May 2023 while he was still a foreign resident, he would make a capital gain of $2m under CGT event A1 at such time.

[17.13] Deceased estates

When a person dies, their assets vest in their legal personal representative—the person nominated under their will to act as the executor of their estate, or the person appointed by a court to act as administrator of their estate. The legal personal representative is responsible for administering the estate and is required to use the assets to discharge any debts of the deceased (including funeral expenses) and to distribute the remaining assets to the beneficiaries of the estate in accordance with the deceased's will (where there is one) or in accordance with statutory rules of intestacy (where the deceased dies without a will).

CGT consequences of death

Although the death of a person would ordinarily result in CGT implications in relation to the assets of the estate, the CGT regime was never intended to operate as a de facto form of death duty. A person's death does not therefore generally result in any CGT liability for their estate. Accordingly, capital gains and capital losses made in respect of CGT events relating to CGT assets that a person owned just before they died are generally disregarded (s 128-10 *ITAA97*).

Capital gains and capital losses made by the deceased's legal personal representative are generally disregarded provided the CGT assets pass to beneficiaries of the deceased estate (s 128-15(3)). A CGT asset passes to a beneficiary of a deceased taxpayer's estate if the beneficiary becomes the owner of the asset:

- under the taxpayer's will, or that will as varied by a court order
- by operation of an intestacy law, or such a law as varied by a court order
- because it is appropriated to the beneficiary by the deceased taxpayer's legal personal representative in satisfaction of a pecuniary legacy or some other interest or share in the estate, or
- under a deed of arrangement, where the beneficiary entered into the deed to settle a claim to participate in the distribution of the estate and any consideration given by the beneficiary for the asset consisted only of the variation or waiver of a claim to an asset of the estate (s 128-20(1)).

A CGT asset does *not* pass to a beneficiary (and the exemption does not apply) where the legal personal representative transfers the CGT asset to a third party (eg where the asset is sold to pay the debts of the estate or is converted into cash).

Where a CGT asset passes to the legal personal representative or beneficiary of a deceased estate, that person is deemed to have acquired the asset on the date of the deceased's death (s 128-15(2)). The first element of the cost base and reduced cost base of the asset to the legal personal representative or beneficiary is determined in accordance with modified rules contained in a table in s 128-15(4). These rules depend on the kind of asset involved. For most assets, the rules operate as follows:

- CGT assets acquired by the deceased on or after 20 September 1985 are deemed to be acquired by the legal personal representative or beneficiary for the relevant cost base or reduced cost base of the asset to the deceased at the date of death (item 1 in the table), and
- CGT assets acquired by the deceased before 20 September 1985 are deemed to be acquired by the legal personal representative or beneficiary for their market value at the date of death (item 4 in the table).

A special rule provides that a dwelling that was a person's main residence just before they died is deemed to be acquired by the legal personal representative or beneficiary for its market value on the date of the deceased's death if the dwelling was not then being used for the purpose of producing assessable income and the deceased was not then an excluded foreign resident (item 3 in the table).

A special rule also applies to trading stock, which is deemed to be acquired for the amount worked out under s 70-105 *ITAA97* [16.6] (item 2 in the table). In addition, assets that were not taxable Australian property of a foreign resident (item 3A in the table) and assets that pass to trustees of disability trusts (item 3B in the table) are deemed to be acquired for their market values on the date of the deceased's death.

Example Darren is an Australian resident who died on 5 January 2023. His assets passed to his legal personal representative, Larry, who is also an Australian resident. Darren's assets included shares which were not trading stock. If Larry sells the shares to pay for the debts of the estate, CGT event A1 will apply. In calculating any gain or loss on the disposal of the shares, Larry will be deemed to have acquired the shares for an amount equal to their market value on 5 January 2023 (if the shares were pre-20 September 1985 assets) or their cost base or reduced cost base on 5 January 2023 (in any other case).

If the shares passed under Darren's will to a beneficiary of the estate, Betty, who is also an Australian resident, any gain or loss made by Larry would be disregarded. Betty would be deemed to have acquired the shares for their market value on 5 January 2023 (if the shares were pre-20 September 1985 assets) or their cost base or reduced cost base on 5 January 2023 (in any other case).

If Betty also acquired a house which was Darren's main residence just before he died, and was not used for producing assessable income, she would be deemed to have acquired this asset for its market value on 5 January 2023.

Section 115-30 determines whether a legal personal representative or beneficiary has held a CGT asset acquired under a deceased estate for at least 12 months for the purposes of entitlement to the CGT discount under div 115 *ITAA97* [17.8]. In general, the legal personal representative or beneficiary is deemed to have acquired the asset when the deceased acquired it (ie they can aggregate the period of ownership). This rule does not, however, apply to a pre-CGT asset of the deceased, which is deemed to be acquired when the deceased died.

Where CGT assets of a deceased estate pass to beneficiaries that are tax-exempt entities, trustees of complying superannuation entities, or foreign residents, capital gains and capital losses can arise under CGT event K3 (s 104-215). In the case of a CGT asset that passes to a foreign resident, CGT event K3 only arises if the deceased was an Australian resident just before dying and the asset is not taxable Australian property of the foreign resident. Under CGT event K3, any capital gains and capital losses are deemed to be made by the deceased just before they died. A capital gain arises if the market value of the asset at the date of death is more than the asset's cost base. A capital loss arises if the market value of the asset at the date of death is less than the asset's reduced cost base. A capital gain or capital loss is disregarded if the deceased acquired the asset before 20 September 1985.

17

Example Liz is an Australian resident who died on 5 May 2023. The beneficiaries of her estate include Kit (a non-resident) and the Salvation Army (an exempt entity). Under her will, Liz gifted shares she owned in X Co to Kit, and shares she owned in Y Co to the Salvation Army. Liz acquired her X Co and Y Co shares for $100,000 each on 1 August 2000. On the date of her death, the market value of her X Co shares was $170,000 and the market value of her Y Co shares was $80,000. Under CGT event K3, Liz is deemed to make a capital gain of $70,000 on her X Co shares and a capital loss of $20,000 on her Y Co shares just before she died.

Co-ownership

Co-ownership arises where two or more entities simultaneously own interests in the same property. Taxpayers can co-own property as either 'tenants in common' or 'joint tenants'. Tenants in common may have equal or different fractional interests in the property, which constitute distinct shares in the property. Their fractional interests form part of the assets of their estates on death and *can* therefore be transferred to the beneficiaries of their estates. Joint tenants, on the other hand, always own equal shares in the property and are subject to the 'principle of survivorship'. This means that their fractional interests automatically devolve to the surviving joint tenants on death and *cannot* be transferred to the beneficiaries of their estates.

It is sometimes difficult to distinguish between a tenancy in common and a joint tenancy. Under the general law, the following 'four unities' must be present for a joint tenancy to exist (*Corin v Patton* (1990) CLR 540; *Mischel v Mischel Holdings Pty Ltd (in liq)* [2012] VCS 292):

- **Unity of possession.** Each co-owner must have the right to possess the entire property.
- **Unity of time.** Each co-owner's interest in the property must be acquired at the same time.
- **Unity of title.** Each co-owner's interest must be derived from the same document or act.
- **Unity of interest.** Each co-owner's interest must be the same in terms of its nature, extent and duration.

For a tenancy in common to exist, only the unity of possession is required. Where one or more of the other unities are missing, the co-ownership is a tenancy in common.

When a tenant in common dies, the general CGT rules apply to their fractional interests in a CGT asset.

When a joint tenant dies, special rules in s 128-50 apply. Under these rules, the survivor is taken to have acquired (on the day of death) the deceased's interest in the asset. If there are more than two survivors, they are deemed to have acquired the interest in equal shares.

The cost base of the interest that each survivor is deemed to have acquired depends on when the deceased acquired their interest in the asset. If the deceased acquired their interest in the asset on or after 20 September 1985, the first element of the cost base or reduced cost base of the interest of each survivor is calculated as follows:

$$\frac{\text{Cost base of the deceased's interest in the asset (worked out on the date of death)}}{\text{Number of survivors}}$$

If the deceased acquired his or her interest in the asset before 20 September 1985, the first element of the cost base or reduced cost base of the interest of each survivor is calculated as follows:

$$\frac{\text{Market value of the deceased's interest in the asset (worked out on the date of death)}}{\text{Number of survivors}}$$

In determining whether a surviving joint tenant has held a deceased's interest in an asset for at least 12 months for the purposes of the CGT discount [17.8], s 115-30 provides that the survivor is deemed to have acquired the asset when the deceased acquired it.

Example On 1 March 1984, Dan and Sally purchased vacant land for \$100,000 as joint tenants. Dan died on 1 May 2023, when the market value of the land was \$250,000. Sally is deemed to have acquired Dan's 50% interest in the land on 1 May 2023 for \$125,000. If she subsequently sold the land on 1 December 2023, she is not subject to CGT on her original 50% interest as it was acquired before 20 September 1985. Sally is, however, subject to CGT on any gain or loss made in respect of the 50% interest that she is deemed to have acquired from Dan. Accordingly, if the land was sold for \$300,000, she is deemed to have made a gain of \$25,000 (ie \$300,000 × 50% – \$125,000).

For the purposes of the CGT discount rules, Sally is taken to have acquired Dan's interest in the land when Dan actually acquired it. This means that she would be eligible to claim the 50% discount, even though she actually acquired his interest less than 12 months ago.

[17.14] Investments

Division 130 *ITAA97* contains special CGT rules that apply to certain kinds of investments. The following discussion focuses on the rules relating to:

- bonus shares and units (sub-div 130-A)
- rights to acquire shares and units (sub-div 130-B), and
- convertible interests (sub-div 130-C).

Bonus shares and units

Subdivision 130-A *ITAA97* modifies the general CGT rules where a taxpayer owns shares in a company or units in a trust ('original equities') and the company issues other shares or the trustee issues other units ('bonus equities') to the taxpayer in relation to the original equities.

The rules in sub-div 130-A determine when the bonus equities are acquired and the first element of their cost base and reduced cost base. Different rules operate depending on:

- whether the original equities were acquired before the introduction of CGT on 20 September 1985 or on or after that date
- whether any amount has been paid for the bonus equities (ie whether or not they are partly paid), and
- whether any part of the bonus equities is a dividend [22.4] or otherwise assessable.

The following diagram summarises how the rules in sub-div 130-A work:

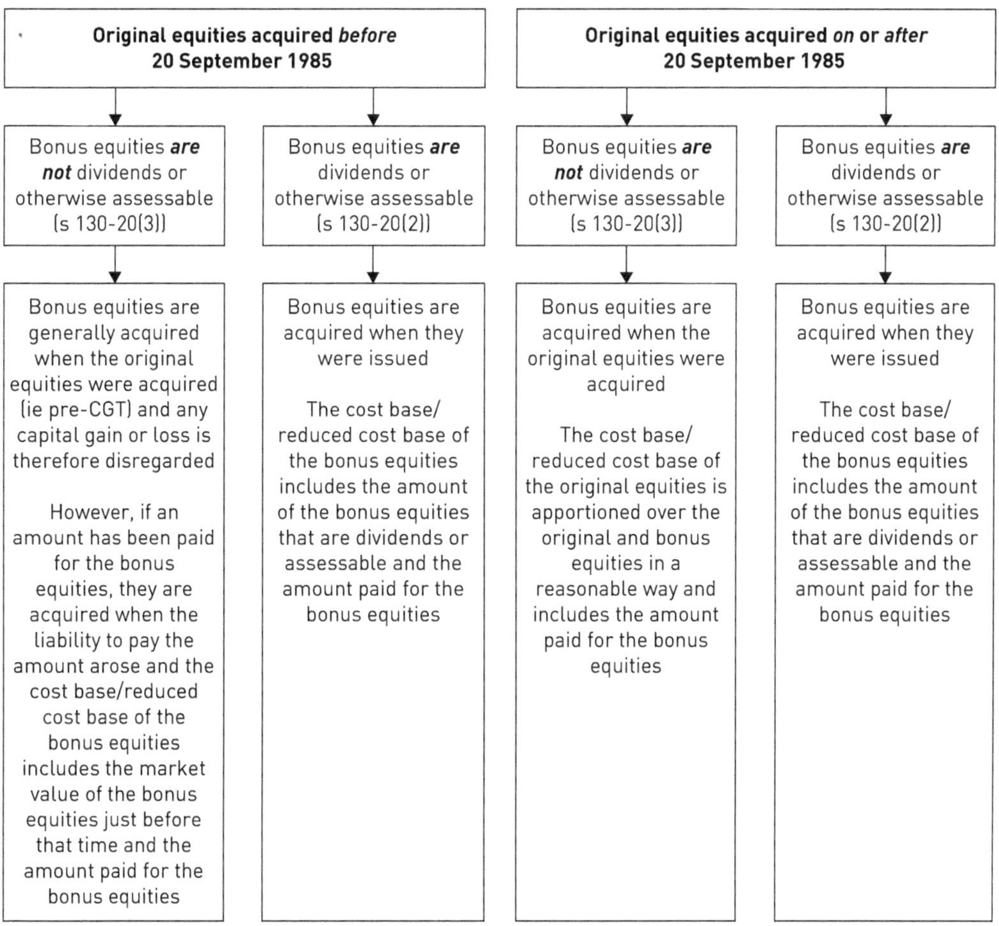

The rules in the diagram are modified by transitional rules in s 130-20 *ITTPA*, which operate as follows:

- If the bonus equities are shares issued on or before 30 June 1987, the taxpayer must work out the cost base and reduced cost base of the Bonus shares without taking into account the amount that is a dividend.
- If the bonus equities were issued on or before 1pm on 10 December 1986 and the taxpayer was required to pay or give something for them, the taxpayer is taken to have acquired the bonus equities when the original equities were acquired.

Example George purchased 1,000 shares in A Co on 10 January 1984 for $5,000 (ie $5 per share). He purchased a further 2,000 shares in A Co on 15 July 2000 for $20,000 (ie $10 per share). On 12 March 2012, A Co issued George with 300 bonus shares, which are not dividends.

The bonus shares are deemed to have been acquired at the time the original shares were acquired. As one-third of the original shares were acquired on 10 January 1984, 100 of the bonus shares are deemed to have been acquired on that date. Any capital gain or loss on these 100 bonus shares is therefore disregarded as they are deemed to be acquired pre-20 September 1985.

As the remaining two-thirds of the original shares were acquired on 15 July 2000, 200 bonus shares are deemed to have been acquired on that date. The first element of their cost base is calculated by apportioning the cost base of the original 2,000 shares ($20,000) over the combined original and bonus shares (2,200 shares). The first element of the cost base of each of the 2,000 original shares and each of the 200 bonus shares is therefore $9.09 (ie $20,000/2,200).

Example Shelly purchased 100 shares in X Co on 2 September 2010 for $5 each. On 7 January 2012, X Co issued Shelly with 100 bonus shares. The bonus shares are assessable as a dividend of $800 under s 44(1) *ITAA36*. On 9 March 2012, X Co made a call of $2 per bonus share, which Shelly paid on that day.

Shelly is deemed to have acquired the 100 bonus shares on 7 January 2012. The first element of the cost base of the 100 bonus shares is $1,000 (ie the sum of $800, being the dividend, and $200, being the amount paid for the bonus shares). The first element of the cost base of each bonus share is therefore $10 (ie $1,000/100).

The acquisition date of the 100 original shares remains 2 September 2010 and the first element of their cost base remains $5.

Subdivision 130-A does not apply to shares acquired under a dividend reinvestment plan [22.5] as such shares are not issued 'in relation to' the original shares (TD 2000/3). Where a shareholder acquires shares under a dividend reinvestment plan, the general CGT rules operate instead. The first element of the cost base or reduced cost base of the shares therefore includes the amount of the dividend applied by the shareholder to acquire the shares (s 110-25(2)) [17.6].

Rights to acquire shares and units

Subdivision 130-B *ITAA97* modifies the general CGT rules where a taxpayer exercises a 'right' to acquire shares, or options to acquire shares, in a company, or units, or options to acquire units, in a unit trust (s 130-40(1)). The subdivision applies to 'options' in the same way that it applies to rights (s 130-50). Separate rules in sub-div 130-D *ITAA97* apply to the exercise of rights under an 'employee share scheme' (ESS). These rules adjust the general CGT rules to align them with the ESS rules in div 83A *ITAA97* [21.2].

Ordinarily, the exercise of rights results in CGT event C2 happening in relation to the rights [17.10]. Subdivision 130-B, however, contains a special rule which provides that any capital gain or capital loss made from the exercise of the rights is disregarded (s 130-40(7)).

Subdivision 130-B also modifies the general cost base and reduced cost base rules [17.6] where certain conditions are met (s 130-40(2)). These conditions differ depending on whether or not the taxpayer paid for the rights. The basic conditions are summarised in the following diagram:

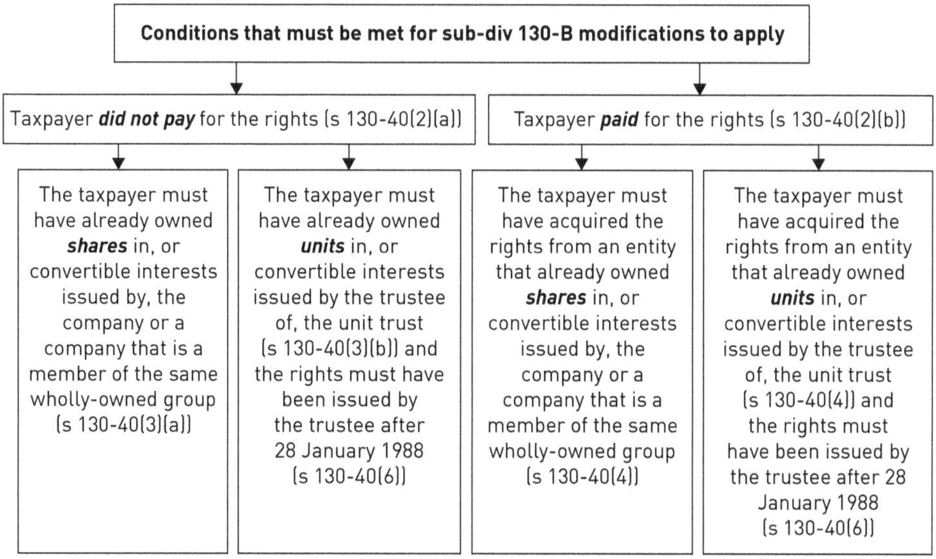

The above conditions operate subject to the following transitional rules in s 130-40 *ITTPA*:

- Where the taxpayer is issued rights by a company before 16 August 1989, the modifications in sub-div 130-B only apply if the taxpayer was a shareholder of that company.
- Where the taxpayer is issued rights by a company after 15 August 1989 and before 1 July 1993 because the taxpayer is a shareholder of another company, the modifications only apply if the companies are members of the same wholly owned group for the whole of the income year concerned.

Where the modifications in sub-div 130-B apply, s 130-40(6) provides that the first element of the cost base or reduced cost base of the newly acquired shares, units or options is the sum of:

(a) either: (i) the cost base of the rights at the time of exercise; or (ii) the market value of the rights at the time of exercise (if the rights were issued to the taxpayer and the taxpayer acquired the original shares, units or convertible interests before 20 September 1985)

(b) any amount paid to exercise the rights (except to the extent that the amount is represented in paragraph (a) above), and

(c) any amount by which a capital gain made from exercising the right has been reduced under s 118-20 [17.5].

Where a taxpayer acquired rights from the company or the trustee of the unit trust, the taxpayer is deemed to have acquired the rights when they acquired the original shares interests (s 130-45(1)). The newly acquired shares, units or options are deemed to have been acquired when the rights are exercised (s 130-45(2)).

Example On 1 October 2022, Rob acquired 600 shares in S Co. On 1 March 2023, S Co made a rights issue to its shareholders offering one new share for every original share held at the price of $5 per share. On 1 April 2023, Rob exercised one-half of these rights and purchased 300 new shares for $1,500. The modifications in sub-div 130-B apply because Rob already owned shares in S Co when he was issued the rights. Although the rights are a CGT asset and their exercise would ordinarily result in CGT event C2 happening, any capital gain or loss in respect of the rights is disregarded by s 130-40(7). The first element of the cost base of Rob's newly acquired 300 S Co shares under s 130-40(6) is $1,500, being the sum of:

(a) $0 (the cost base of the rights)
(b) $1,500 (the amount paid to exercise the rights), and
(c) nil (the amount by which a capital gain made from exercising the right has been reduced under s 118-20).

On 1 May 2023, Rob sold the other half of the rights to Sam (who did not previously own any S Co shares) for $300. Rob is deemed to have acquired the rights when he acquired the original shares on 1 October 2022 (s 130-45(1)). Since Rob did not pay for the rights, the cost base of the rights is nil and he makes a capital gain under CGT event A1 of $300 when he disposes of the rights to Sam.

On 1 June 2023, Sam exercised the rights he acquired from Rob and purchased 300 shares in S Co for $1,500. The modifications in sub-div 130-B apply because Sam provided consideration for the rights, and acquired them from Rob who already owned shares in S Co. The first element of the cost base of Sam's newly acquired shares is $1,800, being the sum of:

(a) $300 (the cost base of the rights)
(b) $1,500 (the amount paid to exercise the rights), and
(c) nil (the amount by which a capital gain made from exercising the right has been reduced under s 118-20).

Example Pete acquired 100 units in a unit trust on 1 August 1983. On 5 March 2023, the trustee of the trust issued rights to acquire units in the trust to all unit holders, offering one new unit for every two units held at a price of $1,000 per unit. Pete immediately exercised the rights and purchased 50 new units for $50,000. On 5 March 2023, the market value of a unit in the trust was $1,200. Subdivision 130-B applies because the rights were issued by the trustee after 28 January 1988 and Pete already owned units in the trust. As Pete acquired the original units before 20 September 1985, the first element of the cost base of each newly acquired unit is $1,200, being the sum of:

(a) $200 (the market value of the rights when exercised, ie $1,200 – $1,000)
(b) $1,000 (the amount paid to exercise the rights), and
(c) nil (the amount by which a capital gain made from exercising the rights has been reduced under s 118-20).

Convertible interests

Subdivision 130-C *ITAA97* modifies the general CGT rules where a taxpayer acquires shares or units by converting a 'convertible interest'.

A 'convertible interest' is defined in s 995-1 *ITAA97* and covers:

- an interest issued by a company that gives the holder (or a connected entity of the holder) a right to be issued with an equity interest in the company (or a connected entity of the company), or
- an interest that will, or may, convert into an equity interest in the company (or a connected entity of the company).

It also covers an interest that has the same or similar effect in relation to a trust.

An example of a convertible interest is a convertible note issued by a company that provides the noteholder with an option to convert a loan into shares in the company.

Where sub-div 130-C applies, any capital gain or capital loss made from converting the convertible interest (eg because of CGT event C2 happening [17.10]) is disregarded (s 130-60(3)).

The new shares or units are deemed to be acquired when the conversion happens (s 130-60(2)). This rule, however, operates subject to a transitional rule which provides that where shares were acquired by the conversion of a convertible note acquired before 20 September 1985 and the taxpayer did not pay or give anything in relation to the conversion, the shares are deemed to be acquired when the convertible note was acquired (s 130-60(3) *ITTPA*).

The first element of the cost base or reduced cost base of the new shares or units is the sum of the cost base of the convertible interest and any additional amount paid to convert the interest (s 130-60(1)). It also includes any amount by which a capital gain made from the convertible interest is reduced under s 118-20 [17.5] (s 130-60(1A)).

The modifications only apply where the taxpayer acquired:

- shares or units by converting a convertible interest that is a 'traditional security' [29.13]
- shares (other than those acquired under an ESS) by converting a convertible interest that is *not* a traditional security, or
- units by converting a convertible interest issued after 28 January 1988 that is *not* a traditional security (s 130-60(1)).

The modifications operate subject to the following transitional rules:

- Where the shares or units were acquired by converting a convertible note that is a traditional security acquired after 10 May 1989 and before 16 August 1989, the first element of the cost base and reduced cost base of the shares or units is the sum of the amount paid or given to acquire the note and any amount paid in relation to the conversion (if that sum was more than the market value of the shares or units at the time of conversion) (s 130-60(1) *ITTPA*).
- Where shares were acquired by converting a convertible note that is not a traditional security acquired before 20 September 1985 and the taxpayer paid or gave something in relation to the conversion, the first element of the cost base and reduced cost base of the shares is the sum of the market value of the note at the time of the conversion and what the taxpayer paid or gave in relation to the conversion (s 130-60(2) *ITTPA*).

[17.15] Options

The grant of an option can result in either CGT event C3 or CGT event D2 happening [17.10]. Division 134 *ITAA97* contains special rules that apply where an option has been exercised. These rules do not apply to the exercise of the following options, which have their own separate rules:

- options acquired under an ESS that are exercised before their 'deferred taxing point' [21.4]
- options issued by companies and trusts that are covered by sub-div 130-B [17.14], or
- options that bind the grantor to dispose of or acquire foreign currency (s 134-1).

Nature of an option

The nature of an option was considered in *FC of T v Guy* 96 ATC 4520, where the Full Federal Court stated (at 4526):

> The word 'option' itself suggests a right in one party unilaterally to require another party to enter a new set of jural relations or to extend or continue an existing jural relationship. Put and call options, options to purchase and options to renew leases are, perhaps, the most common illustrations.

Capital gain or loss on exercise of option disregarded

Under div 134, if an option is exercised, any capital gain or capital loss made by the grantor (s 104-40(5)) or by the grantee (s 134-1(4)) from the exercise of the option is generally disregarded.

Cost base modifications to CGT asset

Where an option to which div 134 applies has been exercised, the general CGT cost base and reduced cost base rules are modified in accordance with special rules contained s 134-1(1). The rules distinguish between 'put' and 'call' options. They generally require grantors and grantees of options to take into account the amounts paid and received in relation to their options in determining the cost base and reduced cost base of the underlying CGT assets that are the subject of the options. More specifically, the modifications operate as follows:

- **Call options.** Where the option binds the grantor to dispose of a CGT asset or to create (eg by granting or issuing) a CGT asset, the following rules apply:
  - For the grantee of the option: the first element of the grantee's cost base and reduced cost base for the CGT asset is what the grantee paid for the option (or to renew or extend it) plus any amount the grantee paid to exercise it. (Note, this rule is modified under div 83A and s 112-97 *ITAA97* for options that are ESS interests [21.3], and under s 134-1 *ITTPA* for options granted before 20 September 1985 but exercised after that date.)
  - For the grantor of the option: the capital proceeds received by the grantor for the disposal of the CGT asset includes any payment received for granting (or renewing or extending) the option (s 116-65).
- **Put options.** Where the option binds the grantor to acquire a CGT asset, the following rules apply:
  - For the grantor of the option: the first element of the grantor's cost base and reduced cost base for the CGT asset is any amount paid to exercise the option reduced by any payment received for the option (or to renew or extend it).
  - For the grantee of the option: the second element of the grantee's cost base and reduced cost base includes any payment the grantee made to acquire the option (or to renew or extend it).

Example On 1 May 2020, Charlie granted Carmel a five-year call option to purchase his land for $500,000. Carmel paid Charlie $20,000 for the option and exercised it on 1 June 2023. The exercise of the option does not result in any capital gain or loss in respect of the option for either Charlie or Carmel. Charlie is deemed to have received $520,000 as capital proceeds for the disposal of the land. The first element of Carmel's cost base and reduced cost base for the land is $520,000.

Example On 5 January 2020, Kate granted Will a five-year put option that requires her to buy his 1,000 shares in J Co for $10,000 if requested to do so. Will paid Kate $500 for the option. On 6 July 2023, Will exercised the option and Kate paid him $10,000 for the shares. The exercise of the option does not result in any capital gain or capital loss in respect of the option for either Kate or Will. The first element of Kate's cost base and reduced cost base for the shares is $9,500 (ie $10,000 – $500). The second element of Will's cost base and reduced cost base for the shares includes the $500 he paid for the option. If he purchased the shares in February 2015 for $3,000, the cost base for his shares would be $3,500 and the capital gain made on the disposal of the shares would be $6,500 (ie $10,000 – $3,500). The capital gain would be a discount capital gain as he has held the shares for more than 12 months [17.8].

[17.16] CGT roll-overs

Capital gains that would otherwise arise as a result of the happening of a CGT event may be deferred where the requirements of certain 'roll-over' provisions have been satisfied. The main roll-over provisions are located in divs 122 to 126 *ITAA97*. There are also special roll-overs that provide CGT relief together with other forms of relief in sub-div 328-G and div 615 *ITAA97*. The roll-overs are complex and apply to a broad range of transactions, including a variety of business, corporate and trust restructure arrangements discussed in Chapter 28. Each roll-over provision contains specific criteria that must be satisfied in order for the roll-over to apply. Some roll-overs operate automatically whereas others require taxpayers to make elections. There are two kinds of roll-overs: 'replacement asset roll-overs' (sub-div 112-C *ITAA97*) and 'same-asset roll-overs' (sub-div 112-D *ITAA97*).

Replacement asset roll-overs

Replacement asset roll-overs involve taxpayers disposing of particular CGT assets and replacing them with other CGT assets. The effect of a replacement asset roll-over is that the taxpayer defers making a capital gain or capital loss from the CGT event until a later CGT event happens (s 112-105). In addition, the attributes of the 'original asset' are deemed to apply to the 'replacement asset'. This means that where the original asset was acquired before 20 September 1985, the replacement asset is also deemed to be acquired before such date (s 124-10). Where the original asset was acquired on or after 20 September 1985, the first element of the replacement asset's cost base or reduced cost base is the same as the original asset's cost base or reduced cost base at the time the replacement asset was acquired (s 112-110).

The table in s 112-115 lists the various kinds of replacement asset roll-overs. For instance, roll-over relief is available where:

17

- assets are transferred to, or created in, a wholly owned company in exchange for shares in the company (sub-div 124-A)
- assets are compulsorily acquired, lost or destroyed and are replaced with new assets (sub-div 124-B)
- statutory licences that end are exchanged for new statutory licences that authorise substantially similar activity (sub-div 124-C)
- ownership interests that give a right to occupy a unit in a building are converted into stratum units as a result of a subdivision by the building's owner (sub-div 124-D)
- shares in companies or units in trusts are exchanged for new shares or new units in the same companies or trusts (sub-div 124-E)
- rights or options to acquire shares in companies or units in trusts are exchanged for new rights or options to acquire shares or units in those companies or trusts (sub-div 124-F)
- bodies incorporated under one law (eg a foreign law) are converted to, or replaced with, bodies incorporated under another law (sub-div 124-I)
- crown leases over land are renewed, extended or converted to an estate in fee simple (sub-div 124-J)
- original prospecting or mining entitlements expire or are surrendered and are replaced by new prospecting or mining entitlements relating to the same land (sub-div 124-L)
- shares in a company, or interests in a trust, that have been acquired on or after 20 September 1985 are exchanged for shares in another company, or interests in another trust, pursuant to a 'scrip for scrip' takeover (sub-div 124-M)
- trusts dispose of all their assets to a company and units and interests in the trust are replaced by shares in the company (sub-div 124-N)

- CGT events happen to ownership interests in the head company of a demerger group under a demerger (div 125), and
- shares in a company or units in a trust are exchanged for shares in an interposed company (div 615).

Same-asset roll-overs

Same-asset roll-overs allow one entity ('the transferor') to disregard a capital gain or capital loss made from disposing of a CGT asset to, or creating a CGT asset in, another entity ('the transferee'). Any gain or loss is deferred until another CGT event happens in relation to the asset in the hands of the transferee (s 112-140). In addition, the attributes of the transferred asset are acquired by the transferee. This means that if the transferor acquired the asset before 20 September 1985, the transferee is also taken to have acquired the asset before that date. If the transferor acquired the asset on or after 20 September 1985, the first element of the asset's cost base or reduced cost base in the hands of the transferee is replaced with the asset's cost base or reduced cost base at the time the transferee acquired it (s 112-145).

The table in s 112-150 lists the various kinds of same-asset roll-overs. For instance, roll-over relief is available where:

- individuals or partnerships dispose of CGT assets to companies in which they own all the shares (sub-divs 122-A and 122-B)
- assets are transferred between spouses on marriage breakdowns (sub-div 126-A), and
- assets are transferred between companies in a wholly owned group where one of the companies is a foreign resident (sub-div 126-B).

[17.17] QUESTIONS

1. What is the difference between a 'net capital gain' and a 'capital gain', and between a 'net capital loss' and a 'capital loss'? Are net capital losses deductible?
2. What is a 'CGT event' and what is a 'CGT asset'? Why are these concepts important?
3. Under which provisions are capital gains and capital losses relating to the following assets disregarded: (a) cars; (b) pre-20 September 1985 assets; (c) collectables acquired for $500 or less; (d) personal use assets acquired for less than $10,000; (e) assets used to produce exempt income; (f) depreciating assets; (g) trading stock; (h) damages for personal injuries; (i) gambling winnings; and (j) the main residence?
4. Mary has a $2,000 carry forward capital loss from the sale of units in a trust in June 2018. In October 2023, she sold an investment property for $180,000, which she had purchased in April 2013 for $160,000 (including stamp duty and legal fees). In November 2023, she held a garage sale at her home and sold the following items:
   - a TV for $8,800 (she bought the TV in May 2018 from an electronics retailer for $5,500)
   - an antique vase for $6,600 (she bought the vase in May 2012 from an antiques store for $9,900)
   - a violin for $14,000 (she bought the violin in May 1983 from a music shop for $11,000)
   - a painting for $11,000 (she bought the painting in June 2013 from an art gallery for $7,700)
   - a fridge for $1,100 (she bought the fridge in April 2012 from a whitegoods retailer for $5,500), and
   - a car for $33,000 (she bought the car in February 2015 from a car retailer for $44,000).

What are the CGT consequences of the transactions?

5. What amounts make up the 'cost base' of a CGT asset and the 'capital proceeds' from a CGT event? When do the market value substitution rules operate? How does GST and ITCs interact with the cost base and capital proceeds rules? In what circumstances may a taxpayer index the cost base of an asset?
6. Theodore is a resident who acquired shares in three companies (A Co, B Co and C Co) for $5,000 each. In the current income year, Theodore sold his shares in A Co and B Co for $6,000 each and he sold his shares in C Co for $4,000. Theodore had held the A Co shares for eight months and the B Co and C Co shares for three years. Calculate Theodore's net capital gain. Would your answer be different if the shares were owned by a company instead of Theodore?
7. Fred is a resident who signed a contract to sell his holiday home in the Blue Mountains in August 2022. The sale was settled in February 2023 when Fred received $800,000 from the purchaser. Fred incurred legal fees of $1,100 (inclusive of GST) and a real estate agent's commission of $9,900 (inclusive of GST) in relation to the sale. Fred purchased the holiday home in March 1987 for $100,000 and paid $2,000 in stamp duty on the transfer and $1,000 in legal fees. In January 1990, Fred engaged a builder to build a garage on the property for $20,000. Calculate Fred's net capital gain for the current year.
8. Ted is 50 years old and established a milk bar business in Melbourne in November 1999. He is planning to sell the business later this year and expects to realise a $600,000 capital gain on the disposal of the goodwill. What conditions must he satisfy to benefit from the small business concessions under div 152 *ITAA97*? Assuming he satisfies the conditions, what CGT small business tax concessions can he claim?
9. Alice and Bob are married residents but often live apart as they are busy professionals. They acquired two houses in 2014: 'house A' and 'house B'. Alice and Bob each held a 50% interest in house A. Bob held an 80% interest in house B and Alice held a 20% interest in house B. In the current income year, they sold both houses. Alice nominated house A as her main residence and Bob nominated house B as his main residence. How does the main residence exemption apply to Alice and Bob if, ignoring the exemption, a capital gain of $1m would arise on the sale of each house?
10. Discuss whether a foreign resident company would be subject to CGT on the disposal of the following assets: (a) shares in a public company listed on the ASX; (b) vacant land in Tasmania; and (c) goodwill of a business carried on through an Australian PE.
11. Peter is an Australian resident who is planning to purchase an apartment in Sydney for $5m from Voula, who is a foreign resident. Advise Peter of his foreign resident capital gains withholding tax obligations.
12. Rachel bought a home on 1 July 1996 for $500,000 and moved into it on the settlement date of 1 December 1996. She lived in the home until 1 July 1998 when she was posted by her employer to Paris to work as a fashion designer. Rachel returned to Australia on 1 July 2006 and immediately moved back into her home. Between 1 July 1998 and 1 July 2006, the property was leased to tenants. On 1 July 2010, Rachel sold her home for $1.5m to Joe who moved in on the settlement date of 1 September 2010. Joe died on 1 December 2014 when the market value of the property was $2m. Monique is the sole beneficiary under Joe's will, and after his death she leased the property to tenants until 1 December 2023 when she sold it for $3m. Discuss the CGT consequences of the transactions.
13. Frank, died in January this year. Under his will, Frank gave his son Ben two properties: his investment property in Sydney and his holiday house on the Gold Coast. Frank acquired the

17

Sydney property in 1980 for $1m and he acquired the Gold Coast property in 1990 for $2m. At the date of Frank's death, each property had a market value of $5m. Ben wants to sell both properties. What are the CGT consequences of doing this?

14. On 10 May 2013, Kim acquired 500 shares in K Co for $5 per share. On 1 June 2014, K Co issued its shareholders rights to acquire one new share for every original share held in the company at a price of $10 per share. On 1 July 2014, Kim exercised one-half of these rights and purchased 250 shares. On the same day she sold the remaining rights to Karl for $250 who immediately exercised the rights. On 1 March 2023, both Kim and Karl sold all their shares in K Co for $12 per share. Discuss the CGT implications of these transactions.
15. On 1 May 2016, Steve purchased a boat for $40,000. On 1 January 2023, he granted Johnny an option to purchase the boat within 12 months for $50,000. Johnny paid Steve $2,000 for the option. What are the consequences of exercising the option?

PART G

FRINGE BENEFITS, SUPERANNUATION AND EMPLOYMENT

18 FRINGE BENEFITS TAX

[18.1] Introduction

This chapter examines FBT, which is a separate Commonwealth tax payable by employers on fringe benefits provided to their employees. Fringe benefits cover most kinds of non-salary benefits provided in respect of employment (eg the use of a car, free housing and discounted goods or services). Australia is one of only two OECD countries (the other is New Zealand) that tax employers on the provision of fringe benefits. Most other countries simply assess employees on the value of the fringe benefits that they receive under their general income tax systems.

Before the introduction of FBT in 1986, Australia used to assess employees on fringe benefits under former s 26(e) *ITAA36* [10.3]. This provision included in a taxpayer's assessable income 'the value to the taxpayer of all allowances, gratuities, compensations, benefits, bonuses and premiums allowed, given or granted to [the taxpayer] in respect of . . . any employment of or services rendered by [the taxpayer]'. FBT was introduced because employees had a poor record of complying with s 26(e) and because the provision suffered from various valuation and other technical problems.

This meant that, in practice, the income tax system did not adequately capture all types of fringe benefits. FBT was also introduced because it is more efficient to administer since there are far fewer taxpayers to deal with. For instance, one employer may have hundreds of employees to whom a range of different fringe benefits are provided. Instead of having to assess each employee separately, as was the case under s 26(e), the ATO now needs to focus its attention on just one taxpayer, being the employer.

FBT is payable by employers on their 'fringe benefits taxable amount' for the year of tax [18.2]. An employer's fringe benefits taxable amount is based on the grossed-up taxable values of the fringe benefits provided during the year in respect of their employees. There are several different kinds of fringe benefit [18.3], and different valuation rules for each of them [18.4]. Some benefits are 'exempt benefits' and therefore excluded from FBT [18.3].

Importantly, the FBT regime is designed to be the exclusive code for taxing fringe benefits. To prevent employees also being assessed under the income tax system on any fringe benefits and exempt benefits they receive, s 23L *ITAA36* deems fringe benefits to be non-assessable non-exempt income and exempt benefits to be exempt income [8.5].

Although employees do not pay income tax on fringe benefits, reportable fringe benefits amounts [8.6] are recorded on their PAYG summaries and are relevant for calculating the employee's reportable fringe benefits total, which is used in calculating their liability for the MLS [8.8] and HELP repayments [8.10] as well as for certain superannuation purposes [19.7].

[18.2] Liability to pay FBT

FBT is assessed under the *Fringe Benefits Tax Assessment Act 1986* (Cth) ('*FBTAA*'). This Act operates in conjunction with the *Fringe Benefits Tax Regulations 2018* (Cth). FBT is imposed under the *Fringe Benefits Tax Act 1986* ('*FBTA*'), which is required to be read as one with the *FBTAA*.

An employer is required to pay FBT on their 'fringe benefits taxable amount' for the 'year of tax' at the rate set out in the *FBTA* (ss 5, 6 *FBTA*; s 66 *FBTAA*). The formula for calculating an employer's FBT liability can therefore be expressed as follows:

$$\text{FBT} = \text{Fringe benefits taxable amount for the year of tax} \times \text{FBT rate}$$

18

In special circumstances, an employer's FBT liability may be calculated under relaxed rules contained in pt XIA *FBTAA* [18.19].

To ensure that Commonwealth Departments are liable for FBT in essentially the same way as other employers, s 4 *Fringe Benefits Tax (Application to the Commonwealth) Act 1986* (Cth) deems that the *FBTAA* applies as if each Commonwealth employee were an employee of the 'responsible Department' and as though the responsible Department were a company.

Fringe benefits taxable amount

An employer's 'fringe benefits taxable amount' is worked out according to complex formulas and method statements contained in s 5B *FBTAA* [18.5]. In order to apply the formulas and method statements, employers need to identify the 'fringe benefits' that have been provided in respect of their employees during the year of tax and calculate their respective 'taxable values'. There are many different kinds of fringe benefit [18.3]. The way in which the taxable value of each fringe benefit is calculated differs depending on the nature of the benefit [18.4].

FBT year of tax

The FBT 'year of tax' (also referred to as the 'FBT year') runs from 1 April to 31 March (s 136(1) *FBTAA*). It therefore differs from the 'income year', which is based on the financial year [8.3].

FBT rate

The FBT rate is designed to mirror the top marginal income tax rate plus ML. It is currently 47%. Importantly, the FBT rate is payable by an employer regardless of the rate of income tax payable by the employee who receives the benefit. In other words, an employer will still be required to pay FBT at the rate of 47% even if its employee pays income tax at a lower rate.

Self-assessment and payment of FBT

Employers are required to self-assess their FBT liability under the *FBTAA*. Employers that are liable to pay FBT for a year of tax must lodge FBT returns by 21 May in the following year of tax, or such later date as the Commissioner allows (s 68).

Employers are generally required to pay FBT by quarterly instalments and report these instalments on their 'activity statements' [40.3] (s 102). Quarterly instalments are not required where the employer's previous year's FBT liability was less than $3,000 (s 111). The date upon which quarterly instalments are due and payable depends on whether or not the employer is classified as a 'deferred BAS payer'. Entities that lodge quarterly GST returns or that are GST instalment payers [7.4] and entities that are not registered for GST but are required to pay quarterly PAYG instalments [39.4] are deferred BAS payers. The relevant payment dates are set out in the following table.

FBT instalment	Payment date	
	General taxpayers	Deferred BAS payers
First instalment for the year of tax	21 July in the year of tax	28 July in the year of tax
Second instalment for the year of tax	21 October in the year of tax	28 October in the year of tax
Third instalment for the year of tax	21 January in the year of tax	28 January in the year of tax
Fourth instalment for the year of tax	21 April in next year of tax	28 April in next year of tax

FBT instalments for a year of tax are based on the employer's 'notional tax amount', which is basically their previous year's FBT liability (ss 109 to 111). Each instalment is generally a quarter of the notional tax amount. Employers can also choose to pay instalments based on an estimate of their current year's FBT liability (s 112). However, the GIC may be payable if instalments based on an estimate are too low (s 112B) [40.8].

FBT instalments are credited against the employer's actual FBT liability for the year (s 105), which becomes due on 21 May in the following year of tax (s 90). The GIC is payable where FBT has not been paid by the due date (s 93) [40.8].

Example E Co is an employer that was liable to pay $40,000 of FBT for the 2022/23 FBT year. It is not a deferred BAS payer and has not chosen to estimate its FBT instalments for the 2023/24 FBT year. E Co must therefore pay FBT instalments for the 2023/24 FBT year of $10,000 on 21 July 2023, 21 October 2023, 21 January 2024 and 21 April 2024. If, when it lodges its return for the 2023/24 FBT year (by 21 May 2024), it has self-assessed that its FBT liability for the year is $55,000, it must pay a balance amount of $15,000 (ie $55,000 – $40,000). However, if it self-assessed that its FBT liability for the year was only $32,000, it would be entitled to a refund of $8,000 (ie $40,000 – $32,000).

Deductibility of FBT instalments

For income tax purposes, the cost of paying FBT (including FBT instalments) is generally deductible to an employer under s 8-1 *ITAA97*, as there is usually a sufficient nexus between the payment of the tax and the employer's income-producing or business activities.

The time at which FBT and FBT instalments are incurred is relevant in determining the income year in which the payments are deductible. According to TR 95/24, FBT is incurred by an employer at the end of the relevant FBT year (as it is at that time that the employer has a fringe benefits taxable amount upon which FBT is payable) and FBT instalments are incurred by an employer when the liability to pay them arises.

[18.3] Fringe benefits

The concept of a 'fringe benefit' lies at the heart of the FBT regime. The term 'fringe benefit' is defined in s 136(1) *FBTAA*. The definition contains both positive and negative limbs.

Positive limbs of the definition of fringe benefit

The positive limbs of the definition of fringe benefit are contained in paras (a) to (ea) of the s 136(1) definition. Under the positive limbs, a fringe benefit arises where:

- a benefit is provided during, or in respect of, the year of tax
- by an employer, an associate of the employer, or a third party under an arrangement with the employer or associate of the employer
- to an employee or an associate of the employee
- in respect of the employment of the employee.

The definition of fringe benefit is intentionally broad. A 'benefit' is defined widely to include any 'right', 'privilege', 'service' or 'facility' (s 136(1)). The term 'associate' is also defined widely, by reference to the definition in s 318 *ITAA36* [8.6], to cover relatives and certain related entities (s 136(1)). Likewise, the terms 'employer' and 'employee' also have broad meanings which include current, former or future employers and employees (s 136(1)). The fact that a fringe benefit can arise under an arrangement made with a third party also significantly extends the scope of a fringe benefit. This is particularly the case given the term 'arrangement' is defined widely in s 136(1).

Example Bob employs Sam. As part of Sam's remuneration package, Bob has an arrangement with his local mechanic to regularly service Sam's wife's car. Even though the benefit (the servicing of the car) is not provided directly by Bob to Sam, it constitutes a fringe benefit as it is provided by a third party (the mechanic) under an arrangement with the employer (Bob) to an associate of the employee (Sam's wife) in respect of Sam's employment.

Whether a benefit is provided 'in respect of' the employment of an employee must be considered in the context of s 148(1) *FBTAA*, which states that the provision of a benefit to a person in respect of the employment of an employee is a reference to the provision of such a benefit:

- whether or not the benefit is also provided in respect of any other matter or thing
- whether the employment will occur, is occurring, or has occurred
- whether or not the benefit is surplus to the needs or wants of the recipient
- whether or not the benefit is also provided to another person
- whether or not the benefit is, to any extent, offset by any inconvenience or disadvantage
- whether or not the benefit is provided or used in connection with that employment
- whether or not the benefit is in the nature of income, or
- whether or not the benefit is provided as a reward for services rendered, or to be rendered, by the employee.

Despite the breadth of the wording used in s 148, not all benefits provided by employers to employees will necessarily be fringe benefits. In *J & G Knowles & Associates Pty Ltd v FC of T* 2000 ATC 4151, the Full Federal Court pointed out that the fact that a benefit must be provided 'in respect of' employment means that there must be 'a nexus, some discernible and rational link, between the benefit and the employment'. A benefit that does not have a sufficient and material connection with an employee's employment would therefore not constitute a fringe benefit (*Starrim Pty Ltd v FC of T* 2000 ATC 4460; *Slade Bloodstock Pty Ltd v FC of T* 2007 ATC 5276). On this basis, a father who employs his daughter in his business would not be subject to FBT as a consequence of simply providing the daughter with a birthday gift, as the gift would not be connected with her employment. This interpretation is supported by the ATO in MT 2016.

For a benefit to constitute a fringe benefit, the benefit must be provided in respect of a particular employee (*Essenbourne v FC of T* 2002 ATC 5201). A fringe benefit does not arise where the identity of the particular employee that is to obtain the benefit is not known at the time the benefit is provided (*FC of T v Indooroopilly Children Services (Qld) Pty Ltd* 2007 ATC 4236).

In *Walstern Pty Ltd v FC of T* 2003 ATC 5076, the Federal Court held that no fringe benefit was provided when an employer made a contribution to a foreign superannuation fund, because the contribution had not been allocated for the benefit of any particular employee at that time. The trust deed provided that an employee would only become a member of the fund upon invitation by the trustee following a recommendation by the employer. The scheme also required the employee to contribute a certain amount to the fund, as determined by the trustee. This amount was then lent to the employee by the trustee (from the contribution received from the employer) and allocated to the employee's account. A fringe benefit nevertheless arose when the trustee (who was found to be an 'arranger' under the scheme) subsequently allocated an amount for the benefit of an employee.

Negative limbs of the definition of fringe benefit

The negative limbs of the definition of fringe benefit are contained in paras (f) to (s) of the s 136(1) definition. The negative limbs exclude 'salary or wages', 'exempt benefits' and a range of 'other benefits' from being fringe benefits.

Salary or wages

Paragraph (f) of the definition of fringe benefit excludes the payment of 'salary or wages' from being a fringe benefit. The reason for this exclusion is that salary or wages are assessed in the hands of employees under the general income tax rules. There is, therefore, no need for FBT to apply to these payments. For FBT purposes, the term 'salary or wages' is defined broadly in s 136(1) *FBTAA* to include certain payments from which amounts must be withheld under the PAYG provisions in the *TAA* [39.4]. The definition specifically mentions payments falling within s 12-35 *TAA*, which covers payments that would not ordinarily be salary or wages, such as 'allowances'.

Exempt benefits

Paragraph (g) of the definition of fringe benefit excludes an 'exempt benefit' from being a fringe benefit. There are many different kinds of exempt benefits under the *FBTAA*. For example, there are a number of specific exemptions that relate to particular categories of benefits; namely:

- exempt car benefits (s 8) [18.7]
- exempt loan benefits (s 17) [18.8]
- exempt expense payment benefits (ss 21, 22) [18.10]
- exempt property benefits (s 41) [18.17], and
- exempt residual benefits (s 47) [18.18].

In addition, there are a number of miscellaneous exempt benefits in div 13 of pt III *FBTAA*, which have their own detailed qualification criteria. Some examples of exempt benefits are listed below:

- car expense, property and residual benefits that relate to a car during a period when a car fringe benefit is provided (eg the provision of fuel) (s 53)
- benefits provided by certain international organisations (s 55)
- benefits provided to religious practitioners who are employees of registered religious institutions (s 57)
- benefits provided by registered public benevolent institutions, public hospitals, hospitals carried on by 'rebatable employers' (ie certain income tax-exempt entities [18.20]), public ambulance service providers and registered health promotion charities (s 57A)
- benefits in respect of employment interviews or selection tests (s 58A)
- engagement of a relocation consultant and removal or storage of an employee's household effects because the employee is required to live away from, or return to, their usual place of residence to perform employment duties (ss 58AA, 58B)
- car parking not at a commercial parking station where the employer is not a public company or government body and is an SBE or would be an SBE if the aggregated turnover threshold for an SBE was $50m (instead of $10m) [8.7] (s 58GA)
- newspapers and periodicals used by an employee for the purpose of gaining their salary or wages (s 58H)
- minor benefits with a taxable value under $300 (eg a small Christmas present) (s 58P)
- portable electronic devices, computer software, protective clothing, briefcases or tools of trade that are primarily for use in the employee's employment (s 58X)
- subscriptions to trade or professional journals and entitlements to use corporate credit cards and airport lounge memberships (s 58Y)
- taxi travel (otherwise than by limousine) beginning or ending at the employee's workplace (s 58Z)
- remote area housing benefits (s 58ZC), and
- education or training to redundant employees for the purpose of assisting them to gain new employment (s 58ZE).

Other benefits

Paragraphs (h) to (s) of the definition of fringe benefit exclude a broad range of other kinds of benefits from being fringe benefits. For instance, the following are excluded:

- benefits under an employee share scheme [21.1]
- deemed dividends [22.4]
- restraint of trade or personal injury payments of a capital nature
- most kinds of termination payments (eg ETPs [20.2], unused annual leave and long service leave payments [20.3], and early retirement scheme and genuine redundancy payments [20.4]), and
- most kinds of superannuation contributions and superannuation benefits.

Categories of benefits

The *FBTAA* recognises the following categories of 'benefits':

- car benefits (defined in s 7) [18.7]
- debt waiver benefits (defined in s 14) [18.8]

- loan benefits (defined in s 16) [18.9]
- expense payment benefits (defined in s 20) [18.10]
- housing benefits (defined in s 25) [18.11]
- living-away-from-home allowance benefits (defined in s 30) [18.12]
- board benefits (defined in s 35) [18.13]
- meal entertainment benefits (defined in s 37AC) [18.14]
- tax-exempt body entertainment benefits (defined in s 38) [18.15]
- car parking benefits (defined in s 39A) [18.16]
- property benefits (defined in s 40) [18.16], and
- residual fringe benefits (defined in s 45) [18.18].

In order for these benefits to constitute 'fringe benefits' and therefore be subject to FBT, they must satisfy the definition of fringe benefit in s 136(1). In other words, they must be provided by an employer (or associate, etc) to an employee (or associate) in respect of the employment of the employee and must not fall within the excluded categories of benefits. Benefits that are not provided in respect of employment, but are provided for some other reason, are therefore not fringe benefits.

[18.4] Calculating the taxable values of fringe benefits

Each fringe benefit has its own valuation rules, which are contained in divs 2 to 12 of pt III *FBTAA* [18.7]–[18.18]. These rules rely on cost price, market values, statutory formulas, benchmark interest rates and other criteria to calculate the taxable values of the particular fringe benefits. Importantly, where the cost of an item is relevant to calculate the taxable value of a fringe benefit, it is the 'GST-inclusive' cost that is used (TR 2001/2).

Although the taxable value of each fringe benefit is calculated differently, there are a number of consistent principles that generally apply throughout the legislation. These principles are outlined below and examined in more detail throughout this chapter.

In-house and external benefits

In some cases, the valuation rules distinguish between 'in-house' and 'external' benefits. Broadly speaking, in-house benefits are those kinds of benefits which the provider also provides in the ordinary course of business to 'outsiders' (eg members of the public). An example of an in-house benefit is the provision of floor stock by a furniture retailer to its employee. External benefits are other kinds of benefits. An example of an external fringe benefit is the provision of a television by a law firm to its employee. As a general rule, more concessional taxation treatment has traditionally been given to in-house benefits than external benefits. However, the legislation was amended in 2013 to remove the concessional treatment for in-house fringe benefits accessed by way of 'salary-packaging arrangements'. A salary-packaging arrangement is an arrangement where the employee receives a benefit:

- in return for a reduction in salary or wages that would not have happened apart from the arrangement, or
- as part of his or her remuneration package, and the benefit is provided in circumstances where it is reasonable to conclude that the employee's salary or wages would be greater if the benefit were not provided (s 136(1)).

This reform is designed to discourage employees from accessing concessionally taxed in-house goods and services out of their 'pre-tax income'.

Unreimbursed recipients contribution

The valuation rules contain internal mechanisms for reducing the taxable value of a fringe benefit by any unreimbursed contribution made by the recipient towards the cost of the benefit. This contribution is known as the 'recipients contribution' (s 136(1)). It is designed to ensure that the employer is only taxed on the net value of the benefit provided to the recipient.

Otherwise deductible rule

In many cases, the valuation rules operate subject to their own internal 'otherwise deductible' rules. Unfortunately, the provisions containing these rules are drafted in extremely long-winded and complex terms. In essence, they are designed to prevent 'double taxation' by reducing the taxable value of a fringe benefit to the extent that the employee has 'lost' a deduction because they have been provided with the fringe benefit instead of incurring the relevant expense themselves. For instance, the otherwise deductible rule would apply where an employer pays for expenditure that the employee could have otherwise claimed as a deduction (eg where the employer pays for the employee's cost of purchasing work-related stationery or attending a work-related conference). Where the otherwise deductible rule applies, the taxable value of a fringe benefit is reduced by a 'notional deduction', which is calculated under special formulas (see the examples at [18.9] and [18.10]).

The otherwise deductible rule only applies to reduce the taxable values of loan fringe benefits [18.9], expense payment fringe benefits [18.10], board fringe benefits [18.13], property fringe benefits [18.17] and residual fringe benefits [18.18]. Moreover, it only operates where the deduction that would otherwise have been allowed to the employee is a 'once-only' deduction (ie a deduction that is wholly allowable in a single income year: s 136(1) *FBTAA*). It does not therefore cover, for example, depreciation deductions that are spread over a number of years.

When calculating the deduction that would otherwise have been allowed to an employee, it is important to consider s 51AJ *ITAA36*, which denies a deduction to the extent that a contribution made by the employee is, in effect, for the private component of the fringe benefit [14.8].

Furthermore, when calculating the 'notional deduction', the substantiation provisions in div 900 *ITAA97* [14.2] are expressly ignored. The *FBTAA*, nevertheless, has its own substantiation provisions which generally only allow employers to use the otherwise deductible rule where they have obtained declarations and certain documentary evidence from their employees specifying the extent to which the expenditure would otherwise have been deductible.

The otherwise deductible rule only applies where a fringe benefit is provided to an employee. Where a fringe benefit is provided jointly to an employee and the employee's associate, the otherwise deductible rule only reduces the taxable value of the benefit to the extent that it relates to the employee's share of the benefit.

Reduction amounts

The taxable values of certain fringe benefits may be reduced by 'reduction amounts' contained in div 14 of pt III *FBTAA*. An example of a reduction amount is s 62, which states that the first $1,000 of the aggregate of any 'in-house fringe benefits' (excluding those under a salary-packaging arrangement) provided to an employee in a particular year of tax is not subject to FBT. There are also reduction amounts relating to:

- remote area residential fuel (s 59)
- remote area housing (s 60)
- remote area holiday transport (ss 60A, 61)
- overseas employment holiday transport (s 61A)
- relocation transport (s 61B)

- temporary accommodation relating to relocation (s 61C)
- temporary accommodation meal fringe benefits (s 61D)
- employment interviews and selection tests (s 61E)
- work-related medical examinations and preventative health care (s 61F)
- living-away-from-home food fringe benefits (s 63)
- entertainment component of certain fringe benefits (s 63A), and
- education of children of overseas employees (s 65A).

Reduction amounts should be distinguished from 'exempt benefits' [18.3]. An exempt benefit is not a fringe benefit and is therefore not subject to FBT. A reduction amount, on the other hand, reduces the taxable value of a fringe benefit. In some cases, it will reduce the taxable value to nil; in other cases, it will only partially reduce the taxable value.

[18.5] Fringe benefits taxable amount

An employer's FBT liability is calculated by multiplying the employer's 'fringe benefits taxable amount' for the year of tax by the FBT rate for the year of tax [18.2]. Calculating an employer's 'fringe benefits taxable amount' is complex as it involves the application of a number of intricate formulas and method statements, which are outlined below and explained further in TR 2001/2.

Subsection 5B(1B) and 5B(1C) amounts

Section 5B(1A) *FBTAA* states that an employer's 'fringe benefits taxable amount' is the sum of the 's 5B(1B) amount' and 's 5B(1C) amount'. These amounts are calculated according to the following formulas (which have been worked out using the 47% FBT rate and 10% GST rate):

$$\text{s 5B(1B) amount} = \begin{array}{c}\text{Type 1 aggregate fringe}\\ \text{benefits amount}\end{array} \times \frac{\text{FBT rate} + \text{GST rate}}{(1-\text{FBT rate}) \times (1+\text{GST rate}) \times \text{FBT rate}}$$

$$= \begin{array}{c}\text{Type 1 aggregate fringe}\\ \text{benefits amount}\end{array} \times 2.0802$$

$$\text{s 5B(1C) amount} = \begin{array}{c}\text{Type 2 aggregate fringe}\\ \text{benefits amount}\end{array} \times \frac{1}{1-\text{FBT rate}}$$

$$= \begin{array}{c}\text{Type 2 aggregate fringe}\\ \text{benefits amount}\end{array} \times 1.8868$$

The terms used in the above formulas have the following meanings:

- **Type 1 aggregate fringe benefits amount.** An employer's 'type 1 aggregate fringe benefits amount' is worked out under the method statement in s 5C(3). Basically, it is the sum of the taxable values of the fringe benefits provided during the year of tax in respect of the employer's employees that are GST-creditable benefits. A 'GST-creditable benefit' is defined in s 149A *FBTAA* and is, essentially, a benefit in respect of which the provider was entitled to an ITC for GST charged on the acquisition or importation of the thing provided as a fringe benefit [7.8]. It also covers a benefit which is a reimbursement for which an ITC is available to the provider under div 111 *GSTA*.
- **Type 2 aggregate fringe benefits amount.** An employer's 'type 2 aggregate fringe benefits amount' is worked out under the method statement in s 5C(4). Essentially, it is the sum of the taxable values of the remaining individual fringe benefits provided during the year of tax in respect of the employer's employees. For instance, it covers those benefits where the provider

is not registered for GST, or where the thing provided as a fringe benefit was acquired by the provider as a GST-free or input taxed supply [7.7].

As can be seen from the above formulas, the type 1 aggregate fringe benefits amount is multiplied by a gross-up rate of 2.0802 and the type 2 aggregate fringe benefits amount is multiplied by a gross-up rate of 1.8868. The gross-up is designed to neutralise the distinction between receiving fringe benefits and being paid salary. Without the gross-up there would be a bias in favour of receiving fringe benefits instead of salary. A higher gross-up rate is used for type 1 benefits to take account of the fact that the provider is entitled to benefit from ITCs as a result of acquiring the thing that is provided as a fringe benefit. If a higher gross-up rate was not used for GST-creditable benefits, this would provide a salary-packaging benefit (see further the discussion and examples at [18.22]). The rationale behind the gross-up is illustrated in the following example.

Example John employs Alex during the 2023/24 FBT year. As part of Alex's remuneration package, John paid Alex's son's secondary school fees, costing $10,000. This is an 'expense payment fringe benefit' that has a taxable value of $10,000. It is a 'type 2' fringe benefit as it relates to the supply of an education course which is GST-free under sub-div 38-C *GSTA* [7.7] and is, therefore, not eligible for ITCs. As a result, the grossed-up taxable value of the fringe benefit is $18,868 (ie $10,000 × 1.8868).

The $18,868 amount corresponds with the income that a taxpayer subject to the top marginal tax rate plus ML would have to earn to have $10,000 available after tax to pay school fees. In other words, if an employee subject to tax at the rate of 47% was paid salary of $18,868, the employee would be required to pay $8,868 in tax on this amount (ie $18,868 × 47%). This would leave the employee with $10,000 after tax to pay for school fees.

Aggregate non-exempt amount

18

Section 5B(1D) *FBTAA* states that if any benefits provided in respect of the employment of an employee are exempt benefits under s 57A *FBTAA*, the employer's fringe benefits taxable amount for the year of tax worked out under s 5B(1A) is increased by the employer's 'aggregate non-exempt amount'.

Section 57A treats as exempt benefits, benefits provided to employees of registered public benevolent institutions, public hospitals, hospitals carried on by rebatable employers, public ambulance service providers and registered health promotion charities [18.3].

The employer's aggregate non-exempt amount is worked out under the method statement in s 5B(1E). Essentially, it is the sum of the grossed-up taxable values of the s 57A exempt benefits provided to each individual employee during the FBT year that exceed the following thresholds:

- $17,000 (for employees involved in duties connected with public hospitals, hospitals carried on by rebatable employers or public ambulance service providers), and
- $30,000 (for employees involved in duties connected with registered public benevolent institutions and registered health promotion charities that are not covered by the $17,000 threshold).

The object of s 5B(1D) is to ensure that employers that provide exempt benefits falling under s 57A only benefit from the exemption up to the respective grossed-up taxable value limits outlined above per employee. Where the grossed-up taxable value of benefits provided to a particular employee exceeds these amounts, FBT will be payable on the excess.

Fringe benefits taxable amount formula

In summary, the various formulas discussed above can be combined into the following generic formula:

$$\text{Fringe benefits taxable amount} = \left[\text{Type 1 aggregate fringe benefits amount} \times 2.0802\right] + \left[\text{Type 2 aggregate fringe benefits amount} \times 1.8868\right] + \text{Aggregate non-exempt amount}$$

Example Dino employs Fred and Barney in his quarrying business. He provides them with the following benefits in addition to salary during the 2023/24 FBT year:

- Fred is given a TV which Dino purchased for $4,400 (inclusive of GST). This constitutes a 'property fringe benefit' which has a taxable value of $4,400 [18.17]. Assuming Dino is registered for GST, Dino is entitled to an ITC for the GST charged on the TV. The benefit is therefore a GST-creditable benefit (ie it is a 'type 1' benefit).
- Barney is reimbursed by Dino for the cost of purchasing an international airline ticket for $3,000 from Qantas. This constitutes an 'expense payment fringe benefit' which has a taxable value of $3,000 [18.10]. No GST has been charged on the supply of the international flight as it is GST-free (div 38-K *GSTA*) [7.7]. Dino is therefore not entitled to an ITC (even though he is registered for GST). The benefit is consequently not a GST-creditable benefit (ie it is a 'type 2' benefit).

Dino's fringe benefits taxable amount for the year is worked out below:

$$\begin{aligned}\text{Fringe benefits taxable amount} &= [\$4{,}400 \times 2.0802] + [\$3{,}000 \times 1.8868] \\ &= \$9{,}152 + \$5{,}660 \\ &= \$14{,}812\end{aligned}$$

Dino's FBT liability for the year is calculated as follows:

$$\begin{aligned}\text{FBT} &= \$14{,}812 \times 47\% \\ &= \$6{,}961\end{aligned}$$

Dino can deduct the FBT as well as the cost of the fringe benefits he has provided under s 8-1 *ITAA97* (except for the amount of the ITC in relation to the TV: s 27-5 *ITAA97*).

[18.6] Steps involved in calculating FBT

The following chart summarises the steps involved in calculating an employer's FBT liability:

1. Determine whether there is a fringe benefit

A fringe benefit arises under s 136(1) *FBTAA* where:

- a benefit is provided during the year of tax
- by an employer, an associate of the employer, or a third party under an arrangement with the employer or associate of the employer
- to an employee or an associate of the employee
- in respect of the employment of the employee.

Certain benefits are excluded (eg salary and wages, most superannuation benefits and exempt benefits).

↓

2. Identify the type of fringe benefit and calculate its taxable value

- Car fringe benefit (s 7) – taxable value (ss 9 or 10)
- Debt waiver fringe benefit (s 14) – taxable value (s 15)
- Loan fringe benefit (s 16) – taxable value (s 18)
- Expense payment fringe benefit (s 20) – taxable value (ss 22A or 23)
- Housing fringe benefit (s 25) – taxable value (s 26)
- Living-away-from-home allowance fringe benefit (s 30) – taxable value (ss 31, 31A or 31B)
- Board fringe benefit (s 35) – taxable value (s 36)
- Meal entertainment fringe benefit (s 37AC) – taxable value (ss 37BA or 37CB)
- Tax exempt body entertainment fringe benefit (s 38) – taxable value (s 39)
- Car parking fringe benefit (s 39A) – taxable value (ss 39C, 39D, 39DA, 39FA or 39GB)
- Property fringe benefit (s 40) – taxable value (ss 42 or 43)
- Residual fringe benefit (s 45) – taxable value (ss 48, 49, 50 or 51)

*Note: the taxable values of certain fringe benefits are reduced by 'reduction amounts' under div 14

↓

3. Calculate the fringe benefits taxable amount

Fringe benefits taxable amount = Type 1 benefits (ie GST-creditable benefits) aggregated and grossed up by 2.0802 + Type 2 benefits (ie other benefits) aggregated and grossed up by 1.8868 + Aggregated non-exempt amount

↓

4. Calculate the employer's FBT liability

FBT = Fringe benefits taxable amount × 47%

[18.7] Car fringe benefits

A 'car fringe benefit' is a fringe benefit that is a 'car benefit' (s 136(1) *FBTAA*). A car benefit arises where a car held by a provider is applied or available for the 'private use' of an employee or their associate. The provider must be the employer, an associate of the employer, or a third party who has a relevant arrangement with the employer or associate (s 7(1) *FBTAA*).

Private use means any use that is not exclusively in the course of gaining or producing assessable income. Where a car is garaged at or near an employee's or associate's place of residence, it is deemed to be available for private use (s 7(2)). This deeming rule does not apply to marked ambulance, fire-fighting or police cars fitted with flashing warning lights and alarms (s 7(2A)).

A car benefit is an 'exempt benefit' if the car is:

- a panel van or utility truck, designed to carry a load of less than one tonne
- used for taxi travel, designed to carry a load of less than one tonne, and is not a limousine, or
- any other road vehicle designed to carry a load of less than 1 tonne (other than a vehicle designed for the principal purpose of carrying passengers), and there was no private use of the car other than work-related travel of the employee and other minor, infrequent and irregular private use by the employee or their associate (s 8(2)).

A car benefit is also an exempt benefit if the car is unregistered and was wholly or principally used directly in connection with the business operations of the employer (or a related company) (s 8(3)).

To encourage the use of electric cars, s 8A treats a car benefit involving a 'zero or low emissions vehicle' (ie a battery, hydrogen fuel cell or plug-in hybrid electric vehicle) provided to a current employee as an exempt benefit. The exemption applies to vehicles that are first held and used on or after 1 July 2022 and only applies if no luxury car tax has been payable on the vehicle (ie its value is below the luxury car tax threshold for fuel efficient cars for the relevant year, being $89,332 in 2023/24) [4.3]. In the 2023 Budget, the Government announced that this exemption will be removed from 1 April 2025.

Taxable value of a car fringe benefit

Employers generally calculate the taxable value of a car fringe benefit according to the 'statutory formula' method contained in s 9 *FBTAA*. They can, however, elect to use the 'cost basis' method contained in s 10 *FBTAA* where it results in a lower taxable value. The way the statutory formula and cost basis methods work is outlined below.

Statutory formula

The statutory formula for calculating the taxable value of a car fringe benefit is (s 9(1)):

$$\text{Taxable value} = \left[0.2 \times \begin{matrix}\text{Base value}\\ \text{of the car}\end{matrix} \times \frac{\begin{matrix}\text{Number of days}\\ \text{during that year of tax}\\ \text{on which the car fringe benefits}\\ \text{were provided by the provider}\end{matrix}}{\begin{matrix}\text{Number of days}\\ \text{in that year of tax}\end{matrix}}\right] - \begin{matrix}\text{Amount}\\ \text{(if any)}\\ \text{of the}\\ \text{recipient's}\\ \text{payment}\end{matrix}$$

Base value of the car

The 'base value of the car' is based on the 'cost price' of the car (if the car is owned by the provider) or the 'leased car value' (if the car is leased by the provider) (s 9(2)). The terms 'cost price' and 'leased car value' are defined in lengthy terms in s 136(1). The cost price includes expenditure that is directly attributable to the acquisition or delivery of the car (other than registration and transfer costs such as stamp duty). It also includes additional expenditure fitting non-business accessories to the car at or about the time the car was acquired (eg an air conditioner).

Where a car has been held by the provider for more than four years at the commencement of the FBT year, the base value of the car is determined by multiplying the cost price or leased car value by two-thirds to reflect the decline in value of the car. For example, if the cost price of a car in Year 1 is \$60,000, its base value in Year 5 and following years is \$40,000 (\$60,000 × 2/3).

0.2 Rate

The statutory formula uses a flat rate of 0.2. This rate replaces four different rates that declined with the increased distance travelled by the car during the FBT year. The new flat rate applies regardless of the distance travelled.

Recipient's payment

The recipient's payment is the sum of any unreimbursed payments made by the recipient as consideration for the provision of the car and any unreimbursed expenses incurred by the recipient in relation to the car (eg fuel, registration, insurance and maintenance costs) (s 9(2)). The recipient must provide the employer with documentary evidence of the expenses (declarations can be used to substantiate fuel and oil expenses).

Cost basis

Under the cost basis method, the taxable value of a car fringe benefit is calculated as follows (s 10(2)):

$$\text{Taxable value} = (C \times (100\% - BP)) - R$$

18

C (operating cost)

'C' is the operating cost of the car (s 10(3)). The operating cost is the sum of any car expenses (eg fuel, maintenance, registration and insurance) relating to the car during the holding period. If the car is owned by the provider, the operating cost includes 'deemed depreciation' and 'deemed interest', which are calculated under special formulas contained in s 11 (illustrated in the example below). If the car is leased by the provider, the operating cost includes lease charges.

BP (business percentage)

'BP' is the business percentage (s 10(3)). It is the percentage of business use of the car during the holding period. Business use is based on the employer's reasonable estimate of the number of business kilometres which the car travels during the holding period. It is deemed to be 'nil' if logbook and odometer records (similar to those required under the substantiation provisions [14.2]) have not been maintained (ss 10A, 10B).

R (recipient's payment)

'R' is the recipient's payment (s 10(3)). The recipient's payment is defined in identical terms to the way in which it is defined for the purposes of the statutory formula method (discussed above).

Example Barry is Sam's employer. On 1 April 2023, Barry purchased a car for $40,000 which he made available for Sam's private use throughout the 2023/24 FBT year. Sam travelled 18,000 km in the car during this period. His car records indicate that the business use of the car was 20%. The fuel, maintenance, registration and insurance costs in relation to the car for the 2023/24 FBT year amounted to $5,000 of which Sam paid $2,000. The way that the taxable value of the car fringe benefit is calculated under the statutory formula and cost basis methods is set out below. Note that the statutory formula method must be used as it produces a lower taxable value than the cost basis method.

$$\text{Statutory formula taxable value} = \left[0.2 \times \text{Base value of the car} \times \frac{\text{Number of days during that year of tax on which the car fringe benefits were provided by the provider}}{\text{Number of days in that year of tax}}\right] - \text{Amount (if any) of the recipient's payment}$$

$$= [0.2 \times \$40{,}000 \times 365/365] - \$2{,}000$$
$$= \$8{,}000 - \$2{,}000$$
$$= \$6{,}000$$

$$\text{Cost basis taxable value} = \big(C \times (100\% - BP)\big) - R$$
$$= \big(\$5{,}000^{(a)} + \$10{,}000^{(b)} + \$3{,}108^{(c)}\big) \times (100\% - 20\%) - \$2{,}000$$
$$= \$18{,}108 \times 80\% - \$2{,}000$$
$$= \$12{,}486$$

(a) $5,000 is the fuel, maintenance, registration and insurance costs in relation to the car for the 2023/24 FBT year.

(b) $10,000 is the 'deemed depreciation' relating to the car for the 2023/24 FBT year which is calculated under the formula in s 11(1) (see below). Element B of the formula is 25%, being the 'deemed depreciation rate'.

$$\frac{ABC}{D} = \frac{\$40{,}000 \times 0.25 \times 365}{365}$$
$$= \$10{,}000$$

(c) $3,108 is the 'deemed interest' relating to the car for the 2023/24 FBT year calculated under the formula in s 11(2) (see below). Element B of the formula is 7.77%, being the 'statutory interest rate' for the 2023/24 FBT year.

$$\frac{ABC}{D} = \frac{\$40{,}000 \times 0.0777 \times 365}{365}$$
$$= \$3{,}108$$

[18.8] Debt waiver fringe benefits

A 'debt waiver fringe benefit' is a fringe benefit that is a 'debt waiver benefit' (s 136(1) *FBTAA*). A debt waiver benefit arises where a person waives the obligation of another person to pay or repay a debt (s 14 *FBTAA*).

Taxable value of a debt waiver fringe benefit

The taxable value of a debt waiver fringe benefit is the amount of the payment or repayment that has been waived (s 15 *FBTAA*).

Example Ian is Larry's employer. On 1 August 2023, Ian released Larry from having to repay 50% of a $2,000 debt owing to Ian. The taxable value of the debt waiver fringe benefit is $1,000.

[18.9] Loan fringe benefits

A 'loan fringe benefit' is a fringe benefit that is a 'loan benefit' (s 136(1) *FBTAA*).

A loan benefit arises where a person makes a loan to another person (s 16(1) *FBTAA*). The concept of a 'loan' is defined widely in s 136(1) and includes an 'advance of money', 'the provision of credit or any other form of financial accommodation' and a transaction 'which in substance effects a loan of money'.

A loan is also deemed to arise where an amount that a person is under an obligation to pay is not paid on the date (s 16(2)).

Furthermore, where a 'deferred interest loan' (ie a loan on which interest is payable at intervals of more than six months) is made, the provider is deemed to have made additional loans of the accrued interest for each six-month period (s 16(3)).

Example An employer provides an employee with an 18-month loan under which interest is payable at the end of the Loan. In addition to the 18-month loan, there are two interest-free deferred interest loans.

- The first deferred interest loan arises at the end of month 6 and lasts 12 months (from the beginning of month 7 to the end of month 18).
- The second deferred interest loan arises at the end of month 12 and lasts six months (from the beginning of month 13 to the end of month 18).

18

A loan benefit is an 'exempt benefit' under the *FBTAA* where:

- The provider carries on a business that includes making loans to the public and the interest rate charged on the loan is not less than the rate charged on similar arm's length loans made in the ordinary course of business to members of the public (different requirements apply to fixed and variable loans) (ss 17(1), (2)).
- The employer makes a loan to a current employee for the sole purpose of enabling the employee to meet expenses incurred in performing duties within six months of the making of the loan (the loan must not substantially exceed the expected expenses and the employee must account for the expenses within six months and repay any amount not accounted for) (s 17(3)).
- The employer makes a loan for the sole purpose of enabling the employee to pay a rental bond, security deposit in respect of electricity, gas or telephone services or any similar amount in relation to temporary accommodation, and the loan is required to be repaid within 12 months (certain additional requirements must also be satisfied) (s 17(4)).

Taxable value of a loan fringe benefit

The taxable value of a loan fringe benefit is the amount (if any) by which the 'notional amount of interest' in relation to the loan in respect of the year of tax exceeds the 'actual amount of interest' that has accrued on the loan in respect of the year of tax (s 18 *FBTAA*).

In the vast majority of cases, the notional amount of interest is the amount of interest that would have accrued on the loan in the year of tax if the interest were calculated on a daily balance based on the 'statutory interest rate' for the year of tax (s 136(1) *FBTAA*). The statutory interest rate is the 'benchmark interest rate' for the FBT year. This rate is based on the Reserve Bank of Australia's indicator variable interest rate for housing loans that is last published before the commencement of the FBT year. The statutory interest rates over the last few FBT years are set out in the following table:

Statutory interest rates					
FBT Year	2019/20	2020/21	2021/22	2022/23	2023/24
Rate	5.37%	4.80%	4.52%	4.52%	7.77%

Special rules apply to the following loans:

- **Fixed interest loans made before 1 July 1986.** For these loans, the notional amount of interest is the lesser of: (a) the statutory interest rate at the time the loan was provided (these rates are set out in the Schedule to the *FBTAA*); and (b) the statutory interest rate for the year of tax.
- **Variable interest housing loans made before 3 April 1986.** For these loans, the notional amount of interest is the lesser of: (a) the statutory interest rate for the year of tax; and (b) 13.5%.

Otherwise deductible rule

Where the loan is used wholly or partly by the employee to produce assessable income (eg to acquire an income-producing property), the otherwise deductible rule in s 19 *FBTAA* reduces the taxable value of the fringe benefit by a 'notional deduction' calculated as follows:

$$\text{Notional deduction} = GD - RD$$

- **GD** is the amount of the once-only deduction to which the employee would have been entitled if he or she had incurred the notional amount of interest in respect of the loan.
- **RD** is the amount of the once-only deduction to which the employee is actually entitled in respect of the loan.

Example Errol lends $10,000 to his employee Brad on the basis that he pays monthly interest at the rate of 2% pa. During the 2023/24 FBT year, Brad pays all interest payments owing under the loan when they become due but does not repay any of the principal sum. He uses 20% of the borrowed funds for income-producing purposes and the balance for private purposes. The taxable value of the loan fringe benefit for the 2023/24 FBT year is calculated as follows:

$$\begin{aligned}\text{Taxable value} &= [\text{Notional amount of interest} - \text{Actual amount of interest}] - [GD - RD]\\ &= [(\$10{,}000 \times 7.77\%) - (\$10{,}000 \times 2\%)] - [(\$10{,}000 \times 7.77\% \times 20\%) - (\$10{,}000 \times 2\% \times 20\%)]\\ &= [\$777 - \$200] - [\$155.40 - \$40]\\ &= \$577 - \$115.40\\ &= \$461.60\end{aligned}$$

[18.10] Expense payment fringe benefits

An expense payment fringe benefit is a fringe benefit that is an 'expense payment benefit' (s 136(1) *FBTAA*).

An 'expense payment benefit' arises where a person pays for or reimburses expenditure incurred by another person (s 20 *FBTAA*).

A reimbursement arises where the recipient is compensated precisely for the whole or part of an expense already incurred, even though it may not necessarily have been disbursed (TR 92/15). As Hill J observed in *Roads & Traffic Authority (NSW) v FC of T* 93 ATC 4508 (at 4514), 'the concept of reimbursement requires that the payment in question be made by reference to actual cost'.

A reimbursement may be contrasted with an 'allowance'. An allowance is not a reimbursement and does not therefore constitute an expense payment benefit. An allowance arises where a person is paid a definite predetermined amount to cover an estimated expense regardless of whether or not the expense is actually incurred. An allowance is generally taxed under the income tax rules instead of the FBT rules, as it falls within the definition of 'salary or wages' in s 136(1) and is therefore not a fringe benefit [18.3].

An expense payment benefit is an 'exempt benefit' under the *FBTAA* where:

- It is covered by a 'no private use' declaration. Such a declaration must be in the approved form and may be made where the employer will only pay or reimburse so much of an expense payment fringe benefit that results in its taxable value being nil (ie the employer will only pay for or reimburses employment-related expenses) (s 20A).
- It relates to expenses that an employee incurs on accommodation for eligible family members and the accommodation is required solely because the employee is required to live away from the employee's usual place of residence to carry out employment duties. To qualify for the exemption, the employee must provide the employer with an appropriate declaration in the approved form (s 21).
- It relates to a reimbursement of certain car expenses relating to a car that is owned or leased by the employee where the reimbursement is based on the distance travelled by the car (eg a cents per kilometre reimbursement) (s 22).

Taxable value of an expense payment fringe benefit

The taxable value of an expense payment fringe benefit depends on whether it is classified as an 'in-house' or 'external' fringe benefit.

There are two kinds of in-house expense payment fringe benefits:

- 'in-house property expense payment fringe benefits'—which arise where the expense relates to the acquisition of property of a kind provided by the employer or an associate of the employer in the ordinary course of their business, and
- 'in-house residual expense payment fringe benefits'—which arise where the expense relates to the acquisition of other benefits of a kind provided by the employer or an associate of the employer in the ordinary course of their business.

All other expense payment fringe benefits are external expense payment fringe benefits (s 136).

The taxable value of an 'in-house property expense payment fringe benefit' is calculated by reference to the valuation rule in s 42 *FBTAA*, which relates to 'in-house property fringe benefits' [18.17] (s 22A(1)).

The taxable value of an 'in-house residual expense payment fringe benefit' is calculated by reference to the valuation rules in ss 48 and 49 *FBTAA*, which relate to 'in-house residual fringe benefits' [18.18] (s 22A(2)).

The taxable value of an external expense payment fringe benefit is the amount of the expenditure that is paid or reimbursed by the provider of the benefit reduced by the recipients contribution (s 23).

Otherwise deductible rule

Where an employee is provided with the benefit and he or she would have been entitled to a once-only deduction if he or she had incurred the payment incurred by the provider of the benefit, the otherwise deductible rule in s 24 *FBTAA* reduces the taxable value of the fringe benefit by a 'notional deduction' calculated as follows:

$$\text{Notional deduction} = \text{GD} - \text{RD}$$

- **GD** is the amount of the once-only deduction to which the employee would have been entitled if he or she had incurred unreimbursed expenditure equal to:
  (a) for an in-house expense payment fringe benefit—the amount that would have been the taxable value of the fringe benefit (ignoring any reductions under div 14 of pt III *FBTAA* or recipients contribution), or
  (b) for an external expense payment fringe benefit—the amount of his or her expenditure.
- **RD** is the amount of the once-only deduction to which the employee is actually entitled in respect of his or her actual expenditure.

Example Daniel is employed as a solicitor in Dorothy's law firm. Daniel purchased an ink cartridge for $500 from his local department store. The ink cartridge is for his home printer, which Daniel uses 60% for work purposes and 40% for private purposes. Dorothy reimburses Daniel the full $500 for the cost of the ink cartridge. The reimbursement is an external expense payment fringe benefit. Its taxable value is calculated as follows:

$$\begin{aligned}\text{Taxable value} &= \text{Amount of reimbursement} - [\text{GD} - \text{RD}]\\ &= \$500 - [(500 \times 60\%) - (\text{Nil} \times 60\%)]\\ &= \$500 - \$300\\ &= \$200\end{aligned}$$

[18.11] Housing fringe benefits

A 'housing fringe benefit' is a fringe benefit that is a 'housing benefit' (s 136(1) *FBTAA*). A housing benefit arises where a 'housing right' has been granted by one person to another person (s 25 *FBTAA*). A housing right is a lease or licence to occupy or use a unit of accommodation as a person's usual place of residence (s 136(1)).

Taxable value of a housing fringe benefit

The taxable value of a housing fringe benefit varies depending on whether the accommodation is outside Australia, in a non-remote part of Australia, or in a remote area of Australia (s 26 *FBTAA*).

If the accommodation is outside Australia, or in an external territory, the taxable value of the housing benefit will be the market value of the accommodation for the time it is occupied during the year, less any rent or other consideration paid.

If the accommodation is in Australia and is not in a remote area, the taxable value of the housing fringe benefit depends on the type of accommodation. If the accommodation is in a hotel, motel, hostel, guesthouse, caravan or mobile home and the provider is in the business of providing similar benefits to the public, the taxable value of the housing fringe benefit is:

- if the provider is not the employer, the market value of the accommodation less any rent paid, or
- if the provider is the employer, 75% of the amount that the public would pay less any rent paid.

For any other type of accommodation in a non-remote area, the taxable value is the 'statutory annual value' of the right to occupy the accommodation, less any rent paid by the employee. In the first year in which the accommodation is used to provide a housing fringe benefit, the statutory annual value is the market value of the right to occupy the accommodation for a year. In subsequent years, the 'statutory annual value' is either:

- the current year's market value, or
- the previous year's market value increased by the relevant indexation factor.

For the 2023/24 FBT year, the indexation factor by which the previous year's market value is to be multiplied is set out in the following table.

NSW	Vic	Qld	SA	WA	Tas	ACT	NT
1.009	1.006	1.046	1.039	1.087	1.055	1.053	1.100

Example As part of his remuneration package, Fred is provided with use of a three-bedroom apartment in Adelaide from 1 April 2022. The market rent for the apartment was $46,800 ($900 per week) in the 2022/23 FBT year and $52,000 ($1,000 per week) in the 2023/24 FBT year.

For the 2023/24 FBT year, the taxable value of the fringe benefit can be calculated as either:

(a) $52,000 (ie the market value for the 2023/24 FBT year), or

(b) $48,625 (ie the market value for the 2022/23 FBT year ($46,800) increased by the indexation factor of 1.039).

The taxable value of the fringe benefit is reduced by any rent paid by Fred. Accordingly, if he paid $200 per week in rent during the 2023/24 FBT year, the taxable value of the fringe benefit would be reduced by $10,400 (ie 52 × $200).

18

If the indexation method is used, then the actual market value must be redetermined at least each tenth year. Likewise, where the accommodation has been materially altered resulting in an increase or decrease of at least 10% in its market value, the accommodation is treated as different accommodation and its market value must be redetermined.

[18.12] Living-away-from-home allowance fringe benefits

A 'living-away-from-home allowance fringe benefit' is a fringe benefit that is a 'living-away-from-home benefit' (s 136(1) *FBTAA*). A living-away-from-home benefit' arises where an employer pays an allowance to an employee, which is in the nature of compensation for additional non-deductible expenses (or additional non-deductible expenses and additional disadvantages) incurred because the employee is required to live away from his or her usual place of residence in order to perform employment duties (s 30 *FBTAA*).

Taxable value of a living-away-from-home allowance fringe benefit

The taxable value of a living-away-from-home allowance fringe benefit is calculated under either ss 31, 31A or 31B *FBTAA*:

- Section 31 applies where:
  - the employee maintains a home in Australia at which they usually reside that continues to be available for their immediate use and enjoyment during the period that their employment duties require them to live away from home, and it is reasonable to expect that they will resume living at that place when the period ends (s 31C)
  - the fringe benefit relates to only the first 12 months that the employee's employment duties require them to live away from home (s 31D), and
  - the employee provides the employer with a declaration about living away from home (s 31F).
- Section 31A applies where:
  - the employee, on a regular and rotational basis, works for a number of days and has a number of days off (which are not the same days in consecutive weeks) and on completion of the work returns to their normal residence (which does not need to be in Australia)
  - the basis of work is customary for employees performing similar duties
  - it is unreasonable to expect the employee to travel between work and their normal residence on a daily basis given the locations of those places
  - it is reasonable to expect that the employee will resume living at their normal residence when their duties no longer require them to live away from home (s 31E), and
  - the employee provides the employer with a declaration about living away from home (s 31F).
- Section 31B applies in any other case not covered by the above sections.

Where either ss 31 or 31A apply, the taxable value of the fringe benefit is the amount of the fringe benefit reduced by the 'exempt accommodation component' and the 'exempt food component':

- The exempt accommodation component is the amount incurred by the employee for the accommodation (s 136(1)).
- The exempt food component is so much of the 'food component' less the 'applicable statutory food total' as equals the total expenses incurred by the employee for food or drink for eligible family members (ie for themselves and their spouse and children living with them) (s 31H). The 'food component' is so much of the fringe benefit as might reasonably be concluded to be compensation for expenses incurred by the employee for food or drink for eligible family members (s 136(1)). The 'applicable statutory food total' is $42 per week for persons aged 12 years or more and $21 per week for persons aged under 12 years (s 136(1)).

The exempt accommodation component and the exempt food component must generally be substantiated (s 31G). However, the exempt food component does not require substantiation if it does not exceed an amount the Commissioner considers reasonable. TD 2023/2 sets out the relevant amounts for the 2023/24 FBT year.

Where s 31B applies, the taxable value of the fringe benefit is simply the amount of the fringe benefit.

In effect, the provisions ensure that living-away-from-home allowance fringe benefits are taxed concessionally if they involve employees who maintain a home in Australia or who have fly-in fly-out and drive-in drive-out arrangements, but not in any other cases.

Example In the current FBT year, Fred works in Perth for 10 weeks. During this period, he lives away from his usual residence in Melbourne, which continues to be available for his use and enjoyment. His employer pays him a living-away-from-home allowance of $850 per week while he works in Perth. The allowance comprises:

- $500 per week for accommodation, and
- $350 per week for food and drink (note: this amount exceeds the amount the Commissioner considers reasonable for a single person to spend per week on food and drink in Australia under TD 2023/2 (ie $316)).

Fred spent the whole $500 per week on leasing a flat in Perth, but he only spent $260 of the $350 per week on food. He can substantiate all his expenses.

The provision of the allowance constitutes a living-away-from-home fringe benefit, which falls within s 31. The taxable value of the fringe benefit is calculated as follows:

Total allowance (per week)		$850
Less:		
Exempt accommodation component (per week)	$500	
Exempt food component* (per week)	$260	
		$760
Taxable value of allowance (per week)		$90
Taxable value of allowance for FBT year ($90 × 10)		$900

* Note: the exempt food component is only $260 as this is less than $308 (ie $350 – $42).

[18.13] Board fringe benefits

A 'board fringe benefit' is a fringe benefit that is a 'board benefit' (s 136(1) *FBTAA*). A board benefit arises where a person provides a 'board meal' to another person. Essentially, a board meal is a meal prepared on eligible premises (eg the employer's premises or a worksite) that is provided by the employer or a related company to an employee or their associate under an industrial award or employment agreement which requires the provision of accommodation and at least two meals per day (s 35 *FBTAA*). 18

Taxable value of a board fringe benefit

The taxable value of a board fringe benefit is $2 per meal (if the recipient was at least 12 years old at the beginning of the FBT year) and $1 per meal (in any other case) reduced by the amount paid by the recipient for the meal (s 36 *FBTAA*).

Example Josh works on an oil rig. Under his employment agreement, he is entitled to accommodation and two meals per day prepared on his employer's premises. Over the year, his employer provides 400 meals to Josh. The taxable value of the board fringe benefits provided to Josh during the year is $800 (ie $2 × 400).

Otherwise deductible rule

Where the employee would have been entitled to an income tax deduction for expenditure on the meal under s 8-1 *ITAA97*, the otherwise deductible rule in s 37 *FBTAA* reduces the taxable value of the fringe benefit by a 'notional deduction' calculated as follows:

$$\text{Notional deduction} = \text{GD} - \text{RD}$$

- **GD** is the amount of the deduction to which the employee would have been entitled under s 8-1 *ITAA97* if he or she had incurred unreimbursed expenditure in respect of the meal equal to what would have been the taxable value of the fringe benefit (ignoring any reductions under div 14 of pt III *FBTAA* or recipients contribution), and
- **RD** is:
  (a) if there is no recipients contribution in relation to the benefit—nil, or
  (b) if there is a recipients contribution in relation to the benefit—the amount of the once-only deduction to which the employee is actually entitled under s 8-1 *ITAA97* in respect of his or her expenditure.

[18.14] Meal entertainment fringe benefits

A 'meal entertainment fringe benefit' is a fringe benefit that is a 'meal entertainment benefit' (s 136(1) *FBTAA*). A meal entertainment benefit arises where an employer provides 'meal entertainment' to a recipient (s 37AC *FBTAA*). Meal entertainment consists of the provision of:

(a) entertainment by way of food or drink
(b) accommodation or travel in connection with, or for the purpose of facilitating, such entertainment, or
(c) the payment or reimbursement of expenses incurred in providing (a) or (b) (s 37AD).

Taxable value of a meal entertainment fringe benefit

Ordinarily, a meal entertainment benefit would be taxed under the appropriate FBT rules discussed elsewhere in this chapter (eg as a property, expense payment or residual fringe benefit depending on how it is provided). However, to reduce compliance costs associated with such benefits, an employer may elect that 'meal entertainment fringe benefits' be taxed in accordance with special rules in div 9A *FBTAA* (in which case they will not be taxed under the other rules).

An employer that elects to use div 9A can choose to calculate the taxable value of meal entertainment fringe benefits for the year of tax under either of the following methods:

- **The 50/50 split method (s 37BA).** Under this method, the taxable value of the meal entertainment fringe benefits is 50% of the expenses incurred by the employer in providing meal entertainment benefits to all persons (ie both employees and other persons) for the FBT year (reduced by unreimbursed amounts paid by employees and their associates).
- **The 12-week register method (s 37BC).** Under this method, the taxable value of the meal entertainment fringe benefits is determined by reference to a 12-week register kept by the employer to determine the employer's percentage of meal entertainment fringe benefits. The taxable value is the 'total meal entertainment expenditure' incurred by the employer on all persons in the year (reduced by unreimbursed amounts paid by employees and their associates) multiplied by the register percentage.

Example An employer's total meal entertainment expenditure in an FBT year is $100,000. The employer maintains a 12-week register which allows the employer to determine that 30% of meal entertainment expenditure was provided as a fringe benefit. The taxable value of meal entertainment fringe benefits provided is $30,000 (ie 30% × $100,000). If no register is maintained, the taxable value of the meal entertainment fringe benefits provided is $50,000 (ie 50% × $100,000).

[18.15] Tax-exempt body entertainment fringe benefits

A 'tax-exempt body entertainment fringe benefit' is a fringe benefit that is a 'tax-exempt body entertainment benefit' (s 136(1) *FBTAA*).

A tax-exempt body entertainment benefit arises where a person incurs 'non-deductible exempt entertainment expenditure' that is wholly or partly in respect of the provision, in respect of the employment of an employee, of 'entertainment' to the employee or his or her associate (s 38 *FBTAA*).

Non-deductible exempt entertainment expenditure is defined as 'non-deductible entertainment expenditure' to the extent to which it is *not* incurred in producing assessable income (s 136(1)). Non-deductible entertainment expenditure is a loss or outgoing to the extent to which s 32-5 *ITAA97* applies to it (or would apply to it if it were incurred in producing assessable income) and that would be deductible under s 8-1 *ITAA97* (or would be deductible if it were incurred in producing assessable income) assuming s 32-20 *ITAA97* had not been enacted [14.4] (s 136(1)).

In basic terms, tax-exempt body entertainment benefits therefore typically arise where income tax-exempt employers provide entertainment (eg a meal at a restaurant) to their employees or their employees' associates.

Taxable value of a tax-exempt body entertainment fringe benefit

The taxable value of a tax-exempt body entertainment fringe benefit is so much of the expenditure referred to in s 38 as is attributable to the provision of the entertainment (s 39 *FBTAA*).

> ***Example*** Charity Co is an income tax-exempt employer. It provides opera tickets together with a meal at a restaurant for one of its employees and a client costing $400 in total. The provision of the tickets and meal for the employee (but not for the client) constitutes a tax-exempt body entertainment fringe benefit. The taxable value of the fringe benefit is $200 (ie $400/2).

[18.16] Car parking fringe benefits

18

A 'car parking fringe benefit' is a fringe benefit that is a 'car parking benefit' (s 136(1) *FBTAA*).

A 'car parking benefit' arises where car parking is provided to an employee at, or in the vicinity of, his or her primary place of employment and used in connection with travel by the employee between such place and his or her residence (s 39A *FBTAA*). The parking must be provided between 7am and 7pm on the provider's 'business premises' or 'associated premises' (for a duration that exceeds four hours). A commercial parking station must be located within 1 km of the premises and the lowest fee charged by the operator in the ordinary course of business to the public for all-day parking on the first business day of the relevant FBT year must be more than the indexed 'car parking threshold' for the year as set out in the table below.

Car parking threshold					
FBT year	2019/20	2020/21	2021/22	2022/23	2023/24
Rate	$8.95	$9.15	$9.25	$9.72	$10.40

Car parking fringe benefits have been considered in a string of cases involving airline employees. In *Virgin Blue Airlines Pty Ltd v FC of T* 2010 ATC ¶20-226, the Full Federal Court held that car parking facilities provided around 2 km from an employee's primary place of employment were not 'in the vicinity of' that place and therefore did not result in a car parking fringe benefit.

Subsequently, in *Qantas Airways Limited v FC of T* 2014 ATC ¶20-477, Qantas had provided its employees that worked at or near airports with car parking at its business or associated premises.

All airports had short-term and long-term car parking facilities within one kilometre of the premises which could be used for a fee. The parking facilities at Canberra airport were special in that the operator imposed a restriction that they were only available to airline passengers and persons meeting and greeting them. Qantas argued that the car parking facilities at the airports were not 'commercial parking stations' for the purposes of s 39A because they were not provided primarily for use by commuters driving their cars to and from work, but rather by travellers and persons greeting them. The AAT, however, rejected this and held that the *FBTAA* did not seek to differentiate car parking facilities by reference to any class of intended primary customers or uses. According to the AAT the provision of car parking facilities (other than those at Canberra) constituted car parking benefits. On appeal, the Full Federal Court held that the provision of parking facilities at *all* airports constituted car parking benefits. According to the Court there was no ambiguity about the word 'public'. The car parking in Canberra was available to the public—the contractual terms imposed by the operator merely meant that there were conditions imposed on the public's use of the car park'.

More recently, in *FC of T v Virgin Australia Airlines Pty Ltd* 2021 ATC ¶20-807, the Full Federal Court held that an airline was liable for FBT on car parking facilities provided to flight and cabin crew near their homebase airports as their primary place of employment was the homebase airport where they worked rather than the aircraft on which they performed their duties.

Taxable value of a car parking fringe benefit

The taxable value of a car parking fringe benefit may be ascertained by using one of the following five methods in the *FBTAA*:

- the commercial parking station method (s 39C)
- the market value method (s 39D)
- the average cost method (s 39DA)
- the statutory formula method (s 39FA), or
- the 12-week record-keeping method (ss 39GA, 39GB).

An employer may choose any of the methods for a year in which a car parking fringe benefit arises. If the employer elects to use either the statutory formula method or the 12-week record-keeping method, the selected method must be used for all benefits covered by the election.

Commercial parking station method

Under the commercial parking station method, the taxable value of a car parking fringe benefit on a particular day is the lowest all-day parking fee charged in the ordinary course of business by any commercial parking station within a 1 km radius of the relevant business premises or associated premises on which the car is parked. The taxable value is reduced by any contribution made by the recipient.

Example Mei's employer provides parking to its employees on 240 days per year. Mei contributes $2 per day towards the parking. The lowest daily commercial parking fee charged by City Carpark (which is 100 metres from the employer's business premises) is $13. The taxable value of the fringe benefits provided to Mei during the year is $2,640 (ie ($13 – $2) × 240).

Market value method

Under the market value method, the taxable value of a car parking fringe benefit on a particular day is the amount that the recipient could reasonably be expected to have been required to pay for the benefit if the provider and the recipient were dealing with each other at arm's length. The relevant market value is to be determined by a suitably qualified arm's length valuer. The taxable value is reduced by any contribution by the recipient.

Example Ruben's employer provides parking to its employees on 240 days per year. Ruben contributes \$2 per day. A qualified valuer determines that the market value of the car parking spaces provided is \$17. The taxable value of the fringe benefits provided to Ruben during the year is \$3,600 (ie (\$17 – \$2) × 240).

Average cost method

Under the average cost method, the taxable value of a car parking fringe benefit is determined by reference to an average of the lowest all-day parking fees charged by any operator of a commercial parking station within a 1 km radius of the employer's premises on the first and last days on which the benefit is provided in the FBT year. The taxable value is reduced by any contribution made by the recipient.

Example Tony's employer provided him with car parking throughout the 2023/24 FBT year. Tony contributed \$2 per day for the parking. There are two commercial parking stations within 1 km of the employer's premises. The daily parking fee charged by X Carpark was \$13 on 1 April 2023 and \$17 on 31 March 2024. The daily fee charged by Y Carpark was \$9 on 1 April 2023 and \$18 on 31 March 2024. The taxable value of each car parking fringe benefit provided to Tony during the year is calculated as follows: \$11 = [(\$9 + \$17)/2] – \$2.

Statutory formula method

Under the statutory formula method, the taxable value of each space for which there is at least one car parking benefit for an employee is calculated by using the formula:

$$\text{Daily rate amount} = \frac{\text{Number of days in availability}}{366} \times 228$$

The 'daily rate amount' is the value of the benefit provided (ie the space) as determined under either the 'average cost method', 'commercial parking station method' or 'market value method', assuming no recipients contribution.

The total taxable value of the car parking fringe benefits under this method will be the sum of each of the taxable values, reduced by any recipients contribution. The employer must record the number of car parking spaces available over the FBT year. If the average number of employees covered by the election is less than the average number of spaces provided, the taxable value of the benefits is reduced on a proportionate basis by the formula contained in s 39FB.

18

Example An employer has 44 employees at the beginning, and 56 at the end, of the FBT year. This is an average of 50 employees (ie (44 + 56)/2) for the FBT year. The employer provides 30 parking spaces. The benefits are provided for only half the FBT year and the taxable value of each benefit calculated under the 'average cost' method is \$10.

Under the statutory formula method, the taxable value of one benefit is calculated as follows:

$$\$1{,}140 = \$10 \times \frac{183}{366} \times 228$$

The total taxable value of the car parking fringe benefits is therefore \$34,200 (ie \$1,140 × 30).

If the employees contributed a total of \$10,000 towards the benefits during the FBT year, the total taxable value of the car parking fringe benefits would be \$24,200 (ie \$34,200 – \$10,000).

12-week record-keeping method

Under the 12-week record-keeping method, an employer must keep a register of the taxable values of the car parking benefits provided during a representative 12-week period and use the register to calculate the total taxable value of the car parking benefits for the FBT year. The taxable value of each car parking benefit provided during the 12-week period must be determined in accordance with either the commercial parking station method, the market value method or the average cost method. The register is generally valid for up to five years. However, it ceases to be valid if the number of car parking fringe benefits increases by more than 10% on any day in the FBT year. The total taxable value of the car parking benefits for the FBT year is calculated using the formula:

$$\text{Total value of car parking benefits (register)} \times \frac{52}{12} \times \frac{\text{Number of days in car parking availability periods}}{366}$$

Example After keeping a register for 12 weeks, an employer determines that 250 car parking benefits, each with a taxable value of $20 (using the commercial parking station method), have been provided to employees during that period. Car parking benefits are provided by the employer from 1 October to the end of the FBT year. The total taxable value of the benefits is calculated as follows: $10,833 = 250 × $20 × 52/12 × 183/366.

[18.17] Property fringe benefits

A 'property fringe benefit' is a fringe benefit that is a 'property benefit' (s 136(1) *FBTAA*). A property benefit arises where a person provides property to another person (s 40 *FBTAA*). 'Property' is defined in s 136(1) to include both 'tangible' and 'intangible' property.

A property benefit is an 'exempt benefit' where it is provided to, and consumed by, the employee on a working day on the employer's (or related company's) business premises. This exemption does not apply to food or drink provided under a salary-packaging arrangement (s 41).

Taxable value of a property fringe benefit

The taxable value of a property fringe benefit depends upon whether it is classified as an 'in-house' or an 'external' property fringe benefit.

An in-house property fringe benefit can only arise in respect of the provision of 'tangible property' and exists where:

- the employer or an associate of the employer provides the property, and the property is of a sort normally sold as part of the provider's business, or
- a third party provides the property, after acquiring it from the employer or an associate of the employer, and the property is of a sort normally sold by both the provider and the person from whom it is acquired as part of their businesses.

All other property fringe benefits are external property fringe benefits (s 136(1)).

The taxable values of in-house and external property fringe benefits are calculated under rules contained in s 42 and s 43 *FBTAA*. Some of these rules refer to the 'notional value' of the property, which is the amount that the person could reasonably be expected to have been required to pay to obtain the property from the provider under an arm's length transaction (s 136(1)).

Special rules apply to an in-house property fringe benefit that is an 'airline transport fringe benefit'. Broadly speaking, such a benefit arises where transport is provided in a passenger aircraft and is subject to the stand-by restrictions that customarily apply in relation to the provision of airline transport to employees in the airline industry (s 136(1)). The taxable value of an airline transport fringe benefit is based on the 'stand-by airline travel value', which is:

- for transport over a domestic route—50% of the carrier's lowest standard single economy airfare for that route as publicly advertised during the year of tax, or
- for transport over an international route—50% of the lowest of any carrier's standard single economy airfare for that route as publicly advertised during the year of tax (s 136(1)).

The rules in ss 42 and 43 are outlined below:

- **In-house property fringe benefits.** The taxable value of an in-house property fringe benefit is calculated as follows:
  - Where the property is provided to the recipient under a salary-packaging arrangement—the taxable value is the notional value of the property at the provision time, reduced by the recipients contribution (s 42(1)(aa)).
  - Where s 42(1)(aa) does not apply and the benefit is an airline transport fringe benefit—the taxable value is 75% of the stand-by airline travel value of the benefit at the time the transport starts, reduced by the recipients contribution (s 42(1)(ab)).
  - Where neither ss 42(1)(a) nor (ab) apply, the taxable value is calculated as follows:
    (i) If the property was manufactured, produced, processed or treated by the provider and identical property was sold by the provider in the ordinary course of business to manufacturers, wholesalers or retailers—the taxable value is the lowest price at which identical property was sold, or could reasonably have been expected to be sold, under an arm's length transaction at the provision time, reduced by the recipients contribution (s 42(1)(a)(i)).
    (ii) If the property was manufactured, produced, processed or treated by the provider and identical property was sold by the provider in the ordinary course of business to the public (but not to manufacturers, wholesalers or retailers) in similar circumstances and identical terms (other than price)—the taxable value is 75% of the lowest price at which identical property was sold to the public, reduced by the recipients contribution (s 42(1)(a)(ii)).
    (iii) If the property was manufactured, produced, processed or treated by the provider and neither (i) nor (ii) above applies—the taxable value is 75% of the notional value of the property at the provision time reduced by the recipients contribution (s 42(1)(a)(iii)).
    (iv) If the property was *not* manufactured, produced, processed or treated by the provider, but was acquired by the provider—the taxable value is the lesser of: (a) the provider's arm's length acquisition price of the property; and (b) the notional value of the property at the provision time, reduced by the recipients contribution (s 42(1)(b)).
    (v) In any other case—the taxable value is 75% of the notional value of the property at the provision time, reduced by the recipients contribution (s 42(1)(c)).
- **External property fringe benefits.** The taxable value of an external property fringe benefit is calculated as follows:
  - Where the provider is the employer (or associate) and the property was purchased under an arm's length transaction—the taxable value is the cost price of the property to the provider, reduced by the recipients contribution (s 43(a)).
  - Where the provider is *not* the employer (or associate) and the employer (or associate) incurred expenditure to the provider under an arm's length transaction in respect of the provision of the property—the taxable value is the amount of the expenditure, reduced by the recipients contribution (s 43(b)).
  - In any other case—the taxable value is the notional value of the property at the provision time, reduced by the recipients contribution (s 43(c)).

> ***Example*** Lucy is employed by a law firm. Her employer provides her with a TV which the firm acquired in an arm's length transaction for $4,000. Lucy contributes $1,000 towards the cost of the TV. The benefit is an external property fringe benefit and its taxable value is $3,000 (ie $4,000 – $1,000).

Otherwise deductible rule

Where the employee is provided with the benefit and would have been entitled to a once-only deduction if he or she purchased the property, the otherwise deductible rule in s 44 *FBTAA* reduces the taxable value of the fringe benefit by a 'notional deduction' calculated as follows:

$$\text{Notional deduction} = GD - RD$$

- **GD** is the amount of the once-only deduction to which the employee would have been entitled if he or she had purchased the property for its taxable value (ignoring any reductions under div 14 of pt III *FBTAA* or recipients contribution), and
- **RD** is the amount of the once-only deduction to which the employee is actually entitled in respect of his or her expenditure to purchase the property.

[18.18] Residual fringe benefits

A 'residual fringe benefit' is a fringe benefit that is a 'residual benefit' (s 136(1) *FBTAA*). A residual benefit arises where the benefit is not covered by any one of the other specific categories of benefits mentioned above (s 45 *FBTAA*).

In *Westpac Banking Corporation v FC of T* 96 ATC 5021, the Full Federal Court held that the provision by a bank of free loan establishment services to its employees constituted a residual benefit.

Likewise, in *Kumagai Gumi Co Ltd v FC of T* 99 ATC 4316, the Federal Court held that a Japanese company that had paid the Australian income tax liabilities of its Japanese executives who had been transferred to Australia had provided 'residual fringe benefits'. The payments were treated as residual fringe benefits because Hill J considered that there was a problem in characterising the payments as 'expense payment benefits' since there were difficulties in characterising the executives' income tax liabilities as 'expenditure incurred' by them for the purposes of s 20.

Other illustrations of residual benefits would be the provision of legal advice by a law firm to one of its employee solicitors and the provision of free gym use by a fitness centre to one of its aerobics instructors.

The following residual benefits are 'exempt benefits' under the FBTAA:

- The provision of transport (otherwise than in an aircraft) to a current employee between their residence and place of employment by an employer or associate that carries on business of providing transport to the public (s 47(1)).
- The provision of public transport to a police officer for travel between their residence and primary place of employment (s 47(1A)).
- The provision to a current employee of recreational and child care facilities located on the business premises of the employer or a related company (s 47(2)).
- The provision to a current employee of the use of property (other than a motor vehicle) located on business premises and used in connection with business operations of the employer or a related company (s 47(3)).
- The provision of accommodation to an employee who is required to live away from his or her usual place of residence in order to perform employment duties so long as the accommodation

is not provided while the employee is undertaking travel in the course of performing their Employment duties (the employee must generally provide the employer with a declaration) (s 47(5)).

- The provision to a current employee of a motor vehicle that is not a car or any other road vehicle designed to carry a load of less than one tonne where the only Private use of the vehicle is for work-related travel or other minor and infrequent use (s 47(6)).
- The provision to a current employee of a motor vehicle that was unregistered throughout the FBT year and that was wholly or principally used directly in connection with business operations of the employer or a related company (s 47(6A)).
- The provision to an employee whose usual place of employment is on an oil rig or other installation at sea or in a remote area of transport between their usual place of employment and usual place of residence (certain other conditions must also be met) (s 47(7)).
- The provision of contributions made under a program administered by the Families Department to obtain priority of access to certain child-minding facilities for children of an employee (s 47(8)).

A residual fringe benefit that is covered by a 'no private use' declaration is also an exempt benefit (s 47A).

Taxable value of a residual fringe benefit

The taxable value of a residual fringe benefit depends upon whether it is classified as:

- an 'in-house non-period residual fringe benefit'
- an 'in-house period residual fringe benefit'
- an 'external non-period residual fringe benefit', or
- an 'external period residual fringe benefit'.

The concept of 'in-house' and 'external' residual fringe benefits is similar to the concept of 'in-house' and 'external' property fringe benefits [18.17]. Accordingly, an in-house residual benefit arises where a residual benefit is provided by an employer whose business includes providing identical or similar benefits in the ordinary course of its business.

18

A 'period' residual fringe benefit is a residual fringe benefit which is provided over a period exceeding one day (s 149 *FBTAA*). Residual fringe benefits provided over a day or less are 'non-period' residual fringe benefits.

The taxable values of in-house non-period and period residual fringe benefits and external non-period and period residual fringe benefits are calculated under rules contained in ss 48 to 51 *FBTAA*. Some of these rules refer to the 'notional value' of the benefit, which is the amount that the person could reasonably be expected to have been required to pay to obtain the benefit from the provider under an arm's length transaction (s 136(1)). Special rules apply to in-house residual fringe benefits that are airline transport fringe benefits [18.17].

The rules in ss 48 to 51 are outlined below:

- **In-house non-period residual fringe benefits.** The taxable value of an in-house non-period residual fringe benefit is calculated as follows:
  - Where the benefit is provided to the recipient under a salary-packaging arrangement—the taxable value is the notional value of the benefit at the comparison time, reduced by the recipients contribution (s 48(aa)).
  - Where s 48(aa) does not apply and the benefit is an airline transport fringe benefit—the taxable value is 75% of the stand-by airline travel value [18.17] of the benefit at the comparison time, reduced by the recipients contribution (s 48(ab)).

   - Where neither s 48(aa) nor s 48(ab) apply and, at or about the comparison time, identical benefits were provided by the provider in the ordinary course of business to members of the public under arm's length transactions and in similar circumstances and subject to identical terms (other than price)—the taxable value is 75% of the lowest price at which an identical benefit was sold to a member of the public, reduced by the recipients contribution (s 48(a)).
   - In any other case—the taxable value is 75% of the notional value of the benefit at the comparison time, reduced by the recipients contribution (s 48(b)).
- **In-house period residual fringe benefits.** The taxable value of an in-house period residual fringe benefit is calculated as follows:
   - Where the benefit is provided to the recipient under a salary-packaging arrangement—the taxable value is the notional value of the benefit at the comparison time, reduced by the recipients contribution (s 49(aa)).
   - Where s 49(aa) does not apply and the benefit is an airline transport fringe benefit—the taxable value is 75% of the stand-by airline travel value [18.17] of the benefit at the comparison time, reduced by the recipients contribution (s 49(ab)).
   - Where neither s 49(aa) nor s 49(ab) apply and, at or about the comparison time, identical overall benefits were provided by the provider in the ordinary course of business to members of the public under arm's length transactions and in similar circumstances and subject to identical terms (other than price)—the taxable value is 75% of the lowest amount payable by any member of the public for an identical overall benefit, reduced by the amount of the recipients contribution (s 49(a)).
   - In any other case—the taxable value is 75% of the notional value of the current benefit, reduced by the recipients contribution (s 49(b)).
- **External non-period residual fringe benefits.** The taxable value of an external non-period residual fringe benefit is calculated as follows:
   - Where the provider is the employer (or associate) and the benefit was purchased under an arm's length transaction—the taxable value is the amount paid or payable by the provider for the benefit, reduced by the recipients contribution (s 50(a)).
   - Where the provider is *not* the employer (or associate) and the employer (or associate) incurred expenditure to the provider under an arm's length transaction in respect of the provision of the benefit—the taxable value is the amount of the expenditure, reduced by the recipients contribution (s 50(b)).
   - In any other case—the taxable value is the notional value of the benefit at the comparison time, reduced by the recipients contribution (s 50(c)).
- **External period residual fringe benefits.** The taxable value of an external period residual fringe benefit is calculated as follows:
   - Where the provider is the employer (or associate) and the overall benefit was purchased under an arm's length transaction—the taxable value is the amount paid or payable by the provider for the benefit, reduced by the recipients contribution (s 51(a)).
   - Where the provider is *not* the employer (or associate) and the employer (or associate) incurred expenditure to the provider under an arm's length transaction in respect of the provision of the current benefit—the taxable value is the amount of the expenditure, reduced by the recipients contribution (s 51(b)).
   - In any other case—the taxable value is the notional value of the current benefit, reduced by the recipients contribution (s 51(c)).

Otherwise deductible rule

Where a residual fringe benefit is provided to an employee and he or she would otherwise have been entitled to a once-only deduction for the cost of acquiring the benefit, the otherwise deductible rule in s 52 *FBTAA* reduces the taxable value of the residual fringe benefit by a 'notional deduction' calculated as follows:

$$\text{Notional deduction} = GD - RD$$

- **GD** is the amount of the once-only deduction to which the employee would have been entitled if he or she had acquired the benefit for its taxable value (ignoring any reductions under div 14 of pt III *FBTAA* or the recipients contribution), and
- **RD** is the amount of the once-only deduction to which the employee is actually entitled in respect of his or her expenditure to acquire the benefit.

In *Roads and Traffic Authority of NSW v FC of T* 93 ATC 4508, a statutory authority had provided accommodation in huts and caravans for its employees at work sites. The Federal Court held that this gave rise to residual fringe benefits whose taxable values could be reduced to nil under s 52 *FBTAA*, as the employees would have been entitled to deduct the cost of the accommodation under former s 51 *ITAA36* if they had paid for the accommodation themselves.

More recently, in *John Holland Group Pty Ltd v FC of T* 2015 ATC ¶20-510, two construction companies provided flights to transport their employees between Perth and Geraldton to work on rail projects. The Full Federal Court held that this also gave rise to residual benefits whose taxable values could be reduced to nil under s 52 *FBTAA*, as the cost of the flights would have been deductible to the employees under s 8-1 *ITAA97* if they had incurred the expenditure themselves [12.7].

[18.19] Relaxed FBT rules

Relaxed liability rules

To reduce compliance costs, pt XIA *FBTAA* (ss 135A to 135L) provides employers, who would otherwise have small FBT liabilities, with the option of using relaxed rules for calculating their FBT liabilities and for keeping their FBT records [40.2]. 18

To qualify for this special treatment, the employer must have established a 'base year' and must not have been given a notice by the Commissioner in the previous FBT year requiring the employer to resume ordinary record-keeping (s 135B).

An FBT year is a 'base year' if:

- the employer has carried on business operations throughout the FBT year
- the employer has lodged an FBT return for the FBT year within the time allowed
- the employer has kept all records for the FBT year as required under s 132 [40.2]
- the employer's aggregate fringe benefits amount for the FBT year does not exceed the indexed 'exemption threshold' for the year ($9,786 for 2023/24), and
- s 135G does not apply to the employer for the FBT year (s 135C).

Where the employer qualifies under pt XIA, the employer can work out their FBT liability for the FBT year under s 66 *FBTAA* [18.2] using the 'aggregate fringe benefits amount' from the 'base year' (s 135G). An employer also has the choice to use the current year's 'aggregate fringe benefits amount' to calculate their FBT liability for the FBT year (eg where this amount is lower).

The aggregate fringe benefits amount from the base year cannot be used if the employer is a government body or is exempt from income tax (s 135J). It also cannot be used where the aggregate fringe benefits amount for the current year is more than 20% greater than the aggregate fringe benefits amount for the most recent base year (unless the difference is less than $100) (s 135K).

Relaxed record-keeping rules

There are numerous provisions in pt III *FBTAA* requiring employees to provide information to their employers about fringe benefits they have received and requiring employers to prepare certain declarations. This has forced employers to create 'statutory evidentiary documents' even though the required information may already exist elsewhere. To reduce compliance costs, the Commissioner has been given the power to make legislative instruments that determine the kinds of alternative records employers may keep in lieu of statutory evidentiary documents (s 123AA).

[18.20] FBT rebate for not-for-profit employers

The cost of paying FBT is generally deductible to most employers under s 8-1 *ITAA97* as it is an outgoing incurred in gaining or producing their assessable income or carrying on their businesses [18.2]. Tax-exempt employers, however, are not entitled to deductions for the payment of FBT. This is because the outgoing is incurred in gaining or producing their exempt income and therefore falls within the third negative limb of s 8-1 *ITAA97* [12.4].

A special FBT rebate exists under s 65J *FBTAA* to compensate certain not-for-profit employers for the fact that they cannot benefit from tax deductions relating to FBT because they are exempt from tax. The rebate is provided to 'rebatable employers', which are defined as employers that are exempt from income tax under any of the provisions set out in the table in s 65J(1) and that satisfy the special conditions in that table. The table covers a range of entities that are exempt from tax under various provisions in div 50 *ITAA97*, including registered charities, scientific and public educational institutions covered by s 50-5 *ITAA97* [11.4].

The FBT rebate is calculated as follows:

$$\begin{matrix}\text{Rebate}\\\text{of FBT}\end{matrix} = \text{FBT rate} \times \left[\begin{matrix}\text{Gross}\\\text{tax}\end{matrix} - \begin{matrix}\text{Aggregate}\\\text{non-rebatable}\\\text{income}\end{matrix}\right] \times \frac{\text{Rebatable days in year}}{\text{Total days in year}}$$

The meanings of the terms used in the above formula are as follows:

- **Gross tax** means the FBT that would otherwise be Payable on the employer's fringe benefits taxable amount for the year of tax assuming s 65J was ignored.
- **Aggregate non-rebatable amount** means the amount calculated in accordance with s 65J(2B).
- **Rebatable days in year** means the number of days in the FBT year during which the employer was engaged in activities covered by ss 65J(1)(a) to (l).
- **Total days in year** means the total number of days in the FBT year.

By subtracting the aggregate non-rebatable amount from the gross tax, the above formula ensures that the FBT rebate does not apply to the individual grossed-up amounts of benefits that exceed $30,000 (ie the higher aggregate non-exempt amount threshold calculated under s 5B(1E) *FBTAA* [18.5]).

[18.21] FBT general anti-avoidance rule

The provisions in the *FBTAA* operate subject to a general anti-avoidance rule contained in s 67 *FBTAA*. Section 67 is designed to deter tax avoidance schemes and has a broadly similar role in respect of FBT as pt IVA *ITAA36* has in respect of income tax [37.3].

In broad terms, the Commissioner can rely on s 67 where an arrangement is entered into for the sole or dominant purpose of reducing an employer's FBT liability. Under s 67, the Commissioner may cancel the tax benefit arising under the arrangement and impose penalty tax under sub-div 284-C of sch 1 *TAA* [41.2].

[18.22] Fringe benefits and salary packaging

It is common for employers to provide their employees with fringe benefits under 'salary-packaging arrangements'. These arrangements are also commonly known as 'salary sacrifice arrangements' as they involve employees agreeing to forgo a portion of the salary that they would otherwise be paid by their employers in exchange for receiving certain benefits that they would otherwise have to purchase out of their after-tax income.

ATO position on salary sacrifice arrangements

TR 2001/10 contains the Commissioner's position on salary sacrifice arrangements. The ruling distinguishes between 'effective' and 'ineffective' salary sacrifice arrangements.

- **Effective salary sacrifice arrangement.** An 'effective' salary sacrifice arrangement arises where the employee entered into the arrangement before they earned the entitlement to receive the salary. Under an effective salary sacrifice arrangement, the employee is not assessed on the sacrificed salary nor the benefit received due to the exemption in s 23L *ITAA36* [8.5].
- **Ineffective salary sacrifice arrangement.** An 'ineffective' salary sacrifice arrangement arises where an employee enters into the arrangement after they have earned the entitlement to receive the salary. Under an ineffective salary sacrifice arrangement, the employee would be assessed on the salary that has been applied to provide the benefit under the constructive receipt rule in s 6-5(4) *ITAA97* [9.9] and the exemption in s 23L *ITAA36* would not apply.

Converting the cost of fringe benefits into an equivalent salary amount

As a general rule, employers will usually be prepared to provide benefits to their employees instead of paying them salary, so long as the employer's cost of providing the benefits is taken into account in calculating the salary component of the employee's remuneration package. As FBT is payable on fringe benefits, employers need to convert the cost of providing fringe benefits into an equivalent salary amount to work out how much to reduce the employee's salary under a salary sacrifice arrangement. The following example illustrates how this is done.

18

Example Chandler is employed by Monica in her coffee shop during the 2023/24 FBT year. As part of Chandler's remuneration package, Monica agrees to reimburse Chandler for the cost of a six-month gym membership costing $1,100 (inclusive of GST). Under their arrangement, Chandler's salary is to be reduced by an appropriate amount that reflects Monica's cost of providing the benefit in equivalent salary terms.

The benefit is an external expense payment fringe benefit that has a taxable value of $1,100 [18.10]. It is a GST-creditable benefit and is therefore a 'type 1 benefit' that must be grossed-up by 2.0802 [18.5]. The grossed-up taxable value of the benefit is therefore $2,288 (ie $1,100 × 2.0802). Monica will therefore have to pay FBT on this benefit of $1,075 (ie $2,288 × 47%).

Assuming Monica is registered for GST, she is entitled to a $100 ITC for the cost of the gym membership as it constitutes a creditable acquisition [7.8]. Her net cost of providing the membership is therefore its GST-exclusive cost of $1,000 plus the $1,075 payable in FBT. As both these amounts are deductible like salary, the salary equivalent cost of the benefit to Monica is therefore $2,075 (ie $1,000 + $1,075). Monica would therefore need to reduce the salary component of Chandler's remuneration package by $2,075.

Situations where salary sacrifice arrangements are not tax-effective

It is important to realise that as fringe benefits are generally taxed at a rate that is equivalent to the top marginal tax rate plus ML, salary-packaging arrangements will often not be of any benefit to employees. This is because, in many cases, the reduction that is required to be made to the employee's salary to compensate the employer for the cost of providing the benefit will be the same amount that it would cost the employee in pre-tax salary to pay for the benefit. In these cases, there will be no benefit in undertaking the salary sacrifice arrangement.

Example Assume that in the previous example, Chandler is subject to income tax at the rate of 47%. If Monica had not reimbursed the cost of Chandler's gym membership, it would have cost Chandler $2,075 in pre-tax salary to pay for the $1,100 gym membership. This is because if he earned $2,075 in salary he would have had to pay tax on this amount of $975 (ie $2,075 × 47%). This would leave him with after-tax income of $1,100 (ie $2,075 – $975). Providing the fringe benefit therefore has no benefit to Chandler, as the reduction in his salary equals his pre-tax cost of acquiring the benefit.

Where the employee is subject to income tax at a rate that is below the FBT rate, salary packaging can actually be detrimental to the employee. This is because the reduction in salary made to compensate the employer for the cost of providing the benefit may be greater than the pre-tax salary required by the employee to pay for the benefit.

Example If, in the previous example, Chandler was subject to tax at the rate of 34.5%, instead of 47%, he would actually be worse off under the salary sacrifice arrangement. This is because his salary would need to be reduced by $2,075 to compensate Monica for the cost of providing the benefit, yet he would only have had to earn pre-tax salary of $1,679 to pay for the $1,100 gym membership. This is because if he earned $1,679 in salary he would have to pay tax on this amount of $579 (ie $1,679 × 34.5%). That would leave him with after-tax income of $1,100 (ie $1,679 – $579).

Situations where salary sacrifice arrangements are tax-effective

In practice, salary sacrifice arrangements are most tax-effective where they involve the provision of 'exempt benefits'. This is because the employer only needs to reduce the employee's salary by the cost of providing the benefit less any ITC available to the employer. There is no FBT payable on an 'exempt benefit' as it is not a fringe benefit [18.3]. As a result, the employer does not need to be compensated for the cost of any FBT. At the same time, as an exempt benefit is exempt income in the hands of the employee under s 23L(1A) [8.5], the employee is not liable to pay income tax on the benefit. The following example illustrates how providing an exempt benefit can be tax-effective.

Example Chandler is subject to income tax at the rate of 47%. His employer, Monica, pays for his taxi travel from home to work during the 2023/24 FBT year at a total cost of $1,100 (inclusive of GST). This benefit is an exempt benefit under s 58Z [18.3]. Monica does not therefore have to pay any FBT. Assuming Monica is entitled to ITCs totalling $100 in relation to the cost of providing the taxi travel, she would only need to reduce the salary component of Chandler's remuneration package by $1,000. Chandler is better off by reducing his pre-tax salary by $1,000 as he would have otherwise had to earn pre-tax salary of $2,075 to pay for the $1,100 benefit. This is because if he earned $2,075 in salary he would have had to pay tax on this amount of $975 (ie $2,075 × 47%). This would then leave him with after-tax income of $1,100 (ie $2,075 – $975) to spend on the taxi travel.

Salary sacrifice arrangements can also be tax-effective where they involve the provision of fringe benefits that have their taxable values calculated on a concessional basis. For instance, this may arise where the taxable value of the fringe benefit is calculated under a concessional formula or where the taxable value of the fringe benefit is reduced by a 'reduction amount'. However, it must be pointed out that the number of fringe benefits which have their taxable values calculated on a concessional basis has been steadily shrinking over the years. In particular, the concessional treatment provided to in-house fringe benefits accessed by way of 'salary-packaging arrangements' has recently been removed [18.4].

Anti-avoidance provisions

When structuring salary sacrifice arrangements, taxpayers need to make sure that their arrangements are not caught by the general anti-avoidance provisions in s 67 *FBTAA* [18.21] or pt IVA *ITAA36* [37.3]. Where these provisions apply, any tax benefits obtained under the arrangements may be cancelled and penalties imposed.

[18.23] QUESTIONS

1. Who pays FBT and what is the FBT tax rate? Are payments of FBT deductible?
2. Discuss the positive and negative elements of the definition of 'fringe benefit'. What are the different categories of fringe benefits? What kinds of benefits are exempt from FBT?
3. George is employed as a journalist. His employer pays him an allowance of $50 per week to cover the costs of any newspapers and magazines he may want to purchase. Is the allowance a fringe benefit?
4. What is the object of the 'otherwise deductible' rule? To which fringe benefits does it apply? What is the difference between a 'reduction amount' and an 'exempt benefit'?
5. Explain the steps involved in calculating an employer's 'fringe benefits taxable amount'. What is the difference between the 'Type 1 aggregate fringe benefits amount' and the 'Type 2 aggregate fringe benefits amount'? Why are these amounts multiplied by different 'gross-up' rates? 18
6. Errol provides his employee with the use of a car for 183 days during the FBT year. During this period the car travelled 16,000 km. Errol purchased the car at the beginning of the FBT year for $50,000. The employee contributed $1,000 towards the cost of running the car and has provided Errol with relevant documentation. Calculate the taxable value of the car fringe benefit using the statutory formula.
7. Terry is given a Porsche by his employer. Is this a car benefit or a property benefit? He is also provided with free accommodation for a month in a house owned by his employer. Is this a housing benefit or a property benefit?
8. Brian is a bank executive. As part of his remuneration package, his employer provided him with a three-year loan of $1m at an interest rate of 1% per annum (payable in monthly instalments). The loan was provided on 1 April 2023. Brian used 40% of the borrowed funds for income-producing purposes and met all his obligations in relation to the interest payments. Calculate the taxable value of this fringe benefit for the 2023/24 FBT year. Would your answer be different if the interest was only payable at the end of the loan rather than in monthly instalments? What would happen if the bank released Brian from repaying the interest on the loan?
9. John is a senior executive with a printing company. As part of his remuneration package, his employer pays his child's school fees of $15,000. His employer also provides him with

accommodation in a Sydney apartment throughout the FBT year. John must pay $100 of rent per week for the apartment. The market value rent for the apartment is $800 per week. Discuss the FBT consequences of John's remuneration package.

10. Discuss the different ways that the taxable value of car parking fringe benefits may be calculated.
11. Gerry is a salesman employed by a furniture retailer. Gerry's employer allowed him to purchase floor stock for $2,200 during the current FBT year. The same floor stock would ordinarily be sold to customers for $8,800. What is the taxable value of this fringe benefit?
12. How does TR 2001/10 distinguish between effective and ineffective salary sacrifice arrangements? Explain how an employer would convert the cost of a fringe benefit into an equivalent salary amount.

SUPERANNUATION 19

[19.1] Introduction

Most developed countries have policies to ensure that their citizens can rely on some form of income in retirement. Australia has adopted a three-pillar retirement income policy consisting of a publicly funded age pension combined with privately funded compulsory and voluntary superannuation. The object of the three-pillar approach is to ensure that retirement income responsibility is shared between the Government and individuals.

The age pension was first introduced in 1909 and is an integral part of the social security system. It is provided by the Government out of public funds on a means-tested basis that takes into account a person's income and assets. To be eligible to receive the age pension, a person must meet residency requirements and have reached the qualifying age (67 years from 1 July 2023). The age pension is a 'safety net' designed to ensure that aged persons have sufficient income to enjoy a minimum standard of living in retirement. It is intended to cover people with low incomes and insufficient retirement savings.

Superannuation is a heavily regulated private savings scheme. Superannuation savings are built up over a person's working life through contributions made to their superannuation funds. Employers are required to provide minimum levels of compulsory superannuation support for their employees under the 'superannuation guarantee' ('SG') scheme. People can also voluntarily make personal superannuation contributions to build up their benefits so they can enjoy a better standard of living in retirement. Making superannuation contributions is encouraged through the provision of various tax concessions and government co-contributions.

Superannuation funds are established as trusts. A small number of superannuation schemes are also established under legislation. Trustees of superannuation funds invest the contributions they receive. Depending on the terms of the fund deed and its investment strategy, contributions may be invested in a broad range of investments, including Australian and international bank deposits, bonds, shares and property. The contributions, together with earnings (less any fees and taxes), are used to pay superannuation benefits to members (on retirement) or to their dependants or trustees of their estates (on death). Superannuation benefits may be paid as 'lump sums' or 'income streams'. In the majority of cases, superannuation benefits paid to persons aged 60 and over are tax-free.

Superannuation is important for Australia as it has an ageing population with one of the longest life expectancies in the world. Australia's life expectancy at birth is 81.3 years (for males) and 85.4 years (for females) (Australian Bureau of Statistics, *Life Tables, States, Territories and Australia, 2019–2021*). The *2021 Intergenerational Report* forecast that the proportion of working age people is expected to fall over the coming years. By 2060/61, it is projected that there will only be 2.7 people of working age to support each Australian aged 65 years and over. This compares with 4 people of working age to support each Australian aged 65 years and over in 2019/20. An ageing population is likely to result in slower economic growth for Australia and increased demand for spending on health, aged care and pensions. More than one-quarter of Australian Government spending is already directed at these areas and this is forecast to rise to almost one-half by 2050.

This chapter examines how Australia's superannuation system operates. It commences with an outline of the superannuation tax concessions [19.2] and a brief history of superannuation [19.3]. This is followed by a discussion of the different types of superannuation entities and the way they are regulated [19.4]. The chapter then proceeds to examine the SG scheme [19.5] and the special ways that superannuation contributions, investments and benefits are taxed [19.6]–[19.18].

[19.2] Outline of the superannuation tax concessions

The Australian Government wants taxpayers to save for their retirement during their working lives rather than have to rely on the publicly funded age pension. It therefore provides generous tax concessions to promote superannuation investment.

Tax-effective nature of superannuation

Superannuation is a tax-effective form of saving for the following reasons:

- **Contributions.** Taxpayers may be entitled to special deductions and tax offsets for their contributions to superannuation funds [19.7].
- **Fund taxation.** Trustees of 'complying superannuation funds' [19.4] generally pay tax at the concessional rate of 15% on the taxable income of the fund [19.14]. This low rate makes superannuation a tax-sheltered environment for growing retirement savings.
- **Benefits.** Superannuation benefits are taxed concessionally in the hands of recipients when they are paid out of a fund as lump sums or income streams. In most cases, benefits paid to persons aged 60 and over are exempt from tax [19.16].

Employers can generally claim deductions for superannuation contributions made to their employees' funds, while members can choose whether or not to claim deductions for superannuation contributions made to their personal funds. Deductible contributions are referred to as 'concessional contributions' (or 'before-tax contributions'), while non-deductible contributions are referred to as 'non-concessional contributions' (or 'after-tax contributions'). Trustees of superannuation funds are generally assessed on concessional contributions, but not on non-concessional contributions.

The major benefit of superannuation investment stems from the difference that exists between a member's personal tax rate and the concessional superannuation fund tax rate. Superannuation investment benefits high-income earners more than low-income earners, as the arbitrage between a member's personal tax rate and the superannuation fund tax rate is obviously greater for high-income earners than for low-income earners. As the following example illustrates, a high-income earner who pays tax at the rate of 47% (ie the top marginal tax rate plus ML) has the potential to generate a 32% benefit by investing in a superannuation fund that pays tax at the rate of 15%.

Example Fred is an employee who earns a salary of $180,000 during the 2023/24 income year. Fred's employer plans to give him a pay rise of $1,000. If the $1,000 is paid to Fred as salary, he will have to pay tax (including ML) of $470 (ie $1,000 × 47%) on the extra income, leaving him with $530 after tax. However, if Fred chooses to 'salary sacrifice' his pay rise by having his employer contribute the $1,000 to his complying superannuation fund, the fund will be required to pay tax of only $150 on the contribution, leaving it with $850 after tax. The net benefit to Fred of the salary sacrifice option is therefore $320 (ie $850 – $530). This reflects the difference between Fred's personal tax rate (47%) and his superannuation fund's tax rate (15%) on the $1,000.

It should also be noted that if Fred received $1,000 as salary, he would only have $530 remaining after tax to invest. If he placed this amount in a bank deposit, he would have to pay tax on the interest at the rate of 47%. In contrast, the superannuation fund could invest the larger amount of $850 in a bank deposit and would only have to pay tax on the interest at the rate of 15%. Superannuation therefore provides a tax-effective environment in which to grow retirement savings. Over many years, the compounding effect of having investments sheltered in a lower tax rate environment provides a substantial benefit. In addition, once Fred is 60 years old, any superannuation benefits paid to him will be tax-free.

The example shows that employees can benefit from entering into 'salary sacrifice arrangements' under which they forgo salary in exchange for superannuation contributions paid directly to their funds by their employers. In practice, employers are generally not concerned whether they pay salary to their employees or make superannuation contributions to their superannuation funds, as both payments are usually deductible. From an employee's perspective, however, salary is taxed at their personal marginal tax rate plus ML, whereas employer superannuation contributions only suffer tax at the rate of 15% in the hands of the trustee of the fund. Salary sacrifice arrangements are therefore very common and are generally acceptable to the ATO as a legitimate tax planning strategy, provided employees forgo their salary *before* they earn the entitlement to receive it (TR 2001/10).

Limits on superannuation concessions

It needs to be recognised that the provision of superannuation tax concessions comes at a considerable cost to the Government in terms of forgone revenue. According to the *Tax Expenditures and Insights Statement* (2023), the superannuation tax concessions constitute some of Australia's most expensive tax expenditures. In 2022/23, the concessional taxation of superannuation entities is estimated to cost $21.5 billion in foregone revenue and the concessional taxation of employer superannuation contributions is estimated to cost $23.3 billion in foregone revenue.

To prevent the cost of superannuation concessions blowing out, the Government has introduced 'contributions caps' [19.9]. These caps limit the amount of concessional and non-concessional contributions that can be tax-effectively made to superannuation funds each year. The concessional contributions cap is $25,000 (for 2017/18 to 2020/21) and $27,500 (for 2021/22 to 2023/24). The non-concessional contributions cap is $100,000 (for 2017/18 to 2020/21) and $110,000 (for 2021/22 to 2023/24).

In addition, from 1 July 2017, non-concessional contributions are no longer permitted to be made to a fund during an income year if immediately before the start of the income year the member's 'total superannuation balance' equals or exceeds the 'general transfer balance cap' for the year [19.15]. The general transfer balance cap is $1.6m (for 2017/18 to 2020/21), $1.7m (for 2021/22 to 2022/23) and $1.9m (for 2023/24). This measure aims to ensure that members cannot continue to build their superannuation savings by making additional non-concessional contributions once they have achieved, what the Government considers to be, an adequate superannuation balance.

[19.3] History of superannuation

Superannuation has existed in Australia in one form or another for more than 100 years. Originally, it was only available to a small group of people, such as senior corporate executives and public servants. By the late 1970s and early 1980s, however, superannuation had become more widespread. The scope of superannuation coverage expanded considerably as a consequence of the 1986 *National Wage Case* in which the Conciliation and Arbitration Commission approved 3% employer superannuation contributions to be made under industrial awards. It was extended even further by the introduction of the SG scheme in 1992 [19.5]. The SG scheme requires employers to provide minimum levels of superannuation support for their employees. Employers that fail to provide such support are liable to pay a non-deductible charge in respect of the shortfall. The minimum level of support was originally set at 3% of an employee's salary or wages and has been incrementally increased over the years. It is 11% for 2023/24 and will increase in 0.5% increments each year until it reaches 12% in 2025/26.

Superannuation growth and performance

The introduction of the SG scheme coupled with the generous tax concessions that have been available in respect of superannuation has resulted in a steady growth in superannuation savings over the last few decades. Statistics published by the Australian Prudential Regulation Authority ('APRA') indicate there were 607,757 superannuation-related entities in existence as at March 2023 holding total assets valued at approximately $3.493 trillion (APRA, *Quarterly Superannuation Performance Statistics March 2022*). The vast majority of these entities (606,217) were 'self-managed superannuation funds' ('SMSFs') [19.4]. Australia's largest superannuation fund, AustralianSuper, manages over $271 billion of superannuation assets for more than 2.2 million members (APRA, *Annual Fund-Level Superannuation Statistics June 2022*). In 2010, the *Super System Report: Final Report* forecast that the superannuation system would grow to around $6.1 trillion by 2035. More recently, Deloitte's 2021 *Dynamics of the Australian Superannuation System* report forecast that superannuation assets would reach $9.2 trillion by 2041.

Despite the steady growth in superannuation over the years, the reality is that many people still do not have sufficient superannuation savings to fund their retirement. People who fall within this category include those who have had lower-paid jobs, those who have only had part-time employment or intermittent working patters (eg because of child raising responsibilities) and those who have been self-employed and therefore have not benefitted from employer SG contributions.

Studies have found a clear gender gap in superannuation savings, with women generally having significantly lower balances than men. According to an industry report, in June 2019, the average superannuation balance for individuals aged 60–64 was $359,870 for men and $279,167 for women, and for individuals aged 65–69 it was $414,380 for men and $370,042 for women (ASFA, *Developments in Account Balances—Superannuation Account Balances for Various Demographic Groups* (2022)). The gender gap in retirement outcomes has been attributed to a number of factors, including that women are more likely to work in lower paid jobs and industries, often on a part-time or casual basis, with career breaks (*Retirement Income Review, Final Report* (2020)). Women also have lower workforce participation—only 62.4% of women compared with 71.1% of men participated in the workforce as at March 2023 (Australian Bureau of Statistics, *Gender Indicators* (2023)).

It is important to be aware that, like other investments, superannuation can generate positive or negative returns. In 2020, the COVID-19 pandemic adversely affected many people's superannuation savings. In particular, people who had a large portion of their superannuation invested in Australian and international share markets were likely to have been negatively affected by the many hundreds of billions of dollars wiped off those markets. People who were approaching retirement or had already retired were the most exposed to the effects of the crisis as they had been saving the longest. Superannuation is a long-term investment; while younger people with long working lives ahead of them will have the opportunity to make up any losses incurred in 2020, it is a lot more difficult for those approaching retirement, or those who have already retired, to recover such losses.

Superannuation reform

Over the last few decades, superannuation has been subject to continual reform as successive governments have placed their individual stamps on the system. This has resulted in the evolution of a complex set of laws that can be quite bewildering for superannuation fund members to understand. Before turning to how the current laws work, it is useful to outline some of the major tax reforms that have taken place since the 1980s.

Hawke Government reforms

The first major overhaul of the superannuation tax rules occurred under the Hawke Labor Government. One of its landmark decisions was to change the way superannuation benefits were taxed. For many years, benefits paid to members had been treated highly concessionally. In particular, former s 26(d) *ITAA36* included only 5% of a lump sum benefit in a taxpayer's assessable income. The Hawke Government repealed s 26(d) from 1 July 1983 and replaced it with a less generous regime contained in ss 27A to 27J *ITAA36*. Under this regime, lump sums were divided into several components, including 'pre-July 83' and 'post-June 83' components, which were each subject to their own particular tax treatment. In addition, to discourage excessive superannuation investment, benefits that exceeded a reasonable benefit limit ('RBL') formed an 'excessive component', which was taxed at the highest marginal rate.

The Hawke Government also started taxing superannuation funds, which had previously been exempt from tax, at the rate of 15% from 1 July 1988. It was also responsible for introducing the SG scheme from 1 July 1992 [19.5].

19

Howard Government reforms

Significant reforms that simplified and streamlined the superannuation tax rules were introduced by the Howard Government from 1 July 2007. The reforms, known as the 'Simpler Super' reforms, are the backbone of the current superannuation system. They are contained in pt 3-30 *ITAA97*, which replaced ss 27A to 27J *ITAA36*. One of the key features of the reforms was that they made most superannuation benefits paid to people aged 60 and over tax-free [19.16]. As a result, most retirees now generally pay no tax on superannuation lump sums and income streams received from their funds.

Another significant feature of the Simpler Super reforms was that they abolished the RBL. There is, therefore, no longer any limit on the amount of concessionally taxed benefits that a person can receive from a superannuation fund. Instead, to prevent over-exploitation of the superannuation concessions, two new taxes, known as 'excess concessional contributions tax' ('ECCT') and 'excess non-concessional contributions tax' ('ENCCT'), were introduced [19.9]. The aim of these taxes was to discourage people from making 'concessional' and 'non-concessional' contributions to superannuation funds that exceeded specified 'caps'. In effect, this meant that instead of having caps on the amount of benefits that could be paid from superannuation funds (as was the case under the RBL rules), caps were placed on the amount of contributions that could be made to superannuation funds. Members of superannuation funds were therefore no longer penalised when they received large benefits simply because their funds had performed well.

Rudd and Gillard Government reforms

The Rudd and Gillard Governments also tinkered with the superannuation tax rules. They made changes to the rules dealing with excess concessional and non-concessional contributions (including abolishing ECCT) and legislated to progressively increase the SGC rate to 12% over coming years [19.5]. They also introduced div 293 tax, which was an additional 15% tax on certain contributions made in respect of members of superannuation funds whose annual income exceeded $300,000 [19.10]. The tax was designed to make the superannuation system fairer by reducing the bias that high-income earners had over low-income earners in relation to superannuation contributions.

Turnbull Government reforms

Major changes to the superannuation tax rules were made by the Turnbull Government. The new measures operate from 1 July 2017 and have added a further layer of complexity to the superannuation regime. The reforms were designed to make the superannuation system more fiscally sustainable by addressing the bourgeoning cost to the Government of providing the tax concessions. The reforms were also designed to improve the integrity of the superannuation system and ensure that it is used to provide income in retirement rather than for tax minimisation and estate planning purposes.

One of the central reforms was the introduction of a 'transfer balance cap' [19.15], which limits the amount that can be transferred to the 'retirement phase' of superannuation. The retirement phase generally commences when a member starts to receive a 'superannuation income stream'. As superannuation funds are exempt from tax on earnings used to fund retirement phase superannuation income streams, the transfer balance cap limits the amount of savings that are eligible for this concession [19.14].

The Turnbull Government also lowered the concessional contributions cap from $30,000 to $25,000 and the non-concessional contributions cap from $180,000 to $100,000 from the 2017/18 income year [19.9]. The lowering of the caps reduced the amounts taxpayers could tax-effectively contribute to superannuation funds. The Turnbull Government also lowered the div 293 tax threshold from $300,000 to $250,000, which exposed more taxpayers to the tax [19.10].

Albanese Government reforms

In 2023, the Albanese Government announced it intends to introduce an additional 15% tax on earnings on superannuation balances in excess of $3m [19.11]. The new tax is proposed to apply from 1 July 2025, which is after the next election and designed to ensure that the Government does not break its pre-2022 election promise not to introduce any new taxes during its current term.

Objectives of the superannuation system

Over the years, various attempts have been made to articulate the core objectives of the superannuation system. In 2013, the Gillard Government established a Charter of Superannuation Adequacy and Sustainability, which delivered a report, entitled *A Super Charter: Fewer Changes, Better Outcomes*. The report concluded that the objectives of the superannuation system were to provide an adequate level of retirement income, relieve pressure on the age pension and increase national savings. It also recommended that an independent Super Council be established to ensure that any future changes to superannuation would be consistent with an agreed Super Charter. However, due to a change of government, this recommendation was never implemented.

Subsequently, the Turnbull Government sought to codify the objectives of the superannuation system in its Superannuation (Objective) Bill 2016. The Bill stated that the primary objective of the superannuation system was 'to provide income in retirement to substitute or supplement the age pension'. It also indicated that the subsidiary objectives of the superannuation system would be contained in regulations. The Bill required any future superannuation laws to be accompanied by a statement assessing their compatibility against the primary and subsidiary objectives. However, the Bill lapsed due to the intervening 2019 federal election.

After the 2019 election, the Morrison Government established a Retirement Income Review to examine Australia's retirement income system. In its 2020 *Final Report*, the Review indicated that clear objectives of the superannuation system were needed to guide policy, improve understanding and provide a framework for assessing its performance. It suggested that the objectives be developed around the goal of delivering 'adequate standards of living in retirement in an equitable, sustainable and cohesive way'. The Review recognised that saving for retirement is a trade-off as it involves taxpayers foregoing consumption in their working years. It also noted that home ownership is the most important component of voluntary savings and is an important factor influencing retirement outcomes. This is because homeowners have lower housing costs and an asset that can be drawn on in retirement.

More recently, in February 2023, the Albanese Government released a consultation paper, *Legislating the Objective of Superannuation*, in which it noted that superannuation has played an important role in combatting old age poverty and lifting retirement standards for Australians. The Government argued that 'it is critical for there to be a clear, shared understanding of the objective of superannuation' and it has suggested the following wording:

> The objective of superannuation is to preserve savings to deliver income for a dignified retirement, alongside government support, in an equitable and sustainable way.

The consultation paper explained that:

- 'preserve savings' indicates that contributions to superannuation should, apart from exceptional circumstances, only be accessed for income in retirement
- 'deliver income' indicates the purpose of the superannuation system is to provide savings that are drawn down in retirement to deliver income that supports retirees' standards of living (rather than for minimising tax on wealth creation or enabling retirees to leave tax-effective bequests), and
- 'dignified' indicates the importance of financial security and wellbeing in retirement while recognising that this does not necessarily equate to the same level of income in retirement for all Australians.

[19.4] Regulation of superannuation

The superannuation system is heavily regulated and contains many prudential rules that are designed to protect members and ensure the efficacy of the regime. Before examining how superannuation investment is taxed, it is important to understand how these rules work. The following discussion outlines the regulatory framework that underpins the superannuation system and the main kinds of entities that operate within it.

Superannuation plan

Superannuation investment takes place via a 'superannuation plan'. A superannuation plan is defined as a 'superannuation fund', 'approved deposit fund' ('ADF') or 'retirement savings account' ('RSA') (s 995-1 *ITAA97*). Superannuation plans are provided by 'superannuation providers' (ie by trustees of superannuation funds and ADFs and by banks and life insurance companies that are RSA providers).

SISA and *SISR*

The main legislation that regulates superannuation entities is the *Superannuation Industry (Supervision) Act 1993* (Cth) ('*SISA*'). The *SISA* is supported by an extensive set of regulations contained in the *Superannuation Industry (Supervision) Regulations 1994* (Cth) ('*SISR*'). The *SISA* does not apply to 'exempt public sector superannuation schemes' (which are regulated under separate Commonwealth, state and territory legislation). It also does not apply to RSAs (which are regulated by APRA under the *Retirement Savings Accounts Act 1997* (Cth) ('*RSAA*') and *Retirement Savings Accounts Regulations 1997* (Cth) ('*RSAR*')).

Superannuation funds

Superannuation funds are the main form of superannuation plan and are the major focus of this chapter. A superannuation fund is defined as an indefinitely continuing 'provident benefit', 'superannuation' or 'retirement' fund, or a 'public sector superannuation scheme' (s 995-1 *ITAA97*; s 10 *SISA*).

The *SISA* divides responsibility for regulating superannuation funds between the ATO, APRA and ASIC. For regulatory purposes, superannuation funds are divided into two broad categories:

- **Self managed superannuation funds ('SMSFs').** SMSFs are regulated by the ATO. These funds were introduced to enable members to take direct control of their superannuation investment decisions and select investments made by the fund. SMSFs must meet certain requirements, including having no more than six members. The trustees of SMSFs (or directors of the corporate trustee) must be the same people as the members of the fund and must not receive any remuneration. In addition, no member may be an employee of another member unless they are relatives (s 17A *SISA*).
- **Registrable superannuation entities ('RSEs').** RSEs are regulated by APRA and ASIC. The trustees of these funds must apply to APRA for RSE licences, which operate subject to various conditions (ss 29C to 29EA *SISA*). If any conditions have been breached, the licences may be cancelled (s 29G *SISA*). The trustees of RSEs select the investments and usually offer their members a number of different investment options. In practice, trustees often invest large portions of their members' savings through fund managers. Some RSEs have only a few members while others have many thousands of members.

Kinds of superannuation funds

There are many different kinds of superannuation funds, including:

- **Personal superannuation funds.** These funds are established by the self-employed and other persons who wish to have their own personal funds. Contributions to these funds are made by the fund members. The vast majority of personal superannuation funds are SMSFs.
- **Employer-sponsored superannuation funds.** These funds (also known as 'corporate funds') are established by employers for the benefit of their employees. Contributions to these funds are made by employers and, in some cases, by employees.
- **Industry superannuation funds.** These funds are established by trade unions and industry organisations and were originally created for the purpose of accepting productivity-based superannuation contributions under industrial awards. They draw their members from employees across particular industries. Examples of such funds include HESTA (for the Healthcare sector), Cbus (for the construction sector) and UniSuper (for the tertiary education sector).
- **Public offer superannuation funds.** These funds (also known as 'retail funds') offer superannuation investment to the public on a commercial basis. They are usually established by financial

institutions and insurance companies. Public offer funds cater for large numbers of unassociated members. Examples of such funds include ANZ Smart Choice Super and AMP SignatureSuper.

Accumulation and defined benefit funds

The vast majority of superannuation funds are 'accumulation funds'. There are, however, also a small number of 'defined benefit funds'. The distinction between these funds stems from the different ways that benefits are calculated:

- **Accumulation funds.** Accumulation funds invest contributions received on behalf of a member and credit earnings (or debit losses) to the member's account. Investments held in a member's account (less fees and taxes) are used to pay benefits to the member on retirement. In accumulation funds, the members bear the investment risk, as their returns depend on the fund's performance.
- **Defined benefit funds.** Defined benefit funds also invest contributions received on behalf of a member, but pay benefits according to a set formula specified in the trust deed (rather than according to actual earnings). The formula is usually based on the member's period of service with the relevant employer, their employment fraction and their salary prior to retirement. In defined benefit funds, employers bear the investment risk, as they may need to make additional contributions to ensure the funds can meet their obligations to members.

Public sector superannuation schemes

Public sector superannuation schemes are established under legislation to provide benefits for certain Commonwealth, state, territory and local government employees (eg politicians, judges and public servants) (s 10 *SISA*). Many public sector superannuation schemes are 'unfunded', which means that benefits are paid out of consolidated revenue rather than from a dedicated fund that has accumulated over time. The 2023 Budget Papers estimated the Commonwealth Government's unfunded superannuation liabilities to be around $275 billion. In 2006, the Commonwealth established a sovereign wealth fund, known as the 'Future Fund', to help pay for these liabilities. The Future Fund's assets were valued at $202 billion as at 31 March 2023.

Public sector superannuation schemes include 'constitutionally protected funds', which are basically funds established under state Acts that are listed in the table in reg 995-1.03 *ITAR21* (s 995-1 *ITAA97*). These funds are exempt from tax under s 50-25 *ITAA97* [11.7].

Unlike ordinary superannuation funds which pay tax on their earnings and are therefore known as 'taxed funds', public sector superannuation schemes that are unfunded or are constitutionally protected superannuation funds do not pay tax and are therefore known as 'untaxed funds'. Benefits paid from untaxed funds are taxed less concessionally in the hands of members than benefits paid from taxed funds [19.16].

Complying and non-complying superannuation funds

It is important to distinguish between 'complying' and 'non-complying' superannuation funds, as concessional tax treatment only applies to 'complying superannuation funds'.

A 'complying superannuation fund' is defined in s 45 *SISA*. To be a complying superannuation fund, the fund must be an 'exempt public sector superannuation scheme' (ie a public sector superannuation scheme that is listed in sch 1AA *SISR*) or it must meet the following requirements:

- **Regulated superannuation fund.** The fund must be a 'regulated superannuation fund' within the meaning of s 19 *SISA*. To satisfy this requirement, the fund must have a trustee and the governing rules of the fund must either require the trustee to be a constitutional corporation or provide that the sole or primary purpose of the fund is to provide old-age pensions. In addition, the trustee must have made an irrevocable election for the *SISA* to apply to the fund.

- **Australian superannuation fund.** The fund must be 'an Australian superannuation fund' within the meaning of s 295-95(2) *ITAA97*. To satisfy this requirement, the following conditions must be fulfilled:
  - the fund must be established in Australia, or any asset of the fund must be situated in Australia
  - the central management and control of the fund must ordinarily be in Australia, and
  - certain member conditions must be satisfied (eg the fund must either have no 'active members' or at least 50% of the superannuation interests held by active members in the fund must be attributable to Australian residents).
- **Compliance notice.** The Regulator must have provided the trustee of the fund with a compliance notice under s 40 *SISA*. Such a notice will be issued if:
  - the fund has not contravened the *SISA* regulatory provisions, or
  - the fund has contravened the *SISA* regulatory provisions but has not failed a 'culpability test' (in the case of non-SMSFs) or has passed a 'compliance test' (in the case of SMSFs) (ss 42, 42A *SISA*).

A fund that does not satisfy the above requirements is a 'non-complying superannuation fund' (*Trustee for the R Ali Superannuation Fund v FC of T* 2012 ATC ¶10-231). An example of such a fund is a superannuation fund that has its central management and control overseas (*CBNP Superannuation Fund v FC of T* 2009 ATC ¶10-105).

Other retirement funds and accounts

Although superannuation funds are the major retirement investment vehicle, a number of related funds and accounts also exist. These are outlined below.

Approved deposit funds ('ADFs')

ADFs are special roll-over funds that were established to 'warehouse' a member's superannuation savings after they had retired or changed employment. The main difference between ADFs and superannuation funds is that ADFs cannot accept employer or personal superannuation contributions as they operate solely as roll-over vehicles. Only a few ADFs remain in existence today and are therefore rarely encountered.

As with superannuation funds, concessional tax treatment only applies to 'complying ADFs'. A complying ADF is a 'resident ADF' that has received a compliance notice from the Regulator (s 40). Generally, to be a complying ADF, the fund must not have contravened the *SISA* regulatory provisions. Alternatively, if a fund has contravened those regulatory provisions, it can still be a complying ADF in certain cases (eg where the contravention is rectified within a specified time, or where the Regulator is satisfied that the seriousness and/or frequency of the contraventions does not warrant the entity being treated as a non-complying ADF) (s 43). All other ADFs are 'non-complying ADFs'.

Retirement savings accounts ('RSAs')

RSAs are special accounts with approved financial and life assurance institutions that are regulated under the *RSAA* and *RSAR*. RSAs represent an alternative low-risk and low-cost option to traditional superannuation investment. RSA deposits are treated in essentially the same manner as superannuation contributions. Likewise, RSA income is taxed in a broadly similar way to superannuation income. Benefits paid from RSAs are treated as if they were superannuation benefits.

Pooled superannuation trusts ('PSTs')

A PST is a special resident unit trust regulated under the *SISA*. PSTs are designed to operate as pooled investment vehicles for superannuation entities. Regulated superannuation funds, ADFs and other PSTs are permitted to own units in PSTs. Individuals, however, cannot own units in PSTs or make contributions to them as they are not superannuation plans.

Superannuation Holding Accounts Special Account ('SHASA')

The SHASA is not a superannuation entity, but rather a statutory account established under the *Small Superannuation Accounts Act 1995* (Cth). The SHASA is administered by the ATO and is used for accepting SG shortfalls [19.5] and 'government co-contributions' [19.8] where a person has not nominated a particular superannuation fund to receive such payments. Before 1 July 2006, employers could also make SG contributions to the SHASA. Personal contributions cannot be made to the SHASA. The SHASA has no administrative fees or charges and pays interest on account balances of up to $1,200.

Operating standards

The *SISA* and *SISR* contain a host of operating standards that superannuation entities must comply with. The standards are designed to protect members and ensure the superannuation system functions as intended. They include a sole purpose test as well as rules about making contributions and releasing benefits. There are also a number of lending, investment and borrowing restrictions placed on funds. Breaches of the rules may result in the imposition of civil or criminal penalties (pt 21 *SISA*). They may also lead to a fund losing its complying status, which results in the fund losing its concessional tax treatment and therefore paying tax at the rate of 45% instead of 15%. The following discussion outlines some of the most important rules.

Sole purpose test

The sole purpose test in s 62 *SISA* requires superannuation funds to be maintained solely for one or more 'core purposes'. Core purposes include the provision of benefits on a member's retirement or on a member attaining a particular age (which must not be less than the age specified in the *SISR*). The sole purpose test is also satisfied where a superannuation fund is maintained for one or more 'core purposes' as well as one or more 'ancillary purposes' (eg the provision of benefits on a member's cessation of work on account of ill-health).

As a consequence of the sole purpose test, a superannuation fund would not be able to acquire a residential property for use by its members as their home or holiday home as this would provide the members with benefits prior to retirement. A frequently cited example of where an earlier version of the sole purpose test was breached is found in *Case* 43/95 95 ATC 374. This case concerned a superannuation fund in which Mr A was the principal member. The fund owned a beachside property, an interest in a family trust that invested in a Swiss chalet, and shares in a private company that owned shares in a golf club. The AAT found that the assets of the fund had been applied for the benefit of Mr A and his associates and that the fund was therefore not maintained solely for the purpose of providing retirement benefits to its members.

The sole purpose test was considered in *Aussiegolfa Pty Ltd (Trustee) v FC of T* 2018 ATC ¶10-471. In this case, the trustee of the Benson SMSF invested in a managed investment scheme which had established a sub-fund that acquired student accommodation. The Federal Court (2017 ATC ¶20-643) concluded that s 62 had been contravened as the accommodation had been leased to the daughter of the SMSF's sole member. On appeal, however, the Full Federal Court reversed this decision and held that the leasing of the property to the daughter did not breach the sole purpose test. The Full Federal Court held that as the property was leased at market rent, no financial benefit had been obtained by the daughter under the *SISA*. Moshinsky J explained (at 176) that 'the statutory context in which s 62 appears does not suggest that a fund will not be treated as being maintained solely for the core purposes, or the core purposes and the ancillary purposes, simply because the trustee enters into a transaction with a related party'. His Honour nevertheless warned (at 178) that the position would

19

have been different if the lease was not at market rent as, in such case, 'an inference would probably readily be drawn that the fund was being maintained for a collateral purpose, namely, to provide discounted accommodation to a relative of a member of the fund, contrary to the sole purpose test'.

Covenants and investment strategy

The *SISA* requires the governing rules of a superannuation fund to contain the covenants set out in s 52. The covenants cover a broad range of matters, including the requirement that the trustees act honestly, with care, skill and diligence and in the best financial interests of the beneficiaries. There is also a covenant requiring the trustees to formulate and give effect to an 'investment strategy' that has regard to the whole of the entity's circumstances, including:

- the risk involved in making, holding and realising, and the likely return from, the entity's investments, having regard to its objectives and its expected cash flow requirements
- the composition of the entity's investments as a whole, including the extent to which the investments are diverse or involve exposure of the entity to risks from inadequate diversification
- the liquidity of the entity's investments, having regard to its expected cash flow requirements, and
- the ability of the entity to discharge its existing and prospective liabilities (reg 4.09 *SISR*).

Contravention of the covenants in s 52 can have civil and criminal consequences (s 54B).

Lending, acquisition and in-house asset restrictions

The *SISA* provides that, subject to certain exceptions, trustees of superannuation funds are generally prohibited from lending money, or giving any form of financial assistance, to members of the fund or their relatives (s 65).

Trustees of superannuation funds are also generally prohibited from acquiring assets from a 'related party' (ss 66, 66A). A related party of a superannuation fund is a member of the fund, a 'standard employer sponsor', or an associate of either entity (s 10). A standard-employer sponsor is essentially an employer that has an arrangement with the trustee of the fund to make contributions to it (s 16). The following related-party acquisitions are, however, specifically permitted:

- the acquisition of listed securities at market value, and
- the acquisition by a fund with no more than six members of real business property at market value.

In addition, pt 8 *SISA* places restrictions on a superannuation fund's ability to acquire 'in-house assets'. In-house assets consist of loans to, or investments in, a standard-employer sponsor or their associate. The acquisition at market value of in-house assets is permitted so long as the acquisition does not breach the 'in-house asset rules'. These rules prescribe that the maximum amount of a fund's in-house assets must generally not exceed 5% of the market value of its total assets.

Borrowing restrictions

The *SISA* generally prohibits trustees of superannuation funds from borrowing money (eg taking out loans or bank overdrafts) (s 67(1)). There are, however, a number of limited exceptions to this restriction. For instance, the following kinds of borrowings are permitted:

- **Borrowings to enable the trustee to pay benefits to members (s 67(2)).** To fall within this exception, the period of the borrowing must not exceed 90 days and the total amount borrowed must not exceed 10% of the value of the fund's assets.
- **Borrowings to enable the trustee to cover the settlement of certain securities transactions (s 67(3)).** To fall within this exception the borrowing must not be of a kind which the Regulator has determined is exempt and it must have been likely, at the time of the investment decision,

that the borrowing would not be needed. The period of the borrowing must not exceed seven days and the total amount borrowed must not exceed 10% of the value of the fund's assets.

- **Limited recourse borrowing arrangements (s 67A).** To fall within this exception, the borrowing must have been applied to acquire a single 'acquirable asset'. The asset must be held on trust giving the superannuation fund trustee a beneficial interest in the asset. The superannuation fund trustee must have a right to acquire legal ownership of the asset by making one or more payments after acquiring the beneficial interest. Most importantly, the rights of the lender against the trustee for default on the borrowing must be limited to rights relating to the acquirable asset. This means that the lender has no recourse to the other assets of the fund. The ATO's views on these arrangements are contained in SMSFR 2012/1.

Investment rules

Trustees of superannuation funds must ensure that when making investments they deal with other parties to the relevant transactions at 'arm's length' (s 109 *SISA*). This does not mean they cannot enter transactions with associates, but such transactions must be made on commercial terms in the same manner as if the other parties were at arm's length.

Trustees of SMSFs must also comply with special rules relating to the making, holding and realising of certain kinds of investments, such as 'collectables' and 'personal use assets' (eg artwork, jewellery, antiques, cars) (s 62A). These kinds of assets must not be leased to related parties or stored in their private homes (reg 13.18AA *SISR*).

Contribution rules

The *SISR* sets out the circumstances in which superannuation funds may accept contributions in respect of a member. Different rules apply depending on the member's age and the nature of the contributions. There are essentially four kinds of contributions:

- **Employer contributions.** These are contributions made by, or on behalf of, an employer-sponsor of the fund (reg 1.03).
- **Mandated employer contributions.** These are contributions made by employers for SG purposes, payments of the shortfall component of the SGC, and contributions made under industrial awards (reg 5.01).
- **Member contributions.** These are contributions made by, or on behalf of, the member of the fund, but do not include 'employer contributions' (reg 5.01).
- **Downsizer contributions.** These are contributions of up to $300,000 from the proceeds of sale of a main residence by persons who are at least 55 years of age (s 292-102 *ITAA97*) [19.12].

19

The following table sets out the general acceptance rules for superannuation contributions (reg 7.04(1)).

Member's age	Contributions the superannuation fund can accept
Under 55	(a) employer contributions, or (b) member contributions
55 to under 75	(a) employer contributions, or (b) member contributions (including downsizer contributions)
75 and over	(a) mandated employer contributions, or (b) downsizer contributions

A special rule provides that a superannuation fund may also accept contributions that are received on or before 28 days after the end of the month in which the member turns 75 and are either employer contributions (other than mandated employer contributions) or member contributions (other than downsizer contributions) (reg 7.04(1A)).

Superannuation funds are prohibited from accepting member contributions if the member's TFN has not been quoted (reg 7.04(2)).

Portability and payment rules

As a general rule, members of regulated superannuation funds and ADFs may transfer (ie 'roll-over') their benefits to another regulated superannuation fund or ADF (reg 6.28 *SISR*). A roll-over must generally take effect within 30 days of a request being made. Trustees may only refuse to make roll-overs in limited circumstances, such as where not all of the member's benefits are sought to be transferred and their residual interest in the fund would amount to less than $5,000. They can also limit the number of transfers that can be made in a 12-month period (reg 6.35).

Allowing members to roll over their superannuation benefits means that benefits are not 'locked into' one fund. This enables members to transfer their benefits to those funds they believe will best serve their needs. It also allows members to consolidate their superannuation, which may reduce administration fees. Portability of superannuation also promotes competition between funds in relation to both fees charged and investment performance.

There is no limit on how long a member can retain benefits in a superannuation fund. Previously, superannuation benefits had to be paid to members once they reached 65 years of age, unless they were still engaged in the workforce, in which case the benefits could be retained in a fund until they reached 75 years of age.

Conditions of release, cashing restrictions and preservation rules

The major drawback of superannuation is that money invested in a superannuation fund is not generally accessible until late in life. As a general rule, benefits must be preserved in a fund (ie they cannot be paid to members) until a 'condition of release' has been satisfied. The conditions of release are specified in sch 1 *SISR*. A number of these conditions operate subject to special 'cashing restrictions'.

The main condition of release is 'retirement'. A member is taken to have retired if an arrangement under which the member was gainfully employed has ended and the trustee is reasonably satisfied that the member intends never to again become gainfully employed on a full-time or part-time basis. In addition, the member must also have reached their 'preservation age' (reg 6.01). As the table below indicates, a member's preservation age is between 55 and 60, depending on when they were born.

Member's birth date	Preservation age
Before July 1960	55
July 1960–June 1961	56
July 1961–June 1962	57
July 1962–June 1963	58
July 1963–June 1964	59
After June 1964	60

Example Brian was born in November 1968. He has resigned from work and does not intend to be gainfully employed in the future. As he has not yet reached his preservation age of 60, he is generally not able to access his superannuation benefits.

Other common conditions of release include death, terminal medical condition, permanent incapacity and attaining 65 years of age. In addition, members can also access their superannuation savings (subject to cashing restrictions) in cases of 'severe financial hardship' or on 'compassionate grounds'.

Members who have reached their preservation age but are still engaged in the workforce may commence receiving non-commutable pensions or annuities or 'transition to retirement income streams'. This allows them to continue in the workforce (often on a part-time basis) while being able to access their superannuation without first having to retire.

Although members generally need to satisfy a condition of release to access their superannuation, special rules allow certain amounts to be released to members who have excess concessional or non-concessional contributions, or div 293 tax liabilities [19.13]. This is designed to help them discharge their tax liabilities.

In addition, to help people deal with the adverse economic effects of the COVID-19 pandemic, the Government introduced a limited early release rule which allowed eligible individuals to access up to $10,000 of their superannuation before 1 July 2020 and up to a further $10,000 before 1 January 2021 (reg 4.22B *RSAR*; reg 6-19B *SISR*).

Superannuation benefits—lump sums and income streams

Different taxation rules apply to 'superannuation lump sum benefits' and 'superannuation income stream benefits' [19.16]. A superannuation lump sum benefit is a superannuation benefit that is *not* a superannuation income stream benefit (s 307-65 *ITAA97*). A superannuation income stream benefit is a superannuation benefit that is paid from a 'superannuation income stream' as defined in reg 307-70.02 *ITAR21* (s 307-70).

Superannuation income streams must comply with standards set out in the *SISR* (regs 1.05 and 1.06). The *SISR* requires superannuation income streams to satisfy various requirements, including minimum annual payment requirements. There is no maximum payment requirement (except for transition to retirement account-based pensions, where annual payments must not exceed 10% of the account balance at the start of each year). The minimum annual payments depend on the kind of income stream involved and are calculated as follows:

- **Non-account-based income streams.** For 'non-account-based income streams' (eg pensions payable for life or life expectancy), the minimum annual payment is calculated by multiplying the 'purchase price' of the income stream by the relevant 'pension factor' corresponding to the beneficiary's age on the commencement day. The pension factor is determined according to Life Tables prepared by the Australian Government Actuary.
- **Account-based income streams.** For 'account-based income streams' (eg allocated pensions), the minimum annual payment is calculated by multiplying the account balance on the commencement day (or 1 July each year) by the relevant 'percentage factor' that corresponds to the beneficiary's age on the commencement day (or 1 July each year) (sch 7 *SISR*). The relevant percentage factors are set out in the following table (note that in response to the COVID-19 pandemic, the Government reduced the 'ordinary' percentage factor by 50% for the 2019/20 to 2022/23 income years).

Age-based percentage factors							
Age	Under 65	65–74	75–79	80–84	85–89	90–94	95 or over
Ordinary percentage	4%	5%	6%	7%	9%	11%	14%
Reduced percentage for 2019/20 to 2022/23	2%	2.5%	3%	3.5%	4.5%	5.5%	7%

19

Example Joe was 64 years of age when he began to receive an allocated pension on 1 July 2022. His account balance was $500,000 at that time. Joe must receive a minimum pension of $10,000 (ie $500,000 × 2%) in 2022/23. On 1 July 2023, he is 65 years of age. In 2023/24, Joe must receive a minimum pension of 5% of his account balance on 1 July 2023.

Bankruptcy protection

Special rules to protect superannuation savings are contained in the *Bankruptcy Act 1966* (Cth). In particular, s 116(2)(d) provides that a bankrupt's interest in a regulated superannuation fund, ADF or exempt public sector superannuation scheme and lump sum payments made from such funds to a bankrupt on or after bankruptcy are excluded from the property that is divisible among the bankrupt's creditors.

Unclaimed and lost superannuation

The *Superannuation (Unclaimed Money and Lost Members) Act 1999* (Cth) requires superannuation providers to report and transfer any 'unclaimed money' they hold to the Commissioner of Taxation (ss 16, 17). Special rules allow state and territory funds to report and transfer amounts to their own authorities. An amount is unclaimed money if it relates to a member who has reached 65 years of age, the superannuation provider has not received an amount in respect of the member within the last two years and, after the end of five years since the superannuation provider last had contact with the member, it has been unable to contact the member after making reasonable efforts (s 12). An amount is also unclaimed money if the member has died, a benefit is immediately payable in respect of the member, the superannuation provider has not received an amount in respect of the member within the last two years and, after making reasonable efforts and after a reasonable period has passed, the provider is unable to ensure that the benefit is received by the person who is entitled to the benefit (s 14).

The Act also requires superannuation providers to report and transfer 'lost member accounts' to the Commissioner (ss 24C, 24E). A lost member account is a small account (ie one with a balance below $6,000) of a lost member, or an account of an unidentifiable lost member where the provider has not received a contribution or roll-over for the member within the last 12 months (s 24B). A lost member is basically a member who is uncontactable or inactive. A member is uncontactable if the provider has never held an address for the member or has on two occasions had mail returned unclaimed and has not received a contribution or roll-over for the member within the last 12 months. A member is inactive if they joined the fund more than two years ago under a 'standard employer-sponsored arrangement' and the provider has not received a contribution or roll-over for the member within the last five years. A member is not a lost member if their address has been confirmed in the past two years, or they have indicated that they want to remain as a member.

The Commissioner is responsible for maintaining an 'unclaimed money register' and a 'lost members register'. Individuals can use the 'myGov' website to locate their unclaimed and lost superannuation [2.5]. Where the Commissioner is satisfied that it is possible to do so, he can pay amounts (together with interest worked out in accordance with the *Superannuation (Unclaimed Money and Lost Members) Regulations 1999* (Cth)) to the member, their superannuation fund, or to a deceased member's beneficiaries or legal personal representative (s 24G). The aim is to reunite members with their unclaimed and lost superannuation and reduce the number of inactive superannuation accounts. The transfer of small account balances also ensures that they are not eroded by fees imposed by superannuation providers.

Rules to make superannuation more competitive

Over recent years, there have been a number of Government reviews into the superannuation system. In its 2014 *Final Report*, the Financial System Inquiry found the superannuation industry had been charging high fees and needed to improve its efficiency, competitiveness and governance arrangements. The Productivity Commission was tasked to undertake further investigations and, in 2018, it released a report, entitled *Superannuation, Assessing Efficiency and Competitiveness*, that identified certain structural flaws in the system. In particular, it found that many people had multiple accounts they did not need, resulting in unnecessary fees. It also noted that there was great variation in fees and performance between funds. Similar concerns were identified by the Hayne Royal Commission into Misconduct in the Banking, Superannuation and Financial Services Industry. The Royal Commission recommended making a number of changes, including only allowing a person to have one 'default fund' so that new accounts are not automatically created every time they commence a new job.

The Government subsequently amended the 'choice of fund' rules in s 32C *SGAA* to provide that if a new employee has an existing 'stapled' superannuation fund when they start a new job and does not choose a fund to receive contributions, their employer is required to make SG contributions to their 'stapled fund' [19.5]. The Government also amended the *SISA* by requiring APRA to undertake an annual performance test of regulated superannuation funds (other than those with no more than six members) (s 60C). The requirements for this test are set out in regulations and include investment return requirements (s 60D). Trustees must notify their members where their products have failed the performance test (s 60E). Funds that have underperformed over two consecutive annual tests are prohibited from receiving new members (unless APRA lifts the prohibition) (s 60F). A new interactive online 'YourSuper comparison tool' has been created to make it easy for people to choose a product based on fees and performance information. The tool is administered by the ATO and ranks products according to formulas determined by APRA (s 60J).

Superannuation supervisory and financial assistance funding levies

As there is a significant cost in regulating the superannuation system, superannuation entities are required to pay an annual 'supervisory levy', which is designed to recover the ATO's and APRA's administration costs of regulating such entities. The levy is deductible under s 25-5 *ITAA97* and differs depending on the nature of the entity:

- **SMSFs.** For SMSFs, the levy is imposed under the *Superannuation (Self-Managed Superannuation Funds) Supervisory Levy Imposition Act 1991* (Cth) and is payable to the ATO. The levy for 2022/23 is $259 under the *Superannuation (Self-Managed Superannuation Funds) Supervisory Levy Imposition Regulations 2018* (Cth).
- **Non-SMSFs.** For non-SMSFs, the levy is imposed under the *Superannuation Supervisory Levy Imposition Act 1998* (Cth) ('*SSLIA*') and is payable to APRA. The Australian Prudential Regulation Authority Supervisory Levies Determination 2023 sets out the levy rates for 2023/24. A flat levy of $590 applies to 'small APRA funds' (ie basically, funds with no more than six members that are not SMSFs). For other funds, the levy is charged on the entity's 'levy base' (basically, the net balance in its audited accounts) and consists of a 'restricted' and 'unrestricted' levy percentage. The restricted levy percentage is 0.00840 (subject to a minimum amount of $12,500 and a maximum amount of $800,000) and the unrestricted levy percentage is 0.003167.

RSE licensees are also required to pay an ASIC supervisory cost recovery levy to recover ASIC's regulatory costs (*ASIC Supervisory Cost Recovery Levy Act 2017* (Cth); *ASIC Supervisory Cost Recovery Levy (Collection) Act 2017* (Cth)). The levy is calculated under the *ASIC Supervisory Cost Recovery Levy Regulations 2017* (Cth).

Superannuation entities (other than SMSFs) must also pay the 'financial assistance funding levy' imposed under the *Superannuation (Financial Assistance Funding) Levy Act 1993* (Cth)). This levy is designed to fund grants of financial assistance under pt 23 *SISA* to superannuation entities that suffer loss due to fraud or theft. The levy is based on the value of the fund's assets. There is a minimum and maximum amount of levy that can be charged. The levy is deductible in the income year that it is incurred (s 295-490 *ITAA97*). Superannuation entities are exempt from tax on any grants of financial assistance they receive (s 295-405 *ITAA97*).

Australian Financial Complaints Authority

The Australian Financial Complaints Authority ('AFCA') was established in 2018 to provide a dispute resolution scheme for dealing with consumer complaints about products and services provided by financial firms. The scheme applies to products and services provided by AFCA members, which includes all RSEs (but not SMSFs). AFCA replaces a number of former dispute resolution schemes, including the Superannuation Complaints Tribunal. A person is not obliged to use AFCA to resolve a dispute and may instead issue court proceedings. AFCA has the power to affirm, vary or set aside a decision-maker's decision. It can also remit all or part of a decision to the decision-maker with directions. AFCA's determinations on questions of law may be appealed to the Federal Court. AFCA must report serious contraventions of the law to APRA, ASIC or the Commissioner of Taxation (s 1052E *Corporations Act 2001* (Cth)).

[19.5] Superannuation guarantee scheme

The superannuation guarantee ('SG') scheme is one of the central pillars of the Government's retirement income policy. It is established under the *Superannuation Guarantee (Administration) Act 1992* (Cth) ('*SGAA*') and is administered by the ATO. The SG scheme is designed to ensure that, subject to limited exceptions, employees are provided with a minimum level of superannuation support from their employers. For 2023/24, this level is 11% of the employee's salary or wages for a quarter (subject to a 'maximum contributions base').

Where employers fail to provide the minimum level of support for a quarter, they are required to pay the SGC. Importantly, unlike ordinary employer superannuation contributions, which are generally deductible under s 290-60 *ITAA97* [19.7], the SGC is not deductible (s 26-95 *ITAA97*).

Employers and employees

As the SG scheme applies to arrangements between 'employers' and 'employees', it is important to define these terms. Section 12(1) *SGAA* states that employer and employee have their ordinary meanings. However, these meanings are extended under ss 12(2) to (11) *SGAA*. For example, company directors are deemed to be employees of their companies (s 12(2)) and members of Commonwealth and state Parliaments and territory Legislatures are deemed to be employees of the respective Commonwealth, states or territories (ss 12(4) to (7)). In addition, s 12(3) provides that a person who 'works under a contract that is wholly or principally for the labour of the person is an employee of the other party to the contract'.

In *Vabu Pty Ltd v FC of T* 96 ATC 4898, the NSW Court of Appeal held that couriers engaged by a courier company to collect and deliver parcels were not employees of the company within either the common law or extended meaning in s 12(3). Rather, they were independent contractors working for themselves. The courier company was therefore not obliged to make SG payments to their superannuation funds. The Court indicated that a prominent factor in determining the nature of the relationship between a person who engages another to perform work and the person so engaged is the degree of control the former can exercise over the latter. The Court, however, went on to point out that control is not the only relevant factor—the totality of the relationship between the parties needs to be considered. Some of the factors that led the Court to conclude that the couriers were not employees included the fact that they were paid for each successful delivery made and used their own vehicles, street directories and equipment to provide the services.

In determining whether a person is an employee or an independent contractor, it is also relevant to take into account the level of integration that the person has in the payer's business organisation. The fundamental question is 'whether the worker has been engaged to serve, or to provide services' (*MWWD v FC of T* 2020 ATC ¶10-553). As the High Court noted in *Hollis v Vabu 2001* ATC 4508 (at 4518), the distinction between an employee and independent contractor is 'rooted fundamentally in the difference between a person who serves his employer in his, the employer's business, and a person who carries on a trade or business of his own'.

The distinction between employees and independent contractors has been considered in cases involving the former PAYE provisions, which required tax instalments to be deducted from 'salary or wages'. Under former s 221A(1) *ITAA36*, 'salary or wages' included any payments made 'under a contract which is wholly or substantially for the labour of the person to whom the payments are made'. As this provision has close similarities with s 12(3) *SGAA*, the cases dealing with it shed light on the potential operation of s 12(3).

The leading case is *Neale (DFC of T) v Atlas Products (Vic) Pty Ltd* (1955) 94 CLR 419, which concerned a supplier of roof tiles that hired tilers to perform particular jobs. The tilers signed contracts for each job that provided they would supply labour and/or material and could do the work themselves or employ others to do it. The Commissioner brought proceedings against the supplier for failing to deduct tax instalments from the payments made to the tilers on the basis that the payments fell within former s 221A(1). The High Court, however, found that the tilers were paid to 'perform a given result' and were therefore independent contractors. The Court stated (at 425):

> If the contract leaves the contractor free to do the work himself or to employ other persons to carry it out the contractual remuneration when paid is not a payment made wholly or at all for the labour of the person to whom the payments are made. It is a payment made under a contract whereby the contractor has undertaken to produce a given result . . .

Similar views were expressed by the NSW Court of Appeal in *World Book (Australia) Pty Ltd v FC of T* 92 ATC 4327, in relation to a company that engaged agents to sell its encyclopaedias and paid them a commission for each order. The agents could sell encyclopaedias themselves or engage others to do so. The Court followed *Atlas Products* and held that the payments did not fall within former s 221A(1) as they were not wholly or principally for the labour of the agents since the essence of the contracts was to achieve a result.

SGR 2005/1 considers a number of the cases outlined above and states that, for the purposes of s 12(3), a contract is wholly or principally for the labour of the individual engaged if the individual is remunerated either wholly or principally for their personal labour and skills, performs the contractual work personally, and is not paid to achieve a result.

The distinction between an employee and independent contractor was recently considered by the High Court in *Construction, Forestry, Maritime, Mining and Energy Union & Anor v Personnel Contracting Pty Ltd* [2022] HCA 1. The case concerned a British backpacker (Mr M) who was on a working holiday in Australia. Mr M was offered a role with a labour-hire company ('Construct') and signed an Administrative Services Agreement ('ASA') in which he was described as a 'self-employed contractor'. In accordance with the ASA, Construct assigned Mr M to work on construction sites run by its client ('Hanssen') under the supervision of Hanssen's employees. The relationship between Construct and Hanssen was governed by a labour hire agreement. There was no contract between Mr M and Hanssen.

A majority of the High Court held that Mr M was Construct's employee notwithstanding that he was described as a 'contractor' under the ASA. This was because the ASA gave Construct the right to determine for whom Mr M would work, Mr M promised Construct that he would cooperate in the supply of his labour, and in return he was entitled to be paid by Construct for the work he performed. Kiefel CJ, Keane and Edelman JJ focused on the contractual terms between the parties and said (at 59):

> Where the parties have comprehensively committed the terms of their relationship to a written contract the validity of which is not in dispute, the characterisation of their relationship as one of employment or otherwise proceeds by reference to the rights and obligations of the parties under that contract.

More recently, in *JMC Pty Ltd v FC of T* 2023 ATC ¶20-861, it was held that a higher education provider was not required to make SG payments in respect of one of its casual lecturers (Mr H) as he was not an employee under either s 12(1) or s 12(3) *SGAA*. Mr H had been engaged under a series of short-term contracts that stated he would be paid an hourly rate for delivering lectures and marking exams. He was required to submit invoices accompanied by time sheets and signed weekly lesson plans and had the right to subcontract or assign his teaching services, subject to obtaining written consent. The Full Federal Court found that Mr H's right to subcontract or assign his teaching services was inconsistent with an employment relationship and this was supported by the manner in which he charged for his services and was required to provide signed lesson plans. The Court noted (at [90]) that *Personnel Contracting* was authority for the proposition that the 'right of a person to control the work of the other is an indicator that a relationship is one of employer and employee'. It concluded that Mr H's contract did not provide the sort of controls over how, when or where he was required to deliver the lectures such as to indicate that he was an employee rather than an independent contractor.

Imposition of the SGC on an employer's SG shortfall

The SGC is imposed on an employer's 'SG shortfall' for the quarter (s 5 *SGCA*). An employer's SG shortfall is calculated under s 17 *SGAA*. It is the sum of:

- the employer's total 'individual SG shortfalls' for the quarter (see below)
- a 'nominal interest component' for the quarter, which is set at the rate of 10% per annum (reg 13 *Superannuation Guarantee (Administration) Regulations 2018* (Cth)) and is calculated from the beginning of the quarter until the date the SGC would be payable under the *SGAA* (ss 31, 46 *SGAA*), and
- an 'administration component' for the quarter, which is $20 for each employee in respect of whom there is an individual SG shortfall (s 32 *SGAA*).

The SGC must be paid by the 28th day of the second month after the end of the quarter (s 46). The GIC applies to any portion of the SGC that is not paid by the due date (s 49) [40.8].

To improve compliance with the SG rules, the Commissioner has the power to direct employers that fail to pay the SGC to complete an approved education course (div 384 of sch 1 *TAA*).

Employer's individual superannuation guarantee shortfall

An employer's individual SG shortfall for a particular employee is calculated by multiplying the 'total salary or wages' paid by the employer to the employee for a quarter by the relevant 'charge percentage' for the quarter (s 19(1) *SGAA*).

If the total salary or wages paid by the employer to the employee for a quarter exceeds the 'maximum contributions base' for the quarter, the total salary or wages to be taken into account is the maximum contributions base (s 19(4)). The maximum contributions base for a quarter in a financial year is generally worked out under ss 15(3) and (4) by multiplying the maximum contributions base for a quarter in the immediately preceding year by the indexation factor for the year. The following table sets out the maximum contributions base for each quarter in the most recent financial years.

Maximum contribution base (per quarter)				
2019/20	2020/21	2021/22	2022/23	2023/24
\$55,270	\$57,090	\$58,920	\$60,220	\$62,270

Example Fred paid his employee, Barney, a salary of \$70,000 for the quarter beginning 1 July 2023. As Barney's salary exceeded the maximum contributions base of \$62,270 for the quarter, the total salary and wages to be taken into account for the purposes of determining any SG shortfall relating to Barney is \$62,270 (not \$70,000). It is therefore sufficient for Fred to contribute \$6,849.70 (ie 11% of \$62,270) to Barney's superannuation fund for the quarter.

A special rule requires the maximum contributions base to be calculated under the following formula in s 15(5) if the amount worked out under the formula is *less* than the maximum contributions base worked out under ss 15(3) and (4):

$$\text{Concessional contributions cap} \times \frac{100}{\text{charge percentage}} \times \frac{1}{4}$$

The aim of this rule is to ensure that if indexation of the maximum contribution base for a quarter requires an employer to make contributions that, if paid over the year, would result in the employee's concessional contributions exceeding the concessional contributions cap [19.9], the maximum contribution base for the quarter is reduced to an amount that does not result in any excess concessional contributions.

Example The rule in s 15(5) does not apply for any quarter in 2023/24 as the maximum contribution base calculated under the formula in s 15(5) is \$65,476.19 (ie \$27,500 × 100/11 × 1/4), which is *more* than the maximum contributions base of \$62,270 worked out under ss 15(3) and (4).

So that an employee does not breach the concessional contributions cap as a result of having SG contributions made on their behalf by multiple employers, the employee is allowed to designate that salary or wages from specified employers be excluded from the standard SG rules. Sections 19AA and 19AB *SGAA* enable an employee to apply to the Commissioner for an 'employer shortfall exemption certificate'. The certificate allows any employer specified on the certificate to treat the maximum contributions base for the quarter in respect of the employee as being nil. It therefore prevents such employers from having SG shortfalls as a result of not making SG contributions for the employee.

Salary or wages

For SG purposes, the term 'salary or wages' takes its ordinary meaning and expressly includes certain payments such as commissions, directors' fees, payments under a contract principally for the labour of a person and remuneration paid to Members of Parliament, government employees and employees (but not office holders) of local governing bodies. It does not, however, include fringe benefits (s 11).

In spite of the broad definition of salary or wages, not all forms of salary or wages are necessarily taken into account for SG purposes. For example, salary or wages paid to an employee who is not an Australian resident for work done outside Australia (s 27(1)(b)) and salary or wages paid by an employer who is not an Australian resident to an employee who is an Australian resident for work done outside Australia (s 27(1)(c)) are ignored. Likewise, salary or wages prescribed under reg 12 *Superannuation Guarantee (Administration) Regulations 2018* (Cth) (eg salary or wages paid to an employee for a period of parental leave) are also ignored (s 27(1)(e)). Previously, salary or wages of less than $450 per month were also not taken into account (former s 27(2)). However, this exemption was removed from 1 July 2022.

Charge percentage

The charge percentage was originally 3% and has progressively increased over the years. From 2002/03 to 2012/13 it was 9%. The Labor Government increased the charge percentage to 9.25% for 2013/14 and 9.5% for 2014/15. The charge percentage was then going to rise by 0.5% each year until it reached 12% in 2019/20. However, the Coalition Government froze the rate at 9.5% from 2014/15 until 2020/21. The rate increased to 10% in 2021/22, 10.5% in 2022/23 and 11% in 2023/24. It will continue to rise in annual increments of 0.5% until it reaches 12% in 2025/26 as set out below.

Superannuation guarantee charge percentage					
2014/15 to 2020/21	2021/22	2022/23	2023/24	2024/25	2025/26
9.5%	10%	10.5%	11%	11.5%	12%

The charge percentage is reduced (until it reaches 0%) by the percentage of actual employer support provided in respect of the quarter. This is measured under the *SGAA* as follows:

- For defined benefit schemes, the percentage of actual employer support is the percentage specified in an actuary's benefit certificate (s 22).
- For accumulation schemes, the percentage of actual employer support is measured by reference to the actual contributions made to the fund expressed as a percentage of the employee's 'ordinary time earnings' (s 23).

An employee's 'ordinary time earnings' for a quarter is the total of the employee's earnings in respect of ordinary hours of work (but not lump sum payments on termination of employment for unused sick, annual or long service leave) and over-award payments, shift loadings or commissions for the quarter. However, if these earnings exceed the maximum contributions base for the quarter, the employee's ordinary time earnings is the maximum contributions base for the quarter (s 6). The Commissioner's guidelines on ordinary time earnings are set out in SGR 2009/2.

The meaning of ordinary time earnings was considered by the Full Federal Court in *Bluescope Steel (AIS) Pty Ltd v Australian Workers' Union* [2019] FCAFC 84. The case concerned an employer's SG obligations in respect of employees who were required under various industrial instruments to work on Sundays and public holidays. The Full Federal Court held that the employer was not liable to pay SG contributions in respect of the additional hours and public holiday components of the salaries paid to its employees. According to the Court, the definition of 'ordinary time earnings', including the phrase 'earnings in respect of ordinary hours of work', had within it 'the well-known conception of ordinary hours at ordinary rates'. The Court explained its reasoning as follows (at 121):

> The superannuation legislation is structured upon standard hours at ordinary rates, where present in an industrial instrument. . . . That legislation is not intended to give superannuation benefits for the total salary. It was and is a system to encourage national savings for retirement based on standard hours at ordinary rates.

> ***Example*** Tom employs Jerry. In the first quarter of 2023/24, Tom contributed $300 to Jerry's accumulation fund. Jerry's ordinary time earnings and salary for the quarter were both $10,000. Tom therefore made superannuation contributions equal to 3% (ie $300/$10,000) of Jerry's ordinary time earnings to his superannuation fund for the quarter. Tom's charge percentage for the quarter is 8% (ie 11% – 3%) and his individual SG shortfall in respect of Jerry for the quarter is $800 (ie $10,000 × 8%).

Contributions can be taken into account for a quarter if they are made by the 28th day *after* the end of the quarter and have not otherwise been taken into account for another period. Any excess contributions made within 12 months *before* the beginning of the relevant quarter can also be taken into account (ss 23(6) to (8)).

Employers can also elect to offset late superannuation contributions (ie contributions made after the 28th day following the end of the relevant quarter) against the interest and shortfall component of their SGC liability for the quarter (s 23A). The election must be made in the approved form within four years after the employer's original assessment for the quarter is made. Late contributions that employers elect to offset in this way are not deductible (s 290-95 *ITAA97*).

In the 2023 Budget, the Government announced it is proposing to require employers to pay their employees' superannuation at the same time as their salary and wages. This reform (called 'payday super') will commence from 1 July 2026.

Payment of shortfall component of the SGC

The Commissioner must generally pay the 'shortfall component' of the SGC to a complying superannuation fund, ADF or RSA nominated by the 'benefiting employee'. This ensures that the employee receives the superannuation support that they should have otherwise received from the employer. If the employee does not make a nomination, the shortfall component must be deposited in the SHASA on behalf of the employee (s 65 *SGAA*). Where there is only one benefiting employee, the shortfall component is the amount of the individual SG shortfall for the employee and the nominal interest component (plus the GIC where late payment is involved) (s 64A). Where more than one benefiting employee is involved, separate shortfall components are worked out for each employee (s 64B).

The Commissioner must pay the shortfall component directly to the employee if the employee is aged 65 or more (s 65A), has a terminal medical condition (s 66A) or has retired due to permanent incapacity (s 66) and the employee has requested him to do so in the approved form. Where an employee has died, the shortfall component must be paid to the employee's legal personal representative (s 67).

Choice of fund rules

Part 3A *SGAA* (ss 32A to 32ZA) contains special 'choice of fund' rules. These rules require employers to make SG contributions to superannuation funds or RSAs that are chosen by their employees (s 32C(1)). The choice of fund rules are also satisfied if employer SG contributions are made in certain other specified situations. For example, they are satisfied if SG contributions are made to the Commonwealth Superannuation Scheme (s 32C(3)) or the Public Sector Superannuation Scheme (s 32C(4)). They are also satisfied if SG contributions are made under certain awards or in accordance with a workplace determination or an enterprise agreement made before 1 January 2021 (s 32C(6)).

Employers must provide their employees, within 28 days of commencing employment, with a 'standard choice form' allowing them to nominate a particular complying superannuation fund or RSA (ss 32N, 32P). If an employee does not choose a particular fund or RSA, the employer can make contributions to an 'eligible choice fund', which is commonly referred to as a 'default fund'. However this rule operates subject to a new rule which provides that, if an employee who commenced employment on or after 1 November 2021 has not chosen a fund and the employer has been notified by the Commissioner that the employee has a 'stapled fund' [19.4], the contributions are required to be made to the stapled fund (s 32C(1A)).

Since 1 January 2014, only a 'MySuper product' qualifies as a default fund. APRA has the role of authorising a MySuper product. To gain authorisation, RSE licensees are required to ensure that their products comply with a broad range of criteria aimed at benefiting members. In general, APRA will only authorise one product per RSE licensee. The objective of MySuper is to provide members with a standardised superannuation product that has a single diversified investment strategy. MySuper products have simpler features, lower costs and increased transparency. They are designed to allow members to more easily understand and compare superannuation products. The kinds of fees that RSE licensees can charge on MySuper products are restricted. While they are able to charge administration, investment and certain switching fees, they are prohibited from charging entry and exit fees. Furthermore, to prevent discrimination, RSE licensees have to adhere to special charging rules (eg they have to base their fees on either a flat fee to all members, a percentage fee to all members or a combination of such fees). Where a member's balance in a MySuper product is below $6,000, the maximum administration and investment fees and prescribed costs that can be charged must not exceed 3% of the account balance.

Where, during a quarter, an employer makes contributions to a superannuation fund or RSA that does not comply with the choice of fund requirements, the employer's individual SG shortfall for the particular employee under s 19(1) may be increased by an amount calculated pursuant to formulas contained in either s 19(2A) (for accumulation funds) or s 19(2B) (for defined benefit funds). Broadly, these formulas increase the employer's individual SG shortfall for the particular employee by 25% of the amount of any shortfall that would have otherwise arisen under s 19(1) if the contributions to the non-choice fund had been ignored. The increase operates subject to a cap of $500 per quarter or 'notice period' (s 19A).

Example Stan employs Oliver, who has ordinary time earnings of $10,000 per quarter. In the quarter beginning 1 July 2023, Stan contributed $700 to Fund A and $400 to Fund B on behalf of Oliver. Although both funds are complying superannuation funds, Oliver has chosen Fund A (which is an accumulation fund) as the fund to which employer contributions are to be made. The total contributions made by Stan on behalf of Oliver for the quarter amount to $1,100. As this amount is 11% of $10,000, there is no individual SG shortfall under s 19(1) as the charge percentage is reduced from 11% to 0%. However, as $400 of the contributions do not comply with the choice of fund rules, Stan's individual SG shortfall in respect of Oliver for the quarter is increased to $100 (ie 25% × $400) under s 19(2A).

To help small employers manage their choice of fund obligations, employers with less than 20 employees or aggregated turnover below $10m can make SG contributions to a central online Small Business Superannuation Clearing House ('SBSCH') administered by the ATO. The SBSCH has the role of passing on contributions to the chosen funds nominated by the employees.

[19.6] Phases in the tax treatment of superannuation

The income tax provisions dealing with superannuation are located in pt 3-30 *ITAA97*. The provisions are complex and span many pages of legislation. In simple terms, they divide the taxation of superannuation into three distinct phases:

- **Phase 1—Contributions phase.** The contributions phase relates to when contributions are made to a superannuation plan [19.7]. Contributions may be made by a range of persons, including the fund's members and their employers. The Government also makes co-contributions to superannuation funds for eligible low-income earners [19.8]. Employers can usually deduct contributions made in respect of their employees (eg SG and salary sacrifice contributions). Members can choose to make either deductible or non-deductible personal contributions. From 1 July 2017, after-tax contributions are not permitted if immediately before the start of the income year a member's 'total superannuation balance' equals or exceeds the 'general transfer balance cap' for the income year [19.15]. Members who have excess concessional contributions or excess non-concessional contributions may be assessed on particular amounts and required to pay certain taxes [19.9]. High-income earners may also be subject to div 293 tax in respect of certain contributions [19.10].
- **Phase 2—Investment phase.** The investment phase relates to when contributions are received and invested by a fund [19.14]. Trustees of complying superannuation funds are generally required to pay tax on the taxable income of the fund at the rate of 15% (the 'non-arm's length component' is taxed at the rate of 45%). Importantly, the assessable income of a fund includes any concessional contributions it receives. The tax payable on concessional contributions is commonly referred to as 'contributions tax'. Where a member has not provided their TFN to the superannuation fund, the trustee may also be subject to 'no-TFN contributions tax' at the rate of 32%.
- **Phase 3—Benefits phase.** The benefits phase relates to when superannuation benefits are paid to members (eg on retirement) or as death benefits (eg to dependants) [19.16]. Superannuation benefits can be paid as lump sums and/or income streams and their taxation treatment depends on the type of benefit received and the age of the member. Benefits may comprise a 'tax-free component' and/or a 'taxable component'. Benefits paid from 'taxed funds' are more concessionally taxed than benefits paid form 'untaxed funds' (eg constitutionally protected funds) [19.4]. As a general rule, benefits paid from taxed funds to members aged 60 or over are tax-free.

The diagram on the following page summarises how the three phases of superannuation are taxed. The diagram deals with contributions made to, and benefits paid from, a taxed accumulation fund. Special rules apply to death benefits and benefits from defined benefit and untaxed funds.

[19.7] Superannuation contributions

To encourage superannuation investment, taxpayers that make contributions to superannuation funds and RSAs may be entitled to deductions or tax offsets for their contributions under div 290 *ITAA97*. Contributions can include not only money, but also transfers of property (in which case the contribution is the market value of the property less any consideration given for the transfer) (s 285-5). Division 290 deals with three distinct kinds of contributions:

- employer contributions (sub-div 290-B)
- personal contributions (sub-div 290-C), and
- spouse contributions (sub-div 290-D).

Deductions for superannuation contributions can only be claimed under div 290 (s 290-10). They cannot therefore be deducted under s 8-1.

Deduction for employer contributions (sub-div 290-B)

Section 290-60 allows employers to deduct contributions made to a superannuation fund or an RSA for the purpose of providing superannuation benefits for persons who are their employees when

Basic Treatment of Superannuation Contributions and Benefits

Phase 1 — Contributions Phase [19.7] to [19.10]

- **Employer contributions for employees (sub-div 290-B)** — Deductible (s 290-60)
- **Personal contributions *with* notice of intention to claim deductions (sub-div 290-C)** — Deductible (s 290-150)
- **Personal contributions *without* notice of intention to claim deductions** — Not deductible
- **Spouse contributions (sub-div 290-D)** — Not deductible, but tax offset may be available (s 290-230)
- **Government co-contributions**

Concessional contributions

Excess concessional contributions are concessional contributions over $27,500 (for 2023/24) (s 291-20)

Members with superannuation balances under $500,000 may be able to carry forward up to 5 years of unused concessional contributions (s 291-20)

Excess concessional contributions are included in a member's assessable income and taxed at their marginal rate (subject to a 15% tax offset) (s 291-15)

Members with income over $250,000 are subject to div 293 tax on their 'taxable contributions' (ie broadly their concessional contributions that are not excess concessional contributions) at the rate of 15% (s 293-15)

Non-concessional contributions

Excess non-concessional contributions are non-concessional contributions over $110,000 (for 2023/24) (s 292-85)

Members under 75 with superannuation balances under $1.9m may be able to bring forward up to 3 years of non-concessional contributions (s 292-85)

Members issued with an excess non-concessional contributions determination can elect to have the total release amount (ie the excess non-concessional contributions and 85% of associated earnings) released from the fund

The released amount is non-assessable non-exempt income (s303-15), but the associated earnings are included in a member's assessable income and taxed at their marginal rate (subject to a 15% tax offset) (ss 292-25, 292-30)

Members who do not elect to have the total release amount released from the fund are subject to ENCCT at the rate of 47% on the excess non-concessional contributions (s 292-80)

Phase 2 — Investment Phase [19.14]

- Employer contributions: Assessable (s 295-160)
- Personal contributions with notice: Assessable (s 295-190)
- Personal contributions without notice: Not assessable
- Spouse contributions: Not assessable (s 295-165)
- Government co-contributions: Not assessable (s 295-170)

Complying Superannuation Fund

'Low tax component' of taxable income is taxed at the rate of 15% (s 26(1) *ITRA*)
'Non-arm's length component' of taxable income is taxed at the rate of 45% (s 26(2) *ITRA*)
'No-TFN contributions income' is taxed at the rate of 32% (s 29 *ITRA*)

Phase 3 — Benefits Phase [19.16]

Tax-free component

The tax-free component comprises:

- a 'contributions segment' (ie contributions made after 30 June 2007 that have not been included in assessable income of the fund) (s 307-220), and
- a 'crystallised segment' (ie certain components that were concessionally taxed under the former rules) (s 307-225)

The tax-free component is non-assessable non-exempt income (s 301-15, s 301-30)

Taxable component

The taxable component is the value of the superannuation interest less the tax-free component (s 307-215). The taxable component is taxed in accordance with the following table:

	Member is 60 or older	Member is between their preservation age and 60	Member is under their preservation age
Lump sum	Non-assessable non-exempt income (s 301-10)	Tax-free up to 'low rate cap amount' ($235,000 for 2023/24) and balance taxed at a rate of no more than 15% (plus ML) (s 301-20)	Taxed at a rate of no more than 20% (plus ML) (s 301-35)
Pension	Non-assessable non-exempt income (s 301-10)	Taxed at marginal rates (plus ML) with 15% tax offset available (s 301-25)	Taxed at marginal rates (plus ML) with 15% tax offset available if a disability benefit (s 301-40)

the contributions are made. Deductions are available in the year the contributions are made and are allowable regardless of whether the benefits are payable to the employee's dependants if they die before or after becoming entitled to receive the benefits.

An entity is only entitled to deductions for contributions under s 290-60 if the following conditions in ss 290-70, 290-75 and 290-80 are satisfied:

- **Employment activity condition.** Section 290-70 requires the employee to be engaged in producing the entity's assessable income, or to be an Australian resident engaged in the entity's business.
- **Complying fund condition.** Section 290-75 requires that if contributions are made to a superannuation fund, at least one of the following conditions must be satisfied:
  (a) the fund must be a complying superannuation fund for the year in which the contributions are made
  (b) at the time of making the contributions, the entity must have had reasonable grounds to believe that the fund was a complying fund, or
  (c) at or before the time of making the contributions, the entity must have obtained a written statement from the fund stating that it was a resident regulated superannuation fund and not subject to a direction preventing it from accepting employer contributions.
- **Age-related condition.** Section 290-80 requires that the contributions must:
  (a) be made on or before the 28th day after the end of the month in which the employee turns 75
  (b) be made under an industrial award, determination or notional agreement preserving state awards, or
  (c) reduce the employer's SGC percentage.

  If a contribution is made after the 28th day following the end of the month in which the employee turns 75, then the deduction cannot exceed the greater of the amount of the contribution required under the relevant industrial award, determination or notional agreement or the amount of the contribution that reduces the employer's SG charge percentage.

Example Alf employs Sam (who is 50 years old) and contributes $10,000 to Sam's complying superannuation fund on 5 July 2023. Alf can deduct the contribution in the 2023/24 income year.

19

Contributions made by employers on behalf of their former employees may also be deductible in certain circumstances, such as where they reduce the employer's SGC percentage [19.5], are one-off payments in lieu of salary or wages that relate to a period when such persons were employees, or are made within four months of such persons ceasing to be employees (s 290-85).

There is also a special rule that allows a person who has a 'controlling interest' in a company to claim deductions for contributions made for the benefit of current or former employees of that company (s 290-90).

Example James owns all the shares in J Co, which employs Alice. If James contributes $1,000 to Alice's complying superannuation fund, he is entitled to a deduction for the contribution as he has a controlling interest in J Co. However, this contribution is not taken into account for J Co's SG purposes as James is not Alice's employer.

Any direct or indirect return of contributions or earnings on contributions made to an employer or controller is included in their assessable income (s 290-100).

Deduction for personal contributions (sub-div 290-C)

Section 290-150 allows a person to claim deductions for contributions made to a superannuation fund or an RSA for the purpose of providing superannuation benefits for themselves. The deductions are available in the year the contributions are made and are allowable regardless of whether the benefits are payable to the person's dependants if the person dies before or after becoming entitled to receive the benefits.

A person is only entitled to deductions under s 290-150 if the following conditions in ss 290-155, 290-165 and 290-170 are satisfied:

- **Complying superannuation fund condition.** Section 290-155 requires that if contributions are made to a superannuation fund, the fund must be a complying superannuation fund in the year in which the contributions are made. In addition, the fund must not be a Commonwealth public sector superannuation scheme in which a person has a defined benefit interest, an untaxed fund or a superannuation fund prescribed by the regulations.
- **Age-related conditions.** Section 290-165 requires that if the person is under 18 at the end of the income year in which the contribution is made, they must have derived income in the income year from employment or carrying on a business. In any other case, the contributions must be made on or before the 28th day after the end of the month in which the person turns 75. In addition, from 1 July 2022, persons aged between 67 and 75 must also meet a 'work test' (ie they must have been gainfully employed for at least 40 hours in any period of 30 consecutive days during the income year in which the contribution was made) or satisfy a 'one-off rule' (ie they must have met the work test in the previous income year, have a total superannuation balance of less than $300,000 at the end of that year, have not already relied on the one off rule in respect of any contribution, and have not made a contribution that falls within a prescribed provision).
- **Notice of intent condition.** Section 290-170 requires the person to give a notice to the trustee of the superannuation fund or the RSA provider of his or her intention to claim a deduction. The notice must be provided by the earlier of the time the person lodges their income tax return for the year and the end of the financial year following the year the contribution was made. In *Khanna v FC of T* [2022] AATA 33, the AAT held that the Commissioner does not have the discretion to extend this time limit. A person cannot deduct more than the amount specified in the notice (s 290-175). Although a notice cannot be revoked or withdrawn, it can be varied in special circumstances (s 290-180).

> ***Example*** Bart is 40 years old and is self-employed. Lisa is 28 years old and an employee. They each contribute $20,000 to their respective complying superannuation funds in 2023/24. Assuming the funds are both taxed funds and not prescribed by the regulations, both Bart and Lisa can deduct the contributions they make in 2023/24 so long as they provide the funds with the requisite notice of their intention to claim the deductions.

Tax offset for spouse contributions (sub-div 290-D)

A person may be entitled to a non-refundable tax offset for contributions made to a complying superannuation fund or RSA for the benefit of their spouse (s 290-230). To be eligible for the tax offset, both the contributor and the spouse must be residents at the time the contribution is made.

In addition, the total of the spouse's assessable income, reportable fringe benefits total and reportable employer superannuation contributions for the year must be less than $40,000.

A tax offset is not available if a deduction is allowable for the contribution under s 290-60 (ie for employer contributions), or if the contributor is living separately from the spouse on a permanent basis (s 290-230(3)). In addition, a tax offset is not available if the taxpayer's spouse's non-concessional contributions for the financial year exceed their 'non-concessional contributions cap' for the year [19.9], or if immediately before the start of the financial year, the spouse's 'total superannuation balance' (defined in s 307-230) equals or exceeds the 'general transfer balance cap' for the income year (ie $1.6m for 2017/18 to 2020/21, $1.7m for 2021/22 to 2022/23 and $1.9m for 2023/24) [19.15] (s 290-230(4A)).

The maximum tax offset available in an income year cannot exceed 18% of the lesser of:

(a) $3,000 reduced by the amount by which the spouse's assessable income, reportable fringe benefits total and reportable employer superannuation contributions for the income year exceeds $37,000, and

(b) the sum of the spouse contributions for the income year (s 290-235).

Example Harry is married to Wendy and they are both 50-year-old Australian residents. In 2023/24, Wendy earns assessable income of $38,000 and does not have any reportable fringe benefits total or reportable employer superannuation contributions. Her total superannuation balance on 30 June 2023 is $1m. Her non-concessional contributions for 2023/24 do not exceed her non-concessional contributions cap for the year.

In July 2023, Harry contributed $3,000 to Wendy's complying superannuation fund. Harry is entitled to a tax offset under s 290-230 in 2023/24 of $360, being the lesser of:

(a) $360 = 18% × ($3,000 – $1,000), and

(b) $540 = 18% × $3,000.

As a consequence, Harry's net cost of contributing $3,000 to Wendy's superannuation fund is only $2,640 (ie $3,000 – $360).

If Wendy's assessable income was $37,000 or less, Harry would be entitled to a $540 tax offset for his contribution. In such case, his net cost of contributing $3,000 to Wendy's superannuation fund would be only $2,460 (ie $3,000 – $540).

Financing costs on loans to fund superannuation contributions

Financing costs incurred to fund superannuation contributions are only deductible if they relate to contributions that are deductible under sub-div 290-B *ITAA97* (s 26-80). This means employers are generally able to claim deductions for interest payments on loans used to fund superannuation contributions made for their employees. Individuals are, however, not able to claim deductions for interest payments on loans used to fund their personal superannuation contributions.

Example Ted runs a business and borrows money to make superannuation contributions for his employees. Ted is allowed deductions for the interest paid on the borrowings. If Ted also borrows money to make personal contributions to his own fund, he is not entitled to deductions for the interest paid on the borrowings.

[19.8] Government co-contributions

To help boost superannuation savings, the Government makes superannuation co-contributions in respect of eligible low-income earners under the *Superannuation (Government Co-contribution for Low Income Earners) Act 2003* (Cth) ('*SGCLIEA*'). There are two distinct kinds of co-contributions:

- co-contributions in respect of non-concessional contributions (eg non-deductible personal contributions), and
- co-contributions in respect of concessional contributions (eg employer contributions and deductible personal contributions).

Co-contributions are generally paid to the relevant person's superannuation fund or RSA. However, they can also be paid to the person (where the Commissioner is satisfied that the person has retired and no longer has an eligible account) or to the person's legal personal representative (where the Commissioner is satisfied that the person has died) (s 15 *SGCLIEA*; reg 7 *Superannuation (Government Co-contribution for Low Income Earners) Regulations 2022* (Cth)).

Co-contribution for non-concessional contributions

The first kind of government co-contribution relates to 'eligible personal superannuation contributions' (ie essentially non-concessional contributions made by a person to their complying superannuation fund or RSA) (s 7 *SGCLIEA*).

To be eligible for co-contributions the following requirements must be met:

- the person must make one or more eligible personal superannuation contributions during the income year
- at least 10% of the person's 'total income' for the year (ie the sum of their assessable income, reportable fringe benefits total and reportable employer superannuation contributions for the year) must be attributable to eligible activities (eg employment or carrying on a business)
- the person's total income for the income year must be less than the 'higher income threshold' for the year (see the table below)
- the person must have lodged an income tax return for the relevant income year
- the person's non-concessional contributions for the financial year must not exceed their non-concessional contributions cap for the financial year (ie $110,000 for 2021/22 to 2023/24) [19.9]
- immediately before the start of that financial year, the person's 'total superannuation balance' must be less than the 'general transfer balance cap' for that financial year (ie $1.7m for 2021/22 and 2022/23 and $1.9m for 2023/24) [19.15]
- the person must be under 71 years of age and must generally not be the holder of a temporary resident visa (unless they are a New Zealand citizen) (s 6).

The government co-contribution is 50% of the eligible personal superannuation contributions that the person makes during the income year (subject to a maximum co-contribution of $500) (ss 9, 10). The co-contribution is phased-out by 3.333 cents for each dollar that the person's 'total income' for the year exceeds the 'lower income threshold' for the year (see the table below) (s 10A).

The following table sets out the most recent co-contributions, thresholds and phase-out rates:

Income year	Maximum co-contribution	Lower income threshold	Higher income threshold	Phase-out rate
2023/24	$500	$43,445	$58,445	3.333 cents per dollar
2022/23	$500	$42,016	$57,016	3.333 cents per dollar

Example James is a 50-year-old resident and a full-time employee whose total income for 2023/24 was $53,445. James made eligible personal superannuation contributions of $4,000 to his complying superannuation fund during the year and did not elect to claim deductions for these contributions. He is entitled to a $167 government co-contribution made to his superannuation fund calculated as follows:

$$\$167 = \$500 - [(\$53{,}445 - \$43{,}445) \times 0.0333]$$

Co-contribution for concessional contributions

The second kind of government co-contribution relates to 'concessional contributions' and is known as the 'low-income superannuation contribution'.

To be eligible for co-contributions, the person's adjusted taxable income [8.6] for the income year must not exceed $37,000 and at least 10% of their 'total income' for the year must be attributable to eligible activities (eg employment or carrying on a business) (s 12C *SGCLIEA*). In addition, they must not be the holder of a temporary resident visa (unless they are a New Zealand citizen).

The co-contribution is calculated by multiplying the concessional contributions made in respect of the person for the income year by 15% (s 12E). The co-contribution aims to compensate low-income earners for the 15% 'contributions tax' paid by their funds on the concessional contributions which are included in the assessable income of the fund [19.9]. The maximum payment that the Government will make in respect of an eligible person for an income year is $500 and the minimum payment is $10 (amounts below this figure are rounded up to $10).

Example Wally is a 50-year-old resident employee who has adjusted taxable income of $30,000 in 2023/24. Wally's employer made $3,000 of SG and salary sacrifice contributions to his complying superannuation fund during the income year. The Government will co-contribute $450 (ie 3,000 × 15%) to Wally's superannuation fund. This compensates for the 15% contributions tax that the trustee of the fund must pay on the concessional contributions received in respect of Wally. If Wally's employer had, instead, contributed $4,000 to his superannuation fund, the government co-contribution would be capped at $500.

[19.9] Excess contributions

The superannuation tax concessions would be extremely costly for the Government if they were left uncapped. In the past, to protect the revenue and ensure that the superannuation tax concessions were not overly generous, RBL rules restricted the amount of superannuation benefits that were eligible for concessional tax treatment. Under these rules, benefits paid by superannuation funds that exceeded annually indexed RBL amounts were taxed at the top marginal rate in the hands of members.

The RBL rules were abolished from 1 July 2007. There is therefore no longer any limit on the amount of concessionally taxed benefits that members of superannuation funds can receive. Instead, to prevent exploitation of the superannuation concessions, special tax consequences arise where 'excess concessional contributions' or 'excess non-concessional contributions' are made to a person's superannuation fund during a financial year. In simple terms, excess concessional contributions and excess non-concessional contributions arise where the 'concessional contributions' and 'non-concessional contributions' made during the year exceed the respective caps set out in the following table. These caps operate subject to carry forward and bring forward rules that are examined further below.

Contributions caps		
Financial year	**Concessional contributions cap**	**Non-concessional contributions cap**
2021/22 to 2023/24	$27,500	$110,000
2017/18 to 2020/21	$25,000	$100,000

Excess concessional contributions

A person has 'excess concessional contributions' for an income year if their 'concessional contributions' for the year exceeds their 'concessional contributions cap' for the year (s 291-20 *ITAA97*).

Concessional contributions

Concessional contributions essentially cover contributions made to a complying superannuation plan in respect of a person that are included in the assessable income of the superannuation provider [19.14] (s 291-25). They include:

- employer contributions (eg SG contributions and salary sacrifice contributions)
- deductible personal contributions, and
- SGC shortfall amounts paid by the ATO to the member's fund.

Special rules apply to contributions made to defined benefit funds because employer contributions are not always attributable to individual members. Concessional contributions for these interests are based on 'notional taxed contributions' calculated under the *ITAR21* (ss 291-155 to 291-175).

Concessional contributions cap

In 2017/18, the concessional contributions cap was set at $25,000 (s 291-20). The cap is indexed annually in line with average weekly ordinary time earnings (s 960-285). Indexation is calculated by multiplying the $25,000 base amount by the relevant indexation factor and rounding the result down to the nearest multiple of $2,500. The cap remained at $25,000 for 2018/19 to 2020/21 and was indexed to $27,500 for 2021/22 to 2023/24.

Example During 2023/24, Sandra's employer made contributions of $29,000 to her complying superannuation fund which is an accumulation fund. Sandra also made $20,000 of non-deductible personal contributions to the fund. Only her employer's contributions are concessional contributions. Sandra therefore has excess concessional contributions of $1,500 (ie $29,000 – $27,500) for 2023/24.

Five-year carry forward of the concessional contributions cap

A special rule allows individuals to make additional 'catch-up' concessional contributions where they have not used all their concessional contributions cap in previous financial years. This rule allows them to carry forward their 'unused concessional contributions cap' amounts from up to five previous financial years provided their 'total superannuation balance' (defined in s 307-230 *ITAA97*) just before the start of the financial year is less than $500,000 (s 291-20(3)). The aim of the rule is to assist people who have experienced interrupted work patterns (eg those taking care of children) accumulate superannuation balances commensurate with those people who have not had breaks from the workforce.

The earliest financial year in which a person could have an unused concessional contributions cap amount was 2018/19. This means that the first financial year in which they were able to make additional concessional contributions was 2019/20. Unused concessional cap amounts that are not utilised after five financial years cannot be carried forward.

Example In each of the 2018/19, 2019/20, 2020/21 and 2021/22 financial years, Debbie's employer made concessional contributions of $10,000 to her complying superannuation fund. No other concessional contributions were made to her fund in those years. As the concessional contributions cap for 2018/19, 2019/20 and 2020/21 was $25,000, Debbie's unused concessional contributions cap amount for each of these financial years was $15,000. As the concessional contributions cap for 2021/22 was $27,500, Debbie's unused concessional contributions cap amount for that year was $17,500.

The concessional contributions cap for 2022/23 was also $27,500. If Debbie's total superannuation balance just before the 2022/23 financial year was less than $500,000, up to $80,000 (ie $15,000 + 15,000 + $15,000 +17,500 + $27,500) of concessional contributions could be made to her fund in 2022/23 without breaching the concessional contributions cap.

Treatment of excess concessional contributions

Individuals that have excess concessional contributions for an income year are required to include the excess concessional contributions in their assessable income and pay tax on those contributions at their respective marginal rates (s 291-15). They are also entitled to a non-refundable tax offset of 15% of the excess concessional contributions. The tax offset compensates them for the fact that 15% contributions tax has been paid on the excess concessional contributions by the superannuation provider. It is therefore designed to prevent double taxation of the contributions (ie once in the hands of the superannuation provider and again in the hands of the member).

Example Errol's employer contributes $37,500 to his superannuation fund in 2022/23. Errol therefore has excess concessional contributions of $10,000 (ie $37,500 – $27,500) for the year. As a consequence, Errol is required to include $10,000 in his assessable income for 2022/23. He is also entitled to a tax offset of $1,500 (ie $10,000 × 15%) to take account of the fact that the trustee of his superannuation fund has paid contributions tax of 15% on the $10,000 excess concessional contributions.

Releasing excess concessional contributions

A person who receives an excess concessional contributions determination for a financial year can request to have up to 85% of the amount of their excess concessional contributions for the year released from their superannuation fund (div 131 of sch 1 *TAA*) [19.13]. The released amount is non-assessable non-exempt income (s 303-15 *ITAA97*).

Example In the previous example, Errol could elect to have $8,500 released from his superannuation fund.

Excess non-concessional contributions

A person has excess non-concessional contributions for a financial year if they have received an 'excess non-concessional contributions determination' for the year (s 292-85(1)(a) *ITAA97*). The Commissioner is required to make such a determination where the person's 'non-concessional contributions' for the financial year exceed their 'non-concessional contributions cap' for the year. The determination must be in writing and state:

- the amount of the excess
- the amount of the 'associated earnings' on the excess (worked out according to the formula in s 97-30 *TAA*), and
- the 'total release amount' (ie the amount of the excess contributions plus 85% of the associated earnings) (s 97-25 *TAA*).

A person will, however, not have excess non-concessional contributions for a year if an amount equal to the excess has been released to the person in response to 'release authorities' [19.13] (s 292-85(1)(b)), or if the Commissioner has made a determination under s 292-467 *ITAA97* that the value of their superannuation interests is nil (eg where they have been paid their benefits in the meantime) (s 292-85(1)(c)).

Non-concessional contributions

Non-concessional contributions generally comprise contributions that are made to a complying superannuation plan in respect of a person and are not included in the assessable income of the superannuation provider (eg non-deductible personal contributions and spouse contributions) [19.14]. They also expressly include any excess concessional contributions (s 292-90).

Non-concessional contributions do not, however, include government co-contributions, roll-over superannuation benefits, certain contributions made to constitutionally protected funds and contributions arising from personal injury structured settlements and orders (ss 292-90, 292-95). In addition, they do not include contributions that do not exceed a lifetime annually indexed 'CGT cap amount' (set out in the table below) and relate to:

- capital gains (of up to $500,000) from CGT events happening to CGT assets that fall within the CGT small business retirement concession in sub-div 152-D *ITAA97* [17.9], or
- capital proceeds from CGT events happening to CGT assets that qualify for the 15-year small business exemption in sub-div 152-B *ITAA97* [17.9], or that would qualify for the exemption except for the fact that the CGT event did not result in a capital gain, related to a pre-CGT asset, or occurred before the expiry of the 15-year time limit due to a person's permanent incapacity (s 292-100).

CGT cap amount				
2019/20	2020/21	2021/22	2022/23	2023/24
$1,515,000	$1,565,000	$1,615,000	$1,650,000	1,705,000

Example During 2023/24, Gavin made $80,000 of non-deductible personal contributions to his superannuation fund. These contributions are ordinarily treated as non-concessional contributions. However, if $50,000 of the contributions related to a capital gain that Gavin made during the year and for which he claimed the small business retirement concession in sub-div 152-D, only $30,000 of the contributions would be non-concessional contributions.

If Gavin also had $37,500 of concessional contributions during the year, he would have excess concessional contributions of $10,000 (ie $37,500 – $27,500). The excess concessional contributions of $10,000 would also be treated as non-concessional contributions. His total non-concessional contributions for the year would therefore be $40,000 (ie $30,000 + $10,000).

Non-concessional contributions cap

From 1 July 2017, the general non-concessional contributions cap is four times the concessional contributions cap (s 292-85(2)). It is therefore $100,000 (ie 4 × $25,000) for 2017/18 to 2020/21 and $110,000 (ie 4 × $27,500) for 2021/22 to 2023/24. However, if immediately before the start of the year, the person's 'total superannuation balance' (defined in s 307-230) equals or exceeds the 'general transfer balance cap for the year' (ie $1.6m for 2017/18 to 2020/21, $1.7m for 2021/22 and 2022/23, and $1.9m for 2023/24) [19.15], the non-concessional contributions cap is nil. This effectively means that individuals that have total superannuation balances of at least $1.9m immediately before the start of the 2023/24 financial year will breach the cap as soon as they make any non-concessional contributions during the year.

Example Tony has a total superannuation balance of $1m on 30 June 2023. His non-concessional contributions cap for 2023/24 is therefore $110,000. However, if his total superannuation balance was $1.9m or more on 30 June 2023, his non-concessional contributions cap for 2023/24 would be nil.

Bring forward non-concessional contributions cap

The non-concessional contributions cap operates subject to a 'bring forward' rule, which allows people to bring forward up to three years of non-concessional contributions into one financial year (the first year) if:

- they are under 75 years of age (or under 67 years of age for contributions made before 1 July 2022) at any time in the first year
- their non-concessional contributions for the first year exceed their general non-concessional contributions cap for that year (ie $110,000 for 2021/22 to 2023/24)
- their total superannuation balance immediately before the first year is less than the general transfer balance cap for the first year (ie $1.7m for 2021/22 and 2022/23 and $1.9m for 2023/24) [19.15]
- the difference between the general transfer balance cap for the first year and their total superannuation balance immediately before the first year (the 'first year cap space') is greater than the general non-concessional contributions cap for the first year, and
- a previous operation of the bring forward rule does not determine their non-concessional contributions cap for the first year (s 292-85(3)).

Example George is 52 years old and his total superannuation balance on 30 June 2023 is $700,000. In 2023/24, George makes $190,000 of non-concessional contributions to his fund. He has not made any non-concessional contributions in earlier years. George can access the bring forward non-concessional contributions cap in 2023/24 because:

- he is under 75 years of age
- his non-concessional contributions for 2023/24 ($190,000) exceeds his general non-concessional contributions cap for 2023/24 ($110,000)
- his total superannuation balance immediately before 2023/24 ($700,000) is less than the 2023/24 general transfer balance cap ($1.9m)
- the difference between the general transfer balance cap for 2023/24 ($1.9m) and his total superannuation balance immediately before 2023/24 ($700,000) is greater than the general non-concessional contributions cap for 2023/24 ($110,000), and
- a previous operation of the bring forward rule does not determine his non-concessional contributions cap for 2023/24.

The amount of non-concessional contributions that an individual may bring forward into a financial year and the bring forward period depends on their 'first year cap space' (ie the difference between the general transfer balance cap for the first year and their total superannuation balance immediately before the first year).

- If the first year cap space is between one and two times the general non-concessional contributions cap, then the bring forward non-concessional contributions cap for the first year is two times the general non-concessional contributions cap for the first year (ie $200,000 for 2017/18 To 2020/21 and $220,000 for 2021/22 to 2023/24) and their bring forward period is two years (s 292-85(5)(a)).
- If the first year cap space is greater than twice the general non-concessional contributions cap, then the bring forward non-concessional contributions cap for the first year is three times their general non-concessional contributions cap (ie $300,000 for 2017/18 to 2020/21 and $330,000 for 2021/22 to 2023/24) and their bring forward period is three years (s 292-85(5)(b)).

Example Ned is 40 years old and has a total superannuation balance of $1.7m on 30 June 2023. If Ned also makes over $110,000 of non-concessional contributions in 2023/24, his bring forward non-concessional contributions cap is $220,000 and his bring forward period is two years. This is because the difference between the general transfer balance cap for 2023/24 ($1.9m) and his total superannuation balance on 30 June 2023 ($1.7m) is between one and two times the general non-concessional contributions cap (ie it is between $110,000 and $220,000).

Kelly is 50 years old. She has a total superannuation balance of $1m on 30 June 2023. If Kelly makes over $110,000 of non-concessional contributions in 2023/24, her bring forward non-concessional contributions cap is $330,000 and her bring forward period is three years. This is because the difference between the general transfer balance cap for 2023/24 ($1.9m) and her total superannuation balance on 30 June 2023 ($1m) is greater than two times the general non-concessional contributions cap ($220,000).

An individual who has a bring forward non-concessional contributions cap may make further non-concessional contributions in the second year of the bring forward period if:

- their total superannuation balance on 30 June of the financial year before the start of the second year is less than the general transfer balance cap in that second year, and
- their non-concessional contributions for the first year fall short of their cap for the first year.

The individual's cap for the second year is the shortfall (ie the unused portion of their cap from the first year) (s 292-85(6)).

If the individual has a three-year bring forward period, they may also make further non-concessional contributions in the third year of the bring forward period if:

- their total superannuation balance on 30 June before the start of the third year is less than the general transfer balance cap in that third year, and
- their non-concessional contributions for the second year fall short of their cap for the second year, or, if their cap for the second year is nil, their non-concessional contributions for the first year fell short of their cap for the first year.

The individual's cap for the third year is the relevant shortfall (ie the unused portion of their cap from the first or second year) (s 292-85(7)).

Example In the previous example, Kelly had a bring forward non-concessional contributions cap of $330,000 in 2023/24 and a bring forward period of three years. If Kelly made non-concessional contributions of $120,000 in 2023/24, the contributions would not exceed her non-concessional contributions cap for the year. Assume that the general transfer balance cap for 2024/25 and 2025/26 remains the same as for 2023/24 ($1.9m). If Kelly's total superannuation balance on 30 June 2024 is less than $1.9m, Kelly can make up to $210,000 of non-concessional contributions in 2024/25 without breaching her non-concessional contributions cap. If she actually makes $130,000 of contributions in 2024/25, she will not breach the cap. On this basis, if her total superannuation balance on 30 June 2025 is less than $1.9m, she will be able to make a further $80,000 of non-concessional contributions in 2025/26 without breaching her non-concessional contributions cap for that year.

The following table summarises the bring forward non-concessional contributions caps and bring forward periods for 2023/24.

Individual's total superannuation balance on 30 June 2023	Non-concessional contributions cap for the first year	Bring forward period
Less than $1.68m	$330,000	3 years
$1.68m to less than $1.79m	$220,000	2 years
$1.79m to less than $1.9m	$110,000	Not applicable
$1.9m or more	Nil	Not applicable

Treatment of excess non-concessional contributions

A person that has been issued an excess non-concessional contributions determination has two options:

- **Release option.** The first option is to elect to have the 'total release amount' stated in the determination released from their superannuation fund [19.13]. The release amount is non-assessable non-exempt income (s 303-15 *ITAA97*). The person must, nevertheless, include the amount of the associated earnings in their assessable income for the year (s 292-25). They are also entitled to a non-refundable tax offset of 15% of the associated earnings (s 292-30). This ensures that they are assessed at their marginal tax rates on the associated earnings subject to a tax offset for the 15% tax paid by the superannuation provider on the earnings.
- **Non-release option.** The second option is to elect not to have the total release amount released from their superannuation fund, in which case they will be liable to pay ENCCT on the excess non-concessional contributions (ss 292-80, 292-85 *ITAA97*). ENCCT is payable at the rate of 47% (s 292-80 *ITAA97*; ss 4, 5 *SENCCTA*). It is due and payable 21 days after the Commissioner gives the person an excess non-concessional contributions tax assessment for the year under s 292-230 (s 292-385). ENCCT is not deductible (s 26-75 *ITAA97*) [14.3].

If a person does not make an election, the ATO will act on their behalf and apply the first option.

Example Sally breaches her excess non-concessional contributions cap by $100,000 in 2023/24. The Commissioner issues her with an excess non-concessional contributions determination stating that the excess is $100,000, the associated earnings is $10,000, and the total release amount is $108,500.

If Sally elects to have the total release amount released, her superannuation provider would be required to pay her $108,500. She would be required to include $10,000 in her assessable income and pay tax on this amount at her marginal rate. She would also be entitled to a tax offset of $1,500 (ie $10,000 × 15%).

If she elects not to have the total release amount released, she would be liable to pay ENCCT of $47,000 (ie $100,000 × 47%).

In practice, it is in a person's interests to have amounts released as this will avoid them becoming liable for ENCCT. Released amounts are required to be paid by superannuation funds to the Commissioner who first applies the money to discharge any outstanding tax debts of the person and then pays any balance over to them.

[19.10] Division 293 tax

High-income earners have traditionally derived a greater benefit than low-income earners from concessional contributions. This is because there is a greater arbitrage between their personal tax rate and the 15% superannuation fund tax rate. To reduce the bias in favour of high-income earners, div 293 *ITAA97* imposes a 15% tax on concessional contributions of people earning income (inclusive of concessional contributions) above a prescribed threshold. From 1 July 2017, the threshold is $250,000. In previous years, it was $300,000.

It is important to understand that div 293 tax is payable by high-income earners on top of the 15% 'contributions tax' already paid by the trustees of their funds on any concessional contributions they receive [19.14]. The tax does not apply to excess concessional contributions as these contributions are already taxed in the hands of members at their marginal rates under the arrangements discussed at [19.9]. The practical effect of div 293 tax is that a high-income earner's concessional contributions are effectively taxed at an overall rate of 30% rather than merely the contributions tax rate of 15%.

Division 293 tax on taxable contributions

Division 293 tax is payable by individuals who have 'taxable contributions' for an income year (s 293-15). The tax is imposed on the individual's taxable contributions at the rate of 15% (s 4 *SSSCCIA*). Division 293 tax is not deductible (s 26-98 *ITAA97*) [14.3].

A person has 'taxable contributions' for an income year where the sum of their 'low-tax contributions' and 'income for surcharge purposes' (disregarding 'reportable superannuation contributions') for the year exceeds $250,000 (s 293-20). Their taxable contributions is the *lesser* of their low-tax contributions and the amount of the excess. Where they do not have any low-tax contributions their taxable contributions are deemed to be nil.

A person's 'low-tax contributions' for an income year are generally the person's 'low-tax contributed amounts' for the year less their 'excess concessional contributions' for the year (s 293-25). In the majority of cases, a person's 'low-tax contributed amounts' for an income year is simply their concessional contributions for the year (eg employer contributions and deductible personal contributions) (s 293-30).

If the person's income excluding concessional contributions is less than the threshold, but their concessional contributions pushes them over the threshold, div 293 tax only applies to the part of the contributions that exceeds the threshold.

Low-tax contributions in relation to defined benefit interests are calculated under modified rules in sub-div 293-D. Broadly, these rules provide that a person's low-tax contributions for an income year is worked out by: first, calculating their low-tax contributed amounts under s 293-30 (but only to the extent that they relate to accumulation interests); second, subtracting their excess concessional contributions; and third, adding their 'defined benefit contributions' as defined in s 293-115 (s 293-105).

Special modifications also apply under sub-div 293-E (to ensure that state office holders do not pay div 293 tax in respect of contributions to constitutionally protected funds unless the contributions are made as part of a salary package) and sub-div 293-F (to ensure that Commonwealth judges do not pay div 293 tax in respect of contributions to a defined benefit interest established under the *Judges' Pensions Act 1968* (Cth)).

Example Butch and Cassie are accumulation superannuation fund members. In 2023/24, Butch's income for surcharge purposes (disregarding reportable superannuation contributions) is $265,000 and Cassie's income for surcharge purposes (disregarding reportable superannuation contributions) is $235,000. Their employers each make $25,000 of contributions to their respective superannuation funds. They therefore each have low-tax contributions of $25,000 for the year.

Butch's total income for surcharge purposes (other than reportable superannuation contributions) and low-tax contributions is $290,000 (ie $265,000 + $25,000). As Butch's low-tax contributions (ie $25,000) is less than the excess of $290,000 over $250,000 (ie $40,000), his taxable contributions for the year is $25,000. He must therefore pay div 293 tax of $3,750 (ie $25,000 × 15%).

Cassie's total income for surcharge purposes (other than reportable superannuation contributions) and low-tax contributions is $260,000 (ie $235,000 + $25,000). As the excess of $260,000 over $250,000 (ie $10,000) is less than her low-tax contributions (ie $25,000), her taxable contributions for the year is $10,000. She must therefore pay div 293 tax of $1,500 (ie $10,000 × 15%).

Assessment and payment of div 293 tax

Division 293 tax is generally due and payable 21 days after the Commissioner gives the taxpayer a notice of assessment of the amount of the tax (s 293-65(1)). However, to the extent that div 293 tax is attributable to defined benefit interests, the liability is deferred under special rules contained in div 133 of sch 1 *TAA* (s 293-65(2)). Under these rules, the Commissioner is required to maintain a debt account for the deferred tax (s 133-60). Debt accounts accrue interest and taxpayers can make voluntary payments to reduce the debit balances in their accounts (ss 133-65, 133-70). The deferred tax must generally be paid 21 days after the taxpayer's 'end benefit' for the superannuation interest is paid (ss 133-110, 133-130). Taxpayers who are assessed to pay div 293 tax may request the Commissioner to release an amount from their superannuation interest (other than a defined benefit interest) to pay their tax [19.13]. Released amounts are non-assessable non-exempt income (s 303-20 *ITAA97*).

[19.11] Tax on earnings on superannuation balances over $3m

The Albanese Government is proposing to introduce a new 15% tax on earnings on superannuation balances in excess of $3m from 1 July 2025 [19.3]. The scope of the proposed changes are outlined in its 2023 consultation paper, *Better Targeted Superannuation Concessions*, and are summarised below.

Application

The tax will apply to individuals with a 'total superannuation balance' (ie combined balances in all their superannuation accounts) in excess of $3m. It will only be payable on earnings on the proportion of an individual's total superannuation balance that exceeds $3m. Accordingly, someone with a total superannuation balance of $4m would only have the additional tax apply to earnings on $1m (not $4m). The tax will be in addition to the 15% tax generally paid by the trustee of the fund on the earnings [19.14]. It will operate similarly to div 293 tax [19.10] in that individuals will be able to pay the tax directly to the ATO or choose to have the money released from their superannuation funds [19.13].

Example Ginger has one superannuation account with a balance of $190,000 at 30 June 2026. Her sister, Mary-Ann, has three superannuation accounts with balances totalling $3.8m at 30 June 2026. The proposed changes will only apply to Mary-Ann as only she has a total superannuation balance of more than $3m.

Calculating tax liability

An individual's tax liability will be calculated according to the following three steps:

1. The earnings in relation to the individual's total superannuation interests will be calculated. This will be the difference between the individual's total superannuation balance for the current year (adjusted for withdrawals and contributions) and their total superannuation balance from the previous financial year as set out below:

$$\text{Earnings} = \left(\text{TSB}_{\text{Current Financial Year}} + \text{Withdrawals} - \text{Net Contributions}\right) - \text{TSB}_{\text{Previous Financial Year}}$$

2. The proportion of earnings attributable to the individual's balance over $3m will be calculated as follows:

$$\text{Proportion of Earnings} = \frac{\text{TSB}_{\text{Current Financial Year}} - \$3\text{ million}}{\text{TSB}_{\text{Current Financial Year}}}$$

3. A flat tax rate of 15% will be applied to the proportion of earnings attributable to the individual's balance over $3m:

$$\text{Tax Liability} = 15\text{ per cent} \times \text{Earnings} \times \text{Proportion of Earnings}$$

Example Pam's total superannuation balance is $3.5m on 30 June 2025 and $4.5m on 30 June 2026. She withdraws $100,000 during the 2025/26 income year.

Under Step 1, her earnings are calculated as follows:

$$\$1.1\text{m} = (\$4.5\text{m} + \$100{,}000) - \$3.5\text{m}$$

Under Step 2, the proportion of her total superannuation balance that is more than $3m is calculated as follows:

$$33.33\% = \frac{\$4.5\text{m} - \$3\text{m}}{4.5\text{m}}$$

Under Step 3, the 15% additional tax will be applied to 33.33% of the $1.1m earnings. Pam's additional tax is therefore calculated as follows:

$$\$55{,}000 = 15\% \times \$1.1\text{m} \times 33.33\%$$

A fund may make investment losses or have expenses that cause the individual's total superannuation balance to be less at the end of a particular financial year than at the end of the previous financial year. Negative earnings will not result in any tax liability and can be carried forward to offset positive earnings in future years.

$3m threshold not indexed

The Government argues its new tax will be a 'small change' to the superannuation system and predicts that in 2025/26 it will only affect around 80,000 people (including some with large balances in excess of $100m), leaving more than 99.5% of individuals with superannuation accounts unaffected. The Government does not intend to index the $3m threshold. It argues this is consistent with the div 293 threshold [19.10] and provides certainty to people when arranging their affairs. However, by ignoring the effect of inflation, the reality is that a far greater number of people will be affected by the tax over time.

[19.12] Superannuation contributions and home ownership

To reduce pressure on housing affordability and make home ownership more achievable, the Government introduced the 'first home super saver' and 'downsizing superannuation contributions' schemes.

First home super saver scheme

The first home super saver scheme is designed to enable people to save for their first home in a concessionally taxed environment. It allows individuals to make voluntary superannuation contributions from 1 July 2017, which they are able to withdraw to purchase or construct their first home (div 138 of sch *1 TAA*).

From 1 July 2022, the maximum amount of contributions that are eligible to be released are $15,000 per financial year up to a total of $50,000 across all years (s 138-35). The contributions can be either concessional or non-concessional contributions and must fall within the relevant contributions caps. To initiate the release process, individuals must request a 'first home super saver determination' from the Commissioner, which specifies their 'FHSS maximum release amount' (ss 138-10, 138-25). Individuals are able to withdraw 100% of their eligible non-concessional contributions, 85% of their eligible concessional contributions and their associated earnings (calculated using a deemed rate of return) (ss 138-30, 138-40).

Individuals are assessed on the concessional contributions and associated earnings withdrawn from their funds but are also eligible for a 30% tax offset of their 'assessable FHSS released amount' (ss 313-15, 313-20, 313-25 *ITAA97*).

Where an individual does not enter into a contract to purchase or construct their first home within a specified period or does not recontribute the required amount into superannuation, they are liable to pay 'first home super saver tax' (s 313-60 *ITAA97*). The tax is 20% the individual's assessable FHSS released amount (s 4 *First Home Saver Tax Act 2017* (Cth)).

Example Meg has made concessional contributions of $10,000 and non-concessional contributions of $12,000 to her superannuation fund since 1 July 2017. If she wants to use her superannuation savings to help pay for her first home, she must request a first home super saver determination from the Commissioner, which specifies her FHSS maximum release amount. Meg will be able to withdraw 100% of her non-concessional contributions (ie $12,000), 85% of her concessional contributions (ie $8,500) and her associated earnings from her fund for this purpose. She will be assessed on the concessional contributions and associated earnings she has withdrawn but will also be entitled to a 30% tax offset on this amount.

Downsizing superannuation contributions scheme

The downsizing superannuation contributions scheme is designed to reduce home downsizing barriers for older people and free up housing stock for younger families. It allows people to make 'downsizer contributions' of up to $300,000 from the proceeds of selling their main residence from 1 July 2018 (s 292-102). Originally, to be eligible to make downsizer contributions, a person had to be at least 65 years of age. However, this was reduced to 60 years of age (from 1 July 2022) and then to 55 years of age (from 1 January 2023). Downsizer contributions must result from the disposal of a main residence owned for 10 or more years and can only be used once. Both members of a couple are able to use the measure in respect of the same home. Downsizer contributions are not counted against the contributions caps and are not deductible (s 290-167).

Example Liz and Phil are a married couple who are both 69 years old. They sell the home which they have jointly owned for 14 years for $2m. Each of them can make downsizer superannuation contributions of up to $300,000 to their respective superannuation funds.

[19.13] Release authorities

Division 131 of sch 1 *TAA* contains a standardised set of rules relating to release authorities. The rules apply where a person has been issued:

- an excess concessional contributions determination [19.9]
- an excess non-concessional contributions determination [19.9]
- a first home super saver determination [19.12], or
- a notice of assessment of an amount of div 293 tax [19.10].

Release authority request

A person who has been issued with a relevant determination or notice may make a request to the Commissioner to release an amount from their superannuation interests (s 131-5). The request is irrevocable and must be made in the approved form within 60 days of the issue of the determination or notice or such further time as the Commissioner allows. It must identify the superannuation interests from which the relevant amount is to be released.

The total amount that a person can request to be released cannot exceed the amounts specified in the following table (s 131-10):

Determination or assessment	Amount
Excess concessional contributions determination	85% of the contributions stated in the determination
Excess non-concessional contributions determination	The total release amount stated in the determination
First home super saver determination	The FHSS maximum release amount stated in that determination
Assessment of an amount of div 293 tax	The amount of div 293 tax

Commissioner's obligation to issue release authority

Upon receiving a valid request from a person under s 131-5, the Commissioner *must* provide a release authority to each superannuation provider that holds a superannuation interest identified in the request (s 131-15(1)).

The Commissioner *may* also provide a release authority to one or more superannuation providers if:

- the person has been issued an excess non-concessional contributions determination and has not made a valid request under s 131-5 within 60 days of the issue of the determination (s 131-15(2))
- the person has been given an excess non-concessional contributions tax assessment (s 131-15(3));
- the person has been given a notice of assessment of an amount of div 293 tax that is not deferred to a tax debt account and on the 60th day after the issue of the notice the sum of any tax paid or liability released falls short of the amount (s 131-15(4)).

Obligation of superannuation provider

A superannuation provider that receives a release authority must pay to the Commissioner within 10 business days after its issue, or such further time as the Commissioner allows, the lesser of the amount specified in the release authority and the value of the superannuation interests (other than defined benefit interests) held by the superannuation provider for the individual (s 131-35). The superannuation provider must also notify the Commissioner in the approved form of the payment in the same time-frame (s 131-50).

Consequences of releasing amounts

If a superannuation provider pays an amount to an individual in respect of a release authority issued under s 131-15, the individual is entitled to a credit for the amount (s 131-65). Where the amount exceeds the individual's tax liability, they are entitled to a refund of the excess. The Commissioner must pay interest if he is late in paying a refund (s 131-70). Released amounts are non-assessable non-exempt income of the individual (ss 303-15, 303-20).

[19.14] Taxation of superannuation entities

Division 295 *ITAA97* contains special rules relating to the taxation of superannuation entities (s 295-5). There are two sets of overlapping rules, one for superannuation funds, ADFs and PSTs and the other for RSA providers that are not life insurance companies (eg banks). RSA providers that are life insurance companies are taxed under separate rules in div 320 *ITAA97* [25.5].

Division 295 does not apply to constitutionally protected superannuation funds, as they are exempt from tax under s 50-25 [11.7]. In addition, it does not impose tax on property belonging to a state (s 295-15).

19

Calculation of tax payable by superannuation funds, ADFs and PSTs

Superannuation providers of complying superannuation entities (ie complying superannuation funds, complying ADFs and PSTs: s 995-1) as well as non-complying superannuation funds and non-complying ADFs are required to work out the tax payable by such entities according to the steps in s 295-10(1). These steps are summarised below:

- **Step 1.** If the entity is a superannuation fund, work out its 'no-TFN contributions income' and apply the applicable rates set out in the *ITRA* to that income.
- **Step 2.** Work out the entity's assessable income and deductions taking account of the special rules in div 295.
- **Step 3.** Work out the entity's taxable income as if its trustee were an Australian resident (or, in the case of a non-complying superannuation fund that is a foreign superannuation fund, as if its trustee were a non-resident).

- **Step 4.** For a complying superannuation entity, work out the 'low tax component' and 'non-arm's length component' of its taxable income.
- **Step 5.** Apply the applicable rates as set out in the *ITRA* to: (a) if step 4 applies to the entity—the components worked out under step 4; or (b) otherwise—the entity's taxable income.
- **Step 6.** Subtract the entity's tax offsets from the step 5 amount or, for a superannuation fund, from the sum of the fund's step 1 and step 5 amounts.

Calculation of tax payable by RSA providers

RSA providers that are not life insurance companies are required to work out their tax payable according to the steps in s 295-10(2). These steps are summarised below (note there is no step 4):

- **Step 1.** Work out the entity's 'no-TFN contributions income' and apply the applicable rates set out in the *ITRA* to that income.
- **Step 2.** Work out the entity's assessable income and deductions taking account of the special rules in div 295.
- **Step 3.** Work out the 'RSA component' and 'non-arm's length component' of the entity's taxable income.
- **Step 5.** Apply the applicable rates as set out in the *ITRA* to the components.
- **Step 6.** Subtract the entity's tax offsets from the sum of the entity's step 1 and step 5 amounts.

No-TFN contributions income

Step 1 in ss 295-10(1) and (2) require the 'no-TFN contributions income' of superannuation funds and RSAs to be calculated. No-TFN contributions income essentially consists of contributions that are included in the assessable income of the fund or RSA provider and are made in respect of members who have not quoted their TFN to their superannuation or RSA provider by the end of the income year in which the contributions are made (s 295-610).

The applicable rate of tax payable by superannuation and RSA providers on no-TFN contributions income is 32% for complying superannuation funds and RSAs and 2% for non-complying superannuation funds (s 295-605 *ITAA97*; s 29 *ITRA*). These rates have been selected because when they are added to the 15% tax rate that applies to the 'low-tax component' of a complying superannuation fund's taxable income, the 15% tax rate that applies to the 'RSA component' of an RSA provider's taxable income, or the 45% tax rate that applies to the taxable income of a non-complying superannuation fund, they ensure that the no-TFN contributions income of these entities is subject to an overall tax rate of 47% (ie the top marginal income tax rate plus ML).

Superannuation providers and RSA providers may be able to obtain tax offsets for tax paid on no-TFN contributions income if a member subsequently quotes their TFN (s 295-675). A tax offset is only available in the 'current year' if the tax was payable by the provider in one of the preceding three income years. The tax offset is the amount of tax payable on no-TFN contributions income for which TFNs have subsequently been quoted (s 295-680).

Example In 2022/23, the trustee of a complying superannuation fund received $10,000 of employer superannuation contributions on behalf of an employee who is a member of the fund and has not quoted their TFN. The $10,000 is included in the assessable income of the fund and is subject to tax at the rate of 15% (see below). The $10,000 is also no-TFN contributions income and is subject to tax at the rate of 32% (ie $3,200). If the employee subsequently quotes their TFN to the trustee in 2023/24, the trustee is entitled to a tax offset for the $3,200 tax paid.

Special rules about assessable income and deductions

Step 2 in ss 295-10(1) and (2) requires a superannuation fund's, ADF's, PST's or RSA provider's assessable income and deductions to be worked out taking account of the special rules in div 295. The following discussion focuses on some of these special rules.

Subdivision 295-B (CGT)

Subdivision 295-B contains special rules to ensure that the CGT regime is the primary code for dealing with CGT events involving CGT assets of complying superannuation entities. This is achieved by virtue of s 295-85, which provides that provisions such as ss 6-5 and 8-1 do not apply to such events. Gains and losses made by these entities on the sale of their assets cannot therefore fall within the general tax rules even though they might occur on a frequent basis. Instead, the CGT regime applies and the entities can therefore benefit from the 33⅓% CGT discount on gains made from assets held for more than 12 months [17.8].

> ***Example*** The trustee of a complying superannuation fund regularly buys and sells shares as part of its investment portfolio. In October 2020, the trustee acquired shares for $10,000. The shares were sold for $40,000 in November 2023. The $30,000 gain on the sale of the shares is treated as a capital gain (rather than ordinary income). As the shares were held for more than 12 months, the capital gain is eligible for the 33⅓% CGT discount, resulting in a discounted capital gain of $20,000.

As superannuation entities only started paying tax from 1 July 1988, a 'freshening-up' rule deems CGT assets owned by complying superannuation entities as at 30 June 1988 to have been acquired on that date (s 295-90). As a result, all CGT assets held by such entities at 30 June 1988 are automatically subject to the CGT regime, even though they may have been acquired before the introduction of CGT on 20 September 1985. The first element of the cost base of a '30 June 1988 asset' is the greater of its market value or cost base at 30 June 1988, and the first element of the reduced cost base of a 30 June 1988 asset is the lesser of its market value or cost base at 30 June 1988 (s 295-85 *ITTPA*).

> ***Example*** The trustee of a superannuation fund acquired shares in a company for $100,000 on 5 June 1984 and sold the shares for $700,000 on 3 July 2023. The trustee is deemed to have acquired the shares on 30 June 1988. If the market value of the shares on that date was $400,000, this would be the first element of the cost base of the shares. The trustee would therefore make a capital gain on the sale of the shares of $300,000 (ie $700,000 – $400,000). The capital gain is a discount capital gain that would be eligible for the 33⅓% CGT discount.

Subdivision 295-C (assessable contributions)

Subdivision 295-C contains special rules that assess superannuation and RSA providers on 'assessable contributions'. Broadly speaking, assessable contributions generally include those contributions made to a fund that are deductible to the contributor (ie 'concessional contributions') and exclude those contributions made to a fund that are not deductible to the contributor (ie 'non-concessional contributions'). More specifically, assessable contributions fall into four broad categories:

- **Contributions made for another person.** Contributions made for another person are assessable contributions of the entities mentioned in the first column of the following table if the contributions fall within the second column of the table and do not fall within the exceptions in the third column of the table.

Contributions made on behalf of someone else		
Assessed entity	**Assessable contributions**	**Major exceptions**
Complying superannuation fund Non-complying superannuation fund that is an Australian superannuation fund RSA provider	Contributions (other than a contribution that is a 'roll-over superannuation benefit') to provide superannuation benefits for someone else (s 295-160)	Contributions that are not deductible and made to a complying superannuation fund or RSA by a person for a spouse that is not living permanently separately and apart from the person (s 295-165) Government co-contributions (s 295-170(1)(a)) Contributions for a child under 18 made by a contributor who is not the child's employer (s 295-170(1)(b))
Non-complying superannuation fund that is a foreign superannuation fund	Contributions (other than a contribution that is a 'roll-over superannuation benefit') to provide superannuation benefits for someone else to the extent that they relate to a period when the person was an Australian resident or a foreign resident who derives withholding payments covered by s 900-12(3) (s 295-160)	
Complying superannuation fund Complying ADF RSA provider	Payments under s 65 *SGAA* (ie payments of the SG shortfall component) (s 295-160)	
Complying superannuation fund RSA provider	Payment made under ss 61 or 61A *Small Superannuation Accounts Act 1995* (ie transfers from the SHASA to complying superannuation fund or RSA) (s 295-160)	Payments to the extent they represent government co-contributions (s 295-170(2))

Example Bill employed Ben in his gardening business and paid him a salary of $35,000 in 2023/24. Bill also contributed $4,000 to Ben's complying superannuation fund and claimed a deduction for this amount under s 290-60 [19.7]. The trustee of Ben's superannuation fund is assessed on the $4,000 contribution under s 295-160.

In the same income year, Ben's wife also made a $3,000 contribution to Ben's superannuation fund and claimed a tax offset of $540 in respect of the contribution under s 290-230 [19.7]. The trustee of Ben's superannuation fund is not assessed on the $3,000 contribution.

- **Personal contributions.** Personal contributions are assessable contributions if they are made to a complying superannuation fund or RSA and the contributor has provided a valid and acknowledged notice to the superannuation provider or RSA provider under s 290-170 indicating that they intend to deduct the contributions [19.7] (s 295-190).

Example Isaac is self-employed and contributes $40,000 to his complying superannuation fund in 2023/24. He notifies the fund that he will be claiming a deduction of $25,000 in respect of the contribution under s 290-150. The trustee of Isaac's superannuation fund will be assessed on the $25,000, but not the balance $15,000.

- **Roll-over superannuation benefits.** Roll-over superannuation benefits that consist of an 'element untaxed in the fund' [19.16] are assessable contributions, but only to the extent that they are not 'excess untaxed roll-over amounts' (ie only to the extent that they do not exceed the 'untaxed plan cap amount' set out at [19.16]) (s 295-190).
- **Transfers from foreign superannuation funds.** Certain amounts transferred from non-resident superannuation funds to Australian superannuation funds also constitute assessable contributions (s 295-200).

Subdivision 295-F (superannuation retirement phase income streams)

Subdivision 295-F provides special exemptions to trustees of complying superannuation funds on their earnings used to fund 'retirement phase superannuation income streams'. The exemptions are designed to encourage individuals to take superannuation benefits as income streams rather than lump sums. They only apply once a fund has reached the retirement phase (ie they do not apply while it is still in the accumulation phase) and they operate subject to the transfer balance cap rules [19.15].

A 'superannuation income stream' is defined in reg 307-70.02 *ITAR21* and covers certain annuities and pensions under the *SISA* and *RSAA* (s 307-70) [19.4]. A superannuation income stream is in the 'retirement phase' if a 'superannuation income stream benefit' is payable from it (s 307-80(1)). A superannuation income stream is also in the retirement phase if it is a 'deferred superannuation income stream' and a superannuation income stream benefit will be payable from it to a person who has retired, has a terminal medical condition, is permanently incapacitated or has attained the age of 65 (s 307-80(2)). However, a superannuation income stream is *not* in the retirement phase if it is a 'transition to retirement income stream' (s 307-80(3)).

There are two distinct exemptions available under sub-div 295-F:

- **Segregated current pension asset exemption.** Section 295-385 provides that complying superannuation funds are exempt from tax on ordinary and statutory income derived from their 'segregated current pension assets' (ie broadly those assets that are held by a fund solely to enable it to discharge its 'retirement phase superannuation income stream benefits': s 307-75).
- **Other assets proportionate exemption.** Section 295-390 provides that complying superannuation funds are exempt from tax on the proportion (determined according to a formula) of their ordinary and statutory income derived from other assets used to meet their current pension liabilities.

The exemptions do not apply to a fund's non-arm's length income or assessable contributions under sub-div 295-C.

There is also a CGT exemption under s 118-320, which provides that capital gains and capital losses made by a complying superannuation entity from CGT events happening in relation to its segregated current pension assets are disregarded.

> ***Example*** Max has retired and is receiving a superannuation income stream from his SMSF. The corporate trustee of his fund has segregated 100% of the fund's assets to pay retirement phase superannuation income stream benefits to Max. The fund is therefore exempt from tax on any income and capital gains it makes from its assets. Accordingly, if the fund received interest on a bank deposit or made a capital gain from selling shares, it would not have to pay any tax on the interest or capital gain.

Subdivision 295-G (deductions)

Subdivision 295-G contains a number of special deductions available to complying superannuation funds and RSA providers. For example, these entities are entitled to deductions for insurance premiums to cover their liability to pay death or disability benefits (ss 295-460, 295-475).

Components of taxable income and applicable tax rates

After a superannuation entity's or RSA provider's assessable income and deductions have been worked out in accordance with the special rules in div 295, the relevant steps in ss 295-10(1) and (2) require the entity's taxable income to be calculated and divided into components, which are taxed at the applicable rates. Generally, the taxable income of superannuation funds, ADFs and PSTs is worked as if the trustee were an Australian resident. However, for non-complying superannuation funds that are foreign superannuation funds, their taxable income is worked out as if the trustee was not an Australian resident.

The taxable income of complying superannuation entities are divided into two components:

- a 'low-tax component', which is taxed at the rate of 15%, and
- a 'non-arm's length component', which is taxed at the rate of 45% (ss 26(1), 27(1), 27A, 35 *ITRA*).

The non-arm's length component comprises the entity's 'non-arm's length income' for the income year less any deductions attributable to that income (s 295-545(2)). Non-arm's length income consists of ordinary or statutory income derived from schemes where the parties were not dealing with each other at arm's length, and the amount of the income is greater than what it would have been had they been dealing at arm's length (s 295-550(1)). It also includes dividends paid by private companies unless the amount is consistent with an arm's length dealing (s 295-550(2)) as well as certain trust distributions (ss 295-550(4), (5)).

The low-tax component is the remaining part of the entity's taxable income (s 295-545(3)). In the vast majority of cases, the taxable income of a complying superannuation entity will consist entirely of a low-tax component, and it will therefore be taxed at the rate of 15%.

The taxable income of non-complying superannuation funds and non-complying ADFs is not divided into any components. Instead, it is simply taxed at the rate of 45% (ss 26(2), 27(2) *ITRA*).

The taxable income of an RSA provider is divided into two components:

- an 'RSA component', which is taxed at the rate of 15%, and
- a 'standard component', which is taxed at the rate of 30% (s 23(3) *ITRA*).

The RSA component of an RSA providers taxable income essentially comprises assessable contributions and other amounts credited to RSAs less amounts paid from RSAs (other than to RSA holders) for the income year (s 295-555(2)). The standard component is the remaining part of the RSA provider's taxable income (s 295-555(4)).

[19.15] Transfer balance cap

From 1 July 2017, a 'transfer balance cap' limits the total amount that individuals can transfer to the tax-exempt retirement phase of superannuation [19.14]. If the balance in an individual's 'transfer balance account' exceeds the cap, they will be required to remove the excess from the retirement phase and pay 'excess transfer balance tax' ('ETBT'). The excess can be transferred to an accumulation account where the earnings are generally taxed at the rate of 15%.

As previously discussed, the transfer balance cap is also relevant for the purposes of determining eligibility for:

- the tax offset for spouse contributions [19.7]
- government co-contributions [19.8]
- the five-year carry forward of the unused concessional cap [19.9], and
- the non-concessional contributions cap [19.9].

Transfer balance account

Transfer balance accounts are used to track the amounts that individuals have transferred to the retirement phase of superannuation and identify whether they have any 'excess transfer balance' (s 294-5). An individual has an excess transfer balance if the transfer balance in their 'transfer balance account' exceeds their 'transfer balance cap' (s 294-30). Each individual who has, at any time, been the 'retirement phase recipient' of a 'superannuation income stream' will have a transfer balance account (s 294-15). The individual's transfer balance account starts on the later of either 1 July 2017 or the day they first start to be a retirement phase recipient of a superannuation income stream. An individual generally starts to be a retirement phase recipient of a superannuation income stream when superannuation income stream benefits start to be payable to them (s 294-20(1)). Special rules apply to 'deferred superannuation income streams' (s 294-20(2)).

Transfer balance

The 'transfer balance' in an individual's transfer balance account is the sum of their 'transfer balance credits' less the sum of their 'transfer balance debits'. As will be discussed below, credits and debits arise in a transfer balance account in a number of situations. In particular, credits arise when an individual becomes the recipient of a superannuation income stream that is in the retirement phase (ie a pension starts to be payable) and debits arise when an income stream ceases to be a superannuation income stream that is in the retirement phase (ie it is commuted to a lump sum).

Transfer balance cap

An individual's transfer balance cap is the 'general transfer balance cap' for the financial year in which they *start* to have a transfer balance. This means that an individual's transfer balance cap will remain the same in future years (subject to special rules, discussed below, relating to proportional indexation where they have an 'unused cap percentage').

General transfer balance cap

The general transfer balance cap was $1.6m in 2017/18 and is indexed in subsequent financial years (s 294-35(3)). Indexation is calculated by multiplying the $1.6m cap by the relevant indexation factor and rounding the figure down to the nearest $100,000. The indexation factor is determined by dividing the CPI number for the quarter ending 31 December in the previous financial year by the CPI number for the base quarter ending on 31 December 2016 (s 960-285). The following table sets out the general transfer balance caps.

General transfer balance cap		
2017/18 to 2020/21	2021/22 to 2022/23	2023/24
$1.6m	$1.7m	$1.9m

Example On 5 December 2015, Adam first became entitled to a superannuation income stream. A transfer balance account is created for Adam on 1 July 2017 and his personal transfer balance cap is $1.6m.

On 1 November 2023, Eve first became entitled to a superannuation income stream. A transfer balance account is created for Eve at that time. Eve's personal transfer balance cap is $1.9m.

Proportional indexation of unused cap percentage

Where an individual's transfer balance is less than their transfer balance cap for a financial year, their 'unused cap percentage' is indexed so that it keeps track proportionately with any indexation of the general transfer balance cap in future years (s 294-40).

Example On 8 October 2017, Betty first became entitled to a superannuation income stream in respect of a superannuation interest valued at $1.2m. As a result, $1.2m is credited to her transfer balance account. Betty has therefore used 75% of her $1.6m transfer balance cap in 2017/18, leaving her with an unused cap percentage of 25%.

As the general transfer balance cap was indexed to $1.9m in 2023/24, Betty's transfer balance cap is increased proportionally to $1.675m. In other words, her transfer balance cap of $1.6m is increased by $75,000 (ie 25% of the $300,000 increase to the general transfer balance cap). She will consequently be able to transfer a further $475,000 to the retirement phase without breaching her transfer balance cap.

Once a proportion of the transfer balance cap has been utilised, it cannot be indexed even if the individual subsequently removes capital from the retirement phase. If this were not the case, individuals could continue to 'top up' the amounts in their retirement phase accounts.

Transfer balance credits and debits

The circumstances in which transfer balance credits and debits arise in a transfer balance account are set out in tables in ss 294-25 and 294-80.

Transfer balance credits

There are three situations in which transfer balance credits arise under s 294-25. The first two of these are where:

- an individual is a retirement phase recipient of a superannuation income stream just before 1 July 2017—in this case, the credit is the value of the superannuation interest that supports the superannuation income stream just before 1 July 2017 and it generally arises on that date; and
- an individual starts to be a retirement phase recipient of a superannuation income stream on or after 1 July 2017—in this case, the credit is the value on the starting day of the superannuation interest that supports the superannuation income stream and it generally arises on the starting day.

The value of a superannuation interest at a particular time is:

- if the regulations specify a method for determining the value of the superannuation interest—that value, or
- otherwise—the total amount of all the superannuation lump sums that could be payable from the interest at that time (s 307-205).

Example Bert commenced receiving a superannuation income stream on 5 May 2015. If the value of the superannuation interest that supported the income stream just before 1 July 2017 was $800,000, he would have an $800,000 credit in his transfer balance account on 1 July 2017. If Bert also commenced to receive another superannuation income stream on 3 November 2017 and the value of the superannuation interest that supported the income stream on that day was $600,000, Bert would have an additional $600,000 credit in his transfer balance account on 3 November 2017. His transfer balance at that time would therefore be $1.4m.

The third situation in which a transfer balance credit arises is where an individual has an excess transfer balance at the end of a day. The credit is the 'excess transfer balance earnings' for that day (calculated under s 294-235) and it arises at the start of the next day. The credit recognises that an individual with an excess transfer balance benefits from earnings on the excess capital. This is therefore taken into account on a daily compounding basis until the breach of the transfer balance cap is rectified (see below).

Transfer balance debits

There are seven situations in which transfer balance debits arise under s 294-80. The main situation is where a superannuation income stream is commuted into a lump sum. In this case, the debit is the amount of the lump sum and it arises when the lump sum is received.

Example On 1 January 2024, Fred starts to receive a pension in relation to a superannuation interest valued at $2.2m. His transfer balance cap for 2023/24 is $1.9m and he therefore has an excess transfer balance of $300,000. If Fred wants to remove the excess transfer balance, he will need to commute part of his pension into a lump sum. If he only does this on 31 January 2024, his transfer balance account will be credited with excess transfer balance earnings in the meantime. If the excess transfer balance earnings over the 30-day period amount to $2,000, his transfer balance on 31 January 2024 will be $2,002,000. Fred would therefore need to partially commute $302,000 of his superannuation interest into a lump sum on that day. This would give rise to a transfer balance debit of $302,000, which would result in his transfer balance being reduced to $1.9m. As Fred has excess transfer balance earnings, he will also be liable to pay ETBT (discussed below).

Excess transfer balance determinations and commutation authorities

Where an individual has an excess transfer balance in their transfer balance account, the Commissioner may make an 'excess transfer balance determination' (s 136-10 *TAA*). A determination does not need to be issued if an individual has already rectified a breach by removing their excess transfer balance (eg by commuting an income stream as discussed above).

The determination must state the 'crystallised reduction amount', which is the value of the individual's superannuation income stream that must be commuted to bring their transfer balance down to the transfer balance cap. It must also include a notice of the 'default commutation authority' that the Commissioner intends to issue, which specifies the superannuation income stream provider and superannuation income stream from which it is intended the crystallised reduction amount will be commuted. Where there is more than one provider or superannuation income stream, the notice must state the amount by which each superannuation income stream is proposed to be commuted, the sum of which cannot exceed the crystallised reduction amount.

Individuals that have more than one superannuation income stream may, within 60 days of being issued a determination, or such further period as the Commissioner allows, make an irrevocable election as to which income stream or streams are to be commuted or partially commuted. The total amount of commutations must equal the crystallised reduction amount (s 136-20 *TAA*).

After the election period has ended, the Commissioner must issue a commutation authority to the relevant provider stating the amount by which the superannuation income stream is to be reduced (s 136-55 *TAA*). If the individual has made an election, the commutation authority must be in accordance with the election. Where there is more than one provider or more than one superannuation income stream, the notice must state the amount by which each superannuation income stream is to be commuted, the sum of which cannot be more than the crystallised reduction amount.

The superannuation income stream provider is obliged to comply with the commutation authority within 60 days (s 136-80 *TAA*). Where they have not done so, the income stream will be deemed *not* to be in the retirement phase and they will consequently not be eligible for the earnings tax exemption [19.14] (s 307-80(4)).

Excess transfer balance tax

An individual is liable to pay ETBT on their excess transfer balance earnings over the period that they have an excess transfer balance (s 294-230). An individual's excess transfer balance earnings for a day is worked out by multiplying the rate specified under s 294-235(2) for that day by the amount of their excess transfer balance at the end of that day (s 294-235(1)).

ETBT is imposed under s 4 *Superannuation (Excess Transfer Balance Tax) Imposition Act 2016* ('*SETBTIA*'). ETBT is based on the person's 'notional earnings' worked out under s 294-230(3) (s 5). It is 15% of the person's notional earnings (for the first breach) and 30% of the person's notional earnings (for subsequent breaches). The 15% tax rate neutralises the benefit of having excess capital in the tax-free retirement phase of superannuation. It reflects the fact that, but for the individual's breach, the excess amount would have been in the accumulation phase where the earnings would have been taxed at the rate of 15%. The 30% rate is punitive to discourage repetitive breaches. ETBT is not deductible (s 26-99).

Modifications for capped defined benefit income streams

Subdivision 294-D makes important modifications to the general rules outlined above in relation to 'capped defined benefit income streams' (s 294-125). Capped defined benefit income streams are income streams that are subject to commutation restrictions under the *SISR* and *RSAR* (s 294-130). They cover lifetime pensions (irrespective of when they started in the retirement phase) as well as lifetime annuities, life-expectancy pensions and annuities, and market linked pensions and annuities (provided they started in the retirement phase before 1 July 2017).

One of the key modifications is contained in s 294-135, which provides that the credit that arises under s 294-25 in an individual's transfer balance account relating to a capped defined benefit income stream is based on the 'special value of the superannuation interest' (instead of the 'value of the superannuation interest'). The special value of a superannuation interest is calculated by multiplying the individual's 'annual entitlement' by a factor of 16. An individual's annual entitlement is worked out by dividing the amount of the first superannuation income stream payment they are entitled to receive from the income stream and dividing this by the number of whole days to which that benefit relates and then multiplying the result by 365. This can be expressed as follows:

$$\text{Annual entitlement} = \frac{\text{first payment}}{\text{days in period}} \times 365$$

Example Ned is the recipient of a lifetime pension of $3,000 per fortnight on 30 June 2023. His annual entitlement is calculated as follows:

$$\$78{,}214.28 = \frac{\$3{,}000}{14} \times 365$$

As a result, the special value of his superannuation interest is worked out as follows:

$$\$1{,}251{,}428.50 = \$78{,}214.28 \times 16$$

The amount of $1,251,428.50 is credited to Ned's transfer balance account on 1 July 2023.

The practical effect of s 294-135 is that a person who has an annual entitlement to capped defined benefit income streams of $100,000 will be taken to have reached the transfer balance cap for the 2017/18 to 2020/21 financial years. This is because $100,000 multiplied by a factor of 16 is $1.6m. For the 2021/22 and 2022/23 financial years, a person who has an annual entitlement to capped defined benefit income streams of $106,250 will be taken to have reached the transfer balance cap for the year. This is because $106,250 multiplied by a factor of 16 is $1.7m. For the 2023/24 financial year, a person who has an annual entitlement to capped defined benefit income streams of $118,750 will be taken to have reached the transfer balance cap for the year. This is because $118,750 multiplied by a factor of 16 is $1.9m.

It is important to note that while capped defined benefit income streams are taken into account for the purposes of determining the balance in an individual's transfer balance account, they are *not* taken into account in determining whether the individual has an excess transfer balance and do not therefore result in any liability for ETBT (s 294-140). Instead, special income tax rules in sub-div 303-A *ITAA97* apply. These rules impose higher taxation on individuals who receive 'defined benefit income streams' in a financial year that exceed their 'defined benefit income cap' for the year. They do this by assessing individuals on additional amounts and denying them tax offsets. The aim of sub-div 303-A is to achieve broadly commensurate taxation treatment to the transfer balance cap rules, while at the same time recognising that because of the commutation restrictions that exist in relation to capped defined benefit income streams, it would be infeasible to require individuals to comply with those rules. Subdivision 303-A is discussed further at [19.16].

[19.16] Taxation of superannuation benefits

As mentioned at [19.2], superannuation benefits are taxed concessionally. A 'superannuation benefit' is defined widely in s 307-5 and includes payments from superannuation funds to their members, payments from RSAs to their account holders and payments from ADFs to their depositors. The way in which superannuation benefits are taxed depends on various factors, including:

- the components of the benefit
- whether the benefits are paid to a member or to a third party as a death benefit

- whether the benefits are paid as lump sums or income streams, and
- the age of the member.

Components of a superannuation benefit

Superannuation benefits may comprise:

- a 'tax-free component', and/or
- a 'taxable component' (s 307-120).

Where only part of a 'superannuation interest' is paid out, the relevant portions of the tax-free component and the taxable component will generally reflect the proportions such components make up of the total value of the superannuation interest (s 307-125).

Tax-free component

The 'tax-free component' of a superannuation interest is the combined value of the following two segments (s 307-210):

- **The contributions segment.** This segment generally includes all contributions made from 1 July 2007 that have not been included in the assessable income of the superannuation provider (ie typically 'non-concessional contributions', such as contributions made out of a member's after-tax income) (s 307-220).
- **The crystallised segment.** This segment relates to certain components that were concessionally taxed under the former 'eligible termination payment' rules (ie the 'undeducted contributions', 'pre-July 1983', 'CGT exempt', 'concessional' and 'post-June 1994 invalidity' components). These components are calculated as if a payment was made just before 1 July 2007 (s 307-225).

Taxable component

The 'taxable component' of a superannuation interest is the value of the interest less the 'tax-free component' (s 307-215). It therefore relates to amounts that have been included in the assessable income of the fund, such as concessional contributions and earnings. The taxable component can include the following elements (s 307-275):

- **Element untaxed in the fund.** This element relates to certain limited kinds of payments, such as payments made from the SHASA, constitutionally protected funds (eg state public sector superannuation plans) and unfunded schemes (ss 307-275(3), 307-280, 307-290, 307-295).
- **Element taxed in the fund.** This element is so much of the taxable component that is not an 'element untaxed in the fund'. In most cases, the taxable component of a superannuation interest will consist entirely of an element taxed in the fund.

Example Ann is a member of a taxed accumulation fund who received a lump sum superannuation benefit of $500,000. The benefit includes an amount of $20,000 which would be the pre-July 1983 component of an eligible termination payment if the benefit was paid before 1 July 2007. Ann made non-concessional contributions of $100,000 to the fund since 1 July 2007. Ann's superannuation benefit therefore consists of a tax-free component of $120,000 (comprising a $100,000 contributions segment and a $20,000 crystallised segment) and a taxable component of $380,000 (comprising an element taxed in the fund).

Taxation of member superannuation benefits (div 301)

Superannuation benefits that are paid to members from a complying superannuation plan are taxed in accordance with rules contained in div 301 *ITAA97*.

Tax-free component

The tax-free component of a member superannuation benefit is non-assessable non-exempt income (ss 301-15, 301-30, 301-90).

Taxable component

The taxable component of a member superannuation benefit is taxed in different ways depending on the member's age and whether it consists of an 'element taxed in the fund' or an 'element untaxed in the fund'.

In the most common case, where the member is over 60 and receives a benefit (either a lump sum or income stream) consisting of an element taxed in the fund, the benefit is non-assessable non-exempt income of the member.

In other cases, the benefit is included in the member's assessable income and the member may be entitled to a tax offset which ensures that the tax payable on the benefit does not exceed certain rates. The rates differ depending on whether the benefit falls within the 'low-rate cap amount' (s 307-345) or 'untaxed plan cap amount' (s 307-350). These amounts are indexed annually (s 960-285). The most recent rates are as follows:

Income year	Low-rate cap amount	Untaxed plan cap amount
2023/24	$235,000	$1,705,000
2022/23	$230,000	$1,650,000

The following table summarises how the taxable component of a member superannuation benefit is taxed:

	Element taxed in the fund (sub-div 301-B)		Element untaxed in the fund (sub-div 301-C)	
Member's age	**Lump sum benefit**	**Income stream**	**Lump sum benefit**	**Income stream**
60 and above	Non-assessable non-exempt income (s 301-10)	Non-assessable non-exempt income (s 301-10)	Included in assessable income Tax offset is available which ensures the rate of tax does not exceed 15% on untaxed plan cap amount The amount above the untaxed plan cap amount is taxed at the top marginal rate (s 301-95)	Included in assessable income Tax offset is available which is equal to 10% of the element untaxed in the fund (s 301-100)
Over preservation age and under 60	Included in assessable income Tax offset is available which ensures: • the rate of tax does not exceed 0% on the low-rate cap amount	Included in assessable income Tax offset is available which is equal to 15% of the taxable component (s 301-25)	Included in assessable income Tax offset is available which ensures: • the rate of tax does not exceed 15% on low-rate cap amount	Included in assessable income (s 301-110)

	Element taxed in the fund (sub-div 301-B)		Element untaxed in the fund (sub-div 301-C)	
Member's age	**Lump sum benefit**	**Income stream**	**Lump sum benefit**	**Income stream**
	• the rate of tax does not exceed 15% on the amount above the low-rate cap amount (s 301-20)		• the rate of tax does not exceed 30% on the amount above the low-rate cap amount up to the untaxed plan cap amount The amount above the untaxed plan cap amount is taxed at the top marginal rate (s 301-105)	
Under preservation age	Included in assessable income Tax offset is available which ensures the rate of tax does not exceed 20% (s 301-35)	Included in assessable income Tax offset is available which is equal to 15% of the taxable component (provided income stream is also a disability superannuation benefit) (s 301-40)	Included in assessable income Tax offset is available which ensures rate of tax does not exceed 30% on the untaxed plan cap amount The amount above the untaxed plan cap amount is taxed at the top marginal rate (s 301-115)	Included in assessable income (s 301-120)

The ML also generally applies to assessable member superannuation benefits. However, no ML applies to the low-rate cap amount that is taxed at 0% under s 301-20 (s 251S(1A) *ITAA36*).

Example On 1 August 2023, Bob retired from the workforce and received a lump sum benefit of $1m from his superannuation fund, consisting of a tax-free component of $300,000 and a taxable component (comprising of an element taxed in the fund) of $700,000.

If Bob was 59 and had reached his preservation age, the tax-free component of $300,000 would be non-assessable non-exempt income and the taxable component of $700,000 would be included in his assessable income. He would be entitled to a tax offset which ensures that the first $235,000 of his taxable component is tax-free and the balance $465,000 of his taxable component is taxed at no more than 15% (plus ML).

If Bob was 61, both the tax-free component and the taxable component would be non-assessable non-exempt income.

Taxation of superannuation death benefits (div 302)

A superannuation benefit that is paid to someone as a result of the death of another person is called a 'superannuation death benefit' (s 307-5 *ITAA97*). Superannuation death benefits that are paid from a complying superannuation plan are taxed according to div 302. The taxation treatment differs depending on whether the death benefit is paid to a person who is a 'death benefits dependant' or a person who is not a 'death benefits dependant'.

A 'death benefits dependant' of a person who has died is:

- the deceased's spouse or former spouse
- the deceased's child aged less than 18
- any other person with whom the deceased had an 'interdependency relationship' just before he or she died
- any other person who was a dependant of the deceased just before he or she died (s 302-195).

An 'interdependency relationship' exists if:

(a) the persons have a close personal relationship
(b) live together
(c) one or each of them provides the other with financial support, and
(d) one or each of them provides the other with domestic support and personal care (s 302-200(1)).

An interdependency relationship also exists if persons have a close personal relationship but do not satisfy one or more of the requirements in (b) to (d) above because either or both of them suffer from a physical, intellectual or psychiatric disability (s 302-200(2)).

Superannuation death benefits are taxed in accordance with the rules set out in following tables.

Death benefits paid to a person who is a death benefits dependant (sub-div 302-B)		
Kind of benefit	**Age of deceased and recipient**	**Tax treatment of tax-free and taxable component**
Lump sum	Any age	Tax-free and taxable component are non-assessable non-exempt income (s 302-60)
Income stream	Deceased and/or recipient aged 60 and above	Tax-free component is non-assessable non-exempt income (s 302-65) Taxable component (element taxed in the fund) is non-assessable non-exempt income (s 302-65) Taxable component (element untaxed in the fund) is assessable income and subject to a tax offset equal to 10% of the element (s 302-85)
	Deceased below 60 and recipient below 60	Tax-free component is non-assessable non-exempt income (s 302-70) Taxable component (element taxed in the fund) is assessable income and subject to a tax offset equal to 15% of the element (ss 302-75, 302-80) Taxable component (element untaxed in the fund) is assessable income (s 302-90)

Death benefits paid to a person who is not a death benefits dependant (sub-div 302-C)		
Kind of benefit	**Age of deceased and recipient**	**Tax treatment of tax-free and taxable component**
Lump sum	Any age	Tax-free component is non-assessable non-exempt income (s 302-140) Taxable component is assessable income, but a tax offset is available which ensures that the rate of tax does not exceed 15% (on the element taxed in the fund) and 30% (on the element untaxed in the fund) (s 302-145)
Income stream	Any age	Not applicable

The ML also generally applies to assessable superannuation death benefits.

> ***Example*** Don died on 5 August 2023 at the age of 56. He provided a binding death benefit nomination to the trustee of his superannuation fund which stated that his wife, Sally, who is aged 54, is entitled to his superannuation on his death. His superannuation benefit was $1m and was paid as a lump sum to Sally. It comprises a tax-free component of $200,000 and a taxable component (consisting of an element taxed in the fund) of $800,000. As Sally is a death benefits dependant, the $1m is non-assessable non-exempt income in her hands.
>
> If Don had instead provided a binding death benefit nomination stating that his daughter, Grace, who is aged 29 and has been living apart from him, is entitled to his superannuation on his death, she would not be a death benefits dependant. The tax-free component of $200,000 would be non-assessable non-exempt income and the taxable component of $800,000 would be assessable, but Grace would be entitled to a tax offset that ensures that the rate of tax on this component does not exceed 15% (plus ML).

Where a superannuation death benefit is paid to the trustee of a deceased estate in their capacity as trustee, it is treated as income to which no beneficiary is presently entitled and is taxed in the hands of the trustee as follows:

- to the extent that one or more beneficiaries of the estate who were death benefits dependants of the deceased have benefited, or may be expected to benefit, from the superannuation death benefit—the benefit is treated as if it were paid to the trustee as a person who was a death benefits dependant of the deceased (see the first table above)
- to the extent that one or more beneficiaries of the estate who were not death benefits dependants of the deceased have benefited, or may be expected to benefit, from the superannuation death benefit—the benefit is treated as if it were paid to the trustee as a person who was not a death benefits dependant of the deceased (see the second table above) (s 302-10).

Special rules for defined benefit income (sub-div 303-A)

The general rules relating to the taxation of superannuation benefits in divs 301 and 302 are modified under sub-div 303-A. The modifications have been introduced because of the transfer balance cap, which applies from 1 July 2017 [19.15]. As discussed, it is not appropriate to apply the transfer balance cap to capped defined benefit income streams because they are subject to commutation restrictions. Accordingly, to create commensurate treatment with the transfer balance cap, sub-div 303-A imposes higher taxation on individuals that have 'defined benefit income' for a financial year that exceeds their 'defined benefit income cap' for the financial year.

An individual's defined benefit income is the superannuation income stream benefits they receive from 'capped defined benefit income streams' [19.15] (s 303-2(2)). Their defined benefit income cap for a financial year is generally equal to the general transfer balance cap for the year divided by 16 (s 303-4(1)). As the table below indicates, it is generally $100,000 (ie $1.6m/16) for 2017/18 to 2020/21, $106,250 (ie $1.7m/16) for 2021/22 and 2022/23 and $118,750 (ie $1.9m/16) for 2023/24. A formula reduces the cap where an individual first becomes entitled to defined benefit income part-way through a financial year (s 303-4(2)).

Defined benefit income cap		
2017/18 to 2020/21	2021/22 to 2022/23	2023/24
$100,000	$106,250	$118,750

The way sub-div 303-A imposes higher taxation on individuals is by including additional amounts in their assessable income and denying them tax offsets as set out below:

- **Additional assessable income.** Section 303-2 applies where an individual receives superannuation income streams that are defined benefit income and would otherwise fall within s 301-10 (which treats superannuation benefits received by individuals who are at least 60 years old as non-assessable non-exempt income) or s 302-65 (which treats superannuation income stream benefits received by individuals because of the death of their death benefits dependent as non-assessable non-exempt income if either the individual or the deceased is at least 60 years old). In these circumstances, if the individual's defined benefit income (other than any elements untaxed in the fund) for the financial year exceeds their defined benefit income cap for the financial year, they are required to include 50% of the excess in their assessable income.

Example Betty is 64 years old and received defined benefit income in the form of a lifetime pension of $140,000 from her taxed defined benefit scheme in 2023/24. As her defined benefit income cap is $118,750 for the financial year, her defined benefit income exceeds her defined benefit income cap by $21,250. She must therefore include $10,625 (ie $21,250 × 50%) in her assessable income under s 303-2.

- **Denial of tax offsets.** Section 303-3 applies where an individual receives superannuation income streams that are defined benefit income and in relation to which they would otherwise be entitled to a 10% tax offset under s 301-100 (which applies to individuals who receive superannuation income stream benefits and are at least 60 years old) or s 302-85 (which applies to individuals who receive superannuation income stream benefits because of the death of their death benefit dependents where the individual or the deceased is at least 60 years old). In these circumstances, if the individual's defined benefit income to which ss 301-10, 301-100, 302-65 or 302-85 apply for the financial year exceeds their defined benefit income cap for the financial year, they are denied the 10% tax offset on the excess amount.

Example Bryan is a 63-year-old retired judge. He received defined benefit income in the form of a lifetime pension of $140,000 from his untaxed defined benefit scheme in 2023/24. Bryan is required to include the $140,000 in his assessable income under s 301-100. As his defined benefit income cap is $118,750 for the financial year, his defined benefit income exceeds this cap by $21,250. Bryan is therefore only entitled to a 10% tax offset on $118,750 under s 301-100. There is no 10% tax offset on the remaining $21,250 by virtue of s 303-3.

Special rules for terminal medical condition

A superannuation lump sum benefit paid to a person who has a 'terminal medical condition' at the time of receiving the payment or within 90 days thereafter is non-assessable non-exempt income (s 303-10 *ITAA97*). A terminal medical condition exists if two registered medical practitioners (one of whom must be a specialist in the relevant area) certify that the person suffers from an illness, or has an injury, that is likely to result in their death within 24 months (reg 995-1.06 *ITAR21*).

Special rules for departing Australia superannuation payments

A 'departing Australia superannuation payment' ('DASP') is a lump sum superannuation benefit made in the circumstances set out in s 301-170 to a person who was previously a temporary resident [30.4] and has departed Australia. Although a DASP is non-assessable non-exempt income of the recipient, tax is required to be paid on the benefit at the rates set out in the *Superannuation (Departing Australia Superannuation Payments Tax) Act 2007* (Cth) (s 301-175). The trustee of the superannuation fund is required to withhold the tax when the benefit is paid under sub-div 12FA of sch 1 *TAA*. The rates of tax are as follows:

Departing Australia superannuation payment tax rates		
Payment component	**Ordinary rates**	**Working holiday maker rates**
Tax-free component	Nil	Nil
Taxable component (taxed element)	35%	65%
Taxable component (untaxed element)	45%	65%

Special rules for excess untaxed roll-over amounts

Where a superannuation benefit is a roll-over superannuation benefit that includes an element untaxed in the fund, the member is taxed at the rate of 47% on the 'excess untaxed roll-over amount' under the *Superannuation (Excess Untaxed Roll-Over Amounts Tax) Act 2007* (Cth) (s 306-15). The 'excess untaxed roll-over amount' is essentially so much of the element untaxed in the fund that exceeds the 'untaxed plan cap amount'. The entity making the payment must withhold the tax from the payment and pay it to the Commissioner on behalf of the member (s 12-312 *TAA*).

Capital gains tax relief

A right to receive benefits from a superannuation fund or RSA is a CGT asset. To prevent the payment of such benefits having CGT consequences for members and their dependants, capital gains and losses happening in relation to such assets are disregarded (ss 118-305, 118-310 *ITAA97*).

Example Sally retired from work and received a lump sum payment from her superannuation fund. As her right to receive the payment has ended, CGT event C2 is triggered [17.10]. However, any gain or loss Sally makes from the CGT event is disregarded under s 118-305.

[19.17] Superannuation contributions splitting

Members of superannuation funds can apply to the trustees of their funds to split 'splittable contributions' with their spouses under div 6.7 *SISR*. Corresponding rules apply to RSA account holders in respect of contributions made to RSAs under div 4.5 *RSAR*. Prior to 1 July 2007, splitting contributions was used as a tax planning strategy to avoid the former RBL rules which applied to excessive superannuation benefits [19.2]. However, now that these rules have been abolished, the main advantage of splitting contributions has been to transfer them from a younger spouse to an older spouse who may be able to access the benefits earlier. From 1 July 2017, splitting contributions can also be used to help a spouse not exceed the general transfer balance cap [19.15].

Trustees of superannuation funds are not obliged to accept an application to split contributions. However, where they do so, they have 90 days to roll over, transfer or allot the relevant amount for the benefit of the receiving spouse (reg 6.45 *SISR*). Only contributions made in the previous financial year (or in the current year where the entire benefit is to be rolled over, transferred or allotted) can be split (reg 6.44 *SISR*).

The two main kinds of 'splittable contributions' are:

- 'taxed splittable contributions' (eg concessional contributions such as employer contributions and deductible personal contributions)

- 'untaxed employer splittable contributions' (eg contributions by the Commonwealth, state or territory to a public sector superannuation scheme) (regs 6.41, 6.42).

An application to split contributions is invalid if the benefits exceed the 'maximum splittable amount' for the year, which is as follows:

- for taxed splittable contributions—85% of the contributions up to the concessional contributions cap, and
- for untaxed splittable employer contributions—100% of the concessional contributions cap (reg 6.40 *SISR*).

> ***Example*** Marius is 40 years old and self-employed. He contributed $60,000 to his superannuation fund in 2023/24. He claimed a deduction of $27,500 (ie the concessional contributions cap for the year) and notified his superannuation fund accordingly. The balance $32,500 of the contribution is not deductible. The $27,500 is a taxed splittable contribution. The maximum amount Marius can split with his spouse is $23,375 (ie $27,500 × 85%).

Where a contribution has been split, a 'contributions-splitting superannuation benefit' arises for the spouse (s 307-5(5) *ITAA97*). If the benefit has been transferred to another fund or to another account in the same fund in the spouse's name, it is treated as a roll-over. The benefit is deemed to comprise a 'taxable component' (s 307-140). If it is paid from a taxed superannuation fund, it consists of an 'element taxed in the fund', otherwise it is an 'element untaxed in the fund' (s 307-275 *ITAA97*) [19.16].

[19.18] Superannuation and marriage breakdown

The Family Court has jurisdiction in the area of 'matrimonial causes', which is defined in s 4 *Family Law Act 1975* (Cth) ('*FLA*') to include proceedings between the parties to a marriage with respect to the property of the parties. The Family Court can make orders in relation to the property of the parties to a marriage under pt VIII *FLA*. The parties to a marriage can also make financial agreements about the division of their property under pt VIIIA *FLA*.

At common law, a person's interest in a superannuation fund was not generally regarded as 'property'. Rather, it was considered to be merely a 'future interest' until a condition of release had been satisfied. As a consequence, it was difficult to apply pt VIII and pt VIIIA to such interests. To address this situation, pt VIIIB *FLA* was introduced in 2002 to deem a superannuation interest to be treated as property for the purposes of the definition of matrimonial causes (s 90MC *FLA*). Part VIIIB also allows for the 'splitting' and 'flagging' of such interests. 19

Superannuation splitting

The parties to a marriage are allowed in their financial agreements to split their superannuation interests (s 90MH). The Family Court also has the power to make orders to split their superannuation interests (s 90MS). These agreements and orders are binding on the trustees of superannuation funds.

Superannuation agreements may only be made in respect of 'splittable payments' as defined in s 90ME. Most superannuation payments are splittable payments. However, certain payments, such as incapacity and hardship payments, are not splittable payments (reg 12 *Family Law (Superannuation) Regulations 2001* (Cth)).

A superannuation fund may pay a splittable payment to a non-member spouse provided he or she satisfies a condition of release. Otherwise, the superannuation fund must create a new interest in the fund for the spouse or transfer the payment to the spouse's roll-over fund.

Superannuation flagging

The parties to a marriage can also enter into a 'flagging agreement' in respect of a superannuation interest. Such an agreement prevents the trustee from making any splittable payments in respect of the interest (s 90ML). In other words, it operates like an injunction that prevents access to superannuation benefits. Flagging agreements continue to have effect until a 'flag-lifting agreement' signed by the parties is served on the trustee (s 90MN) or until it is terminated by a court (s 90MM). The Family Court can also make a 'flagging order' (s 90MU).

The benefit of flagging is that it defers the time at which it is necessary to determine how to split a superannuation interest. This can be particularly useful, if the superannuation interest relates to a defined benefit fund where the benefit is usually based on the member's length of service and salary prior to retirement. It may be difficult to value such an interest at the time of the marriage breakdown and more appropriate to split the payment closer to retirement when the amount of the interest can be more precisely determined.

Taxation consequences

A capital gain or capital loss arising under CGT event C2 or D1 [17.10] relating directly to the making, termination or setting aside of a superannuation agreement is disregarded (s 118-313 *ITAA97*). Likewise, a capital gain or loss arising from the payment of a superannuation benefit under a payment split to a spouse is also disregarded (s 118-305).

Lump sums and income streams resulting from payment splits are taxed in accordance with the general superannuation benefit taxation rules [19.16].

[19.19] QUESTIONS

1. What is the role of superannuation and what kinds of tax concessions exist to encourage superannuation investment?
2. What is a 'complying superannuation fund' and why is this concept important? Explain the difference between 'defined benefit' and 'accumulation' funds and between 'taxed' and 'untaxed' funds. What is an 'ADF', an 'RSA', a 'PST' and the 'SHASA'?
3. Discuss some of the main regulatory requirements imposed under the *SISA* and *SISR*. What borrowing, lending and investment restrictions apply to superannuation funds? In what circumstances may superannuation funds accept contributions in respect of their members? What is meant by the terms 'preservation age' and 'condition of release' and why are these concepts important?
4. What is the object of the SG scheme? What is the current 'maximum contributions base'? How is an employer's SGC calculated?
5. Jerry is employed by Tom. Jerry's salary for the quarter ending 31 December 2023 was $30,000. On 7 December 2022, Tom contributed $3,000 to one of Jerry's complying superannuation funds. However, it was not his 'chosen fund'. What are the consequences of this?
6. Abe (aged 52) runs an accounting practice and employs Betty (aged 30) and Phil (aged 40). Betty is paid an annual salary of $120,000 and Phil is paid an annual salary of $30,000. Abe makes quarterly contributions to their chosen complying superannuation funds of $2,000 and $500 respectively. Discuss the consequences of the contributions.
7. Mark is 45 years old and has a total superannuation balance on 30 June 2023 of $1.5m. During 2023/24, he makes non-concessional contributions of $140,000 to his complying

superannuation fund. Can Mark use the bring forward non-concessional contributions cap? If so, what is his bring forward period and how much non-concessional contributions can he make in the following year?

8. Rob is 35 years old and has a total superannuation balance of $250,000 on 30 June 2023. His current remuneration package is valued at $210,000 and consists of a salary component of $180,000 and a superannuation component of $30,000, which is paid directly by Rob's employer into his complying superannuation fund. Rob wants to salary sacrifice $80,000 of the salary component of his package. His employer is prepared to pay this amount directly to his fund and reduce the salary component of his package to $100,000. Rob also wants to 'top up' his superannuation by making a personal contribution of $300,000 to his fund. Discuss the proposed arrangements.

9. Rick and Liz are 50 years old and married to each other. Rick is a member of the R Complying Superannuation Fund and Liz is a member of the L Complying Superannuation Fund. Liz owns a small business and earned assessable income of $38,000 in 2023/24. Rick is employed by E Co as an engineer and is paid salary of $300,000 in 2023/24. E Co also contributed $5,000 per quarter to the R Complying Super Fund, which is Rick's chosen fund. On 5 January 2024, Rick made a personal contribution of $220,000 to the R Complying Super Fund and provided a notice to the trustee stating that he intends to claim a deduction of $20,000 in respect of the payment. At the same time, Rick also contributed $6,000 to the L Complying Super Fund on behalf of Liz. Liz also made a personal contribution of $4,000 to her fund during 2023/24 but did not provide any notice to the trustee. On 30 June 2023, Rick's total superannuation balance was $1.7m and Liz's total superannuation balance was $1.3m. The last time Rick or Liz made personal contributions to their funds was in 2017. Discuss the tax implications of the contributions.

10. What superannuation measures have been introduced to make home ownership more achievable?

11. Explain why the taxation rules governing superannuation have traditionally benefited high-income earners more than low-income earners. What are some of the reforms that have been introduced to reduce this bias and make superannuation more sustainable in terms of its cost to the Government.

12. What rates of tax do trustees of complying and non-complying superannuation funds pay? Provide examples of the kinds of superannuation contributions that are 'assessable contributions'.

13. What is the purpose of a transfer balance account and in what circumstances do transfer balance credits and debits arise in such an account? What are the consequences of having an excess transfer balance?

14. Ingrid is 61 years old and became entitled to receive a superannuation income stream on 1 August 2023 in respect of a superannuation interest valued at $1m. What entries are required to be made to her transfer balance account in 2023/24? Does she have any 'unused cap percentage' and, if so, what is the consequence of this? What is the total amount of superannuation benefits she will be able to transfer to the retirement phase without breaching her transfer balance cap?

15. Basil has reached his preservation age and received a lump sum benefit of $500,000 from his complying superannuation fund on retirement in August 2023 at the age of 59. Over the years, Basil made non-concessional personal contributions of $50,000 to the fund. His employer also made contributions of $120,000 to his fund. The fund also received government co-contributions

totalling $5,000. Discuss how Basil's superannuation benefit is taxed? Would your answer be different if Basil had retired at the age of 60? Also, would it be different if he had died at the age of 59 and a death benefit was paid in equal shares to his 52-year-old wife and 30-year-old independent son?

16. Rachel is 62 years old and has retired. Since 1 August 2016, she has been receiving a lifetime pension from her taxed defined benefit scheme. In 2023/24, she received a pension of $130,000. How is this amount taxed? Would your answer be different if the pension was from an untaxed defined benefit scheme?

TERMINATION AND UNUSED LEAVE PAYMENTS 20

[20.1] Introduction

The income tax legislation contains special provisions that deal with the taxation of various kinds of termination, unused leave and related payments made to employees and certain other persons (eg their dependants). This chapter discusses the special rules that apply to:

- employment termination payments ('ETPs') (div 82 *ITAA97*) [20.2]
- unused annual leave payments and unused long service leave payments (sub-divs 83-A and 83-B *ITAA97*) [20.3]
- genuine redundancy payments and early retirement scheme payments (sub-div 83-C *ITAA97*) [20.4], and
- foreign termination payments (sub-div 83-D *ITAA97*) [20.5].

The special rules treat certain payments (or components thereof) as non-assessable non-exempt income and other payments (or components thereof) as assessable income. To the extent that a payment is assessable, it may be subject to a tax offset, which ensures that the rate of income tax on the payment does not exceed a specified maximum rate. The ML is also generally payable in respect of assessable payments [8.8].

To prevent overlap with the FBT regime, no FBT is payable in respect of the payments discussed in this chapter as they are all expressly excluded from the definition of fringe benefit (ss 136(1)(la), (lb), (lc), (ld), (le) *FBTAA*) [18.2].

[20.2] Employment termination payments

An ETP is a payment that is received by an employee (or by another person after the employee's death) in consequence of the termination of the employee's employment (eg a golden handshake payment) (s 82-130 *ITAA97*).

For a payment to be an ETP it must generally be received within 12 months after the termination of employment. However, this requirement does not apply if the payment is covered by a determination made by the Commissioner or if it is a genuine redundancy payment or early retirement scheme payment [20.4].

An ETP does not include the kinds of payments mentioned in s 82-135. For example, it excludes superannuation benefits, pensions, annuities, unused annual leave and long service leave payments and the tax-free part of genuine redundancy or early retirement scheme payments.

Meaning of 'in consequence of' the termination of employment

The phrase 'in consequence of' the termination of employment has been considered in several cases dealing with former s 26(d) *ITAA36* (which included 5% of a lump sum amount paid in consequence of retirement in a taxpayer's assessable income). The leading case is *Reseck v FC of T* 75 ATC 4213, in which Gibbs J held (at 4216) that 'a sum is paid in consequence of the termination of employment when the payment follows as an effect or result of the termination'. His Honour added that it is not necessary that the termination should be the dominant cause of the payment.

In *McIntosh v FC of T* 79 ATC 4325, a bank officer commuted half of his pension into a lump sum a week after he retired. The Commissioner included 5% of the lump sum amount in his assessable income under former s 26(d). The taxpayer argued the payment was not in consequence of retirement because it was caused by his decision to commute the pension (rather than his retirement). The Federal Court rejected this and held that the payment was in consequence of retirement because his retirement was 'the occasion of, and a condition of entitlement to the payment' (Brennan J at 4328) and was a 'prerequisite' (Toohey J at 4331) and 'condition precedent' (Lockhart J at 4336) to the payment.

In *Le Grand v FC of T* 2002 ATC 4907, the taxpayer received a payment as a result of accepting an offer of compromise in respect of claims made against his former employer for wrongful dismissal and misleading and deceptive conduct. Goldberg J referred to *Reseck* and *McIntosh* and explained (at 4914) that the 'thrust' of the judgments in those cases was that 'a payment is made "in consequence" of a particular circumstance when the payment follows on from, and is an effect or result, in a causal sense, of that circumstance'. His Honour found that the payment was an effect or result of the termination in the sense that there was a sequence of connected events following the termination which ultimately led to the payment. It was therefore an ETP.

A similar outcome arose in *Stark v FC of T* 2021 ATC ¶10-580, where the AAT held that a payment received in settlement of a claim for wrongful dismissal and deceptive conduct was an ETP. The AAT found that the litigation followed as a consequence of the termination of the taxpayer's employment and the payment was directly linked to the discontinuance of the litigation. The payment was therefore made in consequence of the termination.

TR 2003/13 states that for a payment to be 'in consequence of' the termination of employment, a 'causal connection' must exist between the termination and the payment. The greater the length of time between these events, the more likely the causal connection will be too remote.

Classification of an ETP

An ETP received by the employee whose employment is terminated is called a 'life benefit termination payment' ('LBTP') and an ETP received by another person after the death of the employee is called a 'death benefit termination payment' ('DBTP'). Both LBTPs and DBTPs may consist of a 'tax-free component' and/or a 'taxable component'.

Tax-free component

The 'tax-free component' of an ETP consists of:

- the 'invalidity segment' of the ETP (calculated according to the formula in s 82-150)—this segment is the portion of the ETP that relates to termination due to ill-health (which must be certified by two medical practitioners), and
- the 'pre-July 83 segment' of the ETP (calculated according to the formula in s 82-155)—this segment is so much of the ETP, after taking away the invalidity segment, that relates to the employee's pre-1 July 83 service (s 82-140).

The tax-free component of an ETP (whether a LBTP or a DBTP) is non-assessable non-exempt income (ss 82-10(1), 82-65(1), 82-70(1)).

Taxable component

The 'taxable component' of an ETP is the ETP less the tax-free component (s 82-145).

The treatment of the taxable component of an ETP depends on whether it is a LBTP or a DBTP and whether the taxable component exceeds the 'ETP cap amount' for the relevant year (s 82-160). The ETP cap amounts over recent years are set out in the following table.

ETP cap amount				
2019/20	2020/21	2021/22	2022/23	2023/24
$210,000	$215,000	$225,000	$230,000	$235,000

Taxable component of a LBTP

The taxable component of a LBTP is included in assessable income, but may be subject to a tax offset (ss 82-10(2) to (4)). The tax offset ensures that the rate of tax on so much of the taxable component up to the 'ETP cap amount' (reduced by any previous LBTP received in respect of the same employment termination) does not exceed:

- 15% (if the taxpayer has reached their 'preservation age' [19.4]), or
- 30% (if the taxpayer has not reached their 'preservation age').

The remainder of the taxable component of a LBTP is taxed at the rate of 45%. From 1 July 2012, if the payment is not an 'excluded payment', only that part of the taxable component of an ETP that takes a person's total taxable income (including the ETP) to no more than $180,000 is eligible for the tax offset (s 82-10(4)). An excluded payment covers certain genuine redundancy payments, early retirement scheme payments, invalidity payments and payments paid in connection with a genuine employment-related dispute relating to personal injury, unfair dismissal, harassment, discrimination, or other matter prescribed by the regulations (s 82-10(6)).

Example Lisa retired from work on 1 March 2024 and received an ETP of $200,000 from her employer. The ETP does not contain any tax-free component as there is no invalidity segment or pre-July 1983 segment. As a consequence, the taxable component of the ETP is $200,000. Lisa was 61 years old when she retired and has therefore reached her preservation age [19.4]. In 2023/23, she also derived salary of $70,000. Her taxable income for the year is therefore $270,000 (comprising salary of $70,000 which is assessable under s 6-5 and an ETP of $200,000 which is assessable under s 82-10). Lisa is required to pay tax on the $270,000 at marginal rates (plus ML). However, she is entitled to a tax offset which ensures that the tax she pays on $110,000 of her ETP (ie $180,000 – $70,000) does not exceed 15% (plus ML).

Taxable component of a DBTP

The taxable component of a DBTP is taxed differently depending upon whether or not the person receiving the ETP is a 'death benefits dependant' as defined in s 302-195 [19.16]:

- **Death benefits dependant.** Where the recipient is a death benefits dependant, the taxable component of the DBTP is non-assessable non-exempt income to the extent that it does not exceed the 'ETP cap amount' reduced by any earlier DBTP received in consequence of the same employment termination. The remainder of the taxable component is assessable income and taxed at rate of 45% (s 82-65).

- **Non-death benefits dependant.** Where the recipient is not a death benefits dependant, the taxable component of the DBTP is assessable income. A tax offset ensures that the rate of tax on so much of the taxable component that does not exceed the 'ETP cap amount' reduced by any earlier DBTP received in consequence of the same employment termination does not exceed 30%. The remainder of the taxable component is taxed at rate of 45%.

Where DBTPs are paid to trustees of deceased estates, they are treated as income to which no beneficiary is presently entitled. Such payments are taxed in the hands of the trustees in essentially the same way as the death benefit/non-death benefit beneficiaries of the estate who have benefited, or may be expected to benefit, from such payments would otherwise be taxed (s 82-75).

Other termination payments

Termination payments that would otherwise qualify as ETPs if not for the fact that they are received more than 12 months after the termination of employment are included in assessable income (s 83-295).

[20.3] Unused annual and long service leave payments

Unused annual leave payments

An 'unused annual leave payment' is a payment received by an employee in consequence of termination of their employment for annual leave not used, or a bonus or other additional payment for annual leave not used. It also covers a payment received by an employee in consequence of termination of their employment for annual leave, or a bonus or other additional payment for annual leave, to which they were not entitled just before the termination, but that would have been made available to them if not for the termination. Annual leave includes recreational leave and holiday leave, as well as any other leave made available in similar circumstances (s 83-10).

Unused annual leave payments are included in a taxpayer's assessable income (s 83-10 *ITAA97*). A tax offset applies to ensure that the rate of tax on an unused annual leave payment does not exceed 30%, to the extent that:

- the payment is made in connection with a payment that includes a 'genuine redundancy payment' [20.4], an 'early retirement scheme payment' [20.4], or an 'invalidity segment of an ETP or a superannuation benefit' [20.2], or
- the payment is made in respect of employment before 18 August 1993 (s 83-15).

Unused long service leave payments

An 'unused long service leave payment' is a payment received by an employee on termination of their employment for long service leave not used, or for long service leave to which they were not entitled just before the termination, but that would have been made available to them if not for the termination (s 83-75).

Unused long service leave payments are generally included in a taxpayer's assessable income (s 83-80). However, only 5% of unused long service leave payments that accrued before 16 August 1978 are assessable. A tax offset applies to ensure that the rate of tax on an unused long service leave payment does not exceed 30%, to the extent that:

- the payment is attributable to employment that occurred before 18 August 1993, or
- the payment is attributable to employment that occurred after 17 August 1993 and is made in respect of a payment that includes a genuine redundancy payment, an early retirement scheme payment, or an invalidity segment of an ETP or a superannuation benefit (s 83-85).

[20.4] Genuine redundancy and early retirement scheme payments

'Genuine redundancy payments' and 'early retirement scheme payments' are non-assessable non-exempt income to the extent that such payments do not exceed the amount worked out according to the following formula in s 83-170(3):

Base amount + (Service amount × Years of service)

The 'base amount' and 'service amount' are indexed annually and are set out in the table below. The 'years of service' are the number of 'whole years' in the period of employment to which the payment relates.

Base and service amounts					
Year	2019/20	2020/21	2021/22	2022/23	2023/24
Base amount	$10,638	$10,989	$11,341	$11,591	$11,985
Service amount	$5,320	$5,496	$5,672	$5,797	$5,994

To the extent that a genuine redundancy payment or an early retirement scheme payment exceeds the amount worked out under the formula, it will be treated as an ETP if it falls within the definition in s 82-130 [20.2].

Example Bertha is a 45-year-old resident who receives a genuine redundancy payment of $40,000 from her employer on the termination of her employment on 1 August 2023. She commenced employment with her employer on 1 January 2019.

Bertha may treat $35,961 (ie $11,985 + [4 ×$5,994]) as non-assessable non-exempt income. The balance $4,039 (ie $40,000 – $35,961) is an ETP (ie the taxable component of a LBTP). As Bertha has not reached her preservation age, the $4,039 is included in her assessable income and taxed at no more than 30% plus ML (assuming her taxable income does not exceed $180,000).

Genuine redundancy payment

A 'genuine redundancy payment' is defined as so much of a lump sum payment received by an employee who is dismissed from employment because the employee's position is genuinely redundant as exceeds the amount that could reasonably be expected to be received by the employee in consequence of the voluntary termination of his or her employment at the time of the dismissal (s 83-175(1)).

A genuine redundancy payment must also satisfy the following conditions:

- the employee must be dismissed before the earlier of: (a) the day they reach pension age; or (b) if the employee's employment would have terminated when they reached a particular age or completed a particular period of service, the day they would reach the age or complete the period of service
- if the dismissal was not at arm's length—the payment must not exceed the amount that could reasonably be expected to be made if the dismissal were at arm's length, and
- at the time of the dismissal, there must be no arrangement between the employee and the employer, or between the employer and another person, to employ the employee after the dismissal (s 83-175(2)).

A genuine redundancy payment does not include any part of a payment that was received by the employee in lieu of superannuation benefits to which the employee may have become entitled (s 83-175(3)).

A payment is not a genuine redundancy payment if it is otherwise excluded from the definition of ETP by s 82-135 [20.2] (s 83-175(4)).

Early retirement scheme payment

An 'early retirement scheme payment' is defined as so much of a payment received by an employee because the employee retires under an 'early retirement scheme' as exceeds the amount that could reasonably be expected to be received by the employee in consequence of the voluntary termination of their employment at the time of the retirement (s 83-180(1)).

An early retirement scheme payment must also satisfy the following conditions:

- the employee must retire before the earlier of: (a) the day they reach pension age; or (b) if the employee's employment would have terminated when they reached a particular age or completed a particular period of service, the day they would reach the age or complete the period of service
- if the retirement is not at arm's length—the payment must not exceed the amount that could reasonably be expected to be made if the retirement were at arm's length, and
- at the time of the retirement, there must be no arrangement between the employee and the employer, or between the employer and another person, to employ the employee after the retirement (s 83-180(2)).

A scheme is an 'early retirement scheme' if:

- all the employer's employees who comprise a class of employees approved by the Commissioner may participate in the scheme
- the employer's purpose in implementing the scheme is to rationalise or reorganise the employer's operations by making any change to the employer's operations, or the nature of the work force, that the Commissioner approves, and
- before the scheme is implemented, the Commissioner approves (in writing) the scheme as an early retirement scheme (s 83-180(3)).

Even where the first two conditions are not satisfied, the Commissioner may treat a scheme as an early retirement scheme where he is satisfied special circumstances exist that make it reasonable to approve the scheme (s 83-180(4)).

An early retirement scheme payment does not include any part of a payment that was received by the employee in lieu of superannuation benefits to which the employee may have become entitled (s 83-180(5)).

A payment is not an early retirement scheme payment if it is otherwise excluded from the definition of ETP by s 82-135 [20.2] (s 83-180(6)).

[20.5] Foreign termination payments

A payment is non-assessable non-exempt income if:

- it is received in consequence of the taxpayer's termination of employment in a foreign country
- it is not a superannuation benefit, pension or annuity, and
- it relates only to a period of employment when the taxpayer was not an Australian resident (s 83-235 *ITAA97*).

A payment is also non-assessable non-exempt income if:

- it is received in consequence of the termination of the taxpayer's employment in a foreign country or engagement in qualifying service on an approved project in relation to a foreign country
- it relates only to the period of that employment or engagement

- it is not a superannuation benefit, pension or annuity
- the taxpayer was an Australian resident during the period of employment or engagement
- the payment is not exempt from income tax under the law of the foreign country, and
- the foreign earnings from the employment or remuneration from the engagement were exempt from tax under ss 23AG or 23AF *ITAA36* [31.4] (s 83-240).

[20.6] QUESTIONS

1. What is an ETP, what are the components of an ETP and how are they taxed?
2. On 5 December 2023, Blake resigned from his job at the age of 52 and received a $170,000 golden handshake payment from his employer. Blake also earned salary of $40,000 in 2023/24. Calculate Blake's tax liability for the income year.
3. Kevin is made redundant after 10 years of employment with his employer, John. As a consequence of his termination, John pays Kevin $180,000 (which includes $10,000 relating to his unused annual leave). How is this payment taxed?
4. Fred receives an early retirement scheme payment of $80,000 from his employer with whom he has been continuously employed for 10 years. How is this payment taxed?
5. Oz Co is an Australian resident mining company and employs Jo (a foreign resident) to work in its mine in Papua New Guinea. After two years of working for Oz Co, Jo's employment is terminated and Oz Co pays him a termination payment of $10,000. How is this payment taxed?

EMPLOYEE SHARE SCHEMES 21

[21.1] Introduction

The most common ways employers remunerate their employees are by paying them salary, providing them with fringe benefits and making contributions to their superannuation funds. A special way that a company can remunerate its employees is by allowing them to acquire shares, or rights to acquire shares, in the company at a discount. Issuing shares or rights to employees is a cost-effective form of remuneration as it does not require the company to pay them any money. It also helps a company attract talented staff, increase staff loyalty and reduce staff turnover. By giving employees a stake in the company, the interests of employees are more closely aligned with the interests of their employer. This has the potential to lead to greater employee commitment and boost corporate productivity.

The tax legislation contains special rules that apply where companies provide their employees with shares, or rights to acquire shares, at a discount. These arrangements are commonly known as 'employee share schemes' ('ESSs'). The tax treatment of ESSs was originally dealt with under s 26AAC *ITAA36*. However, this provision was replaced by div 13A of pt III *ITAA36* (which applied to shares, or rights to acquire shares, acquired from 28 March 1995 to 30 June 2009). Division 13A was subsequently replaced with new rules contained in div 83A *ITAA97*, which commenced on 1 July 2009.

The original version of div 83A was heavily criticised on a number of fronts. In particular, it was argued that the tax concessions under div 83A were less generous and more restricted than those previously available under div 13A. Unless special conditions were satisfied, employees were generally taxed on their discounts in the income year in which they acquired their shares or rights rather than in the income year in which they sold their shares or exercised their rights. This made Australian ESSs quite unattractive when compared with overseas schemes, and it placed Australian companies at a competitive disadvantage in international markets. It was also contended that the regime did not distinguish between small and large companies, and that ESSs were expensive to establish and administer, especially for start-ups, because of the costs involved in seeking legal and financial advice and undertaking valuations (especially for unlisted rights).

In its 2010 report, *Review into Elements of the Taxation of Employee Share Arrangements—A Report to the Assistant Treasurer*, the Board of Taxation noted that ESSs were more popular with listed companies than unlisted companies. It also recognised that start-ups had problems with valuing rights as well as satisfying the qualifying criteria for concessional taxation treatment under the regime. The

Board, nevertheless, decided against recommending any special concessions for start-ups because of integrity issues and difficulties in attempting to define which companies should benefit from the concessions.

Continued lobbying from the start-up sector prompted the Labor Government to announce a new review of ESSs in 2013. In its 2013 discussion paper, *Employee Share Schemes and Start-up Companies: Administrative and Taxation Arrangements*, Treasury noted that several industry sectors had concerns that div 83A was 'inconsistent and out of step with global practice' as it generally required tax to be paid on shares or rights at the time of acquisition rather than disposal. Given that few start-ups would actually become sustainable companies, tax was required to be paid on shares and rights that may never have a realised value to employees. It was also noted that employees who were provided with shares or rights for little or no upfront cost may not actually have the cash available to pay the tax on such benefits. The discussion paper identified a range of alternative ways of taxing ESSs. However, before any reforms could be enacted, the 2013 election intervened and a Coalition Government was elected.

The Coalition Government announced in its 2014 *Industry Innovation and Competitiveness Agenda* that it would reform the ESS rules. Amendments were subsequently made to div 83A, which addressed many of the criticisms levelled at the original provisions and removed some of the obstacles that inhibited the practical use of ESSs. The new rules operate in respect of ESS interests acquired on or after 1 July 2015 and include special concessions for employees of start-up companies. This chapter focuses on how these rules work.

[21.2] Overview of div 83A

Application

Division 83A *ITAA97* applies to an 'ESS interest' acquired under an 'ESS' at a discount (s 83A-20(1)).

An 'ESS interest' is a beneficial interest in a share, or a right to acquire a beneficial interest in a share, in a company (s 83A-10(1)).

An 'ESS' is a scheme under which 'ESS interests' in a company are provided to employees, or 'associates' of employees, (including past or prospective employees) of the company or its subsidiaries in relation to the employees' employment (s 83A-10(2)).

An 'associate' is defined widely in accordance with s 318 *ITAA36* and covers persons such as an employee's relatives (s 995-1 *ITAA97*). The term 'discount' is not defined and takes its ordinary meaning.

Importantly, to prevent duplication, div 83A does not apply to a share acquired as a result of the exercise of a right under an ESS (s 83A-20(2)). This recognises that where div 83A has already applied to the right, the share obtained by exercising that right should not also be taxed under the division.

ESS interests are sometimes held through 'employee share trusts'. Where an employee has an interest in an employee share trust that holds shares or rights, the employee is deemed to have a beneficial interest in the relevant number of shares or rights that correspond to their interest in the trust (ss 83A-320, 130-85 *ITAA97*). This effectively means that the rules in div 83A will apply to the employee as if they were absolutely entitled to the relevant shares or rights.

Division 83A applies to stapled securities in the same way as it applies to shares in a company, if at least one of the ownership interests that are stapled together to form the stapled security is a share in the company (s 83A-335).

Objects of div 83A

The objects of div 83A are:

- to ensure that benefits (ie discounts) provided under ESSs are subject to income tax in the hands of employees rather than FBT in the hands of employers
- to increase the extent to which the interests of employees are aligned with those of their employers, by providing a tax concession to encourage lower- and middle-income earners to acquire shares under ESSs, and
- to increase the number of new entrepreneurial companies in Australia by assisting them to attract and retain employees by providing those employees with a tax concession for acquiring shares under such schemes (s 83A-5).

To prevent employers also being subject to FBT on the provision of such benefits, ESS interests do not constitute 'fringe benefits' (s 136(1)(h) *FBTAA*) [18.3].

Upfront and deferred taxation

One of the key issues that arises under div 83A is determining the 'taxing point' of a discount. Depending on the nature of the ESS, discounts may be taxed in the hands of employees on either:

- an 'upfront' basis (ie at the time of acquisition) under sub-div 83A-B [21.3], or
- a 'deferred' basis (ie at the time of the occurrence of a specific event) under sub-div 83A-C [21.4].

As a general rule, discounts are usually taxed upfront. However, where upfront taxation applies, one of two concessions may be available to reduce the amount of the discount that is assessable to an employee provided certain conditions are satisfied.

In special cases, discounts are taxed on a deferred basis. To qualify for deferred taxation, the ESS interest must be at 'real risk of forfeiture', must be a share that is obtained under a 'salary sacrifice arrangement', or must be a right that is subject to a 'genuine disposal restriction'. In addition, certain other conditions must also be satisfied. Where deferred taxation applies, the taxing point can be deferred for a period which, depending on the circumstances, can be up to 15 years (the limit was previously seven years under former div 83A and 10 years under former div 13A of pt III *ITAA36*).

Interaction of div 83A with the CGT regime

Division 83A is the primary regime for taxing discounts arising under an ESS (s 130-75). Capital gains and capital losses arising from CGT events relating to an ESS interest are generally disregarded to the extent that they happen at or before the relevant taxing point (s 130-80(1) *ITAA97*). Subsequent dealings in ESS interests are, however, subject to ordinary CGT treatment. For example, where a share acquired by an employee under an ESS is disposed of, the employee may make a gain or loss that falls within the CGT provisions. Subdivision 130-D *ITAA97* makes certain modifications to the general CGT rules to ensure that they operate consistently with the rules in div 83A.

Benefits provided to associates treated as being acquired by employees

To prevent manipulation of the ESS rules, an ESS interest provided to an employee's associate is treated as if it was acquired by the employee (ss 83A-305, 130-85(3)). For example, if an employee's spouse receives shares under an ESS, the employee (rather than the associate) will include the discount in their assessable income (either on an upfront or deferred basis, depending on the circumstances) as if the employee had acquired the shares. However, when the associate later disposes of the shares any capital gain or loss arising from the CGT event will be made by the associate (s 130-85(3)).

Example Barney is married to Betty and is employed by Rock Co. Betty acquires shares in Rock Co under an ESS. As the shares are provided in respect of Barney's employment with Rock Co, any discount is required to be included in Barney's (not Betty's) assessable income. If Betty subsequently sells the shares, any capital gain or loss arising on the disposal will be made by Betty (not Barney).

Valuing ESS interests

Determining the 'market value' of an ESS interest is a key element in calculating the amount assessable to an employee under div 83A. The term 'market value' generally takes its ordinary meaning. In practice, however, it is often problematic to determine the market value of certain shares and rights. This is particularly the case for unlisted shares and rights, as they are not openly traded on a stock exchange as is the case with listed shares and rights.

To address this problem, s 960-412 *ITAA97* allows the Commissioner to approve methods for working out the market values of particular assets. *Income Tax Assessment (Methods for Valuing Unlisted Shares) Approval 2015* sets out various approved methods for valuing unlisted shares for the purposes of the ESS rules.

In addition, div 83A *ITAR21* contains a set of regulations, which allow special rules to be used to determine the value of unlisted rights. The regulations are made pursuant to s 83A-315 *ITAA97* and are an updated version of similar rules that existed under former div 13A of pt III *ITAA36*. The regulations provide that an employee has the choice of valuing an unlisted right that must be exercised within 15 years of the day when it was acquired at either its market value or the amount determined in accordance with regs 83A-315.02 to 83A-315.09. Regulation 83A-315.02 provides that value of an unlisted right is the greater of:

- the market value, on the day, of the share that may be acquired by exercising the right, less the lowest amount that must be paid to exercise the right to acquire the share, and
- the value determined in accordance with regs 83A-315.05 to 83A-315.09 (which use special formulas and tables to calculate the value of a right).

However, if the lowest amount that must be paid to exercise the right is nil, or cannot be determined, the value of the right is deemed to be the market value of the share on the relevant day (reg 83A-315.03).

Further guidance on determining the market value of shares and rights is provided on the ATO website (see *Market Value of Listed Shares and Stapled Securities* and *Market Value of Unlisted Rights to Acquire Listed Shares and Stapled Securities*).

Corporate reporting and withholding

A company that provides ESS interests to an employee (or associate) during an income year must give the employee (by 14 July after the end of the year) and the Commissioner (by 14 August after the end of the year) a statement in the approved form containing prescribed information relating to the scheme (including details of the company's estimate of the market value of the interest at the time of acquisition) (s 392-5 *TAA*). An administrative penalty applies for non-compliance (s 286-75(2BA) *TAA*).

Withholding tax at the rate of 47% is imposed under the *Income Tax (TFN Withholding Tax (ESS)) Act 2009* (Cth) where employees have not provided their ABN or TFN to the provider of the ESS interests by the end of an income year in which an amount is assessable under div 83A (s 14-155 *TAA*).

Diagram of div 83A

The following diagram outlines the steps involved in applying div 83A:

Step 1
Determine whether div 83A applies

Division 83A applies to the acquisition of an ESS interest by an employee (or their associate) under an ESS (s 83A-10)

Step 2
Determine whether the employee is taxed under the upfront taxation rules in sub-div 83A-B or the deferred taxation rules in sub-div 83A-C

Upfront taxation automatically applies unless the requirements for deferred taxation in s 83A-105 are satisfied

Deferred taxation applies if one of the following three key requirements are satisfied:

- the real risk of forfeiture requirement (s 83A-105(3))
- the salary sacrifice arrangement requirement (s 83A-105(4)), or
- the genuine disposal restriction requirement (s 83A-105(6))

In addition, all of the following conditions must also be satisfied:

- the start-up reduction in s 83A-33 must not apply (s 83A-105(1)(ab))
- the further conditions in ss 83A-45(1), (2), (3) and (6) (ie the employment, ordinary share, integrity, and shareholding and voting conditions) are met (s 83A-105(1)(b)), and
- the broad availability requirement must be met if the ESS interest is a share (s 83A-105(2))

Step 3
Determine the effect of the upfront or deferred taxation rules

Upfront taxation *without* the start-up concession

Employees are assessed at the time of acquisition of the ESS interest on the discount provided in relation to the interest (s 83A-25)

A reduction of up to $1,000 is available for employees earning under $180,000 if the s 83A-45 further conditions along with the non-discriminatory scheme and no real risk of forfeiture requirements are satisfied (s 83A-35)

An equivalent deduction is also available to employers (s 83A-205)

The ESS interest is taken to have been acquired for its market value (s 83A-30)

Upfront taxation *with* the start-up concession

Employees of start-ups reduce the amount assessable under s 83A-25 to nil if the following requirements are satisfied (s 83A-33(1)):

- the ss 83A-33(2) to (6) requirements (ie the unlisted and incorporation, $50m aggregate turnover, market value and Australian resident employer requirements)
- the s 83A-45 further conditions (ie the employment, ordinary share, integrity, minimum holding period, and shareholding and voting power conditions), and
- the s 83A-105(2) broad availability requirements

The ESS interest is taken to have been acquired for its market value (unless the ESS interest is a right, in which case it is taken to have been acquired for the amount paid to acquire the right) (s 83A-30)

Deferred taxation

Employees are assessed at the 'ESS deferred taxing point' on the difference between the market value and cost base of the ESS interest (s 83A-110(1))

The ESS deferred taxing point is the earliest of any of the following:

- when there is no real risk under the ESS of forfeiture or loss of the ESS interest, including in the case of rights the underlying shares acquired through exercise of those rights, and any general restrictions preventing their disposal no longer apply, or
- 15 years after the ESS interest was acquired (ss 83A-115, 83A-120)

The ESS interest is generally taken to have been acquired for its market value immediately after the ESS deferred taxing point (s 83A-125)

[21.3] Upfront taxation

Generally, a discount received under an ESS is included in the employee's assessable income in the year the ESS interest is acquired under sub-div 83A-B. In other words, the discount is ordinarily assessed 'upfront' (s 83A-25(1)). This treatment is designed to promote horizontal equity by ensuring that discounts are assessed consistently with other forms of remuneration (eg salary), which are also ordinarily assessed in the year of receipt. The discount is the market value of the ESS interest less any consideration paid by the employee (or their associate).

To the extent that a discount is attributable to employment outside Australia, it is treated as foreign source income (s 83A-25(2)). A foreign resident is therefore only assessed on that part of the discount that relates to their employment in Australia.

Importantly, employees may be entitled to reduce the amount included in their assessable income under s 83A-25 if they meet one of two sets of conditions. The first set is targeted at employees of start-up companies, and the second set applies in certain other cases where employees earn under $180,000.

Reduction for employees of start-up companies

Theoretically, ESSs should be of greatest benefit to start-up companies as they usually do not have much cash to employ staff. However, as mentioned at [21.1], many start-ups complained about the way the former version of div 83A applied to them. The reforms made to div 83A in 2015 therefore included a new concession targeted specifically at employees of 'start-ups' (although the legislation does not use this term).

The concession, contained in s 83A-33(1), reduces the amount included in the assessable income of an employee under s 83A-25 by the amount that would otherwise be included under that provision. In other words, the assessable discount is reduced to nil and there is therefore no upfront taxation.

To qualify for the reduction, s 83A-33(1) requires three sets of requirements to be fulfilled. The first set of requirements are contained in ss 83A-33(2) to (6):

- **Unlisted and incorporation requirements.** The company in which the ESS interest is issued (including its holding company and any subsidiaries) must not be listed on a stock exchange (s 83A-33(2)) and must be incorporated for less than 10 years before the end of the income year before the ESS was acquired (s 83A-33(3)).
- **$50m aggregated turnover requirement.** The company must have no more than $50m aggregated turnover in the income year before the ESS was acquired (s 83A-33(4)).
- **Market value requirement.** If the ESS interest is a share, the discount must be less than 15% of the market value of the share when it is acquired. If the ESS interest is a right, the amount that must be paid to exercise the right must be greater than or equal to the market value of an ordinary share in the company when the ESS interest is acquired (s 83A-33(5)).
- **Australian resident employer requirement.** The employee's employer (which may not necessarily be the company issuing the ESS interest) must be an Australian resident at the time the taxpayer acquires their ESS interest (s 83A-33(6)).

The second set of requirements comprise the 'further conditions' set out in s 83A-45:

- **Employment condition.** At the time of acquisition of the ESS interest, the acquirer must be employed by the company or a subsidiary of the company that issues the ESS interest (s 83A-45(1)).
- **Ordinary share condition.** At the time of acquisition of the ESS interest, all ESS interests available for acquisition under the scheme must relate to ordinary shares (s 83A-45(2)).

- **Integrity condition.** The predominant business of the company in which the ESS interests are acquired must not be the acquisition, sale or holding of shares, securities or other investments (s 83A-45(3)).
- **Minimum holding period condition.** The ESS must be operated in such a way that every acquirer of an ESS interest is not permitted to dispose of their ESS interest (or any share acquired on exercise of an ESS interest that is a right) before the earlier of: three years (or such earlier time as the Commissioner allows), or the time they cease employment (ss 83A-45(4), (5)).
- **Shareholding and voting power condition.** Immediately after acquiring their ESS interest, the employee must not hold a beneficial interest in more than 10% of the shares in the company or control more than 10% of the voting rights in the company (calculated taking into account any rights the employee holds to acquire shares as if they actually held those shares: s 83A-45(7)) (s 83A-45(6)).

The third set of requirements comprise the 'broad availability requirements' contained in s 83A-105(2) and only apply to ESS interests that are shares (not rights) (s 83A-33(1)(c)). They require that, at the time of acquiring the ESS interest, at least 75% of the permanent employees of the employer who have completed three years of service (whether continuous or non-continuous) and who are Australian residents must be entitled to acquire ESS interests under the scheme or another ESS with the employer or its holding company.

Reduction of up to $1,000 for employees earning under $180,000

Where the start-up reduction in s 83A-33 does not apply, s 83A-35 may allow an employee to reduce the amount of the discount that is otherwise assessable under s 83A-25 by up to $1,000. This reduction is, however, only available if the sum of the employee's taxable income, reportable fringe benefits total, reportable superannuation contributions, and total net investment loss for the income year does not exceed $180,000 (s 83A-35(2)). This ensures that the reduction is targeted at lower- and middle-income earners.

To qualify for the reduction, the further conditions set out in s 83A-45 (discussed above) must be satisfied (ie the employment, ordinary share, integrity, minimum holding period and shareholding and voting conditions). In addition, the following requirements must also be met:

- **Non-discriminatory scheme requirement.** The ESS and any scheme for the provision of financial assistance in respect of acquisitions of ESS interests under the ESS must be operated on a non-discriminatory basis to at least 75% of the permanent employees of the employer who have completed three years of service and are Australian residents (s 83A-35(6)).
- **No real risk of loss or forfeiture requirement.** At the time when the ESS interest is acquired:
  - if the ESS interest is a share—there must be no real risk that, under the conditions of the ESS, the share will be forfeited or lost (other than by disposing of it), or
  - if the ESS interest is a right—there must be no real risk that, under the conditions of the scheme, the right will be forfeited or lost (other than by disposing of it, exercising it or letting it lapse); and, if the right is exercised, there must be no real risk that, under the conditions of the scheme, the share will be forfeited or lost (other than by disposing of it) (s 83A-35(7)).

In order to encourage companies to provide ESSs, a specific deduction (of up to $1,000 per employee) may be available to employers who provide ESS interests under an ESS (s 83A-205). The deduction is equal to the amount of the reduction available to the relevant employee under s 83A-35.

Example Homer is employed by X Co. In August 2023, Homer acquires 50,000 shares in his employer under an ESS for $50,000. The shares have a market value of $90,000 and there is no risk that they will be lost or forfeited. He does not qualify for the reduction under s 83A-33 but does qualify for the reduction under s 83A-35. Homer must include $39,000 (ie the discount of $40,000 less the $1,000 reduction) in his assessable income for the 2023/24 income year under s 83A-25. X Co can also claim a deduction of $1,000 in respect of Homer under s 83A-205.

Acquisition of ESS interests

An ESS interest that is subject to upfront taxation is generally taken to have been acquired for its market value (rather than its discounted value) (ss 83A-30(1), 130-80(4)). The fact that the ESS interest is taken to be acquired for its market value (rather than simply the amount paid for it) recognises that the employee has been assessed on the discount.

A special rule, however, applies to an ESS interest that is a right if the start-up concession in s 83A-33 reduces the amount included in the employee's assessable income (s 83A-30(2)). As the discount on the right is not subject to upfront taxation by virtue of s 83A-33, the right is taken to have been acquired for the amount paid to acquire it (rather than its market value).

Exercise of rights

If rights are exercised, any capital gain or loss arising on their exercise is disregarded (s 134-1(4)). The shares acquired as a result of the exercise of the rights are deemed to be acquired when the rights are exercised (if the start-up concession does not apply) (s 130-45), or when the rights are acquired (if the start-up concession applies) (s 115-30 *ITAA97* (item 9A in the table)). The first element of the cost base of the shares is the amount paid for the rights (determined in accordance with either ss 83A-30(1) or (2)) plus the amount paid to exercise those rights (s 134-1(1)).

Example

Acquisition of shares—no reductions available

In December 2022, under an ESS, Curly acquired 1,000 shares in his employer for $10 per share when the market value of a share was $14. If he is not eligible for any reductions under ss 83A-33 or 83A-35, he will be assessed on the $4,000 discount (ie $14,000 – $10,000) in the 2022/23 income year. He will be deemed to have acquired the 1,000 shares for $14,000. If he sells the shares in November 2023 for $20,000, he will make a capital gain in the 2023/24 income year of $6,000 (ie $20,000 – $14,000).

Acquisition of shares—start-up reduction available

In October 2020, under an ESS, Larry acquired 1,000 shares in his employer (a start-up company) for $9 per share when the market value of a share was $10. If all the requirements of the start-up concession in s 83A-33(1) are satisfied, Larry will not be required to include the $1,000 discount in his assessable income. He will be deemed to have acquired the 1,000 shares for their market value of $10,000. If he sells the shares for $17,000 in October 2023, he will make a capital gain in the 2023/24 income year of $7,000 (ie $17,000 – $10,000), which is a discount capital gain.

Acquisition of rights—start-up reduction available

In September 2020, under an ESS, Mo acquired for no consideration rights to acquire 1,000 shares in his employer (a start-up company) for an exercise price of $15 per right (which exceeds the market value of each share, being $10). The market value of the rights at the time was $3,000. If all the requirements for the start-up concession in s 83A-33 are satisfied, the $3,000 discount which would otherwise be included in his assessable income under s 83A-25 is reduced to nil under s 83A-33(1). If, in October 2023, he exercises the rights, there will be no CGT consequences on their exercise as any gain or loss is disregarded. The cost base of his shares will be deemed to be $15,000. If he sells the shares in the same month for $20,000, he will make a capital gain in the 2023/24 income year of $5,000 (ie $20,000 – $15,000). This is a discount capital gain as the shares are deemed to have been acquired in September 2020 when Mo acquired the rights.

[21.4] Deferred taxation

An employee may be assessed on a discount received under an ESS on a deferred basis under sub-div 83A-C (rather than upfront under sub-div 83A-B) if they satisfy one of three key requirements together with a number of additional conditions outlined below (s 83A-105(1)).

Key requirements

Deferred taxation will only apply if one of the following three key requirements are satisfied:

- **Real risk of forfeiture requirement.** This requirement applies to ESS interests that are either shares or rights and requires that, at the time when the ESS interest is acquired:
  - if the ESS interest is a share—there must be a real risk that, under the conditions of the ESS, the share will be forfeited or lost (other than by disposing of it), or
  - if the ESS interest is a right—there must be a real risk that, under the conditions of the scheme, the right will be forfeited or lost (other than by disposing of it, exercising it or letting it lapse); or, if the right is exercised, there must be a real risk that, under The conditions of the scheme, the share will be forfeited or lost (other than by disposing of it) (s 83A-105(3)).
- **Salary sacrifice arrangement requirement.** This requirement only applies to ESS interests that are shares and requires that:
  - the ESS interest is to be provided in return for a reduction in the employee's salary or wages, or as part of their remuneration package
  - at the time when the ESS interest is acquired, the discount must equal the market value of the ESS interest (ie the employee or associate provided no consideration for the shares) and the governing rules of the ESS must state that deferred taxation applies, and
  - the total market value of the ESS interests acquired in the employer and any holding company of the employer during the year must not exceed $5,000 (s 83A-105(4)).
- **Genuine disposal restriction requirement.** This requirement only applies to ESS interests that are rights and requires that, at the time the ESS interest is acquired, the ESS must genuinely restrict the disposal of the right and the governing rules of the scheme must state that sub-div 83A-C applies to the scheme (s 83A-105(6)).

An ESS interest will be at 'real risk of forfeiture' if, for example, the conditions of the ESS provide that the employee will lose their ESS interest if they have not worked for the employer for a specified period of time or failed to meet particular performance targets. In *Gennai v FC of T* 2020 ATC ¶10-556, rights to acquire shares under an ESS were held to be at real risk of forfeiture because there was a real risk the taxpayer could lose his job within one year and would thereby, under the terms of the ESS, lose his ESS interest. The AAT indicated that the focus should be on the conditions of the scheme and whether under those conditions there is a real risk of forfeiture or loss of the interest.

TD 2022/4 states that disposal restrictions will be 'genuine' where they are 'sufficiently identifiable (real and objectively demonstrable), certain and legally enforceable (not spurious or hypothetical)'. This requires 'serious and enforced consequences when a breach of a scheme's disposal restriction occurs'.

Example Phoebe is employed by a public company, F Co, as a sales representative. F Co issues 1,000 shares under an ESS to the F Employee Share Trust which are held on trust for the benefit of Phoebe. The shares will vest in Phoebe in three years' time provided she is still employed by F Co at that time and has met certain sales targets. In these circumstances, Phoebe's shares are considered to be at real risk of forfeiture.

Additional conditions

In addition to the key requirements mentioned above, to qualify for deferred taxation, the additional conditions contained in s 83A-105 must also be satisfied.

One of these additional conditions is that the employee must not be eligible for the start-up reduction in s 83A-33 [21.3].

Another condition is that the further conditions in ss 83A-45(1), (2), (3) and (6) (ie the employment, ordinary share, integrity, and shareholding and voting conditions) must also be satisfied [21.3]. Note that the minimum holding period condition in ss 83A-45(4) and (5), which is a requirement for both of the reduction concessions under the upfront taxation rules in sub-div 83A-B, does not need to be satisfied for deferred taxation under sub-div 83A-C.

A further condition in s 83A-105(2) must be satisfied if the ESS interest is a share. This condition requires that at the time of acquisition of the ESS interest, 75% of the permanent employees of the employer who have completed three years of service (whether continuous or non-continuous) and who are Australian residents must be entitled to acquire ESS interests under the scheme or another ESS with the employer or its holding company.

ESS deferred taxing point

Where deferred taxation applies, the discount is assessed at the 'ESS deferred taxing point', which is generally determined as follows:

- **ESS deferred taxing point for shares.** In the case of ESS interests that are shares, the ESS deferred taxing point is the earliest of the following times:
  - when there is no real risk under the ESS of forfeiture or loss of the shares (other than by disposal) and any genuine restrictions preventing their disposal no longer apply, or
  - 15 years after the shares were acquired (s 83A-115).
- **ESS deferred taxing point for rights.** In the case of ESS interests that are rights to acquire shares, the ESS deferred taxing point is the earliest of the following times:
  - when (in the case of rights that have not been exercised) there is no real risk under the ESS of forfeiture or loss of the rights (other than by disposal, exercise or lapsing) and any genuine restrictions preventing their disposal no longer apply
  - 15 years after the rights were acquired, or
  - when (in the case of rights that have been exercised) there is no real risk under the ESS of forfeiture or loss of the underlying shares and any genuine restrictions preventing the disposal of the shares no longer apply (s 83A-120).

Previously, the cessation of employment was also an ESS deferred taxing point for both shares and rights. However, it was removed from 1 July 2022.

The above rules operate subject to a '30-day rule', which provides that if the employee disposes of an ESS interest within 30 days of the ESS deferred taxing point, the ESS deferred taxing point is taken to be the date of disposal (ss 83A-115(3), 83A-120(3)). For example, if the deferred taxing point was originally 20 June 2023 and the employee subsequently disposed of their shares on 4 July 2023, the deferred taxing point is moved to 4 July 2023. This demonstrates that, in some cases, the 30-day rule can operate to move the deferred taxing point from one income year to the next.

Assessable amount

For the income year in which the ESS deferred taxing point occurs, the employee must include in their assessable income the market value of the ESS interest at the ESS deferred taxing point, reduced by the cost base of the ESS interest [17.6] (s 83A-110(1)).

Example Pam is employed by B Co. On 1 September 2018, Pam acquired rights under an ESS to acquire 10,000 shares in B Co for $5 per share. She paid $2,000 for the rights, which expire in 10 years. The governing rules of the scheme state that sub-div 83A-C applies to the ESS and that Pam is required to work for B Co for 5 years before she can dispose of the rights. Pam is not taxed on the discount upfront as there is a genuine restriction on disposal of the rights. Assuming she is still working for B Co on 1 September 2023 and assuming the criteria in s 83A-105 are satisfied, the ESS deferred taxing point will be 1 September 2023. On this basis, if the market value of the rights is $20,000 on 1 September 2023, Pam will be assessed on $18,000 (ie $20,000 – $2,000) in the 2023/24 income year.

To the extent that a discount is attributable to employment outside Australia, it is treated as foreign source income (s 83A-110(2)). A foreign resident is therefore only assessed on that part of the discount that relates to their employment in Australia.

Acquisition of ESS interests

An ESS interest that is subject to deferred taxation is taken to have been acquired for its market value immediately after the ESS deferred taxing point (except where the ESS deferred taxing point occurs on the disposal of the interest) (ss 83A-125, 83-80(3)).

Exercise of rights

If rights are exercised, any capital gain or loss arising on their exercise is disregarded (s 134-1(4)). The shares acquired as a result of the exercise of the rights are deemed to be acquired when the rights are exercised (s 130-45). The first element of their cost base is the amount paid for the rights (determined in accordance with s 83A-125) plus the amount paid to exercise those rights (s 134-1(1)).

Special roll-over relief for corporate restructures

Where an employee has a deferred tax liability on a discount, a takeover or corporate restructure of the employer may trigger an ESS deferred taxing point (eg because of the disposal of shares or the breaking of the employment relationship). If this occurs, employees are generally entitled to 'roll over' their ESS deferred taxing point if:

- an arrangement is entered into that results in the original company becoming the subsidiary of another company, or

- a change in ownership of the original company results in ESS interests being replaced, wholly or partly, by ESS interests in one or more other companies (s 83A-130).

The effect of the roll-over is that the employee's new interests are treated as continuations of the old interests. Any consideration paid when the employee acquired the old interests is spread over the new interests (and any remaining old interests) in proportion to their market values immediately after the restructure. This enables the apportionment of the 'cost base' of the discount.

[21.5] Forfeiture of ESS interests

To prevent div 83A operating inappropriately, s 83A-310 deems that the division is generally taken never to have applied to an ESS interest where an employee has been assessed on a discount in respect of the ESS interest, but the ESS interest is subsequently forfeited or lost. The effect of this rule is that the employee will be refunded the tax that they have paid on the discount. However, this rule only applies if the forfeiture did not result from a choice made by the employee (other than a choice to cease employment, or, in the case of a right, a choice not to exercise the right before it lapsed or a choice to allow the right to be cancelled).

Example In the previous example at [21.4], Pam was assessed on $18,000 in the 2023/24 income year as five years had expired since she acquired the rights. If Pam does not exercise the rights by the time they expire on 1 September 2028, div 83A is taken to have never applied and Pam will be able to request the Commissioner to amend her assessment for the 2023/24 income year so that the tax she paid on the $18,000 which was included in her assessable income in that year is refunded.

[21.6] QUESTIONS

1. What is an 'ESS interest'? When is the discount in relation to an ESS interest taxed on an upfront basis and when is it taxed on a deferred basis? Who is taxed on the discount if an ESS interest is provided to an associate of the employee?
2. D Co is a start-up company that employs Ross as a paleontologist. In January 2020, D Co issues Ross, for no consideration, rights to acquire 10,000 shares in the company for $3 per share under an ESS. At the time the rights were issued, the market value of each share in D Co was $2. The ESS meets all the requirements for the start-up concession in s 83A-33. In October 2023, Ross exercises the rights and acquires 10,000 shares in D Co for $30,000. At that time, the shares in D Co had a market value of $8 per share. Six months later Ross sold the 10,000 shares to Rachel for $84,000. Discuss the tax implications of the transactions.
3. C Co is a public company that employs Joe. On 1 December 2020, Joe was provided, for no consideration, rights to acquire 10,000 shares in C Co under an ESS for $1 per share. At that time, the rights were valued at $3,000. The terms of the ESS require Joe to work for C Co until 1 December 2023, otherwise the rights will be forfeited. Joe satisfied this requirement and the rights are valued at $9,000 on 1 December 2023. How does div 83A apply to this arrangement?

PART H

ENTITIES

22 COMPANIES

[22.1] Introduction

Companies are one of the most common forms of legal entity. They are popular business and investment vehicles and are also used for many other purposes. ASIC's website indicates that there were 3,241,836 registered companies in Australia as at July 2023. While some of these have only one member, others have many thousands of members. Many large companies are listed on stock exchanges around the world, and their shares are traded daily. At the time of writing, the largest company listed on the Australian Securities Exchange ('ASX') was the mining company, BHP Group, which had a market capitalisation of around $230 billion. Companies make up the majority of Australia's largest taxpayers. Their importance is highlighted in the 2023 Budget Papers, which estimated that corporate tax receipts would amount to $127.3 billion in 2022/23. Traditionally, Australia has relied heavily on corporate taxation for its tax revenue, and it has one of the highest corporate tax-to-GDP ratios in the OECD.

This chapter examines how the tax law applies to companies and their members (eg shareholders). Special taxation rules apply to certain companies, such as PDFs [27.3], life insurers [25.5], co-operatives [25.6], listed investment companies [25.7], and corporate collective investment vehicles [25.11]. A separate taxation regime also applies to companies that are members of a consolidated group (Chapter 26).

At the outset, it is important to recognise that the tax law operates consistently with the general law in that it treats companies as separate entities from their members [22.2]. This means that companies are independent taxpayers from their shareholders. Companies may therefore be described as 'opaque' entities, as opposed to 'flow-through' entities like partnerships (Chapter 23) and trusts (Chapter 24). Like other taxpayers, companies are required to calculate their taxable income or tax loss for each income year. Companies generally do this in the same way as other taxpayers. There are, however, a number of special rules that apply to companies. For instance, a company's income year is the previous financial year, rather than the current financial year [8.3]. Companies also pay a flat rate of tax on their taxable income [22.3]. In addition, they are subject to special rules relating to their tax losses, including restrictions on their ability to carry them forward [22.22].

Companies often distribute profits to their members by paying them dividends [22.4]. They also sometimes return capital to them [22.9]. The tax treatment of these payments is the major focus of this chapter. The way in which corporate distributions are taxed depends on a number of factors, including the nature of the distribution (eg whether it represents a dividend or a return of capital) and the kind of company and shareholder involved (eg whether they are residents or non-residents).

To prevent a company's profits from being double taxed (once in the hands of the company and again in the hands of shareholders when distributed as dividends), payments of corporate tax are generally credited to shareholders under the 'imputation system' [22.6]. The imputation system allows resident companies to 'frank' dividends (ie impute corporate tax that they have paid to their shareholders) [22.7]. Resident shareholders that receive franked dividends are generally entitled to tax offsets for the franking credits allocated to such dividends [22.8]. As a general rule, non-resident companies cannot frank dividends and non-resident shareholders are not entitled to tax offsets for franking credits.

The corporate tax system is complex and operates subject to a plethora of anti-avoidance measures, including special rules designed to prevent manipulation of the imputation system [22.12]–[22.21].

[22.2] Companies and their members

Companies are regulated by ASIC under the *Corporations Act 2001* (Cth) and related legislation. They are treated as separate legal entities distinct from the persons who own interests in them (ie their members) and the persons who operate them (ie their directors and officers).

Creation of companies under the *Corporations Act*

A company is created by ASIC registering the company following the lodgment of an application for registration (ss 117, 118 *Corporations Act*). Companies can also be established under legislation (eg Monash University is a statutory corporation established under a Victorian Act).

Once registered, a company has all the powers of an individual as well as the powers of a 'body corporate'. This means it can:

- issue and cancel shares (except where it is a company limited by guarantee)
- issue debentures
- grant options over unissued shares
- distribute its property among its members
- give security and grant floating charges over its property

- arrange for its registration in a foreign jurisdiction, and
- do anything else that it is authorised to do under law.

A company continues in existence until it is deregistered. Deregistration can occur in three main ways:

- **Voluntary deregistration.** The members of a company can apply to ASIC to have a company deregistered if it is not carrying on business, its assets are worth less than $1,000, and certain other criteria are met (s 601AA).
- **ASIC initiated deregistration.** ASIC can initiate deregistration in specified situations, such as where the company has not paid certain fees (s 601AB).
- **Court ordered deregistration.** ASIC must deregister a company if a court orders its deregistration following completion of winding up proceedings undertaken by a liquidator (s 601AC).

Types of companies under the *Corporations Act*

The following types of companies can be registered under the *Corporations Act* (s 112):

- **Companies limited by shares.** The liability of the members of these companies is limited to the amounts they have agreed to pay for their shares. The vast majority of Australian companies fall within this category.
- **Unlimited companies.** The liability of the members of these companies is unlimited. The rules of certain professional organisations require the formation of these companies.
- **Companies limited by guarantee.** The liability of the members of these companies is limited by the amounts they have guaranteed to pay. Non-profit organisations, such as sports and social clubs, are sometimes established as these companies.
- **No liability companies.** The members of these companies have no liability. Only mining companies are permitted to form these companies.

Public and proprietary companies under the *Corporations Act*

The *Corporations Act* draws important distinctions between 'public' and 'proprietary' companies. Public companies can be registered as any one of the above types of companies, whereas proprietary companies can only be registered as one the first two types of companies (s 45A).

A public company is defined as a company that is not a proprietary company (s 9). A proprietary company is a company registered as such under the *Corporations Act* (s 45A). Proprietary companies must generally have no more than 50 shareholders (excluding employee shareholders and 'CSF shareholders') (s 113).

A proprietary company is a 'small proprietary company' for a financial year if it meets at least two of the following criteria:

- the consolidated revenue of the company (and any entities it controls) for the financial year is less than $50m
- the value of the consolidated gross assets of the company (and any entities it controls) at the end of the financial year is less than $25m
- the company (and any entities it controls) has fewer than 100 employees at the end of the financial year (s 45A; reg 1.0.02B *Corporations Regulations 2001*).

A proprietary company that does not meet at least two of these criteria for a financial year is a 'large proprietary company'.

Public companies have the most onerous regulatory burdens, followed by large proprietary companies, then small proprietary companies. Public companies are required to have three directors, while proprietary companies are only required to have one director. Public companies and large proprietary companies are required to prepare financial reports and directors' reports annually and have them audited. Small proprietary companies generally do not need to prepare these reports, unless expressly directed to do so by ASIC or by shareholders who have 5% of the voting power in the company.

ASX listed companies

Many companies choose to list on the ASX as this can increase their profile, enable them to raise capital in the market, and allow their securities to be traded on the exchange, which makes them more liquid. To be listed, a company must be a public company and comply with the ASX's listing rules. These rules prescribe minimum admission criteria. For example, upon listing, a company must generally have at least 300 non-affiliated investors with holdings valued at a minimum of $2,000 each. In addition, a company must also satisfy either:

- a 'profit test' (ie it must have at least $1m aggregated profit from continuing operations over the past 3 years and $500,000 consolidated profit from continuing operations over the last year), or
- an 'assets test' (ie it must have net assets of at least $4m or a market capitalisation of at least $15m).

Listed companies are required to report on both a half-yearly and annual basis. They must also comply with continuous disclosure requirements that require them to immediately notify the ASX once they become aware of any information concerning themselves that a reasonable person would expect to have a material effect on the price or value of their securities.

Definition of a company for tax purposes

For tax purposes, the term 'company' is defined in s 995-1 *ITAA97* to mean 'a body corporate' or 'any other unincorporated association or body of persons'. Partnerships are expressly excluded from the definition.

The notion of a company for tax purposes is broader than it is under the general law as it expressly includes unincorporated associations. This means that clubs and co-operatives, which would not be companies under the general law, are nevertheless treated as companies under the tax law.

Public and private companies under the tax law

The tax law sometimes distinguishes between 'public' and 'private' companies. The distinction is different from the distinction between public and proprietary companies under the *Corporations Act*, and is important for the following reasons:

- superannuation funds may be required to include private company dividends in their 'non-arm's length income' [19.14]
- certain loans and payments made by private companies are treated as dividends [22.4], and
- different 'franking periods' apply to private and public companies [22.7].

A company is a 'private company' in relation to a year of income if it is not a 'public company' for the year (s 103A(1) *ITAA36*).

A 'public company' is defined in s 103A(2). Public companies generally include companies that are listed on the Australian or an overseas stock exchange on the last day of the income year. They also include special kinds of companies such as co-operatives, non-profit companies, mutual life assurance companies, and certain bodies established for public purposes under Commonwealth, state or territory law. A subsidiary of a public company is also deemed to be a public company.

Listed companies and co-operatives are not public companies if they have concentrated ownership. This will usually be the case where 20 persons or less have the right to not less than 75% of the capital, dividend or voting rights in the company. A person together with his or her relatives and their nominees are treated as a single person for the purposes of this rule.

The Commissioner has the discretion to treat what would otherwise be a private company as a public company where he considers it reasonable to do so having regard to:

- the number of persons who were, at any time during the year, capable of controlling the company and whether any of those persons was a public company
- the market value of the shares issued by the company before the end of the income year
- the number of persons who beneficially owned shares in the company at the end of the income year, and
- any other matters he thinks relevant (s 103A(5)).

Management of companies

The *Corporations Act* contains a set of 'replaceable rules' that govern the internal management of companies. Some companies may also have their own constitutions, which can exclude some or all of the replaceable rules as well as include additional rules (ss 134 to 141). The replaceable rules and constitution deal with matters such as the appointment and powers of directors and secretaries, the conduct of meetings, and the procedures for issuing and transferring shares. They operate as a contract between the company and each member, the company and each director and secretary, and a member and each other member.

The responsibility for managing a company lies with its directors, who must comply with a broad range of statutory, common law and equitable duties (including an underlying fiduciary obligation to act in good faith and in the best interests of the company). In practice, it is common, especially in the case of larger companies, for the directors to delegate certain functions to the company's 'officers' (eg executives) who routinely deal with daily management issues.

As a company is a separate legal entity, the directors are not ordinarily liable for any of its debts. They may, nevertheless, be exposed to liability if the debts were incurred while the company was insolvent and there were reasonable grounds for suspecting that it was insolvent at the time or would become insolvent as a result of incurring such debts (s 588G). They may also be liable to the company if it suffers loss as a result of a breach of their directors' duties.

Appointment of a public officer

Every company must appoint a 'public officer' within three months of commencing to derive income in Australia (s 252 *ITAA36*). A public officer must be a natural person who has attained the age of 18, is ordinarily resident in Australia and is capable of understanding the nature of their appointment as a public officer. The public officer is answerable for the doing of all things required to be done by the company under the tax legislation and is liable for the same penalties in the case of default. The public officer is, however, not personally liable for the company's tax liabilities.

Shareholders' interests in a company

In a company limited by shares, the members of the company are known as its 'shareholders'. The shareholders are investors in the company. They own shares in the company, but do not own the company's assets, which are the separate property of the company. Shares are CGT assets [17.4], being intangible property in the nature of a 'chose in action' (*Colonial Bank v Whinney* (1886) 11 App Cas 426; *Sydney Futures Exchange Ltd v Australian Stock Exchange Ltd* (1995) 13 ACLC 369). Like other forms of property, shares can be sold, gifted, held on trust or used as security.

In *Archibald Howie Pty Ltd v Commissioner of Stamp Duties (NSW)* (1948) 77 CLR 143, Dixon J described (at 152) the nature of a shareholder's rights as follows:

> While a shareholder has not a proprietary right or interest in the assets of an incorporated company, his 'share' is after all an aliquot proportion of the company's share capital with reference to which he has certain rights. He is entitled among other things to have share capital applied in pursuance of the memorandum and articles of association and, so far as assets are available for the purpose, to have his paid-up capital returned in a liquidation or upon a reduction of capital if that method of returning it is decided upon pursuant to the articles of association.

Companies can determine the terms under which they issue shares and they often issue different classes of shares. Ordinary shares typically carry equal voting and distribution rights (eg the right to receive dividends and return of capital on winding up). Other classes of shares carry either limited or enhanced rights (eg companies may issue preference shares, which give shareholders preferential rights to dividends). Companies can also issue partly paid shares, in which case, the shareholders are liable to pay any amounts unpaid on their shares if called upon to do so.

Capital raising

Companies need capital to carry on their business, investment and other activities. They can raise 'equity capital' by issuing shares for consideration to shareholders. They can also raise capital by issuing 'rights' and 'options' to acquire shares. Ownership of a right or option to acquire shares does not make the owner a member of the company until the right or option is exercised and the person becomes registered as a shareholder. A mere owner of rights or options has quite different rights from an ordinary shareholder—in particular, they do not have any voting or distribution rights.

Companies can also raise 'debt capital' by borrowing money. Lenders (eg banks) do not have equity interests in the company, like shareholders, but merely debt interests, making them creditors. Debt capital can take a variety of forms (eg bonds and notes) and may be issued on the basis that it can be converted into shares in the future (eg convertible notes). While debt capital must be repaid to investors (often with interest), there is no requirement to return equity capital to investors until the company is wound up.

Disclosure requirements

When raising capital, companies must comply with the disclosure requirements in the *Corporations Act* relating to offers of 'securities' (eg shares and debentures). The disclosure requirements in ch 6D require companies to issue disclosure documents (eg a prospectus) and lodge these with ASIC. This is designed to ensure that investors have adequate information to make informed investment decisions. Public companies are generally permitted to issue securities to the public so long as they provide the relevant disclosure documents required under ch 6D. Proprietary companies, on the other hand, must not engage in any activity that would require disclosure under ch 6D (s 113). This means that proprietary companies are generally prohibited from issuing securities to the public. However, this prohibition does not apply to an offer of the company's shares to its existing shareholders, or to its employees or employees of its subsidiaries, or to a 'CSF offer' (see below).

The prohibition also operates subject to the following exceptions:

- **Small-scale personal offer exception.** Offers of securities do not require disclosure if the offer does not result in more than 20 new investors being issued shares in any 12-month period and no more than $2m being raised in any 12-month period (s 708(2)). Advertising of offers is prohibited (s 734).
- **Sophisticated investor exception.** Offers of securities do not require disclosure if the minimum amount payable for the securities is at least $500,000, or if it appears from a certificate

given by a qualified accountant that the person to whom the securities are issued has net assets of at least $2.5m or gross income of at least $250,000 for each of the last two financial years (s 708(8)). Disclosure is also generally not required where the offer is made through a financial services licensee who is satisfied on reasonable grounds that the person to whom the offer is made has previous experience in investing in securities that allows them to make an assessment of the merits of the offer and certain other matters (s 708(10)).

- **Professional investor exception.** Offers of securities do not require disclosure if they are made to a 'professional investor' (s 708(11)). A professional investor includes a financial services licensee, the trustee of a superannuation fund that has net assets of at least $10m, and a person who has or controls at least $10m.
- **Associated persons exception.** Offers of securities do not require disclosure if they are made to a senior manager of the company or a related body, or their spouse, parent, child, brother or sister, or a body controlled by such persons (s 708(12)).

Crowd source funding

Crowd source funding ('CSF') is a special form of fundraising typically used by start-up companies that enables them to raise capital via online platforms operated by 'CSF intermediaries' from a large number of investors who each invest small amounts. Part 6D.3A *Corporations Act* allows 'eligible CSF companies' (ie basically, unlisted public and proprietary companies that have consolidated gross assets and consolidated annual revenue below $25m) to make 'CSF offers'. Eligible CSF companies can raise up to $5m in a 12-month period by issuing ordinary fully-paid shares to the public. CSF offers operate subject to strict regulatory and consumer protection rules, including a per company investor cap of $10,000 for retail clients.

Employee share schemes

To facilitate ESSs, reduced disclosure requirements apply under div 1A of pt 7.12 *Corporations Act* to offers of ESS interests [21.2]. The requirements differ depending on whether or not payment is required to participate in the ESS. If payment is not required, the only requirement is a statement that the offer is made under div 1A of pt 7.12 and there is no limit on the number of ESS interests that may be issued. If payment is required, there are limited disclosure obligations and a cap on the number of ESS interests that may be issued over a three-year period (generally 5% of the issued share capital for a listed company and 20% of the issued share capital for an unlisted company). In addition, a monetary cap applies to unlisted company schemes (participants can generally only outlay up to $30,000 plus 70% of any dividends and bonuses they receive over a 12-month period).

Corporate capital and profits

The money raised by companies from issuing shares is generally credited to their 'share capital accounts' and used to fund their activities. Companies with excess capital are permitted to return capital to their shareholders by undertaking 'capital reductions' in accordance with rules contained in the *Corporations Act* [22.9].

Profits made by a company can be reinvested in the company or distributed to shareholders as 'dividends' [22.4]. Importantly, as companies are 'opaque' entities, the underlying nature of their profits do not flow through to their shareholders when they are paid dividends. This is in marked contrast to the position relating to, for instance, trusts where amounts distributed by trustees to beneficiaries retain their character [24.7]. Accordingly, if a company makes a capital gain which it uses to pay dividends to its shareholders, the shareholders do not receive a capital gain against which they might be able to set off their personal capital losses. Instead, the shareholders simply receive 'dividends' against which they cannot set off their personal capital losses.

Acquisitions and disposals of shares by shareholders

The most common ways shareholders acquire shares in a company are by either subscribing for the shares (eg when the company issues shares for the first time or undertakes a subsequent capital raising) or acquiring the shares from other shareholders (eg by way of purchase or gift).

The most common way shareholders dispose of shares in a company is by transferring the shares (eg by way of sale or gift) to third parties. Disposals can also arise as a consequence of the company cancelling the shares as a result of a capital reduction [22.9] or purchasing the shares under a share buy-back [22.10]. In addition, shares are cancelled when a company is wound up as a result of being placed into liquidation [22.11].

When dealing with acquisitions and disposals of shares, it is important to determine whether shareholders hold their shares on revenue or capital account for the following reasons:

- Shareholders that hold their shares on revenue account (eg as trading stock) are taxed under the general income tax rules. Generally speaking, these shareholders can deduct the cost of acquiring the shares under s 8-1 *ITAA97* [12.3] and are assessed on the proceeds from the disposal of the shares under s 6-5 *ITAA97* [9.4]. They must also account for their trading stock on hand at the end of an income year under div 70 *ITAA97* [16.4].
- Shareholders that hold their shares on capital account (eg as investments) are taxed under the CGT regime. Generally speaking, these shareholders include the cost of acquiring the shares in the cost base or reduced cost base of their shares under ss 110-25 and 110-55 *ITAA97* [17.6] and include the proceeds from the disposal of the shares in their capital proceeds from the CGT event under s 116-20 *ITAA97* [17.7].

Bonus shares

Companies sometimes issue bonus shares to their shareholders. The CGT treatment of bonus shares is dealt with under sub-div 130-A *ITAA97* [17.14]. For general income tax purposes (eg where the shareholder is a share trader), bonus shares are dealt with under s 6BA *ITAA36*. Where the bonus shares are dividends, the consideration for the acquisition of the bonus shares is the amount of the dividends that are included in the shareholder's assessable income (s 6BA(2)). Where the bonus shares are not dividends and are issued for no consideration, the consideration for the acquisition of the original shares is spread over both the original and bonus shares (ss 6BA(3), (4)). Special rules apply where the shareholder has a choice to be paid a dividend or be issued bonus shares and the shareholder chooses to be issued shares (ss 6BA(5), (6)).

> ***Example*** Basil is a share trader who purchased 100 shares in a private company for $3 per share. If the company subsequently issues 50 bonus shares to Basil for no consideration in circumstances where none of the bonus issue is a dividend, the cost of Basil's original shares will be spread across the original and bonus shares. This will result in Basil having 150 shares with a cost of $2 per share.

[22.3] Corporate tax rate

In Australia, companies (both resident and foreign) pay tax at flat rates on their taxable income. Companies that are 'base rate entities' pay tax at the rate of 25% (s 23(2)(a) *ITRA*), while other companies generally pay tax at the rate of 30% (s 23(2)(b) *ITRA*).

Special rates of tax apply to certain companies, such as non-profit companies (s 23(6) *ITRA*), RSA providers (s 23(3) *ITRA*) [19.4], PDFs (ss 23(4), (5) *ITRA*) [27.3] and life insurance companies (s 23A *ITRA*) [25.5].

Where a company acts in the capacity of trustee, the trust tax rates [24.5] apply instead of the corporate tax rates outlined above (s 23(1) *ITRA*).

Base rate entity

According to s 23AA *ITRA*, an entity is a base rate entity for an income year if:

- no more than 80% of its assessable income for the year of income is 'base rate entity passive income', and
- its 'aggregated turnover' for the year of income is less than $50m.

Base rate entity passive income

Base rate entity passive income is defined in s 23AB(1) as assessable income that is any of the following:

- a distribution by a corporate tax entity (other than a 'non-portfolio dividend' [31.6])
- a franking credit on such a distribution [22.8]
- a non-share dividend [29.9]
- interest (or a payment in the nature of interest), royalties and rent
- a gain on a qualifying security [29.12]
- a net capital gain [17.2]
- an amount included in the assessable income of a partner in a partnership or a beneficiary of a trust estate under div 5 [23.3] or div 6 [24.5] of pt III *ITAA36* to the extent that the amount is referable (either directly or indirectly through one or more interposed partnerships or trust estates) to another amount that is base rate entity passive income.

However, assessable income that is interest (or a payment in the nature of interest) and is derived by one of the entities mentioned in s 23AB(2) (eg a financial institution, such as bank) is deemed not to constitute interest (or a payment in the nature of interest) of that entity for the purposes s 23AB(1).

Aggregated turnover

An entity's 'aggregated turnover' is based on the combined annual turnover of the entity, its connected entities and its affiliates for the particular income year (s 328-115) [8.7]. An entity's 'annual turnover' is, broadly speaking, the total ordinary income (excluding GST) that it derives during the income year in the ordinary course of carrying on a business (s 328-120).

Example

Base rate entity

Ruby Co owns a jewellery business and also derives rental income. In 2022/23, it had aggregated turnover under the $50m threshold. Its assessable income was $10m, comprising $8m of trading income from running its business and $2m of rental income. The rental income is base rate entity passive income. Because this income is only 20% of its assessable income, Ruby Co is a base rate entity and pays tax at the rate of 25% for 2022/23.

Not a base rate entity

Emerald Co is an investment company. In 2022/23, it had aggregated turnover under the $50m threshold. Its assessable income was $10m, comprising $2m of interest income and $8m of dividend income. The interest and dividend income are both base rate entity passive income. Because this income is 100% of its assessable income, Emerald Co is not a base rate entity and pays tax at the rate of 30% for 2022/23.

Not a base rate entity
Jade Co is a manufacturing company. In 2022/23, it had assessable income of $80m, which is all trading income from selling products. Although none of its assessable income is base rate entity passive income, it is not a base rate entity as its aggregated turnover is above the $50m threshold. Jade Co therefore pays tax at the rate of 30% for 2022/23.

Corporate tax rates over the years

Australia used to only have a single corporate tax rate. This rate was 49% (from 1986/87 to 1987/88), 39% (from 1988/89 to 1992/93), 33% (from 1993/94 to 1994/95), 36% (from 1995/96 to 1999/2000), 34% (in 2000/01) and 30% (from 2001/02 to the current income year).

In 2015/16, a special lower rate of tax was introduced for companies that were SBEs [8.7]. To be an SBE, a company had to be carrying on a business and its aggregated turnover for the income year had to be below $2m (for 2015/16) or $10m (for 2016/17). Companies that were SBEs paid tax at the rate of 28.5% (for 2015/16) and 27.5% (for 2016/17).

In 2017/18, the concept of a base rate entity was introduced and originally only applied to entities with aggregated turnover of less than $25m. The aggregated turnover threshold was increased in the following income year to $50m. Base rate entities paid tax at the rate of 27.5% (for 2017/18 to 2019/20), 26% (for 2020/21) and 25% (for 2021/22 and subsequent income years).

The following table summarises the corporate tax rates that have applied in Australia since the mid-1980s:

Corporate tax rates			
Income year	**Aggregated turnover threshold**	**Tax rate for base rate entities (or SBEs for 2015/16 to 2016/17)**	**Tax rate for other companies**
2021/22 and subsequent years	$50m	25%	30%
2020/21	$50m	26%	30%
2018/19 to 2019/20	$50m	27.5%	30%
2016/17 to 2017/18	$25m	27.5%	30%
2015/16	$25m	28.5%	30%
2001/02 to 2014/15	Not applicable	Not applicable	30%
2000/01	Not applicable	Not applicable	34%
1995/96 to 1999/2000	Not applicable	Not applicable	36%
1993/94 to 1994/95	Not applicable	Not applicable	33%
1988/89 to 1992/93	Not applicable	Not applicable	39%
1986/87 to 1987/88	Not applicable	Not applicable	49%

Although Australia's corporate tax rate has generally come down over time, it remains relatively high compared with many other jurisdictions. Australia's general corporate tax rate of 30% is the second highest among OECD countries. The country with the highest corporate tax rate in the OECD is Colombia (35%), while the country with the lowest corporate tax in the OECD is Hungary (9%). Australia's general corporate tax rate is higher than the corporate tax rates in several neighbouring countries, including New Zealand (28%), Malaysia (24%), Indonesia (22%) and Singapore (17%). It is also higher than the United States' corporate tax rate (21%).

[22.4] Dividends

Dividends are the most common form of payment that companies make to their shareholders. Dividends have been described as distributions that constitute a 'detachment', 'release' or 'liberation' of a company's profits while it is a going concern (*FC of T v Brewing Investments Ltd (No 2)* 2000 ATC 4431; *Re Crichton's Oil Co* [1902] 2 Ch 86). There is no legal obligation on a company to pay dividends. Under the *Corporations Act*, it is up to the directors of a company to determine whether a dividend is payable and to fix the amount, time and method of payment (s 254U). A company must not pay a dividend unless:

- its assets exceed its liabilities immediately before the dividend is declared and the excess is sufficient for the payment of the dividend
- payment of the dividend is fair and reasonable to the company's shareholders as a whole, and
- payment of the dividend does not materially prejudice the company's ability to pay its creditors (s 254T).

A company is not entitled to a deduction for the payment of dividends. This point was recognised by Hill J in the Federal Court decision in *Macquarie Finance Ltd v FC of T* 2004 ATC 4866, where his Honour observed (at 4879–4880):

> It is accepted without question in the Australian income tax system and indeed in most other systems that a deduction is not available for dividends paid by a taxpayer company on its share capital. It may not be possible to give a clear logical answer as to the reasons . . . One answer might be that dividends are a distribution or division of profit after that profit has been ascertained, which means that they could not be seen to be part of the cost of earning or deriving that profit: *Commissioner of Taxation (WA) v Boulder Perseverance Ltd* (1937) 58 CLR 223. Such an explanation would require it to be said that the declaration of a dividend is not part of the actual business activity but subsequent to it. Another possible explanation might be that a dividend is part of the cost of the fixed capital of the business, thereby related to the business entity or structure rather than the process by which the business operates.

Although dividends are not deductible to a company, the company's shareholders are nevertheless usually assessed on such distributions in accordance with the rules discussed at [22.5].

Definitions of dividend

The tax law contains a general definition of dividend in s 6(1) *ITAA36*. In addition, a number of specific provisions deem certain amounts to constitute dividends. For instance, s 109 and div 7A of pt III *ITAA36* contain special integrity rules that deem private companies to pay dividends in certain cases discussed below. Deemed dividends can also arise where companies undertake 'off-market share buy-backs' (s 159GZZZP *ITAA36*) [22.10] and where liquidators make distributions on winding up companies (s 47 *ITAA36*) [22.11].

General definition of dividend in s 6(1) *ITAA36*

The general definition of dividend in s 6(1) contains both positive and negative elements.

Positive elements

The positive elements of the s 6(1) definition provide that a dividend includes:

- a 'distribution' made by a company to its shareholders, whether in money or other property (para (a)), and
- any amount 'credited' by a company to its shareholders as shareholders (para (b)).

For the purposes of para (a), in order for there to be a 'distribution', a company must generally make a payment. The mere forgiveness of a debt by a company does not satisfy this requirement. This is illustrated in *DFC of T v Black* 90 ATC 4699, where the Federal Court held that a private company that had forgiven a debt owing to it by one of its shareholders had not paid a dividend to the shareholder as it had not made any distribution to them—it only 'forwent the receipt of payment'.

For the purposes of para (b), in order for an amount to be 'credited' by a company to a shareholder, a debt must be created that is recorded in the company's account with the shareholder (*CIR (NZ) v Taylor* (1964) 13 ATD 389). Furthermore, the amount must be credited to a person in their capacity as a 'shareholder' and not in some other capacity. This is also illustrated in *DFC of T v Black*, where it was held that the private company that had forgiven the debt had not credited the shareholder in his capacity as a shareholder but, rather, in his capacity as a debtor of the company.

Negative elements

The most important negative element of the s 6(1) definition is contained in para (d), which provides that a dividend excludes amounts debited against the company's 'share capital account'. A share capital account is an account that a company keeps of its share capital (s 975-300(1) *ITAA97*). Ordinarily, this account reflects the amount the company receives from its members for issuing shares to them.

In *Aurizon Holdings Ltd v FC of T* 2022 ATC ¶20-824, the question arose whether a large amount contributed to a company by the State of Queensland as part of a restructure and privatisation of the Queensland Rail group could qualify as 'share capital' for the purposes of s 975-300 even though it was not made in exchange for an issue of shares. The Federal Court held that while share capital almost invariably refers to the capital contributed to a company in exchange for shares, this is not always the case. Thawley J held that the legal documents indicated that the state contribution was not a gift or a loan, but rather an equity contribution intended to form part of the company's share capital notwithstanding no shares were issued in exchange. The case demonstrates there can be special circumstances (although rare) where share capital arises without the corresponding issue of shares.

A share capital account does not include a 'tainted' share capital account (s 975-300(3) *ITAA97*). A share capital account is tainted if amounts from other accounts have been transferred to it (sub-div 197-A *ITAA97*) [22.21]. As a tainted share capital account is not a 'genuine' share capital account, distributions from tainted share capital accounts are treated as dividends (rather than capital distributions). The tainting rules are designed to stop companies transferring profits to their share capital accounts and thereby disguising the profits as share capital.

> ***Example*** X Co makes a payment of $100 to its shareholders. A portion of the payment ($20) is debited against its share capital account (which is not 'tainted'). The balance of the payment ($80) is from its accumulated profits. Only $80 is treated as a dividend. The remaining $20 is a return of capital. If X Co's share capital account was tainted, the whole $100 would be treated as a dividend.

A dividend also excludes money paid or credited, or property distributed, by a company for the redemption or cancellation of a redeemable preference share if the company gives the shareholder a notice specifying the amount paid-up on the share immediately before cancellation or redemption and the amount is debited to the company's share capital account (para (e)). This exclusion only applies to the extent that the amount of the money or value of the property is not greater than the amount specified in the notice as the amount paid-up on the share. In addition, a dividend also excludes a reversionary bonus on a life assurance policy (para (f)).

Deemed dividends under s 109 *ITAA36*

Section 109 *ITAA36* empowers the Commissioner to deem excessive amounts of remuneration and retiring allowances paid or credited by private companies to 'associated persons' to be non-deductible dividends. In *Case* U158 87 ATC 915, it was noted (at 926) that the section was enacted 'to prevent a company from unreasonably reducing its taxable income by making excessive payments to members and related persons in the guise of remuneration for services or retiring allowances'.

Section 109 operates where a private company pays or credits an amount to an 'associated person' that is, or purports to be:

- remuneration for services rendered by the associated person, or
- an allowance, gratuity or compensation in consequence of the retirement or termination of the associated person from an office or employment in the company.

So much of the amount which exceeds the amount that, in the opinion of the Commissioner, is 'reasonable' is not an allowable deduction to the company. In addition, it is deemed (other than for withholding tax purposes [31.11]) to be a dividend paid by the company to the associated person as a shareholder in the company out of profits derived by the company on the last day of the income year in which the excessive payment or credit is made.

Associated person

An 'associated person' is defined as a person who is, or has been, a shareholder or director in the company, and includes any 'associate' of such persons within the meaning in s 318 *ITAA36* [8.6] (s 109(2)).

Reasonable

In *Risby Forest Industries Pty Ltd v FC of T* 88 ATC 4683, Lockhart J noted that the Commissioner's power to form an opinion under s 109 as to whether a payment is 'reasonable' would seem to be unlimited since no criteria are specified governing the exercise of the discretion. His Honour, nevertheless, cautioned (at 4694) that 'the discretion must be exercised reasonably and in conformity with the purpose for which the power was conferred'. A discretion not exercised in this way would be open to administrative review.

In determining whether a payment is reasonable, the Commissioner should take into account all relevant circumstances. In *Case* U64 87 ATC 406, it was observed that whether remuneration is reasonable depends largely on 'the value of the services rendered by the taxpayer to the relevant company'. IT 2621 sets out a non-exhaustive list of factors the Commissioner considers relevant in determining whether a payment is reasonable, including the terms of the taxpayer's employment, the length of the taxpayer's service, the level of remuneration received during the period of service and commercial practice.

Example P Co is a private company that paid a fee for consulting services of $100,000 to a spouse of one of its directors (ie an associated person). Ordinarily, P Co would be entitled to a deduction for the full amount of the fee. However, if the Commissioner decides under s 109 that 40% of the fee is unreasonable, P Co will be denied a deduction for $40,000. This amount will be treated as a dividend paid by P Co to the director's wife as a shareholder in the company out of profits derived by P Co on the last day of the income year. This is the case even though the director's wife may not actually be a shareholder in the company. The net effect of the arrangement is that the director's wife will be assessed on the full $100,000, while the company only gets a deduction of $60,000.

Deemed dividends under div 7A of pt III *ITAA36*

Division 7A of pt III *ITAA36* (ss 109B to 109ZE) is designed to discourage private companies disguising distributions of profits as non-assessable payments, loans and forgiven debts. It achieves this objective by deeming the relevant amounts to be dividends. In particular, subject to a number of exceptions, div 7A deems a private company to have paid a dividend where it:

- pays an amount to a shareholder or an 'associate' (defined in s 318 *ITAA36* [8.6]) of the shareholder (s 109C)
- makes a loan during an income year to a shareholder or an associate of the shareholder that is not fully repaid by the 'lodgment day' (ie the due date for lodgment of the company's tax return for the year) (s 109D), or
- forgives a debt it is owed by a shareholder or an associate of the shareholder (s 109F).

A private company is also deemed to have paid a dividend where a reasonable person would conclude (having regard to all the circumstances) that the payment or loan is made, or the debt is forgiven, because the relevant entity had been a shareholder or associate at some time.

Payment

The term 'payment' includes crediting an amount and transferring property (s 109C(3)). In the case of a transfer of property, the amount of the payment is the amount that would have been paid for the transfer by the parties dealing at arm's length less any consideration given by the transferee (s 109C(4)).

A payment also includes the provision of an asset for 'use by' an entity (eg where a private company allows a shareholder, or an associate of the shareholder, to use its yacht) (s 109CA(1)). The payment is deemed to be made when the entity first uses the asset with the permission of the provider, or has a right to use the asset when the provider does not have such a right (s 109CA(2)). Where the use or right continues into another income year, the provision of the asset for use in the other year is treated as a separate payment made at the start of that year (s 109CA(3)).

A payment does not, however, arise where the provision of the asset, if it was provided in respect of the employment of an employee, would be a 'minor benefit' under s 58P *FBTAA* (ie a benefit valued at under $300) [18.3] (s 109CA(4)). A payment also does not arise to the extent that, if the entity had incurred and paid expenditure in respect of the asset, a once-only deduction would have been allowable to the entity (s 109CA(5)). In addition, a payment does not arise in limited cases involving the provision of a dwelling (ss 109CA(6), (7)).

Division 7A can also apply where a private company is presently entitled to income of a trust estate (but that income has not been paid to the company) and the trustee of the trust estate makes a payment or loan to, or forgives a debt owed by, the private company's shareholder or an associate of the shareholder (ss 109XA, 109XB).

Excluded payments and loans

Division 7A operates subject to a number of exclusions which ensure that not all payments and loans made by private companies are treated as dividends. For instance, the following kinds of payments and loans are excluded:

- payments of genuine debts (s 109J)
- payments and loans to other companies (s 109K)
- payments and loans that are otherwise assessable income (s 109L), and
- loans made in the ordinary course of business on ordinary commercial terms (s 109M).

To ensure that div 7A is directed at 'non-commercial loans', s 109N provides that a loan is also not caught by div 7A if it is in writing and meets specified minimum interest rate and maximum term requirements. The minimum interest rate requirement is met if the interest rate on the loan equals or exceeds the 'benchmark interest rate' for the relevant year as set out in the following table:

Benchmark interest rates				
2019/20	2020/21	2021/22	2022/23	2023/24
5.37%	4.80%	4.52%	4.77%	8.27%

The maximum term requirement is met if the loan does not exceed 25 years (where the loan is fully secured by a registered mortgage over real property and the market value of the property at the time the loan is made is at least 110% of the loan amount) or 7 years (in other cases).

Deemed dividends cannot exceed distributable surplus

Where the sum of all deemed dividends paid by a private company for a year under div 7A would otherwise exceed the company's 'distributable surplus' for the income year, the deemed dividends are reduced proportionally so that they do not exceed the distributable surplus for the year (s 109Y).

A private company's distributable surplus for an income year is calculated according to the following formula:

$$\text{Distributable surplus} = \text{Net assets} + \text{Division 7A amounts} - \text{Non-commercial loans} - \text{Paid-up share capital} - \text{Repayments of non-commercial loans}$$

Treatment of deemed dividends

Deemed dividends are taken to have been paid to an entity as a shareholder in the private company out of the private company's profits (s 109Z) and are not subject to withholding tax (s 109ZA) or FBT (s 109ZB).

Example P Co is a private company that makes a 20-year interest-free loan of $100,000 to the wife of one of its shareholders (ie an associate) in the current income year. If the loan is not repaid by the time P Co is required to lodge its tax return for the income year, P Co will be deemed to have paid an unfranked dividend of $100,000 to the wife under div 7A (assuming this amount does not exceed P Co's distributable surplus for the year).

If, instead, the loan was made at an interest rate that was at least equal to the benchmark interest rate for the year and was fully secured by a registered mortgage over land which, at the time the loan was made, had a market value of at least $110,000, then the loan would be excluded from div 7A.

[22.5] Taxation of dividends

The tax law contains a complex web of provisions dealing with the taxation of dividends. The most important provision is s 44(1) *ITAA36*. This section operates subject to a number of specific exemptions. It also ties in closely with:

- the imputation system's 'gross-up' and 'credit' rules, which apply to 'franked dividends' (ie dividends paid out of a company's after-tax profits) [22.8], and
- the withholding tax rules, which require resident companies to withhold tax (usually at the rate of 30% or 15%) on certain dividends paid to non-residents [31.11].

Section 44(1)

Section 44(1) requires 'shareholders' to include certain dividends that are 'paid' out of a company's 'profits' in their assessable income. The assessment rules differ depending on whether the shareholder is a resident or non-resident. However, before examining how these rules work, it is necessary to understand the meanings of the key terms used in the provision, namely: 'shareholder', 'paid' and 'profits'. It is also necessary to identify the 'source' out of which a company's profits are paid.

Shareholder

The term 'shareholder' is defined in s 6(1) *ITAA36* to include a 'member' or 'stockholder'. In *Patcorp Investments Ltd & Ors v FC of T* 76 ATC 4225, the High Court held that a person is a 'shareholder' in a company if the person is registered as a shareholder in the company's register or is entitled to be so registered. Where shares are held by nominees on behalf of the beneficial owners of the shares, the beneficial owners are not shareholders in the company.

Example Alf is the trustee of a trust estate and holds shares in X Co on trust for Bob. Alf is the shareholder in X Co even though Bob is beneficially entitled to the dividends paid by X Co.

Paid

The term 'paid' is defined in s 6(1) *ITAA36* to include 'credited' or 'distributed'. These terms were examined, in relation to former legislation, by Latham CJ in *C of T (Vic) v Nicholas* (1938) 59 CLR 230, where his Honour stated (at 238):

> The term 'payment' plainly covers a payment of money owed by the company to a shareholder . . . The term 'distribution', whether or not it includes the payment of money, is wide enough to cover other benefits received from the company by a shareholder, for example, a distribution of assets other than money. The term 'crediting' relates to something of which the shareholder receives the benefit in account with the company, even if there is no payment or distribution of anything to him.

A dividend can be paid even if the shareholder is restricted from accessing it. In *Blankfield v FC of T* 72 ATC 4177, a South African company had declared a dividend in respect of shares owned by a former South African who had migrated to Australia. The company had credited the dividend to an account in the shareholder's name with a South African bank. The High Court held that the dividend had been paid to the shareholder when the amount was credited to his account even though the shareholder was restricted from accessing the account under South African law.

In *Brookton Co-operative Society Ltd v FC of T* 81 ATC 4346, the High Court held that an 'interim dividend', which had been declared by a company but which the directors had the power to rescind, had not been paid or credited to the company's shareholder as the declaration of the dividend did not create an enforceable debt owing by the company.

The ATO treats dividends that are not actually received by shareholders, but which are reinvested in exchange for new shares in the company under 'dividend reinvestment plans' as having been paid to the shareholders (IT 2285).

Example Bill owns shares in a listed company and has taken up the company's offer to participate in its dividend reinvestment plan. Under the plan, a dividend of $50, which would otherwise have been paid to Bill in cash, is applied towards the purchase of six shares in the company with a market value of $8 each. The balance of $2 is credited to a 'dividend reinvestment account' with the company in Bill's name. Bill will be able to apply the amount standing to the credit of this account towards the cost of shares allotted under the plan when dividends are declared in the future. Even though Bill has not received any cash from the company, he will be treated as having been 'paid' a $50 dividend.

Profits

The term 'profits' is not defined in the legislation and therefore has its ordinary meaning. This meaning is based on general accounting and business concepts rather than any special tax concepts. In *Re Spanish Prospecting Co Ltd* [1911] 1 Ch 92, Fletcher Moulton LJ stated (at 98):

> 'Profits' implies a comparison between the state of a business at two specific dates usually separated by an interval of a year. The fundamental meaning is the amount of gain made by the business during the year. This can only be ascertained by a comparison of the assets of the business at the two dates.

The High Court in *FC of T v Slater Holdings Ltd (No 2)* 84 ATC 4883 relied on this passage to conclude that a dividend, which had been sourced partly out of a company's 'capital reserves' (made up of realised non-taxable capital gains made by the company and a gift received by the company), had been paid out of profits and was therefore assessable under s 44(1). This demonstrates that, for the purposes of s 44(1), the term 'profits' includes both the company's revenue and capital profits (irrespective of whether or not those profits have been taxed in the hands of the company).

Source of profits

In *Esquire Nominees Ltd (as Trustee of Manolas Trust) v FC of T* 73 ATC 4114, the High Court indicated that the source of a company's profits is the place where those profits are made [30.3]. This is a question of fact that must be determined by reference to all of the circumstances of the particular case. In *Esquire Nominees*, Barwick CJ acknowledged (at 4117) that the profits of a company may not all be made in the same geographical area, in which case 'it may be necessary to resort to apportionment of the total fund of profits and to assign a different locality to the portions so estimated or calculated'. His Honour went on to state (at 4118) that the source of a company's profits from its investment activities is 'the place where it has its central management and control' whereas the source of a company's manufacturing or trading profits is 'where these activities are carried on'.

Paid out of profits rule

Section 254T of the *Corporations Act* used to provide that dividends could only be paid out of a company's 'profits'. However, reforms introduced in 2010 now technically allow a company to also pay a dividend out of other sources [22.4]. Such a payment would qualify under the s 6(1) *ITAA36* definition of dividend, assuming it does not fall within the negative elements of the definition (eg provided it is not debited to the company's share capital account). It would not, however, technically be assessable under s 44(1), since it is not 'paid out of profits'. To address this situation, s 44(1A) *ITAA36* deems that, for the purposes of the *ITAA36* and *ITAA97*, 'a dividend paid out of an amount other than profits is taken to be a dividend paid out of profits'. This ensures that a dividend for corporations law purposes paid from a non-profit source can be assessable under s 44(1).

Dividends paid to resident shareholders

Section 44(1)(a) provides that the assessable income of a resident shareholder includes dividends paid to the shareholder out of a company's profits, irrespective of whether the company paying the dividend is a resident or a non-resident and irrespective of the source of those profits.

Section 44(1)(a), however, operates subject to a number of exceptions, including:

- s 768-5 *ITAA97*, which treats dividends paid by a foreign company to a resident company that holds 'participation interests' of at least 10% in the foreign company as non-assessable non-exempt income [31.6], and
- ss 23AI and 23AK *ITAA36*, which treat dividends paid to a resident shareholder out of income that has been previously attributed to the shareholder under the CFC and former foreign investment fund ('FIF') accruals taxation regimes as non-assessable non-exempt income [34.5].

Example Bertha is a resident who is paid a $500 dividend by a resident company and a $300 dividend by a non-resident company. Both of these dividends are included in her assessable income under s 44(1)(a) assuming none of the exceptions apply.

Dividends paid to non-resident shareholders

Section 44(1)(b) provides that the assessable income of a non-resident shareholder includes dividends paid to the shareholder by a company to the extent that the dividends are paid out of profits derived by the company from sources *in* Australia.

Section 44(1)(b), however, operates subject to special withholding tax rules [31.11]. In particular, s 128D provides that dividends upon which 'withholding tax' is payable under s 128B, or upon which withholding tax would be payable but for s 128B(3)(ga), constitute non-assessable non-exempt income.

Section 128B(1) states that withholding tax is payable on dividends paid by resident companies to non-residents. Section 128B(1), however, operates subject to a number of exceptions, including s 128B(3)(ga), which provides that withholding tax is not payable on the 'franked' part of a dividend. Withholding tax is required to be withheld by the company from the dividend and paid to the Commissioner under sub-div 12-F of sch 1 *TAA* [31.11]. The rate of withholding tax is 30%, unless the recipient is a resident of a tax treaty country [32.3], in which case it is generally 15% under most DTAs [32.6].

The broad effect of these provisions is that dividends paid by resident companies to non-resident shareholders are not assessable under s 44(1)(b) but may be subject to withholding tax if the dividends are 'unfranked'. This means that, in practice, s 44(1)(b) has a limited scope. It generally only applies to assess dividends paid by non-resident companies to non-resident shareholders to the extent that those dividends are paid out of profits derived by the company from sources in Australia.

An illustration of where s 44(1)(b) applied is found in *Parke Davis & Co v FC of T* (1959) 101 CLR 521. This case concerned a United States parent company that received a deemed dividend under s 47(1) *ITAA36* [22.11] from the liquidator of its United States subsidiary company. The subsidiary company had an Australian branch. The High Court held that the parent company should be assessed on so much of the deemed dividend that represented a distribution of profits arising from its subsidiary's Australian branch operations.

Example Theo is a non-resident who is paid a $1,000 dividend by a resident company. The dividend is 'franked' to the extent of $700 and 'unfranked' to the extent of $300. The unfranked part of the dividend is subject to withholding tax under s 128B(1). The rate of withholding tax is 30% unless Theo is a resident of a tax treaty country, in which case it is generally 15%. The franked part of the dividend is exempt from withholding tax under s 128B(3)(ga). Both the franked and unfranked parts of the dividend are non-assessable non-exempt income under s 128D and are therefore not assessable under s 44(1)(b).

If Theo also received a $1,000 dividend paid by a non-resident company, the dividend would be assessable under s 44(1)(b) to the extent that it is paid from profits derived by the non-resident company from sources in Australia. No withholding tax applies in this case as the dividend is not paid by a resident company.

A special rule applies to a non-resident shareholder that carries on business in Australia through a permanent establishment ('PE') [30.5] in Australia. Under s 44(1)(c), the assessable income of such a shareholder includes dividends paid to the shareholder by a resident company that are attributable to the PE to the extent that the dividends are paid out of profits derived by the company from sources *outside* Australia. To prevent such dividends also being subject to withholding tax, s 128B(3E) provides that s 128B(1) does not apply to dividends paid to a non-resident that carries on business in Australia at or through a PE in Australia that are attributable to the PE [31.11].

Example F Co is a foreign company that carries on an investment business in Australia through a PE in Australia. As part of its business, F Co invested in shares in R Co, a resident company. R Co pays F Co a $1,000 dividend from profits R Co derived overseas. F Co is assessed on the $1,000 dividend under s 44(1)(c). The dividend is not subject to withholding tax under s 128B(1) by virtue of s 128B(3E).

[22.6] Imputation system

The imputation system is the central pillar of Australia's corporate tax system. It has operated since 1 July 1987 and was originally contained in pt IIIAA *ITAA36* (former ss 160APA to 160ASN). However, as these provisions were quite complicated, they were replaced with a 'simplified imputation system' from 1 July 2002. The new imputation system is contained in pt 3-6 *ITAA97* (divs 200 to 220) and applies to 'corporate tax entities' and their members. A corporate tax entity is defined as a 'company', a 'corporate limited partnership' [25.8] or a 'public trading trust' [25.9] (s 960-115 *ITAA97*). Companies are the most common form of corporate tax entity and are the main focus of the following discussion.

Former classical system

The imputation system replaced the former 'classical system' of corporate taxation, which operated until 30 June 1987. Under the classical system, companies and shareholders were taxed as separate entities. This meant that companies were taxed on their profits and shareholders were also taxed on distributions paid out of those profits (ie dividends). Shareholders did not receive any relief for tax paid by companies on their underlying profits as the corporate and shareholder tax systems were not integrated. This ultimately resulted in double taxation of corporate profits and made companies unattractive business and investment vehicles. The following example illustrates how a classical system of corporate taxation works.

Example Assume that a classical system of corporate taxation exists and that Classic Co is a resident company that is required to pay tax at the rate of 30%. Classic Co has taxable income of $10,000 for an income year and is therefore required to pay tax of $3,000 (ie $10,000 × 30%). Classic Co pays all its after-tax profits of $7,000 as a dividend to Clare, a resident who pays tax at the rate of 47% (including ML). Clare is therefore required to pay tax of $3,290 (ie $7,000 × 47%).

The classical system results in $6,290 in overall tax being paid on the $10,000 underlying corporate profits (ie $3,000 at corporate level and $3,290 at shareholder level). This represents an overall tax rate of 62.9%.

Objectives of the imputation system

The imputation system is designed to prevent double taxation of corporate profits. It adopts an integration approach to prevent double taxation by providing a resident corporate tax entity's resident members with credits for Australian tax paid by the entity. The credits are referred to as 'franking credits' and are recorded in the entity's 'franking account'. The entity can allocate its franking credits to 'franked distributions' that it pays its members.

Members who receive franked distributions are ordinarily assessed on such distributions. In addition, they must generally include the franking credits allocated to the distributions in their assessable income and they are entitled to tax offsets for the franking credits. Importantly, this 'gross-up' and 'credit' mechanism generally only applies if they satisfy 'residency requirements' at the time the franked distribution is paid. This means that the gross-up and credit rules do not usually apply to franked distributions paid to non-residents. The gross-up and credit rules also do not generally apply to tax-exempt entities. Special rules, however, allow certain tax-exempt charities and deductible gift recipients to benefit from franking credits.

The way corporate tax entities frank distributions is examined at [22.7] and the way the gross-up and credit rules apply to their members is discussed at [22.8].

Basic features of imputation

Before examining how the imputation rules work, it is useful to consider a simple example that demonstrates the basic features of the gross-up and credit mechanism.

Example R Co is a resident company that pays tax at the rate of 30%. In the current income year, it earned $10,000, upon which it is required to pay tax of $3,000. This leaves R Co with $7,000 to pay dividends. The payment of tax results in $3,000 of franking credits in R Co's franking account, which it can use to frank dividends.

R Co has one shareholder, Frank, who is a resident that pays tax at the rate of 47% (including ML). If R Co pays a $7,000 dividend with $3,000 of franking credits to Frank, he will be taxed as follows:

Dividend	$7,000
Plus gross-up for franking credit	$3,000
Taxable income relating to dividend	$10,000
Tax on dividend at 47%	$4,700
Minus franking credit	$3,000
Net tax payable by Frank	$1,700

A different result would have arisen if Frank's tax rate was less than 47%.

Example Assume the same facts as in the previous example, with the exception that Frank only pays tax at the rate of 21% (including ML). In these circumstances, Frank will be taxed as follows:

Dividend	$7,000
Plus gross-up for franking credit	$3,000
Taxable income relating to dividend	$10,000
Tax on dividend at 21%	$2,100
Minus franking credit	$3,000
Net refund of tax available to Frank	$900

The preceding examples show that imputation is designed to ensure that corporate profits (once distributed) ultimately bear a total tax burden equivalent to the tax that would have been paid by the shareholder on the profits if the shareholder had derived those profits directly (rather than as an after-tax distribution via a company). Thus:

- In the first example, an overall amount of $4,700 in tax was paid on the $10,000 ($3,000 was paid by R Co and $1,700 was paid by Frank). This is the same amount of tax that Frank would have had to pay if he derived the $10,000 directly and was subject to tax at the rate of 47%.
- In the second example, an overall amount of $2,100 in tax was paid on the $10,000 ($3,000 was paid by R Co less the refund of $900 that was available to Frank). This is the same amount of tax that Frank would have had to pay if he derived the $10,000 directly and was subject to tax at the rate of 21%.

Until a company's profits are distributed to its shareholders, the only tax paid on those profits will be corporate tax. By retaining profits in a company, the profits are not exposed to any additional tax at the shareholder level. Tax at the shareholder level will only be paid when the profits are eventually distributed (which might only occur several years in the future). Accordingly, if a company has high-rate shareholders (as in the first example above), it has the ability to shelter its profits at the 30% tax rate until such time as it decides to distribute the profits. In other words, the time at which the profits are ultimately exposed to an additional $1,700 in tax at the shareholder level is deferred, making the retention of profits tax-effective.

By contrast, if a company has shareholders that pay tax at a rate below the corporate tax rate (as in the second example above), it is more tax-effective to distribute the profits to the shareholders. This is because their franking credit entitlements exceed the tax they are required to pay on the grossed-up amount of the dividends, resulting in a net refund of corporate tax to the shareholders.

Imputation applies only to Australian tax (not foreign tax)

In its AFTS report [5.5], the Henry Tax Review found that the imputation system provided a number of integrity and other benefits to Australia, including improved neutrality around financing and entity choices. However, it also found that imputation creates biases, as franking credits do not arise in respect of foreign taxes paid by resident companies operating overseas. As a result, the imputation system effectively encourages domestic investment over foreign investment because it only provides franking credits for payments of Australian tax. The significance of this is illustrated in the example below.

Example A Co is a resident company that is not a base rate entity and therefore pays tax at the rate of 30%. A Co earned the equivalent of $10,000 of income in a foreign country that also imposes corporate tax at the rate of 30% on income sourced in that country. A Co's income is therefore subject to foreign tax of $3,000 as well as Australian tax of $3,000. However, to alleviate double taxation, Australia provides a foreign income tax offset under div 770 *ITAA97* for the payment of foreign tax [31.3]. A Co is therefore entitled to a tax offset of $3,000, meaning that it does not need to pay any Australian tax (only foreign tax). After paying $3,000 foreign tax, it therefore has $7,000 remaining to pay as a dividend.

The problem for A Co is that it is only entitled to franking credits in its franking account for the payment of Australian tax (not foreign tax). This means that while A Co can pay a $7,000 dividend, the dividend cannot be franked. Accordingly, if A Co paid a $7,000 unfranked dividend to Felicity who is a resident shareholder that is subject to tax at the rate of 47% (including ML), Felicity would be required to pay tax of $3,290 (ie $7,000 × 47%).

Felicity's situation may be contrasted with Frank's situation in the first example above. While both Felicity and Frank received the same amount of dividends ($7,000) and pay tax at the same rate (47%), Felicity has after-tax income of only $3,710 (ie $7,000 – $3,290), while Frank has after-tax income of $5,300 (ie $7,000 – $1,700). Felicity is therefore in a worse position than Frank because she does not get the benefit of the gross-up and credit mechanism under the imputation system. This is the case even though both R Co and A Co have each paid the same amount of tax ($3,000). In other words, Frank is better off than Felicity simply because R Co has paid Australian tax (which gives rise to franking credits) while A Co has paid foreign tax (which does not give rise to franking credits).

Other ways of preventing double taxation of corporate profits

Australia has a 'full imputation system' (ie one in which corporate tax is generally fully credited to eligible shareholders). Australia's imputation system is broadly similar to New Zealand's imputation system, subject to the exception that New Zealand does not allow shareholders refunds for excess franking credits. New Zealand does, nevertheless, generally allow excess credits to be carried forward into future income years. It is interesting to note that in its failed 2019 election campaign, Labor had proposed to remove refunds for excess franking credits [5.8]. The Coalition campaigned strongly against this change and some people believe it was one of the factors that contributed to it winning the election. Although Labor subsequently won the 2022 election, it no longer plans to remove refunds for excess franking credits.

Over recent years, many countries have moved away from using full imputation systems. While certain countries still use a classical system, most have implemented some other mechanism for dealing with double taxation of corporate profits. Some of the alternative ways for providing relief against double taxation are outlined below:

- **Single-tier system.** Double taxation of corporate profits can be completely overcome by simply adopting a 'single-tier' corporate tax system. For example, Singapore and Malaysia replaced their imputation systems with single-tier systems in 2003 and 2008 respectively. Under a single-tier system, companies are taxed on their profits, but shareholders are exempt from tax on the dividends they receive. In other words, there is only one layer of tax—corporate profits only attract tax at the corporate rate, irrespective of the rates of tax payable by shareholders. This clearly benefits shareholders who are subject to tax at rates above the corporate tax rate, but not shareholders who are subject to tax at rates below the corporate tax rate (as these shareholders would be entitled to refunds under an imputation system).

- **Partial imputation, preferential and deduction systems.** Double taxation of corporate profits can be partly addressed by providing shareholders a credit for a portion of the tax paid by a company under a 'partial imputation system'. In effect, this approach is a blend between a full imputation and a classical system of corporate taxation. Alternatively, double taxation can also be partly addressed by assessing shareholders on only a portion of the dividends they receive, or by taxing dividends at preferential rates. Another option is to allow companies deductions for all, or part of, the profits distributed to their shareholders.

[22.7] Franking distributions

The concept of 'franking' is central to the operation of Australia's imputation system as it is the process through which tax paid by a company is imputed to its shareholders. Franking involves a company allocating 'franking credits' to 'frankable distributions' paid to its members. This is done via entries made in its 'franking account'.

Franking accounts

Corporate tax entities are required to maintain 'franking accounts' (s 205-10). Franking accounts are made up of 'franking credit' and 'franking debit' entries and enable corporate tax entities to track the extent to which they are in a position to frank distributions they pay to their members.

Most franking credits and franking debits can only arise if the corporate tax entity satisfies the 'residency requirement' for the income year in which the relevant entry occurs (s 205-25). This requirement is satisfied if the company is an Australian resident:

- for more than half of the 12 months immediately preceding the event (if the event occurs before the end of the income year)
- at all times during the income year when the entity exists (if the event occurs after the end of the income year), or
- for more than half of the income year (whether or not the event occurs before the end of the income year).

Companies that are foreign residents throughout the income year do not, therefore, generate franking credits and debits. There is, however, an important exception to this rule, which applies to 'NZ franking companies' (ie New Zealand resident companies that have made a 'NZ franking choice'). These companies are treated as having met the residency requirements and can therefore generate franking credits and debits in their franking accounts under modified rules in div 220 *ITAA97*. Division 220 was introduced under special 'reciprocal imputation arrangements' entered into between Australia and New Zealand. The arrangements were implemented because ordinarily, New Zealand companies that make profits in Australia would not be able to pass on franking credits for tax paid in Australia to their Australian shareholders (resulting in the Australian profits being double taxed). Likewise, Australian companies that make profits in New Zealand would not be able to pass on New Zealand franking credits for tax paid in New Zealand to their New Zealand shareholders (resulting in the New Zealand profits being double taxed). To prevent double taxation, the reciprocal arrangements allow New Zealand companies that pay tax in Australia to allocate Australian franking credits to dividends they pay their Australian shareholders, and they allow Australian companies that pay tax in New Zealand to allocate New Zealand franking credits to dividends they pay their New Zealand shareholders.

Franking credit entries

The circumstances in which corporate tax entities generate franking credits in their franking accounts are set out in the table in s 205-15. The main situations in which franking credits arise are where they:

- pay income tax or PAYG instalments—in such a case, the credit is generally the amount of the payment and it arises on the day the payment is made
- receive franked distributions from another corporate tax entity—in such a case, the credit is the amount of the franking credit on the distribution and it arises on the day the distribution is made
- receive franked distributions indirectly via a partnership or trust—in such a case, the credit is the corporate tax entity's share of the franking credit on the distribution and it arises at the end of the income year of the partnership or trust that made the distribution, or
- incur a liability to pay 'franking deficit tax' (see below)—in such a case, the credit is the amount of the liability and it arises immediately after the liability is incurred.

Franking debit entries

The circumstances in which corporate tax entities generate franking debits in their franking accounts are set out in the table in s 205-30. The main situations in which franking debits arise are where they:

- pay franked distributions—in such a case, the debit is the amount of the franking credit on the distribution and it arises on the day the distribution is made
- receive tax refunds—in such a case, the debit is generally the amount of the refund and it arises on the day the refund is received
- underfrank distributions (see below)—in such a case, the debit is worked out under the formula in s 203-50(2) (see below) and it arises on the day on which the frankable distribution is made, or
- transfer amounts to their share capital account from certain other accounts—in such a case, the debit and the time it arises are worked out under s 197-45 [22.21] (s 205-30).

Franking debits can also arise in special cases, such as where share buy-backs take place [22.10] or anti-avoidance provisions are triggered [22.14]–[22.15].

Franking account illustration

The following table illustrates some typical movements in a company's franking account:

Date	Details	Debit	Credit	Balance
1/7/22	Opening balance of $10,000 (automatically carried forward from previous year)			$10,000
21/7/22	Payment of final PAYG tax instalment for 2021/22 of $40,000		$40,000	$50,000
28/10/22	Payment of first PAYG instalment for 2022/23 of $50,000		$50,000	$100,000
3/11/22	Receipt of a $70,000 dividend with $15,000 of franking credits allocated to it from Company X		$15,000	$115,000
28/2/23	Payment of second PAYG instalment for 2022/23 of $30,000		$30,000	$145,000
5/3/23	Payment of $70,000 dividend with $30,000 of franking credits allocated to the dividend	$30,000		$115,000
16/3/23	Receipt of tax refund of $10,000 relating to the 2019/20 income year	$10,000		$105,000
28/4/23	Payment of third PAYG instalment for 2022/23 of $20,000		$20,000	$125,000

Date	Details	Debit	Credit	Balance
30/6/23	Receipt of trust distribution that includes a $70,000 dividend with $30,000 of franking credits allocated to it		$30,000	$155,000
30/6/23	Closing balance (automatically carried forward to following year)			$155,000

The Commissioner may, by legislative instrument, require a company to give him a franking return for a specified income year (s 214-15). The company must comply with this requirement within the time specified in the notice, or within any further time allowed by the Commissioner.

Frankable distributions

Corporate tax entities can only allocate franking credits to 'frankable distributions'. A 'frankable distribution' is defined as a 'distribution' that is not 'unfrankable' (s 202-40).

A 'distribution' is a dividend (or something that is taken to be a dividend) paid by a company. It also includes a profit distribution made by a corporate limited partnership [25.8] and a unit trust dividend paid by a public trading trust [25.9] (s 960-120).

A distribution is 'unfrankable' if it falls within s 202-45. Unfrankable distributions include:

- distributions from a company's share capital account [22.4]
- deemed dividends falling within s 109 and div 7A of pt III *ITAA36* [22.4]
- 'demerger dividends' [28.4], and
- distributions in respect of 'non-equity shares' [29.9].

Treasury Laws Amendment (2023 Measures No 1) Bill 2023 proposes to extend the list of unfrankable distributions to include, for example, listed public company distributions that are consideration for the cancellation of membership interests in the company as part of a selective reduction of capital [22.9].

Example P Co is a company that distributes $1,500 to its shareholders. This payment comprises a $1,000 dividend under the general definition in s 6(1) and a $500 return of capital sourced from its share capital account. Only the $1,000 dividend is a frankable distribution. The $500 return of capital is unfrankable.

Franking distributions

To be able to frank a distribution, an entity must be a 'franking entity' and satisfy the 'residency requirements' when the distribution is made (s 202-5). An entity is a franking entity at a particular time if it is a corporate tax entity at the time and is not a mutual life insurance company or acting in the capacity as trustee (s 202-15). A corporate tax entity satisfies the residency requirement when making a distribution if it is an Australian resident at the time (s 202-20).

A corporate tax entity franks a distribution by allocating a 'franking credit' to the distribution. In practice, the amount of the franking credit that is allocated to a distribution is determined by the entity's board of directors after examining the balance in the entity's franking account. In other words, it is at the discretion of the board of directors to determine the extent to which a distribution is franked. In the majority of cases, subject to the operation of the 'benchmark rule' (see below), an entity's board of directors will usually choose to 'fully frank' a distribution if the entity has sufficient credits in its franking account to warrant this.

The franking credit on a distribution is generally the amount specified on the 'distribution statement' provided by the entity to its members (see below). However, where this amount exceeds the 'maximum franking credit' for the distribution, the franking credit is equal to the maximum franking credit (ss 202-60, 202-65).

Maximum franking credit, corporate tax gross-up rate and corporate tax rate for imputation purposes

The maximum franking credit for a distribution is calculated according to the following formula in s 202-60(2):

$$\text{Maximum franking credit} = \text{Amount of the frankable distribution} \times \frac{1}{\text{Applicable gross-up rate}}$$

The 'applicable gross-up rate' is the 'corporate tax gross-up rate' of the entity making the distribution for the income year in which the distribution is made (s 202-60(2)).

The way the 'corporate tax gross-up rate' is calculated is as follows (s 995-1):

$$\text{Corporate tax gross-up rate} = \frac{\text{100\% – Corporate tax rate for imputation purposes of the entity for the income year}}{\text{Corporate tax rate for imputation purposes of the entity for the income year}}$$

The 'corporate tax rate for imputation purposes' of an entity for an income year is the entity's corporate tax rate for the income year worked out on the assumptions that:

- its aggregated turnover for the income year is equal to its aggregated turnover for the *previous* income year
- its base rate entity passive income for the income year is equal to its base rate entity passive income for the *previous* income year, and
- its assessable income for the income year is equal to its assessable income for the *previous* year.

However, if the entity did not exist in the previous income year, its corporate tax rate for imputation purposes is deemed to be the base rate entity tax rate (ie 25%) (s 995-1).

This means that the corporate tax gross-up rate for entities that have a corporate tax rate for imputation purposes of 30% is 70/30 (which can also be expressed as a decimal of 2.333333) and the corporate tax gross-up rate for entities that have a corporate tax rate for imputation purposes of 25% is 75/25 (which can also be expressed as a decimal of 3.0).

Correspondingly, the maximum franking credit for a distribution is therefore the amount of the frankable distribution multiplied by either 1/2.333333 (ie 30/70) or 1/3 (ie 25/75) depending on the relevant corporate tax rate.

The following table summarises these rates:

Corporate tax rate for imputation purposes	Corporate tax gross-up rate	Maximum franking credit
30%	2.333333 or 70/30	Frankable distribution × 1/2.333333 or Frankable distribution × 30/70
25%	3.0 or 75/25	Frankable distribution × 1/3 or Frankable distribution × 25/75

Example In 2023/24, A Co has a corporate tax rate for imputation purposes of 30%. If it makes a $7,000 frankable distribution during the year, the maximum franking credit it can pass on to its shareholders is $3,000 (ie $7,000 × 1/2.333333 or $7,000 × 30/70).

In 2023/24, D Co has a corporate tax rate for imputation purposes of 25%. If it makes a $7,000 frankable distribution during the year, the maximum franking credit it can pass on to its shareholders is $2,333.33 (ie $7,000 × 1/3 or $7,000 × 25/75).

It is important to point out that an entity's corporate tax rate for an income year is not necessarily the same as its corporate tax rate for imputation purposes for the year. This is illustrated in the following example.

Example X Co carries on a manufacturing business and has aggregated turnover of $60m in 20232/24 and $20m in 2022/23. For 2023/24, X Co has:

- a corporate tax rate of 30% as its aggregated turnover for 2023/24 is $60m, which is above the base rate entity threshold of $50m, and
- a corporate tax rate for imputation purposes of 25% as its aggregated turnover for 2022/23 was $20m, which is below the base rate entity threshold of $50m.

Accordingly, if it pays a $10,000 frankable distribution in 2023/24, the maximum franking credit it can allocate to the distribution is $3,333.33 (ie $10,000 × 25/75).

Franked and unfranked parts of a distribution

Distributions may be 'fully franked', 'partly franked' or 'unfranked'. The extent to which a distribution is franked depends on the extent to which the company has allocated franking credits to the distribution.

The 'franked part' of a distribution is worked out according to the following formula in s 976-1:

$$\text{Franked part of distribution} = \text{Franking credit on distribution} \times \text{Applicable gross-up rate}$$

The 'applicable gross-up rate' is the 'corporate tax gross-up rate' of the entity making the distribution for the income year in which the distribution is made (see the table above).

The 'unfranked part' of a distribution is the amount of the distribution that is left after deducting the 'franked part' of the distribution (s 976-5).

Example A company paid a $700 dividend and allocated $90 of franking credits to the dividend. If the company has a corporate tax rate for imputation purposes of 30%, the franked part of the dividend is $210 (ie $90 × 70/30) and the unfranked part of the dividend is $490 (ie $700 – $210). However, if the company has a corporate tax rate for imputation purposes of 25%, the franked part of the dividend is $270 (ie $90 × 75/25) and the unfranked part of the dividend is $430 (ie $700 – $270).

Determining the extent to which a dividend is franked is especially important where dividends are paid by resident companies to non-resident shareholders, as the franked part of such dividends is generally non-assessable non-exempt income, whereas the unfranked part of such dividends is generally subject to withholding tax [22.5].

Distribution statement

A distribution statement must generally be provided by a corporate tax entity to its members on or before the day on which it pays them a frankable distribution (s 202-75). Private companies, however, can provide distribution statements up to four months after the end of the income year in which the distribution is made, or at such later time as the Commissioner determines in writing, so long as the franking credits allocated to the distribution do not create or add to a 'franking deficit tax liability' for the entity at the end of the income year.

The distribution statement must be in the approved form and must:

(a) identify the entity making the distribution
(b) state the date on which the distribution is made
(c) state the amount of the distribution
(d) state that there is a franking credit of an amount specified on the distribution
(e) state the franking percentage for the distribution
(f) state the amount of any withholding tax that has been deducted from the distribution by the entity, and
(g) include any other information required by the approved form that is relevant to imputation generally or the distribution.

A sample distribution statement is provided below. The statement indicates that ABCD Ltd has paid Ivan Investor a dividend of $2.80 per share on the 1,000 ordinary shares he held in the company on the record date of 22 September 2023. The dividend is paid on 5 October 2023 and is partly franked. As Ivan is a resident and has quoted his TFN to the company, no withholding tax has been deducted from the payment [39.4].

ABCD Ltd

ABN 123456789
Registered Office 123 Alphabet Ave, Melbourne, 3000

Ivan Investor
Investor Road
Sydney, 2000

TFN/ABN Status: Quoted
Record date: 22 September 2023
Payment date: 5 October 2023

Dividend for the period ended 30 June 2023

Class of shares	**Number of shares**	**Dividends per share**	**Unfranked amount**	**Franked amount**	**Franking credit**	**Withholding tax**
Ordinary shares	1,000	$2.80	$2,100	$700	$300	Nil

Dividend amount: $2,800

Franking information: Franked rate per share: $0.70
Franked percentage: 25%
Company tax rate: 30%

Benchmark rule

To ensure that franked distributions are spread evenly across a corporate tax entity's members and to prevent 'streaming' of franking credits to those members who can benefit most from them, there is a 'benchmark rule'. This rule essentially requires all frankable distributions made by a corporate tax entity during a 'franking period' to be franked to the same extent. More specifically, it provides that a corporate tax entity must not make a frankable distribution if its 'franking percentage' differs from its 'benchmark franking percentage' for the 'franking period' in which the distribution is made (s 203-25).

The franking period for a private company is its income year (s 203-45). Public companies generally have two franking periods during their income year (ie being the first six months of their income year and the balance of their income year) (s 203-40).

The benchmark franking percentage is the same as the franking percentage for the first frankable distribution that the corporate tax entity made during the relevant franking period (s 203-30). The franking percentage for a frankable distribution is calculated according to the following formula and cannot exceed 100% (s 203-35):

$$\text{Franking percentage} = \frac{\text{Franking credit allocated to the frankable distribution}}{\text{Maximum franking credit for the distribution}} \times 100$$

Example The first frankable distribution that a company with a corporate tax rate for imputation purposes of 30% made in a franking period was $700. If it allocated $150 of franking credits to the distribution, its benchmark franking percentage for the period is 50% (ie $150/$300 × 100). In order not to breach the benchmark rule, any subsequent frankable distributions it makes in the same franking period would need to be franked to 50%.

The benchmark rule operates subject to certain exceptions relating to listed public companies (s 203-20). In particular, it does not apply to a listed company that only has a single class of membership interests during the relevant franking period.

In extraordinary circumstances, the Commissioner is permitted to allow an entity to frank a distribution at a franking percentage that differs from its benchmark franking percentage (s 203-55(1)). In exercising this power, the Commissioner must have regard to the matters listed in s 203-55(3).

To assist with identifying potential streaming arrangements, a corporate tax entity must notify the Commissioner if its benchmark franking percentage for a franking period 'differs significantly' (ie by more than 20 percentage points) from the benchmark franking percentage for the last franking period in which a frankable distribution was made (s 204-75).

If a corporate tax entity breaches the benchmark rule it will be subject to either:

- 'over-franking tax' (if the franking percentage of the distribution exceeds the benchmark franking percentage), or
- a 'penalty franking debit' (if the franking percentage for the distribution is less than the benchmark franking percentage) (s 203-50).

The amount of the over-franking tax or penalty franking debit is calculated as follows (s 203-50(2)):

$$\begin{matrix}\text{Over-franking tax or} \\ \text{penalty franking debit}\end{matrix} = \begin{matrix}\text{Amount of the} \\ \text{frankable distribution}\end{matrix} \times \frac{\text{Franking \% differential}}{\text{Applicable gross-up rate}}$$

The 'franking % differential' is the difference between the actual franking percentage for the distribution and either the benchmark franking percentage for the period or the franking percentage determined by the Commissioner where he has made such a determination under s 203-55(1).

The 'applicable gross-up rate' is the corporate tax gross-up rate of the entity making the distribution for the income year in which the distribution is made (see the table above).

Over-franking tax addresses the fact that the entity has passed on more franking credits to its members than it should have under the benchmark rule. The corporate tax entity does not credit its franking account for the payment of over-franking tax (like for ordinary tax). Correspondingly, the penalty franking debit cancels the unused amount of franking credits that the entity should have allocated to the distribution under the benchmark rule. It does not result in any corresponding franking credit being passed on to the entity's members.

Example Suppose the company in the previous example made a subsequent distribution in the same franking period of $1,400. In order not to breach the benchmark rule, it would need to frank the distribution to 50%. If it only allocated $60 of franking credits to the distribution, the franking percentage of the dividend would be 10% (ie $60/$600 × 100). This means that it would have underfranked the distribution, and this would generate a franking debit in its franking account of $240 (ie $1,400 × 40%/2.333333).

Franking deficit tax

Corporate tax entities can determine the extent to which they allocate franking credits to distributions. However, they ultimately need to reconcile the franking credits allocated to distributions with the tax they have paid as disclosed in their franking accounts. Where an entity's franking account is in deficit, this will indicate that it has passed on more franking credits to its members than is warranted by the tax it has paid. 'Franking deficit tax' (FDT) is designed to make up for over-franking and is imposed under the *New Business Tax System (Franking Deficit Tax) Act 2002* (Cth).

An entity is liable to pay FDT if it has a deficit in its franking account at the end of an income year or immediately before it ceases to be a franking entity (s 205-45). The amount of FDT is equal to the deficit in its franking account at such time.

To ensure that an entity does not avoid FDT by deferring the time at which a franking debit occurs in its franking account, a tax refund received within three months after the end of a year is treated as having been received immediately before the end of that year (s 205-50).

FDT is treated as a pre-payment of income tax. Accordingly, the entity obtains a credit for the payment of FDT in its franking account (s 205-15). The entity is also generally entitled to an FDT offset calculated under s 205-70.

Where the entity's FDT liability is greater than 10% of the total franking credits that arise in its franking account for the year, the tax offset is generally reduced by 30%. This is designed as a penalty to discourage substantial over-franking.

Example A company has a franking deficit of $1,000 in its franking account at the end of an income year because it has over-franked dividends paid to its shareholders during the year. It therefore has an FDT liability of $1,000. The payment of FDT results in a credit in its franking account. It also results in the company being entitled to an FDT offset. If the company had a total of $4,000 in franking credits in its franking account for the year, then, since the FDT is greater than 10% of the total franking credits, the FDT offset is reduced by 30% (from $1,000 to $700). The $300 reduction represents the penalty for substantial over-franking.

The 'over-franking penalty' only applies to franking deficits that are attributable to certain franking debits (ie those arising under specified items of the table in s 205-30). For instance, it generally applies to franking deficits arising from payments of franked distributions during the year. However, the penalty does not apply where the Commissioner determines that the deficit has been caused by circumstances 'outside the entity's control'.

Example A company pays franked dividends during the year (resulting in franking debits), but reasonably expects that its future PAYG instalments for the year (resulting in franking credits) will be sufficient to ensure that it does not have a franking deficit at the end of the year. If an unexpected downturn results in its future PAYG instalments being less than expected, the Commissioner could determine not to impose the penalty on the basis that the deficit is outside the company's control.

[22.8] Gross-up and credit mechanism

A key feature of the imputation system is the 'gross-up' and 'credit' mechanism that applies to franked distributions in div 207 *ITAA97*. The general gross-up and credit rules are contained in sub-div 207-A. These rules apply to franked distributions paid 'directly' to individuals, corporate tax entities and complying superannuation entities. They do not apply to franked distributions paid to partnerships and trustees (except those partnerships and trustees that are corporate tax entities or complying superannuation entities). Instead, special 'flow-through' rules in sub-div 207-B operate where franked distributions flow 'indirectly' to an entity or through another entity (eg where entities derive franked distributions via interests they hold in partnerships and trusts). The special flow-through rules are necessary as partnerships and trusts are 'transparent' entities rather than distinct taxpayers.

General rules in sub-div 207-A

Under sub-div 207-A, an entity that receives a franked distribution:

- is required to include in assessable income the amount of the franking credit allocated to the distribution (s 207-20(1)), and
- is entitled to a tax offset for the franking credit (s 207-20(2)).

The amount included in assessable income under s 207-20(1) is in addition to the amount assessable as a dividend under s 44(1) *ITAA36* [22.5].

The tax offset under s 207-20(2) is generally refundable to individuals and trustees of complying superannuation entities, but not to companies and trustees of non-complying superannuation entities (see below).

The way the gross-up and credit mechanism applies to individual shareholders is illustrated below.

Example

Situation 1

X Co is a resident company that has a corporate tax rate for imputation purposes of 30%. It pays a $7,000 dividend with $3,000 of franking credits to each of the following resident shareholders:

- A (an individual whose taxable income is below the tax-free threshold and pays no tax)
- B (an individual whose marginal tax rate is 19% plus ML)
- C (an individual whose marginal tax rate is 32.5% plus ML)

- D (an individual whose marginal tax rate is 37% plus ML)
- E (an individual whose marginal tax rate is 45% plus ML).

The income tax positions of the respective shareholders are as follows:

	A (0%)	B (21%)	C (34.5%)	D (39%)	E (47%)
Dividend (s 44(1)(a))	$7,000	$7,000	$7,000	$7,000	$7,000
Gross-up (s 207-20(1))	$3,000	$3,000	$3,000	$3,000	$3,000
Taxable income	$10,000	$10,000	$10,000	$10,000	$10,000
Basic income tax (plus ML)	Nil	$2,100	$3,450	$3,900	$4,700
Franking credit (s 207-20(2))	$3,000	$3,000	$3,000	$3,000	$3,000
Income tax or (refund)	($3,000)	($900)	$450	$900	$1,700

Situation 2

Y Co is a resident company that has a corporate tax rate for imputation purposes of 25%. Y Co has the same shareholders as X Co and pays a $7,500 dividend with $2,500 of franking credits to each of them. The income tax positions of the respective shareholders are as follows:

	A (0%)	B (21%)	C (34.5%)	D (39%)	E (47%)
Dividend (s 44(1)(a))	$7,500	$7,500	$7,500	$7,500	$7,500
Gross-up (s 207-20(1))	$2,500	$2,500	$2,500	$2,500	$2,500
Taxable income	$10,000	$10,000	$10,000	$10,000	$10,000
Basic income tax	Nil	$2,100	$3,450	$3,900	$4,700
Franking credit (s 207-20(2))	$2,500	$2,500	$2,500	$2,500	$2,500
Income tax or (refund)	($2,500)	($400)	$950	$1,400	$2,200

It is worth noting that in both situations outlined above, the dividend was fully franked [22.7]. This is because the maximum franking credit that X Co could allocate to the $7,000 dividend (assuming its corporate tax rate for imputation purposes was 30%) was $3,000 (ie $7,000 × 30/70), while the maximum franking credit that Y Co could allocate to the $7,500 dividend (assuming its corporate tax rate for imputation purposes was 25%) was $2,500 (ie $7,500 × 25/75).

It is also important to understand that while the respective gross-up and credit amounts in each situation are identical, they do not simply cancel each other out. This is because the gross-up amount is assessable income while the credit amount is a tax offset (rather than a deduction). The gross-up merely increases each shareholder's taxable income by either $3,000 or $2,500, requiring them to pay tax on the additional amount at their respective tax rates. The credit, on the other hand, reduces their tax payable by either $3,000 or $2,500.

Special flow-through rules in sub-div 207-B

Subdivision 207-B contains special flow-through rules that apply where franked distributions are paid to partnerships or trusts. These rules are complex and tie in with the general taxation rules relating to partnerships (Chapter 23) and trusts (Chapter 24).

In simple terms, where franked distributions are paid to a partnership or trust, the franking credits allocated to such distributions must be included in the assessable income of the partnership or trust under s 207-35. This ensures that the franking credits are taken into account in calculating the 'net income' or 'loss' of the partnership or trust and will be reflected in any amounts that flow through to the respective partners and beneficiaries.

An entity to which a franked distribution flows indirectly is entitled to a tax offset under s 207-45 for its 'share of the franking credit' on the distribution if it is an individual, a corporate tax entity, a trustee assessed under ss 98, 99 or 99A *ITAA36*, or a trustee of a superannuation fund, ADF or PST.

An entity's 'share of a franking credit on a franked distribution' is an amount that is notionally allocated to the entity as its share of that credit, whether or not the entity actually receives any of that credit or distribution (s 207-57). The amount of the credit depends on the entity's 'share of the franked distribution' (determined according to the table in s 207-55) and is worked out as follows:

$$\text{Entity's share of the franked distribution} = \text{Amount of the franking credit on the franked distribution} \times \frac{\text{Entity's share of the franked distribution}}{\text{Amount of the franked distribution}}$$

A special formula applies where a beneficiary is 'specifically entitled' to an amount of a franked distribution (ie where 'streaming' has occurred) (s 207-58) [24.8].

The gross-up and credit mechanism under ss 207-35 and 207-45 perform a similar function to the gross-up and credit mechanism under s 207-20. This mechanism, however, needs to be adjusted where a franked distribution flows indirectly to an entity and the entity's share of the distribution would be exempt income or non-assessable non-exempt income. In these circumstances, the franking gross-up and credit generally needs to be removed. For example, this situation would arise where a share of a franked dividend flows indirectly through a partnership to a non-resident partner who would be exempt from tax on their share of the dividend under s 128D [22.5]. In such a case, the partner is entitled to deduct an amount equal to its share of the franking credit on the distribution and is not entitled to a tax offset for its share of the franking credit under s 207-45 (s 207-95).

The broad aim of the flow-through rules is to ensure that the underlying entities that receive franked distributions indirectly through partnerships and trusts also benefit from the appropriate share of the franking credits that have been allocated to those distributions as if those entities had received the distributions directly. The mechanics of the flow-through rules as they apply to trusts is illustrated in the example at [24.8].

Subdivisions 207-A and 207-B operate subject to other subdivisions

It is important to be aware that sub-div 207-A operates subject to sub-divs 207-C, 207-D, 207-E and 207-F and sub-div 207-B operates subject to sub-divs 207-D, 207-E and 207-F. The broad scope of these subdivisions is outlined below:

- **Subdivision 207-C (residency requirement).** Subdivision 207-C provides that the gross-up and credit mechanism in s 207-20 does not apply to an individual or company unless the entity satisfies the 'residency requirement' at the time the distribution is made (s 207-70). The residency requirement will be satisfied where the individual or company is a resident at the time the distribution is made (s 207-75(1)). It will also be satisfied if the individual or company is a non-resident at the time the distribution is made provided the entity carries on business in Australia at or through a PE and the distribution is attributable to the PE (s 207-75(2)).

Example R Co is a resident company that has a corporate tax rate for imputation purposes of 30%. It pays a $700 dividend with $300 of franking credits to Fabio, who is a non-resident that does not carry on business in Australia. As Fabio does not satisfy the residency requirement, sub-div 207-A does not apply to the franked distribution. Consequently, Fabio does not include the franking credit in his assessable income and is not entitled to a tax offset for the franking credit.

- **Subdivisions 207-D and 207-E (exempt entity rules).** Subdivision 207-D provides that the gross-up and credit rules do not apply to franked distributions that are exempt income or non-assessable non-exempt income of an entity (ss 207-90, 207-95). Subdivision 207-D, however, operates subject to sub-div 207-E, which allows an 'exempt institution that is eligible for a refund' to benefit from franking credits (s 207-110). Such institutions include endorsed tax-exempt registered charities [11.4] and deductible gift recipients [13.13] that satisfy the residency requirement (s 207-115). Subdivision 207-E also allows complying superannuation entities that are exempt from tax on their income under ss 295-385 and 295-390 [19.14] to benefit from franking credits (s 207-110).

Example R Co is a resident company that pays a $700 dividend with $300 of franking credits to an endorsed tax-exempt charity. Since the charity's income is exempt from tax, it is not assessed on the dividend or the franking credit. However, as it is an entity that falls within sub-div 207-E, it is nevertheless entitled to a refund of $300 relating to the franking credit. The charity therefore receives a net amount of $1,000, comprising the $700 dividend and the $300 franking credit refund.

- **Subdivision 207-F (anti-avoidance rules).** Subdivision 207-F provides that the gross-up and credit rules do not apply in certain cases where the imputation system has been 'manipulated'. Section 207-145 sets out six circumstances in which entities do not include franking credits in their assessable income and are not entitled to tax offsets for franking credits in respect of franked distributions. These circumstances arise where:
  - the entity is not a 'qualified person' in relation to the distribution for the purposes of former div 1A of pt IIIAA *ITAA36* (ie generally where the entity has not held the shares for at least 45 days) [22.12]
  - the Commissioner has made a determination under s 177EA(5)(b) *ITAA36* that no 'imputation benefit' is to arise in respect of the distribution [22.13]
  - the Commissioner has made a determination under s 204-30(3)(c) *ITAA97* that no 'imputation benefit' is to arise in respect of the distribution [22.14]
  - the distribution is made as part of a 'dividend stripping operation' [22.16], or
  - the distribution is one to which s 207-157 *ITAA97* (relating to 'distribution washing') applies [22.17]
  - the distribution is one to which s 207-158 *ITAA97* (relating to 'foreign income tax deductions') applies.

Refundable tax offset rules

As mentioned above, individuals and trustees of complying superannuation entities are generally entitled to refunds for any excess tax offsets available under div 207 (s 67-25(1)). In other words, these taxpayers are entitled to be refunded so much of their franking credits that exceed their income tax liabilities for a particular year. Refunds for excess franking credits are, however, generally not available to trustees of non-complying superannuation entities (s 67-25(1A)), or to companies (unless they are exempt institutions eligible for refunds, such as endorsed tax-exempt charities) (s 67-25(1C)).

Example Y Co has a corporate tax rate for imputation purposes of 30%. It pays a $7,000 dividend with $3,000 of franking credits to each of the following resident shareholders:

- F (the trustee of a complying superannuation fund subject to tax at the rate of 15%)
- G (the trustee of a non-complying superannuation fund subject to tax at the rate of 45%)
- H (a company that is subject to tax at the rate of 30%)
- I (a company that is a base rate entity and subject to tax at the rate of 25%)
- J (a company that is an endorsed tax exempt charity and is exempt from tax).

The income tax positions of the respective shareholders are as follows:

	F (15%)	G (45%)	H (30%)	I (25%)	J (0%)
Dividend (s 44(1)(a))	$7,000	$7,000	$7,000	$7,000	N/A
Gross-up (s 207-20(1))	$3,000	$3,000	$3,000	$3,000	N/A
Taxable income	$10,000	$10,000	$10,000	$10,000	N/A
Basic income tax (plus ML)	$1,500	$4,500	$3,000	$2,500	N/A
Franking credit (s 207-20(2))	$3,000	$3,000	$3,000	$3,000	$3,000
Income tax or (refund)	($1,500)	$1,500	Nil	Nil	($3,000)

Converting a company's excess franking credits into tax losses

Since companies are generally not entitled to refunds for excess franking credits, the benefit of such credits would ordinarily be wasted. To prevent companies wasting franking credits, special rules allow them to convert their 'excess franking offsets' into equivalent tax loss amounts [13.15].

Broadly speaking, a company has excess franking offsets for an income year where the total amount of its franking credit tax offsets for the year exceeds the tax it would have to pay on its taxable income for the year if it did not have those tax offsets (s 36-55(1)). A company's excess franking offsets are converted into a tax loss in accordance with the method statement in s 36-55(2).

Example Z Co is a resident company that is not a base rate entity and therefore pays tax at the rate of 30%. In 2023/24, it receives a dividend of $14,000 with $6,000 of franking credits allocated to it. It also has deductions of $10,000.

The amount of income tax the company would have to pay on its taxable income if it did not have the $6,000 franking credit tax offset is $3,000 calculated as follows:

$$\$3{,}000 = [(\$14{,}000 + \$6{,}000) - \$10{,}000] \times 30\%$$

As $3,000 is less than the franking credit tax offset of $6,000, Z Co has an excess tax offset of $3,000 for the year under s 36-55(1). The excess tax offset is converted into a tax loss amount calculated under s 36-55(2) as follows:

$$\text{Tax loss} = \begin{array}{c}\text{Amount (if any) that would}\\ \text{have been the entity's tax loss}\\ \text{for the income year if its net}\\ \text{exempt income (if any)}\\ \text{were disregarded}\end{array} + \frac{\text{Excess franking offsets}}{\text{Corporate tax rate for imputation purposes for that year}} - \begin{array}{c}\text{Net exempt}\\ \text{income}\end{array}$$

$$= 0 + \$3{,}000/30\% - 0$$

$$= \$10{,}000$$

Z Co will be able to deduct the $10,000 tax loss in future income years, provided it satisfies the carry forward loss requirements [22.22].

[22.9] Capital returns

Companies sometimes have excess capital that they wish to return to their shareholders who may have better use for those funds. The *Corporations Act* allows companies to reduce their share capital if the reduction is fair and reasonable to the company's shareholders, does not materially prejudice the company's ability to pay its creditors, and is approved by the shareholders (s 256B). Different shareholder approval requirements apply depending on whether the reduction is an 'equal' or 'selective' reduction (s 256C). If the reduction involves the cancellation of shares, it must be approved by a special resolution passed at a meeting of the shareholders whose shares are to be cancelled (ie it must be passed by at least 75% of the votes cast by members entitled to vote on the resolution: s 9).

Where a company returns capital to its shareholders, this will generally give rise to CGT issues for the shareholders in respect of their shares. The CGT implications for a shareholder of a capital reduction depend on whether or not the shareholder's shares are cancelled. The following diagram contains a simplified outline of the basic rules:

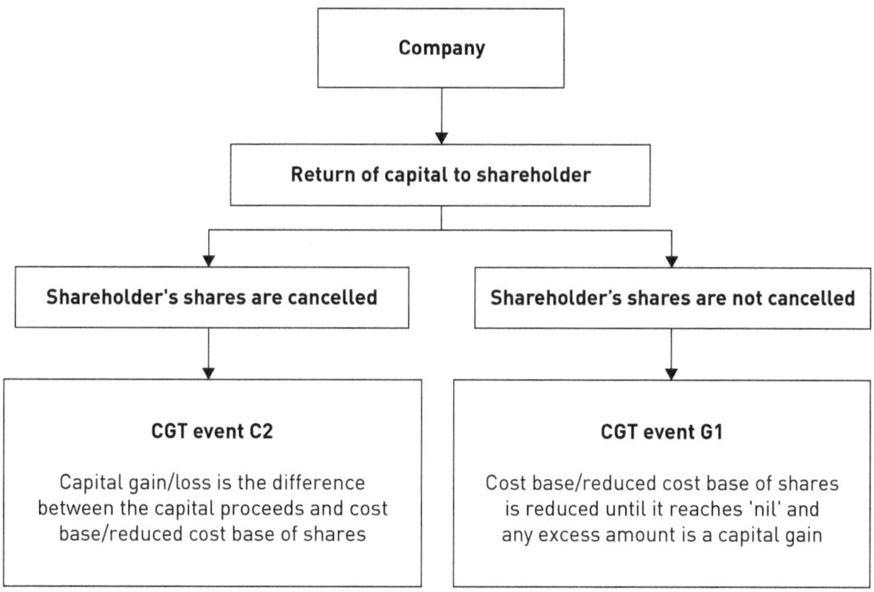

Shareholder's shares cancelled

Where a capital reduction results in the shareholder's shares being cancelled, CGT event C2 applies [17.10].

In such a case, the shareholder is deemed to make a capital gain if the amount returned is more than the cost base of the shares and the shareholder is deemed to make a capital loss if the amount returned is less than the reduced cost base of the shares (s 104-25(3)).

Capital gains and losses are disregarded if they are made in relation to shares acquired prior to 20 September 1985 (s 104-25(5)).

> *Example* Six months ago, Barry acquired a share for $100 in X Co. X Co returned $120 of capital to Barry and cancelled the share. Barry makes a capital gain under CGT event C2 of $20 (ie $120 – $100). If X Co had only returned $90 to Barry, he would make a capital loss of $10 (ie $100 – $90).

Shareholder's shares not cancelled

Where the capital reduction does not result in the shareholder's shares being cancelled, CGT event G1 applies.

In such a case, where the amount returned (excluding any part of the payment that is a dividend) is more than the share's cost base, the share's cost base/reduced cost base is reduced to nil and the excess amount is treated as a capital gain (s 104-135(3)).

Where the amount returned (excluding any part of the payment that is a dividend) is not more than the cost base of the share, the share's cost base/reduced cost base is reduced by such amount (s 104-135(4)).

Capital gains and losses are disregarded if they are made in relation to shares acquired prior to 20 September 1985 (s 104-135(5)).

> *Example* Six months ago, John acquired a share in Y Co for $100. Y Co returned $70 of capital to John but did not cancel his share. The cost base of John's share is reduced to $30 (ie $100 – $70). If John sold the share the next day for $50, he would make a capital gain of $20 (ie $50 – $30).
>
> If Y Co had instead returned $110 to John, the cost base of his share would be reduced to nil and he would make a capital gain of $10. If he sold the share the next day for $50, he would make a capital gain of $50 (ie $50 – nil).

Returns of capital to share traders

Where shareholders are share traders, their shares constitute trading stock. Any capital gains or capital losses made on their shares will therefore be disregarded under s 118-25 [17.5]. These shareholders will, nevertheless, need to be account for returns of capital under the general income tax rules. Returns of capital to share traders would generally be assessable under s 6-5.

[22.10] Share buy-backs

Companies can also return amounts to their shareholders by undertaking 'share buy-backs'. This involves companies buying back shares from their shareholders and results in the cancellation of those shares. Under the *Corporations Act*, companies are permitted to buy back their shares provided the buy-back does not materially prejudice their ability to pay their creditors and the buy-back satisfies the procedures in div 2 of pt 2J.1 (ss 257A to 257J) of the Act. Companies can use their share capital and/or profits to fund a buy-back.

Share buy-backs differ from capital reductions as they only take place when a shareholder agrees to sell their shares to the company. In a capital reduction, the company determines whether or not to cancel the shareholder's shares [22.9].

Division 16K

The rules dealing with the taxation of share buy-backs are contained in div 16K of pt III *ITAA36* (ss 159GZZZIA to 159GZZZS). These rules are complex and depend on whether the buy-back is classified as:

- an 'on-market purchase' (ie a buy-back undertaken in the ordinary course of trading on the stock exchange), or
- an 'off-market purchase' (ie any other buy-back) (s 159GZZZK).

Depending on the kind of buy-back involved and the extent to which the company uses its share capital and/or profits to fund the buy-back, the purchase price may involve a 'consideration component' and/or a 'dividend component'. The consideration component is relevant in calculating whether an amount is assessable or deductible, or gives rise to a capital gain or capital loss, for the seller. The dividend component is generally a frankable distribution and may have franking credits allocated to it which the seller may be able to utilise.

The rationale for treating an on-market purchase differently from an off-market purchase is that, in an on-market purchase, the shareholder may not necessarily be aware that the company is purchasing the shares since the transaction occurs in the ordinary course of trading on a stock exchange. For this reason, shareholders that sell their shares to a company under an on-market purchase are taxed as if they had sold their shares under an 'ordinary sale' to a third party. Even though the company may have used its profits to fund the purchase, no part of the purchase price is treated as a dividend. Instead, the whole amount is treated as consideration for the sale of the shares.

In contrast, in an off-market purchase, shareholders know that the company is the purchaser of their shares since the company would have made a specific offer to buy their shares or invited the shareholders to tender their shares for sale back to the company. Shareholders are therefore in a position to know the extent to which the company has funded the purchase out of its capital and/or profits. As a consequence, subject to special rules that are proposed to apply to buy-backs undertaken by listed public companies (discussed below), the purchase price can include both consideration and dividend components.

Tender-style off-market purchases undertaken by listed public companies

Prior to the announcement of proposed amendments to the share buy-back rules by the Albanese Government in its October 2022 Budget, it was common for listed public companies to structure off-market purchases in ways that took advantage of the tax status of their shareholders. Many well-known companies (including BHP, Commonwealth Bank, Telstra and Woolworths) entered into sophisticated off-market buy-back arrangements in which they returned billions of dollars to their shareholders. Under these buy-backs, the shareholders were given the option of tendering their shares at one or more 'tender prices' set by the company. Shareholders could nominate how many shares they would offer to sell at particular prices, subject to any limits set by the company. It was then up to the company to determine how many of the tendered shares it would buy back.

The tender process created a 'Dutch auction' bidding competition between the shareholders who wanted to participate in the buy-back. It also helped reduce the price at which shares could be purchased by companies, allowing them to buy back a greater number of shares than they might otherwise have been able to purchase on-market.

Tax-exempt shareholders (such as charities) and low-rate shareholders (such as complying superannuation funds) who were eligible to benefit from refundable franking credits were usually keen to participate in these buy-backs because the purchase price would usually include a substantial franked dividend component. These shareholders would, therefore, often be willing to sell their shares at prices below the value at which the shares were being traded on-market to benefit from the franking credits. At the same time, the purchase price would typically have a low consideration component, which meant that they would usually generate losses on the cancellation of their shares.

The shareholders who did not participate in the buy-back (typically high-rate shareholders) also stood to benefit as they would end up with a greater percentage interest in the company after the buy-back was completed, since there would be fewer remaining shareholders.

An important feature of off-market purchases was the 'split' between the dividend and capital components of the purchase price. A split that had a capital component that was too low could result in streaming of dividends and artificial losses. Conversely, a split that had a capital component that was too high could result in the streaming of capital benefits at the expense of dividends. The Commissioner consequently issued PS LA 2007/9, which set out his views on acceptable methodologies for determining the 'split' and whether any anti-avoidance provisions applied.

October 2022 Budget changes: off-market buy-backs by listed public companies

Concerns about the way listed public companies used off-market buy-backs led the Albanese Government to announce in the October 2022 Budget that it would align the tax treatment of off-market purchases undertaken by such companies with the treatment of on-market purchases. Treasury Laws Amendment (2023 Measures No 1) Bill 2023 contains the amendments, which are proposed to be backdated to commence from the time of announcement (ie 7.30pm on 25 October 2022). The amendments are designed to ensure that off-market purchases by listed public companies can no longer give rise to dividends. This effectively prevents them from undertaking the kinds of tender-style buy-backs outlined above. The following discussion examines the tax consequences of share buy-backs under the proposed new rules.

Tax consequences for companies: On-market and off-market purchases

Section 159GZZZN provides that if a company buys back shares from its shareholders, the buy-back and any subsequent cancellation of the shares are disregarded for the purposes of determining whether an amount is included in the company's assessable income or allowed as a deduction, and for the purposes of determining whether the company makes a capital gain or capital loss. In other words, a buy-back generally has no tax implications for a company. It may, nevertheless, have franking implications (see below).

Tax consequences for shareholders: On-market purchase

In an on-market purchase, the purchase price does not include any dividend component (s 159GZZZR). This is the case even though the company may have used its profits to fund the buy-back. For the purposes of determining whether the seller has made any gain or loss on the sale of the share, the seller is deemed to have received as consideration for the sale the purchase price paid for the share (s 159GZZZS).

Example L Co is a listed public company that undertakes an on-market purchase in which it buys back Jill's share on the stock exchange for $20. The company uses $5 from its share capital account and $15 from its accumulated profits to fund the buy-back. Jill does not receive any dividend in respect of the buy-back and is deemed to have disposed of her share for $20. Accordingly, if she purchased the share six months ago for $17 and it was not trading stock, she would make a capital gain of $3 (ie $20 – $17).

Tax consequences for shareholders: Off-market purchase

In an off-market, the purchase price may include a dividend component and/or a consideration component. However, where a listed public company buys back its shares after 7.30pm on 25 October 2022, no part of the purchase price will be a dividend (proposed s 159GZZZPA). As a result, the entire purchase price will be treated as consideration for the sale of the share. This ensures that an off-market purchase undertaken by a listed public company will have the same tax effect for a shareholder as an on-market purchase.

Dividend component

Section 159GZZZP provides that, in an off-market purchase, the difference between the purchase price paid for a share and that part of the purchase price debited against the company's share capital account is treated as a dividend paid to the seller out of profits derived by the company on the day of the buy-back. However, this section will no longer apply to buy-backs undertaken by listed public companies after 7.30pm on 25 October 2022 (proposed s 159GZZZP(3)).

Consideration component

Section 159GZZZQ(1) provides that, in an off-market purchase, the seller is deemed to have received as consideration for the sale the purchase price paid for the share. However, this rule operates subject to the following modifications:

- **Market value uplift.** Where the purchase price is less than the amount that would have been the market value of the share at the time of the buy-back (assuming the buy-back did not occur and was never proposed to occur), the consideration for the sale is deemed to be the market value of the share at that time (s 159GZZZQ(2)). TD 2004/22 contains a formula for calculating the market value of shares in listed companies for the purposes of s 159GZZZQ(2).
- **Reduction amount.** Where there is a 'reduction amount', the consideration for the sale is reduced by that amount (s 159GZZZQ(3)). The reduction amount is basically so much of the purchase price that is a dividend under s 159GZZZP (s 159GZZZQ(4)). However, where the seller is a corporate tax entity and receives a franked dividend as part of the purchase price, then, if it would otherwise generate a loss on the sale of the share, the 'reduction amount' does not include so much of the 'offsetable amount' as does not exceed the 'loss amount' (ss 159GZZZQ(8), (9)). The aim of this rule is to reduce the amount of a loss that would otherwise be available to a company on the sale of a share where the loss is attributable to the franked dividend component of the purchase price. There is, however, no reduction amount if the buy-back is undertaken by a listed public company after 7.30pm on 25 October 2022 (proposed s 159GZZZQ(3A)).

Example U Co is an unlisted company that undertakes an off-market purchase and buys back one of Jack's shares for $20. The company uses $5 from its share capital account to fund the buy-back of the share. The remaining $15 comes from its accumulated profits. At the time of the buy-back, the market value of the share is $21.

Jack is deemed to have received a dividend in respect of the buy-back calculated as follows:

$$\begin{aligned} \text{Dividend} &= \text{Purchase price} - \text{Amount debited to share capital account} \\ \$15 &= \$20 - \$5 \end{aligned}$$

The dividend is a frankable distribution and U Co can therefore allocate franking credits to it [22.7]. The dividend is taxed under the general dividend taxation rules [22.5] and, to the extent that the dividend is franked, it is subject to the franking rules [22.8].

Jack is also deemed to have disposed of his share for the following consideration:

$$\begin{aligned} \text{Consideration} &= \text{Purchase price} + \text{Market value uplift} - \text{Reduction amount} \\ \$6 &= \$20 + 1 - \$15 \end{aligned}$$

If Jack purchased the share six months ago for $17 and it was not trading stock, he would make a capital loss of $11 (ie $17 – $6).

If, on the other hand, the company was a listed public company, no part of the purchase price would be a dividend. As a result, Jack would be deemed to have disposed of his share for $21. He would therefore make a capital gain of $4 (ie $21 – $17).

Franking implications of share buy-backs

On-market purchases

Although an on-market purchase does not give rise to a dividend, the company is required to debit its franking account on the day of the purchase by an amount equal to the debit that would have arisen if:

(a) the purchase of the share were a frankable distribution equal to the one that would have arisen if the company:

   (i) purchased the share off-market, and

   (ii) in the case of a public listed company, were not a listed public company, and

(b) the distribution were franked at the entity's benchmark franking percentage for the franking period in which the purchase was made or, if the entity does not have a benchmark franking percentage for the period, at a franking percentage of 100% (s 205-30 (item 9 of the table)).

Off-market purchases

In the case of an off-market purchase, the dividend component of the purchase price is a frankable distribution (except to the extent that the purchase price exceeds the share's market value) (ss 202-40, 202-45). A company undertaking an off-market purchase must therefore determine the extent to which it franks the distribution and, in doing so, should consider the operation of the benchmark rule [22.7].

Although an off-market purchase undertaken by a listed public company does not give rise to a dividend, listed public companies that undertake such buy-backs after 7.30pm on 25 October 2022 are required to debit their franking account on the day of the purchase by an amount equal to the debit that would have arisen if:

(a) the purchase of the share were a frankable distribution equal to the one that would have arisen if the entity were not a listed public company, and

(b) the distribution were franked at the entity's benchmark franking percentage for the franking period in which the purchase was made or, if the entity does not have a benchmark franking percentage for the period, at a franking percentage of 100% (proposed s 205-30 (item 9A of the table)).

[22.11] Liquidator distributions

When a company is placed into liquidation, a liquidator is appointed to wind up its affairs. The winding up may be 'voluntary' or 'compulsory'. A voluntary winding up is initiated by a special resolution of the company and is either a 'members' voluntary winding up' (where the company is solvent) or a 'creditors' voluntary winding up' (where the company is insolvent). In a members' voluntary winding up, the liquidator is appointed by the members; whereas in a creditors' voluntary winding up the liquidator is appointed by the creditors. A compulsory winding up involves court proceedings instituted by creditors of an insolvent company. In a compulsory winding up, the liquidator is appointed by the court.

Liquidators of a company have several duties, including collecting the company's assets, paying its debts, and distributing any surplus to its shareholders. As the Supreme Court of NSW noted in *Re Partridge; Ex parte McDonald* [1961] SR (NSW) 622 (at 629):

> The liquidator's principal duties, speaking generally, are to take possession of and protect the assets, to make lists of contributories and creditors, to have disputed cases adjudicated upon, to realise the assets and to apply the proceeds in due course of administration amongst the creditors and contributories.

The debts of a company are required to be discharged in a particular order. Secured creditors (eg entities that have a mortgage over the company's real property) have priority to those assets. Liquidators can then use the remaining assets to pay for the costs of liquidation (including their approved fees). If there are residual funds available, these are applied first to pay priority unsecured creditors (eg employees) and then other unsecured creditors (eg contractors and suppliers). Any surplus is then available to be distributed among the shareholders.

The liquidation of a company raises a number of tax consequences for its shareholders. This includes the CGT and dividend issues outlined below.

CGT event C2

On the liquidation of a company, the shareholders' shares in the company are cancelled. This results in the happening of CGT event C2 under s 104-25 *ITAA97* [17.10]. Consequently, where a shareholder acquired shares after 19 September 1985:

- if the amount returned by a liquidator exceeds the cost base of the shares, the shareholder will make a capital gain, and
- if the amount returned by the liquidator is less than the reduced cost base of the shares, the shareholder will make a capital loss (s 104-25(3)).

Where the shareholder acquired shares before 20 September 1985, any capital gain or loss made as a result of the cancellation of the shares is disregarded (s 104-25(5)(a)).

Section 47 deemed dividends

The distribution of a company's profits to its shareholders represents a 'detachment', 'release' or 'liberation' of the profits of the company to them. Under the common law, such a distribution is of an income nature (*Hill v Permanent Trustee Co of New South Wales Ltd* [1930] AC 720). The position is quite different where a company goes into liquidation and its assets are distributed to its shareholders by a liquidator. In such a case, the amount distributed represents capital in the hands of shareholders. As Hill J noted in *FC of T v Brewing Investments Ltd* 2000 ATC 4431 (at 4437):

> In such a case shareholders are returned the ultimate capital value of the intangible property constituted by their shares which no longer exist. Profits are not detached, released or liberated leaving the share intact.

High Court authority for this principle is found in *C of T (NSW) v Stevenson* (1937) 59 CLR 80, where a majority of the Court rejected the Commissioner's argument that, on the winding up of a company, a shareholder should be assessed on a distribution to the extent that it represented undistributed profits of the company. Rich, Dixon and McTiernan JJ drew a distinction (at 103) between 'distributions or detachments of profit by a company as a going concern' and 'distributions in retirement or extinguishment of shares'. Their Honours relied (at 99) on the United Kingdom decision in *IRC v Burrell* [1924] 2 KB 52 for the principle that in a winding up:

> The shareholder simply receives his proper proportion of a total net fund without distinction in respect of the source of its components and he receives it in replacement of his shares.

To ensure that the profits of a company do not escape tax simply because they are distributed in the course of its winding up (rather than while it is a going concern), s 47(1) *ITAA36* was enacted. This provision states that distributions to shareholders of a company by a liquidator in the course of winding up the company, to the extent to which those distributions represent 'income derived by the company' (whether before or during liquidation) other than 'income which has been properly applied to replace a loss of paid-up capital', are 'deemed to be dividends paid to the shareholders by the company out of profits derived by it'.

The object of s 47(1) is to overcome the common law rule established in *Burrell* and *Stevenson* that would otherwise treat distributions by liquidators as capital amounts. It is important to understand, however, that s 47(1) is merely a deeming provision and is not an assessment provision in its own right. The provision, nevertheless, ties in with s 44(1), which generally includes such dividends in a shareholder's assessable income.

Income derived by a company

For the purposes of s 47(1), the term 'income derived by a company' is defined in s 47(1A). The term encompasses any amount included in the company's assessable income (ie both ordinary and statutory income). Net capital gains must, however, be worked out without taking into account any indexation or capital losses.

Example Company X owned three assets: Asset A, Asset B and Asset C. Each asset had a cost base of $1,000 and an indexed cost base of $1,300. Prior to liquidation, Company X disposed of asset A for $900, asset B for $1,200 and asset C for $1,500.

The income derived by Company X is calculated under s 47(1A) by ignoring the $100 loss in respect of Asset A and ignoring indexation. Company X therefore has income under s 47(1A) of $700 (consisting of a $200 gain on Asset B and a $500 gain on Asset C).

To the extent that this $700 amount is distributed by the liquidator to Company X's shareholders and is not applied to replace any loss of Company X's paid-up capital, it will be treated as a dividend.

Application by liquidator

It is up to the liquidator to determine how a company's income is to be applied. This principle is illustrated in *Archer Brothers Pty Ltd v FC of T* (1953) 90 CLR 140. The case concerned 'undistributed profits tax', which used to apply where a private company did not make a sufficient distribution of its profits by way of dividends to its shareholders within a certain period after the end of an income year. The liquidator in *Archer Brothers* had distributed a company's income to its shareholders and treated these amounts as replacements of paid-up capital. The Commissioner assessed the company to undistributed profits tax on the basis that it had not made a sufficient distribution of its profits by way of dividends. The High Court upheld the Commissioner's assessment. In doing so, the Court indicated that it would have been possible for the liquidator to satisfy the sufficient distribution rules if it had not treated the distributions as a replacement of paid-up capital, but rather treated them as dividends. The Court stated (at 155):

> By a proper system of book-keeping the liquidator, in the same way as the accountant of a private company which is a going concern, could so keep his accounts that these distributions could be made wholly and exclusively out of those particular profits or income . . .

This passage from *Archer Brothers* was examined in *Glenville Pastoral Co Pty Ltd (in liq) v FC of T* (1963) 109 CLR 199. In that case, a liquidator had distributed £241,669 of a private company's income to its shareholders as a dividend. The Commissioner formed the view that since the company had a loss of paid-up capital of £159,271, only £82,398 of the distribution should be treated as a dividend and that, as a result, the company had not made a sufficient distribution of its profits and was liable to undistributed profits tax. The High Court, however, rejected this argument, and held that the entire £241,669 amount was a dividend. The Court explained that *Archer Brothers* does not stand for the proposition that a liquidator may capitalise profits, as this can only be done by the company while it is a going concern. *Archer Brothers* merely indicates that a liquidator may select one income source rather than another for the payment of a particular distribution.

In TD 95/10, the ATO considers that the principle to be derived from *Archer Bros* is that 'if a liquidator appropriates (or 'sources') a particular fund of profit or income in making a distribution (or part of a distribution), that appropriation ordinarily determines the character of the distributed amount'.

Territorial limitations

The scope of s 47(1) and whether it operates subject to any territorial limitations was tested in *FC of T v Brewing Investments Ltd* 2000 ATC 4431. The taxpayer was an Australian resident company that beneficially owned all the shares in 'Rowsom' (which, in turn, owned all the shares in 'Clarkson' which, in turn, owned all the shares in 'EIL'). Rowsom, Clarkson and EIL were all non-resident companies that did not derive any Australian source income. Over a period of years, the companies were progressively placed into liquidation and the taxpayer ended up receiving money from Rowsom's liquidator, including an amount in excess of US$27m, which related to Clarkson's and EIL's income reserves that had been paid to Rowsom as a result of their respective liquidations. The Commissioner assessed the taxpayer on this sum pursuant to s 44(1)(a) on the basis that it was a dividend under s 47(1). The taxpayer contended that it should not be assessed as the distributions made by Clarkson's and EIL's liquidators did not constitute income of Rowsom under s 47(1) since Rowsom was a non-resident and the distributions had a foreign source. The Full Federal Court rejected this argument and relied on *Parke Davis & Co v FC of T* (1959) 101 CLR 521 [22.5] for the principle that s 47(1) operates independently of considerations of 'locality'. Hill J explained that s 47(1) has 'no territorial limitation at all' and that the only territorial limitation is found in s 44(1). His Honour stated (at 4445):

> While it is true that s 47(1) cannot operate by itself to make a distribution assessable income, it can operate 'for the purposes of the Act' on its own . . . So, when Clarkson was liquidated, the resultant distribution was treated for the purposes of the Act as a dividend paid out of profits and thus income. Thus when Rowsom was liquidated the resultant distribution was, by the application of s 47(1) to the Clarkson distribution, to be treated as income and in the result there was deemed to be a distribution to [the taxpayer], being a dividend paid out of profits to which the terms of s 44(1) then fell to be applied.

Preventing double taxation

To prevent CGT event C2 and s 47(1) resulting in liquidator distributions being double taxed, s 118-20 *ITAA97* [17.5] reduces the amount of the capital gain arising to the shareholder.

Example A resident individual shareholder acquired a share in Company Y for $10. Shortly thereafter, Company Y was placed into liquidation. The liquidator distributed $18 to the shareholder (which included a deemed dividend of $15 under s 47(1)).

Ordinarily, the shareholder would realise a capital gain of $8 ($18 – $10) under s 104-25 and would be assessed on the $15 deemed dividend under s 44(1). However, s 118-20 reduces the capital gain to nil so that the shareholder is only assessed on $15 [17.5].

[22.12] Franking credit trading schemes

Since franking credits are more beneficial to some taxpayers than others, schemes may be entered into to divert franking credits from the true economic owners of shares to other entities that benefit most from them. This might occur, for example, as a result of franking credit trading schemes under which entities that are not entitled to benefit from franking credits (eg foreign residents) transfer their shares to entities that are entitled to benefit from franking credits (eg resident individuals, complying superannuation funds and certain tax-exempt entities). This is often done for only a short period of time (typically just before a franked dividend is about to be paid). The Government takes the view that it is inappropriate for persons who are not exposed, or who only have a minimal exposure, to the risks of loss and opportunities for gain arising from the ownership of shares, to benefit from franking credits arising in respect of dividends paid in relation to those shares. Special rules to combat franking credit trading schemes were therefore introduced in 1999. These rules were contained in former div 1A of pt IIIAA *ITAA36* (ss 160APHC to 160APHU). Although the provisions were technically repealed in 2006, they remain relevant as s 207-145(1)(a) *ITAA97* continues to refer to the former rules [22.8].

Qualified person

Section 207-145(1)(a) provides that the gross-up and credit mechanism relating to franked dividends in div 207 *ITAA97* [22.8] only applies if the entity that holds shares, or an interest in shares, in respect of which a dividend is paid is a 'qualified person' within the meaning of former div 1A of pt IIIAA *ITAA36*. To be a qualified person, an entity must satisfy a 'related payments rule' and a 'holding period rule'.

Related payments rule

To satisfy the related payments rule, the entity (or an associate of the entity) must not make, or be under an obligation to make, a 'related payment' in respect of the dividend. A related payment is essentially a payment that effectively passes the benefit of the dividend to another person (former s 160APHN).

Holding period rule

To satisfy the holding period rule, the entity must hold the shares, or interests in the shares, in respect of which the franked dividends have been paid for a minimum period of 45 days (90 days for preference shares) (former s 160APHO(2)).

The holding period does not include:

- the day that the shareholder acquired the shares or interests in the shares
- the day the shareholder disposed of the shares or interests in the shares, or
- any day on which the entity has 'materially diminished risks' of loss and opportunities for gain in relation to the shares or interests in the shares.

In broad terms, an entity will have materially diminished risks if the 'net position' of the entity results in it having less than 30% of the risks and opportunities relating to the shares, or interests in the shares.

The holding period rule generally operates on a 'last-in, first-out' basis, which means that entities will be deemed to have disposed of their most recently acquired shares first (former s 160APHI).

Example Sandy acquired shares in T Co on 1 April 2023. On 3 May 2023, she was paid a dividend of $21,000 (which had $9,000 of franking credits allocated to it). On 9 May 2023, Sandy sold her shares.

Sandy fails the holding period rule as she did not hold the shares for at least 45 days. As a consequence, she does not include the $9,000 franking credit in her assessable income under s 207-20(1) and is not entitled to a tax offset of $9,000 for the franking credit under s 207-20(2).

In order to be entitled to the franking gross-up and credit, Sandy would have had to hold on to her shares until 17 May 2023 as this would be a total of 45 days (excluding the acquisition and disposal days).

Special rule for small shareholders

An entity that does not satisfy the holding period rule will, nevertheless, still be treated as a qualified person if the entity is an individual with imputation credit entitlements for the income year that do not exceed $5,000 (former s 160APHT). This exception is designed to exempt 'small shareholders' from the rigours of the holding period rule.

Example In the previous example, Sandy would not qualify for the 'small shareholder' exemption since her franking credit entitlements exceed $5,000. However, if the dividend only had $4,500 in franking credits allocated to it and this was the only dividend Sandy received during the income year, she would be entitled to the franking gross-up and credit as she would qualify for the small shareholder exemption since her imputation credit entitlements would not exceed $5,000 for the year.

Special rule for eligible taxpayers

The rigours of the holding period rule also do not apply to an 'eligible taxpayer' that has elected to adopt a formula-based imputation credit ceiling amount to calculate their franking credit entitlements (former s 160APHR). This exception is designed to allow institutional investors (eg trustees of widely held trusts or complying superannuation funds) who regularly turn over shares a more practical method for determining their franking credit entitlements.

Special rule for beneficiaries of family trusts

Ordinarily, beneficiaries of discretionary trusts would not be able to satisfy the holding period rule, as they do not technically have an interest in the shares owned by the trustee (*Gartside v IRC* [1968] AC 553). There is, however, a special rule which treats beneficiaries of 'family trusts' (ie trusts that have made a 'family trust election' [24.9]) to be holding the relevant shares (former s 160APHL).

[22.13] Imputation benefit membership interest disposition schemes

The general anti-avoidance provisions in pt IVA *ITAA36* were amended in 1998 to include s 177EA [37.2]. The Explanatory Memorandum accompanying the Bill that introduced this provision states that it is a general measure designed to 'prevent abuse of the imputation system through schemes which circumvent the basic rules for the franking of dividends'. Like former div 1A of pt IIIAA *ITAA36* [22.12], s 177EA is also directed at franking credit trading schemes. However, it tackles these schemes in a different manner.

Section 177EA applies to a 'scheme' for the disposition of membership interests or interests in membership interests. The section operates where a franked distribution is paid, payable or flows indirectly to a person (the 'relevant taxpayer') in respect of such interests and where, having regard to the 'relevant circumstances' of the scheme, it would be concluded that a person who entered into the scheme did so for a purpose (other than an incidental purpose) of obtaining an 'imputation benefit' for the relevant taxpayer.

Imputation benefit

An 'imputation benefit' arises if, as a result of the distribution, a person is entitled to a tax offset under div 207 *ITAA97* [22.8] or a credit would arise in a company's franking account [22.7] (s 177EA(16)).

Relevant circumstances

The 'relevant circumstances' of a scheme can include a wide range of matters, such as the duration that the membership interests are held, whether the relevant taxpayer would derive a greater benefit from franking credits than other entities that hold membership interests, and any of the matters referred to in s 177D(2) [37.6] (s 177EA(17)).

Determinations

Where the requirements of s 177EA are satisfied, the Commissioner may make:

- a determination to debit the company's franking account by a particular amount (if it is a party to the scheme) (s 177EA(5)(a)), or
- a determination that no imputation benefit arises in respect of the distribution or part of the distribution to the relevant taxpayer (s 177EA(5)(b)).

Where the Commissioner makes a determination under s 177EA(5), the gross-up and credit mechanism under div 207 does not apply to the relevant shareholder (s 207-145(1)(b)).

[22.14] Imputation benefit streaming schemes

Subdivision 204-D *ITAA97* was introduced to discourage corporate tax entities from streaming 'imputation benefits' to those members that are most able to benefit from them. It applies if an entity 'streams' one or more distributions in such a way that:

- an 'imputation benefit' is, or would be, received by a member of the entity as a result of the distributions
- the member ('favoured member') would derive a greater benefit from franking credits than another member of the entity ('disadvantaged member'), and
- the other member of the entity will receive lesser imputation benefits, or will not receive any imputation benefits, whether or not the other member receives other benefits (s 204-30(1)).

Imputation benefit

A member of an entity receives an 'imputation benefit' as a result of a distribution if:

- the member is entitled to a tax offset under div 207 [22.8]
- an amount would be included in the member's assessable income under s 207-35 [22.8]
- a franking credit would arise in the member's franking account [22.7]

- an 'exempting credit' would arise in the member's 'exempting account' [22.18]
- the member would not be liable to pay withholding tax on the distribution because of s 128B(3)(ga) (ie because the distribution is franked) [22.5], or
- the member is entitled to a tax offset under s 210-170 (ie because the distribution is franked with a 'venture capital credit') [27.3] (s 204-30(6)).

Determinations

Where the requirements of sub-div 204-D are satisfied, the Commissioner may make:

- a determination that a specified franking debit arises in the streaming entity's franking account
- a determination that a specified 'exempting debit' arises in the streaming entity's 'exempting account' [22.18], and/or
- a determination that no imputation benefits arise to the favoured member (s 204-30(3)).

Where the Commissioner makes a determination that no imputation benefit arises to the favoured member, the member cannot benefit from the gross-up and credit mechanism under div 207 *ITAA97* [22.8] (s 207-145(1)(c)).

[22.15] Distribution substitution schemes

Corporate tax entities may stream amounts to their members by entering into certain kinds of 'substitution schemes'. Subdivision 204-B *ITAA97* is designed to combat schemes involving 'linked distributions' and sub-div 204-C *ITAA97* is designed to combat schemes involving 'tax-exempt bonus shares'. Both these subdivisions result in penalty franking debits arising in a company's franking account.

Linked distributions

Subdivision 204-B is designed to prevent exploitation of the 'benchmark rule' [22.7] by schemes involving the substitution of a distribution by one corporate tax entity for a distribution by another corporate tax entity (eg through a 'stapled stock' arrangement).

The subdivision applies where a member of a corporate tax entity (the 'first entity') exercises, or fails to exercise, a choice or selection that has the effect of substituting a distribution by the first entity for a distribution by another corporate tax entity (the 'linked distribution') that is franked at a franking percentage that differs from the 'benchmark franking percentage' of the first entity (s 204-15(1)).

In these circumstances, a franking debit arises on the day the linked distribution is made in the franking account of the entity with the higher benchmark franking percentage for the franking period in which the linked distribution is made (ss 204-15(2), (4)). The debit is equal to the debit that would have arisen in that account if the entity had made a franked distribution equal to the linked distribution, with a franking percentage equal to the benchmark franking percentage for that entity (ss 204-15(3), (4)). If the entity has no benchmark franking percentage for the franking period, the entity's benchmark franking percentage is taken to be 100% (if the linked distribution has a franking percentage of less than 50%) or 0% (if the linked distribution has a franking percentage equal to or greater than 50%) (s 204-15(6)). The debit is in addition to any other debit that arises as a consequence of the linked distribution (s 204-15(5)).

Tax-exempt bonus shares

Subdivision 204-C is designed to prevent exploitation of the corporate tax rules by schemes involving the substitution of 'tax-exempt bonus shares' for franked distributions. A tax-exempt bonus share covers a bonus share issued in the circumstances mentioned in s 6BA(6) [22.2] (s 204-25(4)).

The subdivision applies where a member of a corporate tax entity exercises, or fails to exercise, a choice or selection that has the effect of determining that the entity issues tax-exempt bonus shares to the member or another member in substitution for one or more franked distributions by the entity to the member or another member (s 204-25(1)).

In these circumstances, a franking debit arises in the corporate tax entity's franking account on the day the bonus shares are issued (s 204-25(3)). The debit equals the debit that would have arisen in the entity's franking account if it had made a distribution equal to the franked distributions at its benchmark franking percentage for the franking period in which the shares were issued (or at 100% if it has no benchmark franking percentage for the franking period) (ss 204-25(2), (6)).

[22.16] Dividend stripping schemes

The tax legislation contains anti-avoidance provisions in s 207-145(1)(d) *ITAA97* and s 177E *ITAA36* to deal with 'dividend stripping' arrangements.

Dividend stripping

The term 'dividend stripping' is not defined in the legislation. In *FC of T v Consolidated Press Holdings Ltd & Anor* 2001 ATC 4343, the High Court stated (at 4361):

> 'Dividend stripping' is not a legal term of art having a literal meaning which can be clearly defined apart from its context. It is not defined in Part IVA, presumably because the legislature considered its meaning to be sufficiently clear in the context of schemes to reduce income tax.

Over the years, many cases have examined the concept of dividend stripping in the context of various anti-avoidance provisions (eg *Slutzkin & Ors v FC of T* 77 ATC 4076; *FC of T v Patcorp Investments Limited* 76 ATC 4225; *FC of T v Eller's Motor Sales Pty Ltd* (1972) 128 CLR 602; *Investment & Merchant Finance Corporation Ltd v FC of T* 70 ATC 4001; *Hancock v FC of T* (1961) 108 CLR 258; *Newton v FC of T* (1958) 98 CLR 1; *Bell v FC of T* (1953) 87 CLR 548). The cases demonstrate that dividend stripping can take place in a number of different ways.

In essence, dividend stripping involves a scheme whereby a company with accumulated profits is acquired for the purpose of having its profits 'stripped out' in a tax-effective manner and then having its shares sold off at a loss. A typical dividend stripping scheme might involve an arrangement where a company (the 'stripper') acquires shares in a 'target company' that is 'pregnant' with profits and franking credits. The acquiring company might then 'strip' the profits out of the target company by arranging for it to pay a franked dividend upon which there would ordinarily be no tax payable by the acquiring company (because of the franking credits allocated to the dividends). The acquiring company would then be able to sell the shares in the target company at a loss after having stripped out the profits from the target company. This loss would be recognised under either the general income tax rules or the CGT rules (depending on the circumstances of the scheme).

Section 207-145(1)(d) *ITAA97*

Section 207-145(1)(d) provides that the franking gross-up and credit mechanism in div 207 *ITAA97* does not apply where a franked distribution is made as part of a 'dividend stripping operation'. According to s 207-155, a distribution is taken to be made as part of a dividend stripping operation only if it arose out of, or was made in the course of, a scheme that was 'by way of, or in the nature of, dividend stripping' or that had 'substantially the effect' of such a scheme.

The effect of s 207-145(1)(d) applying to schemes like those mentioned in the illustration above is that it results in the acquiring company being denied access to franking credits. As a consequence, the acquiring company would therefore have to pay tax on the stripped profits.

Section 177E *ITAA36*

Section 177E is a separate anti-avoidance provision dealing with dividend stripping contained in pt IVA *ITAA36* [37.3]. It applies where the following conditions are met:

- as a result of a dividend stripping scheme, or a scheme having substantially the effect of a scheme by way of or in the nature of dividend stripping, any property of the company is disposed of
- the Commissioner is of the opinion that the disposal of the property represents, wholly or in part, a distribution (whether to a shareholder or another person) of profits (whether of the current, a past or a future accounting period) of the company, and
- if, immediately before the scheme was entered into, the company had paid a dividend out of profits of an amount equal to the amount determined by the Commissioner to be the amount of profits represented by the disposal of the property, an amount (the 'notional amount') would have been included, or might reasonably be expected to have been included, by reason of the payment of that dividend, in the assessable income of a taxpayer of a year of income.

Where the above conditions are satisfied, the scheme is taken to be a scheme to which pt IVA applies and the taxpayer is taken to have obtained a 'tax benefit' in connection with the scheme that is referable to the notional amount not included in the taxpayer's assessable income.

Under s 177F, the Commissioner may consequently make a determination to cancel, in whole or part, the tax benefit (being the notional amount) and make any compensating adjustments deemed necessary [37.3].

In *FC of T v Consolidated Press Holdings Ltd & Anor*, it was held that s 177E only applies to schemes that have the sole or dominant purpose of tax avoidance. The High Court held that the provision did not apply to the complex corporate reorganisation entered into by the group of companies in that case as the scheme had been entered into to overcome double taxation issues arising from proposed amendments to the United Kingdom tax law that affected non-resident companies rather than for the dominant purpose of dividend stripping.

It should be noted that s 177E applies not only to a 'dividend striping scheme', but also to a scheme that has 'substantially the effect of a scheme by way of or in the nature of dividend stripping'. The nature of such a scheme was considered in *Lawrence v FC of T* 2009 ATC ¶20-096.

[22.17] Distribution washing schemes

Distribution washing schemes involve taxpayers obtaining the benefit of multiple franking credits in respect of what is essentially a single economic interest. This could be achieved, for example, by a taxpayer selling an interest in shares after an entitlement to a franked distribution has accrued (ie 'ex-dividend') and then immediately purchasing an identical interest in shares with an entitlement to a corresponding franked distribution (ie 'cum dividend'). Distribution washing enables taxpayers to obtain two sets of dividends even though they have only ever substantially held one parcel of shares. This provides taxpayers with a disproportionate amount of franking credits, which is beyond the intent of the imputation system.

To tackle distribution washing schemes, s 207-145(1)(da) provides that where s 207-157 applies to a distribution, the taxpayer is not entitled to benefit from the franking gross-up and credit mechanism in div 207 on the distribution.

Section 207-157 applies to a franked distribution in respect of a membership interest (the 'washed interest') where:

- the washed interest was acquired after the member or a connected entity of the member, disposed of a 'substantially identical membership interest' (defined in s 207-157(3)), and

- a corresponding franked distribution is made to the member or the connected entity in respect of the substantially identical interest (s 207-157(1)(a)).

Where a connected entity disposed of the substantially identical interest, s 207-157 only applies if either the disposal or the acquisition took place only because at least one of the entities expected or believed that the other transaction would occur (s 207-157(2)).

As with the 45-day holding period rule [22.12], s 207-157 does not apply to individuals with franking credit tax offsets that do not exceed $5,000 during an income year (s 207-157(4)).

[22.18] Exempting entity schemes

Since non-resident and tax-exempt entities do not generally obtain tax offsets for franking credits [22.8], it is more likely that franking credit trading schemes would take place in relation to corporate tax entities that are controlled by such persons. To discourage such schemes, div 208 *ITAA97* prevents franking credits being passed on by these entities to those persons that could otherwise benefit from them (eg taxable residents). The division applies to distributions made by 'exempting entities' and 'former exempting entities'.

Exempting entity

A corporate tax entity is an 'exempting entity' if it is 'effectively owned' by 'prescribed persons' (this is the case if not less than 95% of the accountable membership interests in the entity are held directly or indirectly by non-resident and tax-exempt persons) (ss 208-20 to 208-45). The gross-up and credit mechanism in div 207 *ITAA97* does not apply to franked distributions made by exempting entities, unless one of the exceptions in sub-div 208-G applies (eg the recipient is another exempting entity or an employee under an eligible ESS) (s 208-195).

Former exempting entity

A corporate tax entity is a 'former exempting entity' if it ceases to be effectively owned by prescribed persons (s 208-50). To ensure that its franking credits are quarantined, a former exempting entity must transfer any surplus or deficit in its franking account to an 'exempting account' which it is required to maintain under sub-div 208-F. It must also establish a new franking account. The gross-up and credit mechanism under div 207 does not apply to distributions franked with 'exempting credits', unless one of the exceptions in sub-div 208-H applies (eg the recipient is another exempting entity, an employee under an eligible ESS, or an 'eligible continuing substantial member' as defined in s 208-155) (s 208-225).

[22.19] Bonus shares and unfranked dividend streaming schemes

Section 45 *ITAA36* applies where a company streams the provision of shares (other than shares to which s 6BA(5) applies [17.14]) and the payment of 'minimally franked dividends' to its shareholders in such a way that:

- the shares are received by some shareholders but not all shareholders, and
- some or all of the shareholders who do not receive the shares receive minimally franked dividends.

A dividend is 'minimally franked' if it is not franked or is franked to less than 10% (s 45(3)).

Where s 45 applies, the value of the share is deemed to be an unfranked dividend paid out of profits of the company to the shareholder (s 45(2)).

[22.20] Capital benefit streaming schemes

As capital returns are generally taxed more favourably than dividends, schemes may be entered into whereby companies channel capital to particular shareholders who stand to derive the most benefit from such payments. For instance, capital payments might be streamed to:

- shareholders who acquired their shares before 20 September 1985 and therefore disregard any capital gains made on their shares
- shareholders who acquired their shares more than a year ago and are therefore eligible for the 50% CGT discount on any gains made on their shares
- shareholders who have capital losses and are therefore able to offset those losses against any capital gains made on their shares, or
- shareholders who are non-residents and are therefore generally not subject to CGT on gains made on shares as they do not usually constitute 'taxable Australian property' [17.12].

To address various kinds of capital benefit and related schemes, the Commissioner may make determinations under s 45A or s 45B *ITAA36* to treat the amount of the capital benefit as an unfranked dividend (s 45C). The circumstances in which ss 45A and 45B apply are outlined below.

Capital benefit and dividend streaming schemes

Section 45A applies where a company 'streams' the provision of capital benefits and the payment of dividends to its shareholders in such a way that:

- capital benefits are received by shareholders who would derive a 'greater benefit' from the capital benefits than other shareholders (the 'disadvantaged shareholders'), and
- it is reasonable to assume that the other shareholders received or will receive dividends.

Section 45A does not apply where s 45 applies [22.19] (s 45A(1)) or where it is reasonable to assume that the disadvantaged shareholders will receive, or have received, fully franked dividends (s 45A(5)).

There is a 'provision of a capital benefit' to a shareholder if there is a provision of shares in the company to the shareholder, there is a distribution of share capital or share premium to the shareholder, or something is done in relation to the shareholder's shares that has the effect of increasing their value (s 45A(3)).

The circumstances in which a shareholder would derive a 'greater benefit' from capital benefits than another shareholder include the situations specified in s 45A(4) (eg where the shareholder acquired their shares before 20 September 1985 or is a non-resident).

Demerger benefit and capital benefit schemes

Section 45B applies where:

- there is a scheme under which a person is provided with a 'demerger benefit' or a 'capital benefit'
- under the scheme, a taxpayer (the 'relevant taxpayer'), who may or may not be the person provided with the capital benefit, obtains a 'tax benefit', and
- having regard to the 'relevant circumstances' of the scheme, it would be concluded that a person who entered into the scheme did so for a purpose (other than an incidental purpose) of enabling the relevant taxpayer to obtain a 'tax benefit'.

A person is 'provided with a capital benefit' if the person is provided with ownership interests in the company, share capital or share premium is distributed to the person, or something is done in relation to the person's ownership interests that has the effect of increasing their value (s 45B(5)).

A person is 'provided with a demerger benefit' if, in relation to a 'demerger' [28.4], a company provides the person with ownership interests in that or another company, or something is done in relation to the person's ownership interests that has the effect of increasing their value (s 45B(4)).

A relevant taxpayer obtains a 'tax benefit' where the tax payable by the person would be less than the amount that would have been payable (or would have been payable at a later time than it would otherwise have been payable) if the demerger benefit or capital benefit had been an assessable dividend (s 45B(9)).

[22.21] Share capital tainting schemes

Division 197 *ITAA97* contains special 'share capital tainting rules' to discourage companies from entering into schemes designed to disguise their profits as share capital. These rules are complex but are necessary because s 254S *Corporations Act* permits companies to capitalise their profits. Without any special anti-avoidance rules, companies could simply transfer profits to their share capital accounts and then use the amounts standing to the credit of such accounts to make distributions to their shareholders which, under the general corporate tax rules, would be treated as capital payments rather than dividends and would therefore be taxed more concessionally.

Application

Division 197 generally applies where an amount is transferred to a company's share capital account from another account (ie where the company's share capital account is 'tainted') (s 197-5). The division, however, operates subject to a number of exclusions. For example, it does not apply where the transferred amount could at all times before the transfer be identified in the books of the company as share capital (s 197-10). Likewise, it does not apply where the transferred amount is transferred under certain 'debt/equity swap' (s 197-15), 'option premium reserve' (s 197-25) and 'demutualisation' (ss 197-30 to 197-40) arrangements.

Consequences of share capital tainting

There are two consequences that arise where div 197 applies. The first consequence of div 197 applying is that a franking debit is deemed to arise in the company's franking account under s 197-45. This will result in the company wasting its franking credits and not being able to pass them on to its shareholders. The franking debit arises immediately before the end of the franking period in which the transfer occurs and is calculated as follows:

$$\text{Transferred amount} \times \frac{\text{Applicable franking percentage}}{\text{Applicable tax gross-up rate}}$$

The 'applicable franking percentage' is the company's 'benchmark franking percentage' for the franking period in which the transfer occurred, or 100% if it does not have a benchmark franking percentage for the franking period [22.7].

The 'applicable gross-up rate' is the company's 'corporate tax gross-up rate' for the income year in which the franking debit arises [22.7].

The second consequence of div 197 applying is that the account to which the amount has been transferred is deemed not to be a share capital account (s 975-300(3)(b) *ITAA97*). Distributions debited to the account are therefore treated as dividends (rather than capital returns). They are also deemed to be unfrankable (s 202-45 *ITAA97*).

Example Taint Co is a company that has a corporate tax gross-up rate of 30% in the 2023/24 income year. During that year, it transferred \$70,000 to its share capital account from another account, and none of the exclusions in div 197 applied to the transfer. For the franking period in which the transfer occurred, Taint Co's 'benchmark franking percentage' was 80%. As a consequence of the transfer, Taint Co is required to debit its franking account by \$24,000 (ie \$70,000 × 80%/2.333333). In addition, Taint Co's share capital account is no longer treated as a share capital account and any amounts debited to it will be treated as unfranked dividends rather than returns of capital.

Untainting the share capital account

A company's share capital account remains tainted until the company chooses to 'untaint' it (s 197-50(2)). A company can untaint its share capital account by making an irrevocable choice in the approved form given to the Commissioner (s 197-55).

There are two consequences that arise where a company untaints its share capital account. The first consequence is that a franking debit arises under s 197-65 if the applicable franking percentage for the franking period in which the choice to untaint occurs is higher than the applicable franking percentage for the franking period in which the share capital account was tainted. The debit is the amount by which the amount calculated under the following formula in s 197-65 exceeds the amount calculated under the formula in s 197-45 mentioned above:

$$\text{Transferred amount} \times \frac{\text{Applicable franking percentage}}{\text{Applicable tax gross-up rate}}$$

The 'applicable franking percentage' is the company's 'benchmark franking percentage' for the franking period in which the choice to untaint is made, or 100% if it does not have a benchmark franking percentage for the franking period [22.7].

The 'applicable gross-up rate' is the company's 'corporate tax gross-up rate' for the income year in which the franking debit arises [22.7].

Example Assume that Taint Co in the preceding example subsequently decided to untaint its share capital account. At the time of making the choice to untaint the account, its benchmark franking percentage was 90%. The amount calculated under the formula in s 197-65 is \$27,000 (ie \$70,000 × 90%/2.333333). As \$27,000 exceeds \$24,000 (being the amount calculated under the formula in s 197-45), Taint Co must debit its franking account by \$3,000.

The second consequence of a company untainting its share capital account is that the company may be liable to pay 'untainting tax' (s 190-60). Untainting tax is imposed under s 3 *New Business Tax System (Untainting Tax) Act 2006* (Cth) and is due and payable 21 days after the end of the franking period in which the choice to untaint is made (s 197-70). Untainting tax is calculated under the following formula in s 197-60(2):

$$\begin{matrix}\text{Applicable}\\ \text{tax amount}\end{matrix} - \left[\begin{matrix}\text{Section 197-45}\\ \text{franking debits}\end{matrix} + \begin{matrix}\text{Section 197-65}\\ \text{franking debits}\end{matrix}\right]$$

The 'applicable tax amount' is calculated according to the formula in s 197-60(3):

$$\left[\begin{array}{c}\text{Tainting amount}\\\text{at time of choice to untaint}\end{array} + \begin{array}{c}\text{Notional}\\\text{franking amount}\end{array}\right] \times \text{Applicable tax rate}$$

The 'tainting amount' is the sum of the transferred amount that most recently caused the account to be tainted and any other amounts to which div 197 applies that have been transferred to the account since it became tainted (s 197-50(3)).

The 'notional franking amount' is worked out under s 197-60(4) as follows:

$$\begin{array}{c}\text{Tainting amount at time}\\\text{of choice to untaint}\end{array} \times \frac{1}{\text{Applicable gross-up rate}}$$

The 'applicable tax rate' is:

- for a 'company with only lower tax members in relation to the tainting period' (ie a company that is wholly owned by other companies, complying superannuation entities or foreign residents)—the company's corporate tax rate for imputation purposes for the income year in which the choice is made, or
- for a 'company with higher tax members in relation to the tainting period' (ie a company that is *not* a company with only lower tax members)—the rate of 48%.

The 'section 197-45 franking debits' is the total franking debits arising under s 197-45 (see above). The 'section 197-65 franking debits' is the total franking debits arising under s 197-65 (see above).

[22.22] Corporate loss restrictions

To prevent the tax loss rules in div 36 *ITAA97* [13.15] being exploited, special restrictions apply to a company's ability to carry forward its tax losses. The restrictions are designed to prevent taxpayers trafficking in loss companies and are found in sub-div 165-A *ITAA97*. They provide that a company cannot deduct a tax loss unless it satisfies:

- a 'continuity of ownership test' ('COT'), or
- a 'business continuity test' ('BCT') (s 165-10).

The following example illustrates why the restrictions are necessary.

Example L Co has a tax loss of $10m from a previous income year. Without any special restrictions, its shareholders could transfer their shares in the company to a third party who could then inject $10m of income into the company (eg by transferring an income-producing asset to the company). The income would then be sheltered by the deduction available to L Co for its tax loss. This would result in L Co paying no tax and the third party indirectly benefiting even though they held no interest in the company at the time the loss was actually made.

The COT and the BCT are also relevant to determine whether companies may carry forward bad debts (sub-div 165-C) [13.6] and net capital losses (sub-div 165-CA) [17.2].

The COT and BCT operate subject to special modification in div 415 *ITAA97* that allow 'designated infrastructure project entities' to effectively ignore the tests and uplift their tax losses by the long-term government bond rate to prevent their value eroding over time by inflation.

Continuity of ownership test

Primary and alternative tests under the COT

The COT requires a company to satisfy either a 'primary test' or an 'alternative test' for the 'ownership test period' (ie from the start of the loss year to the end of the income year) (s 165-12). The primary test is used unless one or more companies owned shares or interests in shares in the company at any time during the 'ownership test period', in which case the alternative test is used (this test traces ownership through interposed entities).

Broadly speaking, the tests are fulfilled if, at all times during the 'ownership test period', the same persons beneficially owned (either directly or indirectly) shares in the company with:

- rights to more than 50% of the voting power in the company
- rights to more than 50% of the company's dividends, and
- rights to more than 50% of the company's capital distributions.

Example

Primary test

In Year 1, Salt Co incurred a tax loss of $3m. Salt Co has 10 ordinary shares on issue which carry equal voting, dividend and capital distribution rights. Throughout Year 1, the shares in Salt Co were owned as follows:

- Andy (1 share)
- Brian (2 shares)
- Colin (3 shares), and
- David (4 shares).

In Year 2, Salt Co makes assessable income of $4m. During Year 2, Andy and Colin sell their shares to Eric. After the change in ownership, the shares in Salt Co are therefore owned as follows:

- Brian (2 shares)
- David (4 shares), and
- Eric (4 shares).

If there are no other shareholding changes, then the primary test is satisfied since Brian and David together beneficially owned a greater than 50% interest in the ownership rights in Salt Co throughout the ownership test period (ie from the beginning of Year 1 to the end of Year 2). As a result, Salt Co can utilise its tax loss from Year 1 to reduce its taxable income in Year 2 to $1m.

Note that if, at the same time that Andy and Colin sold their shares to Eric, Brian had also sold his shares to Eric, the primary test would not have been satisfied. In such a case, Salt Co would not be able to utilise the tax loss.

Alternative test

In Year 1, Pepper Co incurred a tax loss of $2m. Pepper Co has 10 ordinary shares on issue which carry equal voting, dividend and capital distribution rights. Throughout the year, the shares in Pepper Co were owned as follows:

- A Co (6 shares)—there are 10 ordinary shares on issue in A Co, which are owned by Alan (5 shares) and Angelina (5 shares), and
- B Co (4 shares)—there are 10 ordinary shares on issue in B Co, which are owned by Bill (8 shares) and Ben (2 shares).

In Year 2, Pepper Co has assessable income of $5m. In order to be able to deduct its tax loss from Year 1 against this amount, Pepper Co must pass the alternative test.

Assume that in Year 2:

- Alan sold one of his five shares in A Co to Arnie
- Angelina sold her five shares in A Co to Audrey
- Bill sold one of his eight shares in B Co to Brian, and
- Ben sold his two shares in B Co to Betty.

For Year 1, tracing the relevant ownership interests in Pepper Co through A Co and B Co:

- Alan had an indirect interest in Pepper Co of 30% (60% × 50%), and
- Bill had an indirect interest in Pepper Co of 32% (40% × 80%).

For Year 2, tracing the relevant ownership interests in Pepper Co through A Co and B Co:

- Alan had an indirect interest in Pepper Co of 24% (60% × 40%), and
- Bill had an indirect interest in Pepper Co of 28% (40% × 70%).
- Pepper Co has satisfied the alternative test since, throughout both Year 1 and Year 2, Alan and Bill together held a greater than 50% indirect interest in Pepper Co (ie 62% in Year 1 and 52% in Year 2).

In determining whether the primary or alternative tests have been satisfied, shares can only be taken into account if the *same persons* owned the *same shares* throughout the relevant period (s 165-165).

Anti-avoidance provisions under the COT

The COT operates subject to the following specific anti-avoidance provisions:

- s 165-180, which provides that the Commissioner may treat a person as not having beneficially owned particular shares at a particular time if an arrangement relating to the beneficial interest in the shares, or a right to them, was entered into for the purpose of eliminating or reducing an entity's income tax liability
- s 165-185, which provides that shares are taken not to have carried particular rights during a part of the ownership test period if the Commissioner is satisfied that the shares have stopped, or will or may stop, carrying those rights after the ownership test period because of the company's constitution as in force at some time during the ownership test period or an arrangement entered into before or during the ownership test period, and
- s 165-190, which provides that shares are taken to have carried particular rights at all times during a part of the ownership test period if the Commissioner is satisfied that the shares started, or will or may start, carrying those rights after the ownership test period because of the company's constitution as in force at some time during the ownership test period or an arrangement entered into before or during the ownership test period.

Example The original shareholders in a company that has a tax loss enter into an arrangement with third parties pursuant to which they agree to retain their shares in the company until it has recouped the tax loss (so as to ostensibly satisfy the COT) and then formally transfer their shares to the third parties. The Commissioner may seek to rely on s 165-180 to treat the original shareholders as not having beneficially owned the shares during the relevant period. As a result, the COT will not be satisfied and the company cannot utilise the tax loss.

Concessional tracing rule for shares held by certain entities

Companies must generally trace ownership through to their ultimate beneficial owners when applying the COT. However, a special rule in s 165-202 provides that shares that are beneficially owned by certain entities are taken to be beneficially owned by a person (who is not a company). These entities are: the Commonwealth; a state or a territory; a municipal corporation; a local governing body; a foreign government; a company in which no person has membership interests; a non-profit company; a charity that is not a trust; a complying superannuation fund; an ADF; a foreign superannuation fund; a special company; and an MIS. As a consequence, there is no need to trace ownership through these entities.

Concessional tracing rule for family trusts

It is not possible to trace ownership interests in a company through discretionary trusts as the beneficiaries of such trusts do not have fixed entitlements to the income or capital of the trust [24.2]. Consequently, a company would not be able to satisfy the COT where 50% or more of the rights to voting power, dividends or capital distributions in the company are owned by trustees of discretionary trusts. A concessional tracing rule, however, applies to 'family trusts' (ie trusts that have made a 'family trust election') [24.9]. According to this rule, a 'single notional entity' is taken to own the shares and rights held by the trustee (s 165-207). This ensures that for the purposes of the COT, ownership interests are effectively measured at the 'trustee level' and do not need to be traced through to the beneficiaries.

> *Example* Terry is the trustee of a discretionary trust established for the benefit of the Trevalli family. Terry has made a family trust election and the trust is therefore a 'family trust'. In his capacity as trustee, Terry holds shares in L Co, which is a company that has a tax loss. Throughout the ownership test period, Terry owned 80% of the shares in L Co. L Co can carry forward its tax loss as it has satisfied the COT since a single notional entity is taken to own 80% of its shares.

Concessional tracing rules for widely held and eligible div 166 companies

The COT operates subject to concessional tracing rules contained in div 166. These rules apply to 'widely held companies' and 'eligible div 166 companies':

- **Widely held companies.** These companies essentially comprise: (a) listed companies; and (b) companies with more than 50 members that have 'concentrated ownership' (ie broadly speaking, this covers those companies in which no more than 20 persons held, or had the right to acquire, 75% or more of the value of the shares in the company, 75% of the voting power in the company, or 75% of the entitlement to dividends paid by the company during the relevant income year).
- **Eligible div 166 companies.** These companies are companies that are not widely held companies and in which more than 50% of the voting power, dividend or capital distribution rights are directly or indirectly beneficially owned by one or more of the following entities: widely held companies, complying superannuation funds, complying ADFs, special companies, MISs, non-profit companies, charities, or entities prescribed under the regulations.

A widely held company or eligible div 166 company will satisfy the COT if there is 'substantial continuity of ownership' of the company as between the start of the test period and the end of each income year in that period and the end of each 'corporate change' in that period (s 166-5(3)):

- **Substantial continuity of ownership.** There is substantial continuity of ownership if the conditions in s 166-145 are satisfied. These conditions are satisfied if there are persons (other than companies) who directly or indirectly hold more than 50% of the voting power, rights to dividends and capital distributions in a company at the start of the test period and those persons also hold more than 50% of the voting power, rights to dividends and capital distributions in the company immediately after the other time in the test period.

- **Corporate change**. There is a corporate change in a company where the special circumstances in s 166-175 exist, such as where there is a takeover bid for shares in the company or a scheme of arrangement involving more than 50% of the company's shares has been approved by a court. The corporate change 'ends' when the bid or scheme ends.

Example In Year 1, L Co made a $1m tax loss. L Co has 100 ordinary shares on issue which carry equal voting, dividend and capital distribution rights. Throughout Year 1, the shares in L Co were owned as follows:

- Andrew (60 shares), and
- Barry (40 shares).

In Year 2, Cathy made a takeover bid for L Co. The bid ended on 25 May and Cathy acquired all of Barry's shares as a consequence of the bid. The company's shares were therefore owned as follows:

- Andrew (60 shares), and
- Cathy (40 shares).

In Year 3, L Co made income of $3m. During Year 3, however, Andrew sold 30 of his shares to David. He, nevertheless, purchased 25 of these shares back from David before the end of Year 3.

Although Andrew owned more than 50% of the shares in L Co in Year 1 and Year 2, during part of Year 3, he only owned 30% of the shares in L Co. The primary test has therefore not been satisfied as Andrew did not have a greater than 50% continuity of ownership throughout the whole ownership test period (ie from the beginning of Year 1 to the end of Year 3). On this basis, L Co cannot utilise the tax loss.

However, if it is assumed that L Co is a widely held company, it would be able to utilise the tax loss as it would satisfy the substantial continuity of ownership requirement. This is because, at the beginning of the loss year, Andrew owned more than 50% of the shares in L Co. Andrew continued to own more than 50% of the shares in L Co at the end of each of Year 1, Year 2 and Year 3, as well as immediately after the takeover bid ended in Year 2.

To make it easier for widely held companies and eligible div 166 companies to satisfy the substantial continuity of ownership requirements, concessional tracing rules deem certain entities to hold specified stakes in such companies. This means it is not essential for widely held companies or eligible div 166 companies to trace ownership interests through these entities to the ultimate beneficial owners. The concessional tracing rules operate as follows:

- A direct stake of less than 10% in a widely held company or eligible div 166 company is attributed to a 'single notional entity' (s 166-255).
- An indirect stake of less than 10% in a widely held company or eligible div 166 company is attributed to the top interposed entity (s 166-230).
- A stake of 10% to 50% in a widely held company or eligible div 166 company that is held by another widely held company is attributed to that company (s 166-240).
- A stake in a widely held company or eligible div 166 company that is held through one or more specified interposed entities (ie superannuation funds, ADFs, special companies, MISs, or entities prescribed by the regulations) is generally attributed to the relevant entity (s 166-245).

Example A widely held company has 1,000 ordinary shares on issue which carry equal voting, dividend and capital distribution rights. The company's shareholders include:

- Andrew (2 shares)
- Barry (2 shares)

- Cathy (2 shares)
- Deborah (2 shares)
- Ely (2 shares)
- Fred (2 shares), and
- Super Co (the trustee of a complying superannuation fund with 30 members) (110 shares).

For the purposes of determining substantial continuity of ownership under the concessional tracing rules, a 'single notional entity' will be treated as owning 12 shares and Super Co will be treated as owning 110 shares.

Concessional rules for companies with unequal share structures

Companies may technically be unable to satisfy the COT where they have different classes of shares with unequal rights to dividends, capital distributions or voting power, even though there may be no significant change in underlying beneficial ownership during the ownership test period. Division 167 has been introduced to modify the COT for these companies.

Under sub-div 167-A, if a company is unable to work out whether a condition of the COT is satisfied in respect of dividend or capital distributions for a particular period, it may choose to reconsider the condition in three ways:

1. disregard debt interests (s 167-15)
2. disregard debt interests and certain secondary classes of shares (s 167-20), and
3. disregard debt interests and certain secondary classes of shares and treat each of the remaining shares as having a specified percentage of the rights to receive dividends and capital distributions (s 167-25).

Under sub-div 167-B, if a company has shares that have different voting rights or do not carry all of the voting rights in the company, then voting power at a particular time may be tested solely by reference to the maximum number of votes that could be cast in a poll on the election of a director of the company or an amendment to the company's constitution (other than one altering the rights carried by its shares or other forms of voting power) at that time (s 167-85).

Business continuity test

A company satisfies the BCT if it meets either:

- the 'same business' requirements in s 165-210, or
- the 'similar business' requirements in s 165-211.

The same business requirements in s 165-210 are based on the 'same business test' ('SBT') which was contained in a former version of the provision. The similar business requirements in s 165-211 are new and apply to tax losses incurred by companies for income years starting on or after 1 July 2015.

As explained below, both the same business and similar business requirements compare the business activities of the company:

- at the 'test time' (ie the time before a change in ownership or control occurred), and
- throughout the 'same business continuity test period' ('BCT period') (ie throughout the income year in which the loss is sought to be claimed).

Same business requirements

Under s 165-210(1), a company satisfies the BCT if throughout the BCT period the company carries on the 'same business' as it did before the test time. However, the test is failed if, during the BCT period, the company derives assessable income from:

- a business of a kind that it did not carry on before the test time, or
- a transaction of a kind that it had not entered into in the course of its business operations before the test time (s 165-210(2)).

In addition, a company will not satisfy the BCT if, before the test time, it:

- started to carry on a business it had not previously carried on, or
- in the course of its business operations, entered into a transaction of a kind that it had not previously entered into,

and did so for the purpose, or for purposes including the purpose, of being taken to have carried on throughout the BCT period a business that is similar to the business it carried on immediately before the test time (s 165-210(3)).

The High Court in *Avondale Motors (Parts) Pty Ltd v FC of T* 71 ATC 4101 examined the meaning of 'same business' under former s 80E *ITAA36* (the predecessor of s 165-210). In this case, a company had carried on business selling motor parts prior to a change in its ownership. After the change, it continued to sell motor parts, but did so under a different name, at different premises, and with different directors and employees. Although it continued to acquire parts from its former suppliers, it also acquired different parts from new suppliers and made sales to new customers. Gibbs J held that the company had not satisfied the SBT, as the term 'same business' means 'identical business' (rather than merely the 'same 'kind of' business').

Although Gibbs J adopted a strict approach to the meaning of same business in *Avondale Motors*, it is important to realise that the mere fact that changes have occurred in the way in which a business is carried on after a change in ownership has taken place does not necessarily mean that the business will be a different business. This point is illustrated in *Lilyvale Hotel Pty Ltd v FC of T* 2009 ATC ¶20-094, which concerned a company that owned a hotel business. Originally, the business was operated and managed by an agent for the taxpayer. However, after the taxpayer was taken over by another company, the business was operated and managed directly by the taxpayer. The Full Federal Court held that the SBT had been satisfied as the management of the hotel at different times in different ways had no bearing upon the identification of the business which the taxpayer carried on.

Similar business requirements

Under s 165-211(1), a company satisfies the BCT if throughout the BCT period it carries on a business (its current business) that is 'similar' to the business it carried on immediately before the test time (its former business). In ascertaining whether a company's current business is similar to its former business, the following *must* be taken into account:

- the extent to which the assets (including goodwill) that are used in its current business to generate assessable income throughout the BCT period were also used in its former business to generate assessable income
- the extent to which the activities and operations from which its current business generated assessable income throughout the BCT period were also the activities and operations from which its former business generated assessable income
- the identity of its current business and the identity of its former business, and
- the extent to which any changes to its former business result from development or commercialisation of assets, products, processes, services or marketing or organisational methods of the former business (s 165-211(2)).

The above matters do not limit the matters that may be taken into account in ascertaining whether a company's current business is similar to its former business, and any other relevant matters may therefore also be considered.

However, a company will *not* satisfy the BCT if, before the test time, it:

- started to carry on a business it had not previously carried on, or
- in the course of its business operations, entered into a transaction of a kind that it had not previously entered into,

and did so for the purpose, or for purposes including the purpose, of being taken to have carried on throughout the BCT period a business that is similar to the business it carried on immediately before the test time (s 165-211(3)).

Calculating taxable income where COT and BCT not satisfied

A company that fails the COT and has not satisfied the BCT is required to calculate its taxable income for the year according to special rules in sub-div 165-B (s 165-35) rather than the general rule in s 4-15 [8.3]. The special rules in sub-div 165-B require a company to divide its income year into periods (based on when relevant changes in ownership occurred) and to calculate its notional income or loss for each period (ss 165-45, 165-50). Any notional income amounts are added to arrive at the company's taxable income for the year (s 165-65). Notional losses cannot be set off against this amount. Instead, they form the company's tax loss for the year (s 165-70). Such a tax loss can only be deducted in future years if the requirements of sub-div 165-A are satisfied.

The following flow chart, taken from s 165-30, outlines the circumstances in which sub-div 165-B applies.

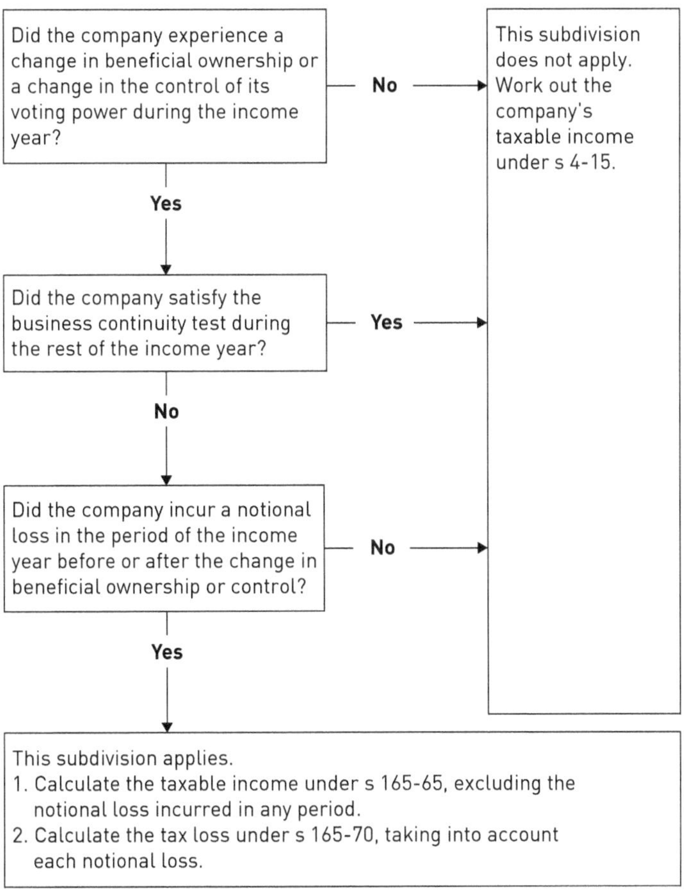

[22.23] Temporary loss carry back tax offset

To assist companies with cashflow during the COVID-19 crisis, the Government introduced a temporary measure to allow the carry back of their tax losses. The measure was designed to support previously profitable companies that fell into a tax loss position due to the weaker economic conditions caused by the pandemic.

The mechanism for allowing companies to carry back their tax losses is contained in div 160 *ITAA97*. Division 160 allows eligible corporate tax entities that incurred tax losses in the 2019/20, 2020/21, 2021/22 or 2022/23 income years to carry back their losses and set them off against their taxed profits in the 2018/19, 2019/20, 2020/21 or 2021/22 income years. The loss carry back is delivered through a refundable 'loss carry back tax offset' ('LCBTO') that is available in the 'current year', rather than by actually requiring corporate tax entities to go back and amend their tax returns to claim deductions in the previous years. The tax offset is a 'proxy' for the tax the entity would save if it deducted the loss in the income year to which the loss is carried back.

Entitlement to the LCBTO

An entity is entitled to a LCBTO for the 'current year' if the following conditions in s 160-5 are satisfied:

(a) the current year is the 2020/21, 2021/22 or 2022/23 income year
(b) the entity is a corporate tax entity throughout the current year
(c) any or all of the 2019/20, 2020/21, 2021/22 and/or 2022/23 income years are loss years
(d) the entity had an income tax liability for any or all of the 2018/19, 2019/20, 2020/21 and/or 2021/22 income years
(e) any of the following requirements are satisfied for the current year and each of the five income years before the current year:
    (i) the entity lodged its income tax return for the year
    (ii) the entity was not required to lodge an income tax return for the year
    (iii) the Commissioner made an assessment of the entity's income tax for the year, and
(f) the entity makes a 'loss carry back choice' for the current year (s 160-5).

The loss carry back choice must be made in the approved form by the day the entity lodges its income tax return for the current year or such later day as the Commissioner allows (s 160-15). It must specify how much of the entity's tax loss for the relevant income year (ie the 2019/20, 2020/21, 2021/22 or 2022/23 income years) is to be carried back to the earlier income years (ie the 2018/19, 2019/20, 2020/21 or 2021/22 income years).

An entity cannot claim the LCBTO unless it was an SBE, or would have been an SBE if the aggregated turnover threshold for an SBE was $5 billion (instead of $10m), for the income year [8.7] (s 160-20).

Calculating the LCBTO

A corporate tax entity's LCBTO is the lesser of:

(a) the sum of the entity's 'loss carry back tax offset components' for the relevant income years (ie the 2018/19, 2019/20, 2021/22 and 2022/23 income years), and
(b) the entity's franking account balance at the end of the current year (s 160-10(1)).

A corporate tax entity's loss carry back tax offset component for an income year is calculated as follows (s 160-10(2)):

- **Step 1.** Start with the amount of the tax loss the entity carries back to the income year.
- **Step 2.** Reduce the step 1 amount by the entity's unutilised net exempt income for the income year.
- **Step 3.** Multiply the step 2 amount by the corporate tax rate for the loss year.

Where more than one tax loss is carried back to an income year, the entity's loss carry back tax offset component is the sum of the amounts calculated above in relation to each of those tax losses.

An entity's loss carry back tax offset component cannot exceed its income tax liability for the income year.

Example X Co has a corporate tax rate of 30%. It has:

- for the 2022/23 income year—a tax loss of \$900,000 and a franking account balance of \$300,000
- for the 2020/21 income year—an income tax liability of \$120,000 and net exempt income of \$5,000, and
- for the 2021/22 income year—an income tax liability of \$210,000.

For the 2022/23 income year (ie the current year), X Co makes a loss carry back choice to carry back \$405,000 of its \$900,000 tax loss to the 2020/21 year and the remaining \$495,000 of that loss to the 2021/22 year. X Co therefore has:

- a loss carry back tax offset component for the 2020/21 income year of \$120,000 (ie (\$405,000 – \$5,000) × 30%), and
- a loss carry back tax offset component for the 2021/22 income year of \$148,500 (ie \$495,000 × 30%).

X Co is entitled to a refundable LCBTO for the 2022/23 income year of \$268,500 (being the sum of the two loss carry back tax offset components of \$120,000 and \$148,500) as this amount is less than its franking account balance of \$300,000 at the end of the 2022/23 income year.

If X Co's franking account balance was only \$200,000 at the end of the 2022/23 income year, its LCBTO would be capped at \$200,000.

[22.24] QUESTIONS

1. L Co and H Co are companies that have less than 80% of their assessable income made up of base rate entity passive income in 2023/24. L Co has aggregated turnover of \$20m and H Co has aggregated turnover of \$60m in the income year. What rates of tax apply to L Co and H Co for the income year?
2. What constitutes a 'dividend' under s 6(1) *ITAA36* and div 7A of pt III *ITAA36*? Discuss the different ways that dividends paid to a company's resident and non-resident shareholders are taxed.
3. Sandy owns 100 shares in X Co. Sandy has elected to participate in the company's dividend reinvestment plan and, as a result, dividends that she would otherwise be entitled to receive are applied towards the cost of purchasing additional shares in the company. In the current income year, X Co declares a dividend of \$1 per share and Sandy is issued with 20 additional shares in the company. Discuss the tax consequences of these arrangement?
4. What is the objective of the imputation system? How does it achieve this objective? Does it apply to distributions made by a non-resident company that pays tax in Australia and makes distributions to Australian resident shareholders?

5. What is the role of a franking account and what are the main kinds of franking credit and debit entries? Do the following result in any franking credit or debit entries in a resident company's franking account:
   - payment of income tax of $300
   - payment of a PAYG instalment of $600
   - payment of GST of $100
   - payment of FBT of $500
   - receipt of a $700 dividend which has $100 of franking credits allocated to it?
6. What is the maximum franking credit that a resident company with a corporate tax rate for imputation purposes of 25% can allocate to a $100,000 dividend?
7. Explain how the following shareholders are taxed on a $10,000 fully franked dividend paid by a company that has a corporate tax rate for imputation purposes of 30%:
   - Tom (a resident who has salary of $60,000)
   - Teresa (a resident who has no other income)
   - R Co (a resident private company that pays tax at the rate of 25%)
   - Super Co (trustee of a complying superannuation fund that has no other income)
   - F Co (a company resident in Canada that has no other income).
8. Bit Co (a resident private company) owns 20% of the shares in Bot Co (a resident public company). Both companies have a corporate tax rate of 30% and a corporate tax rate for imputation purposes of 30%. Bot Co pays Bit Co a $70,000 dividend which has $12,000 of franking credits allocated to it (ie the franking percentage of the dividend is 40%). What are the relevant franking account entries for Bit Co and Bot Co? Assuming this is the only receipt of Bit Co, how much tax will it be required to pay? How would your answer be different if Bit Co was a resident base rate entity? Also, how would your answer be different if Bit Co was a non-resident company?
9. P Co (a resident company that has a corporate tax rate for imputation purposes of 30%) carries on various businesses, including mining gold in Peru. In January 2023, P Co paid a $2.4m dividend that was 20% franked to A Co (a resident company that has a corporate tax rate of 30%). The dividend was paid out of profits P Co made in Peru. This is the only receipt of A Co which has a carry-forward tax loss of $3m from the previous income year. At the same time, P Co also paid a $1.2m dividend that was 20% franked F Co (a company resident in the United States). Discuss the tax consequences of the transactions.
10. Tony acquired 1,000 shares in X Co (a resident public company) for $10 each in August 2000. In January this year, X Co returned $7 of capital to its shareholders in respect of each share they held. The shares were not cancelled. The following month Tony sold all his shares in X Co for $20 each. Discuss the CGT implications of the sale. How would your answer differ if X Co had returned $13 of capital per share instead of $7 or if the shares were cancelled?
11. On 8 May 2001, Mary purchased 1,000 shares in P Co for $40 per share. On 2 February 2023, P Co undertook a capital reduction in which it debited its share capital account and returned $25 to all its shareholders without cancelling any of their shares. On 2 May 2023, Mary gifted her 1,000 shares in P Co to her boyfriend, Gary. The market value of each share at the time was $32. On 15 May 2023, P Co paid Gary a dividend of $4,200 which had $900 of franking credits allocated to it. The following week, Gary sold his shares for $33 per share to G Co (a company resident in Germany). On 7 June 2023, P Co paid G Co a $4,200 dividend that had $900 of franking credits allocated to it. Discuss the tax implications of the transactions.

12. Greta owns 1,000 shares in B Co (a listed public company), which she purchased for $10 each in January 2001. B Co is planning to undertake an off-market buy-back in which it will offer to purchase Greta's shares for $12 each (which is also the market value of the shares). B Co uses $5 of share capital and $7 of profits to fund the purchase price of each share. Discuss the tax implications of the buy-back. Would your answer differ if B Co was an unlisted company or if the buy-back was an on-market buy-back?
13. Fred acquired shares in L Co for $5,000 in January 2002. L Co was placed into liquidation earlier this year and Fred received a distribution of $13,000 from the liquidator on the winding up of the company. The distribution included a $7,000 dividend under s 47(1) *ITAA36* that was unfranked. What are the tax implications of the liquidator's distribution?
14. What requirements must be satisfied for an entity to be classified as a 'qualified person'? Why is this concept important? Explain what is meant by the term 'dividend stripping'. How does the legislation tackle dividend stripping schemes?
15. D Co is a resident company that has divided its shares into two classes: Class A shares belonging to shareholders that acquired their shares before 20 September 1985 and Class B shares belonging to shareholders that acquired their shares on or after that date. During the current year, the company pays a franked dividend to both classes of shareholders. The Class A shareholders receive a slightly lesser dividend than the Class B shareholders, but the Class A shareholders also receive a return of capital to compensate them for the lower dividend. Could any anti-avoidance rules apply to this arrangement?
16. T Co is a company that has transferred $7,000 to its share capital account from another account. At the time of the transfer, T Co's 'benchmark franking percentage' was 40%. What are the consequences of the transfer?
17. Why is it necessary to have a COT and a BCT for companies with tax losses? Discuss the key requirements of the COT and BCT.
18. Z Co is not a base rate entity. It has a tax loss of $90m and a franking account balance of $40m in 2022/23. In 2021/22, it had an income tax liability of $120m and net exempt income of $10m. Z Co chooses to carry back all of its $90m tax loss to 2021/22. Calculate Z Co's LCBTO for 2022/23. Would your answer differ if Z Co only had a franking account balance of $15m at the end of 2022/23?

23 PARTNERSHIPS

[23.1] Introduction

Partnerships are a common and relatively straightforward form of business structure. The general taxation rules dealing with partnerships are contained in div 5 of pt III *ITAA36* (ss 90 to 94). Division 5 ensures that while partnership income and losses are calculated at the partnership entity level, a partnership does not actually pay any tax. Instead, the income and losses 'flow through' to the partners based on their respective interests in the partnership. This ensures that it is the individual partners (rather than the partnership) that are the relevant taxpayers.

The 'look-through' treatment under div 5 is consistent with the general law, which does not recognise a partnership as a separate legal entity distinct from the partners. Under the general law, a partnership is simply a legal relationship that exists between the partners. This relationship is based upon the terms of their agreement with each other and is governed by the law of contract and the Partnership Acts of the various states and territories.

This chapter examines the nature of a partnership [23.2] and focuses on the way that the partnership taxation rules in div 5 operate [23.3]. It also considers how the tax law deals with certain kinds of partnership dealings (eg variations in the constitution of partnerships) [23.4] and how the CGT regime applies to partnership assets [23.5] and assignments of interests in partnerships [23.6].

[23.2] Nature of a partnership

General law definition

Three different kinds of partnerships can be established in Australia: general partnerships, limited partnerships and incorporated limited partnerships.

General partnerships

The most common form of partnership is known as a 'general partnership'. The state and territory Partnership Acts define a partnership as 'the relationship which subsists between persons carrying on business in common with a view of profit'. Companies are specifically excluded from the definition.

The following points are worth mentioning about the definition of partnership:

- **Relationship.** A partnership is simply a 'relationship' that exists between the partners. It does not create any separate legal entity that is distinct from the partners. This makes a partnership quite different from a company, which is a separate legal person from its members.

- **Carrying on business.** A partnership requires persons to be 'carrying on a business'. The mere co-ownership of property does not of itself create a partnership between the co-owners.
- **In common.** A partnership can only exist where a business is carried on 'in common'. A partnership cannot therefore arise where two or more businesses are carried on separately. For example, in *Checker Taxicab Co Ltd v Stone* [1930] NZLR 169, it was held that the owner of cab that rented it to a taxi driver was carrying on a separate business from the taxi driver and they were therefore not in partnership.
- **Profit.** A partnership requires persons to be carrying on a business for 'profit'. Non-profit associations, such as certain clubs, do not therefore constitute partnerships.

Partnerships should be distinguished from other kinds of associations such as 'joint ventures'. In *United Dominions Corp Ltd v Brian Pty Ltd* (1985) 157 CLR 1, Dawson J explained (at 15) that 'the important distinction between a partnership and a joint venture is, for practical purposes, the distinction between an association of persons who engage in a common undertaking for profit and an association of those who do so in order to generate a product to be shared among the participants'.

In *ARM Constructions Pty Ltd v FC of T* 87 ATC 4790, the NSW Supreme Court held that a partnership did not exist where entities entered into an agreement to construct residential buildings, which were then partitioned equally between them after construction so that each could go their separate way. The Court found that the agreement constituted a joint venture to construct buildings, in contrast to an agreement to make profits for sharing among themselves.

Importantly, the name given to an arrangement does not necessarily characterise it. In some cases, arrangements described by the parties as joint ventures may actually constitute partnerships (*Canny Gabriel Castle Jackson Advertising Pty Ltd v Volume Sales (Finance) Pty Ltd* (1974) 131 CLR 321).

The Partnership Acts set out rules that regulate the relations of the partners to one another and their relations to outsiders. These rules are complemented by common law and equitable principles developed by the courts (eg principles of contract law and agency). In practice, the partners each contribute something to the partnership (eg skill, labour and/or property). Partners have a fiduciary obligation to act in the interests of each other and in good faith. They have joint and several liability for the debts and obligations of the 'firm'. Partners are both principals and agents of each other and are liable to outsiders for each other's conduct in relation to the partnership business. Partners are therefore, generally, responsible to third parties for any debts incurred by the partnership during the time that they were partners. The interests of the partners in any partnership property and their rights and duties in relation to the partnership are determined, subject to any express or implied agreement, in accordance with rules contained in the Partnership Acts. These interests, rights and duties may be varied from time to time by agreement of the partners.

In *FC of T v Everett* 80 ATC 4076, the High Court pointed out that a partner's interest in a partnership is an 'equitable interest', being a 'chose in action', that is capable of being assigned in whole or in part to third parties. Barwick CJ, Stephen, Mason and Wilson JJ stated (at 4079):

> Although a partner has no title to specific property owned by the partnership, he has a beneficial interest in the partnership assets, indeed in each and every asset of the partnership . . . His share in the partnership consists of a right to a proportion of the surplus after the realization of the assets and payment of the debts and liabilities of the partnership.

Partnerships are relatively inexpensive to establish. There are no special formalities that need to be complied with in order to create a partnership (although, in many cases, a formal partnership deed is executed by the partners). There may, nevertheless, be professional restrictions associated with the establishment of certain kinds of partnerships, such as medical partnerships, where legislation specifies that only qualified persons may become partners.

The *Corporations Act 2001* (Cth) limits the number of partners in a partnership to 20 persons (s 115). This restriction, however, operates subject to a number of exceptions. For instance, accounting partnerships can have up to 1,000 partners, legal partnerships can have up to 400 partners, pharmaceutical partnerships can have up to 100 partners and medical partnerships can have up to 50 partners (reg 2A.1.01 *Corporations Regulations 2001* (Cth)).

Partnerships continue until they are terminated. Termination can occur in a variety of ways, including by agreement of the partners, by the death or bankruptcy of a partner, by operation of law, or by a court making an order to wind up the partnership. Technically, any change in the membership of the partnership (eg as a consequence of the retirement of a partner or the admission of a new partner) destroys the identity of the original firm and results in a new partnership being created.

Limited partnerships

It is possible under state and territory legislation to establish special kinds of partnerships known as 'limited partnerships'. These partnerships are required to be registered on the relevant state or territory Register of Limited Partnerships. The main distinguishing feature of limited partnerships is that they have both 'general partners' and 'limited partners'. The general partners are in essentially the same position as the partners in a general partnership (ie they are responsible for managing the partnership and have joint and several liability for the debts and obligations of the partnership). The limited partners, on the other hand, cannot participate in the management of the partnership and only invest in the partnership by contributing capital to it. For this reason, their liability is limited to the capital that they have agreed to contribute.

Incorporated limited partnerships

A special form of limited partnership, known as an 'incorporated limited partnership', can also be established under state and territory legislation. These partnerships are required to be registered on the relevant state or territory Register of Incorporated Limited Partnerships. Incorporated limited partnerships are hybrid entities that blend certain features of partnerships and companies. Like other limited partnerships, they have both general and limited partners. However, unlike other partnerships, they are deemed to be companies with separate legal personality from the partners for general law purposes. Incorporated limited partnerships have been specifically designed for use in Australia's venture capital programs [27.4]. As a consequence, only limited partnerships that are registered as venture capital limited partnerships ('VCLPs'), early stage venture capital limited partnerships ('ESVCLPs') or Australian fund of funds ('AFOFs') under the *Venture Capital Act 2002* (Cth) or that are venture capital management partnerships ('VCMPs') under the *ITAA36* can be registered as incorporated limited partnerships.

Tax law definition

Under the tax law, a partnership is defined in s 995-1 *ITAA97* as follows:

(a) an association of persons (other than a company or a limited partnership) carrying on business as partners or in receipt of ordinary income or statutory income jointly, or

(b) a limited partnership.

The tax law definition clearly covers all forms of partnership that are recognised under the general law. It is important to note that the tax law definition of a partnership is actually wider than the general law definition of a partnership. While the general law requires a business to be carried on in order for a partnership to exist, it is clear from para (a) of the above definition that a partnership can arise under the tax law where persons merely receive income jointly irrespective of whether or not they are carrying on business as partners. On this basis, it has been held that the tax law definition of partnership covers mere co-owners of property who jointly derive rental income from the property (*FC of T v McDonald* 87 ATC 4541). Likewise, a partnership can also arise for tax purposes where co-owners derive assessable profits from the sale of property under a profit-making scheme (*Tikva Investments Pty Ltd v FC of T* 72 ATC 4231).

[23.3] Determining tax liability

Most partnerships are taxed under div 5 of pt III *ITAA36*. Division 5 requires partnerships to lodge returns, but does not make them liable to pay tax (s 91). Instead, it is the partners who account for their respective shares in the income or loss of the partnership (s 92). This 'flow-through' approach is consistent with the general law, which treats a partnership as merely a 'relationship' that exists between the partners, rather than as a separate legal entity. There are two steps involved in determining tax liability under div 5. The first step arises at the 'partnership entity level' and the second step arises at the 'partner level'.

First step: calculation of partnership net income, etc

The first step in the application of div 5 is to calculate the partnership's net income, partnership loss, exempt income and/or non-assessable non-exempt income. The terms are defined in s 90 as follows:

- 'Net income' means 'the assessable income of the partnership, calculated as if the partnership were a taxpayer who was a resident, less all allowable deductions except deductions allowable under s 290-150 or div 36 of the *ITAA97*'.
- 'Partnership loss' means 'the excess (if any) of the allowable deductions, other than deductions allowable under s 290-150 or div 36 of the *ITAA97*, over the assessable income of the partnership calculated as if the partnership were a taxpayer who was a resident'.
- 'Exempt income' means 'the exempt income of the partnership calculated as if the partnership were a taxpayer who was a resident'.
- 'Non-assessable non-exempt income' means 'the non-assessable non-exempt income of the partnership calculated as if the partnership were a taxpayer who was a resident'.

Since each of the above amounts is determined 'as if the partnership were a taxpayer who was a resident', income from all sources is taken into account in the calculations under the general jurisdictional rules [30.1]. This is the case, even though the partnership may have non-resident partners.

Example Jack (a resident) and Jill (a non-resident) carry on business as partners selling buckets. They derive assessable income of $100,000 from selling buckets in Australia and $50,000 from selling buckets overseas. They also incur deductions relating to the running of the business amounting to $30,000. For the purposes of calculating the net income of the partnership, income from all sources is taken into account as the partnership is treated as if it was a resident taxpayer. The net income of the partnership is therefore $120,000 (ie $100,000 + $50,000 – $30,000).

It is also important to note that in calculating the net income and partnership loss, deductions under s 290-150 *ITAA97* (personal superannuation contributions [19.7]) and div 36 *ITAA97* (tax losses [13.15]) are specifically ignored. These deductions are 'personal' to the partners and can only be claimed at the partner level, not at the partnership level.

Second step: allocation of net income, etc, to partners

The second step in the application of div 5 is to allocate the net income, partnership loss, exempt income and non-assessable non-exempt income between the partners (s 92).

Partners include their individual interests in these amounts in their respective assessable income, deductions, exempt income or non-assessable non-exempt income for the year of income. A partner's interest in the relevant amounts will be based on the partner's interest in the partnership. It is immaterial how much they actually draw down from the partnership. This is illustrated in *Case 7/2000* 2000 ATC 168, where it was held that the fact that a partner does not withdraw their full profit entitlement is of no consequences for income tax purposes. As the AAT explained (at 172): 'the design of s 92 is to catch the whole of a partner's interest in any year of income rather than merely the amount of his drawings'.

For any period that a partner is a non-resident during the income year, the partner only includes his or her respective interests in such amounts to the extent that they are attributable to sources in Australia. This ensures that the partnership taxation rules operate consistently with the general jurisdictional rules [30.1].

Example R (a resident) and F (a non-resident) are equal partners in a partnership. If the partnership derived net income under s 90 of $100,000 during the year and the net income was 80% attributable to Australian sources and 20% attributable to foreign sources, R and F must include the following amounts in their assessable income under s 92:

R: $50,000 = $100,000 × 50%

F: $40,000 = $80,000 × 50%.

If the partnership had made a partnership loss under s 90 of $100,000 during the year and the loss was 70% attributable to Australian sources and 30% attributable to foreign sources, R and F would be entitled to the following deductions under s 92:

R: $50,000 = $100,000 × 50%

F: $35,000 = $70,000 × 50%.

A special rule limits the amount of losses that limited partners in VCLPs, ESVCLPs, AFOFs or VCMPs are allowed to claim under div 5 (s 92(2AA)) [27.4]. The broad effect of this rule is that the limited partners in these partnerships are prevented from claiming losses that exceed their contributions to the partnership.

Division 5 does not apply to corporate limited partnerships

It is important to be aware that the rules in div 5 (ie the two-step approach outlined above) do not apply to 'limited partnerships', unless they are VCLPs, ESVCLPs, AFOFs or VCMPs [27.4]. Limited partnerships that are *not* one of these partnerships are known as 'corporate limited partnerships'. Corporate limited partnerships are not subject to flow-through taxation like other partnerships and are instead taxed as if they were companies under special rules in div 5A of pt III *ITAA36* [25.8].

Diagram of the general rules in div 5

The following diagram illustrates how the two-step approach under div 5 operates:

Partnership

Step 1: Calculate net income, partnership loss, exempt income and/or non-assessable non-exempt income of the partnership under s 90

Net income	**Partnership loss**	**Exempt income**	**Non-assessable non-exempt income**
Assessable income of the partnership, calculated as if the partnership were a taxpayer who was a resident, less all allowable deductions (except deductions under div 36 and s 290-150)	Excess (if any) of the allowable deductions (except deductions under div 36 and s 290-150) over the assessable income of the partnership calculated as if the partnership were a taxpayer who was a resident	Exempt income of the partnership calculated as if the partnership were a taxpayer who was a resident	Non-assessable non-exempt income of the partnership, calculated as if the partnership were a taxpayer who was a resident

Step 2: Allocate net income, exempt income, non-assessable non-exempt income and/or partnership loss to partners under s 92

S 92(1)—assessable income of a partner includes:	S 92(2)—a partner is allowed to deduct (subject to s 830-45):	S 92(3)—exempt income of a partner includes:	S 92(4)—non-assessable non-exempt income of a partner includes:
(a) so much of the individual interest of the partner in the net income of the partnership of the year of income as is attributable to a period when the partner was a resident, and	(a) so much of the individual interest of the partner in the partnership loss as is attributable to a period when the partner was a resident, and	(a) so much of the individual interest of the partner in the exempt income of the partnership of the year of income as is attributable to a period when the partner was a resident, and	(a) so much of the individual interest of the partner in the non-assessable non-exempt income of the partnership of the year of income as is attributable to a period when the partner was a resident, and
(b) so much of the individual interest of the partner in the net income of the partnership of the year of income as is attributable to a period when the partner was not a resident and is also attributable to sources in Australia	(b) so much of the individual interest of the partner in the partnership loss as is attributable to a period when the partner was not a resident and is also attributable to sources in Australia	(b) so much of the individual interest of the partner in the exempt income of the partnership of the year of income as is attributable to a period when the partner was not a resident and is also attributable to sources in Australia	(b) so much of the individual interest of the partner in the non-assessable non-exempt income of the partnership of the year of income as is attributable to a period when the partner was not a resident and is also attributable to sources in Australia

[23.4] Partnership creation, variation and other dealings

Existence of partnerships

Whether or not a partnership exists is a mixed question of law and fact (*Keith Spicer Ltd v Mansell* (1970) 1 WLR 333). As Lord President Clyde explained in *IRC v Williamson* (1928) 14 TC 335:

> You do not constitute or create or prove a partnership by saying that there is one. The only proof that a partnership exists is proof of the relations of agency and of community of losses and profits and of the sharing in one form or another of the capital of the concern; the only proof of a partnership consists in proof of these things.

According to the Full Federal Court in *Jolley v FC of T* 89 ATC 4197 (at 4205):

> The establishment of mutual assent and intention is an essential element in demonstrating the existence of a partnership although it does not stand alone and must be assessed with regard to all relevant circumstances including the conduct of the parties.

A written agreement to act as partners is not necessary to demonstrate mutual assent and intention—an agreement may be inferred from a course of conduct. While it is not essential for all partners to actively participate in a partnership, such participation supports the existence of a partnership, as do other factors such as the existence of joint bank accounts, joint ownership of business assets and contributions of capital (TR 94/8). However, the mere fact that persons (eg a husband and a wife) may have a joint bank account does not necessarily give rise to a presumption that a partnership exists. As stated in *Case Z7* 92 ATC 131 (at 131):

> A joint account—in the absence of any other evidence—means no more that either party has the authority on behalf of and as agent for both to sign cheques or otherwise withdraw from the account.

In practice, the issue of whether a partnership exists is often most difficult to resolve in situations involving arrangements between spouses. For example, in *Jolley's Case*, the issue was whether a partnership existed between a husband and wife in relation to a business involving the sale of oil drums. The husband originally ran the business and had been advised by his accountant to take on his wife as a partner. The business did not have a separate name and there was no written partnership agreement. Most receipts and purchase orders were made in the husband's name. A joint bank account had nevertheless been established. While the husband operated the account almost exclusively, the wife also had access to it. The parties testified that the wife was entitled to half the profits and spent approximately 20 hours per week from home attending to business matters (eg answering phone calls, doing some banking and mailing some accounts). The Full Federal Court held that the Tribunal that originally decided the matter appeared to have wrongly considered that an oral agreement to conduct business in partnership was insufficient to constitute a partnership. According to the Court, the Tribunal's assessment should have proceeded on the basis that the parties had a mutual intention to act in partnership. The Court pointed out (at 4205):

> A partnership may exist notwithstanding that a partner may have no interest in anything but profits and may be denied the right of participation in management.

Jolley may be contrasted with *Harbutt v FC of T* 2013 ATC ¶10-290, where a husband who was the registered owner of a commercial property failed to convince the AAT that he was carrying on a partnership with his wife and that the rental income from the property, which was paid into his bank account, should therefore be split between them. There was no written partnership agreement or any other evidence supporting the existence of a partnership. The fact that the wife was able to withdraw money from the husband's account merely demonstrated that he allowed her to spend the income—it did not show they jointly received income.

Commencement and termination of partnerships

Determining when a partnership commences and terminates is important because it sets the parameters for when the rules in div 5 apply. It is well established that the time at which a partnership commences and terminates is a question of fact. An agreement to retrospectively create or dissolve a partnership therefore has no effect for taxation purposes.

This is illustrated in *Rowe v FC of T* 82 ATC 4243, which involved a husband and wife who had carried on a farming business in partnership since 1957. On 16 May 1975, they entered into a deed of assignment under which they each assigned 50% of their interest in the partnership from 1 July 1974 to a company that had been incorporated to act as the trustee of their family trust. Immediately afterwards, a supplementary partnership deed was executed which purported to regulate the terms of the new partnership between the taxpayers and the company from 1 July 1974. The taxpayers argued that their original partnership came to an end on 30 June 1974 and a new partnership between them and the company came into existence on 1 July 1974. The Federal Court, however, held that it was not possible to retrospectively terminate the old partnership or create a new partnership from 1 July 1974. The original partnership continued in existence until the execution of the deed of assignment on 16 May 1975, and it was only thereafter that the farming business began to be carried on by the new partnership. As a consequence, the net income of the farming business up to 16 May 1975 was net income of the original partnership and was included in the assessable income of the husband and wife according to their respective interests. The net income of the business for the remainder of the year was net income of the new partnership and was included in the assessable income of the husband, wife and the company according to their respective interests.

A similar situation arose in *FC of T v Happ* (1952) 9 ATD 447. This case concerned four people who carried on a business in partnership. On 22 December 1944, the partners entered into a written agreement to dissolve the partnership. The agreement provided that the taxpayer and Mr Gutkins would retire from the partnership as from 30 June 1944 and that the partnership was dissolved from that date. The taxpayer and Mr Gutkins were to receive a lump sum payment for their interests in the partnership business, which was to be carried on by the remaining two partners. The remaining partners lodged a partnership tax return for the period 1 July 1944 to 22 December 1944 indicating that the partnership had net income for the period of £2,580. One-quarter of this amount, being £645, was allocated to the taxpayer. The taxpayer argued that he should not be assessed on this amount as the partnership had been dissolved from 30 June 1944. The High Court, however, rejected this argument. Williams J found that the partnership had continued in fact until 22 December 1944. His Honour pointed out that 'businesses are carried on by the individuals who are in partnership and not by the firm as a separate conception'. The taxpayer retained an interest in the business and the net income it derived until 22 December 1944 and was therefore properly assessed on one-quarter of the net income.

Variation of partnerships

As a partnership is a 'relationship' that exists between the partners, a variation in the constitution of a partnership (eg through retirement or death of a partner or admission of a new partner) creates a new partnership. This was recognised by the High Court in *Tikva Investments Pty Ltd v FC of T* 72 ATC 4231, where Stephen J stated (at 4238):

> When s 92 refers to 'the partnership' it necessarily refers to the 'association of persons' described in the definition of 'partnership' in s 6(1); with every alteration in the identity of the persons associated together, whether because of the substitution of a new partner for an old

> or the introduction of additional partners, a new association of persons comes into existence, the old association of persons being replaced by the new.

In general, the ATO requires separate returns to be lodged for differently constituted partnerships.

It is important to realise that variations in the composition of partnerships can result in disposals of fractional interests in partnership property by the partners leaving the 'old partnership' and acquisitions of fractional interests in partnership property by the partners joining the 'new partnership'. The CGT consequences of such disposals and acquisition are considered at [23.5]. Special rules also apply where interests in 'depreciating assets' or 'trading stock' change due to variations in the composition of partnerships. The depreciation rules are contained in ss 40-295 and 40-340 *ITAA97* [15.2]. The trading stock rules are contained in s 70-100 *ITAA97* [16.6].

Sharing of profits and losses

Partners carrying on 'general law partnerships' are able, as a matter of contract law, to determine how they allocate profits and losses between themselves. The tax law will usually tax the partners of these partnerships in accordance with their interests under the partnership agreement.

This principle is illustrated in *FC of T v Nandan* 96 ATC 2370, which involved a pharmacy partnership operated by Mr Nandan and Mr Liddy. Pursuant to a partnership deed entered into in 1980, the net profits of the partnership were to be shared between the partners in equal shares. However, on 30 June 1992, they resolved to dissolve the partnership from 1 July 1992 and entered into a deed of dissolution which provided that Mr Nandan was entitled to $15,000 as his share of the undrawn profits of the partnership for the year ending 30 June 1992 and Mr Liddy was entitled to the remainder. The Commissioner assessed Mr Nandan on $35,332 on the basis that this was half of the $70,644 net income of the partnership for the relevant year. The Federal Court, however, held that the partners were entitled to vary their percentage interests in the partnership. Accordingly, by virtue of the deed of dissolution, Mr Nandan was only assessable on $15,000.

In contrast, where taxpayers are involved in 'mere tax partnerships' (ie they are not carrying on any business and are therefore not also partners under the general law), they are required to share their profits and losses for tax purposes in accordance with their interests in the underlying property (TR 93/32). Accordingly, a 50% co-owner of an investment property must account for 50% of the income or losses from the property irrespective of any agreement to the contrary.

This principle is illustrated in *FC of T v McDonald* 87 ATC 4541, where a husband (who was a company manager) and wife (who was engaged in domestic duties) jointly purchased two home units from which they derived rental income. They entered into an agreement which provided that the husband's share of the partnership profits would be 25% and the wife's share would be 75%, and that the husband would absorb all partnership losses. In the relevant income year, the partnership made a loss and the husband sought to deduct the full amount of the loss based on the terms of the agreement. The Federal Court, held, however, that the husband was only entitled to deduct 50% of the loss based on his interest in the properties. The Court concluded that, although the husband and wife were in receipt of income jointly, they were not carrying on any business and were therefore merely partners for taxation purposes.

It is important to note that partners do not need to have partnership profits 'distributed' to them in order to be assessed on their share of the profits. Partners are therefore quite different from shareholders in a company, who must be 'paid' a dividend before they can be assessed on a company's profits [22.4]. As the High Court pointed out in *Rose v FC of T* (1951) 84 CLR 118 (at 124):

> Division 5 . . . is based upon the view that the collective income earned by the partnership belongs according to their shares to the partners regardless of its liberation from the funds of the partnership, that is, its actual distribution.

Partnership 'salary' payments

As a partnership is not a separate legal entity, it cannot technically employ the partners (*Ellis v Joseph Ellis & Co* (1905) 1 KB 324). Partnership agreements, nevertheless, often provide that certain partners are entitled to receive 'salary'. Unlike payments of salary to employees, which are generally deductible to a partnership, payments of salary to partners are really distributions of profits for which no deduction is available to the partnership (*Case S75* 85 ATC 544; *Scott & Ors v FC of T* 2002 ATC 2158). This means that salary payments to partners do not affect the 'net income' or 'partnership loss' calculations made under s 90 *ITAA36*. They nevertheless affect the partners' interests in the partnership and must therefore be taken into account for the purposes of the calculations made under s 92 *ITAA36*.

According to TR 2005/7, an agreement to pay salary to a partner 'takes effect as a contractual agreement among the partners to vary the distribution of partnership profits among the partners so that one partner receives an additional share of the profits'. This principle is illustrated in the following example.

Example Bill and Ben are residents that carry on business manufacturing flowerpots. Under their partnership agreement, Bill is allowed to draw a 'salary' of $30,000 for managing the business and any remaining profits and losses are to be shared equally between Bill and Ben. If the partnership made a net profit (after paying Bill's salary) of $40,000 during an income year, the net income of the partnership would be calculated as follows:

Partnership profit (after deducting salary)	$40,000
Bill's salary	$30,000
Net income of the partnership	$70,000

Bill and Ben would be assessed as follows:

	Bill	**Ben**
Salary	$30,000	Nil
Interest in balance of net income	$20,000	$20,000
Section 92(1) assessable income	$50,000	$20,000

Partnership 'interest' payments

Interest charged by a partnership on a partner's overdrawn current account is not necessarily treated as income of the partnership. Depending on the terms of the partnership agreement, the interest may simply be one of the factors to take into account in allocating profits and losses between the partners in much the same way as salary paid to partners is treated. For instance, in *FC of T v Beville* (1953) 10 ATD 170, the partnership agreement provided that interest at the rate of 6% per annum would be credited or debited on the credit or debit balances in the partners' respective current accounts. One of the partners was charged £151 of interest as a consequence of having a debit balance in his account. The High Court held that the interest was not income of the partnership but was instead a factor to be taken into account in determining the allocation of profits between the partners. In other words, debiting the partner's current account with interest reduced his individual interest in the net income of the partnership.

Partners can, nevertheless, act independently of the partnership and can loan money to the partnership. In such a case, interest paid by the partnership may be treated as a deduction for the purposes of calculating the net income or partnership loss and the interest received by the lending partner is treated as ordinary income (*Leonard v FC of T* (1919) 26 CLR 175). Partnerships may also be able to claim deductions for interest paid to third parties on money borrowed to repay capital advances made by the partners for the purposes of running the partnership business (*FC of T v Roberts & Smith* 92 ATC 4380) [12.12].

Work in progress payments

Partnerships typically account for their business income on an accruals basis [9.9]. Like other taxpayers, they are therefore not usually required to account for uncompleted work, namely 'work in progress' (*Henderson v FC of T* 70 ATC 4016). The reason for this is that the work has not yet matured into a recoverable debt and no income can therefore be said to be derived by the partnership at such time.

An exception to this rule, however, applies where partners leave a partnership and payments are made to the 'retiring partners' by the 'continuing partners' for their share of the work in progress of the firm. The general law treats such payments as income that is derived when received by the retiring partners (*Stapleton v FC of T* 89 ATC 4818; *Crommelin v DFC of T* 98 ATC 4790; *FC of T v Grant & Ors* 91 ATC 4608; *Jamieson v CIR* 74 ATC 6008). The general law does not, however, allow deductions for such payments to the continuing partners on the basis that the payments are capital in nature (*Coughlan & Ors v FC of T* 91 ATC 4505).

This lack of symmetry produced a problem for the continuing partners, as they were eventually assessed on the full amount received for the completed work without any allowance for the work in progress payments made to the retiring partners. To overcome this 'double taxation' problem, specific provisions were introduced in the *ITAA97* to deal with 'work in progress amounts'. For the purposes of these provisions, a work in progress amount is an amount that an entity agrees to pay to a recipient in respect of work that has been partially performed by the recipient for a third entity but not yet completed to the stage where a recoverable debt has arisen in respect of the completion or partial completion of the work (s 25-95(3)).

In line with the common law position, the receipt of a work in progress amount continues to be assessable to the partner who receives it (s 15-50). However, in contrast to the common law position, the payment of a work in progress amount is deductible in the year of payment to the extent that, as at the end of that year, either a recoverable debt has arisen in respect of the work to which the amount related, or it is reasonably expected that a recoverable debt will arise in respect of the completion or partial completion of that work within 12 months after the amount was paid (s 25-95(1)). The remainder of any work in progress amount is deductible in the following year (s 25-95(2)).

Example Alf, Barry and Charles carried on a partnership. On 1 January 2023, Alf retired from the partnership and was paid $20,000 for his share of the work in progress of the firm. This amount is assessable to Alf in the 2022/23 income year under s 15-50.

As at 30 June 2023, $5,000 of the work in progress was billed to clients by the remaining partners. It is also reasonable to expect that a further $7,000 will be billed to clients by 1 January 2024. As a consequence, a total of $12,000 is deductible to the partnership in the 2022/23 income year under s 25-95(1). The remaining $8,000 will be deductible in the 2023/24 income year under s 25-95(2).

Uncontrolled partnership income

To prevent partnerships being used as vehicles for income-splitting, 'penalty tax' applies to a share, or part of a share, of the net income of a partnership that is included in the assessable income of a partner who does not have 'the real and effective control and disposal of that share or of a part of that share' (s 94 *ITAA36*). The section does not apply to a partner that is a company, a trustee or a person under 18 years of age.

The broad aim of s 94 is to prevent situations arising such as where a husband admits his wife into partnership merely to split income with her, in circumstances where the husband retains real and effective control over her share of the net income.

The current wording used in s 94 is designed to remedy weaknesses exposed in the wording of a former version of the provision identified by the High Court in *Robert Coldstream Partnership v FC of T* (1943) 68 CLR 391. The earlier section did not refer to the words 'part of a share' and, on this basis, Latham CJ held that a person could not have the 'real and effective control' of a partner's share of the net income of a partnership until the person had the 'whole control' of that share.

The penalty tax is imposed on what is commonly referred to as the partner's 'uncontrolled partnership income'. The rate of penalty tax is 45% less the average rate of ordinary income tax payable on the partner's total taxable income (calculated ignoring any tax offsets) (s 12(7) *ITRA*).

[23.5] CGT and partnerships

Subdivision 106-A *ITAA97* deals with the CGT rules for partnerships. The subdivision recognises that partners have individual fractional interests in the partnership property. This is consistent with *Rose v FC of T* (1951) 84 CLR 118, where the High Court held that a person who contributes an asset to a partnership in which they are a partner is not disposing of the entire asset, but only a fractional interest in the asset, since they retain a fractional interest themselves. Accordingly, where CGT assets are sold to third parties or where the partners' interests in those assets change due to variations in the constitution of the partnership, the partners are required to separately account for capital gains and losses made in relation to their individual fractional interests in such assets.

Section 106-5 provides that any capital gain or capital loss made from a CGT event happening in relation to a partnership or one of its CGT assets is made by the partners individually. The capital gain or capital loss is therefore not taken into account in calculating the net income of the partnership or partnership loss under s 90 and is not reported on the partnership income tax return. Each partner's gain or loss is calculated by reference to the partnership agreement and each partner has a separate cost base or reduced cost base for their interest in each CGT asset of the partnership.

If a partner leaves a partnership, a remaining partner acquires a separate CGT asset to the extent that the remaining partner acquires a share of the departing partner's interest in the asset. If a new partner is admitted to the partnership, the new partner acquires a share of each partnership asset, and the existing partners are treated as having disposed of part of their interest in each partnership asset to the extent that the new partner has acquired it.

In IT 2540, the Commissioner examined the application of the former CGT provisions in pt IIIA *ITAA36* to partnerships. In considering how these provisions applied to large professional partnerships, the ruling states:

> In the case of large professional partnerships, where the partners' dealings with each other are at arm's length, it will only be where consideration is paid by a partner on entering the partnership or where a partner receives a payment on leaving the partnership that Part IIIA will have any practical effect. Where consideration is neither paid by a person on entering the partnership, nor received on retirement from the partnership, the partner will not realise a capital gain or incur a capital loss on the disposal of particular assets. However, as noted

above, the admission or retirement of a partner may affect the proportionate ownership of the partnership assets by the individual partners and therefore may affect the extent of a continuing partner's interest in the partnership. This would be relevant in the event of a subsequent disposal of the partnership assets for consideration, or where consideration is paid to a partner on retirement from the partnership.

[23.6] Assignments of interests in partnerships

In addition to having interests in the CGT assets of a partnership, a partner also has a separate interest in the partnership itself. *FC of T v Everett* 80 ATC 4076 establishes that this interest is capable of being assigned to third parties. In *Everett*, a partner in a law firm had assigned a 6/13th share in his interest in a legal partnership to his wife. The High Court held that the effect of the assignment was that the partner held the relevant portion of the income from the partnership on trust for his wife (as beneficiary), and the wife (rather than the partner) was therefore liable to pay tax on the income.

As partners do not ordinarily have interests in the net income of a partnership until the accounts are taken at the end of the year, partners can alienate their share of the net income for the year by effecting assignments at any time prior to the end of the year. This is what occurred in *FC of T v Galland* 86 ATC 4885, where a solicitor, on 27 June 1980, assigned 49% of his share in a partnership to the trustee of his family discretionary trust. The High Court followed the decision in *Everett* to conclude that the assignment was effective to assign 49% of the solicitor's share in the entire net income of the partnership for the year ending 30 June 1980 (even though the assignment had only been made three days earlier).

The Commissioner has stated in IT 2501 that assignments 'on all fours' with *Everett* and *Galland* will not be caught by the general anti-avoidance provisions in s 260 or pt IVA *ITAA36* [37.1]. Such assignments may, nevertheless, give rise for a need to apportion deductions available to the assigning partner. In IT 2608, the Commissioner states that where expenditure relates to the partner's proportionate interest in the partnership, deductions are only available for the partner's share of the partnership interest not assigned. For example, where a partner assigns one-third of his interest in the partnership, he would only be entitled to a deduction for two-thirds of any interest expenditure incurred on borrowings used to purchase his interest in the partnership.

Assignments of partnership interests were common many years ago as they enabled partners to split income with their associates. However, as a consequence of the introduction of CGT, it is now dangerous to undertake such assignments where the partnership interest was acquired after 19 September 1985. This is because a partner's interest in a partnership is a form of property and therefore a CGT asset. Consequently, the assignment of such an interest triggers a CGT event. The CGT event is likely to result in adverse tax consequences for the assignor even if they have received no consideration for the assignment, as in such a case the 'market value substitution rule' contained in s 116-30 would deem the assignor to have disposed of the interest in the partnership for its market value [17.7].

The Commissioner has stated in IT 2540 that for the purposes of the former CGT provisions in pt IIIA *ITAA36*, where an *Everett* assignment is not made at arm's length, the valuation method adopted in *Reynolds v C of T* (WA) 86 ATC 4528 is usually appropriate for determining the market value of the assigned interest. Broadly, this involves determining the price that a 'hypothetical buyer' would pay for the assigned interest having regard to the value of the right to the future income of the partnership which is attached to the interest.

[23.7] QUESTIONS

1. How are the general law and tax law definitions of a 'partnership' different? How does div 5 of pt III *ITAA36* deal with the income and losses of partnerships?
2. Fred (a resident) and Wilma (a non-resident) are equal partners in a computer business. The business generates 75% of its income from Australian sources and 25% of its income from foreign sources. Assuming the partnership's net income for the income year is $400,000, how is it taxed?
3. Jack and Jill are married and borrowed money to purchase a rental property as joint tenants. They entered into a written agreement which provided that Jack is entitled to 10% of the profits from the property and Jill is entitled to 90% of the profits from the property. The agreement also provided that if the property generates a loss, Jack is entitled to 100% of the loss. Last year a loss of $10,000 arose. How is this loss allocated for tax purposes? If Jack and Jill decide to sell the property, how should they account for any capital gain or capital loss?
4. Murray, Tony and Greg have been carrying on a business in partnership for many years. Greg decided to leave the partnership on 1 August 2023 and received a payment of $1m in respect of his interest in the work in progress of the partnership. The partners, however, agreed that to make things simpler, they will prepare the partnership's tax returns on the basis that Greg resigned from the partnership on 30 June 2023. Discuss the consequences of this arrangement.
5. Ross, Joe and Chandler are partners in an accountancy partnership. Chandler retires from the partnership on 1 May 2023 and is paid $50,000 for his share of the firm's work in progress. As at 30 June 2023, $30,000 of the work in progress has been billed to clients by Ross and Joe. It is reasonable to expect that a further $15,000 will be billed by 1 May 2023. How is the work in progress payment taxed?
6. Penny has recently become a partner in a law firm and intends to enter into an *Everett*-style assignment of one-half of her interest in the partnership to her husband. What are the consequences of doing this?

24 TRUSTS

[24.1] Introduction

This chapter examines the nature of a trust and discusses how trust estates are taxed.

The general rules relating to the taxation of trust estates are contained in div 6 of pt III *ITAA36* (ss 95AAA to 102) [24.3]–[24.5]. Division 6 calculates the 'net income' of a trust estate and assesses the net income in the hands of either the beneficiaries or the trustees of the estate. The operation of the assessment rules depends on whether a beneficiary is 'presently entitled' to a 'share' of the 'income' of the trust estate and whether the beneficiary is under a 'legal disability'. The rules also operate subject to jurisdictional rules that take into account the concepts of residence [30.2] and source [30.3].

Trusts differ fundamentally from companies in that they are not separate taxpayers. Although s 960-100(1) *ITAA97* refers to a trust as an 'entity', no tax is payable by a trust. This is logical as a trust, like a partnership, is not a separate legal person, but merely a conduit through which persons derive income and capital. Their net income is therefore taxed on a 'flow-through' basis [24.7] in much the same way as the net income of a partnership is taxed [23.3]. Unlike partnerships, however, there is no flow-through of any losses. Losses are locked in the trust estate and can be carried forward to be offset against trust income in future years provided certain tests are satisfied [24.9]. Although trusts are not separate legal entities, trustees must nevertheless furnish tax returns that disclose the net income or loss of their trust estates for an income year.

In 2011, important amendments were made to the general rules dealing with the taxation of trust estates. These reforms were introduced because of a number of longstanding practical problems associated with the operation of div 6. The problems were highlighted by the High Court in *FC of T v Bamford & Ors* 2010 ATC ¶20-170 [24.4]. The 2011 trust reforms are designed to improve the way that the net income of a trust estate is taxed. Under the reforms, div 6 remains the basic regime for dealing with the taxation of the net income of a trust estate. However, where the net income includes capital gains and/or franked distributions, these amounts are now assessed under sub-div 115-C *ITAA97* (for capital gains) and sub-div 207-B *ITAA97* (for franked distributions). To prevent double taxation, the amounts assessable under div 6 are adjusted under div 6E of pt III *ITAA36* (ss 102UW to 102UY). The interaction between divs 6, 6E, sub-divs 115-C and 207-B is complex and is examined at [24.8].

While the general rules in div 6 apply to most trusts, they do not apply to all trusts. In particular, they do not apply to superannuation funds, which are taxed under special rules discussed in Chapter 19. They also do not apply to 'public trading trusts', which are taxed as if they were companies under special rules contained in div 6C of pt III *ITAA36* [25.9].

Special rules also apply to certain widely held trusts, known as 'managed investment trusts' ('MITs'). These trusts have traditionally been taxed under div 6. However, as a consequence of reforms enacted in 2016, div 6 no longer applies to those MITs that are 'attribution MITs' ('AMITs') (s 95AAD). Instead, AMITs are subject to their own special attribution rules contained in div 276 *ITAA97* [25.10].

[24.2] Nature of a trust

Before examining the way trust estates are taxed, it is important to consider the nature of a trust. A 'trust' is an equitable concept that evolved out of principles developed by the English Court of Chancery. These principles had their origins in the medieval 'use', which was a device designed, among other things, to avoid the payment of feudal death duties. Under the use, an estate in land was transferred to X (known as the *feoffee*) for the use of Y (known as the *cestui que use*). X was the legal owner of the land (ie the equivalent of the modern day trustee), while Y was the person who benefited from the land (ie the equivalent of the modern day beneficiary).

The concept of a trust has been defined by legal scholars in a variety of ways. Ford and Lee, for example, in *Principles of the Law of Trusts* (1990) state (at 3):

> A trust may be defined as an obligation enforceable in equity which rests on a person (the trustee) as owner of some specific property (the trust property) to deal with that property for the benefit of another person (the beneficiary) or for the advancement of certain purposes.

In *Raftland Pty Ltd v FC of T* 2006 ATC 4189, Kiefel J referred (at [65]) to the following definition advanced by Jacobs, Meagher and Gummow in *Jacobs' Law of Trusts in Australia* (1997):

> A trust exists when the owner of a legal or equitable interest in property is bound by an obligation, recognised by and enforced in equity, to hold that interest for the benefit of others, or for some object or purpose permitted by law.

It is clear from these definitions that the essential feature of a trust is that it involves the separation of legal and beneficial ownership of property. This means that although a trustee has legal title to the trust property, the trustee cannot deal with the property contrary to the interests of the beneficiaries. Equity imposes a number of fiduciary duties on trustees, and beneficiaries have a variety of remedies if these duties are breached. While trustees are generally personally liable for their actions in respect of the trust property, they have a 'right of indemnity' against the trust property for liabilities properly incurred in the administration of the trust (*Vacuum Oil Co Pty Ltd v Wiltshire* (1945) 72 CLR 319; *Octavo Investments Pty Ltd v Knight* (1979) 144 CLR 360). This means, for example, that a trustee who holds land on trust for certain beneficiaries will be liable to pay rates and other taxes relating to the land, but will also be entitled to be reimbursed for those outgoings (eg from any rent derived from the land).

Kinds of trusts

People can establish trusts during their lifetimes ('inter vivos' trusts) as well as under their wills ('testamentary trusts'). In Australia, many businesses and investments are held in trust structures and, as a result, much private wealth is accumulated in these vehicles. Many trusts are also established for charitable purposes [11.4]. Trusts may be express or implied:

- **Express trusts.** These trusts arise where there is an express intention to create a trust. In the simplest case, an express trust arises where a person declares (either orally or in writing) that they hold property 'on trust' for the benefit of another person. More often, however, the person who creates the trust (the settlor) does this by settling property on another party (the trustee) who agrees to hold the property, in accordance with the terms of the trust, for the benefit of specified persons (the beneficiaries). An express trust can also arise where a court orders money to be held on trust as security for costs (*Dwight v FC of T* 92 ATC 4192) or pending the outcome of a dispute (*Harmer & Ors v FC of T* 91 ATC 5000) [24.4].

- **Implied trusts.** These trusts arise where there is no express declaration of trust, but it is nevertheless appropriate that a trust be implied or construed. For example, if a settlor transfers property to a trustee to hold it for the benefit of the settlor's daughter once she reaches 18, then if the daughter dies before that age, the trustee would hold the property and income earned from it on a 'resulting trust' for the settlor. Similarly, where an employee misappropriates an employer's funds, the employee would hold the funds and any earnings from them on a 'constructive trust' for the benefit of the employer (*Zobory v FC of T* 95 ATC 4251).

It can sometimes be difficult to determine whether a trust actually exists. This is illustrated in *Bosanac v FC of T* [2022] HCA 34, where the Commissioner, in seeking to recover tax owing by a taxpayer, was unsuccessful in claiming that he held a half-interest in property which was in his wife's name and had been purchased with shared funds. The Commissioner argued that where a person advances purchase monies for property, which is held in the name of another person, there is a presumption that they intend to have a beneficial interest in the property under a resulting trust. The High Court, however, held that a resulting trust will not arise where there is evidence that the parties' objective intention was inconsistent with the person obtaining an interest in the property. The Court also stated that in cases of purchases by a husband in the name of a wife, the presumption of a resulting trust operates subject to the presumption of 'advancement', which assumes that the purchaser intends the beneficial interest to pass with the legal interest.

In the commercial world, the most common kinds of trusts are express trusts. The two main kinds of express trusts are 'fixed trusts' and 'discretionary trusts':

- **Fixed trusts.** Under a fixed trust, the beneficiaries' entitlements to income and capital are fixed. A common example of such a trust is a 'unit trust', under which the beneficiaries' entitlements to income and capital are determined by reference to the classes and proportion of units they hold. A beneficiary of a fixed trust has an equitable interest in the trust property (*Baker v Archer-Shee* [1927] AC 844; *Charles v FC of T* (1954) 90 CLR 598).
- **Discretionary trusts.** Under a discretionary trust, the trustee has the discretion how to distribute the trust income and capital. In other words, the trustee selects, from a class of 'objects' (ie potential beneficiaries), the persons who are to receive particular benefits under the trust and the amount of such benefits. The only right a beneficiary of a discretionary trust usually possesses is the equitable right to demand that the trustee properly administer the trust. Until the trustee exercises the discretion to distribute an amount to a particular beneficiary, the beneficiary's interest in the income and capital of a discretionary trust is a 'mere expectancy' (*Gartside v IRC* [1968] AC 553).

The difference between a fixed trust and a discretionary trust was discussed by Gummow J in *FC of T v Vegners* 89 ATC 5274 (at 5278):

> A fixed trust is used to describe a species of express trust where all the beneficiaries are ascertainable and their beneficial interests are fixed, there being no discretion in the trustee or any other person to vary the group of beneficiaries or the quantum of their interests. The expression 'discretionary trust' is used to identify another species of express trust, one where the entitlement of beneficiaries to income, or to corpus, or both, is not immediately ascertainable. Rather, the beneficiaries are selected from a nominated class by the trustee or some other person and this power may be exercisable once or from time to time.

One of the most commonly encountered varieties of trust is a 'family trust'. Family trusts are designed to benefit a particular family group and are usually established as discretionary trusts to allow flexible distributions of the income and capital to be made among the family members from year to year. Family trusts often have a corporate trustee but are usually controlled by the 'family head' who is typically a director of the corporate trustee. Family trusts are traditionally used to invest family assets and operate family businesses. To avoid penalty tax applying under s 102 *ITAA36* [24.6], family trusts are typically established by an independent 'settlor', who is not a family member and does not benefit under the trust or have the right to revoke or alter the trust.

While family discretionary trusts have tax benefits as they allow income and capital to be split and distributed flexibly between family members, they also provide asset protection advantages. These advantages arise because under insolvency law property held by a person as trustee is not available for distribution among their creditors. It is only property that is beneficially held by a person that can be claimed by their creditors if they become insolvent.

The following diagram illustrates a basic trust structure:

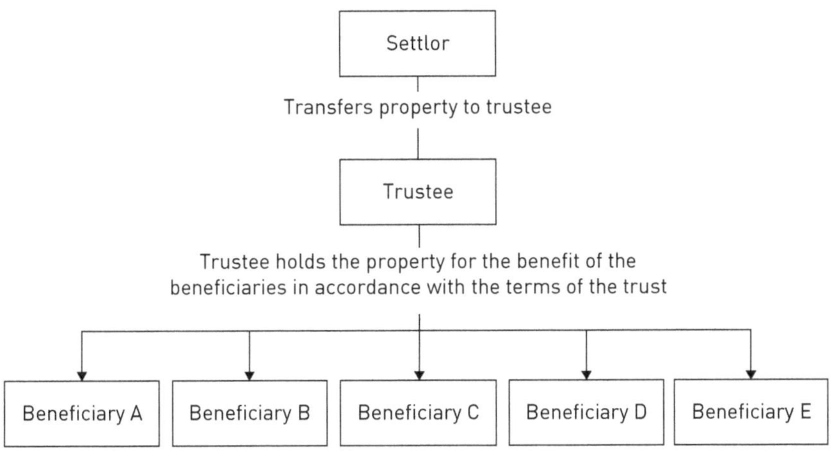

Termination of trusts

Trusts may come to an end in a variety of ways. For example, a trust may terminate as a result of an express term in the trust deed (eg the trust reaching its vesting date). In such case, where there are 'default beneficiaries' specified under the deed, they become absolutely entitled to the remaining trust property. A trust may also be terminated where the trust deed provides the trustee or some other person with the right to revoke the trust and this right is exercised. In certain circumstances, a court may also order the termination of a trust.

A trust terminates automatically when a beneficiary becomes entitled to the entire legal and beneficial interests in the trust property, as there is no longer any division of such interests (*Re Cook*; *Beck v Grant* [1948] 1 All ER 231). In addition, where all the beneficiaries of a trust are *sui juris* (ie adults that are not under any legal disability) and between them absolutely entitled to the trust property, they may call upon the trustee to terminate the trust and transfer the property to them under the rule in *Saunders v Vautier* (1841) 49 ER 282.

The termination of a trust can give rise to several tax issues. In particular, it can trigger CGT events in relation to the trust property [17.10] and result in any unutilised trust losses being wasted [24.9].

As trust deeds often contain wide powers of amendment, this raises the question whether amending a trust can result in the trust being terminated and a new trust being created by way of a 'resettlement'. The High Court considered this question in *FC of T v Commercial Nominees of Australia Ltd* 2001 ATC 4336. The case involved a superannuation fund established in 1988 under a deed that contained wide powers of amendment. In 1993, extensive amendments were made to the deed, including the introduction of a new category of beneficiary and the conversion of the fund from a defined benefit fund to an accumulation fund. The issue in the case was whether losses made by the superannuation fund in income years prior to the amendments could be carried forward and deducted in an income year following the amendments. The Commissioner argued that the losses were not deductible as the amendments resulted in a fundamental alteration in the trust relationship and destroyed the 'necessary continuity' of the taxpayer. The High Court, however, rejected this argument and found that the entity that claimed the losses was the same entity as had incurred the losses. The Court held that the changes to the deed did not destroy the continuity of the trust. In doing so, it pointed out that the trust continued to operate under the terms of the original deed as varied by the amendments, the property which was the subject of the trust did not alter, and the persons who were members of the fund before the amendments remained members after the amendments.

[24.3] Overview of the taxation of trust estates

Basic rules for taxing trust estates

The basic rules for taxing trust estates are contained in div 6 of pt III *ITAA36*. Division 6 has two main roles:

- its first role is to calculate the 'net income' of a trust estate (which is ascertained under s 95), and
- its second role is to determine who is assessed on the net income of the trust estate (which is ascertained under ss 97, 98, 99, 99A and 100).

In broad terms, the 'net income' of a trust estate is generally calculated in much the same way as the taxable income of a resident taxpayer is calculated. In determining who is assessed on the net income of the trust estate and on what amounts they are assessed, it is necessary to determine whether a beneficiary is 'presently entitled' to a 'share' of the 'income' of the trust estate and whether the beneficiary is under a 'legal disability'. These terms all have technical meanings that are explained at [24.4]. The assessment rules also operate subject to jurisdictional rules [24.5] that take into account the concepts of residence [30.2] and source [30.3].

In the simplest cases, subject to the operation of jurisdictional rules, the net income of a trust estate is *generally* assessed as follows:

- where a beneficiary is presently entitled to a share of the income of a trust estate and is not under a legal disability, the beneficiary is assessed on their share of the net income of the trust estate (s 97)
- where a beneficiary is presently entitled to a share of the income of a trust estate but is under a legal disability, the trustee is assessed (on behalf of the beneficiary) on the beneficiary's share of the net income of the trust estate (s 98), and
- where there is a share of the income of a trust estate to which no beneficiaries are presently entitled, the trustee is assessed (in a personal capacity) on any residual net income of the trust estate (s 99A).

Beneficiaries who are assessed under s 97 pay tax at their ordinary tax rates (eg marginal tax rates for individual beneficiaries and the appropriate company tax rate for corporate beneficiaries). Trustees that are assessed under s 98 generally pay tax at rates that are designed to reflect the tax rates of the beneficiaries on behalf of whom they are paying tax. Trustees that are assessed under s 99A pay tax at the rate of 45%. The ML is also payable by certain beneficiaries and trustees [24.5].

Modifications for capital gains and/or franked distributions

Where the net income of a trust estate includes capital gains and/or franked distributions, the basic rules in div 6 are modified under the 2011 trust reforms. In these circumstances, the following special rules apply:

- the capital gains and franked distributions of the trust estate are assessed in the hands of the beneficiaries or trustees in accordance with rules contained in sub-div 115-C and sub-div 207-B *ITAA97*, and
- the amounts that would otherwise be assessable to beneficiaries or trustees under div 6 are adjusted in accordance with modifications contained in div 6E *ITAA36*.

The special rules outlined above are complex and are explained further at [24.8].

[24.4] Meanings of key terms used in div 6

The operation of the rules in div 6 turn on the meanings of the following terms:

- 'trust estate', 'trustee' and 'beneficiary'
- 'income' of the trust estate
- 'net income' of the trust estate
- 'share' of the income and net income of the trust estate
- 'legal disability', and
- 'present entitlement'.

As the discussion at [24.5] will show, these concepts ultimately determine whether it is the trustees or the beneficiaries of a trust estate that are assessed on the net income of the trust estate and the amounts upon which they are assessed.

Meanings of trust estate, trustee and beneficiary

The income tax law does not contain definitions of the terms 'trust estate' or 'beneficiary'. These terms therefore take on their general meanings.

The term 'trustee' is defined in s 6(1) *ITAA36* to include 'an executor or administrator, guardian, committee, receiver, or liquidator' and 'every person having or taking upon himself the administration or control of income affected by any express or implied trust, or acting in any fiduciary capacity, or having possession, control or management of the income of a person under any legal or other disability'. As this definition is merely inclusive, any person who is a trustee under the general law will also be a trustee for tax purposes. Both individuals and companies can be trustees of a trust estate.

Individuals and companies can also be beneficiaries of a trust estate. A beneficiary of a trust estate can also be a trustee of another trust estate (*FC of T v Totledge Pty Ltd* 82 ATC 4168). This means that it is possible to have a 'head trust' with one or more 'sub-trusts' underneath it. Multi-layered trusts are relatively common business and investment structures. For example, a business might be run through a unit trust by two families ('family A' and 'family B'). Some of the units in the trust would be held by the trustee of family A's discretionary trust (for the benefit of family A members) and the remaining units in the trust would be held by the trustee of family B's discretionary trust (for the benefit of family B members).

Meaning of 'income' of the trust estate (trust law income)

The term 'income' of the trust estate is not defined in the legislation and therefore has its ordinary meaning. This meaning is based on principles derived from the general law of trusts. For this reason, the income of the trust estate is often referred to as the 'trust law income' of the trust estate.

In *FC of T v Bamford & Ors* 2010 ATC ¶20-170, the High Court, relying on Sundberg J's judgment in *Zeta Force Pty Ltd v FC of T* 98 ATC 4681, held that the expression 'income of the trust estate' refers to 'distributable income', which is 'income ascertained by the trustee according to appropriate accounting principles and the trust instrument'. *Bamford* is authority for the principle that where a trust instrument permits a trustee to treat a capital gain as 'income' for the purposes of making distributions to the beneficiaries (as is common in many discretionary trust deeds), the capital gain forms 'income of the trust estate' even though it is not income according to ordinary concepts.

Meaning of 'net income' of the trust estate (tax law income)

The term 'net income' of the trust estate is defined in s 95 *ITAA36*. It is the total assessable income of the trust estate, calculated as if the trustee were a resident taxpayer in respect of that income, less all deductions (other than specified excluded deductions). The net income of the trust estate is, therefore, a broadly similar concept to the concept of taxable income. For this reason, it is often referred to as the 'tax law income' of the trust estate.

It is important to understand that the 'net income' of a trust estate can include amounts that are not ordinarily treated as 'income' of the trust estate, such as capital gains and franking credits. Furthermore, as the trustee is treated as a resident taxpayer in respect of the income of the trust estate, income from all sources is included in calculating the net income of the trust estate. Trust losses from previous years can generally be taken into account in determining the net income of a trust estate for a particular year (special rules apply where there are life tenants or beneficiaries who do not have a beneficial interest in the corpus of the trust estate). Trust losses cannot, however, be utilised if a trust fails to satisfy specified ownership or control tests contained in sch 2 F *ITAA36* [24.9].

Meaning of 'share' of the income and net income of the trust estate

Under the basic assessment rules in div 6, a beneficiary's 'share' of the 'income' of a trust estate is used to determine their 'share' of the 'net income' of the trust estate [24.5]. Their share of the net income of the trust estate is the amount upon which they (or the trustee on their behalf) will typically be assessed (subject to jurisdictional rules).

The High Court decision in *FC of T v Bamford & Ors* 2010 ATC ¶20-170 establishes that the term 'share' means 'proportion'. A beneficiary's share of the net income of the trust estate is therefore calculated by reference to the proportion of the income of the trust estate to which the beneficiary is presently entitled. Authority for the use of this proportionate approach can also be found in a number of earlier cases, such as *Davis & Anor v FC of T* 89 ATC 4377; *Zeta Force Pty Ltd v FC of T* 98 ATC 4681; *FC of T v Prestige Motors Pty Ltd (as Trustee of the Prestige Toyota Trust)* 98 ATC 4241; and *Cajkusic & Anor v FC of T (No 2)* 2006 ATC 4752.

The way that the proportionate approach operates is illustrated in the following example.

Example If a resident beneficiary is presently entitled to 40% of the income of a trust estate, the beneficiary would also be assessed on 40% of the net income of the trust estate. Accordingly:

- if the income of the trust estate was \$100 and the net income of the trust estate was \$200, the beneficiary's share of the net income of the trust estate would be \$80 (ie \$200 × 40%), and
- if the income of the trust estate was \$200 and the net income of the trust estate was \$100, the beneficiary's share of the net income of the trust estate would be \$40 (ie \$100 × 40%).

However, if there was no income of the trust estate, but there was nevertheless \$100 of net income, the beneficiary's share of the net income of the trust estate would be nil as there is no share of the income of the trust estate to which the beneficiary is presently entitled.

An important consequence of the proportionate approach is that beneficiaries can technically be assessed under div 6 on amounts that they might not actually receive. This is because their share of the net income of the trust estate is based on their 'proportionate' share of the income of the trust estate rather than the actual 'quantum' of the income that they receive from the trust estate.

Meaning of 'legal disability'

The concept of legal disability is important under div 6 as beneficiaries that are presently entitled to a share of the income of a trust estate, but are under a legal disability, will have their share of the net income of the trust estate assessed in the hands of the trustees of the estate on their behalf.

The term 'legal disability' is concerned with the legal capacity of the beneficiaries of the trust estate. The term is not defined in the legislation, and therefore takes its ordinary meaning. Under the general law, beneficiaries that are unable to give a valid discharge for payments made to them by trustees are regarded as being under a legal disability. This would therefore cover minors, bankrupts and people who are legally incapable due to a mental condition.

Meaning of 'present entitlement'

The concept of present entitlement is central to the operation of div 6 as beneficiaries who are presently entitled to a share of the income of a trust estate are generally assessed on their share of the net income of the trust estate (unless they are under a legal disability, in which case, the trustee is assessed on their behalf).

It is important to note that the concept of present entitlement is concerned with the distributable income of the trust estate (ie the 'trust law income' as opposed to the 'tax law income' of the trust estate) (*FC of T v Bamford & Ors* 2010 ATC ¶20-170; *Zeta Force Pty Ltd v FC of T* 98 ATC 4681). In other words, it relates to a beneficiary's entitlement to the 'income' as opposed to the 'net income' of the trust estate.

The meaning of the term 'present entitlement' is complex and has been considered in several cases. It is also the subject of specific statutory rules. The key principles relating to present entitlement are outlined below.

Position to demand payment

FC of T v Whiting (1943) 68 CLR 199 establishes that in order for a beneficiary to be 'presently entitled' to income of a trust estate, the beneficiary must be in a position to demand payment of the income from the trustee. *Whiting* concerned income of a deceased estate. The deceased's will provided that, after payment of the estate's liabilities, the trustees of the estate were required to use the residue to provide an annuity for the deceased's widow and children. Some 10 years after the deceased's death, the estate's liabilities had not been finalised and it was still uncertain whether there was a sufficient residue to pay the annuity. The High Court held that the beneficiaries were not presently entitled to the income of the estate since they were not entitled to call upon the trustees to pay them the residue. Latham CJ and Williams J stated (at 215):

> The words 'presently entitled to a share of the income' refer to a right to income 'presently' existing—ie, a right of such a kind that a beneficiary may demand payment of the income from the trustee . . . A beneficiary who has a vested right to income (as in this case) but who may never receive any payment by reason of such a right, is entitled to income, but cannot be said to be 'presently entitled' as distinct from merely 'entitled'.

Present entitlement where beneficiary under a legal disability

The above statement in *Whiting* must be considered in the light of subsequent statements made in *Taylor & Anor v FC of T* 70 ATC 4026. The statements in *Taylor* indicate that where a beneficiary is prevented from demanding immediate payment of income from a trustee merely because the beneficiary is under a legal disability, this does not, by itself, prevent the beneficiary from being presently entitled to the income.

Taylor concerned various trusts established for infant beneficiaries. The trust deeds provided that the income from the trust funds was, until the beneficiary attained the age of 21 or died, to be held on trust to be paid to the beneficiary's parents or guardians for the beneficiary's maintenance and education. The balance income not so applied was to be accumulated and invested for the beneficiary absolutely if the beneficiary attained the age of 21 but, if the beneficiary died beforehand, for the beneficiary's personal representative absolutely as part of the beneficiary's estate.

In the relevant income year, the beneficiaries of the respective trusts were alive but had not yet turned 21, and no part of the income had been paid to their parents or guardians. The High Court held that the beneficiaries were, nevertheless, presently entitled to the income of the trust estates as they had an absolutely vested interest in possession in the income and, but for their legal disability, which prevented them from being able to give a valid discharge, they would have succeeded in an action to recover the income from the trustees. Kitto J explained (at 4029):

> Section 98 plainly acknowledges that a beneficiary may be 'presently entitled' to income notwithstanding that he is under a legal disability . . . Since the consequence which the section attaches to the disability is that the trustee is to be assessed instead of the beneficiary, the inference is clearly that the disability is from obtaining from the trustee income to which the beneficiary is presently entitled. It is therefore impossible to suppose that the learned Judges who decided *Whiting's case* meant that a person whose title to a specific amount of income is absolute, but who is under a disability from obtaining payment of it, is for that reason to be held not 'presently entitled' to it.

Subsequently, his Honour went on to conclude (at 4030):

> I think that 'presently entitled' refers to an interest in possession in an amount of income that is legally ready for distribution so that the beneficiary would have a right to obtain payment of it if he were not under a disability.

Present entitlement requires a vested interest

Harmer & Ors v FC of T 91 ATC 5000 is authority for the principle that, to be presently entitled to the income of a trust estate, a beneficiary must have a 'vested interest' (as opposed to a mere 'contingent interest') in the income of the trust estate. *Harmer* concerned a litigation dispute relating to the ownership of a sum of money. The court hearing the dispute had ordered that, pending the outcome of the case, the money should be 'paid into court' and invested in a building society account 'on trust' in the names of the three solicitors acting for the claimants. The solicitors were unsuccessful in arguing that they should not be assessed on the income derived from the building society account on the basis that one or more of the parties to the dispute were presently entitled to the income. The High Court found that none of the claimants was presently entitled to the income, as none of them had a vested interest in the money unless and until an order was made by the court in their favour. Mason CJ, Deane, Dawson, Toohey and McHugh JJ explained (at 5005):

> The respective interests of the individual claimants were, at best, contingent. None had an entitlement to the capital or the income of the fund which was vested either in interest or in possession. *A fortiori*, none had a present legal right to demand or receive payment of either capital or income. It follows that none of the claimants was 'presently entitled' to the income of the fund . . .

According to their Honours (at 5004), a beneficiary is only presently entitled to a share of the income of a trust estate if:

(a) the beneficiary has an interest in the income which is both vested in interest and vested in possession; and

(b) the beneficiary has a present legal right to demand and receive payment of the income, whether or not the precise entitlement can be ascertained before the end of the relevant year of income and whether or not the trustee has the funds available for immediate payment.

The above passage was relied on by the Full Federal Court in *Walsh Bay Developments Pty Ltd & Anor v FC of T* 95 ATC 4378. This case related to an agreement between WB and MSB in respect of a proposed land development project under which WB was granted the right to develop land owned by MSB. The project required WB to make an upfront payment of approximately $74m to MSB. This money was required to be invested in a bank account in the joint names of WB and MSB and held on trust pending the receipt of notification that development approval had been granted, whereupon the $74m and interest earned on that amount would become the property of MSB. However, the agreement also provided that if development approval could not be obtained, the money would be returned to WB and the interest earned would be shared equally between the parties. It also provided that if the agreement was terminated beforehand, the $74m and all interest earned would be returned to WB, less a retention amount of $10m.

For the income year ending 30 June 1989, some $5m of interest was earned on the deposit, but no development approval had been received and the agreement had not been terminated. The Full Federal Court followed *Harmer* to conclude that no beneficiary was presently entitled to the income as at 30 June 1989. The Court found that the interest of the parties in the income at such time was contingent, because it depended on events that 'might or might not have taken place'. For instance, it depended on whether the development approval would be granted and whether the agreement would be terminated beforehand.

Present entitlement determined at the end of the income year

In *FC of T v Carter & Ors* 2022 ATC ¶20-822, the High Court noted that the phrase 'is presently entitled to a share of the income of the trust estate' in s 97(1) was expressed in the present tense. It was therefore directed to the position existing immediately before the end of the income year for the stated purpose of identifying the beneficiaries who were to be assessed with the income of the trust; namely, those beneficiaries who, as well as having an interest in the income of the trust that was vested both in interest and in possession, had a present legal right to demand and receive payment of the income. The Court pointed out that the legislation was drafted to tax a beneficiary by reference to present entitlement, not receipt.

Deemed present entitlement under s 95A(2)

Section 95A(2) *ITAA36* provides that 'where a beneficiary has a vested and indefeasible interest in any of the income of a trust estate but is not presently entitled to that income' (eg because the beneficiary cannot demand immediate payment of the income from the trustee) the beneficiary is, nevertheless, still deemed to be presently entitled to the income.

Section 95A(2) was applied in *Dwight v FC of T* 92 ATC 4192. This case concerned a litigation dispute involving a foreign company. The company had been ordered to deposit money into a bank account as 'security for costs' in the joint names of the solicitors acting for the parties. The Commissioner, relying on *Harmer*, sought to assess the solicitors on the interest earned from the deposits on the basis that no beneficiary was presently entitled to the income. The Federal Court, however, distinguished *Harmer*. Hill J found that the security for costs orders created a trust whereby the money was held by the solicitors on trust for the foreign company, subject to an equitable charge for such sums as should be ordered against it. His Honour explained (at 4200):

> *Harmer* differs from the present case in two respects. The first is that there was no suggestion in *Harmer*, nor could there have been, that the income was income of the party paying the money into court, or formed part of the general property of that person. The argument was a different one. It was submitted that the income was income to which the ultimately successful parties to the litigation were presently entitled, albeit that the identity of those parties and the quantum of their entitlement was ascertained only after the litigation ended. The second is that the moneys in *Harmer* were held not as security for costs which a party may ultimately be entitled to, but to be dealt with in accordance with the order of the court consequent upon its determination of the conflicting claims to the moneys. Both of these matters were critical to the outcome in *Harmer*.

Hill J held that the foreign company was deemed to be presently entitled to the income under s 95A(2) as it had a vested and indefeasible interest in the income. The existence of the charge or lien in favour of the defendants to the proceedings did not result in there being no deemed present entitlement.

Deemed present entitlement under s 101

Where a trustee has the discretion to pay or apply income of a trust for the benefit of specified beneficiaries (eg in the case of a discretionary trust), the beneficiaries in whose favour the trustee exercises that discretion are deemed to be presently entitled to the income under s 101.

It is not necessary that the income be immediately paid to, or applied for, the benefit of a beneficiary in order for s 101 to apply (*Case E47*, 73 ATC 385). The requirements of the provision are satisfied so long as the trustee makes the appropriate resolution. Nevertheless, s 101 can only operate if there is 'distributable income' of a trust estate, otherwise there is nothing upon which the trustee's discretion can be exercised (*Cajkusic & Anor v FC of T (No 2)* 2006 ATC 4752).

A declaration by a trustee that income is to be held for 'the credit of' beneficiaries has been held to constitute an 'application' of the income for their benefit under the New Zealand equivalent of s 101 (*CIR v Ward* 69 ATC 6050).

Interestingly, the effect of s 101 is that a beneficiary may be presently entitled to income of a trust estate even though the beneficiary may have no knowledge of the trust (*Vegners v FC of T* 91 ATC 4213). A beneficiary may, nevertheless, disclaim an entitlement to trust income. In *FC of T v Ramsden* 2005 ATC 4136, the Full Federal Court held that to be effective for tax purposes, a disclaimer would need to occur within a reasonable time of the beneficiary becoming aware of their entitlement and must relate to the whole of their entitlement (not merely part of it).

The decision in *Ramsden* must, however, now be read in the light of the recent decision in *FC of T v Carter & Ors* 2022 ATC ¶20-822, where the High Court held that default beneficiaries that had made disclaimers to income of a trust after the end of the relevant income year could not retrospectively avoid being assessed on the income under s 97. This was because the question of the present entitlement of a beneficiary to income of a trust must be tested and examined at the close of the income year, not some reasonable period of time after the end of that year.

Deemed present entitlement after payment under s 95A(1)

Section 95A(1) provides that a beneficiary that is presently entitled to income is deemed to continue to be presently entitled to that income after it has been paid or applied for the beneficiary's benefit.

Section 95A(1) was introduced to address comments made by Barwick CJ in *Union Fidelity Trustee Co of Australia Ltd v FC of T* 69 ATC 4084 (at 4087) that once income of a trust estate has been paid to a beneficiary, the beneficiary ceases to be presently entitled to it, and therefore might be taxed on the income under former s 26(b) *ITAA36*.

No present entitlement where reimbursement agreement exists under s 100A

Section 100A contains a specific anti-avoidance rule, which deems that a beneficiary who would otherwise be presently entitled to income of a trust estate is not presently entitled to the income if the present entitlement arose in connection with a 'reimbursement agreement'.

A 'reimbursement agreement' is an agreement that provides for the payment of money or the transfer of property to, or the provision of services or other benefits for, a person or persons other than the beneficiary (s 100A(7)). The agreement must be entered into for the purpose of reducing the tax liability of some person (s 100A(8)).

Section 100A was applied by the High Court in *Raftland Pty Ltd v FC of T* 2008 ATC ¶20-029 to a scheme in which a trustee of a trust with losses was introduced as a beneficiary of another trust to absorb the income of the other trust. It was also recently applied in *B&F Investments Pty Ltd v FC of T* 2023 ATC ¶20-865, but not in *FC of T v Guardian AIT Pty Ltd ATF Australian Investment Trust* 2023 ATC ¶20-850 [37.5]. The Commissioner's views on reimbursement agreements are contained in TR 2022/4 and PCG 2022/2.

No present entitlement for exempt entities under ss 100AA and 100AB

To prevent tax-exempt beneficiaries being used to inappropriately reduce the amount of tax payable on the net income of a trust estate, the following two anti-avoidance rules were introduced:

- Section 100AA *ITAA36* applies where an exempt entity that would otherwise be presently entitled to an amount of income of the trust estate has not been notified of their present entitlement within two months of the end of the income year. In this case, the entity is deemed not to be presently entitled, and to have never been presently entitled, to the amount of the income. The aim of this rule is to prevent exempt entities that are not aware of their present entitlement being used to shelter the tax payable on the net income of a trust estate.
- Section s 100AB *ITAA36* applies where an exempt entity's 'adjusted Division 6 percentage' [24.8] share of the income of the trust estate exceeds a prescribed benchmark percentage. In this case, the entity is treated as not being presently entitled to the 'excess'. The aim of this rule is to prevent exempt entities from receiving a disproportionate share of a trust's net income relative to their entitlement to the income of the trust estate.

The above rules do not apply to an exempt entity that is an Australian Government agency. The Commissioner also has the discretion not to apply the rules in certain cases.

No present entitlement for income received after death s 101A

Section 101A(1) provides that where the trustee of a deceased estate receives any amount which would have been assessable income in the hands of the deceased person if it had been received by that person during their lifetime, the amount is included in the assessable income of the trust estate and is deemed to be income to which no beneficiary is presently entitled.

The section was considered in *Single v FC of T* (1964) 110 CLR 177 in relation to the trustee of the estate of a deceased solicitor who, until his death, had been a partner in a law firm and was entitled to 25% of the net income of the firm. After the deceased's death, the trustee received two amounts for fees relating to the deceased's entitlement under the partnership agreement to work in progress which had not been completed or billed to clients during his lifetime, but which had only been completed and paid for after his death.

A majority of the High Court (Menzies and Owen JJ; Kitto J dissenting) held that the amounts received by the taxpayer in respect of the deceased's entitlement to the work in progress of the partnership up to the date of his death constituted assessable income of the trust estate under s 101A. The majority held that it did not matter that the deceased had no actual right to receive the payments during his lifetime because the work had not been completed during his lifetime. Menzies J explained (at 189):

> The object of s 101A is to make any receipts of the character therein specified assessable income of the trustee, that is those which would have been assessable income in the hands of the deceased if received by him during his lifetime. It does not seem to me to matter whether or not the deceased could during his lifetime have received the actual payments which the trustee of his estate received after his death. Nor does it matter that the deceased had no right to receive the payments in question during his lifetime. The section operates upon an assumption, viz. that the payments in question had been received by the deceased during his lifetime, and attributes to receipts by the trustee the character of assessable income if, on the assumption stated, it would have been assessable income in the hands of the deceased.

[24.5] Operation of the basic rules in div 6

The diagram on the following page outlines how the basic rules in div 6 operate. The rules are adjusted where the net income of a trust estate includes capital gains and/or franked distributions [24.8].

Key questions

There are three key questions that need to be addressed in determining how the net income of a trust estate is taxed under the basic rules in div 6:

- Who is assessed on the net income of a trust estate: the beneficiaries or trustees?
- What amounts are the beneficiaries and trustees assessed on?
- What rates of tax do the beneficiaries and trustees pay?

Who is assessed on the net income of a trust estate?

There are five 'basic rules' about who is assessed on the net income of a trust estate under div 6:

1. The beneficiary is assessed where the beneficiary is not under a legal disability and is presently entitled to a share of the income of the trust estate (s 97(1)). This rule does not apply where deemed present entitlement arises under s 95A(2) (see basic rule 3), or where the beneficiary is a non-resident at the end of the income year (see basic rule 4) (s 97(2)).
2. The trustee is assessed (on behalf of the beneficiary) where the beneficiary is under a legal disability and is presently entitled to a share of the income of the trust estate (s 98(1)). The beneficiary is also assessed where the beneficiary is a beneficiary in more than one trust estate or derives income from other sources (s 100(1)). However, in such a case, the beneficiary gets a credit for the tax paid by the trustee (to avoid double taxation) (s 100(2)).
3. The trustee is assessed (on behalf of the beneficiary) where the beneficiary is deemed to be presently entitled under s 95A(2)—ie the beneficiary has a vested and indefeasible interest in the income of the trust estate but is not otherwise presently entitled to the income (s 98(2)). The beneficiary is also assessed where the beneficiary is a beneficiary in more than one trust estate or derives income from other sources (s 100(1)). However, the beneficiary gets a credit for the tax paid by the trustee (to avoid double taxation) (s 100(2)).
4. The trustee is assessed (on behalf of the beneficiary) where the beneficiary is presently entitled to a share of the income of the trust estate and is a non-resident at the end of the income year (ss 98(2A), (3)). The beneficiary is also assessed (s 98A(1)). However, the beneficiary gets a credit for the tax paid by the trustee (to avoid double taxation) (s 98A(2)).
5. The trustee is assessed where there is net income of a trust estate to which no beneficiary is presently entitled (ss 99, 99A).

Step 1: Calculate net income of trust estate (s 95)

Net Income = Total assessable income of trust estate (calculated as if the trustee were a resident taxpayer in respect of the income) – Deductions (other than specified excluded deductions)

Step 2: Determine who pays tax on net income of trust estate

1. Beneficiary is not under a legal disability and is presently entitled to a share of the income of the trust estate

*Does not apply where s 95A(2) applies or where the beneficiary is a non-resident at the end of the income year

→ S 97—beneficiary assessed on:
(a) so much of the beneficiary's share of the net income of the trust estate as is attributable to a period when the beneficiary was a resident, and
(b) so much of the beneficiary's share of the net income of the trust estate as is attributable to a period when the beneficiary was not a resident and is also attributable to sources in Australia

→ Tax payable in accordance with beneficiary's ordinary tax rates

*Medicare levy may also be payable where appropriate

2. Beneficiary is under a legal disability but is presently entitled to a share of the income of the trust estate

→ S 98(1)—trustee assessed (on behalf of beneficiary) on:
(a) so much of the beneficiary's share of the net income of the trust estate as is attributable to a period when the beneficiary was a resident, and
(b) so much of the beneficiary's share of the net income of the trust estate as is attributable to a period when the beneficiary was not a resident and is also attributable to sources in Australia

→ Tax payable in accordance with schs 10 & 12 *ITRA* (eg where beneficiary is a company—trustee taxed at the relevant corporate tax rate; where beneficiary is individual—trustee taxed at prescribed marginal rates; and where beneficiary is a minor—trustee taxed at minor's rates)
*Medicare levy may also be payable where appropriate

→ Beneficiary also assessed where beneficiary is a beneficiary in more than one trust estate or derives income from other sources (s 100(1))

Beneficiary gets a credit for the tax paid by the trustee (s 100 (2))

3. Beneficiary is deemed presently entitled to a share of the income of the trust estate under s 95A(2)

→ S 98(2)—trustee assessed (on behalf of beneficiary) on:
(a) so much of the beneficiary's share of the net income of the trust estate as is attributable to a period when the beneficiary was a resident, and
(b) so much of the beneficiary's share of the net income of the trust estate as is attributable to a period when the beneficiary was not a resident and is also attributable to sources in Australia

→ Tax payable in accordance with schs 10 & 12 *ITRA* (as above)

→ Beneficiary also assessed where beneficiary is a beneficiary in more than one trust estate or derives income from other sources (s 100(1))

Beneficiary gets a credit for the tax paid by the trustee (s 100 (2))

4. Beneficiary is presently entitled to a share of the income of the trust estate and is a non-resident at the end of the income year

→ SS 98(2A) and (3)—trustee assessed (on behalf of beneficiary) on:
(a) so much of the beneficiary's share of the net income of the trust estate as is attributable to a period when the beneficiary was a resident, and
(b) so much of the beneficiary's share of the net income of the trust estate as is attributable to a period when the beneficiary was not a resident and is also attributable to sources in Australia

→ Tax payable in accordance with schs 10 & 12 *ITRA* (as above)

→ Beneficiary also assessed (s 98A(1))

Beneficiary gets a credit for the tax paid by the trustee (s 98A(2))

5. No beneficiary is presently entitled to a share of the income of the trust estate

→ S 99 (applies where s 99A does not apply, eg where trust estate results from a will)—trustee assessed on:
(a) in the case of a resident trust estate—so much of the net income of the trust estate to which no beneficiary is presently entitled, and
(b) in the case of a non-resident trust estate—so much of the net income of the trust estate to which no beneficiary is presently entitled and which is also attributable to sources in Australia

→ Tax payable at marginal rates in accordance with sch 10 *ITRA*

*Medicare levy may also be payable where appropriate

→ S 99A—trustee assessed on:
(a) in the case of a resident trust estate—so much of the net income of the trust estate to which no beneficiary is presently entitled, and
(b) in the case of a non-resident trust estate—so much of the net income of the trust estate to which no beneficiary is presently entitled and which is also attributable to sources in Australia

→ Tax payable at 45% (s 12(9) *ITRA*)

* Medicare levy may also be payable where appropriate

Amounts referable to trust income that have previously been assessed in the hands of trustees are treated as trust capital and are not assessed again when they are subsequently paid to beneficiaries. However, resident beneficiaries may be assessed on amounts that have been paid out of trust capital referable to previously untaxed income where that income would have been assessed if derived by a resident (s 99B). This rule might apply where foreign income of a non-resident trust estate to which no beneficiary was presently entitled in a particular income year is distributed in a subsequent income year to a resident beneficiary.

What amounts are the beneficiaries and trustees assessed on?

The amounts upon which beneficiaries and trustees are assessed depends on which one of the basic rules apply.

Basic rules 1 to 4

Where basic rule 1, 2, 3 or 4 applies, the beneficiary or trustee (as the case requires) is assessed on:

- so much of the beneficiary's share of the net income of the trust estate as is attributable to a period when the beneficiary was a resident, and
- so much of the beneficiary's share of the net income of the trust estate as is attributable to a period when the beneficiary was not a resident and is also attributable to sources in Australia.

Basic rule 5

Where basic rule 5 applies, it is necessary to determine whether s 99 or s 99A applies and whether the trust estate is a resident or non-resident trust estate. Section 99 only applies where s 99A does not apply (s 99(1)). The circumstances in which s 99A does not apply are listed in s 99A(2). Most importantly, s 99A does not apply where:

- the trust estate results from a will or intestacy, or consists of property of a bankrupt or of a kind referred to in s 102AG(2)(c) *ITAA36* (eg specified compensation amounts), and
- the Commissioner considers it would be unreasonable that s 99A apply.

Section 99A therefore operates as the default assessment provision where there is net income of a trust estate to which no beneficiary is presently entitled. Section 99 will only apply in a limited number of specific 'concessional' situations.

In the case of a 'resident trust estate', the trustee is assessed on so much of the net income of the trust estate to which no beneficiary is presently entitled. In the case of a 'non-resident trust estate', the trustee is assessed on so much of the net income of the trust estate to which no beneficiary is presently entitled and that is also attributable to sources in Australia (ss 99, 99A).

A trust estate is a 'resident trust estate' where the trustee was a resident at any time during the income year or where the central management and control of the trust estate was in Australia at any time during the year (s 95(2)). In other circumstances, the trust estate is a 'non-resident trust estate' (s 95(3)).

What rates of tax do the beneficiaries and trustees pay?

Beneficiaries and trustees who are assessed in respect of shares of the net income of the estate under div 6 pay tax at the rates outlined below.

Beneficiary tax rates

Beneficiaries that are assessed on shares of the net income of a trust estate under ss 97, 98A or 100 *ITAA36* [24.5] pay tax on these amounts at their ordinary tax rates [8.8]. Individual beneficiaries therefore pay tax at their respective marginal rates plus ML where applicable (note that special penalty tax rates apply to minors [25.4]). Corporate beneficiaries pay tax at the relevant corporate tax rate [22.3].

Trustees assessed on behalf of beneficiaries under s 98

Trustees that are assessed on behalf of beneficiaries under s 98 generally pay tax at rates that mirror the rates that would apply if the beneficiaries had been personally assessed on such amounts. For example, this means that:

- if the relevant beneficiary is a resident or non-resident individual, tax is payable by the trustee at rates equivalent to the resident or non-resident individual tax rates [8.8]
- if the relevant beneficiary is a company, tax is payable by the trustee at a rate equivalent to the corporate tax rate [22.3], and
- if the relevant beneficiary is a minor, tax is payable by the trustee at rates equivalent to the rates applicable to minors [25.4] (ss 12(6), 13(3) to (4), 15(3) to (5), 28, schs 10, 12 *ITRA*).

Special rates apply where the trustee is assessed under s 99 in respect of an estate of a person who died less than three years before the end of the income year (ss 12(6), 14, sch 10 *ITRA*).

Where a trustee is assessed under s 98 in respect of a share of the net income of a trust estate to which a resident individual beneficiary is presently entitled, the trustee must also generally pay the ML (s 251S(1)(b) *ITAA36*).

Trustees assessed under ss 99 or 99A

Trustees of resident trust estates that are assessed under s 99 generally pay tax at the rates set out in the table below. However, where they are assessed in respect of a deceased estate, they pay tax at ordinary individual marginal rates [8.8] for the first three income years after the deceased's death (s 12(6); sch 10 *ITRA*). Trustees of non-resident trust estates that are assessed under s 99 pay tax at the non-resident individual marginal tax rates [8.8] (s 12(6); sch 10 *ITRA*).

Tax rates for trustees of resident trust estate assessed under s 99		
Net income	**Tax**	**% on excess**
$416	Nil	50%
$670	$127	19%
$45,000	$8,549	32.5%
$120,000	$32,924	37%
$180,000	$55,124	45%

Trustees that are assessed under s 99A pay tax at the rate of 45% (s 12(9) *ITRA*).

In addition, trustees that are assessed under s 99 or s 99A must also generally pay the ML (but not in the case of a deceased estate) (s 251S(1)(c) *ITAA36*).

Illustration of the basic rules in div 6

The following example illustrates how the net income of a trust estate is taxed under the basic rules in div 6.

Example T Co is a resident company that acts as trustee of the Simpson family discretionary trust. In the 2022/23 income year, the trust earned $50,000 in rent from leasing an Australian property and $50,000 of foreign source interest income. The net income of the trust estate for the 2022/23 income year was therefore $100,000 (50% sourced in Australia and 50% sourced overseas) (s 95). Assume this amount was also the income of the trust estate for trust law purposes.

On 30 June 2023, T Co (in accordance with a discretion available to it under the terms of the trust deed) resolved to distribute the income of the trust estate as follows:

- one-quarter to Homer (a resident aged 50)
- one-quarter to Bart (a resident aged 15), and
- one-quarter to F Co (a non-resident company subject to tax at the rate of 30%).

Homer, Bart and F Co are therefore each presently entitled to one-quarter of the income of the trust estate pursuant to s 101.

Homer is assessed on his share of the net income ($25,000) (s 97(1)). He will have to pay tax on this amount at his ordinary marginal rates (plus ML).

As Bart is under a legal disability (being a minor), T Co is assessed on Bart's share of the net income ($25,000) (s 98(1)). T Co will pay tax on this income at the penalty rates applicable to minors (plus ML). If Bart is also presently entitled to income of another trust estate or derives income from any other source, he will also be assessed on the $25,000 and will pay tax at minor's rates (plus ML) (s 100(1)). Bart will, however, be entitled to a credit for the tax paid by T Co (s 100(2)).

As F Co is a non-resident, T Co is assessed on so much of F Co's share of the net income as is attributable to Australian sources ($12,500) (s 98(2A)). T Co will pay tax on such income at the rate of 30%. F Co is also assessed on the $12,500 and will pay tax on this amount at the corporate tax rate (s 98A(1)). F Co will, however, be entitled to a credit for the tax paid by T Co (s 98A(2)).

Assuming no resolution was made in respect of the remaining one-quarter of the income of the trust estate, no beneficiary is presently entitled to such income. As the trust estate is a resident trust estate (since T Co is a resident company), T Co is assessed on the remaining share of the net income ($25,000) and will pay tax on this amount at the rate of 45% (plus ML) (s 99A).

[24.6] Revocable trusts and trusts for a settlor's children

Section 102 *ITAA36* applies where a person who has 'created a trust' (ie the settlor) has the power to revoke, or alter, the trust so as to acquire a beneficial interest in the income or property of the trust. The provision also applies where income of the trust is payable to or accumulated for, or applicable for the benefit of that person's children who are under 18 years of age.

Where s 102 applies, the Commissioner has the discretion to assess the trustee to pay tax equal to the amount by which the tax actually payable by the settlor is less than the tax which would have been payable if the settlor had also received so much of the net income of the trust estate as attributable to the income or property in which he or she has the power to acquire the beneficial interest, or which is payable to or accumulated for, or applicable for the benefit of, his or her children under 18 years of age.

It is important to be aware of the potential impact of s 102 when establishing family trusts. To avoid the operation of the section, family trusts are usually established by an independent settlor (eg a friend of the family). Typically, the trust deed will expressly provide that the settlor does not have the power to revoke or alter the trust, and that neither the settlor nor his or her children are entitled to benefit under the trust. In practice, the independent settlor usually settles only a nominal sum (eg $10) on trust for the benefit of the family. After the trust has been settled, it is common for the family members who are to benefit under the trust to then transfer money and property to the trust for investment by the trustee.

Truesdale v FC of T 70 ATC 4056 is authority for the principle that a person who transfers property to a trust which has already been established is not 'creating' a trust for the purposes of s 102 and will therefore not be caught under the provision. *Truesdale* concerned three trusts established for the unmarried infant children of Mr King. Each of the trusts had been settled by an accountant (employed by Mr King's company). Shortly after settlement, Mr King transferred money to the trustee in respect of each trust and this money was used to buy shares which generated dividends. The Commissioner sought to assess the trustee under s 102 but failed because the High Court found that all that Mr King had done was transfer property to a pre-existing trust. Menzies J stated (at 4059):

> There is an obvious difference between creating a trust in respect of property, on the one hand, and, on the other hand, transferring property to a trustee to hold upon the terms of an established trust.

[24.7] Flow-through nature of a trust and streaming

Flow-through nature of a trust

It is important to appreciate that a trust is merely a 'conduit' rather than a separate legal entity. A trust is therefore a 'flow-through vehicle' (like a partnership) as opposed to an 'opaque vehicle' (like a company).

A key consequence of the flow-through nature of a trust is that amounts that pass through a trust to the beneficiaries of the estate retain the same character in the hands of the beneficiaries as those amounts had in the hands of the estate. This means, for example, that interest, rent, dividends, foreign income or capital gains of a trust estate are also respectively treated as interest, rent, dividends, foreign income or capital gains of the beneficiaries who are entitled to those amounts. In other words, the amounts do not lose their underlying character merely because they pass through a trust.

The way trust distributions are treated differs markedly from the way corporate distributions are treated. Amounts derived by a company lose their underlying character when distributed to shareholders. A company that makes a capital gain will distribute its profits to its shareholders as 'dividends' rather than as a capital gain. The shareholders cannot, therefore, offset their capital losses against such distributions. Beneficiaries who receive the capital gains of a trust, on the other hand, will be able to offset their capital losses against those distributions.

Support for the principle that trusts operate as 'flow-through vehicles' can be found in observations made by the High Court in *Charles v FC of T* (1954) 90 CLR 598. The case concerned the character of distributions made to unit holders in a unit trust. Dixon CJ, Kitto and Taylor JJ drew a distinction between units in a trust and shares in a company, stating (at 609):

> a unit held under this trust deed is fundamentally different from a share in a company. A share confers upon the holder no legal or equitable interest in the assets of the company; it is a separate piece of property; and if a portion of the company's assets is distributed among the shareholders the question whether it comes to them as income or as capital depends upon whether the corpus of their property (their shares) remains intact despite the distribution: *Inland Revenue Commissioners v Reid's Trustees*. But a unit under the trust deed before us confers a proprietary interest in all the property which for the time being is subject to the trust deed: *Baker v Archer-Shee*; so that the question whether moneys distributed to unit holders under the trust form part of their income or of their capital must be answered by considering the character of those moneys in the hands of the trustees before the distribution is made.

Streaming

The flow-through nature of a trust has enabled trustees to 'stream' (ie 'channel') particular classes of income and capital amounts to specific beneficiaries. For streaming to occur, it must be permitted under the terms of the trust. Many discretionary family trust deeds expressly authorise streaming. Streaming is far less common under other kinds of trusts (eg unit trusts).

Where streaming is allowed, it has been common for trustees to allocate certain kinds of income and capital distributions to those beneficiaries who are most able to benefit from them from a tax perspective. In particular, it has been common for trustees to stream capital gains to beneficiaries with capital losses (so that they can utilise their losses) and to stream franked distributions to resident beneficiaries (so that they can benefit from the franking credits).

The ability to stream capital gains and franked distributions has been affected by the 2011 trust reforms. Under these reforms, streaming is now only effective for tax purposes where the beneficiary is 'specifically entitled' to an amount of the capital gain or franked distribution [24.8].

[24.8] The 2011 trust reforms

The 2011 trust reforms have resulted in major changes to the way trust estates are taxed. The reforms *only* apply to trust estates that have capital gains and/or franked distributions. In the past, capital gains and franked distributions of a trust estate were assessed in the hands of the beneficiaries or trustees of the estate under the basic rules in div 6 [24.5]. Under the reforms, there is now an intricate multi-step process involved in determining how such amounts are taxed (div 6 is now only the starting point in this process).

Object of the reforms

The main object of the reforms is to take capital gains and franked distributions (including franking credits) out of the general assessment process in div 6 and instead account for capital gains under sub-div 115-C *ITAA97* and franked distributions under sub-div 207-B *ITAA97*. The rules broadly work as follows:

- capital gains and franked distributions to which a beneficiary is 'specifically entitled' are assessed on a 'quantum basis' in the beneficiary's hands, and
- capital gains and franked distributions to which no beneficiaries are 'specifically entitled' are assessed on a 'proportional basis' in the hands of:
  - the beneficiaries based on their share of the adjusted 'income of the trust estate', or
  - the trustees to the extent that there is adjusted 'income of the trust estate' to which no beneficiaries are presently entitled.

Assessing net income of a trust estate that has capital gains and franked distributions

Under the 2011 trust reforms, there are a number of complex steps involved in assessing the net income of a trust estate that has capital gains and franked distributions. These steps are outlined below and summerised in the diagram on page 704.

- **Step 1.** The first step is to apply the basic assessment rules in div 6.
- **Step 2.** The second step is to calculate the beneficiaries' and trustees' 'adjusted div 6 percentage'. This concept is used to allocate capital gains and franked distributions to the beneficiaries and trustees under Steps 3 and 4. According to s 95(1):
  - a beneficiary's 'adjusted div 6 percentage' is the beneficiary's share of the income of a trust estate to which the beneficiary is presently entitled (the beneficiary's 'div 6 percentage') calculated on the assumption that the amount of any capital gain or franked distribution to which any beneficiary or trustee is specifically entitled were disregarded in working out the income of the trust estate, and

- a trustee's 'adjusted div 6 percentage' is the share of the income of the trust estate to which no beneficiary is presently entitled (the trustee's 'div 6 percentage') calculated on the assumption that the amount of any capital gain or franked distribution to which any beneficiary or trustee is specifically entitled were disregarded in working out the income of the trust estate.

If the income of the trust estate is nil, a beneficiary is deemed to have a 'div 6 percentage' of 0% and the trustee is deemed to have a 'div 6 percentage' of 100%.

- **Step 3.** The third step is to apply sub-div 115-C to the capital gains of the trust estate. Subdivision 115-C allocates capital gains to beneficiaries and trustees based on their 'share' of the capital gains. An entity's 'share' of a capital gain is calculated under s 115-227 as the sum of:
  - the amount of the capital gain to which the entity is 'specifically entitled' (see below), and
  - the amount of the capital gain to which *no one* is 'specifically entitled' multiplied by the entity's 'div 6 percentage' of the income of the trust estate.

  The beneficiary's share of the capital gain is then divided by the total capital gain, which gives their 'fraction' of the capital gain. This fraction is then multiplied by the net income of the trust estate that relates to the capital gain to arrive at the 'attributable gain'. This amount must then be grossed-up for any 50% CGT discount concession [17.8] and/or 50% small business reduction concession [17.9] that has been used to calculate the trust estate's net capital gain. Where none of the concessions apply, there is no gross-up. Where only one of the concessions applies, it must be doubled. Where both concessions apply, the attributable capital gain must be quadrupled (ss 115-215, 115-220, 115-222, 115-225). The gross-up ensures that in calculating their individual net capital gains under s 102-5 [17.2], beneficiaries can apply their personal capital losses and net capital losses against the grossed-up capital gain. An eligible beneficiary (eg an individual) is then entitled to reduce any remaining capital gains by the relevant concessions.

- **Step 4.** The fourth step is to apply sub-div 207-B to the franked distributions of the trust estate. Subdivision 207-B allocates franked distributions between the beneficiaries and trustees of the estate based on the entity's 'share' of the franked distribution, which is calculated under complex rules in s 207-55. In simple terms, a beneficiary's share of a franked distribution is the sum of:
  - the amount of the franked distribution to which the beneficiary is 'specifically entitled', and
  - the amount of the franked distribution to which *no one* is 'specifically entitled' multiplied by the beneficiary's 'div 6 percentage' of the income of the trust estate.

  An entity's share of the franked distribution is then divided by the total franked distribution, which gives their 'fraction' of the franked distribution. This fraction is then multiplied by the amount of the net franked distribution (ie the franked distribution after taking into account deductions that are directly attributable to it) to arrive at the 'attributable franked distribution' (s 207-37). This amount is included in the entity's assessable income (s 207-35(4)(b)(ii)). The entity is also generally assessed on their 'share of the franking credit' (s 207-35(4)(b)(i)) and entitled to a tax offset for their share of the franking credit (s 207-45). Special adjustments ensure that entities are not assessed on their share of franked distributions which are exempt income or non-assessable non-exempt income and that there is no gross-up or tax offset available for their share of the franking credit in such cases (ss 207-90, 207-95). An entity's 'share of the franking credit' is calculated under the following formula in s 207-57:

$$\begin{array}{c}\text{Amount of the franking credit}\\\text{on the franked distribution}\end{array} \times \frac{\text{Entity's share of the franked distribution}}{\text{Amount of the franked distribution}}$$

- **Step 5.** The fifth step is to adjust the amounts otherwise assessable to the beneficiaries and trustees under the basic rules in div 6. This is done pursuant to modifications contained in div 6E of pt III *ITAA36*. The modifications are designed to ensure that the div 6 assessable amounts are calculated as if the trust estate had no capital gains or franked distributions. More specifically, s 102UX provides that the amounts that are assessable under ss 97, 98, 98A, 99, 99A, and 100 must be calculated on the assumptions that:
  - the div 6 'income of the trust estate' is equal to the 'div 6E income' (ie the income of the trust estate calculated ignoring capital gains, franked distributions and franking credits: s 12UY)
  - the div 6 'net income of the trust estate' is equal to the 'div 6E net income' (ie the net income of the trust estate calculated ignoring capital gains, franked distributions and franking credits: s 102UY), and
  - the amount of a beneficiary's present entitlement to the income of the trust estate is equal to the beneficiary's 'div 6E present entitlement to the income of the trust estate' (ie the beneficiary's present entitlement to the income of the trust estate reduced by the beneficiary's 'share' of any capital gains, franked distributions and franking credits: s 102UY).

  The obvious purpose of the div 6E adjustments is to prevent div 6 overlapping with sub-div 115-C and 207-B and giving rise to double taxation.
- **Step 6.** The sixth step is to determine the final combined result of applying the rules in div 6, sub-div 115-C, sub-div 207-B and div 6E.

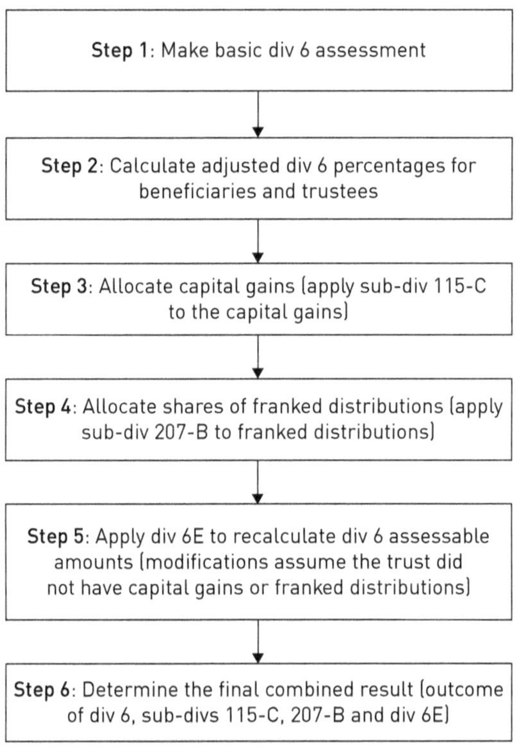

Specific entitlement to an amount of a capital gain or franked distribution

In order to apply steps 3 and 4 above, it is necessary to determine the amount of a capital gain or franked distribution to which a beneficiary is 'specifically entitled', as this is relevant in calculating their share of the capital gain or franked distribution.

The amount of a capital gain made by a trust estate to which a beneficiary is specifically entitled is calculated under the following formula in s 115-228:

$$\text{Capital gain} \times \frac{\text{Share of net financial benefit}}{\text{Net financial benefit}}$$

The amount of a franked distribution made by a trust estate to which a beneficiary is specifically entitled is calculated under the following formula in s 207-58:

$$\text{Franked distribution} \times \frac{\text{Share of net financial benefit}}{\text{Net financial benefit}}$$

The terms used in the above formulas have the following meanings:

- 'Net financial benefit' means:
  - in the case of a capital gain—an amount equal to the financial benefit that is referable to the capital gain (after any application by the trustee of losses, to the extent that the application is consistent with the application of capital losses against the capital gain in accordance with s 102-5(1)), and
  - in the case of franked distributions—an amount equal to the financial benefit that is referable to the franked distribution (after any application by the trustee of expenses that are directly relevant to the franked distribution).
- 'Share of net financial benefit' means:
  - in the case of a capital gain—an amount equal to the financial benefit that, in accordance with the terms of the trust:
    (a) the beneficiary has received, or can be reasonably expected to receive
    (b) is referable to the capital gain (after application by the trustee of losses as set out above)
    (c) is recorded, in its character as referable to the capital gain, in the accounts or records of the trust no later than two months after the end of the income year, and
  - in the case of a franked distribution—an amount equal to the financial benefit that, in accordance with the terms of the trust:
    (a) the beneficiary has received, or can be reasonably expected to receive
    (b) is referable to the franked distribution (after any application by the trustee of expenses that are directly relevant to the franked distribution)
    (c) is recorded, in its character as referable to the franked distribution, in the accounts or records of the trust no later than the end of the income year.

A 'financial benefit' is anything of economic value (s 974-160).

In summary, the formulas ensure that beneficiaries are only specifically entitled to a share of a capital gain or a franked distribution of a trust estate where they receive, or can reasonably be expected to receive, an amount equal to their share of the net financial benefit referable to the capital gain or franked distribution (after taking into account relevant losses and expenses) and the entitlement is recorded in its character in the accounts or records of the trust.

It should be noted that only beneficiaries can normally be specifically entitled to a capital gain or franked distribution. A trustee of a resident trust estate can, nevertheless, choose to be specifically entitled to a capital gain under s 115-230 if no trust property representing the capital gain has been paid or applied for the benefit of a beneficiary.

Example of the 2011 trust reforms

The following example illustrates the way the 2011 trust reforms operate. The figures used in the example are modelled on the figures used in the example at 2.27 in the Explanatory Memorandum accompanying the Bill that introduced the reforms. The example has, nevertheless, been modified and expanded to explain certain key points and link it to the preceding discussion in this chapter.

Example T Co is a resident company that acts as the trustee of the Alphabet Family Discretionary Trust ('AFDT'). The AFDT has four beneficiaries (who are all residents and not under any legal disability):

- Andy Alphabet
- Brandy Alphabet
- Candy Alphabet, and
- Dandy Alphabet.

T Co has the power under the deed to make distributions of both income and capital to the beneficiaries. The AFDT deed does not define the term 'income' (this term has its ordinary meaning).

During the 2022/23 income year, the following amounts were derived by the AFDT:

- Rental income of $100,000.
- A dividend from Company X of $70,000 (with $30,000 franking credits allocated to the dividend). The trust has $50,000 of deductible borrowing expenses that are directly related to the dividend.
- A dividend from Company Y of $70,000 (with $30,000 franking credits allocated to the dividend). The trust has no expenses directly related to the dividend.
- A capital gain of $200,000 on Asset A (that is eligible for the 50% CGT discount).
- A capital gain of $100,000 on Asset B (that is not eligible for the 50% CGT discount).

The trust also has a net capital loss of $50,000 carried forward from the previous year.

Net income of the trust estate under s 95

In calculating the net income of the trust estate under s 95, T Co chooses to set off the $50,000 net capital loss against the $100,000 capital gain on Asset B (ie the asset that is not eligible for the 50% CGT discount). On this basis, the net income of the trust estate is $400,000, calculated as follows:

Description	Amount
Rental income	$100,000
Franked dividend from Company X	$70,000
Franking credit	$30,000
Franked dividend from Company Y	$70,000
Franking credit	$30,000
Capital gain from Asset A ($200,000 × 50% discount)	$100,000
Capital gain from Asset B ($100,000 – $50,000 net capital loss)	$50,000
Deductible expenses (relating to the Company X dividend)	($50,000)
Net income under s 95	$400,000

Division 6E net income under s 102UY

The 'div 6E net income' of the trust estate calculated under s 102UY is $100,000. Only the rental income is included in the calculation as capital gains, franked dividends and franking credits must be ignored.

Income of the trust estate

As the AFDT deed does not define the term 'income', this term has its ordinary meaning and will therefore not include capital gains or franking credits. On this basis, the income of the trust estate is $190,000, calculated as follows:

Description	Amount
Rental income	$100,000
Net franked dividend from Company X ($70,0000 – $50,000)	$20,000
Franked dividend from Company Y	$70,000
Income of the trust estate (ie distributable income)	$190,000

Distributions to beneficiaries

Pursuant to its powers under the deed, T Co resolves to distribute the income of the trust estate as follows:

- Andy: $50,000 of income and $100,000 capital distribution (specified to be attributable to the discount capital gain of $200,000 on Asset A).
- Brandy: $50,000 capital distribution (specified to be attributable to the non-discount capital gain of $100,000 on Asset B [Note: the other $50,000 is retained to replenish the loss of trust corpus attributable to the previous year's capital loss]).
- Candy: $20,000 of income (specified to be attributable to the net franked dividend from Company X).
- Dandy: the balance of distributable income (ie $120,000 = $190,000 – $50,000 – $20,000).

Steps involved in assessing the beneficiaries

The steps involved in working out how the beneficiaries are assessed are outlined below.

Step 1: Apply the basic rules in div 6 (without taking into account div 6E)

Under div 6 (ignoring div 6E), the beneficiaries would be assessed pursuant to s 97 on their share of the 'net income' of the trust estate based on their share (ie div 6 percentage) of the 'income' of the trust estate as follows:

Beneficiary	Present entitlement to income	Div 6 percentage	Section 97 share of net income
Andy	$50,000	26.3% ($50,000/$190,000)	$105,263
Brandy	$0	0% ($0/$190,000)	Nil
Candy	$20,000	10.5% ($20,000/$190,000)	$42,105
Dandy	$120,000	63.2% ($120,000/$190,000)	$252,632
Total	$190,000	100%	$400,000

Step 2: Calculate each beneficiary's 'adjusted div 6 percentage'

A beneficiary's 'adjusted div 6 percentage' is the share of the income of a trust estate to which the beneficiary is presently entitled (calculated on the assumption that it excludes capital gains and franked distributions to which *any* beneficiary or trustee of the trust estate is specifically entitled) (s 95(1)).

As the income of the trust estate is $190,000 and as Candy is specifically entitled to the $20,000 net franked dividend from Company X, the 'adjusted income' of the trust estate used to work out each beneficiary's adjusted div 6 percentage is $170,000 (ie $190,000 – $20,000).

Beneficiary	Present entitlement to 'adjusted income' of the trust estate	Adjusted div 6 percentage
Andy	$50,000	29.4%
Brandy	Nil	Nil
Candy	Nil	Nil
Dandy	$120,000	70.6%
Total	$170,000	100%

Step 3: Apply sub-div 115-C to the capital gains
Subdivision 115-C allocates capital gains to beneficiaries based on their 'specific entitlement' and their 'adjusted div 6 percentage' of the 'adjusted income' of the trust estate.

The following table shows that Andy and Dandy share in the $200,000 discount capital gain on Asset A as they are both entitled to share in the capital distribution relating to that asset. Brandy is exclusively entitled to the $100,000 non-discountable capital gain on Asset B (as she is specifically entitled to all of the capital distribution relating to that asset after taking into account the net capital loss). She is not entitled to any of the capital distribution relating to Asset A. Candy does not share in any capital distribution relating to either Asset A or Asset B.

Concept (provision)	Andy	Brandy	Candy	Dandy
Specific entitlement (s 115-227(a))	$100,000	$100,000	N/A	Nil
Adjusted div 6 percentage share (s 115-227(b))	$ 29,400	Nil	N/A	$70,600
Share of capital gain (amount) (s 115-227)	$129,400	$100,000	N/A	$70,600
Total capital gain in which beneficiary entitled to share (before any reductions under steps 1 to 4 of the s 102-5 method statement)	$200,000	$100,000	N/A	$200,000
Total capital gain reduced by steps 1 to 4 of the s 102-5 method statement (ie after taking into account any losses, 50% CGT discount and 50% small business concession) (s 115-225(1)(a))	$100,000	$50,000	N/A	$100,000
Fraction of the capital gain (s 115-225(1)(b))	64.7%	100%	N/A	35.3%
Attributable gain (s 115-225(1))	$64,700	$50,000	N/A	$35,300
Is the beneficiary required to gross-up the capital gain? (s 115-215(3))	Yes	No	N/A	Yes
Extra capital gain (s 115-215(3))	$129,400	$50,000	N/A	$70,600

Step 4: Apply sub-div 207-B to the franked distributions
Subdivision 207-B allocates franked distributions to beneficiaries based on their 'specific entitlement' and their 'adjusted div 6 percentage' of the adjusted income of the trust estate.

The following table shows that Andy and Dandy share in the $70,000 Company Y franked dividend. Candy is exclusively entitled to the $70,000 Company X franked dividend (which, after taking into account directly related deductible expenses, comes to $20,000). Brandy does not share in any franked dividends.

Concept (provision)	Andy	Brandy	Candy	Dandy
Specific entitlement (s 207-55(4)(a))	Nil	N/A	$ 70,000	Nil
Adjusted div 6 percentage share (s 207-55(4)(b))	$20,580	N/A	Nil	$49,420
Share of franked dividend (amount) (s 207-55 table)	$20,580	N/A	$70,000	$49,420
Fraction of the dividend (s 207-37(1)(b))	29.4%	N/A	100%	70.6%
Amount of net franked dividend (ie franked dividend less deductions directly attributable to it) (s 207-37(1)(a))	$70,000	N/A	$20,000	$70,000
Franking credit included in assessable income (s 207-35(4)(b)(i))	$8,820	N/A	$30,000	$21,180
Franked dividend included in assessable income (s 207-35(4)(b)(ii))	$20,580	N/A	$20,000	$49,420

Step 5: Apply div 6E to recalculate the assessable amounts under div 6

The beneficiaries' assessable amounts under s 97 (calculated under Step 1) are adjusted by the operation of div 6E, which requires the 'div 6E income' of the trust estate, the 'div 6E net income' of the trust estate and the beneficiaries' 'div 6E present entitlement to the income of the trust estate' to be determined under s 102UY.

The 'div 6E income of the trust estate' and the 'div 6E net income of the trust estate' are respectively the 'income of the trust estate' and the 'net income of the trust estate' calculated on the basis that capital gains, franked distributions and franking credits are ignored. On this basis:

- The 'div 6E income' of the trust estate is therefore $100,000 (ie $190,000 – [$70,000 + $20,000]). The div 6E income does not include the amounts included in the income of the trust estate that are attributable to the net franked dividends.
- The 'div 6E net income' is also $100,000 (ie $400,000 – [$100,000 + $50,000 + $70,000 + $20,000 + $30,000 + $30,000]). The div 6E net income does not include the amounts included in the net income of the trust estate that are attributable to the capital gains, franked dividends and franking credits.

A beneficiary's 'div 6E present entitlement to the income of the trust estate' is their present entitlement to the income of the trust estate reduced by the beneficiary's 'share' of any capital gains, franked distributions and franking credits. On this basis:

- Andy's 'div 6E present entitlement to the income of the trust estate' is $29,420, being his present entitlement to income of the trust estate ($50,000) minus his share of the franked dividends ($20,580). His share of the capital gain of the trust is not part of trust income and therefore not part of the calculation.
- Brandy and Candy do not have any 'div 6E present entitlement to the income of the trust estate' as they are only entitled to capital gains and franked distributions respectively.
- Dandy's 'div 6E present entitlement to the income of the trust estate' is $70,580. This is her present entitlement to trust income ($120,000) minus her share of franked dividends ($49,420).

After applying div 6E, the adjusted amounts assessable to the beneficiaries under div 6 are as follows:

Beneficiary	Div 6E present entitlement to income of trust estate	Share of div 6E income	Section 97 assessable income
Andy	$29,420	29.42% ($29,420/$100,000)	$29,420
Brandy	Nil	Nil	Nil
Candy	Nil	Nil	Nil
Dandy	$70,580	70.58% ($70,580/$100,000)	$70,580
Total	$100,000		$100,000

Step 6: Determine the final combined result after applying div 6, sub-divs 115-C, 207-B and div 6E

The table below assumes for simplicity that beneficiaries have no individual capital gains or capital losses and are eligible for the franking credits. The total amount received by the beneficiaries from the trust is $340,000 (ie the trust income of $190,000 plus $150,000 of capital contributions to Andy and Brandy).

Concept (provision)	Andy	Brandy	Candy	Dandy	Total
Section 97 assessable income	$29,420	Nil	Nil	$70,580	$100,000
Section 102-5 net capital gain (this assumes beneficiaries have no individual capital losses or net capital losses to offset against the capital gain and that they have claimed the 50% CGT discount in respect of any discount capital gains)	$64,700	$50,000	Nil	$35,300	$150,000
Section 207-37(1)(a) franked dividend	$20,580	Nil	$20,000	$49,420	$90,000
Section 207-35(4)(b)(i) franking credit	$8,820	Nil	$30,000	$21,180	$60,000
Total assessable income	$123,520	$50,000	$50,000	$176,480	$400,000
Amount received from trust	$150,000	$50,000	$20,000	$120,000	$340,000

[24.9] Trust losses

Trust losses cannot be distributed to the beneficiaries of a trust estate like trust income. Instead, such losses may be carried forward by a trust estate and utilised as deductions in future years provided the relevant carry forward tests in sch 2F *ITAA36* (ss 265-5 to 272-140) are satisfied. The tests are complex and differ depending on the nature of the trust. They also operate subject to special anti-avoidance rules (eg relating to 'income injection schemes').

A trust will satisfy the carry forward loss requirements if it satisfies a '50% stake test' ('family trusts' do not need to satisfy this test). A 'listed widely held trust' that fails the 50% stake test can carry forward its loss if it satisfies a business continuity test ('BCT'). A 'non-fixed trust' that fails the test can carry forward its loss if it satisfies a 'pattern of distributions' or 'control' test.

All trusts—the '50% stake test'

A trust can carry forward its losses if it satisfies a '50% stake test' in sub-div 269-C. The 50% stake test has similarities to the COT applicable to companies [22.22]. Essentially, the test is satisfied if, at all relevant times during the test period:

(a) the same individuals have fixed entitlements, directly or indirectly, to more than 50% of the income of the trust, and

(b) the same individuals have fixed entitlements, directly or indirectly, to more than 50% of the capital of the trust (these individuals need not be the same as those in para (a)).

Example A fixed trust (that is not a family trust) has a loss from Year 1 that it seeks to deduct in Year 2. Throughout Year 1 and part of Year 2:

- John and Lee each have a 50% fixed entitlement to income and a 30% fixed entitlement to capital, and
- Otto and Jenny each have a 20% fixed entitlement to capital.

During Year 2, both John and Lee sold 60% of their fixed entitlements in the trust to Fred. As a result, from the time of the sale, John's and Lee's fixed entitlements to income and capital are each reduced to 20% and 12% respectively, while Fred has a 60% fixed entitlement to income and a 36% fixed entitlement to capital. Before the sale, John, Lee, Otto and Jenny have, between them, 100% of the fixed entitlements to income and capital. After the sale, they have, between them, a fixed entitlement to income of 40% and a fixed entitlement to capital of 64%.

As the original owners of more than 50% of the fixed entitlements have not held more than 50% of the fixed entitlements to income of the trust throughout the test period, the trust fails the 50% stake test and the loss is not deductible.

Family trusts—'family trust election'

Family trusts do not need to satisfy the 50% stake test. A trust is classified as a family trust if a 'family trust election' is in force in respect of the trust (s 272-75). A family trust election is required to be made by the trustee in writing in the approved form and applies from the beginning of the income year specified in the election (s 272-80). The election must nominate an individual (also known as the 'primary individual') whose 'family group' is the subject of the election.

A family trust election can only be made if the trust passes the 'family control test' in s 272-87 at the end of the specified income year. This test is satisfied if the primary individual and/or members of their family are able to control the application of the income and capital of the trust or meet certain other control requirements.

A family group is defined in s 272-90 to include:

- members of the primary individual's family (ie the primary individual's spouse, child, parent, grandparent, brother, sister, nephew or niece, or a lineal descendant of the primary individual's or their spouse's child, nephew or niece: s 272-95)
- a person who was a spouse of the primary individual or a member of their family before a marriage or relationship breakdown
- the trust covered by the family trust election or a trust that has the same primary individual specified in its family trust election
- a company, partnership or trust in which family members and/or family trusts of those persons have fixed entitlements, directly or indirectly, to all of the income and capital of the company, partnership and trust, and
- a company, partnership or trust that has made an 'interposed entity election' under s 272-85 to be included in the family group.

If the trustee of a family trust, or a company, partnership or trust that has made an interposed entity election, distributes income or capital to someone other than the primary individual or a member of their family group, they will be liable to pay 'family trust distribution tax' on the distribution (ss 271-15, 271-20). Family trust distribution tax is imposed under the *Family Trust Distribution Tax (Primary Liability) Act 1998* (Cth) at the rate of 47%.

> ***Example*** W Co is the trustee of the White family trust. In the 2015/16 income year, W Co made a family trust election and named Will White as the primary individual for the purposes of the election. If the trust made a loss in the 2022/23 income year, it does not need to satisfy the 50% stake test to carry forward the loss. The loss can be set off against its assessable income in the 2023/24 income year.
>
> If W Co distributes income or capital to anyone who is not a member of the Will White family group, it will be required to pay family trust distribution tax. Accordingly, if in the 2023/24 income year, Will's wife is presently entitled to all of the income of the trust estate other than an amount of \$10,000 which is distributed to Bruce Black (who is not a member of the Will White family group), W Co will be liable to pay family trust distribution tax of \$4,700 (ie \$10,000 × 47%).

Listed widely held trusts—'business continuity test'

A 'listed widely held trust' is defined as a widely held trust whose units are listed on an approved stock exchange (s 272-115). A listed widely held trust that fails the 50% stake test can carry forward its losses if it passes the BCT in sub-div 269-F. Like the BCT for companies [22.22], sub-div 269-F contains the same business requirement (s 269-100) and a similar business requirement (s 269-105). If a listed widely held trust meets either one of these requirements, it passes the BCT.

Non-fixed trusts—'pattern of distributions' or 'control' test

A 'non-fixed trust' (defined in s 272-70) that fails the 50% stake test can carry forward its losses if it satisfies a 'pattern of distributions' or 'control' test.

The 'pattern of distributions test' is contained in sub-div 269-D. It is satisfied if, within two months of the end of the income year:

- the trust has distributed, directly or indirectly, more than 50% of every 'test year distribution' of income to the same individuals for their own benefit (ie otherwise than as trustee), and
- the trust has distributed, directly or indirectly, more than 50% of every 'test year distribution' of capital to the same individuals for their own benefit (those individuals need not be the same as those to whom income is distributed).

The 'control test' is contained in sub-div 269-E. It requires that no group (ie a person and their associates, whether alone or together) begin to control the non-fixed trust, whether directly or indirectly, in the test period. A group is taken to control a non-fixed trust if:

- the group has the power to obtain the benefit of the income or capital of the trust
- the group is able to control the application of the income or capital of the trust
- the trustee is accustomed to act in accordance with the directions or wishes of the group
- the group is able to remove or appoint the trustee or any of the trustees, or
- the group acquires more than a 50% stake in the income or capital of the trust.

Income injection schemes

Division 270 contains a special anti-avoidance rule that prevents trusts from carrying forward tax losses where they are involved in certain kinds of 'income injection schemes'. These schemes involve income being injected into trusts with deductions (eg from tax losses) so that the tax payable on the income is reduced or eliminated. According to s 270-10, the division applies where:

- a deduction is allowable to a trust for the income year
- there is a scheme under which:
  - the trust derives assessable income
  - an 'outsider to the trust' (defined in s 270-25) directly or indirectly provides a 'benefit' (defined in s 270-20) to the trustee or a beneficiary (or their associates), and
  - the trustee or beneficiary (or their associates) directly or indirectly provides a benefit to the outsider (or to an associate of the outsider)
- it is reasonable to conclude that the assessable income has been derived, or the benefits have been provided, wholly or partly (but not merely incidentally) because the deduction would be allowable, and
- the trust is not a specified kind of 'excepted trust' (eg a complying superannuation fund) (s 270-10).

Division 270 does not apply to family trusts where benefits are provided only to one or more members of the family group (this includes interposed entities that have made an 'interposed entity election' to be included in the family group).

If the requirements of s 270-10 are satisfied, no deduction is allowable in the income year against the scheme's assessable income.

Example A, B and C are a group of individuals who control and benefit from two separate discretionary trusts:

- a Loss Trust that made a $500,000 loss in a previous income year, and
- an Income Trust that made $500,000 of income in the current income year.

The Loss Trust is also a beneficiary of the Income Trust. In the current income year, the trustee of the Income Trust exercises its discretion to allocate the net income of the Income Trust to the Loss Trust in exchange for an amount of $500,000 being lent back as a low-interest loan from the Loss Trust to the Income Trust.

Division 270 is likely to apply to this scheme, unless the trusts made family trust and interposed entity elections.

[24.10] QUESTIONS

1. What is the nature of a trust? Explain the differences between a 'discretionary trust' and a 'fixed trust'.
2. Outline the basic legislative scheme for taxing trust estates. How is the net income of a trust estate calculated? Discuss the difference between the 'tax law' and 'trust law' income of a trust estate and the meanings of the terms 'legal disability', 'present entitlement' and 'resident trust estate'. Why are these concepts important?
3. Contrast *Dwight v FC of T* 92 ATC 4192 and *Harmer & Ors v FC of T* 91 ATC 5000.
4. Minnow Co is a resident company that is trustee of a discretionary trust. During the 2022/23 income year, the trust estate derived $100,000 of interest income from Australian sources and $100,000 of rental income from foreign sources. On 30 June 2023, the directors of the company resolved to distribute one-fifth of the income of the trust estate to each of: Ginger (a 30-year-old

Australian resident), Thurston (a 90-year-old foreign resident), Mary-Anne (a 16-year-old Australian resident), and F Co (a company resident in Fiji). No resolution was made in respect of the balance income. How is the net income of the trust estate taxed?

5. In what circumstances does s 102 *ITAA36* apply? Why did it not apply in *Truesdale v FC of T* 70 ATC 4056?
6. Why were the 2011 trust reforms introduced, and how do they affect the operation of div 6 *ITAA36*?
7. X Co is a resident company that is the trustee of the Blogs family discretionary trust. During the 2022/23 income year, the trust estate derived rent of $30,000 from an investment property. It also derived a dividend of $70,000 (with $30,000 of franking credits allocated to it) and made a net capital gain of $50,000 from selling a property that it had purchased 10 years ago. Under the terms of the trust deed, X Co has the power to distribute the income and capital of the trust estate to members of the Blogs family. The trust deed does not define the term income and does not contain a clause which states that the trustee can treat capital gains as income. On 30 June 2023, the directors of X Co resolved to make a capital distribution of all the gain on the sale of the property to Johnny Blogs, who is a 30-year-old Australian resident. X Co also resolved to distribute 40% of the income of the trust estate for the 2022/23 income year to Xavier Blogs, who is a 25-year-old Australian resident. X Co resolved to distribute the balance 60% of the income of the trust estate for the 2022/23 income year to Penny Blogs, who is a 12-year-old Australian resident. How is the net income of trust estate taxed?
8. Can trust losses be distributed to the beneficiaries of a trust estate? What restrictions are placed on the use of trust losses?

SPECIAL ENTITIES 25

[25.1] Introduction

The tax law contains a number of special regimes that apply to certain kinds of entities. This chapter outlines the special rules relating to:

- primary producers [25.2]
- special professionals [25.3]
- minors [25.4]
- life insurance companies [25.5]
- co-operative companies [25.6]
- listed investment companies [25.7]
- corporate limited partnerships [25.8]
- public trading trusts [25.9]
- managed investment trusts [25.10]
- corporate collective investment vehicles [25.11]
- foreign hybrids [25.12], and
- offshore banking units [25.13].

[25.2] Primary producers

Special tax concessions are available to entities that carry on a 'primary production business'. These entities are often referred to as 'primary producers' and include persons such as farmers.

Primary production business

According to s 995-1 *ITAA97*, an entity carries on a primary production business if it carries on the business of:

(a) cultivating or propagating plants, fungi or their products or parts (including seeds, spores, bulbs and similar things), in any physical environment
(b) maintaining animals for the purpose of selling them or their bodily produce (including natural increase)
(c) manufacturing dairy produce from raw material produced by the entity
(d) conducting operations relating directly to taking or catching fish, turtles, dugong, bêche-de-mer, crustaceans or aquatic molluscs
(e) conducting operations relating directly to taking or culturing pearls or pearl shell
(f) planting or tending trees in a plantation or forest that are intended to be felled
(g) felling trees in a plantation or forest, or
(h) transporting trees, or parts of trees, felled in a plantation or forest to the place where they are first to be milled or processed, or from which they are to be transported to the place where they are first to be milled or processed.

Averaging of tax liability

Individuals who carry on primary production businesses can 'average' their taxable income over periods of up to five years under special rules contained in div 392 *ITAA97*. The broad object of these rules is to ensure that individuals who are primary producers and who have fluctuating levels of taxable income from year to year pay similar amounts of tax to those persons who have the same overall amount of taxable income for the identical period, but who have earned their taxable income on a steady basis over the relevant years. The averaging concession recognises that primary producers may experience radically different 'good' and 'bad' income years due to seasonal and market variations. In good years, their taxable income may be pushed into higher marginal tax brackets. This has a 'bunching effect' in these years and produces an overall higher tax liability for such taxpayers.

To even out an individual primary producer's tax liability, div 392 requires 'averaging adjustments' to be made. These adjustments apply if the tax that would be payable on the 'averaging component' of the primary producer's 'basic taxable income' for an income year at the 'comparison rate' is more or less than the tax that would be payable at 'basic rates'. In simple terms, the adjustments result in primary producers being entitled to tax offsets (in their above-average years of income) or being liable for extra income tax (in their below-average years of income) (s 392-35).

Primary producers can choose to withdraw from the averaging system, in which case the ordinary tax rules will apply (s 392-25). Where such a choice is made, the primary producer must wait 10 years before they can reaccess averaging.

Farm Management Deposit scheme

The Farm Management Deposit ('FMD') scheme, contained in div 393 *ITAA97*, has been established to assist primary producers manage the risks associated with earning uneven amounts of income from year to year. The broad object of the scheme is to encourage such persons to save money in profitable years, which they can then access in unprofitable years.

The FMD scheme allows eligible individual primary producers to establish FMD accounts with banks and certain other financial institutions. Individuals that make deposits to these accounts are entitled to deductions for the deposits in the year in which they are made (s 393-5). The deposits must be at least $1,000 and must total no more than $800,000 (s 393-35).

To be eligible for deductions, the individual must be carrying on a primary production business in Australia during the year and must not have 'taxable non-primary production income' for the year of more than $100,000. Deductions cannot exceed the individual's 'taxable primary production income' for the year. Any part of a deposit that has been repaid within 12 months is generally not deductible (s 393-40).

When deposits are subsequently withdrawn, the amount of the deduction previously allowed is generally included in the primary producer's assessable income (s 393-10).

Example Jock is a primary producer who has taxable primary production income of $50,000 and taxable non-primary production income of $60,000 in Year 1. Jock has a FMD account with a bank and deposits $10,000 in the account in Year 1. He is entitled to claim a deduction for the amount of the deposit in Year 1. In Year 4, Jock withdraws the deposit. The amount is included in his assessable income in Year 4.

Special capital write-offs

Primary producers are also entitled to special capital write-offs under sub-divs 40-F and 40-G *ITAA97* [15.5].

[25.3] Special professionals

Taxpayers engaged in certain professions may, like primary producers [25.2], also experience significant fluctuations in their taxable incomes from year to year. Division 405 *ITAA97* contains 'averaging rules' designed to lessen the impact of these fluctuations on 'special professionals'. Special professionals are individuals who are authors of literary, dramatic, musical or artistic works, inventors, performing artists, production associates, or sportspersons (s 405-25).

Special tax rates

Special professionals who have 'above-average special professional income' during an income year calculate the tax payable on their taxable income according to a rate worked out under a special formula set out in the *ITRA*. The effect of this formula is that the amount of tax payable by a special professional on the top four-fifths of their 'above-average special professional income' is effectively four times what they would have to pay on the bottom fifth of that income at basic income tax rates. This is illustrated in the diagram contained in s 405-5(2):

Income tax treatment of above-average special professional income

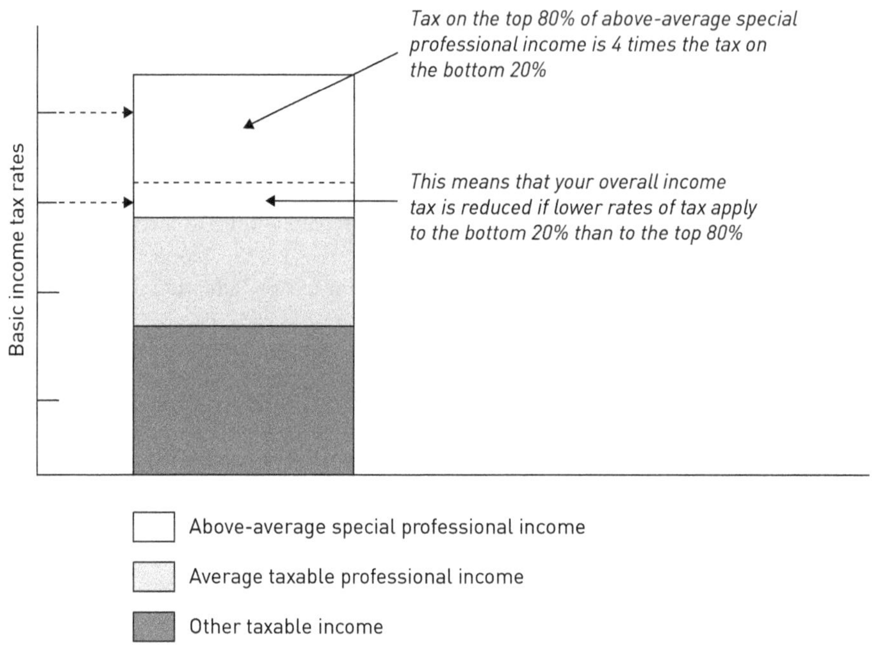

Above-average special professional income

An individual has 'above-average special professional income' during an income year if they have been resident in Australia for all or part of the year and their 'taxable professional income' for the year exceeds their 'average taxable professional income' for the year (s 405-15).

Taxable professional income

A person's taxable professional income for an income year is the amount by which their 'assessable professional income' for the year exceeds their deductions for that year worked out under s 405-45.

A person's assessable professional income consists of:

- assessable income derived as a reward for services or as prizes for their activities as a special professional
- assessable income derived from endorsements and promotions received because they were a special professional
- assessable income derived as consideration for assigning, licensing or granting rights in relation to the copyright in a literary, dramatic, musical or artistic work or a patent for an invention, and
- assessable income derived (as royalties or otherwise) for literary, dramatic, musical or artistic work or for an invention (s 405-20).

Average taxable professional income

A person's average taxable professional income for a year is worked out by dividing their taxable professional income for the preceding four income years by four (s 405-50). Phase-in rules apply where a person has been a special professional for less than four years.

Example Roger is a professional tennis player. During 2022/23, he derived $40,000 in prizes from tennis competitions and $10,000 in endorsements for advertising a sponsor's tennis racquet. He also worked part-time as a waiter and earned $20,000. Roger's taxable income for 2022/23 is $70,000. This amount includes 'taxable professional income' of $50,000.

Roger's taxable professional income over the previous four years was: $20,000 (2021/22), $30,000 (2020/21), $40,000 (2019/20) and $50,000 (2018/19). His 'average taxable professional income' for 2022/23 is therefore $35,000 (ie $140,000/4). His 'above-average professional income' for 2022/23 is calculated as follows:

$$\text{Above-average special professional income} = \text{Taxable professional income} - \text{Average taxable processional income}$$

$$\$15{,}000 = \$50{,}000 - \$35{,}000$$

Calculation of tax payable

The formula used for calculating the rate of tax payable on the taxable income of a special professional who has above-average special professional income for an income year is contained in cl 2 pt I of sch 7 *ITRA* and set out below:

$$\frac{A+B}{C}$$

- A is the amount of tax that ordinarily would be payable by the taxpayer if their taxable income equalled their 'reduced taxable income' (ie their taxable income minus their above-average special professional income).
- B is five times the difference between:
  (a) the tax that would be payable by the taxpayer on their reduced taxable income plus 20% of their above-average special professional income, and
  (b) the tax that would be payable by the taxpayer on their reduced taxable income.
- C is the taxpayer's taxable income.

Example In the previous example, Roger had above-average special professional income of $15,000 for 2022/23. He therefore calculates the rate of tax payable on his taxable income of $70,000 for the income year according to the above formula. For the purposes of this formula:

- A is the tax on $55,000 (ie $70,000 – $15,000). This amount is $8,342.
- B is five times the difference between:
  (a) the tax on $58,000 (ie $55,000 + ($15,000 × 1/5)), and
  (b) the tax on $55,000.
  This amount is $975 (ie $9,317 – $8,342).
- C is $70,000.

Roger's rate of tax is worked out as follows:

$$\text{Rate of tax} = \frac{A+B}{C}$$

$$= \frac{\$8{,}342 + \$975}{\$70{,}000}$$

$$= 0.1331$$

Roger must consequently pay $9,317 in income tax (ie $70,000 × 0.1331). This compares with the $13,217 in income tax that he would otherwise have had to pay on taxable income of $70,000 according to the basic marginal rates of tax.

[25.4] Minors

To discourage adults from splitting income with children, div 6AA of pt III *ITAA36* (ss 102AA to 102AGA) contains special rules that apply to 'prescribed persons'. Where these rules apply, the 'eligible taxable income' of the prescribed person is taxed at penalty rates under ss 13 and 15 *ITRA* rather than ordinary marginal tax rates [8.8].

Prescribed person

A 'prescribed person' is defined in s 102AC(1) as a person who is under the age of 18 years (ie a 'minor') on the last day of the income year and is not an 'excepted person'. A person is an 'excepted person' for an income year if they fall within the categories of persons listed in s 102AC(2). Excepted persons include:

- a minor who was engaged in a full-time occupation on the last day of the year
- a minor in respect of whom a carer allowance or disability support pension was payable under the *Social Security Act 1991* (Cth) ('*SSA*') in respect of a period that included the last day of the year
- a minor who is certified as a disabled child within the meaning of pt 2.19 of the *SSA* or who has a continuing inability to work within the meaning of pt 2.3 of the *SSA*, or who is permanently blind
- a minor who is a principal beneficiary of a special disability trust within the meaning of pt 3.18A of the *SSA*
- a minor in respect of whom a double orphan pension was payable under the *SSA* for a period that included the last day of the year, and
- a minor who is certified as being unlikely to be able to engage in full-time employment by reason of a permanent disability.

Eligible taxable income

A minor's 'eligible taxable income' is basically their 'eligible assessable income' less certain deductions (eg those that relate exclusively to their eligible assessable income) (s 102AD).

A minor's 'eligible assessable income' is so much of their assessable income as is not 'excepted income' (s 102AE(1)). 'Excepted income' includes:

- employment or business income
- certain income derived from property that devolved upon the minor from a deceased estate (eg a testamentary trust), and
- certain other forms of income (eg income from the investment of workers compensation payments) (s 102AE(2)).

A minor's eligible taxable income is, therefore, essentially their net (non-excepted) income. In other words, it consists of, broadly, their net 'passive' income. For this reason, eligible taxable income is sometimes loosely referred to as 'unearned income'. It includes, for example, the net interest income arising from a bank deposit opened in the name of a child by their parent. It also covers the net income received by a child as a beneficiary of a family discretionary trust.

Example Max is 17 years old and works at his local supermarket. During the previous income year, he earned $30,000 in wages. He also received $2,000 in interest from a bank deposit and a $7,000 distribution of income from his family trust. Max's taxable income is $39,000, comprising eligible taxable income of $9,000 and excepted income of $30,000.

Penalty tax rates on minor's eligible taxable income

Resident minors

The eligible taxable income of a resident minor is taxed at the following rates (plus ML where applicable):

- If the minor's eligible taxable income is $416 or less, it is taxed at the ordinary resident individual tax rates (ie no penalty tax rate applies).
- If the minor's eligible taxable income exceeds $416 but does not exceed $1,307, the tax payable on the eligible taxable income is the greater of:
  - 66% of the excess over $416, and
  - the difference between the tax payable at resident individual tax rates on the minor's taxable income and the tax payable at resident individual tax rates on the minor's taxable income excluding eligible taxable income.
- If the minor's eligible taxable income exceeds $1,307, it is taxed at the rate of 45%.

25

Example

1. A resident minor has taxable income of $30,000 (including $400 of eligible taxable income). The income tax payable on the minor's eligible taxable income is calculated according to the ordinary resident individual tax rates.
2. A resident minor has taxable income of $30,000 (including $1,000 of eligible taxable income). The income tax payable on the minor's eligible taxable income of $1,000 is $385, being the greater of:
   $385 = 66% × $584 (ie $1,000 – $416), and
   $190 = $2,242 (ie tax on $30,000) – $2,052 (ie tax on $29,000).
3. A resident minor has taxable income of $30,000 (including $10,000 of eligible taxable income). The income tax payable on the minor's eligible taxable income of $10,000 is $4,500 (ie $10,000 × 45%).

Non-resident minors

The eligible taxable income of a non-resident minor is taxed at the following rates:

- If the minor's eligible taxable income is $416 or less, the tax payable on the eligible taxable income is the greater of:
  - 32.5% of the eligible taxable income, and
  - the difference between the tax payable at non-resident individual rates on the minor's taxable income and the tax payable at non-resident individual rates on the minor's taxable income excluding eligible taxable income.

- If the minor's eligible taxable income exceeds $416 but does not exceed $663, the tax payable on the eligible taxable income is the greater of:
  - $135.20 plus 66% of the excess over $416, and
  - the difference between the tax payable at non-resident individual rates on the minor's taxable income and the tax payable at non-resident individual rates on the minor's taxable income excluding eligible taxable income.
- If the minor's eligible taxable income exceeds $663, the minor's eligible taxable income is taxed at the rate of 45%.

[25.5] Life insurance companies

A life insurance company is a company that is registered under s 21 of the *Life Insurance Act 1995* (Cth) (s 995-1 *ITAA97*). Life insurance companies carry on 'life businesses' (ie they issue life insurance policies and undertake liabilities under those policies). Because of the special nature of their businesses, these entities are subject to special taxation rules.

Under div 320 *ITAA97*, life insurance companies are required to include particular amounts in their assessable income, exempt income and non-assessable non-exempt income, and are allowed deductions for specific kinds of expenditure. For example, they are assessed on life insurance premiums paid by their policy holders and they are entitled to deductions for certain components of life insurance premiums which they pay.

Life insurance companies are also required to divide their taxable income into 'classes'. They must pay tax at the rate of:

- 15% on the 'complying superannuation class' (which relates to the 'RSA component' of their taxable income [19.14]), and
- 30% on the 'ordinary class' (which relates to the rest of their taxable income) (s 23A *ITRA*).

Like other companies, life insurance companies (other than mutual life insurance companies) are required to maintain franking accounts (s 202-15). The circumstances in which franking credits and debits arise in such accounts are, however, modified by div 219 *ITAA97*. The modifications are designed to ensure that franking credits and debits only arise to the extent that payments and refunds of tax are attributable to the 'shareholders' share' of a life insurance company's income tax liability (ss 219-15, 219-30).

[25.6] Co-operative companies

Nature of a co-operative company

A co-operative company is defined in s 117(1) *ITAA36* as a company whose rules limit the number of shares that may be held on behalf of any one shareholder, prohibit the quotation of the shares on a stock exchange or in any public manner, and which is established for the purpose of carrying on any business which has as its primary objective one or more of the following:

- the acquisition of commodities or animals for disposal or distribution among its shareholders
- the acquisition of commodities or animals from its shareholders for disposal or distribution
- the storage, marketing, packing or processing of commodities of its shareholders
- the rendering of services to its shareholders
- the obtaining of funds from its shareholders for the purpose of making loans to its shareholders to enable them to acquire land or buildings to be used for the purpose of residence or of residence and business.

Approved credit unions are deemed not to be co-operative companies (s 117(2)). In addition, a company is not a co-operative if less than 90% of its business is with its members (s 118).

In *Brookton Co-operative Society Ltd v FC of T* 81 ATC 4346, the High Court held that a company that was purportedly established to render services to its shareholders in relation to the purchase of wine, but which was actually engaged in holding shares in subsidiary companies and involved in share trading and dividend stripping activities, was not a co-operative. Gibbs CJ, Mason and Wilson JJ stated that s 117(1) requires two questions to be considered—whether the company is established for the purpose of carrying on any business, and, if so, whether such business has as its primary objects any of those described in the sub-section. According to their Honours, it is the sole or dominant purpose of the company in the relevant income years having regard to its actual activities at that time which needs to be considered. Their Honours went on to conclude that in determining the purpose for which a company is established, it is permissible to look not just at the activities of the taxpayer and its directors, but also the intentions of the promoters.

Taxation of co-operatives and their members

Co-operative companies are taxed under special rules contained in div 9 of pt III *ITAA36*. The assessable income of a co-operative includes all sums received by it (whether from shareholders or other persons), for the storage, marketing, packing or processing of commodities, or for the rendering of services, or in payment for commodities or animals or land sold (s 119).

Unlike other companies, co-operatives can generally claim deductions for amounts paid out of assessable income to their shareholders as rebates or bonuses based on business done, or as interest or dividends (s 120(1)).

A co-operative's shareholders are ordinarily assessed on distributions received from the co-operative. However, rebates and bonuses on purchases from the co-operative are not assessable to the shareholders (except where the purchases are deductible to them) (s 120(2)).

Co-operatives can elect to frank dividends paid to their shareholders (no deductions are available to the co-operative for the payment of such dividends) (ss 120(4), (5)).

[25.7] Listed investment companies

Nature of a listed investment company

A listed investment company ('LIC') is a special kind of company that operates as a managed fund and invests in the financial markets (see TR 2005/23). More specifically, a company is a LIC if it is an Australian resident, it is listed on the ASX or other approved exchange, and at least 90% of the market value of its CGT assets are 'permitted investments' (s 115-290(1)). A 100% subsidiary of a LIC which meets these criteria (other than the listing requirement) is also deemed to be an LIC (s 115-290(2)). A company that fails the 90% test can still qualify as a LIC if the failure was only temporary and caused by circumstances outside its control (s 115-290(3)).

Permitted investments comprise: shares, options, rights or similar interests; financial instruments (eg loans, debts, debentures, bonds promissory notes and futures contracts); certain assets used to derive interest, annuities, rent, royalties or foreign exchange gains; and goodwill (s 115-290(4)).

Taxation of LIC shareholders

Shareholders in LICs are taxed on their LIC dividends in accordance with the general rules discussed in Chapter 22. In addition, eligible shareholders are entitled to a special deduction in respect of dividends which are reasonably attributable to 'LIC capital gains' (s 115-280). LIC capital gains are essentially capital gains made by LICs on permitted investments which have been held for at least 12 months and have been included in their net capital gain and taxable income for the relevant income year (s 115-285). LICs must specify the extent to which dividends are sourced from LIC capital gains in their distribution statements to shareholders [22.7].

The special deduction is designed to be a broad equivalent to the CGT discount that the shareholders would otherwise be entitled to receive if they had made the capital gains themselves [17.8]. LICs, being companies, are not entitled to CGT discounts on their capital gains. Shareholders cannot offset their capital losses against LIC dividends even though they may be attributable to LIC capital gains.

The deduction available to an eligible shareholder is a specified percentage of the 'attributable part', which is calculated as follows:

$$\text{Attributable part} = \text{After tax gain} + \left[\frac{\text{After tax gain} \times \text{Corporate tax rate (at the time of CGT event)}}{1 - \text{Corporate tax rate (at the time of CGT event)}}\right]$$

Shareholders who are Australian resident individuals, foreign resident individuals who have PEs [30.5] in Australia, trusts and partnerships are entitled to a deduction of 50% of the attributable part. Shareholders that are complying superannuation entities are entitled to a deduction of 33⅓% of the attributable part.

Example L Co is a LIC that has a corporate tax rate of 30%. It acquired a CGT asset in May 2015 for \$10,000 and disposed of it in June 2023 for \$30,000, resulting in a capital gain of \$20,000. It also had a capital loss of \$10,000, which it offset against the capital gain of \$20,000, resulting in it having a net capital gain of \$10,000. L Co paid tax of \$3,000 (ie \$10,000 × 30%) on the net capital gain, leaving it with \$7,000 to distribute as a fully franked dividend.

L Co paid each of its shareholders a fully franked dividend of \$7 per share. Larry is a resident who owns one share in the company. The attributable part of the \$7 fully franked dividend paid to Larry is calculated as follows:

$$\$10 = \$7 + \left[\frac{\$7 \times 30\%}{1 - 30\%}\right]$$

Under the general tax rules, Larry must include the \$7 dividend in his assessable income under s 44(1) [22.5] together with the \$3 franking credit under s 207-20(1), and he is also entitled to a tax offset of \$3 for the franking credit under s 207-20(2) [22.8]. In addition, he is entitled to a deduction of 50% of the attributable part of the dividend, being \$5 (\$10 × 50%), under s 115-280.

[25.8] Corporate limited partnerships

Corporate limited partnerships are taxed under special rules in div 5A of pt III *ITAA36* rather than the general partnership rules in div 5 of pt III *ITAA36* [23.3]. The broad object of div 5A is to tax corporate limited partnerships and their members in a similar way to companies and their shareholders, rather than on a flow-through basis like ordinary partnerships. The rationale for this treatment is that limited partnerships are similar to companies in that their limited partners enjoy limited liability like shareholders.

Nature of a corporate limited partnership

A corporate limited partnership is a limited partnership that is *not* a VCLP, ESVCLP, AFOF or VCMP [27.4] (s 94D). The key feature of a limited partnership is that it has both 'general partners' (who manage the partnership and whose liability for partnership debts is unlimited) and 'limited partners' (who merely invest in the partnership and whose liability is limited to the amounts of capital they have agreed to contribute) [23.2].

Taxation treatment

Corporate limited partnerships are deemed *not* to be partnerships for tax purposes (s 94K) and are instead treated as 'corporate tax entities' (s 960-115 *ITAA97*). Division 5A modifies the tax law to ensure that a reference to a 'company' generally includes a reference to a 'corporate limited partnership' (s 94J). Likewise, references to a 'share' and 'shareholder' are respectively deemed to include references to 'an interest in the partnership' and 'a partner in the partnership' (ss 94P, 94Q). In addition, references to a 'dividend' include distributions made by the partnership (s 94L).

Like companies, corporate limited partnerships are required to pay tax on their net income at the rate of 30% unless they are base rate entities in which case they are required to pay tax on their net income at the rate of 25% (s 23 *ITRA*). If a corporate limited partnership pays or credits profits to partners, such amounts are treated as dividends and taxed in accordance with the dividend taxation rules [22.5] (s 94M). As corporate limited partnerships are corporate tax entities, they can frank such distributions under the imputation system [22.6].

The taxation treatment of corporate limited partnerships was recently considered by the Full Federal Court in *FC of T v Resource Capital Fund IV LP* 2019 ATC ¶20-691. The case concerned two limited partnerships that were established in the Cayman Islands. Each partnership had a Cayman Islands general partner (who managed the partnership) and United States limited partners (who provided capital to the partnership). The partnerships made profits from the sale of shares in an Australian company that had lithium mining assets. The sale had taken place pursuant to a scheme of arrangement ordered by the Federal Court of Australia. The Commissioner sought to assess the partnerships on the profits from the sale of the shares on the basis that they had an Australian source.

At first instance (*Resource Capital Fund IV LP v FC of T* 2018 ATC ¶20-647), Pagone J held that although div 5A treats corporate limited partnerships as companies for taxation purposes, they are not converted into companies for other purposes. According to his Honour, the intention of div 5A was not to create a new taxable entity, but to treat a corporate limited partnership as if it was a separate entity for calculation purposes only. On this basis, his Honour held that it was the United States limited partners (not the corporate limited partnerships) that were the taxable entities. However, his Honour went on to conclude that even though the profits had an Australian source, the partners were not subject to Australian tax on those profits as they were entitled to relief from double taxation under Australia's DTA with the United States.

On appeal, the Full Federal Court reversed Pagone J's decision and held that div 5A treated a corporate limited partnership as a company for taxation purposes, and this included it being a taxable entity. Although the Court agreed that the source of the profits was Australia, it held that the corporate limited partnerships could not rely on Australia's DTA with the United States as they were established in the Cayman Islands and were therefore not United States residents. The corporate limited partnerships were therefore assessable on the profits from the sale of shares in Australia.

[25.9] Public trading trusts

Public trading trusts are essentially widely held trusts that carry on trading businesses. These trusts are taxed under special rules in div 6C of pt III *ITAA36* (ss 102M to 102T) rather than the general trust taxation rules in div 6 of pt III *ITAA36* [24.1]. The broad object of div 6C is to tax public trading trusts as separate entities in a similar manner to companies, rather than on a flow-through basis like other trusts.

Nature of a public trading trust

A public trading trust is a unit trust that is a 'resident unit trust', a 'public unit trust' and a 'trading trust' in relation to a year of income (s 102R)

Resident unit trust

A unit trust is a 'resident unit trust' if, at any time during the income year, any property of the trust is situated in Australia or the trustee carries on business in Australia, and the central management and control of the trust is in Australia or persons who hold more than 50% of the beneficial interests in the income or property of the trust are residents (s 102Q).

Public unit trust

A unit trust is a 'public unit trust' if its units are listed on a stock exchange, offered to the public, or held by 50 or more persons (s 102P(1)). A unit trust is, however, not a public unit trust if 20 or fewer persons hold 75% or more of the beneficial interests in the income or property of the trust (s 102P(7)). In certain cases, the Commissioner may nevertheless treat such a trust as a public trading trust (s 102P(5)). A unit trust will also be deemed to be a public unit trust if at any time during the year of income, 'exempt entities' (which do not include exempt institutions that are eligible for a refund of franking credits: s 102MD) beneficially held, or had the right to acquire, 20% or more of the property or income of the trust (s 102P(2)).

Trading trust

A unit trust is a 'trading trust' if the trustee carries on a 'trading business' or controls, or is capable of controlling, another person in respect of the carrying on by that person of a trading business (s 102N). A 'trading business' is a business that does not consist wholly of 'eligible investment business' (s 102M). An 'eligible investment business' consists of:

(a) investing in land for the purpose, or primarily for the purpose, of deriving rent
(b) investing or trading in certain specified products such as loans, securities, shares, and futures contracts, or
(c) investing or trading in financial instruments not covered by (b) above that arise under financial arrangements, other than those arrangements excepted by s 102MA.

Investments in moveable property that are incidental and relevant to the renting of land, customarily supplied or provided in connection with the renting of land, and ancillary to the ownership and use of land are taken to be investments in land (s 102MB(1)). Generally, an entity's investments in land are taken to be primarily for the purpose of deriving rent so long as at least 75% of the gross revenue from those investments consists of rent (other than excluded rent) (s 102MB(2)).

Special taxation treatment

Public trading trusts are deemed *not* to be trust estates for the purposes of div 6 (s 102T *ITAA36*) and are instead treated as corporate tax entities (s 960-115 *ITAA97*).

To ensure that public trading trusts are taxed like companies, trustees of public trading trusts are required to pay tax on the net income of the trust at the rate of 30% unless they are base rate entities in which case they are required to pay tax on their net income at the rate of 25% (s 102S *ITAA36*; s 25 *ITRA*).

'Unit trust dividends' paid by public trading trusts to their unitholders are treated in the same way as dividends paid by companies to their shareholders (s 102T *ITAA36*). A unit trust dividend is defined in s 102M *ITAA36* in a similar way to the way in which a dividend is defined in s 6(1) *ITAA36*

[22.4]. As a consequence, distributions of profits by public trading trusts to their unitholders are taxed under the dividend taxation rules [22.5]. Since public trading trusts are corporate tax entities, they can frank these distributions under the imputation system [22.6].

[25.10] Managed investment trusts

Managed investment trusts ('MITs') are widely held trusts that are used as pooled investment vehicles in the managed funds industry. MITs are different from other trusts as they can elect under div 275 *ITAA97* to have the CGT regime apply as the primary code for taxing gains and losses made on their assets. This allows them to be treated in a similar fashion to superannuation funds, which also have their gains and losses generally taxed under the CGT regime under div 295 *ITAA97* [19.14]. The rules relating to the taxation of trust estates in div 6 of pt III *ITAA36* [24.1] generally apply to MITs. However, these rules do not apply to 'attribution MITs' ('AMITs') (s 95AAD *ITAA36*). AMITs are MITs that meet certain additional criteria and are therefore a 'sub-set' of MITs. AMITs are subject to their own special tax treatment under div 276 *ITAA97*.

Nature of an MIT

A trust is an MIT in relation to an income year if the following conditions in s 275-10 are satisfied:

- at the time the trustee makes the first fund payment for the year, the trustee was an Australian resident, or the central management and control of the trust was in Australia
- the trust is a managed investment scheme ('MIS') and is not a trading trust nor carrying on a trading business within the meaning of div 6C of pt III *ITAA36* [25.9]
- the trust is a 'registered MIS' or has 'wholesale membership' as set out in s 275-15 and satisfies the 'licensing requirements' in s 275-35, and
- the trust satisfies the 'widely held requirements' in ss 275-20 and 275-25 and the 'closely held restrictions' in s 275-30.

Managed investment scheme

An MIS is defined as an entity, with more than 20 members, that is an MIS for the purposes of the *Corporations Act 2001* (Cth), or an entity with a similar status under a foreign law relating to corporate regulation (s 995-1). An MIS is a scheme under which people contribute money to acquire interests to benefits produced by the scheme, the contributions are pooled, and the members do not have day-to-day control over the operation of the scheme (s 9 *Corporations Act*). An MIS must be registered if it has more than 20 members or is promoted by a person who is in the business of promoting MISs (s 601ED(1) *Corporations Act*).

Wholesale membership

Broadly speaking, a trust has wholesale membership under s 275-15 if it is not required to be registered as an MIS and has no more than 20 'retail client' members who have a total 'MIT participation interest' in the trust of no more than 10%. An MIT participation interest is basically the percentage of direct and indirect acquisition, control or distribution interests an entity has in a trust (whichever is greatest) (s 275-40).

Licensing requirements

A trust satisfies the licensing requirements in s 275-35 in a number of circumstances, including if it is operated or managed by a financial services licensee who holds an Australian financial services licence covering it to provide financial services to wholesale clients.

Widely held requirements

A trust satisfies the 'widely held' requirements in ss 275-20 and 275-25 if it satisfies one of the following:

- it has wholesale membership, is a registered MIS and either: (a) has at least 25 members; or (b) one or more entities mentioned in s 275-20(4) that has an 'MIT participation interest' of more than 25% in the trust and no entity, other than an entity covered by s 275-20(4), has an MIT participation interest of more than 60% in the trust
- it does not have wholesale membership, is a registered MIS and either: (a) has at least 50 members; (b) is listed on an approved stock exchange in Australia; or (c) one or more entities mentioned in s 275-20(4) has an MIT participation interest of more than 25% in the trust and no entity, other than an entity covered by s 275-20(4), has an MIT participation interest of more than 60% in the trust, or
- it has wholesale membership, is not a registered MIS and has at least 25 members.

Section 275-20(4) covers specified widely held entities, such as complying superannuation funds with at least 50 members, life insurance companies and MITs.

Closely held restrictions

A trust satisfies the 'closely held' restrictions *unless*, at any time during the income year, any of the following applies:

- if the trust has wholesale membership, 10 or fewer of its members have a total MIT participation interest in the trust of 75% or more (s 275-30(1)(a))
- if the trust does not have wholesale membership, 20 or fewer of its members have a total MIT participation interest in the trust of 75% or more (s 275-30(1)(b)), or
- a foreign resident individual has an MIT participation interest in the trust of 10% or more (s 275-30(1)(c)).

Extended definition of an MIT

A trust is also deemed to be an MIT in relation to an income year where:

- the trustee is an Australian resident, or the central management and control of the trust is in Australia, and the only members of the trust are specified entities covered by s 275-20(4) or other MITs (s 275-45)
- the trustee has not made a fund payment in relation to the income year, but the trust would have been an MIT in relation to the income year if a fund payment had been made on both the first and last days of the income year (s 275-50), or
- the trust would be an MIT in relation to the income year but for a temporary circumstance that arose outside the trustee's control and it is fair and reasonable to treat the trust as an MIT (s 275-55).

Electing CGT regime as the primary code for taxing gains and losses

MITs can elect to have the CGT regime apply as the primary code for calculating gains and losses made on their assets where the following conditions in s 275-100(1) are met:

- a CGT event happens involving a CGT asset owned by an entity that is an MIT, and the CGT event happens because the MIT disposes of, ceases to own, or otherwise realises the asset
- the asset is covered by s 275-105 (ie it is a share or non-share equity interest in a company, a unit in a unit trust, an interest in land, or a right or option to acquire or dispose of any of these assets, and is not a div 230 financial arrangement or a debt interest)

- the MIT meets the requirements in s 275-110 (ie it is not a trading trust [25.9])
- a choice under s 275-115 covering the entity is in force for the income year (ie the trustee of the entity has made an irrevocable choice in writing in the approved form within specified time limits).

Where the above conditions are satisfied, the general taxation rules in ss 6-5 and 8-1 *ITAA97*, as well as a range of other revenue related provisions (eg ss 15-15 [10.3], 25-40 [13.7] *ITAA97*), do not apply to the CGT event (s 275-100(2)).

If an MIT is not covered by a choice under s 275-115, its relevant assets (other than interests in land) are treated as if they were revenue assets (s 275-120).

Special taxation rules for AMITs under div 276 *ITAA97*

As mentioned above, special taxation rules in div 276 apply to AMITs instead of the general trust rules in div 6 of pt III *ITAA36*. A trust is an AMIT for an income year if:

- it is an MIT in relation to the income year
- the interests of its members in the income and capital of the trust are 'clearly defined', and
- the trustee has made an irrevocable choice to be an AMIT in the income year or a previous income year (s 276-10).

Whether particular interests are clearly defined is a question of fact determined by reference to the trust documents. Interests are deemed to be clearly defined where the trust is a registered MIS, or the rights to income and capital arising from each of the membership interests are the same (s 276-15).

Division 276 allows AMITs to:

- be treated as fixed trusts
- attribute amounts of assessable income, exempt income, non-assessable non-exempt income and tax offsets to their members on a fair and reasonable basis, and
- reconcile variances between amounts actually attributed to members for an income year and amounts that should have been attributed to them using an 'unders and overs' regime.

AMIT fixed trust treatment

An AMIT is treated as a 'fixed trust' for income tax purposes (s 276-55(a)). This makes it easier for the trust to satisfy the 'carry forward trust loss rules' [24.9]. In addition, each entity that is a member of an AMIT in respect of an income year is treated as having vested and indefeasible interests in a share of the income and capital of the trust throughout the income year (s 276-55(b)). This assists in complying with the 'holding period rule' in relation to franking credits [22.12].

AMIT attribution rule

Division 276 enables trustees of AMITs to attribute particular amounts to their members on a 'fair and reasonable basis' in accordance with their interests in the trust as set out in its constituent documents. For this purpose, trustees of AMITs are required to identify amounts earned during the year and divide them into 'characters' that relate to:

- assessable income (eg discount and non-discount capital gains from taxable and non-taxable Australian property, franking credit gross-ups, certain withholding amounts and ordinary and statutory income amounts from foreign sources)
- exempt income
- non-assessable non-exempt income, and
- tax offsets (eg franking credits and foreign income tax offsets).

The trustee of an AMIT must create a document that states the 'determined trust components' for each character for an income year (s 276-255). The respective amounts for each character are the 'trust components' for the income year (s 276-260). These amounts, once attributed to members on a fair and reasonable basis in accordance with the trust's constituent documents, are known as 'member components' (s 276-210). The trustee is required to provide members with 'AMMA statements' no later than three months after the end of the income year (s 276-455(2)). The 'determined member components' are the amounts that are attributable to the member on the AMMA statements (s 276-205(2)).

For the purposes of calculating their tax liabilities, members are treated as having derived their respective determined member components (s 276-80). Special rules apply to certain amounts within characters. For example, the amount of a discount capital gain is doubled under s 276-85(4). This ensures that the member can offset their own capital losses against so much of the AMIT's full capital gain (ie the pre-discount amount) as is attributable to them.

To prevent double taxation, a special rule ensures that determined member components are not assessed under more than one provision (s 276-100).

AMIT reconciliation of variances

Division 276 enables trustees of AMITs to use special rules to reconcile variances they have discovered between amounts attributed to their members for an income year and amounts that they should have attributed to them for the year. Discrepancies are common in practice and may arise due to mistakes or incomplete accounting information available to trustees at the end of the income year. Variances are reconciled on a character-by-character basis in the hands of the trust. If a variance occurs in calculating particular AMIT characters, the trustee of an AMIT can:

- apply the 'unders and overs' regime contained in sub-div 276-F to attribute the variance to members in the discovery year by adjusting the trust component of the relevant Character in that year, or
- revise the trust component for the income year to which the variance relates and reissue AMMA statements for the year to members.

A variance is determined by comparing:

- the 'discovery year amount' (ie the AMIT's trust component of that character for the base year worked out at the discovery time), and
- the 'base year running balance' (ie the AMIT's determined trust component of that character for the base year, or as worked out in a previous year) (s 276-345).

If the base year running balance is less than the discovery year amount, the shortfall is an 'under' of that character (s 276-345(4)). If the base year running balance exceeds the discovery year amount, the excess is an 'over' of that character (s 276-345(5)).

The variance is reconciled in the relevant income year (ie the year of discovery) as follows:

- if the AMIT has an under of a particular character in the income year (relating to any earlier income year), the trustee must increase the trust component by the amount of the under (s 276-305(2)), and
- if the AMIT has an over of a particular character in the income year (relating to any earlier income year), the trustee must decrease the trust component by the amount of the over (s 276-305(3)).

Example T Co is the trustee of an AMIT. In the 2022/23 income year (the 'base year'), T Co calculates that the trust has a trust component of $100,000 of an assessable income character (this relates exclusively to a non-discount capital gain made by the trust). T Co states that this amount is the determined trust component for that character. T Co issues AMMA statements to its members and attributes the amount to its members on a fair and reasonable basis in accordance with the trust's constituent documents. Sometime in the 2023/24 income year (the 'discovery time'), T Co discovers that its trust component for the assessable income character for the 2022/23 income year was actually $90,000. T Co may either reissue AMMA statements to the members with the revised trust component for the 2022/23 income year or apply the unders and overs regime in the 2023/24 income year.

If T Co uses the unders and overs regime, it must calculate the variance according to s 276- 345. The 'discovery year amount' for the assessable income character is $90,000 as this is the trust component of that character for the base year worked out at the discovery time. The 'base year running balance' is $100,000 as this is the determined trust component of that character in the base year. Because the base year running balance exceeds the discovery year amount, the $10,000 excess is an 'over' of that character in the 2023/24 income year.

In the 2023/24 income year, T Co calculates that the trust has a trust component of an assessable income character of $50,000 (before taking into account any unders or overs). Because the trust also had an over of such a character in the 2023/24 income year (relating to an earlier year, ie the 2022/23 income year), it must decrease the amount of its trust component for that character by $10,000 under s 276-305(3). Therefore, it actually has a trust component of an assessable income character of $40,000 for the 2023/24 income year.

Trustee liability to tax for AMITs

The trustee of an AMIT will be assessed in certain cases where there has been an under-attribution of income (ss 276-405, 276-415, 276-420) or an over-attribution of tax offsets (ss 276-410, 276-425). Where there has been an under-attribution of income, the trustee will be liable to tax at the rate of 47% (s 12 *ITRA*). Where there has been an over-attribution of tax offsets, the trustee will be liable to tax at the rate of 100% (s 4 *Income Tax (Attribution Managed Investment Trusts—Offsets) Act 2015* (Cth)).

Cost base adjustment for members' interests in AMITs

Membership interests in AMITs are CGT assets that may be subject to special upward and downward cost base adjustments to address potential double taxation and non-taxation issues that may arise from the attribution mechanism. The adjustments occur just before the end of the income year, unless a CGT event happens in relation to the interest before the end of the income year, in which case the adjustments happen just before the time of the CGT event (s 104-107B(4)). Adjustments are required to be specified on AMMA statements provided to members (ss 104-107C, 276-460(2)(b)). Broadly speaking, assessable and non-assessable non-exempt income attributed to members for the income year result in upward adjustments (s 104-107E), and actual payments made to members in the income year as well as tax offsets attributed to members for the income year result in downward adjustments (s 104-107D).

Example Vicky holds one unit in an AMIT, which she acquired for $1,000 on 1 January 2023. On 1 August 2023, T Co (the trustee of the AMIT) issues an AMMA statement to Vicky for the 2022/23 income year, which attributes to her $100 of an assessable income character (this relates exclusively to ordinary income). Because of the operation of s 276-80, Vicky is required to include the $100 in her assessable income for the 2022/23 income year.

Vicky sells her unit to Percy on 1 September 2023 for $1,150. On 1 December 2023, T Co distributes the income of the AMIT. As Percy is now the owner of the unit, he receives the $100. The sale of the unit by Vicky results in CGT event A1 happening and an adjustment must be made to the cost base of the unit (s 104-107B(4)). Because Vicky does not have the right to receive the $100, but has been assessed on this amount, the cost base of her unit is increased by $100 to $1,100. She therefore makes a capital gain of only $50 on the disposal of the unit (rather than $150, which would be the case if the adjustment was not made).

As Percy has received $100, which was assessable to Vicky rather than him, the cost base of his unit must be reduced from $1,150 to $1,050.

If the amount of the downward adjustment exceeds the cost base of the membership interest, CGT event E10 is triggered at the time of the reduction (s 104-107A). The cost base and reduced cost base of the asset are reduced to nil, and there is a capital gain equal to the excess (s 104-107B(2)(a)).

Special rules apply to membership interests that are revenue assets (ss 104-107G, 104-107H).

MIT withholding tax

Trustees of 'withholding MITs' are required to withhold tax on 'fund payments' made to entities whose address, or place of payment, is outside Australia (s 12-385 *TAA*).

Withholding MITs

A trust is a withholding MIT in relation to an income year if it is an MIT in relation to that income year because of ss 275-10(1)(a) or (2)(b) *ITAA97* and a substantial proportion of the investment management activities carried out in relation to the trust in respect of the following assets are carried out in Australia throughout the income year: (i) assets situated in Australia; (ii) taxable Australian property; (iii) shares, units, or interests listed on an approved stock exchange in Australia (s 12-383 *TAA*).

Fund payments

For withholding MITs that are not AMITs, 'fund payments' are the distributions of the trust's net income for the year disregarding 'excluded amounts' (ie dividends, interest, royalties, capital gains and losses in relation to CGT assets that are not taxable Australian property, and foreign source amounts) (s 12-405 *TAA*).

For withholding MITs that are AMITs, fund payments are the sum of:

(a) the 'determined member components' of an assessable income character for the income year disregarding 'excluded components' (ie those components that have the character of discount capital gains from non-taxable Australian property, capital gains from non-taxable Australian property, dividends, interest, royalties, foreign source income, and any other amounts excluded by legislative instrument), and

(b) the AMIT's capital losses from CGT events in respect of non-taxable Australian property for the income year (s 12A-110 *TAA*).

Imposition of MIT withholding tax

Withholding tax is imposed on fund payments under the *Income Tax (Managed Investment Trust Withholding Tax) Act 2008* (Cth). The rate of tax is 30%. However, if the recipient's address or place of payment is in an 'information exchange country' (ie a country listed in reg 34 *TAR17*) the rate is 15%. A concessional 10% rate applies to fund payments by a 'clean building MIT' (ie an MIT that holds certain energy efficient buildings: s 12-425 *TAA*). From 1 July 2024, the 15% rate is also proposed to apply to fund payments made to foreign residents on income from newly constructed residential build-to-rent projects [15.7].

MIT withholding tax is a final tax. Income on which MIT withholding tax is payable is therefore non-assessable non-exempt income (s 840-815(1) *ITAA97*). However, this rule does not apply to

Australian residents who directly or indirectly receive fund payments from AMITs (s 840-815(2)). Australian residents are assessed on such payments and entitled to a credit for the MIT withholding tax that has been paid (s 18-30 *TAA*).

Example The trustee of an MIT that is not an AMIT distributed $100,000 of the trust's net income for the 2022/23 income year to a unitholder who resides in Canada (an information exchange country). The distribution included $90,000 of interest, which was subject to interest withholding tax at the rate of 10% [31.11]. The balance $10,000 of the distribution was a 'fund payment', which was subject to MIT withholding tax at the rate of 15%. The trustee of the MIT is therefore required to withhold a total of $10,500 from the distribution, leaving the Canadian unitholder with a net payment of $89,500 calculated as follows:

Distribution	$100,000
Interest withholding tax ($90,000 × 10%)	$9,000
MIT withholding tax ($10,000 × 15%)	$1,500
Net payment received by unitholder	$89,500

[25.11] Corporate collective investment vehicles

A new type of vehicle, called a 'corporate collective investment vehicle' ('CCIV'), was introduced in Australia from 1 July 2022. The idea for this new vehicle originated in a recommendation of the Australian Financial Centre Forum in its 2009 report, *Australia as a Financial Centre: Building on our Strengths*, and was further informed by work done by the Board of Taxation in its 2011 *Review of Tax Arrangements Applying to Collective Investment Vehicles.*

CCIVs are special kinds of registered investment companies in which investors pool their capital and have them managed by professional fund managers. They were introduced to increase the competitiveness of Australia's managed funds industry and attract offshore investment. Funds management in Australia had traditionally been conducted through MISs, which adopted a trust-based structure [25.10]. Many international investors were, however, unfamiliar with this structure. The introduction of CCIVs enables a more internationally recognisable corporate vehicle to be used for making collective investments.

In contrast to ordinary companies, CCIVs provide flow-through tax treatment for investors while at the same time maintaining investor protection. CCIVs do not have their own bespoke tax regime, but are instead closely aligned with the MIT and AMIT regimes [25.10]. The rules ensure that the tax outcomes for CCIV investors are essentially the same as those for AMIT investors.

CCIV

The framework for registering and regulating CCIVs is contained in ch 8B of the *Corporations Act 2001* (Cth). A company must apply to be registered as a CCIV (s 1222A). ASIC is required to register a company as a CCIV where an application to register has been lodged under s 117 [22.2] and the requirements for registration are met (s 1222C). A CCIV is required to have the expression 'Corporate Collective Investment Vehicle' or 'CCIV' appear at the end of its name (s 1222E).

The requirements for registration are set out in s 1222. The key requirements are that the company must be limited by shares, have a constitution, and have at least one 'sub-fund' each of which must have at least one member. The company must also have a corporate director, which must be a company that holds an Australian financial services licence ('AFSL') authorising it to operate the business and conduct the affairs of the CCIV. The company must also specify whether it is a 'retail' or a 'wholesale' CCIV.

- **Retail CCIV.** A CCIV is a retail CCIV if it satisfies the retail CCIV test or if it notifies ASIC that it is a retail CCIV (s 1222J). A CCIV meets the retail CCIV test if it has at least one member who is a 'protected retail client', a 'protected client under a custodial arrangement' or a 'protected passport fund member' (s 1222K). A person is a protected retail client if the person acquires a security issued by a CCIV as a 'retail client' within the meaning in ch 7 of the *Corporations Act*.
- **Wholesale CCIV.** A CCIV is a wholesale CCIV unless it has at least one investor that acquires securities in the CCIV as a 'retail client'.

Retail CCIVs are subject to a stricter regulatory framework than wholesale CCIVs. Retail CCIVs must provide additional protections for retail investors (eg they must have a compliance plan and comply with special reporting requirements). The same protections are not required for wholesale CCIVs as they are more sophisticated and often have the capacity to negotiate bespoke arrangements with fund managers.

Sub-funds

A key feature of the CCIV regime is that the assets and liabilities of CCIVs are required to be segregated into one or more sub-funds in an umbrella-like structure as illustrated in the diagram below.

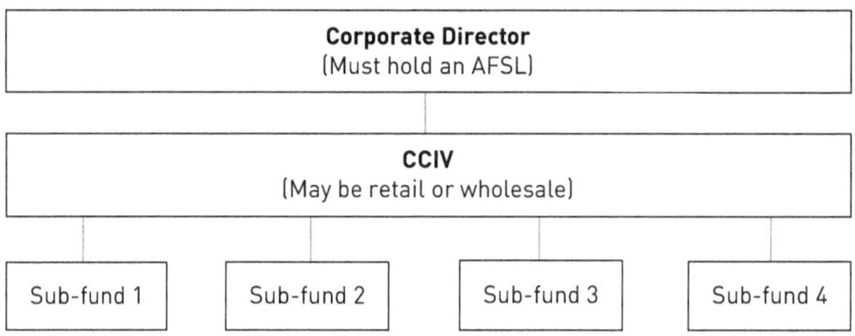

Every CCIV must have at least one sub-fund and each part of the CCIV's business must be referable to one (and only one) sub-fund. Each sub-fund may offer a different investment strategy. The cumulative businesses of all of the sub-funds must constitute the CCIV's entire business. The CCIV must keep financial records for each sub-fund.

A sub-fund of a CCIV is all or part of the business of the CCIV that is registered as a sub-fund under s 1222S (s 1222Q(1)). Although a sub-fund does not have legal personality (s 1222Q(2)), it has its own name and Australian registered fund number ('ARFN'), which must be used on all its public documents (ss 1222V to 1222X).

The assets of a CCIV include the money and property it acquires in carrying on its business and its liabilities include all its debts and expenses. The way in which a CCIV's assets and liabilities are attributed to its sub-funds is determined in accordance with special allocation rules. The corporate director must set up and maintain a register of the assets and liabilities of the sub-funds.

Sub-finds may be voluntarily deregistered on application by the CCIV, the corporate director or a liquidator. ASIC or a Court may also deregister a sub-fund.

Importantly, each security (eg share) that is issued by a CCIV must be referable to a particular sub-fund. A CCIV may distribute dividends to its members on their shares provided the sub-fund to which the share is referable is solvent. Each share in a class of shares has the same dividend rights unless provided for in the CCIV's constitution or by special resolution of the members of the sub-fund to which the shares are referable.

Tax treatment of CCIVs and their investors

The tax treatment of CCIVs and their members is governed by rules in sub-div 195-C *ITAA97*. Underpinning sub-div 195-C is a deeming rule, which creates a 'statutory fiction' that treats a CCIV and its members as having a trust relationship for tax law purposes. Under this deeming rule, a trust relationship is deemed to exist between a CCIV, the business, assets and liabilities referable to a sub-fund and the relevant class of members. Each sub-fund is treated as a separate unit trust (known as the 'CCIV sub-fund trust'). The CCIV is the trustee of the CCIV sub-fund trust and the members of the sub-fund are its beneficiaries (ss 195-110 to 195-115). Each beneficiary of a CCIV sub-fund trust has fixed entitlements to the income and capital of the trust (s 195-115).

The income of a CCIV sub-fund trust for an income year is based on the sub-fund's accounting profits for that income year (s 195-123). A beneficiary of a CCIV sub-fund trust is taken to be presently entitled to a share of the income of the trust estate for an income year if any of the sub-fund's profit for the income year was or is payable to the beneficiary by way of one or more dividends declared during, or within three months after, the income year (s 195-125).

Special rules modify the MIT and AMIT criteria in divs 275 and 276 *ITAA97* [25.10] to enable a CCIV sub-fund trust to be capable of meeting those criteria (ss 195-130, 195-135). Where a CCIV sub-fund trust meets the modified criteria it is treated as an AMIT for that year and the following consequences arise:

- the CCIV sub-fund trust is taken to be a fixed trust and its members are taken to have a vested and indefeasible interest in a share of the income and capital of the trust
- amounts derived or received by the CCIV sub-fund trust that are attributed to members retain the character they had in the hands of the trustee of the CCIV sub-fund trust
- the CCIV sub-fund trust is able to attribute amounts of assessable income, exempt income, non-assessable non-exempt income and tax offsets to members on a fair and reasonable basis
- the CCIV sub-fund trust can elect to have the CGT regime operate as the primary code for calculating gains and losses made on its assets, and
- the CCIV sub-fund trust is able to use the unders and overs regime [25.10].

The withholding tax provisions apply to attribution CCIV sub-fund trusts and their members in the same way that they apply to AMITs, notwithstanding that the CCIV is legally a corporate entity that pays dividends.

If a CCIV sub-fund trust fails to meet the modified AMIT eligibility criteria, it will be taxed in accordance with the general trust provisions in div 6 of pt III *ITAA36* [24.1] (except where it fails the criteria because it is a trading trust, in which case, it will be taxed in accordance with the rules in div 6C of pt III *ITAA36* [25.9]).

[25.12] Foreign hybrids

Division 830 *ITAA97* contains special rules relating to 'foreign hybrids'. Foreign hybrids include certain foreign companies and foreign limited partnerships that are treated as partnerships overseas but would ordinarily be treated as companies under Australia's tax laws. An example of a foreign hybrid company is a United States limited liability company (ID 2006/18) and an example of a foreign hybrid limited partnership is a United Kingdom limited partnership (ID 2006/334).

Foreign hybrids are not taxed in Australia as companies under either the general corporate tax rules or under the corporate limited partnership rules in div 5A of pt III *ITAA36* [25.8]. Instead, they are taxed as if they were partnerships under modified rules in div 830. This means that they are treated as 'flow-through entities' rather than 'opaque entities' and it is the partners who are responsible for any tax liabilities. A special loss limitation rule prevents the partners of a foreign hybrid from benefiting from deductions for tax losses where they are not exposed to those losses due to their limited liability.

The broad object of div 830 is to ensure that foreign hybrids are taxed under Australia's tax laws in a roughly comparable manner to the way in which they are taxed under foreign tax laws.

[25.13] Offshore banking units

To support Australia as a global financial centre and encourage offshore banking activities for non-residents to be conducted through Australia, an 'offshore banking unit' ('OBU') regime was established in 1987. This regime, contained in div 9A of pt III *ITAA36*, allowed banks and certain other companies to apply to the Treasurer to be declared as OBUs. OBUs are taxed concessionally on the income from their 'OB activities', which include certain activities relating to acting as a financial intermediary between offshore lenders and borrowers and providing certain financial services to offshore investors who invest outside Australia (s 121D).

OBUs are generally only assessed on one-third of their 'assessable OB income' (defined in s 121EE) and are generally only allowed deductions for one-third of their 'allowable OB deductions' (defined in s 121EF) (s 121EG). This results in OBUs paying an effective tax rate of only 10% in relation to their OB activities rather than the general corporate tax rate.

OBUs are also subject to special withholding tax treatment under div 11A of pt III *ITAA36* [31.11]. In particular, they are not required to withholding tax from interest paid on offshore borrowings (s 128GB).

In 2018, the OECD determined that Australia's OBU regime was a 'harmful preferential tax regime' as it provided a concessional tax rate and was ring-fenced to exclude domestic transactions from its scope (meaning it was only available in relation to transactions between foreign residents). As a result, the Government closed the regime to new entrants and has removed the tax concessions for existing OBUs from the 2023/24 income year.

[25.14] QUESTIONS

1. Why is it important to determine whether an entity is carrying on a primary production business? What special taxation rules apply to primary producers?
2. Jill plans to withdraw $20,000 from her farm management deposit account with a bank. What are the consequences of this?
3. Mei is a professional artist. In the current income year, she won $20,000 in an art competition and made $30,000 from selling her paintings at an art exhibition. She also has a part-time job as a cook and earns $40,000. Over the preceding four income years, her taxable professional income was respectively: $10,000, $25,000, $15,000 and $35,000. Calculate her tax liability for the current income year.
4. Why are penalty rates of tax imposed on the eligible taxable income of children? How is eligible taxable income calculated?
5. Andy is a 12-year-old resident who earns $40,000 in interest from a bank deposit made in his name by his father. How much tax is he liable to pay?
6. What is special about the way that life insurance companies, co-operative companies and LICs are taxed?
7. How are corporate limited partnerships treated differently from other partnerships and how are public trading trusts treated differently from other trusts?
8. What kinds of trusts fall within the MIT regime? How does div 275 *ITAA97* affect the way MITs are taxed? What is an AMIT, and what special rules apply to them?
9. What is a CCIV and how are CCIVs and their members taxed?

CONSOLIDATED GROUPS 26

[26.1] Introduction

Ordinarily, the income tax law treats distinct legal entities as separate taxpayers. As a result, each entity must determine its own tax liability, irrespective of the liability of any other entity that may be related to it. This principle, however, operates subject to the consolidation regime, which was introduced on 1 July 2002 and is contained in pt 3-90 *ITAA97* (divs 700 to 721).

Under the consolidation regime, a resident head company and all its wholly owned resident subsidiary members may elect to form a consolidated group and be treated as a single entity for income tax purposes. The consequence of electing to become a consolidated group is that the subsidiary members of the group lose their individual identity for tax purposes and are treated as parts of the head company. Although consolidation is not mandatory, many corporate groups have chosen to consolidate because certain concessions that were previously available to corporate groups (such as the ability to transfer losses between group members and obtain CGT roll-over relief for asset transfers between group members) have been removed. Consolidation is also attractive to corporate groups as it facilitates their internal restructures.

Consolidation aims to reduce compliance costs by allowing a consolidated group to lodge a single income tax return. It does not have any effect on a group's other tax liabilities, such as GST and FBT, which remain the responsibility of the individual entities concerned. Consolidation is also designed to improve the integrity of the tax system by reducing the opportunities for tax avoidance through loss creation and value shifting arrangements.

This chapter outlines the basic features of the consolidation regime. Because of the complexity of the regime, it is only possible to discuss the main general rules and not the many intricate exceptions to them. The chapter commences by examining the nature of a consolidated group and how such a group is formed [26.2]. It also discusses a related kind of group, known as an 'MEC group' [26.3]. The chapter then proceeds to examine some of the core rules that exist under the consolidation regime, being the single entity rule, the entry history rule and the exit history rule [26.4]. Other important rules, such as the cost setting rules [26.5] and loss transfer rules [26.6], are also considered. The chapter also discusses the consequences that arise where an entity leaves a consolidated group [26.7]. It concludes with a discussion of the special liability rules that apply to the tax debts of a consolidated group [26.8].

[26.2] Consolidated group

To form a consolidated group, the 'head company' of a 'consolidatable group' must make an irrevocable choice, in writing, to consolidate (s 703-50 *ITAA97*). The consolidated group comes into existence on the date specified in the choice and consists of the head company and *all* its subsidiary members (s 703-5).

Head company

A 'head company' is a resident company that is not a wholly owned subsidiary of another resident company (s 703-15). A head company is therefore the 'highest' resident company in a group of wholly owned entities.

Subsidiary member

A 'subsidiary member' is, broadly, a resident company, a resident trust estate, or a partnership that is a 'wholly owned subsidiary' of the head company (s 703-15). An entity is a 'wholly owned subsidiary' of another entity (the 'holding entity') if all of the 'membership interests' in the entity are beneficially owned by the holding entity and/or its other wholly owned subsidiaries (s 703-30). In determining whether an entity is a wholly owned subsidiary, minor shareholdings under ESSs [21.1] are ignored (s 703-35). Likewise, 'debt interests' are also ignored as they do not constitute 'membership interests' (ss 960-130, 960-135).

Example In the following diagram, Black Co may elect to form a consolidated group with White Co, Blue Trust and Green Co. Red Co cannot be a member of the group as it is a non-resident. Alpha Co cannot be a member of the group as it is not a wholly owned subsidiary of Black Co. Alpha Co can, however, elect to form a separate consolidated group with Beta Co. Gamma Co cannot be a member of this group as it is a non-resident.

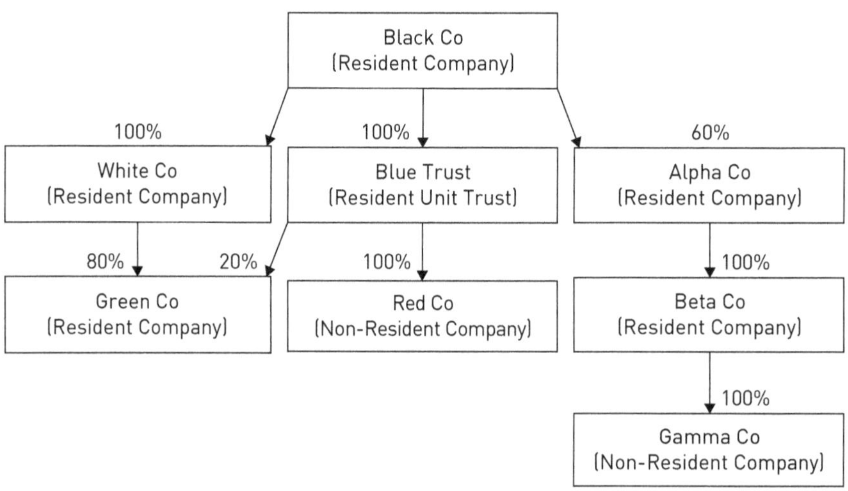

Entities that cannot be members of consolidated groups

Certain entities are prohibited from being members of a consolidated group, such as entities that are exempt from tax under div 50 [11.2], superannuation entities [19.4] and PDFs [27.3] (s 703-20).

Public trading trusts

Subdivision 713-C allows public trading trusts to also make a choice under s 703-50 to form a consolidated group and be treated as the head company of the group provided certain conditions are met.

Existence of consolidated group

Once formed, a consolidated group continues to exist until the head company ceases to be a head company or it becomes a member of an 'MEC group' [26.3] (s 703-5(2)). A consolidated group therefore continues to exist even though new members join the group and old members leave the group, so long as the head company is not liquidated or replaced by another head company that is higher in the 'chain' of companies. A consolidated group would therefore cease to exist where the head company is taken over and becomes a wholly owned subsidiary of another resident company.

[26.3] MEC group

Resident wholly owned subsidiaries of a common foreign parent company that do not have the same head company may be able to form a 'multi-entry consolidated group' ('MEC group'). In general, the consolidation rules will apply to MEC groups in roughly the same way as they apply to consolidated groups.

To form an MEC group, two or more 'eligible tier-1 companies' of a 'top company' must make an irrevocable choice in writing to consolidate (ss 719-5, 719-50, 719-55). An 'eligible tier-1 company' is a resident company that is a wholly owned subsidiary of a 'top company' (ie a non-resident company) and is not a wholly owned subsidiary of another resident company (s 719-20).

The MEC group consists of all those eligible tier-1 companies that have made the choice and all their resident wholly owned subsidiaries. One of the eligible tier-1 companies must be appointed as the 'provisional head company' of the MEC group (s 719-60). This company has essentially a similar role to the head company of a consolidated group.

Example In the following diagram, Pink Co and Orange Co are eligible tier-1 companies of a top company, Grey Co. Pink Co and Orange Co can elect to form an MEC group, in which case one of them must be nominated as the provisional head company of the group. The MEC group will consist of Pink Co, Amber Co, Orange Co and Yellow Co. Scarlet Co cannot be a member of the MEC group as it is a non-resident.

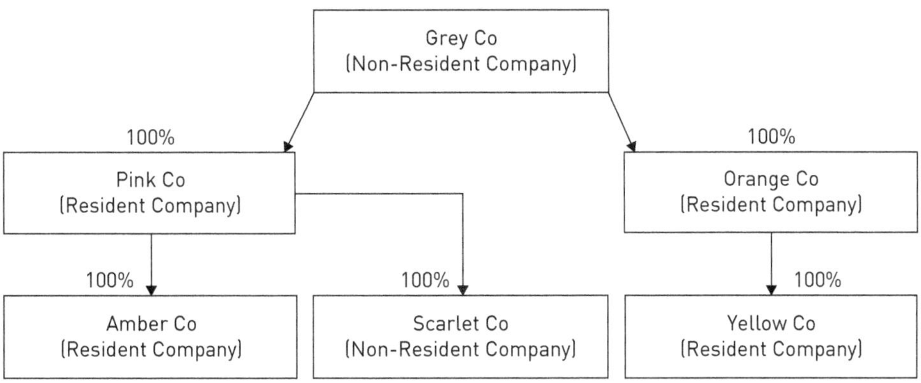

[26.4] Core rules

The consolidation regime is underpinned by three core rules:

- the 'single entity rule'
- the 'entry history rule', and
- the 'exit history rule'.

Single entity rule

The key effect of consolidation is that a consolidated group is treated as a 'single entity' for income tax purposes. This means that the subsidiary members of the group are 'parts' of the head company, rather than separate entities (s 701-1(1) *ITAA97*). The head company is therefore liable for all the group's income tax liabilities and is entitled to the benefit of any losses of the group (s 701-1(2)). The head company is also responsible for lodging a group income tax return.

Some other important consequences that flow from the single entity rule are outlined below:

- **Membership interests ignored.** During the period of consolidation, all membership interests held by the head company and its subsidiary members in entities that are part of the consolidated group are ignored for income tax purposes. Similarly, all intra-group transactions are also ignored for income tax purposes. This means that dividends paid between group members are not assessable and no income tax consequences flow when a subsidiary member undertakes a capital reduction or share buy-back or is liquidated. It also means that assets can be transferred between group members without any CGT or balancing adjustment events occurring. It is only when assets are transferred outside the group that CGT or balancing adjustment events arise.

Example H Co is the head company of a consolidated group that has S1 Co, S2 Co and S3 Co as subsidiary members. H Co owns all the shares in S1 Co. S1 Co owns all the shares in S2 Co. S2 Co owns all the shares in S3 Co.

If S1 Co transfers a CGT asset to S2 Co, this transaction is ignored for income tax purposes and there are consequently no CGT implications arising from the disposal.

If S2 Co pays a dividend to S1 Co, there are no income tax implications (ie no assessable dividends arise under s 44(1) *ITAA36*).

Likewise, there are no income tax implications if S3 Co is placed into liquidation (ie no deemed dividends arise under s 47 *ITAA36* and there are no CGT issues on the cancellation of the shares).

- **Foreign income tax offset.** If a subsidiary member of a consolidated group pays foreign income tax on an amount that is included in the assessable income of the head company, the head company is deemed to have paid the tax and is entitled to the benefit of any foreign income tax offset available under div 770 *ITAA97* [31.3] (s 717-10).

Example H Co is the head company of a consolidated group that includes S Co as a subsidiary member. S Co pays tax in Singapore on its income derived in Singapore. H Co is deemed to have paid this tax and is therefore entitled to any foreign income tax offset under div 770.

- **Pooled franking account.** During the period of consolidation, the head company is required to maintain a single 'pooled' franking account for the group (s 709-55). If a subsidiary member has a surplus in its franking account at the joining time, the surplus is transferred to the head company (s 709-60). If it has a deficit in its franking account at such time, it must pay franking deficit tax (s 709-60). During the period of consolidation, a subsidiary member's franking account is rendered inoperative (s 709-65) and any debits and credits that would otherwise arise in its franking account arise instead in the head company's franking account (ss 709-70, 709-75).

Example H Co is the head company of a consolidated group. On 1 August 2023, it acquired all the shares in T Co, which automatically became a member of the H Co group at that time. Immediately before the 'joining time', H Co had a franking surplus in its franking account of $10m and T Co had a franking surplus in its franking account of $3m. Pursuant to s 709-60, at the joining time, a $3m debit arises in T Co's franking account and a corresponding $3m credit arises in H Co's franking account. The effect of this is that the franking surplus is transferred from T Co to H Co.

T Co's franking account				
Date	**Details**	**Debit**	**Credit**	**Balance**
1/8/23	Balance just before joining time			$3m
1/8/23	Franking surplus transferred to H Co	$3m		Nil

H Co's franking account				
Date	**Details**	**Debit**	**Credit**	**Balance**
1/8/23	Balance just before joining time			$10m
1/8/23	Franking surplus received from T Co		$3m	$13m

If T Co had a $5m franking deficit instead of a $3m franking surplus at the joining time, then a $5m credit would arise in T Co's franking account at the joining time and it would be required to pay $5m of FDT (s 709-60). There would, however, be no corresponding credit in H Co's franking account.

It is important to realise that the single entity rule is a legal fiction specific to the income tax law. Consequently, consolidation does not affect the group's other tax liabilities (eg GST or FBT liabilities) and the members of the group must therefore continue to lodge returns relating to these liabilities. Likewise, the single entity rule does not affect the general law. Group members therefore continue to be treated as separate entities for general law purposes. Accordingly, if a subsidiary member of the group enters into a contract with a third party, the contracting parties would be the subsidiary member and the third party (rather than the head company and the third party). If the third party brings a legal action for breach of contract, it would need to proceed against the subsidiary member rather than the head company. Any tax liability arising from such a breach (eg the payment of damages by the subsidiary member) is, however, attributed to the head company under the consolidation regime.

Entry history rule

The entry history rule provides that when an entity joins a consolidated group as a subsidiary member, the head company 'inherits' its income tax history in that everything that happened to the entity before it became a subsidiary member is taken to have happened to the head company (s 701-5). One consequence of this is that the pre-CGT status of the joining entity's assets will generally be retained in the hands of the head company. Another consequence is that the head company will generally be entitled to any outstanding deductions for expenditure incurred by the joining entity. The entry history rule operates subject to a number of important special rules, including 'cost setting' [26.5] and 'loss utilisation' [26.6] rules.

Exit history rule

The exit history rule provides that when a subsidiary member leaves a consolidated group, it inherits the income tax history of the assets, liabilities and businesses that it takes with it. More specifically, everything that happened to an eligible asset while it was that of the head company is taken to have happened in relation to it as if it had been an eligible asset of the leaving entity (s 701-40). The leaving entity will therefore adopt the head company's tax cost of any assets it takes with it when it leaves the group [26.7].

[26.5] Cost setting rules

Under the single entity rule, the assets of a subsidiary member are treated as the assets of the head company [26.4]. The head company must therefore ascertain its cost for each of these assets in order to determine its income tax position in relation to dealings with them (eg for CGT, trading stock and capital allowance purposes). Although dealings such as the transfer of an asset *within* the group will generally not give rise to any CGT or other income tax issues for the head company, the transfer of an asset *outside* the group (whether by the head company or its subsidiary member) will give rise to such issues for the head company.

The consolidation regime contains 'tax cost setting amount' ('TCSA') rules that reset the cost of a joining entity's assets. The broad object of these rules is to treat the head company's cost for a joining entity's assets as being an amount that reflects the group's cost of acquiring the joining entity.

Tax cost setting amount

The TCSA rules are located in div 705 *ITAA97* and are complex. Subdivision 705-A contains the basic TCSA rules, which operate where a subsidiary member joins an existing consolidated group. These rules are modified to accommodate other situations, such as where a subsidiary becomes a member of the group on formation (sub-div 705-B) or where one consolidated group joins another consolidated group (sub-div 705-C). Groups formed between 1 July 2002 and 30 June 2004 could, in certain cases, elect to use transitional TCSA rules.

There are two key steps in applying the basic TCSA rules:

- the first step is to determine the 'allocable cost amount' ('ACA') for the joining entity, and
- the second step is to spread the ACA over the joining entity's assets.

Step 1: Determining the ACA

The ACA for the joining entity is worked out according to a series of nine steps set out in s 705-60. In basic terms, the steps are designed to ensure that the ACA for the joining entity is based on the cost of the group's membership interests in the joining entity, increased by the joining entity's liabilities and adjusted to take into account various special factors. The steps are summarised in the following table:

Working out the joined groups ACA for the joining entity			
Step	**What the step requires**	**What the step is about**	**Purpose of the step**
1	Work out the Step 1 amount under s 705-65	The cost of membership interests in the joining entity held by members of the group	To ensure that the ACA includes the cost of acquiring the membership interests
2	Add the Step 2 amount worked out under s 705-70 (note that this amount may need to be adjusted under ss 705-75 to 705-85)	The value of the joining entity's liabilities	To ensure that the joining entity's liabilities at the joining time, which are part of the group's cost of acquiring the joining entity, are reflected in the ACA
3	Add the Step 3 amount worked out under: (a) s 705-90, or (b) s 713-25 (if the joining entity is a trust and not a corporate tax entity)	The: (a) undistributed, taxed profits accruing to the group before the joining time, or (b) realised profits accruing to the group before the joining time that could be distributed tax-free	To increase the ACA to reflect: (a) the undistributed, taxed profits and so prevent double taxation, or (b) the undistributed, realised profits that could be distributed tax-free
3A	For each Step 3A amount (if any) under s 705-93: (a) if the Step 3A amount is a deferred roll-over loss—add the Step 3A amount, or (b) if the Step 3A amount is a deferred roll-over gain—subtract the Step 3A amount	Pre-joining time roll-overs	To adjust for certain roll-overs that occurred before the joining time affecting deferred gains and losses
4	Subtract the Step 4 amount worked out under s 705-95	Pre-joining time distributions out of certain profits	To prevent the ACA reflecting a return of part of the amount paid to acquire the membership interests in the joining entity
5	Subtract the Step 5 amount worked out under s 705-100	Losses accruing to the group before the joining time	To prevent: (a) a double benefit arising from the losses, and (b) losses that cannot be transferred to, or are cancelled by, the head company being reinstated
6	Subtract the Step 6 amount worked out under s 705-110	Losses that the joining entity transferred to the head company	To stop the group getting benefits both through higher TCSAs for the joining entity's assets and through losses transferred to the head company

26

Working out the joined groups ACA for the joining entity			
Step	**What the step requires**	**What the step is about**	**Purpose of the step**
7	Subtract the Step 7 amount worked out under s 705-115	Certain deductions to which the head company is entitled	To stop the group getting benefits both through the tax cost of the joining entity's assets being set and through certain tax deductions of the joining entity being inherited by the head company
8	If the remaining amount is positive, it is the joined group's ACA. Otherwise the joined group's ACA is nil.		

In practice, the first two steps are the most important elements that make up the ACA and they are illustrated in the following simplified example.

Example H Co is the head company of a consolidated group. On 1 January 2010, H Co acquired 70 of the 100 shares in J Co for $100m. On 1 July 2023, it acquired the remaining 30 shares in J Co for $60m. J Co therefore becomes a subsidiary member of the group on 1 July 2023. At that time of joining the group, J Co owed $30m to a third party in respect of a loan. The ACA for J Co is therefore $190m (ie $100m + $60m + $30m).

Step 2: Spreading the ACA over the joining entity's assets

Once the ACA for a joining entity has been determined, it is then necessary to spread the ACA over the joining entity's assets to arrive at their respective individual TCSAs. This is done as follows:

- First, the ACA is applied to determine the TCSA of any 'retained cost base assets' (eg Australian currency and rights to receive Australian currency), which generally retain their value (s 705-25).
- Second, the balance of the ACA is then spread over the entity's 'reset cost base assets' (ie other assets) in proportion to their market values to arrive at their TCSAs (s 705-35).

A special rule reduces the TCSA of a reset cost base asset that is a right to receive Australian currency where the market value of the asset is less than its TCSA and the head company makes a capital gain under CGT event L3 [17.3] (s 705-27). Special capping rules also apply to certain other assets, including trading stock, depreciating assets and revenue assets. The TCSA of such assets must generally not exceed the greater of their 'market value' or the joining entity's 'terminating value' for them (ss 705-30, 705-40). Any excess amount is spread over the entity's other reset cost base assets or, where there are no such assets, produces a capital loss under CGT event L4 [17.3].

The basic effect of the TCSA rules is that the group's cost of acquiring an entity is 'pushed down' over the acquired entity's assets to arrive at their respective TCSAs. This is illustrated in the following simplified example.

Example H Co acquired all the shares in S Co for $100 on 1 January 2001. On 1 July 2023, H Co decided to form a consolidated group with S Co. At the joining time, S Co had a liability of $300 owing under a loan. The group's ACA for S Co is therefore $400 ($100 + $300).

S Co owned the following assets at the joining time: cash ($100), trading stock (market value $50) and land (market value $200). The group's TCSA for these assets is calculated as follows:

Asset	Cost base asset type	Market value	TCSA ignoring capping rule	TCSA taking into account capping rule
Cash	Retained	$100	$100	$100
Trading stock	Reset	$50	$50/$250 × $300 = $60	$50 (ie $60 – $10)
Land	Reset	$200	$200/$250 × $300 = $240	$250 (ie $240 + $10)

Correcting errors

As the TCSA rules are complex, errors can be made in the relevant calculations (ie amounts may be overstated or understated). To avoid the time and expense involved in correcting these errors, sub-div 705-E permits a head company, in certain circumstances, to reverse the effect of such errors by simply realising a capital gain or capital loss under CGT event L6 [17.3].

[26.6] Transfer and utilisation of losses

Transfer of losses

Division 707 *ITAA97* allows subsidiary members of a group to transfer their losses to the head company when they join the group. Losses can only be transferred to the extent that the joining entity would have been entitled to use the losses (based on certain assumptions) outside the group during the 'trial year' (s 707-120).

The trial year is generally the period that ends immediately after the joining time and that commences 12 months before the joining time.

Whether a joining entity would have been entitled to use losses outside the group during the trial year is tested by reference to modified 'continuity of ownership' and 'business continuity' tests [22.22] (ss 707-125, 707-130, 707-205, 707-210).

Transferred losses are treated as if they were made by the head company in the year of transfer (ss 707-105(1), 707-140). Any losses that cannot be transferred are wasted and cannot be used even if a subsidiary later leaves the group (ss 707-105(2), 707-150).

Utilisation of transferred losses

Each set of losses (regardless of their 'sort') that are transferred by a joining entity to a group form a 'bundle of losses'. A limit is placed on the amount of each bundle of losses that a head company can utilise in a particular year. The reason for imposing a limit is that a joining entity's losses could, potentially, be used at a faster rate in a consolidated group since they would be able to be applied against the income and gains of the entire group (rather than merely against the income and gains of the entity that actually made the losses).

Available fraction method

The general method for determining the annual utilisation limit for a bundle of losses is known as the 'available fraction method' ('AFM'). This method is contained in sub-div 707-C and is complex. Essentially, the AFM allows a head company to apply a bundle of losses against a fraction of its income and gains that remain after it has used up its other deductions and losses for the year. The fraction reflects the income or gains of the group that are attributed to the joining entity.

More specifically, the AFM sets the limit by reference to the 'available fraction' for the bundle of losses (s 707-310). The available fraction is calculated according to a formula in s 707-320, which divides the transferring entity's 'modified market value' by the head company's 'adjusted market value'. These values are the respective market values of such entities, calculated at the joining time, taking into account certain modifications and assumptions (ss 707-310 to 707-325).

The way in which the AFM broadly operates is illustrated in the following example.

Example H Co, the head company of a consolidated group, acquired all the interests in S Co on 1 July 2023. At the joining time, H Co's adjusted market value was \$10m and S Co's modified market value was \$2m. S Co satisfied the loss transfer tests and is able to transfer a \$200,000 tax loss and a \$10,000 net capital loss to H Co. Ignoring this bundle of losses, H Co has capital gains of \$140,000, capital losses of \$40,000, other assessable income of \$440,000 and deductions of \$40,000 in 2023/24.

H Co's taxable income for 2023/24 is calculated according to the following steps:

Step 1: Identify H Co's bundle of losses and sorts of losses
H Co has a single bundle of losses consisting of a tax loss of \$200,000 and a net capital loss of \$10,000.

Step 2: Calculate H Co's available fraction for the bundle of losses
H Co's available fraction is 0.2 (\$2m/\$10m).

Step 3: Calculate H Co's particular kinds of income and gains for the year before taking into account the transferred losses
Capital gains = \$100,000 (\$140,000 – \$40,000).
Other assessable income = \$400,000 (\$440,000 – \$40,000).

Step 4: Multiply H Co's income and gains (Step 3) by the available fraction (Step 2)
Capital gains = \$20,000 (\$100,000 × 0.2).
Other assessable income = \$80,000 (\$400,000 × 0.2).

H Co can offset the transferred bundle of losses only against the above amounts.

Step 5: Apply the losses in the transferred bundle against H Co's 'notional taxable income' (calculated as if it comprised only the Step 4 amounts)
H Co's 'notional taxable income' is \$100,000 (\$20,000 'notional capital gains' and \$80,000 'notional other assessable income'). This means:

- H Co can utilise the \$10,000 transferred net capital loss and \$10,000 of its \$200,000 transferred tax loss to reduce its notional capital gain from \$20,000 to nil. It is therefore left with an actual capital gain of \$80,000 (\$100,000 – \$20,000) for the year, and
- H Co can utilise \$80,000 of the remaining transferred tax loss of \$190,000 (\$200,000 – \$10,000) to reduce its notional other assessable income from \$80,000 to nil. It is therefore left with actual other assessable income of \$320,000 (\$400,000 – \$80,000) for the year.

Step 6: Calculate H Co's actual taxable income for the year and any remaining bundle of transferred losses
H Co's taxable income for the year is \$400,000 (\$80,000 + \$320,000). It also has a remaining bundle of transferred tax losses of \$110,000 (\$200,000 – \$10,000 – \$80,000), which it can apply in future years under the AFM.

[26.7] Leaving a consolidated group

Due to the single entity rule, the membership interests in a subsidiary are ignored while it is part of a consolidated group. However, when it leaves the group (ie it is no longer wholly owned by the group), the head company must once again recognise the membership interests in the 'leaving entity'. This is particularly important for the purposes of determining whether there are any CGT implications for the head company (eg on sale of the shares in the subsidiary).

Determining the TCSA of the membership interests in the leaving entity

When an entity leaves the group, the head company needs to determine its TCSA of the membership interests in the leaving entity. The TCSA of membership interests in a leaving entity is determined in accordance with rules in div 711 *ITAA97*. These rules require the group's ACA for the leaving entity to be determined pursuant to s 711-20.

In basic situations, the ACA for the leaving entity is simply the 'terminating values' of the assets that the entity takes with it when it leaves the group (s 711-25). The terminating values of the assets that the leaving entity takes with it when it leaves a group are worked out in a similar way to how the terminating values of the assets of a joining entity are worked out [26.5].

The TCSA for a particular membership interest is then calculated by allocating the ACA for the leaving entity to the membership interests (or, where there is more than one class of membership interests, to each class in proportion to the market value of all the membership interests in the class) and then dividing the result by the number of membership interests (or membership interests in the class) (s 711-15). 26

The basic effect of the above rules is that the terminating values of the assets that a leaving entity takes with it when it leaves the group are 'pushed up' to determine the TCSA of the membership interests in the leaving entity. The way in which this works is illustrated in the following example.

Example H Co (the head company of a consolidated group) owns all of the 1,000 shares in L Co (a subsidiary member of the group). H Co sells 500 of its shares in L Co to a third party that is not a member of the group for $5m (ie $10,000 per share). L Co therefore ceases to be a subsidiary member of the H Co group and H Co needs to determine the TCSA of its shares in L Co to determine whether it has made a capital gain or capital loss from their disposal.

If at the time that H Co sold the shares, L Co owned cash of $1m, depreciating asset with a terminating value of $1.5m and land with a terminating value of $2m, H Co's ACA for L Co is $4.5m ($1m + $1.5m + $2m). H Co's TCSA for each share in L Co is therefore $4,500 ($4.5m/1,000). As a consequence, H Co makes a capital gain of $5,500 ($10,000 – $4,500) on the disposal of each share. This results in an overall capital gain of $2.75m ($5,500 × 500) on the sale of the 500 shares.

Pre-CGT proportion of the membership interests in the leaving entity

Some of the membership interests in an entity that joins a consolidated group may have been acquired pre-20 September 1985. To ensure that the pre-CGT status of such membership interests is preserved when an entity leaves the group, it is necessary to work out the 'pre-CGT proportion' for the membership interests in the leaving entity.

The pre-CGT proportion is calculated under s 705-125 as follows:

$$\text{Pre-CGT proportion} = \frac{\text{Market value of pre-CGT membership interests held by members of the group at the joining time}}{\text{Market value of all membership interests held by members of the group at the joining time}}$$

When an entity leaves the group, the number of membership interests in the leaving entity that members of the old group are taken to have acquired pre-CGT is calculated under the following formula in s 711-65 (the number is rounded down to the nearest whole number or to zero if it is less than one):

$$\begin{array}{c}\text{Number of pre-CGT}\\\text{membership interests}\\\text{in leaving entity}\end{array} = \begin{array}{c}\text{Number of membership}\\\text{interests in leaving entity}\\\text{held by the old group}\end{array} \times \begin{array}{c}\text{Leaving entity's}\\\text{pre-CGT}\\\text{proportion}\end{array}$$

Example H Co is the head company of a consolidated group. H Co acquired 30 of the 100 shares in S Co in 1983. On 1 July 2010, H Co purchased the remaining 70 shares in S Co, whereupon S Co became a subsidiary member of the group. On 1 July 2010, the market value of S Co is $1,000 and each share in S Co therefore has a market value of $10. The pre-CGT proportion of H Co's membership interests in S Co is calculated as follows:

$$30\% = \frac{\$10 \times 30}{\$10 \times 100}$$

On 5 August 2023, H Co sold 40 of its 100 shares in S Co to a third party. S Co, therefore, ceases to be a subsidiary member of the group at that time. The number of pre-CGT shares that H Co holds in S Co is 30 (ie 100 × 30%). This means H Co can choose to treat up to 30 of the 40 shares it sold as pre-CGT shares. Assuming H Co chooses to treat 30 of those shares as pre-CGT shares, then the remaining 60 shares H Co continues to hold are all post-CGT shares.

[26.8] Liability rules

An important consequence of the single entity rule is that a head company is primarily responsible for the tax liabilities of the group. However, where a head company fails to pay a 'group liability' by the time it becomes due and payable, special rules in div 721 *ITAA97* apply. Under these rules, a head company's 'contributing members' may become jointly and severally liable for the group liability (ss 721-10, 721-15).

A group liability is a 'tax-related liability' specified in s 721-10(2); namely, a liability for income tax, PAYG instalments and certain other taxes. Pre-consolidation liabilities of group members and other liabilities, such as PAYG withholding, GST or FBT liabilities, are not covered.

An entity is a contributing member if it was a subsidiary member of the group during *any part* of the period to which the group liability relates.

The joint and several liability of a contributing member becomes due and payable 14 days after the Commissioner gives the member notice of the liability (s 721-15(5)).

Tax sharing agreements

The joint and several liability rules do not operate if the liability is covered by a valid 'tax sharing agreement' ('TSA'). In order to constitute a valid TSA, an agreement must be entered into between the head company and one or more of its contributing members before the time the relevant group liability becomes due (s 721-25). A 'contribution amount' must be able to be determined under the agreement for each TSA contributing member and this amount must represent a 'reasonable allocation' of the total amount of the group liability among the head company and those members. If the liability is covered by a valid TSA, the subsidiaries are only liable for the share of the liability allocated to them under the TSA (s 721-30).

A member of a group can also leave the group clear of a liability if it pays the amount it owes under a TSA to the head company prior to leaving (s 721-35).

Example H Co is the head company of a consolidated group. H Co owns all the shares in its three subsidiary members, S1 Co, S2 Co and S3 Co. On 8 May 2022, H Co entered into a valid TSA with its subsidiary members. Under the TSA, 30% of the group's income tax liability is allocated to S3 Co. On 1 July 2023, H Co sold its shares in S3 Co to X Co (a third party). S3 Co therefore ceases to be a member of the H Co group. Prior to leaving the group S3 Co paid $3m to H Co. The $3m represents 30% of the H Co group's $10m income tax liability for the 2022/23 income year. If H Co does not pay its $10m tax liability for the 2022/23 income year, the Commissioner cannot chase S3 Co for any of this amount as it has left the group clear of the tax liability. If, on the other hand, a valid TSA did not exist, S3 Co would remain jointly and severally liable for the entire $10m owed by H Co even though it has left the group.

[26.9] QUESTIONS

1. What requirements must be fulfilled for a group of entities to consolidate? Must all of a head company's subsidiary members be included in the group? What are the consequences of consolidation? How is an MEC group different from a consolidated group?
2. What is the aim of the consolidation TCSA rules? What is the 'ACA' and how is it spread over the assets of a joining entity under the TCSA rules?
3. H Co acquired 80% of the shares in S Co for $100,000 on 1 January 2010 and the remaining 20% of the shares in S Co for $50,000 on 1 August 2011. H Co decided to form a consolidated group with S Co from 1 July 2023. At the joining time, S Co had a liability of $30,000 owing on a bank loan and it owned $50,000 cash, a depreciating asset with an adjustable value of $80,000 and a market value of $100,000, trading stock with a market value of $40,000 and shares in a listed company with a market value of $20,000. Calculate H Co's TCSA in relation to the assets brought into the group.
4. In what circumstances can an entity joining a consolidated group as a subsidiary member transfer its losses to a head company? What restrictions are placed on a head company's ability to utilise transferred losses?
5. What are the tax consequences of a member of a consolidated group leaving the group? What happens to the contributing members if the head company fails to pay a group liability? What happens if the liability is covered by a tax sharing agreement?

PART

TAX INCENTIVES AND RELIEFS

27 INVESTMENT INCENTIVES

[27.1] Introduction

Income tax systems contain a broad range of tax incentives. Tax incentives are tax expenditures [1.5]. They are an indirect form of government spending designed to benefit targeted taxpayers. Based on the income tax formula set out at [8.3], the principal ways that tax incentives may be provided are by granting special exemptions, deductions, tax offsets, or reduced tax rates. The effect of each of these is summarised below:

- **Exemptions and deductions.** Tax incentives that are provided by way of exemptions or deductions reduce a taxpayer's taxable income. As a taxpayer's taxable income is required to be multiplied by their respective tax rate to determine their tax payable, a $1 tax exemption or a $1 tax deduction is worth $1 multiplied by the taxpayer's tax rate. In other words, a $1 tax exemption for a company that pays tax at the rate of 30% reduces its taxable income by $1 and therefore reduces its tax payable by 30 cents. Similarly, a $1 deduction to an individual who pays tax at the rate of 47% (including ML) reduces their taxable income by $1 and therefore reduces their tax payable by 47 cents.
- **Tax offsets.** Tax incentives that are provided by way of tax offsets reduce the tax payable by a taxpayer on their taxable income by the amount of the tax offset. The value of a $1 tax offset is therefore $1 (assuming there is sufficient income tax against which to apply the tax offset or that it is a refundable tax offset).
- **Reduced tax rates.** Tax incentives that are provided by way of a reduction in the taxpayer's tax rate reduce the tax payable on the taxpayer's taxable income by the same percentage as the decrease in tax rate. Accordingly, a 10% reduction in a taxpayer's tax rate reduces their overall tax liability by 10%.

In Australia, tax incentives are provided to taxpayers for a wide variety of reasons. For example, incentives are often used to support entities engaged in public, benevolent and philanthropic activities, such as charities [11.4], community service associations [11.5] and public hospitals [11.8].

They are also used to support particular kinds of taxpayers, such as SBEs [8.7] and primary producers (eg farmers) [25.2]. In addition, many tax incentives are provided to stimulate economic activity in particular areas where market failures are perceived to exist, or where the Government wishes to specifically boost investment.

This chapter examines a number of intricate tax incentive programs that have been established by the Australian Government to encourage certain forms of investment. In particular, it examines various programs that support investment in start-ups and other entrepreneurial 'small and medium enterprises' ('SMEs'). These entities have the potential for rapid growth and play a key role in Australia's innovation system. However, because of their risky nature, they often find it difficult to borrow money and therefore need to rely heavily on equity finance. This form of finance is known as 'venture capital' and traditionally comes from two main sources: angel investors (ie wealthy entrepreneurs and business people) and venture capital funds (ie funds run by professional fund managers). The Government supports angel investment under its early stage investors program [27.2], and it supports venture capital fund investment under its 'pooled development fund' ('PDF') [27.3], 'venture capital limited partnership' ('VCLP') and 'early stage venture capital limited partnership' ('ESVCLP') [27.4] programs.

The Government also supports Australia's innovation system under its 'research and development' ('R&D') program, which provides tax incentives to companies that undertake R&D activities [27.5]. R&D is vital for generating knowledge, making new discoveries and developing new inventions, technologies and products. Companies that invest in R&D are likely to be more innovative and more competitive than other companies, and therefore have greater chance of success.

Tax incentives are also used to support other areas, such as investment in Australian films under the film production program [27.6] and construction of affordable rental accommodation under the National Rent Affordability Scheme ('NRAS') [27.7]. The Government has also recently introduced a number of new tax incentives to support small businesses [27.8] and the development of the digital games industry [27.9].

It is important to appreciate that the Government bears the cost of tax incentives in terms of foregone revenue. In many cases, however, this cost may be offset by ancillary benefits achieved from providing the incentives. For example, if providing tax incentives to encourage venture capital or R&D investment helps a company grow and become successful, the Government will ultimately recoup some or all of the tax revenue that it has foregone when the company eventually pays tax on its income in the future. In addition, by encouraging such investment, the Government is supporting the country's overarching innovation system, which should provide spillover benefits for the broader economy, including the creation of skilled jobs in scientific and technical areas.

[27.2] Early stage investors

As part of its *National Innovation and Science Agenda*, the Turnbull Government introduced special tax incentives for early stage investors in 2016. The incentives are contained in sub-div 360-A *ITAA97* and are designed to encourage angel venture capital investment in small, innovative, unlisted, Australian start-up companies with high growth potential. These companies are known as 'early stage innovation companies' ('ESICs'). Due to their risky nature, they have traditionally struggled to raise capital and have therefore often been unable to undertake R&D and other activities that are essential for their growth. To address the funding gap problem (which is sometimes referred to as the 'valley of death') and to encourage innovation and an entrepreneurial culture, entities that subscribe for shares in ESICs are entitled to special tax incentives in the form of a non-refundable tax offset and modified CGT treatment (including an exemption from CGT for up to 10 years).

Entitlement to the tax offset

Section 360-15(1) provides that an entity is entitled to a tax offset for an income year if:

- the entity is *not* a trust, partnership, widely held company, 100% subsidiary of a widely held company, or an ESVCLP [27.4]
- at a particular time during the income year, a company issues the entity with equity interests that are shares in the company
- s 360-40(1) (which is about ESICs) applies to the company immediately after that time
- the entity and the company are not affiliates [8.6] at that time
- the issue of the shares is not an acquisition of ESS interests under an ESS [21.2], and
- immediately after the issue of the shares, the entity does not hold equity interests in the company, or in an entity connected with the company, that carry the right to:
  - receive more than 30% of any distributions of income by the company or connected entity
  - receive more than 30% of any distributions of capital by the company or connected entity, or
  - exercise, or control the exercise of, more than 30% of the total voting power in the company or connected entity.

Although trusts and partnerships are not entitled to the tax offset, special flow-through rules ensure that their members (ie their beneficiaries and partners) are entitled to respective shares of the tax offset that the trustee or partnership would have been entitled to receive if it was an individual (s 360-15(2)). Trustees that are assessed and liable to pay tax on the net income of a trust estate under ss 98, 99 or 99A [24.5] can also claim the tax offset (s 360-15(3)). The flow-through rules do not, however, apply to members of a partnership that is an ESVCLP [27.4].

Recognising that investments in ESICs are high risk, restrictions apply to limit the exposure of 'retail investors' (ie essentially those investors that do not meet the reduced disclosure requirements that apply to sophisticated and professional investors' under s 708 *Corporations Act* [22.2]). Retail investors are not entitled to any tax offset if their investment exceeds $50,000 (s 360-20).

Early stage innovation companies

Section 360-40(1) applies to a company at a particular time (ie 'test time') in an income year (ie 'current year') if the company meets all the requirements set out below and has not, before the test time, engaged in an activity of a kind prescribed by the regulations:

- **Recent incorporation or registration requirement.** The company must be:
  - (i) incorporated in Australia within the last 3 income years (the latest being the current year)
  - (ii) incorporated in Australia within the last 6 income years (the latest being the current year), and across the last 3 of those income years the company and its 100% subsidiaries must have incurred total expenses of $1m or less, or
  - (iii) registered in the Australian Business Register [39.3] within the last 3 income years (the latest being the current year).
- **Expenses and assessable income requirement.** The company and its 100% subsidiaries must have incurred total expenses of $1m or less in the income year before the current year and must have had total assessable income of $200,000 or less (disregarding any Accelerating Commercialisation Grant) in the income year before the current year.
- **Unlisted requirement.** The company's equity interests must *not* be listed for quotation on any stock exchange at the test time.
- **Innovation requirement.** The company must, at the test time, have at least 100 points under the 'innovation test' in s 360-45 or it must satisfy a set of alternative requirements. The

innovation test lists eight different innovation criteria, each with allocated points. For example, it receives 75 points if it has received an Accelerating Commercialisation Grant or if at least 50% of its total expenses for the previous income year is expenditure on R&D that it can notionally deduct under s 355-205 [27.5]. The alternative requirements are as follows:
  - the company must be genuinely focused on developing for commercialisation one or more new, or significantly improved, products, processes, services or marketing or organisational methods
  - the business relating to those products, processes, services or methods must have a high growth potential
  - the company must demonstrate that it has the potential to successfully scale that business
  - the company must demonstrate that it has the potential to be able to address a broader than local market, including global markets, through that business, and
  - the company must demonstrate that it has the potential to have competitive advantages for that business.
- **Non-foreign company requirement.** The company must not be a foreign company within the meaning of the *Corporations Act 2001* (Cth).

Nature and amount of tax offset

The tax offset that is available to an investor is generally 20% of the amount paid for the shares in the ESIC (s 360-25(1)). Although the tax offset is non-refundable, any excess tax offset may be carried forward into future income years under div 65 *ITAA97* (s 63-10).

Where the investment is made by a trust or partnership, the trustee or partnership may determine the percentage of the notional tax offset to which their respective members are entitled (subject to the proviso that where a member would be entitled to a fixed portion of any capital gain, the percentage must equal that fixed portion) (s 360-30).

The tax offset operates subject to a cap that ensures an investor (together with its affiliates) cannot claim a tax offset in an income year that exceeds $200,000 less the sum of any tax offsets that have been carried forward into the income year (ss 360-25(1A), (2)). This effectively means that investors will be able to claim tax offsets on their combined direct and indirect investments of up to $1m in a particular income year.

Modified CGT treatment

If an entity is entitled to a tax offset for an issue of shares in a company, it will be deemed to hold those shares on capital account (ss 360-50(1), (2)). This means any dealings in relation to the shares automatically fall within the CGT rules rather than within the general income tax rules. The CGT rules, however, operate subject to the following exemptions:

- The entity *must* disregard any capital loss it makes from a CGT event happening in relation to the shares if it has continuously held the shares since their issue and the CGT event happens before the tenth anniversary of the issue of the shares (s 360-50(3)).
- The entity *may* disregard any capital gain it makes from a CGT event happening in relation to the shares if it has continuously held the shares since their issue and the CGT event happens on or after the first anniversary, but before the tenth anniversary, of the issue of the shares (s 360-50(4)).

Where an entity has continuously held the shares since their issue, the first element of their cost base and reduced cost base becomes, on the tenth anniversary of their issue, the market value of the shares at that time (s 360-50(5)). This is designed to ensure that only incremental gains or losses in value that occur *after* 10 years will be taken into account for CGT purposes.

Example Angie is a sophisticated investor. On 1 August 2022, G Co, a green technology start-up company, issued 100 shares to Angie for $100,000. Assuming all the requirements for the tax offset are met, Angie is entitled to claim a tax offset of $20,000 (ie $100,000 × 20%) in respect of her investment in the 2022/23 income year. This means the net cost of her $100,000 investment is only $80,000.

If Angie sells the shares eight years later for $500,000, she can disregard the $400,000 capital gain that she has made. If, on the other hand, she sells the shares 14 years later for $2m, she will be subject to CGT. In these circumstances, if the market value of the shares on 1 August 2032 is $1.7m, she will make a capital gain of $300,000 (ie $2m – $1.7m) in the 2036/37 income year.

ESIC reporting requirements

To assist the ATO administer the tax incentives, ESICs are required to comply with third party reporting rules contained in the Taxable Payments Reporting System ('TPRS') in sub-div 396-B of sch 1 *TAA* [40.6]. These rules place obligations on the company to provide information in the approved form about shares it has issued during a financial year that could give rise to an entitlement to the tax offset or modified CGT treatment for an investor under sub-div 360-A (s 396-55). The approved form requires information concerning:

- the investor's name, address and ABN
- the number of new shares issued to the investor in the company
- the amount paid for the new shares
- the date the shares were issued, and
- the percentage of shares in the company held by the investor immediately after the shares were issued.

The information must be provided on or before the 31st day after the end of the financial year or such other time as the Commissioner specifies by legislative instrument.

The third party reporting rules operate subject to exceptions. In particular, companies do not need to provide information on certain wholesale clients (s 396-65) or entities that have been exempted by the Commissioner under legislative instrument (s 396-70).

[27.3] Pooled Development Funds

The PDF program was introduced in 1992 to address the shortage of funding available to Australian SMEs. The program uses companies that have been registered as PDFs to act as pooled investment vehicles for providing patient equity capital to SMEs that carry on eligible businesses. PDFs are essentially corporate venture capital funds that raise capital from their investors (ie their shareholders) for the purposes of making eligible investments in SMEs.

The *Pooled Development Funds Act 1992* (Cth) ('*PDF Act*') regulates PDFs and places a number of restrictions on them. The activities of PDFs are monitored by an independent statutory board established under s 6 *Industry Research and Development Act 1986* (Cth) ('*IRDA*'). The board's current name is Industry Innovation and Science Australia ('IISA') and was previously known as Innovation and Science Australia ('ISA').

Unless approval has been granted by IISA, investors (other than banks, life offices and widely held complying superannuation funds) are prohibited from owning together with their associates more than 30% of the issued shares in a PDF (s 31). This ensures that a PDF must generally have a minimum of four unassociated investors.

PDFs are required to operate as investment vehicles and cannot carry on any other business. They cannot borrow money and are only allowed to use the capital raised from their shareholders to make the following investments (s 19 *PDF Act*):

- **SME investments.** These investments consist of investments in ordinary shares, non-transferable options and loans in Australian companies that are valued at no more than $50m and are not primarily engaged in excluded activities (ie retail sale operations or land development) (ss 20, 20A, 20B, 23, 24 *PDF Act*; reg 6 *Pooled Development Funds Regulations 2018* (Cth)).
- **Unregulated investments.** These investments consist of bank deposits and investments in the short-term money market (reg 7 *Pooled Development Funds Regulations 2018* (Cth)). Unregulated investments are used by PDFs to 'park' their capital while they identify appropriate SME investments.

PDFs must believe, on reasonable grounds, that their SME investments are made for the purpose of establishing an eligible business to be carried on by the company or substantially expanding its production capacity or markets (s 21 *PDF Act*). To ensure that PDFs channel equity capital to eligible companies, unless IISA approves otherwise, PDFs are prohibited from acquiring 'pre-owned shares' in such entities (s 20 *PDF Act*). In addition, unless IISA approves otherwise, PDFs are also required to hold at least 10% of the total of all amounts paid on the issued shares in an investee company immediately after making the investment (s 27 *PDF Act*). Loans made by PDFs to investee companies cannot exceed 20% of the PDF's shareholders' funds and can only be made if the PDF first holds shares in the investee company that meet the 10% rule (s 20B *PDF Act*).

PDF program superseded by the ESVCLP program

In 2007, the PDF program was superseded by the 'ESVCLP program' [27.4]. As a consequence, it is no longer possible to register new PDFs. The PDF program, nevertheless, continues to apply to companies already registered as PDFs. Over the program's lifetime, a total of 198 PDFs were registered (including a few that were listed on the ASX). PDFs have raised over $1 billion of capital and invested in hundreds of SMEs. At the time of writing, only 18 PDFs remain in existence.

Tax concessions

Participation in the PDF program is encouraged through the provision of a broad range of tax concessions available to PDFs and their shareholders. These concessions are outlined in the diagram on the following page and examined further below.

Concessional tax rates

PDFs pay tax at concessional rates. In order to calculate their tax liabilities, PDFs must divide their taxable income into:

- an 'SME income component' (which relates to income and gains generated from SME investments), and
- an 'unregulated investment component' (which relates to income and gains from unregulated investments).

The SME income component of a PDF's taxable income is taxed at a rate of 15%, while the unregulated investment component of a PDF's taxable income is taxed at a rate of 25% (s 23(5) *ITRA*).

PDF Tax Concessions

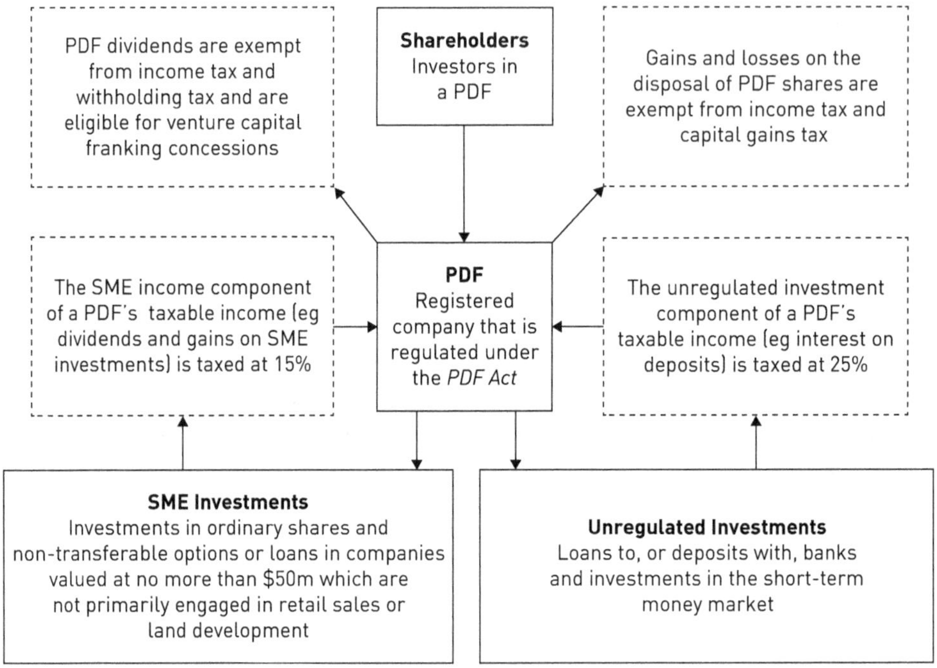

Example A company that is registered as a PDF has taxable income for an income year of $6m. Its taxable income consists of:

- an SME component of $5m (relating to a capital gain it made on the sale of shares that it owned in an SME), and
- an unregulated investment component of $1m (relating to interest that it earned on a bank deposit).

The PDF's tax liability for the year is calculated as follows:

$$\begin{aligned}\text{Tax} &= (\$5\text{m} \times 15\%) + (\$1\text{m} \times 25\%)\\ &= \$750{,}000 + \$250{,}000\\ &= \$1\text{m}\end{aligned}$$

CGT and income tax concessions

Shareholders in PDFs are not subject to income tax or capital gains tax on gains and losses made on the disposal of their PDF shares. Section 124ZN *ITAA36* provides that income derived by a taxpayer from selling shares in a PDF is exempt from tax and s 124ZO provides that shares in a PDF are not trading stock. Section 118-13 *ITAA97* provides that capital gains and losses made from CGT events relating to PDF shares are disregarded.

Example A taxpayer acquired shares in a PDF for $10,000. If the taxpayer subsequently sold the shares for $20,000, the taxpayer would not be taxed on any income or capital gain. Similarly, if the shareholder sold the shares for $5,000, the shareholder would not be entitled to any deduction or capital loss.

Dividend concessions

A PDF's shareholders are exempt from income tax (ss 124ZM(1), (4) *ITAA36*) and withholding tax (ss 128B(3)(ba), (ga)) in respect of PDF dividends. A PDF's resident shareholders may, nevertheless, choose to be assessed on franked PDF dividends (s 124ZM(7)). Making this choice allows them to benefit from the franking credits allocated to such distributions. It is beneficial for those shareholders who pay tax at rates below the PDF tax rates.

Example A PDF has taxable income consisting entirely of an SME income component of $1m. The PDF pays tax of $150,000 on this amount and distributes the balance of $850,000 (together with franking credits of $150,000) as a dividend to its shareholders. Because the PDF's tax rate is 15%, the maximum franking credit it can allocate to the dividend is $150,000 (ie $850,000 × 15/85) (s 202-60 *ITAA97*) [22.7].

One of the PDF's shareholders owns 10% of the shares in the PDF. It receives a dividend of $85,000 with franking credits of $15,000. The franked part of the dividend is therefore $85,000 (ie $15,000 × 85/15) (s 976-1 *ITAA97*) [22.7]. The shareholder can treat the franked dividend as exempt from tax, in which case they are not entitled to any franking credits and receive a 'net return' of $85,000. Alternatively, they may choose to be assessed on the franked dividend, in which case they are entitled to a tax offset for the franking credit. 27

The ways the choice affects a low-rate shareholder (eg a complying superannuation fund that pays tax at the rate of 15%) and a high-rate shareholder (eg a person who pays tax at the rate of 47%) is illustrated below.

	Superannuation fund	Individual
Franked dividend	$850,000	$850,000
Franking credit gross-up	$150,000	$150,000
Taxable income	$1,000,000	$1,000,000
Tax at 15% or 47%	$150,000	$470,000
Franking credit tax offset	$150,000	$150,000
Net tax payable (or net refund)	Nil	$320,000

The complying superannuation fund's net after-tax return is $850,000 (ie the same amount as if it had been exempt from tax on the franked dividend). The resident individual's net after-tax return, on the other hand, is only $530,000 (ie $850,000 – $320,000). The resident individual would therefore have been better off treating the franked dividend as exempt income.

Venture capital franking concessions

PDFs can maintain 'venture capital sub-accounts' under div 210 *ITAA97*. These accounts are sub-accounts of their franking accounts and are credited with income tax that is reasonably attributable to a CGT event arising in relation to their qualifying SME investments (s 210-105). PDFs are able to frank distributions with venture capital franking credits (s 210-120). 'Relevant venture capital investors' (ie non-SMSFs and certain other superannuation entities) are exempt from tax in respect of such distributions (s 124ZM(5) *ITAA36*) and are also generally entitled to tax offsets for the venture capital franking credits (ss 210-160 to 210-175).

Example If, in the previous example, the $850,000 franked part of the dividend was 'venture capital franked' and paid to a non-SMSF, then the fund could treat the entire dividend as exempt from tax yet still benefit from a tax offset of $150,000. This would result in a net return of $1m (ie $850,000 + $150,000).

Restrictions on PDF losses

Special restrictions are placed on tax losses and net capital losses made by PDFs. These losses can only be carried forward and applied in future income years if the company remains registered as a PDF in those years (ss 195-5, 195-25 *ITAA97*).

[27.4] Venture Capital Limited Partnerships and Early Stage Venture Capital Limited Partnerships

Venture capital involves making risky equity investments in unlisted start-up businesses that have high growth potential. These businesses are often 'disruptors' that are engaged in generating new knowledge, scientific discoveries and technological innovations. However, because of their small size and lack of track record, they usually struggle to obtain finance. In Australia, investment in venture capital has traditionally lagged behind many other countries. This has stifled innovation and entrepreneurship and prevented start-ups from being able to grow. To encourage venture capital investment and enhance the development of venture capital fund management expertise in Australia, the Government established the VCLP and ESVCLP programs. The VCLP program was introduced in 2002 to encourage foreign venture capital investment in eligible Australian companies and unit trusts valued at under $250m. In 2007, the VCLP program was extended to include the ESVCLP program, which supersedes the PDF program [27.3] and is designed to encourage early stage venture capital investment in eligible Australian companies and trusts valued at under $50m.

The VCLP and ESVCLP programs are regulated under the *Venture Capital Act 2002* (Cth) ('*VCA*'). They differ from the PDF program in that they use limited partnerships (rather than companies) as investment vehicles. Using these vehicles to act as venture capital funds is consistent with the practice adopted overseas, particularly in the United States, where most venture capital funds are established as limited partnerships.

Special kinds of limited partnership, known as 'incorporated limited partnerships', are formed to make investments under the VCLP and ESVCLP programs. Like other limited partnerships, incorporated limited partnerships have both 'general partners' (who manage the partnership and whose liability for partnership debts is unlimited) and 'limited partners' (who invest in the partnership and whose liability is limited to the amounts of capital they have committed to contribute) [23.2].

To come within the VCLP and ESVCLP programs, partnerships are required to be registered as VCLPs and ESVCLPs by IISA. IISA can also register another kind of limited partnership, known as an AFOF (ie Australian Venture Capital Fund of Funds). VCLPs and ESVCLPs are required to invest in 'eligible venture capital investments' ('EVCIs') (ie investments in companies and unit trusts that satisfy prescribed investment criteria). AFOFs, on the other hand, are 'fund of funds' vehicles (ie funds that invest in other funds) and can invest in VCLPs and ESVCLPs.

In practice, the general partner of a VCLP, ESVCLP or AFOF is typically another kind of limited partnership, known as a 'venture capital management partnership' ('VCMP'), which has its own general and limited partners. VCMPs do not need to be registered by IISA.

For general law purposes, the relevant state Partnership Acts treat incorporated limited partnerships as if they were companies (ie as separate legal entities). The corporate limited partnership rules in div 5A of pt III *ITAA36* [25.8] do not, however, apply to these entities. In contrast to other limited partnerships, VCLPs, ESVCLPs, AFOFs and VCMPs are not treated like companies for tax purposes. Instead, they are treated as 'transparent' entities and their partners are taxed on a 'flow-through' basis under the general partnership rules in div 5 of pt III *ITAA36*.

To encourage participation in the VCLP and ESVCLP programs, special tax concessions are available to the partners in VCLPs, ESVCLPs and AFOFs.

Registration requirements

VCLPs, ESVCLPs and AFOFs must be registered under the *VCA* with IISA. The key registration requirements are summarised below:

- **VCLPs.** To be registered as a VCLP, a limited partnership must be established under the law of Australia or a country with which Australia has a DTA and all the general partners must be residents of such countries. The partnership agreement must provide that the partnership is to remain in existence for a period of between 5 and 15 years and the partnership must have 'committed capital' of at least $10m. Each investment that the partnership holds must be an EVCI or an investment in a company or unit trust in which the partnership owns an EVCI that would have been an EVCI but for certain requirements (contained in ss 118-425(2) and (6) and ss 118-427(3) and (7)) not being fulfilled. The partnership must only carry on activities related to making such investments and every debt interest it owns must be a 'permitted loan' (s 9-1 *VCA*). 27
- **ESVCLPs.** To be registered as an ESVCLP, a limited partnership must meet the same requirements as those set out above for a VCLP. However, in addition, an ESVCLP's committed capital must not exceed $200m and none of the partners may hold (together with their associates) more than 30% of the partnership's committed capital unless IISA approves otherwise. The 30% holding rule does not apply to banks, life insurance companies, public authorities, widely held complying superannuation funds and widely held foreign venture capital funds of funds (s 9-3 *VCA*). Furthermore, each investment that the partnership holds must be in accordance with its approved investment plan, and the partnership must act in accordance with that plan. IISA must be satisfied that the partnership's investment plan is appropriate and that it has access to the skills and resources necessary to implement its investment plan (s 13(1A) *VCA*). In deciding whether an ESVCLP's investment plan is appropriate, IISA is required to consider the extent to which the partnership focuses on 'early stage venture capital' having regard to various factors, including the stages of development of the entities in which it proposes to invest, their cash flows, levels of technology and proportion of intellectual property (s 13-20 *VCA*).
- **AFOFs.** To be registered as an AFOF, a limited partnership must be established under the law of Australia and all the general partners must be Australian residents. The partnership agreement must provide that the partnership is to remain in force for between 5 and 20 years. Each investment that the partnership holds must be: (a) an investment in a VCLP or an ESVCLP; (b) an EVCI in which a VCLP or an ESVCLP, of which the partnership is a partner, owns one or more EVCIs; or (c) an investment in a company or unit trust that would be an EVCI but for certain requirements (contained in ss 118-425(2) and (6) and ss 118-427(3) and (7)) not being fulfilled. The partnership must only carry on activities related to making such investments and every debt interest it owns must be a 'permitted loan' (s 9-5 *VCA*).

A debt interest is a 'permitted loan' if it is a loan made to a company or unit trust in which the VCLP, ESVCLP or AFOF owns at least 10% of the equity interests and debt interests that can be converted into equity interests. A loan that is repaid within six months, or such longer period as IISA allows, is also a permitted loan (s 9-10 *VCA*).

An application for registration must be in writing and include certain prescribed information (s 11-1 *VCA*). Where a partnership does not meet the registration requirements (eg it may not yet have $10m of committed capital to operate as a VCLP or ESVCLP), it may be granted conditional registration if IISA is satisfied that it is likely to meet the registration requirements within two years (ss 13-5, 13-10 *VCA*). Conditional registration lapses if the partnership is not registered within two years. A partnership's registration generally comes into force on the day it is registered (unless it was first conditionally registered, in which case its registration is generally backdated to the day it was conditionally registered) (s 13-20 *VCA*). A conditionally registered VCLP, ESVCLP or AFOF may make investments; however, no tax concessions will be available to the partners until it has become fully registered.

The general partner of a VCLP, ESVCLP or AFOF must submit quarterly and annual returns to IISA and comply with any requests for information that IISA considers necessary for the purposes of administering the *VCA* (ss 15-1 to 15-20 *VCA*). IISA has the power to revoke a partnership's registration as a VCLP, ESVCLP or AFOF if it does not meet certain registration requirements (ss 17-1, 17-20 *VCA*). A general partner can also seek revocation of the partnership's registration (eg this might occur where the partnership wishes to make investments that are not EVCIs) (s 17-25 *VCA*).

At 30 June 2022, there were 108 conditionally and unconditionally registered VCLPs with committed capital of $17.91 billion, and 135 conditionally and unconditionally registered ESVCLPs with committed capital of $4.02 billion (IISA, *Annual Report 2021/22*).

Eligible venture capital investments

As outlined above, VCLPs, ESVCLPS and AFOFs are required to make investments in EVCIs. An EVCI is an investment that satisfies the requirements in s 118-425 *ITAA97* (for investments in companies) or s 118-427 *ITAA97* (for investments in unit trusts). The basic requirements of these provisions are summarised below:

- **Investment requirement.** The investment must be at risk (s 118-430) and be an acquisition of: shares in a company or units in a unit trust; options issued by a company or unit trust to acquire shares or units; or convertible notes (other than those that are debt interests) issued by a company or unit trust. In addition, the total amount that the partnership has invested in all the equity and debt interests in the company or trust and their connected entities must not exceed 30% of the partnership's committed capital (ss 118-425(1), 118-427(1)).
- **Location requirement.** The company must be an Australian resident or the trust must carry on business in Australia and have its central management and control in Australia or more than 50% of the beneficial interests in its income or property held by Australian residents. In addition, if at the time of making the investment the partnership does not own any other investments in the company or trust, the company or trust must have (unless IISA determines otherwise) more than 50% of its assets situated in Australia and more than 50% of its employees performing services in Australia during the 12 months (or such shorter period as IISA allows) from the time the investment is made (ss 118-425(2), 118-427(3)). Note: the location requirement is also deemed to be satisfied if the value of the investment together with the value of all other investments that do not otherwise meet the location requirement does not exceed 20% of the partnership's committed capital (ss 118-425(12A), 118-427(13)).
- **Unlisted requirement.** The company or trust must generally have a registered auditor and must not be listed on a stock exchange at the time the investment is made (or must be delisted within 12 months of making the investment) (ss 118-425(5), (7), 118-427(6), (8))
- **Permitted entity value requirement.** The value of the assets of the company or trust, immediately before the investment is made, must not exceed the permitted entity value (s 118-440),

being $50m (for investments made by an ESVCLP) or $250m (for investments made by a VCLP and an AFOF) (ss 118-425(6), 118-427(7))

- **Predominant activity requirement.** The company or trust must satisfy at least two of the following requirements:

  (a) more than 75% of the assets of the company or trust or their controlled entities must be used primarily in activities that are *not* ineligible activities

  (b) more than 75% of the employees of the company or trust or their controlled entities must be engaged primarily in activities that are *not* ineligible activities, and

  (c) more than 75% of the total income of the company or trust and their controlled entities must come from activities that are *not* ineligible activities (ss 118-425(3), 118-427(4)).

The following activities are 'ineligible activities':

- property development or land ownership
- finance (to the extent that it involves banking, providing capital to others, leasing, factoring or securitisation)
- insurance
- construction or acquisition of infrastructure or related facilities, and
- making investments directed at deriving interest, rent, dividends, royalties or lease payments (ss 118-425(13), 118-427(14)).

27

However, activities that consist of developing technology (or that are ancillary to incidental to developing technology) in relation to finance, insurance or making investments are *not* ineligible activities (ss 118-425(13A), 118-427(14A)). Likewise, an activity relating to finance, insurance or making investments that is covered by a private or public finding from IISA under s 118-432 stating that it is a substantially novel application of technology is *not* an ineligible activity.

Additional investment requirements for ESVCLPs

Special additional investment requirements set out in s 118-428 apply to ESVCLPs. The most important of these relates to the acquisition of a 'pre-owned investment' (eg shares or units that have already been issued to another entity). An ESVCLP can only acquire a pre-owned investment if:

- the ESVCLP already owns an investment in the entity or will be making investments that are not pre-owned investments in the entity, and
- the sum of the value of the pre-owned investment when the ESVCLP makes it and the total value of all the other pre-owned investments that the ESVCLP owns at that time does not exceed 20% of the ESVCLP's committed capital.

The aim of s 118-428 is to ensure that ESVCLPs focus on acquiring new shares and units in investees so that they provide them with fresh equity to grow their businesses.

Tax exemptions for partners

To encourage investment in the VCLP and ESVCLP programs, tax exemptions are provided to:

- partners in ESVCLPs (the exemptions only apply to a general partner if the partner is a resident of Australia or a country with which Australia has a DTA), and
- eligible venture capital partners in VCLPs and AFOFs.

An 'eligible venture capital partner' in a VCLP or AFOF is one of the following entities:

- a 'tax-exempt foreign resident'
- a 'foreign venture capital fund of funds' (provided the sum of its committed capital and the committed capital of any of its 'connected entities' does not exceed 30% of the partnership's committed capital), or
- a 'foreign resident' who is not a general partner of a VCLP or ESVCLP and is not a tax-exempt foreign resident or a foreign venture capital fund of funds (provided the partner's committed capital and the committed capital of any of its 'connected entities' is less than 10% of the partnership's committed capital) (s 118-420).

The following tax exemptions are provided under the VCLP and ESVCLP programs:

- **CGT exemption for EVCI gains and losses.** Partners in ESVCLPs and eligible venture capital partners in VCLPs and AFOFs disregard their shares of capital gains and capital losses arising from CGT events relating to EVCIs that have been owned by the partnership for at least 12 months (ss 118-405, 118-407, 118-410). However, partners in ESVCLPs are only entitled to a partial exemption for capital gains relating to EVCIs where the value of the assets of the relevant company or unit trust exceeds $250m at the end of an income year and the CGT event happens more than six months after the end of that income year (s 118-408).
- **Income tax exemption for EVCI profits and losses.** Partners in ESVCLPs and eligible venture capital partners in VCLPs and AFOFs are also exempt from income tax on their share of profits and are denied deductions for their share of losses from the realisation of EVCIs that have been owned by the partnership for at least 12 months (ss 26-68, 51-54).
- **Income tax exemption for EVCI income.** Partners in ESVCLPs are exempt from income tax on income derived from EVCIs (eg dividends paid by an investee company) (s 51-52). Likewise, partners in AFOFs are exempt from income tax on income derived from EVCIs resulting from their investments in ESVCLPs.

> ***Example*** Johnny is a limited partner who holds a 20% interest in the Hotshot ESVCLP. On 1 December 2022, the ESVCLP made an EVCI by subscribing for shares in a start-up company, G Co, for $5m. On 1 February 2025, the shares are sold for $25m. In the meantime, G Co paid a $100,000 dividend to the ESVCLP. Johnny is able to disregard his share of the gain made in relation to the shares, being $4m (ie $20m × 20%). He is also exempt from tax on his share of the dividend, being $20,000 (ie $100,000 × 20%).

Tax offset for limited partners in ESVCLPs

To encourage greater levels of investment in ESVCLPs, a tax offset is available to limited partners that contribute capital to ESVCLPs (s 61-760). The tax offset is non-refundable, but any excess tax offset may be carried forward into future years under div 65 *ITAA97*.

The amount of the tax offset that a limited partner may claim for an income year is 10% of the lesser of:

- the amounts the partner contributes to the ESVCLP during the income year, reduced by any 'excluded amounts' (ie broadly, any amounts repaid to the partner), and
- the partner's 'investment related amount' (ie broadly, the partner's share of the EVCIs made by the ESVCLP from the beginning of the income year to two months after the end of the income year) (s 61-765).

The tax offset is not available to limited partners that are trusts and partnerships. Special flow-through rules nevertheless ensure that their members are entitled to the respective shares of the tax offset that the trustee or partnership would otherwise have been entitled to if it was an individual (ss 61-760(2), 61-770). A trustee that is assessed and liable to pay tax on the net income of a trust estate under ss 98, 99 or 99A [24.5] can also claim the tax offset (s 61-760(3)).

Example If, in the previous example, Johnny contributed capital of $1m to the ESVCLP in 2022/23 and this money was used by the general partner of the ESVCLP (along with contributions from the other limited partners) to purchase the shares in G Co. Johnny is entitled to a tax offset of $100,000 (ie $1m × 10%) in 2022/23.

Tax treatment of carried interest payments

The general partners in VCLPs, ESVCLPs and AFOFs typically receive management fees as well as 'carried interest' payments for their services. Carried interest payments are distributions from VCLPs, ESVCLPs or AFOFs that are contingent on profits being attained for the limited partners. These payments represent the general partner's 'performance bonus' for making successful investments.

To encourage general partners to participate in the VCLP and ESVCLP programs, special tax treatment applies to their carried interest payments. Carried interest payments are dealt with under the CGT rules rather than under the general income tax provisions. Carried interest payments are therefore not assessable as ordinary income under s 6-5 *ITAA97* (s 118-21 *ITAA97*). Instead, CGT event K9 happens if a general partner in a VCLP, ESVCLP or AFOF or a limited partner in a VCMP receives a carried interest payment [17.3] (s 104-255). Carried interest payments under CGT event K9 are treated as 'discount capital gains' if the partnership agreement was entered into at least 12 months before the CGT event (s 115-25(2A)). Eligible partners may therefore be able to benefit from the CGT discount in respect of their carried interest payments [17.8]. These payments are therefore taxed concessionally compared with, for example, management fees which are usually assessable as ordinary income under s 6-5 *ITAA97*.

As mentioned above, most VCLPs ESVCLPs and AFOFs have VCMPs as their general partners. As VCMPs are incorporated limited partnerships, they also have their own general and limited partners. The general partner of a VCMP is usually a company and the limited partners are usually individuals. Most VCMP partnership deeds provide that management fees received by VCMPs flow through to their general partners, but carried interest payments flow through to their limited partners as only individuals (and not companies) can benefit from the CGT discount [17.8].

Example Manager ILP is a VCMP that is the general partner of the High Growth ESVCLP, which was formed on 1 September 2015. The general partner of Manager ILP is M Co and its limited partners are Bob and Alice. The ESVCLP partnership agreement stipulates that after the limited partners have been repaid their capital contributions, Manager ILP is entitled to a carried interest payment of 20% of the remaining gains made on any investment. On 1 July 2023, the ESVCLP disposed of EVCIs, which resulted in Manager ILP being entitled to receive a carried interest payment of $1m. The $1m is not included in Manager ILP's ordinary income but will instead trigger CGT event K9. As the partnership agreement was entered into more than 12 months before the CGT event, the capital gain is a discount capital gain. If the VCMP partnership agreement provides that Bob and Alice are entitled to receive any carried interest payments of the VCMP, the capital gain under CGT event K9 will flow through to Bob and Alice who will be eligible to claim the 50% CGT discount on their respective shares of the capital gain.

27

Diagram of VCLP and ESVCLP structure and tax concessions

The following diagrams outline how VCLPs and ESVCLPs are typically structured and the nature of the tax incentives available to the respective partners. They also summarise the registration requirements for such entities as well as some of the key requirements for an investment to constitute an EVCI. It is important to be aware that the rules regulating VCLPs and ESVCLPs are complex and operate subject to a number of provisos which, for the sake of brevity, are not all set out in the following diagrams.

VCLP Structure and Tax Concessions

General Partner
Manager of the partnership
(usually a VCMP)

Limited Partners
Investors who commit capital to the partnership
(usually high net worth individuals, banks and superannuation funds)

Limited partners who are eligible venture capital partners

An eligible venture capital partner is one of the following entities:

- A tax exempt foreign resident (ie, an entity which is a foreign resident, is not a general partner of a VCLP/ESVCLP, and whose income is exempt from taxation in its country of residence)
- A foreign venture capital fund of funds whose committed capital in the VCLP does not exceed 30% of the VCLP's committed capital
- A widely-held foreign venture capital fund of funds
- A taxable foreign resident who is not a general partner of a VCLP/ESVCLP and whose committed capital in the VCLP is less than 10% of the VCLP's committed capital (s 118-420)

Limited partners who are not eligible venture capital partners

- Carried interest payments are not assessable income (s 118-21)
- Carried interest payments trigger CGT event K9 (s 104-255) (CGT discount may apply if partnership agreement was entered into at least 12 months before the CGT event) (s 115-25(2A))

- Gains and losses from the disposal of EVCIs owned for at least 12 months are exempt from income tax and not deductible (ss 26-68, 51-54)
- Capital gains and losses from CGT events relating to EVCIs owned for at least 12 months are disregarded (s 118-405)

VCLP Registration requirements (s 9-1 *VCA*)

- Partnership must be established under Australian or DTA country law
- All general partners must be residents of such countries
- Partnership must remain in existence for 5-15 years
- Partnership must have at least $10m of committed capital
- Each investment the partnership holds must be an EVCI (or otherwise permitted investment)
- Partnership only carries on activities that are related to making EVCIs
- Every debt interest the partnership owns must be a permitted loan

EVCI requirements

- Investments must be at risk and be an acquisition of shares, units, options, or convertible notes in a company or unit trust, and the total amount of equity and debt interests that the VCLP owns in the company or unit trust and its connected entities must not exceed 30% of the VCLP's committed capital (ss 118-425(1), 118-427(1))
- The company must be an Australian resident or the trust must carry on business in Australia and must either have its central management and control in Australia or more than 50% of the beneficial interests in its income or property must be held by Australian residents. In addition, if at the time of making the investment the VCLP does not own any other investments in the company or trust, the company or trust must have (unless ISA determines otherwise) more than 50% of its assets situated in Australia and more than 50% of its employees performing services in Australia during the 12 months (or such shorter period as ISA allows) from the time the investment is made (ss 118-425(2), 118-427(3)). Note: these requirements are also taken to be met if the value of the investment does not exceed 20% of the partnership's committed capital (s 118-425(12A)).
- The company or trust must satisfy at least two of the following three requirements: 75% of the company's assets must be used primarily in activities that are not 'ineligible activities'; 75% of its employees must be engaged in activities that are not 'ineligible activities'; 75% of the total assessable income, exempt income, and non-assessable, non-exempt income must come from activities that are not 'ineligible activities' (ss 118-425(3), 118-427(4)). Ineligible activities are property development, land ownership, finance, insurance, construction or acquisition of infrastructure, and making investments directed at deriving interest, rent, dividends, royalties or lease payments (ss 118-425(13), 118-427(14)).
- The company or trust must generally not invest in another company (ss 118-425(4), 118-427(5)), must have a registered auditor (ss 118-425(5), 118-427(6)) and must not be listed on a stock exchange at the time the investment is made (or must be delisted within 12 months of making the investment) (ss 118-425(7), 118-427(8))
- The value of the assets of the company or trust, immediately before the investment is made, must not exceed the permitted entity value of $250m (ss 118-425(6), 118-427(7))

ESVCLP Structure and Tax Concessions

General Partner
Manager of the partnership
(usually a VCMP)

- Carried interest payments are not assessable income (s 118-21)
- Carried interest payments trigger CGT event K9 (s 104-255) (CGT discount may apply if partnership agreement was entered into at least 12 months before the CGT event) (s 115-25(2A))

Limited Partners
Investors who commit capital to the partnership
(usually high net worth individuals, banks and superannuation funds)

- 10% non-refundable tax offset is available for contributing capital to an ESVCLP
- Income from EVCIs is exempt from income tax (s 51-52)
- Capital gains and losses from CGT events relating to EVCIs owned for at least 12 months are disregarded and profits and losses from the disposal of EVCIs are exempt from income tax and not deductible (ss 26-68, 51-54, 118-407). However, only a partial exemption applies where the value of the assets of the company or unit trust exceed $250m at the end of an income year, and the CGT event happens more than 6 months after the end of the year (s 118-408).

ESVCLP Registration requirements (s 9-3 *VCA*)

- Partnership must be established under Australian or DTA country law
- All general partners must be residents of such countries
- Partnership must remain in existence for 5-15 years
- Partnership must have at least $10m and no more than $200m of committed capital
- Each investment the partnership holds must be an EVCI (or otherwise permitted investment)
- Investments must be held in accordance with the partnership's approved investment plan
- Partnership acts in accordance with its approved investment plan
- Partnership only carries on activities that are related to making EVCIs
- Every debt interest the partnership owns must be a permitted loan
- None of the partners have more than 30% of the fund's committed capital. This limit does not apply to certain entities (eg ADIs, widely-held complying superannuation funds, widely-held foreign venture capital fund of funds and life insurance companies). It also does not apply if ISA allows the limit to be exceeded (s 9-4).

EVCI requirements

- Investments must be at risk and be an acquisition of shares, units, options, or convertible notes in a company or unit trust, and the total amount of equity and debt interests that the ESVCLP owns in the company or unit trust and its connected entities must not exceed 30% of the ESVCLP's committed capital (ss 118-425(1), 118-427(1))
- The company must be an Australian resident or the trust must carry on business in Australia and must either have its central management and control in Australia or more than 50% of the beneficial interests in its income or property must be held by Australian residents. In addition, if at the time of making the investment the ESVCLP does not own any other investments in the company or trust, the company or trust must have (unless ISA determines otherwise) more than 50% of its assets situated in Australia and more than 50% of its employees performing services in Australia during the 12 months (or such shorter period as ISA allows) from the time the investment is made (ss 118-425(2), 118-427(3)). Note: these requirements are also taken to be met if the value of the investments do not exceed 20% of the partnership's committed capital (ss 118-425(12A), 118-427(13)).
- The company or trust must satisfy at least two of the following three requirements: 75% of the company's assets must be used primarily in activities that are not 'ineligible activities'; 75% of its employees must be engaged in activities that are not 'ineligible activities'; 75% of the total assessable income, exempt income, and non-assessable, non-exempt income must come from activities that are not 'ineligible activities' (ss 118-425(3), 118-427(4)). Ineligible activities are property development or land ownership, finance and insurance, construction or acquisition of infrastructure, and making investments directed at deriving interest, rent, dividends, royalties or lease payments (ss 118-425(13), 118-427(14)).
- The company or trust must generally not invest in another company (ss 118-425(4), 118-427(5)), must have a registered auditor (ss 118-425(5), 118-427(6)) and must not be listed on a stock exchange at the time the investment is made (or must be delisted within 12 months of making the investment) (ss 118-425(7), 118-427(8))
- The value of the assets of the company or trust, immediately before the investment is made, must not exceed the permitted entity value of $50m (ss 118-425(6), 118-427(7))
- Pre-owned investments can only be acquired if the ESVCLP already owns an investment in the entity or will be making investments that are not pre-owned investments in the entity, and the sum of the value of the pre-owned investments at the time of investment and the value of all other investments that the ESVCLP owns at the time does not exceed 20% of its committed capital (s 118-428)

27

[27.5] Research and development

R&D generates new knowledge and has played a key role in the development of many revolutionary inventions, technologies and products that have changed the world. R&D also supports innovation, economic growth and the creation of skilled jobs that are critical for a country's scientific and technological advancement. Companies that invest in R&D stand to improve their competitiveness and productivity and are more likely to become leaders in their field. The successful commercialisation of R&D can also open new markets for companies and improve their profitability.

However, due to its investigative and experimental nature, R&D is inherently risky and its outcomes uncertain. R&D can also involve considerable costs, including salaries for staff and substantial capital investment in plant and equipment. Many companies may, therefore, be reluctant to undertake such activities without some form of government support.

Over the years, the Australian Government has provided various tax incentives to encourage companies to undertake R&D. However, despite these incentives, investment in R&D remains relatively modest. Australia's gross expenditure on R&D ('GERD') as a proportion of GDP has decreased from 2.11% in 2011/12 to 1.79% in 2019/20 (Australian Bureau of Statistics, *Research and Experimental Development, Businesses, Australia* (2021)). This indicates Australia's R&D intensity is declining, which is concerning as there are often strong correlations between a country's R&D intensity and its wealth. It is also concerning that Australia's GERD as a proportion of GDP is consistently below the OECD average (OECD, *Main Science and Technology Indicators* (2022)). This suggests that Australia is lagging behind its peers in its investment in generating new knowledge.

Division 355 *ITAA97*

Australia's R&D tax incentive is located in div 355 *ITAA97*. Section s 355-5(1) states that the object of div 355 'is to encourage industry to conduct R&D activities that might otherwise not be conducted because of an uncertain return from the activities, in cases where the knowledge gained is likely to benefit the wider Australian economy'. Section 355-5(2) goes on to explain that this object 'is to be achieved by providing a tax incentive for industry to conduct, in a scientific way, experimental activities for the purpose of generating new knowledge or information in either a general or applied form (including new knowledge in the form of new or improved materials, products, devices, processes or services).'

Division 355 was introduced on 1 July 2011 and replaced a set of former tax incentives in ss 73B to 73Z *ITAA36*, which provided eligible companies with a range of special tax deductions, including:

- a 125% deduction for expenditure on R&D activities and salaries
- a 50% deduction for increased R&D expenditure (measured over three years)
- a 100% deduction for core technology (eg a licence to use intellectual property)
- a 125% write-off for plant used for R&D activities, and
- a 2.5% deduction each year over 40 years for expenditure on R&D buildings.

Division 355 provides 'R&D entities' with a tax offset (rather than deductions) for their expenditure on 'R&D activities'. The R&D tax offset favours smaller companies as they are entitled to a greater tax offset than larger companies. It also benefits smaller companies that are not yet producing significant amounts of income (eg start-ups) as the tax offset for these companies is refundable.

R&D entities

An R&D entity is one of the following:

- a corporation incorporated under an Australian law (s 335-35(1)(a))
- a corporation incorporated under a foreign law that is an Australian resident (s 335-35(1)(b)), or

- a corporation incorporated under a foreign law that is a resident of a country with which Australia has a DTA and which carries on business through a PE [30.5] in Australia (s 335-35(2)).

An exempt entity cannot be an R&D entity (s 335-35(3)).

In order to claim the R&D tax offset, an R&D entity must be registered by IISA for its R&D activities for the relevant income year. The registration process is undertaken under div 2 of pt III *IRDA*. Companies have 10 months from the end of their income year to lodge an application for registration of the R&D activities they conducted in the previous year.

To provide R&D entities with greater certainty regarding their entitlement to the R&D tax offset, IISA can make an 'advance finding' about their activities before registration (s 28A *IRDA*). Such a finding is binding on the Commissioner for the purpose of working out the R&D tax offset under div 355 for the year of application and the next two income years (s 355-705 *ITAA97*).

R&D activities

'R&D activities' are defined in s 355-20 as 'core R&D activities' or 'supporting R&D activities'. These terms have the following meanings:

- **Core R&D activities.** Core R&D activities are defined in s 355-25(1) as 'experimental activities':
  (a) whose outcome cannot be known or determined in advance on the basis of current knowledge, information or experience, but can only be determined by applying a systematic progression of work that:
    (i) is based on principles of established science, and
    (ii) proceeds from hypothesis to experiment, observation and evaluation, and leads to logical conclusions, and
  (b) that are conducted for the purpose of generating new knowledge (including new knowledge in the form of improved materials, products, devices, processes or services).

  The following activities are expressly excluded from being core R&D activities under s 355-25(2):
  - market research, market testing or market development, or sales promotion (including consumer surveys)
  - prospecting, exploring or drilling for minerals or petroleum for the purposes of one or more of the following: (i) discovering deposits; (ii) determining more precisely the location of deposits; (iii) determining the size or quality of deposits
  - management studies or efficiency surveys
  - research in social sciences, arts or humanities
  - commercial, legal and administrative aspects of patenting, licensing or other activities
  - activities associated with complying with statutory requirements or standards, including one or more of the following: (i) maintaining national standards; (ii) calibrating secondary standards; (iii) routine testing and analysis of materials, components, products, processes, soils, atmospheres and other things
  - any activity related to the reproduction of a commercial product or process: (i) by a physical examination of an existing system; or (ii) from plans, blueprints, detailed specifications or publicly available information, and
  - developing, modifying or customising computer software for the dominant purpose of use by any of the following entities for their internal administration: (i) the entity for which the software is developed, Modified or customised; (ii) an entity connected with the developer; (iii) an affiliate of the developer, or an entity of which the developer is an affiliate.

- **Supporting R&D activities.** Supporting R&D activities are defined in s 355-30 as activities 'directly related' to core R&D activities (ie activities that have a direct, close and immediate relationship with core R&D activities). However, activities covered by the exclusions in s 355-25(2) or that produce, or are directly related to producing, goods or services are supporting R&D activities only if they are undertaken for the 'dominant' (ie 'prevailing' or 'most influential') purpose of supporting core R&D activities.

The concept of R&D activities was considered in *Moreton Resources Ltd v ISA* 2019 ATC ¶20-700. The case concerned a pilot project to test the viability of existing underground coal gasification technology used to synthesise gas for a facility at a site in Queensland. The pilot project ultimately failed, and the facility broke down causing underground water contamination. The Full Federal Court took a broad view of the object of div 355 and held that core R&D activities could include experimental activities to generate new knowledge to overcome uncertainties in the application of existing technologies to a new site.

By way of contrast, in *Coal of Queensland Pty Ltd v ISA* 2021 ATC ¶20-789, the Full Federal Court held that activities undertaken by a taxpayer to make the mining, processing and handling of highly branded coal seams economically viable were not core R&D or supporting R&D activities, as the evidence indicated that the outcome of the work could have been determined in advance and was not conducted for the substantial purpose of generating new knowledge.

More recently, in *Lakes Oil NL v ISA* 2023 ATC ¶10-667, the AAT held that the activities of an oil mining company were ineligible for registration as R&D activities as they fell within the prospecting, exploring or drilling exclusion in s 355-25(2).

Tax offset based on 'notional deductions'

An R&D entity's tax offset is based on the amounts it can 'notionally' deduct for the income year under the following provisions listed in s 355-100:

- s 355-205 (R&D expenditure on R&D activities)
- s 355-305 (decline in value of depreciating assets used for R&D activities)
- s 355-315 (balancing adjustment for depreciating assets only used for R&D activities)
- s 355-480 (earlier year associate expenditure for R&D activities)
- s 355-520 (partner's proportion of decline in value of R&D partnership depreciating assets used for R&D activities)
- s 355-525 (partner's proportion of balancing adjustment for R&D partnership depreciating assets only used for R&D activities), and
- s 355-580 (contributions to a Cooperative Research Centre).

A special rule limits the amount of the tax offset where an R&D entity's notional deductions are under $20,000 for an income year. Broadly speaking, in such a case, the tax offset only applies to: (a) amounts that the R&D entity can notionally deduct under s 355-205 and are incurred to a non-associated 'research service provider' within the meaning of the *IRDA*; and (b) amounts that the R&D entity can notionally deduct under 355-580 (s 355-100(2)).

R&D activities must generally be conducted in Australia (s 355-210). In certain cases, however, overseas R&D activities may also qualify provided IISA has made a 'finding' that the overseas activities meet the conditions in s 28D *IRDA*. To satisfy these conditions, the overseas activities must have a significant scientific link to Australian core R&D activities and must not be able to be conducted in Australia for particular reasons (eg because of a lack of access to expertise or equipment in Australia). In addition, the total actual and reasonably anticipated expenditure on overseas R&D activities must be less than the total actual and anticipated expenditure on R&D activities conducted in Australia.

As a general rule, an R&D entity is only entitled to notional deductions for expenditure on R&D activities conducted for itself and not for another entity (s 355-210). There are, however, some limited exceptions to this rule (eg certain R&D activities conducted in Australia under a written agreement on behalf of a foreign resident that is connected or affiliated with the R&D entity) (s 355-220).

To prevent abuse, special 'integrity rules' apply where the expenditure is not at 'arm's length' (s 355-400) or 'at risk' (s 355-405).

Calculating the R&D tax offset

For the 2021/22 and later income years, the R&D tax offset is calculated as follows:

- **Small R&D entities.** If the R&D entity's aggregated turnover [8.6] for the income year is less than $20m, it is entitled to a *refundable* tax offset for up to $150m of its notional deductions for the income year at a rate equal to its corporate tax rate for the year plus a 'premium' of 18.5% (s 355-100(1)).
- **Large R&D entities.** If the R&D entity's aggregated turnover for the income year is $20m or more, it is entitled to a *non-refundable* tax offset for up to $150m of its notional deductions for the income year at a rate equal to its corporate tax rate plus an 'intensity premium' of 8.5% (for notional deductions up to 2% of the R&D entity's total expenses calculated under s 355-115) and 16.5% (for notional deductions above 2% of the R&D entity's total expenses calculated under s 355-115) (s 355-100(1A)).

To the extent that an R&D entity's notional deductions for the income year exceed $150m, it is entitled to a non-refundable tax offset at its corporate tax rate for the income year on the excess amount (s 355-100(3)).

Example

Small R&D entity

S Co is a base rate entity that has a corporate tax rate of 25% for 2023/24. It has aggregated turnover of $3m and notional deductions of $10m in 2023/24. As its aggregated turnover is below $20m, its R&D tax offset rate is 43.5% (ie 25% + 18.5%). S Co is therefore entitled to a refundable tax offset of $4.35m (ie $10m × 43.5%).

Large R&D entity

L Co is not a base rate entity and has a corporate tax rate of 30% for 2023/24. It has aggregated turnover of $1,200m in 2023/24. It also has total expenses of $1,000m, which includes notional deductions of $180m, in that year. L Co is therefore entitled to a non-refundable tax offset of $77.15m calculated as follows:

Tier	Notional deductions	R&D premium	Non-refundable tax offset
2% of total expenses (up to $150m)	$20m (ie 2% of $1,000m)	8.5%	$20m × 38.5% = $7.7m
Excess of total expenses (up to $150m)	$130m (ie $150m – $20m)	16.5%	$130m × 46.5% = $60.45m
Excess of total expenses (above $150m)	$30m (ie $180m – $150m)	Nil	$30m × 30% = $9m
Total	$180m		$77.15m

Clawback rules

The R&D tax incentive operates subject to special 'clawback' and 'catch up' rules that aim to protect the integrity of the R&D tax incentive and prevent duplication of benefits. For example, these rules can apply where a balancing adjustment event [15.3] happens to an asset that an R&D entity, or a partnership in which it is a partner, held for R&D purposes (ss 355-446, 355-449, 355-465, 355-468). A clawback can also arise where an R&D entity:

- receives a recoupment (eg a grant) from a government agency of expenditure on R&D activities (s 355-440), or
- incurs expenditure on goods, materials or energy used during R&D activities in producing marketable products or products applied for its own use (s 355-445).

An R&D entity that has a clawback amount is required to include an additional amount in its assessable income calculated under s 355-450. An R&D entity that has a catch-up amount is entitled to a deduction calculated under s 355-475.

[27.6] Film production

Having a strong and vibrant film industry is important to Australia for both economic and cultural reasons. The Australian film industry fosters the arts, creates jobs and promotes national identity. The Government has supported investment in Australian films through the provision of various tax incentives over the years. In the past, these incentives were provided by way of special deductions available under former divs 10B and 10BA of pt III *ITAA36*. A new incentive scheme, contained in div 376 *ITAA97*, applies from 1 July 2007. This scheme provides companies with refundable tax offsets in respect of their 'qualifying Australian production expenditure' ('QAPE').

Tax offsets

There are three kinds of tax offsets available under div 376:

- **Producer offset.** A company is entitled to a refundable tax offset of 40% of its QAPE on an eligible feature film or 30% of its QAPE on other eligible films (ss 376-55 to 376-75).
- **Location offset.** A company is entitled to a refundable tax offset of 16.5% of its QAPE on an eligible film (ss 376-10 to 376-30).
- **PDV offset.** A company is entitled to a refundable tax offset of 30% of its total QAPE on post, digital and visual ('PDV') effects production on an eligible film (ss 376-35 to 376-50).

In order to be able to claim the tax offsets, a company must satisfy certain conditions, including the requirement that it has been issued with a certificate from either the film authority ('Screen Australia') (in the case of the production offset) or the Arts Minister (in the case of the location offset and PDV offset). Certificates are only issued where the film meets specified eligibility criteria and certain conditions are fulfilled.

Qualifying Australian production expenditure

A company's QAPE on a film is its 'production expenditure' incurred on the film to the extent that it is reasonably attributable to:

- goods and services provided in Australia
- the use of land located in Australia, or
- the use of goods located in Australia at the time that they are used in the making of a film (s 376-145).

It also includes specific expenditure mentioned in s 376-150 (eg Australian development expenditure, expenditure incurred in acquiring Australian copyright, expenditure incurred in producing Australian copyrighted promotional material and expenditure incurred in producing additional content).

A company's QAPE also includes:

- for the location offset and PDV offset, the expenditure mentioned in s 376-165 (eg Australian business overheads and expenditure on certain travel to Australia and freighting goods to Australia), and
- for the producer offset, the expenditure mentioned in s 376-170 (eg its Australian business overheads, expenditure on certain travel to Australia and other countries, and expenditure on freighting goods between countries).

However, QAPE does not include expenditure excluded under s 376-155 (eg expenditure incurred when the company is a foreign resident without a PE in Australia and an ABN, and remuneration or travel costs to Australia of a non-cast member entering Australia to work on the film for less than two consecutive weeks).

Production expenditure covers expenditure incurred by a company to the extent that it relates to making the film—this includes pre-production and post-production activities, but not developing the proposal for the film, or distributing or promoting the film (ss 376-125, 376-130). It also includes deductions under div 40 *ITAA97* relating to depreciating assets used in making the film as well as certain other expenditure. The expenditure mentioned in s 376-135 is, however, expressly excluded. For the location offset, production expenditure also excludes expenditure on a television series that is not a feature film or a mini-series of a television drama and expenditure on producing a pilot episode of a television series (s 376-140).

Producer offset

Section 376-55 provides that a company is entitled to claim the producer offset for an income year if:

- it has completed a film in the income year
- the film authority has issued a certificate to the company under s 376-65 for the film, and
- the company is either an Australian resident or a foreign resident with an ABN that has a PE in Australia.

The film authority must issue the company with a certificate if it is satisfied that the film has met certain conditions, including:

- the film has significant Australian content (determined having regard to the matters in s 376-70) or has been made under an arrangement between the Commonwealth and a foreign country
- the film was produced for exhibition to the public in cinemas or via television or as a video recording
- the film is a feature film, a single episode program, series, a season of a series or a short form animation drama
- the film is not an ineligible film (eg an advertising program or commercial, a quiz or panel program, a training film, a computer game, a news or current affairs program or a reality program), and
- the company's total QAPE on the film meets the minimum expenditure threshold (which for most films is either $500,000 or $1m depending on the nature of the film) (s 376-65).

The film authority must issue a written determination of the company's QAPE on the film if a company has applied for a certificate under s 376-65 (s 376-75). The producer offset is currently 40% (for a feature film) or 30% (for other films) of the QAPE determined by the film authority (s 376-60).

> ***Example*** Empire Films is a resident company that incurred expenditure in buying goods and services for a feature film in Australia, which it completed in the income year. The film authority has issued Empire Films with a certificate in respect of the film and determined that its total QAPE is $10m. Empire Films is entitled to claim a $4m tax offset (40% × $10m).

Location offset

Section 376-10 provides that a company is entitled to claim the location offset for an income year in respect of a film if:

- its production expenditure on the film ceased being incurred in the income year
- the Arts Minister has issued a certificate to the company under s 376-20 for the film, and
- the company is either an Australian resident or a foreign resident with an ABN that has a PE in Australia.

The Arts Minister must issue the company with a certificate if it is satisfied that the film has met certain conditions, including the following:

- the film was produced for exhibition to the public in cinemas or via television or as a video recording
- the film is a feature film or film of a like nature, television drama mini-series or other television series
- the film is not an ineligible film (eg a documentary, an advertising program or commercial, a quiz or panel program, a film of a public event, a training film, a computer game), and
- the company's total QAPE on the film is at least $15m (s 376-20).

The Arts Minister must issue a written determination of the company's QAPE on the film if a company has applied for a certificate under s 376-20 (s 376-30). The location offset is 16.5% of the QAPE determined by the Arts Minister (s 376-15). In the 2023 Budget, the Government announced that, from 2024/25, this rate will increase to 30% and companies will need to have total QAPE of $20m instead of $15m.

PDV offset

Section 376-35 provides that a company is entitled to claim the PDV offset for an income year in respect of a film if:

- its QAPE, to the extent that it relates to 'PDV effects production' for the film, ceased during the year
- the Arts Minister has issued a certificate to the company under s 376-45 for the PDV effects for the film, and
- the company is either an Australian resident or a foreign resident with an ABN that has a PE in Australia.

PDV effects production for a film is defined as the creation of audio or visual elements (except principal photography, pick ups or the creation of physical elements such as sets, props or costumes) for the film, the manipulation of audio or visual elements (other than pick ups or physical elements) for the film and any necessarily related activities (s 376-35(2)).

The Arts Minister must issue the company with a certificate for its PDV effects production for a film if it is satisfied that certain conditions have been met, including the following:

- the film was produced for exhibition to the public in cinemas or via television or as a video recording

- the film is a feature film or film of a like nature, television drama mini-series or other television series
- the film is not an ineligible film (eg a documentary, an advertising program or commercial, a quiz or panel program, a film of a public event, a training film or a computer game), and
- the company's total QAPE on PDV effects production is at least $500,000 and the company either carried out, or made the arrangements for the carrying out of, all the activities in Australia that were necessary for the PDV effects production (s 376-45).

The Arts Minister must issue a written determination of the company's QAPE on the PDV effects production for a film if a company has applied for a certificate under s 376-45 (s 376-50). The PDV offset is 30% of the QAPE determined by the Arts Minister (s 376-40).

Example Empire Films is a resident company that incurred $50m in creating audio visual special effects and $20m in creating sets, props and costumes for a television drama which it completed in the income year. The Arts Minister has issued Empire Films with a certificate in respect of the film and provided a written determination that its total QAPE relating to PDV effects production is $50m. Empire Films is entitled to claim a $15m tax offset (30% × $50m).

[27.7] National Rental Affordability Scheme

The NRAS program is a joint Commonwealth–state scheme that was introduced in 2008 to address the shortage of affordable rental accommodation in Australia. The program is regulated under the *National Rental Affordability Scheme Act 2008* (Cth) and the *National Rental Affordability Scheme Regulations 2020* (Cth). Its aims are to increase the supply of new affordable rental housing, reduce rental costs for low- and moderate-income households, and encourage large-scale investment and innovative delivery of affordable housing.

NRAS incentives

The NRAS program provides the following annual incentives over a period of 10 years to approved NRAS participants engaged in constructing eligible accommodation:

- a Commonwealth Government incentive ($8,711.48 per dwelling in 2023/24) in the form of a refundable tax offset available under div 380 *ITAA97* or a direct payment (in the case of tax-exempt entities), and
- a state or territory Government incentive ($2,903.83 per dwelling in 2023/24) in the form of direct or in-kind financial support.

The incentives are indexed annually and provided on the condition that throughout the relevant period the dwelling is rented at 20% below market rates to qualifying NRAS tenants (ie tenants whose household incomes do not exceed specified income thresholds).

State and territory government NRAS payments are non-assessable non-exempt income of the recipients (s 380-35). In addition, any capital gains and losses arising from any incentives are disregarded (s 118-37).

Suspension of NRAS

In the 2014 Budget, the Commonwealth Government announced that it would suspend future NRAS approvals. Existing NRAS participants, however, continue to benefit under the scheme.

[27.8] Small business temporary incentives

The Government recently introduced two new temporary incentives: the 'skills and training boost' and the 'technology investment boost'. The incentives are available to SBEs and entities that would be SBEs if the aggregated turnover threshold for SBEs was $50m (instead of $10m).

Skills and training boost

The skills and training boost gives eligible businesses an additional 20% deduction on expenditure on external training for their employees (s 328-445 *ITTPA*). To qualify for the deduction, the expenditure must be:

- for training employees, either in-person in Australia, or online
- fully deductible under another provision of the taxation law
- charged, directly or indirectly, by a registered training provider (which must not be the small business or their associate) for training within the scope of the provider's registration (except where the provider is a registered higher education provider), and
- incurred between 7.30pm on 29 March 2022 and 30 June 2024 (s 328-450 *ITTPA*).

> ***Example*** C Co is an SBE. In November 2023, it paid $5,000 for one of its employees to undertake external training delivered by a university that is a registered training provider. No GST was charged by the provider as the training was a GST-free education course [7.7]. In addition to being able to claim $5,000 as a deduction under s 8-1 *ITAA97*, C Co is also entitled to a bonus deduction of $1,000 (ie $5,000 × 20%) under s 328-445 *ITTPA*.

Technology investment boost

The technology investment boost gives eligible businesses an additional 20% deduction (up to a maximum deduction cap of $20,000) for expenditure that supports their digital operations (eg expenditure on computers, software, digital marketing and cyber security) (s 328-455 *ITTPA*). To qualify for the deduction, the expenditure must be:

- wholly or substantially for the purposes of the entity's digital operations
- deductible under another provision of the taxation law and must not be excluded under s 328-460(5) (eg salary or wages)
- incurred between 7:30pm on 29 March 2022 and 30 June 2023 and, if it is on a depreciating asset, the asset must be first used or installed ready for use by 30 June 2023 (s 328-460 *ITTPA*).

Energy incentive

In the 2023 Budget, the Government announced that businesses with aggregated turnover of less than $50m will be able to deduct an additional 20% of the cost of depreciating assets that support electrification and more efficient use of energy. The incentive will apply to a range of depreciating assets, including assets that upgrade electrical efficiency (eg energy-efficient fridges) and assets that support electrification (eg electric heating and cooling systems). Certain assets will be excluded (eg electric vehicles, renewable electricity generation assets, capital works, and assets that are not connected to the electricity grid and use fossil fuels). To qualify for the deduction, the eligible assets must be first used or installed ready for use between 1 July 2023 and 30 June 2024. Expenditure of up to $100,000 will be eligible, meaning that the maximum bonus deduction is capped at $20,000.

[27.9] Digital games tax offset

One of the fastest growing industries in the world is the digital games industry. To support the industry and the opportunities it presents for creating digital talent with highly transferrable skills that can be used across the IT sector in Australia, the Government introduced a refundable digital games tax offset ('DGTO') in div 378 *ITAA97*.

The DGTO is available to resident companies and foreign companies with PEs in Australia that have ABNs and that spend at least $500,000 on 'qualifying Australian development expenditure' in completing or porting a digital game or carrying on ongoing development of digital games in an income year (s 378-10). A 'digital game' is defined as a game in electronic form that is capable of generating a display on a portable electronic device, or on a computer monitor, television screen, liquid crystal display or similar medium that allows for the playing of an interactive game (s 378-20). The company must obtain a certificate for the digital game from the Arts Minister for the income year (ss 378-25, 378-30). Certain games (eg those with gambling elements or that contain material likely to lead to the game being refused classification) are not eligible.

The tax offset is the lower of: (a) 30% of the total qualifying Australian development expenditure as determined by the Arts Minister; and (b) $20m (s 378-15).

[27.10] QUESTIONS

1. Angelo is a wealthy angel investor. On 5 May 2023, he subscribed for new shares in S Co, an unlisted start-up company involved in developing a revolutionary new and environmentally friendly weed killer. Angelo paid $40,000 to purchase 20% of the shares in the company. S Co was incorporated two years before Angelo made the investment. It has not yet generated any assessable income but has incurred expenses of $300,000 on clinical trials of its product. Angelo believes S Co has the potential for rapid growth and will be able to use the internet to successfully scale its operations around the world. He also believes the company has no direct competitors. S Co becomes a successful company and, on 5 March 2028, Angelo sells his shares in it for $500,000 to a private equity fund. What are the tax implications for Angelo?
2. Fred is a resident who purchased 100 shares in a PDF for $10,000 at the beginning of the current financial year. A few months later, the PDF paid Fred a $850 dividend with $150 of franking credits allocated to it. Shortly thereafter, Fred sold his shares in the PDF for $14,000. Discuss the tax implications of these transactions.
3. Discuss the differences between the PDF, VCLP and ESVCLP programs and the tax concessions available under them.
4. Bloom ESVCLP is an incorporated limited partnership that was registered as an ESVCLP on 5 May 2023. The general partner of Bloom ESVCLP is Manager ILP, a VCMP. Bloom ESVCLP has 10 limited partners who each own a 10% interest in the partnership. Under the partnership agreement, the general partner is entitled to a carried interest payment of 20% of the profits from the sale of any investments made by the partnership. On 20 September 2023, each of the limited partners contributed $100,000 to the partnership. The general partner used the $1m to subscribe for new shares in an unlisted start-up company, Growth Co. This gave the partnership a 25% interest in the company. Growth Co was involved in developing and commercialising new laser technology and became successful. On 8 June 2028, to regain total control of the company, the founder of Growth Co (who owned the remaining 75% of the shares in the company) purchased Bloom ESVCLP's shares for $10m. This resulted in Bloom ESVCLP making a $9m gain. As a consequence, Manager ILP was paid a carried interest payment of $1.8m and each of the limited partners received a payment of $820,000. Discuss the tax consequences of the transactions for the parties.

5. What conditions must be satisfied to obtain the R&D tax incentive? What kinds of expenditure does it apply to? What rates of tax offset apply?
6. What kinds of tax offsets are available to companies for expenditure on Australian film production and the development of digital games? What conditions must be satisfied for these tax offsets to be available?

BUSINESS AND ENTITY RESTRUCTURE RELIEF 28

[28.1] Introduction

Business and entity restructures are common in the commercial world. To ensure the tax law does not impede or frustrate such activity, special roll-over and other forms of tax relief are available. Without this relief, these restructures might otherwise give rise to a number of adverse CGT and other consequences for the parties involved.

This chapter examines the roll-over relief available for:

- small business restructures [28.2]
- scrip for scrip takeovers [28.3]
- demergers [28.4]
- disposals of assets to, and creation of assets in, wholly owned companies [28.5]
- exchanges of shares or units in the same company or unit trust [28.6], and
- exchanges of shares or units for shares in an interposed company [28.7].

In 2019, the Assistant Treasurer announced that the Board of Taxation would review the roll-over provisions. In February 2020, the Board published a Consultation Guide containing an overview of the provisions and various policy considerations central to improving their framework. In December 2020, it released a Consultation Paper, *Review of CGT Roll-Overs*, in which it sought submissions on its proposal to rationalise and replace some existing roll-overs dealing with common business restructuring transactions with a single comprehensive 'general restructure roll-over'. At the time of writing, the Albanese Government has not indicated whether it plans to make any changes to the rules.

[28.2] Small business restructures

Subdivision 328-G *ITAA97* provides roll-over relief in relation to the restructure of a small business. A roll-over is available in relation to an asset that, under a transaction, is transferred by an entity to one or more other entities where the following requirements are met (s 328-430(1)):

- **Genuine restructure requirement.** The transaction must be part of a genuine restructure of an ongoing business. Whether a restructure is genuine is a question of fact. A transaction is deemed to be a genuine restructure if, in the 3 years after the transaction takes effect, there is no change in the ultimate economic ownership of any of the significant assets of the business (excluding trading stock), those assets continue to be active assets and there is no significant or material use of those assets for private purposes (s 328-435).

- **SBE requirement.** Each party to the transfer must be an entity that: (a) is an SBE; (b) has an affiliate that is an SBE; (c) is connected with an SBE; or (d) is a partner in a partnership that is an SBE [8.7].
- **Ultimate economic ownership requirement.** The transaction must not have the effect of materially changing the ultimate economic ownership of the asset nor the proportionate shares of that ownership. In the case of a non-fixed trust that is a family trust, every individual who had ultimate economic ownership of the asset just before the transfer, and every individual who has ultimate economic ownership of the asset just after the transfer, must be members of the same family group (s 328-440).
- **CGT active asset requirement.** The asset must be a CGT asset (other than a depreciating asset) that is an active asset [17.9].
- **Residency requirement.** Both the transferor and each transferee must: (a) be an Australian resident; (b) be a resident trust for CGT purposes; (c) have at least one partner who is an Australian resident; or (d) be a resident corporate limited partnership under s 94T *ITAA36* (s 328-445).
- **Choice requirement.** Both the transferor and each transferee must choose to apply the roll-over.

The roll-over is not available if the transferor or any transferee is an exempt entity or a complying superannuation entity (s 328-430(2)).

Consequences of the roll-over for assets

If the roll-over applies, the transfer does not generally result in any direct tax consequences (s 328-450). The asset is deemed to have been transferred by the transferor and acquired by the transferee for its 'roll-over cost' (s 328-455(1)), which is determined as follows:

- **CGT assets.** The roll-over cost in relation to a CGT asset (other than trading stock, a revenue asset, or a depreciating asset) is the transferor's cost base for that asset just before the transfer takes effect (s 328-455(2)(a)). Pre-CGT assets are taken to have been acquired by the transferee before 20 September 1985 (s 328-460).
- **Trading stock.** The roll-over cost in relation to an asset that is trading stock is its cost for the transferor, or if it was held as trading stock at the start of the income year, its value for the transferor (s 328-455(2)(b)).
- **Revenue assets.** The roll-over cost of a revenue asset is the amount that would result in the transferor not making a profit or loss on the transfer (s 328-455(2)(c)).

The roll-over does not apply to depreciating assets, which may be subject to separate roll-over relief under s 40-340 *ITAA97* [15.2].

Consequences of roll-over for membership interests

Where membership interests are issued wholly as consideration for the transferred assets under the restructure, the cost base and reduced cost base of those interests is the sum of the roll-over costs of the transferred assets that are neither depreciating assets nor pre-CGT assets plus the adjustable values of the depreciating assets (less any liabilities that a transferee undertakes to discharge in respect of the transferred assets), divided by the number of membership interests (s 328-465(1)). Where membership interests are issued partly as consideration, the amounts are reduced accordingly (s 328-465(2)).

Capital losses from a CGT event arising in relation to membership interests are generally disregarded (except to the extent that that they are attributable to a matter other than the transaction) (s 328-470).

[28.3] Scrip for scrip takeovers

It is common in takeover and merger situations for taxpayers to exchange their interests in a company or trust for replacement interests in another company or trust. This is known as a 'scrip for scrip' exchange. Ordinarily, such an exchange results in CGT consequences for the original interest holders as they are disposing of their original interests in the 'target entity' for new interests in the 'takeover entity'.

Subdivision 124-M *ITAA97* contains scrip for scrip roll-over relief, which allows the original interest holders to defer a capital gain (but not a capital loss) that they would otherwise make from the exchange. If the original interest holders also receive something other than replacement interests (eg cash), they may make a capital gain or capital loss in relation to such 'ineligible proceeds'.

CGT roll-over for original interest holders

A taxpayer may choose the roll-over if they exchange an original interest in a company or trust (the 'original entity') for a replacement interest in another company or trust (the 'replacement entity') and meet the conditions set out in ss 124-780 or 124-781.

The exchange must be in consequence of an arrangement that results in a company or trust (the 'acquiring entity') owning 80% or more of the voting interests in the original entity. The 'replacement entity' must be the acquiring entity (or, if the acquiring entity is a member of a wholly owned group, it must be the ultimate holding company in that group). 28

A number of other conditions must also be satisfied for the roll-over to be available, including the following:

- the original interest holder must have acquired their original interest on or after 20 September 1985 (ie the interest must be a post-CGT asset)
- the original interest holder would, apart from the roll-over, make a capital gain from a CGT event happening in relation to their original interest
- the original interest holder must receive a replacement interest that is similar to their original interest (eg shares for shares or units for units)
- the arrangement must be one in which all holders of voting interests in the original entity are given the option of participating on substantially the same terms, or the arrangement must be a takeover bid, compromise or scheme of arrangement under the *Corporations Act*, and
- if the original interest holder and the acquiring entity did not deal with each other at arm's length, and neither the original entity nor the replacement entity are 'widely held' (ie have at least 300 members), the original interest holder must receive proceeds that are at least substantially the same as the market value of the original interest.

The following diagram illustrates the effect of a scrip for scrip takeover:

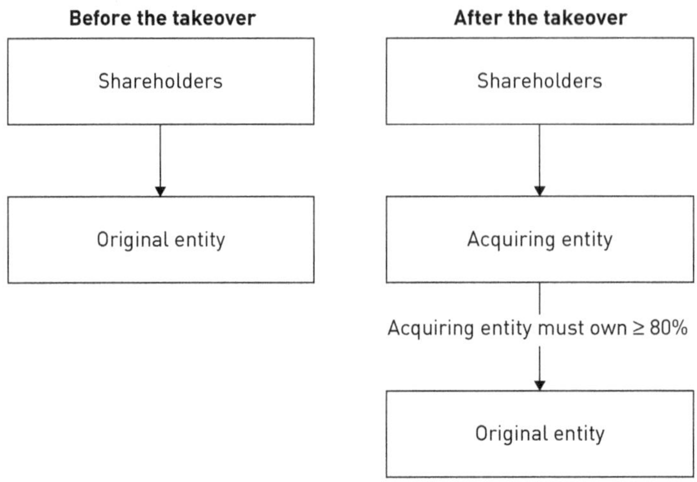

Consequences of the roll-over

If a taxpayer chooses the roll-over, a capital gain made from a CGT event in relation to their original interest is disregarded (s 124-785). The first element of the cost base or reduced cost base of each replacement interest is determined by reasonably attributing to it the cost base of the original interest that it replaced.

Example Lassie owns 300 shares in Red Rover Co, which she acquired in January 2010 for $300 (ie $1 per share). On 1 September 2023, Predator Co made a takeover bid for Red Rover. Under the arrangement, Lassie exchanged her Red Rover shares for 600 Predator shares with a market value of $1,200 (ie $2 per share).

If the conditions in s 124-780 are satisfied and Lassie chose the roll-over, the capital gain she would otherwise make from the disposal of her Red Rover shares is disregarded. For future CGT purposes, the cost base of her Predator shares is $300 (ie $0.50 per share). If she subsequently sells the Predator shares for $2 per share, she will make a capital gain of $900 (ie $1.50 × 600).

Partial roll-over

A taxpayer can obtain only a partial roll-over if the proceeds for their original interest includes something (the 'ineligible proceeds'), which is additional to their replacement interest (s 124-790). This situation commonly arises where the taxpayer also receives cash in addition to scrip. In these circumstances, there is no roll-over for the 'ineligible part' of the taxpayer's original interest (ie the part for which it received ineligible proceeds). In addition, the first element of the cost base or reduced cost base of the replacement interest is reduced by the cost base of the ineligible part. The cost base of the ineligible part is that part of the cost base of the original interest that is reasonably attributable to it.

Example Rinny owns 300 shares in D Co, which he acquired in January 2010 for $300 (ie $1 per share). On 1 August 2023, P Co made a takeover bid for D Co. Under the arrangement, Rinny exchanged his D Co shares for 300 P Co shares with a market value of $600 (ie $2 per share) plus $300 cash.

The ineligible proceeds represent one-third of the total proceeds received for Rinny's original interest. Hence, the cost base of the ineligible part is $100 (one-third of the cost base of Rinny's original interest). Rinny therefore makes a capital gain of $200, being the difference between the ineligible proceeds and the cost base of the ineligible part (ie $300 – $100).

The cost base of his P Co shares is $200, being the cost base of the original interest reduced by the cost base of the ineligible part (ie $300 – $100). Each P Co share therefore has a cost base of $0.67 (ie $200/300). If Rinny subsequently sells his P Co shares for $2 each, he will make a capital gain of $1.33 per share.

Exceptions

A roll-over cannot be obtained for an interest acquired before 20 September 1985. Where a pre-CGT asset is exchanged for an interest in the replacement entity, the first element of the cost base or reduced cost base of the interest in the replacement entity is deemed to be its market value immediately after the exchange (s 124-800).

Additionally, a roll-over cannot be obtained if the exceptions in s 124-795 apply. For example, no roll-over is available if the original interest holder is a foreign resident immediately before the exchange (unless the replacement interest is 'taxable Australian property' [17.12]).

The roll-over also operates subject to a number of integrity measures and other special rules.

[28.4] Demergers

One of the ways that a corporate or trust group can restructure is by undertaking a 'demerger'. A 'demerger' occurs where the group 'spins off' an entity within the group to the owners of the 'head entity', who, after the demerger, own the interests in the 'demerged entity' directly (rather than indirectly via their interests in the head entity).

Ordinarily, such an arrangement can result in CGT liabilities and assessable dividends. To allow for flexible and tax-efficient restructuring, tax relief is available for demergers. Where the requirements of div 125 *ITAA97* are met, the owners of interests in the head entity may obtain CGT 'roll-over' relief under s 125-55 as well as a dividend exemption under s 44(4) *ITAA36*. In addition, capital gains and capital losses made by a demerging entity from CGT events A1, C2, C3 of K6 happening to its ownership interests in a demerged entity are disregarded under s 125-155.

Over the years, many high-profile demergers have taken advantage of these tax relief provisions. Some well-known examples include the demerger of South 32 from BHP Billiton (discussed in CR 2015/40) and the demerger of Endeavour Group from Woolworths (discussed in CR 2021/50).

CGT roll-over for owners of interests

A taxpayer can choose to obtain CGT roll-over relief if, as a result of a 'demerger', a CGT event happens to their original ownership interest in the 'head entity' of a 'demerger group' and they acquire a new interest in the 'demerged entity' (s 125-55(1)).

The roll-over is not available to foreign residents if their new interests are not 'taxable Australian property' [17.12] (s 125-55(2)).

Demerger group, head entity, demerger subsidiary and demerged entity

A 'demerger group' comprises the 'head entity' and one or more 'demerger subsidiaries' (s 125-65(1)).

A company or trust is the 'head entity' if no other member of the group holds ownership interests in it (s 125-65(3)).

A company or trust is a 'demerger subsidiary' if:

- in the case of a company—a member of the demerger group has the right to receive more than 20% of any distribution of income or capital by the company, or the right to exercise, or control the exercise of, more than 20% of the voting power of the company (s 125-65(6)), or

- in the case of a trust—a member of the demerger group has the right to receive more than 20% of any distribution of income or capital by the trustee (s 125-65(7)).

The 'demerged entity' is the company or trust that has been spun off as a result of the demerger (ie it is the entity in which ownership interests are acquired by the interest holders in the head entity) (s 125-70(6)).

Certain entities are precluded from being members of a demerger group (eg complying superannuation entities: s 125-65(2A)).

Demerger

In broad terms, a 'demerger' happens to a demerger group if the following requirements are met (s 125-70):

- there is a restructure of the demerger group pursuant to which at least 80% of the demerger group's ownership interests in a demerger subsidiary is spun off to owners of original interests in the head entity
- under the restructure, whether or not a CGT event happens to original interests of the original owners in the head entity, they acquire new interests and nothing else
- the original owners receive new interests in the demerged entity only because they owned original interests
- the new interests are: (a) if the head entity is a company—ownership interests in a company; or (b) if the head entity is a trust—ownership interests in a trust
- each original owner acquires the same proportion of new interests in the demerged entity as they owned in the head entity just before the demerger, and
- immediately after the demerger, each owner of original interests has the same proportionate market value of interests in the head entity and demerged entity as they owned in the head entity just before the demerger.

The following diagram illustrates the basic requirements and effect of a demerger:

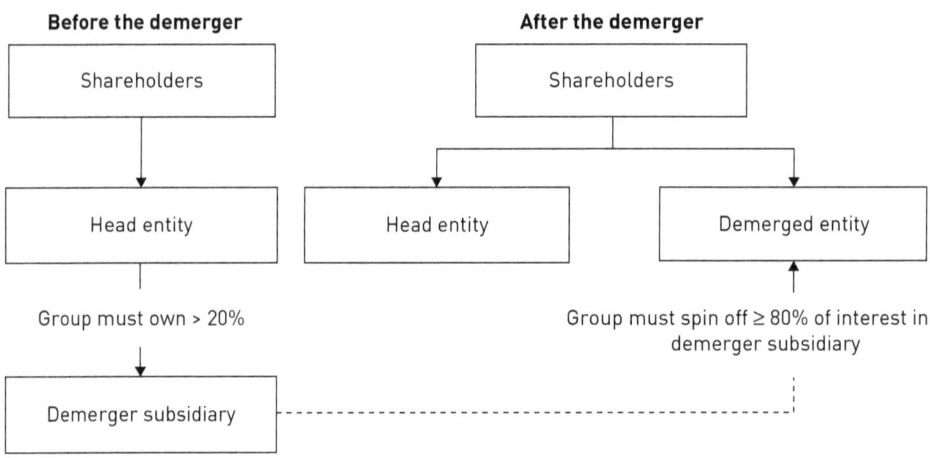

Consequences of the roll-over

If a taxpayer chooses the roll-over, a capital gain or capital loss made from a CGT event in relation to their original interests is disregarded (s 125-80).

The first element of the cost base or reduced cost base of the taxpayer's original interests is apportioned between the original and new interests on the basis of the relative market values of those interests immediately after the demerger.

The new interests will be taken to be pre-CGT assets to the extent that the original interests were acquired before 20 September 1985. For example, if half of the taxpayer's original interests were pre-CGT assets, half of their new interests will be taken to be pre-CGT assets.

Example Sylvester is a resident who purchased 500 of the 2,000 shares in H Co for $1 per share on 1 February 1998. He therefore owns 25% of the shares in H Co.

H Co is the head entity of a group. The H Co group owns 100% of the shares in S Co (which represents 50% of the market value of the group). Under a demerger, S Co is spun off to H Co's shareholders and Sylvester receives 100 S Co shares.

S Co is a demerger subsidiary as H Co holds more than 20% of the relevant rights in S Co. Assuming the conditions in s 125-70 are satisfied and Sylvester chooses the roll-over, no CGT consequences will arise in respect of his H Co shares.

Given that 50% of the market value of H Co has been spun off, the cost base of Sylvester's 500 H Co shares will be reduced from $500 to $250 (ie $500 × 50%). The cost base of his 100 S Co shares will also be $250 (ie $500 × 50%). Therefore, each H Co share will have a cost base of $0.50 (ie $250/500) and each S Co share will have a cost base of $2.50 (ie $250/100).

The following diagram illustrates how the cost base of Sylvester's shares are apportioned between his original and new interests:

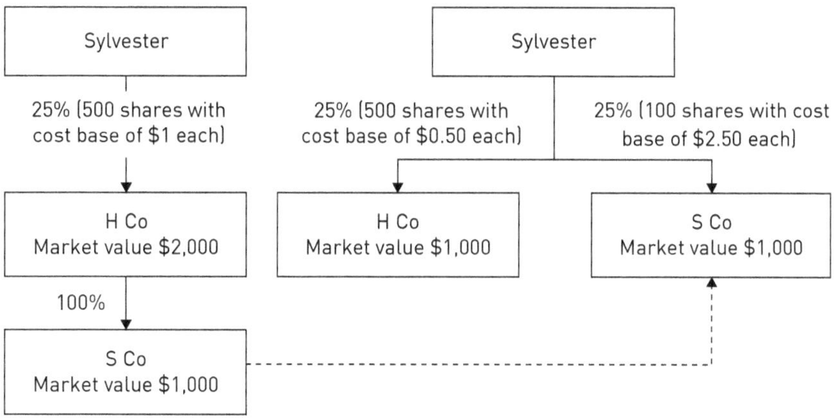

Demerger dividend exemption

Ordinarily, in a corporate demerger, the distribution of the demerging entity's interests in the demerged entity to shareholders in the head entity may constitute a dividend that is assessable under s 44(1) *ITAA36* [22.5]. This is because s 6(1) defines a dividend as including 'any distribution made by a company to any of its shareholders, whether in money or other property' [22.4]. To address this situation, a 'demerger dividend' is deemed not to be paid out of profits (s 44(3)) and is treated as non-assessable non-exempt income (s 44(4)). A 'demerger dividend' is essentially, that part of a 'demerger allocation' that would otherwise be assessable under s 44(1), apart from the operation of ss 44(3), (4) (s 6(1)). A demerger dividend is unfrankable [22.7] (s 202-45(i) *ITAA97*).

Example In the previous example, assuming the distribution of the shares in S Co to Sylvester would constitute a demerger dividend, Sylvester would not be assessed on the dividend.

Section 44(3) and (4) operate subject to the anti-avoidance rule in s 45B *ITAA36*, which applies to schemes under which a person is provided with a 'demerger benefit' [22.20]. Where s 45B applies, the Commissioner may make a determination that s 45BA applies to the whole or part of the 'demerger benefit' (s 45B(3)). The effect of this is that the whole, or relevant part, of the demerger benefit is taken not to be a 'demerger dividend'. As a consequence, ss 44(3) and (4) will not apply.

[28.5] Disposals of assets to wholly owned companies

An individual or trustee of a trust can choose to obtain CGT roll-over relief under sub-div 122-A *ITAA97* for transferring a CGT asset to a wholly owned company, or for creating contractual or other rights in the company, in exchange for shares in the company. The roll-over is available where a 'trigger event' has happened and certain other conditions are satisfied.

Trigger event

A 'trigger event' is any of five different CGT events listed in s 122-15. The two most important trigger events are:

- CGT event A1—where an individual or trustee disposes of a CGT asset, or all the assets of a business, to a company ('disposal case'), and
- CGT event D1—where an individual or trustee creates a contractual or other right (ie a new asset) in the company ('creation case').

Consideration for trigger event

To obtain the roll-over, the consideration the individual or trustee receives for disposing of a CGT asset or assets to the company, or creating a new asset in the company, must be non-redeemable shares in the company and nothing else (s 122-20). However, in a disposal case, the consideration may include the company undertaking to discharge a liability in respect of the asset or assets.

The market value of the shares must be substantially the same as:

- in a disposal case, the market value of the asset or assets disposed of, less any liabilities the company undertakes to discharge in respect of the asset or assets, or
- in a creation case, the market value of the CGT asset created in the company.

The following diagram depicts how the rules work in a disposal case:

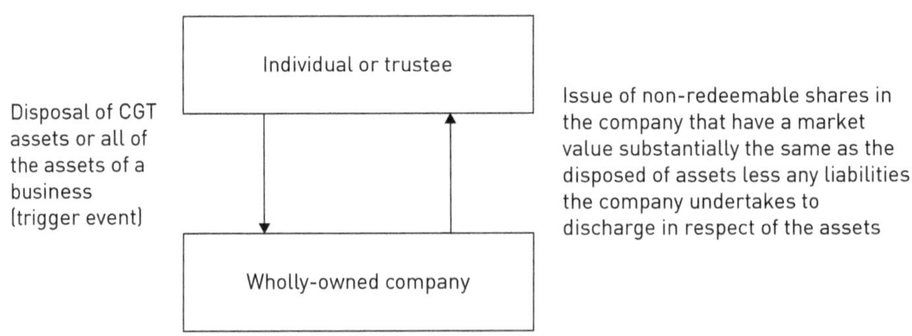

Other requirements for the roll-over

To obtain the roll-over, the following requirements must also be satisfied (s 122-25):

- **Ownership requirement.** The individual or trustee must own all the shares in the company immediately after the trigger event.

- **Residency requirement.** Both the company and the individual or trust must be residents at the time the trigger event happens. Otherwise, each asset disposed of or created, and the shares received for them, must be 'taxable Australian property' [17.12].
- **Asset requirement.** The asset transferred must not be, among other things, a 'collectable' or a 'personal use asset' [17.4]. Furthermore, a 'precluded asset' cannot be rolled over unless it is disposed of as part of all the assets of a business. Precluded assets include trading stock [16.1] and depreciating assets [15.2] (capital gains and losses on these assets are disregarded under ss 118-24 and 118-25 [17.5]).

Consequences of the roll-over to the individual or trustee

If the individual or trustee chooses to use the roll-over, any capital gain or capital loss they make from the disposal or creation of the relevant asset or assets is disregarded (ss 122-40, 122-45, 122-65).

In addition, the following rules apply to the shares acquired in exchange for the relevant asset or assets:

- **Disposal case—single asset.** If the individual or trustee disposed of an asset that they acquired on or after 20 September 1985, the first element of each share's cost base or reduced cost base is the asset's cost base when the individual or trustee disposed of it (less any liabilities the company undertakes to discharge in respect of It), divided by the number of shares. If the asset was acquired before 20 September 1985, the shares are taken to have been acquired before that day (s 122-40).
- **Disposal case—all the assets of a business.** If the individual or trustee disposed of all the assets of a business, then the following rules apply:
  - If all the assets were acquired on or after 20 September 1985, the first element of each share's cost base or reduced cost base is the sum of the market values of the precluded assets and the cost bases of the other assets (less any liabilities the company undertakes to discharge in respect of all those assets), divided by the number of shares (s 122-50).
  - If all the assets were acquired before 20 September 1985, the shares are generally taken to have been acquired before that day. However, if a precluded asset is involved, the number of shares that are taken to have been acquired before 20 September 1985 is the greatest possible number that (when expressed as a percentage of all the shares) does not exceed: the total of the market values of the assets that are not precluded assets (less any liabilities the company undertakes to discharge in respect of those assets), expressed as a percentage of the total of the market values of all the assets (less any liabilities the company undertakes to discharge in respect of those assets) (s 122-55).
  - If some of the assets were acquired on or after 20 September 1985 and some of the assets were acquired before 20 September 1985, the number of shares that are taken to have been acquired before 20 September is the greatest possible number that (when expressed as a percentage of all the shares) does not exceed: the total of the market values of the pre-CGT assets that are not precluded assets (reduced by any liabilities the company undertakes to discharge in respect of those assets), expressed as a percentage of the total of the market values of all the assets at the time of the disposal (reduced by any liabilities the company undertakes to discharge in respect of those assets). The first element of the cost base or reduced cost base of each remaining share (ie post-CGT share) is the sum of the market values of the precluded assets and the cost bases or reduced cost bases of any other post-CGT assets at the time of the disposal (less any liabilities the company undertakes to discharge in respect of those assets), divided by the number of those post-CGT shares (s 122-60).

- **Creation case.** If the individual or trustee created a new asset in the company, the first element of each share's cost base or reduced cost base is the incidental costs incurred by the individual or trustee in creating the asset (eg legal expenses), divided by the number of shares (s 122-65).

Consequences of the roll-over to the wholly owned company

The consequences of the roll-over for the company are as follows:

- **Disposal case.** If the individual or trustee that disposed of the asset to the company acquired the asset on or after 20 September 1985, the first element of the asset's cost base or reduced cost base to the company is the same as the cost base or reduced cost base of the asset to the individual or trustee when they disposed of it. This rule is not relevant to precluded assets as capital gains and losses on such assets are disregarded [17.5]. If the asset was acquired by the individual or trustee before 20 September 1985, the asset is also taken to have been acquired by the company before that date (s 122-70).
- **Creation case.** The first element of the created asset's cost base to the company is the incidental costs incurred by the individual or trustee in creating the asset (s 122-75).

Example Cameron is an Australian resident sole trader who established a shoe retail business three years ago. The assets of the business comprise:

- shop premises (cost base of $400,000 and market value of $600,000)
- depreciating assets (cost base of $80,000 and market value of $100,000), and
- trading stock (cost base of $10,000 and market value of $20,000).

If Cameron disposes of these assets to C Co (a wholly owned company) in exchange for 520,000 non-redeemable shares in C Co and he chooses to use the roll-over, he can disregard the capital gains that he would otherwise make in relation to the assets he disposed of. If the roll-over was not available, Cameron would have made a $200,000 capital gain on the shop premises. He would have also made a $20,000 capital gain on the depreciating asset and a $10,000 capital gain on the trading stock, although these gains would have been disregarded in any case under ss 118-24 and 118-25 [17.5].

The first element of the cost base of each share that Cameron acquires in C Co is $1 (ie ($400,000 + $100,000 + $20,000)/520,000).

For the purposes of determining any subsequent capital gain or capital loss that C Co may make when it subsequently disposes of the shop premises, the first element of the cost base or reduced cost base of the shop premises is $400,000.

Partnership relief

Partners in a partnership can choose to obtain CGT roll-over relief under sub-div 122-B *ITAA97* for transferring a CGT asset to a wholly owned company, or for creating contractual or other rights in the company, in exchange for shares in the company. The requirements for, and consequences of, the roll-over are broadly similar to those pertaining to the roll-over available to individuals and trustees under sub-div 122-A *ITAA97*. The partners must own all the shares in the company just after the time of the 'trigger event' and each partner must own the shares they receive for the trigger event in the same capacity that they owned their interests in the asset or participated in the creation of the asset (s 122-135).

[28.6] Exchanges of shares or units in the same company or unit trust

The cancellation or redemption of shares in a company or units in a unit trust ordinarily triggers CGT event C2 for the shareholders or unitholders [17.10]. Taxpayers can, however, choose to obtain CGT roll-over relief under sub-div 124-E where their shares or units are exchanged for new shares or units in the same company or unit trust.

Requirements for the roll-over

Roll-over relief is available under sub-div 124-E if the following conditions are met:

- the taxpayer owns shares in a company or units in a trust that are of a certain class
- the company or trust redeems or cancels all shares or units in that class
- the company or trust issues the taxpayer new shares or units in substitution of the original shares or units and nothing else
- the market value of the new shares or units immediately after their issue is at least equal to the market value of the original shares or units immediately before their redemption or cancellation
- in the case of shares in a company, the paid-up share capital of the company is at least equal to the market value of the original shares just before their redemption or cancellation, and
- the taxpayer is a resident, or both the original and new shares or units are 'taxable Australian property' [17.12] (ss 124-240, 124-245).

Consequences of the roll-over

28

The consequences of the roll-over are determined under the replacement asset roll-over rules in sub-div 124-A *ITAA97* [17.16]. These rules provide that a capital gain or a capital loss a taxpayer makes from their 'original assets' (ie their original shares or units) is disregarded (s 124-10(2)). In addition, the following rules apply to their 'new assets' (ie their new shares or units):

- If the original assets were all acquired post-CGT, the first element of the cost base or reduced cost base of each new asset is calculated as follows (s 124-10(3)):

$$\frac{\text{Total cost bases of all the original assets}}{\text{Number of new asssets}}$$

- If the original assets were all acquired pre-CGT, the taxpayer is taken to acquire each new asset before that date (s 124-10(4)).
- If some of the original assets were acquired pre-CGT and some were acquired post-CGT, the taxpayer is taken to have acquired a number of new assets that are pre-CGT assets. The number is the maximum possible that does not exceed the amount worked out as follows (s 124-15(5)):

$$\text{Number of new assets} \times \frac{\text{Number of original pre-CGT assets}}{\text{Total number of original assets}}$$

The remaining new assets are treated as post-CGT assets and first element of their cost base or reduced cost base is calculated as follows (s 124-15(6)):

$$\frac{\text{Total cost bases of all the original assets acquired post-CGT}}{\text{Number of remaining new assets}}$$

Example Errol owns 100 shares in a company. The company redeems his shares and issues 10 new shares in substitution of the original shares in circumstances that qualify for roll-over relief under sub-div 124-E. Errol acquired 60 of the 100 original shares before 20 September 1985. The other 40 shares were acquired after that date for $100 each.

The number of new shares that Errol is taken to have acquired pre-CGT cannot exceed 6 (ie 10 × 60/100). This means that six of his new shares will be pre-CGT shares. The remaining four shares will be post-CGT shares. The first element of the cost base of each of these shares is $100 (ie $4,000/40).

[28.7] Exchanges of shares or units for shares in an interposed company

Division 615 *ITAA97* allows taxpayers to choose roll-over relief where their shares or units in an entity are disposed of or cancelled or redeemed, and they acquire shares in an interposed company in exchange for their original shares or units. Division 615 replaces former sub-divs 124-G and 124-H *ITAA97* and is designed to facilitate corporate reorganisations such as those illustrated in the following diagram:

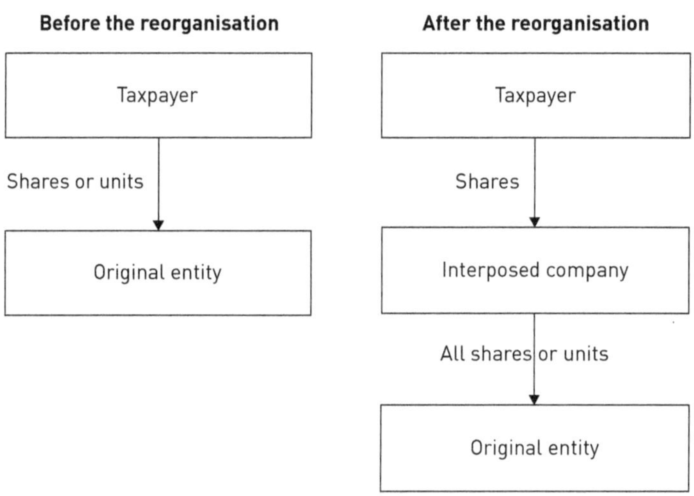

Choosing the roll-over

Taxpayers can choose roll-over relief under div 615 in the following two circumstances:

- **Disposal of shares or units.** A taxpayer can choose to obtain roll-over relief where:
  - the taxpayer is a member of a company or unit trust (the 'original entity')
  - the taxpayer and at least one other entity (the 'exchanging members') own all the shares or units in the original entity
  - under a scheme for reorganising the original entity's affairs, the exchanging members dispose of all their shares or units in the original entity to a company (the 'interposed company') in exchange for shares in the interposed company and nothing else, and
  - the requirements of sub-div 615-B (see below) are satisfied (s 615-5(1)).
- **Cancellation or redemption of shares or units.** A taxpayer can choose to obtain roll-over relief where:

- the taxpayer is a member of a company or unit trust (the 'original entity'), and under a scheme for reorganising its affairs:
  (a) a company (the 'interposed company') acquires one or more, but not all, of the shares or units in the original entity
  (b) these are the first shares or units that the interposed company acquires in the original entity
  (c) the taxpayer and at least one other entity (the 'exchanging members') own all the remaining shares or units in the original entity
  (d) the remaining shares or units in the original entity are redeemed or cancelled, and
  (e) each exchanging member receives shares (and nothing else) in the interposed company in return for the redemption or cancellation of their shares or units in the original entity, and
- the requirements of sub-div 615-B (see below) are satisfied (s 615-10(1)).

Taxpayers are deemed to have chosen to obtain the roll-over if immediately before the 'completion time' (defined in s 615-15), the original entity is the head company of a consolidated group, and immediately after the completion time, the interposed company is the head company of the group (ss 615-5(2), 615-10(2)).

Subdivision 615-B requirements

Subdivision 615-B prescribes the following requirements for obtaining the roll-over:

- **Ownership of original interests.** The interposed company must own all the shares or units in the original entity immediately after the 'completion time' (ie when the exchanging members' shares or units in the original entity are disposed of, redeemed or cancelled) (s 615-15).
- **Percentages.** Immediately after the completion time, each exchanging member must own a whole number of shares in the interposed company and the same percentage of shares in the interposed company as the percentage of shares or units they owned in the original entity and were disposed of, redeemed or cancelled (s 615-20(1)).
- **Ratios.** The ratio of the market value of each exchanging member's shares in the interposed company to the market value of the shares in the interposed company issued to all the exchanging members must equal the ratio of the market value of the member's shares or units in the original entity that were disposed of, redeemed or cancelled to the market value of all the shares or units in the original entity that were disposed of, redeemed or cancelled (s 615-20(2)).
- **Residency.** The exchanging member must be a resident at the time the shares or units were disposed of, redeemed or cancelled. Alternatively, if the exchanging member is a foreign resident, the shares or units in the original entity (before the completion time) and the shares in the interposed company (after the completion time) must be taxable Australian property [17.12] (s 615-20(3)).
- **Shares in interposed company.** The shares issued in the interposed company must not be redeemable shares. In addition, each exchanging member who is issued shares in the interposed company must own the shares from the time they are issued until at least the completion time. The exchanging members must also own all the shares in the interposed company, or other entities must own no more than five shares In the interposed company and the market value of those shares must be such that it is reasonable to treat the exchanging members as owning all the shares (s 615-25).
- **Interposed entity choice.** The interposed entity must choose (within two months after the completion time or such further period as the Commissioner allows) that s 615-65 (outlined below) applies. Alternatively, the interposed entity must choose (within 28 days after the

28

completion time or such further period as the Commissioner allows) that a consolidated group continues in existence with it as its head company if immediately before the completion time, the consolidated group consisted of the original entity as head company and other group members and immediately after the completion time, the interposed company is the head company of a consolidatable group consisting only of itself and the other group members (s 615-30).

Consequences of the roll-over for the members

The CGT consequences of the roll-over are determined under the replacement asset roll-over rules in sub-div 124-A *ITAA97* [17.16]. These rules provide that a capital gain or a capital loss a taxpayer makes from their 'original assets' (ie their shares or units in the original entity) is disregarded (s 124-10(2)). In addition, the following rules apply to the taxpayer's 'new assets' (ie their shares in the interposed company):

- If the original assets were all acquired post-CGT, the first element of the cost base or reduced cost base of each new asset is calculated as follows (s 124-10(3)):

$$\frac{\text{Total cost bases of all the original assets}}{\text{Number of new asssets}}$$

- If all the original assets were all acquired pre-CGT, the taxpayer is taken to acquire each new asset before that date (s 124-10(4)).
- If some of the original assets were acquired pre-CGT and some were acquired post-CGT, the taxpayer is taken to have acquired a number of new assets that are pre-CGT assets. The number is the maximum possible that does not exceed the amount worked out as follows (s 124-15(5)):

$$\text{Number of new assets} \times \frac{\text{Number of original pre-CGT assets}}{\text{Total number of original assets}}$$

The remaining new assets are treated as post-CGT assets and first element of their cost base or reduced cost base is calculated as follows (s 124-15(6)):

$$\frac{\text{Total cost bases of all the original assets acquired post-CGT}}{\text{Number of remaining new assets}}$$

Example Sarah and Phil are Australian residents who acquired 500 shares each in O Co in June 2016 for $100 per share. There are no other shares in O Co. Under a reorganisation of O Co's affairs in December 2023, Sarah and Phil (the 'exchanging members') each dispose of their 500 O Co shares to P Co in exchange for being issued 2,000 P Co shares. If the requirements of div 615 are satisfied and Sarah chooses the roll-over, any capital gain or capital loss she makes from the exchange of shares would be disregarded. The cost base of her P Co shares would be $25 per share, being the total cost base of her O Co shares, divided by the number of her P Co shares (ie $50,000/2,000).

Taxpayers can also obtain special income tax roll-over relief in respect of shares or units in the original entity which they held as trading stock or as revenue assets under ss 615-50 and 615-55.

Consequences of the roll-over for the interposed company

Section 615-65 provides that where the interposed company makes a choice under s 615-30, a number of the shares or units it owns in the original entity are taken to be pre-CGT shares or units if any of the original entity's assets were acquired by it before that day. That number is the greatest possible whole number that does not exceed the market value of the original entity's pre-CGT assets less its liabilities in respect of those assets expressed as a percentage of the market value of all the original entity's assets less all of its liabilities. The first element of the cost base or reduced cost base of the interposed company's shares or units in the original entity that are *not* taken to have been acquired pre-CGT is the total of the cost bases (as at the completion time) of the original entity's assets that it acquired on or after that day less its liabilities in respect of those assets.

[28.8] QUESTIONS

1. What are the requirements for roll-over under sub-div 124-M *ITAA97* and what relief is available?
2. On 1 July 2015, George purchased 1,000 shares for $1 each in T Co (a resident company). On 25 September 2023, R Co (a resident company) made a successful 'scrip and cash' takeover bid for T Co. The takeover satisfied the conditions for roll-over relief in sub-div 124-M *ITAA97*. As a consequence of the takeover, R Co acquired 100% of the shares in T Co and George received $1,000 plus 4 R Co shares (valued at $0.80 per share) for every 1 of his T Co shares. On 2 January 2024, George sold his 4,000 R Co shares for $1.20 each. What are the tax implications of these transactions assuming George chose to use the roll-over?
3. What is a demerger and what kind of roll-over relief is available in respect of demergers?
4. Identify the main requirements that must be met for an individual to obtain roll-over relief under sub-div 122-A *ITAA97*? What is the nature of the roll-over relief?
5. What kinds of transactions are sub-div 124-E and div 615 directed at?

PART J

FINANCIAL TRANSACTIONS

29 FINANCIAL TRANSACTIONS REGIMES

[29.1] Introduction

The tax law contains a number of regimes dealing with financial transactions. These regimes are scattered throughout the *ITAA36* and *ITAA97* and are either superimposed on, or take precedence over, the general taxation rules discussed elsewhere in this book. The regimes are complex and span many pages of legislation. They contain their own unique terminology and are often targeted at addressing particular kinds of tax avoidance arrangements. This chapter focuses on the following regimes:

- the taxation of financial arrangements ('TOFA') regime in div 230 *ITAA97* [29.2]
- the hire purchase agreements regime in div 240 *ITAA97* [29.3]
- the leases of luxury cars regime in div 242 *ITAA97* [29.4]
- the limited recourse debt regime in div 243 *ITAA97* [29.5]
- the forgiveness of commercial debts regime in div 245 *ITAA97* [29.6]
- the capital protected borrowings regime in div 247 *ITAA97* [29.7]
- the assets put to tax preferred use regime in div 250 *ITAA97* [29.8]
- the debt and equity regime in div 974 *ITAA97* [29.9]
- the advance payments regime in sub-div H of div 3 of pt III *ITAA36* (ss 82KZL to 82KZO) [29.10]
- the pre-payment, deferral and recoupment scheme regime in sub-div D of div 3 of pt III *ITAA36* (ss 82KH to 82KL) [29.11]
- the qualifying securities regime in div 16E of pt III *ITAA36* (ss 159GP to 159GZ) [29.12]
- the traditional securities regime in ss 26BB and 70B *ITAA36* [29.13].

[29.2] TOFA regime

Over the years, many new kinds of innovative financial instruments, including complex and sophisticated derivative and hybrid products, have been developed by the finance industry. The general tax rules have struggled to keep up with these products and deal systematically with them. As a result, inconsistencies and anomalies emerged, which enabled taxpayers to exploit various tax arbitrage and timing opportunities. The TOFA regime in div 230 *ITAA97* was introduced to provide an overarching set of rules to address these issues.

The broad aim of div 230 is to bring gains and losses from 'financial arrangements' to account on a 'revenue' basis (ie gains are assessable and losses are deductible) according to a set of specific 'tax-timing methods'. Division 230 is designed to provide greater certainty and ensure that the tax law operates more consistently with accounting principles, rather than being based purely on legal form. It is aimed at reducing compliance costs, removing distortions, and aligning more closely the tax and commercial recognition of gains and losses from financial arrangements.

As a general rule, the TOFA regime is mainly directed at arrangements involving large taxpayers. In certain cases, small taxpayers may nevertheless also come within the regime. The regime generally applies to financial arrangements that start to be held in income years commencing on or after 1 July 2010. It can also apply to financial arrangements held before that date where the taxpayer has made an irrevocable transitional election to have div 230 apply to such arrangements. Where div 230 applies, it takes precedence over any other taxation regimes that might otherwise apply to an arrangement.

Financial arrangements

Division 230 is built around the concept of a 'financial arrangement'. Section 230-45 defines a financial arrangement as a 'cash settlable' legal or equitable right to receive, or obligation to provide, a financial benefit (or a combination of one or more of such rights and/or obligations) under an arrangement.

A right to receive, or an obligation to provide, a financial benefit is 'cash settlable' if:

- the benefit is money or a money equivalent
- in the case of a right—the taxpayer intends to satisfy or settle it by receiving money or a money equivalent or by starting, or ceasing, to have another financial arrangement
- in the case of an obligation—the taxpayer intends to satisfy or settle it by providing money or a money equivalent or by starting, or ceasing, to have another financial arrangement
- the taxpayer has a practice of satisfying or settling similar rights or obligations
- the taxpayer deals with the right or obligation (or similar rights or obligations) in order to generate a profit from short-term fluctuations in price and/or a dealer's margin
- the financial benefit is readily convertible into money or a money equivalent, there is a highly liquid market for the financial benefit, and either:
  - the money or money equivalent is not subject to substantial risk of substantial decrease in value, or
  - the taxpayer's purpose, or one of their purposes, for entering into the arrangement is to receive or deliver the financial benefit to raise or provide finance or so that it may be converted or liquidated into money or a money equivalent (other than as part of the taxpayer's expected purchase, sale or usage requirements), or
- the taxpayer is able to settle the right or obligation and they do not have as their sole or dominant purpose for entering into the arrangement, the purpose of receiving or delivering the financial benefit as part of their expected purchase, sale or usage requirements.

Financial arrangements cover a whole range of debt and derivative products, such as loans, bonds, debentures, promissory notes, hedges, options and swaps. Financial arrangements also expressly include equity interests and rights to receive, or obligations to provide, equity interests (s 230-50) as well as foreign currency and non-equity shares [29.9] (s 230-530). A financial arrangement also includes money owing for goods or services that have been delivered or performed because the only rights and obligations under such an arrangement that subsist following delivery or performance are cash settlable.

Exclusions

Division 230 does not apply to gains and losses from the following financial arrangements:

- **Short-term financial arrangements (s 230-450).** Division 230 does not apply to a financial arrangement where an entity acquired or provided goods, property or services (other than money or a money equivalent) and the financial benefits that the entity is to provide or receive are consideration for those goods, property or services if the period between the time the entity provides or receives the consideration and the time when it acquires or provides the goods, property or services is not more than 12 months. This exclusion only applies if the arrangement is not a derivative financial arrangement, and the fair value election (see below) does not apply.
- **Financial arrangements of individuals and small entities where there is no significant deferral (s 230-455).** Division 230 does not generally apply to gains and losses from financial arrangements of individuals. It also does not apply to gains and losses from financial arrangements of other entities provided their assets or aggregated turnovers are below specified thresholds. For example, superannuation entities and MISs are generally excluded if the value of their assets is less than $100m. For most other entities, their annual turnover must be less than $100m, the value of their financial assets must be less than $100m and the value of their total assets must be less than $300m. The exclusion only applies to arrangements that are to end within 12 months or that are not 'qualifying securities' [29.12]. Taxpayers can make an irrevocable election not to be covered by the exclusion, whereupon div 230 will apply to all financial arrangements acquired in the income year the election is made and later income years.
- **Certain rights and/or obligations (s 230-460).** Division 230 does not apply to gains and losses from financial arrangements to the extent that the taxpayer's rights and obligations fall within specific exceptions, including those outlined below:
  - a right or obligation arising under arrangements to which div 240 *ITAA97* (hire purchase agreements) [29.3], div 242 *ITAA97* (leases of luxury cars) [29.4], or div 250 *ITAA97* (tax preferred use of an asset) [29.8] apply
  - a right that is an interest in a partnership or trust or an obligation that corresponds to such a right
  - a right or obligation under specified insurance policies
  - a right or obligation under a guarantee or indemnity (unless it is subject to a fair value election or a derivative financial arrangement)
  - a right or obligation for the provision of personal services
  - a right or obligation in relation to personal injuries or reputation
  - a right or obligation arising from the administration of a deceased estate
  - a right or obligation in relation to a gift under a deed
  - a right or obligation in relation to certain maintenance arrangements
  - a right or obligation arising from membership of a superannuation or pension scheme
  - a right or obligation arising from the sale of a business
  - a right or obligation in relation to a farm management deposit [25.2], and
  - a right or obligation specified in the regulations.

Taxation of gains and losses

Division 230 requires taxpayers to include gains made from financial arrangements in their assessable income (s 230-15(1) *ITAA97*). It also allows taxpayers deductions for losses made from financial arrangements, but only to the extent that such losses are made in gaining or producing their assessable income or are necessarily made in carrying on a business for the purpose of gaining or producing such income (s 230-15(2)). 'Australian entities' are also entitled to deductions for losses made in deriving foreign source income that is non-assessable non-exempt income under s 768-5 *ITAA97* [31.6] or ss 23AI or 23AK *ITAA36* [34.5] provided the loss is a cost in relation to a debt interest covered by the definition of 'debt deduction' in s 820-40(1)(a) *ITAA97* [33.5] (s 230-15(3)).

To ensure that gains and losses are only taken into account once, gains and losses that fall with div 230 are not assessable or deductible under any other provisions (s 230-20).

Tax-timing methods

Gains and losses that fall within div 230 *ITAA97* are brought to account according to specified tax-timing methods. There are two 'default methods' (the 'accruals' and 'realisation' methods) and four 'elective methods' (the 'fair value', 'foreign exchange retranslation', 'hedging financial arrangement' and 'reliance on financial reports' methods) which operate subject to priority rules set out in ss 230-40(5) to (7). There is also a separate 'balancing adjustment' method that applies where rights and/or obligations under a financial arrangement are transferred or cease.

The accruals and realisation methods are alternative methods—they only apply if the elective methods do not apply and if the financial arrangement is not an equity interest (s 230-40(4)). Taxpayers are required to determine whether the accruals or realisation methods apply at the time they start to have the financial arrangement. They must make 'fresh assessments' of which gains and losses the methods apply to if there is a 'material change' to the terms and conditions of the arrangement or circumstances that affect the arrangement (s 230-185). They must also re-estimate gains and losses as soon as practicable after they become aware of any circumstances that materially affect the amount or value, or the timing, of financial benefits that were taken into account in working out the amount of the gains or losses (s 230-190).

Accruals method (sub-div 230-B)

29

The accruals method applies to a gain or loss from a financial arrangement if it is 'sufficiently certain', at the time the taxpayer starts to have the financial arrangement, that a gain or loss will arise. The gain or loss may be in respect of the overall financial arrangement or a particular financial benefit (s 230-100). An overall gain or loss from a financial arrangement is sufficiently certain if, at the time the taxpayer starts to have the arrangement, it is sufficiently certain that the taxpayer will make an overall gain or loss from the arrangement of a particular amount (s 230-105). A financial benefit is sufficiently certain if it is reasonably expected that the taxpayer will provide or receive the financial benefit and at least some of the amount or value of the benefit is fixed or determinable with reasonable accuracy (s 230-115). The taxpayer must make certain assumptions in determining whether a gain or loss form a financial arrangement or a financial benefit is sufficiently certain, including the assumption that the they will continue to have it for the rest of its life (ie until maturity).

The accruals method requires the gain or loss to be spread over a period that commences when the taxpayer starts to have the financial arrangement and ends when they cease to have the financial arrangement assuming it will be held for the rest of its life (s 230-130). In simple terms, a 'compounding accruals method' that uses intervals not exceeding 12 months and an 'effective interest rate' based on accounting standards operates to spread the gain or loss over the relevant period (ss 230-135, 230-140). Intervals must generally be the same length (although the first and last intervals may be shorter) and where intervals straddle two income years, allocations between those years must be made on a reasonable basis.

Example On 1 July 2020, Z Co acquired a promissory note for $100m. The promissory note has a face value of $133.1m and matures on 1 July 2023. Z Co is expected to make an overall gain of $33.1m from the financial arrangement. Since the gain is 'sufficiently certain', Z Co can use the accruals method to account for the gain. Under this method, the assessable gain that Z Co makes in each of the three years of the financial arrangement may be worked out as follows:

- First, the estimated annual cash flows (see the table below) is determined.
- Second, the effective interest rate ('i') is determined using the formula below:

$$\text{Future Value} = \text{Present Value} \times (1 + i)^n$$
$$\$133.1\text{m} = \$100\text{m} \times (1 + 10\%)^3$$

- Third, the effective interest rate is applied to the cost of the financial arrangement on a compounding basis to determine the annual accrued interest.

Year	Cash flow	Compounding base (at start of each year)	Annual accrued interest (10% pa)
1	- $100m	$100m	$10m
2	$0	$110m	$11m
3	$0	$121m	$12.1m
Total	$133.10m		33.1m

Z Co is therefore assessed on the $33.1m gain over three years: $10m is assessable in 2020/21, $11m is assessable in 2021/22 and $12.1m is assessable in 2022/23.

Realisation method (sub-div 230-B)

The realisation method applies where the accruals method does not apply (s 230-100(5)). This will be the case where it is *not* sufficiently certain that a gain or loss from a financial arrangement will arise. Under the realisation method, gains and losses are simply allocated to the income years in which they occur (s 230-180). This will generally be when the financial benefit is provided or received.

Fair value method (sub-div 230-C)

The fair value method allows taxpayers to elect to calculate gains and losses from financial arrangements based on the increase or decrease in their 'fair value' as stated in financial reports (s 230-230). The election is irrevocable and can be made by taxpayers that prepare audited financial reports in accordance with accounting principles (s 230-210). It applies to financial arrangements that are classified in the financial reports at 'fair value' (s 230-220). The election does not apply to a financial arrangement that is an equity interest if the entity is the issuer of that interest (s 230-225). It also does not apply to the extent that the hedging financial arrangements or reliance on financial reports methods apply (s 230-40(5)).

Foreign exchange retranslation method (sub-div 230-D)

The foreign exchange retranslation method allows taxpayers to elect to account for gains and losses from financial arrangements that are attributable to foreign exchange fluctuations based on the way they are recognised under accounting standards (s 230-280). Taxpayers may make 'general elections' (which apply to foreign exchange gains and losses from all their financial arrangements) or 'qualifying forex accounts elections' (which apply to foreign exchange gains and losses from one or more 'qualifying forex accounts') (s 230-255). The election does not apply to a financial arrangement that is an equity interest (s 230-270(1)). It also does not apply to the extent that the fair value, hedging financial arrangement or reliance on financial reports methods apply (s 230-40(6)).

Hedging financial arrangement method (sub-div 230-E)

The hedging financial arrangement method allows taxpayers that prepare audited financial reports in accordance with accounting principles to elect to align the time they recognise gains or losses from their 'hedging financial arrangements' with the time they recognise gains or losses from the underlying 'hedged item'. The gain or loss from a hedging financial arrangement is also matched to the character of the hedged item (ss 230-300, 230-310). This means, for example, that where the CGT rules apply to the hedged item, the gain or loss from the hedging financial arrangement will produce a capital gain or loss (as opposed to a revenue gain or loss).

A 'hedging financial arrangement' is a financial arrangement that is a 'derivative financial arrangement' (s 230-350(1)) or a 'foreign currency hedge' (s 230-350(2)). The taxpayer must have created, acquired or applied the arrangement for the purpose of hedging risks in relation to assets, liabilities or future transactions and must satisfy certain reporting requirements (s 230-335). The hedge must also be expected to be effective and the taxpayer must determine the basis on which gains or losses are to be allocated according to fair value principles (ss 230-360, 230-365). Where these requirements are not satisfied, the Commissioner may determine the basis for allocating gains and losses in a way that satisfies those requirements (s 230-380).

Taxpayers must make an irrevocable election to use the hedging financial arrangement method (s 230-315). The election generally applies to hedging financial arrangements that a taxpayer starts to have in the year the election is made and in later years (s 230-325). However, it does not generally apply to financial arrangements that are equity interests (s 230-330).

Reliance on financial reports method (sub-div 230-F)

The reliance on financial reports method allows taxpayers to elect to align the tax treatment of their gains and losses from financial arrangements with the accounting treatment that applies to such arrangements based on their financial reports (s 230-420). Taxpayers must make an irrevocable election to use the financial reports method. The method may be used where financial reports are prepared in accordance with accounting principles and auditing requirements are satisfied (s 230-395). The method does not apply to the extent that the hedging financial arrangement method applies (s 230-40(7)).

Balancing adjustment method (sub-div 230-G)

The balancing adjustment method applies where:

- a taxpayer transfers all, or a proportionate share, of their rights and/or obligations under a financial arrangement to another entity
- a taxpayer's rights and/or obligations under a financial arrangement cease, or
- an arrangement ceases to be a financial arrangement (s 230-435).

Balancing adjustments must also be made where elections to use one of the elective methods cease to apply (ss 230-245, 230-290, 230-375, 230-430). They do not, however, apply to equity interests, hedging arrangements, or financial arrangements written off as bad debts (s 230-440).

Balancing adjustment gains and losses are calculated under s 230-445. This section contains a method statement which basically works out the gain or loss by comparing the total financial benefits received and amounts allowable as deductions in respect of the financial arrangement with the total financial benefits provided and amounts included in assessable income in respect of the financial arrangement.

[29.3] Hire purchase agreements regime

Division 240 *ITAA97* applies to arrangements involving 'hire purchase agreements' (s 240-10). A hire purchase agreement is defined in s 995-1 as:

- a contract for the hire of goods where: (i) the hirer has the right, obligation or contingent obligation to buy the goods; (ii) the charge that is or may be made for the hire, together with any other amount payable under the contract (including an amount to buy the goods or to exercise an option to do so), exceeds the price of the goods; and (iii) the title in the goods does not pass to the hirer until the option is exercised, or
- an agreement for the purchase of goods by instalments where title in the goods does not pass until the final instalment is paid.

For all purposes, other than CGT and withholding tax, div 240 treats arrangements involving hire purchase agreements as if they involved a 'notional sale' of the relevant property by the 'notional seller' (ie the actual owner) to the 'notional buyer' (ie the hirer) (ss 240-17, 240-20). The notional sale is deemed to be financed by a 'notional loan' that is subject to interest made by the notional seller to the notional buyer (s 240-25). The arrangement payments are treated as the repayments of the 'notional loan principal' and interest (s 240-25(6)) but are otherwise non-assessable non-exempt income of the notional seller (s 240-40) and are not deductible to the notional buyer (s 240-55). Arrangements that fall within div 240 are expressly excluded from the operation of the TOFA regime (s 230-460) [29.2].

Notional sale

Section 240-20 provides that the notional seller is taken to have disposed of the property by way of sale to the notional buyer, and the notional buyer is taken to have acquired it at the start of the arrangement. The notional buyer is taken to own the property until the arrangement ends. The notional buyer is therefore the 'holder' of the asset under s 40-40 and will be able to claim any deductions available under the capital allowance regime (see TR 2005/20) [15.2].

The consideration for the sale of the property for the notional seller and the cost of acquisition of the property for the notional buyer is generally the cost or value of the property for the purposes of the arrangement. However, if the parties were *not* dealing with each other at arm's length, it is the arm's length value of the property at the start of the arrangement (s 240-25(5)).

If the property is not trading stock of the notional seller and the consideration for the notional sale of the property exceeds what it cost the notional seller to acquire the property, the notional seller is assessable on the excess in the income year of the notional sale (s 240-35(2)).

Example Harry enters into an arm's length hire purchase agreement with L Co on 1 July 2023. The arrangement relates to machinery that Harry will use for income-producing purposes in his business, and it is reasonable to conclude that Harry will acquire the machinery at the end of the arrangement. L Co acquired the machinery for $90,000 and it was not its trading stock. The hire purchase agreement states that the cost of the machinery is $100,000.

L Co is taken to have sold the machinery to Harry, who is treated as the owner of the property and who can therefore claim deductions for its decline in value under div 40 based on its cost of $100,000.

L Co is required to include the profit of $10,000 (ie $100,000 – $90,000) from the notional sale in its assessable income in the 2023/24 income year under s 240-35(2).

Notional loan

Section 240-25 provides that the notional seller is also taken to have made a notional loan to the notional buyer in the amount of the 'notional loan principal' (ie generally the consideration for the sale of the property) which is subject to the payment of interest. The notional loan is for a period that starts at the start of the arrangement and generally ends when it ceases to have effect.

The notional seller is assessable on the 'notional interest' (s 240-35(1)). This is calculated under s 240-60 and is essentially the 'outstanding notional loan principal' at the start of the arrangement payment period multiplied by the 'implicit interest rate' for that period. The notional buyer is entitled to claim deductions for the notional interest to the extent that they would otherwise be entitled to deduct arrangement payments if no part of those payments were capital in nature (s 240-50).

Extensions, renewals and ending of arrangements

When an arrangement is extended or renewed, the original arrangement is treated as having ended and a separate arrangement is treated as having commenced (ss 240-80(1), (2)). There is, however, deemed to be no change in ownership of the property by the notional buyer (s 240-80(3)). The notional loan principal for the renewal or extension is generally the cost or value of the property for the purposes of the renewal or extension. However, if the parties were *not* dealing with each other at arm's length, it is the arm's length value of the property at the time of the extension or renewal (s 240-80(4)).

If the notional buyer pays an amount to the notional seller at or after the end of the agreement to acquire the property, the amount is not included in the notional seller's assessable income and not deductible to the notional buyer. Furthermore, the transfer of legal title from the notional seller to the notional buyer is not taken to be a disposal of the property and the notional buyer is deemed to continue to own the property (s 240-85).

If the arrangement ends without extension or renewal and the notional buyer does not pay any amount to acquire the property, the property is taken to have been sold back by the notional buyer to the notional seller for its market value (s 240-90). If the notional buyer has been claiming deductions under div 40, this will trigger a balancing adjustment event for the notional buyer (s 40-295) [15.3].

If at the end of the arrangement there are differences in the amounts included in the notional seller's assessable income and the actual interest received, special balancing adjustments arise under sub-div 240-G.

[29.4] Leases of luxury cars regime

Division 242 *ITAA97* applies to leases of luxury cars that are not 'short-term hire agreements' or 'hire purchase agreements' [29.3]. A luxury car is basically a car that costs more than the 'car limit' in s 40-230 (ie $68,108 for 2023/24) [15.2]. Division 242 was introduced to ensure that the lease of a luxury car does not result in a better after-tax outcome than if the car had been sold to the lessee. To address this situation, div 242 treats the lease of a luxury car as if the lessor had sold the car to the lessee and lent the lessee the purchase price. If not for div 242, the lessee might be able to deduct the lease payments (thereby effectively avoiding the capital allowance limit for luxury cars). Arrangements that fall within div 242 are expressly excluded from the TOFA regime (s 230-460) [29.2].

Notional sale and loan

Under div 242, the lessor is deemed to have disposed of the car by way of a notional sale to the lessee, which is financed by a notional loan subject to interest for the term of the lease (ss 242-15, 242-25). The consideration for the notional sale, the first element of the cost of the car to the lessee, and the 'notional loan principal' are all deemed to be the market value of the car at the start of the lease (ss 242-20, 240-25).

Lessors are assessable on 'accrual amounts', which represent the interest on the notional loan (these amounts are calculated by multiplying the 'outstanding notional loan principal' at the start of the lease period by the 'implicit interest rate' for that period) (s 242-35).

Lessees can deduct accrual amounts to the extent that they could otherwise have deducted lease payments (s 242-50). They can also claim appropriate deductions under the capital allowance regime in div 40 for the cost of the car (subject to the car limit) [15.2].

The actual lease payments are non-assessable non-exempt income of the lessor and are not deductible to the lessee (ss 242-40, 242-55).

Extensions, renewals and ending of leases

Where a lease is extended or renewed, the original loan is also deemed to end and the lessor is treated as having made a new loan to the lessee, who continues to own the car until the end of the extended or renewed lease (s 242-80).

If actual ownership of the car is transferred to the lessee, the amount paid to acquire the car is not included in the lessor's assessable income and is not deductible to the lessee, and the lessee is deemed to continue to own the car until they dispose of it (s 242-85).

When the lease ends, the lessee is treated as having sold the car back to the lessor for its market value (s 242-90). This may result in balancing adjustments arising under div 40 [15.2].

If at the end of the lease there are differences in the overall nominal gain to the lessor and the nominal interest paid under the lease, special balancing adjustments arise under sub-div 242-D.

[29.5] Limited recourse debt regime

Division 243 *ITAA97* applies where taxpayers have financed the acquisition of property using 'limited recourse debt' arrangements that are terminated before the debt has been fully repaid (s 243-15). The broad aim of the regime is to include an amount in a taxpayer's assessable income where their capital allowance deductions in respect of the property (ie deductions under divs 40, 43 and 328-D *ITAA97*) exceed the amount they have actually repaid under the arrangement.

Limited recourse debt arrangements

A limited recourse debt arrangement arises where a person (ie the 'debtor') has an obligation to pay an amount to another person (ie the 'creditor') in circumstances where the rights of the creditor against the debtor in the event of default in payment of the debt are limited wholly or predominantly to rights relating to the 'debt property', a mortgage or security over the debt property, or rights that arise out of any arrangement relating to the financial obligations of an end user of the 'financed property' to the debtor (s 243-20(1)). The 'financed property' is the property acquired with the funds from the limited recourse debt arrangement and the 'debt property' is the financed property or any other property provided as security for the debt (s 243-30).

A limited recourse debt arrangement also exists where it is reasonable to conclude that a creditor's rights are capable of being limited in the way mentioned above or are in substance or effect wholly or predominantly limited to rights in relation to the debt property (s 243-20(2)). This is designed to address the *FC of T v BHP Billiton Ltd* 2011 ATC ¶20-264 decision, where it was held that s 243-20(1) *ITAA97* was only concerned with contractually limited recourse debt arrangements.

Termination

A limited recourse debt arrangement can be 'terminated' in a variety of ways, including where the debtor's obligation to repay the debt is waived or varied so as to reduce or extinguish the debt, and where the debtor's interest in the property is surrendered to the creditor because of a failure to repay the debt (s 243-25).

Operation of div 243

Where div 243 applies, the debtor is required to include in their assessable income in the income year in which the termination occurs any excessive capital allowance deductions (s 243-40). Excessive capital allowance deductions are, basically, the amount by which the net capital allowance deductions to which the debtor is actually entitled *exceed* the net capital allowance deductions to which they would otherwise be entitled (for past, present and future income years) if their original expenditure on the asset was reduced by the unpaid debt (s 243-35). By including excessive capital allowance deductions in the debtor's assessable income, the debtor is effectively prevented from writing off more than 100% of the amount repaid to the creditor.

Example On 1 July 2020, Deb (the debtor) purchased an income-producing depreciating asset (the debt property) for $100,000, which she intends to depreciate at the prime cost rate of 10% over the 10-year life of the asset. As a result, Deb is entitled to a deduction under s 40-25 of $10,000 per year.

Deb financed the purchase of the asset with a loan from C Bank (the creditor). Under the terms of the loan, Deb is required to make principal repayments of $20,000 on 30 June each year (together with interest) and C Bank's rights in the event of default are limited to seizure and sale of the debt property.

Deb met her repayment obligations on 30 June 2021 and 30 June 2022 (totalling $40,000). However, she failed to meet her repayment obligation on 30 June 2023. The limited recourse debt arrangement was consequently terminated and the property (which had a market value of $50,000 at the time) was surrendered to C Bank.

Over the 2020/21 to 2022/23 income years, Deb claimed total deductions under s 40-25 of $30,000 (ie 3 × $10,000). On 30 June 2023, the 'adjustable value' of the property was $70,000 (ie $100,000 – $30,000) and its 'termination value' was $50,000. This resulted in Deb also being entitled to a deduction of $20,000 (ie $70,000 – $50,000) as a balancing adjustment under s 40-285 in the 2022/23 income year [15.3].

Deb's actual capital allowance deductions of $50,000 (ie $30,000 + $20,000) exceed $40,000 (being the amount that she would otherwise be allowed to deduct in all past, present and future income years if the $100,000 original expenditure on the debt property were reduced by the $60,000 unpaid debt). Deb therefore has excessive capital allowance deductions of $10,000, which must be included in her assessable income in the 2022/23 income year under s 243-40.

[29.6] Forgiveness of commercial debts regime

Division 245 *ITAA97* contains the forgiveness of commercial debts regime. The regime applies where a creditor forgives certain debts (commonly referred to as 'commercial debts') owed by a taxpayer (ie the debtor). The classic example of such a debt is a loan on which the interest payable by the debtor is deductible (eg an ordinary business loan).

Prior to the introduction of div 245 (and its predecessor in sch 2C *ITAA36*), the forgiveness of a commercial debt produced an unbalanced result. The forgiveness of the debt ordinarily gave rise to a deduction or capital loss to the creditor. However, the debtor was not ordinarily assessed on any corresponding gain and did not lose the benefit of any deductions. The aim of div 245 is to provide some 'symmetry' between the tax positions of the creditor and debtor. The Division achieves this by reducing certain amounts that would otherwise lessen the amount of the debtor's taxable income for the relevant year or future years.

Application

Division 245 requires debtors to apply the 'total net forgiven amount' of their 'debts' that are 'forgiven' during an income year in accordance with 'reduction rules' set out in ss 245-115 to 245-195 (s 245-105). The reduction rules reduce the following amounts:

- the tax losses of the debtor
- the net capital losses of the debtor
- the expenditure of the debtor that is deductible under specified provisions, and
- the cost base or reduced cost base of the debtor's CGT assets.

The manner in which the reduction rules apply is examined below. However, before dealing with this issue, it is important to identify the kinds of 'debts' to which div 245 applies and to determine the circumstances in which such debts are taken to be 'forgiven' under the division. It is also necessary to understand how the debtor's 'total net forgiven amount' is calculated.

Debt

Section 245-10 states that div 245 only applies to a debt if:

- the whole or part of the interest paid or payable in respect of the debt is deductible by the debtor
- interest is not payable in respect of the debt but, had interest been charged, it would have been deductible by the debtor, or
- interest could have been deducted by the debtor but for the operation of a provision in the *ITAA36* or *ITAA97* (other than ss 8-1(2)(a), (b) and (c)) that prevents such a deduction.

Example Marge owns a milk bar and borrows $100,000 from a bank at an interest rate of 5% per annum to purchase equipment for her shop. As the loan is used for income-producing purposes, any interest payable on the loan is deductible under s 8-1 *ITAA97*. The $100,000 amount, therefore, constitutes a 'debt' that is covered by div 245.

If the loan to Marge was an interest-free loan, the debt would still be covered by div 245, as interest would have been deductible had it been charged on the loan.

However, if Marge borrowed the money to renovate her home, the debt would not be covered by div 245, as any interest payable on the loan would not be deductible because the borrowings are of a private nature and therefore fall within s 8-1(2)(b) *ITAA97*.

Division 245 also applies to a non-equity share [29.9] issued by a company as if it were a debt to which s 245-10 applies that is owed by the company to the relevant shareholder (s 245-15).

In addition, div 245 applies to part of a debt in the same way as it applies to the whole debt (s 245-20).

Forgiveness

A debt is taken to be forgiven if and when:

- the debtor's obligation to pay the debt is released, waived or otherwise extinguished other than by repaying the debt in full, or
- the debt becomes statute-barred (s 245-35).

A debt is also taken to be forgiven in a number of other specific cases (eg where the debt has been assigned (s 245-36) or where a 'debt-for-equity swap' arrangement takes place (s 245-37)).

The operative rules in div 245 do not, however, apply to the forgiveness of a debt if:

- the debt is waived and the waiver constitutes a fringe benefit
- the amount of the debt is included in the debtor's assessable income in any income year
- the forgiveness arises under an Act relating to bankruptcy
- the forgiveness arises under a will
- the forgiveness arises for reasons of natural love or affection, or
- the debt is a tax-related liability or civil penalty under div 290 of sch 1 *TAA* (s 245-40).

Total net forgiven amount

A debtor's 'total net forgiven amount' for an income year is the total of the 'net forgiven amounts' of all of the debtor's debts that are forgiven in that year (s 245-105(1)).

The 'net forgiven amount' of a debt is the 'gross forgiven amount' of the debt reduced by the following amounts:

- any amount that, under a provision of the legislation (other than div 245), is included in the debtor's assessable income, for any income year as a result of the forgiveness of the debt
- any amount by which, under a provision of the legislation (other than div 245), a deduction that would otherwise be allowable to the debtor has been reduced as a result of the forgiveness of the debt (except under div 727 *ITAA97*), and
- any amount by which the cost base of any of the debtor's assets is reduced as a result of the forgiveness of the debt (s 245-85).

The 'gross forgiven amount' of the debt is generally the 'value' of the debt at the time it is forgiven (s 245-75). The 'value' of a debt at the time it is forgiven is generally the amount that would have been the market value of the debt at the forgiveness time (assuming that the debtor was able to pay all its debts when the debt was incurred and at the forgiveness time). Special rules apply to calculate the value of non-recourse debts (s 245-60) and previously assigned debts (s 245-61).

The value of a debt that is forgiven is reduced by any 'offset amount' calculated pursuant to s 245-65. The offset amount reflects any consideration that the debtor has given to the creditor in respect of the forgiveness (ie the amount of money, or the market value of property, that the debtor has paid, or is required to pay in respect of the forgiveness).

Application of total net forgiven amount

A debtor must apply their total net forgiven amount to reduce the following amounts:

- the tax losses of the debtor (s 245-115)
- the net capital losses of the debtor (s 245-130)
- the expenditure of the debtor that is deductible under specified provisions, which include:
  - div 40 *ITAA97* (capital allowance expenditure) [15.2]
  - s 25-25 *ITAA97* (borrowing expenditure) [13.5]
  - div 355 *ITAA97* (R&D expenditure) [27.5], and
  - s 43-10 *ITAA97* (capital works expenditure) [15.7] (s 245-145)
- the cost base or reduced cost base of the debtor's CGT assets [17.6] (s 245-165).

The relevant amounts are reduced in the order that they appear. Within each of the four classes of amounts, the debtor may choose the order in which the total net forgiven amount reduces the relevant amounts within the particular class so long as it is applied to the maximum extent possible within that class. Once the total net forgiven amount has been applied against all the amounts in a class, any excess is applied against the next class of amounts. After the debtor has applied the total net forgiven amount to the maximum extent possible against the relevant amounts, any excess is disregarded (s 245-195).

Example Flora borrowed $1m from a bank to purchase an outdoor nursery business. Shortly after borrowing the $1m, a cyclone completely destroyed the nursery and Flora is in financial strife as she is not insured. After negotiations with the bank, the bank agrees to forgive the $1m debt Flora owes the bank on the basis that she pays $400,000 immediately to the bank.

As Flora would be able to claim a deduction for interest paid on her loan under s 8-1 *ITAA97*, the $1m is a 'debt' to which div 245 applies (s 245-10). Flora's 'total net forgiven amount' is $600,000 ($1m – $400,000). She must apply this amount against any of the four amounts mentioned above (s 245-105). If she has a carry forward tax loss of $100,000, a net capital loss of $200,000 and shares with a cost base of $500,000, her tax loss and net capital loss would both be reduced to nil and the cost base of her shares would be reduced to $200,000.

[29.7] Capital protected borrowings regime

Division 247 *ITAA97* contains the 'capital protected borrowings' ('CPBs') regime, which was enacted to deal with certain limited recourse loan arrangements, such as those that occurred in *FC of T v Firth* 2002 ATC 4346 (where it was held that just because the terms of a loan may limit a lender's right of recovery against the asset acquired with the borrowed funds does not necessarily mean that part of the interest will be capital in nature) [12.12].

CPBs are borrowing arrangements under which the borrower is wholly or partly protected against a fall in the market value of a protected thing that is acquired with the borrowings or used as security for the borrowings (s 247-10). The protected thing must be a direct or indirect beneficial interest in a share, a unit in a unit trust or a stapled security. Certain shares, units and stapled securities (eg those acquired under ESSs [21.2]) are excluded (s 247-15).

Division 247 applies to CPBs entered into, or extended after, 1 July 2007 if the borrower has an 'excess' calculated under the method statement in s 247-20(3) *ITAA97*. An excess arises where the amount incurred by a borrower on capital protection and interest on the borrowing for the income year exceeds the interest that would have been payable on a similar borrowing for the year using specified 'benchmark rates'. Division 247 also applies to CPBs, or extensions of CPBs, entered into from 16 April 2003 to 30 June 2007 if the borrower has an 'amount that is reasonably attributable to the capital protection' worked out under div 247 *ITTPA*.

Where div 247 applies, the 'excess' or 'amount that is reasonably attributable to the capital protection' (reduced by any amount incurred by the borrower for a specific put option) is treated as if it was incurred for a 'put option' granted under the arrangement (s 247-20(6)). The effect of treating the excess or amount as a put option (rather than interest) is that it will not be deductible under s 8-1 and will instead fall within the CGT regime. The exercise or expiry of the put option may therefore trigger a capital gain or capital loss under CGT event C2 [17.10] (s 247-30).

[29.8] Assets put to tax preferred use regime

Division 250 *ITAA97* contains a special regime that denies or reduces capital allowance deductions in relation to certain financing arrangements involving assets that are put to a 'tax preferred use'. The regime also treats these arrangements as loans that are taxed on a compounding accruals basis.

The aim of div 250 is to combat arrangements whereby taxpayers (eg banks) seek to obtain tax deferral benefits by leasing an asset to a tax preferred end user (eg a tax-exempt entity) and transferring some or all of the risks or benefits associated with the ownership of the asset to that entity.

Under these arrangements, the taxpayer is assessed on the rent and is also entitled to deductions (eg capital allowance deductions) as it is the legal owner of the asset. The tax-preferred entity is not entitled to any deductions relating to the asset even though it is the economic owner of the asset because of its tax-exempt status. Without div 250, tax deferral benefits could arise if the taxpayer charges the tax preferred end user low rent in the initial years of the arrangement. If the rent is less than the deductions available to the taxpayer, this would allow the taxpayer to offset the excess deductions against its other assessable income. While the rent charged in the later years would typically be increased to compensate for the initial low rent, the taxpayer would obtain tax deferral benefits. The tax preferred end user would also obtain a timing benefit from being charged lower initial rent.

Division 250 generally operates where the tax preferred use of the asset commences on or after 1 July 2007 under an arrangement entered into on or after that date. The division replaces s 51AD *ITAA36* and div 16D of pt IIII *ITAA36*, which continue to have residual operation, but do not generally apply to arrangements entered into from 1 July 2007. Arrangements that fall within div 250 are excluded from the TOFA regime in div 230 (s 230-460).

Application

Division 250 applies where:

- an asset is put to 'tax preferred use'
- the 'arrangement period' for the tax preferred use of the asset (ie the period from the start of the tax preferred use to the date on which it is reasonably expected to end (s 250-65) is greater than 12 months
- financial benefits in relation to the tax preferred use of the asset have been, will be, or can be expected to be provided to a taxpayer by a 'tax preferred end user', a 'tax preferred entity' or a foreign resident
- but for the operation of div 250, the taxpayer would be entitled to a capital allowance deduction in respect of the asset, and
- the taxpayer lacks a 'predominant economic interest' in the asset (s 250-15).

Division 250 operates subject to a number of exclusions. For example, it does not apply to an SBE that claims capital allowance deductions under sub-div 328-D [15.2] (s 250-20). It also does not apply where the financial benefits do not exceed a specified minimum amount ($5m indexed annually) (s 250-25). Certain short-term or low-value arrangements are also excluded (s 250-30). The Commissioner may also determine that it is unreasonable to apply the division (s 250-45).

Tax preferred end user and tax preferred use

A 'tax preferred end user' is an 'end user' (defined in s 250-50) that is a 'tax preferred entity' (eg an exempt entity), a foreign resident, or an Australian resident to the extent that it carries on business in a foreign country through a PE [30.5] in that country (s 250-55).

An asset is put to 'tax preferred use' where an end user is a lessee of the asset and the asset is used by or on behalf of a tax preferred entity or used wholly or principally outside Australia by a foreign resident or an Australian resident that carries on business through a PE in a foreign country (s 250-60).

Predominant economic interest

An entity lacks a 'predominant economic interest' in an asset where the arrangement falls within the 'limited recourse debt test' in s 250-115, the 'right to acquire asset test' in s 250-120, the 'effectively non-cancellable, long-term arrangement test' in s 250-125, or the 'level of expected financial benefits test' in s 250-130 (s 250-110).

Operation of div 250

Where div 250 applies, the capital allowance deductions to which a taxpayer would otherwise be entitled in respect of the asset are denied (s 250-145). The deductions are apportioned if only part of the financial benefits provided during the arrangement period are applicable to the tax preferred use of the asset (s 250-150).

In addition, a financial arrangement in the form of a loan arises (s 250-155). The taxpayer receiving the financial benefits in relation to the tax preferred use of the asset is treated as the lender and the amount lent is generally based on the adjustable value of the property. The taxpayer is required to recognise gains and losses from the financial arrangement over the life of the arrangement. The overall gain or loss (ie the difference between the amount of the loan and the sum of all financial benefits subject to deemed loan treatment) is spread over the arrangement period on a compounding accruals basis and allocated to particular income years (ss 250-240 to 250-250). Gains are included in assessable income while losses are deductible to the extent that they are made in gaining or producing assessable income or necessarily made in carrying on a business for the purpose of gaining or producing assessable income (s 250-205). To prevent duplication, gains and losses are not assessable or deductible under any other provisions (s 250-210).

[29.9] Debt and equity regime

In the past, the tax treatment of payments made by companies depended on the 'legal form' of the interest held in the company, rather than the 'substance' of the arrangement. For instance, whether a payment was treated as a 'dividend' (ie a frankable distribution which was not deductible to the company) or as 'interest' (ie a non-frankable distribution which was generally deductible to the company) simply depended on whether it was made in respect of a share or a loan. To ensure that returns made by companies are taxed according to the 'substance' of the arrangement rather than its 'legal form', the debt and equity regime in div 974 was enacted in 2001. The regime has two key functions:

- it prescribes tests for distinguishing between 'debt' and 'equity' interests in companies, and
- it sets out rules for dealing with the taxation treatment of returns made in respect of such interests.

Tests for distinguishing between debt and equity interests

The tests for distinguishing between debt and equity interests are contained in sub-divs 974-B and 974-C *ITAA97*. Interests are classified according to 'schemes' and 'related schemes' (ss 974-150, 974-155) determined at the time they are entered into (ss 974-15, 974-70). However, special rules apply to converting interests (eg convertible notes), which give rise to new interests at the time of conversion. Under these rules:

- if a debt interest is an interest that will or may convert into an equity interest, the conversion is taken to give rise to a new interest (and is not treated as merely a continuation of the debt interest) (s 974-100(1)), and
- if an equity interest is an interest that will or may convert into a debt interest, the conversion is taken to give rise to a new interest (and is not treated as merely a continuation of the equity interest) (s 974-100(2)).

Example A company issues a convertible note to an investor. The note pays interest at the rate of 2% pa and converts into ordinary shares in the company after three years. The convertible note gives rise to a debt interest when it is issued and it becomes an equity interest when it is converted into shares.

In general, for a scheme to fall within div 974, the scheme must be a 'financing arrangement' (ie a scheme entered into to raise finance for the company or connected entity) (s 974-130(1)). Schemes that are generally entered into to raise finance include bills of exchange, income securities and convertible interests that will convert into equity interests (s 974-130(2)). By way of contrast, schemes that are generally *not* entered into to raise finance include derivatives used for managing financial risk and contracts for personal services entered into in the ordinary course of business (s 974-130(3)). Certain leases, bailments, securities lending, insurance and royalty arrangements are deemed not to be entered into to raise finance (s 974-130(4)). The regulations may also specify that particular schemes are not financing arrangements (s 974-130(5)).

In simple terms:

- an interest that gives rise to 'non-contingent returns' is usually classified as a 'debt interest' (provided the returns are at least equal to the issue price of the interest), and
- an interest that gives rise to 'contingent returns' is usually classified as an 'equity interest'.

A return is not contingent merely because it is contingent on the ability of the entity to meet the obligation (s 974-85(1)). Accordingly, the mere fact that repayment of a loan depends on the borrower having funds available to satisfy the debt when it becomes due does not necessarily make the loan an equity interest.

Debt test

According to s 974-15, a scheme gives rise to a 'debt interest' if it satisfies the 'debt test' in s 974-20(1). Broadly, a scheme satisfies the debt test in relation to an entity if it satisfies all of the following requirements:

(a) the scheme is a 'financing arrangement' (this requirement does not need to be fulfilled if the scheme gives rise to an interest that is a share)
(b) the entity (or a connected entity) will receive a 'financial benefit' (s 974-160) under the scheme
(c) the entity (or the entity and a connected entity) has an 'effectively non-contingent obligation' under the scheme to provide a financial benefit to one or more entities, and
(d) it is substantially more likely than not that the 'value provided' under the scheme will be at least equal to the 'value received' under the scheme.

The value provided is the value of the financial benefit (or sum of the financial benefits) provided, or to be provided under the scheme by the entity or its connected entity (s 974-20(2)). The value received is the value of the financial benefit (or sum of the financial benefits) received, or to be received under the scheme by the entity or its connected entity (s 974-20(3)).

The value of a financial benefit provided or received under a scheme is calculated:

- in 'nominal terms' if the interest must end within 10 years after it is issued, or
- in 'present value terms' if the interest must or may end more than 10 years after it is issued (ss 974-35, 974-50).

As a general rule, the value of a financial benefit provided or received under a scheme is calculated assuming it will continue to be held for the rest of its life (s 974-35(2)). However, a special rule applies where a party has the right or option to terminate the scheme early, in which case the relevant interest is deemed to end at the earliest time that the party must exercise the right or option (s 974-40). A party's right or option to terminate a scheme is only taken into account if the party has an 'effectively non-contingent obligation' to exercise the right or option. An 'effectively non-contingent obligation' exists if, having regard to the pricing, terms and conditions of the scheme, there is in substance or effect a 'non-contingent obligation' (ie an obligation that is not contingent on any event, condition or situation, other than the ability or willingness of the entity or a connected entity to meet the obligation) (ss 974-135(1), (3)). The existence of a right to convert an interest into an equity interest does not of itself make the issuer's obligation contingent (s 974-135(4)).

Equity test

According to s 974-70, a scheme gives rise to an 'equity interest' if it satisfies the 'equity test' in s 974-75 and is not characterised as part of a larger interest that is a debt interest. Broadly, a scheme satisfies the equity test if it gives rise to any of the following interests:

(a) an interest that is a share in a company
(b) an interest that is contingent on the economic performance of the company (or a connected entity)
(c) an interest that is subject to a return that is at the discretion of the company (or a connected entity), or
(d) an interest that gives the holder (or a connected entity) a right to be issued an equity interest in the company (or a connected entity).

In all the above situations, other than (a), there is also a requirement that the scheme must be a 'financing arrangement' for the interest to constitute an equity interest.

Tie-breaker rule

If an interest satisfies both the debt and equity tests, it will be treated as a debt interest under a 'tie-breaker rule' (s 974-5(4)).

Example On 1 August 2016, A Co issues redeemable preference shares ('RPS') for $100. The RPS are redeemable for their face value on 1 August 2023. RPS shareholders are entitled to receive dividends equal to 12% of the issue price at the end of every 12 months. These dividends must be paid ahead of any other dividends and are cumulative (ie if A Co does not have sufficient profits to pay RPS dividends in a particular year, the dividends payable in the following year are increased).

- **Equity test.** The RPS satisfy the equity test because they are shares in A Co.
- **Debt test.** The RPS also satisfy the debt test because:
  (a) there is a scheme which is a financing arrangement (being the arrangement between A Co and the RPS shareholders)
  (b) A Co receives a financial benefit under the arrangement (being $100 for each RPS issued)
  (c) A Co has an effectively non-contingent obligation to provide a financial benefit, being the obligation to repay $100 in seven years' time (note: A Co does not have an effectively non-contingent obligation to pay dividends because the payment of dividends is contingent upon it having profits), and
  (d) it is substantially more likely than not that the financial benefit to be provided by A Co ($100 redemption price) will be at least equal to the financial benefit received by A Co ($100 issue price).
- **Tie-breaker rule.** Since the RPS satisfy both the equity and debt tests, they are characterised as debt interests.

Note, if the shares were 'non-redeemable preference shares' (ie there was no right to have them redeemed for $100), then element (c) in the debt test would not be satisfied. Likewise, if the shares were redeemable at a discount to their face value (eg for $80 instead of $100), then element (d) in the debt test would not be satisfied. In both of these cases, the shares would be treated as equity interests.

Treatment of returns on debt and equity interests

The way in which returns made by a company are treated under the debt and equity rules depends on whether they are paid in respect of 'non-equity shares' or 'non-share equity interests'.

Non-equity shares

'Non-equity shares' are shares that give rise to debt interests (s 995-1 *ITAA97*). Returns on non-equity shares are treated in effectively the same manner as returns on debt (eg returns on loans).

Section 25-85 provides that a company can generally deduct dividends paid in respect of non-equity shares to the extent to which the dividends would have been deductible under s 8-1 if they were interest incurred in raising finance. For this purpose, subject to capping rules, a return is expressly not prevented from being deductible merely because it is contingent on the company's economic performance or because it secures a permanent or enduring benefit for the company.

Dividends paid on non-equity shares are generally assessable in the hands of resident shareholders under the general dividend assessment rules in s 44(1) *ITAA36*, but are not frankable (s 202-45(d)). The withholding tax rules can apply to dividends paid in respect of non-equity shares to non-residents [31.11]. However, for withholding tax purposes, the dividends are treated as if they were interest payments (ss 128A(1), (1AB) *ITAA36*). Consequently, the rate of withholding tax is generally 10% [39.4].

> ***Example*** In the example above, the RPS were characterised as debt interests and are therefore 'non-equity shares'. A Co would therefore be able to claim a deduction for the dividend payments but would not be able to frank them. Resident RPS shareholders would be required to include the RPS dividends in their assessable income. Interest withholding tax would generally apply to RPS dividends paid to non-resident shareholders.

Non-share equity interests

'Non-share equity interests' are equity interests in a company that are not solely shares (s 995-1). Returns on non-share equity interests are treated in essentially the same manner as returns on shares. Distributions made by a company on non-share equity interests are referred to as 'non-share distributions' (s 974-115).

Non-share distributions are treated as 'non-share dividends' except to the extent that they are 'non-share capital returns' (ie the company debits them against either its share capital account or its 'non-share capital account', as defined in s 164-10) (ss 974-120, 974-125). Non-share distributions are not deductible to the company (s 26-26).

Non-share dividends are 'frankable distributions' (s 202-40), except to the extent that they exceed the company's 'available frankable profits' worked out under s 215-20 (s 215-15).

The general dividend assessment rules in s 44(1) and the withholding tax provisions in s 128B apply to non-share dividends in the same manner as they apply to dividends (ss 43B, 128AAA). Consequently, non-share dividends paid to residents are generally assessable, while non-share dividends paid to non-residents are generally subject to withholding tax to the extent that they are unfranked [22.5].

[29.10] Advance payments regime

Under the general deduction provision in s 8-1, payments made in advance for things provided in subsequent income years are ordinarily fully deductible in the income year that the payments are made. This is because such outgoings would be considered to be 'incurred' in the year of payment

(*FC of T v Lau* 84 ATC 4929; *FC of T v Raymor (NSW) Pty Ltd* 90 ATC 4461, TR 94/25) [12.5]. However, s 8-1 operates subject to the advance payments regime in sub-div H of div 3 of pt III *ITAA36*, which prevents taxpayers from obtaining the benefit of upfront deductions for certain types of pre-paid expenditure.

Application

The advance payments regime applies to expenditure that is deductible under s 8-1 *ITAA97* [12.2] and that is incurred in return for doing something under an agreement that is not to be wholly done within the year that the expenditure is incurred (s 82KZMA *ITAA36*).

The regime does not apply to 'excluded expenditure' (s 82KZL). Excluded expenditure covers things such as:

- expenditure that is less than $1,000
- expenditure required to be incurred by a Commonwealth, state or territory law or court order, and
- expenditure under a contract of service (eg salary or wages).

General rules

Where the advance payment rules apply, taxpayers are generally required to spread deductions for their expenditure over the 'eligible service period' (s 82KZMD). The eligible service period is, essentially, the period over which the relevant thing is to be done or 10 years (if this is shorter) (s 82KZL).

Special rules

Special rules apply to individuals that incur non-business expenditure and to SBEs and entities that would be SBEs if the aggregated annual turnover threshold for SBEs was $50m (instead of $10m) [8.7]. These taxpayers are generally able to fully deduct pre-paid expenditure in the year it is incurred, provided the eligible service period is not more than 12 months and ends no later than the last day of the income year following the income year in which the expenditure was incurred (s 82KZM).

Example

Situation 1

On 1 June Year 1, an SBE pre-paid $10,000 for three years of computer services to be provided from 1 August in Year 2 to 31 July in Year 5 (a total of 1,095 days). The entity is required to spread the deduction over the eligible service period as follows:

- Year 2: 334/1,095 × $10,000 = $3,050.23
- Year 3: 365/1,095 × $10,000 = $3,333.33
- Year 4: 365/1,095 × $10,000 = $3,333.33
- Year 5: 31/1,095 × $10,000 = $283.11

Situation 2

On 1 June Year 1, an SBE pre-paid $10,000 for one year of computer services to be provided from 1 August Year 2 to 31 July Year 3. Even though the eligible service period is not more than 12 months, since it ends after the last day of the income year following the year in which it was incurred, the entity must spread the deduction over the eligible service period as follows:

- Year 2: 334/365 × $10,000 = $9,150.68
- Year 3: 31/365 × $10,000 = $849.32

Situation 3
On 1 June Year 1, an SBE pre-paid $10,000 for one year of computer services to be provided from 25 June Year 1 to 24 June Year 2. As the eligible service period is not more than 12 months and as it ends before the last day of the income year following the year in which it was incurred, the entity is able to deduct the entire $10,000 in Year 1.

Special rules also apply to pre-paid expenditure incurred under certain tax shelter arrangements (s 82KZME).

[29.11] Pre-payment, deferral and recoupment scheme regime

Subdivision D of div 3 of pt III *ITAA36* contains three separate anti-avoidance provisions that deny deductions for losses or outgoings incurred under certain pre-payment, deferral and recoupment schemes. Although the provisions are highly technical in nature, their key features may be summarised as follows.

Pre-payment schemes

Section 82KJ is designed to discourage taxpayers entering into pre-payment schemes under which they seek to generate deductions in excess of their net outlays on deductible items. Broadly speaking, the provision applies where:

- a loss or outgoing in respect of which a deduction would otherwise be allowable is incurred by a taxpayer under a 'tax avoidance agreement' (defined in s 82KH(1))
- having regard to the benefit secured by the loss or outgoing, the amount of the loss or outgoing exceeds the amount which might reasonably have been expected to have been incurred had it not been incurred as part of a tax avoidance agreement
- property has been, will be, or may reasonably be expected to be, acquired by the taxpayer (or their associate) under the tax avoidance agreement, and
- the consideration that was payable in respect of the acquisition of that property is less than the consideration that might reasonably be expected to have been payable if the loss or outgoing had not been incurred.

29

Where the above conditions apply, the taxpayer is denied a deduction for the loss or outgoing.

The following example illustrates the kinds of schemes to which s 82KJ is directed and is based on an example taken from the Explanatory Memorandum accompanying the Bill that introduced the provision in 1978.

Example Don borrows $1,000 from a money lender, ostensibly for income-producing purposes, and promptly pays $700 as a pre-payment of interest at 14% for 5 years. Upon the pre-payment of interest, Don (or an associate) is entitled to acquire the lender's rights under the loan agreement. Because the terms of the loan provide for a reduced interest rate of 4% once the pre-payment of interest has been made, the loan has a reduced value and can be acquired by Don or his associate for $370.

Ignoring s 82KJ, the effect of the arrangement is that Don claims a deduction for $700 in respect of a net outlay of $70 (ie $700 + $370 – $1,000). The lender, on the other hand, receives $700 interest but will offset against this amount the loss sustained in selling its $1,000 loan for $370. To counter this type of arrangement, s 82KJ denies Don a deduction for the $700.

Deferral schemes

Section 82KK is designed to prevent taxpayers from deferring their tax liabilities by entering into certain arrangements with associates. In essence, the section operates where:

- a taxpayer incurs a loss or outgoing to an associate (defined in s 82KH(1))
- the taxpayer is entitled to a deduction for that loss or outgoing
- the deduction is allowable in the income year in which it is incurred, but all or part of the income will not be included in the assessable income of the associate until a later income year, and
- the loss or outgoing is incurred under an 'agreement' (defined in s 82KH(1)) entered into or carried out for the purpose of securing a deferral in assessability.

Where the loss or outgoing incurred is in respect of the supply of goods or services, the deduction is deferred until the goods or services are actually supplied by the associate. Where the loss or outgoing incurred is not in respect of the supply of goods or services, the deduction is limited to the amount actually paid by the taxpayer to the associate during the relevant income year.

Example Jack and Jill are associates. In Year 1, Jill pays Jack $1m for goods or services to be supplied in Year 2. Jill seeks to deduct the payment in Year 1, but Jack only includes the income in his assessable income in Year 2. If the agreement is entered into for the purpose of deferring Jack's assessable income, Jill will not be entitled to any deduction in Year 1 as no goods or services have been supplied to her in that year.

Recoupment schemes

Section 82KL is designed to prevent taxpayers entering into expenditure recoupment schemes. The provision generally denies a deduction where a taxpayer incurs 'eligible relevant expenditure' and receives an additional benefit which, when combined with the tax saving in relation to the eligible relevant expenditure, exceeds the value of the eligible relevant expenditure.

Broadly speaking, eligible relevant expenditure is the amount of the 'relevant expenditure' incurred under a tax avoidance scheme that relates to benefits received by the taxpayer in addition to the main benefit in respect of which the relevant expenditure was incurred (s 82KH). Relevant expenditure covers specific outgoings such as borrowing expenses, interest and rent (s 82KH).

Example Jonathan is an artist who seeks to rent a studio in an art gallery for his business for $100,000. However, Jonathan agrees with the owner of the art gallery, Betty, that he will instead pay rent of $150,000 and receive a painting valued at $30,000 to display in his home.

Betty is willing to enter into the transaction because she is effectively disposing of a $30,000 painting for $50,000 (ie the increase in rent). Jonathan benefits from the transaction because he would ordinarily obtain a tax deduction of $50,000 for the increased rent, whereas he would not receive any deduction for purchasing the painting as it is for private use.

If Jonathan pays tax at the top rate, his expected tax saving from the increased deduction of $50,000 is $23,500 (ie $50,000 × 47%). The value of this tax saving ($23,500) combined with the value of the additional benefit ($50,000) is $73,500. As this exceeds the $50,000 increase in rent, s 82KL denies a deduction for the increased rent.

[29.12] Qualifying securities regime

Division 16E of pt III *ITAA36* (ss 159GP to 159GZ) was introduced to eliminate timing advantages associated with certain tax-deferral financing schemes. These schemes typically involved taxpayers that were not engaged in the business of lending money issuing discounted or deferred interest securities (eg five-year loans where interest was payable at the end of the loan). Under the general timing rules, the lender would only derive the interest income when it was received at the end of the loan [9.9], while the borrower would be entitled to deductions for the interest expenditure as it accrued over the period of the loan [12.5]. The general timing rules therefore produced a mismatch between the derivation of the income and the incurring of the outgoings.

The aim of div 16E is to ensure that the 'eligible return' from a 'qualifying security' is brought to account on an accruals basis over the term of the security. To ensure symmetry, there is a corresponding rule to ensure that deductions are also spread over such term. Importantly, div 16E is superimposed upon the general tax rules and only applies to amounts that would otherwise be assessable or deductible to a taxpayer under those rules.

As a consequence of the introduction of the TOFA regime, div 16E now only applies where div 230 *ITAA97* does not apply [29.2]. Division 16E can therefore potentially apply to qualifying securities issued prior to the introduction of the TOFA regime (which generally came into force on 1 July 2010) or where the qualifying securities are held by individuals (as individuals are generally excluded from the TOFA regime).

Qualifying securities

'Qualifying securities' are 'securities' (eg deposits with a financial institution, loans, debentures, bonds, promissory notes, bills of exchange and other contracts under which persons are liable to pay amounts) that satisfy the following requirements:

- the securities must be issued after 16 December 1984 and must not be part of an 'exempt series' as defined in s 159GP(9A)
- the securities must have an expected term that exceeds or is likely to exceed 12 months, and
- the securities must have an 'eligible return' and, where the eligible return can be established at the time of issue, the eligible return must be greater than 1.5% of the sum of all payments due under the security multiplied by the number of years of the term of the security (s 159GP(1)).

Eligible return

The 'eligible return' in relation to a security is the amount by which the payments made under the security (other than 'periodic interest') are 'reasonably likely' to exceed the issue price of the security (s 159GP(3)).

Effect of div 16E

Where div 16E applies to a security, the taxpayer is required to divide the term of the security into 'accrual periods' (usually periods of six months) and calculate the 'accrual amount' for each period according to a special formula (ss 159GQA, 159GQB). This accrual amount is then brought to account under s 159GQ.

Example Fred made an eight-year loan of $10m to a company in January 2016. Under the terms of the loan, the company is required to repay the principal and interest at the end of the loan. At such time, Fred will receive $18m (ie $10m principal and $8m interest).

The loan is a qualifying security because:

- it is a 'security' that is issued after 16 December 1984
- its expected term is likely to exceed 12 months, and
- its 'eligible return' ($8m) is more than 1.5% of the sum of all payments made under the security multiplied by the number of years of its term, ie it is more than $2.16m (1.5% × $18m × 8).

Fred must therefore bring the interest income to account on an accruals basis under div 16E.

[29.13] Traditional securities regime

Sections 26BB and 70B *ITAA36* contain special rules relating to the disposal or redemption of 'traditional securities'. The rules only operate where the TOFA regime in div 230 *ITAA97* does not apply [29.2].

Traditional security

A 'traditional security' is defined in s 26BB(1) as a 'security' held by a taxpayer that was acquired after 10 May 1989, is not trading stock, and either:

- does not have an 'eligible return' (defined in div 16E of pt III *ITAA36* [29.12]), or
- has an eligible return that is not more than 1.5% of the sum of the payments (excluding periodic interest) liable to be made under the security multiplied by the number (including fractions) of years in the term of security.

Example Felicity issued a promissory note to Fred for $180,000 on 1 January 2013. The promissory note matured on 1 January in 2023 when it was redeemed for its face value of $200,000. The promissory note is a security that has an eligible return of $20,000 (ie $200,000 – $180,000). The eligible return is not more than $30,000, being 1.5% of the sum of all payments due under the security multiplied by the number of years of its term (ie 1.5% × $200,000 × 10). The promissory note is therefore a traditional security (assuming it is not trading stock).

General tax treatment

Where a taxpayer disposes of a traditional security, or a traditional security is redeemed, the following consequences generally arise:

- the amount of any gain on the disposal or redemption is included in the taxpayer's assessable income in the year of income in which the disposal or redemption takes place (s 26BB(2))
- the amount of any loss on the disposal or redemption is allowable as a deduction to the taxpayer in the year of income in which the disposal or redemption takes place (s 70B(2)).

Example Following on from the preceding example, in the 2022/23 income year, Felicity is required to include the $20,000 gain made on the redemption of the promissory note in her assessable income under s 26BB(2) and Fred is entitled to a deduction for the $20,000 loss on the redemption of the promissory note under s 70B(2).

Where the Commissioner is satisfied that the parties to the disposal or redemption transaction were not dealing with each other at arm's length, he may, for the purposes of determining any gain or loss, substitute an arm's length amount as the consideration for the transaction (ss 26BB(3), 70B(3)).

Special rules relating to losses

Deductions are not allowable under s 70B(2) for the following losses:

- losses on the disposal or redemption of traditional securities that are segregated exempt assets of a life assurance company or segregated current pension assets of a complying superannuation fund [19.14] (s 70B(2A)), and
- losses to the extent that they are of a capital nature on the disposal or redemption of traditional securities (other than marketable securities acquired and disposed of in the ordinary course of trading on a securities market) where, having regard to specified matters, it would be concluded that a reason for the disposal or redemption of the security was an apprehension or belief that the issuer would be unable or unwilling to discharge its liability to pay amounts under the security (s 70B(4)).

Convertible or exchangeable interests

Sections 26BB(2) and 70B(2) do not apply to a gain or a loss on the disposal or redemption of a traditional security if:

- it is issued on the basis that it will or may convert into ordinary shares in the issuer of the security or a connected entity, and the disposal or redemption occurs because the traditional security is converted into such shares (ss 26BB(4), 70B(2B))—in these circumstances, the traditional security is a 'convertible interest' and special rules in sub-div 130-C *ITAA97* apply [17.15], or
- it is in exchange for ordinary shares in a company that is neither the issuer of the security nor a connected entity, and the traditional security was issued on the basis that it will or may be redeemed or disposed of to the issuer or connected entity in exchange for ordinary shares in the company (ss 26BB(5), 70B(2B))—in these circumstances, the traditional security is an 'exchangeable interest' and special rules in sub-div 130-E *ITAA97* apply.

[29.14] QUESTIONS

1. What is a 'financial arrangement' under div 230 *ITAA97*? How are gains and losses from financial arrangements treated under div 230?
2. On 1 July 2018, R Co acquired a promissory note for $100m with a face value of $150m that matures on 30 June 2023. How does div 230 deal with the promissory note?
3. What kinds of arrangements fall within divs 240 and 242 *ITAA97*? How do the notional sale and loan rules apply under these divisions?
4. On 5 May 2022, Lease Co acquired manufacturing equipment for $500,000. On 1 July 2023, it entered into a five-year hire purchase agreement with George. George will use the equipment in his manufacturing business and it is reasonable to conclude that he will acquire the equipment at the end of the arrangement. The agreement states that the cost of the equipment is $600,000. How does div 240 apply to this arrangement?
5. What is a limited recourse debt arrangement and how does div 243 *ITAA97* tax such arrangements?

6. Barry owes $100,000 to Les for a loan used by Barry to renovate his business premises. In the current income year, Les releases Barry from having to repay half the debt. During the income year, Barry makes $80,000 of income from his business as well as a net capital loss of $20,000. He also owns a CGT asset with a cost base of $15,000. How do the rules in div 245 apply to Barry?
7. When does div 247 *ITAA97* apply and what is its effect? How does div 247 address the situation encountered in *FC of T v Firth* 2002 ATC 4346?
8. Why is it important to distinguish between 'debt' and 'equity' interests? Discuss the key elements of the debt and equity tests. What are 'non-equity shares' and 'non-share equity interests'? How are returns on such shares and interests taxed?
9. On 1 January 2020, R Co (a resident public company) issued redeemable preference shares ('RPS'), which are redeemable for their face value issue price of $10 on 1 January 2024. RPS holders are entitled to receive dividends at the end of each year of 70 cents per share. R Co must pay such dividends before it pays any dividends on its ordinary shares. The dividends are 'cumulative' (ie if R Co does not have sufficient profits to pay RPS dividends in a particular year, the dividends payable in the following year will be increased appropriately). Discuss whether the RPS are debt or equity interests and how payments are taxed. Would your answer differ if the RPS were redeemed for $8?
10. A firm of architects occupies a large building in the city. It engages N Co, a small cleaning company, to service their offices on a weekly basis for the next seven years. Under the arrangement, the firm is required to pay N Co a lump sum amount of $220,000 on signing the contract. How should the parties account for their income and outgoings under this arrangement?
11. On 1 January 2016, Larry made a loan of $10m to Betty who used the funds to purchase an investment property. Pursuant to the loan agreement, the interest and principal was repaid at the end of the loan on 1 January 2024. At such time, Larry received $18m from Betty. How should they account for the interest?

PART K

INTERNATIONAL TAXATION

30 GENERAL JURISDICTIONAL RULES

[30.1] Introduction

This chapter focuses on the concepts of 'residence' [30.2] and 'source' [30.3]. These concepts are important because they underpin Australia's 'general jurisdictional rules', which apply to a taxpayer's ordinary and statutory income. Under these rules:

- residents are assessed on their ordinary and statutory income from all sources (ss 6-5(2), 6-10(4) *ITAA97*), and
- foreign residents are assessed on their ordinary and statutory income from Australian sources (ss 6-5(3)(a), 6-10(5)(a) *ITAA97*).

Example Hans is an Australian resident and Gretel is a foreign resident. Each of them earns $30,000 of Australian source income and $50,000 of foreign source income during the income year. Under Australia's general jurisdictional rules, Hans is assessed on $80,000 while Gretel is assessed on only $30,000.

The general jurisdictional rules recognise that there must be some territorial link between Australia and either the taxpayer or the source of the income in order for Australia to exercise its taxing rights. Foreign residents are therefore generally not taxed on their foreign income as there is a complete lack of connection with Australia.

It is important to be aware that the general jurisdictional rules operate subject to numerous exceptions. For instance, in special cases, foreign residents may be assessed on ordinary and statutory income on some basis other than the income having an Australian source (ss 6-5(3)(b), 6-10(5)(b)). The general jurisdictional rules also operate subject to a range of exemptions (discussed in Chapter 31) as well as special rules contained in Australia's DTAs (discussed in Chapter 32). Special rules also apply to 'temporary residents' [30.4] and taxpayers that carry on business through permanent establishments ('PEs') [30.5].

The residency status of a taxpayer is important because different rates of tax are payable by resident and non-resident individuals [8.8]. In addition, only resident individuals pay the ML and MLS [8.8] and only resident individuals are entitled to certain tax offsets [8.9]. Residency is also relevant for the purposes of various international tax regimes, such as the withholding tax [31.11], controlled foreign company [34.2], and transferor trust [34.3] regimes. It is also important for CGT purposes, as foreign residents generally disregard capital gains and capital losses relating to CGT assets that are not taxable Australian property [17.12] and they are generally no longer entitled to benefit from the CGT discount [17.8] or main residence exemption [17.11].

[30.2] Residence

An 'Australian resident' is defined in s 995-1 *ITAA97* as a person who is a resident for the purposes of the *ITAA36*. The *ITAA36* definition of 'resident' is located in s 6(1). This provision contains separate definitions for individuals (para (a)) and companies (para (b)). The respective definitions are outlined in the following diagram and discussed further below.

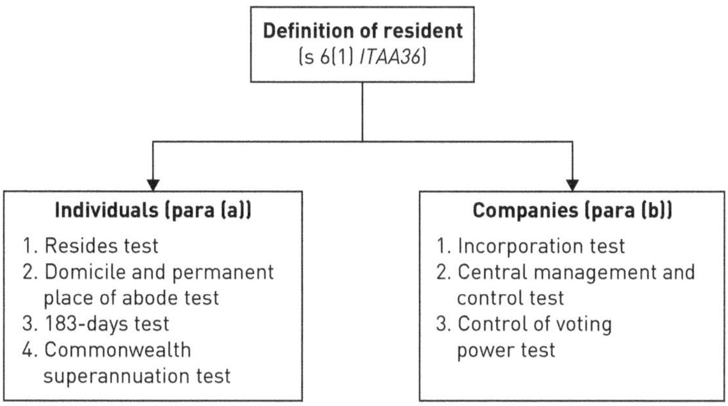

Residence of individuals

There are four circumstances in which an individual is a resident of Australia according to the definition in s 6(1)(a) *ITAA36*. Each one of these circumstances (referred to as 'tests' of residence) is examined below.

1. Resides test

An individual is a resident of Australia if the person resides in Australia. The term 'resides' is not defined in the legislation and therefore takes its ordinary meaning. The *Shorter Oxford English Dictionary* defines the term to mean 'to dwell permanently or for a considerable time, to have one's settled or usual abode, to live, in or at a particular place'.

Ultimately, the place where a person resides is a question of fact (*FC of T v Miller* (1946) 73 CLR 93). It must be determined by reference to all the circumstances of the case. Many different factors may need to be considered and weighed against each other. No single factor is paramount.

TR 2023/1 recognises there is a difference between 'staying' in Australia and 'residing' in Australia. The resides test looks at whether a taxpayer's presence in Australia is 'usual and settled' in contrast to 'temporary and casual'. This is informed by the nature, duration and quality of the person's physical presence and their intention to treat Australia as their home. TR 2023/1 outlines some common, often overlapping, factors that the Commissioner considers are relevant in determining whether a taxpayer resides in Australia:

- **Physical presence in Australia.** The time that a person spends in Australia is important, but not necessarily determinative. If the person's stay is short and subject to visa limitations, they are unlikely to reside in Australia. Stays of less than six months are generally considered insufficient to support residency because of a lack of a durable connection to Australia. However, a short presence is less relevant if the person previously spent a long time in the country and retained a continuity of association with Australia. Where a person's presence in Australia overlaps income years, their full period of presence needs to be taken into account.

- **Intention or purpose of presence.** Having a settled purpose for being in Australia (eg undertaking long-term employment or a course of education) supports the inference that a person resides in Australia. A person's subjective intention, while important, is not decisive—residency is not established merely by asserting an intention to live permanently in Australia and it is not shed merely by asserting an intention to never again live in Australia. Objectively observable factors and behaviours as well as contemporaneous statements (eg those included on passenger cards and visa documents) are relevant in assessing intention or purpose.
- **Behaviour in Australia.** The way that a person regularly lives (ie their routine and habits) is relevant. A person with long-term accommodation, employment, extracurricular activities and children attending schools in Australia is likely to reside in Australia. This is the case even though they may maintain a house in their country of domicile. Conversely, a person that usually lives overseas and travels around Australia on holidays is unlikely to reside in Australia.
- **Family and business or employment ties.** A person's connection with Australia is informed by the presence, or absence, of family members in the country. If a person's family is living with them in Australia or the person has their business or employment in Australia, this often indicates that they reside in Australia. An individual that works overseas but returns at intervals to an established family and social life will also generally reside in Australia.
- **Social and living arrangements.** A person's social and living arrangements reflect how they interact with their surroundings and their routines and habits. Where a person joins sporting associations in Australia, enrols his or her children at a school in Australia, and redirects mail to Australia, this suggests they reside in Australia.
- **Maintenance and location of assets.** The residency of a person is also informed by where their assets are maintained and located. If they own a dwelling in Australia in which they live and have other assets such as cars, superannuation and bank accounts in Australia, this supports the inference that they reside in Australia. However, the relevance given to holding Australian assets must be considered in context (eg opening an Australian bank account may be merely done for convenience to deposit locally acquired earnings to fund a holiday).

In *Joachim v FC of T* 2002 ATC 2088, a mariner who had migrated from Sri Lanka to Australia with his family in 1994 was employed by a Sri Lankan maritime agency and spent 316 days during the relevant income year outside Australia on Sri Lankan vessels. Throughout this period, he kept his Australian permanent residency and maintained a home in Australia for his wife and children to which he returned between contracts. The AAT concluded that he was a resident of Australia, stating (at 2090):

> Physical presence and intention will coincide for most of the time but few people are always at home. Once a person has established a home in a particular place, even involuntary, a person does not necessarily cease to be resident there because he or she is physically absent. The test is, whether the person has retained a continuity of association with the place, together with an intention to return to that place and an attitude that the place remains home.

A similar conclusion was reached in *Sneddon v FC of T* 2012 ATC ¶10-264 in respect of a taxpayer who commenced work in Qatar in April 2008 as a supervisor with an engineering company. During the 2008/09 income year, the taxpayer returned to Australia three times for a total period of just over seven weeks. The AAT concluded that despite his physical absence from Australia during most of the year, he maintained a 'continuity of association' with Australia and therefore resided in Australia. The taxpayer's salary was paid in Australian dollars into an Australian bank account, and he continued to use his money to cover expenses on his mortgage on his Perth residence and car loan. He also left personal items at his residence and retained his internet and telephone account at his residence. All his personal ties were in Australia—his only tie to Qatar was his employment.

Likewise, in *Pillay v FC of T* 2013 ATC ¶10-324, an Australian citizen who worked as a doctor in East Timor for between nine and 11 months each year and who returned to Australia for around six to eight weeks each year was found to reside in Australia. When he returned to Australia, the taxpayer lived in his property at Sapphire Beach and visited his children and grandchildren. He also owned a property in Bali where he spent some time and planned to divide his time between Bali and Australia when he retired. The Tribunal found that the taxpayer had retained a 'continuity of association' with Australia and did not treat East Timor as his home as his connection with that country was based almost entirely on employment.

A continuity of association with Australia was also found to exist in *Nordern v FC of T* 2013 ATC ¶10-329 in relation to a taxpayer who was born in Australia and worked in Asia for over 200 days during the relevant income year. Some of the factors that led the AAT to conclude that the taxpayer was an Australian resident included that he was an Australian citizen and not a citizen of any other country; he spent relatively short periods overseas; he lived and worked on oil rigs and his overseas living expenses were covered by his employer; he had no overseas assets and his income was paid into an Australian bank account; he was physically present in Australia for approximately 35% of the year and when he returned between periods of work, he lived with his family in the home jointly owned with his wife; and he stated that he was an Australian resident temporarily departing Australia on his immigration cards.

Ordinarily, visiting a country on holidays would be insufficient to demonstrate residency of that country (TR 2023/1). Likewise, staying for a short time in a country purely for work purposes would generally be unlikely to establish residency there. This principle is supported by *FC of T v Pechey* 75 ATC 4083, which involved an Australian public servant who lived in the Territory of Cocos (Keeling) Islands for four weeks while acting as its Official Representative. The taxpayer's residence was in Canberra and his family members did not accompany him. The NSW Supreme Court held that, due to the short and temporary nature of his stay in the Territory, he should not be regarded as a resident of the Territory for that period.

Early United Kingdom cases indicate that the regularity of visits to a country can be important in determining where a taxpayer resides. In *Levene v IRC* [1928] AC 217, a United Kingdom subject, who had always lived in London, left England to live abroad on medical advice. The taxpayer surrendered the lease on his house and, from 1919 to 1925, had no fixed abode, living in hotels in Monaco and France. During this period, he also returned to England for around five months each year (again living in hotels) to obtain medical advice, visit family and attend to various business and religious matters. The House of Lords confirmed that it was open to the Inland Revenue Commissioners to conclude that the taxpayer was an 'ordinary resident' of the United Kingdom for the relevant period based on his habits of life, the regularity of his visits, his ties with England and the freedom of his attachments abroad.

Likewise, in *IRC v Lysaght* [1928] AC 234, a taxpayer that had retired as managing director of an English company moved with his family from England to Ireland to live on a large estate. The taxpayer was subsequently appointed as an advisory director of the English company and was required to visit England for approximately one week every month. When in England, the taxpayer stayed in hotels or at his brother's house. The House of Lords again held that it was open to the Inland Revenue Commissioners to treat the taxpayer as an 'ordinary resident' of the United Kingdom on the facts of the case. Viscount Sumner held that the fact that the taxpayer had a home in Ireland and no established home in England was not incompatible with him being a resident of the United Kingdom if there was other sufficient evidence to support this conclusion.

2. Domicile and permanent place of abode test

An individual is a resident of Australia if the person's domicile is in Australia, unless the Commissioner is satisfied that the person's permanent place of abode is outside Australia (s 6(1)(a)(i) *ITAA36*).

Domicile is a complex legal concept that is determined in accordance with the *Domicile Act 1982* (Cth) ('*DA*') and common law. A person acquires a 'domicile of origin' at birth. A person under 18 who is not married is not capable of having an independent domicile (s 8 *DA*). Under the common law, a child generally acquires their father's domicile, or their mother's domicile if the father is deceased or unknown. Where the parents are separated, a child acquires the domicile of the parent with whom they have their principal home (s 9 *DA*). A person retains their domicile of origin until they acquire a 'domicile of choice' elsewhere (eg by choosing to make another country their home), or until they acquire another domicile by operation of law (eg a child's domicile changes when their parent's domicile changes). A person must intend to make their home indefinitely in a foreign country to acquire a domicile of choice in the country (s 10 *DA*). A person always has a domicile and can only have one domicile at any point in time (*Udny v Udny* (1869) LR 1 HL 441).

An example of where a taxpayer established a domicile of choice in Australia is found in *Ellwood v FC of T* 2012 ATC ¶10-287. The taxpayer was a New Zealand citizen who left New Zealand in 1975 and worked for extended periods abroad. He lived and worked mainly in Australia until 1993 when he started working on overseas construction projects. Except for a period in the 1980s when he worked on New Zealand projects, his wife and daughters lived continuously in Australia. In the 2008/09 income year, he spent only 99 days in Australia and the balance of time working mainly in Qatar. The taxpayer argued that he was not an Australian resident during the income year because he was seldom in the country and only returned to visit his wife. He submitted that he had maintained his New Zealand domicile of origin and had never acquired a domicile of choice in Australia. The AAT, however, found that although the taxpayer may have wished to return to New Zealand, he had done nothing about this—he had no place to live in New Zealand, no New Zealand investments and no plans for retiring in New Zealand. The taxpayer had a well-established home, substantial real estate investments, immediate family in Australia and a long history of returning to Australia to visit them. On this basis, he had made a home in Australia for the foreseeable future and had established a domicile of choice in Australia well before the 2008/09 income year.

A person's 'place of abode' is the place where they live (ie the place where the person has their home). In *R v Hammond* (1852) 117 ER 1477, Campbell CJ stated (at 1480):

> A man's residence, where he lives with his family and sleeps at night, is always his place of abode in the full sense of that expression.

Whether or not a place of abode is 'permanent' has been considered in a number of cases. The cases indicate that the term 'permanent' is not taken to mean 'everlasting', but rather something 'more than temporary or transitory'. Authority for this principle comes from *FC of T v Applegate* 79 ATC 4307, which concerned an Australian lawyer who had been posted by his firm to establish a branch office in the New Hebrides. It was originally anticipated that the taxpayer would stay in the New Hebrides for a substantial, but indefinite, period. He left no assets in Australia, surrendered the lease on his Sydney flat and took his wife with him. The lawyer was found to have a permanent place of abode outside Australia, even though he ultimately intended to return to Australia (and in fact did so after a period of two years due to ill-health). Northrop J explained (at 4314):

> The word 'permanent' can have many shades of meanings. This is illustrated by a reference to the *Shorter Oxford English Dictionary*. And as was said by du Parcq LJ in *Henriksen (Inspector of Taxes) v Grafton Hotel Ltd* (1942) 2 KB 184 at p 196:

> '"Permanent" is indeed a relative term, and is not synonymous with "everlasting".'
>
> . . . The word 'permanent' as used in para. (a)(i) of the extended definition of 'resident', must be construed as having a shade of meaning applicable to the particular year of income under consideration. In this context it is unreal to consider whether a taxpayer has formed the intention to live or reside or to have a place of abode outside of Australia indefinitely, without any definite intention of ever returning to Australia in the foreseeable future. . . . What is of importance is whether the taxpayer has abandoned any residence or place of abode he may have had in Australia. Each year of income must be looked at separately. If in that year a taxpayer does not reside in Australia in the sense in which that word has been interpreted, but has formed the intention to, and in fact has, resided outside Australia, then truly it can be said that his permanent place of abode is outside Australia during that year of income. This is to be contrasted with a temporary or transitory place of abode outside Australia.

Even if a taxpayer's stay outside Australia is only for a fixed period, the taxpayer can still have a permanent place of abode outside Australia, provided the stay is for a substantial duration. This is illustrated in *FC of T v Jenkins* 82 ATC 4098, where a bank officer had been transferred from Australia with his wife and family to work in the bank's New Hebrides office for a three-year term (although he returned early due to ill-health). Relying on Applegate, the Supreme Court of Queensland held that for the period that he worked in the New Hebrides, the taxpayer's permanent place of abode was in that country rather than Australia.

A taxpayer will not, however, have a permanent place of abode outside Australia if they have not abandoned their home in Australia (*Case Q68* 83 ATC 343). In such a case, the taxpayer's stay outside Australia will be regarded as merely temporary or transitory. As TR 2023/1 states, if a taxpayer takes up an employment opportunity overseas or commences living overseas with no fixed timeframe in mind (but as a tentative venture), it is unlikely they will have their permanent place of abode overseas.

By contrast, where a taxpayer has a settled intention to make another country their home, their permanent place of abode will be outside Australia. In *Dempsey v FC of T* 2014 ATC ¶10-363, an Australian project manager went to work in Saudi Arabia in 2007 under a contract of indefinite duration. He was initially unsure whether he would make Saudi Arabia his home and wanted to first see whether he enjoyed working there. He kept his house on the Gold Coast and occasionally returned on holidays and caught up with his children in Canberra. The AAT found that by the start of the 2009 income year, the taxpayer had established a permanent place of abode in Saudi Arabia as by then his settled intention was to make the kingdom his home for the indefinite future. His presence in Saudi Arabia was 'hardly casual or passing'.

A similar outcome was reached in *Mynott v FC of T* 2011 ATC ¶10-195 in relation to an engineer who left Australia in 1997. While working in Malaysia, the taxpayer formed a relationship with a Philippines national, and they subsequently moved to the Philippines where they rented an apartment. However, as the taxpayer could not obtain work in the Philippines, he pursued work in other countries. Prior to leaving Australia, the taxpayer sold a home unit and, in 1999, he sold his personal residence. He nevertheless retained a vacant block of land in Queensland and maintained an Australian bank account. The taxpayer visited Australia several times to stay with his parents and he also regularly visited the Philippines to see his partner. He eventually returned to Australia on 29 January 2002 after the relationship with his partner ended. The Commissioner assessed the taxpayer on the foreign income he earned in the years ending 30 June 1999 to 30 June 2002 on the basis that he was a resident of Australia. The Commissioner contended that the taxpayer had not left Australia permanently and maintained links with the country. The AAT, however, rejected this and held that the taxpayer did not reside in Australia prior to his return on 29 January 2002 as he did not work in Australia and did not have a home in Australia. According to the AAT, up until that date his permanent place of abode was the Philippines.

Harding v FC of T 2019 ATC ¶20-685 demonstrates that so long as a person has definitely abandoned their residence in Australia, it is not necessary for them to have a particular house or flat overseas to have a permanent place of abode outside Australia. The reference to 'place' in the phrase 'outside Australia' is not a reference to a person's specific dwelling but can instead be the town or country in which the person is physically residing permanently. In this case, the taxpayer had moved to Bahrain in 2009 to work in nearby Saudi Arabia, while his wife and son remained in Australia. The taxpayer initially planned to have his wife and son join him in Bahrain. In 2011, he made four visits to Australia totalling 91 days and stayed with his family. However, in October 2011, the taxpayer and his wife separated, and he formed a new relationship and continued to live in Bahrain. The Full Federal Court held that the taxpayer was not a resident of Australia in the 2011 income year as his permanent place of abode was Bahrain. The Court pointed out that although the taxpayer lived in a serviced apartment in Bahrain, as distinct from permanent lodgings, this did not prevent him from having a permanent place of abode outside Australia. The quality and nature of his connections with Australia supported the conclusion that he had abandoned his residence in Australia.

TR 2023/1 indicates that the Commissioner considers the following factors relevant in determining whether a taxpayer has a permanent place of abode overseas:

- the length of the overseas stay (eg the longer the stay, the more permanent it is likely to be)
- the nature of the accommodation and conditions upon which it is occupied (eg staying in temporary accommodation such as hotels or campsites usually indicates overseas presence is not permanent), and
- the durability of association and strength of connections maintained overseas and retained in Australia (eg retaining the family home in Australia and consistently returning to it is usually inconsistent with living permanently overseas).

TR 2023/1 states that, 'as a broad rule of thumb', a stay of two years or more in another country would generally be regarded as a substantial period for the purposes of determining the permanency of the taxpayer's stay in that country. The ruling explains that if a taxpayer's intended length of stay is less than two years, they are unlikely to be able to establish that their permanent place of abode is outside Australia. Whether a stay of two years or longer results in them having a permanent place of abode outside Australia will depend on the circumstances. The 'critical question is whether a person has in fact abandoned Australian residency and commenced to live in a permanency overseas'.

3. 183-days test

An individual is a resident of Australia if he 'has actually been in Australia, continuously or intermittently, during more than one-half of the year of income, unless the Commissioner is satisfied that his usual place of abode is outside Australia and that he does not intend to take up residence in Australia' (s 6(1)(a)(ii) *ITAA36*).

According to TR 2023/1, a person's usual place of abode is the place they 'usually live or would live but for being absent from it due to, for example, a transient lifestyle or other temporary circumstances'. For instance, if a person has lived overseas most of their life, travels to Australia to spend 18 months experiencing the country in transient accommodation and employment, and then returns overseas, the person will still have their usual place of abode overseas.

Case S19 85 ATC 225 indicates that the 183-days test does not apply to an individual who has been a resident during the year, but subsequently leaves Australia before the end of the year and is no longer a resident under the domicile test (discussed above) for the remainder of the year. The taxpayer in this case had accepted a two-year posting as a bank manager to the New Hebrides and left Australia with his family on 14 April 1978. The Board of Review found that, at the time of leaving Australia, the taxpayer intended to remain abroad for an indefinite period and had abandoned his place of abode in Australia, making the New Hebrides his home. On this basis, the Board held that, even though the taxpayer had spent more than 183 days of the 1977/78 income year in Australia, he was not a resident of Australia for the year as his place of abode was outside Australia. According to the Board, the 183-days test 'is in aid of determining whether a person has commenced residing in Australia' and is not relevant for taxpayers that are departing Australia.

It is important to note that the fact that an individual spends more than 183 days outside Australia does not necessarily mean they cannot be a resident of Australia. In *Gunawan v FC of T* 2012 ATC ¶10-234, the AAT held that a person who spent more than half the year working in Indonesia selling properties was an Australian resident as his home (ie his settled place of abode) was in Australia. He was therefore a resident under the resides test discussed above.

Likewise, it is also important to note that the fact that an individual does not have a usual place of abode within Australia does not necessarily mean that they have a usual place of abode elsewhere. As Emmett J pointed out in *FC of T v Executors of the Estate of Subrahmanyam* 2002 ATC 4001 (at 4015), although the legislation appears to contemplate that there will be only one usual place of abode, it does not necessarily follow that every person must have a usual place of abode.

4. Commonwealth superannuation test

An individual is a resident of Australia if he or she is:

(a) a member of a superannuation scheme established under the *Superannuation Act 1990* (Cth)
(b) an eligible employee for the purposes of the *Superannuation Act 1976* (Cth), or
(c) a spouse, or a child under 16, of a person covered by (a) or (b) (s 6(1)(a)(iii) *ITAA36*).

This test covers certain Commonwealth public servants (eg foreign diplomats living abroad) as well as their spouses and children under 16 years of age.

In *Baker v FC of T* 2012 ATC ¶10-240, an Australian citizen took leave without pay from the Department of Defence and left Australia in 2009. The taxpayer resided and worked as a contractor in the Philippines and married a Philippines national. He did not intend to return to live in Australia and eventually resigned from the Department of Defence in 2011. The AAT ruled that the taxpayer was a resident of Australia as he remained a member of an Australian superannuation scheme established under the *Superannuation Act 1990*. This was the case even though he had ceased to contribute to the fund and was unable to contribute while on leave.

Proposed residency rules for individuals

In 2016, the Board of Taxation commenced a self-initiated review of the residency rules for individuals. In 2017, it published a report, *Review of the Income Tax Residency Rules for Individuals*, which found that the current rules are no longer appropriate and require modernisation and simplification. The Board also noted that there was an integrity risk where individuals manipulate the residency rules to become 'residents of nowhere'. The Board recommended replacing the current rules with a 'primary days count test' (which is based on the number of days an individual is present in Australia) and a 'secondary objective test' (which applies where the primary test is not satisfied and involves an analysis of the individual's particular circumstances against a list of objective factors).

Although many stakeholders supported the tests, the Board concluded that further consultation was necessary. This took place in late 2018 and was followed by the release of a report to the Treasurer in 2019, entitled *Reforming Individual Tax Residency Rules—A Model for Modernisation*. The report contains a new model for determining the residency of individuals and is based on four guiding principles:

- **Adhesive residency.** The new rules should make it harder to cease residency than establish it.
- **Certainty.** The new rules should provide clear and consistent outcomes.
- **Simplicity.** The new rules should remove complexity.
- **Integrity.** The new rules should not make it easier for individuals with close ties to Australia to manipulate the system and not pay their fair share of tax in Australia.

The Board states that its new model will address the high level of uncertainty that exists under the current rules, significantly reduce compliance costs (particularly for businesses with mobile workforces), lead to a more efficient taxation system through more consistent and predictable outcomes, and protect Australia's tax base by reducing opportunities for manipulation.

In the 2021 Budget, the Coalition Government announced it would introduce new residency rules for individuals based on the Board's 2019 report. However, it was unable to enact legislation before the 2022 election. In July 2023, the Labor Government released a consultation paper, *Modernising the Individual Tax Residency Rules*, seeking feedback on the Board's proposal. If the Government decides to implement the proposal, an individual's residency will be based around two tests:

- **Primary bright line test.** This test provides that an individual who spends 183 days or more in Australia during an Income year is a resident.
- **Secondary test.** This test provides that an individual who does not spend 183 days in Australia during an income year is a resident if they meet the 'commencing residency test' and do not fall within the 'ceasing residency test':
  - **Commencing residency test.** This test applies to individuals who *were not* residents in the preceding income year to determine whether they commence residency. The test is satisfied if an individual is physically present in Australia for 45 days or more in the current income year and they satisfy *two or more* factors under the 'factor test' (see below).
  - **Ceasing residency test.** This test applies to individuals who *were* residents in the preceding income year to determine whether they cease residency. Different rules apply to long-term and short-term residents:
    - A long-term resident (ie an individual who has been a resident for three or more income years) ceases residency if they spend less than 45 days in Australia in the current income year and less than 45 days in Australia in each of the two preceding income years.
    - A short-term resident (ie an individual who has been a resident for less than three income years) ceases residency if they satisfy *less than two* of the factors in the 'factor test' (see below).

The factor test is designed to determine whether an individual has specific identifiable connections to Australia. There are four factors to consider. An individual will meet these factors if they have:

- the right to reside permanently in Australia for immigration purposes
- the right to access Australian accommodation
- Australian family (ie a spouse or child under 18 years of age located in Australia), or
- Australian economic connections (ie they are employed in Australia, actively participate in carrying on business in Australia or have interests in 'Australian assets').

The new model also proposes to replace the Commonwealth superannuation test with a new test for overseas Government officials. Under this test, an individual deployed overseas in the service of the Commonwealth, state or territory governments is deemed to be a tax resident for the duration of their deployment.

The following flowchart, adapted from the Board's report, summarises the steps involved under the proposed new residency rules for individuals:

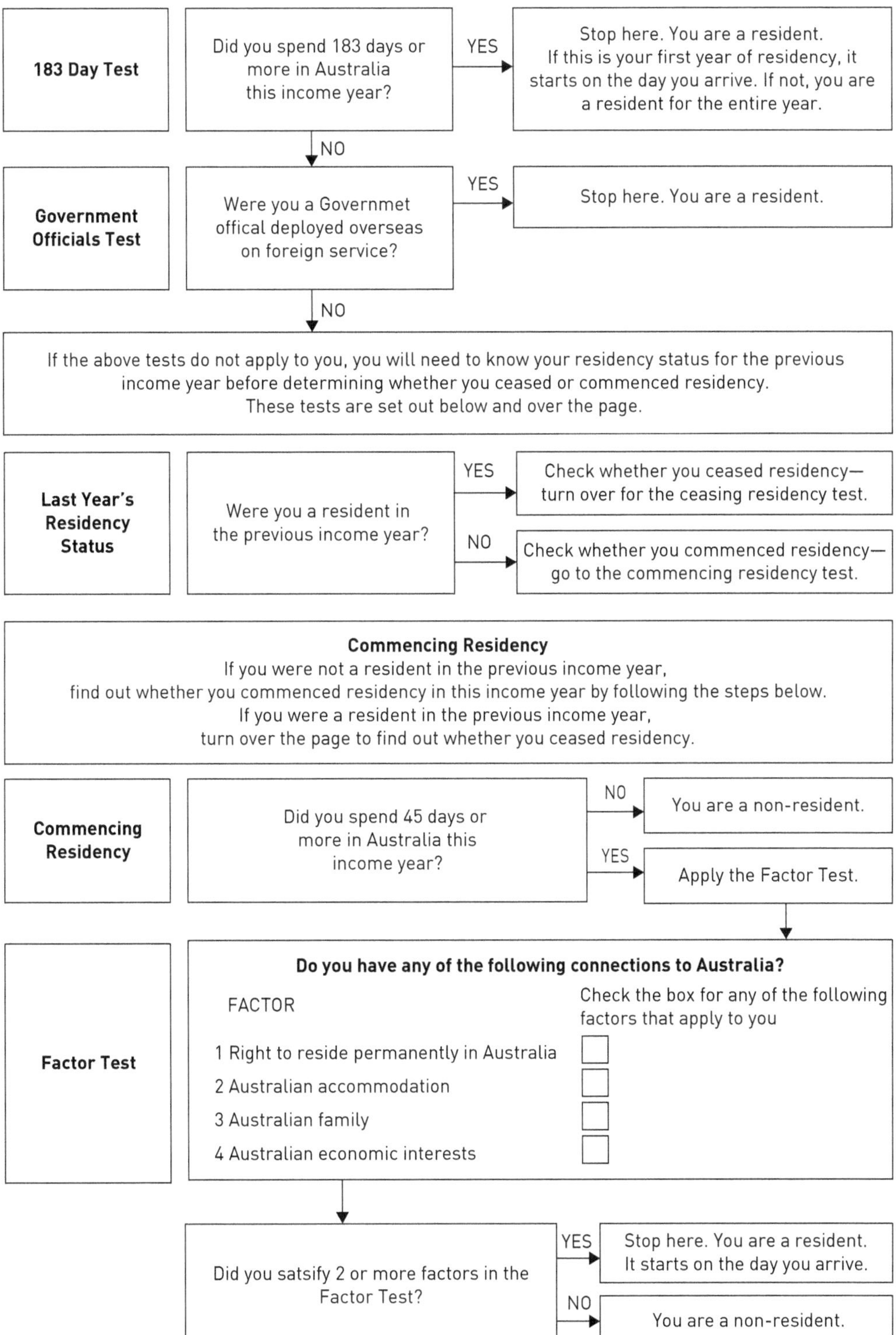

30

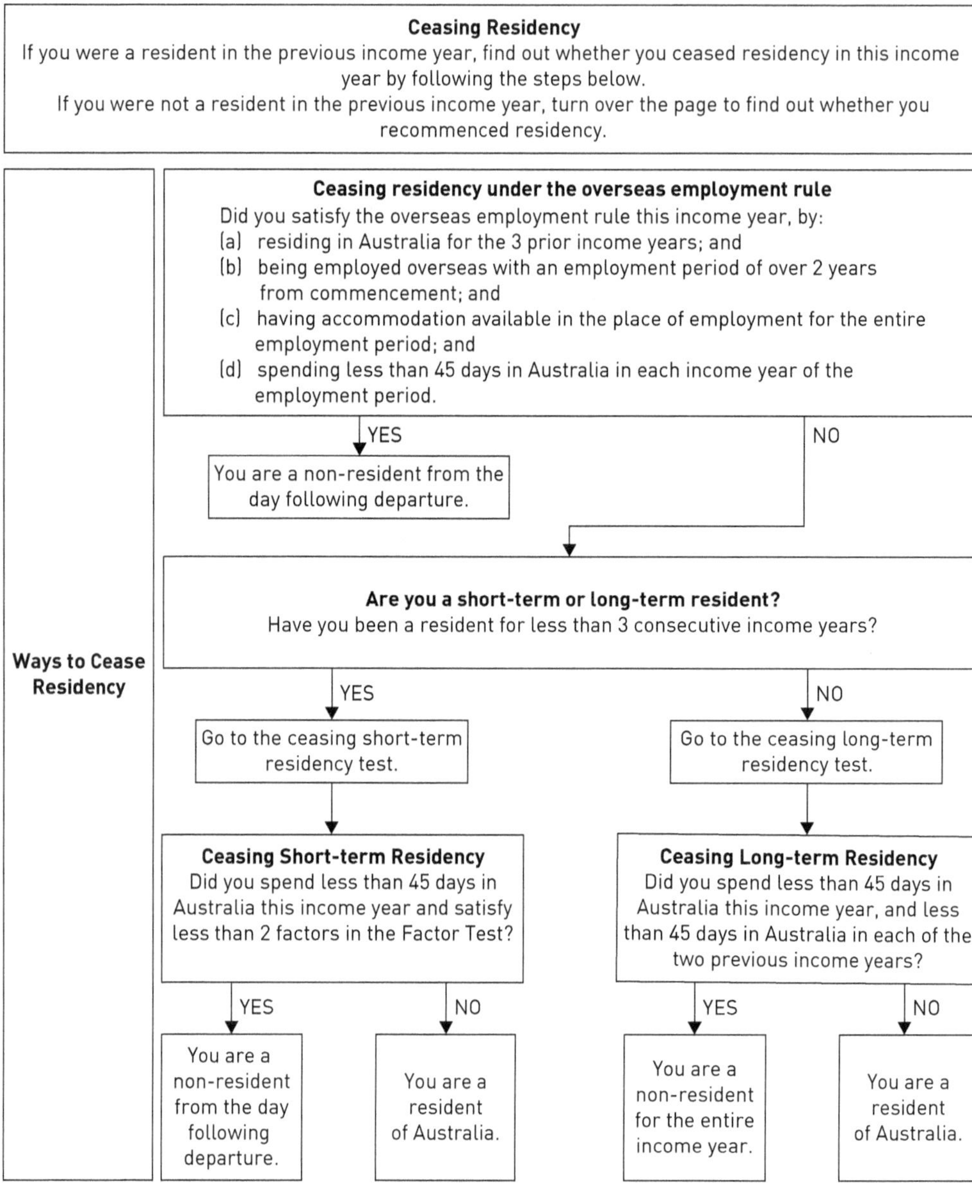

Residence of companies

There are three circumstances in which a company is treated as a resident of Australia according to the definition in s 6(1)(b) *ITAA36*. Each of these circumstances (also referred to as 'tests' of residence) is examined below.

1. Incorporation test

A company is a resident of Australia if it is 'incorporated in Australia'. This is the case even if the company is controlled by foreign shareholders, is managed overseas and carries on its business overseas. The rationale for treating a company incorporated in Australia as a resident is that the company owes its existence to its incorporation in this country.

2. Central management and control test

A company is a resident of Australia if it is not incorporated in Australia but 'carries on business in Australia' and has its 'central management and control' in Australia.

The place where a company carries on business and the place where its central management and control are located are both questions of fact (*Malayan Shipping Company Ltd v FC of T* (1946) 71 CLR 156).

A company's central management and control is located where its operations are controlled and directed (*Koitaki Para Rubber Estates Ltd v FC of T* (1941) 64 CLR 241). Ordinarily, this will be where the company's board of directors' meetings are held. This principle can be traced to *De Beers Consolidated Mines Ltd v Howe* [1906] AC 455, which concerned a company incorporated in South Africa that carried on business mining and selling diamonds. The company had its head office and mines in South Africa but was nevertheless found to have its central management and control in the United Kingdom. The House of Lords held that the company's central management and control was in the United Kingdom as the seat and directing power of the taxpayer's affairs were located at its offices in London since this was where the directors met (and where, incidentally, most lived). It was where the chief operations of the taxpayer were controlled, managed and directed.

Where, however, the decisions relating to a company are actually made by its parent company, the company's central management and control will be where the parent company's board of directors' meetings are held (*Unit Construction Co Ltd v Bullock* [1959] 3 All ER 831).

The fact that a company's board of directors may act on advice provided by third parties does not necessarily mean that central management and control of the company is not with its board. In *Esquire Nominees Ltd v FC of T* 72 ATC 4076, the High Court held that a Norfolk Island company that acted as the trustee of a trust and whose directors resided and met in Norfolk Island did not have its central management and control in Australia even though the directors invariably acted in accordance with the advice provided to them by a firm of Australian accountants.

The position is, however, quite different where a company's board of directors abrogates its decision-making powers and does not exercise any independent judgment. This is illustrated in *Bywater Investments Ltd & Ors v FC of T* 2016 ATC ¶20-589, which concerned several companies that were incorporated overseas and whose directors resided outside Australia. The High Court found that despite the directors' meetings all being held overseas, the companies were actually controlled by an accountant in Sydney (Mr Gould). The boards had mechanically followed Mr Gould's directions and had abrogated their decision-making powers. On this basis, the companies were treated as residents of Australia, as this was where their central management and control was located. French CJ, Kiefel, Bell and Nettle JJ explained (at [41]):

30

> Ordinarily . . . it will be found that a company is resident where the meetings of its board are conducted. But, contrary to the appellants' submissions, it does not follow that the result should be the same where a board of directors abrogate its decision-making power in favour of an outsider and operates as a puppet or cypher, effectively doing no more than noting and implementing decisions made by the outsider as if they were in truth decisions of the board.

The issue of central management and control had also been considered earlier, in *Malayan Shipping Company Ltd v FC of T*. This case concerned a company that had been incorporated in Singapore by Mr Sleigh, who lived in Melbourne. Mr Sleigh held 2,498 shares in the company and two Singapore nominee directors each held one share in the company. Under the company's articles of association, Mr Sleigh was managing director and had the power to remove the other directors. The articles also provided that no resolution would be effective without his agreement. Mr Sleigh had organised for the company to charter a tanker in London and then sub-charter it to himself. The charter documents were executed in London through shipping agents under instructions from Mr Sleigh. The sub-charter documents were prepared in Melbourne by Mr Sleigh and sent to Singapore for execution. The High Court held that the company was a resident of Australia. Williams J found that the central management and control of the company was in Australia since Mr Sleigh exercised complete control over its business operations. His Honour also held that this meant that the company was carrying on business in Australia since the essence of its business was his decision to charter and sub-charter the tanker.

The Commissioner's views on central management and control test following the *Bywater Investments* case are now set out in TR 2018/5. The ruling makes the following points:

- Central management and control refers to the control and direction of a company's operations. The key element is the making of high-level decisions that set the company's general policies and determine the direction of its operations and the types of transactions it will enter.
- A company will be controlled and directed where those making its high-level decisions do so as a matter of fact and substance (not where the decisions are merely recorded and formalised or where the Directors reside or live).
- Central management and control can be exercised by setting investment and operational policy, deciding to buy and sell significant assets, appointing company officers and agents and determining how profits are used and dividends are declared.
- The control and direction of a company is different from the day-to-day conduct and management of its Activities and operations.
- Company administration matters (eg keeping the share register and accounts) are not acts of central management and control.
- Just because a person is a majority shareholder, or has the power to appoint those who control and direct a company's operations, does not, by itself, mean the person controls and directs a company's operations.
- A person without any legal power or authority to control or direct a company may nevertheless exercise management and control. While merely being able to influence the directors is not enough, if an outsider actually dictates or controls their decisions, the outsider will be seen as exercising central management and control.

Importantly, TR 2018/5 states that '[i]f a company carries on business and has its central management and control in Australia, it will carry on business in Australia within the meaning of the central management and control test'. The ruling goes on to state that '[i]t is not necessary for the substantive trading or investment activities of the business that generate its profits to take place in Australia'. This view is quite different to the earlier view expressed in TR 2004/15, which was withdrawn on 15 March 2016, and stated that 'a company that has major operational activities relative to the whole of its business carries on business wherever those activities take place and not necessarily where its CM&C is likely to be located'. Guidelines on applying the principles in TR 2018/5 and identifying where a company's central management and control is located are contained in PCG 2018/9.

3. Control of voting power test

A company is a resident of Australia if it is not incorporated in Australia but 'carries on business in Australia' and has its 'voting power controlled by shareholders who are residents of Australia'.

A person is a 'shareholder' in a company if the person is registered as a shareholder in the company's register or is entitled to be so registered. Mere beneficial ownership of shares by itself is not sufficient to make the beneficial owner a shareholder in the company (*Patcorp Investments Ltd & Ors v FC of T* 76 ATC 4225).

Proposed corporate residency reforms

Based on a recommendation in the 2020 Board of Taxation's *Review of Corporate Tax Residency* report, the Morrison Government announced it would amend the residency test to ensure that companies incorporated offshore will be treated as Australian residents where they have a 'significant economic connection to Australia'. The test will be satisfied where both the company's core commercial activities are undertaken in Australia and its central management and control is in Australia. At this stage, no legislation to implement this reform has been introduced by the Albanese Government.

Dual residence

It is technically possible for taxpayers to be resident in multiple jurisdictions if they satisfy the residency rules of more than one country. Early House of Lords authority for this principle can be found in *Swedish Central Railway Co Ltd v Thompson* [1925] AC 495, where a company incorporated in the United Kingdom to construct and operate a railway in Sweden was found to be resident in both the United Kingdom and Sweden.

The principle that a taxpayer can be a dual resident was accepted in Australia in *North Australian Pastoral Company Ltd v FC of T* (1946) 71 CLR 623. In this case, a company incorporated in the Northern Territory also had a branch office in Queensland. The company claimed it was exempt from tax under former s 23(m) *ITAA36*, which exempted Northern Territory residents from tax on income derived from primary production in the Territory. The Commissioner argued that, as the company had its branch office in Queensland where board meetings were held and company documents were kept, it had become a Queensland resident and was not eligible for the exemption. The High Court rejected this argument and held that the facts supported the taxpayer being a resident of both the Northern Territory and Queensland.

The fact that dual residency can occur had been recognised five years earlier in *Koitaki Para Rubber Estates Ltd v FC of T* (1941) 64 CLR 241. However, the High Court found that the relevant company was only resident in Australia (where it was incorporated and its directors resided and met) and not also in Papua (where it conducted its day-to-day operations of producing and shipping rubber). Rich ACJ explained (at 244):

> It is true that a company may reside in more than one place . . . But the facts in the present case show conclusively . . . that there is no divided control . . . Sydney is the pivot or axis . . . on which the operations of the company hinge. There matters of policy and finance are determined and all the direction, control and management take place. There it has its life and being. In Papua the company's operations fall into an auxiliary or subordinate position of a purely local as opposed to a central nature.

30

Importantly, the principle that a taxpayer can be a resident of two countries operates subject to the terms of any DTA that exists between those countries. DTAs generally contain 'tie-breaker rules' that specify the country in which a taxpayer who would otherwise be a resident of both countries is deemed to be resident [32.5].

[30.3] Source

The concept of 'source' was considered by Issacs J in *Nathan v FC of T* (1918) 25 CLR 183, where he stated (at 190):

> The Legislature in using the word 'source' meant, not a legal concept, but something which a practical man would regard as a real source of income. Legal concepts must, of course, enter into the question when we have to consider to whom a given source belongs. But the ascertainment of the actual source of a given income is a practical, hard matter of fact.

Although *Nathan* concerned the former *Income Tax Assessment Act 1915*, Isaacs J's comments have been approved in many subsequent High Court cases, including *FC of T v Mitchum* (1965) 113 CLR 401 and *Esquire Nominees Ltd (as Trustee of Manolas Trust) v FC of T* 73 ATC 4114. His Honour's comments have also been adopted overseas by the Privy Council in *Rhodesia Metals Ltd (In Liq) v Taxes Commissioner* [1940] 3 All ER 422 and by the New Zealand Court of Appeal in *CIR (NZ) v NV Philips Gloeilampenfabrieken* [1955] NZLR 868.

In *CIR v Lever Brothers & Unilever Ltd* (1946) 14 SATC 1, a South African Court recognised that 'source' has many meanings. The Court held, that to identify the source of income, it was necessary to determine its 'originating cause'. This will usually be based on the work the taxpayer does to earn the income, and need not necessarily all occur in one place.

In *Esquire Nominees*, Barwick CJ noted that the income tax legislation contemplates that 'all income is derived from some source having a geographical location'. His Honour, nevertheless, went on to explain (at 4117) that there was no universal rule for determining the source of income:

> I do not think that any single verbal formula can be devised which by its mere mechanical application to any given factual situation will yield the answer to the problem of the location of the source of some item of income.

Accordingly, unless a specific statutory provision exists to deem income to have a particular source, the source of income will need to be determined by reference to the particular facts of each case. It is therefore necessary to weigh up the different factors involved in producing the income in question to ascertain its source.

Where income is derived from a series of operations that occur in different places, its source is usually apportioned between those locations (*Australian Machinery & Investment Co Ltd v DFC of T* (1946) 180 CLR 9; *C of T v Kirk* [1900] AC 588; *C of T (NSW) v Hillsdon Watts Ltd* (1937) 57 CLR 36; *FC of T v W Angliss & Co Pty Ltd* (1931) 46 CLR 417). As the High Court noted in *FC of T v Lewis Berger & Sons (Australia) Ltd* (1927) 39 CLR 468, there is no 'rigid formula' for determining apportionment—it depends on business judgment and experience applied to the facts of the particular case, the nature of the business, and the mode in which it is actually carried on.

The following discussion examines the approaches taken by the courts in determining the source of certain kinds of income.

Services income

The courts have usually found that the source of services income is located at the place where the services are performed. An early illustration is *C of T (NSW) v Cam & Sons Ltd* (1936) 36 SR (NSW) 544, which involved a taxpayer that operated a fishing trawling business and engaged fishermen to work off the coasts of NSW and Victoria. Under the *Special Income and Wages Tax (Management) Act 1933* (NSW), the taxpayer was required to deduct wages tax from the wages derived by its employees from sources within NSW. The Supreme Court of NSW held that that the proportion of wages derived by the employees from NSW should be determined by reference to the proportion of time they spent earning their wages in its territorial waters. Jordan CJ explained (at 547–548):

> In the ordinary case of the employment of a seaman . . . where there is nothing special in the circumstances of the contract of employment or in the payment . . . the all-important factor is the doing of the work; and the contract of employment and the payment are relatively insignificant and formal elements.

The decision in *Cam & Sons Ltd* was approved by the High Court in *FC of T v French* (1957) 98 CLR 398. This case concerned an Australian engineer who was employed by an Australian company under a contract made in Australia, and whose wages were paid into a Sydney bank account. Each year, the taxpayer was required to work for two to three weeks in New Zealand. The High Court held that, for the period that he worked in New Zealand, the source of his wages was New Zealand. This was important for the taxpayer as former s 23(q) *ITAA36* exempted from Australian tax foreign income derived by an Australian resident that was not exempt from tax in the country in which it was derived [31.3].

Another case that illustrates the importance of the place where services are performed in determining the source of income is *FC of T v Efstathakis* 79 ATC 4256. In this case, a Greek national who was employed by the Greek Government to work for the Greek Press and Information Service in Australia was held to derive her income from sources in Australia. The Full Federal Court held that although the circumstances under which the taxpayer obtained her employment and was paid her salary included some factors occurring outside Australia, they were not significant enough to outweigh the importance of the performance of the services in Australia, which was central to her earning of income.

Despite the cases outlined above, there have been occasions where the courts have been prepared to overlook the place where services are performed and instead determine the source of income according to other criteria, such as the place where the relevant contract was entered into or where relevant payments were made. For example, in *FC of T v Mitchum* (1965) 113 CLR 401, an American actor who had entered into an agreement with a Swiss company to act in certain films was required to work for 11 weeks in Australia on a film called 'The Sundowners'. Under the agreement, the taxpayer's salary was paid to him in the United States. The High Court held that there is no rule of law that the source of salary or wages is where the work is performed. On this basis, it concluded that it was open to the Board of Review that heard the case to decide that the taxpayer's income did not have an Australian source.

Likewise, in *Evans v FC of T* 81 ATC 4512, an academic employed by the University of Adelaide was granted a period of study leave to work in Switzerland. The academic received a study leave grant from the university and his salary was paid into his Adelaide bank account and then remitted to a Swiss bank account. The Supreme Court of Queensland held that both the study leave grant and the salary had an Australian source.

Business income

The source of business income depends on the nature of the business and the mode in which it is carried on (*FC of T v Lewis Berger & Sons (Australia) Ltd* (1927) 39 CLR 468). In general, the source of business income will be where the business is transacted (*FC of T v United Aircraft Corporation* (1943) 68 CLR 525).

Accordingly, in the case of the sale of goods, the source of the income will usually be where the goods are sold. This is illustrated in *C of T (WA) v D & W Murray* (1929) 42 CLR 332, where the High Court held that a United Kingdom company that exported goods to Australia and carried on a wholesaling business through branches in various states, including Western Australia, made all its profits from the sale of goods in Western Australia from sources within that state. Likewise, where a taxpayer carries on a share trading business, the source of its income will usually be where the trading activities take place. This is illustrated in *Picton Finance Ltd v FC of T* 2013 ATC ¶10-298, where the AAT held that a Vanuatu company that traded in shares in an Australian company listed on the ASX made its income in Australia, as its trading activities took place in Australia because that was where the contracts were concluded. 30

The importance of identifying where business is transacted for the purpose of determining the source of income is illustrated in *Cliffs International Inc v FC of T* 85 ATC 4374. This case concerned a non-resident company that was the world representative for the sale of iron ore produced by a joint venture project in Western Australia. The taxpayer received a commission for negotiating contracts for the sale of iron ore to overseas steel mills. The Western Australian Supreme Court held that the taxpayer was not subject to Australian tax on its commission income as it was derived from sources outside Australia as all negotiations and work done to ensure the contracts were carried out took place overseas. The Court held that the fact the taxpayer maintained an office in Western Australia played only a minimal role in the process and the fact the contracts were actually executed in Australia was a mere formality.

Property income

The source of income from the sale of interests in real property will usually be the place where the property is located. Support for this proposition is found in *Rhodesia Metals Ltd (In Liq) v Taxes Commissioner* [1940] 3 All ER 422, where an English company derived profits from the sale of mining claims in Southern Rhodesia. The Privy Council held that even though the claims were sold to another English company under a contract made in England, the profit had its source in Southern Rhodesia. The Privy Council explained (at 426–427):

> their Lordships find themselves dealing with a case where the sole business operation of an English company is the purchase of immoveable property in Southern Rhodesia and its development in that territory for purposes of transfer in that territory at a profitable price. . . . As a hard matter of fact, the only proper conclusion appears to be that the company received the sum in question from a source within the territory, namely, the mining claims which they had acquired and developed there for the very purpose of obtaining the particular receipt.

Interest income

The source of interest arising from a loan will usually be the place where the loan agreement is entered into and the money is lent (*FC of T v Spotless Services Ltd & Anor* 95 ATC 4775). For example, in *CIR (NZ) v NV Philips Gloeilampenfabrieken* [1955] NZLR 868, a Dutch company entered into a loan with a New Zealand company to convert a trading debt owed by the New Zealand company for the supply of goods. The New Zealand Court of Appeal held that the interest payable on the loan did not have a New Zealand source, even though it was paid by a New Zealand company, as the loan was made in the Netherlands.

The source of interest arising under the terms of a business contract will usually be the place where the business is transacted. This is illustrated in *Studebaker Corporation of Australasia Ltd v C of T* (NSW) (1921) 29 CLR 225, which concerned an American car manufacturer that sold cars to a NSW company. The agreement between the parties allowed the manufacturer to charge interest on money owing on cars that had been delivered, but which had not been paid for within a certain period. The High Court held that the interest received by the manufacturer flowed from the agreement, which was made in America. As it arose from business transacted in America, it had a source in America rather than in New South Wales.

Rental income

The source of rent from the lease of fixed property (eg land) is ordinarily based on where the property is located. The source of rent from the lease of moveable property (eg chattels), on the other hand, is likely to be based on where the lease agreement is entered into and the goods are taken. Support for this proposition can be found in *James Fenwick & Co Ltd v FC of T* (1921) 29 CLR 164, which concerned a company that had received a compensation payment on account of hire charges for its steam tugs which had been requisitioned by the Government for use in World War I. The tugs were requisitioned in Australian waters but were subsequently sent outside Australian waters as part of the war effort. The High Court held that the compensation payments arose because the tugs had been requisitioned in Australia and the income therefore had an Australian source. It was immaterial where the tugs were used, as 'the real practical source' of the income was the 'taking of the tugs in Australia'.

Royalty income

The source of royalties arising from the supply of know-how was considered in *FC of T v United Aircraft Corporation* (1943) 68 CLR 525. The taxpayer was an American company that granted an Australian company a licence to manufacture engines and parts in Australia and New Zealand. The taxpayer supplied the Australian company with drawings and other information in exchange for being paid a lump sum amount together with royalties of US$500 per engine and 7.5% of the list price of parts manufactured. A majority of the High Court held that the royalties did not have an Australian source as they were not derived from property of the taxpayer located in Australia, nor were they earned from any services or other acts performed by the taxpayer in Australia. Instead, the royalties were held to be produced under an agreement made and performed in the United States.

The United Aircraft Corporation decision must, however, now be considered in the context of s 6C *ITAA36*, which contains a specific statutory source rule. In broad terms, the provision deems royalties paid or credited to non-residents to have an Australian source to the extent that they are:

- outgoings incurred by a resident that are not incurred in carrying on a business at or through a PE outside Australia, or
- outgoings incurred by a non-resident that are incurred in carrying on a business at or through a PE in Australia.

If s 6C had been enacted at the time of the *United Aircraft Corporation Case*, the royalties would have been deemed to have an Australian source.

Dividend income

The source of dividend income was discussed in *Esquire Nominees Ltd (as Trustee of Manolas Trust) v FC of T* 73 ATC 4114. The taxpayer in this case was a Norfolk Island company that acted as the trustee of a trust. The taxpayer owned shares in a Norfolk Island company ('MCL'), which owned shares in another Norfolk Island company ('PIL'). PIL owned shares in an Australian company ('MPPL'), which paid it dividends. PIL used the dividends it received from MPPL to pay dividends to MCL. MCL, in turn, used these dividends to pay dividends to the taxpayer. The High Court held that the dividends paid to the taxpayer were sourced in Norfolk Island and were therefore not assessable to the taxpayer under s 99 *ITAA36* [24.5] as they had a foreign source. In arriving at this conclusion, the Court held that the source of the dividends should not be determined by tracing the various distributions through the entire chain of companies back to MPPL. Rather, the source of the dividends had to be determined according to the source of the fund of profits out of which the dividends were paid. As MCL derived its profits from its investment in PIL, the source of the dividends paid by MCL to the taxpayer was Norfolk Island.

[30.4] Temporary residents

Subdivision 768-R *ITAA97* contains special taxation rules relating to temporary residents. A 'temporary resident' is essentially a person who:

- holds a temporary visa
- is not an Australian resident under the *Social Security Act 1991* (Cth), and
- does not have an Australian resident spouse (s 995-1 *ITAA97*).

The broad aim of sub-div 768-R is to tax temporary residents (who might otherwise be treated as residents under the rules discussed at [30.2]) in generally the same way as if they were foreign residents. The foreign source income of a temporary resident will therefore generally be treated as non-assessable non-exempt income (s 768-910). Likewise, temporary residents will also generally be entitled to disregard capital gains and capital losses made from CGT events in relation to CGT assets that are not 'taxable Australian property' (s 768-915) [17.12].

[30.5] Permanent establishments

The tax law contains special rules that apply where taxpayers carry on business through an Australian or overseas PE. For instance, there are:

- withholding tax exemptions that operate where dividends are paid to non-residents that carry on business through an Australian PE (s 128B(3E) *ITAA36*) [31.11], and
- income tax and capital gains tax exemptions that apply to resident companies that derive foreign income from carrying on business through a foreign PE (s 23AH *ITAA36*) [31.5].

In addition, entities that carry on business through Australian PEs are required to comply with special record-keeping requirements under sub-div 820-L *ITAA97*.

General *ITAA36* definition

A PE is defined in s 6(1) *ITAA36* as 'a place at or through which' a person 'carries on any business' (ie a branch). The definition of a PE also expressly includes:

(a) a place where the person is carrying on business through an agent

(b) a place where the person has, or is using or installing substantial equipment or machinery

(c) a place where the person is engaged in a construction project, and

(d) a place where goods are manufactured, assembled, processed, packed or distributed (provided certain criteria are met by the person).

The definition, however, expressly excludes the following places:

(e) a place where the person is engaged in business dealings through a bona fide commission agent or broker who, in relation to those dealings, acts in the ordinary course of his business as a commission agent or broker and does not receive remuneration otherwise than at a rate customary in relation to dealings of that kind, not being a place where the person otherwise carries on business

(f) a place where the person is carrying on business through an agent:

  (i) who does not have, or does not habitually exercise, a general authority to negotiate and conclude contracts on behalf of the person, or

  (ii) whose authority extends to filling orders on behalf of the person from a stock of goods or merchandise situated in the country where the place is located, but who does not regularly exercise that authority, not being a place where the person otherwise carries on business, or

(g) a place of business maintained by the person solely for the purpose of purchasing goods or merchandise.

TR 2002/5 examines the concept of 'a place at or through which' a person 'carries on any business'. The ruling states that such a place 'must have an element of permanence both geographic and temporal'. It also indicates that permanence 'must be construed in the context of each particular business and is a question of fact and degree'. While permanent does not mean 'forever', the business presence must not be of a 'purely temporary nature'. The following two examples illustrate these points and are based on examples contained in the ruling.

Example

Situation 1
Alex is a Ukrainian resident who carries on business as a professional tennis player. He visits Australia to compete in a professional tennis tournament, which is held at a major tennis centre and runs for a week. Alex spends two weeks in Australia, including two practice days and five rest days. In order for the tennis centre to constitute a place at or through which he carries on his tennis business, his professional activities would need to be both geographically and temporally permanent. Although the activities at the tennis centre are undertaken at a single location which is geographically permanent, Alex only plays tennis there for nine days (including practice days). As a result, a sufficient temporal permanence is not established and the tennis centre is therefore not a place at or through which he carries on business for the purposes of the s 6(1) definition of a PE.

Situation 2
B Co is a Moroccan dance company that visits Australia and performs at a Sydney theatre for one year. The company has a place at or through which it carries on its business in Australia under the s 6(1) definition of a PE because it satisfies the geographic and temporal permanence requirements. However, if B Co was merely touring Australia and giving 'one-off' performances at cities around the country over a period of three months under separate contracts with local venues, it would not have a place at or through which it carries on business in Australia in either a geographic or temporal sense.

Double Taxation Agreement definitions

Australia's DTAs contain their own definitions of a PE [32.5], which are important for the purposes of applying the 'distributive articles' under the respective agreements [32.6].

[30.6] QUESTIONS

1. Why are the concepts of 'residence' and 'source' important? Discuss the residency tests for individuals and companies.
2. Kit is a permanent resident of Australia. He was born in Peru and retains his Peruvian citizenship. Kit spends most of the year working off the coast of Indonesia on an oil rig for a United States company. He was recruited for this job in Australia and signed a contract with the company in Sydney. For the last four years, Kit's wife has lived in Australia with their two children. They purchased a home in Australia three years ago. Kit and his wife have a joint account with Westpac Bank. Kit's salary is paid directly into this account. All of the family's other investments, including a share portfolio that generates dividend income, remain in Peru. Kit gets one month off from work every third month and, on these occasions, he meets with his family either in Australia or on holidays in South America (usually in Peru, where his parents reside). Discuss whether Kit is a resident of Australia and how his salary and investment income is taxed.
3. Pablo is a Portuguese resident employed by a Portuguese company. He is sent to Australia to work on a short-term project to assist with the establishment of a branch office in Australia. Pablo worked in Australia for one month. Throughout this period, his salary was paid into his Portuguese bank account. Does Pablo have to pay Australian tax on salary?
4. Jean is a temporary resident who derives both Australian and foreign source income. How is her income taxed?

5. Why is the definition of a PE in s 6(1) *ITAA36* important? Provide examples of places that would, and would not, be PEs.
6. US Co is a company resident in the United States that manufactures cars. It enters into an agreement in the United States to provide A Co, an Australian resident company, with drawings and other intellectual property that A Co can use under a licence agreement to produce motors in Melbourne. A Co is required to pay a royalty to US Co under the arrangement. What is the source of the royalty? Would your answer differ if A Co used the drawings and intellectual property in carrying on a business that it operated through a PE in Malaysia?

INTERNATIONAL EXEMPTIONS, OFFSETS AND WITHHOLDING TAXES 31

[31.1] Introduction

International taxation is a broad concept that covers the taxation of transactions with jurisdictional links to more than one country. These transactions, sometimes referred to as 'cross-border transactions', pose particular challenges and problems for taxpayers and taxation authorities. For instance, there is the obvious potential for double taxation to arise (ie the same income being taxed in more than one jurisdiction). The potential also exists for income to be diverted and sheltered in low-tax jurisdictions (ie tax havens), which raises concerns about tax evasion and tax avoidance.

It is important to realise that as taxation is a sovereign right, there is no general overarching body of international law that deals with the taxation of cross-border transactions. In other words, there is no 'supernational' taxation law. Instead, each country must develop its own set of rules to deal with cross-border transactions and any jurisdictional conflicts that may arise. In order to protect their revenue bases, it is natural for countries to want to adopt broad-based international taxation rules to ensure that they collect as much tax as possible. However, as countries will have competing interests in relation to international transactions, double taxation will inevitably arise unless they are prepared to make compromises. Ideally, from a global perspective, it would be desirable for countries to design international tax laws that are compatible with each other and that promote the principles of worldwide tax equity and neutrality, as this would ensure that the revenue from cross-border economic activities is shared fairly between the countries concerned and business and investment choices are not based on discriminatory or preferential tax rules. However, despite increased economic cooperation between nations, it has been difficult for governments to harmonise their international tax policies. Although many countries adopt similar broad principles of international taxation, individual approaches for taxing particular kinds of cross-border transactions vary considerably.

Australia's income tax legislation contains hundreds of pages of international tax rules. These rules are complex and are superimposed on top of the general jurisdictional rules discussed in Chapter 30. Over recent years, Australia's international tax rules have been reformed on several occasions. Many of the reforms have been aimed at increasing the competitiveness of Australian entities operating overseas and encouraging foreign entities to invest in Australia. This chapter examines a number of Australia's commonly encountered international tax rules and focuses on some of the measures that Australia has adopted to tackle the problem of double taxation. In particular, it examines the foreign income tax offset [31.3] and a number of specific exemptions that apply to foreign income [31.4]–[31.10]. It is important to be aware that, like many other countries around the world, Australia also tackles double taxation issues under its DTAs. Australia's general tax rules operate subject to the terms of these DTAs, which are discussed in Chapter 32.

Withholding taxes also play an important role in the operation of Australia's international tax rules. This chapter examines some of the withholding tax regimes that apply to payments made to foreigners [31.11]. Entities that make payments that fall within these regimes are required to 'withhold' a specified portion of the payments and remit them to the ATO. The aim is to collect tax 'at source' from payers in order to avoid the practical problems the ATO would otherwise face in collecting tax from recipients located overseas and from whom it might otherwise be difficult to recover tax.

[31.2] International double taxation

International transactions involve the intersection of the tax laws of two (or sometimes more) jurisdictions and therefore give rise to the potential for double (or even multiple) taxation. International double taxation can have a major impact on global commerce as taxpayers will be reluctant to enter into transactions if they end up being taxed twice. Countries that do not deal adequately with the problem of international double taxation are at risk of discouraging their residents from expanding overseas and missing out on foreign investment. This can have a significant negative impact on their economic competitiveness.

International juridical double taxation

The potential for international double taxation is particularly acute for Australian residents as they are ordinarily taxed on both their Australian and foreign source income [30.1]. At the same time, their foreign source income is also often taxed in the country of source (ie the jurisdiction where the income is derived). This overlap results in what is described as 'international juridical double taxation', which is defined in the OECD *Model Tax Convention on Income and on Capital* as 'the imposition of comparable taxes in two (or more) states on the same taxpayer in respect of the same subject matter and for identical periods'.

International juridical double taxation can also arise where an entity is treated as a resident of more than one jurisdiction. For instance, a company incorporated in one country may have its central management and control in another country, resulting in both countries asserting that the company is a resident of their respective jurisdiction. In addition, international juridical double taxation can arise where countries adopt different views of the source of income, with each country treating the income as having a source within their respective jurisdiction.

The following diagram outlines the three main circumstances in which international juridical double taxation conflicts typically arise:

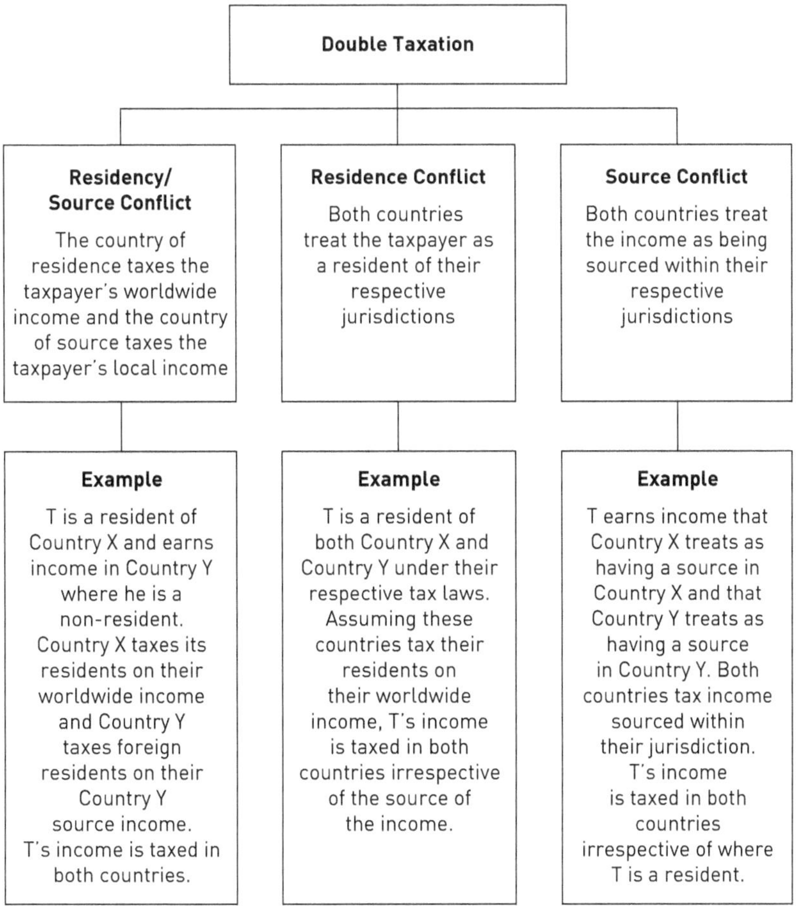

International juridical double taxation should be distinguished from 'international economic double taxation', which arises where the same underlying transaction is taxed in two (or more) countries, but in the hands of different taxpayers.

Preventing international juridical double taxation

International juridical double taxation can be alleviated through bilateral arrangements entered into by countries under their DTAs (Chapter 32). Alternatively, countries can also unilaterally deal with international juridical double taxation by enacting specific rules to address particular problem areas. There are three main methods that a country can use to prevent (or at least limit) international juridical double taxation:

- **The credit method.** This method addresses double taxation by providing credits for tax paid overseas.
- **The exemption method.** This method addresses double taxation by exempting certain kinds of foreign source income from tax.
- **The deduction method.** This method addresses double taxation by providing a deduction for tax paid overseas.

The following example illustrates how the respective methods produce different results.

31.2

Example A company earns income of $90,000 in its country of residence (Country R) and income of $10,000 in a foreign country (Country F). Country R subjects resident companies to tax on their worldwide income at the rate of 30%. Country F subjects foreign companies to tax on income earned in Country F at the rate of 25%. The way in which the different methods would work to limit double taxation is outlined below:

	Credit method	**Exemption method**	**Deduction method**
Domestic income	$90,000	$90,000	$90,000
Foreign income	$10,000	$10,000	$10,000
Total income	$100,000	$100,000	$100,000
Exemption for foreign income		($10,000)	
Deduction for foreign tax			($2,500)
Taxable income	$100,000	$90,000	$97,500
Basic income tax at 30%	$30,000	$27,000	$29,250
Credit for foreign tax	($2,500)		
Income tax after tax credit for foreign tax	$27,500	$27,000	$29,250
Foreign tax paid at 25%	$2,500	$2,500	$2,500
Total domestic and foreign tax paid	$30,000	$29,500	$31,750

If no relief was available to limit double taxation, the company would be subject to total domestic and foreign tax of $32,500 (ie $30,000 + $2,500).

In the above scenario, the rate of tax paid in Country F (25%) was less than the rate of tax paid in Country R (30%). In practice, countries do not usually allow credits to the extent that the foreign tax paid on the foreign income exceeds the amount of domestic tax paid on the foreign income. Accordingly, assuming the facts were the same as in the above scenario, with the exception that Country F subjected foreign resident companies to tax on income earned in Country F at the rate of 40% (rather than 25%), the way in which the different methods would work to limit double taxation is as follows:

	Credit method	**Exemption method**	**Deduction method**
Domestic source income	$90,000	$90,000	$90,000
Foreign source income	$10,000	$10,000	$10,000
Total income	$100,000	$100,000	$100,000
Exemption for foreign income		($10,000)	
Deduction for foreign tax			($4,000)
Taxable income	$100,000	$90,000	$96,000
Basic income tax at 30%	$30,000	$27,000	$28,880
Credit for foreign tax (limited to $3,000)	($3,000)		
Income tax after tax credit for foreign tax	$27,000	$27,000	$28,880
Foreign tax paid at 40%	$4,000	$4,000	$4,000
Total domestic and foreign tax paid	$31,000	$31,000	$32,880

If no relief was available to limit double taxation, the company would be subject to total domestic and foreign tax of $34,000 (ie $30,000 + $4,000).

Australia uses both the credit and the exemption methods but does not use the deduction method. It provides tax credits both to Australian residents and to foreign residents under its 'foreign income tax offset' regime contained in div 770 *ITAA97* [31.3]. It also provides Australian residents with a number of specific tax exemptions, including the following:

- the 'foreign service income exemption' (s 23AG *ITAA36*) [31.4]
- the 'foreign branch income and CGT exemption' (s 23AH *ITAA36*) [31.5]
- the 'foreign equity distribution exemption' (s 768-5 *ITAA97*) [31.6], and
- the 'CGT participation exemption' (sub-div 768-G *ITAA97*) [31.7].

In addition, Australia provides foreign residents with the following tax exemptions:

- the 'foreign government officials exemption' (s 768-100 *ITAA97*) [31.8]
- the 'conduit foreign income exemption' (sub-div 802-A *ITAA97*) [31.9], and
- the 'investment manager regime exemption' (sub-div 842-I *ITAA97*) [31.10].

It is important to realise that by providing credits and exemptions, Australia is effectively granting foreign jurisdictions taxing preferences over income that Australia would otherwise have the jurisdiction to tax. The provision of these tax concessions therefore comes at a cost in the form of lost revenue for the government. This cost can, nevertheless, be justified on the basis that the concessions promote international fiscal equity and prevent international double taxation, which, in theory, should promote international trade and commerce and make Australia a more desirable place for investment.

[31.3] Foreign income tax offset

In the past, to prevent double taxation of foreign source income, former s 23(q) *ITAA36* exempted resident taxpayers from Australian tax on foreign income that was taxed overseas. This exemption applied even though only small amounts of foreign tax may have been payable on the foreign income. For example, if foreign income was subject to only 1% tax overseas, the entire income was exempt from Australian tax even though it would have otherwise suffered much higher tax rates in Australia. Australian residents were therefore treated very favourably under this exemption and it was, not surprisingly, exploited under various tax avoidance arrangements.

In 1986, the s 23(q) exemption was replaced by a less favourable 'foreign tax credit' ('FTC') contained in former s 160AF *ITAA36*. This provision granted resident taxpayers credits for payments of foreign tax. The amount of the credit was essentially limited to the lesser of the amount of the Australian or foreign tax paid on the foreign source income. The FTC operated subject to quarantining rules in relation to certain kinds of income (such as interest). On 1 July 2008, the FTC was replaced with a 'foreign income tax offset' ('FITO') contained in div 770 *ITAA97*. The FITO provides a tax offset for payments of foreign tax. It differs from the FTC in that it applies to both Australian and foreign residents and is not subject to quarantining rules.

Division 770

The key provision in div 770 is s 770-10, which provides that a taxpayer is entitled to a tax offset for an income year for foreign income tax. Foreign income tax is defined as a tax that is imposed by a law other than an Australian law, and is a tax on income, a tax on profits or gains of an income or capital nature, or a tax that is subject to an agreement having the force of law under the *International Tax Agreements Act 1953* (Cth) (eg a DTA) (s 770-15(1)). An amount of foreign income tax counts towards the tax offset for an income year if the taxpayer paid it in respect of an amount that is all or part of an amount included in their assessable income for the year (s 770-10(1)). In addition, an amount of foreign income tax also counts towards the tax offset if the taxpayer paid it in respect of an amount that is non-assessable non-exempt income under ss 23AI or 23AK *ITAA36* [34.5] (s 770-10(2)).

Calculating the FITO

The FITO generally equals the foreign income tax paid (s 770-70). However, it operates subject to an 'offset limit' (s 770-75). The offset limit is essentially the greater of:

- $1,000, and
- the amount of Australian income tax payable by the taxpayer for the income year *less* the amount of Australian income tax that would have been payable for the year if the following assumptions were made:
  - that the taxpayer's assessable income did not include:
    (i) assessable income in respect of which foreign tax was paid, and
    (ii) other amounts of ordinary or statutory income from a foreign source, and
  - that the taxpayer was not entitled to:
    (i) debt deductions attributable to an overseas PE, or
    (ii) other deductions that are reasonably related to assessable income in respect of which foreign tax was paid or are reasonably related to other amounts of ordinary or statutory income from a foreign source.

In broad terms, the offset limit is designed to ensure that the FITO does not generally exceed the amount of Australian tax that would have otherwise been payable on the foreign income. This approach is consistent with the approach adopted overseas where tax credits are not usually provided for foreign taxes paid on foreign income beyond the amount of domestic tax paid on such income.

Example A Co is a resident company that pays tax at the rate of 30% and has $30m of taxable income, consisting of:

- $20m of Australian income, and
- $10m of foreign income (which is taxed overseas at the rate of 40%).

The amount of Australian tax payable on A Co's taxable income (ignoring any FITO) is $9m ($30m × 30%).

The amount of foreign tax payable on A Co's foreign income is $4m (ie $10m × 40%).

A Co's FITO cannot exceed the offset limit of $3m, being:

- the amount of Australian income tax payable (ie $9m less)
- the amount of Australian income tax that would have been payable assuming the taxpayer's assessable income did not include the $10m of foreign income, ie $6m ($20m × 30%).

A Co is therefore entitled to a FITO of $3m (not $4m). This shows that the FITO will generally be the lesser of the Australian or foreign tax payable on the foreign source income.

The total Australian tax payable by A Co on its taxable income of $30m is therefore $6m (ie $9m - $3m). As A Co is also liable to $4m of foreign tax, it will have paid total worldwide tax of $10m.

The FITO was recently considered in *Burton v FC of T* 2019 ATC ¶20-709. In this case, the taxpayer made gains in the United States from the disposal of investments which were taxed in the United States. The gains were also subject to CGT in Australia, but were eligible for the 50% CGT discount [17.8]. The taxpayer claimed the FITO in respect of the whole of the United States tax paid, but the Full Federal Court held that the taxpayer should only be allowed a tax offset for half the foreign tax. The reason for this was that the United States tax was payable on double the amount included in the taxpayer's assessable income in Australia. Therefore, only half of the United States tax could be said to be 'in respect of' an amount included in the taxpayer's assessable income. The case illustrates that where an Australian resident pays foreign income tax on the whole of a foreign capital gain which is only partly assessable in Australia due to the CGT discount, only a proportionate share of the foreign income tax counts towards the FITO under s 770-10.

Payment

The FITO applies only if foreign income tax has been paid. Subdivision 770-C contains special rules that deem foreign income tax to have been paid in certain circumstances (ss 770-130, 770-135). It also contains an anti-avoidance rule that deems foreign income tax not to have been paid where the entity is entitled to a refund of the foreign income tax or gets some other benefit worked out by reference to the amount of foreign income tax (s 770-140).

In addition, sub-div 770-D contains a special rule that allows a taxpayer's assessment to be amended where foreign tax is paid in an income year after the foreign income was included in their assessable income (s 770-190). The amendment period is four years from the time of payment and is designed to ensure that taxpayers are not deprived of the tax offset merely because they pay foreign income tax in an income year that does not coincide with the income year in which they derive the foreign income.

Exceptions

Foreign income tax does not count towards the FITO in the following situations:

- **Residence-based taxes.** The FITO is not available for foreign income tax paid to a foreign country in which the taxpayer is a resident in respect of an amount derived from a source outside that country (s 770-10(3)). For example, a resident of a foreign country that imposes a worldwide tax system (like Australia) does not get a tax offset for tax paid in the foreign country on income earned in another foreign country.
- **Credit absorption and unitary taxes.** The FITO is not available in respect of 'credit absorption' or 'unitary' taxes (s 770-10(5)). A credit absorption tax is a tax imposed under a foreign law that would not have been payable by an entity if the entity (or another entity) had not been entitled to a tax offset in respect of the tax (s 770-15(2)). A unitary tax is essentially a foreign tax that, for the purposes of taxing a company on its income derived from sources in the country, takes into account the company's (or its associated company's) income and outgoings derived from sources outside the country (s 770-15(3)).

[31.4] Foreign service income exemption

Section 23AG(1) *ITAA36* provides that resident individuals who have been engaged in 'foreign service' for a 'continuous period of not less than 91 days' are exempt from tax on 'foreign earnings' derived from that foreign service.

The exemption is quite limited as it is only available if the foreign service is directly attributable to any of the following:

- the delivery of Australian official development assistance (ie assistance delivered through a government overseas aid program) by the individual's employer (except where that employer is an Australian Government agency)
- the activities of the individual's employer in operating a developing country relief fund or a public disaster relief fund
- the activities of the individual's employer being a prescribed charitable or religious institution that is exempt from Australian income tax

- the individual's deployment outside Australia as a member of a disciplined force by the Commonwealth, a state or a territory (or an authority thereof), or
- an activity of a kind specified in the regulations (s 23AG(1AA)).

Foreign service and earnings

'Foreign service' is defined as 'service in a foreign country as the holder of an office or in the capacity of an employee' (s 23AG(7)).

In *Chaudhri v FC of T* 2001 ATC 4214, the Full Federal Court held that an officer who served aboard merchant ships was not engaged in 'foreign service' while the ships travelled across the high seas and was therefore not entitled to benefit under the s 23AG exemption. According to the Court, the term 'foreign country' should be interpreted according to its ordinary meaning. Hill, Drummond and Goldberg JJ stated (at 4220) that the modern usage of the expression foreign country 'looks to a political entity, be that a tract of land, a district, or a group of islands' and 'does not extend to an ocean or region of the sea'.

'Foreign earnings' is defined as 'income consisting of earnings, salary, wages, commission, bonuses or allowances' (s 23AG(7)). It also includes amounts assessable under the ESS rules in div 83A *ITAA97* [21.1]. Certain payments are, however, expressly excluded from the definition of foreign earnings, such as payments that are assessable under div 82 (ETPs) [19.2], or divs 301, 302, 304 or 305 *ITAA97* (superannuation benefits) [19.16].

Continuous period of not less than 91 days

The 'continuous period of not less than 91 days' of foreign service is measured quite liberally. For example, there is no requirement that the 91-day period must occur in the same income year—it can straddle two income years. This means, for example, that where the period of service commences in Year 1 and ends in Year 2, the entire period of service will be counted in determining the application of the exemption for each year even though there may not be a continuous period of at least 91 days of foreign service in each year.

Furthermore, where a person is, in accordance with the terms and conditions of their foreign service, absent from work due to recreation leave (subject to certain exceptions) or because of accident or illness, the period of absence is included in the period of foreign service (s 23AG(6)).

In addition, periods of temporary absence will not break the continuous service requirement, provided the absences do not exceed one-sixth of the total number of days of foreign service (s 23AG(6A)).

Example Trish and Tom are Australian residents who are employed to assist with their employer's delivery of a government overseas aid program in Indonesia.

Trish commenced work in Indonesia on 1 June 2023 and continued until 1 September 2023. Trish's period of foreign service includes 30 days of work in 2022/23 and 62 days of work in 2023/24. She has therefore been engaged in a continuous period of foreign service of 92 days. Her foreign earnings for both the 2022/23 and 2023/24 income years are therefore exempt from tax under s 23AG.

Tom commenced work in Indonesia on 10 July 2023. On 18 July 2023, he caught influenza, leaving him unable to work until 1 August 2023. Under his employment contract, he is entitled to sick leave. The 14 days of sick leave is taken into account in determining his period of foreign service. Tom continued to work in Indonesia until 12 October 2023. Tom has a continuous period of foreign service of 95 days (from 10 July 2023 to 12 October 2023). His foreign earnings for the 2023/24 income year are therefore exempt from tax under s 23AG.

Exclusions

The exemption in s 23AG(1) does not apply to foreign earnings that are exempt from income tax in the foreign country *only* because any one or more of the matters listed in s 23AG(2) applies, namely:

- the foreign earnings are exempt under a DTA or foreign law giving effect to a DTA
- the laws of a foreign country exempt income derived in the capacity of an employee, income from personal services, or similar income, or
- a foreign law corresponding to the *International Organisations (Privileges and Immunities) Act 1963* (Cth), or an international agreement to which Australia is a party dealing with privileges and immunities of diplomats or consuls or of persons connected with international organisations applies.

Effect of exemption

The exemption under s 23AG is known as an 'exemption with progression' because while it exempts foreign earnings from tax, the foreign earnings are nevertheless taken into account in determining the rate of tax payable on the taxpayer's non-exempt income. Section 23AG(3) requires the tax payable on the taxpayer's non-exempt income to be calculated according to a special formula. This formula essentially calculates the tax payable on the non-exempt income by reference to the average rate of tax that would be payable on the taxpayer's taxable income assuming it included both the exempt income and non-exempt income.

[31.5] Foreign branch income and CGT exemption

Section 23AH *ITAA36* contains the 'foreign branch income and CGT exemption'. The exemption applies to resident companies that carry on business through a PE [30.5] in a foreign country. The broad aim of s 23AH is to exempt amounts that are taxed overseas on a comparable basis to Australia. The rationale for the exemption is that if the amounts were assessable in Australia, the FITO would provide a credit for the foreign tax paid on such amounts [31.3]. The exemption therefore provides similar relief without requiring taxpayers to undertake any FITO calculations.

Key concepts

The operation of s 23AH is based around complex concepts that are adapted from the CFC regime contained in pt X *ITAA36* [34.2]. In particular, the scope of s 23AH depends on technical terms such as 'listed country' and 'unlisted country', 'active income test', 'tainted asset', 'adjusted tainted income' ('ATI'), and 'eligible designated concession income' ('EDCI'), which are all defined in s 317 *ITAA36* and explained at [34.2].

Branch income exemption

The foreign branch income exemption is contained in s 23AH(2). This provision states that foreign income derived by a resident company in carrying on a business through a PE in a foreign country is non-assessable non-exempt income. The exemption operates differently depending on whether the PE is in a listed or an unlisted country:

- If a resident company that carries on business through a PE in a 'listed country' fails the 'active income test', the exemption does not apply to foreign income that is both ATI and EDCI (s 23AH(5)).
- If a resident company that carries on business through a PE in an 'unlisted country' fails the active income test, the exemption does not apply to foreign income that is ATI (s 23AH(7)).

Example A Co is a resident company that carries on business through a PE in France (a listed country). If A Co passes the active income test, any income derived from its French PE will be non-assessable non-exempt income. If it fails the 'active income test', income derived from its French PE that is both ATI and EDCI will not qualify for the exemption.

Branch CGT exemption

The foreign branch CGT exemption is contained in ss 23AH(3) and (4). According to these provisions, a resident company disregards capital gains and capital losses arising in respect of CGT assets that are not taxable Australian property [17.12] and that are used wholly or mainly for the purpose of producing foreign income in carrying on a business through a PE in a foreign country.

However, a resident company must not disregard a capital gain or capital loss happening in relation to a 'tainted asset' that is used wholly or mainly for the purpose of producing foreign income through a PE in a listed country where:

- in the case of a capital gain, the gain is EDCI, or
- in the case of a capital loss, the loss would be EDCI if it were a capital gain (s 23AH(6)).

Likewise, a resident company must not disregard a capital gain or capital loss happening in relation to a 'tainted asset' that is used wholly or mainly for the purpose of producing foreign income through a PE in an unlisted country (s 23AH(8)).

Example R Co is a resident company that carries on business through a PE in Germany (a listed country). R Co owns a German building that it uses exclusively to store its equipment. The building is not a tainted asset and is not taxable Australian property. R Co sells the building and realises a capital gain of $100,000. As the building is used wholly for the purpose of producing foreign income in carrying on R Co's business through its German PE, the capital gain is disregarded.

[31.6] Foreign equity distribution exemption

In the past, former s 23AJ *ITAA36* treated a 'non-portfolio dividend' paid to a resident company by a company that was *not* a 'Part X Australian resident' as non-assessable non-exempt income. A non-portfolio dividend is a dividend paid to a company that has at least a 10% voting interest in the company paying the dividend (s 317 *ITAA36*).

Section 23AJ was intended to help foreign subsidiaries of Australian resident companies operating overseas compete on an equal footing with other businesses located overseas. There were, however, a number of problems with s 23AJ. One of these was that it could apply to returns on debt interests (eg dividends on redeemable preference shares), which had unintended consequences for thin capitalisation purposes [33.5]. Another problem was that it only applied to dividends received directly from a foreign company and not to dividends received through interposed entities (eg trusts). To remedy these issues, s 23AJ was replaced by s 768-5 *ITAA97* in 2014.

Section 768-5 exemption

Section 768-5 provides that a 'foreign equity distribution' is non-assessable non-exempt income of an Australian resident corporate tax entity if, at the time the distribution is made, the entity satisfies the 'participation test' in s 768-15 in relation to the company that made the distribution and does not receive the distribution in the capacity of a trustee.

A 'foreign equity distribution' is a distribution or non-share dividend made by a company that is a foreign resident in respect of an equity interest in the company (s 768-10).

An Australian resident corporate tax entity satisfies the 'participation test' in s 768-15 in relation to another entity if the sum of the direct and indirect participation interests (disregarding rights on winding up) that it has in the other entity is at least 10%. The concepts of direct and indirect participation interests are defined in ss 960-185 and 960-190 *ITAA97* and are based on the 'control' tests under the CFC regime [34.2].

Example R Co (a resident company) has a 40% participation interest in F Co (a foreign company). F Co pays R Co a dividend of $1,000 during the current income year. The dividend is non-assessable non-exempt income of R Co under s 768-5. If R Co only had a 5% participation interest in F Co, the dividend would be assessable income of R Co under s 44(1)(a) [22.5].

Foreign source non-assessable non-exempt income debt deductions

Section 8-1 *ITAA97* does not allow a deduction for a loss or outgoing to the extent that it relates to gaining or producing non-assessable non-exempt income [12.1]. However, a specific deduction is available under s 25-90 *ITAA97* for losses or outgoings incurred by an entity in earning foreign source income that is non-assessable non-exempt income under s 768-5 *ITAA97* or under ss 23AI or 23AK *ITAA36* [34.5]. To be deductible, the amount must be a 'debt deduction' (eg interest) as defined in s 820-40(1)(a) *ITAA97* [33.5].

Example R Co (a resident company) borrows money from a bank to purchase 70% of the shares in F Co (a foreign company), giving it a 70% participation interest in F Co. Dividends paid by F Co to R Co constitute non-assessable non-exempt income under s 768-5. R Co cannot therefore deduct the interest it pays on the loan under s 8-1. R Co can, nevertheless, deduct the interest under s 25-90 as the dividends fall within s 768-5 and the interest constitutes a debt deduction under s 820-40(1)(a).

[31.7] CGT participation exemption

Subdivision 768-G *ITAA97* contains the 'CGT participation exemption'. This exemption applies where:

- a resident company makes a capital gain or capital loss from specified CGT events (ie CGT event A1, B1, C2, E1, E2, G3, J1, K4, K6, K10 or K11) that happen in relation to shares it owns in a foreign company, and
- the resident company holds a direct voting percentage of at least 10% in the foreign company for a continuous period of at least 12 months in the 24 months before the CGT event.

Where the above criteria are satisfied, the gain or loss that would otherwise arise from the CGT event is reduced by the 'active foreign business asset percentage' (s 768-505).

The 'active foreign business asset percentage' is the percentage value of the foreign company's 'active foreign business assets' relative to all its assets (s 768-510). However, where this percentage would otherwise be less than 10%, it is deemed to be zero, and where it would otherwise be 90% or more, it is deemed to be 100%.

The term 'active foreign business asset' is defined in s 768-540 and covers assets used by a foreign company in carrying on a business that are not taxable Australian property [17.12].

Example In July 2020, R Co (a resident company) acquired shares carrying 25% of the voting rights in F Co (a foreign company) for $8m. In September 2023, R Co sold the shares for $9m. At the time of the CGT event, 30% of F Co's total assets were active foreign business assets. The $1m capital gain that R Co would have otherwise made on the sale of the shares is therefore reduced by F Co's 'active foreign business asset percentage' of 30%. R Co's capital gain is therefore $700,000 (ie $1m × (100% – $30%)).

[31.8] Foreign government officials exemption

Section 768-100 *ITAA97* treats as exempt income the official salary and the ordinary and statutory income from a source outside Australia of:

- foreign government representatives and their official staff who are neither Australian citizens nor ordinarily resident in Australia, and
- officers of the government of a Commonwealth of Nations country who are temporarily in Australia to render services on behalf of that country, or an Australian Government agency.

The exemption only applies to foreign government representatives and their official staff if the foreign country grants a similar exemption in relation to Australian representatives and neither the *Vienna Convention on Diplomatic Relations* nor the *Vienna Convention on Consular Relations* applies. Where these conventions apply, the person's income may be exempt under the *Diplomatic Privileges and Immunities Act 1967* (Cth) or the *Consular Privileges and Immunities Act 1972* (Cth).

The exemption only applies to officers of the government of a Commonwealth of Nations country if the country exempts Australian Government officers from income tax on their salaries under a similar arrangement.

[31.9] Conduit foreign income exemption

The term 'conduit foreign income' is used to describe certain kinds of income which would ordinarily be subject to Australian tax in the hands of foreign residents purely because it is channelled through Australia (eg because it is deemed to have an Australian source or is attributable to an Australian PE). To create greater certainty for foreign residents and improve Australia's position as an international financial services centre, Australia introduced sub-div 802-A *ITAA97*, which exempts foreign residents from having to pay Australian income tax on their conduit foreign income.

Subdivision 802-A *ITAA97* was introduced to remove the impediments that would otherwise exist for foreign residents who invest in Australian companies and who are paid unfranked distributions by such companies out of exempt foreign profits. Without a specific exemption, such distributions would ordinarily be subject to withholding tax because they are unfranked [31.11]. This is the case even though, had the foreign resident derived the income directly (rather than via an Australian company), the income would have been exempt from Australian tax.

The key provision is s 802-15, which provides that so much of an unfranked distribution made by an Australian corporate tax entity that it declares in its distribution statement to be 'conduit foreign income' is non-assessable non-exempt income of a foreign resident, and is not subject to dividend withholding tax [31.11].

An Australian corporate tax entity's 'conduit foreign income' is calculated according to ss 802-30 to 802-55 (s 802-25). In broad terms, conduit foreign income consists of certain kinds of foreign income which are not ordinarily included in the assessable income of the Australian corporate tax entity and which would otherwise be distributed by it as an unfranked dividend. In particular, it covers foreign branch income and capital gains derived by an Australian company that fall within s 23AH *ITAA36* [31.5] foreign equity distributions received by an Australian company that fall within s 768-5 *ITAA97* [31.6].

> ***Example*** R Co (a resident company) has a participation interest of 40% in F Co (a foreign company). F Co pays R Co a $5,000 dividend. The dividend is non-assessable non-exempt income of R Co under s 768-5 *ITAA97*. R Co uses the $5,000 to pay an unfranked dividend and declares that this amount is conduit foreign income in its distribution statement. If the dividend is paid to a foreign shareholder, the dividend will be exempt from both income tax and withholding tax under s 802-15.

[31.10] Investment manager regime exemption

In 2008, the Government established the Australian Financial Centre Forum to examine ways of positioning Australia as a leading regional financial services centre. In its 2009 report, *Australia as a Financial Centre: Building on our Strengths*, it noted that Australia's tax system could act as an impediment to cross-border activities, including certain investments made into Australia by foreign investors though foreign managed funds or intermediary Australian fund managers. It was therefore recommended that an Investment Manager Regime ('IMR') be introduced to provide foreign investors with exemptions from Australian tax in respect of certain investments.

Object of sub-div 842-I *ITAA97*

The IMR regime is contained in sub-div 842-I *ITAA97*. The object of the subdivision is to encourage certain forms of investment made into or through Australia by foreign entities that have wide membership, or that use independent Australian fund managers (s 842-205). It achieves this by providing tax exemptions to certain foreign investors.

Application of sub-div 842-I *ITAA97*

Subdivision 842-I applies to 'IMR entities' in relation to 'IMR financial arrangements' if the requirements in either ss 842-215(3) or 842-215(5) are met in relation to an income year (s 842-215(1)).

An entity is an 'IMR entity' for an income year if it is not an Australian resident and not a resident trust for CGT purposes for the income year (s 842-220). An 'IMR financial arrangement' is any financial arrangement other than one that relates to a CGT asset that is taxable Australian real property (s 855-20) or an indirect Australian real property interest (s 855-25) [17.12] (s 842-225).

Section 842-215(3) contains 'direct investment requirements', which will generally be met if:

- the IMR entity is an 'IMR widely held entity'
- its returns from the IMR financial arrangement are not attributable to a PE in Australia
- its interest in the issuer of the arrangement does not pass the 'non-portfolio interest test', and
- it does not carry on a trading business in Australia relating to the arrangement.

Section 842-215(5) contains 'indirect investment requirements', which will generally be met if:

- the IMR financial arrangement is made on the IMR entity's behalf by an 'independent Australian fund manager'
- if the issuer of the arrangement is an Australian resident, the interest in the issuer must *not* pass the 'non-portfolio interest test', and
- the IMR entity does not carry on a trading business in Australia relating to the arrangement.

An IMR entity is an 'IMR widely held entity' if it is a foreign life assurance company, is covered by ss 12-402(3)(a) to (h) *TAA* (eg it is an MIT or a foreign superannuation fund with at least 50 members), or is specified in the regulations (s 842-230(1)). An IMR entity is also an IMR widely held entity if no entity has a total participation interest in the entity of 20% or more, or there are *not* five or fewer other entities whose total participation interests in the entity is 50% or more (s 842-230(2)).

An independent Australian fund manager is, broadly, an Australian resident that carries out investment management activities for an IMR entity for arm's length remuneration and meets certain other tests contained in s 842-245.

The 'non-portfolio interest test' is contained in s 960-195. The test is passed if a 'holding entity' and its associates have direct participation interests (defined in s 960-190) in a 'test entity' of 10% or more. As a consequence, the test will *not* be passed by an IMR entity that together with its associates has direct participation interests of less than 10% in the issuer.

The requirement that an IMR entity not to be carrying on a trading business is designed to ensure that sub-div 842-I is directed at passive (rather than active business) investments. The nature of a trading business is defined in s 102M *ITAA36* [25.9].

Tax exemptions under sub-div 842-I *ITAA97*

Where sub-div 842-I applies, the IMR entity is entitled to tax exemptions in relation to its gains and losses from disposing or otherwise realising the IMR financial arrangement. Specifically, amounts that would otherwise be assessable income to the IMR entity from disposing or realising the arrangement are deemed non-assessable non-exempt income, and amounts that would otherwise be deductible to the IMR entity from disposing or realising the arrangement are deemed not deductible. Similarly, any capital gains and capital losses made by the IMR entity from CGT events that relate to the arrangement are disregarded (s 842-215).

[31.11] Withholding taxes

Withholding taxes are a key feature of most countries' international tax regimes. They require payers to withhold tax 'at source' from certain payments made to foreigners. This is designed to overcome the practical problems revenue authorities would otherwise face in collecting tax from recipients located overseas.

Australia has a number of withholding tax regimes, including:

- the dividend, interest, and royalty withholding tax regime
- the foreign residents withholding tax regime, and
- the Pacific Australia Labour Mobility Program withholding tax regime.

These regimes are complemented by other withholding tax regimes, such as the foreign residents capital gains withholding tax regime [17.12] and the MIT withholding tax regime [25.10].

Some of Australia's withholding taxes operate as 'final taxes', whereas others are merely prepayments of tax that are credited against the taxpayer's actual tax liability at the end of the income year. Where withholding taxes are final taxes, foreign residents are not required to lodge income tax returns or pay income tax in respect of the payments. In other words, they do not interact any further with the Australian tax system.

Dividend, interest and royalty withholding tax

Subdivision 12-F of sch 1 *TAA* requires certain entities that make dividend, interest, and royalty payments to foreign residents to withhold amounts from such payments. Withholding is only required under sub-div 12-F if 'withholding tax' is payable on the dividends, interest, or royalties (s 12-300). 'Withholding tax' is defined as income tax payable under s 128B *ITAA36* (s 995-1 *ITAA97*). Section 128B makes non-residents liable to income tax on dividends (s 128B(4)), interest (s 128B(5)), and royalties (s 128B(5A)) that fall within the provisions in div 11A of pt III *ITAA36*.

Withholding tax is imposed at the rates prescribed under the *Income Tax (Dividends, Interest and Royalties Withholding Tax) Act 1974* (Cth) ('*ITDIRWTA*') and is due and payable at the expiration of 21 days after the end of the month in which the income was derived by the non-resident (s 128C).

Where a DTA limits the Australian withholding tax payable, the withholding tax must be reduced in accordance with the DTA (s 17A *International Tax Agreements Act 1953* (Cth)).

Amounts that have been subject to withholding tax, as well as certain amounts that are specifically excluded from withholding tax, constitute non-assessable non-exempt income (s 128D). This means that the non-resident is not also assessed on such amounts under the general tax rules (eg s 6-5 *ITAA97* or s 44(1) *ITAA36*). Withholding tax on dividend, interest, and royalty payments is therefore a final tax. To prevent any potential double taxation, an entity is entitled to a credit if their ordinary or statutory income includes dividends interest or royalties and they have borne all or part of an amount withheld from the payment (s 18-30 *TAA*).

The specific circumstances in which withholding tax applies to dividends, interest, and royalties, and the relevant rates of withholding tax that apply to such payments, are outlined below.

Dividend withholding tax

Dividends derived by a non-resident are generally subject to withholding tax if they are paid by a resident company (ss 128B(1), (4) *ITAA36*; s 12-210 *TAA*).

Withholding tax does not apply to dividends paid by a resident company to a non-resident carrying on business in Australia through a PE in Australia that are attributable to the PE (s 128B(3E)). This is because such dividends are ordinarily assessable under the general dividend taxation rules in s 44(1)(c) *ITAA36* [22.5].

Withholding tax also does not apply to franked dividends [22.7] and dividends franked with exempting credits [22.18] (s 128B(3)(ga)). This is because such dividends are paid out of profits that have already been subject to corporate tax in Australia. In addition, withholding tax does not apply to so much of an unfranked dividend that is 'conduit foreign income' [31.9] (s 802-15 *ITAA97*).

Withholding tax is imposed on dividends at the rate of 30% (s 7(a) *ITDIRWTA*). However, if the recipient is a resident of a tax treaty country [32.3], the rate cannot exceed the maximum rate set out under the relevant DTA. Under most DTAs, the maximum rate is 15% (although there are a number of exceptions to this rule) [32.6].

Example R Co (a resident company) pays a $20,000 dividend, which is 50% franked, to Felix who is a resident of Singapore (a tax treaty country [32.3]). The $10,000 unfranked part of the dividend is subject to withholding tax at the rate of 15% (ss 128B(1), (4) *ITAA36*). The $10,000 franked part of the dividend is exempt from withholding tax (s 128B(3)(ga) *ITAA36*). R Co will be required to withhold tax of $1,500 from the dividend (s 12-210 *TAA*) [39.4]. As a result, Felix will receive a net payment of $18,500 (ie $20,000 – ($10,000 × 15%)). He will not be personally liable to pay any Australian tax on the dividend as it is non-assessable non-exempt income (s 128D *ITAA36*).

Interest withholding tax

31

Interest derived by a non-resident is generally subject to withholding tax if it is paid by:

- a resident (provided the interest is not wholly incurred by the resident in a business carried on in a foreign country at or through a PE in that country), or
- a non-resident (provided the interest is wholly or partly incurred by the non-resident in carrying on business in Australia at or through a PE in Australia) (ss 128B(2), (5) *ITAA36*; s 12-245 *TAA*).

For withholding tax purposes, 'interest' includes amounts that are 'in the nature of interest' and certain amounts 'in substitution of interest' or 'in exchange of interest' (s 128A(1AB) *ITAA36*). A dividend paid in respect of a 'non-equity share' [29.9] is also deemed to be interest rather than a dividend (ss 128A(1), (1AB) *ITAA36*).

In *FC of T v Century Yuasa Batteries Pty Ltd* 98 ATC 4380, the Full Federal Court found that 'gross-up' amounts required to be paid in respect of withholding tax by a borrower under its loan agreement with a non-resident bank were not 'interest' or 'in the nature of interest' but were an 'indemnity' against withholding tax. The additional amounts did not have the character of a return or profit to the lender for the use of the money advanced. Instead, their purpose was to ensure the effective rate of interest earned by the bank was not reduced by withholding tax.

Withholding tax does not apply to certain forms of interest, such as interest paid by a temporary resident [30.4] (s 768-980 *ITAA97*) or interest paid before 1 January 2024 by an OBU on offshore borrowings [25.9] (s 128GB *ITAA36*).

Withholding tax also does not apply to interest paid by eligible companies and unit trusts on debentures and debt interests they issue as long as they satisfy a 'public offer test' (ss 128F, 128FA *ITAA36*). Companies generally qualify for the exemption if they are residents at the time of issue and payment, or if they are non-residents at the time of issue and payment and the issue and payment arise in carrying on their business through a PE in Australia (ss 128F(1), (1A) *ITAA36*). The public offer test is satisfied if the debentures or debt interests are offered in the circumstances specified in s 128F(2). These circumstances include situations where they are offered to:

- at least 10 persons carrying on business of providing finance or dealing in securities in the financial markets
- at least 100 investors whom it was reasonable to regard as either having acquired debentures or debt interests in the past or likely to be interested in acquiring debentures or debt interests, or
- a dealer, manager or underwriter for the purpose of placement of the debentures or debt interest.

The public offer test is also satisfied if the debentures or debt interests are 'global bonds' (ss 128F(4), (10) *ITAA36*).

Withholding tax has also been removed from interest on debentures and debt interests issued by the Commonwealth, states and territories or their relevant authorities (s 128F(7) *ITAA36*). This is to increase the attractiveness of government securities (eg government bonds) in global markets and to ensure they are taxed similarly to how such securities are taxed overseas (eg in the United States and the United Kingdom).

Withholding tax is imposed on interest at the rate of 10% (s 7(b) *ITDIRWTA*). However, if the recipient is a resident of a tax treaty country [32.3], the rate cannot exceed the maximum rate set out under the relevant DTA. Under most DTAs, the maximum rate is generally also 10% (although there are a number of exceptions to this rule) [32.6].

Example An Australian resident bank pays interest of $1,000 to Pablo who is a non-resident that resides in Uruguay and has a term deposit with the bank. The interest is subject to withholding tax (s 128B(2) *ITAA36*). The bank is required to withhold $100 from the interest paid to Pablo (s 12-245 *TAA*) [39.4]. Pablo is not required to pay any Australian income tax on the interest as it is non-assessable non-exempt income (s 128D *ITAA36*).

Royalty withholding tax

Royalties derived by a non-resident are generally subject to withholding tax if they are paid by:

- a resident (provided the royalty is not wholly incurred by the resident in a business carried on in a foreign country at or through a PE in that country), or
- a non-resident (provided the royalty is wholly or partly incurred by the non-resident in carrying on business in Australia at or through a PE in Australia) (ss 128B(2B), (5A) *ITAA36*; s 12-280 *TAA*).

Withholding tax is imposed on royalties at the rate of 30% (s 7(c) *ITDIRWTA*). However, if the recipient is a resident of a tax treaty country [32.3], the rate cannot exceed the maximum rate set out under the relevant DTA. Under most DTAs, the maximum rate is generally 10% (although there are a number of exceptions to this rule) [32.6].

Example Jo is a non-resident author who resides in Monaco. She writes books that are published by an Australian resident publisher in Melbourne. The publisher paid Jo a royalty of $10,000 relating to the sale of her books. The royalty is subject to withholding tax (s 128B(2B) *ITAA36*). The publisher is required to withhold $3,000 from the payment (s 12-280 *TAA*). Jo is not subject to Australian income tax on the royalty as it is non-assessable non-exempt income (s 128D *ITAA36*).

Foreign residents withholding tax

Subdivision 12-FB of sch 1 *TAA* contains a withholding tax regime that applies to certain payments made to foreign residents by an entity in the course of carrying on its enterprise (s 12-315 *TAA*). The payments must be of a kind set out in the *Taxation Administration Regulations 2017* (Cth) ('*TAR17*'), namely:

- payments for promoting casino junket tours (withholding tax applies at the rate of 3%: regs 31, 49)
- payments for entertainment and sports activities (withholding tax applies at the appropriate non-resident tax rates: regs 32, 50), and
- payments for construction and related activities (withholding tax applies at the rate of 5%: regs 33, 51).

The regime does not apply to excluded payments (eg dividends, interest and royalties). It also does not apply to payments made to, or received for, entities covered by an exemption under s 12-319 *TAA*. To obtain such an exemption, the Commissioner must be satisfied that the relevant entity has an established history of complying with the tax laws and is likely to continue to comply with its obligations.

Non-residents are not entitled to income tax exemptions in respect of payments that fall within the withholding tax rules in sub-div 12-FB. This means that, in contrast to dividend, interest, and royalty withholding tax, the tax is not a 'final tax'. Non-residents are, nevertheless, entitled to credits against their income tax liabilities for amounts withheld under the regime (s 18-15 *TAA*).

Example A Co is an Australian resident building company. It agrees to pay $1m to F Co, a foreign company, to help it construct power generation infrastructure for a plant that A Co is building for one of its clients in Australia. If F Co is not covered by an exemption under s 12-319, A Co must withhold $50,000 (ie $1m × 5%) from the $1m payment. F Co is assessed on the $1m payment. However, it gets a credit under s 18-15 of $50,000 for the tax withheld by A Co.

Pacific Australia Labour Mobility Program withholding tax

The Pacific Australia Labour Mobility Program is a government program that supports labour mobility within the Pacific region. Subdivision 840-S *ITAA97* and sub-div 12-FC of sch 1 *TAA* contain a withholding tax regime that applies to payments made to foreign workers participating in this program. Withholding tax at the rate of 15% applies to payments made to foreign resident workers that hold a Temporary Work (International Relations) Visa (subclass 403) (s 840-905 *ITAA97*; s 4 *Income Tax (Labour Mobility Program Withholding Tax) Act 2012* (Cth)). The withholding tax is payable 21 days after the end of the income year in which the income is derived by the worker (s 840-910

ITAA97). It is a final tax as the payments are non-assessable non-exempt income in the hands of the foreign workers (s 840-915 *ITAA97*).

[31.12] QUESTIONS

1. Describe the circumstances in which international juridical double taxation conflicts arise. What methods can be used for dealing with international juridical double taxation?
2. What is the role of the FITO? Why was the taxpayer in *Burton v FC of T* 2019 ATC ¶20-709 only allowed a FITO for half of the foreign tax paid?
3. Oz Co is a resident company that pays tax at the rate of 30%. Last year it derived $400m of Australian source income and $200m of foreign source income. The foreign source income was subject to foreign income tax at the rate of 20%. Calculate Oz Co's Australian tax liability, taking into account the FITO.
4. Ted is a resident who owns shares in a foreign company. Each year, the company pays Ted dividends that are subject to 15% foreign withholding tax. In the current year, Ted received a net dividend of $8,500 from the company. How are the dividends taxed in Australia?
5. Bill is a resident who is subject to tax at the top marginal rate. Bill deposited $100,000 with a foreign bank overseas. The bank paid him interest of $10,000 during the current income year, but has deducted $1,000 of foreign withholding tax, leaving him with only $9,000. How is the interest taxed in Australia?
6. Sam is an Australian resident who is employed as a nurse. He spends six months in Africa working for his employer on a public disaster relief fund project. How does the Australian tax law apply to his income? Would your answer be different if he had worked in Africa for only two months?
7. R Co (a resident company) owns 30% of the shares in F Co (a non-resident company). F Co pays R Co a dividend of $85,000 after deducting withholding tax of $15,000 from the payment. How is the dividend taxed in Australia? Would your answer differ if R Co only owned 5% of the shares in F Co?
8. In what circumstances does the CGT participation exemption apply?
9. On 5 May 2021, White Co (a resident company) acquired shares carrying 40% of the voting rights in Black Co (a foreign company) for $500,000. On 7 August 2023, White Co sold the Black Co shares for $800,000. At the time of sale, 25% of Black Co's assets were active foreign business assets. Calculate White Co's capital gain on the sale of the shares.
10. R Co (a resident company) receives a $10,000 dividend from F Co (a foreign company), which is non-assessable non-exempt income of R Co under s 768-5 *ITAA97*. R Co uses the $10,000 to pay an unfranked dividend of $5,000 to each of its two shareholders, Jack (a foreign resident) and Jill (a resident). R Co declares in its distribution statement that the dividend is conduit foreign income. How does sub-div 802-A apply to the distributions?
11. In what circumstances does withholding tax apply to dividends, interest, and royalty payments? What rates of tax generally apply? What is the effect of s 128D *ITAA36* on such payments?
12. Res Bank is a resident company that carries on a banking business. How does the withholding tax regime apply to dividends and interest it pays to its non-resident shareholders and depositors?
13. X Co is a resident company that pays a dividend of $10,000 that is franked to the extent of $9,000 to Pierre (a French resident). Explain how withholding tax applies to the dividend.

DOUBLE TAXATION AGREEMENTS 32

[32.1] Introduction

The Australian Government has negotiated bilateral tax agreements (also known as 'treaties' or 'conventions') with the governments of more than 40 nations. These agreements are often referred to as Double Taxation Agreements ('DTAs') since one of their main functions is to prevent international juridical double taxation. DTAs deal with double taxation issues by allocating taxing rights in relation to cross-border transactions between Australia and the respective 'Contracting States'. DTAs also assist with the prevention of tax evasion through the exchange of information between the relevant tax authorities. They also indirectly serve to promote trade and investment between Australia and the Contracting States, as they reduce the uncertainty of international tax treatment of cross-border transactions.

As discussed in Chapter 31, international juridical double taxation essentially arises where two countries tax an entity on the same amount. This can occur due to the different kinds of conflicts outlined in the diagram at [31.2]. For instance, double taxation can arise because it is common for countries to tax residents on their worldwide income and non-residents on income sourced within their territories. Residents of Australia operating overseas could therefore be subject to tax in both Australia and overseas on their foreign source income (ie a 'residence/source conflict'). Double taxation can also arise where there is overlap in countries' tax laws, resulting in an entity being treated as a resident of more than one jurisdiction (ie a 'residence conflict'), or income being treated as having its source in more than one jurisdiction (ie a 'source conflict').

This chapter examines how Australia's DTAs deal with double taxation conflicts as well as certain other related issues. As Australia's DTAs are broadly based on the OECD *Model Tax Convention on Income and on Capital* ('OECD MTC'), the chapter begins with a discussion of the historical origins of the convention [32.2]. This is followed by an outline of the legislative framework that underpins Australia's DTAs [32.3] and a discussion of a special multilateral instrument that enables countries to expeditiously upgrade their DTAs [32.4]. Some of the key terms used in DTAs are examined at [32.5]. The way that Australia's DTAs deal with allocating taxing rights in respect of specific kinds of income is discussed at [32.6]. There is also discussion of how the DTAs deal with taxation discrimination

[32.7], the resolution of disputes [32.8] and the exchange of information between tax authorities [32.9]. Interpretation issues relating to DTAs are considered at [32.10].

[32.2] Historical background to DTAs

International tax agreements have a history that dates back more than 100 years. The first bilateral income tax treaty was entered into in 1899 between Prussia and Austria-Hungary. Since then, many hundreds of tax treaties have been executed around the world.

League of Nations Draft Models

The origins of modern style tax treaties can be traced back to an initiative undertaken by the League of Nations shortly after World War I. In the early 1920s, the League of Nations, through its Financial Committee consisting of government tax officials, commenced an investigation into international double taxation. The work of this committee eventually resulted in the publication of a Draft Model *Bilateral Convention for the Prevention of Double Taxation* in 1928 (known as the 'Geneva Model'). A revised Draft Model (known as the 'Mexico Model') was published in 1943. This was followed by another Draft Model (known as the 'London Model'), which was published in 1946.

The Mexico Model generally treated the 'source country' as having primary taxing rights, while the London Model gave a number of taxing rights back to the 'residence country'. For instance, under the London Model, a resident of one country could only be taxed on its business profits in the source country if it had a PE in the source country. Since the Mexico Model focused on source, it generally tended to favour capital-importing countries (typically developing countries). The London Model, on the other hand, generally tended to favour capital-exporting countries (typically developed countries).

During the late 1940s and early 1950s, the United Nations (which had replaced the League of Nations after World War II) tried to design a new Draft Model that would reconcile the competing interests of developing and developed countries. However, as an acceptable compromise could not be reached, the project was suspended.

OECD Model Tax Convention

In the late 1950s, the Organisation for European Economic Cooperation (which was formed in 1948 to revitalise the Western European economies after World War II and which was transformed into the OECD in 1960) established a Fiscal Committee to work on designing its own model tax treaty. In 1963, the OECD published a *Draft Double Taxation Convention on Income and Capital* which was largely based on the London Model. The convention was revised in 1977, resulting in publication of the OECD MTC. The OECD MTC was updated in 1992 and has continued to be revised periodically ever since (most recently in 2017). The OECD MTC is widely used by developed countries as the basis of their DTAs. It is accompanied by detailed commentary explaining the articles.

United Nations Model Tax Convention

In addition to the OECD MTC, a number of other DTAs are used around the world. This includes, most notably, the United Nations *Model Tax Convention Between Developed and Developing Countries* ('UN MTC'). This convention and its accompanying commentary were first published in 1980 and last updated in 2021. Developing countries, which were effectively excluded from having input into the OECD MTC, had a significant role in the design of the UN MTC. Although much of the UN MTC is based on the OECD MTC, it has some important differences. For instance, it adopts a broader definition of a PE and allows the source country additional taxing rights in respect of business profits. The UN MTC has been adopted by many developing countries as the basis for their DTAs. Some developed countries (typically capital-importing countries) have also adopted certain articles from the convention in their DTAs.

United States Model Tax Convention

The United States also has its own *Model Income Tax Convention* ('US MTC') which was first published in 1996 and was last updated in 2016. As the United States is a capital-exporting country, it is not surprising that the articles in the US MTC, like the OECD MTC, tend to favour the country of residence.

[32.3] Legislative framework of Australia's DTAs

Australia's first DTA was entered into with the United Kingdom in 1947. This DTA was terminated in the late 1960s and replaced with a new DTA which came into force in 1968. The 1968 DTA was eventually superseded by the current DTA which came into force in 2003.

Since the late 1960s, Australia has executed a substantial number of DTAs. Over this period, several of these DTAs have been renegotiated or amended by 'protocols'. A few early agreements were confined to dealing with only airline profits. The following table contains a list of Australia's DTAs as well as the dates they were signed and entered into force. It is important to note that the articles in a number of these treaties have recently been modified under the *Multilateral Convention to Implement Tax Treaty Related Measures to Prevent Base Erosion and Profit Shifting* [32.4]. The modified treaties are marked with an asterisk (*) in the table.

Jurisdictions with which Australia has comprehensive DTAs		
Jurisdiction	**Date of signing agreement**	**Date of entry into force**
Argentina	27 August 1999	30 December 1999
Austria	8 July 1986	1 September 1988
Belgium*	13 October 1977 20 March 1984 (First Protocol) 24 June 2009 (Second Protocol)	1 November 1979 20 September 1986 12 May 2014
Canada*	21 May 1980 23 January 2002 (First Protocol)	29 April 1981 18 December 2002
Chile*	10 March 2010	22 March 2013
China*	22 November 1985 (Airline Profits) 17 November 1988 (Full Agreement)	14 November 1986 28 December 1990
Czech Republic*	28 March 1995	27 November 1995
Denmark*	1 April 1981	27 October 1981
Fiji	15 October 1990	28 December 1990
Finland*	20 November 2006	10 November 2007
France*	20 June 2006	1 June 2009
Germany	12 November 2015	7 December 2016
Greece	5 May 1977 (Airline Profits)	7 April 1981
Hungary*	29 November 1990	10 April 1992
Iceland	12 October 2022	Not yet in force
India*	25 July 1991 16 December 2011 (First Protocol)	30 December 1991 2 April 2013
Indonesia*	22 April 1992	14 December 1992
Ireland*	31 May 1983	21 December 1983
Israel	28 March 2019	6 December 2019

32

Jurisdictions with which Australia has comprehensive DTAs		
Jurisdiction	**Date of signing agreement**	**Date of entry into force**
Italy	13 April 1972 (Airline Profits) 14 December 1982 (Full Agreement)	9 April 1976 5 November 1985
Japan*	31 January 2008	3 December 2008
Kiribati	25 March 1991	28 June 1991
Korea*	12 July 1982	1 January 1984
Malaysia*	20 August 1980 2 August 1999 (First Protocol) 28 July 2002 (Second Protocol) 24 February 2010 (Third Protocol)	26 June 1981 27 June 2000 23 July 2003 8 August 2011
Malta*	9 May 1984	20 May 1985
Mexico	9 September 2002	31 December 2003
Netherlands*	17 March 1976 (DTA and First Protocol) 30 June 1986 (Second Protocol)	27 September 1976 1 May 1987
New Zealand*	26 June 2009	19 March 2010
Norway*	8 August 2006	12 September 2007
Papua New Guinea	24 May 1989	29 December 1989
Philippines	11 May 1979	17 June 1980
Poland*	7 May 1991	4 March 1992
Romania*	2 February 2000	11 April 2001
Russia*	7 September 2000	17 December 2003
Singapore*	11 February 1969 18 October 1989 (First Protocol) 8 September 2009 (Second Protocol)	4 June 1969 5 January 1990 22 December 2010
Slovakia*	24 August 1999	22 December 1999
South Africa	1 July 1999 31 March 2008 (First Protocol)	21 December 1999 12 November 2008
Spain*	24 March 1992	10 December 1992
Sri Lanka	18 December 1989	21 October 1991
Sweden	14 January 1981	4 September 1981
Switzerland	30 July 2013	14 October 2014
Taiwan	29 May 1996	21 October 1996
Thailand*	31 August 1989	27 December 1989
Turkiye	28 April 2010	5 June 2013
United Kingdom*	21 August 2003	17 December 2003
United States	6 August 1982 27 September 2001 (First Protocol)	31 October 1983 13 May 2003
Vietnam	13 April 1992 22 November 1996 (Amended by exchange of notes) 5 August 2002 (Amended by exchange of letters)	10 December 1992 23 July 1997 11 February 2003

DTA negotiations

The process for negotiating tax treaties can often take around two years, or even longer, and usually only starts after each country has undertaken a due diligence exercise in which it analyses the other country's tax system, tax treaties and trade relations. The official process ordinarily commences with the governments of the respective countries exchanging their model tax treaties, which are then used as the basis for negotiating a draft DTA that is mutually acceptable to both countries. The draft DTA is usually settled following formal negotiations between government officials. It is then signed by the respective governments. In Australia, the standard practice is for the Treasurer to sign DTAs.

Although the terms of Australia's DTAs are broadly based on the OECD MTC, as Australia has historically been a capital-importing country, its DTA policy has emphasised source-based taxing rights with the result that some of the articles in its DTAs are closer to those contained in the UN MTC. In its 2003 report, *International Taxation—A Report to the Treasurer*, the Board of Taxation recommended that Australia should consider heading towards a more residence-based treaty policy (Recommendation 3.5). An illustration of where such an approach was adopted is the 2001 United States Protocol, which amended the United States DTA.

Incorporation of DTAs into domestic law

As DTAs are international agreements entered into by the governments of the Contracting States, it is up to the government of each country to incorporate DTAs into their domestic tax laws. Australia's DTAs are tabled in Parliament and scrutinised by the Joint Standing Committee on Treaties. Until recently, treaties were incorporated as schedules to the *International Tax Agreements Act 1953* (Cth). For example, sch 2 contained the United States convention and sch 2A contained the United States protocol that amends the United States convention. The many schedules to the Act, however, made it a very long piece of legislation. In 2011, the *International Tax Agreements Act 1953* was amended and streamlined. As a result, the majority of schedules have been removed from the Act. The treaties are now simply defined in the Act (in country alphabetical order) by reference to their full title together with a note stating that the relevant treaty is published in the *Australian Treaty Series*.

Once a DTA has been incorporated into Australia's tax laws, the Government informs the other country that it has been ratified. It is only once this has taken place that the agreement 'enters into force'. The terms of the agreement will thereupon have effect from the particular application date specified in the agreement. It is common for agreements to refer to different application dates for Australia and the other country (this is often done for convenience to ensure that the DTA only commences to operate from the beginning of each country's financial year). Some agreements also have different commencement dates for particular parts of the agreement (eg the withholding tax articles in certain DTAs sometimes apply from a different date to the other articles in the agreement).

Termination of DTAs

A DTA continues in effect indefinitely, until one of the countries terminates the agreement by providing notice to the other country in accordance with the relevant termination article contained in the DTA.

Reading the *International Tax Agreements Act 1953* with other Acts

The *ITAA36* and *ITAA97* are incorporated and required to be 'read as one' with the *International Tax Agreements Act 1953* (s 4(1) *International Tax Agreements Act 1953*). Similarly, the *FBTAA* is incorporated and required to be 'read as one' with the *International Tax Agreements Act 1953* (s 4AA(1) *International Tax Agreements Act 1953*). To the extent that there is any inconsistency, the provisions in the DTAs generally prevail over any conflicting provisions in the *ITAA36*, *ITAA97* or *FBTAA*. An important exception to this rule is that the DTAs do not limit the operation of the general anti-avoidance provisions in pt IVA *ITAA36* [37.3] or s 67 *FBTAA* [18.21] (ss 4(2), 4AA(2) *International Tax Agreements Act 1953*; s 177B *ITAA36*).

DTA articles

Although each DTA has similar features, their terms are not identical since each DTA has evolved out of separate negotiations between Australia and the respective Contracting States. Moreover, while the individual articles in the DTAs are modelled on those in the OECD MTC, there are many variations to these articles. It is therefore necessary to consult the specific articles of a particular DTA to resolve any issues that may arise under it. Typically, there are around 30 articles in each DTA. Some of the main areas covered by these articles and the approaches they adopt are outlined below.

Application articles

Each DTA commences with a set of articles that specify who the DTA applies to and the kinds of Australian and foreign taxes that are covered by the DTA. In general, each DTA applies to 'persons who are residents of one or more of the Contracting States'. All of Australia's DTAs are concerned with income tax. Some of the more recent DTAs also cover PRRT and FBT. In addition, the DTAs also expressly apply to 'any identical or substantially similar taxes' imposed after the signing of the agreement.

Definition articles

The DTAs contain a number of articles that define the meanings of key terms, such as 'resident' and 'permanent establishment' [32.5]. The concept of a resident is important as the DTAs apply to residents of the Contracting States. The concept of a PE is important as it is used to determine whether a Contracting State has the right to tax the profits of an enterprise of the other Contracting State.

Distributive articles

The bulk of the articles in DTAs are distributive articles. The object of these articles is to allocate taxing rights between the Contracting States in respect of particular categories of income (eg business profits, income from employment, dividends, interest and royalties) [32.6]. Allocations are achieved by the Contracting States agreeing to reciprocally restrict the operation of their general tax laws in accordance with the terms of the relevant agreement. In this regard, the DTAs operate purely as a 'shield' to prevent double taxation, not as a 'sword' to provide countries with additional taxing rights. As Lindgren J explained in *Undershaft No 1 Ltd v FC of T*; *Undershaft No 2 BV v FC of T* 2009 ATC ¶20-091 (at [46]):

> A DTA does not give a Contracting State power to tax, or oblige it to tax an amount over which it is allocated the right to tax by the DTA. Rather, a DTA avoids the potential for double taxation by restricting one Contracting State's taxing power.

In some cases, the DTAs allocate taxing rights exclusively to the country in which the taxpayer is resident. In other cases, both the country of residence and the country of source are allowed to share taxing rights. To provide relief against double taxation in such cases, the DTAs generally require a Contracting State to provide its residents with credits for tax paid in the other Contracting State.

Other articles

The DTAs also contain a variety of other articles. For example, certain DTAs contain articles to prevent taxation discrimination based on nationality [32.7]. Some DTAs also contain a 'mutual agreement procedure' ('MAP') for resolving DTA disputes outside a country's normal tax appeal and review process [32.8]. The DTAs also generally contain articles that require the competent authorities of the Contracting States to exchange information with each other to help tackle international tax avoidance and evasion [32.9]. In addition, some recent DTAs, such as the Australia-New Zealand DTA, include an article that requires the Contracting States to 'lend assistance to each other in the collection of revenue claims'. The way in which Australia addresses its obligations under this article is discussed at [33.10].

Additional Benefits and Tax Information Exchange Agreements

In addition to entering into DTAs with the countries mentioned in the table above, Australia has also entered into Additional Benefits Agreements ('ABAs') and Tax Information Exchange Agreements ('TIEAs') with many of the jurisdictions that it does not have DTAs.

ABAs are essentially mini DTAs that only cover discrete and limited topics. They are therefore nowhere near as comprehensive as DTAs. Australia has ABAs with Aruba, the British Virgin Islands, the Cook Islands, Guernsey, Isle of Man, Jersey, the Marshall Islands, Mauritius and Samoa.

TIEAs are designed to assist the 'Contracting Parties' with the exchange of information relevant for the administration and enforcement of their tax laws and assist with identifying secretive activities undertaken in tax havens. Australia has TIEAs with the 36 jurisdictions listed in the table at [33.2].

[32.4] Multilateral convention

A number of Australia's DTAs have been modified under the *Multilateral Convention to Implement Tax Treaty Related Measures to Prevent Base Erosion and Profit Shifting* ('MLI') [32.3]. The MLI is a multilateral instrument developed by the OECD to enable countries to upgrade provisions in their existing treaties to combat international 'base erosion and profit shifting' ('BEPS') [33.3]. The MLI contains articles that address certain BEPS actions and allows countries to expeditiously transpose the MLI articles into their existing DTAs. As at May 2023, 100 jurisdictions have signed the MLI (although 19 of these jurisdictions still need to ratify it). Australia signed the MLI on 7 June 2017 and ratified it on 26 September 2018. The *Treasury Laws Amendment (OECD Multilateral Instrument) Act 2018* (Cth) amended the *International Tax Agreements Act 1953* to give the MLI the force of law in Australia from 1 January 2019.

Countries can tailor adoption of the MLI articles to suit their particular circumstances. While some articles are mandatory (eg art 7 relating to treaty abuse), most articles are optional. Countries may choose to only adopt the mandatory articles. Alternatively, they may choose to cherry-pick one or more optional articles, which they can also adopt with or without reservations. A DTA is only modified by the MLI where both treaty partners have nominated the DTA to be a 'Covered Tax Agreement'. Where this is not the case, the DTA is unaffected by the MLI. Countries must notify the OECD of their MLI position (ie they must identify their Covered Tax Agreements and the articles they wish to adopt with details of any reservations they choose to make to those articles). It is only where there is a bilateral match that the MLI modifies the relevant articles in the DTA.

As each country may choose to adopt different articles in the MLI, the effect on their DTAs depends on the MLI positions adopted by their treaty partners. For example, although Australia's treaties with both New Zealand and the United Kingdom have been modified by the MLI, only Australia and New Zealand have ratified art 8 (relating to dividend transfer transactions). Consequently, it is only Australia's treaty with New Zealand (and not its treaty with the United Kingdom) that is modified by art 8.

Worldwide, around 1,850 DTAs are covered by the MLI. To date, Australia's DTAs with the following countries have been modified by the MLI: Belgium, Canada, Chile, China, Czech Republic, Denmark, Finland, France, Hungary, India, Indonesia, Ireland, Japan, Korea, Malaysia, Malta, the Netherlands, New Zealand, Norway, Poland, Romania, Russia, Singapore, Slovakia, Spain, Thailand and the United Kingdom. The Government has prepared synthesised texts of Australia's modified DTAs to make them easier to read. These are available from the Treasury website [2.5].

[32.5] Key terms used in DTAs

The DTAs contain definitions of a number of key terms that are crucial to the interpretation of the agreements. Two of the most important terms used in the DTAs are 'resident' and 'permanent establishment'.

Definition of 'resident'

Under the DTAs, an entity's residence is determined according to the ordinary residency rules of the Contracting States (see art 4 OECD MTC). However, where this results in an overlap, the DTAs contain 'tie-breaker rules' to prevent dual residency. The nature of the tie-breaker rules differs under the various DTAs. The rules operate on a hierarchical or cascading basis and generally work as follows:

- **Individuals.** In the case of individuals, the tie-breaker rule generally provides that where the individual would otherwise be a resident of both Contracting States, the individual is treated as a resident solely of the Contracting State in which he or she has a 'permanent home'. If the individual has a permanent home in both Contracting States or does not have a permanent home in either of them, he or she is usually deemed to be a resident solely of the Contracting State in which he or she has an 'habitual abode'. If the individual has an habitual abode in both Contracting States, or does not have an habitual abode in either of them, he or she is usually deemed to be a resident solely of the Contracting State with which his or her 'personal and economic relations' are closer. If this cannot be determined, then he or she will usually be a resident solely of the Contracting State in which he or she is a 'national'. If the individual is a national of both Contracting States, or neither of them, then the Contracting States are usually required to settle the matter by agreement.
- **Other entities.** In the case of other entities (eg companies), the tie-breaker rule generally provides that where the entity would otherwise be a resident of both Contracting States, the entity will be a resident solely of the Contracting State in which its 'place of effective management' is situated. Where this cannot be determined, then the Contracting States are usually required to settle the matter by agreement.

A tie-breaker rule was applied in *Tan v FC of T* 2016 ATC ¶10-443. In this case, the taxpayer qualified as a resident of Australia in the 2014/15 income year under both the 'resides test' and '183-days test' in s 6(1) *ITAA36* [30.2]. However, he also qualified as a resident of Malaysia under s 7(1)(a) of the *Income Tax Act 1967* (Malaysia) on the basis that he was in Malaysia for more than 182 days of the 2015 calendar year. As he was a resident of both Australia and Malaysia under the respective countries' domestic tax laws, the tie-breaker rule in art 4 of the Australia–Malaysia DTA needed to be considered. The AAT found that the taxpayer had both a 'permanent home' and an 'habitual home' in Australia and Malaysia, but as his 'personal and economic relations' were closer to Australia, he was deemed to be an Australian resident under the DTA. This meant his entire income (including foreign income) was subject to tax in Australia.

Some of the factors that demonstrated the taxpayer's personal and economic relations with Australia were that he was an Australian citizen and had an Australian passport. His wife was a permanent resident and purchased a home in Australia. Their baby was born in Australia and the taxpayer's parents lived in Australia. The taxpayer also identified himself as a resident returning to Australia on immigration cards and stated that he intended to live in Australia for 12 months. He had an ABN and his main business location was in Australia. He kept a car in Australia, held an Australian driver's licence, and did not hold a licence from any other country. He was also registered on the Australian Electoral Roll and entitled to Medicare benefits.

More recently, in *FC of T v Pike* 2020 ATC ¶20-764, the Full Federal Court considered the tie-breaker rule in art 4 of the Australia–Thailand DTA. The Court held that although the taxpayer was a resident of Australia according to ordinary concepts, he should be deemed a resident of Thailand under the tie-breaker rule as his personal and economic relations were closer to Thailand than Australia. Davies, White and Steward JJ explained (at 39) that the use of the expression 'personal and economic relations' in the tie-breaker rule 'poses a composite test and in each case it will be a matter of fact and degree as to whether a taxpayer's personal and economic relations, viewed as a whole, support ties closer to one contracting state over the other contracting state'. Their Honours also examined the terms 'permanent home' and 'habitual abode' as used in the tie-breaker rule. They noted that rented accommodation can constitute a permanent home and there is no warrant for imputing that a person's habitual abode is the place where they have spent the most days.

The term 'resident' should be distinguished from the term 'national', which is also used in the tie-breaker rules. A national of a Contracting State is not necessarily also a resident of that Contracting State. Rather, a national is simply an individual who possesses the nationality or citizenship of the Contracting State, or any legal person, company partnership or association that derives its status as such from the laws in force in the Contracting State. The concept of a national is also important for the purposes of the government service [32.6] and non-discrimination [32.7] articles.

Definition of 'permanent establishment'

Under the DTAs, a PE is generally defined as a 'fixed place of business through which the business of an enterprise is wholly or partly carried on' (see art 5 OECD MTC). This definition, however, operates subject to a long list of inclusions and exclusions. For instance, the DTAs generally deem certain places to be PEs (eg a place of management, a branch, an office, a factory, a workshop, a mine and an agricultural property). A building site that lasts for a specified period (eg typically six or nine months) can also constitute a PE. Likewise, the maintenance of substantial equipment in a jurisdiction can sometimes give rise to a PE in that jurisdiction. By way of contrast, the use of facilities solely for the purpose of storage of goods will usually not constitute a PE.

An enterprise will usually have a PE in a Contracting State where it carries on business in that state through an agent who has authority to conclude contracts on behalf of the enterprise and habitually exercises that authority in that state. However, the enterprise will not have a PE in the state where it merely carries on business in that state through an independent agent who is acting in the ordinary course of business.

[32.6] Distributive articles in DTAs

The distributive articles in DTAs allocate taxing rights between the Contracting States in respect of particular categories of income. They use two key expressions ('shall be taxable only' and 'may be taxed') to allocate taxing rights. A Contracting State has *exclusive* taxing rights in relation to a particular kind of income where the income 'shall be taxable only' in the Contracting State. A Contracting State has *non-exclusive* taxing rights in relation to a particular kind of income where the income 'may be taxed' in the Contracting State.

Broad approaches

In essence, the DTAs use two broad approaches to prevent double taxation:

- The first (less common) approach reserves the right to tax certain classes of income solely to the country in which the recipient of the income resides.
- The second (more common) approach allows the country of source to tax certain classes of income, subject to the proviso that if the country in which the recipient of the income resides also taxes the income, the country of residence is required to provide a credit for tax paid in the country of source.

The approach used depends on the kind of income concerned. The different ways that Australia's DTAs *generally* deal with some common forms of income are briefly outlined below. The headings in the discussion refer to relevant article numbers contained in the most recent version of the OECD MTC. The article numbers are provided purely for reference purposes and do not necessarily correspond to the article numbers in Australia's DTAs, as many of the DTAs are based on earlier versions of the OECD MTC. It should also be noted that the terms of the DTAs do not always correspond exactly with the terms in the OECD MTC. In addition, many DTAs have been modified by the *MLI* [32.4].

Real property (art 6 OECD MTC)

The DTAs provide that income from real property (which includes leasehold interests and mining rights) may be taxed in the country in which that property is situated.

Example Inga is a resident of Norway. She owns an office building in Australia that is leased to tenants. As the building is situated in Australia, the rent she earns from it can be taxed in Australia.

Business profits (art 7 OECD MTC)

The DTAs provide that the business profits of an 'enterprise' resident in one country shall be taxable only in that country, unless the enterprise carries on business through a PE situated in the other country. If the enterprise carries on business through a PE situated in the other country, the profits may generally only be taxed in the other country to the extent that they are attributable to the particular PE.

Example US Co is a company that is a resident of the United States. It carries on part of its business through a PE in Australia. Australia can tax US Co's business profits to the extent that those profits are attributable to its PE in Australia.

If US Co did not have a PE in Australia, Australia would not be able to tax any of its business profits, even though those profits might have an Australian source.

International shipping and transport profits (art 8 OECD MTC)

The DTAs provide that international shipping and air transport profits shall be taxable only in the respective operator's country of residence. There are, however, certain exceptions to this rule. For instance, some DTAs provide that the profits may be taxed in the other country where they are from operations of ships or aircraft confined solely to places in that country.

Example S Co is a company that is a resident of Switzerland. It operates an international air transport business under which it transports freight by air between Switzerland and various other countries (including Australia). Its profits relating to freight transported between Australia and Switzerland cannot be taxed in Australia.

Dividends (art 10 OECD MTC)

The DTAs allow dividends to be taxed in both the country in which the beneficial owner of the dividends (eg the shareholder) is a resident as well as the country in which the company paying the dividends is a resident. However, this rule operates subject to the proviso that the tax in the country in which the company paying the dividends is a resident cannot exceed a prescribed amount.

Under most DTAs, the prescribed amount is 15% of the gross amount of the dividends. However, depending on the circumstances, it can be higher or lower than this amount under certain DTAs. For example, the prescribed amount under Australia's DTAs with Fiji and Kiribati is 20%. By way of contrast, under Australia's DTAs with Canada, Finland, Israel, New Zealand, Norway, the United States and the United Kingdom, the prescribed amount is generally reduced to 5% if the shareholder is a company which holds directly at least 10% of the voting power in the company paying the dividends. Australia's DTAs with Finland, New Zealand, Norway, the United States and the United Kingdom also generally exempt dividends from tax if the shareholder is a company and it owned shares representing 80% or more of the voting power of the company paying the dividends for a 12-month period ending on the date the dividend is declared.

Example Aussie Co is an Australian company that pays an unfranked dividend of $10,000 to US Co (a United States resident company) and Don (a United States resident individual) who each hold 12% of the voting power in Aussie Co. Both Australia and the United States may tax the dividends. However, in the case of the dividend paid to US Co, the amount of Australian tax cannot exceed $500 (ie 5% × $10,000), whereas, in the case of the dividend paid to Don, the amount of Australian tax cannot exceed $1,500 (ie 15% × $10,000). The Australian tax is collected under the withholding tax regime [31.11].

Interest (art 11 OECD MTC)

The DTAs allow interest to be taxed in the country in which the recipient is resident as well as the country in which the interest arises (ie has its source), subject to the proviso that the tax in the country in which the interest arises cannot exceed a prescribed amount.

The prescribed amount is generally 10% of the gross amount of the interest. However, it is 12% under Australia's DTA with Argentina and 15% under Australia's DTAs with Korea, Malaysia and Malta. In addition, some DTAs have two prescribed amounts depending on the nature of the entity deriving the interest. These amounts are 5% and 10% under Australia's DTAs with Chile and Israel, 10% and 15% under Australia's DTAs with Mexico and the Philippines, and 10% and 25% under Australia's DTA with Thailand. Furthermore, while the prescribed amount under Australia's DTAs with South Africa, the United Kingdom and the United States is 10%, the DTAs exempt specified kinds of interest from being taxed in the country of source.

Example F Co is a French company that has deposited money with A Co, an Australian bank. A Co pays F Co $100,000 of interest on the deposit. Both Australia and France may tax the interest. However, the amount of Australian tax on the interest cannot exceed $10,000 (ie 10% of the interest). The Australian tax is collected under the withholding tax regime [31.11].

Royalties (art 12 OECD MTC)

The DTAs allow royalties to be taxed in the country in which the recipient is resident as well as the country in which the royalties arise (ie have their source), subject to the proviso that the tax in the country in which the royalties arise cannot exceed a prescribed amount.

The prescribed amount is generally 10% of the gross amount of the royalties. However, it is 5% under Australia's DTAs with Finland, France, Germany, Israel, Japan, New Zealand, Norway, South

Africa, Switzerland, the United Kingdom and the United States; 12.5% under Australia's DTA with Taipei; and 15% under Australia's DTAs with Kiribati, Korea and Malaysia. In addition, some DTAs have two prescribed amounts depending on the nature of the royalties. These amounts are 5% and 10% under Australia's DTA with Chile; 10% and 15% under Australia's DTAs with Argentina, India and Indonesia; and 15% and 25% under Australia's DTA with the Philippines.

Example P Co is an Australian publisher that publishes a book written by Steve who is a New Zealand resident. Steve is entitled to royalties of $10,000 relating to sales of the book. Both Australia and New Zealand may tax the royalties. However, the Australian tax payable on the royalties cannot exceed $500 (ie 5% of the royalties). The Australian tax is collected under the withholding tax regime [31.11].

Alienation of property (art 13 OECD MTC)

Australia's DTAs generally contain an alienation of property article. The article provides that income, profits or gains derived by a resident of one country from the alienation of real property situated in the other country may be taxed in that other country.

It also usually provides that income, profits or gains derived by a resident of one country from the alienation of any shares or comparable interests deriving more than 50% of their value directly or indirectly from real property situated in the other country may be taxed in that other country.

In addition, the article also typically states that income, profits or gains from the alienation of property, other than real property, that forms part of the business property of a PE which an enterprise of one country has in the other country may be taxed in that other country. This also expressly extends to income, profits or gains from the alienation of the PE itself.

Independent personal services income (former art 14 OECD MTC)

Many of Australia's earlier DTAs contain an independent personal services income article that is based on former art 14 of the OECD MTC (which was removed from the MTC in 2000). According to this article, independent personal services income (eg the income of a self-employed lawyer) shall be taxable only in the country in which the recipient is resident. Importantly, however, such income may also be taxed in the country of source in specified cases, such as where:

- the recipient is present in the source country for more than 183 days in the income year, or
- the income is attributable to a fixed base regularly available to the recipient in the source country.

The latest DTAs no longer contain an independent personal services income article. Instead, personal services income is dealt with under the business profits article (art 7 OECD MTC).

Income from employment (art 15 OECD MTC)

The DTAs generally provide that salary, wages and similar remuneration shall be taxable only in the country in which the recipient is a resident, unless the employment is exercised in the other country. However, even if the employment is exercised in the other country, such income is generally taxable only in the country of residence if:

- the duration of the recipient's visit in the source country does not exceed a specified limit (usually 90 or 183 days)
- the salary is paid by a non-resident of the source country, and

- the remuneration is not deductible in determining the profits attributable to a PE of the employer in the other country.

Under certain DTAs, visiting academics and teachers are exempt from tax on their remuneration in the source country provided their visit does not exceed two years.

> ***Example*** Albert is an Australian resident who is employed by an Australian company. He is posted to New Zealand to work on a project for seven months and is paid salary by his Australian employer. Both Australia and New Zealand can tax him on his salary.
>
> If, on the other hand, Albert was posted to New Zealand for only one month, then, provided his salary is not deductible in determining the taxable profits of a PE of his Australian employer in New Zealand, his income is only taxable in Australia.

Directors' fees (art 16 OECD MTC)

The DTAs usually provide that directors' fees and similar payments derived by a resident of a country in their capacity as a member of the board of directors of a company which is a resident of the other country may be taxed in the other country.

> ***Example*** Amanda is an Irish resident. She is a director of an Australian resident company and attends board meetings six times a year in Australia. Her director fees relating to these meetings may be taxed in Australia.

Entertainers (art 17 OECD MTC)

The DTAs generally provide that income derived by entertainers (eg theatre, motion picture, radio or television artistes and musicians and sportspersons) from their personal activities as entertainers may be taxed in the country in which the activities are exercised. This article is typically expressed in such a way that it prevails over the more general business profits article and the income from employment article.

Some DTAs, however, contain exceptions to the rule. For example, Australia's DTA with New Zealand provides that it does not apply to sportspersons who are members of a recognised team that regularly plays in a league competition organised and conducted in both Contracting States, except in respect of performance as a member of a national representative team of either Contracting State. Where the exception applies, the business profits or income from employment articles apply instead.

> ***Example*** Taylor is a singer who is resident of the United States. She visits Australia for a month to perform at various concerts. Her income from these performances may be taxed in Australia.

Pensions and annuities (art 18 OECD MTC)

The DTAs generally provide that pensions and annuities paid to a resident of a Contracting State shall be taxable only in that state. There are, however, some exceptions to this rule. For example, Australia's DTA with Canada provides that pensions or annuities arising in a Contracting State may be taxed in the other Contracting State, subject to the proviso that the tax charged shall not exceed the lesser of 15% of the pension or annuity, or the tax that would be payable in respect of the pension of annuity if the recipient were a resident of the Contracting State in which the pension or annuity arises.

> ***Example*** Pasquale moved to Australia from Italy several years ago and has become an Australian resident. He receives a pension from Italy. The pension is taxable only in Australia.

Government service (art 19 OECD MTC)

The DTAs provide that remuneration paid by a Contracting State to individuals in respect of services rendered to the state is generally taxable only in that state. However, where the services are rendered in the other state and the official is a resident and national of the other state, the remuneration is generally taxable only in the other state (provided the individual did not become a resident of that state solely for the purposes of rendering the services).

> ***Example*** Rod is an Australian national who works as an Austrade representative for the Australian Government in New Zealand. His remuneration is taxable only in Australia. Arie is a national and resident of Israel who works for the Australian Government as an interpreter in Israel. His remuneration is taxable only in Israel.

Other income (art 21 OECD MTC)

The DTAs generally contain an article that deals with other income not specifically mentioned in the other articles. Other income is generally only taxable in the country of residence unless it is effectively connected with a PE in the other country, in which case it may also be taxed in the other country.

[32.7] Non-discrimination article

A number of DTAs contain a 'non-discrimination article' which is modelled on art 24 OECD MTC. This article is designed to prevent taxation discrimination based on 'nationality'. It provides that 'nationals' of a Contracting State shall not be subject to any taxation or any requirement connected therewith, which is other or more burdensome than the taxation and other requirements to which nationals of the other Contracting State in the same circumstances, in particular, with respect to residence, may be subjected.

A breach of this article will arise, for example, if two persons who are residents of the same country are treated differently because one is an Australian national while the other is a New Zealand national. There is, however, no breach merely because different taxation treatment is accorded to a New Zealand resident compared to an Australian resident as the two taxpayers are not in the same circumstances since they are residents of different countries. Similarly, the article is not breached if, for example, one country taxes the income of non-residents at a higher rate than the income of its residents or provides imputation credits only to residents and not to non-residents.

The non-discrimination article was considered in *Addy v FC of T* 2021 ATC ¶20-803. This case concerned a national of the United Kingdom who travelled to Australia on a British passport and held a subclass 417 (Working Holiday) visa. The taxpayer lived and worked in Australia between August 2015 and May 2017. During the 2017 income year, she earned $26,576 of taxable income from casual employment as a waitress. The Commissioner found that the taxpayer was an Australian resident during the income year and taxed her at the special rates applicable to working holiday makers under pt III of sch 7 *ITRA* (which applied a 15% tax rate on the first $37,000 of working holiday taxable income) [8.8]. The taxpayer argued that taxing her under these rates contravened the non-discrimination article located in art 25 of the Australia–United Kingdom DTA and submitted that she should have instead been taxed at the ordinary resident rates under pt I of sch 7 *ITRA* (which included a tax-free threshold on the first $18,200 of taxable income) [8.8].

The High Court held that imposing the special rates of tax under pt III of sch 7 *ITRA* on the taxpayer contravened art 25 of the DTA. The High Court noted that this article requires a comparison between a United Kingdom national and an Australian national who is, otherwise than with respect to nationality, 'in the same circumstances, in particular with respect to residence'. The Court held that the 'same circumstances' cannot include being or not being the holder of a working holiday visa, because that status depends on the person's nationality. As an Australian national deriving taxable income from the same source during the same period would have been taxed at a lower rate under pt I of sch 7 *ITRA*, more burdensome taxation was imposed on the taxpayer owing to her nationality.

It is important to understand that the outcome in *Addy* does not mean that the special rates of tax in pt III of sch 7 *ITRA* are invalid. The special rates were not applicable in that case due to the existence of the non-discrimination article in the Australia–United Kingdom DTA, which prevails over Australia's domestic tax laws to the extent of any inconsistency. Nationals of countries with which Australia does not have a DTA and nationals of countries with which Australia has a DTA that does not contain a similar non-discrimination article are unaffected by the decision. The Commissioner has stated he considers that *Addy* will only be relevant to working holiday visa holders that are both Australian tax residents and nationals of either Chile, Finland, Germany, Israel, Japan, Norway, Turkiye or the United Kingdom (DIS S25/2021).

[32.8] Mutual agreement procedure

Many DTAs contain a 'mutual agreement procedure' ('MAP') modelled on art 25 of the OECD MTC for resolving DTA disputes. The MAP lies outside a country's domestic laws, as it operates in addition to its normal tax appeal and review process.

Article 25 of the OECD MTC provides that where a person considers that the actions of one or both of the Contracting States result, or will result, for the person in taxation not in accordance with the provisions of the DTA, they may, irrespective of the remedies provided by the domestic law of those States, present their case to the 'competent authority' of the Contracting State of which they are a resident. The competent authorities are typically the relevant revenue authorities of the respective Contracting States. In the case of Australia, it is the Commissioner of Taxation. Australian residents can apply to a special division with the ATO, known as the 'Australian Competent Authority', for assistance with MAP disputes.

Under art 25, a case must be presented to a competent authority within three years from the first notification of the action resulting in taxation not in accordance with the provisions of the DTA. If the competent authority is not itself able to arrive at a satisfactory solution, it is required to resolve the case by mutual agreement with the competent authority of the other Contracting State. For this purpose, art 25 provides that the competent authorities 'may communicate with each other directly, including through a joint commission consisting of themselves or their representatives'.

The MAP has been designed to be used in situations where the Contracting States take different views on the application of a DTA to a particular case. For example, it has been used where Contracting States adopt different views of the attribution of income or expenses of an enterprise to a PE resulting in double taxation (which is precisely what the DTAs were designed to avoid). In practice, the MAP has significant shortcomings as it only requires the competent authorities to 'endeavour' to resolve a dispute. There is no obligation to actually arrive at a resolution, nor any deadline for a resolution to take place. There is also no arbitrator involved. This places taxpayers in a relatively weak position as they have no way of forcing the competent authorities to reach agreement.

[32.9] Exchange of information

One of the important roles of DTAs is to assist countries prevent international tax avoidance and evasion. The DTAs therefore contain exchange of information articles that are generally based on art 26 of the OECD MTC. According to these articles, the Contracting States are required to exchange information that is 'foreseeably relevant' to the administration and enforcement of their domestic tax laws or the provisions of their respective DTAs. The exchange of information is not limited to information about residents of the respective Contracting States.

Information received by a Contracting State is treated as secret in the same manner as information obtained by the Contracting State under its domestic tax laws. It can only be disclosed to persons and authorities (including courts) concerned with the assessment, collection, enforcement or prosecution of its relevant tax laws.

[32.10] Interpretation of DTA articles

Since DTAs are international agreements, they raise special interpretation issues. The ATO's position on a number of these issues is outlined in TR 2001/13.

A leading Australian case dealing with the interpretation of DTAs is *Thiel v FC of T* 90 ATC 4717. The issue in this case was whether profits made by a Swiss resident from the sale of certain units and shares were assessable under former s 26AAA *ITAA36*. The outcome depended on whether the taxpayer's activities constituted an 'enterprise of one of the Contracting States' under the Australia-Switzerland DTA. The High Court found that there was no established meaning of the term 'enterprise' under Australian tax law and that it was appropriate to use the OECD Commentary to interpret the articles in the DTA. The Court also held (at 4727) that, as the DTAs are international treaties, they are 'to be interpreted in accordance with the rules of interpretation recognised by international lawyers'. These rules are codified in the *Vienna Convention on the Law of Treaties*, to which Australia is a party.

In *FC of T v Lamesa Holdings BV* 97 ATC 4752, the Full Federal Court was required to interpret Australia's DTA with the Netherlands. The Court relied on McHugh J's judgment in *Applicant A v Minister for Immigration and Ethnic Affairs* (1997) 190 CLR 225, where his Honour considered the *Vienna Convention on the Law of Treaties* and laid down a number of principles for interpreting treaties. The key principles may be summarised as follows:

- Courts should adopt a 'holistic approach' in interpreting treaties.
- Courts should focus on the 'four corners of the actual text' of the treaty—the text is the starting point in interpreting treaties and necessarily has 'primacy' in the interpretation process.
- Courts should, in addition to having regard to the text, also have regard to the 'context, object and purpose' of the treaty provisions.
- Courts should interpret treaties in a more 'liberal manner' than they construe domestic legislation—the lack of precision in treaties means that they 'cannot be expected to be applied with taut logical precision'.

[32.11] QUESTIONS

1. In what circumstances might double taxation arise and how do the DTAs prevent double taxation? What do the DTA articles cover and what happens if there is an inconsistency between the articles and the provisions in the *ITAA36* or *ITAA97*? What is the role of the MLI and what is its effect on Australia's DTAs?

2. How do the DTAs define a 'resident'? Why is it important to determine whether an enterprise is carried on through a PE in a Contracting State?
3. Oskar is an Australian resident employed by an Australian company as an engineer. He is sent to work in Singapore for nine months. While in Singapore, he also takes on a part-time job as a tutor at the National University of Singapore. He derives rent from leasing out his Australian home and purchases a Singapore apartment which he leases to tenants. All of Oskar's rent is paid into a Singapore bank account on which he earns interest. How is Oskar's income taxed?
4. What is the role of a non-discrimination article in a DTA? Did it apply in *Addy v FC of T* 2021 ATC ¶20-803?
5. Discuss the role of the MAP in a DTA.
6. What exchange of information requirements do DTAs usually contain? How can this information be used by the Contracting States?

33 BASE EROSION AND PROFIT SHIFTING AND INTERNATIONAL TAX ENFORCEMENT

[33.1] Introduction

This chapter focuses on the problem of 'base erosion and profit shifting' ('BEPS'). BEPS typically involves large multinational enterprises ('MNEs') entering into transactions that exploit gaps, loopholes, and mismatches in the tax rules of different jurisdictions to artificially shift profits from high to low tax locations. International tax havens are commonly used for this purpose [33.2].

To help countries tackle BEPS, the OECD implemented the 'BEPS project', which has over 100 participating jurisdictions [33.3]. As a consequence of this project, Australia has introduced several new measures to strengthen its tax system. These measures complement its existing transfer pricing [33.4] and thin capitalisation [33.5] regimes.

One of the most significant aspects of the BEPS project has been the development of a 'two-pillar solution on global tax reform' [33.6]. This initiative aims to re-allocate profits of large MNEs to the jurisdictions where they are earned and ensure that MNEs pay a worldwide minimum corporate tax rate of at least 15%. Australia, like many other countries, is planning to implement this reform. This chapter outlines how the new rules are proposed to operate.

The chapter also discusses a number of BEPS measures that relate to 'significant global entities' [33.7]. In addition, as financial secrecy is a key feature of tax haven activity various reporting regimes designed to assist revenue authorities collect information about international transactions in order to effectively administer their tax laws are also examined [33.8]–[33.9]. The chapter concludes with a discussion of the challenges faced by revenue authorities in collecting international tax debts and examines the reciprocal enforcement arrangements implemented to address this problem [33.10].

[33.2] Tax havens

The ability to invest and relocate businesses overseas has become much easier in recent years due to a number of factors, including:

- the rapid globalisation of the world economy
- the progressive breakdown of trade and investment barriers

- the explosive growth in electronic commerce and banking, and
- the evolution of an increasingly mobile workforce.

As a consequence, it is not surprising that there is a great deal of international movement of capital and resources. In order to generate the highest possible returns, investors and businesses have a natural tendency to gravitate towards jurisdictions with low tax rates or attractive tax incentives. As low taxation can attract capital inflows into a country and discourage capital outflows from a country, it is not surprising that significant tax competition exists between nations and that several tax havens have sprung up around the world.

What is a 'tax haven'?

Although the term 'tax haven' is widely used, it is difficult to precisely define. A tax haven is usually described in the literature in vague and nebulous terms as a country or territory that engages in unfair tax competition and harmful tax practices. According to the Tax Justice Network—an organisation that opposes tax havens and promotes transparency in international finance—a tax haven is generally 'a country or jurisdiction that enables multinational corporations and individuals to escape the rule of law in the countries where they operate and live, and to pay less tax than they should in those countries'.

Tax havens generally share a number of features:

- they impose very low (or nil) tax rates
- they provide tax concessions to persons who do not have a substantive local presence or undertake any real economic activity in the relevant country or territory
- they lack transparent legal systems and do not readily exchange tax information with foreign revenue authorities, and
- they actively promote themselves as offshore banking and financial centres.

Tax havens are often small island nations or principalities whose economies are heavily driven by their status as low-tax jurisdictions with secretive financial systems rather than by more fundamental economic factors.

Problems with tax havens

Higher-taxing countries argue that tax havens undermine fair tax competition and erode public confidence in their tax systems. They contend that tax havens siphon revenue from their coffers, distort investment and business decisions, interfere with international trade and commerce and facilitate tax avoidance and money laundering.

It is impossible to quantify the revenue lost by higher-taxing countries to tax havens. This is particularly the case given the secrecy that usually surrounds their activities (especially banking transactions). Various organisations have, nevertheless, attempted to provide rough estimates of the cost of tax havens to higher-taxing countries. For example, the Tax Justice Network has estimated that MNEs are shifting over US$1 trillion in profits every year to tax havens.

While revenue leakage is clearly a problem for higher-taxing countries, it is important to realise that not all transactions associated with tax havens involve tax evasion or avoidance. Many lawful commercial transactions also take place in these jurisdictions. Revenue authorities are principally concerned with those transactions that use tax havens illegitimately for concealment. As the ATO stated in its 2009 publication, *Tax Havens and Tax Administration* (at 11):

> Concealment is our main concern—in particular, those schemes and arrangements that use secrecy laws to conceal assets and income that are subject to Australian tax.

The Corporate Tax Haven Index, published by the Tax Justice Network, uses various measures to rank the jurisdictions considered to be the most complicit in facilitating companies to underpay income tax. In 2021, the top 10 jurisdictions were (in order): the British Virgin Islands, the Cayman Islands, Bermuda, the Netherlands, Switzerland, Luxembourg, Hong Kong, Jersey, Singapore and the United Arab Emirates.

OECD response to combating tax haven activity

In order to protect their revenue bases, higher-taxing countries have sought the assistance of international organisations, such as the OECD, to combat illegitimate tax haven activity. Over the years, the OECD has released several reports on harmful tax practices and has urged its members to adopt a concerted approach towards curbing tax haven activity. In particular, it has suggested that higher-taxing countries should consider disallowing deductions, exemptions and credits to residents of countries that are involved in harmful tax practices. It has also recommended that higher-taxing countries introduce special anti-avoidance measures such as:

- transfer pricing rules (which adopt arm's length prices in relation to transactions that inappropriately shift profits overseas)
- thin capitalisation rules (which restrict debt deductions available to certain entities with high levels of debt compared to equity), and
- accruals taxation rules (which tax residents on income sheltered in low-tax countries through controlled entities).

Australia has adopted all of these measures. The transfer pricing rules are discussed at [33.4], the thin capitalisation rules are discussed at [33.5], and the accruals taxation rules are discussed in Chapter 34. In addition, as mentioned above, Australia is actively involved in the OECD's BEPS project and it has implemented a number of BEPS actions [33.3].

Tax Information Exchange Agreements

Tax havens are traditionally uncooperative about sharing financial information with other countries and hide behind their banking secrecy rules. As information sharing is central in the battle against harmful tax competition, the OECD established the 'Global Forum on Transparency and Exchange of Information' in 2000. The Global Forum has been instrumental in developing internationally accepted standards on the exchange of information for tax purposes.

As a consequence of work undertaken by the Global Forum, a *Model Agreement on Exchange of Information on Tax Matters* was released in 2002. This document was designed to improve transparency of international financial arrangements through the use of model TIEAs. It was developed by the OECD in cooperation with non-OECD countries and it has been endorsed by the G20 Finance Ministers and Central Bank Governors as well as the United Nations Committee of Experts on International Cooperation in Tax Matters.

TIEAs are bilateral agreements that specify rules and procedures for exchanging information between the competent authorities in the Contracting States. They require the Contracting States to have appropriate frameworks in place to exchange information that is foreseeably relevant to the determination, assessment and collection of their taxes, the recovery and enforcement of tax claims, and the investigation or prosecution of tax matters. Information is only required to be exchanged between the authorities 'on request'. This means that a jurisdiction is not required to provide information it has not been asked for by the other jurisdiction. The request for information can include information held by banks and other financial institutions as well as information regarding the ownership of companies, partnerships and trusts. A Contracting State is, however, not obligated to provide information that is neither held by its authorities nor in the possession or control of persons within its territorial jurisdiction. TIEAs complement the information-sharing rules in DTAs [32.9]. However, unlike DTAs, they do not contain provisions relating to the allocation of taxing rights. Higher-taxing countries have been strongly encouraged to enter into TIEAs with those jurisdictions with which they do not have DTAs. There is considerable international pressure on low-tax countries to enter TIEAs, as it usually leads to their removal from a higher-taxing country's list of tax havens and can enhance their reputation as legitimate offshore financial centres. Over 500 TIEAs have been entered into globally. Australia has TIEAs with the jurisdictions listed below.

Jurisdictions with which Australia has TIEAs		
Jurisdiction	**Date of signing agreement**	**Date of entry into force**
Andorra	24 September 2011	3 December 2012
Anguilla	19 March 2010	17 February 2011
Antigua and Barbuda	30 January 2007	14 December 2009
Aruba	16 December 2009	17 August 2011
Bahamas	30 March 2010	11 January 2011
Bahrain	15 December 2011	15 December 2012
Belize	31 March 2010	11 January 2011
Bermuda	10 November 2005	6 August 2007
British Virgin Islands	27 October 2008	19 April 2010
Brunei	6 August 2013	25 February 2016
Cayman Islands	30 March 2010	14 February 2011
Cook Islands	27 October 2009	2 September 2011
Costa Rica	1 July 2011	4 February 2013
Dominica	30 March 2010	8 December 2011
Gibraltar	25 August 2009	26 July 2010
Grenada	30 March 2010	9 January 2012
Guatemala	26 September 2013	20 January 2018
Guernsey	7 October 2009	27 July 2010
Isle of Man	29 January 2009	5 January 2010
Jersey	10 June 2009	5 January 2010
Liberia	11 August 2011	23 May 2012
Liechtenstein	21 June 2011	21 June 2012
Macao	12 July 2011	18 May 2012
Marshall Islands	12 May 2010	25 November 2011
Mauritius	8 December 2010	25 November 2011
Monaco	1 April 2010	13 June 2011
Montserrat	23 November 2010	25 November 2011
Netherlands Antilles	1 March 2007	4 April 2008
Samoa	16 December 2009	24 February 2012
San Marino	4 March 2010	11 January 2011
St Christopher and Nevis	5 March 2010	11 January 2011

Jurisdictions with which Australia has TIEAs		
Jurisdiction	**Date of signing agreement**	**Date of entry into force**
St Lucia	30 March 2010	10 February 2011
St Vincent and the Grenadines	18 March 2010	11 January 2011
Turks and Caicos Islands	30 March 2010	25 January 2011
Uruguay	10 December 2012	1 July 2014
Vanuatu	21 April 2010	1 September 2011

International pressure on tax havens

The issue of tax competition is extremely controversial, as it is intimately connected with the broader issue of national sovereignty. Low-taxing nations argue that their ability to offer tax incentives to attract foreign investment is critical to their economic survival, and they contend that it is unfair for them to be subjected to international pressure from powerful foreign governments to change their domestic tax laws. Higher-taxing countries nevertheless continue to maintain concerted pressure on tax havens to reform their laws. Much of this is achieved through the work of international organisations such as the OECD, the EU, the G7, the G20, the Financial Actions Taskforce and the International Monetary Fund.

The EU, for example, established a *Code of Conduct* for business taxation in 1997 under which Member States agreed to roll back their harmful tax practices and refrain from introducing them in the future. In 2009, it issued a *Communication* identifying actions that Member States should take to promote 'good governance' in the tax area. The *Communication* emphasised the importance of tax cooperation between Member States and taking action against 'uncooperative third countries'. It also focused on the issues of greater transparency and exchange of information. In 2017, the EU published its first blacklist of uncooperative third countries. This list originally consisted of 17 countries which were considered to fail tax good governance standards and encourage abusive tax practices. Some countries have since been removed from the list after committing to make certain changes, while others have been added. As at February 2023, the list covered: American Samoa, Anguilla, Bahamas, British Virgin Islands, Costa Rica, Fiji, Guam, Marshall Islands, Palau, Panama, Russian Federation, Samoa, Trinidad and Tobago, Turks and Caicos Islands, US Virgin Islands and Vanuatu.

As a consequence of the sustained international pressure on tax havens, considerable progress has been made over recent years in curbing tax haven activity. In particular, several former tax havens have reformed their laws and entered into TIEAs so that they are no longer blacklisted. Tax haven activity nevertheless continues to exist, and remains a concern for the broader international community.

ATO's approach to dealing with tax havens

The ATO has traditionally relied heavily on the Australian Transaction Reports and Analysis Centre ('AUSTRAC') [39.5] to identify tax haven activity and it has used Project Wickenby and the Serious Financial Crimes Taskforce [36.2] to investigate tax haven avoidance and evasion schemes. The ATO also gathers much intelligence about tax havens from its international information exchange arrangements under DTAs and TIEAs and from its involvement with special international organisations, such as the Joint International Taskforce on Shared Information and Collaboration ('JITSIC'), which is a network of over 40 of the world's tax administrations established to collaborate on ways to deal with tax avoidance more effectively.

The Panama and Paradise Papers

The potential scale of worldwide tax evasion was highlighted by the 2016 'Panama Papers' scandal, which involved an anonymous leak of over 11 million confidential documents from the Panamanian law firm Mossack Fonseca. The amount of data leaked (over 2.5 terabytes) was even larger than the 2010 WikiLeaks leak. The documents were first released to a German newspaper, which enlisted the support of the International Consortium of Investigative Journalists ('ICIJ'), a group of journalists and news agencies from around the world, to help verify their authenticity. The documents contained sensitive banking and other information of more than 200,000 offshore shell companies and trust structures in more than 20 jurisdictions and demonstrated how some wealthy individuals and corporations have used tax havens.

The scale and inner workings of the tax haven industry were further revealed in a subsequent leak of over 13 million documents in 2017. The documents covered transactions spanning over half a century and included bank statements, emails, deeds, agreements and other records. While the documents came from a number of different sources, about half of them related to the law firm Appleby, founded in Bermuda. Like the Panama Papers, the documents were shared with the ICIJ. They have become known as the 'Paradise Papers', reflecting the idyllic tax haven locations where many of the offshore companies and trusts are located (eg the Cayman Islands, the British Virgin Islands and Mauritius).

The Panama and Paradise Papers shed light on the secretive and elaborate structures that have been used by some well-known MNEs and high-profile people from around the world. The documents expose the financial affairs of royalty, politicians, government officials and wealthy individuals. While the identification of a person in the documents does not necessarily implicate them in any illegal activities, the leaks have provided revenue authorities and enforcement agencies with an unprecedented amount of information that may potentially be useful in their broader tax evasion and money laundering investigations. AUSTRAC has analysed data from the leaks and the ATO has identified hundreds of taxpayers who are likely to be subject to further investigation and compliance action.

[33.3] Base erosion and profit shifting

BEPS typically involves MNEs playing one country's tax system off against another's by exploiting gaps and mismatches in the tax laws of different jurisdictions to minimise their overall tax liabilities. One of the ways this is done is through 'transfer pricing' arrangements, whereby MNEs artificially shift their profits from high-tax jurisdictions to low-tax jurisdictions [33.4]. Another common approach is to use thin capitalisation techniques, whereby MNEs fund their operations in high-tax countries with high levels of debt (rather than equity) to generate valuable deductions in those jurisdictions [33.5].

BEPS can also be achieved by taxpayers inappropriately gaining benefits under tax treaties. This is often achieved through 'treaty shopping' arrangements, which typically involve an entity that is not a resident of either of the countries that have signed a DTA obtaining benefits under the DTA. These benefits are typically obtained indirectly and could include, for example, lower withholding tax rates on dividends or royalties.

Example Country A and Country B have not entered into a DTA, but Country B and Country C have entered into a DTA. An entity in Country A that might otherwise earn income directly from an entity in Country B could interpose an entity in Country C and earn the income through that interposed entity. This would enable the entity in Country A to benefit from the favourable tax treatment that exists under the DTA between Country B and Country C, especially where the income can be tax-effectively repatriated to the entity in Country A from the entity in Country C due to special features of their tax systems.

OECD BEPS Action Plan

It is widely recognised that BEPS is one of the greatest threats to national tax systems. The OECD conservatively estimated that BEPS practices cost countries between $US100 to $US240 billion in lost revenue annually. BEPS has become more prevalent in recent years because of the increase in international trade, the rise of the digital economy, and the ease with which capital can be mobilised across borders. The aggressive tax planning strategies adopted by some of the world's largest MNEs have been the subject of much adverse media attention. It has become clear that despite making huge profits, many high-profile MNEs pay low effective rates of tax simply because of the way they have been structured. This has fuelled much public criticism and placed considerable political pressure on governments to tackle BEPS. However, the reality is that many countries have struggled to deal with BEPS because of inadequacies in their tax laws and failures in international cooperation to stamp it out. Recognising that BEPS is a global problem requiring global solutions, the OECD has formulated coordinated strategies to help revenue authorities combat BEPS to ensure that profits are taxed where the economic activities generating them occur. In 2013, the OECD issued a report, *Addressing Base Erosion and Profit Shifting*, together with an *Action Plan on Base Erosion and Profit Shifting*. The Action Plan identified the following 15 key actions to address BEPS:

- Action 1—Address the tax challenges of the digital economy
- Action 2—Neutralise the effects of hybrid mismatch arrangements
- Action 3—Strengthen CFC rules
- Action 4—Limit base erosion via interest deductions and other financial payments
- Action 5—Counter harmful tax practices more effectively, taking into account transparency and substance
- Action 6—Prevent treaty abuse
- Action 7—Prevent the artificial avoidance of PE status
- Actions 8 to 10—Assure that transfer pricing outcomes are in line with value creation in relation to intangibles (Action 8), risks and capital (Action 9) and other high-risk transactions (Action 10)
- Action 11—Establish methodologies to collect and analyse data on BEPS and the actions to address it
- Action 12—Require taxpayers to disclose their aggressive tax planning arrangements
- Action 13—Re-examine transfer pricing documentation and country-by-country reporting
- Action 14—Make dispute resolution mechanisms more effective, and
- Action 15—Develop a multilateral instrument that can be used to implement various treaty-related measures.

In October 2015, the OECD released a package of 13 Final Reports to address the 15 actions in the BEPS Action Plan. The measures in the Final Reports are being adopted by OECD, G20, and other countries through amendments to their domestic tax legislation and treaty provisions. The *OECD/G20 Inclusive Framework on BEPS* has brought over 140 jurisdictions together to collaborate on the implementation of the BEPS Action Plan. The objective is to establish an international tax framework that ensures profits are taxed where economic activity and value creation occur.

One of the aims of the BEPS project is to counter jurisdictions entering into harmful tax practices. To support Action 5, the OECD established a Forum on Harmful Tax Practices, which, by the end of 2022, had reviewed close to 320 tax regimes in various jurisdictions to determine whether they were compliant with OECD standards. As a consequence, over 100 regimes have been abolished.

Australia is one of the countries that has been at the forefront of the international response to BEPS. For example, to address the tax challenges of the digital economy (Action 1), Australia has amended its GST laws by introducing the 'Netflix tax' in sub-div 84-B *GSTA* [7.18]. In addition, to address various other BEPS actions, it has extended the scope of its general anti-avoidance provisions in pt IVA *ITAA36* by introducing a 'multinational anti-avoidance law' ('MAAL') [37.8] and a 'diverted profits tax' ('DPT') [37.9]. It has also recently enacted div 832 *ITAA97* to deal with hybrid mismatch arrangements (Action 2). These arrangements exploit differences in the tax treatment of an entity or financial instrument under the laws of two or more jurisdictions. For example, they can apply where a payment is deductible in one jurisdiction and non-assessable in the other jurisdiction, or where a payment is deductible in two or more jurisdictions. Division 832 *ITAA97* neutralises hybrid mismatches by cancelling an entity's deductions or including amounts in its assessable income.

Australia was also one of the first countries to sign the *Multilateral Convention to Implement Tax Treaty Related Measures to Prevent Base Erosion and Profit Shifting* ('MLI') [32.4]. The MLI was developed by the OECD in accordance with Action 15 to assist countries to expeditiously amend their DTAs and bring them up-to-date with international standards to prevent BEPS. The MLI contains a broad range of integrity measures, including articles that prevent treaty abuse (Action 6), prevent artificial avoidance of PE status (Action 7), and make dispute resolution more effective (Action 14).

[33.4] Transfer pricing

Transfer pricing is one of the oldest and most common tax avoidance techniques. It involves inappropriately shifting the prices of goods and services between related entities (or branches) operating in different jurisdictions to exploit the tax laws in those jurisdictions. MNEs are in the ideal position to engage in transfer pricing arrangements. The members of these groups might try to siphon profits from high-tax to low-tax jurisdictions to benefit the overall tax position of the group. For example, if an Australian subsidiary paid a higher than normal price for goods from its parent company (that is resident in a low-tax foreign country) the group overall could benefit. This is because the parent would be taxed on the excessive income at low rates, while the subsidiary would obtain greater deductions in Australia which could be applied to reduce income that attracts high tax rates. Likewise, an Australian company could sell goods at a lower than normal price to a related company in a low-tax jurisdiction, which could then supply the goods to customers at market prices. This would shift the profits from the Australian company to the related company which is subject to lower rates of tax.

For many years, Australia's tax laws have contained anti-avoidance rules to discourage international transfer pricing practices. These rules have allowed the Commissioner to tax transactions between connected entities as if arm's length consideration was charged. The transfer pricing rules were initially located in div 13 of pt III *ITAA36*. In 2012, div 13 was supplemented with additional anti-avoidance measures contained in sub-div 815-A *ITAA97*, which were given retrospective effect from 1 July 2004. Both div 13 and sub-div 815-A were recently considered by the Full Federal Court in *Chevron Australia Holdings Pty Ltd v FC of T* 2017 ATC ¶20-615. From 1 July 2013, div 13 and sub-div 815-A have been replaced with new rules contained in sub-divs 815-B and 815-C *ITAA97* (discussed below).

Inter-entity transfer pricing rules (sub-div 815-B)

Subdivision 815-B *ITAA97* was introduced to align Australia's transfer pricing rules with modern international transfer pricing standards. The object of sub-div 815-B is to ensure the amount brought to tax in Australia from cross-border conditions between entities is not less than it would be if those conditions reflected:

- the arm's length contribution made by Australian operations through functions performed, assets used and risks assumed, and
- the conditions that might be expected to operate between entities dealing at arm's length.

This is achieved by specifying that, where an entity would otherwise get a tax advantage from actual conditions that differ from arm's length conditions, the arm's length conditions are taken to operate for income tax and withholding tax purposes (s 815-105).

The key provision in sub-div 815-B is s 815-115(1), which provides that if an entity gets a 'transfer pricing benefit' from conditions that operate between the entity and another entity in connection with their commercial or financial relations, those conditions are taken not to operate and instead the 'arm's length conditions' are taken to operate.

Transfer pricing benefit

An entity gets a transfer pricing benefit from conditions that operate between the entity and another entity in connection with their commercial or financial relations if:

- those conditions differ from 'arm's length conditions'
- the actual conditions satisfy a 'cross-border test', and
- had the arm's length conditions operated, instead of the actual conditions, one or more of the following would otherwise apply:
  - the amount of the entity's taxable income for an income year would be greater
  - the amount of the entity's loss of a particular 'sort' (ie a tax loss, film loss or capital loss) for an income year would be less
  - the amount of the entity's tax offsets for an income year would be less
  - an amount of withholding tax payable in respect of interests or royalties by the entity would be greater (s 815-120(1)).

Cross-border test

The cross-border test is satisfied if the conditions that operate between the entity and another entity in connection with their commercial or financial relations meet the 'overseas requirement' for either or both entities. If one of the entities is an Australian resident, a resident trust estate or a partnership in which all of the partners are Australian residents or resident trust estates, the overseas requirement is met where the conditions operate at or through an overseas PE of that entity. In the case of other entities, the overseas requirement is met where the conditions do not operate solely at or through an Australian PE of the entity. The cross-border test is also satisfied if the conditions operate in connection with a business that the entity carries on in an area covered by an 'international tax sharing treaty' (s 815-120(3)).

Arm's length conditions

Arm's length conditions are defined as conditions that might be expected to operate between independent entities dealing wholly independently with one another in comparable circumstances (s 815-125(1)). In identifying the arm's length conditions, the method or combination of methods that are most appropriate and reliable must be used. The methods are chosen having regard to all relevant factors, including the following:

- the respective strengths and weaknesses of the possible methods in their application to the actual conditions
- the circumstances, including the functions performed, assets used, and risks borne by the entities
- the availability of reliable information required to apply a particular method, and

- the degree of comparability between the actual circumstances and the comparable circumstances, including the reliability of any adjustments to eliminate the effect of material differences between those circumstances (s 815-125(2)).

The arm's length conditions must be based on the commercial or financial relations in connection with which the actual conditions operate and have regard to both the form and substance of those relations (s 815-130(1)). There are, however, a number of exceptions to this approach:

- The form of the actual commercial or financial relations is disregarded to the extent that it is inconsistent with the substance of those relations (s 815-130(2)).
- If independent entities dealing wholly independently with one another in comparable circumstances would have entered into other commercial or financial relations instead of entering into the actual commercial or financial relations, and those other commercial or financial relations differ in substance from the actual or commercial relations, the identification of the arm's length conditions must be based on those other commercial or financial relations (s 815-130(3)).
- If independent entities dealing wholly independently with one another in comparable circumstances would not have entered into commercial or financial relations, the identification of the arm's length conditions is to be based on that absence of commercial or financial relations (s 815-130(4)).

Importantly, the identification of the arm's length conditions must be done so as to best achieve consistency with the OECD's *Transfer Pricing Guidelines for Multinational Enterprises and Tax Administrations* and any other document prescribed by the regulations (s 815-135).

OECD's Transfer Pricing Guidelines

The OECD's guidelines provide a detailed framework for determining arm's length prices. They set out five distinct methods outlined below. These are not the only methods that may be used—where an alternative method (or combination of methods) produces a more appropriate arm's length outcome, that alternate method (or combination of methods) may be used.

1. **The comparable uncontrolled price method.** This method compares the price that is actually charged for property or services transferred in a 'controlled transaction' (ie between associated enterprises) with the price charged for property or services transferred in a comparable 'uncontrolled transaction' (ie between unrelated enterprises) in comparable circumstances. The arm's length price is set by reference to the comparable dealing.
2. **The cost plus method.** This method begins with the costs incurred by a supplier in providing property or services to a related purchaser. An appropriate mark-up is then added to this cost to make an appropriate profit in light of the functions performed and the market conditions. The result is treated as the arm's length price. The mark-up should ideally be established by reference to the mark-up that the taxpayer earns in comparable uncontrolled dealings. If there are no comparable uncontrolled dealings, the mark-up may be able to be based on comparable dealings by independent enterprises.
3. **The resale price method.** This method is based on the price at which a product that has been purchased from an associated enterprise is resold to an independent enterprise, reduced by an independent resale price margin (determined by reference to the supplier's resale price margins in comparable dealings with independent parties). The balance (after adjustment for certain other costs such as customs duties) is the arm's length price.
4. **The transactional net margin method.** This method is based on a comparison at the net profit level between the taxpayer and independent parties dealing wholly independently in relation to comparable transactions.

5. **The transactional profit-split method.** This method identifies the combined profits for the associated enterprises from a controlled transaction or transactions. It then splits the profits between the associated enterprises according to an economically valid basis that approximates the division of profits that would have been anticipated and reflected in an agreement made between independent parties.

Consequential adjustments

Where the arm's length conditions are taken by s 815-115 to operate, the Commissioner may make a determination in relation to another entity (the 'disadvantaged entity') to adjust its taxable income, loss of a particular sort, or tax offset for an income year or its withholding tax payable in respect of interest or royalties (ss 815-145(1), (2)). The Commissioner can only make such a determination where he considers that if the arm's length conditions (instead of the actual conditions) had operated:

- the amount of the disadvantaged entity's taxable income for the income year might have been expected to be less than its actual amount
- the amount of the disadvantaged entity's loss for the income year might have been expected to be greater than its actual amount
- the amount of the disadvantaged entity's tax offsets for the income year might have been expected to be greater than its actual amount, or
- an amount of withholding tax payable in respect of interest or royalties by the disadvantaged entity might have been expected to be less than its actual amount.

The Commissioner must also consider it is fair and reasonable that the actual amounts be adjusted accordingly.

The Commissioner may take any action necessary to give effect to a determination and must give a copy of a determination to the disadvantaged entity (although a failure to comply with this requirement does not undermine the validity of the determination) (ss 815-145(3) to (5)).

An entity may also give the Commissioner a written request to make a determination in relation to it. The Commissioner must decide whether or not to grant the request and notify the entity of his decision (s 815-145(7)). If the entity is dissatisfied with the decision, it may object against that decision under pt IVC *TAA* [38.5] (s 815-145(8)).

Time limit for amending assessments

An amended assessment to give effect to s 815-115 must be made within seven years after the day on which the Commissioner gives notice of the assessment to the entity (s 815-150(1)). There is no time limit for amending an assessment to give effect to a consequential adjustment under s 815-145 (s 815-150(2)).

Permanent establishment transfer pricing rules (sub-div 815-C)

Subdivision 815-C *ITAA97* applies the internationally accepted arm's length principle discussed above in the context of PEs. The object of sub-div 815-C is to ensure the amount brought to tax in Australia by entities operating PEs is not less than if the PE were a distinct and separate entity engaged in the same or comparable activities under the same or comparable circumstances but dealing wholly independently with the other part of the entity (s 815-205).

The key provision in sub-div 815-C is s 815-215(1), which provides that if an entity obtains a 'transfer pricing benefit' from the attribution of profits to a PE of the entity, the amount of profits actually attributed to the PE is taken not to have been so attributed and instead the 'arm's length profits' are taken to have been attributed to the PE.

Transfer pricing benefit

An entity gets a transfer pricing benefit from the attribution of profits to a PE of the entity if:

- the amount of profits (the 'actual profits') attributed to the PE differs from the arm's length profits for the PE, and
- had the arm's length profits, instead of the actual profits, been attributed to the PE, one or more of the following would otherwise apply:
  - the amount of the entity's taxable income for an income year would be greater
  - the amount of the entity's loss of a particular 'sort' (ie a tax loss, film loss or capital loss) for an income year would be less
  - the amount of the entity's tax offsets for an income year would be less (s 815-220(1)).

Arm's length profits

The 'arm's length profits' for a PE of an entity are calculated by allocating the actual expenditure and income of the entity between the PE and the entity so that the profits attributable to the PE equal the profits the PE might be expected to make if:

- the PE were a distinct and separate legal entity
- the activities and circumstances of the PE, including the functions performed, assets used and risks borne by the PE, were those of that separate legal entity, and
- the conditions that operated between that separate entity and the entity of which it is a PE were the arm's length conditions (s 815-225).

Special source rules provide that the arm's length profits for a PE in Australia are taken to be attributable to sources in Australia, and that the arm's length profits for a PE in an area covered by an international tax sharing treaty are taken to be attributable to sources in that area (s 815-230).

The calculation of arm's length profits and the identification of arm's length conditions must be done so as to best achieve consistency with the documents specified in s 815-235 (ie the OECD's MTC and Commentary, its *Transfer Pricing Guidelines for Multinational Enterprises and Tax Administrations*, and any other documents prescribed by the regulations).

Time limit for amending assessments

An amended assessment to give effect to s 815-215 must be made within seven years after the day on which the Commissioner gives notice of the assessment to the entity (s 815-240).

Administrative penalty

Where an entity is liable to pay additional tax as a consequence of an adjustment under sub-divs 815-B or 815-C, it will also be liable to an administrative penalty under div 284 of sch 1 *TAA* (s 284-145(2B) *TAA*) [41.2].

Advance pricing arrangements

Taxpayers are able to negotiate 'advance pricing arrangements' ('APAs') with the ATO. An APA is an agreement reached between a taxpayer and the ATO regarding the use of transfer pricing methodologies that result in an appropriate allocation of income and expenses between related businesses. The object of an APA is to provide certainty on how arm's length consideration is to be determined in future transactions. Guidelines on the policies and procedures for APAs are found in PS LA 2015/4.

APAs may be 'unilateral', 'bilateral' or 'multilateral'. A unilateral APA only involves the taxpayer and the ATO. In a bilateral or multilateral APA, the ATO negotiates with one or more foreign tax authorities to arrive at an agreed position in relation to transfer pricing methodologies. Bilateral and multilateral APAs are designed to address international double taxation issues and are concluded under the mutual agreement procedure articles in DTAs [32.8]. The basic structure of a bilateral APA is illustrated in the following diagram:

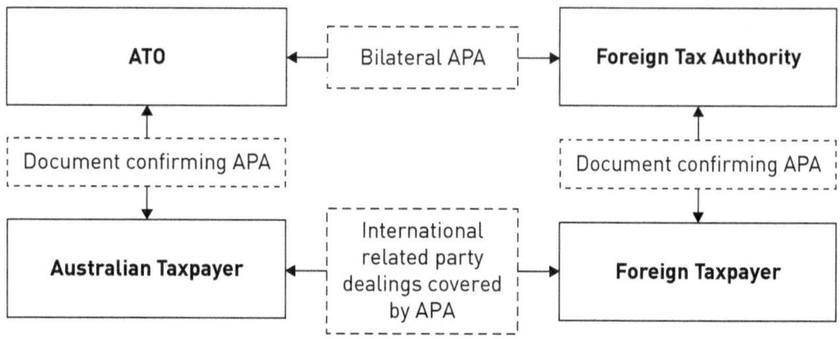

[33.5] Thin capitalisation regime

MNEs have an incentive to use debt to fund their Australian investments and focus their equity investments overseas. This is because deductions are generally available for debt financing costs (eg payments of interest), but not for equity financing costs (eg payments for shares). Special rules have been introduced in div 820 *ITAA97* to restrict entities from obtaining debt deductions where they are too highly 'geared'. The aim is to prevent MNEs shifting profits out of Australia by assigning excessive amounts of debt to their Australian operations. In essence, div 820 applies where an entity's assets are funded by high levels of debt compared to equity, making it 'thinly capitalised'. More specifically, it operates where an entity's 'debt-to-equity ratio' exceeds specified statutory limits.

Operation of div 820

Division 820 limits debt deductions used to finance the Australian operations of:

- outward investing entities (ie Australian entities that control foreign entities or that operate through an overseas PE) (s 820-185), and
- inward investing entities (ie Australian entities that are foreign controlled and foreign entities that invest in Australia or operate through an Australian PE) (s 820-185).

Special rules ensure that deductions are not denied to certain entities, such as:

- an entity that (together with associates) claims no more than $2m in debt deductions (s 820-35), or
- an outward investing entity whose average Australian assets (and those of its associates) are 90% or more of its (and its associates) average total assets (s 820-37).

A 'debt deduction' covers certain costs incurred in connection with a 'debt interest' (defined in sub-div 974-B [29.9]) issued by an entity, which would be deductible if div 820 did not apply (s 820-40). The relevant costs are:

- interest, amounts in the nature of interest, or other amounts that are calculated by reference to the time value of money
- the difference between the financial benefits received and the financial benefits provided under schemes that give rise to debt interests
- amounts directly incurred in obtaining or maintaining those financial benefits, and
- any other expenses specified in the regulations.

The rules in div 820 operate differently depending on whether the entity is an 'inward' or 'outward' investor and whether it is an 'ADI' (ie an authorised deposit-taking institution under the *Banking Act 1959* (Cth), such as a bank), or a 'non-ADI' (ie any other entity). In the case of a non-ADI, different rules apply depending on whether it is a 'financial entity' as defined in s 995-1 *ITAA97* (eg a finance company or securities dealer) or a 'general entity'.

The following discussion considers how div 820 applies to non-ADIs and does not examine its effect on ADIs. Because of the highly technical nature of the rules, which span almost 100 pages of legislation, the discussion merely provides a simplified introduction to the provisions.

Application of div 820 to non-ADIs

Division 820 disallows a debt deduction to a non-ADI for an income year if its 'adjusted average debt' for the year exceeds its 'maximum allowable debt' for the year (ss 820-85, 820-185). The amount of the debt deduction that is disallowed is calculated as follows (ss 820-115, 820-220):

$$\text{Disallowed debt deduction} = \text{Debt deduction} \times \frac{\text{Excess debt}}{\text{Average debt}}$$

Adjusted average debt

A non-ADI's adjusted average debt is calculated differently for outward and inward investing entities and depends on whether or not it is a financial entity. For an outward investor, it is generally the average value of the entity's debt capital that gives rise to debt deductions (disregarding debt attributable to an overseas PE) less the average value of debt owed to associated entities and controlled foreign entities (s 820-85). For an inward investor, it is generally the average value of the entity's debt capital that gives rise to debt deductions reduced by the average value of debt owed to associated entities (s 820-185).

Maximum allowable debt

The maximum allowable debt for a year of both an inward and outward investing non-ADI is generally the greatest of the 'safe harbour debt amount', the 'arm's length debt amount' and the 'worldwide gearing debt amount' (ss 820-90, 820-190). The way these amounts are calculated is complex and outlined in basic terms below:

- **Safe harbour debt amount.** The safe harbour debt amount is calculated differently for outward and inward investing entities and depends on whether the entity is a financial entity. For non-ADIs that are not financial entities, it is basically 3/5 of the average value of the entity's Australian assets (ss 820-95, 820-195). For non-ADIs that are financial entities, it is basically 15/16 of the average value of the entity's Australian assets (ss 820-100, 820-200).
- **Arm's length debt amount.** The arm's length debt amount is a notional amount of debt which, in the light of specified factual assumptions and factors, would be attributable to the entity's Australian business and would have been available from non-associated commercial lending institutions on arm's length terms (ss 820-105, 820-215).
- **Worldwide gearing debt amount.** The worldwide gearing debt amount is based on the level of gearing of the Australian entity's worldwide group. It is designed to allow the entity's Australian operations to be geared at up to 100% of the gearing of the worldwide group (s 820-110).

Example A Co is an outward investing non-ADI that is not a financial entity. It holds $30m equity in a foreign company that it controls (F Co). It also has 'adjusted average debt' of $80m for the year relating to a bank loan on which interest is payable at 10% per annum (ie the debt deduction would ordinarily be $8m).

If the average value of A Co's Australian assets is \$100m, the safe harbour debt amount is \$60m (ie \$100m × 3/5). Assume the safe harbour debt amount is greater than the arm's length debt amount and the worldwide gearing debt amount.

A Co's adjusted average debt (\$80m) exceeds its maximum allowable debt (\$60m) by \$20m. This means that debt deductions amounting to \$2m (ie \$8m × \$20m/\$80m) are disallowed under div 820.

The example shows that the thin capitalisation rules typically apply to a non-ADI that is not a financial entity if its debts exceed 60% of the net value of its Australian assets.

Proposed amendments

In the October 2022 Budget, the Government announced it would amend div 820 to strengthen its operation. The reforms are contained in Treasury Laws Amendment (Making Multinationals Pay Their Fair Share—Integrity and Transparency) Bill 2023 and are based on the OECD's best practice guidance.

The amendments replace the existing safe harbour and worldwide gearing rules for certain entities and limit the arm's length debt amount to external third-party debt. They apply to 'general class investors' (ie entities that are not ADIs or financial entities). ADIs and financial entities continue to be subject to the existing rules (subject to the proviso that the new external third-party debt test will also apply to financial entities). The measures are proposed to apply on or after 1 July 2023 and result in the following changes:

- **Fixed ratio test.** The safe harbour debt amount will be replaced with a new test that limits an entity's debt deductions to 30% of its profits (measured by reference to EBITDA (ie earnings before income tax, depreciation and amortization). Excess debt deductions will be able to be carried forward for up to 15 years.
- **Group ratio test.** The worldwide gearing debt amount will be replaced with a new test that allows an entity to claim debt deductions up to the level of the worldwide group's net interest expense as a share of earnings.
- **Third-party debt test.** The arm's length debt amount will be retained but will only apply to an entity's external (third-party) debt. Deductions for related party debt will be entirely disallowed.

[33.6] Two-pillar solution on global tax reform

The rules governing the taxation of international business profits developed over the 20th century have struggled to keep pace with globalisation and the growing scale of cross-border trade in electronic services. One reason for this is that international tax laws have traditionally focused on where entities have their physical presence (eg their PEs) to determine where their income is taxed. Digital technology allows entities to operate in countries without necessarily having a physical presence in them and it is not surprising this has provided opportunities for MNEs (particularly large technology companies) to engage in BEPS.

Many MNEs have found ingenious ways of structuring their affairs to enable them to earn significant amounts of income in a jurisdiction without necessarily having to pay substantial amounts of corporate tax in that jurisdiction. They have often achieved this by having their headquarters and physical presence located in another jurisdiction and diverting their profits to subsidiaries in low-tax jurisdictions through licensing their intellectual property and entering into sophisticated schemes (such as treaty shopping arrangements) that exploit loopholes in various tax regimes.

A classic example of this was the infamous 'double Irish with a Dutch sandwich' tax avoidance scheme that involved MNEs channelling their profits through a combination of Irish and Dutch subsidiaries to tax havens in jurisdictions such as Bermuda. While legislative reforms have now shut down this scheme, opportunities continue to exist for MNEs to minimise their tax.

Digital services taxes

To address weaknesses in the ways their tax systems have traditionally dealt with the business profits of international technology companies, a number of jurisdictions introduced digital services taxes ('DSTs'). Although Australia does not have a DST, DSTs have been popular in several countries. DSTs are imposed on specific revenue streams of large MNEs (eg income from search engines, online advertising, digital marketplaces and social media services). The aim is to ensure the profits made by large technology companies (such as Google, Apple and Amazon) from their digital transactions are taxed in the jurisdictions where their consumers are located, rather than where their intellectual property or physical presence may be situated. In essence, DSTs seek to address the misalignment that often exists between the places where value is created and the places where profits are ultimately taxed. There is, however, no harmonisation of how DSTs operate or the rates at which they are levied. DSTs also risk causing trade tensions between nations, which can result in retaliatory tariffs. As a consequence, DSTs have been criticised as ad-hoc, discriminatory, and inadequate responses to tackling what are essentially fundamental problems with the basic way the international tax rules operate.

Two-pillar solution

To bring the international tax system into the 21st century and ensure that an MNE's income from its digital transactions is taxed where it is earned (rather than where its intellectual property or physical presence is located), the OECD/G20 Inclusive Framework on BEPS issued its *Statement on a Two-Pillar Solution to Address the Tax Challenges Arising from the Digitalisation of the Economy* on 8 October 2021. The statement addresses BEPS Action 1 [33.3]. It followed years of intensive negotiations and arose as a result of a landmark in-principle agreement on global tax reform entered into on 5 June 2021 by the Finance Ministers from Canada, France, Germany, Italy, Japan, the United Kingdom and the United States (the 'G7'). The statement adopts a two-pillar solution to tackle BEPs by large MNEs and has, so far, been accepted by over 135 jurisdictions (including Australia).

The two-pillar solution aims to:

1. reallocate profits of the largest and most profitable MNEs to those countries where the profits are earned ('Pillar One'), and
2. ensure MNEs will be subject to a worldwide minimum corporate tax rate of at least 15% ('Pillar Two').

The OECD estimates that Pillar One will result in the reallocation of around US$200 billion of profits to market jurisdictions each year and Pillar Two will generate around US$220 billion in additional global tax revenue each year. It expects that additional benefits will come from stabilisation of the international tax system and increased tax certainty for taxpayers and tax administrations.

The OECD has been consulting with stakeholders on the regime and the Australian Treasury released its own consultation paper in 2022: *Global Agreement on Corporate Taxation: Addressing the Tax Challenges Arising from the Digitalisation of the Economy*. In the 2023 Budget, the Government confirmed it will implement key aspects of the two-pillar solution on or after 1 January 2024.

Pillar One (allocation of taxing rights)

Pillar One is designed to provide a fairer allocation of taxing rights to the profits of MNEs. It proposes to revise the standard international tax rules that determine which jurisdiction has the right to tax such profits. Under Pillar One, some of the taxing rights over MNEs will be relocated from their 'home countries' to those markets where they have their business activities and earn profits, regardless of where they may be physically present. Detailed rules for specific categories of transactions will be developed to ensure that MNE profits are sourced in the end market jurisdictions where their goods or services are used or consumed.

Pillar One will apply to a 'Covered Group'. Basically, a Covered Group consists of a MNE with global turnover above €20 billion per annum and a profit-before-tax to revenue ratio above a 10% threshold. These entities will have 25% of their profit above the 10% threshold (referred to as 'Amount A') reallocated among market jurisdictions based on the share of revenue sourced from each of those jurisdictions. Detailed revenue sourcing rules provide a methodology for determining the jurisdictions in which the revenues of a Covered Group are generated.

Market jurisdictions will then apply their domestic corporate tax laws to tax the allocated residual profits, while 'relieving jurisdictions' will relinquish their taxing rights over those profits. A special purpose nexus rule will permit the allocation of Amount A to a market jurisdiction when the MNE derives at least €1m in revenue from that jurisdiction. A lower threshold of €250,000 will apply for jurisdictions with GDP of less than €40 billion.

Pillar One will not apply to profits from extractive activities (eg mining) and regulated financial services. Treasury's consultation paper explains that this reflects 'the policy goals of excluding economic rents from location-specific non-renewable extractive resources and the returns on risk borne by firms that are subject to regulated capital adequacy requirements'.

The taxing rights under Pillar One will be implemented through a multilateral convention ('MLC') being developed by the OECD's Task Force on the Digital Economy. The MLC will require all parties to remove their DSTs and commit not to introduce such measures. The OECD estimates that approximately 100 MNEs will initially fall within the scope of Pillar One. Treasury believes that no Australian headquartered companies will fall within this initial group, but this could change depending on economic conditions and profitability levels.

The following diagram outlines the basic steps involved in allocation taxing rights under Pillar One:

Step 1: Determine whether the MNE is in scope
The MNE must be a Covered Group (ie it must have more than €20 billion in revenues per annum and profitability exceeding 10%). Revenues and profits from extractive activities and regulated financial services are excluded.

↓

Step 2: Determine the market jurisdictions eligible to tax a portion of Amount A
A market jurisdiction will be eligible to tax a portion of Amount A if the Covered Group derives more than €1 million in revenues from that jurisdiction (or €250,000, if that jurisdiction's GDP is lower than €40 billion). Revenue sourcing rules will determine how much revenue is derived from each jurisdiction.

↓

Step 3: Determine the profit of the Covered Group
The profit of the Covered Group is determined by reference to its consolidated financial statements, which may then be adjusted for certain items to arrive at an 'Adjusted Profit Before Tax' amount

↓

Step 4: Allocate Amount A to eligible market jurisdictions
The Amount A profit allocated to an eligible market jurisdiction (Step 2) is determined by taking 25% of the Adjusted Profit Before Tax amount (Step 3) that is in excess of 10% of the Covered Group's revenues and then allocating it to the market jurisdiction in proportion to the amount of revenues the Covered Group derives from that jurisdiction (see Step 2)

↓

Step 5: Eliminate double taxation
Special mechanisms will eliminate double taxation arising from the application of Amount A

Pillar Two (worldwide minimum corporate tax rate)

Pillar Two establishes a global minimum corporate tax rate of 15% on MNEs with consolidated annual revenues over €750m per annum. This is designed to stop countries undercutting each other in a 'race to the bottom' on corporate tax rates. It discourages them from using lower corporate tax rates to compete with each other to attract mobile capital and aims to create a more level playing field by placing a floor on tax competition. Pillar Two consists of:

- a set of domestic 'global anti-base erosion rules' ('GloBE rules'), and
- a treaty-based 'subject to tax rule' ('STTR').

Global anti-base erosion rules ('GloBE rules')

The OECD released model GloBE rules on 20 December 2021 in its publication, *Tax Challenges Arising from Digitalisation of the Economy—Global Anti-Base Erosion Model Rules (Pillar Two)*. The model rules have been designed to accommodate a diverse range of tax systems and provide a template that countries can translate into their domestic laws.

The model rules apply to 'constituent entities' that are members of an 'MNE group' that has annual revenue of €750m or more in the consolidated financial statements of the 'ultimate parent entity' ('UPE') in at least two of the four fiscal years immediately preceding the tested fiscal year.

A constituent entity is an entity within an MNE group or a PE of an entity within an MNE group. A constituent entity does not include an excluded entity (eg a government entity, an international or non-profit organisation, or a pension, investment or real estate fund). A constituent entity is located in the jurisdiction where it is resident or, in the case of a PE, the jurisdiction where the PE is located.

The primary GloBE rule is the 'income inclusion rule' ('IIR') which imposes 'top-up tax' on a parent entity in respect of the low taxed income of its constituent entities in a jurisdiction. The IIR is supported by an 'undertaxed payment rule' ('UTPR') which is a back-up mechanism that makes a 'UTPR adjustment' where there is residual low tax income that is not subject to tax under the IIR.

Top-up tax is designed to bring the total amount of taxes paid on an MNE group's profits in a jurisdiction up to the minimum rate of 15%. The top-up tax rate payable by the parent entity is the difference between the 15% minimum tax rate and the effective tax rate of all its constituent entities in the jurisdiction. The effective tax rate is determined by dividing the amount of covered taxes by the amount of each constituent entity's income on a blended jurisdictional basis. Parent entities will be required to pay top-up tax in their home jurisdiction in proportion to their ownership interests in those entities that have low-taxed income.

The GloBE rules allow for the development of safe harbours and contain a *de minimis* exclusion for jurisdictions where MNEs have relatively small amounts of income.

> ***Example*** A Co is an Australian company headquartered in Sydney. It is the UPE of an MNE group with consolidated revenues over €750m per annum. A Co has a number of foreign subsidiaries operating in a jurisdiction where those companies pay an effective tax rate of only 10%. Under the IIR, subject to the operation of any specific exclusions, A Co would be required to pay top-up tax equivalent to 5% of its foreign subsidiaries' profits in Australia.

The following diagram outlines the key steps involved in determining an MNE's top-up tax liability:

Step 1: Scope
Determine whether the MNE group is within the scope of the GloBE rules and identify the location of each of each of its constituent entities

↓

Step 2: GloBE income
Determine the income of each constituent entity

↓

Step 3: Covered taxes
Determine the taxes attributable to each constitutent entity's income

↓

Step 4: Effective tax rate and top-up tax
Determine the effective tax rate of all constituent entities located in the same jurisdiction and determine the top-up tax

↓

Step 5: IIR and UTPR
Impose top-up tax on the UPE under the IIR or UTPR

Subject to tax rule ('STTR')

The STTR will be made available to developing countries to protect their treaty networks from BEPS and will be implemented through changes made to their DTAs. In essence, it overrides benefits available under existing treaties in respect of certain payments where those payments are not subject to a minimum level of tax in the recipient jurisdiction. The OECD's 2020 publication, *Tax Challenges Arising from Digitalisation—Report on the Pillar Two Blueprint*, explains that the STTR 'is based on the rationale that a source jurisdiction that has ceded taxing rights in the context of an income tax treaty should be able to apply a top up tax to the agreed minimum rate where, as a result of BEPS structures relating to intragroup payments, the income that benefits from treaty protection is not taxed or is taxed at below the minimum rate in the other contracting jurisdiction'.

The STTR targets intragroup payments that exploit treaty provisions in order to shift profits from source countries to jurisdictions where those payments are taxed at low rates. For example, it will prevent companies avoiding tax by making deductible intragroup payments which benefit from reduced withholding tax rates under a developing country's tax treaty that are also concessionally taxed under its treaty partner's tax laws. The STTR will give source jurisdictions the right to tax related party interest, royalty, and other specified payments that are taxed below a minimum rate of 9%. The rate of top-up tax will be limited to the difference between the rate of tax payable and the minimum 9% rate. By restoring taxing rights to the source country, the STTR aims to protect their tax bases.

[33.7] Significant global entities

Governments face the greatest risks from BEPS where large MNEs engage in international tax avoidance. For example, there have been many cases where MNEs have entered into sophisticated transfer pricing arrangements and schemes under which they seek to avoid having a taxable presence in the countries in which they operate so that they can divert profits to tax havens. As these activities are likely to involve large sums of money, they can result in substantial revenue leakage for governments if not addressed. To combat these arrangements, the Australian Government introduced special reporting and anti-avoidance rules (discussed below) that apply to 'significant global entities'. These entities are also subject to higher penalties in certain cases [41.2].

Significant global entity

A 'significant global entity' is defined in sub-div 960-U *ITAA97*. An entity is a 'significant global entity' for a period if:

- it is a global parent entity whose annual global income for the period is $1 billion or more, or in relation to whom the Commissioner makes a determination under s 960-555(3) (s 960-555(1))
- it is a member of a group of entities that are consolidated for accounting purposes and the global parent entity of the group has annual global income for the period of $1 billion or more (s 960-555(2)), or
- it is a member of a 'notional listed company group' and one of the other members of the group is a global parent entity whose annual global income for the period is $1 billion or more, or in relation to whom the Commissioner makes a determination under s 960-555(3) (s 960-555(2A)).

A 'global parent entity' is an entity that is not controlled by another entity according to accounting principles, or, where accounting principles do not apply, commercially accepted principles (s 960-560).

A 'notional listed company group' is essentially a group of entities that would be required to be consolidated as a single group for accounting purposes, if an entity of that group was a listed company (s 960-575).

A global parent entity's 'annual global income' for a period is the total annual income of the entity as shown in its latest 'global financial statements' (defined in s 960-570) for that period (s 960-565). However, where it is a member of a group of entities that are consolidated for accounting purposes, its annual global income for a period is the total annual income of all the members of the group as shown in its latest 'global financial statements' for that period.

Country-by-country reporting

To address transfer pricing concerns and implement BEPS Action 13 [33.3], the OECD created special country-by-country ('CbC') reporting standards. These standards require MNEs to provide certain information to tax administrators and implement related government-to-government report exchange mechanisms. The measures are designed to increase transparency and give national tax administrators a complete understanding of how MNEs structure their global operations. They require MNEs to provide aggregate information relating to their profits and losses and income taxes paid in each jurisdiction where they operate. They also require details of the location of economic activities, information about which entities do business in particular jurisdictions, and the relevant activities they engage in. The measures are contained in the *Multilateral Competent Authority Agreement for Country-by-Country Reporting*, which has been signed by over 90 countries.

To implement the CbC reporting measures, the Australian Government inserted sub-div 815-E *ITAA97* into its transfer pricing regime [33.4]. Subdivision 815-E applies to significant global entities that are Australian residents or have PEs in Australia. These entities must, within 12 months of the end of the income year (or replacement reporting period), provide certain statements to the Commissioner unless exempted to do so by him (ss 815-355, 815-365). There are three statements that must be provided. Each of these has a different focus and is based on OECD guidelines and explained further in LCR 2015/3:

- **Master file.** This statement relates to the global operations, activities and transfer pricing policies of the entity's MNE group. It provides a high-level description of the group's global business operations, including its organisational structure and use of intangibles and intercompany financial activities.
- **Local file.** This statement relates to the entity's operations, activities, dealings and transactions. It provides information about its management structure and business strategy, its cross-border related party transactions, and its financial information.
- **CbC report.** This statement relates to the allocation between countries of the MNE group's income, activities, and taxes paid. It provides an indication of where the group's economic activity takes place.

Multinational tax transparency reporting

To increase transparency and help the public better assess whether an entity's economic presence in a jurisdiction aligns with the amount of tax they pay in that jurisdiction, the Government is proposing to introduce a multinational tax transparency reporting requirement that uses publicity as a means of discouraging tax avoidance. The new measure is contained in proposed s 3D *TAA* (Exposure Draft Taxation Laws Amendment (Measures for Future Bills) Bill 2023: Multinational Tax Transparency—Tax Changes). It will apply to a 'CbC reporting parent' (defined in s 815-375 *ITAA97*) where, at any time during the income year, it, or a member of its 'CBC reporting group' (defined in s 815-380 *ITAA97*), is an Australian resident or a foreign resident that operates a PE in Australia. The CBC reporting parent is required to publish specified information within 12 months after the end of the income year (unless exempted by the Commissioner). Failure to publish the information will be an offence under s 8C *TAA* that is subject to penalties under s 8E *TAA* [41.3].

To comply with the publication requirements, the CbC reporting parent must provide the Commissioner with a document in the approved form containing certain information. The Commissioner is then required to make the information available to the public on an Australian Government website. The CbC reporting parent must provide details of the names of each entity in the CBC reporting group and a description of the group's approach to tax. In addition, for each jurisdiction the CBC reporting group operates in, it must provide details of:

- main business activities
- number of employees
- revenue from unrelated parties
- revenue from related parties
- expenses from related party transactions
- profit and loss before income tax
- tangible and intangible assets (including their value)
- income tax paid (on cash basis)
- income tax accrued (current year)
- effective tax rate
- the reasons for the difference between income tax accrued (current year) and the amount of income tax due if the income tax rate applicable to the jurisdiction were applied to profit and loss before income tax, and
- the currency used in calculating and presenting the above information.

Anti-avoidance rules

To counter certain BEPS arrangements entered into by large MNEs, a multinational anti-avoidance law ('MAAL')) and a diverted profits tax ('DPT') have been inserted into the general anti-avoidance provisions in pt IVA *ITAA36*.

Multinational anti-avoidance law

The MAAL was introduced in 2016 and is contained in s 177DA *ITAA36* [37.8]. It applies to significant global entities that are foreign entities and is designed to combat schemes where such entities use artificial or contrived arrangements to avoid having a taxable presence in Australia. Basically, s 177DA applies if under, or in connection with, a scheme:

- the foreign entity supplies goods or services to an Australian customer
- an Australian entity, that is an associate of, or is commercially dependent on, the foreign entity, undertakes activities directly in connection with the supply
- some or all of the ordinary or statutory income derived by the foreign entity is not attributable to an Australian PE of the foreign entity, and
- the principal purpose, or one of the principal purposes, of a person that entered into the scheme, was to enable a relevant taxpayer to obtain a tax benefit or reduce their foreign tax liabilities.

Diverted profits tax

DPT was introduced in 2017 and is contained in ss 177H to 177R *ITAA36* [37.9]. It applies to significant global entities and is designed to ensure that the Australian tax payable by such entities properly reflects the economic substance of the activities that they carry on in Australia. In particular, the provisions seek to prevent them from reducing the amount of Australian tax they pay by diverting profits offshore through contrived related party arrangements. DPT basically applies if under, or in connection with, a scheme:

- a relevant taxpayer has obtained a tax benefit
- the principal purpose, or one of the principal purposes, of a person who entered into or carried out the scheme, was to enable the relevant taxpayer to obtain a tax benefit or both obtain a tax benefit and reduce their foreign tax liabilities
- a foreign associate of the relevant taxpayer is involved in entering into, or carrying out, the scheme or is otherwise connected with the scheme, and
- none of the exceptions in ss 177K to 177M apply.

Payments to associates for intangibles in low corporate tax jurisdictions

In the October 2022 Budget, the Government announced it would introduce a new anti-avoidance rule to prevent significant global entities from claiming tax deductions for payments made to related parties for intangibles held in low corporate tax jurisdictions. The reform is contained in Exposure Draft Treasury Laws Amendment (Measures for Consultation) Bill 2023: Deductions for Payments Relating to Intangible Assets Connected with Low Corporate Tax Jurisdictions, which proposes to introduce s 26-110 *ITAA97*.

Proposed s 26-110 denies a deduction for a payment a significant global entity makes to their associate, to the extent that the payment is attributable to a right to exploit an intangible asset, if:

- as a result of the arrangement under which the entity makes the payment, or a related arrangement, the entity or its associate acquires the intangible asset, acquires a right to exploit the intangible asset or exploits the intangible asset, and
- this results in the associate, or another associate of the entity, deriving income in a low corporate tax jurisdiction directly or indirectly from exploiting the intangible asset, or from a related intangible asset.

A low corporate tax jurisdiction is defined in proposed s 960-258 *ITAA97* as a jurisdiction with a tax rate of less than 15% or nil, or that the Minister has determined has a tax preferential patent box regime without sufficient economic substance.

[33.8] Third-party reporting of financial information

In order to detect international tax evasion, it is useful for revenue authorities to identify taxpayers who have money in overseas accounts with foreign financial institutions. In practice, it has been difficult to obtain this information. Accordingly, to assist revenue authorities with their investigations, certain third-party reporting regimes have been developed.

Foreign Account Tax Compliance Act

In 2010, the United States Congress enacted the *Foreign Account Tax Compliance Act* ('*FATCA*'), which is designed to assist the United States Internal Revenue Service ('IRS') to detect United States citizens who use accounts with foreign financial institutions to conceal income and assets overseas.

From 1 July 2014, *FATCA* requires financial institutions outside the United States to enter agreements with the IRS under which they agree to periodically report certain information about United States accountholders. Financial institutions that fail to comply with *FATCA* are subject to a 30% United States withholding tax on their United States source income.

As many Australian financial institutions operate or invest in the United States, the imposition of a 30% United States withholding tax on their United States income is a strong incentive to comply with *FATCA*. However, as Australia's domestic tax laws (like those of many other countries) would otherwise prevent financial institutions from fully complying with *FATCA*, an intergovernmental agreement was entered into between the United States and Australia on 28 April 2014 to facilitate compliance with the regime. As a consequence of this agreement, the Australian Government enacted sub-div 396-A of sch 1 *TAA*. Subdivision 396-A requires 'Reporting Australian Financial Institutions' to collect information relating to their 'US Reportable Accounts' (ie accounts held by their customers who are likely to be United States citizens or tax residents) and provide relevant details (eg the account holders' names and account balances) to the ATO. The ATO is then required to pass these details on to the IRS in accordance with the exchange of information provision in art 25 of the Australia–US DTA. By requiring Australian financial institutions to deal with the ATO instead of the IRS, various issues that would otherwise arise under Australia's privacy and other laws are avoided.

Common Reporting Standard

The OECD and non-OECD G20 countries have also developed a Common Reporting Standard ('CRS') which is designed to operate as a global mechanism for collecting, reporting and exchanging financial account information of foreign residents. It requires financial institutions to identify the financial accounts of foreign residents and to report this to local tax authorities, who are required to exchange the information with the tax authorities of the foreign residents. Over 100 jurisdictions have committed to the CRS.

Australia enacted sub-div 396-C of sch 1 *TAA* to implement the CRS. The subdivision operates from 1 July 2017 and imposes similar kinds of obligations to those under *FATCA*. 'Reporting Financial Institutions' are required to report to the Commissioner on 'Reportable Accounts'. The ATO exchanges information reported about foreign residents with the relevant foreign tax authorities and, in return, receives information on Australian tax residents that hold financial accounts overseas. The CRS assists Australia to comply with its obligations under international agreements, such as the multilateral *Convention on Mutual Administrative Assistance in Tax Matters* [33.10].

[33.9] Public beneficial ownership register

While it is usually easy to identify the legal owners of an entity, it is often difficult to identify its beneficial owners, especially when this requires tracing through several layers of complex international structures. Australia is not ranked highly against international benchmarks for collecting and disclosing beneficial ownership information. Accordingly, as part of its multinational tax integrity package, the Government proposes to introduce a public beneficial ownership register designed to record who ultimately owns, controls, and receives benefits from a company or legal vehicle operating in Australia. The register aims to increase transparency and discourage the use of complex structures that avoid legal requirements and obscure tax liabilities. It is designed to support law enforcement, tackle money laundering, tax and financial crime, and assist with foreign investment applications.

In November 2022, the Government released a consultation paper, *Multinational Tax Integrity: Public Beneficial Ownership Register*, seeking comments on the register which it proposes to introduce in phases. The first phase is proposed to apply to specific unlisted entities regulated under the *Corporations Act*. These regulated entities include proprietary companies [22.2], unlisted Australian public companies [22.2], unlisted Australian registered MISs [25.10], and CCIVs [25.11]. Regulated entities will be required to include on their beneficial ownership register entities or individuals who either:

- hold, directly or indirectly, 20% of shares or units in the regulated entity
- hold, directly or indirectly, 20% of the voting rights in the regulated entity
- hold the right, directly or directly, to:
  - appoint or remove a majority of the board of directors (where the regulated entity is an unlisted proprietary or unlisted public company)
  - appoint or remove the regulated entity's responsible entity (where the regulated entity is an MIS)
  - appoint or remove the regulated entity's corporate director (where the regulated entity is a CCIV), or

- have the right to exercise, or actually exercise, significant influence or control over the regulated entity.

In future phases, the Government will consult on approaches to the disclosure of beneficial ownership of property held through other entities, such as trusts.

[33.10] International tax enforcement

As a general rule, countries reserve the right to tax any income earned within their territories, irrespective of who earns that income. There are no general rules of international law that restrict countries to taxing only their own citizens. Countries are therefore technically free to assert taxing rights over foreigners who reside outside their national borders. There are, nevertheless, practical limitations on a country's ability to enforce its tax laws against foreigners. This was recognised long ago in *Planché v Fletcher* (1779) 1 Douglas 251, where Lord Mansfield stated (at 253): 'One nation does not take notice of the revenue laws of another.'

The principle that one country will not enforce the revenue laws of another country is illustrated in *In re Visser* [1928] 1 Ch 877, where a United Kingdom court refused to enforce a claim made in England by the Queen of Holland for succession duty relating to the estate of a Dutch subject who was domiciled in Holland and died there. As Lord Tomlin explained (at 884):

> there is a well recognized rule, which has been enforced for at least 200 years or thereabouts, under which these Courts will not collect the taxes of foreign States for the benefit of the sovereigns of those foreign States.

A similar outcome was reached by the House of Lords in *Government of India, Ministry of Finance (Revenue Division) v Taylor* [1955] AC 491. In that case, the Indian Government sought to recover tax purportedly owed by a United Kingdom company that had been trading in India. It was held that claims to recover taxes due under Indian laws were unenforceable before the English courts.

The *Government of India* decision was applied in Australia in *Jamieson v Commissioner for Internal Revenue* [2007] NSWSC 324, where the NSW Supreme Court determined that an executor of a will could distribute the assets of her deceased father's estate without recognising the United States Commissioner for Internal Revenue as a creditor. This was the case even though the Commissioner had obtained judgment in a United States Tax Court against the estate for unpaid United States taxes. Gzell J held that the decision of the United States Tax Court was unenforceable in Australia.

Reciprocal enforcement arrangements

The practical problems associated with international tax recovery have prompted countries to enter 'reciprocal enforcement arrangements'. In 2003, the OECD MTC was amended to include art 27, which requires the Contracting States to 'lend assistance' to each other in the collection of revenue claims. This article has been included in some of Australia's recent DTAs (eg the New Zealand and Norwegian DTAs). However, the bulk of Australia's DTAs do not contain this article.

To support the new article, Australia enacted div 263 of sch 1 *TAA*. Division 263 operates where a DTA requires Australia to provide assistance in the collection of foreign revenue claims. Under div 263, foreign revenue claims that have been entered on the 'Foreign Revenue Claims Register' become pecuniary liabilities owed to the Commonwealth and can be enforced in the Australian courts by the Commissioner of Taxation against the debtor. Where a foreign revenue claim is recovered, the amount must be remitted to the relevant foreign authority.

Convention on Mutual Administrative Assistance in Tax Matters

International tax enforcement has also been substantially bolstered through the OECD's *Convention on Mutual Administrative Assistance in Tax Matters*, which is a multilateral agreement designed to promote international tax cooperation between signatory countries. The convention was amended by a protocol which came into force on 1 July 2011. The protocol brings the convention in line with a new international standard and opens it to all countries (including non-OECD countries). More than 140 jurisdictions, including Australia, have signed the convention.

The convention provides the parties with mutual assistance powers and obligations in relation to the exchange of information and recovery of tax debts. It covers a broad range of taxes, including taxes on income, capital gains and goods and services. As a consequence of the convention coming into force in Australia on 1 December 2012, the Commissioner now has a duty to provide assistance in tax recovery matters to a much wider range of countries (ie not just those countries with which Australia has a DTA containing a reciprocal enforcement article). Equally, these countries have an obligation to assist in collecting Australian tax debts overseas.

Article 11 of the convention deals with the recovery of tax and provides that at the request of the 'applicant State', the 'requested State' shall 'take the necessary steps to recover tax claims of the first-mentioned state as if they were its own tax claims.' The article generally only applies to tax claims which 'form the subject of an instrument permitting their enforcement' (eg an assessment) and which are 'uncontested'. However, a special rule exists under art 12, which requires a requested state to adopt 'conservancy' measures (eg seek a 'garnishee order') where requested to do so by an applicant state, even in cases where the tax claim is contested or is not yet subject to an instrument permitting enforcement.

[33.11] QUESTIONS

1. What are the characteristics of a 'tax haven'? Why are higher-taxing countries concerned about tax havens and how have these countries tried to curb tax haven activity?
2. What is the role of a TIEA?
3. How have the Panama and Paradise Papers leaks helped revenue authorities?
4. What is BEPS and how is the international community seeking to address it?
5. What is the aim of the transfer pricing rules? Provide examples of how transfer pricing might occur. What are the different circumstances in which sub-divs 815-B and 815-C *ITAA97* operate? How are 'arm's length conditions' and 'arm's length profits' determined?
6. What is an 'APA' and why might a taxpayer enter into such an agreement with the ATO? Describe how a bilateral APA works.
7. What is the object of the thin capitalisation rules in div 820 *ITAA97*?
8. What are each of the pillars of the two-pillar solution on global tax reform designed to achieve?
9. What is a significant global entity and what special rules apply to such entities?
10. Why is it important for Australian financial institutions to comply with *FATCA*?
11. What is the role of sub-div 396-C of sch 1 *TAA* and what obligations does it place on financial institutions?
12. What practical problems exist in recovering tax from foreigners? What have some countries done to tackle the problems?

34 ACCRUALS TAXATION

[34.1] Introduction

The income tax legislation contains complex accruals regimes that attribute income earned by foreign entities to Australian resident taxpayers who control them or have transferred value to them. Attribution occurs even though these taxpayers have not actually received the relevant income. This chapter outlines the basic features of the accruals regimes and the way they attribute income to certain taxpayers.

The accruals regimes were introduced in the early 1990s and are based on United States measures that were originally developed in the 1960s. They are designed to prevent the deferral advantages associated with having certain kinds of income sheltered offshore in tax havens through interests held by taxpayers in foreign entities. Ordinarily, such income would be able to accumulate at low (or zero) tax rates in such entities until repatriated to Australia. The accruals measures operate to bring forward the point at which such income is taxed. Essentially, resident controllers and transferors are taxed on income earned by the relevant entities (eg companies or trusts) as those entities earn the income (ie on an accruals basis), rather than only when those entities subsequently distribute amounts (eg by way of dividends or trust distributions).

The accruals regimes are important anti-avoidance measures that support the integrity of Australia's tax system, which generally taxes resident taxpayers on their worldwide income [30.2]. The measures are basically targeted at capturing concessionally taxed tainted and passive income stored offshore by residents through foreign entities in which they hold relevant interests.

There are presently two accruals regimes, the CFC regime (contained in pt X *ITAA36*) [34.2] and the transferor trust regime (contained in div 6AAA of pt III *ITAA36*) [34.3]. A third accruals regime, the FIF regime (contained in former pt XI *ITAA36*), was repealed from 1 July 2010 [34.4].

[34.2] Controlled foreign company regime

The CFC regime is designed to assess resident shareholders that control foreign companies on certain income derived by such entities that is not taxed in Australia or comparably taxed overseas. The way the regime operates differs depending on the country in which the CFC is resident.

The CFC regime distinguishes between 'listed countries' and 'unlisted countries'. The following countries (which have tax systems that are considered closely comparable to Australia's tax system) are listed countries: Canada, France, Germany, Japan, New Zealand, the United Kingdom and the United States (reg 19 *ITAR15*). All other countries are unlisted countries (s 320).

In broad terms, subject to the operation of an 'active income test', the CFC regime is aimed primarily at assessing 'attributable taxpayers' on:

- the 'adjusted tainted income' ('ATI') of a CFC resident in an unlisted country, and
- the ATI that is 'eligible designated concession income' ('EDCI') of a CFC resident in a listed country.

Attribution rule

The key provision in the CFC rules is s 456 *ITAA36* which provides that where a 'CFC' has 'attributable income' for a 'statutory accounting period' in respect of an 'attributable taxpayer', the taxpayer's 'attribution percentage' of the attributable income is included in the taxpayer's assessable income in the income year in which the end of the statutory accounting period occurs.

CFC

Broadly, a company is a CFC at a particular time if it is a resident of a listed or unlisted country (ie it is a foreign company) and one of the following applies:

- a group of five or fewer 'Australian entities' (defined in s 336) (each of which has at least a 1% control interest) have an aggregate 'associate-inclusive control interest' of at least 50% in the company
- a single Australian entity has an associate-inclusive control interest of at least 40% in the company and the company is not controlled by any unrelated entities, or
- a group of five or fewer Australian entities either alone or together with associates control the company (s 340).

Example

Situation 1—strict control
A, B and C are Australian residents who each own shares in a foreign company, F1 Co. The remainder of the shares are owned by foreign residents. A has 30% of the associate-inclusive control interests in the company, B has 15% of the associate-inclusive control interests in the company and C has 5% of the associate-inclusive control interests in the company. F1 Co is a CFC because a group of 5 or fewer Australian entities hold 50% of the associate-inclusive control interests in the company.

Situation 2—assumed control
D is an Australian resident who owns shares in a foreign company, F2 Co. The remainder of the shares are owned by foreign residents. If D's associate-inclusive control interest in F2 Co is 42%, F2 Co is a CFC because a single Australian entity has an associate-inclusive control interest of at least 40% in the company.

Situation 3—de facto control
E is an Australian resident who owns shares in a foreign company, F3 Co. The remainder of the shares are owned by foreign residents. Under F3 Co's articles of association, E has the exclusive power to appoint the company's directors. Even if E only has an associate-inclusive control interest of 10% in F3 Co, F3 Co is likely to be a CFC as E would be regarded as controlling the company.

Associate-inclusive control interest

The associate-inclusive control interest that an entity holds in another entity is the sum of the 'direct' and 'indirect' control interests that the entity and their associates (defined in s 318 [8.6]) hold in the entity (s 349).

Broadly speaking, an entity's direct control interest in a company is the greatest percentage of its: (a) rights to paid-up share capital; (b) rights to vote; (c) rights to distributions of capital or profits on winding-up; or (d) rights to distributions of capital or profits otherwise than on winding-up (s 350). An entity's direct control interest in a trust is the greatest percentage of the income or corpus of the trust to which the entity is entitled (s 351).

Indirect control interests are calculated by tracing interests through interposed entities. Indirect control interests can only be traced through 'controlled foreign entities' ('CFEs') (s 352). A CFE is a CFC, a 'controlled foreign partnership' (as defined in s 341) or a 'controlled foreign trust' (as defined in s 342) (s 339). Where an entity is a CFE, the 'control tracing interest' is deemed to be 100% (irrespective of the actual percentage of control) (ss 353 to 356).

Statutory accounting period

A CFC's statutory accounting period is generally a period of 12 months ending on 30 June (s 319). However, a CFC can elect to use an alternative balancing date for determining its statutory accounting period if it regularly uses such date for complying with foreign tax laws or reporting to shareholders.

Attributable taxpayer

An attributable taxpayer is, broadly, an Australian resident who has at least either:

- a 10% associate-inclusive control interest in the CFC, or
- a 1% associate-inclusive control interest in the CFC and is one of five or fewer entities that control the CFC (s 361).

Attribution percentage

The attribution percentage of an attributable taxpayer is the sum of the 'direct' (s 356) and 'indirect' (s 357) attribution interests held by the taxpayer in the CFC (s 362). Indirect attribution interests can only be traced through controlled foreign entities and are calculated by multiplying attribution tracing interests (ss 358 to 360).

Attributable income of a CFC

The attributable income of a CFC is calculated separately for each attributable taxpayer at the end of the CFC's 'statutory accounting period' (s 381). Essentially, the attributable income of a CFC is the CFC's taxable income for the period (based on notional calculations of assessable income, exempt income and deductions) taking into account certain basic assumptions (s 382).

The basic assumptions include the assumptions that the CFC is a resident for the entire period and that its taxable income is calculated according to specified modifications (set out in ss 388 to 431A) (s 383). Importantly, a further assumption is that a particular CFC's notional assessable income consists of only certain amounts, which depend on the kind of foreign country in which the CFC is resident and whether or not it has passed an 'active income test' (see below).

Very broadly, the general effect of this is as follows:

- **Unlisted country CFC.** The attributable income of an unlisted country CFC consists of its:
  (a) ATI (note: if the CFC passes the active income test, ATI is not attributable income)
  (b) trust income, and
  (c) income attributed under the trust transferor rules (s 384).
- **Listed country CFC.** The attributable income of a listed country CFC consists of its:
  (a) ATI that is EDCI (note: if the CFC passes the active income test, ATI that is EDCI is not attributable income)

(b) income that is derived from sources outside the listed country, is not EDCI, and is ATI which is not taxed in a listed country

(c) trust income that is not taxed in the listed country or is taxed in the listed country and is 'designated concession income', and

(d) income attributed under the transferor trust rules (s 385).

There is a *de minimis* exemption which excludes certain forms of income from the attributable income of a listed country CFC provided it does not exceed the lesser of $50,000 or 5% of the CFC's gross turnover for the relevant period (s 385(4)).

Adjusted tainted income

A CFC's ATI (s 386) consists of its:

- passive income (eg dividends, tainted interest income, rent, royalties and net gains from the disposal of tainted assets as defined in s 317) (s 446)
- tainted sales income (eg income from the sale of certain goods to an associate) (s 447), and
- tainted services income (eg income from providing services either to an Australian resident other than in connection with an overseas PE, or to a non-resident in connection with a PE in Australia) (s 448).

Tainted interest income includes interest or a payment in the nature of interest as well as certain other forms of income (s 317). A tainted asset is defined widely to include loans, debentures, bonds, bills of exchange, promissory notes, shares in companies, interests in trusts or partnerships, futures contracts, life insurance policies, rights or options in respect of such items and similar financial instruments (s 317).

Eligible designated concession income

Broadly speaking, the EDCI of a listed country CFC consists of 'designated concession income' that is not taxed in a listed country or taxed at reduced rates in a listed country (s 317). Designated concession income comprises income or profits of a kind specified in the table in reg 17 *ITAR15* (s 317). The table refers to particular kinds of income or profits that are concessionally taxed in the various listed countries.

Active income test

To pass the active income test in relation to a statutory accounting period, a CFC must have:

- been in existence at the end of the statutory accounting period and been resident of a listed or unlisted country at all times during the period it existed
- carried on business through a PE in its country of residence at all times during the period
- maintained accounts prepared according to commercially accepted accounting principles which give a true and fair view of its financial position, and
- a 'tainted income ratio' for the statutory accounting period of less than 0.05 (s 432).

A CFC will have a tainted income ratio for a statutory accounting period of less than 0.05 if less than 5% of its gross turnover for the statutory accounting period is gross tainted turnover (ie passive income, tainted sales income and tainted services income) (ss 433 to 435).

Diagram

The following diagram summarises the key questions that need to be answered and the basic steps involved in calculating an attributable taxpayer's assessable income under the CFC regime:

Is there a CFC?

A CFC is a foreign company in relation to which any one of the following applies:

1. A group of five or fewer 'Australian entities', each with at least 1% control interest, have an aggregate 'associate-inclusive control interest' of at least 50% or more in the company
2. A single Australian entity has an associate-inclusive control interest of at least 40% in the company and the company is not controlled by any unrelated entities, or
3. A group of five or fewer Australian entities either alone or together with an associate control the company (s 340).

An associate-inclusive control interest is, broadly, the sum of the direct (ss 350, 351) and indirect (s 352) control interests held by a taxpayer and their associates (s 349).

No → The CFC regime does not apply

Yes ↓

Is the taxpayer an attributable taxpayer in respect of the CFC?

An attributable taxpayer is, broadly, an Australian resident who has at least either:

1. A 10% associate-inclusive control interest in the CFC, or
2. A 1% associate-inclusive control interest in the CFC and is one of five or fewer entities that control the CFC (s 361)

No → The CFC regime does not apply

Yes ↓

What is the attributable income of the CFC?

The attributable income of a CFC depends on whether it is a resident of a 'listed country' (ie Canada, France, Germany, Japan, New Zealand, the United Kingdom and the United States) or an 'unlisted country' (ie any other country) (s 320; reg 19 *ITAR15*)

Unlisted country CFC

The attributable income of an unlisted country CFC is generally the sum of its:

1. Adjusted tainted income (ie passive income, tainted sales income and tainted services income)
2. Trust income, and
3. Income attributed under the transferor trust rules (s 384).

However, if the CFC passes the active income test, its adjusted tainted income is not attributable income.

Listed country CFC

The attributable income of a listed country CFC is generally the sum of its:

1. Adjusted tainted income that is 'eligible designated concession income' (EDCI) (reg 17 *ITAR15*)
2. Adjusted tainted income derived from sources outside the listed country that is neither EDCI nor taxed in a listed country
3. Trust income that is not taxed in a listed country or is taxed in a listed country and is 'designated concession income', and
4. Income attributed under the transferor trust rules.

However, if the CFC passes the active income test, adjusted tainted income that is eligible designated concession income is not attributable income.

What is included in the attributable taxpayer's assessable income?

An attributable taxpayer must include its 'attribution percentage' of a CFC's attributable income in its assessable income (s 456)

An attributable taxpayer's attribution percentage is the sum of the direct (s 356) and indirect (s 357) attribution interests held by the taxpayer in the CFC (s 362)

[34.3] Transferor trust regime

The transferor trust regime contained in div 6AAA of pt III *ITAA36* attributes the income of a non-resident trust estate (s 102AAB) to residents that have transferred property or provided services to the trust (ss 102AAJ, 102AAK).

Attribution rule

A resident entity that is an 'attributable taxpayer' in relation to a non-resident trust estate is required to include in assessable income the 'notional attributable income' ('NAI') of the trust estate (or a pro rata portion of the NAI if the taxpayer is a resident for only part of the income year) (s 102AAZD(1)). The NAI of a trust estate is its 'attributable income' for the year (unless the income years of the taxpayer and non-resident trust do not start at the same time, in which case the NAI is based on a formula) (s 102AAZD(2)).

If more than one person has transferred property or provided services to the trust, the Commissioner may reduce the amount included in a particular attributable taxpayer's assessable income to reflect this (so long as the taxpayer has provided the requisite information to make the adjustment) (s 102AAZD(3)). However, if it would be unreasonable to expect the taxpayer to obtain such information, the amount included is calculated by reference to a formula based on the indexed value of the property transferred or services provided multiplied by a statutory interest rate (s 102AAZD(4)).

Attributable taxpayer

Generally, an entity is an attributable taxpayer in respect of a trust estate if it has transferred property or provided services to the trust before or during the entity's current year of income. In the case of a 'non-discretionary trust estate' (defined in s 102AAB) the property transferred or services provided must have occurred after 12 April 1989 and must have been for no consideration or less than arm's length consideration.

Attributable income

The calculation of the attributable income of a non-resident trust estate depends on whether or not it is a listed country trust estate (ie a trust estate which has each item of its income subject to tax in a listed country or Australia, or treated as 'designated concession income': s 102AAE).

The attributable income of a non-resident trust estate is, broadly, its 'net income' (for a listed country trust estate, its net income is calculated by reference to only its EDCI and FIF income) reduced by specified amounts (eg amounts assessable under ss 97, 98, 99 or 99A; amounts that have previously been attributed under the transferor trust, CFC or FIF rules; and any foreign or Australian tax paid by the trustee or beneficiaries on the reduced net income) (s 102AAU).

De minimis exemption

No amount is attributable in respect of a listed country trust estate if the total attributable income from all non-resident trusts in respect of which the taxpayer is an attributable taxpayer does not exceed the lesser of: (a) $20,000; or (b) 10% of the total net income of each of those trust estates (s 102AAZE).

[34.4] Former foreign investment fund regime

The FIF regime in former pt XI *ITAA36* was designed to address certain deferral opportunities not covered by the CFC or transferor trust measures. The FIF regime was extremely complex and had certain unintended effects, which resulted in its repeal from 1 July 2010.

Attribution rule

The FIF regime applied to persons who were residents at any time during an income year and who held 'interests' in FIFs (ie foreign companies and foreign trusts) at the end of an income year, or who held interests in 'FLPs' (foreign life assurance policies) at any time during the year (former ss 481 to 483).

Under former s 529, a resident taxpayer was assessed on the FIF income which accrued to the taxpayer from a FIF or FLP during the FIF's or FLP's notional accounting period. Where the taxpayer was a resident for only part of the FIF's or FLP's notional accounting period, the taxpayer was only assessed on a pro rata proportion of the FIF income. The assessable amount was reduced in certain cases (eg where the FIF or FLP made assessable distributions or paid exempt dividends under former s 23AJ to the taxpayer during the relevant period: former s 530).

The FIF income that accrued to a taxpayer from a FIF was calculated, where practicable, according to a market value method (former ss 538 to 542). Otherwise, it was calculated according to a 'deemed rate of return method', unless the taxpayer elected to use a 'calculation method' (former ss 542 to 583). The FIF income that accrued to a taxpayer from a FLP was calculated according to a deemed rate of return method, unless the taxpayer elected to use a 'cash surrender value method' (former ss 584 to 600).

Exemptions from the FIF regime

There were a number of exemptions from the FIF regime. For instance, it did not apply to an interest held by a taxpayer in a foreign company that was principally engaged in 'eligible activities' (ie business activities other than excluded activities) (former ss 495 to 501). The regime also did not apply to interests held by individuals that (together with their associates' interests) did not exceed $50,000 (former s 515). Furthermore, it did not apply where the taxpayer's non-exempt FIF interests were 10% or less of the total value of all the taxpayer's FIF interests (former s 525). Complying superannuation entities were also excluded from the FIF rules.

[34.5] Preventing double taxation of attributed income

Income that has been attributed to taxpayers under the accruals taxation regimes should not be taxed again when it is eventually distributed to them (eg as dividends or trust distributions), as this would produce double taxation of the same underlying amounts.

To prevent double taxation occurring as a consequence of the operation of the CFC and former FIF regimes, special accounts are used to trace the extent to which CFC income or former FIF income has been attributed to taxpayers. These accounts give rise to credit and debit entries and are known as 'attribution accounts' for CFC purposes (div 4 of pt X *ITAA36*) and 'FIF attribution accounts' for FIF purposes (former div 19 of pt XI *ITAA36*). Under the CFC rules, for example, an 'attribution credit' arises where an amount is attributed to a taxpayer under s 456 (s 371) and an 'attribution debit' arises where an 'attribution account payment' (eg a dividend) is made to a taxpayer under s 365 (s 372). Payments that are debited to attribution accounts and FIF attribution accounts are non-assessable non-exempt income in the hands of taxpayers under ss 23AI and 23AK *ITAA36*.

Likewise, payments out of income that has been attributed to a transferor under the transferor trust rules are generally exempt from tax when they are paid to a resident beneficiary of a trust under ss 99B(2)(d) and (e) (note that an interest charge may nevertheless apply to such income to take into account the benefit of deferral: s 102AAM).

Example A Co (an Australia resident company) owns all of the shares in F Co (a CFC resident in an unlisted country). F Co had attributable income of $50,000 for the statutory accounting period ending 30 June 2023. This amount is attributed to A Co and included in its assessable income for 2022/23 under s 456 [34.2]. It also results in an attribution credit of $50,000 arising in F Co's attribution account under s 371. F Co subsequently pays a dividend of $50,000 to A Co in the following income year. The dividend is an attribution account payment which gives rise to an attribution debit of $50,000 under s 372. As a result, to prevent double taxation, the dividend is non-assessable non-exempt income of A Co under s 23AI.

[34.6] QUESTIONS

1. What is 'accruals taxation' and what is the object of the accruals taxation regimes?
2. What is the difference between a listed country and an unlisted country? Why is this distinction important under the CFC rules?
3. What is a CFC? How is the income of a CFC attributed to taxpayers?
4. Discuss the concepts of ATI and EDCI and their relevance.
5. Describe the broad features of the trust transferor regime.
6. What rules exist to prevent double taxation of previously attributed income?

35 FOREIGN EXCHANGE

[35.1] Introduction

Many transactions that affect taxpayers may occur in foreign currency. For example, an Australian resident employed by an international company may be paid his or her salary in euros. Likewise, an exporter that sells its goods to overseas purchasers might be paid in US dollars. To deal with situations like these, the *ITAA97* has special rules for translating foreign currency into Australian currency [35.2]. The aim of these rules is to ensure that transactions that occur in foreign currency are converted into Australian dollars ('A$') so that a standard unit of account is used for calculating a taxpayer's Australian income tax liabilities.

It is important to be aware that transactions that occur in foreign currency can also result in taxpayers making exchange gains and exchange losses as a result of currency fluctuations. A special forex regime is contained in the *ITAA97* for dealing with the tax treatment of such gains and losses [35.3].

[35.2] Currency translation regime

The currency translation rules are located in div 960 *ITAA97* and consist of a general translation rule (sub-div 960-C) and a functional currency rule (sub-div 960-D). They apply to 'foreign currency', which is defined as a currency other than Australian currency, digital currency or anything prescribed by the regulations (s 995-1 *ITAA97*). Digital currency has the same meaning as it does under the *GSTA* [7.6].

General translation rule

The general translation rule requires 'amounts' in a foreign currency to be translated into Australian currency at the exchange rate applicable at the times specified in the table in s 960-50(6). The table contains the following translation rules:

- The amount of an obligation to pay foreign currency that has ceased in circumstances where 'forex realisation event 4' happens is translated at the exchange rate applicable at the 'tax recognition time' [35.3].
- The cost of a depreciating asset is translated at the exchange rate applicable when the taxpayer began to hold the asset or satisfied the liability to pay for it (whichever occurs first).
- The value of trading stock on hand at the end of an income year that is valued at 'cost' is translated at the exchange rate applicable at the time when the item became on hand.
- The value of trading stock on hand at the end of an income year that is valued at 'market selling value' or 'replacement value' is translated at the exchange rate applicable at the end of the income year.

- The amount of money, or the market value of property, relating to transactions or events under the CGT rules is translated at the exchange rate applicable at the time of the transaction or event.
- The amount of ordinary income is translated at the exchange rate applicable at the time of its derivation or receipt (whichever occurs first).
- The amount of statutory income (other than an amount included in assessable income under the CGT rules in div 102 *ITAA97*) is translated at the exchange rate applicable at the time of receipt or at the time when the requirement first arose to include it in assessable income (whichever occurs first).
- The amount of a deduction (other than a deduction arising under div 40 *ITAA97*, ie the capital allowance regime) is translated at the exchange rate applicable at the time of payment or the time the amount becomes deductible (whichever occurs first).
- The amount that is relevant to quantifying a company's expenditure on a film for the purposes of div 376 *ITAA97* [27.6] is translated at one of three different exchange rates depending on what it relates to.
- The amount required to be withheld from a payment under the PAYG provisions is translated at the exchange rate applicable at the time when the amount is required to be withheld.
- The amount of any other payment or receipt is translated at the exchange rate applicable at the time of the payment or receipt.

The above rules operate subject to any modifications in the regulations (s 960-50(7)). Subdivision 960-C *ITAR21* permits foreign currency to be translated into Australian dollars using various rates, including average rates, daily rates and rates used in preparing audited financial reports. This is designed to provide flexibility so that it is not necessary for taxpayers to always use the prevailing 'spot rate' each time that an amount needs to be translated into Australian dollars.

Example T Co manufactures tractors in Australia and exports them to customers in the United States. T Co sold a tractor for US$7,000 on 15 May 2023 (when A$1.00 = US$0.70). T Co received payment for the tractor on 1 August 2023 (when A$1.00 = US$0.90).

T Co accounts for its income on an accruals basis and it therefore derived the US$7,000 on 15 May 2023. T Co must translate the US$7,000 into Australian dollars at the exchange rate applicable at the time of derivation. T Co's income from the sale of the tractor is therefore A$10,000 (US$7,000 × 1.00/0.70). This amount must be brought to account in the 2022/23 income year.

Note that when T Co receives payment for the tractor, this will result in a 'forex realisation event' happening, which has separate tax implications discussed at [35.3].

Functional currency rules

To reduce compliance costs, certain entities that keep their accounts solely or predominantly in a particular foreign currency, the 'applicable functional currency' ('AFC') (s 960-70), may choose to work out their relevant tax liabilities in the AFC and then simply translate the net figure into Australian dollars (s 960-60). Allowing entities to use the AFC overcomes the need for them to separately translate every amount relevant to each transaction that is denominated in a foreign currency into Australian dollars, as would ordinarily be required under the general translation rule.

The following entities may choose to use their AFC for the following purposes (s 960-60):

- An Australian resident required to prepare financial reports under s 292 of the *Corporations Act* (eg a public company) can use the AFC to work out so much of its taxable income or tax loss as is not Covered by any other choices outlined below.

- An Australian resident carrying on an activity or business through an overseas PE and A foreign resident carrying on an activity or business through an Australian PE can use the AFC to work out the taxable income or tax loss derived from the activity or Business carried on through the PE.
- An offshore banking unit can use the AFC to work out its total assessable OB income and its total allowable OB deductions [25.13].
- An attributable taxpayer of a CFC can use the AFC to work out the CFC's total 'attributable income' [34.2].
- A transferor trust can use the AFC to work out its 'attributable income' [34.3].

A choice to use the AFC must be made in writing and continues to have effect until a written withdrawal of the choice takes effect.

Amounts are translated according to 'translation rules' contained in s 960-80 (which operate subject to special rules in s 960-85). Generally, the translation rules require all relevant amounts that are not in the AFC (including Australian dollars) to be translated into the AFC. The relevant tax liability is then worked out in the AFC. This amount is then finally translated into Australian dollars.

[35.3] Forex regime

Division 775 *ITAA97* contains the 'forex regime', which sets out special rules for dealing with foreign currency exchange gains and losses. The forex regime generally applies to transactions entered into from 1 July 2003 (ss 775-155, 960-55).

Forex regime supersedes general tax rules

The aim of the forex regime is to tax currency exchange gains and losses under a set of standard statutory rules. Such gains and losses can arise where the price in a contract is expressed in a foreign currency. If the exchange rate between the Australian dollar and the foreign currency changes between the time the contract is entered into and the time the consideration is paid or received, the taxpayer will be required to pay, or will be entitled to receive, a different Australian dollar amount than the Australian dollar amount originally brought to account as assessable income or as a deduction. This difference represents the respective exchange gain or loss.

The forex regime supersedes the traditional approach of dealing with exchange gains and losses under the 'general tax rules' (ie under the ordinary income and general deduction provisions). Under these rules, exchange gains were assessable and exchange losses were deductible where they arose on 'revenue account'. For example, in *International Nickel Australia Ltd v FC of T* 77 ATC 4383, a nickel supplier was assessed on exchange gains and was entitled to deductions for exchange losses made in relation to its nickel contracts. Similarly, in *AVCO Financial Services Ltd v FC of T* 82 ATC 4246, a finance company was assessed on exchange gains and was entitled to deductions for exchange losses arising from overseas borrowings that it used to provide loans to its customers. By way of contrast, in *Commercial & General Acceptance Ltd v FC of T* 77 ATC 4375, a finance company that had borrowed money to strengthen its capital base was not assessed on exchange gains made on its borrowings as the gains were of a capital nature. To reverse the outcome in situations such as those that occurred in *Commercial & General Acceptance Ltd*, div 3B of pt III *ITAA36* was enacted. Basically, the object of div 3B was to assess taxpayers on exchange gains and allow them deductions for exchange losses that were of a capital nature where they had an income-producing or business character. Division 3B was repealed upon the introduction of the forex regime.

Under the general tax rules, exchange gains and losses were only recognised if amounts in one currency had actually been converted into another currency. This is demonstrated by *FC of T v Energy Resources of Australia Ltd* 96 ATC 4536, where the High Court held that a mining company that had financed its operations by issuing discounted Euronotes in US dollars, which were subsequently paid out at face value in US dollars, had not made any exchange gains or losses, since only one currency was involved in the relevant transactions. The Court held (at 4540):

> This case has nothing to do with currency gains and losses, for the simple reason that the taxpayer dealt only in US dollars. The taxpayer made no currency gains or losses because it never converted any of the proceeds of the notes into Australian dollars. For Australian tax purposes, the only relevant conversion was the cost in Australian dollars of the loss made in US dollars when the taxpayer incurred its liability to pay the face value of the notes.

It is important to be aware that the introduction of the currency translation regime has meant that amounts in foreign currency must now generally be translated into Australian dollars at the exchange rate applicable at the times specified in the table in s 960-50(6) [35.2]. This means that exchange gains and losses can, therefore, technically now arise even though no foreign currency has actually been converted into Australian dollars.

Basic forex rules

The foreign currency exchange gain and loss rules require taxpayers to include a 'forex realisation' gain ('FRG') in their assessable income (s 775-15(1)) and allow them a deduction for a 'forex realisation loss' ('FRL') (s 775-30(1)). Certain FRGs and FRLs are excluded from these basic rules (eg certain gains and losses of a private or domestic nature) (ss 775-15(2), 775-30(2)).

To prevent duplication with the other tax laws, to the extent that a FRG is included in assessable income or a FRL is deductible, the gain is not included in assessable income and the loss is not deductible under any other taxation provision (ss 775-15(4), 775-30(4)). This ensures that the forex regime is an 'exclusive code' that takes precedence over the general tax rules (discussed above).

Forex realisation events

A FRG or a FRL can only arise as a result of the happening of a 'forex realisation Event' ('FRE'). There are five basic kinds of FRE:

- FRE 1 happens when CGT event A1 applies to an entity that disposes of foreign currency, or a right to foreign currency, to another entity (s 775-40).
- FRE 2 happens when an entity ceases to have a right to receive foreign currency (eg where an entity has a right to be paid in foreign currency and receives payment in that currency) (s 775-45).
- FRE 3 happens when an entity ceases to have an obligation to receive foreign currency where the obligation was assumed in return for the creation or acquisition of a right to pay either foreign currency or Australian currency (eg where an entity has granted a 'put option' that requires the entity to acquire foreign currency from another entity and the Option is exercised or expires) (s 775-50).
- FRE 4 happens when an entity ceases to have an obligation to pay foreign currency (eg where an entity is obliged to pay an amount in foreign currency and pays the amount) (s 775-55).
- FRE 5 happens when an entity ceases to have a right to pay foreign currency and the right is created or acquired in return for the assumption of an obligation to pay either foreign currency or Australian currency (eg where an entity has a 'call option' requiring another entity to acquire its foreign currency and the option is exercised or expires) (s 775-60).

The basic rules outlined above operate subject to special rules relating to 'short-term' FRGs and FRLs. In addition, in certain circumstances, entities are permitted to make particular elections that result in the basic FREs being disregarded and replaced with special FREs. There are four special FREs:

- FRE 6 and FRE 7 provide an entity that issues 'eligible securities' in respect of a 'facility agreement' with roll-over relief (sub-div 775-C)
- FRE 8 allows an entity to use a 'retranslation rule' in respect of its 'qualifying forex accounts' (sub-div 775-E), and
- FRE 9 allows an entity to use a 'retranslation rule' where it has made a 'foreign exchange retranslation election' under sub-div 230-D (sub-div 775-F) [29.2].

Multiple forex realisation events

It is technically possible for one transaction to produce multiple FREs. For instance, an agreement to sell one foreign currency in exchange for another foreign currency in the future will involve both a right or obligation to receive foreign currency and a right or obligation to pay foreign currency. Where more than one FRE can potentially apply, s 775-65 specifies which FREs are to be ignored. The object of s 775-65 is to ensure that a taxpayer only makes one FRG or FRL from a single transaction.

Amount of a forex realisation gain or loss

The way a FRG or a FRL is calculated depends on the nature of the FRE. In general, the amount of the gain or loss is calculated according to the 'currency exchange rate effect' (ie the currency fluctuation that has arisen under the event). This is usually the difference between the A$ cost of the foreign currency or right and the A$ proceeds for its disposal.

Alternatively, the gain or loss may be based on the difference between the A$ cost of a right or obligation to receive or pay foreign currency at its 'tax recognition time' and the A$ amount paid or received in satisfaction of that right or obligation. The 'tax recognition time' is generally the time that the right or obligation is first recognised under the tax system (eg as income, a deduction, a cost, etc).

Example

FRE 1 (entity disposes of foreign currency)

Brian acquired US$1m on 1 March 2022 (when A$1 = US$0.80). He used the US$1m to purchase shares in a US company on 1 April 2023 (when A$1 = US$0.50).

CGT event A1 happened when Brian disposed of the foreign currency to purchase the shares. The cost base of the foreign currency is A$1.25m (US$1m × 1.00/0.80). The capital proceeds from the disposal of the foreign currency is the market value of the shares received for the disposal of the foreign currency, ie A$2m (US$1m × 1.00/0.50). Brian has therefore made a FRG under FRE 1 of A$750,000 (A$2m – A$1.25m), which he must include in his assessable income for the 2022/23 income year.

FRE 2 (entity ceases to have right to receive foreign currency)

On 1 March 2022 (when A$1 = US$0.80), Ted, a tennis racquet manufacturer, entered into a contract to supply tennis racquets to a customer in the United States for US$10,000. As a result of entering into the contract, Ted has a right to receive foreign currency. The forex cost base of the right is determined at the tax recognition time, which occurs when the income is derived (ie 1 March 2022). It is therefore A$12,500 (US$10,000 × 1.00/0.80). This amount is included in Ted's assessable income under s 6-5 *ITAA97* for the 2021/22 income year.

The customer paid Ted for the racquets on 1 April 2023 (when A$1 = US$0.50). At such time, Ted ceases to have the right to receive the foreign currency because the debt has been satisfied. FRE 2 therefore happens on 1 April 2023. The A$ amount that Ted receives in respect of the event is A$20,000 (US$10,000 × 1.00/0.50). As this amount is greater than the forex cost base of the right (A$12,500), Ted makes a FRG of A$7,500, which he must include in his assessable income for the 2022/23 income year.

FRE 4 (entity ceases to have obligation to pay foreign currency)

On 1 March 2022 (when A$1 = US$0.80), Gino, a dentist, purchased some dental products for his surgery from an overseas supplier for US$1,000. Gino therefore assumed an obligation to pay foreign currency and is entitled to a deduction of A$1,250 (US$1,000 × 1.00/0.80). This amount is deductible to Gino in the 2021/22 income year under s 8-1 *ITAA97*.

On 1 April 2023 (when A$1 = US$0.50), Gino pays his supplier US$1,000. As a consequence, FRE 4 happens as Gino ceases to have an obligation to pay the foreign currency. As the A$ amount Gino pays in respect of the event (A$2,000 = US$1,000 × 1.00/0.50) exceeds the proceeds of assuming the obligation (A$1,250), he makes a FRL of A$750, which he can deduct in the 2022/23 income year.

Special short-term forex realisation gain and loss rules

The basic forex realisation rules discussed above operate subject to special 'short-term' rules. Very broadly, these rules apply to FRGs and FRLs that arise under FRE 2 and FRE 4 in the circumstances specified in the tables in ss 775-70 and 775-75. Most importantly, they operate in respect of gains and losses that occur as a result of:

- a right to receive foreign currency arising from disposing a CGT asset
- an obligation to pay foreign currency for acquiring a CGT asset, and
- an obligation to pay foreign currency for a depreciating asset.

In the first two cases, the short-term rules apply if a CGT asset is acquired or disposed of and the time between the acquisition or disposal of the asset and the date for payment or receipt of the foreign currency is not more than 12 months. In the third case, the short-term rules apply if the time between a depreciating asset beginning to be held and the date for payment of the foreign currency is not more than 12 months before or 12 months after the date the asset began to be held.

Taxpayers may make an irrevocable written election to exclude the short-term rules, in which case the basic rules in ss 775-15 and 775-30 will operate instead (s 775-80).

Where the short-term rules operate, the treatment of any FRG or FRL is integrated into the tax treatment of the underlying asset rather than being brought to account separately as assessable income or as a deduction under the basic rules in ss 775-15 and 775-30. The broad way in which this occurs is summarised in the following table:

Short-term forex realisation gain	Short-term forex realisation loss
Where the taxpayer makes a FRG from FRE 2 and the right to receive foreign currency was created in return for the disposal of a CGT asset (other than a depreciating asset), the FRG is not assessable under s 775-15. Instead, CGT event K10 occurs when the FRE happens and the taxpayer makes a capital gain equal to the FRG.	Where the taxpayer makes a FRL from FRE 2 and the right to receive foreign currency was created in return for the disposal of a CGT asset (other than a depreciating asset), the FRL is not deductible under s 775-30. Instead, CGT event K11 occurs when the FRE happens and the taxpayer makes a capital loss equal to the FRL.
Where the taxpayer makes a FRG from FRE 4 and the obligation to pay foreign currency was incurred in return for the acquisition of a CGT asset (other than a depreciating asset), the FRG is not assessable under s 775-15. Instead, the cost base and reduced cost base of the CGT asset is reduced by the amount of the FRG.	Where a taxpayer makes a FRL from FRE 4 and the obligation to pay foreign currency was incurred in return for the acquisition of a CGT asset (other than a depreciating asset), the FRL is not deductible under s 775-30. Instead, the cost base and reduced cost base of the CGT asset is increased by the FRL.

Short-term forex realisation gain	Short-term forex realisation loss
Where the taxpayer makes a FRG from FRE 4 and the obligation to pay foreign currency was incurred in return for acquiring a depreciating asset, the FRG is not assessable under s 775-15. Instead, the asset's cost, its adjustable value, or the opening value of the pool in which the asset resides is reduced by the FRG (but not below zero) and any excess is included in assessable income.	Where the taxpayer makes a FRL from FRE 4 and the obligation to pay foreign currency was incurred in return for acquiring a depreciating asset, the FRL is not deductible under s 775-30. Instead, the asset's cost, its adjustable value, or the opening value of the pool in which the asset resides is increased by the amount of the FRL.

Qualifying forex accounts

The following FREs can occur where a taxpayer maintains a bank account in a foreign currency:

- FRE 1 can occur whenever the taxpayer deposits foreign currency into the account (this is because the taxpayer has disposed of foreign currency).
- FRE 2 can occur whenever the taxpayer Withdraws foreign currency from the account at a time when it has a credit balance (this is because the taxpayer's right to receive foreign currency from the bank ceases to the extent of the withdrawal).
- FRE 4 can occur whenever the taxpayer deposits foreign currency into an account at a time when it has a debit balance (this is because the taxpayer's obligations to pay foreign currency to the bank ceases to the extent of the deposit).

Taxpayers can elect to use the 'limited balance election' (sub-div 775-D) or the 'retranslation election' (sub-div 775-E) to minimise their compliance costs in relation to their 'qualifying forex accounts' ('QFAs'). A QFA is defined as a credit card account, or an account held for the primary purpose of facilitating transactions, that is denominated in a foreign currency (s 995-1).

Limited balance election (sub-div 775-D)

Where a taxpayer has made a 'limited balance election' in respect of a QFA under s 775-230, FRGs and FRLs that arise as a result of FRE 2 or FRE 4 happening in respect of the QFA are disregarded, provided the 'limited balance test' is passed (s 775-250). This test is passed if the combined credit and debit balances of all the accounts covered by the taxpayer's election is not more than the foreign currency equivalent of A$250,000 (a 'buffer exception' allows the combined balance of the accounts to be no more than A$500,000 for up to two 15-day periods in an income year) (s 775-245).

Where a taxpayer breaches the limited balance test, FRE 2 and FRE 4 can apply to subsequent deposits and withdrawals. A taxpayer can re-enter the regime without making a fresh election if it subsequently satisfies the limited balance test. A notional realisation rule, however, applies in this situation to ensure that any gain or loss made during the intervening breach period is brought to account on re-entry (s 775-255).

Retranslation election (sub-div 775-E)

Where a taxpayer has made a 'retranslation election' in respect of a QFA under s 775-270, FRGs and FRLs that arise as a result of FRE 2 or FRE 4 happening in respect of the QFA are disregarded (s 775-280) and FRE 8 applies in respect of the QFA (s 775-285).

FRE 8 requires a taxpayer to determine the 'retranslation amount' in respect of the QFA for the 'retranslation period' (ordinarily the income year) using the following formula:

$$\begin{array}{c}\text{Closing balance}\\ \text{of account for}\\ \text{the retranslation}\\ \text{period}\end{array} - \begin{array}{c}\text{Opening balance}\\ \text{of account for}\\ \text{the retranslation}\\ \text{period}\end{array} - \begin{array}{c}\text{Total deposits made}\\ \text{to account during}\\ \text{the retranslation}\\ \text{period}\end{array} - \begin{array}{c}\text{Total withdrawals made}\\ \text{from account during}\\ \text{the retranslation}\\ \text{period}\end{array}$$

In calculating the elements in the formula, the following exchange rates are used:

- **closing balance**—the exchange rate at the end of the retranslation period
- **opening balance**—the exchange rate at the beginning of the retranslation period
- **deposits**—the exchange rate at the time each deposit is made, and
- **withdrawals**—the exchange rate at the time each withdrawal is made.

A taxpayer makes a FRG under FRE 8 if there is a positive retranslation amount for the retranslation period. The taxpayer makes a FRL under FRE 8 if there is a negative retranslation amount for the retranslation period. The amount of the FRG or FRL is the respective positive or negative retranslation amount.

[35.4] QUESTIONS

1. What is the aim of the currency translation rules? What is the role of the table in s 960-50(6) *ITAA97*? What is the role of the 'functional currency rule' in s 960-60?
2. Discuss the relationship between the forex regime in div 775 and the general tax rules for dealing with exchange gains and losses.
3. Can foreign exchange gains and losses arise under div 775 where no foreign currency has actually been converted into Australian dollars?
4. What are the consequences of taxpayers making foreign exchange gains and foreign exchange losses?
5. What is a 'forex realisation event'? In what circumstances do such events arise and why is it important to determine whether they occur?
6. Softie Co is an exporter of computer software. On 1 May 2022 (when A$1 = US$0.80), Softie entered into a contract to supply products to a customer in the United States for US$10,000. Softie's customer paid Softie US$10,000 on 1 August 2023 (when A$1 = US$0.50). How do the forex rules apply to this transaction?
7. What is the object of the short-term FRG and FRL rules?

PART L

TAX AVOIDANCE

36 TAX AVOIDANCE

[36.1] Introduction

Tax avoidance is one of the most controversial and widely debated topics in taxation law. This chapter examines the concept of tax avoidance and distinguishes it from the concepts of tax evasion and tax planning with which it is sometimes confused [36.2]. It also discusses various judicial and legislative responses to tax avoidance. In particular, it focuses on the specific anti-avoidance provisions in div 6A of pt III *ITAA36* [36.4] and pt 2-42 *ITAA97* [36.5], which have been enacted to address certain income alienation schemes designed to divert income from taxpayers who are subject to high rates of tax to their associates (eg family members and related entities) who are subject to lower rates of tax. It also discusses service entity arrangements, which have been used by some professional firms to split income [36.6].

[36.2] Distinguishing tax avoidance from tax evasion and tax planning

Tax avoidance is a distinct and nebulous concept that lies somewhere between the concepts of tax evasion and tax planning. For the purposes of general discussion, these concepts may be described as follows:

- **Tax evasion.** Tax evasion involves the illegal underpayment of tax. It typically involves non-disclosure of a liability or a fraudulent claim for benefits. For example, it would include failing to declare income or claiming deductions for outgoings that have not been incurred.
- **Tax avoidance.** Tax avoidance involves entering into legal arrangements that are designed to exploit unintended defects and loopholes in the legislation. These arrangements are often contrived and artificial and designed to circumvent the 'spirit' of the tax law. They also sometimes involve transactions or steps that appear to have little or no substantial commercial purpose other than to create a situation that would give rise to some form of tax benefit.
- **Tax planning.** Tax planning involves entering into legal arrangements in order to exploit legitimate opportunities available under the tax law to minimise tax liabilities. These arrangements often involve taxpayers exercising specific choices available under the legislation to enable them to benefit from various concessions.

Although (once detected) tax evasion is usually clear-cut, the line that separates tax avoidance from tax planning (sometimes also referred to as 'tax minimisation' or 'tax mitigation') is not as obvious, and in borderline cases can be quite blurred. In the United Kingdom decision of *IRC v Willoughby* [1997] 4 All ER 65, Lord Nolan attempted to explain the essential difference between these concepts as follows (at 73):

> The hallmark of tax avoidance is that the taxpayer reduces his liability to tax without incurring the economic consequences that Parliament intended to be suffered by any taxpayer qualifying for such reduction in his tax liability. The hallmark of tax mitigation, on the other hand, is that the taxpayer takes advantage of a fiscally attractive option afforded to him by the tax legislation, and genuinely suffers the economic consequences that Parliament intended to be suffered by those taking advantage of the option.

Combating tax evasion

Tax evasion is one of the greatest challenges confronting revenue authorities around the world. Governments need to prevent tax evasion, as it not only results in them collecting less revenue, but also places a greater overall burden on law-abiding members of society to fund public spending. The fact that some people evade tax can cause considerable resentment in the community at large and, if not addressed, can lead to a loss of confidence in the integrity of the tax system. This can have significant social, economic and political consequences.

The seriousness of tax evasion was recognised in *DPP (Commonwealth) v Goldberg* (2001) 184 ALR 387, where it was stated:

> Tax evasion is not a game, or a victimless crime. It is a form of corruption and is, therefore, insidious. In the face of brazen tax evasion, honest citizens begin to doubt their own values and are tempted to do what they see others do with apparent impunity. At the very least, they are left with a legitimate sense of grievance, which is itself divisive. Tax evasion is not simply a matter of failing to pay one's debt to the government. It is theft and tax evaders are thieves.

Dealing with tax evasion is naturally always a high priority for Governments, not only because it decreases their revenue, but also because it is often linked to other crimes. The Australian Government combats tax evasion by imposing pecuniary penalties and jail terms on offenders. For instance, tax evaders can be prosecuted for committing a range of offences under the *Tax Administration Act 1953* (Cth) and the *Criminal Code Act 1995* (Cth) [41.3].

The obvious problem with tax evasion is that it can be difficult to detect because of its covert nature. If tax evasion is not addressed, it can escalate and have an adverse impact on taxpayer compliance. If the community sees that tax evaders are not prosecuted, there is a real risk that more people will be tempted to evade tax. It is therefore important for revenue authorities to highlight the actions they are taking to curb tax evasion so as to deter others from becoming involved. The ATO is continually warning taxpayers about its serious stance on tax evasion on its website and in its publications (eg *Targeting Tax Crime—A Whole-of-Government Approach*).

As a general rule, it is easier for those dealing in cash to engage in tax evasion. As a consequence, a major focus of the ATO over the years has been tackling tax evasion in the 'cash economy' (sometimes also referred to as the 'black economy'). In 1996, the Commissioner established the ATO's Cash Economy Taskforce. The taskforce released three reports (*Improving Tax Compliance in the Cash Economy* (1997); *Improving Tax Compliance in the Cash Economy* (1998); and *The Cash Economy under the New Tax System* (2003)). The reports identified various issues relating to the cash economy and made recommendations on strategies to combat tax evasion. In its first report, the taskforce stated (at 8):

> The very existence and nature of cash provides the opportunity for evading tax. It is difficult to trace as it often leaves no audit trail. The Task Force is of the view that there is a risk that tax evasion may occur in any business that has the opportunity to deal in cash. However, the risks appear to be greater in those businesses with high cash turnover and little internal or external controls. In the absence of such controls, tax evasion can occur through simple techniques such as skimming a percentage of cash receipts 'off the top' or falsely recording wages paid to 'ghost employees'. These practices often flow through to other taxpayers as the tax evader seeks to disguise his or her activities by paying cash wages to employees or making cash payments to other businesses for goods and services. In turn, these taxpayers have the opportunity to evade their tax obligations by not declaring these payments as income.

In 2016, the Black Economy Taskforce was established to look at strategies to crack down on taxpayers operating outside the tax system. In its *Interim Report* the taskforce stated (at 1):

> Black economy activities: undermine the community's trust in the tax system; create an unfair commercial environment which penalises businesses and individuals doing the right thing; enable and entrench the exploitation of vulnerable workers; undermine tax revenue; and enable abuse of the welfare system. If unchecked, increasing black economy participation can lead to a dangerous dynamic. It can foster a culture which legitimises and supports this participation, spurring its further growth. As revenues fall, those remaining in the formal economy may ultimately be faced with higher tax burdens, giving them a greater incentive to move into the shadows. All other OECD countries are grappling with the black economy issue. Australia is not alone.

In its *Final Report*, delivered in October 2017, the taskforce found that there had been significant undocumented cash payments for things such as houses, renovations, agricultural crops, commodities, school fees, cars, jewellery, boats and luxury goods. To address this concern, the Morrison Government's Currency (Restrictions on the Use of Cash) Bill 2019 proposed to make it an offence for entities to make or accept cash payments of $10,000 or more. However, due to various criticisms, the Bill was withdrawn.

To address the challenges of the black economy and help the ATO identify taxable transactions, a Taxable Payments Reporting System ('TPRS') is contained in sub-div 396-B of sch 1 *TAA* [40.6]. Under the TPRS, the entities mentioned in the table in s 396-55 are required to provide information about certain transactions they have with other entities (eg payments made to contractors). The TPRS applies to a wide range of entities including those involved in building and construction, courier and road freight, cleaning, security and surveillance, information technology services and electronic distribution platforms. These entities must provide annual reports of relevant transactions to the ATO, which can then be used for data matching and audit purposes.

Tax evasion sometimes also involves the use of offshore tax havens and money laundering activities that are often hard to trace. Persons unlawfully engaged in such activities may be prosecuted under various Acts, including the *Anti-Money Laundering and Counter-Terrorism Financing Act 2006* (Cth) (eg ss 136 to 143 in relation to providing false statements or documents, using false identities and conducting transactions to avoid reporting requirements) [39.5] and the *Criminal Code Act 1995* (Cth) (eg s 400 in relation to dealing with the proceeds of crime) [41.3]. To address tax evasion and money laundering, the Government established 'Project Wickenby' in 2006. Project Wickenby combined the powers and resources of five government agencies: the ATO, ASIC, the Australian Crime Commission ('ACC'), the Australian Federal Police ('AFP'), and the Commonwealth Director of Public Prosecutions ('DPP'). These agencies were supported by the Attorney-General's Department ('AGD'), the Australian Government Solicitor ('AGS') and the Australian Transaction Reports and Analysis Centre ('AUSTRAC') [39.5]. According to the ATO website, Project Wickenby resulted in

4,520 audits, raised $2.297 billion in tax liabilities, and achieved 46 convictions by the time it closed on 30 June 2015. Some of the cases that came before the courts as a result of Project Wickenby include *Hili v R; Jones v R* [2010] HCA 45; *R v Lynette Liles* [2012] NSWSC 1249; and *R v Hawkins* [2013] NSWCCA 208.

Building on the work done by Project Wickenby, the Government established the Serious Financial Crime Taskforce. This taskforce commenced operating from 1 July 2015 and involves the following agencies: the ATO, ACC, AFP, AUSTRAC, ASIC, DPP, AGD and the Australian Border Force. According to the ATO website, as at 31 March 2023, the taskforce had undertaken 1,770 audits, raised $1.647 billion in tax liabilities, and produced 21 convictions.

As tax crime is a global problem, in 2018, the ATO joined the revenue agencies of Canada, the United States, the United Kingdom and the Netherlands to form the Joint Chiefs of Global Tax Enforcement ('J5'). The J5 is an international alliance that targets tax crime and money laundering. By working together, the agencies are better equipped to share information and handle sophisticated international tax evasion investigations.

The Government has gone to great lengths to protect the revenue and prosecute those involved in tax crimes. A recent high-profile illustration of this is Operation Elbrus, which was an investigation led by the AFP (with assistance from the ATO and Serious Financial Crime Taskforce) into a large-scale and organised $105m tax fraud and money laundering conspiracy conducted by a syndicate over a period of 3 years. A company, known as Plutus Payroll, lay at the heart of the scheme and was alleged to have siphoned off PAYG and GST amounts that should have been paid to the ATO. After a lengthy trial lasting almost a year, the NSW Supreme Court found several people guilty of their roles in the syndicate, including a solicitor who was sentenced to 14 years imprisonment for knowingly dealing with the proceeds of crime.

For the sake of expediency, the ATO sometimes offers taxpayers who have evaded tax limited amnesties. For example, to encourage taxpayers to declare offshore income and assets that had not been correctly reported in the past, the ATO established 'Project DO IT' ('disclose offshore income today'). Project DO IT was announced in March 2014, prior to a global crackdown on international tax havens. It provided eligible taxpayers with a 'last chance' opportunity to disclose offshore income and assets before 19 December 2014 in return for receiving reduced penalties and various assurances about how their affairs would be treated by the ATO.

The ATO relies on many avenues to detect tax evasion, including 'tip offs' from the community, and it has established a Tax Integrity Centre as a single point of contact for reporting illegal activities. Tip offs can be made online or via a dedicated telephone hotline (1800 060 062). The ATO website indicates that, during the 2019/20 income year, nearly 56,000 reports of suspected tax evasion, the black economy or illegal phoenix activity were received. More than half of the tip-offs related to alleged failures to declare income.

In order to protect people that disclose information to the ATO relating to breaches of the tax law or tax misconduct within entities, the Government has introduced special protections for 'whistleblowers' in pt IVD of the *TAA* (ss 14ZZT to 14ZZZE). The regime applies to a 'disclosure of information' that 'qualifies for protection' under pt IVD (s 14ZZT). The disclosure must be made by an 'eligible whistleblower' in relation to an entity (s 14ZZU). Such a person includes an individual who is, or has been, an officer or employee of the entity, who supplies goods or services to the entity, or who is an associate of the entity.

The disclosure is protected if it is made to the Commissioner and the discloser considers that the information may assist the Commissioner in performing his functions or duties under a taxation law in relation to the entity or its associate. Alternatively, the disclosure is also protected if it is made to an 'eligible recipient' (eg an auditor or tax agent of the entity) where the discloser has reasonable grounds to suspect that the information indicates misconduct or improper circumstances in relation to the tax affairs of the entity or its associate, and the discloser considers that the information may assist the eligible recipient to perform functions or duties in relation to the tax affairs of the entity or its associate.

The regime makes it an offence to disclose a whistleblower's identity (s 14ZZW), and protects whistleblowers against any civil, criminal or administrative liabilities for making disclosures (s 14ZZX). It also makes victimisation of whistleblowers an offence (s 14ZZY) and provides a court with the power to make an order for compensation and other remedies where victimisation has occurred (s 14ZZZ). For example, a court may make such an order where a person has engaged in conduct that causes detriment, or threatens to cause detriment, to another person because that other person may have made, or proposes to make, a disclosure that qualifies for protection under pt IVD.

Combating tax avoidance

Obviously, the most effective way of combating tax avoidance is to ensure that the law is framed in such a way that it does not have loopholes which allow it to be exploited or manipulated. In reality, however, it is not always possible to design 'ironclad' tax legislation, as many tax avoidance arrangements are unforeseen at the time that legislation is introduced. As a result, the legislature combats tax avoidance by enacting general and specific anti-avoidance provisions. Where anti-avoidance provisions apply to a scheme, they can have a significant negative impact on its effectiveness as they usually operate to cancel any tax benefits obtained and result in the imposition of substantial penalties for those involved.

From the Government's perspective, the advantage of general anti-avoidance provisions over specific ones is that general anti-avoidance provisions can apply to a broad range of arrangements, many of which might not even have been specifically contemplated at the time of enacting the provisions. In contrast, specific anti-avoidance provisions are usually reactive responses to particular arrangements that have been able to circumvent the law. They are therefore designed to close down specific schemes as opposed to dealing with wide-ranging tax avoidance arrangements.

The general anti-avoidance provisions in the income tax legislation are contained in pt IVA *ITAA36* [37.3]. General anti-avoidance provisions that are loosely modelled on pt IVA are also contained in the GST legislation (div 165 *GSTA*) [7.19] and the FBT legislation (s 67 *FBTAA*) [18.21].

There are many specific anti-avoidance provisions peppered throughout the income tax legislation. Some of these consist of only a single section (eg s 100A *ITAA36*, which is designed to combat schemes involving reimbursement agreements [24.4]), while others consist of entire regimes made up of many provisions (eg pt 2-42 *ITAA97*, which is designed to combat schemes involving the alienation of 'personal services income' [36.5]).

To help the Commissioner deal with tax avoidance, the Government established a Tax Avoidance Taskforce in 2016. The taskforce works closely with other government agencies to enable the ATO to undertake enhanced compliance activities targeting multinationals, large public and private groups and high-wealth individuals. The ATO website states that the taskforce raised $22.9 billion in tax liabilities from these entities up to June 2021.

Tax planning

Nobody is required to pay any more tax than they are legally obliged to pay. There is no legal requirement for taxpayers to arrange their affairs in ways that produce the greatest tax revenue for their governments. This concept has been colourfully encapsulated in a frequently cited Morgan Stanley advertisement:

> You must pay taxes. But there's no law that says you gotta leave a tip.

It is quite natural for taxpayers to want to organise their affairs in such a way as to legitimately minimise their tax liabilities, and it is a generally acceptable practice for them to seek tax planning advice on how to achieve this under the law. Tax is part of the commercial landscape, and, in economic terms, there is no difference between a dollar of tax saved and any other dollar. In many instances, the tax legislation itself gives taxpayers express choices and options which can lead to quite different outcomes. Governments also often specifically encourage taxpayers to undertake particular kinds of activities by providing incentives under various tax expenditure programs. Taking advantage of such options is not an abuse of the tax system and is generally regarded as acceptable tax planning.

As income tax is payable under the formula set out at [8.3], income tax planning typically involves arrangements that:

- reduce assessable income
- increase deductions
- increase tax offsets, and/or
- reduce tax rates.

Since income tax is an annual tax, taxpayers can also derive timing benefits from deferring the derivation of assessable income into subsequent years or bringing forward deductions into the current year.

Many different kinds of tax planning strategies have been developed by taxpayers and their advisers over the years. For instance, it has been common for high-income-earning employees to engage in 'salary sacrifice arrangements' under which they receive less salary in exchange for superannuation contributions or fringe benefits provided by their employers. The benefit of an effective salary sacrifice arrangement involving superannuation contributions is illustrated in the example at [19.2]. Salary sacrifice arrangements involving fringe benefits are discussed at [18.22]. TR 2001/10 states that the ATO generally accepts salary sacrifice arrangements provided employees forgo an expected entitlement to salary *before* that entitlement has been earned. Where an employee has performed services and is already entitled to receive salary, but subsequently arranges for the employer to provide a benefit instead (eg an overseas holiday), the arrangement would not be an 'effective' salary sacrifice arrangement as it would be caught by the constructive receipt rule in s 6-5(4) *ITAA97* [9.9]. The Commissioner would therefore treat the employee as having derived salary income which has been applied on behalf of the employee to purchase the overseas holiday.

It has also been common for high-income earners who operate businesses to do so through companies or trusts, as this may enable them to benefit from sheltered tax rates and provide them with opportunities for income splitting. The ATO's views on the use of family companies and trusts in income-splitting arrangements are contained in various rulings such as IT 2121 and IT 2330 [36.5].

It is crucial to be aware that any tax planning strategy needs to be carefully considered in the light of the taxpayer's individual circumstances to ensure that it is not caught by pt IVA or a specific anti-avoidance provision. It is also important to realise that an income tax planning strategy may sometimes have adverse flow-on effects, such as adverse stamp duty or GST implications. It may also sometimes result in taxpayers transferring assets to others and therefore losing control of those assets, which may have other undesirable consequences (eg for estate planning purposes). Great care therefore needs to be undertaken in implementing any kind of tax planning arrangement to ensure that it is effective and does not have any unintended consequences. There is often a fine line that separates legitimate tax planning and illegitimate tax avoidance. The distinction between these concepts lies at the heart of many philosophical debates about taxation and raises important professional and ethical issues for tax advisers.

Importantly, just because a particular strategy is being used by one taxpayer does not mean that it actually works as intended or that it is appropriate to be used by another taxpayer with different circumstances. The attitude of the Commissioner to particular kinds of strategies can also change over time, and it is therefore important to consult up-to-date taxation rulings to determine the ATO's attitude to specific kinds of arrangements. Taxpayers should also be aware that the ATO is particularly concerned about 'aggressive tax planning' and that it publishes media releases, which can be accessed via the ATO website, detailing its views on particular arrangements.

Furthermore, it is important to be aware that many tax planning arrangements have not been tested by the courts and their effectiveness may therefore be questionable. Legislative developments may have also occurred in the meantime, and this may impact on the effectiveness of a particular strategy. It is therefore prudent for taxpayers to periodically review their arrangements to make sure that they remain effective.

[36.3] Judicial responses to tax avoidance

Before examining how Parliament has dealt with tax avoidance schemes under its anti-avoidance legislation, it is appropriate to first consider how the courts have responded to these schemes.

Form and substance

Early cases indicate that when dealing with tax avoidance arrangements, the courts have traditionally focused on the 'form' of the arrangements rather than their 'substance'. One of the clearest illustrations of this approach is found in the famous United Kingdom case of *IRC v Duke of Westminster* [1936] AC 1, which concerned the character of certain payments made by the Duke of Westminster to his employees. Under the *Income Tax Act 1918* (UK), taxpayers were not allowed deductions for the payment of salaries and wages for the purposes of calculating their liability to 'surtax'. The Act did, however, allow deductions for annual payments or annuities. On this basis, the Duke entered into deeds with his employees altering the payments made to them from salaries and wages to annual payments. For example, in a deed made with a gardener, the Duke undertook to pay the gardener (in weekly instalments) annual sums of money for seven years. The weekly instalments were approximately equal to the gardener's previous wages. Although the annual sums would be paid regardless of whether the gardener continued to work for the taxpayer, the gardener acknowledged in writing that he would be content not to claim any remuneration in addition to these payments.

The Inland Revenue Commissioners denied deductions for the payments made by the Duke on the basis that they were, in substance, salary and wages. The House of Lords, however, adopted a 'form over substance' interpretation and held that the payments were annuities and therefore deductible. In a famous passage, Lord Tomlin made the following remark (at 19):

> Every man is entitled if he can to order his affairs so as that the tax attaching under the appropriate Acts is less than it otherwise would be. If he succeeds in ordering them so as to secure this result, then, however unappreciative the Commissioners of Inland Revenue or his fellow taxpayers may be of his ingenuity, he cannot be compelled to pay an increased tax. This so-called doctrine of 'the substance' seems to me to be nothing more than an attempt to make a man pay notwithstanding that he has so ordered his affairs that the amount of tax sought from him is not legally claimable.

A similar observation was made by Lord Clyde less than a decade earlier in *Ayrshire Pullman Services v IRC* (1929) 14 TC 754, where he stated (at 763):

> No man in this country is under the smallest obligation, moral or other, so to arrange his legal relations to his business or to his property as to enable the Inland Revenue to put the largest possible shovel into his stores. The Inland Revenue is not slow—and quite rightly—to take every advantage which is open to it under the taxing statutes for the purpose of depleting the taxpayer's pocket. And the taxpayer is, in like manner, entitled to be astute to prevent, so far as he honestly can, the depletion of his means by the Revenue.

In the *Duke of Westminster Case*, the Court focused on the legal situation created by the parties rather than their intention. As the discussion at [37.2] reveals, the *Duke of Westminster* doctrine had an important influence on the Australian courts throughout the 1970s, which was the peak of the tax avoidance era in Australia. During this time, the courts tended to adopt a highly literal approach to interpreting tax statutes. This contributed to the development of a culture of tax avoidance, which resulted in the proliferation of many notorious schemes, including the infamous 'bottom of the harbour' schemes. Bottom of the harbour schemes essentially involved companies with accumulated profits being stripped of their assets before their tax liabilities arose, leaving them unable to pay their tax assessments. These schemes were eventually dealt with legislatively by the introduction of the *Crimes (Taxation Offences) Act 1980* (Cth), which made it a criminal offence for any person to enter into an arrangement with the intention of making a company or trust unable to pay its tax. It also made it an offence for a person to aid or abet any person to do so [41.3].

Purposive approach

Frustrated by the blatant schemes engineered in the 1970s, it is not surprising that by the 1980s and 1990s, the Australian courts began adopting a much broader approach to dealing with tax avoidance. This change in attitude followed the resignation of Sir Garfield Barwick as Chief Justice of the High Court who, as the discussion at [37.2] reveals, was a staunch 'literalist'. The progressive approach of the courts is evidenced in cases like *Ure v FC of T* 81 ATC 4100; *FC of T v Ilbery* 81 ATC 4661; and *Fletcher & Ors v FC of T* 91 ATC 4950 [12.3] . These cases are illustrations of situations where the courts were prepared to characterise arrangements by reference to the taxpayer's purpose rather than simply by reference to form alone. Nowadays, the *Duke of Westminster* doctrine has been largely overshadowed by the modern 'purposive approach' to statutory interpretation outlined at [2.5]. The doctrine should therefore be approached with extreme caution as modern courts are less likely to give paramountcy to form over substance. In *FC of T v Spotless Services Limited & Anor* 96 ATC 5201, the High Court expressly indicated that the doctrine is irrelevant for the purposes of determining whether the general anti-avoidance rules in pt IVA *ITAA36* apply to a transaction as s 177D *ITAA36* expressly requires both form *and* substance to be considered [37.3].

Shams

The Commissioner does not need to rely on anti-avoidance provisions to defeat 'shams'. As Issacs J observed in *Jaques v FC of T* (1924) CLR 328 (at 358):

> A sham transaction is inherently worthless, and needs no enactment to nullify it.

Shams are therefore mere cloaks or facades that have no legal effect. As Jordan CJ explained in *The Estate of William Vicars Deceased* (1944) 45 SR (NSW) 85 (at 93):

> It is now well settled that the substance, in law, of a transaction can be determined only by ascertaining what the transaction really was. If the ostensible transaction is a sham, a mere facade concealing a different transaction, it must be disregarded, and legal rights and liabilities determined according to the real transaction.

Essentially, a sham is an arrangement which gives the impression of creating legal rights and obligations between parties that are different from the legal rights and obligations that actually exist between them. In *Snook v London and West Riding Investments Ltd* [1967] 2 QB 786, Diplock JJ described a sham (at 802) in the following terms:

> [Sham] means acts done or documents executed by the parties to the 'sham' which are intended by them to give to third parties or to the court the appearance of creating between the parties legal rights and obligations different from the actual legal rights and obligations

> (if any) which the parties intend to create . . . [F]or acts or documents to be a 'sham' . . . all the parties thereto must have a common intention that the acts or documents are not to create the legal rights and obligations which they give the appearance of creating.

In *Sharrment Pty Ltd v Official Trustee in Bankruptcy* (1988) 18 FCR 449, Lockhart J stated (at 454):

> A 'sham' is . . . for the purposes of Australian law, something that is intended to be mistaken for something else or that is not really what it purports to be. It is a spurious imitation, a counterfeit, a disguise or a false front. It is not genuine or true, but something made in imitation of something else or made to appear to be something which it is not. It is something which is false or deceptive.

Illustrations of sham transactions are found in *Alloyweld Pty Ltd v FC of T* 84 ATC 4328 and *Cranstoun v FC of T* 84 ATC 4876. In both these cases, the Supreme Court of Queensland disallowed deductions for pre-paid interest on the basis that the purported loan transactions under which the interest was payable were shams. In *Cranstoun*, Carter J found that the written documents were not intended to have legal efficacy and stated (at 4882):

> If two persons sign a document which on its face purports to be a loan agreement evidencing a loan from one to the other . . . but it is agreed either expressly or impliedly that the document is intended to give the appearance only of a loan transaction then it is, in my view, a sham; it is something devised to delude, it is a trick or a hoax, an imposture, it is something that is intended to be mistaken for something else, it is not really what it purports to be, it is a spurious imitation or a counterfeit.

In *Raftland Pty Ltd v FC of T* 2008 ATC ¶20-029, the High Court held that a purported distribution of income from a discretionary trust to a recently acquired unit trust which had accumulated tax losses was a sham because it was never the intention of the parties that the unit trust would truly benefit from the income under the arrangement. Gleeson CJ, Gummow and Crennan JJ indicated that a sham can exist where there is a discrepancy between the legal rights and obligations provided for on the face of a document and the actual transactions that take place in circumstances where the evidence suggests that the parties brought the document into existence as 'a mere piece of machinery' for serving some purpose other than that of constituting the whole of the arrangement. Kirby J came to a similar conclusion stating (at [145]–[146]):

> The key to finding a sham is the demonstration, by evidence or available inference, of a disparity between the transaction evidenced in the documentation (and the related conduct of the parties) and the reality disclosed elsewhere in the evidence. Where, for example, the evidence shows a discordance between the parties' legal rights or obligations as described in the documents and the actual intentions which those parties are shown to have had as to their legal rights and obligations, a conclusion of sham will be warranted . . .
>
> The test as to the parties' intentions is subjective . . . In essence, the parties must have intended to create rights and obligations different from those described in their documents. Such documents must have intended to mislead third parties in respect of such rights and obligations . . .

Fiscal nullity

In the absence of general anti-avoidance provisions in the United Kingdom tax legislation, the United Kingdom courts developed a common law doctrine, known as 'fiscal nullity', to strike down tax avoidance arrangements. This doctrine was developed in three leading cases: *WT Ramsay Ltd v IRC* [1982] AC 300; *IRC v Burmah Oil Co Ltd* (1982) STC 30; and *Furniss v Dawson* [1984] AC 474.

In *Furniss v Dawson*, Lord Brightman explained that the doctrine applies where there is a pre-ordained series of transactions with steps inserted that have no commercial purpose other than the avoidance of tax. Where these criteria exist, the United Kingdom courts have been prepared to disregard the inserted steps in determining a taxpayer's true tax position.

Since the Australian tax law contains general anti-avoidance provisions, it has been held by the Full Federal Court in *Oakey Abattoir Pty Ltd v FC of T* 84 ATC 4718 and by the High Court in *John v FC of T* 89 ATC 4101 that the doctrine of fiscal nullity does not apply in Australia. In *John*, Mason CJ, Wilson, Dawson, Toohey and Gaudron JJ explained the reason for this as follows (at 4110):

> If any such or similar principle is to be applied in relation to the Act, it is one that must be capable of implication consonant with the general rules of statutory construction. One such general rule, expressed in the maxim *expressum facit cessare tacitum*, is that where there is specific statutory provision on a topic there is no room for implication of any further matter on that same topic. The Act, in s 260 and now in Part IVA, makes specific provision on the topic of what may be called tax minimisation arrangements and thereby excludes any implication of a further limitation upon that which a taxpayer may or may not do for the purpose of obtaining a taxation advantage.

[36.4] Alienation of income from property

Dispositions of property

An obvious way that a taxpayer might seek to minimise their tax liability is by transferring the whole, or part, of an income-producing asset (eg land or shares) to their associate. Alternatively, the taxpayer may declare that the whole, or part, of the asset is held on trust for their associate. This is what occurred in *DFC of T v Purcell* (1921) 29 CLR 464, where the owner of a pastoral property executed a deed in which he declared that he held the property on trust for himself, his wife and his daughter in equal shares. The High Court held that the taxpayer was only assessable on one-third of the income from the property rather than the whole amount. Former s 53 *ITAA22* (which was the predecessor of former s 260 *ITAA36* [37.2]) did not strike down the arrangement as it was held that the section did not operate to render a genuine gift of property void against the Commissioner.

Assignments of the right to income from property

In many instances, a taxpayer may wish to retain ownership of an asset and only alienate the income from it. To achieve this, the taxpayer needs to assign the underlying 'right to income' to their associate. Obviously, to be tax-effective, an assignment of a right to income must occur before the relevant income has been derived, otherwise it would already be included in the assignor's assessable income. Furthermore, at the time the assignment is made, there must be some proprietary interest in existence that is capable of being assigned. By itself, an assignment of a 'mere expectancy' is not effective for tax purposes to alienate income from the assignor. This is illustrated in *Norman v FC of T* (1963) 109 CLR 9, where a husband executed a deed under which he voluntarily assigned, among other things, future dividends that he expected to receive on certain shares. The High Court held that the assignment was not effective for tax purposes to alienate the income from the husband to the wife, as the future dividend was a 'mere expectancy' and did not constitute an existing proprietary interest in the form of a 'chose in action'.

A similar outcome was reached in *Howard v FC of T* 2014 ATC ¶20-457, where the High Court held that a taxpayer was assessable in respect of a share of damages awarded for losses relating to a joint venture. The taxpayer argued that the damages had been tax-effectively alienated to a company under a litigation agreement. However, the Court found that the litigation agreement only provided for the assignment of the proceeds of the action rather than the 'underlying rights to receive those sums'. Accordingly, the taxpayer had merely assigned 'future income' without the associated underlying proprietary interest.

By way of contrast, in *Shepherd v FC of T* (1965) 113 CLR 385, the High Court held that a taxpayer was able to tax-effectively alienate royalty income by assigning a percentage of his rights to royalties under an existing licensing agreement to five assignees. Similarly, in *FC of T v Everett* 80 ATC 4076, the High Court held that a partner in law firm was able to tax-effectively alienate partnership income by assigning a fractional share in his interest in the partnership to his wife. In these cases, the assignments were effective for tax purposes because the rights under the licensing agreement and the interest in the partnership were both existing choses in action as opposed to 'mere expectancies'. As a consequence, in both cases, it was the assignees (as opposed to the assignors) who were liable to pay tax on the relevant income.

Division 6A treatment of transfers of rights to income from property

To combat income alienation schemes involving transfers of rights to income from property, specific anti-avoidance measures have been inserted in div 6A of pt III *ITAA36*. The two most important provisions are:

- s 102B, which applies to transfers made for short periods to 'associates' (as defined in s 318 *ITAA36* [8.6]), and
- s 102CA, which applies to transfers made for consideration that do not fall within s 102B.

Section 102B—short-term transfers to associates

Section 102B applies where a right to receive income from property is transferred (otherwise than by will or codicil) by a person to their associate for a period that will, or may, for any reason other than the death of any person or the associate becoming under a legal disability, terminate within seven years.

Where s 102B applies, the transfer is treated for tax purposes as if it had not been made and any income derived from the property is therefore deemed to be derived by the transferor rather than the associate.

Section 102B operates subject to a number of exceptions. For instance, it does not apply to a transfer of a right to receive income from property if the transferor does not own an interest in the property. The section also does not apply if at least arm's length consideration has been received, or is receivable, in respect of the transfer of the right (s 102B(2)). In addition, it has no application in respect of income derived after the transferor dies (in the case of a natural person) or ceases to exist (in the case of a company) (s 102B(3)).

Importantly, the seven-year requirement under s 102B is only satisfied if the right that is transferred is one which by its nature will subsist for at least seven years. In *Booth v FC of T* 87 ATC 5100, the High Court held that assignments for periods exceeding seven years of the right to rent under three separate three-year leases did not satisfy this requirement. The fact that the leases were for periods of less than seven years meant that they would necessarily terminate within that time and therefore fell within s 102B.

Likewise, in *Davis & Anor v FC of T* 89 ATC 4377, it was held that an assignment for a period exceeding seven years of the right to rent under a 20-year sublease also failed to satisfy the seven-year requirement. This was because a clause in the sublease provided that it could be terminated any time the rent was in arrears by 14 days. As a result, the right was one which *may* terminate within the prescribed period.

Example Don made an interest-bearing loan of $1m to a company for a period of 10 years. Immediately after entering into the loan, Don assigned the right to receive the first five years of interest under the loan to his sister Marie for no consideration. Section 102B applies as Don has transferred a right to receive income from property that will terminate within seven years to his associate. Don is consequently assessed on the interest instead of Marie.

Section 102CA—transfers for consideration not falling within s 102B

Section 102CA provides that where a right to receive income from property is transferred (otherwise than by will or codicil) and s 102B does not apply to the transfer (eg because the transfer is for a period of greater than seven years or is made to someone who is not an associate), then any consideration that has been received or is receivable in respect of the transfer is assessable to the transferor in the income year in which the right is transferred.

Section 102CA operates subject to a number of exceptions. For instance, like s 102B, it does not apply to a transfer of a right to receive income from property if the transferor does not own an interest in the property. It also does not apply to a right that is a div 230 financial arrangement [29.2].

Section 102CA was introduced to address the kind of scheme that was entered into in *FC of T v The Myer Emporium Ltd* 87 ATC 4363 [9.5]. The issue in that case was whether a taxpayer that had assigned its right to receive interest under a loan it made to a shelf company for a period of just over seven years should be assessed on the $45.37m consideration that it received for the assignment from the third party assignee. The High Court held that the consideration was income according to ordinary concepts and was therefore assessable under former s 25(1) *ITAA36*. In arriving at this conclusion, the High Court reversed the earlier decision of the Full Federal Court (85 ATC 4601) which held that the consideration was a non-assessable capital receipt. Section 102CA was specifically enacted to reverse the effect of the Full Federal Court decision and remains in the legislation even though the High Court subsequently overturned that decision.

Example If, in the preceding example, Don had assigned the right to receive the first five years of interest under the loan to a third party for its arm's length value (say $50,000), s 102B would not apply to the assignment. This is because it is made to a non-associated person and is for arm's length consideration. Section 102CA would, nevertheless, apply to assess Don on the $50,000 amount in the income year in which he transferred the right.

CGT consequences of assignments

As a right to receive income from property is a chose in action, it constitutes a proprietary interest which is a CGT asset [17.4]. Where a person assigns a right to receive income to another person, the assignor will trigger a CGT event, such as CGT event A1 or CGT event E1 [17.10]. Accordingly, taxpayers that enter into assignments, such as those that occurred in *Shepherd*, *Everett* and *Myer*, would therefore nowadays be subject to CGT (assuming they acquired their choses in action on or after 20 September 1985). As div 6A would also usually apply to these assignments, to prevent double taxation, s 118-20 *ITAA97* [17.5] requires any capital gain resulting from the assignment to be reduced to the extent that an amount is also assessable under div 6A.

> ***Example*** In the previous examples, to prevent double taxation, the amount of any capital gain made by Don from the relevant assignments would be reduced by the amounts assessable to him under ss 102B or 102CA.

[36.5] Alienation of personal services income

Taxpayers have often sought to alienate income to associates by purporting to derive such income through interposed entities, such as trusts and companies. It is particularly common for these arrangements to involve discretionary trusts as these entities provide income-splitting opportunities. The Commissioner has conceded that it is possible to tax-effectively operate 'business income' through a trust structure (IT 2330). Indeed, many businesses in Australia, particularly family businesses, are owned by trustees of trusts. The Commissioner has, nevertheless, generally challenged schemes under which individuals have attempted to channel their 'personal services income' ('PSI') through trusts.

These schemes, typically, involve an individual who had been deriving salary or wages income forming a family company that acts as the trustee of their family trust. The trustee then engages the individual as an 'employee' of the trust and subcontracts their services to a third party (eg often their former employer). After paying the individual a portion of the income received from the subcontracting arrangement as salary, the trustee distributes the balance income to the individual's family members who are beneficiaries of the trust. In this way, income that might otherwise have been earned entirely by the individual is split between the individual and their family members.

For a long time, the Commissioner has been of the view that these kinds of arrangements are ineffective, and that the individual continues to be assessable on payments made to the trust for the services rendered by the individual (IT 2121). The Commissioner has generally been successful in striking down these kinds of income-splitting schemes under the general anti-avoidance provisions. For example, the Full Federal Court held that former s 260 *ITAA36* applied to strike down income-splitting arrangements involving the use of family trusts for services rendered by an insurance agent in *Tupicoff v FC of T* 84 ATC 4851 and by a computer consultant in *Bunting v FC of T* 89 ATC 5245. Likewise, the High Court held that s 260 applied to strike down income-splitting arrangements entered into by doctors who provided their services through various trust structures in *FC of T v Gulland*; *Watson v FC of T*; *Pincus v FC of T* 85 ATC 4765. Part IVA *ITAA36* has also applied to similar kinds of schemes involving consultancy arrangements in Case W58 89 ATC 524 and Case Y13 91 ATC 191.

Earlier on, in *Peate v FC of T* (1966) 116 CLR 38, the Commissioner also succeeded in applying former s 260 to strike down a scheme under which a doctor provided his services through a company. The obvious benefit of operating through a company is that any income not distributed to the doctor would be sheltered at the corporate tax rate.

It is important to be aware, however, that in spite of the cases mentioned above, there is no general principle that a person acting in the capacity of trustee and carrying on a business involving the performance of personal services, must derive the income beneficially (*Liedig v FC of T* 94 ATC 4269). As a consequence, the Commissioner has traditionally had to rely on the general anti-avoidance provisions to combat schemes involving the alienation of PSI using interposed entities such as trusts and companies. However, as these provisions had to be applied on a case-by-case basis and required the use of extensive ATO resources, a specific anti-avoidance regime, known as the 'PSI regime', was introduced on 1 July 2000 to combat these schemes.

The PSI regime in pt 2-42 *ITAA97*

The PSI regime is contained in pt 2-42 *ITAA97* (divs 84 to 87) and has two broad roles:

- its first role is to ensure that individuals who earn PSI are generally entitled to only those deductions that employees would otherwise be entitled to claim (ie they are not entitled to business deductions), and
- its second role is to ensure that PSI derived through a personal services entity ('PSE') is assessed in the hands of the individual who earns the income rather than the entity.

The broad features of the PSI regime are outlined below. Cases falling outside the scope of the PSI regime can still be challenged by the Commissioner under pt IVA *ITAA36* [37.3].

Application

The PSI regime applies to PSI earned directly by individuals as well as PSI earned indirectly by individuals through interposed entities, known as PSEs.

'PSI' is defined as ordinary or statutory income that is *mainly* a reward for the personal efforts or skills of an individual taxpayer (s 84-5).

A 'PSE' is a company, partnership or trust whose ordinary or statutory income consists of PSI of one or more individuals (s 86-15(2)).

According to TR 2022/3, the word 'mainly' means 'chiefly', 'principally' or 'primarily'. This means that for the PSI regime to apply, more than 50% of the ordinary or statutory income earned must be a reward for the personal efforts and skills of an individual rather than from the use of assets, the supply of goods or a business structure.

It is the substance of the arrangement between the parties that determines whether an amount received by an individual or PSE is mainly a reward for the personal efforts or skills of the individual. TR 2022/3 states that where the substance of the arrangement gives rise to a single set of obligations, they should be considered together. This is illustrated in the ruling (at 47–48):

> For example, where a sole trader or PSE provides plumbing services to replace a faulty tap, all the activities associated with those services would be looked at as one source of income rather than separate sources of income for labour and replacement parts. The supply of the tap in this case is integral to the plumbing services. If the income from the supply of the tap is less than 50% of the income received for the service overall, the whole amount is PSI.
>
> If, however, the income received by the plumber for supplying the replacement tap was more than 50% of the income received for the service overall, then the whole of the amount received is not PSI but is mainly for the sale or supply of goods.

Example Felix is a computer programmer who is employed by his family company, F Co, to provide programming services to a client. Felix works on the client's premises and uses the client's computer equipment to perform the services. The fees paid by the client to F Co constitute the PSI of Felix, since they are received for his personal efforts and skills. F Co is therefore a PSE.

Oscar is a taxi driver who is also employed by his family company, O Co, to provide taxi services. O Co owns a limousine which Oscar uses to transport clients. The fares paid to O Co by the clients are not the PSI of Oscar since they are produced mainly from the use of the limousine. O Co is therefore not a PSE.

Rob is a carpenter who designs and constructs bespoke furniture which he sells at a local market. Although Rob's personal efforts and skills are required to make the furniture, the amounts he receives would be treated as payments for the sale of the furniture as they are made by customers to acquire the relevant items rather than for his personal efforts or skills. The income derived by Rob is therefore not PSI.

Pierre operates a welding partnership with his wife, Marie. Although Marie does not perform any of the welding work, she assists with book-keeping, preparing quotes and arranging appointments. Pierre supplies the welding work with the assistance of 4 full-time employees. The partnership has a trade name and over 100 clients. It also owns 2 trucks and special tools. The income is derived from the business structure of the partnership and is therefore not PSI.

Deduction restrictions for individuals

The broad aim of pt 2-42 *ITAA97* is to put taxpayers who earn income in ways that are analogous to employees in the same tax position as employees (TR 2003/10). Accordingly, s 85-10(1) provides that individuals who earn PSI are generally restricted to claiming only those deductions relating to their PSI that would be available to an employee. Section 85-10(1), however, operates subject to s 85-10(2), which states that individuals are not prevented from deducting amounts to the extent that they relate to:

- gaining work (eg advertising)
- insuring against loss of income (eg disability insurance)
- insuring against liability for acts or omissions in the course of earning income (eg professional indemnity insurance)
- engaging an entity that is not an associate to perform work
- engaging an associate to perform work that forms part of the principal work for which the individual gains or produces PSI
- making personal superannuation contributions
- meeting workers compensation obligations, or
- meeting obligations under the GST law.

Individuals are, nevertheless, expressly prevented from deducting rent, mortgage interest, rates or land tax for their (or their associate's) residence to the extent that it relates to gaining or producing their PSI (s 85-15).

Likewise, payments to an associate (s 85-20) and superannuation contributions made for an associate (s 85-25), to the extent that they relate to gaining or producing the individual's PSI, are also not deductible. However, this rule does not apply to the extent that the payments or contributions relate to the performance of work by the associate which forms part of the 'principal work' for which the individual gains their PSI. TR 2022/3 states that principal work is work that is central to meeting obligations under an agreement with the service acquirer. It does not include associated clerical or administrative work (such as bookkeeping and answering phones), unless the principal work is administrative in nature. Deductions for an associate's superannuation contributions cannot exceed the amount required to ensure that the individual does not have a SG shortfall [19.5].

Importantly, the deduction restrictions outlined above do not apply to income derived by an individual from conducting a 'personal services business' ('PSB') (see below) (s 85-30).

Example Adam is an architect who employs his wife, Eve, to provide general secretarial services. Unless Adam is carrying on a PSB, he is not entitled to deductions for salary paid to Eve or for superannuation contributions made to Eve's superannuation fund.

Deduction restrictions for PSEs

A PSE is generally not entitled to deductions for amounts to the extent that they relate to earning PSI of an individual unless either:

- the individual could have otherwise deducted the amount if the entity's circumstances had applied instead to the individual, or
- the PSE receives the PSI in the course of carrying on a PSB (see below) (s 86-60).

There are a number of exceptions to this rule. For instance, it does not apply to:

- entity maintenance deductions (eg fees for operating bank accounts and tax-related expenses under s 25-5 [13.2]) (s 86-65)
- specified car expenses (s 86-70)
- superannuation contributions for the benefit of the individual (subject to certain limitations) (s 86-75), or
- salary or wages that have been paid before the end of the 14th day after the PAYG payment period during which the amount became income of the entity (s 86-80).

Attribution of PSI derived by PSEs to individuals

The PSI regime contains special attribution rules which ensure that, after taking into account certain allowable deductions incurred by a PSE (s 86-20), the PSI derived by a PSE is included in the assessable income of the individual who performs the services, rather than the assessable income of the PSE (s 86-15(1)). This is achieved by treating the PSI as non-assessable non-exempt income of the PSE (s 86-30).

To prevent double taxation, PSI that is assessable under s 86-15(1) in the hands of an individual is not assessed again when it is subsequently paid by the PSE to the individual (s 86-35).

The attribution rules do not apply to:

- a PSE that conducts a PSB (see below) (s 86-15(3))
- an amount that a PSE pays to an individual as an employee as salary or wages (provided it is paid before the end of the 14th day after the PAYG payment period during which the amount became income of the entity) (s 86-15(4)), or
- an amount that is not assessable income (eg GST charged on a supply made by a PSE) (s 86-15(5)).

Example T Co is a PSE that does not carry on a PSB. T Co employs Terry to provide computer programming services to one of its clients. The client pays T Co $110,000 (inclusive of GST) for these services. Assuming that the fees paid to T Co are PSI of Terry, Terry is required to include $100,000 (ie $110,000 less $10,000 GST charged by T Co) in his assessable income under s 86-15(1). To prevent double taxation, this amount is non-assessable non-exempt income of T Co under s 86-30.

An illustration of where the Commissioner successfully applied the PSI rules to income earned through a PSE is found in *Fowler v FC of T* 2008 ATC ¶20-022. The case involved a computer consultant that held all the shares in, and was sole director and employee of, a company that derived income from entering into contracts with labour hire firms for the supply of his services at an hourly rate to end-users. The work was usually performed at the end-user's premises with the use of their equipment and software. While the company derived income of $156,444, $155,084 and $56,648 during the 2000/01 to 2002/03 income years, the consultant only included $86,624, $60,000 and $6,000 in his assessable income as salary or wages over those years. The Federal Court upheld the AAT's decision that the Commissioner had correctly applied s 86-15 to assess the consultant on the income received by the company (less certain deductions to which it was entitled). The Court concluded that the amounts in question were the consultant's PSI and were ordinary income of the company, which was a PSE that was not conducting a PSB as the criteria of s 87-15 (discussed below) were not met.

Personal services business

As mentioned above, the PSI deduction restrictions and attribution rules do not apply to income derived from conducting a PSB. A PSB is conducted by an individual if a 'PSB determination' is in force relating to the individual's PSI. A PSB is conducted by a PSE if a PSB determination is in force relating to an individual whose PSI is included in the PSE's ordinary or statutory income (s 87-15(1)). PSB determinations are issued by the Commissioner under sub-div 87-B *ITAA97*. The Commissioner can only make a PSB determination if he is satisfied that specified conditions in s 87-60 (in the case of individuals) or s 87-65 (in the case of PSEs) have been met.

An individual or PSE also conducts a PSB if one of the following four PSB tests are satisfied (ss 87-15(1)(c), (2)):

- **The results test (s 87-18).** This test is satisfied by an individual if in relation to at least 75% of the individual's PSI (other than PSI received as an employee, office holder or religious practitioner) during the year:
  (a) the income is for producing a result
  (b) the individual is required to supply the equipment, etc, needed to produce the result, and
  (c) the individual is liable for the cost of rectifying any defect in the work performed.

  The test is satisfied by a PSE if in relation to at least 75% of the PSI of one or more individuals that is included in the PSE's ordinary or statutory income during the year:
  (a) the income is for producing a result
  (b) the PSE is required to supply the equipment, etc, needed to produce the result, and
  (c) the PSE is liable for the cost of rectifying any defect in the work performed.

  TR 2022/3 notes that in contracts for producing a result, payment is usually made for a negotiated price to achieve a specified outcome (as opposed to payment for the hours worked) and is usually made when the result has been fulfilled.
- **The unrelated clients test (s 87-20).** This test is satisfied if:
  (a) the individual or PSE gains PSI from two or more entities that are not associates of each other, the individual or the PSE, and
  (b) the services are provided as a direct result of making offers or invitations (eg by advertising), to the public at large or to a section of the public, to provide the services.

  TR 2022/3 states that to satisfy the test, there must be a direct causal effect between the offers or invitations and obtaining the work. If the services are provided through an intermediary (eg a labour-hire firm), the test is not satisfied as offers or invitations have not been made to the public at large or a section of the public. Likewise, a word-of-mouth referral does not generally meet the test.
- **The employment test (s 87-25).** This test is satisfied by an individual if he or she engages one or more unassociated entities to perform work which is at least 20% (by market value) of the entity's 'principal work' for the year. The test is satisfied by a PSE if it engages one or more entities (other than individuals whose PSI is included in the entity's ordinary or statutory income or associates of the entity who are not individuals) to perform work which is at least 20% (by market value) of the entity's 'principal work' for the year.
- **The business premises test (s 87-30).** This test is satisfied if at all times during the year, the individual or PSE maintains and uses business premises:
  (a) at which the individual or PSE mainly conducts activities from which PSI is produced
  (b) of which the individual or PSE has exclusive use

(c) that are physically separate from any premises that the individual or PSE (or any associate) uses for private purposes, and

(d) that are physically separate from the premises of the entity (or associate) to which the individual or PSE provides services.

TR 2022/3 points out that while an individual or PSE is not required to maintain and use the same business premises throughout the whole year, they need to have business premises at all times during the year. An individual or sole trader must have exclusive possession of the premises in order to have exclusive use of them. If they share the premises with another entity, or if they merely have a licence (as opposed to a lease), they will not have exclusive use of the premises.

Importantly, a special rule provides that if 80% or more of an individual's PSI (other than PSI received as an employee, office holder or religious practitioner) during an income year is income from the same entity (or from one entity and its associates) and the individual does not meet the results test (above), the individual's PSI is not taken to be from conducting a PSB, unless when that income is produced a PSB determination under sub-div 87-B is in force (s 87-15(3)).

The following diagram from s 87-5 shows how to ascertain whether PSI is income from conducting a PSB:

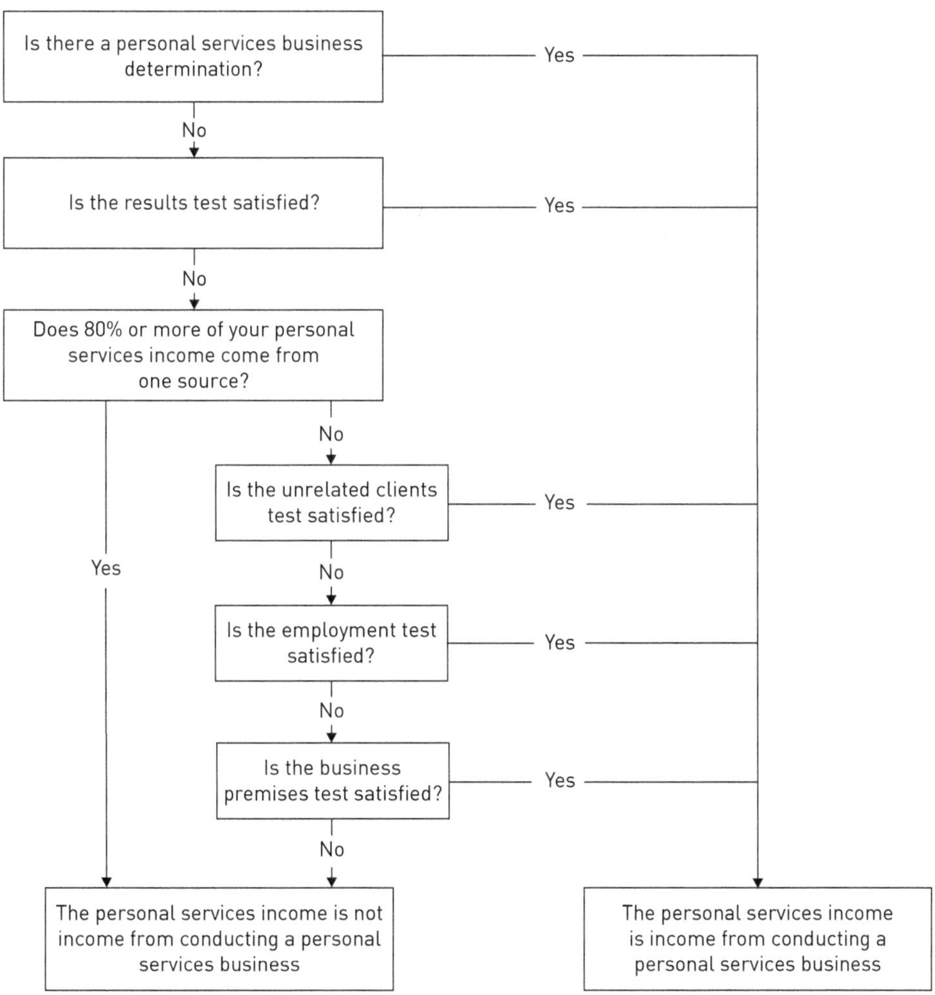

Personal services business determination

Subdivision 87-B *ITAA97* contains the rules for making PSB determinations. Under these rules, the Commissioner may make a PSB determination in relation to an individual (s 87-60). He can also make a PSB determination in relation to a PSE whose ordinary or statutory income includes an individual's PSI (s 87-65). The individual or PSE must apply for a PSB determination in the approved form to the Commissioner who may request the applicant to provide specified information or documents that he needs to decide the application (s 87-70). A PSB determination is effective from the day specified in the notice or, if a day is not specified, the day on which the notice is given. The PSB determination ceases to have effect at the end of the earliest day on which one or more of the following occurs:

- one or more conditions to which the determination is subject are not met
- the Commissioner revokes the determination, or
- the period for which the determination has effect comes to an end (s 87-75).

The Commissioner must not make a PSB determination in relation to an individual unless he is satisfied that one or more of the following conditions are met in the income year during which the determination first has effect:

- the individual could reasonably be expected to meet, or met, one or more of the results test, the employment test or the business premises test and the individual's PSI could reasonably be expected to be, or was, from the individual conducting activities that met one or more of those tests (s 87-60(3A))
- but for unusual circumstances applying to the individual in that year, the individual could reasonably have been expected to meet, or would have met, one or more of the results test, the employment test or the business premises test and the PSI of the individual was, or could reasonably be expected to be, from the individual conducting activities that met one or more of those tests (s 87-60(3B))
- the individual could reasonably be expected to meet, or met, the unrelated clients test but because of unusual circumstances 80% or more of the PSI of the individual could reasonably have been expected to be, or would have been, from the same source and the PSI of the individual could reasonably be expected to be, or was, from the individual conducting activities that met the unrelated clients test (s 87-60(5)), or
- but for unusual circumstances applying to the individual in that year, the individual could reasonably have been expected to meet, or would have met, the unrelated clients test and if 80% or more of the individual's PSI could reasonably have been expected to be, or would have been, from the same entity, this was only because of unusual circumstances applying to the individual in the income year and the individual's PSI could reasonably be expected to be, or was, from the individual conducting activities that met the unrelated clients test (s 87-60(6)).

Likewise, the Commissioner must not make a PSB determination in relation to a PSE unless broadly corresponding conditions are met (ss 87-65(3) to (6)).

TR 2022/3 states that a 'reasonable expectation' of an event requires 'more than a possibility, risk or chance of the event occurring'. It also states that 'unusual circumstances' are circumstances that are 'not usual', 'not common' and 'out of the ordinary' and that they must be 'temporary, rather than a new mode of operation'.

[36.6] Service entity arrangements

It is common for professional partnerships (eg law and accounting firms) to enter into service entity arrangements. These arrangements (illustrated in the diagram below) typically involve the establishment of a separate service entity that is controlled by the partners of the partnership.

The entity is usually the corporate trustee of a unit trust, whose beneficiaries are associates of the partners (eg the trustees of their family discretionary trusts who can distribute income to the partners' family members). The service entity provides certain business services to the partnership, such as the lease of premises and equipment, the provision of secretarial and support staff, and the provision of administrative and debt collection services. These services are typically provided at a 'mark-up', which results in the service entity generating net income from the arrangement and the partnership incurring greater deductions than it would otherwise have incurred. The net income made by the service entity is then distributed to the beneficiaries of the trust. An effective service entity arrangement, therefore, enables income to be 'split' from the partners to their associates.

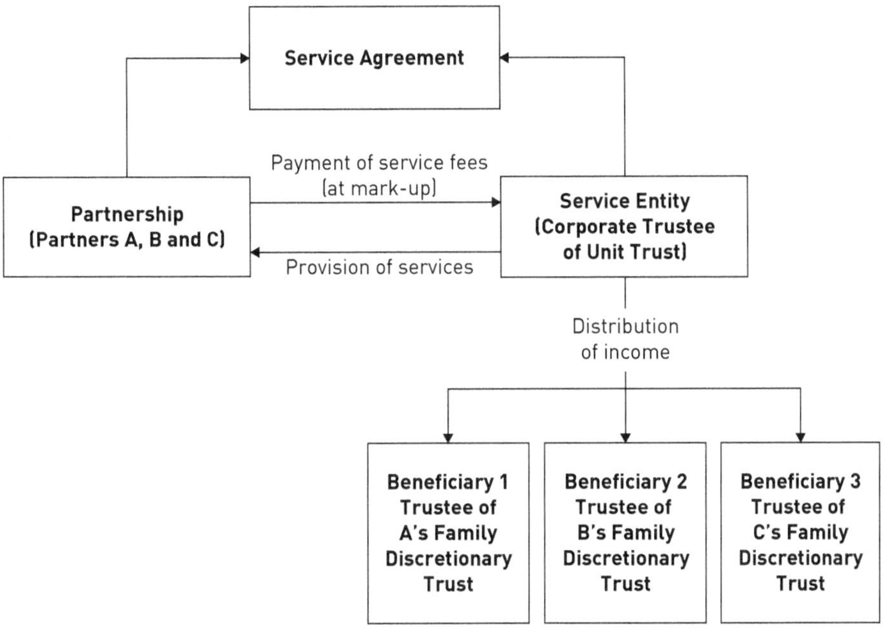

The leading case dealing with service entity arrangements is *FC of T v Phillips* 78 ATC 4361 [12.3], where the Full Federal Court held that the Commissioner was not able to deny deductions under s 51(1) *ITAA36* to an accounting firm for the mark-ups charged by its service entity. This outcome was justified on the basis that the mark-ups charged in the case were 'commercially realistic'. Where mark-ups charged for services provided by a service entity are found to be 'commercially unrealistic', it is unlikely that deductions would be allowed for the excessive portion of the charges.

In TR 2006/2, the Commissioner indicates that he is prepared to apply the general anti-avoidance provisions in pt IVA [37.3] to strike down service entity arrangements that are not commercially realistic (eg where service fees are disproportionate to the benefits conferred under the arrangement). The circumstances in which the Commissioner considers fees charged by service entities are acceptable are set out in the ATO publication, *Your Service Entity Arrangements*. Further guidelines dealing with the potential application of pt IVA to a range of common arrangements entered into by professional firms are contained in the ATO publication, *Assessing the Risk: Allocation of Profits Within Professional Firms*.

[36.7] QUESTIONS

1. What is the difference between tax evasion, tax avoidance and tax planning? Provide some examples of activities that might constitute each of these things.
2. What principle was established in *IRC v Duke of Westminster* [1936] AC 1 and how relevant is it today in Australia?
3. What is a sham, and what is the effect of a sham? What is the fiscal nullity principle and does it apply in Australia?
4. George is an author who wrote a best-selling novel last year. The contract with his publisher provides that the publisher must pay him a royalty of 10% of the sale price of all books it sells. George has recently executed a deed of assignment under which he assigned (for no consideration) 50% of his right to receive royalties under the contract to his wife for a period of four years. What are the consequences of the assignment? What would have happened if George had instead assigned his entire future right to receive royalties under the contract to a bank for $1m?
5. Why is it important under the PSI rules to determine whether a PSB is being conducted? What requirements must be fulfilled for an entity to pass the 'results test', the 'unrelated clients test', the 'employment test' and 'the business premises test'?
6. Felicity has been employed by Zip Co as a computer programmer for many years. Her annual salary is $200,000 plus SG contributions. Felicity, who is the only income earner in her family, has a plan which she thinks will help reduce her tax liability. She proposes to resign from work and arrange for Zip Co to engage the trustee of her family discretionary trust to provide it with computer programming services for an annual fee of $222,000 (plus GST). Felicity would do all the computer programming work as an employee of the trust and she would be paid an annual salary of $50,000 plus SG contributions. The trust would also employ her retired husband to perform secretarial services for which he would be paid an annual salary of $40,000 plus SG contributions. The remaining income of the trust would be distributed equally between Felicity's twins (aged 22) who are full-time university students. Will Felicity's plan be tax-effective?

GENERAL ANTI-AVOIDANCE PROVISIONS 37

[37.1] Introduction

Australia's income tax legislation has always contained some form of general anti-avoidance rule. As Pagone stated in his article, 'Part IVA: The General Anti-Avoidance Provisions in Australian Taxation Law' (2003) 27 *MULR* 770 (at 771):

> General anti-avoidance provisions occupy a very special role in tax laws because their role is to underpin the effectiveness of the primary operative provisions when those primary provisions fail to achieve their purpose.

Australia's general anti-avoidance provisions are located in pt IVA *ITAA36*. Part IVA replaced the former general anti-avoidance provision contained in s 260 *ITAA36*, which applied to arrangements that were made or entered into up to 27 May 1981. Part IVA applies to 'schemes' entered into after that date.

Part IVA is a complex statutory regime that consists of a number of interconnected provisions. The provisions have been amended on several occasions over the years and currently comprise ss 177A to 177R. This chapter discusses the background to the introduction of pt IVA [37.2] and focuses on the operation of its core provisions [37.3]–[37.7]. It is important to be aware that significant amendments to pt IVA were introduced by *Tax Laws Amendment (Countering Tax Avoidance and Multinational Profit Shifting) Act 2013* (Cth). These amendments were designed to address certain weaknesses in the provisions that had been identified in various cases. They apply to schemes other than those that were entered into, or commenced to be carried out, before 16 November 2012.

Part IVA also contains a number of special provisions that operate alongside its core provisions to tackle particular kinds of tax avoidance schemes. This chapter examines the special provisions in s 177DA (dealing with the 'multinational anti-avoidance law' ('MAAL')) [37.8] and ss 177H to 177R (dealing with diverted profits tax' ('DPT')) [37.9]. Chapter 22 considers the special provisions in s 177E (dealing with dividend stripping schemes) [22.16] and ss 177EA and 177EB (dealing with imputation benefit schemes) [22.13].

[37.2] Background to the general anti-avoidance provisions

In order to appreciate the context in which pt IVA was introduced, it is useful to first examine its predecessor, s 260, and some of the challenges this section faced in its chequered history before the courts. At the same time, it is also important to recognise that pt IVA is quite different from s 260. One must therefore be mindful of the caution expressed by the High Court in *FC of T v Spotless Services Limited & Anor* 96 ATC 5201, where Brennan CJ, Dawson, Toohey, Gaudron, Gummow and Kirby JJ stated (at 5205):

> Part IVA is to be construed and applied according to its terms, not under the influence of 'muffled echoes of old arguments' concerning other legislation.

Section 260

Section 260 provided as follows:

> Every contract, agreement, or arrangement made or entered into, orally or in writing, whether before or after the commencement of this Act, shall so far as it has or purports to have the purpose or effect of in any way, directly or indirectly:
>
> (a) altering the incidence of any income tax;
>
> (b) relieving any person from liability to pay any income tax or make any return;
>
> (c) defeating, evading, or avoiding any duty or liability imposed on any person by this Act; or
>
> (d) preventing the operation of this Act in any respect,
>
> be absolutely void, as against the Commissioner, or in regard to any proceeding under this Act, but without prejudice to such validity as it may have in any other respect or for any other purpose.

Despite being drafted in broad terms, the Commissioner encountered a number of significant difficulties in applying s 260. The inadequacies of s 260 were especially exposed in a string of landmark decisions handed down by the Privy Council and the High Court in the 1950s to the 1970s. The courts in these cases considerably read down s 260. A narrow interpretation of s 260 was perhaps a natural reaction to the fact that the provision was drafted in wide terms and was 'self-executing' (ie the Commissioner did not have any discretion as to its application). In commenting on s 260's predecessor (s 53 *Income Tax Assessment Act 1915* (Cth)), Knox CJ stated in *DFC of T v Purcell* (1921) 29 CLR 464 (at 466) that the section 'if construed literally would extend to every transaction whether voluntary or for value which had the effect of reducing the income of any taxpayer'.

Some of the main limitations that were experienced by s 260 are outlined below.

Annihilation limitation

Section 260 was construed by the courts as an 'annihilating provision' that simply rendered an arrangement void as against the Commissioner. It did not, therefore, allow the Commissioner to restructure the arrangement and tax some other alternative transaction. In other words, it had a 'vacuum' effect, whereby the Commissioner could only tax whatever was left behind after the arrangement was eliminated. In *Bell v FC of T* (1953) 87 CLR 548, Dixon CJ, Williams, Webb, Fullagar and Kitto JJ explained (at 573):

> The section is, of course, an annihilating provision only. It has no further or other operation than to eliminate from consideration for tax purposes such contracts, agreements and arrangements as fall within the descriptions it contains. It assists the Commissioner . . . only if, when all contracts, agreements and arrangements having such a purpose or effect as the section mentions are obliterated, the facts which remain justify the Commissioner's assessment.

Predication limitation

In *Newton v FC of T* (1958) 98 CLR 1, the Privy Council held that s 260 applied only to arrangements that were explicable by reference to tax avoidance and not to ordinary business or commercial dealings. Lord Denning explained this as follows (at 8):

> In order to bring the arrangement within the section you must be able to predicate—by looking at the overt acts by which it was implemented—that it was implemented in that particular way so as to avoid tax. If you cannot so predicate, but have to acknowledge that the transactions are capable of explanation by reference to ordinary business or family dealing, without necessarily being labelled as a means to avoid tax, then the arrangement does not come within the section.

Antecedent transaction limitation

In order for there to be an alteration in the incidence of tax for the purposes of s 260, there had to be some form of 'antecedent transaction' that had been altered by the relevant contract, agreement or arrangement. On this basis, s 260 did not apply to completely 'fresh' transactions that did not alter any antecedent situation. As Barwick CJ observed in *Mullens & Ors v FC of T* (1976) 135 CLR 290 (at 302):

> Though the section speaks of the purpose in entering into the transaction, it can have no relevance if, being effective, the transaction does not alter the incidence of tax, as that expression has come to be understood . . . It would be otherwise if there had been some antecedent transaction between the parties, for which the transaction under attack was substituted in order to obtain the benefit of the particular provision of the Act.

Choice limitation

One of the most significant limitations on s 260 was the 'choice limitation'. According to this limitation, s 260 could not be used to deny a taxpayer a choice allowed under the legislation. On this basis, in *WP Keighery Pty Ltd v FC of T* (1957) 100 CLR 66, the High Court held that s 260 did not apply to a company that had restructured itself as a public company, instead of a private company, in order to avoid former 'undistributed profits tax'. Dixon CJ, Kitto and Taylor JJ stated (at 92):

> the section intends only to protect the general provisions of the Act from frustration, and not to deny to taxpayers any right of choice between alternatives, which the Act itself lays open to them.

The choice limitation was based on the *Duke of Westminster* doctrine [36.3] and was applied to a dividend stripping scheme in *Slutzkin & Ors v FC of T* 77 ATC 4076, where Barwick CJ stated (at 4079):

> the choice of the form of transaction by which a taxpayer obtains the benefit of his assets is a matter for him: he is quite entitled to choose that form of transaction which will not subject him to tax, or subject him only to less tax than some other form of transaction might do. *IRC v Duke of Westminster* (1936) AC 1, too easily forgotten, is still basic in this area of law.

The choice limitation also applied in *Cridland v FC of T* 77 ATC 4538, where a university student who received $1 of income as a result of holding a unit in a mass-marketed trust that carried on the business of primary production was allowed to average his entire income under the primary production rules. Mason J (with whom Barwick CJ, Stephen, Jacobs and Aickin JJ concurred) took a broad view of the choice limitation stating (at 4542):

> It is not confined to cases in which the Act offers two alternative bases of taxation; it proceeds on the footing that the taxpayer is entitled to create a situation by entry into a transaction which will attract tax consequences for which the Act makes specific provision and that the validity of the transaction is not affected by s 260 merely because the tax consequences which it attracts are advantageous to the taxpayer and he enters into the transaction deliberately with a view to gaining that advantage.

Resurrection of s 260 after the introduction of pt IVA

As a consequence of the introduction of pt IVA, s 260 has no effect in relation to contracts, agreements or arrangements entered into after 27 May 1981. Ironically, although pt IVA was introduced to address the shortcomings of s 260, after s 260 had been replaced, the Commissioner succeeded in applying the provision to a number of tax avoidance schemes that were still being litigated before the courts.

The first significant victory for the Commissioner arose in *Tupicoff v FC of T* 84 ATC 4851, where the Commissioner succeeded in applying s 260 to strike down an income-splitting arrangement entered into by an insurance agent. The agent had interposed a family company between himself and the insurance company that paid him commissions. The family company then began to employ the agent and paid him a salary out of part of the commissions it now received from the insurance company. The family company also acted as the trustee of the agent's family discretionary trust and distributed the balance of its income among the taxpayer's family. The Full Federal Court held that the arrangements had the main purpose of splitting income between the taxpayer and his family members and that s 260 therefore rendered the arrangements void. Interestingly, Fisher J held (at 4853) that the choice limitation did not protect the taxpayer as 'although the taxpayer attempted to cease deriving income, he did not cease "the personal exertion" activities which heretofore had been the undoubted source of his income'.

The most high-profile case in which s 260 was successfully applied is *FC of T v Gulland*; *Watson v FC of T*; *Pincus v FC of T* 85 ATC 4765. This case involved income-splitting arrangements entered into by three doctors. Under the arrangements, the doctors had sold their respective medical practices to trustees of unit trusts. The units in these trusts were owned by the doctors' family discretionary trusts. The doctors also entered into service arrangements with the trustees of the unit trusts under which they continued to work in the medical practices as employees, but at salaries that were lower than what they would have received from their former practices. A majority of the High Court held that s 260 operated to render the arrangements void as against the Commissioner, with the effect that each of the doctors was treated as receiving the income from his respective medical practice. It was held that the arrangements entered into by the doctors were not ordinary business or family dealings and that the choice limitation did not apply. In this regard, Gibbs CJ stated (at 4773):

> it is simply not right to say that the Act allows a taxpayer the opportunity to have his own income from personal exertion taxed as though it were income derived by a trust and held for the benefit of a number of beneficiaries.

The change in attitude to s 260 in the 1980s coincided with changes to the membership of the High Court, particularly the retirement in 1981 of Sir Garfield Barwick CJ, whose attitude to tax avoidance was closely aligned with, and influenced by, the *Duke of Westminster* doctrine. Critics of Barwick CJ argued that his judgments fuelled the rampant tax avoidance industry that flourished in the 1970s. In his memoirs, *A Radical Tory: Reflections and Recollections* (The Federation Press, 1996), the former Chief Justice responded to these accusations in the following terms (at 229):

> The liability to pay income tax is wholly derived from the law imposing and providing for the assessment of that tax. The obligation to pay it is a legal one. Some politicians try to treat it

as a moral obligation. But it is not. The citizen is bound to pay no more tax than the statute requires him to pay according to the relevant state of his affairs.

Consistently with this view, it has long been a principle of the law of income taxation that the citizen may so arrange his affairs as to render him less liable to pay tax than would be the case if his affairs were cast in some different form. In the language of the layman, the citizen is entitled to minimise his liability to pay tax. This is sometimes expressed as a right to avoid tax, an expression which is in contradiction to the evasion of tax, a failure to pay tax which is properly due.

On this principle, I regularly acted. Provided the citizen's transactions were not shams, pretences, the form of his transactions and their legal consequences would affect his liability to tax, even though that form might be unusual and adopted for the express purpose of limiting the liability to pay tax.

Differences between pt IVA and s 260

The Bill that inserted pt IVA into the *ITAA36* in 1981 was introduced by John Howard (who was then Treasurer and subsequently became Prime Minister). The Bill was drafted with the assistance of two highly respected Queen's Counsel: Murray Gleeson (who later became Chief Justice of the High Court) and Graham Hill (who later became a Justice of the Federal Court).

It is evident from the Explanatory Memorandum to the Bill that introduced pt IVA that the provisions were designed to overcome many of the limitations faced by s 260 and strike at tax avoidance schemes that are 'blatant, artificial or contrived'. In this regard, the Explanatory Memorandum stated:

> Part IVA . . . is designed to overcome these difficulties and provide—with paramount force in the income tax law—an effective general measure against those tax avoidance arrangements that—inexact though the words be in legal terms—are blatant, artificial or contrived. In other words, the new provisions are designed to apply where, on an objective view of the particular arrangement and its surrounding circumstances, it would be concluded that the arrangement was entered into for the sole or dominant purpose of obtaining a tax deduction or having an amount left out of assessable income.

Part IVA was not, however, designed to apply to ordinary business or family dealings, indicating an intention to preserve what is, in effect, the predication limitation identified in *Newton* (see above). In this respect, the Explanatory Memorandum expressly stated that 'arrangements of a normal business or family kind, including those of a tax planning nature, will be beyond the scope of Part IVA'.

The intent that the new provisions would not extend to normal commercial transactions was also acknowledged by the Treasurer in his second reading speech where he stated:

> The proposed provisions . . . seek to give effect to a policy that such measures ought to strike down blatant, artificial or contrived arrangements, but not cast unnecessary inhibitions on normal commercial transactions by which taxpayers legitimately take advantage of opportunities available for the arrangement of their affairs. For example, a husband and wife who choose to run a business as partners will need have no fear of having their arrangements affected by Part IVA. There will be no question, either, of the new provisions impeding a parent who wishes to pass to a spouse or to children the use and enjoyment of some income-producing assets.

Part IVA approaches tax avoidance from a different perspective to s 260. As the Privy Council recognised in *Newton*, s 260 was not concerned with the motives of the taxpayer or any other person who entered into the arrangement, but rather the purpose or effect of the arrangement itself.

In contrast, the purpose of a person who enters into a 'scheme' is relevant for the purposes of pt IVA, and this purpose is determined according to a set of objective criteria.

[37.3] Core provisions in pt IVA

The central provision in pt IVA is s 177D. This section was restructured under amendments made in 2013, although the substance of the provision remains largely unchanged. The rewritten version of s 177D was designed to make it clear that the provision is the 'fulcrum' or 'pivot' around which pt IVA is based. As noted in the Explanatory Memorandum to the Bill that inserted the rewritten provision:

> The question whether Part IVA applies to a scheme starts with a consideration of whether any person participated in the scheme for the sole or dominant purpose of securing for the taxpayer a tax benefit in connection with the scheme.

The new version of s 177D(1) provides that pt IVA applies to a 'scheme' if it would be concluded (having regard to the matters in s 177D(2)) that the person, or one of the persons, who entered into or carried out the scheme or any part of the scheme did so for the 'purpose' of:

(a) enabling a 'relevant taxpayer' to obtain a 'tax benefit' in connection with the scheme, or

(b) enabling the 'relevant taxpayer' and another taxpayer (or other taxpayers) each to obtain a tax benefit in connection with the scheme,

whether or not that person who entered into or carried out the scheme or any part of the scheme is the relevant taxpayer or is the other taxpayer or one of the other taxpayers.

As with the former version of pt IVA, the new version of pt IVA can apply to a scheme that has been entered into or carried out in Australia or outside Australia or partly in Australia and partly outside Australia (s 177D(5)).

Where a tax benefit has been obtained by a taxpayer in connection with a scheme to which pt IVA applies, the Commissioner is empowered under s 177F to make a determination to cancel all or part of the tax benefit [37.7]. He may also make compensating adjustments relating to other taxpayers. Guidelines on how the ATO applies pt IVA are detailed in PS LA 2005/24.

Importantly, where pt IVA applies to a scheme, penalty tax is also imposed under sub-div 284-C of sch 1 *TAA* [41.2]. The base penalty amount is 50% of the 'scheme shortfall amount' (or 25% of the scheme shortfall amount where the taxpayer has a reasonably arguable case that pt IVA does not apply) (s 284-160). The base penalty amount is increased by 20% if the taxpayer was involved in obstructing the Commissioner, resulting in a maximum penalty of 60% (ie 50% + (50% × 20%)).

Key issues

Four key issues need to be considered under pt IVA:

1. The first issue involves identifying the particular 'scheme' [37.4].
2. The second issue involves determining whether the 'relevant taxpayer' has obtained a 'tax benefit' in connection with the scheme [37.5].
3. The third issue involves ascertaining whether it would be concluded (having regard to the matters in s 177D(2)) that a person who entered into the scheme, or any part of it, did so for the 'purpose' of enabling the relevant taxpayer to obtain a tax benefit in connection with the scheme [37.6].
4. The fourth issue involves the exercise of the Commissioner's determination to cancel the tax benefit under s 177F [37.7].

However, before discussing these issues, it is important to make the point that, being a general anti-avoidance rule, pt IVA is a measure of 'last resort'. It therefore only applies to schemes that have legal effect (ie that are not shams) and that are not otherwise caught under specific anti-avoidance provisions.

Furthermore, as pt IVA can only apply where there is a tax benefit, it obviously has no work to do if the underlying scheme does not produce any tax benefit. Accordingly, in *Vincent v FC of T* 2002 ATC 4742, the Full Federal Court did not need to apply pt IVA to strike down deductions claimed in respect of a cattle breeding scheme because the outgoings were of a capital nature and therefore not deductible under s 51(1) *ITAA36*. Likewise, in *Macquarie Finance Limited v FC of T* 2005 ATC 4829, the Full Federal Court held that it was unnecessary to apply pt IVA to deny deductions for interest paid under a stapled security arrangement as the interest was of a capital nature and therefore not deductible under s 8-1 *ITAA97*.

[37.4] Scheme

The starting point in dealing with pt IVA is to identify the relevant 'scheme' to which pt IVA applies. Identification of the scheme is critical for the reasons expressed by Gleeson CJ and McHugh J in *FC of T v Hart & Anor* 2004 ATC 4599 (at 4602):

> the definition of the scheme is important, because any tax benefit identified must be related to the scheme, as must any conclusion of dominant purpose, and also the ultimate determination . . . It is central to the application of ss 177C, 177D and 177F.

The concept of 'scheme' is defined broadly in s 177A(1) to mean:

(a) any agreement, arrangement, understanding, promise or undertaking, whether express or implied and whether or not enforceable, or intended to be enforceable, by legal proceedings, and
(b) any scheme, plan, proposal, action, course of action or course of conduct.

A scheme also expressly includes a 'unilateral' scheme, plan, proposal, action, course of action, or course of conduct (s 177A(3)). This means that a scheme can be carried out by only one person. This contrasts with s 260 *ITAA36* which required there to be a 'contract, agreement or arrangement'.

In *FC of T v Peabody* 94 ATC 4663, the High Court indicated that the Commissioner may identify alternative schemes including wider and narrower schemes provided this does not cause 'undue embarrassment or surprise to the other side'. The High Court, however, went on to explain (at 4670) that pt IVA must be applied to an entire scheme rather than merely part of a scheme:

> pt IVA does not provide that a scheme includes part of a scheme and it is possible, despite the very wide definition of a scheme, to conceive of a set of circumstances which constitutes only part of a scheme and not a scheme in itself. That will occur where the circumstances are incapable of standing on their own without being 'robbed of all practical meaning' . . .

In *FC of T v Hart & Anor* 2004 ATC 4599, Gummow and Hayne JJ were of the opinion that, in the above passage, the words 'where the circumstances are incapable of standing on their own without being "robbed of all practical meaning"' were directed at the issue of 'procedural fairness'. On this basis, their Honours had no trouble in concluding (at 4610) that a scheme may not always permit the precise identification of 'all of the integers' of the particular scheme and that there is nothing in pt IVA that requires a scheme to have 'some commercial or other coherence'. This represents a very wide view of what constitutes a scheme and is a more liberal interpretation of the term than was given by, for instance, Cooper J in the Full Federal Court decision in *FC of T v Spotless Services Limited & Anor* 95 ATC 4775, where his Honour stated (at 4805):

> In my view, the definition in s 177A requires that the parties to the scheme, insofar as they are known, must be identified and the terms or content of any agreement, arrangement, understanding, promise or undertaking and the steps or stages of any course of action or

> proposal, insofar as they are relevant, be identified. It is not sufficient to identify a scheme by reference to a hoped for fiscal outcome.

In theory, the more narrowly a scheme is defined by the Commissioner, the more likely he will be able to focus on tax matters to identify the purpose of a person who entered into the scheme. In contrast, if a scheme is defined widely, it is likely that there will be several non-tax aspects of the scheme and it may therefore be more difficult for the Commissioner to establish that pt IVA applies.

[37.5] Tax benefit

For pt IVA to operate, a taxpayer (referred to as the 'relevant taxpayer' in s 177D) must have obtained, or would but for s 177F (see below) have obtained, a 'tax benefit' in connection with the scheme.

The term tax benefit is defined in s 177C. This section has been amended on several occasions over the last few years by adding additional categories of tax benefits. The main categories of tax benefits that arise under the current version of the provision are summarised below.

Under s 177C, a taxpayer obtains a tax benefit in connection with a scheme if:

- an amount is not included in the taxpayer's assessable income for an income year where that amount would have been included, or might reasonably be expected to have been included, in the taxpayer's assessable income for the year if the scheme had not been entered into or carried out (s 177C(1)(a))
- a deduction is allowable to the taxpayer in relation to an income year where the whole or a part of that deduction would not have been allowable, or might reasonably be expected not to have been allowable, to the taxpayer in the income year if the scheme had not been entered into or carried out (s 177C(1)(b))
- a capital loss is incurred by the taxpayer during an income year where the whole or part of that loss would not have been incurred, or might reasonably be expected not to have been incurred, by the taxpayer during the year if the scheme had not been entered into or carried out (s 177C(1)(ba))
- a LCBTO [22.23] is allowable to the taxpayer where the whole or part of that offset would not have been allowable, or might reasonably be expected not to have been allowable, to the taxpayer if the scheme had not been entered into or carried out (s 177C(1)(baa))
- a FITO [31.3] is allowable to the taxpayer where the whole or part of that offset would not have been allowable, or might reasonably be expected not to have been allowable, to the taxpayer if the scheme had not been entered into or carried out (s 177C(1)(bb))
- an innovation tax offset (ie a tax offset under sub-divs 61-P [27.4] or 360-A [27.2]) is allowable to the taxpayer where the whole or part of that offset would not have been allowable, or might reasonably be expected not to have been allowable, to the taxpayer if the scheme had not been entered into or carried out (s 177C(1)(bbaa))
- withholding tax is not payable by the taxpayer on an amount where the taxpayer would have, or might reasonably be expected to have, been liable to pay withholding tax on the amount if the scheme had not been entered into or carried out (s 177C(1)(bc)), or
- a refundable or non-refundable R&D tax offset [27.5] is allowable to the taxpayer where the whole or part of that offset would not have been allowable, or might reasonably be expected not to have been allowable, to the taxpayer if the scheme had not been entered into or carried out (s 177C(1)(bd)).

Importantly, s 177C(2) states that a tax benefit does not arise in connection with a scheme if the benefit is attributable to the making of an agreement, choice, declaration, election or selection, the giving of a notice, or the exercise of an option, expressly provided for by the legislation. However, this exclusion does not apply if the scheme was entered into or carried out for the purpose of creating the circumstances necessary to enable the making of the agreement, choice, declaration, etc.

Ultimately, the concept of a tax benefit turns on what 'would have' occurred, or what 'might reasonably be expected' to have occurred, if the scheme had not been entered into or carried out. In determining what 'might reasonably be expected' to have occurred, it is necessary to make a prediction as to what would have otherwise reasonably taken place. This requires comparing what has actually occurred with some 'counterfactual', 'alternative postulate' or 'alternative hypothesis'.

In the Full Federal Court decision in *Peabody v FC of T* 93 ATC 4104, Hill J stated (at 4112):

> The determination under s 177C(1)(a) requires a finding based upon 'reasonable expectation'. In the context, expectation is not used in the sense of prediction as to the future but rather in the sense of supposition or hypothesis. But what is clear is that the expectation must be one which is reasonable and not one which is unreasonable, irrational or absurd.

Subsequently, on appeal in *FC of T v Peabody* 94 ATC 4663, the High Court held (at 4671):

> A reasonable expectation requires more than a possibility. It involves a prediction as to events which would have taken place if the relevant scheme had not been entered into or carried out and the prediction must be sufficiently reliable for it to be regarded as reasonable.

The issue in *Peabody* was whether pt IVA applied to a complex scheme designed to avoid the operation of former s 26AAA *ITAA36*, which assessed taxpayers on profit arising from the sale of property within 12 months of its purchase. The High Court held that pt IVA did not apply to the scheme as it could not be reasonably concluded that the relevant taxpayer (a beneficiary of a discretionary trust) would have received the amount on which she was assessed by the Commissioner if the scheme had not been implemented.

In contrast, in *FC of T v Spotless Services Ltd & Anor* 96 ATC 5201, the Commissioner successfully applied pt IVA to assess the relevant taxpayers on certain amounts of interest obtained under a scheme involving a Cook Islands bank deposit. Under the scheme, the taxpayers had invested $40m with a Cook Islands bank, which paid them interest that was subject to Cook Islands withholding tax at the rate of 5%. The taxpayers argued that the interest fell within former s 23(q) *ITAA36*, which provided that income derived by an Australian resident from foreign sources was exempt from tax so long as the income was taxable in the country of source [31.3]. The taxpayers submitted that no tax benefit existed because without the scheme (ie if the Cook Islands deposit had not been made) the relevant amount would not have existed (ie no Cook Islands interest would have been earned). In essence, the taxpayers contended that the phrase 'an amount' in s 177C(1)(a) referred to a specific kind of assessable income. The High Court, however, rejected this narrow argument and held that the reference to 'an amount' was 'quantitative' rather than 'qualitative'. On this basis, the Court concluded that the taxpayers received a tax benefit in an amount equal to the interest less withholding tax which they received from the investment which, but for the operation of pt IVA, had not been included in their assessable income.

The concept of a tax benefit was also considered in *RCI Pty Ltd v FC of T* 2011 ATC ¶20-275. This case concerned the reorganisation of the James Hardie group of companies and the movement of its centre of operations to the United States. The taxpayer was an Australian company that was a member of the group. It owned all the shares in a United States company (JHH). JHH had revalued shares it held in another United States company, resulting in a US$318m increase in their value. JHH declared a dividend (which was exempt from tax under former s 23AJ *ITAA36* [31.6]) in favour of the taxpayer equal to this amount. As a consequence, the value of the JHH shares was correspondingly reduced. The taxpayer subsequently disposed of its shares in JHH and included a capital gain in its assessable income. The Commissioner formed the view that a scheme had been entered into by the taxpayer to reduce the market value of its shares in JHH prior to their disposal. The Commissioner maintained that, if the scheme had not been entered into, the taxpayer would have nevertheless proceeded with the disposal of the shares, which would have resulted in a larger capital gain being included in its assessable income. On this basis, he relied on pt IVA to include an additional $478m in the taxpayer's assessable income.

The Full Federal Court, however, held that the taxpayer had not obtained a tax benefit in connection with a scheme. The Court found that pt IVA did not apply because, if the scheme had not been entered into, it was reasonable to assume that the taxpayer would *not* have disposed of its shares since this would have given rise to additional transaction cost of $172m. The Court concluded that the Commissioner's counterfactual could not be supported by the evidence as there was no possibility that the taxpayer would have proceeded with the disposal due to the increase in its transaction cost. Edmonds, Gilmour and Logan JJ were of the view that (at [150]):

> if the scheme . . . had not been entered into or carried out, the reasonable expectation is that the relevant parties would have either abandoned the proposal, indefinitely deferred it, altered it so that it did not involve the transfer by [the taxpayer] of its shares . . . but they would not have proceeded . . . at a tax cost of $172 million.

A similar outcome was also reached in *FC of T v Futuris Corporation Ltd* 2012 ATC ¶20-306. This case concerned a scheme involving a company that had sold shares in one of its subsidiaries in a public float. Prior to the sale, various transfers had occurred between members of the corporate group for less than their cost base or market value. This ultimately resulted in the specific anti-avoidance provisions in former div 19A of pt IIIA *ITAA36* operating to increase the cost base of the taxpayer's shares (thereby reducing its capital gain). The Commissioner submitted that the taxpayer had obtained a tax benefit in connection with a scheme to which pt IVA applied and that an additional net capital gain of $82.95m would have accrued to the taxpayer on the disposal of the shares had it not entered into the scheme. The Full Federal Court, however, held that there was no tax benefit as it was not reasonable to conclude that the taxpayer would have carried out the float in the way postulated in the Commissioner's counterfactual because it would have resulted in significant adverse tax consequences and was not commercially feasible.

The Government was concerned about the outcomes in *RCI* and *Futuris* and announced that it would amend pt IVA to ensure that taxpayers would not be able to overcome the operation of the provisions by arguing that they did not get a tax benefit because, if they had not entered into the scheme, they would not have entered into an arrangement that attracted tax (eg because they could have entered into another scheme that also avoided tax, deferred their arrangements, or done nothing at all) (Assistant Treasurer, *Media Release No 10* (2012)).

The insertion of s 177CB into pt IVA in 2013 makes it clear that the 'would have' and 'might reasonably be expected to have' limbs of the definition of tax benefit in s 177C(1) represent separate and distinct bases upon which the existence of a tax benefit can be demonstrated. Section 177CB prescribes the following two approaches for determining the alternative postulate for the purposes of s 177C:

- **Annihilation approach.** The first approach is an 'annihilation approach' and applies where a 'tax effect *would have* occurred if the scheme had not been entered into or carried out'. The annihilation approach requires the postulate to comprise only the events or circumstances that actually happened or existed (other than those that Form part of the scheme) (s 177CB(2)).
- **Reconstruction approach.** The second approach is a 'reconstruction approach' and applies where a 'tax effect *might reasonably be expected to have* occurred if the scheme had not been entered into or carried out'. The reconstruction approach requires the postulate to be based on a reasonable alternative to entering into the scheme (s 177CB(3)).

Importantly, under the reconstruction approach, in determining whether a postulate is a reasonable alternative, a court is required to have particular regard to the substance of the scheme and any result or consequence for the taxpayer that is or would be achieved by the scheme (other than a result in relation to the operation of the *ITAA36* or *ITAA97*) (s 177CB(4)(a)). Furthermore, any result in relation to the operation of the legislation that would be achieved by the postulate for any person (whether or not a party to the scheme) is expressly ignored (s 177CB(4)(b)).

It is clear from s 177CB(4) that for the purposes of identifying a reasonable alternative postulate, the focus must be on the scheme's financial, commercial and economic substance (ignoring tax results) rather than its legal form. By expressly ignoring tax results in the consideration, Parliament has tried to address the kinds of arguments that were raised by the taxpayers in *RCI* and *Futuris*. So, for example, in *FC of T v Guardian AIT Pty Ltd ATF Australian Investment Trust* 2023 ATC ¶20-850, the Full Federal Court held that, in determining what might reasonably be expected to have happened had a scheme involving certain trusts not been entered into or carried out, the primary judge should have disregarded the higher Australian income tax cost that would have applied if income had been distributed directly to a particular beneficiary.

The Explanatory Memorandum to the Bill that introduced s 177CB contains the following illustration of the reconstruction approach.

Example Mr and Mrs Heginbothom want to borrow money to acquire both a family home and a holiday house that they plan to rent to holiday makers. They borrow the money under an arrangement in which the repayments are applied exclusively to the borrowing in relation to the family home. The result is that the deductible interest payments are increased for the holiday home borrowing and the non-deductible interest payments for the family home borrowing are minimised.

Merely annihilating the scheme would not leave a sensible result because there would be no borrowing at all, so some reconstruction is necessary. It is therefore necessary to consider what might reasonably be expected to have happened if the scheme had not been entered into. A reasonable alternative in this case might be that the Heginbothoms took out two loans, one for each of the homes they wished to acquire, each of which was entered into on normal commercial terms.

[37.6] Purpose

The concept of 'purpose' lies at the heart of s 177D. In contrast to s 260, s 177D requires a conclusion to be made as to the purpose of a particular person rather than a particular scheme. It is the purpose of a person who entered into or carried out the scheme, or any part of the scheme, that is relevant in determining whether pt IVA applies. Importantly, this person does not necessarily have to be the same person as the person who obtains the tax benefit (ie the 'relevant taxpayer') in connection with the scheme. The person may, for example, be an 'adviser' (*FC of T v Consolidated Press Holdings Ltd & Anor* 2001 ATC 4343) or a 'promoter' (*Vincent v FC of T* 2002 ATC 4742) of the scheme.

Section 177A(5) makes it clear that the purpose referred to in s 177D is the 'dominant purpose'. In *FC of T v Spotless Services Ltd & Anor* 96 ATC 5201, the High Court held (at 5206) that 'dominant purpose' means 'the ruling, prevailing or most influential purpose'.

Purpose is determined objectively by reference to the following eight matters listed in s 177D(2) (formerly ss 177D(b)(i) to (viii)):

(a) the manner in which the scheme was entered into or carried out
(b) the form and substance of the scheme

(c) the time at which the scheme was entered into and the length of the period during which the scheme was carried out
(d) the result in relation to the operation of the Act that, but for this Part, would be achieved by the scheme
(e) any change in the financial position of the relevant taxpayer that has resulted, will result, or may reasonably be expected to result, from the scheme
(f) any change in the financial position of any person who has, or has had, any connection (whether of a business, family or other nature) with the relevant taxpayer, being a change that has resulted, will result or may reasonably be expected to result, from the scheme
(g) any other consequence for the relevant taxpayer, or for any person referred to in (f), of the scheme having been entered into or carried out, and
(h) the nature of any connection (whether of a business, family or other nature) between the relevant taxpayer and any person referred to in (f).

In the Full Federal Court decision in *Peabody v FC of T* 93 ATC 4104, Hill J indicated (at 4113) that the Commissioner must have regard to each of these matters. This does not, however, mean that each matter must point to a relevant tax avoidance purpose for pt IVA to apply—some matters may point in one direction and others in another. The conclusion reached must, nevertheless, be based on an evaluation of all the relevant matters. As his Honour observed (at 4114):

> It is the evaluation of these matters, alone or in combination, some for, some against, that s 177D requires in order to reach the conclusion to which s 177D refers.

The High Court in *FC of T v Hart & Anor* 2004 ATC 4599 has confirmed (at 4612) that all eight factors must be considered. Callinan J, however, noted (at 4626):

> It is not necessary of course that every one of them be relevant to every scheme. Indeed the presence or overwhelming weight of one factor alone may of itself in an appropriate case be of such significance as to expose a relevant dominant purpose.

In examining the Commissioner's conclusion as to purpose, it is not necessary for a judge to refer to each of the matters separately in his or her judgment. It is sufficient if the judgment demonstrates that all the specified matters have been taken into account in forming a 'global assessment of purpose' (*FC of T v Consolidated Press Holdings Ltd & Anor* 2001 ATC 4343 at 4360).

Importantly, the Commissioner must not have regard to a matter that is not listed in s 177D(2). In *Peabody v FC of T* 93 ATC 4104, Hill J pointed out (at 4113) that 'the actual subjective purpose of any relevant person' is not a relevant matter to be considered since it is not listed in the provision. This was confirmed in *Eastern Nitrogen Ltd v FC of T* 2001 ATC 4164, where the Full Federal Court, in determining whether pt IVA applied to a sale and leaseback arrangement relating to an ammonia plant, held that the trial judge had erred in taking into account a participant's actual subjective purpose in entering into the scheme.

In *FC of T v Consolidated Press Holdings Ltd & Anor* 2001 ATC 4343, the High Court pointed out that s 177D does not depend on the 'fiscal awareness' of a taxpayer and that the purpose of a professional adviser can be attributed to the taxpayer. The case concerned the takeover of a foreign company by a corporate group. Acting on professional advice, a complex financing scheme was implemented to circumvent the operation of former s 79D *ITAA36* which would have otherwise quarantined deductions for interest expenditure. In concluding that pt IVA applied to the scheme, the High Court said (at 4360):

> It is to be expected that those who participate in a complex, international, commercial transaction will be concerned about its tax implications, and will seek expert advice. Attributing the purpose of a professional adviser to one or more of the corporate parties in the present

> case is both possible and appropriate. In some cases, the actual parties to a scheme subjectively may not have any purpose, independent of that of a professional adviser, in relation to the scheme or part of the scheme, but that does not defeat the operation of s 177D. If, in the present case, there had been evidence which showed that no director or employee of any member of the Group had ever heard of s 79D, that would not conclude the matter in favour of the taxpayer. One of the reasons for making s 177D turn upon the objective matters listed in the section, it may be inferred, was to avoid the consequence that the operation of pt IVA depends upon the fiscal awareness of a taxpayer.

In *Consolidated Press*, the High Court held that it is possible to conclude that a person has entered into a scheme for the dominant purpose of enabling the relevant taxpayer to obtain a tax benefit and for this purpose to be consistent with the pursuit of a commercial gain. The High Court relied on *FC of T v Spotless Services Ltd & Anor* for this proposition. In *Spotless*, the High Court had held that a rational commercial transaction in which a taxpayer seeks a greater after-tax return on an investment can fall within pt IVA. Brennan CJ, Dawson, Toohey, Gaudron, Gummow and Kirby JJ stated (at 5206):

> A particular course of action may be, to use a phrase found in the Full Court judgments, both 'tax driven' and bear the character of a rational commercial decision. The presence of the latter characteristic does not determine the answer to the question whether, within the meaning of pt IVA, a person entered into or carried out a 'scheme' for the 'dominant purpose' of enabling the taxpayer to obtain a 'tax benefit'.

The fact that pt IVA can apply to a scheme that also has commercial imperatives is illustrated in *FC of T v Hart & Anor* 2004 ATC 4599. This case concerned a 'split loan' financing facility that had been marketed to the taxpayers by Austral. Under the arrangement, the taxpayers had borrowed money to finance the acquisition of a private residence and refinance an income-producing property. The loan was split into two portions: a 'home loan account' and an 'investment loan account'. The taxpayers had the option, which they exercised, of paying off the home loan account before the investment loan account. The documents indicated that the benefit of doing this was that the home loan account would be paid off sooner and the amount of interest paid on the home loan account would be less than would have been the case. This interest was, of course, not deductible as it was of a private nature. Correspondingly, the interest on the investment loan account would be greater than it would otherwise be, and it would include 'additional interest' as well as 'compound interest' on the additional interest. The taxpayers sought deductions for all of these interest payments. The Commissioner, however, disallowed deductions for the additional and compound interest on the basis that it constituted a tax benefit under a scheme to which pt IVA applied.

The High Court confirmed that the Commissioner had properly applied pt IVA. In doing so, the Court held that the fact that a scheme was directed at a commercial end (the borrowing of money to finance the properties), did not preclude the operation of pt IVA. In this regard, Gummow and Hayne JJ stated (at 4613): 'The presence of a discernible commercial end does not determine the answer to the question posed by s 177D.' Their Honours emphasised that s 177D requires the drawing of a conclusion about purpose from the eight objective matters listed, and they concluded (at 4614):

> There could be no doubt in these matters that the terms on which the loan was made available were explicable only by the taxation consequences for the respondents. If the scheme was identified as 'all the steps leading to, and the entering into, and the implementation of the loan arrangements' the manner in which that scheme was entered into strongly suggested that the respondents (each a relevant taxpayer) entered into that scheme for the dominant purpose of obtaining a tax benefit. Further, if the scheme was identified in this way, the respondents, by giving the directions they did, carried out the scheme for that same

> dominant purpose. But so too, if the scheme is identified more narrowly (as the making of the relevant provisions in the loan agreement and the giving of directions under those provisions) the like conclusion would be reached. Both the manner in which that (narrower) scheme was entered into, and the manner in which it was carried out, strongly suggested the conclusion described.

The decision in *Hart* may be contrasted with *Mochkin v FC of T* 2003 ATC 4272 where it was held that pt IVA did not apply to a taxpayer who had entered into a commission-sharing arrangement with a firm of stockbrokers through a family discretionary trust. The trust structure was used because the taxpayer had previously been sued by a firm of stockbrokers for losses arising from client defaults. The Commissioner sought to apply pt IVA to assess the taxpayer on the commissions that had been paid to the trust over a number of years. The Full Federal Court, however, held that although the trust structure had tax advantages, the facts indicated that these were 'subsidiary' to the commercial objectives of avoiding personal liability for client defaults. In reaching the conclusion that the taxpayer's dominant purpose in entering the scheme was to avoid personal liability, Sackville, Merkel and Kenny JJ stated (at 4287):

> It is undoubtedly true that the discretionary trust structure adopted by the Taxpayer had substantial tax advantages when compared with other structures that might have been adopted to achieve the same commercial objectives. The primary Judge, with respect, was clearly correct in accepting that one of the purposes of the Taxpayer in entering into the Ledger scheme was to obtain a tax benefit in the form of the ability to have the net income generated by the stockbroking consultancy business distributed in a tax effective way to the beneficiaries of the discretionary trusts. But, as *Eastern Nitrogen* and *Hart* show, the fact that aspects of the scheme are tax driven does not establish that the 'dominant purpose' of the relevant person, objectively assessed, was to obtain a tax benefit. Unlike *Spotless*, the scheme in the present case, even without the tax benefits, would have made commercial sense.

[37.7] Commissioner's discretion to make a determination

Section 177F gives the Commissioner the discretion whether or not to apply pt IVA. This should be contrasted with s 260, which was a 'self-executing' provision [37.2]. The Commissioner may make the following determinations under s 177F relating to the tax benefits outlined at [37.4]:

- if the tax benefit relates to an amount not being included in the taxpayer's assessable income—determine that the whole or part of that amount is included in the taxpayer's assessable income
- if the tax benefit relates to a deduction being allowable to the taxpayer—determine that the whole or part of the deduction is not allowable to the taxpayer
- if the tax benefit relates to the incurring of a capital loss by the taxpayer—determine that the whole or part of the loss was not incurred by the taxpayer
- if the tax benefit relates to a LCBTO being allowable to the taxpayer—determine that the whole or part of the LCBTO is not allowable to the taxpayer
- if the tax benefit relates to a FITO being allowable to the taxpayer—determine that the whole or part of the FITO is not allowable to the taxpayer
- if the tax benefit relates to an innovation tax offset being allowable to the taxpayer—determine that the whole or part of the offset is not allowable to the taxpayer
- if the tax benefit relates to withholding tax on an amount—determine that the taxpayer is subject to withholding tax on the whole or part of that amount
- if the tax benefit relates to a refundable or non-refundable R&D tax offset—determine that the whole or part of the tax offset is not allowable to the taxpayer.

Where the Commissioner has made a determination under s 177F to cancel the whole or part of a tax benefit obtained by a taxpayer, he is also empowered to make a fair and reasonable compensating adjustment in respect of any other taxpayer. This is designed to address any injustice which might otherwise result from the cancellation of the tax benefit (eg to prevent double taxation).

[37.8] Multinational anti-avoidance law

The MAAL is one of the Government's tools for dealing with BEPS [33.3] and was inserted in pt IVA by the *Tax Laws Amendment (Combating Multinational Tax Avoidance) Act 2015* (Cth). The MAAL is contained in s 177DA and builds on the existing architecture of pt IVA. It targets schemes entered into by significant global entities [33.7] that make supplies to Australian customers where activities are undertaken in Australia directly in connection with the supplies by an Australian entity, or through an associated Australian PE, and some or all of the income is not attributable to an Australian PE of the foreign entity. It operates from 1 January 2016, irrespective of when or where the relevant scheme was entered into or carried out.

The MAAL contains a 'principal' (rather than 'dominant') purpose test and takes into account schemes that involve not just Australian tax benefits, but also reductions in foreign tax. The object of this is to overcome arguments that the existing rules in pt IVA cannot apply to schemes entered into for the dominant purpose of avoiding foreign tax.

Where the requirements of s 177DA are satisfied, the Commissioner can make a determination under s 177F to cancel the tax benefit and he can also make compensating adjustments [37.7].

Section 177DA—schemes that limit a taxable presence in Australia

Section 177DA(1) states that, without limiting s 177D [37.3], pt IVA also applies to a scheme if:

(a) under, or in connection with, the scheme:
  (i) a foreign entity makes a supply to an Australian customer of the foreign entity; and
  (ii) activities are undertaken in Australia directly in connection with the supply; and
  (iii) some or all of those activities are undertaken by an Australian entity who, or are undertaken at or through an Australian PE of an entity who, is an associate of or is commercially dependent on the foreign entity; and
  (iv) the foreign entity derives ordinary income, or statutory income, from the supply; and
  (v) some or all of that income is not attributable to an Australian PE of the foreign entity;

(b) it would be concluded (having regard to the matters in sub-section (2)) that the person, or one of the persons, who entered into or carried out the scheme or any part of the scheme did so for a principal purpose of, or for more than one principal purpose that includes a purpose of:
  (i) enabling a taxpayer (a ***relevant taxpayer***) to obtain a tax benefit, or both to obtain a tax benefit and to reduce one or more of the relevant taxpayer's liabilities to tax under a foreign law, in connection with the scheme; or
  (ii) enabling the relevant taxpayer and another taxpayer (or other taxpayers) to obtain a tax benefit, or both to obtain a tax benefit and to reduce one or more of their liabilities to tax under a foreign law, in connection with the scheme;

  whether or not that person who entered into or carried out the scheme or any part of the scheme is the relevant taxpayer or is the other taxpayer or one of the other taxpayers; and

(c) the foreign entity is a significant global entity for a year of income in which the relevant taxpayer, or one or more other taxpayers, would (but for this Part):

(i) obtain a tax benefit; or

(ii) reduce one or more of their liabilities to tax under a foreign law;

in connection with the scheme.

Section 177DA(2) provides that the Commissioner must have regard to the following matters for the purposes of reaching the conclusion in s 177DA(1)(b):

- the matters in subsection 177D(2) [37.6]
- the extent to which the activities that contribute to bringing about the contract for the supply are performed, and are able to be performed, by the foreign entity, another entity referred to in s 177DA(1)(a)(iii), or any other entities
- the result, in relation to the operation of any foreign law relating to taxation, that (but for pt IVA) would be achieved by the scheme.

[37.9] Diverted profits tax

DPT was introduced by the *Treasury Laws Amendment (Combating Multinational Tax Avoidance) Act 2017* (Cth) as another prong in the Government's response to BEPS [33.3]. The DPT provisions are contained in ss 177H to 177R of pt IVA. Like the MAAL, these provisions build on the existing architecture in pt IVA and only apply to significant global entities [33.7].

The primary objects of the DPT provisions are to:

- ensure that the Australian tax payable by significant global entities properly reflects the economic substance of the activities that those entities carry on in Australia, and
- prevent those entities from reducing the amount of Australian tax they pay by diverting profits offshore through contrived arrangements between related parties (s 177H).

Application

The DPT provisions apply to 'DPT tax benefits' for income years starting on or after 1 July 2017. The key provision is s 177J(1), which provides that pt IVA applies to a scheme in relation to a tax benefit (the 'DPT tax benefit') if:

- a relevant taxpayer has obtained, or would but for s 177F obtain, a DPT tax benefit in connection with the scheme in an income year
- it would be concluded (having regard to the matters in s 177J(2)) that the person, or one of the persons, who entered into or carried out the scheme or any part of the scheme did so for a principal purpose of, or for more than one principal purpose that includes a purpose of:
  - enabling the relevant taxpayer to obtain a tax benefit, or both to obtain a tax benefit and reduce one or more foreign tax liabilities; or
  - enabling the relevant taxpayer and another taxpayer (or other taxpayers) to obtain a tax benefit, or both to obtain a tax benefit and reduce one or more foreign tax liabilities
- the relevant taxpayer is a significant global entity for the income year
- a foreign entity that is an associate of the relevant taxpayer is the person, or one of the persons, who entered into or carried out the scheme or any part of the scheme, or is otherwise connected with the scheme or any part of the scheme
- the relevant taxpayer is not: an MIT, a foreign collective investment vehicle with wide membership, a foreign entity owned by a foreign government, a complying superannuation entity, or a foreign pension fund, and
- it is reasonable to conclude that none of the following sections apply in relation to the relevant taxpayer, in relation to the DPT tax benefit:

  - s 177K (this section contains the '$25m income test', which applies if the sum of the assessable income, exempt income and non-assessable non-exempt income of the relevant taxpayer, the assessable income of any other associated entities that are members of the same global group and, if the DPT tax benefit relates to an amount not being included in assessable income, the amount of the DPT tax benefit, does not exceed $25m)
  - s 177L (this section contains the 'sufficient foreign tax test', which applies if the increase in the foreign tax liabilities of foreign entities resulting from the scheme is 80% or more of the reduction in the Australian tax liability of the relevant taxpayer), or
  - s 177M (this section contains the 'sufficient economic substance test', which applies if the profit made as a result of the scheme by the relevant taxpayer and their associated entities, reasonably reflects the economic substance of their activities in connection with the scheme).

The matters the Commissioner must have regard to under s 177J(2) are:

- the matters in s 177D(2) [37.6]
- the extent to which non-tax financial benefits that are quantifiable have resulted, will result, or may reasonably be expected to result, from the scheme
- the result, in relation to the operation of any foreign law relating to taxation, that (but for pt IVA) would be achieved by the scheme, and
- the amount of the tax benefit.

37

Assessment and imposition of DPT

If the DPT provisions apply to a scheme, the Commissioner may issue a DPT assessment to the relevant taxpayer under div 145 *TAA* requiring them to pay DPT. DPT is due 21 days after the notice has been issued and is imposed on the 'DPT base amount' at the rate of 40% under the *Diverted Profits Tax Act 2017* (Cth) (s 177P).

[37.10] QUESTIONS

1. What limitations did former s 260 *ITAA36* encounter? In what ways is pt IVA *ITAA36* different?
2. Discuss the meanings of 'scheme' and 'tax benefit'. Why are these concepts important?
3. What is the role of s 177CB *ITAA36*?
4. What is the relevance of 'purpose' under pt IVA? Whose purpose is relevant and how is purpose ascertained?
5. Discuss why pt IVA applied in *FC of T v Spotless Services Ltd & Anor* 96 ATC 5201 and *FC of T v Hart & Anor* 2004 ATC 4599 and why it did not apply in *FC of T v Peabody* 94 ATC 4663 and *RCI Pty Ltd v FC of T* 2011 ATC ¶20-275.
6. What is the role of s 177F *ITAA36* and what consequences flow if pt IVA applies to a scheme?
7. Outline the kinds of schemes to which the MAAL and DPT are targeted.

PART M

TAX ADMINISTRATION

38 INCOME TAX RETURNS, ASSESSMENTS, RULINGS, APPEALS AND AUDITS

[38.1] Introduction

This chapter focuses on some important aspects of income tax administration. It commences with an examination of the obligation on taxpayers to lodge income tax returns [38.2] followed by a discussion of the assessment process [38.3] and the taxation ruling system [38.4]. The chapter examines the special rules for objecting to assessments and private rulings under pt IVC *TAA* [38.5]. It also discusses the limited avenues for challenging assessments outside these rules [38.6] and various other aspects of tax litigation [38.7]. The chapter concludes with a discussion of the Commissioner's audit and investigatory powers [38.8] and his attitude to tax compliance [38.9].

[38.2] Income tax returns

Income tax returns are used for reporting purposes and are a central feature of the income tax system. As a general rule, taxpayers are assessed on the basis of the information contained in their returns [38.3].

Requirement to lodge returns

Taxpayers must lodge income tax returns if required to do so by the Commissioner (s 161 *ITAA36*). Each year, the Commissioner issues legislative instruments specifying the categories of taxpayers that should lodge returns (eg Notice of Requirement to Lodge a Return for the Income Year Ended 30 June 2023).

In general, most taxpayers are required to lodge tax returns. However, an exception applies to resident individuals with taxable income below the tax-free threshold of $18,200. These persons must, nevertheless, still lodge returns in certain cases, such as where they carry on a business or are under 18 years of age and have more than $416 of eligible taxable income.

The Commissioner also has power to require taxpayers to lodge:

- 'further returns' (eg where he is not satisfied with the original return) (s 162), and

- 'special returns' (eg where a taxpayer is planning to leave Australia before the end of the income year) (s 163).

Administrative penalties apply where taxpayers fail to lodge their income returns on time (div 286 of sch 1 *TAA*) [41.2].

Forms

The ATO produces different return forms for different kinds of entities. There are separate forms for individuals (Form I), companies (Form C), trusts (Form T), partnerships (Form P), and superannuation funds (Form F). Depending on the taxpayer's circumstances, the taxpayer may be required to complete additional schedules detailing specific information. For example, schedules relating to business and professional items, employment termination payments, superannuation lump sum payments, and capital gains tax.

Lodgment of returns

Over the last few years, individuals have been required to lodge their income tax returns by 31 October following the end of the income year. To assist individuals in lodging their returns, the ATO publishes a guide entitled *Individual Tax Return Instructions* (which replaces the former *TaxPack* guide). Taxpayers can also now lodge returns electronically using 'myTax' via the 'myGov' website, which is the single point for government online services [2.5]. The myTax product contains a useful pre-filling service to assist taxpayers to complete their returns. The pre-filling service populates a taxpayer's return with information that the ATO already possesses about them, obtained from organisations such as employers, banks, companies and government agencies.

Special arrangements apply where taxpayers use tax agents to lodge their returns. Tax agents must lodge returns in accordance with their specific lodgment programs. Lodgment programs are designed to allow tax agents to spread their workload over the year. Most tax agents use the ATO's electronic lodgment system to lodge their clients' returns. However, before using this system for a client, a tax agent must obtain a written authority from the client to do so.

Taxpayers are required to sign their returns and declare that the information provided is 'true and correct'. A return lodged electronically must contain the taxpayer's electronic signature. Where the return is lodged electronically by a tax agent, it must contain the electronic signature of the tax agent. Penalties apply where information has been misstated in the return [41.2].

[38.3] Assessments

Underpinning the Australian income tax system is the 'assessment' process. Since 1986, a 'self-assessment regime' has operated in Australia. Before this time, taxpayers were required to make full disclosure of all relevant material in their income tax returns. This was cumbersome and required ATO officers to spend a long time scrutinising returns. Under the self-assessment regime, the ATO generally accepts statements made by taxpayers in their returns and issues assessments based on such information. Assessments are not issued to companies and superannuation entities, as these taxpayers are subject to a 'full self-assessment regime' under which they assess themselves [8.11].

The Commissioner has wide audit powers that enable him to check that the information provided by taxpayers in their returns is correct [38.8]. Where he believes that a taxpayer has been wrongly assessed, he has the power to amend the taxpayer's assessment subject to certain limitations.

Importance of assessments

Assessments effectively 'crystallise' a taxpayer's tax liability for a particular tax period and are important because:

- the Commissioner can generally only recover tax from a taxpayer after a valid notice of assessment has been served on the taxpayer and a prescribed period of time has elapsed after the making of the assessment, and
- there are limited time periods within which assessments may be amended and limited time periods within which taxpayers can object to assessments.

Nature of an assessment

An 'assessment' is defined in s 6(1)(a) *ITAA36* as:

> the ascertainment of taxable income (or that there is no taxable income) and of the tax payable on that taxable income (or that no tax is payable).

The words in parentheses in this definition were inserted to overcome arguments raised in cases such as *FC of T v Ryan* 2000 ATC 4079 and *DFC of T v Sheehan* 86 ATC 4718 that the former definition of assessment did not apply to a document that indicated no tax was payable. The current definition makes it clear that a notice specifying that no tax is payable is just as much an assessment as a notice specifying a positive tax liability.

The assessment process is only complete once the assessment is served on the taxpayer under s 174 *ITAA36* (*Batagol v FC of T* (1963) 109 CLR 243). The Commissioner may serve the assessment on the taxpayer by leaving a copy at his or her preferred address for service, posting a copy to that address, or delivering an electronic copy to the taxpayer's preferred electronic address.

The nature of an assessment was described in *R v DFC of T; ex parte Hooper* (1926) 37 CLR 368 by Issacs J (at 373) in the following terms:

> An 'assessment' is not a piece of paper; it is an official act or operation; it is the Commissioner's ascertainment, on consideration of all relevant circumstances, including sometimes his own opinion, of the amount of tax chargeable to a given taxpayer. When he has completed his ascertainment of the amount, he sends by post a notification thereof called 'a notice of assessment'. . . . But neither the paper sent nor the notification it gives is the 'assessment'. That is and remains the act or operation of the Commissioner.

It is clear from these words that the essence of an assessment is that it is an administrative process under which the Commissioner has reached a final conclusion regarding a taxpayer's tax position (which, under the new definition of assessment, may be either a positive tax liability or a nil tax liability).

An assessment must be 'definitive' as opposed to 'provisional' (*FC of T v S Hoffnung Company Ltd* (1928) 42 CLR 39). It must also be made 'bona fide' for the purposes of the Act (*DFC of T v Richard Walter Pty Ltd* 95 ATC 4067). The Commissioner cannot therefore 'pluck a figure out of the air' to assess a taxpayer (*Briggs v DFC of T* 85 ATC 4569). He can, nevertheless, base an assessment on a reasoned estimate and he often makes 'asset betterment' assessments on this basis (*L'Estrange v FC of T* 78 ATC 4744). There is no requirement on the Commissioner to make inquiries from the taxpayer or their agent prior to issuing an assessment, and a failure to do so does not vitiate an assessment (*McCleary v FC of T* 97 ATC 4266).

Just because the facts of a particular case are uncertain does not invalidate a bona fide attempt made by the Commissioner to assess a taxpayer. However, where a purported assessment is made on the basis of facts known to the Commissioner to be untrue, this is not a bone fide exercise of the power of assessment (*Darrell Lea Chocolate Shops Pty Ltd v FC of T* 97 ATC 4040).

Alternative assessments in respect of the same taxpayer for a particular income year are invalid since they do not fix any definitive liability and are merely tentative. This is illustrated in *FC of T v Stokes* 97 ATC 4001, where three different notices of assessments were served on a taxpayer at the same time relating to the identical year of income. The Full Federal Court found that the notices reflected three alternative positions and it could not therefore be said that the taxpayer's liability for the year had been precisely determined.

The Commissioner can, nevertheless, issue assessments against more than one taxpayer in relation to the same income for the same income year (*Richardson v FC of T* (1932) 48 CLR 192; *DFC of T v Richard Walter Pty Ltd* 95 ATC 4067). A recent illustration of this is found in *Hyder & Ors v FC of T* 2023 ATC ¶20-854, where the Full Federal Court rejected the taxpayers' contention that the scheme of the income tax legislation was such that the Commissioner could not lawfully assess more than one taxpayer in respect of income from the same source.

Kinds of assessments

The most common type of assessment that the Commissioner makes is known as an 'ordinary assessment'. This assessment is based on information provided in a taxpayer's return and any other information in the Commissioner's possession (s 166 *ITAA36*).

The Commissioner also has the power to make 'default assessments' (eg where a taxpayer fails to furnish a return) (s 167 *ITAA36*).

In addition, he can make 'special assessments' relating to taxable income derived during part of an income year (s 168 *ITAA36*). In *DFC of T v Jones & Anor* 99 ATC 4373, the Full Federal Court held that this provision could be used to assess a taxpayer who had become bankrupt in respect of taxable income derived in that part of the income year ending with the bankruptcy and separately in respect of taxable income covering the period from the bankruptcy to the end of the income year.

Full self-assessment taxpayers

Companies as well as trustees of superannuation funds, ADFs, PSTs and public trading trusts are treated as 'full self-assessment taxpayers' (s 6(1) *ITAA36*) [8.11]. The Commissioner is deemed to have made an assessment of the taxable income or net income and tax payable by these entities on the day that they lodge their returns (s 166A(3) *ITAA36*). As a result, unlike individuals, these entities do not receive formal notices of assessment from the Commissioner. They are required to calculate their income tax liability and pay tax when they lodge their returns.

Amendment of assessments

The Commissioner has the power to amend an income tax assessment subject to prescribed time limits (s 170 *ITAA36*). In practice, the Commissioner amends assessments where he has discovered some irregularity following an audit.

The Commissioner has four years after giving a taxpayer their notice of assessment to amend the assessment (s 170(1) (item 4 in the table)). However, a shorter amendment period of two years applies to individuals that are not carrying on a business and to individuals, companies, or trustees that are SBEs or that would be SBEs if the aggregated turnover threshold for SBEs was $50m (instead of $10m) (s 170(1) (items 1, 2 and 3 in the table)). The two-year amendment period does not apply if it is reasonable to conclude that any person entered into or carried out a scheme (either alone or with others) for the sole or dominant purpose of obtaining a 'scheme benefit' (as defined in s 284-150 *TAA*) in relation to income tax from the scheme.

Where fraud or evasion is involved, the Commissioner can amend an assessment at any time (s 170(1) (item 5 in the table)). The Commissioner can also amend an assessment at any time to give effect to a decision on an appeal or review or as a result of an objection made by the taxpayer (s 170(1) (item 6 in the table)).

Tax receipt

The Commissioner is required to provide individual taxpayers with a tax receipt under div 70 of sch 1 *TAA* if their assessed income tax for a year exceeds $100. The tax receipt must include information about how the total tax paid is notionally used to finance different categories of Commonwealth expenditure and is designed to provide greater transparency of how a taxpayer's money is spent.

[38.4] Taxation rulings

Australia's tax system, like those of many other countries around the world, contains a 'rulings system' [2.3]. Under this system, the Commissioner has the power to issue rulings that set out his interpretation of the operation of the tax laws. The rulings system complements the self-assessment regime as it informs taxpayers about the Commissioner's views on particular matters that may affect them. Taxpayers often rely on the Commissioner's rulings when contemplating potential transactions and completing their tax returns.

Binding rulings system

Australia introduced a binding rulings system in 1992. Rulings issued before this time were not binding. The binding rulings system was initially contained in pt IVAAA *TAA*. However, it has since been replaced by a new system contained in pt 5-5 of sch 1 *TAA*. To ensure the continued operation of former rulings, a ruling in force under the old rules is taken to have effect as if it was made under the new rules.

The rulings system contains a set of common rules in div 357 *TAA* which allow the Commissioner to make rulings on a range of taxes, including income tax, withholding tax, FBT and the ML (s 357-55). From 1 July 2010, the rulings system has been extended to also cover GST, LCT, WET and excise duty. Previously, the *TAA* contained separate rules dealing with 'indirect tax rulings'. By harmonising indirect tax rulings with the general rulings system, there is consistent treatment across the tax laws.

Section 357-5 states that the object of the rulings system is:

> to provide a way for you to find out the Commissioner's view about how certain laws administered by the Commissioner apply to you so that the risks to you of uncertainty when you are self-assessing or working out your tax obligations or entitlements are reduced.

A ruling binds the Commissioner if the ruling applies to a person and that person relies on the ruling by acting (or omitting to act) in accordance with the ruling (s 357-60). As a consequence, a taxpayer that relies on a ruling is protected against any 'tax shortfall' (ie underpaid tax), penalties or interest that would otherwise be payable under the law. This protection operates even if the ruling subsequently turns out to be incorrect. A ruling is, however, only binding in relation to the specific schemes stated in the ruling (*Bellinz Pty Ltd & Ors v FC of T* 98 ATC 4634).

Although there is no penalty for failing to follow a ruling, such a failure may be relevant to determine any penalties under the tax shortfall provisions in div 284 [41.2] (s 357-65).

Special rules operate to resolve conflicts where rulings are inconsistent with each other (s 357-75).

Binding rulings fall into three categories:

- **Public rulings.** These rulings are issued in writing and apply to the kinds of taxpayers and schemes identified in the rulings (see further TR 2006/10).
- **Private rulings.** These rulings are also issued in writing but only apply to the specific taxpayers who have requested them (see further TR 2006/11).
- **Oral rulings.** These rulings are made orally and apply only to individuals with simple tax matters.

Public rulings

The Commissioner may make 'public rulings' on the way in which a tax law applies to:

- entities generally or to a class of entities
- entities in relation to a class of schemes, or
- entities in relation to a particular scheme.

A ruling is a public ruling if it is published and states that it is a public ruling (s 358-5). A public ruling may specify the time at which it ceases to apply. If it does not do this, it continues to apply until it is withdrawn (s 358-15). The Commissioner may withdraw a public ruling (in whole or part) by publishing a notice of withdrawal. The public ruling, nevertheless, continues to apply to schemes that have begun to be carried out before the withdrawal (s 358-20). There is no right of objection against a public ruling.

The Commissioner publishes a range of different binding public rulings, including the TR, GSTR, PR, CR and LCR series discussed at [2.3]. Before a public ruling is issued, a draft ruling reflecting the ATO's preliminary views on the relevant topic is usually circulated for public comment. Draft rulings are not binding and are signified by a 'D' appearing before the ruling numbers (eg TR 2012/D1). A special Public Rulings Panel considers draft rulings. The panel comprises senior ATO officers and consultants from the profession and academia.

Private rulings

The Commissioner may make a private ruling on the way in which he considers a tax law applies to a taxpayer in relation to a specified scheme (s 359-5). An application for a private ruling must be made in the approved form (s 359-10). The Commissioner makes a private ruling by recording the ruling in writing and providing the applicant with a copy of the ruling (s 359-15). The ruling must state that it is a private ruling and must identify to whom it applies as well as the relevant scheme and relevant provision to which it relates (s 359-20).

Private rulings are 'taxation decisions' and rulees dissatisfied with private rulings may object against them under the procedures set out in pt IVC *TAA* [38.5] (s 359-60).

The Commissioner must make a private ruling in response to an application, unless he considers that making the ruling would prejudice or unduly restrict the administration of a taxation law, or the matter sought to be ruled on has been considered by him. He may also decline to make a private ruling if the matter sought to be ruled on relates to how he would exercise a power under a relevant provision and he has already decided whether or not to exercise that power. If the Commissioner considers that further information is required to make a private ruling, he must request the applicant to give the information to him, and he may decline to make a ruling if the applicant does not give the information within a reasonable time (s 357-105). Where the Commissioner considers that the correctness of a private ruling would depend on which assumptions were made about a future event or other matter, he may decline to make the ruling or make such assumptions as he considers most appropriate (s 357-110; see also *FC of T v Hacon Pty Ltd & Ors* 2017 ATC ¶20-639).

The Commissioner must give the applicant written reasons for declining to make a private ruling (s 359-35). If the Commissioner has neither made a ruling nor informed the applicant that he has declined to make the ruling, the applicant may, 60 days after making the application, give the Commissioner a written notice requiring him to make the ruling. If the ruling is not made within 30 days thereafter, the applicant may object against the Commissioner's failure to make the ruling in the manner set out in pt IVC *TAA* [38.5] (s 359-50).

Oral rulings

Individuals and their legal personal representatives are entitled to apply to the Commissioner for oral rulings about the way in which he considers a relevant provision applies in relation to a scheme. The Commissioner must give an oral ruling unless he considers that the advice sought relates to a 'business matter' or a 'complex matter' or is already being, or has been, considered by him for the relevant person. The applicant is not entitled to a written record of the ruling. The Commissioner must, however, include a registration identifier for the ruling (s 360-5). Applicants cannot object against oral rulings.

[38.5] Objections, reviews and appeals

Taxpayers may be dissatisfied with their assessments, particularly where the Commissioner has issued an amended assessment following an audit. In the interests of justice, it is important for taxpayers to have proper channels to challenge assessments that they believe to be incorrect. Likewise, it is also important for taxpayers to have the ability to contest adverse private rulings. The principal avenue for challenging an assessment or a private ruling is through the objection, review and appeal procedures contained in pt IVC *TAA*.

Objections

A taxpayer can object to an assessment or a private ruling in the manner prescribed in pt IVC *TAA* (s 175A *ITAA36*; s 359-60 *TAA*). The taxpayer must lodge an objection in the approved form within a specified time. This is usually four years from the time that the taxpayer was served with the assessment, unless the Commissioner has granted an extension. The taxpayer must state 'fully and in detail' the grounds of the objection (ss 14ZU, 14ZW, 14ZX *TAA*). Once an objection has been lodged, the Commissioner must decide whether to allow the objection (in full or part) or disallow it (s 14ZY *TAA*). This process is known as an 'internal review' for administrative law purposes.

Taxpayers need to make sure that they have complied with the 'fully and in detail' requirement in drafting their objections. A statement that an assessment is 'excessive' without providing specific grounds would not seem to satisfy this requirement. A taxpayer may, nevertheless, incorporate relevant information by reference in their letter of objection (eg by referring to information in their tax returns). For example, in *Szajntop v FC of T* 93 ATC 4307, a taxpayer had been assessed based on an 'assets betterment statement' prepared by the ATO following an audit. The taxpayer's tax agent sent a short letter to the ATO which objected to the assessments and stated:

> On the 5th August 1987 we lodged income tax returns . . . and in each case it indicated that there was no tax payable at all. The assessments were raised from a betterment statement produced by one of your Officers on completely erroneous information.

A majority of the Full Federal Court held that the letter constituted a valid objection as it was more than a 'general complaint' and contained an intelligible ground of objection. Black CJ and Burchett J pointed out (at 4313) that the letter 'tells the Commissioner the extent to which the taxpayer contends the assessments are excessive, why she says they are excessive and precisely what the taxpayer says her true income from all sources was for the years in question'. Their Honours also noted that by referring to her tax returns, 'the objection also tells the Commissioner what the taxpayer says are the sources of what she contends was her only income for the years in question'.

Reviews and appeals

If a taxpayer is dissatisfied with the Commissioner's objection decision, the taxpayer may apply to the AAT for review of the decision or appeal to the Federal Court against the decision (s 14ZZ *TAA*).

In December 2022, the Government announced it will replace the AAT with a new federal administrative review body. The Government is consulting on the new body's design and is expected to introduce enabling legislation in 2023.

The AAT is an administrative body that undertakes a 'merits review'. This means that it makes a fresh decision on the evidence before it and can stand in the Commissioner's shoes and exercise all powers and discretions provided to him under the legislation. The AAT can (a) affirm the decision; (b) vary the decision; or (c) set aside the decision and either make a substituted decision or remit the matter for reconsideration by the Commissioner in accordance with any directions or recommendations it makes (s 43 *AATA*). The Federal Court, on the other hand, is a judicial body that undertakes 'judicial review'. This means that it is concerned purely with the legality of the decision and can only interfere with a discretion exercised by the Commissioner where it was unlawfully made (eg where it breaches the rules of natural justice because it was made *mala fides*). If the Federal Court finds that the decision was unlawful, it will generally set aside the decision and remit the matter to the Commissioner for action according to law.

Proceedings before the AAT are generally less costly and less formal than proceedings before the Federal Court (s 33 *AATA*). Taxpayers often appear before the AAT in person without legal representation. The AAT must follow the rules of natural justice and procedural fairness but is not bound by the rules of evidence. Taxpayers can request that hearings before the AAT be made private to preserve their anonymity (s 14ZZE *TAA*). The AAT can make orders prohibiting or restricting the disclosure of information that reveals the identity of a party or witness to the proceedings or evidence relating to the proceedings (s 35 *AATA*). Federal Court proceedings, on the other hand, usually involve legal representation and operate subject to the rules of evidence. The proceedings generally occur in open court, which means that the taxpayer's identity will be disclosed, unless the court issues a suppression order (*Herald & Weekly Times v Williams* 2003 ATC 4868). Another difference between AAT and Federal Court proceedings is that in AAT proceedings, the taxpayer and the Commissioner usually bear their own costs, while in Federal Court proceedings, it is common for the Court to award costs against the unsuccessful party.

Appeals can be made from the AAT to the Federal Court on questions of law, but not of fact (s 44 *AATA*). An appeal can nevertheless involve mixed questions of law and fact (*Haritos & Anor v FC of T* 2015 ATC ¶20-513). However, in such case, it is the question of law, and it alone, that is the subject matter of an appeal (*FC of T v Brixius* 87 ATC 4963). The Court hearing an appeal must rely on the facts found by the AAT. Usually, appeals from the AAT are heard by a single judge of the Federal Court. However, where one of the members of the AAT is a judge (eg the President of the Tribunal), the appeal is heard by the Full Federal Court. An appeal must be instituted within 28 days after the day on which a document setting out the AAT's decision is given to the applicant, or such further time as the Federal Court allows.

Appeals can be made from decisions of a single judge of the Federal Court to the Full Federal Court (consisting of three judges) (ss 24, 25 *Federal Court of Australia Act 1976* (Cth)). An appeal must be lodged within 21 days of the judgment being handed down, or such further time as the Full Federal Court allows.

From the Full Federal Court, it is possible to appeal to the High Court provided special leave has been granted (s 33 *Federal Court of Australia Act 1976*). An application for special leave must be filed within 28 days of the judgment, or such further time as the High Court allows. High Court cases may be determined by up to all of the seven High Court judges (although usually five judges hear each case).

Diagram of the objection, review and appeal process

The following diagram illustrates the basic steps in the objection, review and appeal process:

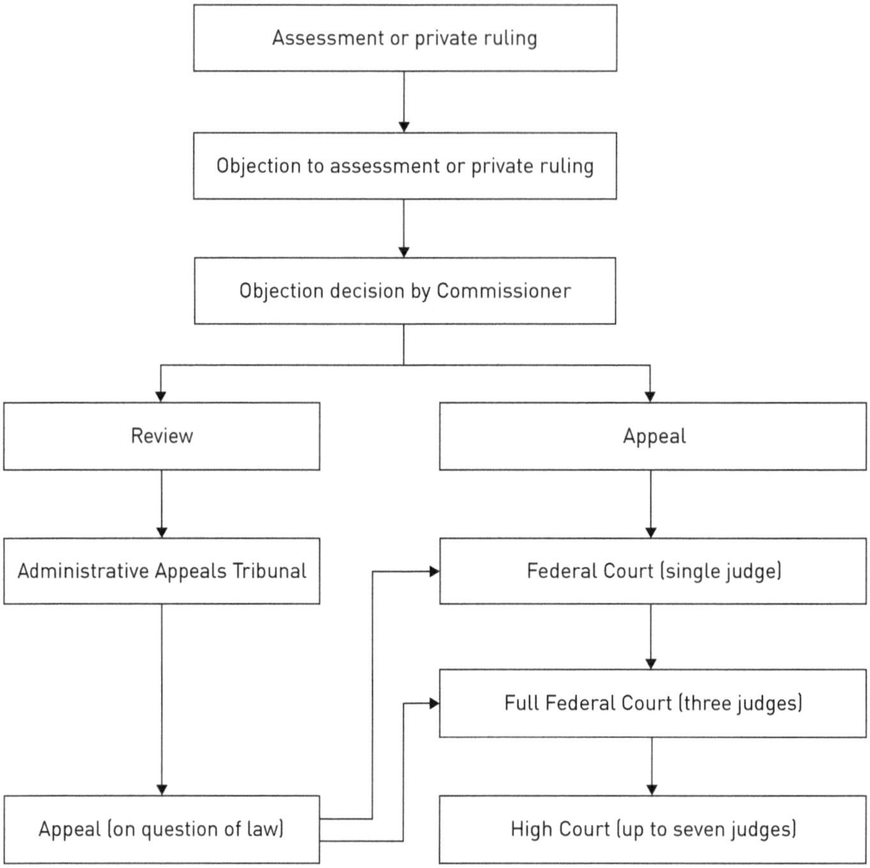

Onus of proving an assessment is excessive

Importantly, the onus of proving that an assessment is excessive lies on the taxpayer (ss 14ZZK, 14ZZO). The taxpayer must prove their case to the court on the 'balance of probabilities' (*Binetter v FC of T*; *FC of T v Bai* 2016 ATC ¶20-593). In *Bosanac v FC of T* 2019 ATC ¶20-720, the High Court explained (at [29]) that this means that the onus is on the taxpayer 'to adduce evidence sufficient to establish on the balance of probabilities the true amount of their taxable income . . . and thereby that the amount of taxable income as determined by the Commissioner exceeded the true amount'. In reaching the conclusion that the plaintiff had failed to discharge its onus of proof, Nettle J noted (at [10]) the comments of the primary judge (see *Bosanac v FC of T* [2018] FCA 946) who had stated:

> Where a taxpayer fails to retain records which evidence the course of a business, or fails to create such documents, he or she may well face a great difficulty in demonstrating excessiveness.

Earlier on, in *FC of T v Dalco* 90 ATC 4088, which involved a challenge to amended assessments issued under s 167 *ITAA36*, the High Court pointed out that the amount of an assessment may not be excessive even though the reasons which led to the assessment are erroneous. As Brennan J observed (at 4091):

> The burden which rests on a taxpayer is to prove that the assessment is excessive and that burden is not necessarily discharged by showing an error by the Commissioner in forming a judgment as to the amount of the assessment.

[38.6] Challenges outside the appeal process

The ability to challenge an assessment outside the review and appeal provisions in pt IVC *TAA* [38.5] is severely curtailed by s 175 *ITAA36* and s 350-10 *TAA* (which replaces former s 177 *ITAA36*).

Section 175 provides that the validity of an assessment shall not be affected by reason that a provision in the legislation has not been complied with.

Section 350-10 provides that the production of a notice of assessment under a taxation law (or copy thereof) is conclusive evidence that the assessment was properly made and, except in proceedings under pt IVC on a review or appeal relating to the assessment, that the amounts and particulars of the assessment are correct.

In *FJ Bloemen Pty Ltd v FC of T* 81 ATC 4280, the High Court held that the effect of former s 177 was that once the Commissioner produces a copy of an assessment in court, the taxpayer is precluded from contesting that the Commissioner has made an assessment or arguing that in making the assessment he has failed to comply with the relevant statutory formalities.

As a general rule, a taxpayer cannot therefore challenge the substance of an assessment in, for example, recovery proceedings instituted by the Commissioner. In other words, the Commissioner can technically commence proceedings before the courts to recover tax due and payable in spite of the fact that the taxpayer may have a genuine dispute about the assessment which is awaiting review under pt IVC proceedings [38.5]. For example, in *FC of T v Broadbeach Properties Pty Ltd & Ors* 2008 ATC ¶20-045, the High Court held that the Commissioner could proceed with statutory demands to recover debts owing by a company despite there being a dispute about those debts.

38

The courts, nevertheless, have an inherent discretion to grant a stay of proceedings or a stay of execution of judgment on conditions which they consider appropriate (*DFC of T v Mackey* 82 ATC 4540; *DFC of T v Gergis* 91 ATC 4510). The taxpayer has the onus of convincing a court that such a stay is warranted and the courts will generally only grant a taxpayer's request in exceptional circumstances (*Snow v DFC of T* 87 ATC 4078).

Challenges under s 39B of the *Judiciary Act 1903*

In limited cases, a taxpayer may be permitted to challenge an 'assessment' by way of 'judicial review' under s 39B of the *Judiciary Act 1903* (Cth). Section 39B confers on the Federal Court jurisdiction with respect to any matter in which a writ of mandamus or prohibition or an injunction is sought against an officer or officers of the Commonwealth. To succeed under s 39B, an applicant must establish 'jurisdictional error' (ie they must establish that there was an error of law in the decision-making process that infected the decision so that it cannot be regarded as having been made according to law). For instance, s 39B can be relied on where it is alleged that the 'assessment' has been made in 'bad faith' or for an 'improper purpose' and is, therefore, not a 'valid assessment' (*DFC of T v Richard Walter Pty Ltd* 95 ATC 4067; cf *David Jones Finance & Investments Pty Ltd & Anor v FC of T* 91 ATC 4315).

In *FC of T v Futuris Corporation Ltd* 2008 ATC ¶20-039, the High Court held that a taxpayer could not rely on s 39B to challenge an amended assessment in which its taxable income had allegedly been double counted. The Court found that the assessment was protected under s 175 *ITAA36* as it was neither tentative nor provisional and there was no conscious maladministration or lack of *bona fides* on the part of the Commissioner. The Court pointed out that if the Commissioner had deliberately failed to comply with the provisions of the Act, or knowingly acted in excess of his powers, the assessment would have been affected by jurisdictional error and would, therefore, have been reviewable. However, there was no evidence that this had occurred in the case. Gummow, Hayne, Heydon and Crennan JJ warned that allegations of administrative corruption or the deliberate abuse of power 'should not be made or upheld lightly'.

Challenges under the *Administrative Decisions (Judicial Review) Act 1977*

Certain decisions that are of an 'administrative character' can also be challenged under the *Administrative Decisions (Judicial Review) Act 1977* (Cth) ('*ADJRA*'). The *ADJRA* was enacted to streamline the review of Commonwealth administrative decisions and codify the grounds for judicial review. The legislation allows persons who are aggrieved by a decision of an administrative character made under an enactment to apply to the Federal Court for an 'order of review' in respect of the decision on specified grounds (ss 3(1), 5). The grounds of review are as follows:

- that there has been a breach of the rules of natural justice in connection with the making of the decision
- that procedures that were required by law to be observed in connection with the making of the decision were not observed
- that the person who purported to make the decision did not have jurisdiction to make the decision
- that the decision was not authorised by the enactment in pursuance to which it was purported to be made
- that the making of the decision was an improper exercise of the power conferred by the enactment in pursuance of which it was made
- that the decision involved an error of law, whether or not the error appears on the record of the decision
- that the decision was induced or affected by fraud
- that there was no evidence or other material to justify the making of the decision
- that the decision was otherwise contrary to law.

The *ADJRA* also allows applications for review of conduct relating to the making of decisions (s 6) and applications for review of failures to make decisions (s 7).

Cases in which challenges have been brought under the *ADJRA* include:

- *Ahern v DFC of T* 86 ATC 4023 (relating to the Commissioner's refusal to grant an extension of time to pay tax)
- *Briggs v DFC of T* 85 ATC 4569 (relating to the Commissioner's decision to issue a departure prohibition order under s 14S *TAA*)
- *Balnaves v DFC of T* 85 ATC 4592 (relating to the Commissioner's refusal to grant a tax agent extensions of time for lodging returns under the tax agent lodgment program)
- *Southern Farmers Group Ltd v DFC of T & Ors* 90 ATC 4056 (relating to the Commissioner's decision to issue notices under former s 263 *ITAA36*)
- *DFC of T v Clarke & Kann* 84 ATC 4273 (relating to the Commissioner's decision to issue notices under former s 264 *ITAA36*)
- *Edelsten v Wilcox & Anor* 88 ATC 4484 (relating to the Commissioner's decision to issue a notice under former s 218 *ITAA36* requiring a third party to pay money owing to the taxpayer directly to the Commissioner)
- *Powell v Evreniades & Ors* 89 ATC 4415 (relating to a decision not to release a taxpayer from paying tax due to 'serious hardship')
- *Stergis & Ors v FC of T & Anor* 89 ATC 4442 (relating to the Commissioner's decision to prosecute a taxpayer for certain offences), and
- *Terrule Pty Ltd v DFC of T* 85 ATC 4173 (relating to the Commissioner's decision to sue for the recovery of tax).

It is important to note that certain decisions cannot be challenged under the *ADJRA* because of the exclusion contained in para (e) of sch 1. This paragraph provides that the *ADJRA* does not apply to the following decisions under specified Acts (including the *ITAA36*, *ITAA97* and *GSTA*):

- decisions making, or forming part of the process of making, or leading up to the making of, assessments or calculations of tax, charge or duty,
- decisions disallowing objections to assessments or calculations of tax, charge or duty, or
- decisions amending, or refusing to amend, assessments or calculations of tax, charge or duty.

In *Independent Holdings Ltd v DFC of T* 92 ATC 4599, the Federal Court held that the exclusion applied to prevent a taxpayer from being able to seek review of a 'threatened assessment'.

Likewise, in *Meredith v FC of T & Ors* 2002 ATC 4730, the Full Federal Court held that the making of a determination to cancel a tax benefit under s 177F of pt IVA *ITAA36* [37.3] was part of the process of making an assessment and was therefore not reviewable under the *ADJRA*.

It is nevertheless possible, in certain circumstances, to have an appeal under pt IVC *TAA* and a review of a decision under the *ADJRA* heard together. In *Buddhist Society of Western Australia Inc v FC of T* [2020] FCA 1126, the applicant had its endorsement as a deductible gift recipient revoked by the Commissioner. The applicant objected to the decision, which was subsequently affirmed by the Commissioner. Section 426-60 *TAA* allowed an entity that was dissatisfied with the revocation of its endorsement to object to the revocation under pt IVC *TAA*. The applicant appealed to the Federal Court against the revocation under pt IVC *TAA* and, at the same time, also challenged the validity of the objection decision under s 5 *ADJRA* on the basis that it was not properly made and should be set aside. The Federal Court held that its statutory jurisdiction to review decisions under both Acts can be invoked in a single proceeding. McKerracher J pointed out (at [36]) that: 'Multiple causes of action claiming different remedies for different reasons but referable to the same "matter" is not uncommon.' It is important to note that the exclusion in para (e) of sch 1 *TAA* did not apply in this case because the decision did not relate to the making of an assessment. Rather, it concerned the making of a decision to revoke endorsement as a deductible gift recipient, which is not excluded by para (e).

[38.7] Tax litigation

Each year, the Commissioner is involved in an extensive number of disputes with taxpayers. These disputes involve complex legal issues and significant sums of money. They can take several years to ultimately resolve under the appeal process discussed at [38.5].

From a taxpayer's perspective, tax litigation is a critical part of the tax system as it allows for independent review of ATO decisions under the legal process. Tax litigation also contributes to the broader development of taxation law through the many judgments handed down by the courts and tribunals which provide valuable precedents under the common law.

However, not all tax disputes proceed to a hearing, as many disputes are settled. In 2021/22, for example, the ATO entered into 453 settlements (Commissioner of Taxation, *Annual Report 2021/22*). A large portion of settlements occur at the audit and objection stages. Factors that can influence the ATO to settle a dispute include high litigation risks (eg evidentiary difficulties), uncertainty about the application of the law, and complex factual situations with limited precedential value. PS LA 2015/1 sets out the ATO's policy on the settlement of tax disputes. In determining whether or not to settle, the ATO will consider the relative strength of the parties' positions, the costs versus the benefits of continuing the dispute, and the impact on future compliance. The ATO will generally not settle where a contentious point of law requires clarification, it is in the public interest to litigate, or there is a need to send a strong message to the community.

Litigation costs

Tax litigation can be extremely costly. It is common in significant tax cases for both the Commissioner and taxpayers to each be represented in court by a team of lawyers, including both junior and senior counsel. In 2021/22, the ATO spent $92,021,889 on legal services (Commissioner of Taxation, *Annual Report 2021/22*).

As a general principle, taxpayers are responsible for funding the costs of their litigation with the ATO. A court may, nevertheless, order that some or all of a taxpayer's costs be paid by the Commonwealth. This usually occurs where the taxpayer is successful in the dispute before the court. In tribunal cases, the parties generally bear their own costs.

The Commonwealth will also usually agree to pay a taxpayer's reasonable costs if an appeal is instituted by the Commissioner against a tribunal or court decision (provided the case does not involve tax avoidance).

Test Case Litigation Program

The ATO operates a Test Case Litigation Program under which it provides financial assistance to a small number of selected taxpayers. The aim of the program is to support the development of legal precedent on issues that require clarification and are likely to be important to the administration of the tax system. Only those cases that meet strict funding criteria are selected. A Test Case Litigation Panel (whose membership includes accounting and legal professionals) advises the ATO on which cases to fund. Cases selected for funding must involve:

- issues that involve uncertainty about how the law operates
- issues that are of significance to a significant section of the public or that have significant commercial implications for an industry, and
- issues that are in the public interest to litigate.

Litigation conduct

Guidelines on the ATO's approach to litigation are set out in PS LA 2009/9, which states (at [6]–[7]):

> The Tax Office conducts and manages litigation in accordance with its obligations under the law, the Attorney-General's *Legal Services Directions 2005* . . . (in particular the model litigant obligation), relevant court and tribunal rules and directions, and other relevant internal and external policies and guidelines. The Tax Office strives to have all disputes brought to finality in a fair, timely and equitable manner consistent with the law. The Tax Office supports the appropriate use of alternative dispute resolution techniques to limit the need for litigation and to simplify and/or reduce the cost of litigation. In taxation disputes, the Tax Office argues its cases consistently with its published view of the tax law. The Tax Office recognises that recourse to the courts and tribunals not only provides final, fair and independent resolution of disputes, it will in some cases, achieve law clarification benefits for Government and the community.
>
> The Tax Office's approach to litigation is never to win at all costs. The Tax Office strives to ensure that legislation is given its intended effect as best as can be discerned from the law, informed by its knowledge of the underlying policy.

The 'model litigant obligation' mentioned above requires the ATO to act 'with propriety, fairness and in accordance with the highest professional standards' and to handle its cases 'efficiently and effectively in accordance with their responsibility to the community to safeguard public revenue and also to fulfil their responsibilities to other litigants and the justice system'.

[38.8] Audit powers

To ensure that taxpayers comply with the income tax laws, the Commissioner is armed with wide audit and investigative powers. These powers allow him to gather information in order to check that taxpayers have been properly assessed. The Commissioner's main powers are located in ss 353-10 and 353-15 *TAA*. Section 353-10 contains an 'information' and 'production' power, while s 353-15 contains an 'access' and 'inspection' power. In 2015, s 353-10 replaced former s 264 *ITAA36* and s 353-15 replaced former s 263 *ITAA36*. While the new and old provisions are drafted in slightly different terms, they are intended to operate in essentially the same manner. The case law dealing with the former provisions therefore generally continues to be relevant for the purposes of the interpretation of the new provisions. The following discussion examines the new provisions in the light of the case law dealing with former ss 263 and 264.

Information and production power

Section s 353-10 states that the Commissioner may by notice in writing require a person to do all or any of the following:

(a) give the Commissioner any information that he requires for the purpose of the administration or operation of a taxation law
(b) attend and give evidence before the Commissioner, or an individual authorised by the Commissioner, for the purpose of the administration or operation of a taxation law, and
(c) produce to the Commissioner any documents in their custody or under their control for the purpose of the administration or operation of a taxation law.

The Commissioner may require the information or evidence to be given on oath or affirmation and to be given orally or in writing. Failure to comply with s 353-10 can constitute an offence under s 8C or 8D of the *TAA*.

Importantly, s 353-10 does not require that the information, evidence or documents relate to the tax affairs of the person providing them. They might, for instance, relate to the tax affairs of another person (eg a family member or business associate).

In commenting on former s 264 in *Grant & Ors v DFC of T* 2000 ATC 4649, the Full Federal Court noted (at 4652) that while the section 'interferes with personal freedoms', Parliament found it necessary to give the Commissioner power to make wide-ranging enquiries due to the many and varied devices employed to avoid tax. The Court concluded 'the intention was to give the Commissioner an effective, but not an oppressive or unfair, power of investigation'.

Access and inspection power

Section 353-15 states that for the purposes of a taxation law, the Commissioner, or an individual authorised by the Commissioner for the purposes of the section:

(a) may at all reasonable times enter and remain on any land, premises or place
(b) is entitled to full and free access at all reasonable times to any documents, goods or other property
(c) may inspect, examine, make copies of, or take extracts from, any documents, and
(d) may inspect, examine, count, measure, weigh, gauge, test or analyse any goods or other property and, to that end, take samples.

An individual authorised by the Commissioner for the purposes of s 353-15 (eg an ATO officer) is not entitled to enter or remain on any land, premises or place if, after having been requested by the occupier to produce proof of his or her authority, does not produce an authority signed by the Commissioner stating that they are authorised to exercise powers under this section.

The occupier of the land, premises or place commits an offence if they do not provide 'all reasonable facilities and assistance' for the effective exercise of the powers under s 353-15.

The words 'full and free access' used in former s 263 were examined in *FC of T & Ors v Citibank Ltd* 89 ATC 4268. French J indicated (at 4287) that it is clear that the rights conveyed by the provision are wide. According to his Honour, 'full access' conveys that the availability of entry or examination extends to all parts of the relevant place or building and to the whole of the relevant documents and other papers, while 'free' conveys an absence of physical obstruction.

In *O'Reilly & Ors v Commissioners of the State Bank of Victoria & Ors* 83 ATC 4156, it was held that the Commissioner did not have full and free access to documents held in a bank where the door to the room which held the records was locked as this constituted physical obstruction.

Audit powers must be exercised for the purpose of the legislation

The powers under ss 353-10 and 353-15 must be exercised in good faith for the purposes of the legislation.

In *Industrial Equity Ltd & Anor v DFC of T & Ors* 90 ATC 5008, the High Court held that it was a legitimate use of former s 263 by the Commissioner to gain access to records held by Bankers Trust in respect of a 'random audit' conducted in relation to a 'top 100' company.

Similarly, in *FC of T v Australia and New Zealand Banking Group Ltd* and *Smorgon & Ors v FC of T & Ors* 79 ATC 4039, the High Court held that the Commissioner could use his powers under former s 264 to make a 'roving enquiry' into the income of a person (ie to 'fish' for information), and to require a bank to produce documents held in a safety deposit box which it held in its custody and control.

Audit powers override the privilege against self-incrimination

Cases dealing with former s 264 indicate that the Commissioner's powers in s 353-10 would seem to override the privilege against self-incrimination (*Stergis & Ors v FC of T & Anor* 89 ATC 4442; *Donovan v FC of T* 92 ATC 4114; *De Vonk v DFC of T* 95 ATC 4538; *Binetter v DFC of T (No 4)* 2012 ATC ¶20-345). A person served with a notice cannot therefore refuse to furnish information or answer questions on the basis that the answers might tend to incriminate him or her.

The policy rationale for abrogating the privilege against self-incrimination was expressed in *DeVonk v FC of T* by Hill and Lindgren JJ (at 4835) as follows:

> If the argument were to prevail that the privilege against self-incrimination was intended to be retained in tax matters, it would be impossible for the Commissioner to interrogate a taxpayer about sources of income since any question put on that subject might tend to incriminate the taxpayer by showing that the taxpayer had not complied with the initial obligation to return all sources of income. Such an argument would totally stultify the collection of income tax.

While it would seem that s 353-10 does not operate subject to the privilege against self-incrimination, it does operate subject to the doctrine of contempt of court. In *De Vonk*, Hill and Lindgren JJ went on to state (at 4839):

> On the whole we think that the legislature should not be taken in s 264 of the Act . . . to have authorised the compulsory interrogation of persons in circumstances where so to do might constitute an interference with the administration of justice, civil or criminal . . .

Audit powers override duty of confidentiality owed to third parties

In *ANZ v Konza & Anor (No 2)* 2012 ATC ¶20-347, the Commissioner issued s 264 notices to a bank requiring it to provide information about customers who held accounts with the bank or its subsidiaries in Vanuatu. The bank submitted that the notices were invalid because they required it to breach common law confidentiality obligations owed to customers as well as certain secrecy provisions enacted in Vanuatu. The Full Federal Court held that the s 264 notices abrogated any contractual and equitable obligations of confidentiality that the recipient might owe to third parties under Australian or Vanuatu law. The Court also held that there was no requirement that the notices must be limited to information directly relating to the assessable income of Australian taxpayers—it was enough that the information was required for the purposes of the *ITAA36* or *ITAA97*.

Audit powers subject to legal professional privilege

The Commissioner's audit powers must be exercised subject to the doctrine of 'legal professional privilege'. This doctrine applies to confidential communications made between lawyers and their clients for the *dominant* purpose of giving or receiving legal advice, or for use in legal proceedings (*Esso Australia Resources Ltd v FC of T* 2000 ATC 4042). The privilege belongs to the client (not the lawyer) and extends to documents created by third parties that are brought into existence for the dominant purpose of obtaining legal advice (*Pratt Holdings Pty Ltd & Anor v FC of T* 2004 ATC 4526). Legal professional privilege is lost where it is waived by the client expressly or impliedly (*Case 29/97* 97 ATC 327; *Rio Tinto Ltd v FC of T* [2005] FCA 1336).

38

The rationale for legal professional privilege was expressed by Stephen, Mason and Murphy JJ (at 685) in *Grant v Downs* (1976) 135 CLR 674 as follows:

> The rationale for this head of privilege, according to traditional doctrine, is that it promotes the public interest because it assists and enhances the administration of justice by facilitating the representation of clients by legal advisers, the law being a complex and complicated discipline. This it does by keeping secret their communications, thereby inducing the client to retain the solicitor and seek his advice, and encouraging the client to make a full and frank disclosure of the relevant circumstances to the solicitor.

In *Daniels Corporation International Pty Ltd v ACCC* (2002) 213 CLR 543, it was held that a provision of the *Trade Practices Act 1974* (Cth) which gave power to require the production of documents did not abrogate legal professional privilege. The High Court emphasised that legal professional privilege is a rule of 'substantive law' and 'an important common law immunity'.

The fact that legal professional privilege is an immunity was recently confirmed in *Glencore International AG & Ors v FC of T & Ors* 2019 ATC ¶20-708. In this case, companies within the global Glencore group had unsuccessfully applied for an injunction restraining the Commissioner and ATO officers from using documents, and any information contained in or derived from such documents, that had come into their possession as a consequence of the 'Paradise Papers' leak [33.2]. The relevant documents had been created by the Bermuda law firm, Appleby, for the sole or dominant purpose of providing legal advice to the plaintiffs in relation to the restructure of their corporate group. They had been stolen from the firm's electronic system and provided to the International Consortium of Investigative Journalists and further disseminated. The High Court held that legal professional privilege was granted to render a person immune from being required to produce documents and was not a legal right capable of founding a cause of action. The Court explained (at 13) that the plaintiffs had sought to 'transform the nature of the privilege from an immunity into an ill-defined cause of action which may be brought against anyone with respect to documents which may be in the public domain'.

FC of T & Ors v Citibank Ltd 89 ATC 4268 demonstrates that, in certain cases, the Commissioner may be required to suspend a search to allow a claim for legal professional privilege to be made. In *Citibank*, more than 30 tax officers relied on s 263 notices to raid a bank which was believed to hold documents relating to certain tax avoidance schemes. Over a four-hour period, several documents were inspected, copied and taken away. The Full Federal Court held that the Commissioner was obliged to ensure that the bank had adequate opportunity to determine in respect of which documents a claim for privilege would be made; and it found that, in most instances, this opportunity had been denied. Due to the lack of warning and the intensity of the search, the Court found that it was unreasonable for the taxation officers to refuse to suspend the search pending the obtaining of legal advice and the Commissioner's powers under s 263 had therefore been improperly exercised.

Legal professional privilege does not apply in respect of mere 'evidentiary' documents (eg most transactional documents, like contracts of sale). In *Allen Allen & Hemsley v DFC of T & Ors* 89 ATC 4294 and *Packer & Ors v DFC of T* 84 ATC 4666, the Full Federal Court and Full Supreme Court of Queensland respectively held that legal professional privilege did not apply to a firm of solicitors' trust accounts. Likewise, in *FC of T v Coombes (No 2)* 99 ATC 4634, the names of a lawyer's clients were held not to be subject to legal professional privilege.

Legal professional privilege also does not apply to communications made between non-lawyers (eg accountants) and their clients. The Commissioner, nevertheless, has special guidelines for dealing with documents held by accountants in his *Access and Information Gathering Manual*. He indicates that he will seek full access to 'source documents' (eg evidentiary documents that record transactions), but will only seek access to 'restricted source documents' (eg advices entered into before a transaction that are likely to shed light on a transaction) and 'non-source documents' (eg certain other advices) in exceptional cases (eg where fraud or evasion is involved or where other avenues have been exhausted).

The Australian Law Reform Commission, in its 2007 report *Privilege in Perspective: Client Legal Privilege and Federal Investigations*, recommended extending legal professional privilege to 'tax advice documents' prepared by accountants. In April 2011, the Assistant Treasurer released a discussion paper, *Privilege in Relation to Tax Advice*, which explored this recommendation in further detail. The discussion paper outlined the rationale for introducing a 'tax advice privilege' and summarised the position in other jurisdictions, such as the United States, where such a privilege exists. It set out arguments for and against establishing such a privilege and discussed the kind of regime that could be established in Australia if the Government ever decided to head down this path.

The issue of whether a claim for legal professional privilege can exist in relation to documents prepared by multi-disciplinary practices that provide legal and non-legal services was considered in *FC of T v PricewaterhouseCoopers* 2022 ATC ¶20-821. The case concerned 'PWC Australia'—a partnership that had partners who were Australian legal practitioners as well as those that were not. The Commissioner issued a notice to produce documents under s 353-10, but the partnership claimed many of the documents were subject to legal professional privilege. Due to the large number of documents involved, the Federal Court only considered a sample 116 documents. Moshinsky J held that the terms of engagements and the services provided by the firm could give rise to a lawyer and client relationship. It was therefore necessary to consider each sample document to determine whether it was made for the dominant purpose of giving or obtaining legal advice from one or more legal practitioners employed by PWC. The Court noted this was to be determined by reference to the content of the document, its context, and the evidence relating to it. A critical part of the context was that the services were provided by a multi-disciplinary partnership and the team carrying out the work comprised both lawyers and non-lawyers. It was also relevant that overseas PWC firms were involved in many of the same projects (under separate engagements) and were not able to provide legal advice. Ultimately, the Court concluded that 49 documents were privileged, 6 documents were partly privileged, and 61 documents were not privileged.

In 2022, the ATO published a protocol, *Compliance with Formal Notices—Claiming Legal Professional Privilege in Response to Formal Notices*, to assist those making claims for legal professional privilege. The protocol sets out the approach the ATO uses in identifying communications covered by the privilege and the steps practitioners should work through in making such claims.

[38.9] ATO approach to tax compliance

Compliance model

The ATO adopts a broad range of strategies to protect the Australian tax system, including taking firm action against people who commit tax crimes, removing opportunities for repeat offences and advising the government on areas of the law that require reform. The ATO website contains the following diagram which sets out taxpayer attitudes to compliance and the ATO's compliance strategy:

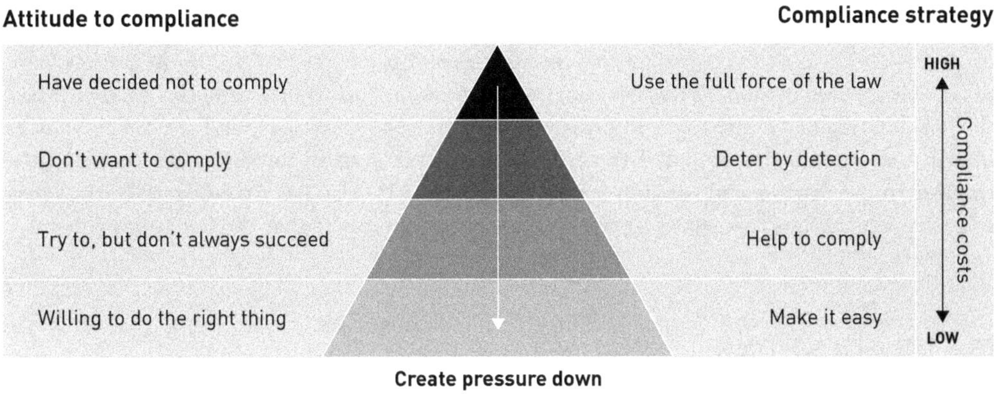

Risk-management approach

The ATO recognises that detecting and dealing appropriately with non-compliance deters others from not complying with the tax laws. As the ATO has finite resources, it uses a risk-management approach in monitoring tax compliance. The Commissioner of Taxation's *Annual Report 2009–10* states (at 77):

> How intensively we scrutinise a taxpayer's affairs depends on the level of risk to the effective operation of the tax and superannuation systems. Where we identify a serious or widespread risk, we increase our level of attention . . .
>
> We also use a range of mechanisms to identify and evaluate emerging risks. For example, large businesses come under closer scrutiny given the size and complexity of their transactions. At the smaller end of the market we rely heavily on our program of data matching to identify potential non-compliance. At all times we aim to differentiate, in accordance with our compliance model, between taxpayers who are trying to do the right thing and those who are not. In determining the right balance of responses, we take into account the causes of non-compliance, the circumstances of the taxpayer, and the level of culpability.

In allocating resources, the ATO gives priority to 'the most complex or significant technical issues based on risk to revenue or impact on confidence in the tax or superannuation systems'. Special attention is devoted to certain kinds of taxpayers. For instance, significant resources are dedicated to auditing Australia's largest companies because of their complex transactions and the amount of potential revenue at stake.

Detecting non-compliance

The ATO relies heavily on strategic intelligence and sophisticated electronic data resources to detect non-compliance. It obtains information from many third-party sources about a broad range of transactions. Some of the main forms of data collected by the ATO that are matched against information provided by individuals in their returns include:

- salary and wage information received from employers under the PAYG system
- interest and dividend information from financial institutions and public companies, and
- pension and allowance information from government departments.

The ATO has extensive information-matching capabilities. According to the ATO website, it matches over 600 million transactions annually. Each year, the ATO's access to data is growing due to technological advances and its increasing number of partnerships with local and international government agencies.

The ATO is required to comply with strict laws when collecting data from other agencies and organisations under its data matching programs. These laws include the secrecy provisions in div 355 of sch 1 *TAA* [6.3] as well as the privacy provisions in the *Privacy Act 1988* (Cth). The ATO also adheres to the Privacy Commissioner's *Guidelines on Data Matching in Australian Government Administration*.

The ATO regularly exchanges information with its treaty partners, and it obtains valuable information on cases of potential tax avoidance and tax evasion through leaks such as those revealed in the Panama and Paradise Papers [33.2]. The ATO also has a confidential online form and telephone hotline that allows a person to report taxpayers who they think may be deliberately evading tax [36.2].

[38.10] QUESTIONS

1. Who must lodge tax returns? What is an assessment? Why are assessments important? Explain how the assessment process operates for an individual. How is this different from the process applicable to companies? What time limits apply to the amendment of assessments?
2. Discuss the different kinds of tax rulings issued by the ATO. What is a 'binding ruling' and what is the effect of such a ruling?
3. Discuss the key features of the objection and appeal process. In what circumstances can a taxpayer challenge an assessment outside the ordinary appeal process in pt IVC *TAA*?
4. What kinds of powers does the Commissioner have under s 353-10 and s 353-15 *TAA*? Are they limited in any way?
5. Provide some examples of communications that are subject to legal professional privilege.
6. Discuss the ATO's approach to monitoring tax compliance.

IDENTIFICATION AND PAYMENT SYSTEMS 39

[39.1] Introduction

This chapter examines some of the important identification and payment systems that underpin the Australian tax system. The key identification systems are the TFN [39.2] and ABN [39.3] systems. The main payment system is the PAYG system [39.4]. The administration and enforcement of the tax laws is also supported by the financial transaction reporting regime [39.5], which assists the government identify tax evaders by tracking suspicious financial dealings and the movement of large amounts of cash.

[39.2] The TFN system

The TFN system is contained in pt VA *ITAA36*. TFNs are personal reference numbers that identify taxpayers. They are used for audit and data-matching purposes by the ATO and appear on a taxpayer's returns and assessments. Taxpayers can apply in the approved form to the Commissioner for a TFN (s 202B). Where the Commissioner is satisfied that a taxpayer's identity has been established, he is required to issue a TFN (s 202BA). The Commissioner may also issue a TFN without an application being made where it is necessary for the performance of his functions under the tax law.

When TFNs must be quoted

Taxpayers are required to quote their TFN in a limited number of situations. In particular, a TFN must be quoted before social security payments can be received under the *Social Security Act 1991* (Cth). In addition, in order to be eligible to obtain a HELP loan for a tertiary course, students who do not pay their fees upfront are required to quote their TFN when enrolling at the relevant institution [8.10].

PAYG consequences of not quoting TFNs

Although there is no general obligation to quote a TFN, taxpayers nevertheless typically choose to quote their TFNs where the opportunity arises because of the adverse PAYG withholding consequences that follow if they do not do this.

For instance, where an employee has not quoted their TFN on a TFN declaration lodged with their employer, the employer is generally required to withhold tax from salary paid to the employee at a rate equivalent to the top marginal tax rate plus ML (where applicable). The withholding tax rate is 47% (for resident employees) and 45% (for non-resident employees) [39.4].

Likewise, where an investor has not quoted their TFN to an investment body in relation to a 'Part VA investment', the investment body must generally withhold tax under the PAYG system from investment income (excluding franked dividends) payable to the investor at the rate of 47% (for resident investors) and 45% for (non-resident investors) [39.4]. A 'Part VA investment' is an investment that falls within the table in s 202D *ITAA36*. It includes the following investments:

- interest-bearing deposits and accounts with financial institutions
- loans to companies and government bodies
- units in unit trusts, and
- shares in public companies.

Example Bob is an Australian resident who has a deposit with a bank and owns shares in a public company. He has not provided the bank or the company with his TFN. If the bank pays him interest of $1,000, the bank is required to withhold tax of $470 from the payment. If the company pays him a $100 unfranked dividend, the company must withhold $47 tax. If, however, the dividend was fully franked, then the company would not need to withhold any tax.

It is also in the interests of members of superannuation funds to quote their TFNs to their superannuation providers. The reason is that superannuation funds that receive assessable contributions in respect of members who have not quoted their TFNs are required to include such contributions in their 'no-TFN contributions income', which is taxed at the rate of 32% in the case of a complying superannuation fund [19.14].

[39.3] The ABN system

The ABN system is contained in the *A New Tax System (Australian Business Number) Act 1999* (Cth) and operates independently of the TFN system. Under the ABN system, registered entities are provided with ABNs (comprising 11 digits). ABNs are designed to make it easier for businesses to conduct dealings with the Australian Government, including the ATO (s 3). They are also used extensively in commercial transactions to help people identify the businesses they are dealing with.

The ABN system is based around the Australian Business Register, which is maintained by the Commissioner of Taxation as Registrar (ss 24, 28). The Australian Business Register contains details of a registered entity's name, ABN and date of registration (s 25). It also contains additional details as prescribed in the *A New Tax System (Australian Business Number) Regulations 2020* (Cth).

An entity is entitled to an ABN if they:

- are carrying on an enterprise in Australia, or
- in the course of carrying on an enterprise make supplies that are connected with the ITZ [7.6] (s 8(1)).

Companies falling within the *Corporations Act* are also entitled to an ABN (s 8(2)). Government entities (eg departments and branches) and superannuation funds can also have an ABN (s 5).

An entity's ABN information can be accessed at ABN Lookup on the Australian Business Register website [2.5]. According to this website, there are over 9 million active ABNs. The majority of these are in the names of individuals or companies.

Although it is not compulsory to have an ABN, having an ABN is important for the following reasons:

- **GST.** Registered entities must quote their ABNs on tax invoices under the GST system [7.11].

- **Investments.** Entities that make investments in the course of an enterprise may quote their ABNs in place of their TFNs to avoid PAYG withholding (s 12-155 *TAA*) [39.4].
- **Deductible gift recipients.** Entities that wish to be endorsed as 'deductible gift recipients' in order to be eligible to receive tax deductible gifts are required to have ABNs (ss 30-120, 30-125 *ITAA97*) [13.13].
- **Supplies.** Entities that make supplies in in the course of enterprises they carry on in Australia (irrespective of whether or not they are registered for GST) should quote their ABNs on invoices. If they do not do so, persons who make payments to them are generally required to withhold tax from such payments at the rate of 47% (s 12-190 *TAA*) [39.4]. There are, however, several important exceptions to this general rule. For instance, it does not apply to:
  - payments made otherwise than in the course of furtherance of an enterprise carried on by the payer
  - payments for a supply that do not exceed $75 in total (disregarding GST), and
  - payments relating to a supply that is wholly input taxed.

Example Eric is an electrician who runs his own electrical contracting business. He charges Mal, who owns a milk bar, $100 for repairing the broken fridge used in Mal's shop for storing milk. If Eric does not provide Mal with an invoice quoting his ABN, Mal is required to withhold $47 from the payment.

If, however, the fee charged by Eric was $75 or less (disregarding GST), Mal would not need to withhold any tax from the payment. Likewise, if instead of repairing the fridge in Mal's shop, Eric repaired Mal's home fridge, Mal would not need to withhold tax as the payment does not relate to any enterprise carried on by Mal.

[39.4] The PAYG system

The PAYG system, contained in pt 2-5 and 2-10 of sch 1 *TAA*, is a special tax collection system which replaced a number of former tax collection systems that existed prior to 1 July 2000 (including the former Pay As You Earn and Provisional Tax systems).

The object of the PAYG system is to collect tax from taxpayers during the income year. Amounts collected under the PAYG system are then credited against the taxpayer's actual tax liability for the year once they have been assessed at the end of the year. The broad aim of the PAYG system is to ensure that tax is collected progressively over the period that income is earned. This ensures that the Government has early access to tax revenue and does not have to wait until the income year has closed to collect tax from taxpayers. It also prevents taxpayers being in the position of not being able to pay their tax at the end of the year because they have spent their income in the meantime.

There are two mutually exclusive PAYG regimes:

- the PAYG withholding regime (pt 2-5), and
- the PAYG instalment payment regime (pt 2-10).

PAYG withholding

The PAYG withholding regime requires entities that make certain payments to taxpayers during the income year to withhold tax from such payments and remit the tax to the ATO. The PAYG withholding regime applies to the 'withholding payments' listed in s 10-5 *TAA*. Certain payments (eg payments that are exempt income, living-away-from-home allowance benefits or expense payment benefits) are excluded from PAYG withholding (s 12-1).

Withholding payments and rates

Division 12 sets out the obligation to withhold amounts from particular payments. The rates of withholding are generally calculated under the *TAR17* or special withholding schedules made by the Commissioner under s 15-25 (s 15-10 *TAA*). Some of the more important withholding payments and rates are outlined in the following table:

<table>
<tr><th>Withholding payment</th><th>Withholding rate</th></tr>
<tr><td>Payments of salary, wages, commissions, bonuses or allowances to an employee (s 12-35)</td><td rowspan="9">Progressive rates based on withholding schedules (see Taxation Administration Withholding Schedules 2023)

If the payee has not quoted their TFN, the rate is 47% (for Australian residents) or 45% (for foreign residents)</td></tr>
<tr><td>Payments of remuneration to a company director (s 12-40)</td></tr>
<tr><td>Payments of salary, wages, commissions, bonuses or allowances to Members of Parliament, local governing bodies, the defence force or a police force (s 12-45)</td></tr>
<tr><td>Return to work payments (s 12-50)</td></tr>
<tr><td>Payments under labour hire arrangements (s 12-60)</td></tr>
<tr><td>Payments of superannuation pensions or annuities (s 12-80)</td></tr>
<tr><td>Superannuation lump sum and ETPs (s 12-85)</td></tr>
<tr><td>Unused leave payments (s 12-90)</td></tr>
<tr><td>Social security payments (s 12-110)</td></tr>
<tr><td>Payments arising from pt VA ITAA36 investments where the payee does not quote its TFN or ABN (s 12-140)</td><td>47% (in the case of dividend payments, this rate only applies to the unfranked part of the dividend) (reg 35 TAR17)</td></tr>
<tr><td>Payments for supplies where the payee does not quote its ABN (s 12-190)</td><td>47% (reg 38 TAR17)</td></tr>
<tr><td>Payments of dividends to overseas persons (does not apply if no withholding tax is payable under div 11A of pt III ITAA36 [31.11]) (s 12-210)</td><td>If the recipient is not a resident of a tax treaty country the rate is 30%. If the recipient is a resident of a tax treaty country the rate is the rate specified in the DTA (generally 15%) [32.6] (reg 40 TAR17).</td></tr>
<tr><td>Payments of interest to overseas persons (does not apply if no withholding tax is payable under div 11A of pt III ITAA36 [31.11]) (s 12-245)</td><td>10% (reg 41 TAR17)</td></tr>
<tr><td>Payments of royalties to overseas persons (does not apply if no withholding tax is payable under div 11A of pt III ITAA36 [31.11]) (s 12-280)</td><td>If the recipient is not a resident of a tax treaty country the rate is 30%. If the recipient is a resident of a tax treaty country the rate is the rate specified in the DTA (generally 10%) [32.6] (reg 42 TAR17).</td></tr>
</table>

The Commissioner may, in special cases, vary the amount required to be withheld by an entity (s 15-15).

Withholding payment dates and methods of payment

Division 16-B imposes an obligation on entities that withhold amounts under div 12 to pay those amounts to the Commissioner. Amounts withheld must be paid to the Commissioner by due dates which vary depending on whether the payer is classified as a 'large', 'medium' or 'small' withholder. In broad terms:

- an entity is a large withholder for a particular month if it withheld more than $1m in a preceding financial year ending at least two months before the current month (s 16-95)
- an entity is a medium withholder for a particular month if it withheld more than $25,000 in a preceding financial year ending before the current month (s 16-100), and
- an entity is a small withholder if it is neither a large nor a medium withholder (s 16-105).

The Commissioner has the power to vary a withholder's status under s 16-110 or s 16-115.

Amounts withheld are recorded on the withholding entity's activity statement [40.3] and must be paid in accordance with the following table:

Withholder (ss 16-95 to 16-105)	Date amounts withheld must be paid to the Commissioner (s 16-75)	Method of payment (s 16-85)
Small	The 28th day after the end of the quarter in which the payment is made	Electronic or other means approved by the Commissioner
Medium	For withholders who are 'deferred BAS payers' (ie entities that have other quarterly BAS obligations, such as entities that are required to report GST on a quarterly basis)—the 28th day after the end of the month (28th February for payments made in December)	Electronic or other means approved by the Commissioner
	For other withholders—the 21st day after the end of the month	
Large	Amounts withheld on a Saturday or Sunday must be paid on the second Monday after that day	Electronic
	Amounts withheld on a Monday or Tuesday must be paid on the first Monday after that day	
	Amounts withheld on a Wednesday must be paid on the second Thursday after that day	
	Amounts withheld on a Thursday or Friday must be paid on the first Thursday after that day	

Payment summaries

An entity that makes a withholding payment to a person during a financial year must, unless exempted, provide the payee with a 'payment summary' within 14 days of the end of the year (s 16-155). A 'payment summary' is a written statement that:

- names the payer and recipient
- states the recipient's TFN or ABN (where these have been provided to the payer)
- states the total of the withholding payments (if any) that it covers and the total of the amounts withheld by the payer from those withholding payments
- specifies the financial year in which the withholding payments were made
- specifies the reportable fringe benefits amount (if any) that it covers and the income year to which that amount relates

- specifies the reportable employer superannuation contributions (if any) that it covers and the income year to which those contributions relate, and
- is in the approved form (s 16-170).

The Commissioner has exercised his discretion under s 16-180 to exempt entities that report under the 'single touch payroll' ('STP') regime from having to provide payment summaries [40.4].

Credits for PAYG amounts withheld

Payees that have PAYG amounts withheld from payments made to them are entitled to credits for these amounts when they are assessed for their income tax liabilities for the income year (s 18-15).

> ***Example*** Jen is employed by Ross. In 2022/23, Jen was paid salary of $80,000, from which Ross withheld $18,000 under the PAYG system. Jen must include her gross salary of $80,000 in her assessable income for the income year. She will be required to pay tax on her taxable income for the year but will get a credit for the $18,000 withheld by Ross. If the amount withheld exceeds the tax payable by Jen on her taxable income for the year, she will receive a refund of the excess amount.

PAYG instalments

The PAYG instalment regime applies to companies and superannuation entities, as well as individuals in relation to their business and investment income. Taxpayers pay tax under the PAYG instalment regime progressively over the income year. However, as a taxpayer's actual tax liability for a particular year cannot be determined until after the end of the year, the instalments are based on notional or estimated amounts. PAYG instalments are reported on a taxpayer's activity statement [40.3].

Payment of instalments

The PAYG instalment regime only applies where a taxpayer has received an 'instalment rate' from the Commissioner (s 45-15). Taxpayers with 'notional tax' under $8,000 that are not registered for GST may generally elect to pay an annual PAYG instalment (sub-div 45-E). Most other taxpayers pay quarterly instalments (sub-div 45-B). These instalments are due within 21 days after the end of the quarter, unless the taxpayer is a 'deferred BAS payer', in which case, instalments are due within 28 days after the end of the quarter (except for the December quarter, for which the due date is 28 February). A deferred BAS payer is essentially an entity that lodges quarterly GST returns or is a GST instalment payer [7.4] (s 995-1 *ITAA97*).

Entities that have a 'base assessment instalment income' of $20m or more are required to pay PAYG instalments on a monthly basis (sub-div 45-DA). However, to ease compliance burdens, monthly instalments do not apply to entities that have base assessment instalment income of less than $100m and are not a head company of a consolidated group [26.2] or a provisional head company of an MEC group [26.3].

Calculating the amount of the instalments

The way in which PAYG instalments are calculated is complex. In broad terms, PAYG instalments may be based on:

- **The taxpayer's 'GDP-adjusted notional tax' (sub-div 45-L).** This is calculated by the Commissioner and is essentially the taxpayer's 'notional tax' for the base year (usually the previous income year) uplifted by a 'GDP adjustment factor' (6% for 2023/24) (ss 45-320, 45-325). An entity's notional tax is basically its adjusted tax on its 'adjusted taxable income' for the base year reduced by its adjusted tax on its 'adjusted withholding income' for the base year. Its adjusted taxable income, is calculated ignoring any net capital gains (except for superannuation entities) (s 45-330). Its adjusted withholding income is basically its assessable income subject to PAYG withholding (s 45-335). Adjusted tax is calculated using a multi-step process that disregards certain tax offsets and makes various other adjustments (s 45-340).

- **The taxpayer's estimate of its 'benchmark tax' (sub-div 45-M).** This is essentially the taxpayer's estimate of its actual tax liability for the year ignoring (except for Superannuation entities) any tax payable in respect of a net capital gain.
- **The taxpayer's 'instalment income' for the period multiplied by an instalment rate (sub-div 45-F).** The taxpayer's instalment income consists of the ordinary income derived by the taxpayer for the relevant period (s 45-120(1)). The instalment income of complying superannuation funds (but not companies and individuals) also includes statutory income such as capital gains (s 45-120(2)). Withholding payments (except 'non-quotation withholding payments') made to a taxpayer are excluded from instalment income (s 45-120(3)). The instalment rate is calculated by the Commissioner in accordance with sub-div 45-J. A taxpayer may elect to vary this rate (s 45-205).

To prevent taxpayers avoiding their PAYG instalment obligations, penalties may apply where taxpayers make variations or estimates which are too low (sub-div 45-G).

Credits for PAYG instalments

Amounts paid under the PAYG instalment regime are credited against the taxpayer's actual tax liability for the year (s 45-30).

Example X Co pays four PAYG instalments of $1m each in respect of an income year. When it lodges its tax return for the year and self-assesses its tax liability, X Co is entitled to a credit for the $4m it has paid in PAYG instalments. If X Co's actual tax liability for the year is $6m, it will only have to pay the balance $2m.

[39.5] Financial transaction reporting

Australia has a financial transaction reporting regime, which assists with the administration and enforcement of the tax laws by requiring certain entities to report financial transactions. The regime is contained in the *Anti-Money Laundering and Counter-Terrorism Financing Act 2006* (Cth) ('*AMLCTFA*'). The *AMLCTFA* seeks to fulfil Australia's international obligations to combat money laundering and financing of terrorism and it targets areas such as the cash economy, financial crime and tax evasion (s 3). AUSTRAC is the statutory authority responsible for administering the regime. AUSTRAC operates as Australia's anti-money laundering and counter-terrorism financing regulator and specialist financial intelligence unit.

Reporting entities

The *AMLCTFA* applies principally to 'reporting entities'. A 'reporting entity' is defined as an entity that provides a 'designated service' (s 5 *AMLCTFA*). A 'designated service' is defined in s 6 *AMLCTFA* and covers, for instance, situations where a bank or other member of the financial services industry opens an account, allows a transaction to be conducted in relation to an account, accepts a deposit, or performs some other specified financial service.

Before providing a designated service to a customer, a reporting entity must verify the identity of the customer in accordance with the procedures in the *Anti-Money Laundering and Counter-Terrorism Financing Rules* (Cth) ('*AMLCTFR*') (s 32).

Reporting obligations

The following is a summary of some of the main reporting obligations in the *AMLCTFA*:

- **Threshold transaction reporting.** A reporting entity that is party to a 'threshold transaction' (ie a transaction involving the transfer of not less than $10,000 in cash) must submit a report in the approved form to AUSTRAC within 10 business days (s 43).
- **International funds transfer reporting.** A reporting entity must submit a report to AUSTRAC if they send or receive an 'international funds transfer instruction' (s 45). An 'international funds transfer instruction' is an instruction to transfer funds into or Outside Australia electronically or under a remittance arrangement (s 46).
- **Cross-border physical currency movement reporting.** Where a person moves physical currency of an amount not less than $10,000 into or out of Australia, the person must submit a report to AUSTRAC (s 53).
- **Suspicious matter reporting.** A reporting entity must submit a report to AUSTRAC if it suspects on reasonable grounds that:
  - a person to whom it provides a designated service, or the person's agent, is not who they claim to be, or
  - information concerning the provision of a designated service may be relevant to the investigation or prosecution of a person for tax evasion or other illegal conduct, including money laundering and terrorist financing (s 41).

Offences

It is an offence under the *AMLCTFA* to:

- provide false or misleading information (s 136)
- forge an identification document (s 137)
- make a false document (s 138), or
- provide or receive a designated service using a false name or anonymity (ss 139, 140).

It is also an offence to structure a transaction to avoid a reporting obligation by entering into two or more non-reportable transactions (ss 142, 143). This arises where, having regard to matters such as the manner in which the transactions were conducted, it would be reasonable to conclude that the person conducted the transactions in that manner for the sole or dominant purpose of avoiding the threshold transaction reporting obligation or the cross-border physical currency movement reporting obligation.

DPP v Ho & Ors (Ruling No 16) [2009] VSC 233 and *Lee v R* (2007) 170 A Crim R 287 examined similar provisions in the former *Financial Transaction Reports Act 1988* (Cth). The cases establish that 'sole or dominant purpose' refers to the 'actuating purpose' of the conduct, rather than an intention to bring about the result of avoiding a reporting obligation. It is, therefore, enough if the person conducted the cash transactions in such a way as to ensure that each transaction would be less than $10,000.

Example Z Co is an Australian bank and is therefore a reporting entity for the purposes of the *AMLCTFA*. On 1 August 2023, Shifty opens an account with the Perth branch of Z Co. As he is a new customer and opening an account is a 'designated service', his identity must be verified in accordance with the *AMLCTFR*. Shifty transfers $180,000 into the new account. This is a 'threshold transaction' involving the transfer of more than $10,000 cash. As such, s 43 obliges Z Co to report the transaction to AUSTRAC. If Shifty then attempts to transfer the money in 30 instalments of

$6,000 to a bank account in Sydney, he would breach s 142. It would be reasonable to conclude that the sole or dominant purpose for transferring the $180,000 in that manner was to ensure that none of the transactions would exceed $10,000. As Z Co would have reasonable grounds to suspect that information about the transaction would aid the investigation or prosecution of illegal conduct, Z Co must provide a suspicious matter report under s 41 to AUSTRAC.

[39.6] QUESTIONS

1. What is the difference between a TFN and an ABN? In what circumstances should TFNs and ABNs be quoted?
2. Ted is employed by a large department store. He has not provided his employer with a TFN declaration. What are the consequences of this for Ted and his employer?
3. Pete is a plumber who charges Felicity, the owner of a restaurant, $500 for installing a dishwasher in her restaurant's kitchen. Pete does not provide his ABN on the invoice provided to Felicity for his services. What are the tax implications for Pete and Felicity?
4. Discuss the differences between the PAYG withholding and PAYG instalment regimes.
5. Jenny has a deposit with a bank and owns shares in a public company. She has not provided either the bank or the public company with her TFN. What is the consequence of this in relation to the interest and dividend payments she receives?
6. Discuss the main reporting obligations under the *AMLCTFA*. What kinds of offences exist under the *AMLCTFA*?

40 TAX RECORD-KEEPING, REPORTING AND RECOVERY

[40.1] Introduction

This chapter discusses a range of miscellaneous matters relating to the administration of the tax system. In particular, it focuses on the special rules relating to record-keeping [40.2], activity statements [40.3], single touch payroll reporting [40.4], running balance accounts [40.5], taxable payments reporting [40.6] and the recovery of tax [40.7]. It also examines the special interest payment regimes that exist under the tax system [40.8].

[40.2] Record-keeping

The tax laws contain important rules requiring taxpayers to retain written records about their tax affairs. Records in English (or that are readily convertible into English) must be kept for specified periods of time (typically five years) so that the ATO has the opportunity to inspect those records if it conducts an audit. Taxpayers that fail to properly keep records may be subject to administrative penalties [41.2] or may be guilty of committing tax offences [41.3].

Income tax records

Persons carrying on business must generally keep records that record and explain all transactions and other acts engaged in by the person that relate to their income tax liabilities for five years after the later of the date those records were prepared or the completion of the transaction to which those records relate (s 262A *ITAA36*). Details of the kinds of records that the Commissioner will accept (eg credit card summaries) are set out in TR 96/7 and TR 2018/2.

Records relating to work expenses, car expenses and business travel expenses that are required to be maintained under the substantiation rules [14.2] must also be kept for five years (s 900-165 *ITAA97*).

GST records

GST records relating to supplies, importations and acquisitions (eg tax invoices and adjustment notes) must be kept for five years after the completion of the transactions or acts to which they relate (s 382-5 *TAA*).

FBT records

Employers are required to keep records that record and explain all transactions and other acts engaged in by the employer or any other person that are relevant for ascertaining the employer's FBT liability (s 132 *FBTAA*). An associate who provides benefits to an employer's employee must also keep records for the relevant transactions and other acts and must give the employer a copy of the records within 21 days after the end of the relevant year. Records must be kept for a period of five years after the completion of the transactions or acts to which they relate.

Employers do not need to keep records under s 132 if they fall within pt XIA *FBTAA*, which applies where an employer's FBT liability for a year of tax is calculated by reference to a previous 'base year' under the relaxed FBT rules [18.19] (s 135E). In these circumstances, an employer must, nevertheless, keep records for the base year for five years after the end of the last FBT year for which the base year is relevant (s 135F).

[40.3] Activity statements

Activity statements are used by taxpayers for reporting and paying their periodic tax obligations. The Business Activity Statement ('BAS') is used by taxpayers to report and pay their GST [7.4], FBT [18.2] and PAYG [39.4] liabilities. Taxpayers with PAYG and/or FBT liabilities that are not registered for GST are required to report and pay their tax liabilities using an Instalment Activity Statement ('IAS') instead of a BAS. The BAS and IAS do not replace the need for taxpayers to lodge income tax returns [38.2] and FBT returns [18.2], or for GST instalment payers to complete annual GST returns [7.4].

[40.4] Single touch payroll

Division 389 of sch 1 *TAA* contains the 'single touch payroll' ('STP') regime, which applies to all employers, other than those exempted by the Commissioner under s 389-10 (s 389-5). The regime requires employers to report the salary and wages, PAYG withholding amounts, and superannuation information relating to their employees to the ATO at the same time as they operate their payroll cycle. Employers are required to use their business reporting payroll software systems to digitally notify the Commissioner of the relevant amounts. The Commissioner must be notified on or before the day the payments are made or, in the case of PAYG withholding amounts, on or before the day they are required to be withheld.

[40.5] Running balance accounts

A running balance account ('RBA') system is contained in pt IIB *TAA* (ss 8AAZA to 8AAZN). A RBA is a special account maintained by the ATO that is designed to record a taxpayer's overall tax liabilities and payments in a single account with a consolidated balance. Under the RBA system, 'primary tax debts' (ie amounts due under the taxation laws) are debited to RBAs whereas payments of tax liabilities are credited to RBAs.

Taxpayers must pay the GIC on deficit balances in their RBAs (s 8AAZF) [40.8]. The Commissioner is required to refund credit surpluses and must generally pay interest on any refunds not paid within 14 days in accordance with the *Taxation (Interest on Overpayments and Early Payments) Act 1983* (Cth) and *Taxation (Interest on Overpayments and Early Payments) Regulations 2018* (Cth) [40.8].

[40.6] Taxable payments reporting

The Taxable Payments Reporting System ('TPRS') in sub-div 396-B of sch 1 *TAA* contains special third-party reporting requirements designed to help the Commissioner identify taxable payments. Specified entities (eg those involved in building and construction, courier and road freight, cleaning, security and surveillance, information technology services, and electronic distribution platforms) are required to report certain transactions they have made during the financial year (eg payments made to their contractors) (s 396-55). They must provide this information in an annual report in the approved form by 28 August following the end of the financial year. The information required is listed in s 396-60 and operates subject to the exemptions contained in ss 396-65 and 396-70.

[40.7] Tax recovery

The power to enforce the payment of taxes is critical to any government. Without effective enforcement powers, a tax system is open to abuse and will inevitably be exploited. A general regime for the collection and recovery of tax is contained in pt 4-15 of sch 1 *TAA* (ss 250-1 to 260-150). This regime applies to all Commonwealth 'tax-related liabilities'.

Tax-related liabilities

Section 250-10 lists the many kinds of tax-related liabilities that exist under the tax legislation. These include liabilities relating to:

- income tax (s 5-5 *ITAA97*)
- withholding tax (s 128C *ITAA36*)
- PAYG (ss 16-75, 45-61, 45-70 in sch 1 *TAA*)
- SGC (s 46 *SGAA*)
- ENCCT (s 292-385 *ITAA97*)
- ETBT (ss 294-240, 294-245 *ITAA97*)
- div 293 tax (ss 293-65, 293-70 *ITAA97*)
- GIC (s 8AAE *TAA*)
- GST (including LCT and WET) (ss 33-3, 33-5, 33-15 *GSTA*), and
- FBT (s 90 *FBTAA*).

Tax-related liabilities constitute debts to the Commonwealth

A tax-related liability constitutes a debt due to the Commonwealth, which is payable to the Commissioner (s 255-5(1)). The Commissioner has the power to sue taxpayers in the courts to recover the amount of a tax-related liability that remains unpaid after it has become due and payable (s 255-5(2)).

Power to defer payment

The Commissioner has the power to defer the time for payment of a tax-related liability and to permit taxpayers to make payments by instalments (ss 255-10, 255-15). The fact that the Commissioner has a deferral power does not necessarily confer upon the debtor any right to its exercise. In PS LA 2011/14, the Commissioner states that he will generally not defer the time for payment unless the debtor can demonstrate that:

- payment cannot be made by the original due date because of circumstances beyond their control and they have taken reasonable steps to mitigate the effects of those circumstances
- payment in full can be made at a later time, once the circumstances that led to non-payment have been alleviated, and
- once the circumstances are under control, continuing tax-related liabilities will be paid as and when they fall due (and accordingly, the debt will not escalate after that time).

Power to release in cases of serious hardship

The Commissioner also has the power to release individuals (and trustees of deceased estates) from all or part of a tax liability where the taxpayer (or the dependants of the deceased individual) would suffer 'serious hardship' (s 340-5). Serious hardship is not defined in the legislation. In PS LA 2011/17, the Commissioner states that he considers serious hardship to exist 'where the payment of a tax liability would result in a person being left without the means to afford basics such as food, clothing, medical supplies, accommodation or reasonable education'. In *Powell v Evreniades* 89 ATC 4415, Hill J considered the meaning of the term under former s 265 *ITAA36*. While he indicated (at 4421) that it was 'inappropriate to endeavour in the abstract to state tests of what will and what will not constitute serious hardship', his Honour nevertheless went on to state:

> Clearly there would be severe financial hardship if the dependants of a deceased person were left destitute without any means of support. That is not to say that in any particular case something less than that will not constitute serious hardship.

In *Wood v FC of T* 2021 ATC ¶20-801, the Federal Court upheld an AAT decision that a medical practitioner would not suffer serious hardship if required to pay his tax liabilities. The Court confirmed that that the onus is on the applicant to prove serious hardship. It held that, in determining whether a tax liability would cause serious hardship, the AAT had correctly decided that the applicant's household assets and liabilities needed to be considered and it was necessary to take into account not only the applicant's resources but also those of their partner. The Court concluded that the AAT was entitled to find that the applicant had not established that his or his wife's income might not increase in the future, and it had not erred in finding that it would have been open to the applicant to find adequate, cheaper accommodation for his family.

Similarly, in *Dua v FC of T* 2022 ATC ¶10-631, a medical practitioner failed to discharge the onus of proving serious hardship. The AAT found the applicant had expenses that were not 'necessities according to normal community standards' (including annual school fees of almost $50,000) and that reducing his household expenditure (eg by sending his children to public schools) would allow him to meet his tax liabilities in a reasonable time without impacting upon his ability to provide reasonable accommodation, food, clothing, medical supplies and education for himself and his family.

40

By way of contrast, a carpenter was granted a partial release from his tax liabilities (comprising outstanding PAYG instalments of $126,480 and GIC of $54,351) on the grounds of serious hardship in *Shaw v FC of T* 2022 ATC ¶10-619. The applicant had suffered a relationship breakdown and had a previous drug and gambling addiction. He had been forced to sell his house, had his car seized by a bailiff, and had various other unpaid debts. At the time of the hearing, he had around $4,000 in his bank account, was employed, and had a surplus of approximately $1,097 per fortnight after living expenses. He also had two daughters living with him (one of whom was earning $1,725 per fortnight). The AAT held that releasing him from the payment of the GIC would be sufficient to avoid serious hardship and would allow him to repay the balance of the tax liabilities within a more reasonable time.

Other cases in which serious hardship was found to exist include *FC of T v Taxpayer* 2006 ATC 4393 and *FC of T v Milne* 2006 ATC 403.

Power to bring forward time of liability and require security

Where the Commissioner suspects that a taxpayer is about to leave Australia before a tax-related liability becomes due and payable, he has the power to bring forward the time at which the liability arises (s 255-20).

The Commissioner can also require a taxpayer to give security (eg by way of a bond) for the payment of an existing or future tax-related liability (s 255-100). For instance, he may require this where a taxpayer plans to temporarily carry on an enterprise in Australia and leave without returning, or where he considers it is otherwise appropriate (eg where a taxpayer has a history of non-compliance).

Commissioner's recovery powers generally not restricted by appeals or reviews

The Commissioner's recovery powers are extremely wide. The fact that a taxpayer may have commenced review or appeal proceedings in relation to an assessment will generally not affect the Commissioner's ability to proceed with recovery action against the taxpayer (eg commencement of bankruptcy proceedings). A special exception to this rule applies to SBEs, which can apply for an order under s 41 *AATA* to stay recovery actions for debts disputed in the AAT until the underlying dispute has been resolved (s 14ZZM(2) *TAA*).

A court may also exercise its inherent power to stay recovery proceedings in appropriate cases. The discretion to use this power will usually only be exercised by a court in exceptional circumstances (*Snow v DFC of T* 87 ATC 4078; *DFC of T v Palumbo & Anor* 92 ATC 4358). Factors that a court might take into account in considering whether or not to grant a stay include the merits of the taxpayer's case on appeal and the effect of any hardship that recovery action may cause the taxpayer.

Commissioner's recovery powers not restricted by state legislation

The Commissioner's recovery powers are also not restricted by the time limits for the recovery of debts imposed under state limitation of action legislation. This is illustrated in *DFC of T v Moorebank Pty Ltd* 88 ATC 4443, which concerned whether the Commissioner could recover income tax and a penalty for non-payment of income tax outside the periods specified by the *Limitation of Actions Act 1974* (Qld). This Act provided that an action to recover a sum under an enactment had to be commenced within six years from the date on which the cause of action accrued and that an action to recover a penalty had to be commenced within two years from the date on which the cause of action accrued. The High Court held that the Commissioner's right to recover the income tax and the penalty was not limited by the Queensland legislation due to s 109 of the *Commonwealth Constitution*, which provides that a Commonwealth law prevails over a state law to the extent of any 'inconsistency' [3.3]. According to the High Court, the Commonwealth recovery of tax provisions were intended to 'cover the field' and left no room for the state legislation to operate.

The decision in *Moorebank* was followed in *DFC of T v DTR Securities Pty Ltd* 88 ATC 4442 and *MUC v DFC of T (No 2)* 2008 ATC ¶20-032 in relation to the *Limitation Act 1969* (NSW). It has also been applied in the context of state judgment debt recovery legislation, which allows taxpayers to apply to the courts for orders that a judgment debt be paid by instalments. For instance, in *DFC of T v Zarzycki* 90 ATC 4707, O'Bryan J held that the income tax recovery legislation covered the field so as to exclude the operation of the *Judgment Debt Recovery Act 1984* (Vic). Similar outcomes were reached in *Re Mazuran; Ex parte DFC of T* 90 ATC 4814; *DFC of T v Homewood* 91 ATC 4633; and *Re Pollack; Ex parte DFC of T* 91 ATC 4925.

Commissioner should not act oppressively

In *Hyder & Ors v FC of T* 2023 ATC ¶20-854, the Full Federal Court held (at [84]) that while it is 'well-established that the Commissioner can issue alternative assessments to different taxpayers when uncertain as to who is correctly to be assessed', the Commissioner 'cannot act oppressively by seeking to recover the full amount owed under each and every alternative assessment'. The Full Federal Court found support for this principle in *DFC of T v Moorebank Pty Ltd* 88 ATC 4443, where the High Court said (at 4448):

> There will inevitably be cases in which it would be oppressive for the Commissioner to seek to enforce payment of the full amount due under a notice of assessment . . . before the final resolution of a genuine dispute about the correctness of the assessment . . . A case in which the Commissioner issues a number of assessments on an alternative basis to different taxpayers in respect of the same income provides an obvious example.

In *Hyder*, the Court noted (at [84]) that 'what amounts to oppressive conduct will necessarily depend on the circumstances of a given case'. However, as the Commissioner had given an undertaking not to seek to recover under the alternative assessments that were in issue in the case until their correctness had been judicially determined, he had agreed not to engage in oppressive conduct. It was therefore not necessary to issue an injunction to restrain him from seeking to recover tax.

Collection of tax from third parties

To assist with tax collection, the Commissioner is given special powers under sub-div 260-A of sch 1 *TAA* to recover tax indirectly from third parties.

Section 260-5 provides that where a tax-related liability is payable to the Commonwealth by a taxpayer, the Commissioner may give a third party who owes money to the taxpayer (or holds money for, or on account of, the taxpayer) a written notice requiring the third party to pay the money to the Commissioner.

A third party that fails to comply with the notice commits an offence for which the maximum penalty is 20 penalty units [41.1] (s 260-20).

A third party that makes a payment pursuant to a notice issued by the Commissioner is taken to be authorised to make the payment by the debtor and is indemnified for the amount paid (s 260-15). This prevents the debtor from later suing the third party for the amount paid to the Commissioner.

In *Burton Holdings Pty Ltd (In Liq) v FC of T & Anor* 2009 ATC ¶20-125, the High Court held that s 260-5 could not be used by the Commissioner in relation to a tax debt owed by a company in liquidation. Instead, special recovery procedures, contained in sub-div 260-B, apply to liquidators.

Separate recovery rules apply to receivers (sub-div 260-C), resident agents that wind up businesses for non-resident principals (sub-div 260-D) and trustees of deceased estates (sub-div 260-E).

Departure prohibition orders

There is a risk that taxpayers with outstanding tax liabilities may leave Australia in order to avoid having to pay tax. It is obviously difficult for the Commissioner to recover tax debts from taxpayers who are no longer in the jurisdiction. The Commissioner therefore has the power under pt IVA *TAA* to issue 'departure prohibition orders' where he believes there are reasonable grounds for doing so to prevent taxpayers leaving Australia before they discharge their tax liabilities (s 14S).

It is an offence (punishable by penalty and/or imprisonment) for a person in respect of whom a departure prohibition order is in force, and who knows that such an order is in force, to depart from Australia (s 14R). This does not apply where the departure is authorised by a 'departure authorisation certificate' (s 14U). The Commissioner may revoke or vary a departure prohibition order (s 14T).

A person may appeal to the Federal Court or state Supreme Court against the making of a departure prohibition order (s 14V).

In *Skase v FC of T* 92 ATC 4001, the Federal Court set aside a departure prohibition order because it was used for the improper purpose of pressuring the taxpayer into filing a petition for bankruptcy and was unlikely to affect the collection of the large tax debt he owed as he had few assets. The Court held that a departure prohibition order must be used for a proper purpose and can only be justified if recoverability of the tax debt will be affected by the departure of the taxpayer from Australia. Pincus J pointed out that s 14S was *not* a 'weapon of general character' that the Commissioner can apply in any case.

The decision in *Skase* was referred to in *Troughton v DFC of T* 2008 ATC ¶20-001, where Jessup J explained (at [22]):

> The purpose of s 14S, and accordingly a central purpose of Part IVA, is not the prevention of persons (owing tax) from leaving Australia *simpliciter*: it is the prevention of such persons from leaving Australia where, in the Commissioner's belief reasonably arrived at, the recovery of tax would or might thereby be impaired.

Mareva injunctions

The Commissioner sometimes applies to the court for 'Mareva injunctions' against taxpayers who have outstanding tax debts (*DFC of T v Ousley & Ors* 92 ATC 4168). A Mareva injunction prevents a person from dealing with assets under their control (*Mareva Compania Naviera SA v International Bulkcarriers SA, The Mareva* [1980] 1 All ER 213). It is a 'freezing order' designed to prevent a debtor from abusing the legal system by disposing of assets to third parties or taking them outside the jurisdiction in order to become 'judgment proof'.

The injunction is an equitable remedy granted at the discretion of the court and may be sought before recovery proceedings have commenced. In *DFC of T v Rosenthal & Ors* 85 ATC 4031, O'Bryan J pointed out that the Commissioner must establish three matters before an injunction will be granted:

1. there must be a sufficiently strong case to justify the relief pending the determination of the claim
2. there must be a risk of the defendant removing assets from the jurisdiction or dissipating assets, and
3. the balance of convenience must require the making of the order.

The Commissioner obtained a freezing order against a company in *FC of T v Regent Pacific Group Limited & Ors* [2013] FCA 36. The Commissioner had argued that:

- the company had liquid assets in the form of shares listed on the ASX, which it could easily sell and transmit the proceeds overseas
- the company did not have a TFN in Australia indicating it had never filed returns in Australia
- the company was registered in the Cayman Islands and had a business office in Hong Kong, and neither of these jurisdictions had a bilateral collection process with Australia or recognised foreign revenue debts, and
- the company had a significant tax debt of approximately $12.7m which was not due to be paid for 11 months.

The Federal Court held that these circumstances were sufficient to support an inference that there was a danger that the failure to grant the order would result in the Commissioner not being able to recover the tax debt.

In *DFC of T v Huang* 2021 ATC ¶20-814, the Commissioner was successful in obtaining a worldwide freezing order against a taxpayer who relocated to China after the ATO commenced an audit into his tax affairs. The order was made under r 7.32 of the *Federal Court Rules* and was challenged by the taxpayer on the basis there was no realistic possibility that the judgment would be enforced in China or Hong Kong. A majority of the High Court held that the granting of a freezing order in respect of assets located outside Australia does not require proof of a realistic possibility of enforcement of a judgment debt against the assets in each foreign jurisdiction to which the order relates.

Recovery of estimates of PAYG and SGC amounts

Division 268 of sch 1 *TAA* enables the Commissioner to make a reasonable estimate, having regard to anything he considers relevant, of any unpaid amounts owing by a person under the PAYG withholding system [39.4] or as an SGC [19.5] (s 268-10). The Commissioner must notify the person in writing of the estimate (s 268-15). A person who receives such a notice is required to pay the Commissioner the amount of the estimate (s 268-20). The amount is due and payable at the time the notice is provided. The amount owing is reduced if the person who receives the notice can show that the liability never existed, has been discharged or is less than the estimate (ss 268-40, 268-90).

Recovery of a company's unpaid PAYG and SGC liabilities from directors

Division 269 of sch 1 *TAA* contains rules designed to ensure that a company either:

- meets its div 268, PAYG withholding [39.4] and SGC [19.4] obligations, or
- goes promptly into voluntary administration or liquidation (s 269-5).

Division 269 applies from 1 July 2010 and replaces broadly similar rules contained in former div 9 of pt VI *ITAA36* (ss 222ANA to 222AQD). The previous rules did not, however, apply to SGC obligations which were only added to div 269 in 2012.

Division 269 imposes a statutory obligation on directors to cause their companies to comply with their PAYG withholding, div 268 and SGC obligations (ss 269-10, 269-15). If a company has not complied with its obligations by the due day and an administrator has not been appointed or winding-up proceedings have not commenced, the Commissioner can recover the relevant amounts from the directors as a 'penalty'.

If a person becomes a director after the due day, they become liable for the penalty 30 days after becoming a director (s 269-20). The Commissioner is required to give 21 days' notice before commencing recovery proceedings against a director (s 269-25).

If the Commissioner recovers an amount from a director by way of penalty, the director has a right of indemnity from the company or contribution from other directors against whom the Commissioner was entitled to recover the penalty (s 269-45).

It is a defence against recovery proceedings if the director can prove that:

- because of illness or some other good reason, it would have been unreasonable to expect the director to take part, and the director did not actually take part, in the management of the company at any time when they were a director and the directors were under the relevant obligations under s 269-15, or
- the director took all reasonable steps to ensure that the directors caused the company to comply with its obligations, or no such steps could have been taken (s 269-35).

Cases dealing with former div 9 have indicated that it can be difficult to satisfy the requirements of these defences. For example, in *DFC of T v George* 2002 ATC 4930, the court held that to come within the first defence, a director must establish good reason for a failure to take part in the management of a company for the *entire* period that they were a director and the relevant obligation existed.

Likewise, in *DFC of T v Saunig* 2002 ATC 5135, the court held that a director could not rely on the second defence, as he failed to demonstrate that he had taken all reasonable steps to ensure compliance since he could have caused the company to begin to be wound up and had not obtained appropriate professional advice at a sufficiently early stage.

The stringency of the rules is further illustrated by *Fitzgerald v DFC of T* 95 ATC 4587, which highlights that the onus is on new directors to make appropriate inquiries regarding the tax obligations of a company. In this case, a person was a director of a company for only 17 days. He had been appointed two months after the amounts owing by the company were due and received a notice from the Commissioner under former div 9 several months after ceasing to be a director. The District Court of Western Australia, nevertheless, held that he was liable for the penalty under former div 9. French DCJ stated (at 4590):

> Although he was not aware of the company's financial position or the moneys due to the [Commissioner] this is not sufficient to provide a defence . . . it is the responsibility of a new director at or prior to taking up his appointment to make inquiries of the relevant officers of the company as to whether there were any moneys owing by the company to the [Commissioner].

His Honour also made the following comments by way of *obiter dictum* (at 4590):

> If there was evidence to suggest that upon such enquiry a director was not given correct information then it may be that he would be able to establish a defence to the [Commissioner's] claim for penalty.

There was, however, no evidence to suggest that this had occurred in this case.

Estoppel against the Commissioner's recovery powers

The Commissioner has a public duty to protect the revenue (*Ellison v DFC of T* 99 ATC 4576). As a general rule, he cannot be estopped from performing his legislative functions, such as issuing assessments and collecting tax (see *FC of T v Wade* (1951) 84 CLR 105, 117 (Kitto J); *AGC (Investments) Ltd v FC of T* 91 ATC 4180, 4195 (Hill J)). As Gobbo J indicated in *DFC of T v Tropitone Furniture Co Pty Ltd* (1991) 22 ATR 361 (at 364): 'save for well known exceptions, estoppel cannot lie against a statutory body charged with carrying out the performance of its duties'.

It is therefore only in extraordinary situations that a taxpayer would be able to successfully argue estoppel against the Commissioner. A rare example of where this occurred is found in *FC of T v Winters* 97 ATC 4967. In this case, the Commissioner sought summary judgment against directors of a company that had been issued penalty notices under former div 9 of pt VI *ITAA36* for group tax that the company had failed to remit. The Commissioner was required to provide 14 days' notice before commencing recovery proceedings. The directors submitted that before this period ended (on 16 April 1996), a tax officer had led them to believe that the time for compliance with the penalty notices would be extended. The directors argued that this induced them not to appoint an administrator until 17 June 1996 (ie outside the 14-day notice period). In dismissing the Deputy Commissioner's application for summary judgment, the Supreme Court of Queensland distinguished *AGC* and *Tropitone* and held that, depending on the resolution of the factual issues in their favour, the directors were capable of making out the elements of estoppel. Moynihan J explained:

> It may be accepted as a matter of general principle that estoppel will not prevent the exercise of a statutory obligation . . . It is however by no means clear that the principle extends to the circumstances here so as to prevent the defendants from raising the limited estoppel on which they rely. Assuming all else in the defendants favour they simply seek to preclude the plaintiff from relying on the consequences of their failure to take steps to avoid the effect of the penalty notices within fourteen days of their receipt; that is in light of an administrator effectively being appointed on 17 June.

Another case where estoppel was raised is *Chamberlain v DFC of T* 88 ATC 4323. In this case, the taxpayer was sued for an amount of $255,579.20 relating to tax owing under various assessments. However, due to a preparation error, the writ only disclosed a balance of $25,557.92. A solicitor employed by the taxpayer contacted the ATO and said that the taxpayer 'would like to pay the total on the writ and costs, subject to a judgment by consent'. After the ATO was informed by the solicitor that the amount paid was the full amount claimed, consent orders were executed and the Supreme Court subsequently entered judgment in favour of the Deputy Commissioner. A few days later, the Deputy Commissioner realised the error and commenced proceedings to recover the balance tax.

In these proceedings, the Deputy Commissioner did not seek to have the judgment set aside. Rather, he simply argued that he was empowered to recover the balance tax. The High Court, however, held that the Commissioner was estopped from recovering the tax due to the doctrine of *res judicata* (which provides that a matter which has been finally adjudicated by a court of competent jurisdiction cannot be reopened by the parties).

The Deputy Commissioner subsequently commenced new proceedings in the Federal Court seeking to have the consent order set aside. On appeal, in *Chamberlain v DFC of T* 91 ATC 4175, the Full Federal Court acknowledged that the tax officer had acted under the mistaken apprehension that the payment was for the full amount of the claim. The Court also indicated that as the mistake related to the subject matter of the consent, which the taxpayer took advantage of, the Deputy Commissioner would normally be entitled to have the judgment set aside. Nevertheless, the Court refused to set aside the judgment because the Deputy Commissioner had chosen not to pursue such a course of action in the earlier proceedings. As a consequence, he was estopped from alleging that the sums claimed were recoverable. Davies, Ryan and Foster JJ pointed out (at 4178) that '[a]n issue which ought to have been raised in one proceeding cannot subsequently be raised between the same parties in a subsequent proceeding'.

[40.8] Interest regimes

Interest on late payments of tax

Taxpayers that fail to pay their tax liabilities on time are usually required to pay interest on the amounts owing. The relevant provisions are found in the GIC regime contained in pt IIA *TAA* (ss 8AAA to 8AAH). The GIC is designed to 'compensate' the Government for not having access to money owed by taxpayers. It effectively treats the amount of any unpaid tax and interest accruing thereon as if it was a loan made by the Government to the relevant taxpayer. The GIC encourages taxpayers to pay their tax on time by making it unprofitable for them to delay their payments. It also promotes equity by ensuring that taxpayers who meet their tax obligations are not disadvantaged in comparison to those that do not.

The GIC applies where certain taxes, including the following, have not been paid by the due date (s 8AAB):

- income tax (s 5-15 *ITAA97*)
- withholding tax (s 128C *ITAA36*)
- FBT (s 93 *FBTAA*)
- GST (s 105-80 in sch 1 *TAA*)
- SGC (s 49 *SGAA*)
- ENCCT (s 292-390 *ITAA97*)
- div 293 tax (s 293-75 *ITAA97*)
- ETBT (s 294-250 *ITAA97*).

The GIC also applies to deficit balances in RBAs [40.5] (s 8AAZF *TAA*).

The GIC for a day is calculated on the unpaid amount of tax and GIC (s 8AAC). This means the GIC is calculated on a daily 'compounding basis'. The GIC rate for a day is worked out by adding seven percentage points to the 'base interest rate' for the day and then dividing this total by the number of days in the calendar year (s 8AAD). The base interest rate for a day is calculated quarterly by reference to the monthly average yield of 90-day bank accepted bills published by the Reserve Bank. The following table sets out the GIC rates for the respective quarters in 2022/23.

Quarter	Annual GIC rate	Daily GIC rate
April–June 2023	10.46	0.02865753%
January–March 2023	10.06%	0.02756164%
October–December 2022	9.31%	0.02550685%
July–September 2022	8.00%	0.02191781%

Example Barry has a \$100,000 tax liability that is due on 28 October 2022, but which he only pays on 15 November 2022. As he is late in paying tax, he is subject to the GIC at the daily interest rate of 0.02550685% (which is the daily rate applicable for the October–December 2022 quarter). The GIC is payable for each day starting on 28 October 2022 and ending on 15 November 2022 (ie for 18 days).

The GIC for 28 October 2022 is \$25.50 (ie \$100,000 × 0.02550685%). As the GIC is worked out on a daily compounding basis, the GIC for subsequent days is based on the \$100,000 outstanding tax liability plus the GIC from each of the previous days. The total amount Barry has to pay to discharge his tax and GIC liability on 15 November 2022 may be calculated using a compound interest formula as follows:

$$\$100{,}460.18 = \$100{,}000 \times (1 + 0.02550685\%)^{18}$$

His total GIC for the 18-day period therefore amounts to \$460.18 (ie \$100,460.18 – \$100,000).

The Commissioner has the power to remit all or part of the GIC (s 8AAG). However, if a person is liable to pay the GIC because an amount is overdue, the Commissioner may only remit all or a part of the GIC if he is satisfied that:

- the circumstances that contributed to the delay in payment were not caused directly or indirectly by an act or omission of the person and they have taken reasonable action to mitigate those circumstances or their effects
- the circumstances that contributed to the delay in payment were caused directly or indirectly by an act or omission of the person, they have taken reasonable action to mitigate those circumstances or their effects, and having regard to those circumstances, it would be fair and reasonable to remit all or a part of the GIC, or
- there are special circumstances which make it fair and reasonable to remit all or a part of the GIC or it is otherwise appropriate to do so.

Guidelines on the remission of the GIC are found in PS LA 2011/12.

Taxpayers can claim deductions for their GIC payments (s 25-5(1)(c) *ITAA97*) [13.2].

Interest on early payments and overpayments of tax

Taxpayers that pay income tax (but not FBT or GST) more than 14 days before it becomes due are entitled to receive interest from the Commissioner under the *Taxation (Interest on Overpayments and Early Payments) Act 1983*.

Interest is also payable by the Commissioner on overpayments of tax (eg where a taxpayer receives a tax refund as a consequence of a successful objection, review or appeal).

Interest is calculated on a daily basis at the 'base interest rate' (ie the 90-day bank accepted bill rate). It should be noted that this rate is less than the GIC rate payable to the Commissioner on late payments of tax.

Interest payable to a taxpayer under the *Taxation (Interest on Overpayments and Early Payments) Act 1983* constitutes assessable income when it is paid to the taxpayer (s 15-35 *ITAA97*) [10.3].

[40.9] QUESTIONS

1. What record-keeping requirements must taxpayers comply with?
2. What are the roles of the BAS and the IAS?
3. How does the STP regime work and to whom does it apply?
4. What is a running balance account?
5. What can the Commissioner do to recover an unpaid tax debt?
6. In what circumstances can departure prohibition orders be issued?
7. What is the object of div 269 of sch 1 *TAA*? How does it potentially affect directors of companies?
8. What happens if a taxpayer is late paying their tax? How is the GIC calculated?

41 TAX PENALTIES AND OFFENCES

[41.1] Introduction

To promote compliance with the tax laws and discourage tax avoidance and tax evasion, the Australian tax system is supported by various administrative and criminal penalty regimes. These regimes contain important sanctions and integrity measures that underpin the operation of the whole tax system. The rationale for having such rules was explained by the Supreme Court of South Australia in *Taplin v Pickford* 90 ATC 4067, where Olsson J said (at 4073):

> To many it may appear that the various 'penal' provisions of the revenue legislation are Draconian, but it must not be forgotten that, particularly under current bases of administration (including the 'self-assessment' concept) much of the efficacy of the income tax administration depends upon the honesty of individual taxpayers. There is a very real prospect that, if the total levels of penalty are not such as to render it extremely unprofitable for individuals to cheat on their fellow citizens, the system could either break down or alternatively become extremely difficult or expensive to administer. The legislature has rendered it quite clear that those minded to attempt to defraud the revenue will do so at their considerable peril.

This chapter focuses on the following regimes:

- the administrative penalty regime contained in pt 4-25 of sch 1 *TAA* [41.2]
- the tax offences regime contained in div 2 of pt III *TAA* [41.3], and
- the promoter penalty regime contained in div 290 of sch 1 *TAA* [41.4].

Penalties imposed under these regimes vary considerably depending on the nature of the offence. Where financial penalties are imposed, they are usually set by reference to penalty units. A penalty unit is $313 from 1 July 2023 and is subject to indexation every three years (s 4AA *Crimes Act 1914* (Cth)).

[41.2] Administrative penalty regime

A general administrative penalty regime is located in pt 4-25 of sch 1 *TAA*. This regime contains standardised administrative penalties that the Commissioner can impose for breaches of the tax laws, including the income tax, GST and FBT laws. The broad objective of the administrative penalty regime is to deter culpable behaviour by imposing a uniform set of penalties where a taxpayer has understated tax or failed to comply with their tax obligations.

There are penalties for a range of prohibited forms of conduct, including:

- making false or misleading statements, adopting positions under the tax laws that are not reasonably arguable, and entering into certain tax avoidance schemes (div 284)
- failing to lodge documents (eg tax returns) on time (div 286), and
- miscellaneous breaches, such as failure to keep requisite records (div 288).

The penalties for making false and misleading statements are contained in sub-div 284-B. Under sub-div 284-B, the 'base penalty amount' is generally a specified percentage (determined according to s 284-90(1)) of the 'shortfall amount' (ie broadly, the understated tax: s 284-80) (s 284-85). However, if there is no shortfall amount, the penalty is simply based on a specified number of penalty units [41.1]. Different penalties apply depending on whether 'intentional disregard of a taxation law', 'recklessness' or 'failure to take reasonable care' is involved. Recklessness means 'more than the failure to exercise reasonable care but less than an intentional disregard of the Act' (*Hart v FC of T* 2003 ATC 4665). It is 'more than mere negligence and must amount to gross carelessness' (*BRK (Bris) Pty Ltd v FC of T* 2001 ATC 4111). Special rules apply to significant global entities [33.7], which must pay double the base penalty amount in certain circumstances (s 284-90(1A)).

The penalties for entering into certain tax avoidance schemes are contained in sub-div 284-C. Under sub-div 284-C, the 'base penalty amount' is a specified percentage of the 'scheme shortfall amount' (s 284-160). The penalty depends on whether the taxpayer's position is 'reasonably arguable' and whether the 'scheme benefit' falls within the general anti-avoidance provisions (eg pt IVA *ITAA36* [37.3] or div 165 *GSTA* [7.19]) or is a transfer pricing benefit (div 815 *ITAA97* [33.4]). The base penalty amount is doubled if the taxpayer is a significant global entity that does not have a reasonably arguable position (s 284-155(3)).

A taxpayer's position is reasonably arguable if it would be concluded in the circumstances, having regard to relevant authorities, that what is argued for is about as likely to be correct as incorrect, or is more likely to be correct than incorrect (s 284-15(1)). The test is objective (*FC of T v Traviati* 2012 ATC ¶20-321; *Thomas & Ors v FC of T* 2015 ATC ¶20-526; *Orica Ltd v FC of T* 2015 ATC ¶20-547). A taxpayer may have a reasonably arguable position even if what they argue is wrong, so long as their argument could objectively be argued on rational grounds to be right (*FC of T v R&D Holdings Pty Ltd* 2007 ATC 4731). An assumption about the way the Commissioner would exercise a discretion is only reasonably arguable if, had the Commissioner exercised the discretion in the way assumed, a court would be about as likely as not to decide that the exercise of the discretion was in accordance with law (s 284-15(2)).

An entity gets a 'scheme benefit' from a scheme where a tax-related liability of the entity for an accounting period is, or could reasonably be expected to be, less than it would be apart from the scheme, or where the amount of the credit the Commissioner must pay to the entity under a taxation law is, or could reasonably be expected to be, more than it would be apart from the scheme (s 284-150).

The base penalty amounts under both sub-divs 284-B and 284-C may be reduced or increased under sub-div 284-D. For example, the base penalty is reduced if the taxpayer applies the law in a way that is consistent with advice received from the Commissioner, general administrative practice, or a statement in an approved publication (s 284-224). The base penalty amount is also reduced if the taxpayer voluntarily discloses the shortfall amount (the amount of the reduction differs depending on whether the disclosure is made before or after notification of an examination of the taxpayer's affairs) (s 284-225). It is increased if the taxpayer prevents or obstructs the Commissioner from finding out about the shortfall amount, or if they have been previously penalised for similar behaviour (s 284-220).

The penalties under divs 286 and 288 are imposed by reference to penalty units [41.1]. In cases involving a failure to lodge returns or other documents, the penalty generally increases with the size of the entity (ie depending on whether it is a 'small', 'medium' or 'large' withholder [39.4]).

The Commissioner is required to provide written notice to taxpayers of their penalties (s 298-10) specifying the due date for payment (which must be at least 14 days after the notice is given) (s 298-15). Where a penalty is not paid by the due date, the GIC applies (s 298-25) [40.8].

The Commissioner has the power to remit all or part of a penalty (s 298-20). Guidelines on the remission of penalties are contained in PS LA 2012/4 and PS LA 2012/5.

The following tables summarise some of the main administrative penalties that exist under divs 284, 286 and 288.

Penalties relating to statements where there is a shortfall amount (sub-div 284-B)				
	Standard base penalty amount	**Increased base penalty amount (obstruction, prevention or previous penalty)**	**Decreased base penalty (voluntary disclosure *after* notification of examination)**	**Decreased base penalty (voluntary disclosure *before* notification of examination)**
Shortfall due to making false or misleading statement resulting from intentional disregard of taxation law	75%	90%	60%	15%
Shortfall due to making false or misleading statement resulting from recklessness	50%	60%	40%	10%
Shortfall due to making false or misleading statement resulting from failure to take reasonable care	25%	30%	20%	5%
Shortfall due to applying the law in a way that is not reasonably arguable	25%	30%	20%	5%

Note 1: In the final column, the decreased base penalty is reduced to nil if the voluntary disclosure is made before an audit and the shortfall is less than $1,000.

Note 2: The base penalty amount is doubled for significant global entities [33.7] (s 284-90(1A)).

Penalties relating to statements where there is no shortfall amount (sub-div 284-B)				
	Standard base penalty amount	**Increased base penalty amount (obstruction, prevention or previous penalty)**	**Decreased base penalty (voluntary disclosure *after* notification of examination)**	**Decreased base penalty (voluntary disclosure *before* notification of examination)**
False or misleading statement because of intentional disregard of taxation law	60 penalty units	72 penalty units	48 penalty units	Nil
False or misleading statement because of reckless disregard of taxation law	40 penalty units	48 penalty units	32 penalty units	Nil
False or misleading statement because of failure to take reasonable care	20 penalty units	24 penalty units	16 penalty units	Nil

Note: The base penalty amount is doubled for significant global entities [33.7] (s 284-90(1A)).

Penalties relating to tax avoidance schemes (sub-div 284-C)				
	Standard base penalty amount	**Increased base penalty amount (obstruction, prevention or previous penalty)**	**Decreased base penalty (voluntary disclosure *after* notification of examination)**	**Decreased base penalty (voluntary disclosure *before* notification of examination)**
Tax avoidance scheme	50% or 25%	60% or 30%	40% or 20%	10% or 5%
Transfer pricing benefit (dominant purpose of tax avoidance)	50% or 25%	60% or 30%	40% or 20%	10% or 5%
Transfer pricing benefit (no dominant purpose of tax avoidance)	25% or 10%	30% or 12%	20% or 8%	5% or 2%

Note 1: Taxpayers can use the lower rates in each box where their position is 'reasonably arguable'.

Note 2: The base penalty amount is doubled for significant global entities [33.7] (s 284-155(3)).

Note 3: The penalties do not apply if a DPT assessment is made (this is because the 40% DPT rate is taken to include a penalty component) [37.9].

Penalties for failure to lodge returns and other documents (div 286)	
Size of withholder	**Penalty**
Small withholder (s 286-80(2))	Base penalty amount of one penalty unit for each 28-day period or part thereof not lodged (up to a maximum of five penalty units)
Medium withholder (s 286-80(3))	Base penalty amount multiplied by two
Large withholder (s 286-80(4))	Base penalty amount multiplied by five

Note: The base penalty amount is multiplied by 500 for significant global entities [33.7] (s 286-80(4A)).

Penalties for other miscellaneous breaches of the taxation law (div 288)	
Breach	**Penalty**
Failure to lodge return electronically (s 288-10)	5 penalty units
Failure to pay amount electronically (s 288-20)	5 penalty units
Failure to keep or retain records (s 288-25)	20 penalty units
Failure to retain or produce declarations (s 288-30)	20 penalty units
Preventing access to authorised officer (s 288-35)	20 penalty units
Failure to register or cancel registration for GST (s 288-40)	20 penalty units
Failure to issue tax invoice for GST (s 288-45)	20 penalty units
Failure to give release authority for ENCCT (s 288-90)	20 penalty units
Failure to comply with release authority (s 288-95)	20 penalty units

Tax-records education direction

As an alternative to imposing an administrative penalty, the Commissioner has recently been given the power to issue a 'tax-records education direction' requiring an entity to complete an approved record-keeping course where he reasonably believes that there has been a failure to comply with one or more specified record-keeping obligations under a taxation law (s 384-12 *TAA*). The tax-records education direction seeks to address record-keeping knowledge gaps and reduce non-compliance by helping entities better understand their tax-related record-keeping obligations. PS LA 2005/2 states tax-records education directions are best suited for SBEs.

[41.3] Tax offences

Offences under the *Taxation Administration Act 1953* (Cth)

The *TAA* contains a number of specific tax offences. These offences are located in div 2 of pt III of the Act (ss 8A to 8ZN). The Commissioner has the power to prosecute offenders for these offences in a court of summary jurisdiction (or the state Supreme Court where the maximum penalty for the offence exceeds 50 penalty units for individuals or 250 penalty units for companies). Prosecutions for tax offences take precedence over the administrative penalty regime discussed at [41.2]. If a prosecution is instituted in relation to a tax offence, the offender is *not* liable to pay any administrative penalty relating to the offence (s 8ZE).

A person who is convicted of a tax offence may be fined or imprisoned. Offences that are not punishable by imprisonment are treated as being of a civil (rather than criminal) nature. In these cases, the elements of the offence must be proved on the 'balance of probabilities' (rather than 'beyond reasonable doubt', which is the burden of proof in criminal trials).

Offences and maximum penalties

The table below briefly outlines the main offences and their maximum penalties. Fines are calculated by reference to 'penalty units' [41.1]. Where a taxation offence is committed by a company and the offence, if committed by a natural person, is punishable by imprisonment, the maximum fine is usually five times the maximum fine that applies to an individual (s 8ZF). This rule does not, however, apply in the case of a 'prescribed offence' (eg an offence under ss 8C, 8D, 8N or 8Q), unless the prescribed offence is a third or subsequent offence under ss 8C or 8D or a second offence under ss 8N or 8Q.

Offence	Maximum penalty (natural person)	Maximum penalty (company)
Person refuses or fails to comply with the requirements under a tax law to furnish an approved form, give information, lodge an instrument, produce documents, or attend before the Commissioner (s 8C). (Note: this offence does not apply to the extent that the person is incapable of complying with the relevant requirements)	20 penalty units (first offence) 40 penalty units (second offence) 50 penalty units and/or 12 months' imprisonment (third and each subsequent offence) (s 8E)	20 penalty units (first offence) 40 penalty units (second offence) 250 penalty units (third and each subsequent offence) (ss 8E, 8ZF)
Person, when attending before the Commissioner or another person pursuant to a taxation law, refuses or fails to answer a question or produce documents as required under a taxation law (s 8D). (Note: this offence does not apply to the extent that the person is incapable of complying with the relevant requirements)	20 penalty units (first offence) 40 penalty units (second offence) 50 penalty units and/or 12 months' imprisonment (third and each subsequent offence) (s 8E)	20 penalty units (first offence) 40 penalty units (second offence) 250 penalty units (third and each subsequent offence) (ss 8E, 8ZF)
Person convicted under s 8C or s 8D refuses or fails to comply with a court order (s 8G)	50 penalty units and/or 12 months' imprisonment (s 8H)	250 penalty units (ss 8H, 8ZF)
Person makes a statement to a taxation officer that is false or misleading in a material particular. (Note: it is a defence if the person did not know and could not reasonably be expected to have known that the statement was false or misleading)	20 penalty units (first offence) 40 penalty units (second and each subsequent offence) (s 8M)	20 penalty units (first offence) 40 penalty units (second and each subsequent offence) (s 8M)

Offence	Maximum penalty (natural person)	Maximum penalty (company)
Person incorrectly keeps records that are required to be kept under a taxation law (s 8L). (Note: it is a defence if the person did not know and could not reasonably be expected to have known that the records were incorrect)	20 penalty units (first offence) 40 penalty units (second and each subsequent offence) (s 8M)	20 penalty units (first offence) 40 penalty units (second and each subsequent offence) (s 8M)
Person recklessly makes a statement to a taxation officer that is false or misleading in a material particular or omits something from a statement which makes it misleading in a material particular (s 8N)	30 penalty units (first offence) 50 penalty units and/or 12 months' imprisonment (second and each subsequent offence) (s 8R)	30 penalty units (first offence) 250 penalty units (second and each subsequent offence) (ss 8R, 8ZF)
Person who is required to keep accounts or records under a taxation law recklessly keeps incorrect accounts or records (s 8Q)	30 penalty units (first offence) 50 penalty units and/or 12 months' imprisonment (second and each subsequent offence) (s 8R)	30 penalty units (first offence) 250 penalty units (second and each subsequent offence) (ss 8R, 8ZF)
Person falsifies, conceals, destroys or alters records with the intention of deceiving, misleading, hindering or obstructing the Commissioner or a particular tax officer, or hindering or obstructing the investigation of a taxation offence or administration or execution of a taxation law (s 8T)	50 penalty units and/or 12 months' imprisonment (first offence) 100 penalty units and/or 2 years' imprisonment (second and each subsequent offence) (s 8V)	250 penalty units (first offence) 500 penalty units (second and each subsequent offence) (ss 8V, 8ZF)
Person engages in conduct that results in the falsification or concealing of the identity or address of a person with the intention of deceiving or obstructing the Commissioner or a particular tax officer, or hindering or obstructing the investigation of a taxation offence or administration or execution of a taxation law (s 8U)	50 penalty units and/or 12 months' imprisonment (first offence) 100 penalty units and/or 2 years' imprisonment (second and each subsequent offence) (s 8V)	250 penalty units (first offence) 500 penalty units (second and each subsequent offence) (ss 8V, 8ZF)
Person requires or requests another person to quote their TFN in circumstances that are unauthorised (s 8WA)	100 penalty units and/or 2 years' imprisonment (s 8WA)	500 penalty units (ss 8WA, 8ZF)
Person records, uses or divulges another person's TFN in circumstances that are unauthorised (s 8WB)	100 penalty units and/or 2 years' imprisonment (s 8WB)	500 penalty units (ss 8WB, 8ZF)
Person who is an investor in two or more investments of a similar kind conducts their affairs so as to avoid TFN requirements (s 8WC)	100 penalty units and/or 2 years' imprisonment (s 8WC)	500 penalty units (ss 8WC, 8ZF)

Offence	Maximum penalty (natural person)	Maximum penalty (company)
Person takes unauthorised action to obtain information about another person's affairs that are contained in records in the possession of the Commissioner or held by the Commissioner for the purposes of a taxation law (s 8XA)	100 penalty units and/or 2 years' imprisonment (s 8XA)	500 penalty units (ss 8XA, 8ZF)
Person records, divulges or uses tax information relating to another person that was disclosed or obtained by the person in breach of a provision of the taxation law (s 8XB)	100 penalty units and/or 2 years' imprisonment (s 8XB)	500 penalty units (ss 8XB, 8ZF)

Court ordered payments in addition to penalties

Where a person is convicted of an offence against ss 8K, 8L, 8N or 8Q relating to making false or misleading statements or the keeping of incorrect records and the court is satisfied that the tax liability of the person or another person exceeds the amount that would have been the amount of the tax liability if it was assessed on the basis that the statement made was not false or misleading or the relevant records were correct, the court may in addition to imposing a penalty on the person, order them to pay the Commissioner an amount not exceeding double the amount of the tax avoided (or, in the case of a second or subsequent offence against ss 8N or 8Q, treble the amount of the tax avoided) (s 8W(1)).

Similarly, where a person has been convicted of an offence against ss 8T or 8U and the court is satisfied that the purpose, or one of the purposes, of the act or omission was to facilitate the avoidance of tax, the court may in addition to imposing a penalty on the person, order them to pay the Commissioner an amount not exceeding double the amount of the tax avoided (or, in the case of a second or subsequent offence, treble the amount of the tax avoided) (s 8W(2)).

Liability of company managers

Where a company does, or omits to do, an act or thing that constitutes a taxation offence, any person who is concerned in, or takes part in, the management of the company is deemed to have committed the offence (s 8Y(1)). It is a defence to a prosecution under this provision if the person proves that they did not aid, abet, counsel or procure the act or omission and were not in any way directly or indirectly concerned in, or party to, the act or omission (s 8Y(2)).

Offences under the *Criminal Code Act 1995* (Cth)

Prosecutions for tax offences can also be instituted under the *Criminal Code Act 1995* (Cth). The *Criminal Code* contains a range of offences, including a number of offences involving dishonesty and fraudulent conduct. For instance, it is an offence under s 134.2 of the *Criminal Code* for a person, by a deception, to dishonestly obtain a financial advantage from the Commonwealth. It is also an offence under s 135.4 of the *Criminal Code* for a person to conspire with another person with the intention of dishonestly obtaining a gain from the Commonwealth (*DPP (Cth) v Gregory* [2011] VSCA 145, *R v Willmott* [2023] NSWSC 474).

Offences under the *Crimes (Taxation Offences) Act 1980* (Cth)

The *Crimes (Taxation Offences) Act 1980* deals with criminal offences relating to company and trust 'stripping' arrangements aimed at rendering entities incapable of paying their tax liabilities. This Act was introduced to tackle what infamously became known in the 1970s as 'bottom of the harbour' schemes [36.3].

Offences under the *Corporations Act 2001* (Cth)

The *Corporations Act* contains special measures to combat illegal 'phoenix' activities. According to the ASIC website, illegal phoenix activity arises 'where a new company is created to continue the business of an existing company that has been deliberately liquidated to avoid paying outstanding debts, including taxes, creditors and employee entitlements'.

The legislation imposes criminal offences and civil penalties on:

- company officers that fail to prevent a company from making creditor-defeating dispositions, and
- other persons that facilitate a company making creditor-defeating dispositions.

A 'creditor-defeating disposition' is essentially a disposition of the company's property for less than its market value (or best price reasonably obtainable) that has the effect of preventing, hindering or significantly delaying the property becoming available to meet the demands of the company's creditors in winding-up. Special safeguards ensure that legitimate businesses and commercial transactions are not affected by the rules. To protect creditors, special rules allow liquidators and ASIC to recover property that is subject to a creditor-defeating disposition.

[41.4] Promoter penalty regime

Over the years, various kinds of mass-marketed tax exploitation schemes have been established by tax advisers. Division 290 of sch 1 *TAA* was introduced in 2006 to deter the promotion of these kinds of schemes. The division allows the Commissioner to apply to the Federal Court for civil penalties and injunctions against 'promoters' of 'tax exploitation schemes'. The maximum civil penalty is the greater of:

- 5,000 penalty units for an individual or 25,000 penalty units for a company, and
- twice the consideration receivable by the promoter and its associates under the scheme (s 290-50).

In *FC of T v Rowntree & Ors* 2021 ATC 20-786, Rares J explained (at 58) the objectives of div 290 in the following terms:

> There is an obligation of all persons in a society to pay taxation on their assessable income to meet the common need to finance the activities that are necessary for the government to operate and provide the services that the community's elected representatives have voted to support in the Parliament. Avoidance or evasion of taxation throws the burden of financing the government meeting the common needs of society onto only those who are willing to obey the taxation laws. No society can conduct its affairs effectively if persons perceive that there will not be substantial penalties applied by the courts to deter conduct that is intended to facilitate the avoidance or evasion of taxation or other imposts that the Parliament has imposed. Division 290 is intended to achieve its objects, namely the deterrence of tax avoidance and tax evasion, by conferring power on the Court to impose appropriately severe penalties, within the range provided in s 290-50(4), on promoters of schemes.

Tax exploitation schemes

'Tax exploitation schemes' are essentially schemes that exploit the tax system through avoidance or evasion. At the time the scheme is promoted, it must be reasonable to conclude that an entity that entered into or carried out the scheme has the sole or dominant purpose of obtaining a 'scheme benefit' from the scheme and it must not be reasonably arguable that the scheme benefit is available under the tax law (s 290-65).

Promoter

An entity is a 'promoter' of a tax exploitation scheme if:

- the entity markets or otherwise encourages the growth of the scheme
- the entity (or its associate) receives directly or indirectly consideration in respect of that marketing or encouragement, and
- having regard to all relevant matters it is reasonable to conclude that the entity had a substantial role in respect of that marketing or encouragement.

However, an entity is not a promoter of a tax exploitation scheme merely because the entity provides advice about the scheme (s 290-60). In practice, the difficulty that can arise for persons such as lawyers and accountants is determining whether they are merely involved in providing advice about a particular scheme or are actually encouraging the scheme.

Illustrations of where persons were found to be promoters of tax exploitation schemes can be found in the following cases:

- *FC of T v Ludekens* 2013 ATC ¶20-415 (which involved the promotion of a complicated forestry MIS designed to provide investors with tax benefits in the form of GST refunds and income tax deductions)
- *FC of T v Arnold & Ors* 2015 ATC ¶20-486 (which involved the promotion of an artificial charitable donations scheme)
- *FC of T v Bogiatto & Ors* 2020 ATC ¶20-757 (which involved the promotion of schemes to obtain refundable R&D tax offsets where the claims were not reasonably arguable), and
- *FC of T v Rowntree & Ors* 2021 ATC ¶20-786 (which involved the promotion of schemes to obtain tax deductions relating to carbon credits).

Exceptions

There are a number of exceptions to the promoter penalty rules. For instance, an entity is not liable for a civil penalty if its conduct was due to a reasonable mistake of fact, or if the scheme treats the taxation law as applying in a way that accords with a statement given to the entity by the Commissioner (eg in a tax ruling) (s 290-55).

[41.5] QUESTIONS

1. How does the general administrative penalty regime apply to breaches of the tax law?
2. Discuss the various tax offences and penalties that apply under the *TAA*. What are the consequences for persons who have been convicted of an offence? Are the penalties greater for subsequent offences?
3. What is the relationship between the administrative penalty regime and the tax offences regime under the *TAA*? Which regime takes precedence?
4. What types of offences may arise under the *Criminal Code* for tax fraud?
5. What is a tax exploitation scheme and who is a promoter of such a scheme? What powers does the Commissioner have against promoters of tax exploitation schemes?

TABLE OF CASES

All cases involving revenue or taxation authorities are listed alphabetically according to the name of the taxpayer.

A

C

F

G

H

I

J

K

L

M

N

S

X

Y

Z

TABLE OF LEGISLATION

COMMONWEALTH LEGISLATION AND REGULATIONS

188-15	7.3
188-20	7.3
190-1	7.17
195-1	2.6, 7.6, 7.7, 7.12, 7.14, 7.17
sch 1	7.7
sch 2	7.7

A New Tax System (Goods and Services Tax Imposition—Customs) Act 1999 ('GSTICA')

SECTION	PARAGRAPH
Generally	3.6, 4.3, 7.3

A New Tax System (Goods and Services Tax Imposition—Excise) Act 1999 ('GSTIEA')

SECTION	PARAGRAPH
Generally	3.6, 4.3, 7.3

A New Tax System (Goods and Services Tax Imposition—General) Act 1999 ('GSTIGA')

SECTION	PARAGRAPH
Generally	3.6, 4.3, 7.3

A New Tax System (Goods and Services Tax) Regulations 2019 ('GST Regs')

SECTION	PARAGRAPH
Generally	7.3
23-14.01	7.5
23-14.02	7.5
29-80.01	7.11
40-5.06	7.13
40-5.08	7.13
40-5.09	7.13
40-5.10	7.13
40-5.12	7.13
70-5.02	7.13
70-5.02A	7.13
70-5.03	7.13

A New Tax System (Goods and Services Tax Transition) Act 1999 ('GSTTA')

SECTION	PARAGRAPH
Generally	4.3
6	7.20
7	7.20
11	7.20
12	7.20
13	7.20
14	7.20
15	7.20
15A to 15M	7.20
19	7.20

A New Tax System (Luxury Car Tax) Act 1999 ('LCTA')

SECTION	PARAGRAPH
Generally	4.3

A New Tax System (Luxury Car Tax Imposition—Customs) Act 1999 ('LCTICA')

SECTION	PARAGRAPH
Generally	4.3

A New Tax System (Luxury Car Tax Imposition—Excise) Act 1999 ('LCTIEA')

SECTION	PARAGRAPH
Generally	4.3

A New Tax System (Luxury Car Tax Imposition—General) Act 1999 ('LCTIGA')

SECTION	PARAGRAPH
Generally	4.3

A New Tax System (Medicare Levy Surcharge—Fringe Benefits) Act 1999 ('MLSFBA')

SECTION	PARAGRAPH
Generally	4.3
10 to 16	8.8

A New Tax System (Wine Equalisation Tax) Act 1999 ('WETA')

SECTION	PARAGRAPH
Generally	4.3

A New Tax System (Wine Equalisation Tax Imposition—Customs) Act 1999 ('WETICA')

SECTION	PARAGRAPH
Generally	4.3

A New Tax System (Wine Equalisation Tax Imposition—Excise) Act 1999 ('WETIEA')

SECTION	PARAGRAPH
Generally	4.3

A New Tax System (Wine Equalisation Tax Imposition—General) Act 1999 ('WETIGA')

SECTION	PARAGRAPH
Generally	4.3

Acts Interpretation Act 1901

SECTION	PARAGRAPH
Generally	3.3
15A	2.6
15AA	2.6
15AB	2.6
15AC	2.6
15AD	2.6

Administrative Appeals Tribunal Act 1975

SECTION	PARAGRAPH
33	38.5
41	40.7
43	38.5
44	38.5

Administrative Decisions (Judicial Review) Act 1977 ('ADJRA')

SECTION	PARAGRAPH
3	38.6
5	38.6
6	38.6
7	38.6
sch 1	38.6

Anti-Money Laundering and Counter-Terrorism Financing Act 2006 ('AMLCTFA')

SECTION	PARAGRAPH
Generally	36.2
3	39.5
5	39.5
6	39.5
41	39.5
43	39.5
45	39.5
46	39.5
53	39.5
136	39.5
137	39.5
138	39.5
139	39.5
140	39.5
142	39.5
143	39.5

Anti-Money Laundering and Counter-Terrorism Financing Rules ('AMLCTFR')

SECTION	PARAGRAPH
32	39.5

ASIC Supervisory Cost Recovery Levy Act 2017

SECTION	PARAGRAPH
Generally	19.4

ASIC Supervisory Cost Recovery Levy (Collection) Act 2017

SECTION	PARAGRAPH
Generally	19.4

ASIC Supervisory Cost Recovery Levy Regulations 2017

SECTION	PARAGRAPH
Generally	19.4

Australia Act 1986

SECTION	PARAGRAPH
Generally	3.2, 3.3

Australian Charities and Not-for-profits Commission Act 2012

SECTION	PARAGRAPH
Generally	11.4

Australian Charities and Not-for-profits Commission (Consequential and Transitional) Act 2012

SECTION	PARAGRAPH
Generally	11.4

Banking Act 1959

SECTION	PARAGRAPH
Generally	4.3, 7.13

Bankruptcy Act 1966

SECTION	PARAGRAPH
Generally	17.5
116	19.4

1222S	25.11
1222Q	25.11
1222V	25.11
1222X	25.11

Corporations Regulations 2001

SECTION	PARAGRAPH
1.02.02B	22.2
2A.1.01	23.2

Crimes Act 1914

SECTION	PARAGRAPH
4AA	41.1
400	36.2

Crimes (Taxation Offences) Act 1980

SECTION	PARAGRAPH
Generally	3.3, 36.3, 41.3

Criminal Code Act 1995

SECTION	PARAGRAPH
Generally	36.2
133.2	41.3
134.4	41.3

Customs Act 1901 (CA)

SECTION	PARAGRAPH
Generally	4.3, 7.16, 7.18
13-5	7.16

Customs Tariff Act 1995 ('CTA')

SECTION	PARAGRAPH
Generally	4.3, 7.16

Diplomatic Privileges and Immunities Act 1967

SECTION	PARAGRAPH
Generally	31.8

Diverted Profits Tax Act 2017

SECTION	PARAGRAPH
9	30.2
10	30.2

Domicile Act 1982

SECTION	PARAGRAPH
Generally	30.2

Excise Act 1901 ('EA')

SECTION	PARAGRAPH
Generally	4.3

Excise Tariff Act 1921 ('ETA')

SECTION	PARAGRAPH
Generally	4.3

Extension of Charitable Purpose Act 2004

SECTION	PARAGRAPH
Generally	11.4

Family Law Act 1975

SECTION	PARAGRAPH
4	19.18
90MC	19.18
90ME	19.18
90MH	19.18
90ML	19.18
90MM	19.18
90MN	19.18
90MS	19.18
90MU	19.18

Family Law (Superannuation) Regulations 2001

SECTION	PARAGRAPH
12	19.18

Family Trust Distribution Tax (Primary Liability) Act 1998

SECTION	PARAGRAPH
Generally	24.9

Federal Court of Australia Act 1976

SECTION	PARAGRAPH
24	38.5
25	38.5
33	38.5

Federal Financial Relations Act 2009

SECTION	PARAGRAPH
Generally	4.4

Financial Management and Accountability Act 1997

SECTION	PARAGRAPH
Generally	6.3

Higher Education Support Act 2003 ('HESA')

Income Tax Act 1986 ('ITA')

Income Tax Assessment Act 1936 ('ITAA36')

Income Tax Assessment Act 1997 ('ITAA97')

Income Tax Assessment (1936 Act) Regulation 2015 ('ITAR15')

Income Tax Assessment (1997 Act) Regulations 2021 ('ITAR21')

Income Tax (Attribution Managed Investment Trusts-Offsets) Act 2015

Privacy Act 1988

SECTION	PARAGRAPH
Generally	38.9

Private Health Insurance Act 2007

SECTION	PARAGRAPH
Generally	11.8

Public Service Act 1999

SECTION	PARAGRAPH
Generally	6.3

Retirement Savings Accounts Act 1997 ('RSAA')

SECTION	PARAGRAPH
Generally	7.13, 19.4, 19.14

Retirement Savings Accounts Regulations 1997 ('RSAR')

SECTION	PARAGRAPH
Generally	19.4, 19.15
4.22B	19.4

Senate (Representation of Territories) Act 1973

SECTION	PARAGRAPH
Generally	3.3

Small Superannuation Accounts Act 1995

SECTION	PARAGRAPH
Generally	19.4
61	19.14
61A	19.14

Social Security Act 1991 ('SSA')

SECTION	PARAGRAPH
Generally	9.4, 25.4, 39.2

States Grants (Income Tax Reimbursement) Act 1942

SECTION	PARAGRAPH
Generally	3.9, 4.2

Statute of Westminster Adoption Act 1942

SECTION	PARAGRAPH
Generally	3.2, 3.3

Student Loans (Overseas Repayment Levy) Act 2015

SECTION	PARAGRAPH
4	8.10

Superannuation Act 1990

SECTION	PARAGRAPH
Generally	30.2

Superannuation (Departing Australia Superannuation Payments Tax) Act 2007

SECTION	PARAGRAPH
Generally	19.16

Superannuation (Excess Non-Concessional Contributions Tax) Act 2007 ('SENCCTA')

SECTION	PARAGRAPH
4	19.9
5	19.9

Superannuation (Excess Transfer Balance Tax) Imposition Act 2016 ('SETBTIA')

SECTION	PARAGRAPH
Generally	4.3
4	19.15
5	19.15

Superannuation (Excess Untaxed Roll-over Amounts Tax) Act 2007

SECTION	PARAGRAPH
Generally	19.14

Superannuation (Financial Assistance Funding) Levy Act 1993

SECTION	PARAGRAPH
Generally	19.4

Superannuation (Government Co-contribution for Low Income Earners) Act 2003 ('SGCLIEA')

SECTION	PARAGRAPH
6	19.8
7	19.8
8	19.8
9	19.8
10	19.8
10A	19.8
12C	19.8

16	19.4
17A	19.4
19AA	19.4
19AB	19.4
23	19.4
29C to 29EA	19.4
29G	19.4
40	19.4
42	19.4
42A	19.4
43	19.4
45	19.4
52	19.4
54B	19.4
62	19.4
62A	19.4
65	19.4
66	19.4
66A	19.4
67	19.4
67A	19.4
109	19.4

Superannuation Industry (Supervision) Regulations 1994 ('SISR')

SECTION	PARAGRAPH
Generally	19.15
1.05	19.4
1.06	19.4
4.09	19.4
5.01	19.4
6.01	19.4
6.19B	19.4
6.28	19.4
6.35	19.4
6.40	19.17
6.41	19.17
6.42	19.17
6.44	19.17
6.45	19.17
7.01	19.4
7.04	19.4
12.18AA	19.4

Superannuation Supervisory Levy Imposition Act 1998 ('SSLIA')

SECTION	PARAGRAPH
Generally	19.4

Taxation Administration Act 1953 ('TAA')

SECTION	PARAGRAPH
3B	6.3
3C	6.3
4	6.3
4A	6.3
5	6.3
8	6.3
8AAA	40.8
8AAC	40.8
8AAD	40.8
8AAG	40.8
8AAH	40.8
8AAZA	40.5
8AAZF	40.5, 40.8
8AAZN	40.5
8A	41.3
8C	38.8, 41.3
8D	38.8, 41.3
8K	41.3
8L	41.3
8N	41.3
8Q	41.3
8T	41.3
8U	41.3
8W	41.3
8Y	41.3
8ZE	41.3
8ZF	41.3
8ZN	41.3
14R	40.7
14S	38.6, 40.7
14T	40.7
14U	40.7
14V	40.7
14ZU	38.5
14ZW	38.5
14ZX	38.5
14ZY	38.5
14ZZ	38.5
14ZZK	38.5
14ZZM	40.7
14ZZO	38.5
14ZZT	36.2
14ZZU	36.2
14ZZW	36.2
14ZZX	36.2
14ZZY	36.2

Taxation Administration Regulations 2017 ('TAR')

Tax Agent Services Act 2009

Land Tax Act 1915 (Qld)

SECTION	PARAGRAPH
Generally	4.4

Land Tax Act 1936 (SA)

SECTION	PARAGRAPH
Generally	4.4

Land Tax Act 1956 (NSW)

SECTION	PARAGRAPH
Generally	4.4

Land Tax Act 2000 (Tas)

SECTION	PARAGRAPH
Generally	4.4

Land Tax Act 2002 (WA)

SECTION	PARAGRAPH
Generally	4.4

Land Tax Act 2005 (Vic)

SECTION	PARAGRAPH
Generally	4.4

Land Tax Assessment Act 2002 (WA)

SECTION	PARAGRAPH
Generally	4.4

Land Tax Management Act 1956 (NSW)

SECTION	PARAGRAPH
Generally	4.4

Land Tax Rating Act 2000 (Tas)

SECTION	PARAGRAPH
Generally	4.4

Payroll Tax Act 1971 (Qld)

SECTION	PARAGRAPH
Generally	4.4

Payroll Tax Act 2002 (WA)

SECTION	PARAGRAPH
Generally	4.4

Payroll Tax Act 2007 (NSW)

SECTION	PARAGRAPH
Generally	4.4

Payroll Tax Act 2007 (Vic)

SECTION	PARAGRAPH
Generally	4.4

Payroll Tax Act 2008 (Tas)

SECTION	PARAGRAPH
Generally	4.4

Payroll Tax Act 2009 (NT)

SECTION	PARAGRAPH
Generally	4.4

Payroll Tax Act 2009 (SA)

SECTION	PARAGRAPH
Generally	4.4

Payroll Tax Act 2011 (ACT)

SECTION	PARAGRAPH
Generally	4.4

Stamp Duties Act 1923 (SA)

SECTION	PARAGRAPH
Generally	4.4

Stamp Duties Act 1978 (NT)

SECTION	PARAGRAPH
Generally	4.4

INDEX

K

L

M

N

Q

R

S

T

Z

For EU product safety concerns, contact us at Calle de José Abascal, 56–1°,
28003 Madrid, Spain or eugpsr@cambridge.org.

www.ingramcontent.com/pod-product-compliance
Lightning Source LLC
LaVergne TN
LVHW081956200926
848481LV00010B/2752
* 9 7 8 1 0 0 9 4 5 8 8 3 2 *